Ethics

Theory and Contemporary Issues

Ninth Edition

Barbara MacKinnon
University of San Francisco, Professor of Philosophy, Emerita

Andrew Fiala
California State University, Fresno, Professor of Philosophy

CENGAGE
Learning·

Australia • Brazil • Mexico • Singapore • United Kingdom • United States

Ethics: Theory and Contemporary Issues, **Ninth Edition**

Barbara MacKinnon, Andrew Fiala

Product Director: Paul Banks

Product Manager: Debra Matteson

Content Development Manager: Megan Garvey

Content Developer: Adrienne Zicht Devlin

Project Manager: Julia Giannotti

Content Development Project Manager: Matt Gervais, Lumina Datamatics, Inc.

Associate Content Developer: Ryan McAndrews

Product Assistant: Staci Eckenroth

Marketing Manager: Jillian Borden

Senior Content Project Manager: Margaret Park Bridges

Art Director: Marissa Falco

Manufacturing Planner: Julio Esperas

IP Analyst: Alex Ricciardi

IP Project Manager: Nick Barrows

Production Service: Cenveo® Publisher Services

Compositor: Cenveo® Publisher Services

Text designer: Cenveo® Publisher Services

Cover designer: Gary Ragaglia

Design credit: Illustrart/Shutterstock.com

Cover Images:

© Samir Hussein/Getty Images

© Photos.com/Getty Images

© Cengage Learning

© Georgios Kollidas/Alamy Stock Photo

© Rob Melnychuk/Digital Vision/Getty Images

© Joseph Sohm/Shutterstock.com

© AP Images/Matthew Putney

© Scott Peterson/Getty Images News/Getty Images

© Jose Luis Cereijido/EPA/Newscom

For product information and technology assistance, contact us at
Cengage Learning Customer & Sales Support, 1-800-354-9706

For permission to use material from this text or product, submit all requests online at **www.cengage.com/permissions.**
Further permissions questions can be emailed to
permissionrequest@cengage.com.

The Library of Congress Control Number: 2016953085

Student Edition:
ISBN: 978-1-305-95867-8

Loose-leaf Edition:
ISBN: 978-1-305-95958-3

Cengage Learning
20 Channel Center Street
Boston, MA 02210
USA

Cengage Learning is a leading provider of customized learning solutions with employees residing in nearly 40 different countries and sales in more than 125 countries around the world. Find your local representative at **www.cengage.com.**

Cengage Learning products are represented in Canada by Nelson Education, Ltd.

To learn more about Cengage Learning Solutions, visit **www.cengage.com.**

Purchase any of our products at your local college store or at our preferred online store **www.cengagebrain.com.**

Printed at CLDPC, USA, 04-17

Contents

This ninth edition of *Ethics: Theory and Contemporary Issues* contains a substantial revision of the text and extensive update of the empirical material contained in the chapters focused on contemporary issues. Andrew Fiala joined as coauthor on the eighth edition. In the ninth edition, we have included new learning apparatus, especially tables that outline possible moral positions with regard to the issues considered. As in past editions, each chapter begins with a detailed, accessible introduction that prepares the student to read accompanying selections from important and influential philosophers. The book remains a comprehensive introduction to ethics in theory and practice. It also continues to emphasize pedagogy through clear summaries, engaging examples, and various study tools—such as review exercises and discussion cases. Each chapter begins with a list of learning objectives, and the book ends with an extensive glossary of key terms.

ADDITIONS AND CHANGES

Although the basic elements remain the same, this new ninth edition includes the following additions and changes from the eighth edition. Each chapter in Part I has been revised to focus on readability. All introductory and empirical material in each chapter in Part II has been updated to incorporate the latest information about contemporary issues and current affairs. These updates include recent statistics, relevant cases, and contemporary examples.

This edition offers expanded and continued coverage of the following topics: global (non-Western) philosophy and religion, the prisoner's dilemma and the tragedy of the commons, social justice and economic inequality, mass incarceration and decarceration, restorative justice, environmental justice, biotechnology and bioengineering, gene editing, vegetarianism and the ethics of hunting, circuses, race and racism, pacifism, gay marriage, global poverty, LGBT and transgender issues, Black Lives Matter, Syrian refugees, the precautionary principle, and climate change. This edition includes some familiar readings from previous editions and some new additions. In some cases, older readings have been shortened to make room for new readings and short excerpts by a more diverse set of authors, including some emerging voices. New readings include: John Lachs on relativism, Hilde Lindemann on feminism, a new essay on abortion by Bertha Alvarez Manninen, U.S. Supreme Court Obergefell Decision, Naomi Zack on Black Lives Matter, Iris Marion Young's "Five Faces of Oppression," Pope Francis and Ayn Rand on economic issues, Michelle Alexander on the New Jim Crow, Tom Regan on animal rights, the Transhumanist declaration, Andrew Fitz-Gibbon on peace, and Garret Hardin on global poverty.

Key Elements

Each chapter of *Ethics: Theory and Contemporary Issues* contains an extended summary of key concepts and issues written in clear, accessible prose. These detailed summaries go beyond the short introductions found in most ethics anthologies to provide students with a thorough grounding in the theory and practical application of philosophical ethics.

As previously noted, these discussions have been thoroughly updated to include detailed information on current events, statistics, and political and cultural developments.

The theory chapters in Part I present detailed summaries of the theories and major concepts, positions, and arguments. The contemporary issues chapters in Part II include summaries of:

> current social conditions and recent events, with special emphasis on their relevance to students' lives
> conceptual issues, such as how to define key words and phrases (for example, *cloning*, *terrorism*, and *distributive justice*)
> arguments and suggested ways to organize an ethical analysis of each topic
> tables outlining possible moral positions, linked to normative theories and key authors.

Throughout this text, we seek to engage readers by posing challenging ethical questions and then offering a range of possible answers or explanations. The aim is to present more than one side of each issue so that students can decide for themselves what position they will take. This also allows instructors more latitude to emphasize specific arguments and concepts and to direct the students' focus as they see fit.

Where possible throughout the text, the relation of ethical theory to the practical issues is indicated. For example, one pervasive distinction used throughout the text is between consequentialist and non-consequentialist considerations and arguments. The idea is that if students are able to first situate or categorize a philosophical reason or argument, then they will be better able to evaluate it critically in their thinking and writing. Connections to related concepts and issues in other chapters are also highlighted throughout the text to help students note similarities and contrasts among various ethical positions.

Pedagogical Aids This text is designed as an accessible, "user-friendly" introduction to ethics. To aid both instructor and student, we have provided the following pedagogical aids:

> a list of learning objectives at the beginning of each chapter (new to this edition)
> a real-life event, hypothetical dialogue, or updated empirical data at the beginning of each chapter
> diagrams, subheadings, and boldface key terms and definitions that provide guideposts for readers and organize the summary exposition
> study questions for each reading selection
> review exercises at the end of each chapter that can be used for exams and quizzes
> a glossary of definitions of key terms (new to this edition)
> discussion cases that follow each chapter in Part II and provide opportunities for class or group discussion
> topics and resources for written assignments in the discussion cases
> tables outlining moral positions (new to this edition).

A Digital Solution for Students and Instructors:

MindTap for Philosophy for Ethics: Theory and Contemporary Issues is a personalized, online digital learning platform providing students with an immersive learning experience that builds critical thinking skills. Through a carefully designed chapter-based learning path, MindTap allows students to easily identify the chapter's learning objectives; draw connections and improve writing skills by completing essay assignments; read short, manageable sections from the e-book; and test their content knowledge with critical thinking Aplia™ questions.

> **Chapter e-Book:** Each chapter within MindTap contains the narrative of the chapter, offering an easy to navigate online reading experience.
> **Chapter Quiz:** Each chapter within MindTap ends with a summative Chapter Test covering the chapter's learning objectives and ensuring

students are reading and understanding the material presented.

> **Chapter Aplia Assignment:** Each chapter includes an Aplia assignment that provides automatically graded critical thinking assignments with detailed, immediate feedback and explanations on every question. Students can also choose to see another set of related questions if they did not earn all available points in their first attempt and want more practice.

> **Ethics Simulations:** Each chapter offers an interactive simulated ethical dilemma, allowing students to make decisions and see the implications of their choices.

> **Chapter Essay Question:** Every chapter ends with essay prompts that ask students to explore and reflect on concepts from the chapter and build writing and critical thinking faculties.

> **KnowNOW! Philosophy Blog:** The KnowNOW! Philosophy Blog connects course concepts with real-world events. Updated twice a week, the blog provides a succinct philosophical analysis of major news stories, along with multimedia and discussion-starter questions.

MindTap also includes a variety of other tools that support philosophy teaching and learning:

> The Philosophy Toolbox collects tutorials on using MindTap and researching and writing academic papers, including citation information and tools, that instructors can use to support students in the writing process.

> Questia allows professors and students to search a database of thousands of peer-reviewed journals, newspapers, magazines, and full-length books—all assets can be added to any relevant chapter in MindTap, and students can

> Kaltura allows instructors to create and insert inline video and audio into the MindTap platform.

> ReadSpeaker reads the text out loud to students in a voice they can customize.

> Note-taking and highlighting are organized in a central location that can be synced with Ever-Note on any mobile device a student may have access to.

> Digital flash cards are premade for each chapter, and students can make their own by adding images, descriptions, and more.

MindTap gives students ample opportunities for improving comprehension and for self-evaluation to prepare for exams, while also providing faculty and students alike a clear way to measure and assess student progress. Faculty can use MindTap as a turnkey solution or customize by adding YouTube videos, RSS feeds, or their own documents directly within the e-book or within each chapter's Learning Path. MindTap goes well beyond an e-book and a homework solution. It is truly a Personal Learning Experience that allows instructors to synchronize the reading with engaging assignments. To learn more, ask your Cengage Learning sales representative to demo it for you—or go to www.Cengage.com/MindTap.

Instructor's Resources:

The Instructor's Companion Site features an Instructor's Manual, PowerPoint Lecture Slides, and a robust Test Bank (Cengage Learning Testing powered by Cognero).

The Instructor's Manual provides useful suggestions for lectures and classroom activities, based directly on the content in this book. Answers to many review exercises or study questions are provided, as well as questions for further thought.

The PowerPoint Lecture Slides offer a chapter-by-chapter breakdown **Cengage Learning Testing, powered by Cognero**, new to this edition, allows instructors to author, edit, and manage Test Bank content. Instructors can create multiple test versions and instantly deliver them through their learning management system right to the classroom.

Interested instructors can find and access all this content by adding the ninth edition of this book to their bookshelf on Cengage.com.

IN SUMMARY

We have sought to make this ninth edition of *Ethics: Theory and Contemporary Issues* the most comprehensive ethics text available. It combines theory and issues, text and readings, as well as up-to-date empirical information about contemporary moral problems. It is designed to be flexible, user-friendly, current, pedagogically helpful, and balanced.

> The flexible structure of the text allows instructors to emphasize only those theories and applied ethical topics which best suit their courses.
> The text is user-friendly, while at the same time philosophically reliable. It employs pedagogical aids throughout and at the end of each chapter, and provides extensive examples from current events and trends. The exposition challenges students with stimulating questions and is interspersed with useful diagrams, charts, and headings.
> The text not only provides up-to-date coverage of developments in the news and in scientific journals but also on ethical issues as they are discussed in contemporary philosophy.
> It offers a balanced collection of readings, including both the ethical theories and contemporary sources on the issues.
> *Ethics: Theory and Contemporary Issues*, ninth edition, is accompanied by a broad range of online and textual tools that amplify its teachability and give instructors specific pedagogical tools for different learning styles.

ACKNOWLEDGMENTS

We wish to thank the many people who have made valuable suggestions for improving the ninth edition of the text, including Marie Gaudio-Zaccaria, Georgia Perimeter College; K.C. Warble III, University of South Carolina; Dusan Galic, College of DuPage; Erin Anchustegu, Boise State University; Christina Tomczak, Cedar Valley College; Susan Brown, University of West Florida; Philip Cronce, Chicago State University; William Rodriguez, Bethune Cookman University; Robert Arp, Johnson County Community College; Jason Gooch, Yakima Valley Community College; Jason Flato, Georgia Perimeter College; and Eric Severson, Seattle Pacific University.

Barbara MacKinnon especially wants to thank the students in her classes at the University of San Francisco. Over the years, they have contributed greatly to this text by challenging her to keep up with the times and to make things more clear and more interesting. She also appreciates the support of her husband and fellow philosopher, Edward MacKinnon. She dedicates this book to her two wonderful daughters, Jennifer and Kathleen. Andrew Fiala is thankful for Barbara's hard work throughout the previous editions of this book and for the opportunity to transform his classroom teaching experience into a useful text for teaching ethics.

We also wish to acknowledge the many professional people from Cengage Learning and its vendors who have worked on this edition, including: Debra Matteson, Product Manager; Adrienne Devlin, Content Developer; Megan Garvey, Content Development Manager; Lauren MacLachlan, Production Manager; Margaret Park Bridges, Senior Content Project Manager; Marissa Falco, Art Director; and Kritika Kaushik, Project Manager, at Cenveo Publisher Services.

Ancient

500 B.C.E.	400	300	200	100	0	100 C.E.	200

Sappho
637–577

Socrates
469–399

Plato
427–347

Buddha
557–477

Aristotle
384–322

Confucius
552–479

Zeno
351–270

Jesus
? 4 B.C.E.–C.E. 29

Philo Judaeus
20 B.C.E.–C.E. 40

Sextus Empiricus
60–117

Marcus Aurelius
121–180

Plotinus
205–270

Medieval

C.E. 300	400	500	600	700	800	900	1000	1100	1200	1300

Augustine
345–400

Boethius
480–524

Mohammed
570–632

Anselm
1033–1109

Abelard
1079–1142

Avicebron
1021–1058

Maimonides
1135–1204

Avicenna
980–1037

Averroes
1126–1198

Aquinas
1224–1274

Scotus
1265–1308

Ockham
1285–1347

Modern

1500	1600	1700	1800	1900	2000

Bacon
1561–1626

Hobbes
1588–1679

Locke
1632–1704

Leibniz
1646–1716

Spinoza
1632–1677

Hume
1711–1776

Kant
1724–1804

Rousseau
1712–1778

Wollstonecraft
1759–1797

Bentham
1748–1832

Kierkegaard
1813–1851

Marx
1818–1883

Hegel
1770–1831

Mill
1806–1873

Gandhi
1869–1948

James
1846–1910

Moore
1873–1958

Rawls
1921–2002

Nietzsche
1844–1900

Sartre
1905–1979

Singer
b. 1946–

Noddings
b. 1929–

DeBeauvoir
1908–1986

Habermas
1929–

Dewey
1859–1952

Ethics and Ethical Reasoning

Jack Hollingsworth/Photodisc/Getty Images

Learning Outcomes

After reading this chapter, you should be able to:

- Describe the philosophical study of ethics.
- Discuss the difference between normative and descriptive claims.
- Define key terms: intuitionism, emotivism, objectivism, and subjectivism.
- Explain the difference between metaethics and normative ethics.
- Decide whether naturalistic explanations of ethics commit the naturalistic fallacy.

- Differentiate between instrumental and intrinsic values.
- Distinguish consequentialist from nonconsequentialist approaches to ethics.
- Use the distinctions among motives, acts, and consequences to analyze ethical phenomena.

MindTap® For more chapter resources and activities, go to MindTap.

WHY STUDY ETHICS?

It is clear that we often disagree about questions of value. Should same-sex marriage be legal? Should women have abortions? Should drugs such as marijuana be legalized? Should we torture terrorists in order to get information from them? Should we eat animals or use them in medical experiments? These sorts of questions are sure to expose divergent ideas about what is right or wrong.

Discussions of these sorts of questions often devolve into unreasonable name-calling, foot-stomping, and other questionable argument styles. The philosophical study of ethics aims to produce good arguments that provide reasonable support for our opinions about practical topics. If someone says that abortion should (or should not) be permitted, he or she needs to explain why this is so. It is not enough to say that abortion should not be permitted because it is wrong or that women should be allowed to choose abortion because it is wrong to limit women's choices. To say that these things are wrong is merely to reiterate that they should not be permitted. Such an answer *begs the question*. Circular, question-begging arguments are fallacious. We need further argument and information to know *why* abortion is wrong or *why* limiting free choice is wrong. We need a theory of what is right and wrong, good or evil, justified, permissible, and unjustifiable, and we need to understand how our theory applies in concrete cases. The first half of this text will discuss various theories and concepts that can be used to help us avoid begging the question in debates about ethical issues. The second half looks in detail at a number of these issues.

It is appropriate to wonder, at the outset, why we need to do this. Why isn't it sufficient to simply state your opinion and assert that "x is wrong (or evil, just, permissible, etc.)"? One answer to this question is that such assertions do nothing to solve the deep conflicts of value that we find in our world. We know that people disagree about abortion, same-sex marriage, animal rights, and other issues. If we are to make progress toward understanding each other, if we are to make progress toward establishing some consensus about these topics, then we have to understand *why* we think certain things are right and others are wrong. We need to make arguments and give reasons in order to work out our own conclusions about these issues and in order to explain our conclusions to others.

It is also insufficient to appeal to custom or authority in deriving our conclusions about moral issues. While it may be appropriate for children to simply obey their parents' decisions, adults should strive for more than conformity and obedience to authority. Sometimes our parents and grandparents are wrong—or they disagree among themselves. Sometimes the law is wrong—or laws conflict. And sometimes religious authorities are wrong—or authorities do not agree. To appeal to authority on moral issues, we would first have to decide which authority is to be trusted and believed. Which religion provides the best set of moral rules? Which set of laws in which country is to be followed? Even within the United States, there is currently a conflict of laws with regard to some of these issues: some states have legalized medical marijuana or physician assisted suicide, others have not. The world's religions also disagree about a number of issues: for example, the status of women, the permissibility of abortion, and the question of whether war is justifiable. And members of the same religion or denomination may disagree among themselves about these issues. To begin resolving these conflicts, we need critical philosophical inquiry into basic ethical questions. In Chapter 2, we discuss the world's diverse religious traditions and ask whether there is a set of common ethical ideas that is shared by these traditions. In this chapter, we clarify what ethics is and how ethical reasoning should proceed.

WHAT IS ETHICS?

On the first day of an ethics class, we often ask students to write one-paragraph answers to the question, "What is ethics?"

How would you answer? Over the years, there have been significant differences of opinion among our students on this issue. Some have argued that ethics is a highly personal thing, a matter of private opinion. Others claim that our values come from family upbringing. Other students think that ethics is a set of social principles, the codes of one's society or particular groups within it, such as medical or legal organizations. Some write that many people get their ethical beliefs from their religion.

One general conclusion can be drawn from these students' comments: We tend to think of ethics as the set of values or principles held by individuals or groups. I have my ethics and you have yours; groups—professional organizations and societies, for example—have shared sets of values. We can study the various sets of values that people have. This could be done historically and sociologically. Or we could take a psychological interest in determining how people form their values. But philosophical ethics is a critical enterprise that asks whether any particular set of values or beliefs is better than any other. We compare and evaluate sets of values and beliefs, giving reasons for our evaluations. We ask questions such as, "Are there good reasons for preferring one set of ethics over another?" In this text, we examine ethics from a critical or evaluative standpoint. This examination will help you come to a better understanding of your own values and the values of others.

Ethics is a branch of *philosophy*. It is also called *moral philosophy*. In general, philosophy is a discipline or study in which we ask—and attempt to answer—basic questions about key areas or subject matters of human life and about pervasive and significant aspects of experience. Some philosophers, such as Plato and Kant, have tried to do this systematically by interrelating their philosophical views in many areas. According to Alfred North Whitehead, "Philosophy is the endeavor to frame a coherent, logical, necessary system of general ideas in terms of which every element of our experience can be interpreted."[1] Some contemporary philosophers have given up on the goal of building a system of general ideas, arguing instead that we must work at problems piecemeal, focusing on one particular issue at a time. For instance, some philosophers might analyze the meaning of the phrase *to know,* while others might work on the morality of lying. Some philosophers are optimistic about our ability to address these problems, while others are more skeptical because they think that the way we analyze the issues and the conclusions we draw will always be influenced by our background, culture, and habitual ways of thinking. Most agree, however, that these problems are worth wondering about and caring about.

We can ask philosophical questions about many subjects. In the philosophical study of **aesthetics**, philosophers ask basic or foundational questions about art and objects of beauty: what kinds of things do or should count as art (rocks arranged in a certain way, for example)? Is what makes something an object of aesthetic interest its emotional expressiveness, its peculiar formal nature, or its ability to reveal truths that cannot be described in other ways? In the philosophy of science, philosophers ask whether scientific knowledge gives us a picture of reality as it is, whether progress exists in science, and whether the scientific method discloses truth. Philosophers of law seek to understand the nature of law itself, the source of its authority, the nature of legal interpretation, and the basis of legal responsibility. In the philosophy of knowledge, called **epistemology**, we try to answer questions about what we can know of ourselves and our world, and what it means to know something rather than just to believe it. In each area, philosophers ask basic questions about the particular subject matter. This is also true of moral philosophy.

> Ethics, or moral philosophy, asks basic questions about the good life, about what is better and worse, about whether there is any objective right and wrong, and how we know it if there is.

One objective of ethics is to help us decide what is good or bad, better or worse. This is generally called **normative ethics**. Normative ethics defends a thesis about what is good, right, or just. Normative ethics can be distinguished from **metaethics**. Metaethical inquiry asks questions about the nature of ethics, including the meaning of ethical terms and judgments. Questions about the relation between philosophical ethics and religion—as we discuss in Chapter 2—are metaethical. Theoretical questions about ethical relativism—as discussed in Chapter 3—are also metaethical. The other chapters in Part I are more properly designated as ethical theory. These chapters present concrete normative theories; they make claims about what is good or evil, just or unjust.

From the mid 1930s until recently, metaethics predominated in English-speaking universities. In doing metaethics, we often analyze the meaning of ethical language. Instead of asking whether the death penalty is morally justified, we would ask what we meant in calling something "morally justified" or "good" or "right." We analyze ethical language, ethical terms, and ethical statements to determine what they mean. In doing this, we function at a level removed from that implied by our definition. It is for this reason that we call this other type of ethics *metaethics—meta* meaning "beyond." Some of the discussions in this chapter are metaethical discussions—for example, the analysis of various senses of "good." As you will see, much can be learned from such discussions.

ETHICAL AND OTHER TYPES OF EVALUATION

"That's great!" "Now, this is what I call a delicious meal!" "That play was wonderful!" All of these statements express approval of something. They do not tell us much about the meal or the play, but they do imply that the speaker thought they were good. These are evaluative statements. Ethical statements or judgments are also *evaluative*. They tell us what the speaker believes is good or bad. They do not simply *describe* the object of the judgment—for example, as an action that occurred at a certain time or that affected people in a certain way. They go further and express a positive or negative regard for it. Of course, factual matters are relevant to moral evaluation. For example, factual judgments about whether capital punishment has a deterrent effect might be relevant to our moral judgments about it. So also would we want to know the facts about whether violence can ever bring about peace; this would help us judge the morality of war. Because ethical judgments often rely on such *empirical* information, ethics is often indebted to other disciplines such as sociology, psychology, and history. Thus, we can distinguish between empirical or **descriptive claims**, which state factual beliefs, and evaluative judgments, which state whether such facts are good or bad, just or unjust, right or wrong. Evaluative judgments are also called **normative judgments**. Moral judgments are evaluative because they "place a value," negative or positive, on some action or practice, such as capital punishment.

- Descriptive (empirical) judgment: Capital punishment acts (or does not act) as a deterrent.
- Normative (moral) judgment: Capital punishment is justifiable (or unjustifiable).

We also evaluate people, saying that a person is good or evil, just or unjust. Because these evaluations also rely on beliefs in general about what is good or right, they are also normative. For example, the judgment that a person is a hero or a villain is based upon a normative theory about good or evil sorts of people.

"That is a good knife" is an evaluative or normative statement. However, it does not mean that the knife is morally good. In making ethical judgments, we use terms such as *good, bad, right, wrong, obligatory,* and *permissible.* We talk about what we ought or ought not to do. These are evaluative terms. *But not all evaluations are moral in nature.* We speak of a good knife without attributing moral goodness to it. In so describing the knife, we are probably referring to its practical usefulness for cutting. Other evaluations refer to other systems of values. When people tell us that a law is legitimate or unconstitutional, that is a legal judgment. When we read that two articles of clothing ought not to be worn together, that is an aesthetic judgment. When religious leaders tell members of their communities what they ought to do, that is a religious matter. When a community teaches people to bow before elders or use eating utensils in a certain way, that is a matter of custom. These various normative or evaluative judgments appeal to practical, legal, aesthetic, religious, or customary norms for their justification.

How do other types of normative judgments differ from moral judgments? Some philosophers believe that it is a characteristic of moral "oughts" in particular that they override other "oughts," such as aesthetic ones. In other words, if we must choose between what is aesthetically pleasing and what is morally right, then we ought to do what is morally right. In this way, morality may also take precedence over the law and custom. The doctrine of civil disobedience relies on this belief, because it holds that we may disobey certain laws for moral reasons. Although moral evaluations differ from other normative evaluations, this is not to say that there is no

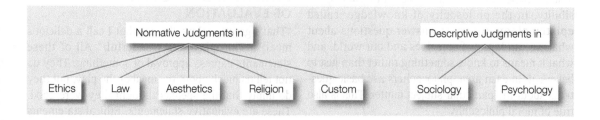

relation between them. In fact, moral reasons often form the basis for certain laws. But law—at least in the United States—results from a variety of political compromises. We don't tend to look to the law for moral guidance. And we are reluctant to think that we can "legislate morality," as the saying goes. Of course, there is still an open debate about whether the law should enforce moral ideas in the context of issues such as gay marriage or abortion.

There may be moral reasons supporting legal arrangements—considerations of basic justice, for example. Furthermore, the fit or harmony between forms and colors that ground some aesthetic judgments may be similar to the rightness or moral fit between certain actions and certain situations or beings. Moreover, in some ethical systems, actions are judged morally by their practical usefulness for producing valued ends. For now, however, note that ethics is not the only area in which we make normative judgments.

SOCIOBIOLOGY AND THE NATURALISTIC FALLACY

The distinction between descriptive and normative claims is a central issue for thinking about ethics. We often confuse these issues in our ordinary thinking, in part because we think that what we ordinarily do is what we ought to do. Many people are inclined to say that if something is natural to us, then we ought to do it. For example, one might argue that since eating meat is natural for us, we ought to eat meat. But vegetarians will disagree. Indeed, there is no necessary relation between what is ethical and what is natural or customary. It is thus not true that what is natural is always good. But people often make the mistake of confusing facts of nature and value judgments. Most of the time, we are not attentive to the shift from facts to values, the shift from *is* to *ought*. Consider an example used by the eighteenth-century philosopher David Hume, who noticed that incest appears to be quite natural—animals do it all the time. But human beings condemn incest. If it is natural, why do we condemn it? Hume pointed out the problem of deriving an *ought* from an *is*; philosophers after Hume named the rule

against simplistically deriving an *ought* from an *is* **Hume's law**. From this perspective, it is not logical, for example, to base our ideas about how we ought to behave from a factual account of how we actually do behave. This logical mistake was called the **naturalistic fallacy** by G. E. Moore, an influential philosopher of the early twentieth century. Moore maintained that moral terms such as *good* are names for nonempirical properties that cannot be reduced to some other natural thing. Moore claimed that to attempt to define *good* in terms of some mundane or natural thing such as pleasure is to commit a version of this fallacy. The problem is that we can ask whether pleasures are actually good. Just because we desire pleasure does not mean that it is good to desire pleasure. As Moore suggested, there is always an open question about whether what is natural is also good.

Now, not everyone agrees that appeals to nature in ethics are fallacious. There are a variety of naturalistic approaches to thinking about ethics. One traditional approach to ethics is called **natural law** ethics (which we discuss in detail in Chapter 7). Natural law ethics focuses on human nature and derives ethical precepts from an account of what is natural for humans. Natural law ethicists may argue, for example, that human body parts have natural functions and that by understanding these natural functions, we can figure out certain moral ideas about sexuality or reproduction. Opponents might argue that this commits the naturalistic fallacy, since there is no obvious moral content to be seen in the structure and function of our body parts.

A more recent version of naturalism in ethics focuses on evolutionary biology and cognitive science. From this perspective, to understand morality, we need to understand the basic functions of our species, including the evolutionary reasons behind moral behavior. We also need to understand how our brains function in order to explain how pleasure works, why some people are psychopathic, and why we struggle to balance egoistic and altruistic motivations. One version of this naturalism is known as **sociobiology**—an idea that was introduced by the biologist E. O. Wilson.[2] "If the brain evolved

Does animal behavior provide a guide for human ethical behavior?

by natural selection, even the capacities to select particular esthetic judgments and religious beliefs must have arisen by the same mechanistic process," Wilson explained.[3] The basic idea of sociobiology is that human behaviors result from the pressures of natural selection. Understanding human morality involves understanding the adaptive advantage of certain behaviors, which can be studied by comparing human behaviors with the behavior of other social animals—from insects to chimpanzees.

Sociobiology attempts to understand altruism, for example, in terms of evolutionary processes. From this perspective, altruistic concern develops through natural selection because altruistic animals will help each other survive. Biologist Richard Dawkins explains a related idea in terms of "the selfish gene."

Dawkins's idea is that our genes use our altruistic and other behaviors to spread themselves. Thus, when we cooperate within groups that share a genetic endowment, we help to preserve the group and help to disseminate our shared genetic characteristics, often in competition with rival genetic groups.[4]

In discussing sociobiology and interpreting biological evidence, we must be careful, however, not to anthropomorphize.[5] When we look at the natural world, we often interpret it in anthropomorphic terms, seeing in animals and even in genes themselves the motivations and interests that human beings have. In other words, we must be careful that our value judgments do not cloud or confuse our description of the facts.

While the naturalistic approach of sociobiology is provocative and insightful, we might still worry that it commits the naturalistic fallacy. Just because altruistic behavior is natural and useful in the evolutionary struggle for survival does not mean that it is good, just, or right. To see this, let us return to Hume's example of incest. Incest might be useful as a method for disseminating our genetic material—so long as the negative problems associated with inbreeding are minimized. We do inbreed animals in this way in order to select for desirable traits. But it is still appropriate to ask whether incest is morally permissible for human beings—the question of *ought* might not be settled by what *is*.

ETHICAL TERMS

You might have wondered what the difference is between calling something "right" and calling it "good." Consider the ethical meaning for these terms. Right and wrong usually apply to actions, as in "You did the right thing," or "That is the wrong thing to do." These terms prescribe things for us to do or not to do. On the other hand, when we say that something is morally good, we may not explicitly recommend doing it. However, we do recommend that it be positively regarded. Thus, we say things such as "Peace is good, and distress is bad." It is also interesting that with "right" and "wrong" there seems to be no in-between; it is either one or the other. However, with "good" and "bad" there is room for degrees, and some things are thought to be better or worse than others.

Other ethical terms require careful consideration. For example, when we say that something "ought" or "ought not" to be done, there is a sense of urgency and obligation. We can refrain from doing what we ought to do, but the obligation is still there. On the other hand, there are certain actions that we think are permissible but that we are not obligated to do. Thus, one may think that there is no obligation to help someone in trouble, though it is "morally permissible" (i.e., not wrong) to do so and even "praiseworthy" to do so in some cases. Somewhat more specific ethical terms include *just* and *unjust* and *virtuous* and *vicious*.

To a certain extent, which set of terms we use depends on the particular overall ethical viewpoint or theory we adopt. This will become clearer as we discuss and analyze the various ethical theories in this first part of the text.

ETHICS AND REASONS

When we evaluate something as right or wrong, good or bad, we appeal to certain norms or reasons. If I say that affirmative action is unjustified, I should give reasons for this conclusion; it will not be acceptable for me to respond that this is merely the way I feel. If I have some intuitive negative response to preferential treatment forms of affirmative action, then I will be expected to delve deeper to determine whether there are reasons for this attitude. Perhaps I have experienced the bad results of such programs. Or I may believe that giving preference in hiring or school admissions on the basis of race or sex is unfair. In either case, I will be expected to push the matter further and explain *why* it is unfair or even what constitutes fairness and unfairness.

Reason-giving is essential in philosophical ethics. However, this does not mean that making ethical judgments is and must be purely rational. We might be tempted to think that good moral judgments require us to be objective and not let our feelings, or emotions, enter into our decision making. Yet this assumes that feelings always get in the way

of making good judgments. Sometimes this is surely true, as when we are overcome by anger, jealousy, or fear and cannot think clearly. Biases and prejudice may stem from such strong feelings. We think prejudice is wrong because it prevents us from judging rightly. But emotions can often aid good decision making. We may, for example, simply feel the injustice of a certain situation or the wrongness of someone's suffering. Furthermore, our caring about some issue or person may, in fact, direct us to more carefully examine the ethical issues involved. However, some explanation of why we hold a certain moral position is still required. Simply to say "X is just wrong" without explanation, or to merely express strong feelings or convictions about "X," is not sufficient.

INTUITIONISM, EMOTIVISM, SUBJECTIVISM, OBJECTIVISM

Philosophers differ on how we know what is good. They also differ on the question of whether moral judgments refer to something objective or whether they are reports of subjective opinions or dispositions.

To say that something is good is often thought to be different from saying that something is yellow or heavy. The latter two qualities are empirical, known by our senses. However, good or goodness is held to be a nonempirical property, said by some to be knowable through intuition. A position known as **intuitionism** claims that our ideas about ethics rest upon some sort of intuitive knowledge of ethical truths. This view is associated with G. E. Moore, whom we discussed earlier.[6] Another philosopher, W. D. Ross, thinks that we have a variety of "crystal-clear intuitions" about basic values. These intuitions are clear and distinct beliefs about ethics, which Ross explains using an analogy with mathematics: just as we see or intuit the self-evident truth of "2 + 2 = 4," we also see or intuit ethical truths: for example, that we have a duty to keep our promises. As Ross explains,

> Both in mathematics and in ethics we have certain crystal-clear intuitions from which we build up all that we can know about the nature of numbers and the

nature of duty…we do not read off our knowledge of particular branches of duty from a single ideal of the good life, but build up our ideal of the good life from intuitions into the particular branches of duty.[7]

A very important question is whether our intuitions point toward some objective moral facts in the world or whether they are reports of something subjective. A significant problem for intuitionism is that people's moral intuitions seem to differ. Unlike the crystal-clear intuitions of mathematics—which are shared by all of us—the intuitions of ethics are not apparently shared by everyone.

Another view, sometimes called **emotivism**, maintains that when we say something is good, we are showing our approval of it and recommending it to others rather than describing it. This view is associated with the work of twentieth-century philosophers such as A. J. Ayer and C. L. Stevenson. But it has deeper roots in a theory of the moral sentiments, such as we find in eighteenth-century philosophers Adam Smith and David Hume. Hume maintains, for example, that reason is "the slave of the passions," by which he means that the ends or goals we pursue are determined by our emotions, passions, and sentiments. Adam Smith maintains that human beings are motivated by the experience of pity, compassion, and sympathy for other human beings. For Smith, ethics develops out of natural sympathy toward one another, experienced by social beings like ourselves.

Emotivism offers an explanation of moral knowledge that is subjective, with moral judgments resting upon subjective experience. One version of emotivism makes ethical judgments akin to expressions of approval or disapproval. In this view, to say "murder is wrong" is to express something like "murder—yuck!" Similarly, to say "courageous self-sacrifice is good" is to express something like "self-sacrifice—yay!" One contemporary author, Leon Kass, whom we study in Chapter 18, argues that there is wisdom in our experiences of disgust and repugnance—that our emotional reactions to things reveal deep moral insight. Kass focuses especially on the "yuck factor" that many feel about advanced biotechnologies such as cloning.

One worry, however, is that our emotions and feelings of sympathy or disgust are variable and relative. Our own emotional responses vary depending upon our moods and these responses vary among and between individuals. Emotional responses are relative to culture and even to the subjective dispositions of individuals. Indeed, our own feelings change over time and are not reliable or sufficient gauges of what is going on in the external world. The worry here is that our emotions merely express internal or subjective responses to things and that they do not connect us to an objective and stable source of value.

Other moral theories aim for more objective sources for morality. From this standpoint, there must be objective reasons that ground our subjective and emotional responses to things. Instead of saying that the things we desire are good, an **objectivist** about ethics will argue that we ought to desire things that are good—with an emphasis on the goodness of the thing-in-itself apart from our subjective responses. The ancient Greek philosopher Plato was an objectivist in this sense. Objectivists hold that values have an objective reality—that they are objects available for knowledge—as opposed to **subjectivists**, who claim that value judgments merely express subjective opinion. Plato argues that there is some concept or idea called "the Good" and that we can compare our subjective moral opinions about morality with this objective standard. Those who want to ground morality in God are objectivists, as are those who defend some form of natural law ethics, which focuses on essential or objective features of bodies and their functions. Interestingly, the approach of sociobiology tends not to be objectivist in this sense. Although the sociobiologist bases her study of morality on objective facts in the world, the sociobiologist does not think that moral judgments represent moral facts. Instead, as Michael Ruse puts it,

Objective ethics, in the sense of something written on tablets of stone (or engraven on God's heart) external to us, has to go. The only reasonable thing that we, as sociobiologists, can say is that morality is something biology makes us believe in, so that we will further our evolutionary ends.[8]

One of the issues introduced in Ruse's rejection of objectivity in ethics is the distinction between **intrinsic** and **instrumental** goods. Instrumental goods are things that are useful as instruments or tools—we value them as means toward some other end. Intrinsic goods are things that have value in themselves or for their own sake. For example, we might say that life is an intrinsic good and fundamentally valuable. But food is an instrumental good because it is a means or tool that is used to support life. From Ruse's perspective, morality itself is merely an instrumental good that is used by evolution for other purposes. Morality is, from this perspective, simply a tool that helps the human species to survive. The selfish gene hypothesis of Richard Dawkins understands individual human beings instrumentally, as carriers of genetic information: "We are survival machines—robot vehicles blindly programmed to serve the selfish molecules known as genes."[9] This runs counter to our usual moral view, which holds that human beings have intrinsic or inherent value. The idea that some things have intrinsic value is an idea that is common to a variety of approaches that claim that ethics is objective. The intrinsic value of a thing is supposed to be an objective fact about that thing, which has no relation to our subjective response to that thing. Claims about intrinsic value show up in arguments about human rights and about the environment. Do human beings, ecosystems, or species have intrinsic value, or is the value of these things contained within our subjective responses and in their instrumental uses? This question shows us that the metaethical theories are connected to important practical issues.

ETHICAL REASONING AND ARGUMENTS

It is important to know how to reason well in thinking or speaking about ethical matters. This is helpful not only in trying to determine what to think about controversial ethical matters but also in arguing for something you believe is right and in critically evaluating positions held by others.

The Structure of Ethical Reasoning and Argument

To be able to reason well in ethics you need to understand what constitutes a good argument. We can do this by looking at an argument's basic structure. This is the structure not only of ethical arguments about what is good or right but also of arguments about what is the case or what is true.

Suppose you are standing on the shore and a person in the water calls out for help. Should you try to rescue that person? You may or may not be able to swim. You may or may not be sure you could rescue the person. In this case, however, there is no time for reasoning, as you would have to act promptly. On the other hand, if this were an imaginary case, you would have to think through the reasons for and against trying to rescue the person. You might conclude that if you could actually rescue the person, then you ought to try to do it. Your reasoning might go as follows:

Every human life is valuable.
Whatever has a good chance of saving such a life should be attempted.
My swimming out to rescue this person has a good chance of saving his life.
Therefore, I ought to do so.

Or you might conclude that you could not save this person, and your reasoning might go like this:

Every human life is valuable.
Whatever has a good chance of saving such a life should be attempted.
In this case, there is no chance of saving this life because I cannot swim.
Thus, I am not obligated to try to save him (although, if others are around who can help, I might be obligated to try to get them to help).

Some structure like this is implicit in any ethical argument, although some are longer and more complex chains than the simple form given here. One can recognize the reasons in an argument by their introduction through key words such as *since*, *because*, and *given that*. The conclusion often contains terms such as *thus* and *therefore*. The reasons supporting the conclusion are called **premises**. In a sound argument, the premises are true and the conclusion follows from them. In the case presented earlier, then, we want to know whether you can save this person and also whether his life is valuable. We also need to know whether the conclusion actually follows from the premises. In the case of the earlier examples, it does. If you say you ought to do what will save a life and you can do it, then you ought to do it. However, there may be other principles that would need to be brought into the argument, such as whether and why one is always obligated to save someone else's life when one can.

To know under what conditions a conclusion actually follows from the premises, we would need to analyze arguments in much greater detail than we can do here. Suffice it to say, however, that the connection is a logical connection—in other words, it must make rational sense. You can improve your ability to reason well in ethics first by being able to pick out the reasons and the conclusion in an argument. Only then can you subject them to critical examination in ways we suggest here.

Evaluating and Making Good Arguments

Ethical reasoning can be done well or done poorly. Ethical arguments can be constructed well or constructed poorly. A good argument is a **sound argument**. It has a **valid** form in which the conclusion actually follows from the premises, and the premises or reasons given for the conclusion are true. An argument is poorly constructed when it is fallacious or when the reasons on which it is based are not true or are uncertain. An ethical argument always involves some claim about values—for example, that saving a life is good. These value-based claims must be established through some theory of values. Part I of this book examines different theories that help establish basic values.

Ethical arguments also involve conceptual and factual matters. Conceptual matters are those that relate to the meaning of terms or concepts. For example, in a case of lying, we would want to know

what lying actually is. Must it be verbal? Must one have an intent to deceive? What is deceit itself? Other conceptual issues central to ethical arguments may involve questions such as, "What constitutes a 'person'?" (in arguments over abortion, for example) and "What is 'cruel and unusual punishment'?" (in death penalty arguments, for example). Sometimes, differences of opinion about an ethical issue are a matter of differences not in values but in the meaning of the terms used.

Ethical arguments often also rely on factual claims. In our example, we might want to know whether it was actually true that you could save the drowning person. In arguments about the death penalty, we may want to know whether such punishment is a deterrent. In such a case, we need to know what scientific studies have found and whether the studies themselves were well grounded. To have adequate factual grounding, we will want to seek out a range of reliable sources of information and be open-minded. The chapters in Part II of this book include factual material that is relevant to ethical decisions about the topics under consideration.

It is important to be clear about the distinction between facts and values when dealing with moral conflict and disagreement. We need to ask whether we disagree about the values involved, about the concepts and terms we are employing, or about the facts connected to the case.

There are various ways in which reasoning can go wrong or be fallacious. We began this chapter by considering the fallacy of **begging the question** or **circular argument**. Such reasoning draws on the argument's conclusion to support its premises, as in "abortion is wrong because it is immoral." Another familiar problem of argumentation is the **ad hominem** fallacy. In this fallacy, people say something like, "That can't be right because just look who is saying it." They look at the source of the opinion rather than the reasons given for it. You can find out more about these and other fallacies from almost any textbook in logic or critical thinking.

You also can improve your understanding of ethical arguments by making note of a particular type of reasoning that is often used in ethics: **arguments**

from analogy. In this type of argument, one compares familiar examples with the issue being disputed. If the two cases are similar in relevant ways, then whatever one concludes about the first familiar case one should also conclude about the disputed case. For example, Judith Jarvis Thomson (as discussed in Chapter 11) once asked whether it would be ethically acceptable to "unplug" someone who had been attached to you and who was using your kidneys to save his life. If you say that you are justified in unplugging, then a pregnant woman is also justified in doing the same with regard to her fetus. The reader is prompted to critically examine such an argument by asking whether or not the two cases were similar in relevant ways—that is, whether the analogy fits.

Finally, we should note that giving reasons to *justify* a conclusion is also not the same as giving an *explanation* for why one believes something. A woman might explain that she does not support euthanasia because that was the way she was brought up or that she is opposed to the death penalty because she cannot stand to see someone die. To justify such beliefs, one would need rather to give reasons that show not why one does, in fact, believe something but why one should believe it. Nor are rationalizations justifying reasons. They are usually reasons given after the fact that are not one's true reasons. *Rationalizations* are usually excuses, used to explain away bad behavior. These false reasons are given to make us look better to others or ourselves. To argue well about ethical matters, we need to examine and give reasons that support the conclusions we draw.

ETHICAL THEORY

Good reasoning in ethics usually involves either implicit or explicit reference to an ethical theory. An *ethical theory* is a systematic exposition of a particular view about what is the nature and basis of good or right. The theory provides reasons or norms for judging acts to be right or wrong; it provides a justification for these norms. These norms can then be used as a guide for action. We can diagram the relationship between ethical theories and moral decision making as follows.

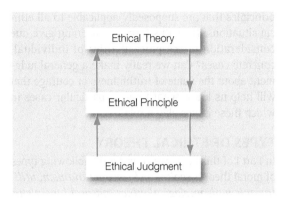

We can think of the diagram as a ladder. In practice, we can start at the ladder's top or bottom. At the top, at the level of theory, we can start by clarifying for ourselves what we think are basic ethical values. We then move downward to the level of principles generated from the theory. The next step is to apply these principles to concrete cases. We can also start at the bottom of the ladder, facing a particular ethical choice or dilemma. We can work our way back up the ladder, thinking through the principles and theories that implicitly guide our concrete decisions. Ultimately and ideally, we come to a basic justification, or the elements of what would be an ethical theory. If we look at the actual practice of thinking people as they develop their ethical views over time, the movement is probably in both directions. We use concrete cases to reform our basic ethical views, and we use the basic ethical views to throw light on concrete cases.

An example of this movement in both directions would be if we start with the belief that pleasure is the ultimate value and then find that applying this value in practice leads us to do things that are contrary to common moral sense or that are repugnant to us and others. We may then be forced to look again and possibly alter our views about the moral significance of pleasure. Or we may change our views about the rightness or wrongness of some particular act or practice on the basis of our theoretical reflections. Obviously, this sketch of moral reasoning is quite simplified. Feminists and others have criticized this model of ethical reasoning, partly because it claims that ethics is governed by general principles that are supposedly applicable to all ethical situations. Does this form of reasoning give due consideration to the particularities of individual, concrete cases? Can we really make a general judgment about the value of truthfulness or courage that will help us know what to do in particular cases in which these issues play a role?

TYPES OF ETHICAL THEORY

In Part I of this book, we consider the following types of moral theory: *egoism* and *contractarianism*, *utilitarianism*, *deontological ethics*, *natural law*, *virtue ethics*, and *feminist ethics*. These theories differ in terms of what they say we should look at in making moral judgments about actions or practices. For example, does it matter morally that I tried to do the right thing or that I had a good motive? Surely it must make some moral difference, we think. But suppose that in acting with good motives I violate someone's rights. Does this make the action a bad action? We would probably be inclined to say yes. Suppose, however, that in violating someone's rights, I am able to bring about a great good. Does this justify the violation of rights? Some theories judge actions in terms of their motive, some in terms of the character or nature of the act itself, and others in terms of the consequences of the actions or practices.

We often appeal to one of these types of reason. Take a situation in which I lie to a person, Jim. We can make the following judgments about this action. Note the different types of reasons given for the judgments.

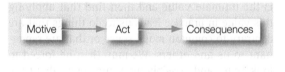

That was good because you intended to make Jim happy by telling him a white lie—or it was bad because you meant to deceive him and do him harm. (Motive)
That was good because it is good to make people happy—or it was bad because it is always wrong to tell a lie. (Act)

That was good because it helped Jim develop his self-esteem—or it was bad because it caused Jim to believe things about himself that were not true. (Consequences)

Although we generally think that a person's motive is relevant to the overall moral judgment about his or her action, we tend to think that it reflects primarily on our moral evaluation of *the person*. We also have good reasons to think that the results of actions matter morally. Those theories that base moral judgments on consequences are called **consequentialist** or sometimes **teleological** moral theories (from the Greek root *telos*, meaning "goal" or "end"). Those theories that hold that actions can be right or wrong regardless of their consequences are called **nonconsequentialist** or **deontological** theories (from the Greek root *deon*, meaning "duty").

One moral theory we will examine is *utilitarianism*. It provides us with an example of a consequentialist moral theory in which we judge whether an action is better than alternatives by its actual or expected results or consequences; actions are then judged in terms of the promotion of human happiness. Kant's moral theory, which we will also examine, provides us with an example of a nonconsequentialist theory, according to which acts are judged right or wrong independently of their consequences; in particular, acts are judged by whether they conform to requirements of rationality and human dignity. The other ethical theories that we will examine stress human nature as the source of what is right and wrong. Some elements of these theories are deontological and some teleological. So, also, some teleological theories are consequentialist in that they advise us to produce some good. But if the good is an ideal, such as virtue or self-realization, then such theories differ from consequentialist theories such as utilitarianism. As anyone who has tried to put some order to the many ethical theories knows, no theory completely and easily fits one classification, even those given here. Feminist theories of care provide yet another way of determining what one ought to do (see Chapter 9). In Part II of this text, we will examine several concrete ethical issues.

As we do so, we will note how various ethical theories analyze the problems from different perspectives and sometimes reach different conclusions about what is morally right or wrong, better or worse.

CAN ETHICS BE TAUGHT?

It would be interesting to know just why some college and university programs require their students to take a course in ethics. Does this requirement stem from a belief that a course in ethics or moral philosophy can actually make people good?

When asked whether ethics can be taught, students have given a variety of answers. "If it can't be taught, then why are we taking this class?" a student wondered. Another student responded, "Look at the behavior of certain corporate executives who have been found guilty of criminal conduct. They surely haven't learned proper ethical values." Still others disagreed with both views. Although certain ideals or types of knowledge can be taught, ethical behavior cannot be taught because it is a matter of individual choice, they said.

The ancient Greek philosopher Plato thought that ethics could be taught. He argues that "All evil is ignorance." In other words, we do what is wrong because we do not know or believe it is wrong; and if we truly believe that something is right, we should necessarily do it. Now, we are free to disagree with Plato by appealing to our own experience. If I know that I should not have that second piece of pie, does this mean that I will not eat it? Ever? Plato might attempt to convince us that he is right by examining or clarifying what he means by the phrase *to know*. If we were really convinced with our whole heart and mind that something is wrong, then we might be highly likely (if not determined) not to do it. However, whether ethics courses should attempt to convince students of such things is surely debatable.

Another aspect of the problem of teaching ethics concerns the problem of motivation. If one knows something to be the right thing to do, does there still remain the question of why we should do it? One way to motivate people to be ethical may be to show them that it is in their own best interest to do the right thing.

Most moral philosophers think that a course on ethics is ethically useful. It should help students understand the nature of ethical problems and help them think critically about ethical matters by providing conceptual tools and skills. It should enable them to form and critically analyze ethical arguments. It is up to the individual, however, to use these skills to reason about ethical matters. A study of ethics should also lead students to respect opposing views because it requires them to analyze carefully the arguments that support views contrary to their own. It also provides opportunities to consider the reasonableness of at least some viewpoints that they may not have considered.

In this opening chapter, we have learned something about what the philosophical study of ethics is. We have considered a few metaethical issues. We have provided a description of ethical reasoning and arguments. We have briefly considered the nature of ethical theories and the role they play in ethical reasoning. We will examine these theories more carefully in the chapters to come, and we will see how they might help us analyze and come to conclusions about particular ethical issues.

The reading selections for this chapter come from David Hume's *Treatise of Human Nature,* first published in 1739, and from C. L. Stevenson, a philosopher associated with the Anglo-American tradition in twentieth-century philosophy. The excerpt from Hume discusses the problem of deriving normative claims from descriptive claims, the problem of deriving an *ought* from an *is*, with a particular focus on the question of the morality of incest. Stevenson discusses the difficulty of connecting ethics and natural science, while also outlining an emotivist approach to understanding ethical terms.

NOTES

1. Alfred North Whitehead, *Process and Reality* (New York: Macmillan, 1929), p. 4.
2. E. O. Wilson, *Sociobiology: The New Synthesis* (Cambridge, MA: Harvard University Press, 1975).
3. E. O. Wilson, *On Human Nature* (Cambridge, MA: Harvard University Press, 1978), p. 2.

4. See Richard Dawkins, *The Selfish Gene* (Oxford: Oxford University Press, 1989).

5. See Frans de Waal, *Good Natured: The Origins of Right and Wrong in Humans and Other Animals* (Cambridge, MA: Harvard University Press, 1996). Also see Morton Hunt, *The Compassionate Beast: What Science Is Discovering about the Human Side of Humankind* (New York: William Morrow, 1990).

6. G. E. Moore, *Principia Ethics* (Buffalo, NY: Prometheus, 1903).

7. W. D. Ross, *Foundations of Ethics* (Oxford: Clarendon Press, 1939), pp. 144–45.

8. Michael Ruse, *Sociobiology: Sense or Nonsense?* (New York: Springer, 1985), p. 237.

9. Richard Dawkins, *The Selfish Gene*, 30th Anniversary Edition (Oxford: Oxford University Press, 2006), p. xxi.

READING

Ethical Judgments and Matters of Fact*

DAVID HUME

MindTap For more chapter resources and activities, go to MindTap.

Study Questions

As you read the excerpt, please consider the following questions:

1. How does Hume employ the fact of animal incest to advance his argument that morality does not consist merely of "matters of fact" and that morality is not merely an "object of reason"?
2. Explain Hume's idea that morality is a matter of feelings and sentiments.
3. Why does Hume have a problem with deducing an *ought* from an *is*?

I would fain ask any one, why incest in the human species is criminal, and why the very same action, and the same relations in animals have not the smallest moral turpitude and deformity? If it be answered, that this action is innocent in animals, because they have not reason sufficient to discover its turpitude; but that man, being endowed with that faculty which ought to restrain him to his duty, the same action instantly becomes criminal to him; should this be said, I would reply, that this is evidently arguing in a circle. For before reason can perceive this turpitude, the turpitude must exist; and consequently is independent of the decisions of our reason, and is their object more properly than their effect. According to this system, then, every animal, that has sense, and appetite, and will; that is, every animal must be susceptible of all the same virtues and vices, for which we ascribe praise and blame to human creatures. All the difference is, that our superior reason may serve to discover the vice or virtue, and by that means may augment the blame or praise: But still this discovery supposes a separate being in these moral distinctions, and a being, which depends only on the will and appetite, and which, both in thought and reality, may be distinguished from the reason. Animals are susceptible of the same relations, with respect to each other, as the human species, and therefore would also be susceptible of the same morality, if the essence of morality consisted in these relations. Their want of a sufficient degree of reason may hinder them from perceiving the duties and obligations of morality, but can never hinder these duties from existing; since they must antecedently exist, in order to their being perceived. Reason must find them, and can never produce them. This argument deserves to be weighed, as being, in my opinion, entirely decisive.

From David Hume, *A Treatise on Human Nature*, (1739; Project Gutenberg, 2010), bk. III, pt. 1, sec. 1, http://www.gutenberg.org/files/4705/4705-h/4705-h.htm

*Title supplied by the editor.

Nor does this reasoning only prove, that morality consists not in any relations, that are the objects of science; but if examined, will prove with equal certainty, that it consists not in any *matter of fact*, which can be discovered by the understanding. This is the *second* part of our argument; and if it can be made evident, we may conclude, that morality is not an object of reason. But can there be any difficulty in proving, that vice and virtue are not matters of fact, whose existence we can infer by reason? Take any action allowed to be vicious: Willful murder, for instance. Examine it in all lights, and see if you can find that matter of fact, or real existence, which you call *vice*. In which-ever way you take it, you find only certain passions, motives, volitions and thoughts. There is no other matter of fact in the case. The vice entirely escapes you, as long as you consider the object. You never can find it, till you turn your reflection into your own breast, and find a sentiment of disapprobation, which arises in you, towards this action. Here is a matter of fact; but it is the object of feeling, not of reason. It lies in yourself, not in the object. So that when you pronounce any action or character to be vicious, you mean nothing, but that from the constitution of your nature you have a feeling or sentiment of blame from the contemplation of it. Vice and virtue, therefore, may be compared to sounds, colours, heat and cold, which, according to modern philosophy, are not qualities in objects, but perceptions in the mind: And this discovery in morals, like that other in physics, is to be regarded as a considerable advancement of the speculative sciences; though, like that too, it has little or no influence on practice. Nothing can be more real, or concern us more, than our own sentiments of pleasure and uneasiness; and if these be favourable to virtue, and unfavourable to vice, no more can be requisite to the regulation of our conduct and behaviour.

I cannot forbear adding to these reasonings an observation, which may, perhaps, be found of some importance. In every system of morality, which I have hitherto met with, I have always remarked, that the author proceeds for some time in the ordinary way of reasoning, and establishes the being of a God, or makes observations concerning human affairs; when of a sudden I am surprized to find, that instead of the usual copulations of propositions, *is*, and *is not*, I meet with no proposition that is not connected with an *ought*, or an *ought not*. This change is imperceptible; but is, however, of the last consequence. For as this *ought*, or *ought not*, expresses some new relation or affirmation, it is necessary that it should be observed and explained; and at the same time that a reason should be given, for what seems altogether inconceivable, how this new relation can be a deduction from others, which are entirely different from it. But as authors do not commonly use this precaution, I shall presume to recommend it to the readers; and am persuaded, that this small attention would subvert all the vulgar systems of morality, and let us see, that the distinction of vice and virtue is not founded merely on the relations of objects, nor is perceived by reason.

READING

Emotivism and Ethics

C. L. STEVENSON

MindTap®   For more chapter resources and activities, go to MindTap.

Study Questions

As you read the excerpt, please consider the following questions:

1. What does Stevenson mean when he says that ethical terms are not (or not simply) descriptive?
2. How does the example of stealing illustrate Stevenson's understanding of the meaning of ethical terms?
3. What does he mean by the "emotive meaning" of ethical terms?

I. FACTS AND VALUES

I want to "place" [my work] within ethics as a whole—as I can best do by mentioning the three branches into which the subject is commonly divided.

First, there is "descriptive" ethics, which studies the moral practices and convictions that have been current among these or those peoples, and thus studies what has been implicitly or explicitly considered good, obligatory, etc. At the present time this part of ethics is developed less by philosophers (though philosophers must of course study it) than by social scientists.

Second, there is "normative" ethics, which seeks to reach conclusions about the justice of this or that law, for instance, or the value of this or that type of conduct, and which often (though not always) attempts to systematize these conclusions under general principles, such as the greatest happiness principle of Bentham and Mill, or the categorical imperative of Kant. Normative ethics differs from descriptive ethics in an obvious way: it does not seek conclusions about what others have implicitly or explicitly considered good, etc., but instead seeks well founded conclusions that are intended to supplement, back up, or stand in opposition to what others have considered good. In a somewhat similar way, a research worker in medicine does not recount what others have considered to be cures for a disease, but instead seeks well founded conclusions that supplement, back up, or stand in opposition to what others have considered cures.

Third, there is a branch of ethics that surveys normative ethic with the intent of clarifying its problems and its terminology, and with the intent, in particular, of examining the sorts of reasons by which its conclusions can be supported. It is called "analytical" ethics though it also goes under alternative names such as "meta-ethics" and "critical" ethics. Socrates was engaged in analytical ethics when he asked, for instance, whether virtue is knowledge, whether virtue, like knowledge, can be taught. It is

accordingly an old branch of the subject; and writers on normative ethics have rarely been content to ignore it, simply because normative ethic has been thought to need the near-logical discipline that analytical ethics has sought to provide....

The need of such a specialized approach to ethics is readily seen when we say that so and so is good, etc., we usually try to avoid dogmatism by giving reasons for what we say, and in many cases we have a dependable half-knowledge of how to go about this. But we are not always aware of the potential complexity of the reasons, or of the extent to which the reasons we manage to give can be supplemented by further reasons. Nor do we clearly understand just what is involved in saying that our reasons "justify" our conclusions. An analytical study, temporarily letting us see our issues in a neutral perspective, is needed to provide us with something rather more than this sort of half-knowledge—doing so not by attempting to give further support to some given conclusion, but rather by pointing out what general kind of support is possible.

An unanalyzed half-knowledge may have one of two effects. It may lead us to an illusory conviction of having said the last word on a normative issue, this conviction being attended by a contempt for those who fail to see the "obvious cogency" of our arguments. Or it may lead us, when controversies attending our "last word" eventually become discouraging, to a growing conviction that reasoning about ethical matters is never really worthwhile. Such convictions are not easily dispelled; but it is not too much to say, I think, that they spring in good measure from ignorance, and from a kind of ignorance that analytical ethics can hope to correct....

By what methods of argument or inquiry may disagreement about matters of value be resolved? It will be obvious that to whatever extent an argument involves disagreement in belief, it is open to the usual methods of the sciences. If these methods are the only rational methods for supporting beliefs— as I believe to be so, but cannot now take time to discuss—then scientific methods are the only rational methods for resolving the disagreement in belief that arguments about values may include.

From C. L. Stevenson, *Facts and Values* (New Haven, CT: Yale University Press, 1963), pp. v–vii; 6–8; 16–18; 21, 23–25.

But if science is granted an undisputed sway in reconciling beliefs, it does not thereby acquire, without qualification, an undisputed sway in reconciling attitudes. We have seen that arguments about values include disagreement in attitude, no less than disagreement in belief, and that in certain ways the disagreement in attitude predominates. By what methods shall the latter sort of disagreement be resolved?

The methods of science are still available for that purpose, but only in an indirect way. Initially, these methods have only to do with establishing agreement in belief. If they serve further to establish agreement in attitude, that will be due simply to the psychological fact that altered beliefs may cause altered attitudes. Hence scientific methods are conclusive in ending arguments about values only to the extent that their success in obtaining agreement in belief will in turn lead to agreement in attitude.

In other words, the extent to which scientific methods can bring about agreement on values depends on the extent to which a commonly accepted body of scientific beliefs would cause us to have a commonly accepted set of attitudes.

How much is the development of science likely to achieve, then, with regard to values? To what extent would common beliefs lead to common attitudes? It is, perhaps, a pardonable enthusiasm to hope that science will do everything—to hope that in some rosy future, when all men know the consequences of their acts, they will all have common aspirations and live peaceably in complete moral accord. But if we speak not from our enthusiastic hopes but from our present knowledge, the answer must be far less exciting. We usually do not know, at the beginning of any argument about values, whether an agreement in belief, scientifically established, will lead to an agreement in attitude or not. It is logically possible, at least, that two men should continue to disagree in attitude even though they had all their beliefs in common, and even though neither had made any logical or inductive error, or omitted any relevant evidence. Differences in temperament, or in early training, or in social status, might make the men retain different attitudes even

though both were possessed of the complete scientific truth. Whether this logical possibility is an empirical likelihood I shall not presume to say; but it is unquestionably a possibility that must not be left out of account.

...I conclude, therefore, that scientific methods cannot be guaranteed the definite role in the so-called normative sciences that they may have in the natural sciences. Apart from a heuristic assumption to the contrary, it is possible that the growth of scientific knowledge may leave many disputes about values permanently unsolved. Should these disputes persist, there are nonrational methods for dealing with them, of course, such as impassioned, moving oratory. But the purely intellectual methods of science, and, indeed, all methods of reasoning, may be insufficient to settle disputes about values even though they may greatly help to do so. For the same reasons I conclude that normative ethics is not a branch of any science. It deliberately deals with a type of disagreement that science deliberately avoids. Ethics is not psychology, for instance; for although psychologists may, of course, agree or disagree in belief about attitudes, they need not, as psychologists, be concerned with whether they agree or disagree with one another in attitude. Insofar as normative ethics draws from the sciences, in order to change attitudes via changing people's beliefs, it draws from all the sciences; but a moralist's peculiar aim—that of redirecting attitudes—is a type of activity, rather than knowledge, and falls within no science. Science may study that activity and may help indirectly to forward it; but is not identical with that activity.

I can take only a brief space to explain why the ethical terms, such as "good," "wrong," "ought," and so on, are so habitually used to deal with disagreement in attitude. On account of their repeated occurrence in emotional situations they have acquired a strong emotive meaning. This emotive meaning makes them serviceable in initiating changes in a hearer's attitudes. Sheer emotive impact is not likely, under many circumstances, to change attitudes in any permanent way; but it begins a process that can then be supported by other means....

II. THE EMOTIVE MEANING OF ETHICAL TERMS

... [Some traditional] theories hold that ethical statements are *descriptive* of the existing state of interests—that they simply *give information* about interests. (More accurately, ethical judgments are said to describe what the state of interests is, was, or will be, or to indicate what the state of interests *would* be under specified circumstances.) It is this emphasis on description, on information, which leads to their incomplete relevance. Doubtless there is always *some* element of description in ethical judgments, but this is by no means all. Their major use is not to indicate facts, but to *create an influence*. Instead of merely describing people's interests, they *change* or *intensify* them. They recommend an interest in an object, rather than state that the interest already exists.

For instance: When you tell a man that he oughtn't to steal, your object isn't merely to let him know that people disapprove of stealing. You are attempting, rather, to get *him* to disapprove of it. Your ethical judgment has a quasi-imperative force which, operating through suggestion, and intensified by your tone of voice, readily permits you to begin to *influence*, to *modify*, his interests. If in the end you do not succeed in getting *him* to disapprove of stealing, you will feel that you've failed to convince him that stealing is wrong. You will continue to feel this, even though he fully acknowledges that you disapprove of it, and that almost everyone else does. When you point out to him the consequences of his actions—consequences which you suspect he already disapproves of—these *reasons* which support your ethical judgment are simply a means of facilitating your influence. If you think you can change his interests by making vivid to him how others will disapprove of him, you will do so; otherwise not. So the consideration about other people's interest is just an additional means you may employ, in order to move him, and is not a part of the ethical judgment itself. Your ethical judgment doesn't merely describe interests to him, it directs his very interests. The difference between the traditional interest theories and my view is like the difference between describing a desert and irrigating it....

Thus ethical terms are *instruments* used in the complicated interplay and readjustment of human interests. This can be seen plainly from more general observations. People from widely separated communities have different moral attitudes. Why? To a great extent because they have been subject to different social influences. Now clearly this influence doesn't operate through sticks and stones alone; words play a great part. People praise one another, to encourage certain inclinations, and blame one another, to discourage others. Those of forceful personalities issue commands which weaker people, for complicated instinctive reasons, find it difficult to disobey, quite apart from fears of consequences. Further influence is brought to bear by writers and orators. Thus social influence is exerted, to an enormous extent, by means that have nothing to do with physical force or material reward. The ethical terms facilitate such influence. Being suited for use in *suggestion*, they are a means by which men's attitudes may be led this way or that. The reason, then, that we find a greater similarity in the moral attitudes of one community than in those of different communities is largely this: ethical judgments propagate themselves. One man says "This is good"; this may influence the approval of another person, who then makes the same ethical judgment, which in turn influences another person, and so on. In the end, by a process of mutual influence, people take up more or less the same attitudes. Between people of widely separated communities, of course, the influence is less strong; hence different communities have different attitudes....

The emotive meaning of a word is a tendency of a word, arising through the history of its usage, to produce (result from) *affective* responses in people. It is the immediate aura of feeling which hovers about a word. Such tendencies to produce affective responses cling to words very tenaciously. It would be difficult, for instance, to express merriment by using the interjection "alas". Because of the persistence of such affective tendencies (among other reasons) it becomes feasible to classify them as "meanings"....

...Consider the case of a mother who says to her several children, "One thing is certain, *we all like to be neat*". If she really believed this, she wouldn't bother to say so. But she is not using the words descriptively. She is *encouraging* the children to like neatness. By telling them that they like neatness, she will lead them to *make* her statement true, so to speak. If, instead of saying "We all like to be neat" in this way, she had said "It's a good thing to be neat", the effect would have been approximately the same....

Strictly speaking, then, it is impossible to define "good" in terms of favourable interest if emotive meaning is not to be distorted. Yet it is possible to say that "This is good" is *about* the favourable interest of the speaker and the hearer or hearers, and that it has a pleasing emotive meaning which fits the words for use in suggestion. This is a rough description of meaning, not a definition. But it serves the same clarifying function that a definition ordinarily does; and that, after all, is enough.

A word must be added about the moral use of "good". This differs from the above in that it is about a different kind of interest. Instead of being about what the hearer and speaker *like*, it is about a stronger sort of approval. When a person *likes* something, he is pleased when it prospers, and disappointed when it doesn't. When a person *morally approves* of something, he experiences a rich feeling of security when it prospers, and is indignant, or "shocked" when it doesn't. These are rough and inaccurate examples of the many factors which one would have to mention in distinguishing the two kinds of interest. In the moral usage, as well as in the non-moral, "good" has an emotive meaning which adapts it to suggestion.

REVIEW EXERCISES

1. Determine whether the following statements about the nature of ethics are true or false. Explain your answers.
   a. Ethics is the study of why people act in certain ways.
   b. The solution to moral conflicts and ethical disputes is to accurately describe the way the world actually is.
   c. The statement "Most people believe that cheating is wrong" is an ethical evaluation of cheating.
2. Label the following statements as either *normative* (N) or *descriptive* (D). If normative, label each as *ethics* (E), *aesthetics* (A), *law* (L), *religion* (R), or *custom* (C).
   a. One ought to respect one's elders because it is one of God's commandments.
   b. Twice as many people today, as compared to ten years ago, believe that the death penalty is morally justified in some cases.
   c. It would be wrong to put an antique chair in a modern room.
   d. People do not always do what they believe to be right.

   e. I ought not to turn left here because the sign says "No Left Turn."
   f. We ought to adopt a universal health insurance policy because everyone has a right to health care.
3. Discuss the differences between the ideas that ethics is subjective and that it is objective.
4. Explain emotivism and intuitionism in ethical theory.
5. Discuss the advantages and disadvantages of using naturalistic explanations in ethics.
6. As they occur in the following statements, label the reasons for the conclusion as appeals to the *motive* (M), the *act* (A), or the *consequences* (C).
   a. Although you intended well, what you did was bad because it caused more harm than good.
   b. We ought always to tell the truth to others because they have a right to know the truth.
   c. Although it did turn out badly, you did not want that, and thus you should not be judged harshly for what you caused.

MindTap® For more chapter resources and activities, go to MindTap.

2

Religion and Global Ethics

Learning Outcomes

After reading this chapter, you should be able to:

- Describe the challenge of developing a global ethical perspective.
- Explain the idea of universal human rights.
- Define key terms: cosmopolitan, civil disobedience, pluralism, secularism, humanism, and Eurocentrism.
- Evaluate the divine command theory of ethics.

- Differentiate between humanistic and religious approaches to ethics.
- Apply the argument made in Plato's *Euthyphro*.
- Defend your own ideas about ethics, religion, and global cultural diversity.

MindTap® For more chapter resources and activities, go to MindTap.

We live in an increasingly integrated world. With the click of the mouse, you can instantly interact with people from a variety of cultures and religions. It is inspiring to see how well we human beings get along despite our differences. But we should also admit that diversity—especially religious diversity—can create tension and difficulty.

Religious tension has become a major concern. Religious fundamentalists of various denominations have asserted the supremacy of their preferred religious texts, traditions, and interpretations. Politicians have asserted claims of cultural and religious supremacy. Some religious people have resorted to violence in defense of their faith. Other religious people proclaim that religion ought to be tolerant and peaceful, despite the intolerance of some radicals.

One solution to religious tension is respect for persons grounded on basic claims about human rights, including the right to freedom of religious belief (we discuss human rights in more detail in Chapter 7). The idea of religious freedom is enshrined in the First Amendment to the Constitution of the United States. Religious freedom is also featured in international agreements and institutions. In 1948, the United Nation's member nations ratified the Universal Declaration of Human Rights, which lays out a set of basic moral principles. The nations of the world are supposed to share these principles despite our vast cultural, religious, and political differences.

The preamble to the UN Declaration begins by affirming the "inherent dignity" and "inalienable rights" of all members of the human family. It explains that disregard for these rights has resulted in barbarous acts that outrage the moral conscience of mankind. It continues, "the advent of a world in which human beings shall enjoy freedom of speech and belief and freedom from fear and want has been proclaimed as the highest aspiration of the common people." It goes on to state that the purpose of the United Nations is to promote universal respect for human rights and fundamental freedoms.[1]

The UN Declaration aims for global agreement about basic rights, the inherent dignity of human beings, and equal rights for men and women, with the broader goals of fostering world peace and harmony. As ongoing religious and cultural disputes illustrate, however, there are outstanding disagreements about the nature of these basic rights. The UN document asserts the importance of freedom of speech and freedom of religion. Article 18 of the UN Declaration explicitly states, "Everyone has the right to freedom of thought, conscience and religion; this right includes freedom to change his religion or belief, and freedom, either alone or in community with others and in public or private, to manifest his religion or belief in teaching, practice, worship and observance."

But does freedom of speech run up against a limit when such speech defames important religious figures (say, when a cartoonist draws a caricature of a saint or prophet)? Does freedom of speech hit a limit when such speech advocates for practices and social arrangements that are viewed by religious people as immoral (say, when it advocates abortion, gay marriage, or other practices that some religious people reject)? In some parts of the world, freedom of religion is viewed as leading to apostasy and blasphemy, which is a punishable offense. In previous centuries, Christians burned witches and heretics alive. And today, according to some interpretations of Islam, blasphemy and apostasy are punishable by death. One famous example of this is the *fatwa* or religious decree announced by the Iranian cleric and supreme leader Ayatollah Ruhollah Khomeini,

which called for the death of novelist Salman Rushdie in 1989 for writing a novel the Ayatollah considered blasphemous. Meanwhile major political candidates, such as Donald Trump, have called for a ban on Muslim immigration to the United States. And some religious leaders, such as the Reverend Franklin Graham, have claimed that Islam is not compatible with American values.[2]

While the example of Islam in the United States has been in the forefront, we should understand that religious diversity is a challenge across the globe. There have been clashes between Sikhs and Hindus in India, between Tibetan Buddhists and Chinese forces in Tibet, and between Israelis and Palestinians. And in previous centuries, Christian sects fought against one another, while Jews were persecuted and exterminated. These examples suggest a serious clash of values, with the basic idea of freedom of expression and respect for religious diversity running up against rigid religious convictions and religious bigotry. Religious differences continue to be flashpoints for conflict. From some religious perspectives, the basic ideas of toleration and freedom of religion may be seen as immoral. It might be that the ideas we find in the First Amendment to the American Constitution or in the UN Declaration only make sense within the context of Western secular democracies. Are these values shared by people who adhere to Buddhism, Confucianism, Islam, or other traditions in the world's vast array of faiths? And which set of values is more fundamental: the secular value of respect for religious liberty or the sectarian values that are dear to the religious faithful?

This points to the important question of how ethics relates to religion. While recent events continue to bring these matters to the forefront, there are deep historical precedents for this discussion. Socrates—the father of the Western philosophical tradition—ran into trouble with the religious and political authorities of Athens. Socrates asked people how they defined moral terms, trying to understand ideas such as justice, courage, love, and friendship. But his philosophical inquiries were tinged with skepticism. He questioned traditional religion, traditional political authority, and conventional wisdom.

He called himself a "gadfly," by which he meant that he buzzed around Athens, nipping at and probing things. He believed that his effort would help Athenians understand morality and help to make them virtuous. Many Athenians found Socrates to be offensive and even immoral. Some viewed him as a dangerously subversive figure. Eventually, he was brought to court and formally charged with not believing in the gods of the city and with corrupting its youth. Many suspected him of being an atheist. As a result, he was sentenced to death.

FREEDOM, COSMOPOLITANISM, AND THE EUROPEAN ENLIGHTENMENT

The story of Socrates demonstrates the inherently controversial nature of philosophical inquiry and the complicated relationship between philosophy and religion. If it is difficult for us to imagine how Socrates could have been sentenced to death for asking questions about Athenian morality and religion, it is because we are used to extensive freedom when it comes to religion and morality. Americans like to believe that our freedom is unique—a product of a distinctly Western tradition of tolerance and pluralism. However, we should be careful when making sweeping generalizations about history. There have been many tolerant and open-minded epochs in the history of the world. The Buddhist emperor Ashoka is known for sponsoring a tolerant regime, as is the Muslim emperor Akbar. And under Confucianism, China was tolerant toward a variety of religious perspectives. We forget that China proclaimed an "Edict of Toleration" in 1692, which permitted Christian missionary work—at around the same time that Protestants were still being persecuted in Europe. Indeed, at the time, the philosopher Leibniz and other Europeans praised China and Confucianism for its open and tolerant spirit.

World history includes a number of free thinkers—both within the lineage that follows after Socrates and in others of the world's traditions. Nonetheless, much of our terminology for understanding these sorts of issues is rooted in Western thinking. The terms *philosophy*, *politics*, and *ethics* come to us from the Greek language. And we still tend to tell a Eurocentric or Western-focused story about the development of tolerance, liberty, and individual rights.

That standard story often begins with Socrates, his trial and execution, and the development of his ideas by his student, Plato, and Plato's student, Aristotle. One of Socrates's other followers was Diogenes the Cynic, a free spirit who refused to conform to social conventions and had an antagonistic relationship with the authorities of his time. One ancient legend explains that when Alexander the Great was a young man, about to embark on his conquest of the ancient world, he went to see Diogenes, who was lounging in the sun. After demanding that the young prince stop blocking his sunbath, Diogenes asked Alexander what he was up to. Alexander explained that he was about to depart with his armies to conquer the world. Diogenes asked, "Then what?" and Alexander said that he supposed he would relax after that. Diogenes said, "Why not sit in the sun with me now and relax, and save yourself all of the trouble?" When the astonished Alexander asked Diogenes where he was from, Diogenes replied, "I am a cosmopolitan," which means a citizen of the world.

In this anecdote, Diogenes displays skepticism toward conventional authority, while asserting his freedom and claiming independence from any particular nation or culture—values that we have come to associate with the Western philosophical approach. This approach emphasizes individual freedom over traditional hierarchies and universal morality over local customs and traditions. Like Diogenes, it makes a **cosmopolitan** claim: it aspires for a single moral community of humanity not bound by national, cultural, or, in many cases, religious traditions. And it questions many things we take for granted. Why do we salute superior officers? Why do we drive on the right? Why do we eat with knives and forks? Or, for that matter, why do we adopt certain religious beliefs and practices rather than others? Is it simply a matter of where and to whom we were born?

While it is true that there are a variety of differences across the globe, including vast religious differences, the cosmopolitan perspective holds that certain ethical principles are universally valuable, such as respect for life and for liberty. In the Western world, we have institutionalized these ideas in the laws of the modern nation state. And a growing body of international law, including the UN Declaration, emphasizes a set of basic ideas about individual liberties and human rights.

Although we've noted that toleration and freedom are not uniquely Western values, the usual historical account emphasizes the development of these values during the seventeenth and eighteenth centuries in Europe. This era is known as **the Enlightenment**. It is the period during which many of the philosophers we'll discuss in the book were active: Locke, Hume, Kant, Bentham, and others. These philosophers tended to think that liberty and tolerance were key values. They were optimistic that history was developing in a progressive direction. They thought that progress would occur through the employment of human reason. And they were interested in discovering common values and learning from other cultures. Also during this time, many philosophical ideas were put into practice in revolutionary politics, as was the case in the American and French revolutions.

The American Revolution can be seen to begin with a famous phrase from the Declaration of Independence: "We hold these truths to be self-evident, that all men are created equal, that they are endowed by their Creator with certain unalienable Rights, that among these are Life, Liberty and the pursuit of Happiness." Drawing on the natural law tradition as developed by John Locke (see Chapter 7), the Declaration enshrines individual liberties at the core of American society. The Constitution of the United States goes further, detailing areas of individual liberty upon which government must not intrude. The most important example, for our purposes, is the First Amendment to the Constitution, which reads, "Congress shall make no law respecting an establishment of religion, or prohibiting the free exercise thereof; or abridging the freedom of speech, or of the press; or the right of the people peaceably to assemble, and to petition the Government for a redress of grievances." The First Amendment makes religious

liberty the law of the land (in the so-called "free exercise" clause), while also prohibiting government from getting involved in religion (in the so-called "establishment clause"). The American system can thus be seen to explicitly reject the kind of society that executed Socrates, where an "established" state religion allowed the authorities to punish (by death) speech perceived to be blasphemous. We've come a long way from ancient Athens.

It should not be surprising that philosophers emphasize individual liberty. Philosophical speculation involves wide-ranging inquiry into an ever-expanding set of topics. We cannot philosophize properly unless we are free to question, argue, and think. Nor is it surprising that philosophical reflection on morality points in a cosmopolitan direction. When Jefferson claims that "all men are created equal," he implies that inalienable rights—of life, liberty, and the pursuit of happiness—are the endowment of all people, from all cultures (despite the sexist language that uses the word "men" for what we should properly call "humanity").

A quick glance at world history or today's paper makes it clear that no such consensus exists. For a long time, even in the United States, there was a substantial disagreement about whether all "men" really were created equal, with slavery, racism, and sexism as obvious problems. Even after slavery was abolished, we continued to disagree about the status of women. In the global context, these issues are far from resolved.

Philosophical freedom can lead to conflicts with authority, especially religious authorities. At around the same time that the American revolutionaries were fighting in the name of liberty, the German philosopher Immanuel Kant defined enlightenment in terms of freedom. He thought that progress would occur when we were permitted freedom to argue and when we were courageous enough to use this freedom to imagine ways to improve society. Kant wrote,

> Enlightenment is man's emergence from his self-incurred immaturity. Immaturity is the inability to use one's own understanding without the guidance of another. This immaturity is self-incurred if its cause is

not lack of understanding, but lack of resolution and courage to use it without the guidance of another. The motto of enlightenment is therefore: *Sapere Aude!* (dare to know) "Have courage to use your own understanding!"[3]

Kant thought that history would develop in a cosmopolitan direction, with European nations forming a confederation based upon shared moral ideas. This federation—an idea that foreshadowed the development of the United Nations—would ensure perpetual peace. It would take two long centuries of war and misery for Europe and the rest of the world to finally achieve Kant's idea. And the idea still seems a bit naive, given remaining cultural and religious differences across the globe.

RELIGION, CIVIC LIFE, AND CIVIL DISOBEDIENCE

Like Socrates, Kant advocated gradual reform through public argument about morality, politics, and religion. This philosophical approach can seem naive when faced with entrenched and powerful unjust systems, such as slavery, serfdom, colonialism, and apartheid. What if the rulers simply have no interest in listening to the ruled?

After Kant, a variety of thinkers and activists—from Henry David Thoreau to Mohandas K. Gandhi to Martin Luther King, Jr.—concluded that principled resistance to an unjust system required something more than argument. Rather than advocate the violent overthrow of the regime, these thinkers called for **civil disobedience**, the open, nonviolent refusal to obey unjust law, with the intent of accepting the penalty and arousing the conscience of the community as a whole. King developed his ideas about nonviolent civil disobedience from Gandhi, the Indian political activist and religious leader who advocated **ahimsa** (or nonviolence) as a key to the struggle for Indian independence. King also drew inspiration from Jesus and from Socrates. King argues in his "Letter from Birmingham Jail" that Socrates and other philosophers are gadflies who nonviolently point out conflicts within society. In King's era, those conflicts had a lot to do with racial injustice. In a sense, King is an heir to the Enlightenment dream,

by which individuals and societies strive to achieve moral maturity through rational inquiry. Like Socrates, King expresses faith in logical questioning of accepted dogmas as a means of overcoming injustice. And like Kant, King also sees his efforts in explicitly cosmopolitan terms, as a quest for universal justice. But King combined philosophical critique with nonviolent civil disobedience. It is important to note, however, that advocates of civil disobedience criticize existing traditions and institutions while also demonstrating a kind of loyalty to those traditions and institutions: they break the law—and accept punishment—as a way of pointing out injustices and failures in the system. The critical stance and civil disobedience of the civil rights movement was not merely negative. It had the positive goal of helping the United States realize the full promise of its founding documents, while remaining faithful to the moral ideals of American political, moral, and religious ideology.

Martin Luther King Jr. in his Atlanta office, standing in front of a portrait of Mohandas K. Gandhi.

This last point is particularly important to bear in mind as we consider the relationship between philosophical inquiry and religious traditions and institutions. Sometimes, it might seem that the most serious impediment to free-ranging philosophical criticism is religion—especially those forms of religious belief that want to limit freedom in the name of conformity to the will of God. With regard to morality, it is often thought that what is required is obedience to God's commandments, his laws, his prophets, and the institutions that have developed to defend and disseminate the faith. (We will hear more about this view of morality in the next section.) And it may seem that philosophy has nothing to offer a faith-centered worldview, that it has no interest in the sacred, and views human life in exclusively secular terms. (A recent survey of nearly one thousand philosophers indicates that 15 percent of the philosophers surveyed accept or lean toward *theism* [belief in the existence of god or gods], while 73 percent accept or lean toward atheism.[4])

But such a stark opposition between philosophy and religion ignores that, for most of human history, the two subjects have been deeply intertwined or even indistinguishable. Both are concerned with the most fundamental questions of human existence: Why are we here? What is the meaning of life? How should we treat one another? And both have frequently challenged ruling powers and conventional ways of thinking. The example of Martin Luther King is a case in point; King was a devout Baptist minister who also thought that philosophical critique was necessary to make moral progress. King drew his primary inspiration from Jesus's teachings on poverty, tolerance, and love. King also valued Socrates's example. It is not necessarily true that philosophical ethics is atheistic or opposed to religious belief. The philosophers mentioned here— Socrates, Locke, and Kant—remained committed to some form of theistic belief.

Religion remains at the center of many of the applied ethical topics that we will discuss later in this text: same-sex marriage, euthanasia, abortion, the status of women, the death penalty, to name a few. Religious perspectives on such topics are not easy to categorize as "liberal" or "conservative." Religion is not one thing. There are a variety of sects and denominations, just as there are a variety of religious people who belong to these sects and denominations. And this reminds us of the importance of religious liberty. Religious liberty along with the freedom of philosophical inquiry is essential in a world that includes a wide variety of people who disagree about religious, political, and moral questions.

ETHICS, RELIGION, AND DIVINE COMMAND THEORY

Many people get their ethical or moral views from their religion. Although religions include other elements, most do have explicit or implicit requirements or ideals for moral conduct. In some cases, they contain explicit rules or commandments: "Honor thy father and mother" and "Thou shalt not kill." Some religions recognize and revere saints or holy people who provide models for us and exemplify virtues we should emulate. And most religions have a long history of internal arguments and interpretations about the nature and content of moral law.

Most contemporary philosophers, however, believe that ethics does not necessarily require a religious grounding. Rather than relying on holy books or religious revelations, philosophical ethics uses reason and experience to determine what is good and bad, right and wrong, better and worse. In fact, even those people for whom morality is religiously based may want to examine some of their views using reason. They may want to examine various interpretations of their religious principles for internal consistency or coherence. Or they may want to know whether elements of their religious morality— some of its rules, for example—are good or valid ones given that other people have different views of what is right and wrong, and given that the problems of contemporary times may be different from those of the past.

If right and wrong can only be grounded in religious belief, then nonbelievers could not be said to have moral views or make legitimate moral arguments. But even religious believers should want to be able to engage in constructive dialogue with nonbelievers and evaluate their claims. In fact, even religious believers regularly make moral judgments that are not based strictly on their religious views but rather on reflection and common sense.

Thinking further about religious morality also raises challenges to it. A key element of many religious moralities is the view that certain things are good for us to do because this is what God wants. This conception is often referred to as the **divine command theory**. The idea is that certain actions are right because they are what God wills for us. The reading at the end of this chapter from Plato's dialogue *Euthyphro* examines this view. In this dialogue, Socrates asks whether things are good because they are approved by the gods or whether the gods approve of them because they are good. To say that actions are good simply because they are willed or approved by the gods or God seems to make morality arbitrary. God could decree anything to be good—lying or treachery, for example. It seems more reasonable to say that lying and treachery are bad, and for this reason, the gods or God condemns or disapproves of them and that we should also. One implication of this view is that morality has a certain independence; if so, we should be able to determine whether certain actions are right or wrong in themselves and for what reason.

This argument does not imply, however, that religion cannot provide a motivation or inspiration to be moral. Many believe that if life has some eternal significance in relation to a supreme and most perfect being, then we ought to take life and morality extremely seriously. This is not to say that the only reason religious persons have for being moral or doing the morally right thing is so that they will be rewarded in some life beyond this one. Such a view might be seen to undermine morality, since it suggests that we should be good only if we are "bribed" to do so. Rather, if something is morally right, then this is itself a reason for doing it. Thus, the good and conscientious person is the one who wants to do right simply because it is right.

Questions about the meaning of life, however, often play a significant role in a person's thoughts about the moral life. Some people might even think that atheists have no reason to be moral or to be concerned with doing the morally right thing. However, this is not necessarily so. For example, a religious person may be inclined to disregard the moral stakes of what occurs in this life if he or she thinks of it as fleeting and less important than the afterlife. And an atheist who believes that this life is all there is may in fact take this life more seriously and care more about living morally. Furthermore, religious and nonreligious people live together in contemporary society and have pressing practical reasons to think clearly and reason well about morality.

For at least three reasons, we should all seek to develop our moral reasoning skills. First, we should be able to evaluate critically our own or other views of what is thought to be good and bad or just and unjust, including religious views. Second, believers of various denominations as well as nonbelievers ought to be able to discuss moral matters together. Third, the fact that many of us live in organized secular communities, cities, states, and countries requires that we be able to develop and rely on widely shared reason-based views on issues of justice, fairness, and moral ideals. This is especially true in political communities with some separation of church and state, where no state religion is mandated, and where one has freedom to practice a chosen religion or practice no religion at all. In these settings, it is important to have nonreligiously based ways of dealing with moral issues. This is one goal of philosophical ethics.

The Russian novelist Fyodor Dostoevsky provides the kernel of one argument that is often used in defense of divine command ethics. Dostoevsky's writings contain the famous claim that, "If God is dead, then everything is permissible."[5] This expresses the worry that if there were no God, then there would be no morality. There are two concerns here: one about religion as the source of morality and another about religion as providing a motivation for morality. The first concern is that without God as a source for morality, there would be no eternal, absolute, or objective basis for morality. We will deal with the first worry in more detail in Chapter 3 when we consider *relativism*—which is the claim that there are no eternal, absolute, or objective values. Theists often hold that God is the source of moral law, provided through the words of a prophet, such as Moses, who receives the moral law directly from God. Some theists worry that if that prophetic origin of morality is denied, we are left without any objective moral principles. Most of the rest of the first half of this book focuses on providing an account of values that avoids this criticism; the ethical theories we will study try to provide reasons and justifications for ethical principles without reference to God.

The second concern is that without a divine judge who gives out punishments and rewards in the afterlife, there would be no motivation to be ethical. A version of this concern led Kant to postulate God and immortality as necessary for morality—so that we might at least hope that moral actions would be rewarded (and immoral actions would be punished) in an afterlife. In response, atheists might argue that the demands, rewards, and punishments of human social life are sufficient to provide motivation to be ethical. We turn to the issue of motivation in our discussion of egoism in Chapter 4. In that chapter, we consider a story from Plato about Gyges, a man who can literally get away with murder. If you were able to do whatever you wanted without fear of getting caught, would you commit immoral deeds? Or do you think that we need some idea of a God who observes our deeds and punishes us or rewards us accordingly?

One of the most important problems for defenders of divine command ethics is the fact of religious diversity. Even if we agree with Dostoevsky that God is required for ethics, we still have to figure out which God or religious story is the one that provides the correct teaching about morality. Saying that ethics is based in religion does not really help us that much because we must also determine which religion is the correct one. Given the incredible amount of religious diversity in the world, it is easy to see that the divine command approach is not really very helpful without a much broader inquiry into the truth of various religions.

Pope Francis and the Dalai Lama represent the wide range of religious diversity in the world.

The problem of diversity holds even within specific religious traditions. This problem was recognized at the time of Socrates and Plato. Plato asks us to consider which versions of the Greek religious stories are the correct or proper ones. The same consideration applies to contemporary religions. Not only do we have to determine which religion is correct, we also have to determine which version of this religion is the correct one. Consider, for example, that Christianity includes a range of denominations: Eastern Orthodox, Roman Catholic, and Protestant (which includes a range of groups from Mennonites and Quakers to Methodists, Presbyterians, and Southern Baptists). Similar diversity can be found within Islam, Judaism, and the religious traditions that come out of South Asia. Even if we think that ethics comes from God, how can we decide which account of God's commands is the correct one? The philosophical approach reminds us that we would have to use reason and experience—including especially our own human insight into ethics—to decide among the world's religious traditions.

PLURALISM AND THE GOLDEN RULE

One approach to resolving the problem of diversity is to look for common ground among the world's cultural and religious traditions. This general idea is known as **religious pluralism**. A more specific philosophical view is often called **value pluralism**, which argues that there are multiple and conflicting goods in the world, which cannot be reduced to some other good. (We will discuss pluralism again when we deal with relativism in Chapter 3.) Pluralists about religion often make a different sort of argument. Religious pluralists, such as John Hick, claim that there is a common core of ideas found among the world's religious traditions. As Hick puts it, quoting the Islamic poet Rumi, "the lamps are many, but the light is one."[6]

The usual candidate for this common core among religions is something like the **Golden Rule**: "Do unto others as you would have them do unto you" or "treat others as you would like to be treated." Many people have claimed that each of the world's religious and cultural systems includes something

like the Golden Rule. John Hick argues that, "all the great traditions teach the moral ideal of generous goodwill, love, compassion, epitomized in the Golden Rule."[7] The Tibetan Buddhist leader, the Dalai Lama, put it this way: "All of the different religious faiths, despite their philosophical differences, have a similar objective. Every religion emphasizes human improvement, love, respect for others, sharing other people's suffering. On these lines every religion has more or less the same viewpoint and the same goal."[8] The reading from Gandhi that follows at the end of this chapter makes a similar point. The religious pluralist idea is a friendly and optimistic one; it hopes to be able to reconcile the world's religious traditions around an ethical core. Indeed, there is some evidence for such a convergence in the existence of interfaith organizations that promote

In this image, American painter Norman Rockwell imagined that the common idea of all the world's cultures and religions was the Golden Rule: *Do unto others as you would have them do unto you."*

religious diversity and pluralism. One example of this is the Parliament of the World's Religions, which is a group dedicated to creating peaceful and harmonious relations between the world's religions.

Unfortunately, this hopeful reconciliation must ignore much; the very deep differences that exist among religions, the fact of apparently immoral elements in some of the world's religious traditions, the reality of religious conflict, and the moral importance of our deep differences over metaphysical questions. As religion scholar Stephen Prothero suggests, the idea that all religions are basically the same "is a lovely sentiment but it is dangerous, disrespectful, and untrue."[9]

Consider for example, the Hindu idea of *dharma*, which is a complex concept that refers to laws of natural order, justice, propriety, and harmony. The idea of dharma is connected to the traditional Indian caste system. Now there are parallels between the idea of destiny and caste in India and medieval Christian ideas about natural law and the great chain of being. But the differences between these ideas are as important as the similarities. The end goal of Hindu ethics is to attain some form of self-realization and connection with the eternal soul of Brahman. While this may sound like the kind of insight and beatification (or holiness) that occurs in Christian unity with God, the differences are again quite important. Other differences and similarities exist among the world's traditions. For example, Islam emphasizes *zakat,* or alms-giving, as one of its five pillars. This includes a universal duty to build a just society, help the poor, and eliminate oppression. While this sounds quite a bit like the idea of charity and tithing in the Christian tradition, *zakat* may be more important and more obligatory than mere charity—closer to a tax than a gift. And so on. The differences are as important and pervasive as the similarities among the world's traditions.

Optimistic religious pluralists want to reduce all of these differences to common values such as love, compassion, and the Golden Rule. But it is easy to see that religious ethics is not simply about love and compassion. If all the world's religions agree about compassion, love, and the Golden Rule, then how do we explain holy wars and religious violence? If all religions are basically variations on the theme of love and compassion, then how do we explain religious texts and ideas that are not very compassionate? Would a purely compassionate and loving God destroy the earth with a flood, threaten punishment in Hell, or require gruesome tests of faith? Would compassionate and loving religious believers stone adulterers and homosexuals and burn witches alive? While interpreters of religion can explain these things in various ways, the specific details of religious ethics matter as much as the general principle of compassion or love.

THE PROBLEM OF EVIL AND FREE WILL

A further ethical question arises in the context of thinking about religion and ethics: the **problem of evil**. This issue provides a concrete example of the problem of religious diversity, since different religions will deal with the problem of evil in different ways. How do we explain the presence of suffering and evil in the world? Buddhists explain that life is characterized by suffering, or *dukha*. They explain that suffering comes from attachment to the fleeting goods of this world and from wrongful actions. Christians also struggle with the problem of evil. But for Christians, the existence of evil creates a metaphysical problem. How can evil exist in a world that is supposedly created by a benevolent and all-powerful God? The Christian tradition developed elaborate **theodicies**, or arguments that attempt to justify God as all-powerful and all-knowing, despite the problem of evil. Important thinkers such as Augustine and Leibniz responded to this problem by focusing on sin and on freedom of the will. For Augustine, **original sin** is passed down from Adam to the rest of us. Leibniz clarifies that God provided us with free will so that we might choose between good and evil and argues that the best of all possible worlds is one that contains both freedom and the related possibility of evil.

Humanistic philosophers have subjected these sorts of disputes to skeptical criticism. How do we know that all life is suffering and that suffering is caused by attachment? How do we know that there is a God, that this God created freedom, and that original sin is passed down? The metaphysical complexities introduced by religion point toward mysteries and paradoxes that give humanistic philosophers reasons to be skeptical.

Consider the question of free will. If we are not free, then we are not responsible for our actions—in which case, the enterprise of moral philosophy begins to seem shaky. As the well-known atheist author Sam Harris explains,

> Morality, law, politics, religion, public policy, intimate relationships, feelings of guilt and personal accomplishment—most of what is distinctly human about our lives seems to depend upon our viewing one another as autonomous persons, capable of free choice....Without free will, sinners and criminals would be nothing more than poorly calibrated clockwork, and any conception of justice that emphasized punishment (rather than deterring, rehabilitating, or merely containing them) would appear utterly incongruous.[10]

Despite this admission, Harris denies the idea of free will—based upon natural scientific account of human beings—while still arguing that morality makes sense. (We will read a brief excerpt from Harris regarding religion at the end of this chapter.) Philosophers have pondered the problem of free will for millennia. Some deny that there is free will in an entirely deterministic universe. Others have argued that free will remains compatible with determinism.

Free will is a puzzle even within Christianity, where there are questions about how much freedom we can have in a universe that is created by an omnipotent (all-powerful) and omniscient (all-knowing) God. Different Christian denominations have different ideas about this issue, with some emphasizing the idea of predestination, by which God ordains things in advance, and others responding to this issue differently. Other religions have responded to the problem of free will in a variety of ways. Buddhists and Hindus, for example, appear to believe in free will—although there are differences within these vast and complex traditions. But Buddhists, at least, do not believe in a God who punishes evil. Rather, they believe that suffering results from the laws of *karma,* the law of continuity between causes and effects: bad deeds lead to suffering and good ones lead to reward—whether in this life or the next. Whether the idea of karma is compatible with free will is an open question. The Confucian and Taoist traditions also maintain that human beings have the freedom to choose. But Confucianism holds that such free choices are constrained by destiny or fate, while the Taoists emphasize freedom experienced in harmony with nature. In the Chinese traditions, there is, again, no God who judges or punishes.

As noted, the idea of religious pluralism focuses on the ethical "core" of the world's religions. But it is difficult to see how such radically different ideas could converge. As Stephen Prothero acknowledges, "the world's religious traditions do share many ethical precepts.... The Golden Rule can be found not only in the Christian Bible and the Jewish Talmud but also in Confucian and Hindu books."[11] But the Golden Rule is a very weak common link. Philosophers have also subjected the Golden Rule to criticism. One problem for the Golden Rule is that if it tells us to love our neighbors as ourselves, we need a definition of "neighbors." Does this mean we should love only those who are related to us—our co-religionists, for example? Or do we have obligations to distant human beings and future generations who do not live in our geographic (or temporal) neighborhood? Even if we all accept the Golden Rule as a basic moral starting point, there are still very difficult questions of application. How does the Golden Rule apply to sexual ethics, abortion, euthanasia, or the death penalty? And what does the Golden Rule tell us to do about evil? Should we punish evildoers? Or should we follow Jesus, who explained that in addition to loving our neighbors, we should love our enemies and refrain from returning evil for evil? The problem of responding to wrongdoing and evil is a complex moral issue, one that is subject to multiple interpretations even within specific religious traditions. Different traditions—even different sects and denominations within the same tradition—give divergent answers about these applied ethical issues, including the very deep question of where evil comes from and how we should deal with it.

We will see that the normative theories defended by philosophers also suffer from a similar problem: they appear to conflict and can be applied in various ways. But the conflicts among the different theories in philosophical ethics may be easier to reconcile, since philosophical arguments are usually not subject to the same ambiguities of interpretation and translation that tend to plague ancient scriptural sources.

It may be possible to imagine a pluralistic convergence of the world's religions around certain key moral principles and central human values. However, until this convergence occurs, we will have to find some way to coexist despite our differences. The challenge of coexistence is exacerbated by our growing diversity. As more and different religious people come to share our common life, we have to find some set of values that can allow us to live together even though we disagree about religion.

SECULAR ETHICS AND TOLERATION

The effort to find ways to coexist despite our religious differences gives rise to **secular ethics**. *Secular* means "based in this world or this age" (as opposed to the eternal and otherworldly focus of religion). When we say that an ethical idea or theory is secular, we mean that it is divorced from any source in religion. A secular ethic can develop out of religious conflict, as members of different religious groups agree to coexist despite their differences. Indeed, this is how the secular system that we currently have in the Western world developed through the course of several centuries of religious wars beginning with the Protestant Reformation.

By the end of the seventeenth century, European philosophers of the Enlightenment era were arguing that public **toleration** of religious diversity was necessary. A hallmark of secularism is the idea of freedom of religion and toleration of religious diversity. For many, the progress of **secularization** is a central aspect of modernization: as cultures and polities modernize, they also become more secular. One recent study concludes that secularization "suggests a trend, a general tendency toward a world in which religion matters less and various forms of secular reason and secular institutions matter more. It is a trend that has been expected at least since modernity and has been given quasi-scientific status in sociological studies advancing a secularization thesis."[12] While this same study presents a somewhat critical perspective on the secularization thesis, the idea does help to explain much of recent history, including the spread of secular cosmopolitan ideas such as those we find in the UN document discussed at the outset of this chapter. Of course, in some parts of the world (even in some parts of the United States), religious fundamentalism—whether it be Christian, Muslim, Jewish, Hindu, or the like—still remains a potent force, with some religious leaders arguing for the subordination of women, arguing against scientific naturalism, and trying to defend traditional ideas from previous centuries.

One of the most important philosophical sources for thinking about secularism is John Locke, who is discussed in greater detail in Chapter 7. In the 1680s, Locke published his influential "Letter Concerning Toleration," which has served as an important touchstone. Locke argues that the state should tolerate religious dissenters. For Locke, religious belief must be a matter of inward persuasion, which is not amenable to the use of force. Locke's basic point is that force is simply not effective to produce genuine religious belief. If that's the case, then political efforts to establish conformity of belief by the use of coercion will ultimately be ineffective. Locke goes on to argue that spiritual and civil authorities must operate in wholly different spheres—the former through persuasion and conversion and the latter through laws backed by coercive force. Religions are to be left alone to deal with spiritual issues. And the state is supposed to focus only on issues related to public order. This argument forms the basis of the constitutional doctrine that is often called "separation of church and state."

Locke's ideas had a significant impact on Jefferson and the other founders of the United States—and they have gone on to influence ethical and political thought, including the ideas found in the UN Declaration of Human Rights. The question of toleration and religion has also been taken up by a number of important philosophers. The great American political philosopher John Rawls has argued that societies need to work to develop "overlapping consensus" among people who adhere to divergent religious and moral worldviews. He calls these deeply held worldviews "comprehensive doctrines." According to Rawls, societies should focus on agreement in the political realm, instead of trying to force a deeper agreement about these comprehensive moral and religious ideas. This leads to a theory of political justice that Rawls calls "political liberalism," as well as a basic conception of human rights that emphasizes toleration for religious diversity.

Rawls's goal is to find a way to establish peaceful coexistence in a just society among people who disagree about the highest good. Rawls's solution is to suggest that there can be "overlapping consensus" among people who disagree about religion. This overlapping consensus about political issues would leave us with something like a secular ethic: a system of values and fair rules that can be agreed upon by people who come from quite different religious traditions or by people who have no religion at all. (Rawls's influential theory of justice is discussed in greater detail in Chapters 4 and 14.)

In contrast to Rawls's view, there are some who have a more radical understanding of the term *secular* that equates it with atheism. Some religious people denounce "secular humanism" as nothing more than atheism. One of the most influential proponents of the idea of secular humanism, Paul Kurtz, has worked hard to clarify that secular humanism can remain open to religious believers, even though it is grounded in a nonreligious approach to ethics. Kurtz has recently focused on what he calls "neo-humanism," which is an attempt to reconcile atheists and religious believers around a global ethics. Kurtz's "Neo-Humanist Manifesto" states, "The challenge facing humankind is to recognize the basic ethical principle of planetary civilization—that every person on the planet has equal dignity and value as a person, and this transcends the limits of national, ethnic, religious, racial, or linguistic boundaries or identities."[13] Kurtz's idea hearkens back to the Enlightenment ideal of a cosmopolitan world grounded in shared ethical values.

CRITICISMS OF SECULARISM AND GLOBAL ETHICS

The dream of global consensus around secular principles may seem like an appealing solution to centuries of violent conflict and contention over religion. But it remains an open question as to whether this is possible. One significant problem is that some religious people reject any taint of secularism on doctrinal grounds. For religious believers who think that God requires absolute obedience to his commandments, or that those commandments must be embodied in the laws of the state, a secular ethic that does not explicitly embrace God as the source of morality will appear to be morally suspect and blasphemous.

Such responses can present advocates of tolerance with a problem called the **paradox of toleration**. The paradox revolves around the question of whether there is a good reason to tolerate those who are intolerant or those who reject the very idea of toleration. Some defenders of toleration simply bite the bullet here and admit that there are limits to toleration. Locke, for example, did not extend toleration to atheists or to Catholics. He thought atheists were untrustworthy since they did not believe in God, and he thought that Catholics were too loyal to Rome to be trusted. Although Locke defended toleration, he clearly thought that there were some people who could not be tolerated. We've come a long way since the time of Locke. But the rise of new fundamentalist movements within such religions as Judaism, Christianity, and Islam has posed new challenges for the idea of tolerance. (**Fundamentalism** is characterized by rigid adherence to a literal interpretation of religious doctrines and a reaction against compromise with secularism and modernity.) The political philosopher

Jürgen Habermas argues that "a fundamentalism that leads to a practice of intolerance is incompatible with the democratic constitutional state."[14] He concludes, "in multicultural societies, the national constitution can tolerate only forms of life articulated within the medium of such non-fundamentalist traditions."[15] Habermas is saying that we cannot tolerate those who reject liberal-democratic principles of toleration on fundamentalist religious grounds. Indeed, it is not difficult to imagine circumstances in which religious fundamentalists violate the shared principles of secular ethics. What do we do about religious pacifists who refuse to serve in the military or pay their taxes, pastors who think that it is acceptable for thirteen-year-old girls to be married to older men, or religious communities that mutilate the genitals of their daughters? And what of religious groups who get involved in democratic politics to advance intolerant agendas—or who may be explicitly opposed to democracy itself? In many cases, even those who want to embrace religious diversity will have to say that there are ethical limits to what they are willing to tolerate in terms of religious belief and practice.

A further problem is that secularization, cosmopolitanism, and modernization sometimes appear to spring directly from the post-Reformation philosophy and politics of the West. One charge against secular and cosmopolitan ethics is that it is Eurocentric, meaning that it is an idea that makes sense only within the context of European culture and history. As the sociologist of religion, José Casanova, explains,

> Cosmopolitanism remains a faithful child of the European Enlightenment.[16]

A significant point of such a criticism has to do with the role of political and economic power. According to this way of thinking, European culture, with its emphasis on individualism and the separation of church and state, spread across the world along with European colonial power. While some may think that this is a progressive development, critics will view it as an imposition of European culture and values that come at the expense of alternative ideas about morality and politics. A related criticism develops from Karl Marx's critique of "bourgeois morality" as the product of a certain strand of European thinking, associated with the ruling class. (Marxists, by the way, tend to view religion as "the opiate of the people," that is, as a drug that reconciles oppressed people to the injustices of the social order by promising an otherworldly reward.) More recently, scholars such as Enrique Dussel have expanded this critical perspective to argue that **Eurocentrism** is at the heart of continual cultural divisions and economic inequalities that plague the globe (as we discuss in more detail in Chapter 20). An influential Latin American philosopher, Dussel critiques the traditional Anglo-American and European approach to philosophy and ethics. For Dussel, European philosophy begins with conquest—as the colonial conquests of the Americas, Asia, and Africa coincide with the dawning of European Enlightenment.[17] Dussel gives voice to the concern that there may be a connection between European imperialism and European ethics—that moral ideas about a variety of topics from sex and gender to individualism and human rights, to the use of drugs and the morality of war have a lot to do with the economic and political power structures at work in the world.

For people who identify with non-Western religions and cultures, the approaches to ethics that we are taking in this book can appear to be Eurocentric. From this standpoint, one might argue that the approach of this book reflects the biases of a predominantly Christian and European worldview. Indeed, the main normative traditions discussed in this book—utilitarianism, virtue ethics, natural law, and Kantian deontology—are rooted in the ideas of European philosophers.

In response, one might admit that even though the goal of understanding ethics in an objective and universal fashion, without reference to religion, is a goal that is widely shared by many in the Western world, this goal is not uniquely Christian or European. Indeed, it is a goal that is shared by many people around the world. As Amartya Sen and others have pointed out, the move toward philosophical and cosmopolitan ethics is also deeply rooted in non-Western intellectual traditions. It is true that we must be sensitive to the diverse cultural and religious starting points from which we begin reflecting on ethics. But this does not mean that we should not attempt to move beyond narrow allegiances and prejudices toward a broader, more impartial, and more objective perspective—that is, toward a cosmopolitan and pluralist point of view that would incorporate the insights of the world's great moral and religious traditions. Whether we can attain this goal is an open question. In Chapter 3, we confront this problem more directly as a question of relativism. The question of that chapter will be whether there really is such a thing as a universal, objective point of view or whether we are hopelessly stuck within a perspective and worldview that we inherit from our culture or religion.

The first reading for this chapter is from Plato, who offers a critique of religious ethics in his dialogue, *Euthyphro*. In this dialogue, Socrates discusses religion with Euthyphro, a young man who claims to know what piety demands. Socrates suggests that the idea of what is good is somehow prior to our understanding of what religion requires. Following this is a short excerpt from an essay by Sam Harris, which outlines a contemporary argument against religion and about the need to evolve beyond religion. The next reading is from Mohandas K. Gandhi, who argues for a pluralistic convergence of religious ideas. In this essay, Gandhi considers the idea that the world's religions converge around a common ethical core.

NOTES

1. http://www.un.org/en/documents/udhr/
2. http://www.cnn.com/2015/12/15/politics/franklin-graham-halt-all-immigration/ (Accessed January 5, 2016).
3. Immanuel Kant, "An Answer to the Question: 'What Is Enlightenment?'" in *Kant: Political Writings* (Cambridge: Cambridge University Press, 1991), p. 54.
4. http://philpapers.org/surveys/results.pl
5. Although this claim is often attributed to Dostoevsky, it is not directly stated by any one of Dostoevsky's characters. Nonetheless, it is the basic idea of his atheist characters: Ivan Karamazov in *The Brothers Karamazov* and Kirilov and Stavrogin in *Devils*.
6. John Hick, *An Interpretation of Religion: Human Responses to the Transcendent*, 2nd ed. (New Haven, CT: Yale University Press, 2005), p. xl.
7. Hick, *An Interpretation of Religion*, p. 316.
8. Dalai Lama, *Kindness, Clarity, and Insight* (Ithaca, NY: Snow Lion Publications, 2006), p. 58.
9. Stephen Prothero, *God Is Not One: The Eight Rival Religions That Run the World—And Why Their Differences Matter* (New York: HarperCollins, 2010), p. 2.
10. Sam Harris, *Free Will* (New York: Free Press, 2012), p. 1.
11. Prothero, *God Is Not One*, p. 2.
12. Craig Calhoun, Mark Juergensmeyer, and Jonathan VanAntwerpen, *Rethinking Secularism* (New York: Oxford University Press, 2011), p. 10.
13. Paul Kurtz, "Neo-Humanist Statement of Secular Principles and Values," http://paulkurtz.net/
14. Jürgen Habermas, "Struggles for Recognition in the Democratic Constitutional State," in *Multiculturalism: Examining the Politics of Recognition,* ed. Amy Gutmann (Princeton, NJ: Princeton University Press, 1994), pp. 132–33.
15. Jürgen Habermas, "Struggles for Recognition," p. 133.
16. José Casanova, "Public Religions Revisited," in *Religion: Beyond a Concept,* ed. Hent de Vries (New York: Fordham University Press, 2007), p. 119.
17. See Enrique Dussel, *Beyond Philosophy: Ethics, History, Marxism, and Liberation Theology* (Lanham, MD: Rowman & Littlefield, 2003).

READING

Euthyphro

PLATO

MindTap® For more chapter resources and activities, go to MindTap.

Study Questions

As you read the excerpt, please consider the following questions:
1. Do the gods have different conceptions about what is good and evil, just and unjust? Why does this pose a problem for Euthyphro's account?
2. Which comes first: being pious or being loved by the gods?
3. What does Socrates suggest is yet needed to give a definition of piety or goodness?

Euthyphro. Piety . . . is that which is dear to the gods, and impiety is that which is not dear to them.

Socrates. Very good, Euthyphro; you have now given me the sort of answer which I wanted. But whether what you say is true or not I cannot as yet tell, although I make no doubt that you will prove the truth of your words.

Euthyphro. Of course.

Socrates. Come, then, and let us examine what we are saying. That thing or person which is dear to the gods is pious, and that thing or person which is hateful to the gods is impious, these two being the extreme opposites of one another. Was not that said?

Euthyphro. It was.

Socrates. And well said?

Euthyphro. Yes, Socrates, I thought so; it was certainly said.

Socrates. And further, Euthyphro, the gods were admitted to have enmities and hatreds and differences?

Euthyphro. Yes, that was also said.

Socrates. And what sort of difference creates enmity and anger? Suppose for example that you and I, my good friend, differ about a number; do differences of this sort make us enemies and set us at variance with one another? Do we not go at once to arithmetic, and put an end to them by a sum?

Euthyphro. True.

Socrates. Or suppose that we differ about magnitudes, do we not quickly end the differences by measuring?

Euthyphro. Very true.

Socrates. And we end a controversy about heavy and light by resorting to a weighing machine?

Euthyphro. To be sure.

Socrates. But what differences are there which cannot be thus decided, and which therefore make us angry and set us at enmity with one another? I dare say the answer does not occur to you at the moment, and therefore I will suggest that these enmities arise when the matters of difference are the just and unjust, good and evil, honourable and dishonourable. Are not these the points about which men differ, and about which when we are unable satisfactorily to decide our differences, you and I and all of us quarrel, when we do quarrel?

Euthyphro. Yes, Socrates, the nature of the differences about which we quarrel is such as you describe.

Socrates. And the quarrels of the gods, noble Euthyphro, when they occur, are of a like nature?

Euthyphro. Certainly they are.

Socrates. They have differences of opinion, as you say, about good and evil, just and unjust, honourable and dishonourable: there would have been

From Plato, *Euthyphro*, trans. B. Jowett. (Project Gutenberg, 2008), http://www.gutenberg.org/files/1642/1642-h/1642-h.htm

no quarrels among them, if there had been no such differences—would there now?

Euthyphro. You are quite right.

Socrates. Does not every man love that which he deems noble and just and good, and hate the opposite of them?

Euthyphro. Very true.

Socrates. But, as you say, people regard the same things, some as just and others as unjust—about these they dispute; and so there arise wars and fightings among them.

Euthyphro. Very true.

Socrates. Then the same things are hated by the gods and loved by the gods, and are both hateful and dear to them?

Euthyphro. True.

Socrates. And upon this view the same things, Euthyphro, will be pious and also impious?

Euthyphro. So I should suppose.

Socrates. Then, my friend, I remark with surprise that you have not answered the question which I asked. For I certainly did not ask you to tell me what action is both pious and impious: but now it would seem that what is loved by the gods is also hated by them. And therefore, Euthyphro, in thus chastising your father you may very likely be doing what is agreeable to Zeus but disagreeable to Cronos or Uranus, and what is acceptable to Hephaestus but unacceptable to Heré, and there may be other gods who have similar differences of opinion.

Euthyphro. But I believe, Socrates, that all the gods would be agreed as to the propriety of punishing a murderer: there would be no difference of opinion about that.

Socrates. Well, but speaking of men, Euthyphro, did you ever hear any one arguing that a murderer or any sort of evil-doer ought to be let off?

Euthyphro. I should rather say that these are the questions which they are always arguing, especially in courts of law: they commit all sorts of crimes, and there is nothing which they will not do or say in their own defence.

Socrates. But do they admit their guilt, Euthyphro, and yet say that they ought not to be punished?

Euthyphro. No; they do not.

Socrates. Then there are some things which they do not venture to say and do: for they do not venture to argue that the guilty are to be unpunished, but they deny their guilt, do they not?

Euthyphro. Yes.

Socrates. Then they do not argue that the evil-doer should not be punished, but they argue about the fact of who the evil-doer is, and what he did and when?

Euthyphro. True.

Socrates. And the gods are in the same case, if as you assert they quarrel about just and unjust, and some of them say while others deny that injustice is done among them. For surely neither God nor man will ever venture to say that the doer of injustice is not to be punished?

Euthyphro. That is true, Socrates, in the main.

Socrates. But they join issue about the particulars—gods and men alike; and, if they dispute at all, they dispute about some act which is called in question, and which by some is affirmed to be just, by others to be unjust. Is not that true?

Euthyphro. Quite true.

Socrates. Well then, my dear friend Euthyphro, do tell me, for my better instruction and information, what proof have you that in the opinion of all the gods a servant who is guilty of murder, and is put in chains by the master of the dead man, and dies because he is put in chains before he who bound him can learn from the interpreters of the gods what he ought to do with him, dies unjustly; and that on behalf of such a one a son ought to proceed against his father and accuse him of murder. How would you show that all the gods absolutely agree in approving of his act? Prove to me that they do, and I will applaud your wisdom as long as I live.

Euthyphro. It will be a difficult task; but I could make the matter very clear indeed to you.

Socrates. I understand; you mean to say that I am not so quick of apprehension as the judges: for to them you will be sure to prove that the act is unjust, and hateful to the gods.

Euthyphro. Yes indeed, Socrates; at least if they will listen to me.

Socrates. But they will be sure to listen if they find that you are a good speaker. There was a notion that came into my mind while you were speaking; I said to myself: "Well, and what if Euthyphro does prove to me that all the gods regarded the death of the serf as unjust, how do I know anything more of the nature of piety and impiety? For granting that this action may be hateful to the gods, still piety and impiety are not adequately defined by these distinctions, for that which is hateful to the gods has been shown to be also pleasing and dear to them." And therefore, Euthyphro, I do not ask you to prove this; I will suppose, if you like, that all the gods condemn and abominate such an action. But I will amend the definition so far as to say that what all the gods hate is impious, and what they love pious or holy; and what some of them love and others hate is both or neither. Shall this be our definition of piety and impiety?

Euthyphro. Why not, Socrates?

Socrates. Why not! Certainly, as far as I am concerned, Euthyphro, there is no reason why not. But whether this admission will greatly assist you in the task of instructing me as you promised, is a matter for you to consider.

Euthyphro. Yes, I should say that what all the gods love is pious and holy, and the opposite which they all hate, impious.

Socrates. Ought we to enquire into the truth of this, Euthyphro, or simply to accept the mere statement on our own authority and that of others? What do you say?

Euthyphro. We should enquire; and I believe that the statement will stand the test of enquiry.

Socrates. We shall know better, my good friend, in a little while. The point which I should first wish to understand is whether the pious or holy is beloved by the gods because it is holy, or holy because it is beloved of the gods.

Euthyphro. I do not understand your meaning, Socrates.

Socrates. I will endeavour to explain; we speak of carrying and we speak of being carried, of leading and being led, seeing and being seen. You know that in all such cases there is a difference, and you know also in what the difference lies?

Euthyphro. I think that I understand.

Socrates. And is not that which is beloved distinct from that which loves?

Euthyphro. Certainly.

Socrates. Well; and now tell me, is that which is carried in this state of carrying because it is carried, or for some other reason?

Euthyphro. No; that is the reason.

Socrates. And the same is true of what is led and of what is seen?

Euthyphro. True.

Socrates. And a thing is not seen because it is visible, but conversely, visible because it is seen; nor is a thing led because it is in the state of being led, or carried because it is in the state of being carried, but the converse of this. And now I think, Euthyphro, that my meaning will be intelligible; and my meaning is, that any state of action or passion implies previous action or passion. It does not become because it is becoming, but it is in a state of becoming because it becomes; neither does it suffer because it is in a state of suffering, but it is in a state of suffering because it suffers. Do you not agree?

Euthyphro. Yes.

Socrates. Is not that which is loved in some state either of becoming or suffering?

Euthyphro. Yes.

Socrates. And the same holds as in the previous instances; the state of being loved follows the act of being loved, and not the act the state.

Euthyphro. Certainly.

Socrates. And what do you say of piety, Euthyphro: is not piety, according to your definition, loved by all the gods?

Euthyphro. Yes.

Socrates. Because it is pious or holy, or for some other reason?

Euthyphro. No, that is the reason.

Socrates. It is loved because it is holy, not holy because it is loved?

Euthyphro. Yes.

Socrates. And that which is dear to the gods is loved by them, and is in a state to be loved of them because it is loved of them?

Euthyphro. Certainly.

Socrates. Then that which is dear to the gods, Euthyphro, is not holy, nor is that which is holy loved of God, as you affirm; but they are two different things.

Euthyphro. How do you mean, Socrates?

Socrates. I mean to say that the holy has been acknowledged by us to be loved of God because it is holy, not to be holy because it is loved.

Euthyphro. Yes.

Socrates. But that which is dear to the gods is dear to them because it is loved by them, not loved by them because it is dear to them.

Euthyphro. True.

Socrates. But, friend Euthyphro, if that which is holy is the same with that which is dear to God, and is loved because it is holy, then that which is dear to God would have been loved as being dear to God; but if that which is dear to God is dear to him because loved by him, then that which is holy would

have been holy because loved by him. But now you see that the reverse is the case, and that they are quite different from one another. For one (qeojtlez) is of a kind to be loved because it is loved, and the other (oston) is loved because it is of a kind to be loved. Thus you appear to me, Euthyphro, when I ask you what is the essence of holiness, to offer an attribute only, and not the essence—the attribute of being loved by all the gods. But you still refuse to explain to me the nature of holiness. And therefore, if you please, I will ask you not to hide your treasure, but to tell me once more what holiness or piety really is, whether dear to the gods or not (for that is a matter about which we will not quarrel); and what is impiety?

Euthyphro. I really do not know, Socrates, how to express what I mean. For somehow or other our arguments, on whatever ground we rest them, seem to turn round and walk away from us.

READING

Letter to a Christian Nation

SAM HARRIS

MindTap   For more chapter resources and activities, go to MindTap.

Study Questions

As you read the excerpt, please consider the following questions:
1. Why does Harris suggest that it is a "ludicrous obscenity" to raise children to believe that they are Christian, Muslim, or Jewish?
2. What kind of evolutionary purpose may religion have served?
3. Is religion an impediment to building a global society?

One of the greatest challenges facing civilization in the twenty-first century is for human beings to learn to speak about their deepest personal concerns—about ethics, spiritual experience, and the inevitability of human suffering—in ways that are not flagrantly irrational.

We desperately need a public discourse that encourages critical thinking and intellectual honesty.

Nothing stands in the way of this project more than the respect we accord religious faith.

. . . .

If we ever do transcend our religious bewilderment, we will look back upon this period in human

Sam Harris, *"Letter to a Christian Nation"* (New York: Knopf, 2006), pp. 87–89.

history with horror and amazement. How could it have been possible for people to believe such things in the twenty first century? How could it be that they allowed their societies to become so dangerously fragmented by empty notions about God and Paradise?

....

Clearly, it is time we learned to meet our emotional needs without embracing the preposterous. We must find ways to invoke the power of ritual and to mark those transitions in every human life that demand profundity—birth, marriage, death—without lying to ourselves about the nature of reality. Only then will the practice of raising our children to believe that they are Christian, Muslim, or Jewish be widely recognized as the ludicrous obscenity that it is. And only then will we stand a chance of healing the deepest and most dangerous fractures in our world.

...

It is important to realize that the distinction between science and religion is not a matter of excluding our ethical intuitions and spiritual experiences from our conversation about the world; it is a matter of our being honest about what we can

reasonably conclude on their basis. There are good reasons to believe that people like Jesus and the Buddha weren't talking nonsense when they spoke about our capacity as human beings to transform our lives in rare and beautiful ways. But any genuine exploration of ethics or the contemplative life demands the same standards of reasonableness and self-criticism that animate all intellectual discourse.

As a biological phenomenon, religion is the product of cognitive processes that have deep roots in our evolutionary past. Some researchers have speculated that religion itself may have played an important role in getting large groups of prehistoric humans to socially cohere. If this is true, we can say that religion has served an important purpose. This does not suggest, however, that it serves an important purpose now. There is, after all, nothing more natural than rape. But no one would argue that rape is good, or compatible with a civil society, because it may have had evolutionary advantages for our ancestors. That religion may have served some necessary function for us in the past does not preclude the possibility that it is now the greatest impediment to our building a global civilization.

READING

Religion and Truth

MOHANDAS K. GANDHI

MindTap® For more chapter resources and activities, go to MindTap.

Study Questions

As you read the excerpt, please consider the following questions:
1. How does Gandhi describe "the religion that underlies all religions"?
2. Why does Gandhi think that *ahimsa* (nonviolence) and self-purification are important?
3. What is the one unifying element of the world's diverse religions, according to Gandhi?

By religion, I do not mean formal religion, or customary religion, but that religion which underlies all religions, which brings us face to face with our Maker.

Let me explain what I mean by religion. It is not the Hindu religion which I certainly prize above all other religions, but the religion which transcends Hinduism, which changes one's very nature, which binds one indissolubly to the truth within and which ever purifies. It is the permanent element in human nature which counts no cost too great in order to find full expression and which leaves the soul utterly restless until it has found itself, known its Maker and appreciated the true correspondence between the Maker and itself.

I have not seen Him, neither have I known Him. I have made the world's faith in God my own, and as my faith is ineffaceable, I regard that faith as amounting to experience. However, as it may be said that to describe faith as experience is to tamper with truth, it may perhaps be more correct to say that I have no word for characterizing my belief in God.

There is an indefinable mysterious Power that pervades everything. I feel it, though I do not see it. It is this unseen Power which makes itself felt and yet defies all proof, because it is so unlike all that I perceive through my senses. It transcends the senses. But it is possible to reason out the existence of God to a limited extent.

I do dimly perceive that whilst everything around me is ever-changing, ever-dying, there is underlying all that change a Living Power that is changeless, that holds all together, that creates, dissolves, and re-creates. That informing Power or Spirit is God. And since nothing else I see merely through the senses can or will persist, He alone is.

And is this Power benevolent or malevolent? I see it as purely benevolent. For I can see that in the midst of death life persists, in the midst of untruth truth persists, in the midst of darkness light persists. Hence I gather that God is Life, Truth, Light. He is Love. He is the Supreme God.

I know, too, that I shall never know God if I do not wrestle with and against evil even at the cost of life itself. I am fortified in the belief by my own humble and limited experience. The purer I try to become the nearer to God I feel myself to be. How much more should I be near to Him when my faith is not a mere apology, as it is today, but has become

as immovable as the Himalayas and as white and bright as the snows on their peaks?

This belief in God has to be based on faith which transcends reason. Indeed, even the so-called realization has at bottom an element of faith without which it cannot be sustained. In the very nature of things it must be so. Who can transgress the limitations of his being? I hold that complete realization is impossible in this embodied life. Nor is it necessary. A living immovable faith is all that is required for reaching the full spiritual height attainable by human beings. God is not outside this earthly case of ours. Therefore, exterior proof is not of much avail, if any at all. We must ever fail to perceive Him through the senses, because He is beyond them. We can feel Him, if we will but withdraw ourselves from the senses. The divine music is incessantly going on within ourselves, but the loud senses drown the delicate music, which is unlike and infinitely superior to anything we can perceive or hear with our senses.

But He is no God who merely satisfies the intellect, if He ever does. God to be God must rule the heart and transform it. He must express Himself in every the smallest act of His votary. This can only be done through a definite realization more real than the five senses can ever produce. Sense perceptions can be, often are, false and deceptive, however real they may appear to us. Where there is realization outside the senses it is infallible. It is proved not by extraneous evidence but in the transformed conduct and character of those who have felt the real presence of God within. Such testimony is to be found in the experiences of an unbroken line of prophets and sages in all countries and climes. To reject this evidence is to deny oneself.

To me God is Truth and Love; God is ethics and morality; God is fearlessness. God is the source of Light and Life and yet He is above and beyond all these. God is conscience. He is even the atheism of the atheist. . . . He transcends speech and reason. . . . He is a personal God to those who need His personal presence. He is embodied to those who need His touch. He is the purest essence. He simply *is* to those who have faith. He is all things to all men. He is in us and yet above and beyond

From Mohandas K. Gandhi, *All Men Are Brothers* (Lausanne, SA: Unesco, 1969). Reprinted by permission of Navajivan Trust.

us. . . . He is long-suffering. He is patient but He is also terrible. . . . With Him ignorance is no excuse. And withal He is ever forgiving for He always gives us the chance to repent. He is the greatest democrat the world knows, for He leaves us 'unfettered' to make our own choice between evil and good. He is the greatest tyrant ever known, for He often dashes the cup from our lips and under the cover of free will leaves us a margin so wholly inadequate as to provide only mirth for Himself. . . . Therefore Hinduism calls it all His sport.

To see the universal and all-pervading Spirit of Truth face to face one must be able to love the meanest of creation as oneself. And a man who aspires after that cannot afford to keep out of any field of life. That is why my devotion to truth has drawn me into the field of politics; and I can say without the slightest hesitation, and yet in all humility, that those who say that religion has nothing to do with politics do not know what religion means.

Identification with everything that lives is impossible without self-purification; without self-purification the observance of the law of *ahimsā* must remain an empty dream; God can never be realized by one who is not pure of heart. Self-purification therefore must mean purification in all walks of life. And purification being highly infectious, purification of oneself necessarily leads to the purification of one's surroundings.

But the path of self-purification is hard and steep. To attain to perfect purity one has to become absolutely passion-free in thought, speech and action; to rise above the opposing currents of love and hatred, attachment and repulsion. I know that I have not in me as yet that triple purity, in spite of constant, ceaseless striving for it. That is why the world's praise fails to move me, indeed it very often stings me. To conquer the subtle passions seems to me to be far harder than the physical conquest of the world by the force of arms.

I am but a poor struggling soul yearning to be wholly good—wholly truthful and wholly non-violent in thought, word and deed; but ever failing to reach the ideal which I know to be true. It is a painful climb, but the pain of it is a positive pleasure

to me. Each step upward makes me feel stronger and fit for the next.

I am endeavouring to see God through service of humanity, for I know that God is neither in heaven, nor down below, but in every one.

Indeed religion should pervade every one of our actions. Here religion does not mean sectarianism. It means a belief in ordered moral government of the universe. It is not less real because it is unseen. This religion transcends Hinduism, Islam, Christianity, etc. It does not supersede them. It harmonizes them and gives them reality.

Religions are different roads converging to the same point. What does it matter that we take different roads, so long as we reach the same goal? In reality, there are as many religions as there are individuals.

If a man reaches the heart of his own religion, he has reached the heart of the others too.

So long as there are different religions, every one of them may need some distinctive symbol. But when the symbol is made into a fetish and an instrument of proving the superiority of one's religion over other's, it is fit only to be discarded.

After long study and experience, I have come to the conclusion that: (1) all religions are true; (2) all religions have some error in them; (3) all religions are almost as dear to me as my own Hinduism, in as much as all human beings should be as dear to one as one's own close relatives. My own veneration for other faiths is the same as that for my own faith; therefore no thought of conversion is possible.

God has created different faiths just as He has the votaries thereof. How can I even secretly harbour the thought that my neighbour's faith is inferior to mine and wish that he should give up his faith and embrace mine? As a true and loyal friend, I can only wish and pray that he may live and grow perfect in his own faith. In God's house there are many mansions and they are equally holy.

Let no one even for a moment entertain the fear that a reverent study of other religions is likely to weaken or shake one's faith in one's own. The Hindu system of philosophy regards all religions as containing the elements of truth in them and enjoins an attitude of respect and reverence towards them all. This of course presupposes regard for one's own religion. Study and appreciation of other religions need not cause a weakening of that regard; it should mean extension of that regard to other religions.

It is better to allow our lives to speak for us than our words. God did not bear the Cross only 1,900 years ago, but He bears it today, and He dies and is resurrected from day to day. It would be poor comfort to the world if it had to depend upon a historical God who died 2,000 years ago. Do not then preach the God of history, but show Him as He lives today through you.

I do not believe in people telling others of their faith, especially with a view to conversion. Faith does not admit of telling. It has to be lived and then it becomes self-propagating.

Divine knowledge is not borrowed from books. It has to be realized in oneself. Books are at best an aid, often even a hindrance.

I believe in the fundamental truth of all great religions of the world. I believe that they are all God-given, and I believe that they were necessary for the people to whom these religions were revealed. And I believe that, if only we could all of us read the scriptures of the different faiths from the standpoint of the followers of those faiths, we should find that they were at the bottom all one and were all helpful to one another.

Belief in one God is the corner-stone of all religions. But I do not foresee a time when there would be only one religion on earth in practice. In theory, since there is one God, there can be only one religion. But in practice, no two persons I have known have had the same identical conception of God. Therefore, there will, perhaps, always be different religions answering to different temperaments and climatic conditions.

I believe that all the great religions of the world are true more or less. I say "more or less" because I believe that everything that the human hand touches, by reason of the very fact that human beings are imperfect, becomes imperfect. Perfection is the exclusive attribute of God and it is indescribable, untranslatable. I do believe that it is possible for every human being to become perfect even as God is perfect. It is necessary for us all to aspire after perfection, but when that blessed state is attained, it becomes indescribable, indefinable. And, I, therefore, admit, in all humility, that even the Vedas, the Koran and the Bible are imperfect word of God and, imperfect beings that we are, swayed to and fro by a multitude of passions, it is impossible for us even to understand this word of God in its fullness.

I do not believe in the exclusive divinity of the Vedas. I believe the Bible, the Koran and the Zend Avesta, to be as much divinely inspired as the Vedas. My belief in the Hindu scriptures does not require me to accept every word and every verse as divinely inspired....I decline to be bound by any interpretation, however learned it may be, if it is repugnant to reason or moral sense.

REVIEW EXERCISES

1. Describe the challenge of developing a global ethical perspective in light of religious and national differences.

2. What is the history of the idea of universal human rights? How is this history susceptible to the charge that it is Eurocentric?

3. If you could develop a global ethic, what would its basic values be?

4. Explain arguments in favor of the divine command theory of ethics, as well as arguments against that theory. Is it true that if there were no God, then everything would be permitted?

5. Is the humanistic or secular approach to ethics better than religious approaches to ethics? How so? Is the humanistic or secular approach antagonistic to religion?

6. What does Socrates mean when he says in *Euthyphro* that the holy or pious is holy or pious because it is loved by the gods? Do you agree with his argument?

7. Are you optimistic about our ability to develop a global ethical consensus across our national and religious differences? Why or why not?

8. Do you think that all religions are pointing in a similar direction, or are there irreconcilable differences among the world's religions?

MindTap® For more chapter resources and activities, go to MindTap.

3

Ethical Relativism

Learning Outcomes

After reading this chapter, you should be able to:

- Describe the difference between descriptive relativism and metaethical relativism.
- Discuss criticisms of objectivism, subjectivism, relativism, and moral realism.
- Explain how relativism poses a problem for moral judgment.
- Explain the connections between relativism and pluralism.

- Evaluate the arguments in favor of and against relativism.
- Differentiate between relativism and a commitment to tolerance.
- Explain how relativism might come up in conversations about concrete moral issues.
- Defend your own ideas about relativism.

MindTap® For more chapter resources and activities, go to MindTap.

Chapter 2 introduced the difficulty of trying to discover a set of universal values that are valid for people who come from diverse religious and cultural backgrounds. This points toward the problem of relativism. Relativism means that our judgments about ethics are relative to (or dependent upon) something else. Cultural relativism holds that ethical judgments are relative to cultural contexts. Individualistic versions of relativism hold that judgments about morality are relative to an individual's point of view. In saying that judgments are relative to individuals or cultures, we mean that they are a function of, or dependent on, what those individuals or cultures happen to believe. Relativism can be based upon **epistemological** claims about what we know. Relativism can also be based upon a claim about the nature of values (as discussed in Chapter 1). The epistemological approach maintains that knowledge about values is derived from or dependent upon a cultural context or worldview. A metaphysical approach claims that there are no absolute, transcendent, or universal values. For the metaphysical relativist, there are only individual perspectives and culturally defined values—there are no absolute or objective values.

Relativism is a very difficult metaethical issue. It asks us to consider how we know things in the realm of morality. And it asks us to consider the ultimate nature or reality of moral values. The belief that guides this text—indeed, the belief that guides most philosophical discussions of ethics—is that better and worse choices can be made, and that morality is not simply a matter of what we feel to be morally right or wrong; nor is morality simply a matter of what our culture tells us. If this were not the case, then there would not seem to be much point in studying ethics. The purpose of studying ethics, as noted in Chapter 1, is to improve one's ability to make good ethical judgments. If ethical relativism were true, then this purpose could not be achieved.

DESCRIPTIVE VERSUS NORMATIVE ETHICAL RELATIVISM

Ethical relativism is a kind of skepticism about ethical reasoning—it is skeptical of the idea that there are right and wrong answers to ethical questions. There are some good reasons why we might be skeptical about the existence of universal or objective values (or that we can know what the objective or universal values are). One reason for skepticism is the empirical and historical fact that different cultures disagree about moral values. As a descriptive fact, relativism appears to be true: it is evident that there are different ideas about ethics at large in the world. What we call **descriptive ethical relativism** is the factual or descriptive claim that there are different ideas about values.

In support of descriptive relativism, we might list some of the ways that cultures vary with regard to morality. Some societies hold bribery to be morally acceptable, but other societies condemn it. Views on appropriate sexual behavior and practices vary widely. Some societies believe that cannibalism, the eating of human flesh, is good because it ensures tribal fertility or increases manliness. Some groups of the Inuit, the native peoples of northern Canada and Alaska, believed that it was appropriate to abandon their elderly when they could no longer travel with the group, whereas other groups once practiced ritual strangulation of the old by their children. The anthropologist Ruth Benedict documented the case of a Northwest Indian group that believed it was justified in killing an innocent person for each member of the group who had died. This was not a matter of revenge but a way of fighting death. In place of bereavement, the group felt relieved by the second killing.[1]

There are a variety of examples of descriptive relativism. In some countries, it is acceptable for women to wear short skirts; in others, women are expected to cover their legs and hair. Indeed, relativism shows up in the language we use to describe contested practices. Consider the practice of cutting women's genitals. Those who are sympathetic to the practice might call it *female circumcision*. But that practice is illegal in other societies, which condemn it by calling it *female genital mutilation* (as we discuss in Chapters 9 and 12). You should be able to think of many other examples of such differences.

Descriptive relativism might appear to lead to a normative rule of thumb, that "When in Rome," we should "do as the Romans do." This saying originated from a discussion between Augustine and Ambrose—two important Christian saints of the fourth century. Augustine noticed that the Christians in Rome fasted on a different day than the Christians in Milan. Ambrose explained that when in Rome, he does what the Romans do. In many cases, it does appear to be wise to go along with local practices. The issue of the appropriate day for fasting is a minor point and it is easy enough to "go along" with such minor details. But should we also go along with local practices that could include slavery, female genital mutilation, child sacrifice, or cannibalism?

Different cultures do have different values. But it might still be the case that some of these cultures are wrong about certain values. Recall the "fact/value" distinction discussed in Chapter 1. Just because something is a fact of the world (as descriptive relativism is a fact) does not mean that it is a good thing. It is possible that we *ought* to strive to overcome our cultural differences. And it is possible that some cultures (or individuals) are wrong—despite the fact that cultures and individuals vary in their moral judgments. We want to say, for example, that cultures that practice slavery (as the United States did until the 1860s) are wrong to do so. The mere fact that cultures disagree about values should not immunize cultures from moral criticism. But to say that a culture is wrong, we need an objective or non-relativist account of the values that would allow us to criticize that culture.

A stronger version of relativism goes beyond merely descriptive relativism and claims that there are no objective or absolute values that would allow us to make such criticisms. We call this version of relativism **metaethical relativism**. Metaethical relativism holds that there are no universal or objective norms (or that human beings cannot know such objective values). Rather, from this point of view, values are simply the beliefs, opinions, practices, or feelings of individuals and cultures. In saying that values are "relative" to individuals or societies, we mean that they are a function of, or dependent on, what those individuals or societies do, in fact, believe. According to metaethical relativism, there is no objective right and wrong. The opposite point of view, that there is an objective right and wrong, is often called **objectivism**, or sometimes simply nonrelativism.

We can understand more about ethical relativism by comparing ethics with science. Most people believe that the natural sciences (biology, chemistry, physics, geology, and their modern variants) tell us things about the natural world. Throughout the centuries, and in modern times, in particular, science seems to have made great progress in uncovering the nature and structure of our world. Moreover, science seems to have a universal validity. Regardless of a person's individual temperament, background, or culture, the same natural world seems accessible to all who sincerely and openly investigate it. Modern science is thought to be governed by a generally accepted method and seems to produce a gradually evolving common body of knowledge. Although this is the popular view of science, philosophers hold that the situation regarding science is much more complex and problematic. And it is possible for there to be relativism with regard to theories of the natural world. Not everyone agrees, for example, that Western biomedicine holds all the answers to good health. Nevertheless, it is useful to compare the ordinary view of science as providing objective truth about the physical world with common understandings of morality.

Morality, in contrast to science, does not seem so objective. Not only is there no general agreement about what is right and wrong, but some people doubt that ethical judgments are the sorts of things about which we could agree. Some people think of morality as a matter of subjective opinion. This is basically the conclusion of ethical relativism: morality is simply a function of the moral beliefs that people have. There is nothing beyond this. Specifically, no category of objective moral truth or reality exists that is comparable to that which we seem to find in the world of nature investigated by science.

INDIVIDUAL VERSUS CULTURAL RELATIVISM

In further exploring the nature of ethical relativism, we should note that it has two basic and different forms.[2] According to one form, called personal or **individual relativism** (also called **subjectivism**), ethical judgments and beliefs are the expressions of the moral outlook and attitudes of individual persons. Rather than being objective, such judgments are subjective. I have my ethical views, and you have yours; neither my views nor yours are better or more correct. I may believe that a particular war was unjust, and you may believe it was just. Someone else may believe that all war is wrong. According to this form of relativism, because no objective right or wrong exists, no particular war can be said to be really just or unjust, right or wrong, nor can *all* wars. We each have our individual histories that explain how we have come to hold our particular views or attitudes. But they are just that—our own individual views and attitudes. We cannot say that they are correct or incorrect because to do so would assume some objective standard of right and wrong against which we could judge their correctness. Such a standard does not exist, according to ethical relativism.[3]

The second form of ethical relativism, called social or **cultural relativism**, holds that ethical values vary from society to society and that the basis for moral judgments lies in these social or cultural views. For an individual to decide and do what is right, he or she must look to the norms of the society. People in a society may, in fact, believe that their views are the correct moral views. However, a cultural relativist holds that no society's views are better than any other in a transcultural sense. Some may be different from others, and some may not be the views generally accepted by a wider group of societies, but that does not make these views worse, more backward, or incorrect in any objective sense.

MindTap° For more chapter resources and activities, go to MindTap.

STRONG AND WEAK RELATIVISM

While it is obvious that different cultures or societies often have different views about what is morally right and wrong, ethical relativism goes further. For the stronger versions of ethical relativism, what is morally right for one just depends on what his or her society holds is right. There are no transcultural moral principles, even ideally. One author often associated with relativism is Friedrich Nietzsche. Nietzsche maintains that words like *good* and *evil* are defined by different people based upon their own perspectives on the world. Indeed, Nietzsche is often viewed as a proponent of **perspectivism**, the idea that there are only perspectives on the world—and nothing beyond these perspectives. Nietzsche also thinks that moral judgments reflect power relations and basic instinctual needs. For example, those who are in power tend to call themselves "good" because they instinctively view themselves as superior to those who are less powerful. As Nietzsche explains, "It is our needs that interpret the world; our drives and their For and Against. Every drive is a kind of lust to rule; each one has its perspective that it would like to compel all the other drives to accept as a norm."[4] For Nietzsche, there is no truth beneath these perspectives, instincts, and drives other than the "will to power." Such a strong version of relativism makes it quite difficult to judge or criticize across cultural divides.

A weaker version of relativism holds that there are some abstract and basic norms or values that are shared but that these abstract values are expressed in different cultures in different ways. Thus, different cultures may share the idea that "life should be valued," for example, but they will disagree about what counts as "life" and what counts as "valuing life." It might be that both human and animal lives count and so no animal lives can be taken in order to support human beings. Or it might be that some form of ritual sacrifice could be justified as a way of valuing life.

One version of this kind of "weak relativism" or "soft universalism" is the "capabilities approach" to ethics and human welfare—as developed by the economist Amartya Sen and the philosopher Martha Nussbaum. Nussbaum maintains that there are certain central features of human flourishing or human well-being, including life, bodily health, bodily integrity, and so on. But she admits the possibility of "multiple realization" of these basic capabilities. As Nussbaum explains, "each of the capabilities may be concretely realized in a variety of different ways, in accordance with individual tastes, local circumstances, and traditions."[5] Nussbaum's approach

Philosopher Martha C. Nussbaum during an event at Oveido University in Spain.

leads to a sort of pluralism. Nussbaum writes that "legitimate concerns for diversity, pluralism, and personal freedom are not incompatible with the recognition of universal norms; indeed, universal norms are actually required if we are to protect diversity, pluralism, and freedom, treating each human being as an agent and an end."[6] But critics will argue that so long as there is no universal agreement about the specific sorts of values that count for human flourishing and an ethical life, we are still left with a kind of relativism.

Nussbaum's Central Capabilities[7]

1. Life
2. Bodily health
3. Bodily integrity
4. Senses, imagination, and thought
5. Emotions
6. Practical reason
7. Affiliation
8. Other species
9. Play
10. Control over one's environment: political and material

REASONS SUPPORTING ETHICAL RELATIVISM

There are many reasons for believing that ethical relativism is true. We will first summarize the three most commonly given reasons and then evaluate their related arguments.[8]

The Diversity of Moral Views

One reason most often given to support relativism is the existence of moral diversity among people and cultures. In fields such as science and history, investigation tends to result in general agreement despite the diversity among scientists. But we have not come to such agreement in ethics. Philosophers have been investigating questions about the basis of morality since ancient times. With sincere and capable thinkers pursuing such a topic for millennia, one would think that some agreement would have been reached. But this seems not to be the case. It is not only on particular issues such as abortion that sincere people disagree but also on basic moral values or principles.

Tolerance and Open-Mindedness

Related to the fact of diversity is the desire to be tolerant and open-minded. Often people maintain relativism in an attempt to refrain from judging and condemning others. Since we know that there are problems with regard to ethnocentrism and bias in judging, we may want to prevent these problems by espousing relativism. From this perspective, the idea is that since there are a variety of cultures with different values, we are in no place to judge which culture is right and wrong. Furthermore, a defender of relativism may argue that those who try to judge are being ethnocentric, closed-minded, and intolerant.

Moral Uncertainty

Another reason to believe that what relativism holds is true is the great difficulty we often have in knowing what is the morally right thing to believe or do. We don't know what is morally most important. For example, we do not know whether it is better to help one's friend or do the honest thing in a case in which we cannot do both. Perhaps helping the friend is best in some circumstances, but being honest is best in others. We are not sure which is best in a particular case. Furthermore, we cannot know for sure what will happen down the line if we choose one course over another. Each of us is also aware of our personal limitations and the subjective viewpoint that we bring to moral judging. Thus, we distrust our own judgments. We then generalize and conclude that all moral judgments are simply personal and subjective viewpoints.

Situational Differences

Finally, people and situations, cultures and times differ in significant ways. The situations and living worlds of different people vary so much that it is difficult to believe that the same things that would be right for one would be right for another. In some places, overpopulation or drought is a problem; other places have too few people or too much water. In some places, people barely have access to the basic necessities of life; in other places, food is plentiful and the standard of living is high. Some individuals are healthy, while others are seriously ill. Some are more outgoing, while others are more reserved. How can the same things be consistently right or wrong under such different circumstances and for such different individuals? It seems unlikely, then, that any moral theory or judgment can apply in a general or universal manner. We thus tend to conclude that they must be relative to the particular situation and circumstance and that no objective or universally valid moral good exists.

ARE THESE REASONS CONVINCING?

Let us consider possible responses by a nonrelativist or objectivist to the preceding three points.

The Diversity of Moral Views

We can consider the matter of diversity of moral views from two different perspectives. First, we can ask, how widespread and deep is the disagreement? Second, we may ask, what does the fact of disagreement prove?

How Widespread and Deep Is the Disagreement?
If two people disagree about a moral matter, does this always amount to a moral disagreement? For example, Bill says that we ought to cut down dramatically on carbon dioxide emissions, while Jane says that we do not have a moral obligation to do this. This looks like a basic moral disagreement, but it actually may result from differences in their factual, rather than ethical, beliefs. Bill may believe that the current rate of carbon emissions is causing and will cause dramatically harmful global climate effects, such as rising sea levels and more severe weather. Jane may see no such connection because she believes that scientists' assessments and predictions are in error. If they did agree on the factual issues, then Bill and Jane would agree on the moral conclusion. It turns out that they both agree on the basic moral obligation to do what we can to improve

the current human condition and prevent serious harm to existing and future generations.

Many apparent moral disagreements are not moral disagreements at all but disagreements about factual or other beliefs. But suppose that at least some of them are about moral matters. Suppose that we do disagree about the relative value, for example, of health and peace, honesty and generosity, or about what rights people do and do not have. It is this type of disagreement that the moral relativist would need to make his or her point.

What Would Disagreement about Basic Moral Matters Prove?   In past years, we have asked students in our ethics classes to tell us in what year George Washington died. A few brave souls venture a guess: 1801, or at least after 1790? No one is sure. Does this disagreement or lack of certitude prove that he did not die or that he died on no particular date? Belief that he did die and on a particular date is consistent with differences of opinion and with uncertainty. So also in ethics: people can disagree about what constitutes the right thing to do and yet believe that there is a right thing to do. "Is it not because of this belief that we try to decide what is right and worry that we might miss it?" the nonrelativist would ask.

Or consider the supposed contrast between ethics and science. Although a body of knowledge

Arguments over moral matters often stem from factual disagreements, such as whether CO_2 emissions from cars and other sources are causing catastrophic climate change.

exists on which those working in the physical sciences agree, those at the forefront of these sciences often profoundly disagree. Does such disagreement prove that no objectivity exists in such matters? If people disagree about whether the universe began with a "big bang" or about what happened in its first millisecond, then does this prove that no answer is to be found, even in principle, about the universe's beginning? Not necessarily.

Tolerance and Open-Mindedness

While some people think that relativism goes hand in hand with tolerance and open-mindedness, it is not necessarily true that these things are mutually implied. It is possible to hold that since there are a variety of different cultures, we should simply ignore the other cultures or show them no respect whatsoever. If relativism holds that there are no universal norms that tell us how to deal with cross-cultural interaction, then tolerance and open-mindedness themselves must be seen as culturally relative values, no more legitimate than intolerance or aggression. Moreover, if Nietzsche is correct that the moral world consists of perspectives and struggles for power, then there is no good reason to remain open-minded and tolerant. Indeed, relativism might be used to support the use of power in order to defend and expand your own worldview or perspective when it comes into conflict with others.

Moral Uncertainty

Let us examine the point that moral matters are complex and difficult to determine. Because of this, we are often uncertain about what is the morally best thing to do. For example, those who "blow the whistle" on unscrupulous employers or coworkers must find it difficult to know whether they are doing the right thing when they consider the potential costs to themselves and others around them. However, this sort of dilemma is not strictly a question of relativism but of **skepticism**. Skepticism is the view that it is difficult, if not impossible, to know something. However, does the fact that we are uncertain about the answer to some question, even a moral question, prove that it lacks an answer? One reason for skepticism might be the belief that we can see things only from our own perspective and thus, in ethics and other inquiries, can never know things as they are. This is a form of subjectivism (as defined earlier). The nonrelativist could argue that in our very dissatisfaction with not knowing and in our seeking to know what we ought to do, we behave as though we believe that a better or worse choice can be made.

In contrast, matters of science and history often eventually get clarified and settled. We can now look up the date of George Washington's death (1799), and scientists gradually improve our knowledge in various fields. "Why is there no similar progress in ethical matters?" relativists might respond. Answers to that question will depend upon a variety of issues, including our ideas about ethical theory (as discussed in the first half of this book) and ideas about progress on social issues (as discussed in the second half). The fact of continued disagreement about moral theory and moral issues reminds us that ethical inquiry is different from inquiry in history and the social sciences or in the natural sciences.

Situational Differences

Do dramatic differences in people's life situations make it unlikely or impossible for them to have any common morality? Suppose that health is taken as an objective value. Is it not the case that what contributes to the health of some is different from what contributes to the health of others? Insulin injections are often good for the diabetic but not for the nondiabetic. A nonrelativist might reply as

Basic Moral Agreement	Factual Disagreement	Different Moral Conclusions
We ought not to harm.	CO_2 emissions harm.	We ought to reduce emissions.
We ought not to harm.	CO_2 emissions do not harm.	We need not reduce emissions.

follows: even though the good in these specific cases differs, there is still a general value—health—that is the goal. Similarly, justice involves "giving to each his or her due"; but what is due people is not always strictly the same. Those who work hard may deserve something different from those who do not, and the guilty deserve punishment that the innocent do not. These different applications of justice do not mean that justice is not an objective moral value. (See the table below.)

One reason situational differences may lead us to think that no objective moral value is possible is that we may be equating objectivism with what is sometimes called **absolutism**. Absolutism is the view that moral rules or principles have no exceptions and are context-independent. One example of such a rule is "Stealing is always wrong." According to absolutism, situational differences such as whether or not a person is starving would make no difference to moral conclusions about whether that person is justified in stealing food—if stealing is wrong.

However, an objectivist who is not an absolutist can argue that although there are some objective goods—for example, health or justice—what is good in a concrete case may vary from person to person and circumstance to circumstance. She or he could hold that stealing might be justified in some circumstances because it is necessary for life, an objective good, and a greater good than property. Opposing absolutism does not necessarily commit one to a similar opposition to objectivism.

One result of this clarification should be the realization that what is often taken as an expression of relativism is not necessarily so. Consider this statement: "What is right for one person is not necessarily right for another." If the term *for* means "in the view of," then the statement simply states the fact that people do disagree. It states that "What is right in the view of one person is not what is right in the view of the other." However, this is not yet relativism. Relativism goes beyond this in its belief that this is all there is. Relativists will claim that there only are various points of view and that there is no way to reconcile what's right for one person with what's right for another. Similarly, if *for* is used in the sense "Insulin injections are good for some people but not for others," then the original statement is also not necessarily relativistic. It could, in fact, imply that health is a true or objective good and that what leads to it is good and what diminishes it is bad. For ethical relativism, on the other hand, there is no such objective good.

IS RELATIVISM SELF-CONTRADICTORY?

One significant argument against relativism is that it is self-contradictory. If relativists claim that all values or truths are relative, then it is possible to ask whether the claim of relativism is itself merely a relative truth or value judgment. But it might be that such an argument against relativism sets up a **straw man**, an easy-to-defeat version of the opposing position. The philosopher Richard Rorty argued that there are no relativists in the sense that is aimed at by this sort of an argument. Rorty explains,

> Relativism is the view that every belief on a certain topic, or perhaps about any topic, is as good as every other. No one holds this view. Except for the occasional cooperative freshman, one cannot find anybody who says that two incompatible opinions on an important topic are equally good. The philosophers who get called 'relativists' are those who say that the grounds for choosing between such

Objective Value	Situational Differences	Different Moral Conclusions
Health	Diabetic.	Insulin injections are good.
Health	Nondiabetic.	Insulin injections are not good.
Justice	Works hard.	Deserves reward.
Justice	Does not work hard.	Does not deserve reward.

opinions are less algorithmic than had previously been thought.[9]

Rorty does not claim that any belief is as good as any other. Instead, he says that it is not so easy to figure out what is better or worse—as he puts it here, there are no "algorithms" that can be used to give precise answers about these things. His version of relativism attempts to avoid the charge of self-contradiction by connecting relativism to skepticism. Rorty has described his approach to things as "pragmatism" or "anti-foundationalism," by which he means that we find ourselves in the middle of things without access to any final account of ultimate reality or absolute values. For pragmatists such as Rorty, our judgments about things (including our judgment about ideas such as relativism) are provisional and embedded in contexts, cultures, and ways of life.

A related objection holds that a relativist has no way to define the group or perspective to which things are relative. With which group should my moral views coincide: my country, my state, my family, or myself and my peers? And how would we decide? Different groups to which I belong may have different moral views. Moreover, if a society changes its views, does this mean that morality changes? If 52 percent of its people once supported some war but later only 48 percent, does this mean that earlier the war was just but it became unjust when the people changed their minds about it?

One problem that individual relativism faces is whether its view accords with personal experience. According to individual relativism, it seems that I should turn within and consult my moral feelings to solve a personal moral problem. This is often just the source of the difficulty, however; for when I look within I find conflicting feelings. I want to know not how I *do* feel but how I *ought* to feel and what I *ought* to believe. But the view that there is something I possibly ought to believe would not be relativism.

As we saw above, a problem for both types of relativist lies in the implied belief that relativism is a more tolerant position than objectivism. The cultural relativist can hold that people in a society should be tolerant only if tolerance is one of the dominant values of their society. He or she cannot hold that all

people should be tolerant because tolerance cannot be an objective or transcultural value, according to relativism. We can also question whether there is any reason for an individual relativist to be tolerant, especially if being tolerant means not just putting up with others who disagree with us but also listening to their positions and arguments. Why should I listen to another who disagrees with me? If ethical relativism is true, then it cannot be because the other person's moral views may be better than mine in an objective sense, for there is no objectively better position. Objectivists might argue that their position provides a better basis for both believing that tolerance is an objective and transcultural good and that we ought to be open to others' views because they may be closer to the truth than ours are.

Relativism is sometimes simply a kind of intellectual laziness or a lack of moral courage. Rather than attempting to give reasons or arguments for my own position, I may hide behind some statement such as, "What is good for some is not necessarily good for others." I may say this simply to excuse myself from having to think about or be critical of my own ethical positions. Those who hold that there is an objective right and wrong may also do so uncritically. They may simply adopt the views of their parents or peers without evaluating those views themselves.

The major difficulty with an objectivist position is the problem it has in providing an alternative to the relativist position. The objectivist should give us reason to believe that there is an objective good. To pursue this problem in a little more detail, we will briefly examine two issues discussed by contemporary moral philosophers. One is the issue of the reality of moral value—**moral realism**; and the other concerns the problem of deciding among plural goods—**moral pluralism**.

MORAL REALISM

Realism is the view that there exists a reality independent of those who know it. Most people are probably realists in this sense about a variety of things. We think, for example, that the external world is real in the sense that it actually exists, independently of our awareness of it. If a tree falls in the woods and no one is there, the event is still real and it still makes a sound. The sound waves are real, even if the subjective perception of them depends upon a variety of contingent factors.

Now compare this to the situation regarding ethics. If I say that John's act of saving a drowning child was good, then what is the object of my moral judgment? Is there some real existing fact of goodness that I can somehow sense in this action? I can observe the actions of John to save the child, the characteristics of the child, John, the lake, and so forth. But in what sense, if any, do I observe the goodness itself? The British philosopher G. E. Moore (discussed in Chapter 1) held that goodness is a specific quality that attaches to people or acts.[10] According to Moore, although we cannot observe the goodness of acts (we cannot hear, touch, taste, or see it), we intuit its presence. Philosophers like Moore have had difficulty explaining both the nature of the quality and the particular intuitive or moral sense by which we are supposed to perceive it.

Some moral philosophers who seek to support a realist view of morality attempt to explain moral reality as a relational matter—perhaps as a certain fit between actions and situations or actions and our innate sensibilities.[11] For example, because of innate human sensibilities, some say, we just would not be able to approve of torturing the innocent. The problem, of course, is that not everyone agrees. To continue with this example, some people would be willing to torture an innocent person if they thought that by torturing that person they could elicit information about a terrorist attack or send a message to frighten would-be terrorists. And some activities that we might describe as torture—starvation, sleep deprivation, even beatings—can be viewed as valuable in religious contexts, in cultural initiation rituals, and even in hazing that occurs on sports teams or fraternities. Moral realists will claim that such disagreements can be resolved by consulting the real objects of morality which are supposed to make judgments about good and evil true. But relativists wonder whether there are any actual or objective qualities of actions that are intuited in the same way by all observers, just as they doubt that moral truth rests upon objective moral reality.

MORAL PLURALISM

Another problem nonrelativists or objectivists face is whether the good is one or many. According to some theories, there is one primary moral principle by which we can judge all actions. However, suppose this were not the case, that there were instead a variety of equally valid moral principles or equal moral values. For example, suppose that autonomy, justice, well-being, authenticity, and peace were all equally valuable. In this case, we would have a plurality of values. One version of pluralism is grounded in the claim that human beings are different and diverse, and that they should be allowed to flourish in their own way. As John Lachs explains in the essay that follows at the end of the chapter, "sanity and toleration demand that we allow each person to pursue his own, possibly unique form of fulfillment."[12] Another version of pluralism is Nussbaum's capabilities approach, discussed earlier. Nussbaum implies that a variety of basic goods can be realized in multiple ways in different cultural contexts. Another version is W. D. Ross's account of what he calls *prima facie* duties. According to Ross, there are a variety of duties—listed below. To say that these duties are **prima facie** (which means "at first face" or "on first look") means that they are duties that are important and valuable at first blush, all other things being equal. It might be, however, that these duties conflict—because there are more than one of them. The fact of a plurality of goods or duties means that there will be conflicts of values.

W. D. Ross's Prima Facie Duties[13]
1. Fidelity
2. Reparation
3. Gratitude
4. Beneficence
5. Nonmaleficence
6. Justice
7. Self-improvement

The difficulty of this pluralistic account is that we face a problem when we are forced to choose between competing duties or values. For example, what do we do when we've made a promise to someone (and have a duty of fidelity) but that promise conflicts with the opportunity to do something good for someone else (in order to fulfill the duty of beneficence)? In such cases when duties or values conflict, we may be forced simply to choose one or the other for no reason or on the basis of something other than reason. Whether some rational and non-arbitrary way exists to make such decisions is an open question. Whether ultimate choices are thus subjective or can be grounded in an assessment of what is objectively best is a question not only about how we do behave but also about what is possible in matters of moral judgment.

Pluralism about morality may be understood as a form of relativism, which holds that there is no single objective or universal standard. In response, pluralists might hold that there are several equally plausible standards of value. But—as we saw in our discussion of religious pluralism in Chapter 2—it is possible for a pluralist to hold that there is some sort of convergence toward something unitary and universal in the realm of values. It might be that there is a hierarchy of values. But genuine pluralism points toward a sort of equality among values, which does not admit to a hierarchical organization of duties.

In subsequent chapters, we will examine several major ethical theories—utilitarianism, deontology, natural law theory, and the ethics of care. These theories are articulated from an objectivist or nonrelativist standpoint: defenders of these theories claim that the theory presents a substantive definition of what is good. But the problem of relativism returns as soon as we ask whether there is some way to compare or unite these normative theories—or whether we are left with incompatible accounts of the good.

In this chapter's reading selection, Louis Pojman presents an argument against relativism and in favor of a version of universalism. Pojman outlines the difference between descriptive or cultural relativism and the stronger claim about ethical relativism.

He concludes that there may in fact be universal values that transcend cultures. In the second reading, John Lachs offers a defense of a form of relativism that is pluralistic and tolerant and that is grounded in a claim about the diversity of human natures.

NOTES

1. Ruth Benedict, "Anthropology and the Abnormal," *Journal of General Psychology* 10 (1934), pp. 60–70.
2. We could also think of many forms of ethical relativism from the most individual or personal to the universal. Thus, we could think of individual relativism, or that based on family values, or local community or state or cultural values. The most universal, however, in which moral values are the same for all human beings, would probably no longer be a form of relativism.
3. According to some versions of individual ethical relativism, moral judgments are similar to expressions of taste. We each have our own individual tastes. I like certain styles or foods, and you like others. Just as no taste can be said to be correct or incorrect, so also no ethical view can be valued as better than any other. My saying that this war is or all wars are unjust is, in effect, my expression of my dislike of or aversion to war. An entire tradition in ethics, sometimes called emotivism (as discussed in Chapter 1), holds this view.
4. Friedrich Nietzsche, *Will to Power* (New York: Random House, 1968) no. 481, p. 267.
5. Martha C. Nussbaum, *Women and Human Development* (Cambridge: Cambridge University Press, 2001), p. 105.
6. Ibid., p. 106.
7. Ibid., pp. 78–80.
8. These are not necessarily complete and coherent arguments for relativism. Rather, they are more popular versions of why people generally are inclined to what they believe is relativism.
9. Richard Rorty, "Pragmatism, Relativism, and Irrationalism," *Proceedings and Addresses of the American Philosophical Association* 53, no. 6 (1980), p. 727.
10. G. E. Moore, *Principia Ethica* (Cambridge: Cambridge University Press, 1903).

11. Bruce W. Brower, "Dispositional Ethical Realism," *Ethics* 103, no. 2 (January 1993), pp. 221–49.
12. John Lachs, "Relativism and Its Benefits" *Soundings* 56:3 (Fall 1973), p. 319.
13. W. D. Ross, *The Right and the Good* (Oxford: Oxford University Press, 1930), Chapter 1.

READING

Who's to Judge?

LOUIS POJMAN

MindTap® For more chapter resources and activities, go to MindTap.

Study Questions

As you read the excerpt, please consider the following questions:
1. How does Pojman link ethnocentrism to relativism?
2. How does Pojman explain the way that the diversity thesis and the dependency thesis lead to relativism?
3. How does Pojman explain the connection (or lack thereof) between cultural relativism and the idea of tolerance?

There is one thing a professor can be absolutely certain of: almost every student entering the university believes, or says he believes, that truth is relative. If this belief is put to the test, one can count on the students' reaction: they will be uncomprehending. That anyone should regard the proposition as not self-evident astonishes them, as though he were calling into question 2 + 2 = 4. ... The danger they have been taught to fear from absolutism is not error but intolerance. Relativism is necessary to openness; and this is the virtue, the only virtue, which all primary education for more than fifty years has dedicated itself to inculcating. (Alan Bloom, The Closing of the American Mind)

In an ancient writing, the Greek historian Herodotus (485–430 BC) relates that the Persian King Darius once called into his presence some Greeks and asked them what he should pay them to eat the bodies of their fathers when they died. They replied that no sum of money would tempt them to do such a terrible deed; whereupon Darius sent for certain people of the Callatian tribe, who eat their fathers, and asked them in the presence of the Greeks what he should give them to burn the bodies of their fathers at their decease [as the Greeks do]. The Callatians were horrified at the thought and bid him desist in such terrible talk. So Herodotus concludes, "Culture is King o'er all."

Today we condemn ethnocentrism, the uncritical belief in the inherent superiority of one's own culture, as a variety of prejudice tantamount to racism and sexism. What is right in one culture may be wrong in another, what is good east of the river may be bad west of the same river, what is a virtue in one nation may be seen as a vice in another, so it behooves us not to judge others but to be tolerant of diversity.

This rejection of ethnocentrism in the West has contributed to a general shift in public opinion about morality, so that for a growing number of Westerners, consciousness-raising about the validity of other ways of life has led to a gradual erosion of belief in moral *objectivism*, the view that there are universal moral principles, valid for all people at all times and climes. For example, in polls taken in my ethics and introduction to philosophy classes over the past several years (in three different universities in three areas of the country) students by a two-to-one ratio

---

"Who's to Judge?", by Louis Pojman. From *Vice and Virtue in Everyday Life*, 6e, Sommers & Sommers. © 2003 Cengage Learning. Reprinted by permission of Gertrude "Trudy" Pojman.

affirmed a version of *moral relativism* over *moral absolutism* with hardly 3 percent seeing something in between these two polar opposites. Of course, I'm not suggesting that all of these students have a clear understanding of what relativism entails, for many of those who say that they are ethical relativists also state on the same questionnaire that "abortion except to save the mother's life is always wrong," that "capital punishment is always morally wrong," or that "suicide is never morally permissible." The apparent contradictions signal an apparent confusion on the matter.

In this essay I want to examine the central notions of ethical relativism and look at the implications that seem to follow from it. After this I want to set forth the outlines of a very modest objectivism, which holds to the objective validity of moral principles but takes into account many of the insights of relativism.

AN ANALYSIS OF RELATIVISM

Ethical relativism is the theory that there are no universally valid moral principles, but that all moral principles are valid relative to culture or individual choice. It is to be distinguished from moral skepticism, the view that there are no valid moral principles at all (or at least we cannot know whether there are any), and from all forms of moral objectivism or absolutism. The following statement by the relativist philosopher John Ladd is a good characterization of the theory.

> *Ethical relativism is the doctrine that the moral rightness and wrongness of actions varies from society to society and that there are no absolute universal moral standards binding on all men at all times. Accordingly, it holds that whether or not it is right for an individual to act in a certain way depends on or is relative to the society to which he belongs. (John Ladd, Ethical Relativism)*

If we analyze this passage, we derive the following argument:

1. What is considered morally right and wrong varies from society to society, so that there are no moral principles accepted by all societies.
2. All moral principles derive their validity from cultural acceptance.

3. Therefore, there are no universally valid moral principles, objective standards which apply to all people everywhere and at all times.

1. The first thesis, which may be called the *Diversity Thesis* and identified with *Cultural Relativism*, is simply an anthropological thesis, which registers the fact that moral rules differ from society to society. As we noted in the introduction of this essay, there is enormous variety in what may count as a moral principle in a given society. The human condition is malleable in the extreme, allowing any number of folkways or moral codes. As Ruth Benedict has written:

> *The cultural pattern of any civilization makes use of a certain segment of the great arc of potential human purposes and motivations. ... [A]ny culture makes use of certain selected material techniques or cultural traits. The great arc along which all the possible human behaviors are distributed is far too immense and too full of contradictions for any one culture to utilize even any considerable portion of it. Selection is the first requirement.* (Patterns of Culture, New York, 1934, p. 219)

It may or may not be the case that there is not a single moral principle held in common by every society, but if there are any, they seem to be few, at best. Certainly, it would be very hard to derive one single "true" morality on the basis of observation of various societies' moral standards.

2. The second thesis, the *Dependency* Thesis, asserts that individual acts are right or wrong depending on the nature of the society from which they emanate. Morality does not occur in a vacuum, but what is considered morally right or wrong must be seen in a context, depending on the goals, wants, beliefs, history, and environment of the society in question. As William Graham Sumner says, "We learn the [morals] as unconsciously as we learn to walk and hear and breathe, and they never know any reason why the [morals] are what they are. The justification of them is that when we wake to consciousness of life we find them facts which already hold us in the bonds of tradition, custom, and habit."[1] Trying to see things from an independent, non-cultural point of view would be like taking out our eyes in order to examine their contours

and qualities. We are simply culturally determined beings.

We could, of course, distinguish a weak and a strong thesis of dependency. The nonrelativist can accept a certain relativity in the way moral principles are *applied* in various cultures, depending on beliefs, history, and environment. For example, Orientals show respect by covering the head and uncovering the feet, whereas Occidentals do the opposite, but both adhere to a principle of respect for deserving people. They just apply the principle of respect differently. Drivers in Great Britain drive on the left side of the road, while those in the rest of Europe and the United States drive on the right side, but both adhere to a principle of orderly progression of traffic. The application of the rule is different but the principle in question is the same principle in both cases. But the ethical relativist must maintain a stronger thesis, one that insists that the very validity of the principles is a product of the culture and that different cultures will invent different valid principles. The ethical relativist maintains that even beyond the environmental factors and differences in beliefs, there is a fundamental disagreement between societies.

In a sense, we all live in radically different worlds. Each person has a different set of beliefs and experiences, a particular perspective that colors all of his or her perceptions. Do the farmer, the real estate dealer, and the artist, looking at the same spatiotemporal field, see the *same* field? Not likely. Their different orientations, values, and expectations govern their perceptions, so that different aspects of the field are highlighted and some features are missed. Even as our individual values arise from personal experience, so social values are grounded in the peculiar history of the community. Morality, then, is just the set of common rules, habits, and customs which have won social approval over time, so that they seem part of the nature of things, as facts. There is nothing mysterious or transcendent about these codes of behavior. They are the outcomes of our social history.

There is something conventional about *any* morality, so that every morality really depends on a level of social acceptance. Not only do various societies adhere to different moral systems, but the very same society could (and often does) change its moral views over time and place. For example, the southern United States now views slavery as immoral whereas just over one hundred years ago, it did not. We have greatly altered our views on abortion, divorce, and sexuality as well.

3. The conclusion that there are no absolute or objective moral standards binding on all people follows from the first two propositions. Cultural relativism (the Diversity Thesis) plus the Dependency Thesis yields ethical relativism in its classic form. If there are different moral principles from culture to culture and if all morality is rooted in culture, then it follows that there are no universal moral principles valid for all cultures and people at all times.

SUBJECTIVE ETHICAL RELATIVISM (SUBJECTIVISM)

Some people think that even this conclusion is too tame and maintain that morality is not dependent on the society but on the individual him or herself. As students sometimes maintain, "Morality is in the eye of the beholder." Ernest Hemingway wrote, "So far, about morals, I know only that what is moral is what you feel good after and what is immoral is what you feel bad after and judged by these moral standards, which I do not defend, the bullfight is very moral to me because I feel very fine while it is going on and have a feeling of life and death and mortality and immortality, and after it is over I feel very sad but very fine."[2]

This form of moral subjectivism has the sorry consequence that it makes morality a useless concept, for, on its premises, little or no interpersonal criticism or judgment is logically possible. Hemingway may feel good about killing bulls in a bull fight, while Albert Schweitzer or Mother Teresa may feel the opposite. No argument about the matter is possible. The only basis for judging Hemingway or anyone else wrong would be if he failed to live up to his own principles, but, of course, one of Hemingway's principles could be that hypocrisy is morally permissible (he feels good about it), so that it would be impossible for him to do wrong. For Hemingway hypocrisy and non-hypocrisy are both morally permissible. On the basis of Subjectivism it could very easily turn out that Adolf Hitler is as moral as Gandhi, so long as each believes he is living by his chosen principles. Notions of moral good and bad, right or wrong, cease to have interpersonal evaluative meaning.

In the opening days of my philosophy classes, I often find students vehemently defending subjective relativism. I then give them their first test of the reading material—which is really a test of their relativism. The next class period I return all the tests, marked with the grade "F" even though my comments show that most of them are of very high quality. When the students explode with outrage (some of them have never before seen this letter on their papers) at this "injustice," I explain that I too have accepted subjectivism for purposes of marking exams, in which case the principle of justice has no objective validity and their complaint is without merit.

You may not like it when your teacher gives you an F on your test paper, while she gives your neighbor an A for one exactly similar, but there is no way to criticize her for injustice, since justice is not one of her elected principles.

Absurd consequences follow from Subjective Ethical Relativism. If it is correct, then morality reduces to aesthetic tastes over which there can be no argument nor interpersonal judgment. Although many students say that they hold this position, there seems to be a conflict between it and other of their moral views (e.g., that Hitler is really morally bad or capital punishment is always wrong). There seems to be a contradiction between Subjectivism and the very concept of morality, which it is supposed to characterize, for morality has to do with "proper" resolution of interpersonal conflict and the amelioration of the human predicament. Whatever else it does, it has a minimal aim of preventing a state of chaos where life is "solitary, poor, nasty, brutish, and short." But if so, Subjectivism is no help at all in doing this, for it doesn't rest on social *agreement* of principle (as the conventionalist maintains) or on

an objectively independent set of norms that bind all people for the common good.

Subjectivism treats individuals as billiard balls on a societal pool table where they meet only in radical collisions, each aiming for its own goal and striving to do the other fellow in before he does you. This atomistic view of personality is belied by the fact that we develop in families and mutually dependent communities, in which we share a common language, common institutions, and habits, and that we often feel each other's joys and sorrows. As John Donne said, "No man is an island, entire of itself; every man is a piece of the continent."

Radical individualistic relativism seems incoherent. If so, it follows that the only plausible view of ethical relativism must be one that grounds morality in the group or culture. This form of relativism is called "conventionalism," and to it we now turn.

CONVENTIONAL ETHICAL RELATIVISM (CONVENTIONALISM)

Conventional Ethical Relativism, the view that there are no objective moral principles but that all valid moral principles are justified by virtue of their cultural acceptance, recognizes the social nature of morality. That is precisely its power and virtue. It does not seem subject to the same absurd consequences which plague Subjectivism. Recognizing the importance of our social environment in generating customs and beliefs, many people suppose that ethical relativism is the correct ethical theory. Furthermore, they are drawn to it for its liberal philosophical stance. It seems to be an enlightened response to the sin of ethnocentricity, and it seems to entail or strongly imply an attitude of tolerance towards other cultures. As Benedict says, in recognizing ethical relativity "we shall arrive at a more realistic social faith, accepting as grounds of hope and as new bases for tolerance the coexisting and equally valid patterns of life which mankind has created for itself from the raw materials of existence."[3] The most famous of those holding this position is the anthropologist Melville Herskovits, who argues even more explicitly than Benedict that ethical relativism entails intercultural tolerance:

1. If Morality is relative to its culture, then there is no independent basis for criticizing the morality of any other culture but one's own.
2. If there is no independent way of criticizing any other culture, we ought to be *tolerant* of the moralities of other cultures.
3. Morality is relative to its culture.

Therefore,

4. we ought to be tolerant of the moralities of other cultures.[4]

Tolerance is certainly a virtue, but is this a good argument for it? I think not. If morality simply is relative to each culture then if the culture does not have a principle of tolerance, its members have no obligation to be tolerant. Herskovits seems to be treating the *principle of tolerance* as the one exception to his relativism. He seems to be treating it as an absolute moral principle. But from a relativistic point of view there is no more reason to be tolerant than to be intolerant, and neither stance is objectively morally better than the other.

Not only do relativists fail to offer a basis for criticizing those who are intolerant, but they cannot rationally criticize anyone who espouses what they might regard as a heinous principle. If, as seems to be the case, valid criticism supposes an objective or impartial standard, relativists cannot morally criticize anyone outside their own culture. Adolf Hitler's genocidal actions, so long as they are culturally accepted, are as morally legitimate as Mother Teresa's works of mercy. If Conventional Relativism is accepted, racism, genocide of unpopular minorities, oppression of the poor, slavery, and even the advocacy of war for its own sake are as equally moral as their opposites. And if a subculture decided that starting a nuclear war was somehow morally acceptable, we could not morally criticize these people.

Any actual morality, whatever its content, is as valid as every other, and more valid than ideal moralities—since the latter aren't adhered to by any culture.

There are other disturbing consequences of ethical relativism. It seems to entail that reformers are always (morally) wrong since they go against the tide of cultural standards. William Wilberforce was wrong in the eighteenth century to oppose slavery; the British were immoral in opposing suttee in India (the burning of widows, which is now illegal in India). The Early Christians were wrong in refusing to serve in the Roman army or bow down to Caesar, since the majority in the Roman Empire believed that these two acts were moral duties. In fact, Jesus himself was immoral in breaking the law of his day by healing on the Sabbath day and by advocating the principles of the Sermon on the Mount, since it is clear that few in his time (or in ours) accepted them.

Yet we normally feel just the opposite, that the reformer is the courageous innovator who is right, who has the truth, against the mindless majority. Sometimes the individual must stand alone with the truth, risking social censure and persecution. As Dr. Stockman says in Ibsen's *Enemy of the People*, after he loses the battle to declare his town's profitable polluted tourist spa unsanitary, "The most dangerous enemy of the truth and freedom among us—is the compact majority. Yes, the damned, compact, and liberal majority. The majority has *might*—unfortunately—but *right* it is not. Right are I and a few others." Yet if relativism is correct, the opposite is necessarily the case. Truth is with the crowd and error with the individual....

There is an even more basic problem with the notion that morality is dependent on cultural acceptance for its validity. The problem is that the notion of a culture or society is notoriously difficult to define. This is especially so in a pluralistic society like our own where the notion seems to be vague with unclear boundary lines. One person may belong to several societies (subcultures) with different value emphases and arrangements of principles. A person may belong to the nation as a single society with certain values of patriotism, honor, courage, laws (including some which are controversial but have majority acceptance, such as the law on abortion). But he or she may also belong to a church which opposes some of the laws of the State. He may also be an integral member of a socially mixed community where different principles hold sway, and he may belong to clubs and a family where still other rules are adhered to. Relativism would seem to tell us that where he is a member of societies with conflicting moralities he must be judged both wrong and not-wrong whatever he does. For example, if Mary is a U.S. citizen and a member of the Roman Catholic Church, she is wrong (qua Catholic) if she chooses to have an abortion and not-wrong (qua citizen of the U.S.A.) if she acts against the teaching of the Church on abortion. As a member of a racist university fraternity, KKK, John has no obligation to treat his fellow Black student as an equal, but as a member of the University community itself (where the principle of equal rights is accepted) he does have the obligation; but as a member of the surrounding community (which may reject the principle of equal rights) he again has no such obligation; but then again as a member of the nation at large (which accepts the principle) he is obligated to treat his fellow with respect. What is the morally right thing for John to do? The question no longer makes much sense in this moral Babel. It has lost its action-guiding function.

Perhaps the relativist would adhere to a principle which says that in such cases the individual may choose which group to belong to as primary. If Mary chooses to have an abortion, she is choosing to belong to the general society relative to that principle. And John must likewise choose between groups. The trouble with this option is that it seems to lead back to counter-intuitive results. If Gangland Gus of Murder, Incorporated, feels like killing Bank President Ortcutt and wants to feel good about it, he identifies with the Murder, Incorporated society rather than the general public morality. Does this justify the killing? In fact, couldn't one justify anything simply by forming a small subculture that approved of it? Charles Manson would be morally pure in killing innocents simply by virtue of forming a little coterie. How large must the group be in order to be a legitimate subculture or society? Does it need ten or fifteen people? How about just three? Come to think about it, why can't my burglary partner and I found our own society with

a morality of its own? Of course, if my partner dies, I could still claim that I was acting from an originally social set of norms. But why can't I dispense with the inter-personal agreements altogether and invent my own morality—since morality, on this view, is only an invention anyway? Conventionalist Relativism seems to reduce to Subjectivism. And Subjectivism leads, as we have seen, to the demise of morality altogether.

However, while we may fear the demise of morality, as we have known it, this in itself may not be a good reason for rejecting relativism; that is, for judging it false. Alas, truth may not always be edifying. But the consequences of this position are sufficiently alarming to prompt us to look carefully for some weakness in the relativist's argument. So let us examine the premises and conclusion listed at the beginning of this essay as the three theses of relativism.

1. *The Diversity Thesis* What is considered morally right and wrong varies from society to society, so that there are no moral principles accepted by all societies.
2. *The Dependency Thesis* All moral principles derive their validity from cultural acceptance.
3. *Ethical Relativism* Therefore, there are no universally valid moral principles, objective standards which apply to all people everywhere and at all times.

Does any one of these seem problematic? Let us consider the first thesis, the Diversity Thesis, which we have also called Cultural Relativism. Perhaps there is not as much diversity as anthropologists like Sumner and Benedict suppose. One can also see great similarities between the moral codes of various cultures. E. O. Wilson has identified over a score of common features, and before him Clyde Kluckhohn has noted some significant common ground.

> *Every culture has a concept of murder, distinguishing this from execution, killing in war, and other "justifiable homicides." The notions of incest and other regulations upon sexual behavior, the prohibitions upon untruth under defined circumstances, of restitution and reciprocity, of mutual obligations between parents and children— these and many other moral concepts are altogether universal. ("Ethical Relativity: Sic et Non," Journal of Philosophy, LII, 1955)*

And Colin Turnbull, whose description of the sadistic, semi-displaced Ik in Northern Uganda, was seen as evidence of a people without principles of kindness and cooperation, has produced evidence that underneath the surface of this dying society, there is a deeper moral code from a time when the tribe flourished, which occasionally surfaces and shows its nobler face.

On the other hand, there is enormous cultural diversity and many societies have radically different moral codes. Cultural Relativism seems to be a fact, but, even if it is, it does not by itself establish the truth of Ethical Relativism. Cultural diversity in itself is neutral between theories. For the objectivist could concede complete cultural relativism, but still defend a form of universalism; for he or she could argue that some cultures simply lack correct moral principles.

On the other hand, a denial of complete Cultural Relativism (i.e., an admission of some universal principles) does not disprove Ethical Relativism. For even if we did find one or more universal principles, this would not prove that they had any objective status. We could still *imagine* a culture that was an exception to the rule and be unable to criticize it. So the first premise doesn't by itself imply Ethical Relativism and its denial doesn't disprove Ethical Relativism.

We turn to the crucial second thesis, the Dependency Thesis. Morality does not occur in a vacuum, but what is considered morally right or wrong must be seen in a context, depending on the goals, wants, beliefs, history, and environment of the society in question. We distinguished a weak and a strong thesis of dependency. The weak thesis says that the application of principles depends on the particular cultural predicament, whereas the strong thesis affirms that the principles themselves depend on that predicament. The nonrelativist can accept a certain relativity in the way moral principles are *applied* in various cultures, depending on beliefs, history, and environment. For example, a raw environment with scarce natural resources may justify the Eskimos' brand of euthanasia to the objectivist, who in another environment would consistently reject that practice. The members of a tribe in the Sudan throw their deformed children into the river

because of their belief that such infants *belong* to the hippopotamus, the god of the river. We believe that they have a false belief about this, but the point is that the same principles of respect for property and respect for human life are operative in these contrary practices. They differ with us only in belief, not in substantive moral principle. This is an illustration of how nonmoral beliefs (e.g., deformed children belong to the hippopotamus) when applied to common moral principles (e.g., give to each his due) generate different actions in different cultures. In our own culture the difference in the nonmoral belief about the status of a fetus generates opposite moral prescriptions. So the fact that moral principles are weakly dependent doesn't show that Ethical Relativism is valid. In spite of this weak dependency on non-moral factors, there could still be a set of general moral norms applicable to all cultures and even recognized in most, which are disregarded at a culture's own expense.

What the relativist needs is a strong thesis of dependency, that somehow all principles are essentially cultural inventions. But why should we choose to view morality this way? Is there anything to recommend the strong thesis over the weak thesis of dependency? The relativist may argue that in fact we don't have an obvious impartial standard from which to judge. "Who's to say which culture is right and which is wrong?" But this seems to be dubious. We can reason and perform thought experiments in order to make a case for one system over another. We may not be able to *know* with certainty that our moral beliefs are closer to the truth than those of another culture or those of others within our own culture, but we may be *justified* in believing that they are. If we can be closer to the truth regarding factual or scientific matters, why can't we be closer to the truth on moral matters? Why can't a culture simply be confused or wrong about its moral perceptions? Why can't we say that the society like the Ik which sees nothing wrong with enjoying watching its own children fall into fires is less moral in that regard than the culture that cherishes children and grants them protection and equal rights? To take such a stand is not to commit the fallacy of ethnocentrism, for we are seeking to derive principles through critical reason, not simply uncritical acceptance of one's own mores....

In conclusion I have argued (1) that Cultural Relativism (the fact that there are cultural differences regarding moral principles) does not entail Ethical Relativism (the thesis that there are no objectively valid universal moral principles); (2) that the Dependency Thesis (that morality derives its legitimacy from individual cultural acceptance) is mistaken; and (3) that there are universal moral principles based on a common human nature and a need to solve conflicts of interest and flourish.

So, returning to the question asked at the beginning of this essay, "Who's to judge what's right or wrong?" the answer is: *We are.* We are to do so on the basis of the best reasoning we can bring forth and with sympathy and understanding.

NOTES

1. *Folkways*, New York, 1906, section 80. Ruth Benedict indicates the depth of our cultural conditioning this way: "The very eyes with which we see the problem are conditioned by the long traditional habits of our own society" ("Anthropology and the Abnormal," in *The Journal of General Psychology* [1934], pp. 59–82).
2. Ernest Hemingway, *Death in the Afternoon* (New York: Scribner's, 1932), p. 4.
3. *Patterns of Culture* (New American Library, 1934), p. 257.
4. Melville Herskovits, *Cultural Relativism* (New York: Random House, 1972).

READING

Relativism and Its Benefits

JOHN LACHS

MindTap® For more chapter resources and activities, go to MindTap.

Study Questions

As you read the excerpt, please consider the following questions:
1. What is Lachs's problem with the idea that we have firm ethical intuitions or that there are self-evident truths?
2. How is Lachs's account of the variety of human natures connected to his defense of tolerance?
3. What are the benefits of relativism, as imagined by Lachs?

Perhaps it is our animal urge for security that turns us into dogmatists in manners and morals. As dogmatists we live in glorious and safe ignorance of alternatives; we find it not unlikely but actually inconceivable that a style of life and a form of behavior—perhaps even a mode of dress and a fashion of wearing hair—different from ours could have any legitimacy or value. Being essentially insecure, the dogmatist pounces with fury upon each innocent change and contrary current; he senses danger, opposition, or conspiracy everywhere, and fights each deviation from his norms as if his life depended on it. The steadfast dogmatist is, therefore, immune to external change. He may be destroyed, but he will not change his mind; he would sooner lose his life than his illusions. In putting his life on the line in their defense, he will fancy

John Lachs, "Relativism and Its Benefits", in *Soundings: An Interdisciplinary Journal*, Vol. 56, No. 3 (Fall 1973), pp. 312–322. Published by Penn State University Press.

Chapter 3 « Ethical Relativism 63

himself the defender of all that is good and wholesome; the collapse of his cause and his inability to impose his will on the rest of this restless world will seem to him a tragic defeat of everything true and noble.

Faced with the need to show that his own ultimate values are universal and defensible, the dogmatist can rely on two strategies. He may say that certain ultimate values stand in no need of being justified: they are self-evident and shine by their own light. Alternatively, he may admit that every moral judgment must be vindicated. Specific ones can be supported by showing their relation to more general principles we hold. General principles, in turn, are justified in terms of some being or attitude or non-moral state of affairs.

Will these strategies work? Not much can be said for the first of them. It is reassuring to think that there are universal moral standards that can be known merely by reflection. If there were such principles, self-evident and knowable by mere intuition, moral disagreements could result only from haste in judgment or a clouding of the moral sense; nothing, surely, that sound education and a clear head could not cure.

Bishop Joseph Butler, the great eighteenth-century British moralist, writes as if he believed this when he recommends that to be sure our judgments are right we reflect on them "in a cool afternoon." But is the matter quite so simple as that? We are all familiar with what it is like to be totally convinced of the legitimacy of a value or the universal applicability of a moral standard. Yet the very firmness of the conviction makes it suspect. Could it not be the expression and result of our gullibility? Does it really have the marks of objective truth?

What response can the defender of such ethical intuitions make to the man who is unable to see the self-evidence of some principle? What reply is possible to the philosopher who, after many earnest attempts, cannot see the universal truth of *any* moral judgment? What we want to say is that persons, actions, and consequences are good or bad as objectively as physical objects are red or green or blue. The colors are there for everyone to see. Similarly, the moral features of things are open to every sensitive person's scrutiny. Those who cannot recognize them are simply blind to the moral hues of life.

The analogy of color vision is striking and inventive. But in reality it does not work to the intuitionist's advantage. The color any given object appears to have is only partly the result of its objective properties. The light in which we bathe it and the nature and condition of the sensory mechanism involved are equally indispensible determining conditions. The color varies with changes in any one of these three factors, at least one of which is the psychological and physiological condition of the subject.

This is sometimes countered by the claim that although an object may appear to have a variety of colors, its *real* color is that which an observer with normal sense organs operating under standard lighting conditions will perceive. This objection is, of course, worthless. The very fact that we have to stabilize the variables of lighting and sensory organs by calling them "standard" and "normal" constitutes an admission that all color determinations are relative to them. And what we shall call "normal" is perfectly arbitrary. Standard lighting conditions are those that resemble sunshine. But what if our sun were a red star? Normal observers are those that can see a "full" spectrum of colors, including red. But what if the bulk of the population were red-green color defective? We simply cannot talk of colors without tacit or explicit reference to the nature and condition of the perceiver. The shrill insistence of the majority cannot make the color they see the *real* color of the object. Though I may have to heed their view, it will always remain a fact that the object appears red to many but a rich brown to me.

The case of values is analogous. What appears good is only partly a result of the objective features of the action or event. The principles or categories in terms of which a given culture or subculture views an action are in some respects similar to the lighting conditions we may use on an object of perception. And the nature and condition of the sensory mechanism is paralleled by those of the mechanisms of desire and preference in the agent.

Pleasure may appear good to some and evil to others. We cannot infer from this that one or the other side must be right though, as G.E. Moore generously conceded, it may be very difficult to establish which one. If disagreement is genuine and ultimate, as in morals it often is, pleasure will seem as genuinely good for Aristippus as it is bad for Cotton Mather. The natural conclusion to draw is that "good" and "bad" are relational terms: as with colors, we cannot meaningfully speak of the value of persons, actions, and consequences without reference to the categories of a culture and the standards and commitments of the man who judges. The moral hue of the world of action will change with changes in our social milieu and in the organ of our moral sight.

It is clear, then, that there are no self-evident objective—that is, universally true—moral principles. But if absolute values are, after all, in need of justification, where shall we look for the principles that might support them? There are four areas to which we may turn for the foundation of morals: (1) society with its rules and attitudes and institutions, (2) human nature with its structure and laws of operation, (3) nature and its purposive constitution and (4) God as the Infinite Lawgiver of creation.

Let me remark at once that if social rules and attitudes were to serve as the foundation upon which the structure of morality is erected, we could not legitimately say that values are absolute and unchanging. Persons, actions, and consequences would then be good as a result of their relation to socially established norms. While every society would have *some* values, there is no reason to suppose that the values of any one would coincide with those of any other.

One might attempt to argue for the universality at least of such generic values as social cooperation and the survival of the members of the group. Yet this is a verbal gloss: it is a way of reading identity into diverse views and values by the expedient of calling them by the same name. "Social cooperation" among primitive Eskimos involves different values and fundamentally diverse modes of behavior from what is required for it in a tour-group from Hoboken or in the Pentagon. And even today "survival of the members of the group" means radically different things in Washington and Peking. Generalities sometimes reach the stage of becoming vacuous and verbal: there is no better example of this than the

claim that all societies share a single vision of the good. Values, if social in origin, vary with societies. If they do, the similarity of societies is the measure of the uniformity of the good.

A similar observation should be made about the view that locates the source of values in human nature. If the view is true, values are uniform only to the extent that individual human natures coincide. It is clear, therefore, that absolute values could not be grounded this way without the ancillary tenet of a shared and unchanging human nature. Questions about the nature of man are notoriously difficult to handle. In any case, this would be no place to handle them, even if I could. There are a few things, however, that need to be said. They can be said briefly and with a reasonable degree of certainty. The question of what we shall be satisfied to call the nature of man is partly a definitional, and hence conventional, and partly an impirical matter. We always have the option of permitting our definitions to be guided by our preconceptions or our changing whims. We can go so far as to take the heroic course of disregarding most of the empirical evidence in our steadfast conviction that many of those who appear human do not properly deserve the compliment. If, however, we allow the suggestions of good sense to guide our concept formation, we shall find ourselves overwhelmingly committed to the view that human nature is no constant and that what we are dealing with is, at best, a wide spectrum of resembling individuals who do not share a single common essence. If human nature is to serve as the foundation of morals, the more reason we have to doubt the uniformity of man, the more we are entitled to deny the existence of universal values.

This leaves us with only two possible foundations for absolutistic morals. The first is the possibly infinite realm of facts we call Nature. Our dogmatist might take a cosmic perspective and assert that the world is saturated with potentialities that demand actualization. It is a law of nature, we might think, that beings with specific potencies must strive to reach fruition: perfection consists in having what is latent discharged. Actualized being is both the aim and the result of potentiality; without it everything would be frustrated and incomplete. Thus value is or is grounded in the actuality which lures matter to create it.

The lawlike and natural connection between fact and fulfillment would amply suffice as the foundation of morals, were it not for the fact that it does not exist. The view that Nature is replete with potentialities aiming at self-realization and values that, although they do not yet exist, charm the world to make them actual is perhaps the most colorful of human fables. There is struggle and striving in the natural world. But who would want to say that each of a plenitude of beings aims at achieving some minor element of the cosmic good? We *can* look at things this way, just as we *can* see shadows as giants and each frog as a metamorphosed minor royalty. But in doing so we commit a great blunder: tacitly we impute aim and consciousness to every natural impulse. The flux of nature has direction and frequently results in the production of some value. But to suppose that direction implies an aim, that motion requires an underlying love of the beautiful and the good to generate it, is to view simple physical fact as if it had an element of mind animating it at every turn.

If we examine the facts calmly and free of the persistent drive to find more rationality in the world than it in fact displays, we will be struck less by the remarkable adaptation of means to ends and the direction of every impulse at its own actualization than by the spectacle of the mindless impartiality with which nature fulfills or frustrates its own potentials. There are millions of acorns for every tree: the phenomenon of discharged potency is the exception rather than the rule. Why should we disregard the wide compass of dysteleology and the plenitude of crushed potentials in nature? If we must see purposes in the flux, we might agree with the disenchanted Schopenhauers of the world that perpetual frustration of the will is the rule in nature and actualized good is for most a rare and furtive joy. In any case, to ground the concrete values of the moral life in some hypothetical cosmic principle which reads vestiges of mind into a mindless flux is as implausible as it is ill-advised.

Let me finally speak of God's decrees as a possible support for human values. It is obvious that in grounding the good in divine commands we are presupposing the existence of a God who can make laws, proclaim rules of behavior and create values as he sees fit. The existence of such a God seems highly dubious to me. I say this not as a person who believes in the existence of no deity at all, nor as one who refuses to accept the reality of a Christian God. My objection to the conception of God as an untrammelled creator of values and laws is precisely that it is not Christian enough, that it introduces the disturbing and religiously unacceptable element of arbitrary power into the concept of a Being of pure love.

One could dwell on the grave philosophical difficulties of such a concept of God. But that is another story. For now it is enough to make two points. If God is the source of all values, in one important sense they are not objective or absolute. At a minimum, they are binding values only because God chooses them. It is, to spell this out, only because of their relation to God that they are values at all. This should incline those who object to everything relative to mend their ways or at least to realize that it is not relativity they quarrel with but its terms. They think it all right for values to be relative to the whim of God, but not to the will of man.

Secondly, what are the conditions requisite for making the commands of an Infinite Being relevant to our finite lives? No command, whatever its source, could be binding on a person who lacked the intelligence to grasp it or the capacity to act on it. One cannot command a stone, nor an Eskimo in Latin, no matter how elegant or fluent. Commands and values must suit the station and the circumstances, the nature and the capacities of the person who is to act on them or adopt them. Hence even if all Values have their source in God, their uniformity is not guaranteed. If human nature is varied, commands and values relevant to one man may be unsuited, perhaps even unintelligible, to others. The uniformity of God's effective commands thus becomes dependent on the uniformity of human nature.

Was Protagoras, then, right in the end and is nothing good but thinking makes it so? There are a few things farther from the truth, but not many. We do not think or act as if mere thoughts and feelings could make much difference to what is good or bad. And if Protagoras were right, we could never be mistaken in our aims and values: whatever we desired at any time would then be good, *for us*. Yet what could be a more painful or pervasive fact of life than moral error in choosing our goals? Inadequate self-knowledge frequently makes us adopt ends that do not satisfy. And who has not chosen the lesser over the greater, the nearer over the remote, the apparent over the real good?

Such short-sighted and inhumane relativism could never account for the bitter complexity of moral experience. But there is a relativism that many candid and tolerant minds spontaneously believe. Human nature is various: this variety, due to biological, social and psychological conditions, must be construed not as a threat or an evil, but as a God-given bounty of being. A variety of natures implies a variety of perfections. Only the egotist, committed to seeing pale replicas of himself everywhere in the world, would want to impose the same values and the same mode of behavior on every living soul. Sanity and toleration demand that we allow each person to pursue his own, possibly unique form of fulfillment; if we had even a vestige of Christian love, we would rejoice in seeing the growth of any man toward his goal.

Values vary with the individual's nature. The good, therefore, is not a question of what we think or how we feel but of who we are. A person's nature, though not unchanging, is perfectly definite. This makes it possible for him to progress in self-knowledge. It also renders the goals that would fulfill him definable and his values precise. These values may differ from the ideal of the next man, but they are not less vital or legitimate.

Would moral or social anarchy not flow if we acted as though this view were true? Not in the least. If the nature of the individual determines his values, similar natures yield similar commitments. The fact that human beings live in cooperative societies is the best evidence that their natures are similar or at least compatible. This is assured by processes of socialization which are, on occasion, so successful that even people left free to do precisely what they want continue to do their usual, useful tasks. What

little self-realization there may be that interferes with the fulfillment of others can be readily controlled by threats or a measure of force. In an orchestra each instrument plays its own tune; is this reason for saying that there is anarchy in the pit? The fact that values are individual does not entail that people must fail to agree on common goods and goals.

Consider the benefits that would accrue if we could make this relativism generally accepted. The view is a secular variant of the beautiful thought of many theologians that even the least of his creatures has dignity and justification in the eyes of God. If sincerely believed, this thought could transform the soul. It would help allay our suspicion of all things alien. It could render us more modest and loving by showing the monstrous egotism displayed in judging another. As a result, we may develop a more tolerant and helpful attitude toward life-styles and values different from those we like or admire: we could then begin to appreciate moral variety or the bounty of fulfillment and perfection open to humans. The personalities shaped by such beliefs and attitudes would be attuned to the beauty and harmony of life. The vast energy we consume in hate and in trying to shove our desires down reluctant throats could be harnessed to enhance our appreciation and joy. If such attitudes were dominant in it, human personality may for the first time reach the stage of not being disgusting.

If private improvement would be extensive, public benefits would likely be immense. Children could be brought up with fewer useless precepts and damaging attitudes. Education, both of intellect and of character, could at last lose some of its rigidity. Human relations could be infused with an element of humanity and understanding, and cooperation may well take the place of blind antagonism. Condemnation of other persons or nations becomes difficult in proportion as we see the legitimacy of differing ideals. Moral pseudo-justifications of much hatred and war would, therefore, at once be closed off to those who take the relativity of values seriously.

The greatest beneficiary of the universal acceptance of moral relativism would, without doubt, be human liberty. There is a shrill, constrictive tone to many of our laws. They impinge on fields where compulsory social prescriptions are inappropriate. Most of the laws we loosely group as designed to enforce the uniformity of morals would be seen as unjustified, if we were all relativists. This would increase the scope of human choice and render all manner of human action free.

Evidently the firmest social or state controls are necessary to protect persons from the real harm others would do them. But due allowance must be made for the difficulty of generalizing about what is to count as harm. The experience that would be harmful to a child may well mean fulfillment to an adult homosexual. If we forbid that children be tempted into such actions, must we also forbid it to consenting adults? And what is the imaginary public interest requiring that monogamy be the sole law of the land? Attention to differences in desires and temperaments would reveal such restrictions on human interaction as intolerant, if not insane.

Society would not collapse if we were to let a hundred flowers bloom. To be sure, it would be different in structure and operation from what it is today. But I cannot count myself among those who think there can be no improvement of the way things are.

But if believing and acting on moral relativism would have such profound impact on the nature of men and society, is it a mere accident that we have not yet accepted it? I cannot think so. Our beliefs and acts surely express our nature; what violates the integrity of our being or would tend to change it is difficult to embrace. Instinctive dogmatists will find it hard to see the merits of relativism on intellectual grounds alone.

Our best hope to escape egotism is by appealing to it. The individual's choice of making the world or even a small segment of it live by his values is negligible. With the increase in social regimentation and the growth of large impersonal institutions each person finds, in fact, ever more trouble in freely conforming even his own conduct to his ideals. A cutback in scope promises increase in intensity: sound self-interest demands that each attend to his own life and leave the moral state of others their sole business. The alternative is to lose control even of one's self, a frequent condition of ambitious egotists.

At stake is the eternal hope to tame human nature. Benevolence may be too high an ideal. Toleration of others would be enough or, as an absolute minimum, indifference to how they shape their fate. If we could only believe moral relativity, we would have the intellectual foundation of such indifference. Our nature could then be changed enough to merit being called human. We might even render our lives joyous and our survival assured. When shall we go to work?

REVIEW EXERCISES

1. Explain the definition of ethical relativism given in the text: "the view that there is no objective standard of right and wrong, even in principle."
2. What is the difference between individual and social or cultural relativism?
3. What is the difference between the descriptive claim that people do differ in their moral beliefs and the metaethical theory of relativism?
4. What are the differences among the three reasons for supporting ethical relativism given in this chapter? In particular, what is the basic difference between the first and second? Between the first and third?
5. How would you know whether a moral disagreement was based on a basic difference in moral values or facts? As an example, use differences about the moral justifiability of torture.
6. What is moral realism? How does your understanding about the reality of the external world differ from your intuitions about morality?

4

Egoism, Altruism, and the Social Contract

Learning Outcomes

After reading this chapter, you should be able to:

- Describe the differences between descriptive (or psychological) egoism and ethical egoism.
- Explain criticisms of altruism and the importance of reciprocal altruism.
- Evaluate disputes about the sources of morality and reasons to be moral.
- Explain the prisoner's dilemma and how it relates to the discussion of egoism and the social contract.

- Discuss how egoism is connected to laissez-faire capitalism and economics.
- Evaluate the challenge that egoism poses for the moral point of view.
- Defend your own ideas about egoism, altruism, and the social contract.

Morality seems to require that individuals sacrifice their own selfish interests for the benefit of others. We tend to praise altruists and condemn egoists. **Altruism** means, most basically, concern for the well-being of others. Some versions of altruism may even appear to hold that truly self-sacrificial behavior is the peak of moral development. Unlike altruists, egoists are primarily concerned with their own well-being. Sometimes egoists are purely selfish, even to the point of being willing to take advantage of others. But less selfish defenders of egoism may claim that egoism is not about taking advantage or being uncaring. Rather, egoism may be a descriptive thesis about human behavior, which claims that even apparently altruistic behavior is ultimately motivated by self-interest. From this perspective, people behave altruistically because they hope to gain something in return, even behaving altruistically in hope of developing social relations of cooperation, which are valuable in the long run. A further form of egoism holds that we would all be better off if people just looked out for themselves and left other people alone. From an egoistic perspective, social rules can be understood as resulting from agreements among rational and self-interested individuals. That idea is known as the **social contract theory**. This chapter considers egoism, altruism, and the theory of the social contract.

Popular culture is full of examples of the conflict between egoism and altruism. Television programs like *Survivor* create circumstances in which people are forced to forge short-term alliances to maximize their own self-interest. The film and book *The Hunger Games* shows us a life-and-death competition in which children struggle for survival in a war of all against all. In these contexts, egoism is to be expected and altruism is an exceptional and heroic virtue.

Disagreements about ethics and political life often rest upon divergent ideas about human nature. We wonder whether people are basically egoistic or altruistic, whether we are motivated by self-interest, or whether we are able to genuinely concern ourselves with the interests of others. Our conception of social organizations, politics, and the law often rests upon what we think about the motives of individuals. Are individuals basically cooperative or competitive? Are individuals motivated primarily by egoistic or altruistic concerns? Should social organizations be set up to minimize the dangers of an inevitable cutthroat competition? Or is there a more cooperative and altruistic basis for social cooperation?

To think about these issues, we need to consider a basic empirical question: Are people basically selfish and primarily motivated by self-interest or are people altruistic and motivated by concern for others? We also have to ask a normative question: Is selfishness good or bad? These two issues illustrate two different versions or meanings of egoism and altruism. One version is descriptive and answers the empirical question. According to this version, egoism (or altruism) is a theory that describes what people are like. Simply put, **descriptive egoism** holds that people are basically self-centered or selfish; that is, people primarily pursue their own self-interest. It is a view about how people behave or why they do what they do. It is often referred to as **psychological egoism**.

Egoism is opposed to altruism. Altruism is often viewed as pure concern for the well-being of others. Sometimes altruism is thought to require entirely unselfish behavior, even to the point at which we sacrifice ourselves for others. But a broader conception of altruism involves a variety of what psychologists call **pro-social behaviors**—that is, behaviors that are not primarily self-interested and that are motivated by basic concern for others.

The empirical question of whether human beings are motivated by self-interest or by non-self-interested concern for others is not so easy to answer. How do we really know what motivates others? Indeed, are you sure that you know what motivates *you* all of the time? Scientists have examined this question from various perspectives. Psychological studies, including accounts of developmental psychology, can give us some insight into what actually motivates people. Another line of inquiry looks at pro-social behavior from an evolutionary perspective. It turns out that pro-social cooperation produces an evolutionary advantage, especially in social species of animals such as our own. Individuals who cooperate with others tend to be able to pass on their genes better than selfish egoists and those who cheat. This is especially true when we cooperate with and support those who are related to us. Our genes get passed on when we are altruistic toward our close relations, helping those who share our genes to survive. This might explain why parents are willing to sacrifice for their own children—but not so willing to sacrifice for children to whom they are not related. It might also explain why we may be more willing to help a cousin than a stranger. Such an evolutionary explanation points toward instinctive forces that lie below the surface of our more explicit motivations and intentions.

Of course, an account of human behavior that is solely focused on the ways that pro-social behavior functions in evolutionary contexts fails to consider the subjective side of experience and human freedom. Sometimes our motivations and intentions run at cross-purposes to attitudes and behaviors that provide evolutionary advantage. Furthermore, it is possible to ask a normative question with regard to the descriptive science of pro-social behavior. We may be instinctively motivated to help those to whom we are more closely related. But should we really help our close relations and only our close relations? The term **nepotism** is used to condemn those who show favoritism to their close relations.

Films such as *The Hunger Games* illustrate conflicts between egoism and altruism.

Maybe we should ignore everyone else and focus only on our own needs and interests. Or maybe we should focus our concern more broadly on humanity at large, possibly even extending moral concern to members of other species.

We must, then, ask a moral question with regard to the empirical science of egoism and altruism. *Should* we be motivated by self-interest or *should* we be concerned with the well-being of others? As a normative theory, **ethical egoism** holds that it is good for people to pursue their own self-interest. Some versions of ethical egoism also hold that altruism is misguided and wrong. In this view, people should pursue their own self-interest, while minding their own business and ignoring others. In defense of this idea, ethical egoists may argue that altruism breeds dependency and undermines the self-esteem of those who receive benefits and gifts from do-gooder altruists.

Various authors have defended egoism. One of the most influential is the novelist and essayist Ayn Rand. Rand's ideas have had a significant influence on the thinking of a variety of American politicians—including former Texas Congressman

Ron Paul (who ran for president in 2012); his son, Kentucky Senator Rand Paul (a presidential candidate in 2016); and Wisconsin Congressman Paul Ryan (who was Mitt Romney's vice presidential running mate in 2012 and Speaker of the House of Representatives in 2016). Paul Ryan has explained that his reading of Ayn Rand is "the reason I got involved in public service."[1] These politicians tend to hold to a libertarian ideology, which emphasizes laissez-faire capitalism and limited government intervention (these political and economic issues are discussed in more detail in Chapter 14).

A fiercely individualistic émigré from Bolshevik Russia, Ayn Rand thought that altruism was pernicious. She argues that altruistic morality "regards man as a sacrificial animal" and that altruism "holds that man has no right to exist for his own sake, that service to others is the only justification of his existence, and that self-sacrifice is his highest moral duty, virtue and value." Her argument goes on to present the altruistic idea of self-sacrifice as a kind of death wish: "altruism holds *death* as its ultimate goal and standard of value—and it is logical that renunciation, resignation, self-denial, and every other form of suffering, including self-destruction, are the virtues it advocates."[2]

While Rand condemns altruism, most mainstream moralists tend to hold that altruism is better than egoism. We tend to praise self-sacrifice. And we tend to agree with the basic principle of altruism that is outlined in the Golden Rule—that you should "do unto others as you would have them do unto you." One might say that the moral point of view is one that involves some basic level of altruism. While altruists need not go to the extremes that Rand criticizes—in advocating suicidal self-sacrifice, for example—most people tend to think that pro-social and cooperative behavior are morally praiseworthy. Indeed, philosophers such as Kurt Baier, James Sterba, and Alan Gewirth have argued in various ways that egoism is basically inconsistent. As Gewirth explains, the egoist's moral claims do not apply to all other people in the same way that they apply to himself.[3] Furthermore, one might

claim that the moral point of view simply ought to point toward altruism. Baier explains that one of our "most widely held moral convictions" is that "in certain circumstances it is morally wrong to promote one's own best interest or greatest good."[4] We tend to think that morality involves overcoming egoism and learning to develop an altruistic (or at least impartial and non-self-interested) point of view.

A further issue has to do with the question of how social cooperation is supposed to occur. Defenders of altruism can argue that there is something natural about developing and nurturing caring relationships with others—perhaps grounded in an account of natural family bonds or group belonging. It may appear to be more difficult for egoists to explain how self-interested egoists can avoid brutal and counterproductive competition and develop a system of cooperation. But cooperation can be explained as paying off in terms of self-interest. From the perspective of egoism, it is rational for self-interested persons to cooperate, since cooperation tends to produce good outcomes for those who cooperate. One way of describing this is in terms of **reciprocal altruism**, which holds that altruistic behavior makes sense for self-interested persons when it is repaid in kind. A more elaborate development of reciprocal altruism is found in the social contract theory, which holds that it is in each person's self-interest to join with others in a social contract that helps us each to maximize our self-interest in community with others. We discuss the social contract theory in more detail at the end of this chapter.

PSYCHOLOGICAL EGOISM

What Is Psychological Egoism?

Psychological egoism is a descriptive theory about our motivations and interests. In one interpretation, it might be taken to say that people are basically selfish. Here, psychological egoism holds that people usually or always act for their own narrow and short-range self-interest. But a different formulation of this theory asserts that although people do act for their own self-interest, this self-interest is to be understood more broadly and as being more concerned with long-term outcomes. Thus, we might

Ayn Rand (1905–1982) was a well-known proponent of egoism.

distinguish between acting selfishly and acting in our own self-interest.

In the broader view, many things are in a person's interest: good health, satisfaction in a career or work, prestige, self-respect, family, and friends. Moreover, if we really wanted to attain these things, we would need to avoid shortsighted selfishness. For example, we would have to be self-disciplined in diet and lifestyle to be healthy. We would need to plan long-term for a career. And we would need to be concerned about others and not be overbearing if we wanted to make and retain friends.

However, a friendly egoist does not actually need to be concerned about others but only to *appear* to be concerned. In this view, doing good to others would be not for the sake of others but, rather, to enable one to call on those friends when they are needed. This would be helping a friend not for the friend's sake but for one's own sake.

Putting the matter in this way also raises another question about how to formulate this theory. Is psychological egoism a theory according to which people always act in their own best interests? Or does it hold that people are always motivated by the desire to attain their own best interests? The first version would be easily refuted; we notice that people do not always do what is best for them. They eat too much, choose the wrong careers, waste time, and so forth. This may be because they do not have sufficient knowledge to be good judges of what is in their best interests. Or it may be because of a phenomenon known as **weakness of will**. For example, I may want to lose weight or get an *A* in a course but may fail to do what I have to do in order to achieve my goal. Philosophers have puzzled over this problem, which is also called the problem of **akrasia** (to use the Greek term for the problem of weakness of will). This is a complex issue in moral psychology; to treat it adequately would take us beyond what we can do here.[5] But the basic concern is why we fail to do the things we know we ought to do. If we really know what we ought to do, it might seem that we would never fail to do what we ought.

On the other hand, it might be true that people always do what they *think* is best for them. Another version of psychological egoism asserts that human beings act for the sake of their own best interests. In this version, the idea is not that people sometimes or always act in their own interests, but that this is the only thing that ultimately motivates people. If they sometimes act for others, it is only because they think that it is in their own best interests to do so. A stronger version of psychological egoism asserts that people cannot do otherwise than act for the sake of their own interests. But how would we know this? We know how people act, but how could we show that they cannot act otherwise?

> MindTap° For more chapter resources and activities, go to MindTap.

Is Psychological Egoism True?

In the early 1990s, a study was done in which people were asked whether they believed in or supported the jury system; that is, should people be judged guilty or not guilty by a group of peers? Most responded that they do support the jury system. However, when asked whether they would serve on a jury if called, significantly fewer said they would.[6] Those who answered the two questions differently might have wanted justice for themselves but were not willing to extend it to others. Some of our most cherished social values may involve more selfish motivation than we generally like to admit. Consider the following story about Abraham Lincoln.[7] It is reported that one day as he was riding in a coach over a bridge he heard a mother pig squealing. Her piglets were drowning after having fallen into the creek and she could not get them out. Lincoln supposedly asked the coachman to stop, waded into the creek, and rescued the piglets. When his companion cited this as an example of unselfishness, Lincoln responded that it was not for the sake of the pigs that he acted as he did. Rather, it was because he would have no peace later when he recalled the incident if he did not do something about it now. In other words, although it seemed unselfish, his action was quite self-centered. Advocates for psychological egoism often draw on such accounts of underlying selfish motivations to bolster their arguments.

But how are we to evaluate the claims of psychological egoism? As a theory about human motivation, it is difficult, if not impossible, to prove. How do we assess the motivations of people? We cannot just assume that apparently altruistic individuals are acting for the sake of the selfish satisfaction they receive from what they do. Nor can we ask them, for individuals are often poor judges of what actually motivates them. We commonly hear or say to ourselves, "I don't know why I did that!"

Furthermore, it is difficult to distinguish different sources of our motivations. Are we innately egoistic or altruistic—that is, are we born with a tendency toward egoism or altruism? Or do our cultural values contribute to our egoistic (or altruistic) tendencies? For example, we might consider differences in socialization between boys and girls. It might be that female children are expected to be altruistic and caring, while male children are taught to be independent and self-motivated. And it might be that these differences in socialization are also dependent upon other cultural differences, with boys and girls from different cultures growing up with divergent dispositions toward altruism or egoism.

Leaving aside the issue of socialization, suppose that people do, in fact, get satisfaction from helping others. This is not the same thing as acting for the purpose of getting that satisfaction. What psychological egoism needs to show is not that people get satisfaction from what they do, but that achieving such satisfaction is their aim. Now, we can find at least some examples in our own actions to test this theory. Do we read the book to get satisfaction or to learn something? Do we pursue that career opportunity because of the satisfaction that we think it will bring or because of the nature of the opportunity? Do we volunteer to help the sick or the needy because we think it will give us personal satisfaction or because we think it will actually help someone? In addition, directly aiming at satisfaction may not be the best way to achieve it. Henry Sidgwick described this as the **paradox of hedonism**: "The impulse toward pleasure, if too predominant, defeats its own aim."[8] We probably have a better chance of being happy if we do not aim at happiness itself, but

obtain happiness while pursuing other worthwhile objects.

Thus, we have seen that the most reasonable or common form of psychological egoism, a theory about human motivation, is especially difficult to prove. It also can't be disproved or falsified. Even if it were shown that we *often* act for the sake of our own interest or satisfaction, this is not enough to prove that psychological egoism is true. According to this theory, we must show that people *always* act to promote their own interests. Next, we need to consider whether this has any relevance to the normative question of how we *ought* to act.

ETHICAL EGOISM
What Is Ethical Egoism?

Ethical egoism is a normative theory. It is a theory about what we *ought* to do, how we *ought* to act. As with psychological egoism, we can formulate ethical egoism in different ways. One version is *individual ethical egoism*. According to this version, I ought to look out only for my own interests. I ought to be concerned about others only to the extent that this concern also contributes to my own interests. A slightly broader formulation of ethical egoism, sometimes called *universal ethical egoism*, maintains that people ought to look out for and seek only their own best interests. As in the individual form, in this second version, people ought to help others only when and to the extent that it is in their own best interests to do so. It is possible to explain cooperation from this perspective as a kind of reciprocal altruism: we cooperate because we each see that it is in our own self-interest to cooperate. As the saying goes, I'll scratch your back, if you scratch mine. From this point of view, what I really want is to get my back scratched (something I cannot do for myself) and I realize that in order to get what I want, I have to give you something you want in return.

Is Ethical Egoism a Good Theory?

We can evaluate ethical egoism in several ways. We will consider its grounding in psychological egoism and its consistency or coherence. We will also consider how it explains social cooperation in the social contract theory as well as its derivation from economic theory. Finally, we will consider its conformity to commonsense moral views.

Grounding in Psychological Egoism Let us consider first whether psychological egoism, if true, would provide a good foundation for ethical egoism. It might be that we should affirm ethical egoism because people are basically and unavoidably egoistic. But recall the discussion of the naturalistic fallacy in Chapter 1: it is not clear that we can derive the *value* of ethical egoism from the *fact* of psychological egoism. If people were in fact always motivated by their own interests, then would this be a good reason to hold that they *ought* to be so motivated? It seems superfluous to tell people that they ought to do what they always do anyway or will do, no matter what. One would think that at least sometimes one of the functions of moral language is to try to motivate ourselves or others to do what we are not inclined to do. For example, I might tell myself that even though I could benefit by cheating on a test, it is wrong, and so I should not do it.

Furthermore, the fact that we do behave in a certain way seems a poor reason for believing that we ought to do so. If people always cheated, would that make cheating right? Thus, although it may at first seem reasonable to rely on a belief about people's basic selfishness to prove that people ought to look out for themselves alone, this seems far from convincing.

Consistency or Coherence Universal ethical egoism may be inconsistent or incoherent. Ethical egoism holds that everyone ought to seek his or her own best interests. But could anyone consistently support such a view? Wouldn't this mean that we would want our own best interests served and, at the same time, be willing to allow that others serve their interests—even to our own detriment? If food was scarce, then I would want enough for myself, and yet, at the same time, I would have to say that I should not have it for myself when another needs it to survive. This view seems to have an internal inconsistency. We might compare it to playing a game in which I can say that the other player ought to block my move, even though, at the same time, I hope that she or he does not do so.

The Prisoner's Dilemma A serious problem plaguing agreements that are made among egoists is the temptation to cheat. If I agree to scratch your back after you scratch mine, what guarantee do you have that I will follow through on my promise once I've gotten my back scratched? If we are both convinced that human beings are basically egoistic, then you will suspect that I will cheat (and I'll suspect that you will cheat), in which case it will be difficult to cooperate. For this reason, there is a worry that egoism will lead to conflict and war. To prevent this from happening, even egoists might agree that we need something external to ourselves to guarantee that we do not renege on our promises. This is the basis for the development of the social contract, which can be interpreted as an agreement made by self-interested persons who want to establish a legal system that ensures promises are kept and that prevents cheating by egoists.

The problem for egoism can be clarified with reference to a thought experiment known as **the prisoner's dilemma**. Imagine that the cops arrest two suspects, X and Y. The cops have the prisoners in two separate rooms. They offer each prisoner the following deal: If you betray the other suspect, you will go free instead of getting a twenty-year term in prison; but if you both betray each other, you will each end up with ten years in prison. On the other hand, if both prisoners keep their mouths shut and refuse to betray each other, there will be no conviction and they will both go free. The choices look like this:

	Y betrays X	Y does not betray X
X betrays Y	Each ends up with 10 years	X goes free; Y gets 20 years
X does not betray Y	Y goes free; X gets 20 years	Each goes free

For the prisoners, the best option is if they coordinate their choices and both refuse to betray each other. But if the prisoners suspect each other of being self-interested egoists, they will not trust each other. Each will suspect that the other prisoner will betray him or her in pursuit of a better deal. And so, it is likely that self-interested prisoners will end up with less-than-optimal outcomes. Each prisoner will suspect the other of operating out of self-interested motives that will lead toward cheating and reneging on prior promises. The prisoner's dilemma thought experiment is often used as a model to show why we need some larger structure to ensure that we do not break our promises. It might be that morality itself provides that larger structure: if we would just agree to comply with the dictates of morality, we would be able to guarantee cooperation. But if there are egoists who would break moral rules when they think that they can get away with it, we might need something stronger than morality—we might need an enforcement mechanism, that is, something like a legal and political system that helps to guarantee cooperation. It is possible, then, that rational, self-interested individuals would agree to something like a social contract.

The Social Contract

A justification of the legal system can be grounded in the rational self-interest of human beings. The idea of the social contract is that it is rational for self-interested individuals to join together and submit to the rule of law in order to ensure that promises are kept and that social cooperation will occur. One of the earliest versions of this idea is found in the writings of the seventeenth-century English philosopher Thomas Hobbes. Hobbes holds that individuals are self-interested; that is, they seek to fulfill their interests and desires and above all seek self-preservation. Hobbes maintains that in the state of nature, individuals would be equal in terms of strength, since even weak individuals can band together with others or use sneak attacks to overpower stronger individuals. Conflict arises when these equally powerful individuals seek the same thing. The competing individuals will thereby become enemies. As a result, the state of nature will be one of war, of all against all, and the results, as Hobbes describes them, are quite bleak,

> In such condition there is no place for industry, because the fruit thereof is uncertain, and consequently, not culture of the earth, no navigation, nor the use of commodities that may be imported by sea, no commodious building, no instruments of moving and removing such things as require much force, no knowledge of the face of the earth, no account of time, no arts, no letters, no society, and which is worst of all, continual fear and danger of violent death, and the life of man, solitary, poor, nasty, brutish, and short.[9]

The solution is peace via an agreement in which one gives up as much liberty "as against other men, as he would allow other men against himself."[10] For Hobbes, the social contract is an agreement to give up certain things to better secure one's own self-interest. Thus, individuals will agree to certain rules, which would be in each individual's best interest to accept and obey. To secure the peace and ensure that these rules are obeyed, Hobbes believes that an absolute sovereign ruler is required.

Hobbes's social contract theory is based on a desire of each person to secure his own advantage while agreeing to social rules enforced by a sovereign; it is a view of how society should function and thus both a political and a moral position. Other versions of the social contract idea were proposed by philosophers such as John Locke and Jean-Jacques Rousseau. Contemporary moral and political theories that appeal to contract ideas can be found in the works of Thomas Scanlon, David Gauthier, and John Rawls.[11] Gauthier's idea is that we should imagine basic moral rules that rational, self-interested parties would voluntarily agree to. Gauthier suggests that rational, self-interested agents would recognize the need for mutual restraint: it is in the interest of self-interested agents to agree to restrain the unbridled pursuit of self-interest. John Rawls imagines an ideal form of the social contract. He asks what rational self-interested people would agree to, in terms of justice, if they did not know if they were young or old, rich or poor, male or female, healthy or disabled.

Rawls's influential ideas are considered in more detail in Chapter 14.

Derivation from Economic Theory   One argument for ethical egoism is taken from economic theory—for example, that proposed by Adam Smith. He and other proponents of **laissez-faire capitalism** (a form of capitalism with minimal government regulation or intervention) argue that self-interest provides the best economic motivation. The idea is that when the profit motive or individual incentives are absent, people will either not work or not work as well. If it is my land or my business, then I will be more likely to take care of it than if the profits go to others or to the government. In addition, Smith believes that in a system in which each person looks out for his or her own economic interests, the general outcome will be best, as though an "invisible hand" were guiding things.[12]

Although this is not the place to go into an extended discussion of economic theory, it is enough to point out that not everyone agrees on the merits of laissez-faire capitalism. Much can be said for the competition that it supports, but it does raise questions, for example, about the breakdown of "winners" and "losers" in such a competition. Is it acceptable if the same individuals, families, or groups consistently win or lose, generation after generation? What if there are many more economic "losers" and a few extremely wealthy "winners"? And what about those with innate or inherited disadvantages that prevent them from competing? Is care for these people a community responsibility? Recent community-oriented theories of social morality stress just this notion of responsibility and oppose laissez-faire capitalism's excessive emphasis on individual rights.[13] (Further discussion of capitalism can be found in Chapter 14.) In any case, a more basic question can be asked about the relevance of economics to morality. Even if an economic system worked well or efficiently, would this prove that morality ought to be modeled on it? Is not the moral life broader than the economic life? Are all human relations economic relations?

Furthermore, the argument that everyone ought to seek his or her own best interests because this contributes to the general well-being is not ethical egoism at all—since self-interest is merely used here as a means to pursuing a broader collective value. As we will come to see more clearly when we examine it, this is a form of utilitarianism (see Chapter 5).

Conformity to Commonsense Morality   Finally, is ethical egoism supported by commonsense morality? Some elements of ethical egoism seem to be contrary to commonsense morality. For example, egoism seems to assume that anything is all right as long as it serves an individual's best interests. Torturing human beings or animals would be permitted so long as this served one's interests. When not useful to one's interests, traditional virtues of honesty, fidelity, and loyalty would have no value. Ethical egoists could argue on empirical or factual grounds that the torturing of others is never in one's best interests because this would make one less sensitive, and being sensitive is generally useful to an individual's objectives. Similarly, they might argue that the development of traditional virtues is often in one's own best interests because these traits are valued by society. For example, possessing these traits may enable me to get what I want more readily. Whether these are good enough reasons to value these virtues or condemn torture is something you must judge for yourself.

Part of the intuitive appeal of egoism may derive from the sense that people ought to take better care of themselves. By having a high regard for ourselves, we increase our self-esteem. We then depend less on others and more on ourselves. We might also be stronger and happier. These are surely desirable traits. The altruist, moreover, might be too self-effacing. He or she might be said to lack a proper regard for himself or herself. There is also some truth in the view that unless one takes care of oneself, one is not of much use to others. This view implies not ethical egoism, however, but again a form of utilitarianism.

THE MORAL POINT OF VIEW

Suppose that a person cares for no one but himself or herself. Would you consider that person to be a moral person? This is not to ask whether the person is a morally good person, but rather whether one can think of that person as even operating in the moral realm, so to speak. In other words, the question concerns not whether the person's morality is a good one, but whether he or she has any morals at all.

Suppose we want to know whether a person has been given a moral education.[14] A woman might answer that she had because she had been taught not to lie, to treat others kindly, not to drink to excess, and to work hard. When asked what reasons she had been given for behaving thus, suppose she responded that she was taught not to lie because others would not trust her if she did. She was taught to treat others well because then they would treat her well in return. She was taught to work hard because of the satisfaction this brought her or because she would then be better able to support herself. Would you consider her to have been given a moral education?

It might be that this woman was given counsels of *prudence*, not morality. She was told what she should do to succeed in life in order to secure her own self-interest. But morality seems to imply more than prudence. We don't lie because it is wrong to do so, or because others have a right to know the truth. We treat others well because they deserve to be so treated, or because it would be wrong to do otherwise. It seems that moral education cannot be merely egoistic. Do you agree?

Taking the moral point of view appears to involve being able to see beyond ourselves and our own interests. It may also mean that we attempt to see things from another's point of view; or that we attempt to be impartial. Morality seems to require that moral rules apply equally to all, or that we have to give reasons why some persons are treated differently than others.

But this view of morality as a set of neutral and impartial social rules raises a number of tricky questions. We usually do not think that we have to justify treating those close to us differently and more favorably than others. If we are nepotistic and care more for our own children or our own friends than we do for strangers, does this mean that we are not

operating in the moral domain? Questions can be raised about the extent to which impartiality influences the moral domain or is required in order to be moral. Some feminists, for example, would rather define morality in terms of sympathy and caring. (See Chapter 9 for further treatment of this issue.)

WHY BE MORAL?

Let us assume that morality does involve considering other people's points of view and treating people equally or impartially. Why should anyone do that, especially when it is not in one's best interests to do so? In other words, are there any reasons we can give to show why one should be moral? One reason is that doing what one ought to do is just what being moral means. But how can we explain why we ought to do what we ought to do?

We could argue that it is generally better for people to have and follow moral rules. Without such rules, our social lives would be pretty wretched. As Hobbes suggests, a life of egoism in the state of nature would be one of constant conflict and war. However, this does not answer the question concerning why I should be moral when it is not in my best interests to do so.

If you were trying to convince a man why he should be moral, how would you do it? You might appeal to his fear of reprisal if he did not generally follow moral rules. If he is not honest, then he will not be trusted. If he steals, he risks being punished. In the selection from Plato's *Republic* that appears in this chapter, Glaucon tells the story of a shepherd named Gyges. Gyges comes into possession of a ring that makes him invisible. He proceeds to use his invisibility to take what he wants from others. Glaucon then asks whether we all would not do the same if we, like Gyges, could get away with it. He believes we would. But is he right? Is avoiding punishment the only reason that people do the right thing?

There are other more positive but still self-interested reasons you might offer someone to convince that person that he or she ought to be moral. You might tell the individual that being virtuous is to one's own advantage. You might recall some of the advice from Benjamin Franklin's *Poor Richard's*

Almanac.[15] "A stitch in time saves nine." "Observe all men, thyself most." "Spare and have is better than spend and crave." Many of the moral aphorisms put forward by motivational speakers and self-help gurus—from Dr. Phil and Oprah Winfrey to Deepak Chopra—are focused on maximizing self-interest. These are the self-interested counsels of a practical morality. It turns out that most of the traditional virtues are usually in our own best interests. It is in our interest to be temperate, courageous, thrifty, kind, honest, and so on—because these virtues help us live a stable life in a world that we share with others. Indeed, it does appear to be in our interests to be altruistic, since concern for others is often reciprocated.

You might go even further in thinking about reasons to be moral. You might make the point that being moral is ennobling. Even when it involves sacrifice for a cause, being a moral person gives one a certain dignity, integrity, and self-respect. Only humans are capable of being moral, you might say, and human beings cannot flourish without being moral. You can give more thought to this question when you read about Kant's moral theory in Chapter 6. For Kant, human dignity and worth is wholly bound up with being able to act for moral reasons.

Nevertheless, one can point to many examples in which people who successfully break the moral rules seem to fare better than those who follow them. "Nice guys [and gals?] finish last," as baseball great Leo Durocher put it. If being moral seems too demanding, then some say this is too bad for morality. We ought to have a good life, even if it means sacrificing something of morality. In another view, if being moral involves sacrificing something of the personally fulfilling life and perhaps even "finishing last" sometimes, then this is what must be done. No one ever said being moral was going to be easy![16]

The discussion of egoism, altruism, and the social contract is an old one that extends throughout the history of philosophy. The reading selections for this chapter span that history. In the first reading, Plato's characters in *The Republic* explore the contention that we always act in our own interests—one of the reasons given in support of an egoist theory. Plato offers a thought experiment involving invisibility and a magic ring to help us think about what we would really do if no one was looking. In the second reading, the English philosopher Thomas Hobbes provides an answer to the question of what people would do if they were not regulated by social rules. He argues not only that all human beings tend to pursue their own safety and interests—but also why it is rational for self-interested individuals to create a social contract that furthers the goal of self-protection. Finally, drawing on the resources of modern biological science, Steven Pinker offers an account of how selfishness and pro-social behavior are related to the social contract.

NOTES

1. Stephen Prothero, "You Can't Reconcile Ayn Rand and Jesus," *USA Today*, June 5, 2011, accessed March 13, 2013, http://usatoday30.usatoday.com/news/opinion/forum/2011-06-05-Ayn-Rand-and-Jesus-dont-mix_n.htm

2. Ayn Rand, "The Objectivist Ethics," available at the Ayn Rand Institute website: http://www.aynrand.org/site/PageServer?pagename=ari_ayn_rand_the_objectivist_ethics

3. Alan Gewirth, *Reason and Morality* (Chicago: University of Chicago Press, 1981), p. 85.

4. Kurt Baier, *The Rational and the Moral Order* (Open Court, 1995), p. 159. Also see James P. Sterba, "Morality and Self-Interest," *Philosophy and Phenomenological Research* 59, no. 2 (June 1999).

5. For a discussion of "weakness of will," see Gwynneth Matthews, "Moral Weakness," *Mind* 299 (July 1966), pp. 405–19; Donald Davidson, "How Is Weakness of the Will Possible?" in *Moral Concepts*, ed. Joel Feinberg (New York: Oxford University Press, 1970), pp. 93–113.

6. Amitai Etzioni, a presentation at the University of San Francisco, December 1, 1992.

7. From the *Springfield Monitor* (ca. 1928), cited in Louis Pojman, *Ethics* (Belmont, CA: Wadsworth, 1990), p. 41.

8. Henry Sidgwick, *The Methods of Ethics* (London: MacMillan and Co., 1884), p. 47.

9. Thomas Hobbes, *Leviathan*, in *The English Works of Thomas Hobbes*, ed. Sir William Molesworth (London: John Bohn, 1839), pp. 2:38–41, 85.

10. Ibid., Chapter 14.

11. Tom Scanlon, *What We Owe Each Other* (Cambridge, MA: Harvard University Press, 1998); David Gauthier, *Morals by Agreement* (Oxford: Oxford University Press, 1987); John Rawls, *A Theory of Justice* (Cambridge, MA: Harvard University Press, 1971).

12. See Adam Smith, *The Wealth of Nations* (New York: Edwin Cannan, 1904).

13. See the communitarian views in Robert Bellah, *Habits of the Heart* (Berkeley: University of California Press, 1985); and Amitai Etzioni, *The Spirit of Community: Rights, Responsibilities, and the Communitarian Agenda* (New York: Crown, 1993).

14. See W. D. Falk, "Morality, Self, and Others," in *Morality and the Language of Conduct*, ed. Hector-Neri Castaneda and George Nakhnikian (Detroit: Wayne State University Press, 1963), pp. 25–67.

15. Benjamin Franklin, "Poor Richard's Almanac," in *American Philosophy: A Historical Anthology*, ed. Barbara MacKinnon (New York: State University of New York Press, 1985), pp. 46–47.

16. See Thomas Nagel's discussion of these different possibilities of the relation between the good life and the moral life in "Living Right and Living Well," in *The View from Nowhere* (New York: Oxford University Press, 1986), pp. 189–207. Also see David Gauthier, "Morality and Advantage," *The Philosophical Review* (1967), pp. 460–75.

READING

The Ring of Gyges

PLATO

MindTap® For more chapter resources and activities, go to MindTap.

Study Questions

As you read the excerpt, please consider the following questions:

1. What view of morality is described using the story of the ring of Gyges?
2. How does this story describe the difference between appearing just and being just?
3. According to the story, what do parents (and religions, myths, and poetry) teach their children and us about morality?

Glaucon *(to Socrates)*. They say that to do injustice is, by nature, good; to suffer injustice, evil; but that the evil is greater than the good. And so when men have both done and suffered injustice and have had experience of both, not being able to avoid the one and obtain the other, they think that they had better agree among themselves to have neither; hence there arise laws and mutual covenants; and that which is ordained by law is termed by them lawful and just. This they affirm to be the origin and nature of justice;—it is a mean or compromise, between the best of all, which is to do injustice

and not be punished, and the worst of all, which is to suffer injustice without the power of retaliation; and justice, being at a middle point between the two, is tolerated not as a good, but as the lesser evil, and honoured by reason of the inability of men to do injustice. For no man who is worthy to be called a man would ever submit to such an agreement if he were able to resist; he would be mad if he did. Such

From Plato, *The Republic*, bk. 2, in *The Dialogues of Plato*, 3rd ed., trans. B. Jowett (Oxford: Oxford University Press, 1892), pp. 357a–369.

is the received account, Socrates, of the nature and origin of justice.

Now that those who practise justice do so involuntarily and because they have not the power to be unjust will best appear if we imagine something of this kind: having given both to the just and the unjust power to do what they will, let us watch and see whither desire will lead them; then we shall discover in the very act the just and unjust man to be proceeding along the same road, following their interest, which all natures deem to be their good, and are only diverted into the path of justice by the force of law. The liberty which we are supposing may be most completely given to them in the form of such a power as is said to have been possessed by Gyges the ancestor of Croesus the Lydian. According to the tradition, Gyges was a shepherd in the service of the king of Lydia; there was a great storm, and an earthquake made an opening in the earth at the place where he was feeding his flock. Amazed at the sight, he descended into the opening, where, among other marvels, he beheld a hollow brazen horse, having doors, at which he stooping and looking in saw a dead body of stature, as appeared to him, more than human, and having nothing on but a gold ring; this he took from the finger of the dead and reascended. Now the shepherds met together, according to custom, that they might send their monthly report about the flocks to the king; into their assembly he came having the ring on his finger, and as he was sitting among them he chanced to turn the collet of the ring inside his hand, when instantly he became invisible to the rest of the company and they began to speak of him as if he were no longer present. He was astonished at this, and again touching the ring he turned the collet outwards and reappeared; he made several trials of the ring, and always with the same result—when he turned the collet inwards he became invisible, when outwards he reappeared. Whereupon he contrived to be chosen one of the messengers who were sent to the court; where as soon as he arrived he seduced the queen, and with her help conspired against the king and slew him, and took the kingdom. Suppose now that there were two such magic rings, and the

just put on one of them and the unjust the other; no man can be imagined to be of such an iron nature that he would stand fast in justice. No man would keep his hands off what was not his own when he could safely take what he liked out of the market, or go into houses and lie with any one at his pleasure, or kill or release from prison whom he would, and in all respects be like a God among men. Then the actions of the just would be as the actions of the unjust; they would both come at last to the same point. And this we may truly affirm to be a great proof that a man is just, not willingly or because he thinks that justice is any good to him individually, but of necessity, for wherever any one thinks that he can safely be unjust, there he is unjust. For all men believe in their hearts that injustice is far more profitable to the individual than justice, and he who argues as I have been supposing, will say that they are right. If you could imagine any one obtaining this power of becoming invisible, and never doing any wrong or touching what was another's, he would be thought by the lookers-on to be a most wretched idiot, although they would praise him to one another's faces, and keep up appearances with one another from a fear that they too might suffer injustice. Enough of this.

Now, if we are to form a real judgment of the life of the just and unjust, we must isolate them; there is no other way; and how is the isolation to be effected? I answer: Let the unjust man be entirely unjust, and the just man entirely just; nothing is to be taken away from either of them, and both are to be perfectly furnished for the work of their respective lives. First, let the unjust be like other distinguished masters of craft; like the skilful pilot or physician, who knows intuitively his own powers and keeps within their limits, and who, if he fails at any point, is able to recover himself. So let the unjust make his unjust attempts in the right way, and lie hidden if he means to be great in his injustice (he who is found out is nobody): for the highest reach of injustice is, to be deemed just when you are not. Therefore I say that in the perfectly unjust man we must assume the most perfect injustice; there is to be no deduction, but we must allow him, while doing the most unjust acts, to have acquired the greatest reputation for justice. If he have taken a false step he must be able to recover himself; he must be one who can speak with effect, if any of his deeds come to light, and who can force his way where force is required by his courage and strength, and command of money and friends. And at his side let us place the just man in his nobleness and simplicity, wishing, as Aeschylus says, to be and not to seem good. There must be no seeming, for if he seem to be just he will be honoured and rewarded, and then we shall not know whether he is just for the sake of justice or for the sake of honours and rewards; therefore, let him be clothed in justice only, and have no other covering; and he must be imagined in a state of life the opposite of the former. Let him be the best of men, and let him be thought the worst; then he will have been put to the proof; and we shall see whether he will be affected by the fear of infamy and its consequences. And let him continue thus to the hour of death; being just and seeming to be unjust. When both have reached the uttermost extreme, the one of justice and the other of injustice, let judgment be given which of them is the happier of the two.

Socrates. Heavens! my dear Glaucon, I said, how energetically you polish them up for the decision, first one and then the other, as if they were two statues.

Glaucon. I do my best. And now that we know what they are like there is no difficulty in tracing out the sort of life which awaits either of them. This I will proceed to describe; but as you may think the description a little too coarse, I ask you to suppose, Socrates, that the words which follow are not mine.—Let me put them into the mouths of the eulogists of injustice: They will tell you that the just man who is thought unjust will be scourged, racked, bound—will have his eyes burnt out; and, at last, after suffering every kind of evil, he will be impaled: Then he will understand that he ought to seem only, and not to be, just; the words of Aeschylus may be more truly spoken of the unjust than of the just. For the unjust is pursuing a reality; he does not live with a view to appearances—he wants to be really unjust and not to seem only—

"His mind has a soil deep and fertile,
Out of which spring his prudent counsels."

In the first place, he is thought just, and therefore bears rule in the city; he can marry whom he will, and give in marriage to whom he will; also he can trade and deal where he likes, and always to his own advantage, because he has no misgivings about injustice; and at every contest, whether in public or private, he gets the better of his antagonists, and gains at their expense, and is rich, and out of his gains he can benefit his friends, and harm his enemies; moreover, he can offer sacrifices, and dedicate gifts to the gods abundantly and magnificently, and can honour the gods or any man whom he wants to honour in a far better style than the just, and therefore he is likely to be dearer than they are to the gods. And thus, Socrates, gods and men are said to unite in making the life of the unjust better than the life of the just.

Adeimantus. Socrates, you do not suppose that there is nothing more to be urged?

Socrates. Why, what else is there?

Adeimantus. The strongest point of all has not been even mentioned.

Socrates. Well, then, according to the proverb, "Let brother help brother"—if he fails in any part do you assist him; although I must confess that Glaucon has already said quite enough to lay me in the dust, and take from me the power of helping justice.

Adeimantus. Nonsense. But let me add something more: There is another side to Glaucon's argument about the praise and censure of justice and injustice, which is equally required in order to bring out what I believe to be his meaning. Parents and tutors are always telling their sons and their wards that they are to be just; but why? not for the sake of justice, but for the sake of character and reputation; in the hope of obtaining for him who is reputed just some of those offices, marriages, and the like which Glaucon has enumerated among the advantages accruing to the unjust from the reputation of justice. More, however, is made of appearances by this class of persons than by the others; for they throw in the good opinion of the gods, and will tell you of a shower of benefits which the heavens, as they say, rain upon the pious; and this accords with the testimony of the noble Hesiod and Homer, the first of whom says, that the gods make the oaks of the just—

> "To bear acorns at their summit, and bees in the middle; And the sheep are bowed down with the weight of their fleeces,"[1]

and many other blessings of a like kind are provided for them. And Homer has a very similar strain; for he speaks of one whose fame is—

> "As the fame of some blameless king who, like a god, Maintains justice; to whom the black earth brings forth Wheat and barley, whose trees are bowed with fruit, And his sheep never fail to bear, and the sea gives him fish."[2]

Still grander are the gifts of heaven which Musaeus and his son[3] vouchsafe to the just; they take them down into the world below, where they have the saints lying on couches at a feast, everlastingly drunk, crowned with garlands; their idea seems to be that an immortality of drunkenness is the highest meed of virtue. Some extend their rewards yet further; the posterity, as they say, of the faithful and just shall survive to the third and fourth generation. This is the style in which they praise justice. But about the wicked there is another strain; they bury them in a slough in Hades, and make them carry water in a sieve; also while they are yet living they bring them to infamy, and inflict upon them the punishments which Glaucon described as the portion of the just who are reputed to be unjust; nothing else does their invention supply. Such is their manner of praising the one and censuring the other.

Once more, Socrates, I will ask you to consider another way of speaking about justice and injustice, which is not confined to the poets, but is found in prose writers. The universal voice of mankind is always declaring that justice and virtue are honourable, but grievous and toilsome; and that the pleasures of vice and injustice are easy of attainment, and are only censured by law and opinion. They say also that honesty is for the most part less profitable than dishonesty; and they are quite ready to call wicked men happy, and to honour them both

in public and private when they are rich or in any other way influential, while they despise and overlook those who may be weak and poor, even though acknowledging them to be better than the others. But most extraordinary of all is their mode of speaking about virtue and the gods: they say that the gods apportion calamity and misery to many good men, and good and happiness to the wicked. And mendicant prophets go to rich men's doors and persuade them that they have a power committed to them by the gods of making an atonement for a man's own or his ancestor's sins by sacrifices or charms, with rejoicings and feasts; and they promise to harm an enemy, whether just or unjust, at a small cost; with magic arts and incantations binding heaven, as they say, to execute their will. And the poets are the authorities to whom they appeal, now smoothing the path of vice with the words of Hesiod—

> "Vice may be had in abundance without trouble; the way is smooth and her dwelling-place is near. But before virtue the gods have set toil,"[4]

and a tedious and uphill road: then citing Homer as a witness that the gods may be influenced by men; for he also says—

> "The gods, too, may be turned from their purpose; and men pray to them and avert their wrath by sacrifices and soothing entreaties, and by libations and the odour of fat, when they have sinned and transgressed."[5]

And they produce a host of books written by Musaeus and Orpheus, who were children of the Moon and the Muses—that is what they say—according to which they perform their ritual, and persuade not only individuals, but whole cities, that expiations and atonements for sin may be made by sacrifices and amusements which fill a vacant hour, and are equally at the service of the living and the dead; the latter sort they call mysteries, and they redeem us from the pains of hell, but if we neglect them no one knows what awaits us.

And now when the young hear all this said about virtue and vice, and the way in which gods and men regard them, how are their minds likely to be affected, my dear Socrates,—those of them, I mean, who are quickwitted, and, like bees on the wing, light on every flower, and from all that they hear are prone to draw conclusions as to what manner of persons they should be and in what way they should walk if they would make the best of life? Probably the youth will say to himself in the words of Pindar—

"Can I by justice or by crooked ways of deceit ascend a loftier tower which may be a fortress to me all my days?"

For what men say is that, if I am really just and am not also thought just, profit there is none, but the pain and loss on the other hand are unmistakeable. But if, though unjust, I acquire the reputation of justice, a heavenly life is promised to me. Since then, as philosophers prove, appearance tyrannizes over truth and is lord of happiness, to appearance I must devote myself. I will describe around me a picture and shadow of virtue to be the vestibule and exterior of my house; behind I will trail the subtle and crafty fox, as Archilochus, greatest of sages, recommends. But I hear some one exclaiming that the concealment of wickedness is often difficult; to which I answer, Nothing great is easy. Nevertheless, the argument indicates this, if we would be happy, to be the path along which we should proceed. With a view to concealment we will establish secret brotherhoods and political clubs. And there are professors of rhetoric who teach the art of persuading courts and assemblies; and so, partly by persuasion and partly by force, I shall make unlawful gains and not be punished. Still I hear a voice saying that the gods cannot be deceived, neither can they be compelled. But what if there are no gods? or, suppose them to have no care of human things—why in either case should we mind about concealment? And even if there are gods, and they do care about us, yet we know of them only from tradition and the genealogies of the poets; and these are the very persons who say that they may be influenced and turned by "sacrifices and soothing entreaties and by offerings." Let us be consistent then, and believe both or neither. If the poets speak truly, why then we had better be unjust, and offer of the fruits of injustice; for if

we are just, although we may escape the vengeance of heaven, we shall lose the gains of injustice; but, if we are unjust, we shall keep the gains, and by our sinning and praying, and praying and sinning, the gods will be propitiated, and we shall not be punished. "But there is a world below in which either we or our posterity will suffer for our unjust deeds." Yes, my friend, will be the reflection, but there are mysteries and atoning deities, and these have great power. That is what mighty cities declare; and the children of the gods, who were their poets and prophets, bear a like testimony.

On what principle, then, shall we any longer choose justice rather than the worst injustice? when, if we only unite the latter with a deceitful regard to appearance, we shall fare to our mind both with gods and men, in life and after death, as the most numerous and the highest authorities tell us. Knowing all this, Socrates, how can a man who has any superiority of mind or person or rank or wealth, be willing to honour justice; or indeed to refrain from laughing when he hears justice praised? And even if there should be some one who is able to disprove the truth of my words, and who is satisfied that justice is best, still he is not angry with the unjust, but is very ready to forgive them, because he also knows that men are not just of their own free will; unless, peradventure, there be some one whom the divinity within him may have inspired with a hatred of injustice, or who has attained knowledge of the truth—but no other man. He only blames injustice who, owing to cowardice or age or some weakness, has not the power of being unjust. And this is proved by the fact that when he obtains the power, he immediately becomes unjust as far as he can be.

The cause of all this, Socrates, was indicated by us at the beginning of the argument, when my brother and I told you how astonished we were to find that of all the professing panegyrists of justice— beginning with the ancient heroes of whom any memorial has been preserved to us, and ending with the men of our own time—no one has ever blamed injustice or praised justice except with a view to the glories, honours, and benefits which flow from them. No one has ever adequately described either in verse or prose the true essential nature of either of them abiding in the soul, and invisible to any human or divine eye; or shown that of all the things of a man's soul which he has within him, justice is the greatest good, and injustice the greatest evil. Had this been the universal strain, had you sought to persuade us of this from our youth upwards, we should not have been on the watch to keep one another from doing wrong, but every one would have been his own watchman, because afraid, if he did wrong, of harbouring in himself the greatest of evils. I dare say that Thrasymachus and others would seriously hold the language which I have been merely repeating, and words even stronger than these about justice and injustice, grossly, as I conceive, perverting their true nature. But I speak in this vehement manner, as I must frankly confess to you, because I want to hear from you the opposite side; and I would ask you to show not only the superiority which justice has over injustice, but what effect they have on the possessor of them which makes the one to be a good and the other an evil to him. And please, as Glaucon requested of you, to exclude reputations; for unless you take away from each of them his true reputation and add on the false, we shall say that you do not praise justice, but the appearance of it; we shall think that you are only exhorting us to keep injustice dark, and that you really agree with Thrasymachus in thinking that justice is another's good and the interest of the stronger, and that injustice is a man's own profit and interest, though injurious to the weaker. Now as you have admitted that justice is one of that highest class of goods which are desired indeed for their results, but in a far greater degree for their own sakes—like sight or hearing or knowledge or health, or any other real and natural and not merely conventional good—I would ask you in your praise of justice to regard one point only: I mean the essential good and evil which justice and injustice work in the possessors of them. Let others praise justice and censure injustice, magnifying the rewards and honours of the one and abusing the other; that is a manner of arguing which, coming from them, I am ready to tolerate, but from you who have spent your whole life in the consideration of this question, unless I hear the contrary from your own lips, I expect something better. And therefore, I say, not only prove to us that justice is better than injustice, but show what they either of them do to the possessor of them, which makes the one to be a good and the other an evil, whether seen or unseen by gods and men.

Socrates. Sons of an illustrious father, that was not a bad beginning of the Elegiac verses which the admirer of Glaucon made in honour of you after you had distinguished yourselves at the battle of Megara—

"'Sons of Ariston,' he sang, 'divine offspring of an illustrious hero.'"

The epithet is very appropriate, for there is something truly divine in being able to argue as you have done for the superiority of injustice, and remaining unconvinced by your own arguments. And I do believe that you are not convinced—this I infer from your general character, for had I judged only from your speeches I should have mistrusted you. But now, the greater my confidence in you, the greater is my difficulty in knowing what to say. For I am in a strait between two; on the one hand I feel that I am unequal to the task; and my inability is brought home to me by the fact that you were not satisfied with the answer which I made to Thrasymachus, proving, as I thought, the superiority which justice has over injustice. And yet I cannot refuse to help, while breath and speech remain to me; I am afraid that there would be an impiety in being present when justice is evil spoken of and not lifting up a hand in her defence. And therefore I had best give such help as I can.

Glaucon and the rest entreated me by all means not to let the question drop, but to proceed in the investigation. They wanted to arrive at the truth, first, about the nature of justice and injustice, and secondly, about their relative advantages. I told them, what I really thought, that the enquiry would be of a serious nature, and would require very good eyes. Seeing then, I said, that we are no great wits, I think that we had better adopt a method which I may illustrate thus; suppose that a short-sighted person had been asked by some one to read small letters from a distance; and it occurred to some one else that they might be found in another place which was larger and in which the letters were larger—if they were the same and he could read the larger letters first, and then proceed to the lesser—this would have been thought a rare piece of good fortune.

Adeimantus. Very true. But how does the illustration apply to our enquiry?

Socrates. I will tell you. Justice, which is the subject of our enquiry, is, as you know, sometimes spoken of as the virtue of an individual, and sometimes as the virtue of a state.

Adeimantus. True.

Socrates. And is not a State larger than an individual?

Adeimantus. It is.

Socrates. Then in the larger the quantity of justice is likely to be larger and more easily discernible. I propose therefore that we enquire into the nature of justice and injustice, first as they appear in the State, and secondly in the individual, proceeding from the greater to the lesser and comparing them.

Adeimantus. That is an excellent proposal.

NOTES

1. Hesiod, *Works and Days*, p. 230.
2. Homer, *Od*, xix, p. 109.
3. Eumolpus.
4. Hesiod, *Works and Days*, p. 287.
5. Homer, *Iliad*, ix, p. 493.

READING

Self Love*

THOMAS HOBBES

MindTap°   For more chapter resources and activities, go to MindTap.

Study Questions

As you read the excerpt, please consider the following questions:

1. In what ways are men equal and unequal? Which is more significant?
2. What does Hobbes mean when he says that nature has given everyone a right to all? What is the result of this?
3. Beyond society and its rules, is there any right or wrong, or just or unjust, according to Hobbes?

There be in animals, two sorts of *motions* peculiar to them: one called vital; begun in generation, and continued without interruption through their whole life; such as are the *course* of the *blood*, the *pulse*, the *breathing*, the *concoction, nutrition, excretion*, etc. to which motions there needs no help of imagination: the other is *animal motion*, otherwise called *voluntary motion*; as to *go*, to *speak*, to *move* any of our limbs, in such manner as is first fancied in our minds. That sense is motion in the organs and interior parts of man's body, caused by the action of the things we see, hear, etc.; and that

fancy is but the relics of the same motion, remaining after sense.... And because *going, speaking*, and the like *voluntary motions*, depend always upon a precedent thought of *whither, which way*, and *what*; it is evident, that the imagination is the first internal beginning of all voluntary motion. And although unstudied men do not conceive any motion

From Thomas Hobbes, *Leviathan*, in *The English Works of Thomas Hobbes*, ed. Sir William Molesworth (London: John Bohn, 1839), pp. 2:38–41, 85.

*Title supplied by the editor.

at all to be there, where the thing moved is invisible; or the space it is moved in is, for the shortness of it, insensible; yet that doth not hinder, but that such motions are. For let a space be never so little, that which is moved over a greater space, whereof that little one is part, must first be moved over that. These small beginnings of motion, within the body of man, before they appear in walking, speaking, striking, and other visible actions, are commonly called ENDEAVOR.

This endeavor, when it is toward something which causes it, is called APPETITE, or DESIRE; the latter, being the general name; and the other oftentimes restrained to signify the desire of food, namely *hunger* and *thirst*. And when the endeavor is fromward something, it is generally called AVERSION. These words, *appetite* and *aversion*, we have from the Latins; and they both of them signify the motions, one of approaching, the other of retiring.... For nature itself does often press upon men those truths, which afterwards, when they look for somewhat beyond nature, they stumble at. For the schools find in mere appetite to go, or move, no actual motion at all: but because some motion they must acknowledge, they call it metaphorical motion; which is but an absurd speech: for though words may be called metaphorical; bodies and motions cannot.

That which men desire, they are also said to LOVE: and to HATE those things for which they have aversion. So that desire and love are the same thing; save that by desire, we always signify the absence of the object; by love, most commonly the presence of the same. So also by aversion, we signify the absence; and by hate, the presence of the object.

Of appetites and aversions, some are born with men; as appetite of food, appetite of excretion, and exoneration, which may also and more properly be called aversions, from somewhat they feel in their bodies; and some other appetites, not many. The rest, which are appetites of particular things, proceed from experience, and trial of their effects upon themselves or other men. For of things we know not at all, or believe not to be, we can have no further

desire, than to taste and try. But aversion we have for things, not only which we know have hurt us, but also that we do not know whether they will hurt us, or not.

Those things which we neither desire, nor hate, we are said to *contemn*; CONTEMPT being nothing else but an immobility, or contumacy of the heart, in resisting the action of certain things; and proceeding from that the heart is already moved otherwise, by other more potent objects; or from want of experience of them.

And because the constitution of a man's body is in continual mutation, it is impossible that all the same things should always cause in him the same appetites, and aversions: much less can all men consent, in the desire of almost any one and the same object.

But whatsoever is the object of any man's appetite or desire, that is it which he for his part calleth *good*: and the object of his hate and aversion, *evil*; and of his *contempt, vile* and inconsiderable. For these words of good, evil, and contemptible, are ever used with relation to the person that useth them: there being nothing simply and absolutely so; nor any common rule of good and evil, to be taken from the nature of the objects themselves....

Felicity of this life consisteth not in the repose of a mind satisfied. For there is no such *finis ultimus*, utmost aim, nor *summum bonum*, greatest good, as is spoken of in the books of the old moral philosophers. Nor can a man any more live, whose desires are at an end, than he, whose senses and imaginations are at a stand. Felicity is a continual progress of the desire, from one object to another; the attaining of the former, being still but the way to the latter. The cause whereof is, that the object of man's desire, is not to enjoy once only, and for one instant of time; but to assure for ever, the way of his future desire....

So that in the first place, I put for a general inclination of all mankind, a perpetual and restless desire of power after power, that ceaseth only in death. And the cause of this, is...that a man...cannot assure the power and means to live well, which he hath present, without the acquisition of more....

Nature hath made men so equal, in the faculties of the body, and mind; as that though there be found one man sometimes manifestly stronger in body, or of quicker mind than another; yet when all is reckoned together, the difference between man, and man, is not so considerable, as that one man can thereupon claim to himself any benefit, to which another may not pretend, as well as he. For as to the strength of body, the weakest has strength enough to kill the strongest, either by secret machination, or by confederacy with others, that are in the same danger with himself.

And as to the faculties of the mind, setting aside the arts grounded upon words, and especially that skill of proceeding upon general, and infallible rules, called science; which very few have, and but in few things; as being not native faculty, born with us; nor attained, as prudence, while we look after somewhat else, I find yet a greater equality amongst men, than that of strength. For prudence, is but experience; which equal time, equally bestows on all men, in those things they equally apply themselves unto. That which may perhaps make such equality incredible, is but a vain conceit of one's own wisdom, which almost all men think they have in a greater degree, than the vulgar; that is, than all men but themselves, and a few others, whom by fame, or for concurring with themselves, they approve. For such is the nature of men, that howsoever they may acknowledge many others to be more witty, or more eloquent, or more learned; yet they will hardly believe there be many so wise as themselves; for they see their own wit at hand, and other men's at a distance. But this proveth rather that men are in that point equal, than unequal. For there is not ordinarily a greater sign of the equal distribution of any thing, than that every man is contented with his share.

From this equality of ability, ariseth equality of hope in the attaining of our ends. And therefore if any two men desire the same thing, which nevertheless they cannot both enjoy, they become enemies; and in the way to their end, which is principally their own conservation, and sometimes their delectation only, endeavor to destroy, or subdue one another. And from hence it comes to pass, that where an invader hath no more to fear, than another man's single power; if one plant, sow, build, or possess a convenient seat, others may probably be expected to come prepared with forces united, to dispossess, and deprive him, not only of the fruit of his labor, but also of his life, or liberty. And the invader again is in the like danger of another.

And from this diffidence of one another, there is no way for any man to secure himself, so reasonable, as anticipation; that is, by force, or wiles, to master the persons of all men he can, so long, till he see no other power great enough to endanger him: and this is no more than his own conservation requireth, and generally allowed. Also because there be some, that taking pleasure in contemplating their own power in the acts of conquest, which they pursue farther than their security requires; if others, that otherwise would be glad to be at ease within modest bounds, should not by invasion increase their power, they would not be able, long time, by standing only on their defense, to subsist. And by consequence, such augmentation of dominion over men being necessary to a man's conservation, it ought to be allowed him.

Again, men have no pleasure, but on the contrary a great deal of grief, in keeping company, where there is no power able to overawe them all. For every man looketh that his companion should value him, at the same rate he sets upon himself: and upon all signs of contempt, or undervaluing, naturally endeavors, as far as he dares, (which amongst them that have no common power to keep them in quiet, is far enough to make them destroy each other), to extort a greater value from his contemners, by damage; and from others, by the example.

So that in the nature of man, we find three principal causes of quarrel. First, competition; secondly, diffidence; thirdly, glory.

The first, maketh men invade for gain; the second, for safety; and the third, for reputation. The first use violence, to make themselves masters of other men's persons, wives, children, and cattle; the second, to defend them; the third, for trifles, as a word, a smile, a different opinion, and any other sign of undervalue, either direct in their persons, or by reflection in their kindred, their friends, their nation, their profession, or their name.

Hereby it is manifest, that during the time men live without a common power to keep them all in awe, they are in that condition which is called war; and such a war, as is of every man, against every man. For WAR, consisteth not in battle only, or the act of fighting; but in a tract of time, wherein the will to contend by battle is sufficiently known: and therefore the notion of time, is to be considered in the nature of war; as it is in the nature of weather. For as the nature of foul weather, lieth not in a shower or two of rain; but in an inclination thereto of many days together: so the nature of war, consisteth not in actual fighting; but in the known disposition thereto, during all the time there is no assurance to the contrary. All other time is PEACE.

Whatsoever therefore is consequent to a time of war, where every man is enemy to every man; the same is consequent to the time, wherein men live without security, than what their own strength, and their own invention shall furnish them withal. In such condition, there is no place for industry; because the fruit thereof is uncertain: and consequently no culture of the earth; no navigation, nor use of the commodities that may be imported by sea; no commodious building; no instruments of moving, and removing, such things as require much force; no knowledge of the face of the earth; no account of time; no arts; no letters; no society; and which

is worst of all, continual fear, and danger of violent death; and the life of man, solitary, poor, nasty, brutish, and short....

It may peradventure be thought, there was never such a time, nor condition of war as this; and I believe it was never generally so, over all the world: but there are many places, where they live so now. For the savage people in many places of America, except the government of small families, the concord whereof dependeth on natural lust, have no government at all; and live at this day in that brutish manner, as I said before. Howsoever, it may be perceived what manner of life there would be, where there were no common power to fear, by the manner of life, which men that have formerly lived under a peaceful government, use to degenerate into, in a civil war.

But though there had never been any time, wherein particular men were in a condition of war one against another; yet in all times, kings, and persons of sovereign authority, because of their independency, are in continual jealousies, and in the state and posture of gladiators; having their weapons pointing, and their eyes fixed on one another; that is, their forts, garrisons, and guns upon the frontiers of their kingdoms; and continual spies upon their neighbors; which is a posture of war. But because they uphold thereby, the industry of their subjects; there does not follow from it, that misery, which accompanies the liberty of particular men....

READING

The Social Contract and Altruism

STEVEN PINKER

MindTap®   For more chapter resources and activities, go to MindTap.

Study Questions

As you read the excerpt, please consider the following questions:

1. How are "nepotistic altruism" and "reciprocal altruism" explained in evolutionary terms?
2. What is the problem with people caring more for their close relations or with parents preferring to save their own children instead of the children of others?
3. How does the modern theory of evolution fall "smack into the social contract tradition?"

It's no mystery why organisms sometimes harm one another. Evolution has no conscience, and if one creature hurts another to benefit itself, such as by eating, parasitizing, intimidating, or cuckolding it, its descendants will come to predominate, complete with those nasty habits. All this is familiar from the vernacular sense of "Darwinian" as a synonym for "ruthless" and from Tennyson's depiction of nature as red in tooth and claw. If that were all there was to the evolution of the human condition, we would have to agree with the rock song: Life sucks, then you die. But of course life doesn't always suck. Many creatures cooperate, nurture, and make peace, and humans in particular find comfort and joy in their families, friends, and communities. This, too, should be familiar to readers of *The Selfish Gene* and the other books on the evolution of altruism that have appeared in the years since.

There are several reasons why organisms may evolve a willingness to do good deeds. They may help other creatures while pursuing their own interests, say, when they form a herd that confuses predators or live off each other's by-products. This is called mutualism, symbiosis, or cooperation. Among humans, friends who have common tastes, hobbies, or enemies are a kind of symbiont pair. The two parents of a brood of children are an even better example. Their genes are tied up in the same package, their children, so what is good for one is good for the other, and each has an interest in keeping the other alive and healthy. These shared interests set the stage for compassionate love and marital love to evolve.

And in some cases organisms may benefit other organisms at a cost to themselves, which biologists call altruism. Altruism in this technical sense can evolve in two main ways. First, since relatives share genes, any gene that inclines an organism toward helping a relative will increase the chance of survival of a copy of itself that sits inside that relative, even if the helper sacrifices its own fitness in the

generous act. Such genes will, on average, come to predominate, as long as the cost to the helper is less than the benefit to the recipient discounted by their degree of relatedness. Family love—the cherishing of children, siblings, parents, grandparents, uncles and aunts, nieces and nephews, and cousins—can evolve. This is called nepotistic altruism.

Altruism can also evolve when organisms trade favors. One helps another by grooming, feeding, protecting, or backing him, and is helped in turn when the needs reverse. This is called reciprocal altruism, and it can evolve when the parties recognize each other, interact repeatedly, can confer a large benefit on others at small cost to themselves, keep a memory for favors offered or denied, and are impelled to reciprocate accordingly. Reciprocal altruism can evolve because cooperators do better than hermits or misanthropes. They enjoy the gains of trading their surpluses, pulling ticks out of one another's hair, saving each other from drowning or starvation, and baby-sitting each other's children. Reciprocators can also do better over the long run than the cheaters who take favors without returning them, because the reciprocators will come to recognize the cheaters and shun or punish them. The demands of reciprocal altruism can explain why the social and moralistic emotions evolved. Sympathy and trust prompt people to extend the first favor. Gratitude and loyalty prompt them to repay favors. Guilt and shame deter them from hurting or failing to repay others. Anger and contempt prompt them to avoid or punish cheaters. And among humans, any tendency of an individual to reciprocate or cheat does not have to be witnessed firsthand but can be recounted by language. This leads to an interest in the reputation of others, transmitted by gossip and public approval or condemnation, and a concern with one's own reputation. Partnerships, friendships, alliances, and communities can emerge, cemented by these emotions and concerns.

Many people start to get nervous at this point, but the discomfort is not from the tragedies that [Robert] Trivers explained. It comes instead from two misconceptions, each of which we have encountered before. First, all this talk about genes that influence behavior does not mean that we are cuckoo clocks or player pianos, mindlessly executing the dictates of DNA. The genes in question are those that endow us with the neural systems for conscience, deliberation, and will, and when we talk about the selection of such genes, we are talking about the various ways those faculties could have evolved. The error comes from the Blank Slate and the Ghost in the Machine: if one starts off thinking that our higher mental faculties are stamped in by society or inhere in a soul, then when biologists mention genetic influence the first alternatives that come to mind are puppet strings or trolley tracks. But if higher faculties, including learning, reason, and choice, are products of a nonrandom organization of the brain, there have to be genes that help do the organizing, and that raises the question of how those genes would have been selected in the course of human evolution. The second misconception is to imagine that talk about costs and benefits implies that people are Machiavellian cynics, coldly calculating the genetic advantages of befriending and marrying. To fret over this picture, or denounce it because it is ugly, is to confuse proximate and ultimate causation. People don't care about their genes; they care about happiness, love, power, respect, and other passions. The cost-benefit calculations are a metaphorical way of describing the selection of alternative genes over millennia, not a literal description of what takes place in a human brain in real time. Nothing prevents the amoral process of natural selection from evolving a brain with genuine big-hearted emotions. It is said that those who appreciate legislation and sausages should not see them being made. The same is true for human emotions. So if love and conscience can evolve, where's the tragedy? Trivers noticed that the confluence of genetic interests that gave rise to the social emotions is only partial.

Because we are not clones, or even social insects (who can share up to three-quarters of their genes), what ultimately is best for one person is not identical to what ultimately is best for another. Thus every human relationship, even the most devoted and intimate, carries the seeds of conflict. In the movie "Antz", an ant with the voice of Woody Allen complains to his psychoanalyst:

> It's this whole gung-ho superorganism thing that I just can't get. I try, but I just don't get it. What is it, I'm supposed to do everything for the colony and … what about my needs?

The humor comes from the clash between ant psychology, which originates in a genetic system that makes workers more closely related to one another than they would be to their offspring, and human psychology, in which our genetic distinctness leads us to ask, "What about my needs?" Trivers, following on the work of William Hamilton and George Williams, did some algebra that predicts the extent to which people should ask themselves that question.

The rest of this chapter is about that deceptively simple algebra and how its implications overturn many conceptions of human nature. It discredits the Blank Slate, which predicts that people's regard for their fellows is determined by their "role," as if it were a part assigned arbitrarily to an actor. But it also discredits some naïve views of evolution that are common among people who don't believe in the Blank Slate. Most people have intuitions about the natural state of affairs. They may believe that if we acted as nature "wants" us to, families would function as harmonious units, or individuals would act for the good of the species, or people would show the true selves beneath their social masks, or, as Newt Gingrich said in 1995, the male of our species would hunt giraffes and wallow in ditches like little piglets.

Understanding the patterns of genetic overlap that bind and divide us can replace simplistic views of all kinds with a more subtle understanding of the human condition. Indeed, it can illuminate the human condition in ways that complement the insights of artists and philosophers through the millennia.

The most obvious human tragedy comes from the difference between our feelings toward kin and our feelings toward non-kin, one of the deepest divides in the living world. When it comes to love and solidarity among people, the relative viscosity of blood and water is evident in everything from the clans and dynasties of traditional societies to the clogging of airports during holidays with people traveling across the world to be with their families.

It has also been borne out by quantitative studies. In traditional foraging societies, genetic relatives are more likely to live together, work in each other's gardens, protect each other, and adopt each other's needy or orphaned children, and are less likely to attack, feud with, and kill each other.

Even in modern societies, which tend to sunder ties of kinship, the more closely two people are genetically related, the more inclined they are to come to one another's aid, especially in life-or-death situations.

But love and solidarity are relative. To say that people are more caring toward their relatives is to say that they are more callous toward their non-relatives. The epigraph to Robert Wright's book on evolutionary psychology is an excerpt from Graham Greene's "The Power and the Glory," in which the protagonist broods about his daughter: "He said, 'Oh god, help her. Damn me, I deserve it, but let her live forever.' This was the love he should have felt for every soul in the world: all the fear and the wish to save concentrated unjustly on the one child. He began to weep....He thought: This is what I should feel all the time for everyone." Family love indeed subverts the ideal of what we should feel for every soul in the world. Moral philosophers play with a hypothetical dilemma in which people can run through the left door of a burning building to save some number of children or through the right door to save their own child.

If you are a parent, ponder this question: Is there any number of children that would lead you to pick the left door? Indeed, all of us reveal our preference with our pocketbooks when we spend money on trifles for our own children (a bicycle, orthodontics, an education at a private school or university) instead of saving the lives of unrelated children in the developing world by donating the money to charity. Similarly, the practice of parents bequeathing their wealth to their children is one of the steepest impediments to an economically egalitarian society. Yet few people would allow the government to confiscate 100 percent of their estate, because most people see their children as an extension of themselves and thus as the proper beneficiaries of their lifelong striving. Nepotism is a universal human bent and a universal scourge of large organizations. It is notorious for sapping countries led by hereditary dynasties and for bogging down governments and businesses in the Third World. A recurring historic solution was to give positions of local power to people who had no family ties, such as eunuchs, celibates, slaves, or people a long way from home.

A more recent solution is to outlaw or regulate nepotism, though the regulations always come with tradeoffs and exceptions. Small businesses or, as they are often called, "family businesses" or "Mom-and-Pop businesses" are highly nepotistic, and thereby can conflict with principles of equal opportunity and earn the resentment of the surrounding community.

The sciences of human nature are pressing on two political hot buttons, not just one. The first is how we conceptualize the entity known as "society." The political philosopher Roger Masters has shown how sociobiology (and related theories invoking evolution, genetics, and brain science) inadvertently took sides in an ancient dispute between two traditions of understanding the social order.

In the sociological tradition, a society is a cohesive organic entity and its individual citizens are mere parts. People are thought to be social by their very nature and to function as constituents of a larger super organism. This is the tradition of Plato, Hegel, Marx, Durkheim, Weber, Kroeber, the sociologist Talcott Parsons, the anthropologist Claude Levi-Strauss, and postmodernism in the humanities and social sciences. In the economic or social contract tradition, society is an arrangement negotiated by rational, self-interested individuals. Society emerges when people agree to sacrifice some of their autonomy in exchange for security from the depredations of others wielding their autonomy. It is the tradition of Thrasymachus in Plato's *Republic*, and of Machiavelli, Hobbes, Locke, Rousseau, Smith, and Bentham. In the twentieth century it became the basis for the rational actor or "economic man" models in economics and political science, and for cost-benefit analyses of public choices. The modern theory of evolution falls smack into the social contract tradition. It maintains that complex adaptations, including behavioral strategies, evolved to benefit the individual (indeed, the genes for those traits within an individual), not the community, species, or ecosystem.

Social organization evolves when the long-term benefits to the individual outweigh the immediate costs. Darwin was influenced by Adam Smith, and many of his successors analyze the evolution of sociality using tools that come right out of economics, such as game theory and other optimization techniques. Reciprocal altruism, in particular, is just the traditional concept of the social contract

restated in biological terms. Of course, humans were never solitary (as Rousseau and Hobbes incorrectly surmised), and they did not inaugurate group living by haggling over a contract at a particular time and place. Bands, clans, tribes, and other social groups are central to human existence and have been so for as long as we have been a species. But the logic of social contracts may have propelled the evolution of the mental faculties that keep us in these groups. Social arrangements are evolutionarily contingent, arising when the benefits of group living exceed the costs.

With a slightly different ecosystem and evolutionary history, we could have ended up like our cousins the orangutans, who are almost entirely solitary. And according to evolutionary biology, all societies "animal and human" seethe with conflicts of interest and are held together by shifting mixtures of dominance and cooperation.

REVIEW EXERCISES

1. Explain the basic difference between psychological egoism and ethical egoism.
2. Give two different formulations or versions of psychological egoism and ethical egoism.
3. Is psychological egoism true, and what must be shown to prove its truth?
4. How is psychological egoism supposed to provide support for an argument for ethical egoism? What is one problem for this argument?
5. Summarize the arguments regarding the consistency or inconsistency of ethical egoism.
6. In what sense does the argument for ethical egoism based on economics support not egoism but

utilitarianism—in other words, the view that we ought to do what is in the best interest of all or the greatest number?
7. Explain how the prisoner's dilemma can be used in discussions of egoism and cooperative endeavor.
8. What is meant by taking the "moral point of view?"
9. How does the example of the "ring of Gyges" illustrate the question: "Why be moral?"
10. Is Hobbes' proposed solution to the problem of egoism, via the social contract, acceptable?
11. How does the discussion of evolution (in Pinker) inform your understanding of the conflict between egoism and altruism?

MindTap® For more chapter resources and activities, go to MindTap.

Utilitarianism and John Stuart Mill

Getty Images/Photos.com

Learning Outcomes

After reading this chapter, you should be able to:

- Explain differences between utilitarianism and egoism as kinds of consequentialism.
- Explain the difference between act utilitarianism and rule utilitarianism.
- Describe the trolley problem and how it exemplifies the challenge of utilitarianism.
- Identify key components of the utilitarian assessment of pleasure: intensity, duration, fruitfulness, and likelihood.

- Articulate ways that utilitarianism is connected with hedonism and Epicureanism.
- Apply utilitarian reasoning to a variety of cases in the real world.
- Provide an overview of John Stuart Mill's defense of utilitarianism.
- Defend your own thesis with regard to the value of utilitarianism.

MindTap®   For more chapter resources and activities, go to MindTap.

In 2015, the global population exceeded 7.3 billion people. The United Nations predicts that another billion people will be added to the world's population by 2030, with the population increasing to over 9 billion by 2050.[1] The increase in human population during the past two centuries has been explosive. Causes for this growth include industrialization, a revolution in agriculture and other technologies, and better political organization. This growing population has created problems, however, as soils are depleted, oceans are overfished, and pollution has increased. Industrialization and technology have led to massive use of carbon-based fuels, which contribute to global climate change. If the world's population keeps growing at the current pace—and if the growing human population eats, drives, and consumes at current rates—we may be headed for a worldwide environmental and humanitarian crisis. A recent United Nations report concluded, "should the global population reach 9.6 billion by 2050, the equivalent of almost three planets could be required to provide the natural resources needed to sustain current lifestyles."[2]

Some argue that a prudent solution would be to take steps to limit consumption, population growth, or both. The means that are used to control population might include morally controversial technologies such as abortion. Moral concerns also haunt proposals to limit consumption: each of us wants the freedom to earn, spend, and consume as we wish. Even though individuals enjoy expanding their families and consuming products, the cumulative choices of individuals pursuing their own happiness can lead to less happiness for all—as the overall increase in population, pollution, and environmental degradation may well decrease opportunities and life prospects for everyone. When we think about issues from this perspective—one that takes into account the general happiness of everyone—we are adopting a utilitarian point of view.

Large social engineering projects are often grounded in utilitarian concerns. Consider the effort in China to control population growth by limiting reproduction to one child per family. Critics of the policy argued that this violates a fundamental right to reproduce. Can limitations on basic rights be justified by the larger utilitarian concerns of social policies? Utilitarian efforts to maximize good consequences require that we adjust our policies in light of changing circumstances. The one-child policy created outcomes that rippled across Chinese society, including, for example, a shift in family structure and gender ratios. As the Chinese government has adjusted its

population policies, it has struggled to manage costs and benefits. Should morality be focused on complex and changing consequences or should it be concerned with abstract and invariable moral principles?

Utilitarian reasoning can be used to justify a variety of actions and policy decisions. How do we justify speed limits on the highways? It might seem that each of us should be free to go as fast as we want. However, unbridled speed would result in more accidents, which not only kill people but also slow the rest of us down. Speed limits satisfy the utilitarian goal of maximizing the greatest happiness for the greatest number. Some will be unhappy because they can't drive 100 mph. But when we each drive at 65 mph and arrive safely, we are each more likely to be better off. Some may be less happy because they are forced to drive more slowly, but overall, more of us are happier.

Some uses of utilitarian reasoning are controversial because they seem to run counter to our intuitions about basic principles of right and wrong. Consider, for example, the use of torture in interrogations of

Crowded village ferry crossing the River Hooghly, West Bengal, India.

Annie Owen/Robert Harding World Imagery/Corbis

terror suspects. If a terrorist had planted a bomb in a public place that would threaten to kill thousands of innocent people, would it be justifiable to torture the terrorist to force him to reveal the location of the bomb? On the one hand, some assert that torture is never permissible because it violates basic moral principles. The Geneva Conventions regulating warfare prohibit torture and define it as "any act by which severe pain or suffering, whether physical or mental, is intentionally inflicted on a person for such purposes as obtaining from him or a third person information or a confession."[3] On the other hand, suppose, for example, that torture could save many lives. Would it then be justified? Former Vice President Dick Cheney maintained that "enhanced interrogation techniques" including waterboarding (a process that simulates drowning) produced useful information. According to the *New York Times,* the CIA waterboarded terror suspect Khaled Sheikh Mohammed 183 times.[4] In a speech on the tenth anniversary of September 11, Cheney claimed that by waterboarding terrorists such as Mohammed, information was extracted that led to the assassination of Osama bin Laden.[5] Cheney and other members of the Bush administration justified torture on utilitarian grounds. Their view is shared by many. A Pentagon study of "the ethics of troops on the front line" in Iraq found that 41 percent said that "torture should be allowed to save the life of a soldier or Marine," and about the same number said that it "should be allowed to gather important information from insurgents."[6] From a utilitarian standpoint, it may make good sense to inflict pain on someone to prevent pain that would be inflicted on a greater number of others. From the same standpoint, however, one may argue that practices such as torture cause greater harm than good—by extracting false confessions and lowering a country's standing with potential allies. In any event, the question remains: Does a good end justify otherwise objectionable means?

WEIGHING CONSEQUENCES

One way of thinking about this is to compare the benefits and costs of each alternative. Whichever has the greater net benefit is the best alternative.

Such an approach begins with the belief that we can measure and compare the risks and benefits of various actions. The idea is that actions are morally better or worse depending on whether they produce pleasure or pain or, more abstractly, on how they affect human well-being and happiness. Unlike egoism, utilitarianism focuses on the *sum* of individual pleasures and pains. It is not my pleasures or pains that matter—but the cumulative happiness of a number of people.

Another aspect of utilitarianism is the belief that each of us counts equally. Peter Singer, an influential contemporary defender of utilitarianism, derives utilitarianism from the basic idea that each person's interests ought to be given equal consideration. Related to this is the idea that "my own interests cannot count for more, simply because they are my own, than the interests of others."[7] The basic procedure for utilitarianism is to add up the interests of everyone who is affected by an action without privileging the interests of anyone in particular. Utilitarianism is thus opposed to racist or sexist ideas, for example, which often hold that the interests of some people matter more than the interests of others.

Utilitarianism suggests that we ought to consider the totality of consequences of a policy or action. Forms of utilitarianism will differ depending on how we understand what sorts of consequences or interests matter. Complexities arise in defining key concepts such as happiness, interest, and well-being. Singer, for example, wants to focus on *interests* instead of pleasures or happiness. This indicates that it is possible that some pleasures are not really in our interest. For example, drug use can produce pleasure, but it is not in anyone's long-term interest to be addicted to cocaine or heroin. We might also focus on people's *preferences*—that is, what people themselves state that they prefer. But again there is an important question of whether our preferences actually coordinate with our interests—or can we prefer things that are not in our interest? In different terms, we might wonder whether pleasure is a good thing or whether genuine happiness can be reduced to pleasure. In any case, utilitarians have to provide an account of what matters when we try to add up benefits and harms—whether it is subjective feeling, taste, and preference, or whether it is something deeper and more objective such as well-being or other interests (in health, longevity, fulfillment, accomplishment, etc.).

Utilitarianism has to provide an account of *whose* interests or happiness matters. Jeremy Bentham, one of the founding fathers of utilitarianism, extended his utilitarian concern in a way that included all suffering beings, including nonhuman animals. Peter Singer would agree. He is well-known as an advocate of animal welfare. Like Bentham, he claims that the interests of nonhuman animals ought to be taken into account. (We discuss the issue of animal ethics further in Chapter 17.)

One important point to bear in mind when discussing utilitarianism is that utilitarians generally do not think that actions or policies are good or bad in themselves. Rather, for the utilitarian, the goodness or badness of an action is solely a function of its consequences. Thus, even killing innocent people may be acceptable if it produces an outcome that saves a greater number of others from harm.

HISTORICAL BACKGROUND
Jeremy Bentham and John Stuart Mill

The classical formulation of utilitarian moral theory is found in the writings of Jeremy Bentham (1748–1832) and John Stuart Mill (1806–1873). Jeremy Bentham was an English-born student of law and the leader of a radical movement for social and legal reform based on utilitarian principles. His primary published work was *Introduction to the Principles of Morals and Legislation* (1789). The title indicates his aim: to take the same principles that provide the basis for morals as a guide for the formation and revision of law. Bentham believed that the same principles guided both social and personal morality.

James Mill, the father of John Stuart Mill, was an associate of Bentham's and a supporter of his views. John Stuart was the eldest of James's nine children. He was educated in the classics and history at home. By the time he was twenty, he had read Bentham and had become a devoted follower of

his philosophy. The basic ideas of utilitarian moral theory are summarized in Mill's short work *Utilitarianism*, in which he sought to dispel the misconception that morality has nothing to do with usefulness or utility or that morality is opposed to pleasure. Mill was also a strong supporter of personal liberty, and in his pamphlet *On Liberty* he argued that the only reason for society to interfere in a person's life was to prevent him or her from doing harm to others. People might choose wrongly, but he believed that allowing bad choices was better than government coercion. Liberty to speak one's own opinion, he believed, would benefit all. However, it is not clear that utility is always served by promoting liberty. Nor is it clear what Mill would say about cases in which liberty must be restricted to promote the general good, as in the case of speed limits or airport security rules. In his work, *On the Subjection of Women*, Mill also emphasized the general good and criticized those social treatments of women that did not allow them to develop their talents and contribute to the good of society. Consistent with these views, he also supported the right of women to vote. Later in life he married his longtime companion and fellow liberal,

A portrait of the utilitarian philosopher John Stuart Mill (1806–1873).

Harriet Taylor. Mill also served in the British Parliament from 1865 to 1868.

The original utilitarians were democratic, progressive, empiricist, and optimistic. They were democratic in the sense that they believed that social policy ought to work for the good of all persons, not just the upper class. They believed that when interests of various persons conflicted, the best choice was that which promoted the interests of the greater number. The utilitarians were progressive in that they questioned the status quo. For example, they believed that if the contemporary punishment system was not working well, then it ought to be changed. Social programs should be judged by their usefulness in promoting the greatest happiness for the greatest number. Observation would determine whether a project or practice succeeded in this goal. Thus, utilitarianism is part of the empiricist tradition in philosophy, which holds that we know what is good only by observation or by appeal to experience. Bentham and Mill were also optimists. They believed that human wisdom and science would improve the lot of humanity. Mill wrote in *Utilitarianism*, "All the grand sources of human suffering are in a great degree, many of them almost entirely, conquerable by human care and effort."[8]

THE PRINCIPLE OF UTILITY

The basic moral principle of utilitarianism is called the **principle of utility** or the **greatest happiness principle**. As John Stuart Mill explained it (and as you will see in the reading that follows) "actions are right in proportion as they tend to promote happiness, wrong as they tend to produce the reverse of happiness."

Utilitarianism is a form of consequentialism. It focuses on the consequences of actions. Egoism is also a form of consequentialism. But unlike egoism, utilitarianism focuses on the consequences for all persons impacted by an action. Consider the diagram used to classify moral theories provided in Chapter 1.

According to classical utilitarian moral theory, when we evaluate human acts or practices, we consider neither the nature of the acts or practices nor the motive for which people do what they do. As Mill puts it, "He who saves a fellow creature from drowning does what is morally right, whether his motive be duty or the hope of being paid for his trouble."[9] It is the result of one's action—that a life is saved—that matters morally. According to utilitarianism, we ought to decide which action or practice is best by considering the likely or actual consequences of each alternative. For example, over the years, people have called for a suicide barrier on the Golden Gate Bridge to prevent people from using it to commit suicide. More than 1,600 people have jumped from the bridge to their deaths.[10] Building a suicide barrier on a bridge is neither good nor bad in itself, according to utilitarianism. Nor is it sufficient that people supporting the building of such a barrier be well intentioned. The only thing that matters for the utilitarian is whether, by erecting such a barrier, we would actually increase happiness by preventing suicides. After much dispute, officials have agreed to build a suicide barrier—a net to catch would-be jumpers—on the bridge.

PLEASURE AND HAPPINESS

Of course, there is an open question about whether suicide is good or bad. Some will argue that there is something inherently or intrinsically wrong with suicide. The deontologist Immanuel Kant provides this sort of argument, as you will see in Chapter 6, maintaining that suicide is wrong in principle. But utilitarians cannot argue that suicide is intrinsically wrong—since they do not focus on the intrinsic rightness or wrongness of acts. Instead, utilitarians have to consider the impact of suicide on the happiness of all those it affects.

Since utilitarians reject the idea that certain acts are intrinsically good or evil, they are open to experimentation and evidence. And they are open to various ways of conceiving the goodness of consequences. Any sort of consequences might be considered good—for example, power, fame, or fortune. However, classical utilitarianism is a *pleasure* or *happiness* theory, meaning that it tends to reduce all other goods to some form of pleasure or happiness. Utilitarianism was not the first such theory to appear in the history of philosophy. Aristotle's ethics, as we shall see in Chapter 8, also focuses on happiness, although it is different from utilitarianism in its focus on virtue. Closer to utilitarianism is the classical theory that has come to be known as **hedonism** (from *hedon*, the Greek word for pleasure) or **Epicureanism** (named after Epicurus, 341–270 BCE). Epicurus held that the good life was the pleasant life. For him, this meant avoiding distress and desires for things beyond one's basic needs. Bodily pleasure and mental delight and peace were the goods to be sought in life.

Utilitarians believe that pleasure or happiness is the good to be produced. As Bentham puts it, "Nature has placed mankind under the governance of two sovereign masters, *pain* and *pleasure*. It is for them alone to point out what we ought to do, as well as to determine what we shall do."[11] Things such as fame, fortune, education, and freedom may be good, but only to the extent that they produce pleasure or happiness. In philosophical terms, they are **instrumental goods** because they are useful for attaining the goals of happiness and pleasure. Happiness and pleasure are the only **intrinsic goods**—that is, the only things good in themselves.

In this explanation of utilitarianism, you may have noticed the seeming identification of pleasure and happiness. In classical utilitarianism, there is no difference between pleasure and happiness. Both terms refer to a kind of psychic state of satisfaction. However, there are different types of pleasure of which humans are capable. According to Mill, we experience a range of pleasures or satisfactions from the physical satisfaction of hunger to the personal satisfaction of a job well done. Aesthetic pleasures, such as the enjoyment of watching a beautiful sunset, are yet another type of pleasure. We also can experience intellectual pleasures such as the peculiar satisfaction of making sense out of something. Mill's theory includes the idea that there are higher, uniquely human pleasures—as we will explain below.

In Mill's view, we should consider the range of types of pleasure in our attempts to decide what the best action is. We also ought to consider other aspects of the pleasurable or happy experience. According to the greatest happiness or utility principle, we must measure, count, and compare the pleasurable experiences likely to be produced by various alternative actions in order to know which is best.

CALCULATING THE GREATEST AMOUNT OF HAPPINESS

Utilitarianism is not an egoistic theory. As we noted in Chapter 4's presentation on egoism, those versions of egoism that said we ought to take care of ourselves because this works out better for all in the long run are actually versions of utilitarianism, not egoism. Some philosophers have called utilitarianism *universalistic* because it is the happiness or pleasure of all who are affected by an action or practice that is to be considered. We are not just to consider our own good, as in egoism, nor just the good of others, as in altruism. Sacrifice may be good, but not in itself. As Mill puts it, "A sacrifice which does not increase or tend to increase the sum total of happiness, (utilitarianism) considers as wasted."[12] Everyone affected by some action is to be counted equally. We ourselves hold no privileged place, so our own happiness counts no more than that of others. I may be required to do what displeases me but pleases others. Thus, in the following scenario, Act B is a better choice than Act A:

Act A makes me happy and two other people happy.
Act B makes me unhappy but five others happy.

In addition to counting each person equally, Bentham and his followers identified five elements that are used to calculate the greatest amount of happiness: the net amount of pleasure or happiness, its intensity, its duration, its fruitfulness, and the likelihood of any act to produce it.[13]

Pleasure Minus Pain Almost every alternative that we choose produces unhappiness or pain as well as happiness or pleasure for ourselves, if not for others. Pain is intrinsically bad, and pleasure is intrinsically good. Something that produces pain may be accepted, but only if it causes more pleasure overall. For instance, if the painfulness of a punishment deters an unwanted behavior, then we ought to punish, but no more than is necessary or useful. When an act produces both pleasure or happiness and pain or unhappiness, we can think of each moment of unhappiness as canceling out a moment of happiness so that what is left to evaluate is the remaining or *net* happiness or unhappiness. We are also to think of pleasure and pain as coming in bits or moments. We can then calculate this net amount by adding and subtracting units of pleasure and displeasure. This is a device for calculating the greatest amount of happiness even if we cannot make mathematically exact calculations. The following simplified equation indicates how the net utility for two acts, A and B, might be determined. We can think of the units as either happy persons or days of happiness:

Act A produces twelve units of happiness and six of unhappiness (12 − 6 = 6 units of happiness).
Act B produces ten units of happiness and one of unhappiness (10 − 1 = 9 units of happiness).

On this measure, Act B is preferable because it produces a greater net amount of happiness, namely, nine units compared with six for Act A.

Intensity   Moments of happiness or pleasure are not all alike. Some are more intense than others. The thrill of some exciting adventure—say, running river rapids—may produce a more intense pleasure than the serenity we feel standing before a beautiful vista. All else being equal, the more intense the pleasure, the better. All other factors being equal, if I have an apple to give away and am deciding which of two friends to give it to, I ought to give it to the friend who will enjoy it most. In calculations involving intensity of pleasure, a scale is sometimes useful. For example, we could use a positive scale of 1 to 10 degrees, from the least pleasurable to the most pleasurable. In the following scenario, then, Act B

is better (all other things being equal) than Act A, even though Act A gives pleasure to thirty more people; this result is because of the greater intensity of pleasure produced by Act B:

Act A gives forty people each mild pleasure (40 × 2 = 80 degrees of pleasure).
Act B gives ten people each intense pleasure (10 × 10 = 100 degrees of pleasure).

Duration   Intensity is not all that matters regarding pleasure. The more serene pleasure may last longer. This also must be factored in our calculation. The longer lasting the pleasure, the better, all else being equal. Thus, in the following scenario, Act A is better than Act B because it gives more total days of pleasure or happiness. This is so even though it affects fewer people (a fact that raises questions about how the number of people counts in comparison to the total amount of happiness):

Act A gives three people each eight days of happiness (3 × 8 = 24 days of happiness).
Act B gives six people each two days of happiness (6 × 2 = 12 days of happiness).

Fruitfulness   A more serene pleasure from contemplating nature may or may not be more fruitful than an exciting pleasure such as that derived from running rapids. The fruitfulness of experiencing pleasure depends on whether it makes us more capable of experiencing similar or other pleasures. For example, the relaxing event may make one person more capable of experiencing other pleasures of friendship or understanding, whereas the thrilling event may do the same for another. The fruitfulness depends not only on the immediate pleasure, but also on the long-term results. Indulging in immediate pleasure may bring pain later on, as we know only too well. So also the pain today may be the only way to prevent more pain tomorrow. The dentist's work on our teeth may be painful today, but it makes us feel better in the long run by providing us with pain-free meals and undistracted, enjoyable mealtime conversations.

Likelihood If before acting we are attempting to decide between two available alternative actions, we must estimate the likely results of each before we compare their net utility. If we are considering whether to go out for some sports competition, for example, we should consider our chances of doing well. We might have greater hope of success trying something else. It may turn out that we ought to choose an act with lesser rather than greater beneficial results if the chances of it happening are better. It is not only the chances that would count, but also the size of the prize. In the following equation, A is preferable to B. In this case, "A bird in the hand is worth two in the bush," as the old saying goes:

Act A has a 90 percent chance of giving eight people each five days of pleasure (40 days × 0.90 = 36 days of pleasure).

Act B has a 40 percent chance of giving ten people each seven days of pleasure (70 days × 0.40 = 28 days of pleasure).

MindTap® For more chapter resources and activities, go to MindTap.

QUANTITY VERSUS QUALITY OF PLEASURE

Bentham and Mill are in agreement that the more pleasure or happiness, the better. However, there is one significant difference between them. According to Bentham, we ought to consider only the *quantity* of pleasure or happiness brought about by various acts: how much pleasure, to how many people, how intense it is, how long-lasting, how fruitful, and how likely the desired outcome will occur. Consider Bentham's own comment on this point: The "quantity of pleasure being equal, pushpin (a children's game) is as good as poetry."[14] The aesthetic or intellectual pleasure that one might derive from reading and understanding a poem is no better in itself than the simple pleasure of playing a mindless game.

Mill agreed with Bentham that the greater amount of pleasure and happiness, the better. But Mill believed that the *quality* of the pleasure should also count. In his autobiography, Mill describes a personal crisis in which he realized that he had not found sufficient place in his life for aesthetic experiences; he realized that this side of the human personality also needed developing and that these pleasures were significantly different from others. This experience and his thoughts about it may have led him to focus on the quality of pleasures. Some are intrinsically better than others, he believed. For example, intellectual pleasures are more valuable in themselves than purely sensual pleasures. Although he does not tell us how much more valuable they are (twice as valuable?), he clearly believed this greater value ought to be factored into our calculation of the "greatest amount of happiness." Although I may not always be required to choose a book over food (for example, I may now need the food more than the book), the intellectual pleasures that might be derived from reading the book are of a higher quality than the pleasures gained from eating.

Mill attempts to prove or show that intellectual pleasures are better than sensual ones. We are to ask people who have experienced a range of pleasures whether they would prefer to live a life of a human, despite all its disappointments and pains, or the life of an animal, which is full of pleasures but only sensual pleasures. He believes that people generally would choose the former. They would prefer, as he puts it, "to be a human being dissatisfied than a pig satisfied; better to be Socrates dissatisfied than a fool satisfied."[15] Socrates was often frustrated in his attempts to know certain things. He struggled to get a grasp on true beauty and true justice. Because human beings have greater possibilities for knowledge and achievement, they also have greater potential for failure, pain, and frustration. The point of Mill's argument is that the only reason we would prefer a life of fewer net pleasures (the dissatisfactions subtracted from the total satisfactions of human life) to a life of a greater total amount of pleasures (the life of the pig) is that we value something other than the *amount* (quantity) of pleasures;

we value the *kind* (quality) of pleasures as well.[16] When considering this argument, you might ask yourself two questions. First, would people generally prefer to be Socrates than a pig? Second, if Mill is correct in his factual assessment, then what does this fact prove? Could it be that people are mistaken about what kinds of pleasures are the best, as Socrates himself often implied? This points us back to the question of whether happiness is merely a subjective preference or whether happiness resides in a more objective standard.

EVALUATING UTILITARIANISM

The following are just some of the many considerations raised by those who wish to determine whether utilitarianism is a valid moral theory.

Application of the Principle

One reaction that students often have to calculating the greatest amount of happiness is that this theory is too complex. When we consider all of the variables concerning pleasure and happiness that are to be counted when trying to estimate the "greatest amount of pleasure or happiness," the task of doing so looks extremely difficult. We must consider how many people will be affected by alternative actions, whether they will be pleased or pained by them, how pleased or pained they will be and for how long, and the likelihood that what we estimate will happen, will, in fact, come to be. In addition, if we want to follow Mill rather than Bentham, we must consider whether the pleasures will be the lowlier sensual pleasures, the higher more intellectual pleasures, or something in between. However, in reality, we may at any one time have to consider only a couple of these variables, depending on their relevance to the moral question we are considering.

The point of this criticism is that no one can consider all of the variables that utilitarianism requires us to consider: the probable consequences of our action to all affected in terms of duration, intensity, fruitfulness, likelihood, and type or quality of pleasure. It also requires us to have a common unit of measurement of pleasure. (Elementary units called *hedons* have been suggested.) The difficulty is finding a way to reduce pleasures of all kinds to some common or basic unit of measurement. A utilitarian could respond to these criticisms by arguing that while this complexity indicates that no one can be a perfect judge of utility, we do make better judgments if we are able to consider these variables. No moral theory is simple in its application.

A more difficult problem in how to apply the principle of utility comes from Mill's specific formulation of it. It may well be that in some cases, at least, one cannot both maximize happiness and make the greatest number of people happy. Thus, one choice may produce 200 units of happiness—but for just one person. The other alternative might produce 150 units of happiness, 50 for each of three people. If the maximization of overall happiness is taken as primary, then we should go with the first choice; if the number of people is to take precedence, then we should go with the second choice. Most readings of Mill, however, suggest that he would give preference to the overall maximization of utility. In that case, how the happiness was distributed (to one versus three) would not, in itself, count.

Utilitarianism and Personal Integrity

A more substantive criticism of utilitarianism concerns its universalist and maximizing agenda—that we should always do that which maximizes overall happiness. Many critics have noted that utilitarian theory does not allow us to privilege our own happiness over that of others. Nor can we privilege the happiness of those we love. In determining what to do, I can give no more weight to my own projects or my own children than other people's similar projects or their children. For some philosophers, the idea that I must treat all persons equally is contrary to common sense, which tells us that we ought to care for our own children more than we care for the children of distant others. Utilitarians might respond that we should probably give more attention to our own projects and our own children, but only because this is likely to have better results overall. We know better how to promote our own projects and have more motivation to do so. Thus, giving preference to ourselves will probably be more effective.

A further objection maintains that there is something wrong if utilitarianism requires us to not give preference to ourselves and to our own personal moral commitments. Utilitarianism appears to be an affront to our personal integrity.[17] The idea is that utilitarianism seems to imply that I am not important from my own point of view. However, a utilitarian might respond that it is important that people regard themselves as unique and give due consideration to their own interests because this will probably have better consequences both for these individuals and the broader society.

Ends and Means

A second criticism concerns utilitarianism's consequentialist character. You may have heard the phrase "The end justifies the means." People often utter this phrase with a certain amount of disdain. Utilitarianism, as a consequentialist moral theory, holds that it is the consequences or ends of our actions that determine whether particular means to them are justified. This seems to lead to conclusions that are contrary to commonsense morality. For example, wouldn't it justify punishing or torturing an innocent person, a "scapegoat," in order to prevent a great evil or to promote a great good? Or could we not justify on utilitarian grounds the killing of some individuals for the sake of the good of a greater number, perhaps in the name of population control? Or could I not make an exception for myself from obeying a law, alleging that it is for some greater long-term good? Utilitarians might respond by noting that such actions or practices will probably do more harm than good, especially if we take a long-range view. In particular, they might point out that practices allowing the punishment of known innocents would undermine the legitimacy and deterrent effect of the law—and thus reduce overall utility.

THE TROLLEY PROBLEM

One particular problem for utilitarianism is exemplified by what has come to be called the trolley problem.[18] According to one version of this scenario, imagine you find yourself beside a train track, on which a trolley is speeding toward a junction. On the track ahead of the trolley are five workers who will all be killed if the trolley continues on its current course. You have access to a switch, and if you pull it, the trolley will be diverted onto another track where it will kill only one worker. According to utilitarianism, if nothing else is relevant, you would not only be permitted but *required* to pull the switch, which would result in one death and five lives saved. From a utilitarian standpoint, it is obvious that you should pull the switch, since not pulling the switch would result in greater net loss of life. Now, compare this scenario with another. In this case, you find yourself on a bridge over a single trolley track with the five workers below you. Next to you on the bridge is an enormously fat man. The only way to stop the trolley in this case is to push the fat man off the bridge and onto the tracks ahead of the workers. Would you be permitted to do this? In both cases, five lives would be saved and one lost. But are the cases the same morally? It would seem that according to utilitarianism, in which only the results matter, the cases would be morally the same. However, it is the intuition of most people that the second case is significantly different. You can't kill one person to save five. To take another example, it seems clear that a doctor who has five patients needing organ transplants to save their lives should not be permitted to take those organs out of another healthy patient, causing his or her death.

It is important to note that versions of the trolley problem have been employed by psychologists to probe human decision-making procedures. Some of this research examines how different parts of the brain are involved in different ways of making decisions that involve moral dilemmas.[19] This sort of research investigates the psychological sources of our decisions—whether emotional responses predominate, whether we actually do calculate costs and benefits, and whether we tend to feel bound to abstract moral rules. One study used a virtual reality version of the trolley problem to pursue this question. It found that 89 percent of people chose the utilitarian option when confronted with at 3-D virtual reality representation of a run-away boxcar that threatened to crash into a group of people.[20] One issue exposed by these sorts of studies is that people respond differently when confronted with the choice of doing something (pulling the lever to divert the train into the group of people) or not doing something (allowing the train to crash into the group). One conclusion of this sort of research is that sometimes there are conflicts in how we actually react and how we think we *should* react to morally fraught situations. Other inquiries have considered whether utilitarian calculation involves a sort of "coldness" that runs counter to empathy and other emotional responses.[21] Another study by Daniel Bartels and David Pizarro concludes, "participants who indicated greater endorsement of utilitarian solutions had higher scores on measures of psychopathy, Machiavellianism, and life meaninglessness."[22] This conclusion appears to follow from the fact that the utilitarian decision—to kill one in order to save others—asks us to overcome an emotional or instinctual aversion to harming others. And yet, it might be that—from the utilitarian point of view—this is exactly what we should do in order to bring about greater happiness for the greatest number. The psychological research into the dilemmas generated by utilitarianism is interesting.

But the normative or moral question remains. Moral philosophy is not merely interested in the psychological question of how we react in these situations, it is also concerned with the question of how we *ought* to react.

ACT AND RULE UTILITARIANISM

Utilitarianism may appear to justify any action just so long as it has better consequences than other available actions. Therefore, cheating, stealing, lying, and breaking promises may all seem to be justified, depending on whether they maximize happiness in some particular case. In response to this type of criticism, contemporary utilitarians often focus on general rules instead of on individual acts. The version of utilitarianism that focuses on rules is usually called **rule utilitarianism**. This is contrasted with **act utilitarianism**, which focuses solely on the consequences of specific individual acts.

Both are forms of utilitarianism. They are alike in requiring us to produce the greatest amount of happiness for the greatest number of people. They differ in what they believe we ought to consider in estimating the consequences. Act utilitarianism states that we ought to consider the consequences of *each act separately*. Rule utilitarianism states that we ought to consider the consequences of the act performed as a *general practice*.[23]

One version of the trolley problem.

© Cengage Learning

Take the following example. Sue is considering whether to keep or break her promise to go out to dinner with Ken. She believes that if she breaks this promise in order to do something else with other friends, then Ken will be unhappy—but she and the other friends will be happier. According to act utilitarianism, if the consequences of her breaking the promise are better than keeping it, then she ought to break it.

Act utilitarianism: Consider the consequences of some particular act such as keeping or breaking one's promise.

A rule utilitarian, on the other hand, would tell Sue to consider what the results would be if everyone broke promises or broke them in similar situations. The question "What if everyone did that?" is familiar to us. According to rule utilitarianism, Sue should ask what the results would be if breaking promises in similar circumstances became a general practice or a general rule that people followed. It is likely that trust in promises would be weakened. This outcome would be bad, she might think, because if we could not trust one another to keep promises, then we would generally be less capable of making plans and relating to one another—two important sources of human happiness. So, even if there would be no general breakdown in trust from just this one instance of promise-breaking, Sue should still probably keep her promise according to rule utilitarian thinking.

Rule utilitarianism: Consider the consequences of some practice or rule of behavior—for example, the practice of promise-keeping or promise-breaking.

Another way to understand the method of reasoning used by the rule utilitarian is the following: I should ask what would be the best practice. For example, regarding promises, what rule would have the better results when people followed that rule? Would it be the rule or practice: "Never break a promise made"? At the other end of the spectrum would be the rule or practice: "Keep promises only if the results of doing so would be better than breaking them." (This actually amounts to a kind of act utilitarian reasoning.) However, there might be a better rule yet, such as: "Always keep your promise unless doing so would have very serious harmful consequences." If this rule was followed, then people would generally have the benefits of being able to say, "I promise," and have people generally believe and trust them. The fact that the promise would not be kept in some limited circumstances would probably not do great harm to the practice of making promises.

Some utilitarians go further and ask us to think about sets of rules. It is not only the practice of promise-keeping that we should evaluate, but also a broader set of related practices regarding truthfulness and bravery and care for children (for example). Moreover, we should think of these rules as forming a system in which there are rules for priority and stringency. These rules would tell us which practices are more important and how important they are compared to the others. We should then do what the best system of moral rules dictates, where *best* is still defined in terms of the maximization of happiness.[24]

Which form of utilitarianism is better is a matter of dispute. Act utilitarians can claim that we ought to consider only what will or is likely to happen if we act in certain ways—not what *would* happen if we acted in certain ways but will not happen because we are not going to so act. Rule utilitarians can claim that acts are similar to one another and so can be thought of as practices. My lying in one case to get myself out of a difficulty is similar to others' lying in other cases to get themselves out of difficulties. Because we should make the same judgments about similar cases (for consistency's sake), we should judge this act by comparing it with the results of the actions of everyone in similar circumstances. We can thus evaluate the general practice of "lying to get oneself out of a difficulty." You can be the judge of which form of utilitarian reasoning is more persuasive.

"PROOF" OF THE THEORY

One of the best ways to evaluate a moral theory is to examine carefully the reasons that are given to support it. Being an empiricist theory, utilitarianism must draw its evidence from experience. This is what Mill does in his attempt to prove that the principle of utility is the correct moral principle. His argument is as follows: Just as the only way in which we know that something is visible is its being seen, and the only way we can show that something is audible is if it can be heard, so also the only proof that we have that something is desirable is its being desired. Because we desire happiness, we thus know it is desirable or good. In addition, Mill holds that happiness is the only thing we desire for its own sake. All else we desire because we believe it will lead to happiness. Thus, happiness or pleasure is the only thing good in itself or the only intrinsic good. All other goods are instrumental goods; in other words, they are good insofar as they lead to happiness. For example, reading is not good in itself but only insofar as it brings us pleasure or understanding (which is either pleasurable in itself or leads to pleasure).

There are two main contentions in this argument. One is that good is defined in terms of what people desire. The other is that happiness is the only thing desired for itself and is the only intrinsic good. Critics have pointed out that Mill's analogy between what is visible, audible, and desirable does not hold up under analysis. In all three words, the suffix means "able to be," but in the case of *desirable*, Mill needs to prove not only that we can desire happiness (it is able to be desired), but also that it is *worth* being desired. Furthermore, just because we desire something does not necessarily mean that we *ought* to desire it or that it is good. There is a risk of the naturalistic fallacy (as defined in Chapter 1) here. Is this a case of illegitimately deriving an *ought* from an *is*?

Mill recognizes the difficulty of proving matters in ethics and that the proofs here will be indirect rather than direct. On the second point, Mill adds a further comment to bolster his case about happiness. He asserts that this desire for happiness is universal and that we are so constructed that we can desire nothing except what appears to us to be or to bring happiness. You may want to consider whether these latter assertions are consistent with his empiricism. Does he know these things from experience? In addition, Mill may be simply pointing to what we already know rather than giving a proof of the principle. You can find out what people believe is good by noticing what they desire. In this case, they desire to be happy or they desire what they think will bring them happiness.[25]

Utilitarianism is a highly influential moral theory that also has had significant influence on a wide variety of policy assessment methods. It can be quite useful for evaluating alternative health care systems, for example. Whichever system brings the most benefit to the most people with the least cost is the system that we probably ought to support. Although Mill was perhaps too optimistic about the ability and willingness of people to increase human happiness and reduce suffering, there is no doubt that the ideal is a good one. Nevertheless, utilitarianism has difficulties, some of which we have discussed here. You will know better how to evaluate this theory when you can compare it with those treated in the following chapters.

The reading selection in this chapter is from the classical work *Utilitarianism* by John Stuart Mill. Mill considers the importance of happiness—and the need to consider the happiness of others. His work remains one of the important touchstones for thinking about utilitarianism.

NOTES

1. United Nations Department of Economic and Social Affairs, http://esa.un.org/unpd/wpp/publications/files/key_findings_wpp_2015.pdf (accessed January 13, 2016).

2. United Nations, Sustainable Development Goals: Goal 12: Ensure Sustainable Consumption and Production Patterns http://www.un.org/sustainabledevelopment/sustainable-consumption-production/ (accessed January 13, 2015).

3. Office of the United Nations High Commissioner for Human Rights, "Convention Against Torture and Other Cruel, Inhuman, or Degrading Treatment or Punishment," http://www.un.org/millennium/law/iv-9.htm

4. Scott Shane, "Waterboarding Used 266 Times on 2 Suspects," *New York Times,* April 19, 2009, http://www.nytimes.com/2009/04/20/world/20detain.html?_r50

5. Chris McGreal, "Dick Cheney Defends Use of Torture on Al-Qaida Leaders," *Guardian,* September 9, 2011, http://www.guardian.co.uk/world/2011/sep/09/dick-cheney-defends-torture-al-qaida

6. *San Francisco Examiner,* February 2, 1993, A4; *San Francisco Chronicle,* May 5, 2007, p. A5.

7. Peter Singer, *Writings on an Ethical Life* (New York: HarperCollins, 2001), p. 16.

8. John Stuart Mill, *Utilitarianism,* ed. Oskar Priest (Indianapolis, IN: Bobbs-Merrill, 1957), p. 20.

9. Ibid., p. 24.

10. John Bateson, "The Golden Gate Bridge's fatal flaw" *Los Angeles Times,* May 25, 2012, http://articles.latimes.com/2012/may/25/opinion/la-oe-adv-bateson-golden-gate-20120525 (Accessed January 13, 2016).

11. Jeremy Bentham, *An Introduction to the Principles of Morals and Legislation* (New York: Oxford University Press, 1789).

12. Mill, *Utilitarianism,* p. 22.

13. These elements for calculation of the greatest amount of happiness are from Bentham's *Principles of Morals and Legislation.*

14. Bentham, *Principles of Morals and Legislation.*

15. Mill, *Utilitarianism,* p. 14.

16. Note that this is an empiricist argument. It is based on an appeal to purported facts. People's actual preferences for intellectual pleasures (if true) are the only source we have for believing them to be more valuable.

17. J. J. C. Smart and Bernard Williams, *Utilitarianism: For and Against* (New York: Cambridge University Press, 1973). Also see Samuel Scheffler, *The Rejection of Consequentialism* (New York: Oxford University Press, 1984). In *The Limits of Morality* (New York: Oxford University Press, 1989). Shelley Kagan distinguishes the universalist element of utilitarianism—its demand that I treat all equally—from the maximizing element—that I must bring about the most good possible. The first element makes utilitarianism too demanding, whereas the second allows us to do anything as long as it maximizes happiness overall.

18. Philippa Foot, "The Problem of Abortion and the Doctrine of Double Effect," in *Virtues and Vices* (Oxford: Basil Blackwell, 1978); and Judith Jarvis Thomson, "Killing, Letting Die, and the Trolley Problem," *The Monist* (1976), pp. 204–17.

19. See, for example, work done by Joshua Greene and the Moral Cognition Lab at Harvard University, http://wjh.harvard.edu/~mcl/

20. C. David Navarrete, Melissa M. McDonald, Michael L. Mott, and Benjamin Asher, "Virtual Morality: Emotion and Action in a Simulated Three-Dimensional 'Trolley Problem,'" *Emotion* 12, no. 2 (April 2012), pp. 364–70.

21. K. Wiech, G. Kahane, N. Shackel, M. Farias, J. Savulescu, and I. Tracey, "Cold or Calculating? Reduced Activity in the Subgenual Cingulate Cortex Re?ects Decreased Emotional Aversion to Harming in Counterintuitive Utilitarian Judgment," *Cognition* 126, no. 3 (March 2013), pp. 364–72.

22. Daniel M. Bartels and David A. Pizarro, "The Mismeasure of Morals: Antisocial Personality Traits Predict Utilitarian Responses to Moral Dilemmas," *Cognition* 121, no. 1 (October 2011), pp. 154–61.

23. See, for example, the explanation of this difference in J. J. C. Smart, "Extreme and Restricted Utilitarianism," *Philosophical Quarterly* (1956).

24. Richard Brandt, "Some Merits of One Form of Rule Utilitarianism," in *Morality and the Language of Conduct,* ed. H. N. Castaneda and George Nakhnikian (Detroit: Wayne State University Press, 1970), pp. 282–307.

25. This explanation is given by Mary Warnock in her introduction to the Fontana edition of Mill's *Utilitarianism,* pp. 25–26.

READING

Utilitarianism

JOHN STUART MILL

MindTap For more chapter resources and activities, go to MindTap.

Study Questions

As you read the excerpt, please consider the following questions:

1. How does Mill describe the basic moral standard of utilitarianism?
2. How does he defend himself against those who accuse utilitarianism of being a crass pleasure theory similar to Epicureanism?
3. How do we know that happiness is a good in itself or as an end?

WHAT UTILITARIANISM IS

The creed which accepts as the foundation of morals "utility" or the "greatest happiness principle" holds that actions are right in proportion as they tend to promote happiness; wrong as they tend to produce the reverse of happiness. By happiness is intended pleasure and the absence of pain; by unhappiness, pain and the privation of pleasure. To give a clear view of the moral standard set up by the theory, much more requires to be said; in particular, what things it includes in the ideas of pain and pleasure, and to what extent this is left an open question. But these supplementary explanations do not affect the theory of life on which this theory of morality is grounded—namely, that pleasure and freedom from pain are the only things desirable as ends; and that all desirable things (which are as numerous in the utilitarian as in any other scheme) are desirable either for pleasure inherent in themselves or as means to the promotion of pleasure and the prevention of pain.

Now such a theory of life excites in many minds, and among them in some of the most estimable in feeling and purpose, inveterate dislike. To suppose that life has (as they express it) no higher end than pleasure—no better and nobler object of desire and pursuit—they designate as utterly mean and groveling, as a doctrine worthy only of swine, to whom the followers of Epicurus were, at a very early period, contemptuously likened; and modern holders of the doctrine are occasionally made the subject of equally polite comparisons by its German, French, and English assailants.

When thus attacked, the Epicureans have always answered that it is not they, but their accusers, who represent human nature in a degrading light, since the accusation supposes human beings to be capable of no pleasures except those of which swine are capable. If this supposition were true, the charge could not be gainsaid, but would then be no longer an imputation; for if the sources of pleasure were precisely the same to human beings and to swine, the rule of life which is good enough for the one would be good enough for the other. The comparison of the Epicurean life to that of beasts is felt as degrading, precisely because a beast's pleasures do not satisfy a human being's conceptions of happiness. Human beings have faculties more elevated than the animal appetites and, when once made conscious of them, do not regard anything as happiness which does not include their gratification. I do not, indeed, consider the Epicureans to have been by any means faultless in drawing out their scheme of consequences from the utilitarian principle. To do this in any sufficient manner, many Stoic, as well as Christian, elements require to be included. But there

---

From John Stuart Mill, *Utilitarianism*, (London: Parker, Son, and Bourn, 1863), chaps. 2 and 4.

*Headings added by the editor.

is no known Epicurean theory of life which does not assign to the pleasures of the intellect, of the feelings and imagination, and of the moral sentiments a much higher value as pleasures than to those of mere sensation. It must be admitted, however, that utilitarian writers in general have placed the superiority of mental over bodily pleasures chiefly in the greater permanency, safety, uncostliness, etc., of the former—that is, in their circumstantial advantages rather than in their intrinsic nature. And on all these points utilitarians have fully proved their case; but they might have taken the other and, as it may be called, higher ground with entire consistency. It is quite compatible with the principle of utility to recognize the fact that some kinds of pleasure are more desirable and more valuable than others. It would be absurd that, while in estimating all other things quality is considered as well as quantity, the estimation of pleasure should be supposed to depend on quantity alone.

Some Pleasures Are Better Than Others*

If I am asked what I mean by difference of quality in pleasures, or what makes one pleasure more valuable than another, merely as a pleasure, except its being greater in amount, there is but one possible answer. Of two pleasures, if there be one to which all or almost all who have experience of both give a decided preference, irrespective of any feeling of moral obligation to prefer it, that is the more desirable pleasure. If one of the two is, by those who are competently acquainted with both, placed so far above the other that they prefer it, even though knowing it to be attended with a greater amount of discontent, and would not resign it for any quantity of the other pleasure which their nature is capable of, we are justified in ascribing to the preferred enjoyment a superiority in quality so far outweighing quantity as to render it, in comparison, of small account.

Now it is an unquestionable fact that those who are equally acquainted with and equally capable of appreciating and enjoying both do give a most marked preference to the manner of existence which employs their higher faculties. Few human creatures would consent to be changed into any of the lower animals for a promise of the fullest allowance of a beast's pleasures; no intelligent human being would consent to be a fool, no instructed person would be an ignoramus, no person of feeling and conscience would be selfish and base, even though they should be persuaded that the fool, the dunce, or the rascal is better satisfied with his lot than they are with theirs. They would not resign what they possess more than he for the most complete satisfaction of all the desires which they have in common with him. If they ever fancy they would, it is only in cases of unhappiness so extreme that to escape from it they would exchange their lot for almost any other, however undesirable in their own eyes. A being of higher faculties requires more to make him happy, is capable probably of more acute suffering, and certainly accessible to it at more points, than one of an inferior type; but in spite of these liabilities, he can never really wish to sink into what he feels to be a lower grade of existence. We may give what explanation we please of this unwillingness; we may attribute it to pride, a name which is given indiscriminately to some of the most and to some of the least estimable feelings of which mankind are capable; we may refer it to the love of liberty and personal independence, an appeal to which was with the Stoics one of the most effective means for the inculcation of it; to the love of power or to the love of excitement, both of which do really enter into and contribute to it; but its most appropriate appellation is a sense of dignity, which all human beings possess in one form or other, and in some, though by no means in exact, proportion to their higher faculties, and which is so essential a part of the happiness of those in whom it is strong that nothing which conflicts with it could be otherwise than momentarily an object of desire to them. Whoever supposes that this preference takes place at a sacrifice of happiness—that the superior being, in anything like equal circumstances, is not happier than the inferior—confounds the two very different ideas of happiness and content. It is indisputable that the being whose capacities of enjoyment are low has the greatest chance of having them fully satisfied; and a highly endowed being will always feel that any happiness which he can look for, as the world is constituted, is imperfect. But he can learn to bear its imperfections, if they are at all bearable; and they will not make him envy the being who is indeed unconscious of the imperfections, but only because he feels not at all the good which those imperfections qualify. It is better to be a human being dissatisfied than a pig satisfied; better to be Socrates dissatisfied than a fool satisfied. And if the fool, or the pig, are of a different opinion, it is because they only know their own side of the question. The other party to the comparison knows both sides.

It may be objected that many who are capable of the higher pleasures occasionally, under the influence of temptation, postpone them to the lower. But this is quite compatible with a full appreciation of the intrinsic superiority of the higher. Men often, from infirmity of character, make their election for the nearer good, though they know it to be the less valuable; and this no less when the choice is between two bodily pleasures than when it is between bodily and mental. They pursue sensual indulgences to the injury of health, though perfectly aware that health is the greater good. It may be further objected that many who begin with youthful enthusiasm for everything noble, as they advance in years, sink into indolence and selfishness. But I do not believe that those who undergo this very common change voluntarily choose the lower description of pleasures in preference to the higher. I believe that, before they devote themselves exclusively to the one, they have already become incapable of the other. Capacity for the nobler feelings is in most natures a very tender plant, easily killed, not only by hostile influences, but by mere want of sustenance; and in the majority of young persons it speedily dies away if the occupations to which their position in life has devoted them, and the society into which it has thrown them, are not favorable to keeping that higher capacity in exercise. Men lose their high aspirations as they lose their intellectual tastes, because they have not time or opportunity for indulging them; and they addict themselves to inferior pleasures, not because they deliberately prefer them, but

because they are either the only ones to which they have access or the only ones which they are any longer capable of enjoying. It may be questioned whether anyone who has remained equally susceptible to both classes of pleasures ever knowingly and calmly preferred the lower, though many, in all ages, have broken down in an ineffectual attempt to combine both.

From this verdict of the only competent judges, I apprehend there can be no appeal. On a question which is the best worth having of two pleasures, or which of two modes of existence is the most grateful to the feelings, apart from its moral attributes and from its consequences, the judgment of those who are qualified by knowledge of both, or, if they differ, that of the majority among them, must be admitted as final. And there needs be the less hesitation to accept this judgment respecting the quality of pleasures, since there is no other tribunal to be referred to even on the question of quantity. What means are there of determining which is the acutest of two pains, or the intenser of two pleasurable sensations, except the general suffrage of those who are familiar with both? Neither pains nor pleasures are homogeneous, and pain is always heterogeneous with pleasure. What is there to decide whether a particular pleasure is worth purchasing at the cost of a particular pain, except the feelings and judgment of the experienced? When, therefore, those feelings and judgment declare the pleasures derived from the higher faculties to be preferable in kind, apart from the question of intensity, to those of which the animal nature, disjoined from the higher faculties, is susceptible, they are entitled on this subject to the same regard.

The Moral Standard

I have dwelt on this point as being a necessary part of a perfectly just conception of utility or happiness considered as the directive rule of human conduct. But it is by no means an indispensable condition to the acceptance of the utilitarian standard; for that standard is not the agent's own greatest happiness, but the greatest amount of happiness altogether; and if it may possibly be doubted whether a noble character is always the happier for its nobleness, there can be no doubt that it makes other people happier, and that the world in general is immensely a gainer by it. Utilitarianism, therefore, could only attain its end by the general cultivation of nobleness of character, even if each individual were only benefited by the nobleness of others, and his own, so far as happiness is concerned, were a sheer deduction from the benefit. But the bare enunciation of such an absurdity as this last renders refutation superfluous.

According to the greatest happiness principle, as above explained, the ultimate end, with reference to and for the sake of which all other things are desirable—whether we are considering our own good or that of other people—is an existence exempt as far as possible from pain, and as rich as possible in enjoyments, both in point of quantity and quality; the test of quality and the rule for measuring it against quantity being the preference felt by those who, in their opportunities of experience, to which must be added their habits of self-consciousness and self-observation, are best furnished with the means of comparison. This, being according to the utilitarian opinion the end of human action, is necessarily also the standard of morality, which may accordingly be defined "the rules and precepts for human conduct," by the observance of which an existence such as has been described might be, to the greatest extent possible, secured to all mankind; and not to them only, but, so far as the nature of things admits, to the whole sentient creation....

OF WHAT SORT OF PROOF THE PRINCIPLE OF UTILITY IS SUSCEPTIBLE

It has already been remarked that questions of ultimate ends do not admit of proof, in the ordinary acceptation of the term. To be incapable of proof by reasoning is common to all first principles, to the first premises of our knowledge, as well as to those of our conduct. But the former, being matters of fact, may be the subject of a direct appeal to the faculties which judge of fact—namely, our senses and our internal consciousness. Can an appeal be made to the same faculties on questions of practical ends? Or by what other faculty is cognizance taken of them?

Questions about ends are, in other words, questions [about] what things are desirable. The utilitarian doctrine is that happiness is desirable, and the only thing desirable, as an end; all other things being only desirable as means to that end. What ought to be required of this doctrine, what conditions is it requisite that the doctrine should fulfill—to make good its claim to be believed?

The only proof capable of being given that an object is visible is that people actually see it. The only proof that a sound is audible is that people hear it; and so of the other sources of our experience. In like manner, I apprehend, the sole evidence it is possible to produce that anything is desirable is that people do actually desire it. If the end which the utilitarian doctrine proposes to itself were not, in theory and in practice, acknowledged to be an end, nothing could ever convince any person that it was so. No reason can be given why the general happiness is desirable, except that each person, so far as he believes it to be attainable, desires his own happiness. This, however, being a fact, we have not only all the proof which the case admits of, but all which it is possible to require, that happiness is a good, that each person's happiness is a good to that person, and the general happiness, therefore, a good to the aggregate of all persons. Happiness has made out its title as one of the ends of conduct and, consequently, one of the criteria of morality.

But it has not, by this alone, proved itself to be the sole criterion. To do that, it would seem, by the same rule, necessary to show, not only that people desire happiness, but that they never desire anything else. Now it is palpable that they do desire things which, in common language, are decidedly distinguished from happiness. They desire, for example, virtue and the absence of vice no less really than pleasure and the absence of pain. The desire of virtue is not as universal, but it is as authentic a fact as the desire of happiness. And hence the opponents of the utilitarian standard deem that they have a right to infer that there are other ends of human action besides happiness, and that happiness is not the standard of approbation and disapprobation.

Happiness and Virtue

But does the utilitarian doctrine deny that people desire virtue, or maintain that virtue is not a thing to be desired? The very reverse. It maintains not only that virtue is to be desired, but that it is to be desired disinterestedly, for itself. Whatever may be the opinion of utilitarian moralists as to the original conditions by which virtue is made virtue, however they may believe (as they do) that actions and dispositions are only virtuous because they promote another end than virtue, yet this being granted, and it having been decided, from considerations of this description, what is virtuous, they not only place virtue at the very head of the things which are good as means to the ultimate end, but they also recognize as a psychological fact the possibility of its being, to the individual, a good in itself, without looking to any end beyond it; and hold that the mind is not in a right state, not in a state conformable to utility, not in the state most conducive to the general happiness, unless it does love virtue in this manner—as a thing desirable in itself, even although, in the individual instance, it should not produce those other desirable consequences which it tends to produce, and on account of which it is held to be virtue. This opinion is not, in the smallest degree, a departure from the happiness principle. The ingredients of happiness are very various, and each of them is desirable in itself, and not merely when considered as swelling an aggregate. The principle of utility does not mean that any given pleasure, as music, for instance, or any given exemption from pain, as for example health, is to be looked upon as means to a collective something termed happiness, and to be desired on that account. They are desired and desirable in and for themselves; besides being means, they are a part of the end. Virtue, according to the utilitarian doctrine, is not naturally and originally part of the end, but it is capable of becoming so; and in those who live it disinterestedly it has become so, and is desired and cherished, not as a means to happiness, but as a part of their happiness.

To illustrate this further, we may remember that virtue is not the only thing originally a means, and which if it were not a means to anything else would be and remain indifferent, but which by association with what it is a means to comes to be desired for itself, and that too with the utmost intensity. What, for example, shall we say of the love of money? There is nothing originally more desirable about money than about any heap of glittering pebbles. Its worth is solely that of the things which it will buy; the desires for other things than itself, which it is a means of gratifying. Yet the love of money is not only one of the strongest moving forces of human life, but money is, in many cases, desired in and for itself; the desire to possess it is often stronger than the desire to use it, and goes on increasing when all the desires which point to ends beyond it, to be compassed by it, are falling off. It may, then, be said truly that money is desired not for the sake of an end, but as part of the end. From being a means to happiness, it has come to be itself a principal ingredient of the individual's conception of happiness. The same may be said of the majority of the great objects of human life: power, for example, or fame, except that to each of these there is a certain amount of immediate pleasure annexed, which has at least the semblance of being naturally inherent in them— a thing which cannot be said of money. Still, however, the strongest natural attraction, both of power and of fame, is the immense aid they give to the attainment of our other wishes; and it is the strong association thus generated between them and all our objects of desire which gives to the direct desire of them the intensity it often assumes, so as in some characters to surpass in strength all other desires. In these cases the means have become a part of the end, and a more important part of it than any of the things which they are means to. What was once desired as an instrument for the attainment of happiness has come to be desired for its own sake. In being desired for its own sake it is, however, desired as part of happiness. The person is made, or thinks he would be made, happy by its mere possession; and is made unhappy by failure to obtain it. The desire of it is not a different thing from the desire of happiness any more than the love of music or the desire of health. They are included in happiness. They are some of the elements of which the desire of happiness is made up. Happiness is not an abstract idea but a concrete whole; and these are some of its parts. And the utilitarian standard sanctions and approves their being so. Life would be a poor thing, very ill provided with sources of happiness, if there were not this provision of nature by which things originally indifferent, but conducive to, or otherwise associated with, the satisfaction of our primitive desires, become in themselves sources of pleasure more valuable than the primitive pleasures, both in permanency, in the space of human existence that they are capable of covering, and even in intensity.

Virtue, according to the utilitarian conception, is a good of this description. There was no original desire of it, or motive to it, save its conduciveness to pleasure, and especially to protection from pain. But through the association thus formed it may be felt a good in itself, and desired as such with as great intensity as any other good; and with this difference between it and the love of money, of power, or of fame—that all of these may, and often do, render the individual noxious to the other members of the society to which he belongs, whereas there is nothing which makes him so much a blessing to them as the cultivation of the disinterested love of virtue. And consequently, the utilitarian standard, while it tolerates and approves those other acquired desires, up to the point beyond which they would be more injurious to the general happiness than promotive of it, enjoins and requires the cultivation of the love of virtue up to the greatest strength possible, as being above all things important to the general happiness.

Happiness the Only Intrinsic Good

It results from the preceding considerations that there is in reality nothing desired except happiness. Whatever is desired otherwise than as a means to some end beyond itself, and ultimately to happiness, is desired as itself a part of happiness, and is not desired for itself until it has become so. Those who desire virtue for its own sake desire it either because the consciousness of it is a pleasure, or because the consciousness of being without it is a pain, or for both reasons united; as in truth the pleasure and pain seldom exist separately, but almost always together—the same person feeling pleasure in the degree of virtue attained, and pain in not having attained more. If one of these gave him no pleasure, and the other no pain, he would not love or desire virtue, or would desire it only for the other benefits which it might produce to himself or to persons whom he cared for.

We have now, then, an answer to the question, of what sort of proof the principle of utility is susceptible. If the opinion which I have now stated is psychologically true—if human nature is so constituted as to desire nothing which is not either a part of happiness or a means of happiness—we can have no other proof, and we require no other, that these are the only things desirable. If so, happiness is the sole end of human action, and the promotion of it the test by which to judge all human conduct; from whence it necessarily follows that it must be the criterion of morality, since a part is included in the whole.

REVIEW EXERCISES

1. State and explain the basic idea of the principle of utility or the greatest happiness principle.
2. What does it mean to speak of utilitarianism as a consequentialist moral theory?
3. What is the difference between intrinsic and instrumental good? Give examples of each.

4. Which of the following statements exemplify consequentialist reasoning? Can all of them be given consequentialist interpretations if expanded? Explain your answers.
   a. Honesty is the best policy.
   b. Sue has the right to know the truth.

c. What good is going to come from giving money to a homeless person on the street?

d. There is a symbolic value present in personally giving something to another person in need.

e. It is only fair that you give him a chance to compete for the position.

f. If I do not study for my ethics exam, it will hurt my GPA.

g. If you are not honest with others, you cannot expect them to be honest with you.

5. Is utilitarianism a hedonist moral theory? Why or why not?

6. Using utilitarian calculation, which choice in each of the following pairs is better, X or Y?

a. X makes four people happy and me unhappy. Y makes me and one other person happy and three people unhappy.

b. X makes twenty people happy and five unhappy. Y makes ten people happy and no one unhappy.

c. X will give five people each two hours of pleasure. Y will give three people each four hours of pleasure.

d. X will make five people very happy and three people mildly unhappy. Y will make six people moderately happy and two people very unhappy.

7. What is Mill's argument for the difference in value between intellectual and sensual pleasures?

8. Which of the following is an example of act utilitarian reasoning and which is an example of rule utilitarian reasoning? Explain your answers.

a. If I do not go to the meeting, then others will not go either. If that happens, then there would not be a quorum for the important vote, which would be bad. Thus, I ought to go to the meeting.

b. If doctors generally lied to their patients about their diagnoses, then patients would lose trust in their doctors. Because that would be bad, I should tell this patient the truth.

c. We ought to keep our promises because it is a valuable practice.

d. If I cheat here, I will be more likely to cheat elsewhere. No one would trust me then. So I should not cheat on this test.

MindTap® For more chapter resources and activities, go to MindTap.

6

Deontological Ethics and Immanuel Kant

Georgios Kollidas/Alamy Stock Photo

Learning Outcomes

After reading this chapter, you should be able to:

- Explain the difference between consequentialist and non-consequentialist approaches to ethics.
- Describe different deontological approaches to ethics.
- Explain the difference between hypothetical and categorical imperatives.
- Describe two formulations of the categorical imperative.
- Explain the difference between perfect and imperfect duties.
- Apply Kantian reasoning to a variety of cases in the real world.
- Defend your own thesis with regard to the value of deontological ethics.

MindTap® For more chapter resources and activities, go to MindTap.

Between 1932 and 1972, experiments were conducted in Tuskegee, Alabama, in which 390 poor and illiterate African American men who had syphilis were followed in order to determine the progress of the disease, whether it was always fatal, and how it was spread. The researchers even failed to give the men penicillin treatment for syphilis, when it became available in the early 1940s. The study was ended in 1972 when it became public and a source of major controversy. The reasons were by now obvious; these men had not been treated with respect but had been used for the purpose of obtaining information.

According to utilitarian thinking, the Tuskegee experiments could perhaps be justifiable. If the harm done to the participants was minimal and the study had no other negative effects, and if the knowledge gained was valuable in reducing overall suffering, then the study might be justified. However, since the post–World War II trials of Nazi war criminals held in Nuremberg, Germany, standards for treatment of human research subjects have become widely accepted. One of the most basic principles of the Nuremberg Code is, "The voluntary consent of the human subject is absolutely essential."[1] Consent must be informed and uncoerced. Implied in this principle is the belief that persons are autonomous, and that autonomy ought to be respected and protected even if it means that we cannot do certain types of seemingly beneficial research.

Subjects in the infamous Tuskegee syphilis experiments.

This emphasis on autonomy and the idea that people ought not to be used as they were in the Tuskegee experiments are central tenets in the moral philosophy of Immanuel Kant, which we examine in detail in this chapter. Kant maintains that there are certain things we ought not do, even if these things would produce the greatest happiness for the greatest number.

DEONTOLOGY AND THE ETHICS OF DUTY

Kant's theory of ethics is best described as a deontological theory. The word *deontology* means "theory of duty" (the Greek word *deon* means "duty"). Deontological ethics focuses on duties, obligations, and rights. The term *deontological* was coined by the utilitarian philosopher Jeremy Bentham, who described it as "knowledge of what is right or proper."[2] Bentham thought that deontology points in the direction of the principle of utility. But contemporary philosophers use the term *deontological* to indicate a contrast with the utilitarian focus on the consequences of actions. Instead of focusing on consequences, deontological ethics focuses on duties and obligations: things we ought to do regardless of the consequences. One way of describing this is to say that deontological theories emphasize the *right* over the *good*, by which we mean that deontology focuses on right actions and right intentions, while downplaying the importance of the goods or benefits that are produced by these actions.

While utilitarian ethics focuses on producing the greatest happiness for the greatest number, deontological ethics focuses on what makes us worthy of happiness. For Kant, as for the Stoics and others who emphasize duty, we are worthy of happiness only when we do our duty. As Kant explained, morality "is not properly the doctrine of how we are to make ourselves happy but of how we are to become worthy of happiness."[3] For Kant, morality is not a "doctrine of happiness" or set of instructions on how to become happy. Rather, morality is the "rational condition of happiness."

There are a variety of deontological theories. Divine command ethics, as discussed in Chapter 2, is deontological in the sense that obedience to God's command is a duty that must be followed no matter what the consequences. The biblical story of Abraham and Isaac (in Genesis 22) provides an example of duty. Out of obedience to God's command, Abraham is willing to sacrifice his own son. In this story, religious duty must be done despite the consequences and the unhappiness that is produced.

This episode shows us one of the problems for divine command ethics—a problem that has been recognized since Socrates discussed it with Euthyphro in Plato's dialogue (see Chapter 2). How is morality related to God's commands? And how are we to know that it is, in fact, God who commands us and not the voice of our culture or our own selfish motives or even mental illness? The Abraham and Isaac episode famously prompted Kant to suggest that Abraham should have questioned God as follows: "That I ought not to kill my good son is quite certain. But that you, this apparition, are God—of that I am not certain, and never can be, not even if this voice rings down to me from heaven."[4] For Kant, the commands of ethics are clear, certain, and without exception—and they do not include the command to kill our own children. In response to this sort of criticism, the Danish philosopher Søren Kierkegaard suggested that the story of Abraham shows us that there may be religious duties that transcend the duties of ethics. Kant rejects such a claim. For Kant, moral duties are universal and absolute, and we should use our knowledge of morality to criticize and interpret religious stories and ideas.

Another form of deontological ethics can be found in the ancient Greek and Roman philosophy of **Stoicism**. The Stoics emphasized doing your duty and playing your part as determined by the natural order of things. Rather than struggling against *external* circumstances that we cannot control, the Stoics argue that the key to morality and happiness is *internal*, a matter of how we orient our will and intentions. According to this view, duty is its own reward. Epictetus, a Stoic philosopher who died in 135 CE, explains, "As Zeus has ordained, so act: if you do not act so, you will feel the penalty, you will be punished. What will be the punishment? Nothing else than not having done your duty: you will lose the character of fidelity, modesty, propriety. Do not look for greater penalties than these."[5]

The typical image of a Stoic is of a sternly disciplined, courageous, and emotionally composed individual who acts solely for the sake of duty—and whose commitment to obedience and duty infuses every part of life. We often associate Stoic ethics

The story of Abraham and Isaac is an example of how religious duties may conflict with ethical duties.

with the kind of courageous and selfless obedience to duty that is typical of soldiers. This image of military service and duty was embodied in the Roman Stoic Emperor Marcus Aurelius, who describes the life of Stoic duty as follows: "It is thy duty to order thy life well in every single act; and if every act does its duty, as far as is possible, be content; and no one is able to hinder thee so that each act shall not do its duty."[6] He imagines someone objecting to the rigors of duty by claiming that some external circumstances stand in the way of the fulfillment of duty. But he replies, "Nothing will stand in the way of thy acting justly and soberly and considerately." As Marcus explains elsewhere, "it is thy business to do thy duty like a soldier in the assault on a town."[7] The basic idea of Stoicism is that we can control our own intentions and actions, even when we cannot control the consequences and external circumstances. From this standpoint, you fulfill your moral obligation by doing what you know is right, even if the external world makes that difficult.

Although Immanuel Kant admired the Stoics' emphasis on "strength of the soul,"[8] he also believed they underestimated the difficulty of being moral. One problem is that we are confused about moral duty—because we often confuse moral duties with other more practical concerns, including the concerns of happiness. To clarify this, Kant focused on the logical and rational structure of duty itself—apart from considerations of happiness, prudence, or the natural order of things.

While it is easy enough to state in general that there are duties and obligations that we ought to fulfill, it is more difficult to establish exactly what those duties and obligations are. Is patriotism an obligation—and does it include patriotism to an unjust or corrupt state? Is the duty to our parents and ancestors primary, as it is in the morality of Confucius? Do we have obligations of compassion and concern for all sentient beings, as many Buddhists argue? These questions remind us that deontological ethics might need to be supplemented with a broader theory of "the good," which tells us how the theory of duty should apply to personal, social, and political affairs. Indeed, this criticism of deontological ethics was noted by John Stuart Mill, who criticized Kant for defining a theory of duty that was so abstract that it could not rule out immoral actions.

As we turn to a discussion of Kant, bear this accusation in mind. Is Kant's conception of duty too abstract? Or does the Kantian theory help to specify our duties in sufficient detail to avoid this charge?

IMMANUEL KANT

Immanuel Kant (1724–1804) was a German philosopher who is now regarded as a central figure in the history of modern philosophy. Modern philosophy itself is sometimes divided into pre-Kantian and post-Kantian periods. Although he is renowned for his moral philosophy, he wrote on a variety of matters including science, geography, beauty, and war and peace. He was a firm believer in the ideas of the Enlightenment (as discussed in Chapter 2), especially reason and freedom, and he was also a supporter of the American Revolution.

Two of the main questions that Kant believed philosophy should address are: "What can I know?" and "What ought I do?"[9] While Kant's theory of knowledge is important and influential, our concern here is his moral philosophy.

One way to begin your examination of Kant's moral theory is to think about how he would answer the question, *What gives an act moral worth?* It is not the consequences of the act, according to Kant, that matters most. Suppose, for example, that I try to do what is right by complimenting a man on his achievements. Through no fault of my own, my action ends up hurting that person because he misunderstands my efforts. According to Kant, because I intended and tried to do what I thought was right, I ought not to be blamed for things having turned out badly. The idea is that we generally ought not to be blamed or praised for what is not in our control. The consequences of our acts are not always in our control, and things do not always turn out as we want. However, Kant believed that our motives are in our control. We are responsible for our intention to do good or bad, and thus it is for this that we are held morally accountable.

Kant also objected to basing morality on the consequences of our actions for another reason. To make morality a matter of producing certain states of affairs, such as happy experiences, seems to approach morality backwards. In such a view, actions and even human beings could be thought of as merely having *use value*. We would be valued to the extent that we were instrumental in bringing about what itself was of greater value, namely, happy states or experiences. However, in Kant's view, we should not be used in this way for we are rational beings or *persons*. Persons have intrinsic or inherent value, according to Kant, not mere instrumental value. The belief that *people ought not to be used*, but ought to be regarded as having the highest intrinsic value, is central to Kant's ethics, as is having *a motive to do what is right*. As we shall see in the next two sections, Kant uses this second idea to answer the question: What gives an act moral worth?

What Is the Right Motive?

Kant believed that an act has moral worth only if it is done with a right intention or motive.[10] He

A portrait of Immanuel Kant (1724–1804).

referred to this as having a "good will." Kant writes that the only thing that is unconditionally good is a good will. Everything else needs a good will to make it good. Without a right intention, such things as intelligence, wit, and control of emotions can be bad and used for evil purposes. Having a right intention means doing what is right (or what one believes to be right) just because it is right. In Kant's words, it is to act "out of duty," out of a concern and respect for the moral law. Kant was not a relativist. He believed that there is a right and a wrong thing to do, whether or not we know or agree about it.

To explain his views on the importance of a right motive or intention, Kant provides the example of a shopkeeper who does the right thing, who charges her customers a fair price and charges the same to all. But what is her motive? Kant discusses three possible motives: (1) The shopkeeper's motive or reason for acting might be because it is a good business practice to charge the same to all. It is in her own best interest that she do this. Although not

necessarily wrong, this motive is not praiseworthy. (2) The shopkeeper might charge a fair and equal price because she is sympathetic toward her customers and is naturally inclined to do them good. Kant said that this motive is also not the highest. We do not have high moral esteem or praise for people who simply do what they feel like doing, even if we believe they are doing the right thing. (3) If the shopkeeper did the right thing just because she believed it was right, however, then this act would be based on the highest motive. We have a special respect, or even a moral reverence, for people who act out of a will to do the right thing, especially when this comes at great cost to themselves. An act has moral worth only when it is motivated by concern for the moral law.

Now, we do not always *know* whether our acts are motivated by self-interest, inclination, or pure respect for morality. Also, we often act from mixed motives. We are more certain that the motive is pure, however, when we do what is right even when it is not in our best interest (when it costs us dearly) and when we do not feel like doing the right thing. In these cases, we can know that we are motivated by concern to do the right thing because the other two motives are missing. Moreover, this ability to act for moral reasons, while resisting other inclinations, is one reason that human beings have a unique value and dignity. The person who says to himself, "I feel like being lazy (or mean or selfish), but I am going to try not to because it would not be right," is operating out of the motive of respect for morality itself. This ability to act for moral reasons or motives, Kant believes, is one part of what gives human beings dignity and worth.

What Is the Right Thing to Do?

For our action to have moral worth, according to Kant, we must not only act out of a right motivation but also do the right thing. Consider again the diagram that we used in Chapter 1.

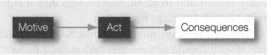

As noted earlier, Kant does not believe that morality is a function of producing good consequences. We may do what has good results, but if we do so for the wrong motive, then that act has no moral worth. However, it is not only the motive that counts for Kant. We must also do what is right. The act itself must be morally right. Both the act and the motive are morally relevant. In Kant's terms, we must act not only "out of duty" (have the right motive) but also "according to duty" or "as duty requires" (do what is right). How then are we to know what is the right thing to do? Once we know this, we can try to do it just because it is right.

To understand Kant's reasoning on this matter, we need to examine the difference between what he calls a **hypothetical imperative** and a **categorical imperative**. First of all, an imperative is simply a form of statement that tells us to do something, for example, "Stand up straight" and "Close the door" and also "You ought to close the door." Some, but only some, imperatives are moral imperatives. Other imperatives are hypothetical. For example, the statement: "If I want to get there on time, I ought to leave early" does not embody a moral "ought" or a moral imperative. What I ought to do in that case is a function of what I happen to want—to get there on time—and of the means necessary to achieve this—leaving early. Moreover, I can avoid the obligation to leave early by changing my goals. I can decide that I do not need or want to get there on time. Then, I need not leave early. These ends may be good or bad. Thus, the statement, "If I want to harm someone, then I ought to use effective means" also expresses a hypothetical "ought." These "oughts" are avoidable, or, as Kant would say, contingent. They are contingent or dependent on what I happen to want or the desires I happen to have, such as to please others, to harm someone, to gain power, or to be punctual.

These "oughts" are also quite individualized. What I ought to do is contingent or dependent on my own individual goals or plans. These actions serve as means to whatever goals I happen to have (or whatever goals my particular community or society happens to approve). Other people ought to do different things than I because they have different goals and plans. For example, I ought to take introduction to sociology because I want to be a sociology major, while you ought to take a course on the philosophy of Kant because you have chosen to be a philosophy major. These are obligations only for those who have these goals or desires. Think of them in this form: "If (or because) I want X, then I ought to do Y." Whether I ought to do Y is totally contingent or dependent on my wanting X.

Moral obligation, on the other hand, is quite different in nature. Kant believed that we experience moral obligation as something quite demanding. If there is something I morally ought to do, I ought to do it no matter what—whether or not I want to, and whether or not it fulfills my desires and goals or is approved by my society. Moral obligation is not contingent on what I or anyone happens to want or approve. Moral "oughts" are thus, in Kant's terminology, unconditional or necessary. Moreover, whereas hypothetical "oughts" relate to goals we each have as individuals, moral "oughts" stem from the ways in which we are alike as persons, for only persons are subject to morality. This is because persons are rational beings, and only persons can act from a reason or from principles. These "oughts" are thus not individualized but universal as they apply to all persons. Kant calls moral "oughts" *categorical imperatives* because they tell us what we ought to do no matter what, under all conditions, or categorically.

It is from the very nature of categorical or moral imperatives, as unconditional and universally binding, that Kant derives his views about morality. In fact, he uses the term *the categorical imperative* to describe the basic moral principle by which we determine what we ought and ought not to do.

THE CATEGORICAL IMPERATIVE

The categorical imperative, Kant's basic moral principle, is comparable in importance for his moral philosophy to the principle of utility for utilitarians. It is Kant's test for right and wrong. Several formulations of the categorical imperative are found in Kant's writings. We will concentrate on just two and call them the first and second forms of the categorical imperative. The others, however, do add different elements to our understanding of his basic moral principle and will be mentioned briefly.

The First Form

Recall that moral obligation is categorical; that is, it is unconditional and applies to all persons as persons rather than to persons as individuals. It is in this sense universal. Moreover, because morality is not a matter of producing good consequences of any sort (be it happiness, knowledge, or peace), the basic moral principle will be formal, without content. It will not include reference to any particular good. Knowing this, we are on the way to understanding the first form of the categorical imperative, which simply requires that we do only what we can accept or will that everyone do. Kant's own statement of it is basically the following:

Act only on that maxim that you can will as a universal law.

In other words, whatever I consider doing, it must be something that I can consistently will or accept that all others do. To will something universally is similar to willing it as a law, for a law by its very nature has a degree of universality. By *maxim*, Kant means a description of the action or policy that I will put to the test. This is expressed in the form of a rule or principle. For example, I might want to know whether "being late for class" or "giving all my money to the homeless" describes a morally permissible action. I need only formulate some maxim or rule and ask whether I could will that everyone follow that maxim. For example, I might ask whether I could will the universal maxim or general rule, "Whenever I have money to spare, I will give it to the homeless." However, this needs further clarification.

How do I know what I can and cannot will as a universal practice? As a rational being, I can only will what is noncontradictory. What do we think of a person who says that it is both raining and not raining here now? It can be raining here and not there, or now and not earlier. But it is either raining here or it is not. It cannot be both. So also we say that a person who wants to "have his cake and eat it, too"

is not being rational. "Make up your mind," we say. "If you eat it, it is gone."

How I know whether I can will something universally without contradiction can be explained by using one of Kant's own examples. He asks us to consider whether it is morally permissible for me to "make a lying or false promise in order to extricate myself from some difficulty." Thus, I would consider the maxim, "Whenever I am in some difficulty that I can get out of only by making a lying or false promise, I will do so." To know whether this would be morally acceptable, it must pass the test of the categorical imperative. If I were to use this test, I would ask whether I could will that sort of thing for all. I must ask whether I could will a general practice in which people who made promises—for example, to pay back some money—could make the promises without intending to keep them. If people who generally made such promises did so falsely, then others would know this and would not believe the promises. Consider whether you would lend money to a woman if she promised to pay you back but you knew she was lying. The reasoning is thus: If I tried to will a general practice of false promise-making, I would find it impossible to do so because by willing that promises could be false, I would also will a situation in which it would be impossible to succeed in making a lying promise. Everyone would know that all promises were potential lies. No one could then make a promise, let alone a false promise, because no one would believe him or her. Part of being able to make a promise is to have it believed. The universal practice of false promise-making is self-contradictory and could not exist. If everyone made such lying promises, no one could!

Now consider the example at the beginning of this chapter: the Tuskegee syphilis experiments, in which people were used as medical test subjects without their full knowing consent. Using Kant's categorical imperative to test this, one would see that if it were a general practice for researchers to lie to their subjects in order to get them into their experiments, they would not be able to get people to participate. A general practice of deceiving potential research subjects would undermine the credibility of all researchers. The only way a particular researcher could lie would be if most other researchers told the truth. Only then could he or she get prospective subjects to believe him or her. But this would be to make himself or herself an exception to the universal rule. Like false promising, a universal practice in which researchers lied to their prospective subjects is self-contradictory and cannot be willed with consistency. Therefore, lying to prospective research subjects fails the test of the categorical imperative and is morally impermissible.

In some ways, Kant's basic moral principle, the categorical imperative, is a principle of fairness. I should not do what I am not able to will that everyone do. For me to succeed in making a lying promise, others must generally make truthful promises so that my lie will be believed. This would be to treat myself as an exception. But this is not fair. In some ways, the principle is similar to the so-called Golden Rule, which requires us only to do unto others what we would be willing for them to do unto us. However, it is not the same, for Kant's principle requires our not willing self-canceling or contradictory practices, whereas the Golden Rule requires that we appeal in the final analysis to what we would or would not like to have done to us. Kant explains that the Golden Rule

> …cannot be a universal law, for it does not contain the principle of duties to oneself, nor of the duties of benevolence to others (for many a one would gladly consent that others should not benefit him, provided only that he might be excused from showing benevolence to them), nor finally that of duties of strict obligation to one another, for on this principle the criminal might argue against the judge who punishes him, and so on.[11]

To explain, the Golden Rule is only about what I or you like or don't like (what we would have others "do unto us"). But this fails to get us to the level of universal duty that is central to Kant's moral theory.

The Second Form

The first form of Kant's categorical imperative requires universalizing one's contemplated action or policy. In the second form, we are asked to consider what constitutes proper treatment of persons as persons. According to Kant, one key characteristic of persons is their ability to set their own goals. Persons are autonomous (from the Greek *auto*, meaning "self," and *nomos*, meaning "rule" or "law"). They are literally self-ruled, or at least capable of being self-ruled. As persons, we choose our own life plans, what we want to be, our friends, our college courses, and so forth. We have our own reasons for doing so. We believe that although our choices are influenced by our circumstances and by the advice and opinions of others, we knowingly allow ourselves be so influenced, and thus, these choices are still our own choices. In this way, persons are different from things. Things cannot choose what they wish to do. We decide how we shall use things. We impose our own goals on things, using wood to build a house and a pen or computer to express our ideas. It is appropriate to use things for our ends, but it is not appropriate to use persons as though they were things purely at our disposal and without wills of their own. Kant's statement of this second form of the categorical imperative is as follows:

> Always treat humanity, whether in your own person or that of another, never simply as a means but always at the same time as an end.

This formulation tells us how we ought to treat ourselves as well as others, namely, as ends rather than merely as means. Kant believes that we should treat persons as having value in themselves and not just as having instrumental value. People are valuable, regardless of whether they are useful or loved or valued by others. We should not simply use others or let ourselves be used. Although I may in some sense use a woman—for example, to paint my house—I may not *simply* use her. The goal of getting my house painted must be shared by the painter, who is also a person and not just an object to be used by me for my own ends. She must know what is involved in the project. I cannot lie to manipulate her into doing something to which she otherwise would not agree. And she must agree to paint the house voluntarily rather than be coerced into doing it. These and similar requirements are necessary for treating another person as an end rather than merely as a means to my ends or goals.

We can use this second form of the categorical imperative to evaluate the examples we considered for the first form. The moral conclusions should be the same whether we use the first or second form. Kant believes that in lying to another person—for example, saying that we will pay back money when we have no intention of doing so—we would be attempting to manipulate another person against that person's will. (He or she is presumably unwilling to just give us the money.) This would violate the requirement not to use persons. Similarly, in the Tuskegee experiments, the deceptive researchers used the subjects as means to an end rather than as ends in themselves.

We noted that Kant provided more formulations of his categorical imperative than the two discussed here. In another of these formulations, Kant relies on his views about nature as a system of everything that we experience because it is organized according to laws. Thus, he says that we ought always to ask whether some action we are contemplating could become a universal law of nature. The effect of this version is to emphasize morality as universal and rational, for nature necessarily operates according to coherent laws. Other formulations of the categorical imperative stress autonomy. We are to ask whether we could consider ourselves as the author of the moral practice that we are about to accept. We are both subject to the moral law and its author because it flows from our own nature as a rational being. Another formulation amplifies what we have here called the second form of the categorical imperative. This formulation points out that our rationality makes us alike as persons, and together, we form a community of persons. He calls the community of rational persons a **kingdom of ends**—that is, a kingdom in which all persons are authors as well as subjects of the moral law. Thus, we ask whether the action we are contemplating would be fitting for and promote such a community. These formulations of the categorical imperative involve other interesting elements of Kant's philosophy, but they also involve more than we can explore here.

MindTap® For more chapter resources and activities, go to MindTap.

EVALUATING KANT'S MORAL THEORY

There is much that is appealing in Kant's moral philosophy, particularly its central aspects—its focus on motives, its emphasis on fairness, its aim of consistency, and its basic idea of treating persons as autonomous and morally equal beings. Kant's deontological approach is quite different from that exemplified by utilitarianism, with its emphasis on the maximization of happiness and the production of good consequences. To more fully evaluate Kant's theory, consider the following aspects of his thought.

The Nature of Moral Obligation

One of the bases on which Kant's moral philosophy rests is his view about the nature of moral obligation. He believes that moral obligation is real and strictly binding. According to Kant, this is how we generally think of moral obligation. If there is anything that we morally ought to do, then we simply ought to do it. Thus, this type of obligation is unlike that which flows from what we ought to do because of the particular goals that we each have as individuals. To evaluate this aspect of Kant's moral philosophy, you must ask yourself whether this is also what you think about the nature of moral obligation. This is important for Kant's moral philosophy because acting out of respect for the moral law is required for an action to have moral worth. Furthermore, being able to act out of such a regard for morality is also the source of human dignity, according to Kant.

The Application of the Categorical Imperative

Critics such as Mill (as noted previously) have pointed out problems with the universalizing form of the categorical imperative. For example, some have argued that when using the first form of the categorical imperative, there are many things that I could will as universal practices that would hardly seem to be moral obligations. I could will that everyone write their names on the top of their test papers. If everyone did that, it would not prevent anyone from doing so. There would be no contradiction involved if this were a universal practice. Nevertheless, this would not mean that people have a moral obligation to write their names on their test papers. A Kantian might respond that to write your name on your test paper is an example of a hypothetical, not a categorical, imperative. I write my name on my paper because I want to be given credit for it. If I can will it as a universal practice, I then know it is a morally permissible action. If I cannot will it universally, then it is impermissible or wrong. Thus, the categorical imperative is actually a negative test—in other words, a test for what we should not do, more than a test for what we ought to do. Whether or not this is a satisfactory response, you should know that this is just one of several problems associated with Kant's universalizing test.

Concern for the universality of moral rules is not unique to Kantian ethics. We saw in Chapter 5 that rule utilitarianism is focused on the general utility of rules. Although Kantians and rule utilitarians are both interested in universalized rules, there is a difference in how Kantian and rule utilitarian reasoning proceeds. Rule utilitarians require that we consider what the *results* would be if some act we are contemplating were to be a universal practice. Reasoning in this way, we ask what would be the results or consequences of some general practice, such as making false promises, or whether one practice would have better results than another. Although in some sense Kant's theory requires that we consider the possible consequences when universalizing some action, the determinant of the action's morality is not whether it has good or bad consequences, but whether there would be anything contradictory in willing the practice as a universal law. Because we are rational beings, we must not will contradictory things.

The second form of the categorical imperative also has problems of application. In the concrete, it is not always easy to determine whether one is using a person—for example, what is coercion and what is simply influence, or what is deception and what is not. When I try to talk a friend into doing something for me, how do I know whether I am simply providing input for my friend's own decision-making or whether I am crossing the line and becoming coercive? Moreover, if I do not tell the whole truth or withhold information from another person, should

this count as deception on my part? Although these are real problems for anyone who tries to apply Kant's views about deceit and coercion, they are not unique to his moral philosophy. Theories vary in the ease of their use or application. Difficulty of application is a problem for most, if not all, moral philosophies.

Duty

Some of the language and terminology found in Kant's moral theory can sound harsh to modern ears. Duty, obligation, law, and universality may not be the moral terms most commonly heard today. Yet if one considers what Kant meant by duty, the idea may not seem so strange to us. Kant was not advocating any particular moral code or set of duties held by any society or group. Rather, duty is what reason tells us is the right thing to do. However, Kant might acknowledge that there is a streak of *absolutism* in his philosophy. Absolutists think that morality consists of a set of exceptionless rules. Kant does, at times, seem to favor absolutism. He provides examples in which it seems clear that he believes it is always wrong to make a false promise or to lie deliberately. There is even one example in which Kant himself suggests that if a killer comes to the door asking for a friend of yours inside whom he or she intends to kill, you must tell the truth. But Kant's moral theory provides only one exceptionless rule, and that is given in the categorical imperative. We are never permitted to do what we cannot will as a universal law or what violates the requirement to treat persons as ends in themselves. Even with these two tests in hand, it is not always clear just how they apply. Furthermore, they may not give adequate help in deciding what to do when they seem to produce contradictory duties, as in the conflict between telling the truth and preserving a life.

Moral Equality and Impartiality

One positive feature of Kant's moral theory is its emphasis on the moral equality of all persons, which is implied in his view that the nature of moral obligation is universally binding. We should not make exceptions for ourselves; we should only do what we can will for all. Moral obligation and morality itself flow from our nature as rational and autonomous persons. Morality is grounded in the ways in which we are alike as persons, rather than the ways in which we are different as individuals. This provides a source for those who want to argue for moral equality and equal moral rights. If we do not treat others as equal persons, we are disrespecting them. If we are not willing to make the same judgment for cases similar to our own, or if we are not willing to have the same rules apply to all, we can be accused of hypocrisy. When we criticize hypocrisy, we act in the spirit of Kant.

Another feature of Kant's moral philosophy is its spirit of impartiality. For an action to be morally permissible, we should be able to will it for all. However, persons differ in significant ways. Among these are differences in gender, race, age, and talents. In what way does morality require that all persons be treated equally, and in what way does it perhaps require that different persons be treated differently?[12]

Some critics have wondered about Kant's stress on the nature of persons as rational and autonomous beings. It might be that human beings are not best conceived as rational autonomous beings, such as Kant describes. Kant seems to forget our emotions and our dependency on relationships. But Kant might reply that we often have no control over how we feel and thus that our feelings should not be a key element of our moral lives. He might also argue that it is the common aspects of our existence as persons, and not the ways in which we are different and unique, that give us dignity and are the basis for the moral equality that we possess. In short, even if we are often not fully autonomous or rational, we ought to consider ourselves as autonomous and rational—and treat others as if they were autonomous and rational—for this is the source of human dignity.

PERFECT AND IMPERFECT DUTIES

In his attempt to explain his views, Kant provides us with several examples. We have already considered one of these: making a false promise. His conclusion is that we should not make a false or lying promise, both because we could not consistently will it for all and because it violates our obligation to treat persons as persons and not to use them only for our own purposes. Kant calls such duties **perfect duties** (they are sometimes described as *necessary* duties). As the term suggests, perfect duties are absolute. We can and should absolutely refrain from making false or lying promises. From the perspective of the first form of the categorical imperative, we have a perfect duty not to do those things that could not even exist and are inconceivable as universal practices. Using the second form of the categorical imperative, we have a perfect duty not to do what violates the requirement to treat persons as ends in themselves.

However, some duties are more flexible. Kant calls these duties **imperfect duties** (sometimes also called *meritorious* duties). Consider another example he provides: egoism. Ethical egoism is the view that we may rightly seek only our own interest and help others only to the extent that doing so also benefits us (see Chapter 4). Is this a morally acceptable philosophy of life? Using the first form of Kant's categorical imperative to test the morality of this practice, we must ask whether we could will that everyone was an egoist. If I try to do this, I would need to will that I was an egoist as well as others, even in those situations when I needed others' help. In those situations, I must allow that they not help me when it is not in their own best interest. But being an egoist myself, I would also want them to help me. In effect, I would be willing contradictories; that they help me (I being an egoist) and that they not help me (they being egoists). Although Kant admits that a society of egoists could indeed exist, no rational person could will it, for a rational person does not will contradictories. We have an imperfect or meritorious duty, then, not to be egoists but to help people for their own good and not just for ours. However, just when to help others and how much to help them is a matter of some choice. There is a certain flexibility here. One implication of this view is that there is no absolute duty to give one's whole life to helping others. We, too, are persons and thus have moral rights and also can at least sometimes act for our own interests.

The same conclusion regarding the wrongness of egoism results from the application of the second form of the categorical imperative. If I were an egoist and concerned only about myself, I might argue that I was not thereby committed to using other people. I would simply leave them alone. But according to Kant, such an attitude and practice would still be inconsistent with the duty to treat others as persons. As persons, they also have interests and plans, and to recognize this, I must at least sometimes and in some ways seek to promote their ends and goals. Thus, avoiding egoism appears to be an imperfect duty, according to Kant's theory. The distinction between perfect and imperfect duties will have implications for handling conflicts among different duties. Perfect duties will take precedence over imperfect ones; we cannot help some by violating the rights of others.

VARIATIONS ON KANT AND DEONTOLOGY

Just as there are contemporary versions of and developments within the utilitarian tradition, there are also many contemporary versions of Kantian and deontological moral theory. One is found in the moral philosophy of W. D. Ross, who also held that there are things we ought and ought not do regardless of the consequences.[13] We discussed Ross in Chapter 3 in relation to pluralism. According to Ross, we have duties not only of beneficence, but also to keep promises, pay our debts, and be good friends and parents and children. Contrary to Kant, Ross believed that we can know through moral intuition in any instance what we ought to do. Sometimes, we are faced with a conflict of moral duties. It seems intuitive that we ought to be both loyal and honest, but we cannot be both. We have *prima facie*, or conditional duties, of loyalty and honesty. In case of conflicting duties, according to Ross, we have to consider which duty is the stronger—that is, which has the greater balance of rightness over wrongness. In choosing honesty in some situations, however, one does not negate or forget that one also has a duty to be loyal. Obvious problems arise for such a theory. For example, how does one go about determining the amount of rightness or wrongness

involved in some action? Don't people have different intuitions about the rightness or wrongness of any particular action? This is a problem for anyone who holds that intuition is the basis for morality.

One of the most noted contemporary versions of Kant's moral philosophy is found in the political philosophy of John Rawls. In *A Theory of Justice*, Rawls applies some aspects of Kantian principles to issues of social justice. According to Rawls, justice is fairness.[14] To know what is fair, we must put ourselves imaginatively in the position of a group of free and equal rational beings who are choosing principles of justice for their society. In thinking of persons as free and equal rational beings in order to develop principles of justice, Rawls is securely in the Kantian tradition of moral philosophy. Kant also stresses autonomy. It is this aspect of our nature that gives us our dignity as persons. Kant's categorical imperative also involves universalization. We must do only those things that we could will that everyone do. It is only a short move from these notions of autonomy and universalization to the Rawlsian requirement to choose those principles of justice that we could accept no matter which position in society we happen to occupy. For details about Rawls' principles, see Chapter 14. Kantian and other versions of deontology continue to be influential. You will be able to better evaluate the Kantian theory as you see aspects of it applied to issues in Part Two of this text.

The reading selection in this chapter from Kant's *Fundamental Principles of the Metaphysic of Morals* contains the key elements of his moral philosophy. As the title implies, Kant is trying to establish the foundations of morality. He begins by claiming that the only thing that is good without qualification is a good will. He goes on to explain duty and the categorical imperative, while applying these ideas to some basic examples.

NOTES

1. From *Trials of War Criminals before the Nuremberg Military Tribunals under Control Council Law No. 10, Vol. 2* (Washington, D.C.: U.S. Government Printing Office, 1949), pp. 181–82.

2. Jeremy Bentham, *Deontology or the Science of Morality* (Edinburgh, William Tait, 1834), vol. 1, Chapter 2.

3. Immanuel Kant, *Critique of Practical Reason*, in *Practical Philosophy* (Cambridge: Cambridge University Press, 1999), 5: 130, p. 244.

4. Immanuel Kant, *The Conflict of the Faculties*, in *Religion and Rational Theology*, ed. A.W. Wood and G. di Giovanni (Cambridge: Cambridge University Press, 1996), p. 283.

5. Epictetus, *Discourses*, 3.7 (Internet Classics Archive: http://classics.mit.edu//Epictetus/discourses.html).

6. Marcus Aurelius, *Meditations* (Internet Classics Archive: http://classics.mit.edu//Antoninus/meditations.html), bk. 8.

7. Aurelius, *Meditations*, bk. 7.

8. Kant, *Critique of Practical Reason* 5: 127, p. 242. Also see J. B. Schneewind, "Kant and Stoic Ethics," in *Essays on the History of Moral Philosophy* (Oxford University Press, 2009).

9. Immanuel Kant, *Critique of Pure Reason*, trans. Norman Kemp Smith (New York: St. Martin's, 1965), p. 635.

10. We will not distinguish here *motive* and *intention*, although the former usually signifies that out of which we act (an impetus or push) and the latter that for which we act (an aim or objective).

11. Kant, *Fundamental Principles of the Metaphysics of Morals* trans. Abbott (Project Gutenburg: http://www.gutenberg.org/cache/epub/5682/pg5682.html), second section.

12. See also the criticism of Kantian theories of justice in the treatment of gender and justice in Susan Moller Okin, *Justice, Gender, and the Family* (New York: Basic Books, 1989), pp. 3–22. See also Marilyn Friedman, "The Social Self and the Partiality Debates," in *Feminist Ethics*, ed. Claudia Card (Lawrence: University of Kansas Press, 1991).

13. W. D. Ross, *The Right and the Good* (Oxford: Oxford University Press, 1930).

14. John Rawls, *A Theory of Justice* (Cambridge, MA: Harvard University Press, 1971).

READING

Fundamental Principles of the Metaphysic of Morals

IMMANUEL KANT

MindTap®   For more chapter resources and activities, go to MindTap.

Study Questions

As you read the excerpt, please consider the following questions:

1. How does Kant state his basic moral principle?
2. What is the difference between a rule of skill, a counsel of prudence, and a command of morality?
3. Explain how Kant uses the categorical imperative in his four examples. Make sure you understand his application of both forms of the categorical imperative.

THE GOOD WILL*

Nothing can possibly be conceived in the world, or even out of it, which can be called good without qualification, except a good will. Intelligence, wit, judgment, and the other *talents* of the mind, however they may be named, or courage, resolution, perseverance, as qualities of temperament, are undoubtedly good and desirable in many respects; but these gifts of nature may also become extremely bad and mischievous if the will which is to make use

From Immanuel Kant, *Fundamental Principles of the Metaphysic of Morals*, trans. Thomas Kingsmill Abbott, (1879; Project Gutenberg 2004), secs. 1 and 2, http://www.gutenberg.org/ebooks/5682

*Headings added by the editor.

*Some notes have been deleted and the remaining ones renumbered.

of them, and which, therefore, constitutes what is called *character*, is not good. It is the same with the *gifts of fortune*. Power, riches, honor, even health, and the general well-being and contentment with one's condition which is called *happiness*, inspire pride, and often presumption, if there is not a good will to correct the influence of these on the mind, and with this also to rectify the whole principle of acting and adapt it to its end. The sight of a being who is not adorned with a single feature of a pure and good will, enjoying unbroken prosperity, can never give pleasure to an impartial rational spectator. Thus a good will appears to constitute the indispensable condition even of being worthy of happiness.

There are even some qualities which are of service to this good will itself, and may facilitate its action, yet which have no intrinsic unconditional value, but always presuppose a good will, and this qualifies the esteem that we justly have for them, and does not permit us to regard them as absolutely good. Moderation in the affections and passions, self-control and calm deliberation are not only good in many respects, but even seem to constitute part of the intrinsic worth of the person; but they are far from deserving to be called good without qualification, although they have been so unconditionally praised by the ancients. For without the principles of a good will, they may become extremely bad, and the coolness of a villain not only makes him far more dangerous, but also immediately makes him more abominable in our eyes than he would have been without it.

A good will is good not because of what it performs or effects, not by its aptness for the attainment of some proposed end, but simply by virtue of the volition, that is, it is good in itself, and considered by itself is to be esteemed much higher than all that can be brought about by it in favour of any inclination, nay even of the sum total of all inclinations. Even if it should happen that, owing to special disfavour of fortune, or the niggardly provision of a step-motherly nature, this will should wholly lack power to accomplish its purpose, if with its greatest efforts it should yet achieve nothing, and there should remain only the good will (not, to be sure, a mere wish, but the summoning of all means in our power), then, like a jewel, it would still shine

by its own light, as a thing which has its whole value in itself. Its usefulness or fruitlessness can neither add nor take away anything from this value. It would be, as it were, only the setting to enable us to handle it the more conveniently in common commerce, or to attract to it the attention of those who are not yet connoisseurs, but not to recommend it to true connoisseurs, or to determine its value....

ACTING FROM DUTY

We have then to develop the notion of a will which deserves to be highly esteemed for itself, and is good without a view to anything further, a notion which exists already in the sound natural understanding, requiring rather to be cleared up than to be taught, and which in estimating the value of our actions always takes the first place, and constitutes the condition of all the rest. In order to do this we will take the notion of duty, which includes that of a good will, although implying certain subjective restrictions and hindrances. These, however, far from concealing it, or rendering it unrecognizable, rather bring it out by contrast, and make it shine forth so much the brighter. I omit here all actions which are already recognized as inconsistent with duty, although they may be useful for this or that purpose, for with these the question whether they are done from duty cannot arise at all, since they even conflict with it. I also set aside those actions which really conform to duty, but to which men have no direct inclination, performing them because they are impelled thereto by some other inclination. For in this case we can readily distinguish whether the action which agrees with duty is done from duty, or from a selfish view. It is much harder to make this distinction when the action accords with duty, and the subject has besides a direct inclination to it. For example, it is always a matter of duty that a dealer should not overcharge an inexperienced purchaser, and wherever there is much commerce the prudent tradesman does not overcharge, but keeps a fixed price for every one, so that a child buys of him as well as any other. Men are thus honestly served; but this is not enough to make us believe that the tradesman has so acted from duty and from principles of honesty: his own advantage required it; it is out of the question in this case to suppose that he might besides have a direct inclination in favour of the buyers, so that, as it were, from love he should give no advantage to one over another. Accordingly the action was done neither from duty nor from direct inclination, but merely with a selfish view.

On the other hand, it is a duty to maintain one's life; and, in addition, every one has also a direct inclination to do so. But on this account the often anxious care which most men take for it has no intrinsic worth, and their maxim has no moral import. They preserve their life *as duty requires*, no doubt, but not *because duty requires*. On the other hand, if adversity and hopeless sorrow have completely taken away the relish for life; if the unfortunate one, strong in mind, indignant at his fate rather than desponding or dejected, wishes for death, and yet preserves his life without loving it—not from inclination or fear, but from duty—then his maxim has a moral worth.

To be beneficent when we can is a duty; and besides this, there are many minds so sympathetically constituted that without any other motive of vanity or self-interest, they find a pleasure in spreading joy around them, and can take delight in the satisfaction of others so far as it is their own work. But I maintain that in such a case an action of this kind, however proper, however amiable it may be, has nevertheless no true moral worth, but is on a level with other inclinations, e.g., the inclination to honour, which, if it is happily directed to that which is in fact of public utility and accordant with duty, and consequently honourable, deserves praise and encouragement, but not esteem. For the maxim wants the moral import, namely, that such actions be done *from duty*, not from inclination. Put the case that the mind of that philanthropist were clouded by sorrow of his own, extinguishing all sympathy with the lot of others, and that while he still has the power to benefit others in distress he is not touched by their trouble because he is absorbed with his own; and now suppose that he tears himself out of this dead insensibility, and performs the action without any inclination to it, but simply from duty, then first has his action its genuine moral worth. Further still; if nature has put little

sympathy in the heart of this or that man; if he, supposed to be an upright man, is by temperament cold and indifferent to the sufferings of others, perhaps because in respect of his own he is provided with the special gift of patience and fortitude, and supposes, or even requires, that others should have the same— and such a man would certainly not be the meanest product of nature—but if nature had not specially framed him for a philanthropist, would he not still find in himself a source from whence to give himself a far higher worth than that of a good-natured temperament could be? Unquestionably. It is just in this that the moral worth of the character is brought out which is incomparably the highest of all, namely, that he is beneficent, not from inclination, but from duty.

To secure one's own happiness is a duty, at least indirectly; for discontent with one's condition under a pressure of many anxieties and amidst unsatisfied wants might easily become a great temptation to *transgression of duty*....

It is in this manner, undoubtedly, that we are to understand those passages of Scripture also in which we are commanded to love our neighbour, even our enemy. For love, as an affection, cannot be commanded, but beneficence for duty's sake; even though we are not impelled to it by any inclination, nay, are even repelled by a natural and unconquerable aversion. This is *practical* love, and not *pathological*, a love which is seated in the will, and not in the propensions of sense, in principles of action and not of tender sympathy; and it is this love alone which can be commanded.

The second proposition[1] is: That an action done from duty derives its moral worth, *not from the purpose* which is to be attained by it, but from the maxim by which it is determined, and therefore does not depend on the realization of the object of the action, but merely on the *principle of volition* by which the action has taken place, without regard to any object of desire. It is clear from what precedes that the purposes which we may have in view in our actions, or their effects regarded as ends and springs of the will, cannot give to actions any unconditional or moral worth. In what then can their worth lie, if it is not to consist in the will and in reference to its expected effect? It cannot lie anywhere but in the *principle of the will* without regard to the ends which can be attained by the action. For the will stands between its *a priori* principle which is formal, and its *a posteriori* spring which is material, as between two roads, and as it must be determined by something, it follows that it must be determined by the formal principle of volition when an action is done from duty, in which case every material principle has been withdrawn from it.

RESPECT FOR THE MORAL LAW

The third proposition, which is a consequence of the two preceding, I would express thus: *Duty is the necessity of acting from respect for the law*. I may have inclination for an object as the effect of my proposed action, but I cannot have respect for it, just for this reason, that it is an effect and not an energy of will. Similarly, I cannot have respect for inclination, whether my own or another's; I can at most if my own, approve it; if another's, sometimes even love it; i.e., look on it as favorable to my own interest. It is only what is connected with my will as a principle, by no means as an effect—what does not subserve my inclination, but overpowers it, or at least in case of choice excludes it from its calculation—in other words, simply the law of itself, which can be an object of respect, and hence a command. Now an action done from duty must wholly exclude the influence of inclination, and with it every object of the will, so that nothing remains which can determine the will except objectively the *law*, and subjectively *pure respect* for this practical law, and consequently the maxim[2] to follow this law even to the thwarting of all my inclinations.

Thus the moral worth of an action does not lie in the effect expected from it, nor in any principle of action which requires to borrow its motive from this expected effect. For all these effects—agreeableness of one's condition, and even the promotion of the happiness of others—could have been also brought about by other causes, so that for this there would have been no need of the will of a rational being; it is in this, however, alone that the supreme and unconditional good can be found. The preeminent good which we call moral can therefore consist in nothing else *than the conception of law* in itself, *which certainly is only possible in a rational being*, in so far as this conception, and not the expected effect, determines the will. This is a good which is already present in the person who acts accordingly, and we have not to wait for it to appear first in the result.[3]

THE CATEGORICAL IMPERATIVE

But what sort of law can that be, the conception of which must determine the will, even without paying any regard to the effect expected from it, in order that this will may be called good absolutely and without qualification? As I have deprived the will of every impulse which could arise to it from obedience to any law, there remains nothing but the universal conformity of its actions to law in general, which alone is to serve the will as a principle, i.e., *I am never to act otherwise than so that I could also will that my maxim should become a universal law*. Here now, it is the simple conformity to law in general, without assuming any particular law applicable to certain actions, that serves the will as its principle, and must so serve it, if duty is not to be a vain delusion and a chimerical notion. The common reason of men in its practical judgments perfectly coincides with this, and always has in view the principle here suggested. Let the question be, for example: May I when in distress make a promise with the intention not to keep it? I readily distinguish here between the two significations which the question may have: Whether it is prudent, or whether it is right, to make a false promise. The former may undoubtedly often be the case. I see clearly indeed that it is not enough to extricate myself from a present difficulty by means of this subterfuge, but it must be well considered whether there may not hereafter spring from this lie much greater inconvenience than that from which I now free myself, and as, with all my supposed cunning, the consequences cannot be so easily foreseen but that credit once lost may be much more injurious to me than any mischief which I seek to avoid at present, it should be considered whether it would not be more prudent to act herein according to a universal maxim, and to make it a habit to promise nothing except with the intention of keeping it.

But it is soon clear to me that such a maxim will still only be based on the fear of consequences. Now it is a wholly different thing to be truthful from duty, and to be so from apprehension of injurious consequences. In the first case, the very notion of the action already implies a law for me; in the second case, I must first look about elsewhere to see what results may be combined with it which would affect myself. For to deviate from the principle of duty is beyond all doubt wicked; but to be unfaithful to my maxim of prudence may often be very advantageous to me, although to abide by it is certainly safer. The shortest way, however, and an unerring one, to discover the answer to this question whether a lying promise is consistent with duty, is to ask myself, Should I be content that my maxim (to extricate myself from difficulty by a false promise) should hold good as a universal law, for myself as well as for others? and should I be able to say to myself, "Every one may make a deceitful promise when he finds himself in a difficulty from which he cannot otherwise extricate himself"? Then I presently become aware that while I can will the lie, I can by no means will that lying should be a universal law. For with such a law there would be no promises at all, since it would be in vain to allege my intention in regard to my future actions to those who would not believe this allegation, or if they over hastily did so would pay me back in my own coin. Hence my maxim, as soon as it should be made a universal law, would necessarily destroy itself.

I do not therefore need any far-reaching penetration to discern what I have to do in order that my will may be morally good. Inexperienced in the course of the world, incapable of being prepared for all its contingencies, I only ask myself: Canst thou also will that thy maxim should be a universal law? If not, then it must be rejected, and that not because of a disadvantage accruing from it to myself or even to others, but because it cannot enter as a principle into a possible universal legislation, and reason extorts from me immediate respect for such legislation. I do not indeed as yet discern on what this respect is based (this the philosopher may inquire), but at least I understand this, that it is an estimation of the worth which far outweighs all worth of what is recommended by inclination, and that the necessity of acting from pure

respect for the practical law is what constitutes duty, to which every other motive must give place, because it is the condition of a will being good in itself, and the worth of such a will is above everything.

Thus then, without quitting the moral knowledge of common human reason, we have arrived at its principle. And although no doubt common men do not conceive it in such an abstract and universal form, yet they always have it really before their eyes, and use it as the standard of their decision....

MORAL AND NONMORAL IMPERATIVES

Everything in nature works according to laws. Rational beings alone have the faculty of acting according *to the conception of laws*, that is according to principles, i.e., have a will. Since the deduction of actions from principles requires *reason*, the will is nothing but practical reason. If reason infallibly determines the will, then the actions of such a being which are recognised as objectively necessary are subjectively necessary also; i.e., the will is a faculty to choose *that only* which reason independent of inclination recognises as practically necessary, i.e., as good. But if reason of itself does not sufficiently determine the will, if the latter is subject also to subjective conditions (particular impulses) which do not always coincide with the objective conditions; in a word, if the will does not in itself completely accord with reason (which is actually the case with men), then the actions which objectively are recognised as necessary are subjectively contingent, and the determination of such a will according to objective laws is obligation, that is to say, the relation of the objective laws to a will that is not thoroughly good, is conceived as the determination of the will of a rational being by principles of reason, but which the will from its nature does not of necessity follow.

The conception of an objective principle, in so far as it is obligatory for a will, is called a command (of reason), and the formula of the command is called an Imperative.

All imperatives are expressed by the word *ought* (or *shall*), and thereby indicate the relation of an objective law of reason to a will, which from its subjective constitution is not necessarily determined by it (an obligation). They say that something would be good to do or to forbear, but they say it to a will which does not always do a thing because it is conceived to be good to do it. That is practically *good*, however, which determines the will by means of the conceptions of reason, and consequently not from subjective causes, but objectively, that is, on principles which are valid for every rational being as such. It is distinguished from the *pleasant*, as that which influences the will only by means of sensation from merely subjective causes, valid only for the sense of this or that one, and not as a principle of reason, which holds for every one.[4]

A perfectly good will would therefore be equally subject to objective laws (viz., of good), but could not be conceived as *obliged* thereby to act lawfully, because of itself from its subjective constitution it can only be determined by the conception of good. Therefore no imperatives hold for the Divine will, or in general for a *holy* will; *ought* is here out of place, because the volition is already of itself necessarily in unison with the law. Therefore imperatives are only formulae to express the relation of objective laws of all volition to the subjective imperfection of the will of this or that rational being, e.g., the human will.

Now all imperatives command either *hypothetically* or *categorically*. The former represent the practical necessity of a possible action as means to something else that is willed (or at least which one might possibly will). The categorical imperative would be that which represented an action as necessary of itself without reference to another end, that is, as objectively necessary.

Since every practical law represents a possible action as good, and on this account, for a subject who is practically determinable by reason as necessary, all imperatives are formulae determining an action which is necessary according to the principle of a will good in some respects. If now the action is good only as a *means to something else*, then the imperative is *hypothetical*; if it is conceived as good in itself and consequently as being necessarily the principle of a will which of itself conforms to reason, then it is *categorical*.

Thus the imperative declares what action possible by me would be good, and presents the practical rule in relation to a will which does not forthwith perform an action simply because it is good, whether because the subject does not always know that it is good, or because, even if it know this, yet its maxims might be opposed to the objective principles of practical reason.

Accordingly the hypothetical imperative only says that the action is good for some purpose, *possible* or *actual*. In the first case it is a *problematical*, in the second an *assertorical* practical principle. The categorical imperative which declares an action to be objectively necessary in itself without reference to any purpose, that is, without any other end, is valid as an *apodictic* (practical) principle.

Whatever is possible only by the power of some rational being may also be conceived as a possible purpose of some will; and therefore the principles of action as regards the means necessary to attain some possible purpose are in fact infinitely numerous. All sciences have a practical part consisting of problems expressing that some end is possible for us, and of imperatives directing how it may be attained. These may, therefore, be called in general imperatives of skill. Here there is no question whether the end is rational and good, but only what one must do in order to attain it. The precepts for the physician to make his patient thoroughly healthy, and for a poisoner to ensure certain death, are of equal value in this respect, that each serves to effect its purpose perfectly. Since in early youth it cannot be known what ends are likely to occur to us in the course of life, parents seek to have their children taught a *great many things*, and provide for their skill in the use of means for all sorts of arbitrary ends, of none of which can they determine whether it may not perhaps hereafter be an object to their pupil, but which it is at all events possible that he might aim at; and this anxiety is so great that they commonly neglect to form and correct their judgment on the value of the things which may be chosen as ends.

There is *one* end, however, which may be assumed to be actually such to all rational beings (so far as imperatives apply to them, viz., as dependent beings), and, therefore, one purpose which they not merely may have, but which we may with certainty assume that they all actually have by a natural necessity, and this is *happiness*. The hypothetical imperative which expresses the practical necessity of an action as means to the advancement of happiness is *assertorical*. We are not to present it as necessary for an uncertain and merely possible purpose, but for a purpose which we may presuppose with certainty and *a priori* in every man, because it belongs to his being. Now skill in the choice of means to his own greatest well-being may be called *prudence*,[5] in the narrowest sense. And thus the imperative which refers to the choice of means to one's own happiness, that is, the precept of prudence, is still always *hypothetical*; the action is not commanded absolutely, but only as means to another purpose.

Finally, there is an imperative which commands a certain conduct immediately, without having as its condition any other purpose to be attained by it. This imperative is *categorical*. It concerns not the matter of the action, or its intended result, but its form and the principle of which it is itself a result; and what is essentially good in it consists in the mental disposition, let the consequence be what it may. This imperative may be called that of *morality*.

There is a marked distinction also between the volitions on these three sorts of principles in the dissimilarity of the obligation of the will. In order to mark this difference more clearly, I think they would be most suitably named in their order if we said they are either *rules* of skill, or *counsels* of prudence, or *commands* (laws) of morality. For it is law only that involves the conception of an unconditional and objective necessity, which is consequently universally valid; and commands are laws which must be obeyed, that is, must be followed, even in opposition to inclination. Counsels, indeed, involve necessity, but one which can only hold under a contingent subjective condition, viz., they depend on whether this or that man reckons this or that as part of his happiness; the categorical imperative, on the contrary, is not limited by any condition, and as being absolutely, although practically, necessary may be quite properly called a command. We might also call

the first kind of imperatives *technical* (belonging to art), the second *pragmatic*[6] (belonging to welfare), the third moral (belonging to free conduct generally, that is, to morals).

Now arises the question, how are all these imperatives possible? This question does not seek to know how we can conceive the accomplishment of the action which the imperative ordains, but merely how we can conceive the obligation of the will which the imperative expresses. No special explanation is needed to show how an imperative of skill is possible. Whoever wills the end wills also (so far as reason decides his conduct) the means in his power which are indispensably necessary thereto....

We shall therefore have to investigate *a priori* the possibility of a categorical imperative, as we have not in this case the advantage of its reality being given in experience, so that (the elucidation of) its possibility should be requisite only for its explanation, not for its establishment. In the meantime it may be discerned beforehand that the categorical imperative alone has the purport of a practical law; all the rest may indeed be called principles of the will but not laws, since whatever is only necessary for the attainment of some arbitrary purpose may be considered as in itself contingent, and we can at any time be free from the precept if we give up the purpose; on the contrary, the unconditional command leaves the will no liberty to choose the opposite, consequently it alone carries with it that necessity which we require in a law....

In this problem we will first inquire whether the mere conception of a categorical imperative may not perhaps supply us also with the formula of it, containing the proposition which alone can be a categorical imperative; for even if we know the tenor of such an absolute command, yet how it is possible will require further special and laborious study; which we postpone to the last section.

When I conceive a hypothetical imperative in general, I do not know before hand what it will contain, until I am given the condition. But when I conceive a categorical imperative I know at once what it contains. For as the imperative contains, besides the law, only the necessity of the maxim[7] conforming to this law, while the law contains no condition restricting it, there remains nothing but the general statement that the maxim of the action should conform to a universal law, and it is this conformity alone that the imperative properly represents as necessary.

There is therefore but one categorical imperative, namely this: *Act only on that maxim whereby thou canst at the same time will that it should become a universal law.*

Now if all imperatives of duty can be deduced from this one imperative as from their principle, then although it should remain undecided whether what is called duty is not merely a vain notion, yet at least we shall be able to show what we understand by it and what this notion means.

APPLYING THE CATEGORICAL IMPERATIVE

Since the universality of the law according to which effects are produced constitutes what is properly called *nature* in the most general sense (as to form), that is the existence of things so far as it is determined by general laws, the imperative of duty may be expressed thus: *Act as if the maxim of thy action were to become by thy will a Universal Law of Nature.*

We will now enumerate a few duties, adopting the usual division of them into duties to ourselves and to others, and into perfect and imperfect duties.[8]

1. A man reduced to despair by a series of misfortunes feels wearied of life, but is still so far in possession of his reason that he can ask himself whether it would not be contrary to his duty to himself to take his own life. Now he inquires whether the maxim of his action could become a universal law of nature. His maxim is: From self-love I adopt it as a principle to shorten my life when its longer duration is likely to bring more evil than satisfaction. It is asked then simply whether this principle of self-love can become a universal law of nature. Now we see at once that a system of nature of which it should be a law to destroy life by the very feeling which is designed to impel to the maintenance of life would contradict itself, and therefore could not exist as a system of nature; hence that maxim cannot possibly exist as a universal law of nature and consequently would be wholly inconsistent with the supreme principle of all duty.

2. Another finds himself forced by necessity to borrow money. He knows that he will not be able to repay it, but sees also that nothing will be lent to him, unless he promises stoutly to repay it in a definite time. He desires to make this promise, but he has still so much conscience as to ask himself: Is it not unlawful and inconsistent with duty to get out of a difficulty in this way? Suppose however that he resolves to do so: then the maxim of his action would be expressed thus: When I think myself in want of money, I will borrow money and promise to repay it, although I know that I never can do so. Now this principle of self-love or of one's own advantage may perhaps be consistent with my whole future welfare; but the question now is, Is it right? I change then the suggestion of self-love into a universal law, and state the question thus: How would it be if my maxim were a universal law? Then I see at once that it could never hold as a universal law of nature, but would necessarily contradict itself. For supposing it to be a universal law that every one when he thinks himself in a difficulty should be able to promise whatever he pleases, with the purpose of not keeping his promise, the promise itself would become impossible, as well as the end that one might have in view in it, since no one would consider that anything was promised to him, and would ridicule all such statements as vain pretenses.

3. A third finds in himself a talent which with the help of some culture might make him a useful man in many respects. But he finds himself in comfortable circumstances, and prefers to indulge in pleasure rather than to take pains in enlarging and improving his happy natural capacities. He asks, however, whether his maxim of neglect of his natural gifts, besides agreeing with his inclination to indulgence, agrees also with what is called duty. He sees then that a system of nature could indeed subsist with such a universal law, though men (like the South Sea islanders) should let their talents rust, and resolve to devote their lives merely to idleness, amusement, and propagation of their species, in a word to enjoyment; but he cannot possibly will that this should be a universal law of nature, or be implanted in us as such by a natural instinct. For, as a rational being, he

necessarily wills that his faculties be developed, since they serve him for all sorts of possible purposes, and have been given him for this.

4. A fourth, who is in prosperity, while he sees that others have to contend with great wretchedness and that he could help them, thinks: What concern is it of mine? Let every one be as happy as heaven pleases or as he can make himself; I will take nothing from him nor even envy him, only I do not wish to contribute anything either to his welfare or to his assistance in distress! Now no doubt if such a mode of thinking were a universal law, the human race might very well subsist, and doubtless even better than in a state in which every one talks of sympathy and good will, or even takes care occasionally to put it into practice, but on the other side, also cheats when he can, betrays the rights of men or otherwise violates them. But although it is possible that a universal law of nature might exist in accordance with that maxim, it is impossible to will that such a principle should have the universal validity of a law of nature. For a will which resolved this would contradict itself, inasmuch as many cases might occur in which one would have need of the love and sympathy of others, and in which by such a law of nature, sprung from his own will, he would deprive himself of all hope of the aid he desires.

These are a few of the many actual duties, or at least what we regard as such, which obviously fall into two classes on the one principle that we have laid down. We must be *able to will* that a maxim of our action should be a universal law. This is the canon of the moral appreciation of the action generally. Some actions are of such a character, that their maxim cannot without contradiction be even *conceived* as a universal law of nature, far from it being possible that we should *will* that it should be so. In others this intrinsic impossibility is not found, but still it is impossible to *will* that their maxim should be raised to the universality of a law of nature, since such a will would contradict itself. It is easily seen that the former violate strict or rigorous (inflexible) duty; the latter only laxer (meritorious) duty. Thus it has been completely shown how all duties depend as regards the nature of the obligation (not the object of the action) on the same principle.

If now we attend to ourselves on occasion of any transgression of duty, we shall find that we in fact do not will that our maxim should be a universal law, for that it is impossible for us; on the contrary we will that the opposite should remain a universal law, only we assume the liberty of making an exception in our own favour or (just for this time only) in favour of our inclination....

The will is conceived as a faculty of determining oneself to action *in accordance with the conception of certain laws*. And such a faculty can be found only in rational beings. Now that which serves the will as the objective ground of its self-determination is the *end*, and if this is assigned by reason alone, it must hold for all rational beings. On the other hand, that which merely contains the ground of possibility of the action of which the effect is the end, this is called the *means*. The subjective ground of the desire is the *spring*, the objective ground of the volition is the *motive*; hence the distinction between subjective ends which rest on springs, and objective ends which depend on motives that hold for every rational being. Practical principles are *formal* when they abstract from all subjective ends, they are *material* when they assume these, and therefore particular springs of action. The ends which a rational being proposes to himself at pleasure as *effects* of his actions (material ends) are all only relative, for it is only their relation to the particular desires of the subject that gives them their worth, which therefore cannot furnish principles universal and necessary for all rational beings and for every volition, that is to say practical laws. Hence all these relative ends can give rise only to hypothetical imperatives.

PERSONS AS ENDS

Supposing, however, that there were something *whose existence has in itself* an absolute worth, something which being *an end in itself*, could be a source of definite laws, then in this and this alone would lie the source of a possible categorical imperative, i.e., a practical law. Now I say, man and generally any rational being exists as an end in himself, *not merely as a means* to be arbitrarily used by this or that will, but in all his actions, whether they concern himself or other rational beings, must always be regarded at the same time as an end. All objects of the inclinations have only a conditional worth, for if the inclinations and the wants founded on them did not exist, then their object would be without value. But the inclinations themselves being sources of want, are so far from having an absolute worth for which they should be desired, that on the contrary it must be the universal wish of every rational being to be wholly free from them. Thus the worth of any object which *is to be acquired* by our action is always conditional. Beings whose existence depends not on our will but on nature's, have nevertheless, if they are irrational beings, only a relative value as means, and are therefore called *things*; rational beings on the contrary, are called *persons*, because their very nature points them out as ends in themselves, that is as something which must not be used merely as means, and so far therefore restricts freedom of action (and is an object of respect). These, therefore, are not merely subjective ends whose existence has a worth for us as an effect of our action, but *objective ends*, that is things whose existence is an end in itself; an end moreover for which no other can be substituted, which they should subserve *merely* as means, for otherwise nothing whatever would possess *absolute worth*; but if all worth were conditioned and therefore contingent, then there would be no supreme practical principle of reason whatever.

If then there is a supreme practical principle or, in respect of the human will, a categorical imperative, it must be one which, drawn from the conception of that which is necessarily an end for every one because it is *an end in itself*, constitutes an objective principle of will, and can therefore serve as a universal practical law. The foundation of this principle is: *rational nature exists as an end in itself*. Man necessarily conceives his own existence as being so; so far then, this is a *subjective* principle of human actions. But every other rational being regards its existence similarly, just on the same rational principle that holds for me:[9] so that it is at the same time an objective principle, from which as a supreme practical law all laws of the will must be capable of being

deduced. Accordingly the practical imperative will be as follows: *So act as to treat humanity, whether in thine own person or in that of any other, in every case as an end withal, never as a means only....*

We will now inquire whether this can be practically carried out.

To abide by the previous examples:

First, under the head of necessary duty to oneself: He who contemplates suicide should ask himself whether his action can be consistent with the idea of humanity *as an end in itself*. If he destroys himself in order to escape from painful circumstances, he uses a person merely as a *means* to maintain a tolerable condition up to the end of life. But a man is not a thing, that is to say, something which can be used merely as means, but must in all his actions be always considered as an end in himself. I cannot, therefore, dispose in any way of a man in my own person so as to mutilate him, to damage or kill him. (It belongs to ethics proper to define this principle more precisely, so as to avoid all misunderstanding, for example, as to the amputation of the limbs in order to preserve myself; as to exposing my life to danger with a view to preserve it, etc. This question is therefore omitted here.)

Secondly, as regards necessary duties, or those of strict obligation, towards others: He who is thinking of making a lying promise to others will see at once that he would be using another *man merely as a means*, without the latter containing at the same time the end in himself. For he whom I propose by such a promise to use for my own purposes cannot possibly assent to my mode of acting towards him, and therefore cannot himself contain the end of this action. This violation of the principle of humanity in other men is more obvious if we take in examples of attacks on the freedom and property of others. For then it is clear that he who transgresses the rights of men intends to use the person of others merely as means, without considering that as rational beings they ought always to be esteemed also as ends, that is, as beings who must be capable of containing in themselves the end of the very same action.[10]

Thirdly, as regards contingent (meritorious) duties to oneself: It is not enough that the action does not violate humanity in our own person as an end in itself, it must also *harmonize with it*.... Now there are in humanity capacities of greater perfection which belong to the end that nature has in view in regard to humanity in ourselves as the subject; to neglect these might perhaps be consistent with the *maintenance* of humanity as an end in itself, but not with the advancement of this end.

Fourthly, as regards meritorious duties towards others: The natural end which all men have is their own happiness. Now humanity might indeed subsist although no one should contribute anything to the happiness of others, provided he did not intentionally withdraw anything from it; but after all, this would only harmonize negatively, not positively, with *humanity as an end in itself*, if everyone does not also endeavor, as far as in him lies, to forward the ends of others. For the ends of any subject which is an end in himself ought as far as possible to be my ends also, if that conception is to have its full effect with me.

NOTES

1. The first proposition was that to have moral worth an action must be done from duty.
2. A *maxim* is the subjective principle of volition. The objective principle (i.e., that which would also serve subjectively as a practical principle to all rational beings if reason had full power over the faculty of desire) is the practical *law*.
3. It might here be objected to me that I take refuge behind the word *respect* in an obscure feeling instead of giving a distinct solution of the question by a concept of the reason. But although respect is a feeling, it is not a feeling *received* through influence, but is *self-wrought* by a rational concept, and, therefore, is specially distinct from all feelings of the former kind, which may be referred either to inclination or fear. What I recognise immediately as a law for me, I recognise with respect. This merely signifies the consciousness that my will is *subordinate* to a law, without the intervention of other influences on my sense. The immediate determination of the will by the law, and the consciousness of this is called *respect*, so that this is regarded as an *effect* of

the law on the subject, and not as the *cause* of it. Respect is properly the conception of a work which thwarts my self-love. Accordingly it is something which is considered neither as an object of inclination nor of fear, although it has something analogous to both. The *object* of respect is the *law* only, and that, the law which we impose on *ourselves*, and yet recognise as necessary in itself. As a law, we are subjected to it without consulting self-love; as imposed by us on ourselves, it is a result of our will. In the former respect it has an analogy to fear, in the latter to inclination. Respect for a person is properly only respect for the law (of honesty, & c.), of which he gives us an example....

4. The dependence of the desires on sensations is called inclination, and this accordingly always indicates a *want*. The dependence of a contingently determinable will on principles of reason is called an *interest*. This, therefore, is found only in the case of a dependent will which does not always of itself conform to reason; in the Divine will we cannot conceive any interest. But the human will can also *take an interest* in a thing without therefore acting *from interest*. The former signifies the *practical* interest in the action, the latter the *pathological* in the object of the action. The former indicates only dependence of the will on principles of reason in themselves; the second, dependence on principles of reason for the sake of inclination, reason supplying only the practical rules how the requirement of the inclination may be satisfied. In the first case the action interests me; in the second the object of the action (because it is pleasant to me). We have seen in the first section that in an action done from duty we must look not to the interest in the object, but only to that in the action itself, and in its rational principle (viz., the law).
5. The word *prudence* is taken in two senses: in the one it may bear the name of knowledge of the world, in the other that of private prudence. The former is a man's ability to influence others so as to use them for his own purposes. The latter is the sagacity to combine all these purposes for his own lasting benefit. This latter is properly that to which the value even of the former is reduced, and when a man is prudent in the former sense, but not in

the latter, we might better say of him that he is clever and cunning, but, on the whole, imprudent.

6. It seems to me that the proper signification of the word *pragmatic* may be most accurately defined in this way. For *sanctions* are called pragmatic which flow properly, not from the law of the states as necessary enactments, but from *precaution* for the general welfare. A history is composed pragmatically when it teaches prudence, that is, instructs the world how it can provide for its interests better, or at least as well as the men of former time.

7. A maxim is a subjective principle of action ... the principle on which the subject acts; but the law is the objective principle valid for every rational being, and is the principle on which it *ought to act* that is an imperative.

8. It must be noted here that I reserve the division of duties for a *future metaphysic of morals*; so that I give it here only as an arbitrary one (in order to arrange my examples). For the rest, I understand by a perfect duty, one that admits no exception in favour of inclination, and then I have not merely external but also internal perfect duties.

9. This proposition is here stated as a postulate. The ground of it will be found in the concluding section.

10. Let it not be thought that the common: *quod tibi non vis fieri,* etc., could serve here as the rule or principle. For it is only a deduction from the former, though with several limitations; it cannot be a universal law, for it does not contain the principle of duties to oneself, nor of the duties of benevolence to others (for many a one would gladly consent that others should not benefit him, provided only that he might be excused from showing benevolence to them), nor finally that of duties of strict obligation to one another, for on this principle the criminal might argue against the judge who punishes him, and so on.

REVIEW EXERCISES

1. Explain why we might not want to locate an action's moral worth in its consequences.
2. When Kant refers to "a good will" or "good intention," does he mean wishing others well? Explain.
3. What does Kant mean by "acting out of duty?" How does the shopkeeper exemplify this?
4. What is the basic difference between a categorical and a hypothetical imperative? In the following examples, which are hypothetical and which are categorical imperatives? Explain your answers.
   a. If you want others to be honest with you, then you ought to be honest with them.
   b. Whether or not you want to pay your share, you ought to do so.
   c. Because everyone wants to be happy, we ought to consider everyone's interests equally.
   d. I ought not to cheat on this test if I do not want to get caught.
5. How does the character of moral obligation lead to Kant's basic moral principle, the categorical imperative?
6. Explain Kant's use of the first form of the categorical imperative to argue that it is wrong to make a false promise. (Make sure that you do not appeal to the bad consequences as the basis of judging it wrong.)
7. According to the second form of Kant's categorical imperative, would it be morally permissible for me to agree to be someone's slave? Explain.
8. What is the practical difference between a perfect and an imperfect duty?

MindTap For more chapter resources and activities, go to MindTap.

7

Natural Law and Human Rights

Learning Outcomes

After reading this chapter, you should be able to:

- Describe the idea of natural law and how it relates to the idea of human rights.
- Explain how natural law theory is related to the law of peoples and norms of international law.
- Identify the contributions to natural law theory made by key thinkers such as Cicero, Thomas Aquinas, and John Locke.
- Explain the importance of teleology for thinking about natural law.

- Clarify how natural law arguments are grounded in claims about the essence of human nature.
- Provide an overview of the natural law argument against relativism.
- Defend your own thesis with regard to the value of natural law theory and the idea of human rights.

MindTap® For more chapter resources and activities, go to MindTap.

In 1776, Thomas Jefferson wrote in the Declaration of Independence, "We hold these truths to be self-evident, that all men are created equal, that they are endowed by their Creator with certain inalienable rights, that among these are life, liberty and the pursuit of happiness."[1] Jefferson had read the work of English philosopher John Locke, who had written in his *Second Treatise on Government* that all human beings were of the same species, born with the same basic capacities.[2] Locke argues that because all humans have the same basic nature, they should be treated equally. This argument should sound familiar from our previous discussion of Kant and deontology. Kant emphasizes respect for human persons as ends in themselves. Locke and Jefferson fill in this abstract idea with a list of natural human rights, including the right to life and liberty. Locke also thought that there was a natural right to own property, while Jefferson thought that there was a right to the pursuit of happiness. These natural rights are supposed to be grounded in self-evident truth. This self-evidence is found in "the Laws of Nature and Nature's God," as the first sentence of the Declaration of Independence puts it.

Discussions of human rights remain important today. We saw in Chapter 2 that the United Nations issued a Universal Declaration of Human Rights, which began by asserting "the inherent dignity and . . . the equal and inalienable rights of all members of the human family." These rights are said to be shared by all human beings,

Detainees in a holding area at Camp X-Ray at Guantanamo Bay, Cuba.

regardless of cultural, religious, or political differences. But in reality, respecting and upholding human rights is not always a simple task for societies and governments, including that of the United States.

For example, following the 2001 terrorist attacks on the World Trade Center and the Pentagon, and with the U.S. invasion of Afghanistan, questions arose about the legal status and treatment of individuals captured by the U.S. forces. In our discussion of utilitarianism in Chapter 5, we mentioned that the United States government endorsed the use of torture (referred to as "enhanced interrogation techniques") for some of these individuals. This would seem to be a violation of Article 5 of the UN Declaration of Human Rights, which states, "No one shall be subjected to torture or to cruel, inhuman or degrading treatment or punishment."

Furthermore, since 2004, many of these suspected terrorists have been transferred to a prison at Guantanamo Bay in Cuba, a U.S. naval base on the southeastern side of the island. (The United States still holds a lease to this land because of the 1903 Cuban–American Treaty.) It was thought that these individuals were members, supporters, or sympathizers of al Qaeda or the Taliban. It was said that these prisoners were not part of any army of any state and thus not prisoners of war but, rather, "enemy combatants" not covered by any of the protections of the Geneva Conventions. These individuals were not given the protections of U.S. laws. And they were denied such basic human rights as knowing the charges against them and being allowed to defend themselves in court. This treatment would seem to violate Article 6 of the UN Declaration, which states, "Everyone has the right to recognition everywhere as a person before the law."

In recent years—and after intense legal and humanitarian scrutiny of Guantanamo's detainment policies—many hundreds of the detainees have been sent back to their countries of origin. Some were finally allowed lawyers, although not of their own choosing. U.S. courts have also ruled that the detainees must be given trials in U.S. military, rather than civilian, courts. As of mid-2016, 91 prisoners still remained in the Guantanamo detention facility, a number have died in custody.[3] Some may be brought to trial and some held indefinitely, either there or in maximum security prisons in the United States. Some of these prisoners went on a hunger strike in 2013 to protest their treatment. Prison officials force-fed them—by inserting feeding tubes up their noses. Critics argued that it was a violation of international law and a human rights violation to force-feed prisoners in this way.[4]

In this and many other contemporary situations, we may ask what is meant by "human rights"—and does every person possess such rights, even enemy combatants? This is one of the fundamental questions addressed in this chapter.

A related question is how the idea of rights applies in situations in which there is no legal or political system to enforce them. Is there a system of "natural law" that is more fundamental than the laws of any particular legal or political system? While the idea of natural law is an ancient one, the concept has been an object of renewed interest, especially now that we are aware that states can

Child labor seems to be a human rights violation.

commit crimes against their own people, including war crimes and genocide. If there is something that we might call natural law, we would suppose that it would at least include a law against genocide.

The Nuremberg trials were trials of Nazi war criminals held in Nuremberg, Germany, from 1945 to 1949. There were thirteen trials in all. In the first trial, Nazi leaders were found guilty of violating international law by starting an aggressive war. Nine of them, including Hermann Goering and Rudolf Hess, were sentenced to death. In other trials, defendants were accused of committing atrocities against civilians. Nazi doctors who had conducted medical experiments on those imprisoned in the death camps were among those tried. Their experiments maimed and killed many people, all of whom were unwilling subjects. For example, experiments for the German air force were conducted to determine

how fast people would die in very thin air. Other experiments tested the effects of freezing water on the human body. The defense contended that the military personnel, judges, and doctors were only following orders from their superiors in the Nazi regime. However, the prosecution argued successfully that even if the experimentation did not violate the defendants' own laws, they were still "crimes against humanity." The idea was that a law more basic than civil laws exists—a moral law—and these doctors and others should have known what this basic moral law required. (We discuss war crimes further in Chapter 19.)

The idea that the basic moral law can be known by human reason is a central tenet of natural law theory. Some treatments of human rights also use human nature as a basis. According to this view, human rights are those things that we can validly claim because they are essential for human beings to function well. These natural human rights are the same for all human beings, since, on this theory, all human beings share a common essence or human nature.

NATURAL LAW THEORY

The **natural law theory** is a theory of ethics that holds that there are moral laws found in nature and discernable by the use of reason. The way the term is used in discussions of ethics should not be confused with those other "laws of nature" that are the generalizations of natural science. The laws of natural science are *descriptive* laws. They describe how nature behaves. For example, gases expand with their containers and when heat is applied. Boyle's law about the behavior of gases does not tell gases how they *ought* to behave. In fact, if gases were found to behave differently from what we had so far observed, then the laws would be changed to match this new information. Simply put, scientific laws are descriptive generalizations of fact.

Moral laws, on the other hand, are *prescriptive* laws. They tell us how we *ought* to behave. The natural law is the moral law written into nature itself. What we ought to do, according to this theory, is determined by considering certain aspects of nature.

In particular, we ought to examine our nature as human beings to see what is essential for us to function well as members of our species. We look to certain aspects of our nature to know what is good and what we ought to do.

Civil law is also prescriptive. As an expression of the moral law, however, natural law is supposed to be more basic or higher than the laws of any particular society. Although laws of particular societies vary and change over time, the natural law is supposed to be universal and stable. In *Antigone*, an ancient Greek tragedy by Sophocles, the protagonist disobeys the king and buries her brother's body—thereby breaking the law of her monarchical society. She does so because she believes that she must follow a higher law, which requires that her brother be buried. In the play, Antigone loses her life for obeying this higher law. In the Nuremberg trials, prosecutors also argued that there was a higher law that all humans should recognize—one that takes precedence over national laws and customs.

People today sometimes appeal to this moral law in order to argue which civil laws ought to be instituted or changed. This is the basic idea behind the theory of civil disobedience as outlined and practiced by Henry David Thoreau, Mohandas K. Gandhi, and Martin Luther King Jr. (as discussed in Chapter 2). When Thoreau was imprisoned for not paying taxes that he thought were used for an unjust war, he defended his actions by appealing to a system of rights and wrongs that is superior to the civil law. In his famous essay, "Civil Disobedience," he writes, "Must the citizen ever for a moment, or in the least degree, resign his conscience to the legislator? Why has every man a conscience, then? I think that we should be men first, and subjects afterward. It is not desirable to cultivate a respect for the law, so much as for the right."[5]

HISTORICAL ORIGINS

The tradition of natural law ethics is a long one. Aristotle was among the first to develop a complex ethical philosophy based on the view that certain actions are right or wrong because they are suited to or go against human nature (we discuss Aristotle in

more detail in Chapter 8). Aristotle had a profound influence on the medieval Christian philosopher and Dominican friar Thomas Aquinas (1224–1274). Aquinas is often credited as a primary source for natural law ethics.

The natural law tradition has deep roots, however, in ideas found in a variety of other ancient Greek thinkers, especially the Stoics, who held that we have a duty to obey the basic laws of nature. (The Stoics were discussed in Chapter 6.) The key moral principle for the Stoics was to "follow nature." This means that nature has a goal or *telos* for human beings, which we ought to pursue. They also believed that there are laws to which all people are subject, no matter what their local customs or conventions. Early Roman jurists believed that a common element existed in the codes of various peoples: a *jus gentium*, or "law of peoples."

One of the most important of the Roman authors associated with the natural law tradition is Cicero. In his *Republic*, Cicero explained the natural law as follows:

> True law is right reason conformable to nature, universal, unchangeable, eternal, whose commands urge us to duty, and whose prohibitions restrain us from evil. Whether it enjoins or forbids, the good respect its injunctions, and the wicked treat them with indifference. This law cannot be contradicted by any other law, and is not liable either to derogation or abrogation. Neither the senate nor the people can give us any dispensation for not obeying this universal law of justice. It needs no other expositor and interpreter than our own conscience. It is not one thing at Rome, and another at Athens; one thing today, and another tomorrow; but in all times and nations this universal law must forever reign, eternal and imperishable. It is the sovereign master and emperor of all beings. God himself is its author, its promulgator, its enforcer. And he who does not obey it flies from himself, and does violence to the very nature of man. And by so doing he will endure the severest penalties even if he avoid the other evils which are usually accounted punishments.[6]

Cicero's point is that the natural law transcends time and place: it is eternal and imperishable, the same today and tomorrow, the same in Rome as in

Athens. Moreover, Cicero maintains that the natural law comes from God himself. It is not surprising that Cicero and his ideas had a profound impact, for example, on Thomas Jefferson and the authors of the founding documents of the United States.

During the medieval period, Greek and Roman philosophy died out in Western Europe, although these ideas were preserved in the East, especially in the work of Islamic scholars. Medieval Islamic and Christian traditions tended to think that morality was primarily derived from scripture. Greek and Roman ideas eventually reentered European culture and were distilled and connected to Christianity by Aquinas. Aquinas's goal was to find a way to synthesize faith and reason, to connect the insights of reason with the commands of faith. While the natural law tradition is often connected to religion, it is not merely a version of divine command theory, since it holds that reason can discover the moral law independent of scripture.

Aquinas was a theologian who held that the natural law is part of the divine law or plan for the universe. The record of much of what he taught can be found in his work the *Summa Theologica* (an excerpt is provided in the reading selection at the end of this chapter).[7] Aquinas maintains that "the natural law shares in the eternal law." He recognizes that this may make it seem that there is no need for human law. But Aquinas argues that particular human laws are a reflection or incomplete manifestation of the divine law. Aquinas indicated his debt to Cicero by quoting him several times in his discussions of law and justice. For example, "Human law originally sprang from nature. Then things became customs because of their rational benefit. Then fear and reverence for law validated things that both sprang from nature and were approved by custom."[8] The point here is that human laws reflect both the natural law and the developed expression of these laws in the customs and positive laws made by humans.

Echoing the views of Aristotle, Aquinas held that the moral good consists in following the innate tendencies of our nature. We are biological beings. Because we tend by nature to grow and mature,

A portrait of Thomas Aquinas (1225–1274).

we ought to preserve our being and our health by avoiding undue risks and doing what will make us healthy. Furthermore, as sentient animals, we can know our world through the physical senses. We ought to use our senses of touch, taste, smell, hearing, and sight; we ought to develop and make use of these senses to appreciate those aspects of existence that they reveal to us. We ought not to do things that injure these senses. Like many nonhuman animals, we reproduce our kind through intercourse. This is what nature means for us to do, according to this version of natural law theory. (See further discussion of this issue in Chapter 12.)

Unique to persons are the specific capacities of knowing and choosing freely. Thus, we ought to treat ourselves and others as beings that are capable of understanding and free choice. Those things that help us pursue the truth, such as education and freedom of public expression, are good. Those things that hinder pursuit of the truth are bad. Deceit and lack of access to the sources of knowledge are morally objectionable simply because they prevent us from fulfilling our innate natural drive or orientation to know the way things are.[9] Moreover, whatever enhances our ability to choose freely is good. A certain amount of self-discipline, options from which to choose, and reflection on what we ought to choose are among the things that enhance freedom. To coerce people and to limit their possibilities of choosing freely are examples of what is inherently bad or wrong.

Finally, natural law theory argues that we ought to find ways to live well together, for this is a theory that emphasizes the interconnectedness of human beings in which no man—or woman—is an island. We are social creatures by nature. Thus, the essence of natural law theory is that we ought to further the inherent ends of human nature and not do what frustrates human fulfillment or flourishing. These ideas can be developed into a concern for social justice, including care for the poor and disabled, the right to decent work and living conditions, and even the right to health care.

> MindTap° For more chapter resources and activities, go to MindTap.

After Aquinas and throughout the modern period of European history, the idea of natural law and natural right became more widespread and more secular. One of the important authors who developed ideas about the natural law was Hugo Grotius, a Dutch jurist who was working during the early part of the seventeenth century. Grotius explained the development of natural law from out of human nature as follows:

> For the mother of right, that is, of natural law, is human nature; for this would lead us to desire mutual society, even if it were not required for the supply of other wants; and the mother of civil laws, is obligation by mutual compact; and since mutual compact derives its force from natural law, nature may be said to be the grandmother of civil laws.[10]

Grotius is known as one of the founders of international law. His ideas about international law had a practical application, for example, in his discussion of the rules of war. Grotius maintained that there was a common law among nations, which was valid even in times of war. We will return to this topic in Chapter 19, where we will discuss the *just war theory*. Note that the idea of natural law may give us grounds to criticize the treatment of the prisoners at Guantanamo Bay, the case with which we began this chapter. If we think that all human beings have basic rights and that these rights obtain even in time of war, then perhaps we ought to provide these rights to the prisoners at Guantanamo.

EVALUATING NATURAL LAW THEORY

Natural law theory has many appealing characteristics. Among them are its belief in the objectivity of moral values and the notion of the good as human flourishing. Various criticisms of the theory have also been advanced, including the following:

First, according to natural law theory, we are to determine what we ought to do by deciphering the moral law as it is written into nature—specifically, human nature. One problem that natural law theory must address concerns our ability to read nature. The moral law is supposedly knowable by human reason. However, throughout the history of philosophy, various thinkers have read nature differently. Aristotle, for example, thought that slavery could be justified in that it was in accord with nature.[11] Natural law arguments can also be used in support of gender inequality. Is it natural, for example, for fathers to rule within the family or men to rule over women? Today, people might argue against slavery and gender inequality on natural law grounds that emphasize basic human equality. Defenders of the natural law theory may argue that those who defend slavery or gender oppression on a natural law basis are simply wrong in their interpretation of the natural law. Such a defense of natural law would maintain that slavery, racism, and sexism are wrong based on natural equality among the races and genders.

A further problem is that traditional natural law theory has picked out highly positive traits of human nature: the desire to know the truth, to choose the good, and to develop as healthy mature beings. Not all views of the essential characteristics of human nature have been so positive, however. Some philosophers have depicted human nature as deceitful, evil, and uncontrolled. This is why Hobbes argued that we need a strong government. Without it, he wrote, life in a state of nature would be "nasty, brutish, and short."[12] (We discussed Hobbes in Chapter 4.) A further problem is that if nature is taken in the broader sense—meaning *all* of nature—and if a natural law as a moral law were based on this, then the general approach might even endorse such theories as **social Darwinism**. This view holds that because the most fit organisms in nature are the ones that survive, so also the most fit should endure in human society and the weaker ought to perish. When combined with a belief in capitalism, social Darwinism justified, for example, arguments that it was only right and according to nature that wealthy industrialists at the end of the nineteenth century were disproportionally rich and powerful. It also implied that the poor were impoverished by the designs of nature, and thus, we ought not interfere with this situation.

Another question for natural law theory is the following: Can the way things are by nature provide the basis for knowing how they *ought* to be? On the face of it, this may not seem right. Just because something exists in a certain way does not necessarily mean that it is good. Floods, famine, and disease all exist, but that does not make them good. As we saw in Chapter 1, in our discussion of the naturalistic fallacy and Hume's law, it is not easy to derive an *ought* from an *is*. Evaluations cannot simply be derived from factual matters. Other moral philosophers have agreed. Henry Veatch, for example, worried that natural law and the related idea of natural rights were undermined by this problem: "the entire doctrine of natural rights and natural law would appear to rest on nothing less than a patent logical fallacy."[13]

In response to this objection, defenders of natural law might claim that what they are really focused on is a set of basic or intrinsic goods. Or they may deny, as Ralph McInerny has, that there is anything fallacious about deriving an ought from an is: "The concern not to infer value from fact,

Ought from Is, is a symptom of false fastidiousness. Worse, it is to take at face value one of the most fundamental errors of modern moral thought."[14] According to McInerny, the value of things is connected to the purpose and function of those things. McInerny maintains that natural law makes best sense in a theistic framework, where the purpose of things is embedded in these things by God. Other authors have clarified that natural law is connected to a theory of basic goods that are known self-evidently: "they cannot be verified by experience or deduced from any more basic truths through a middle term. They are self-evident."[15] This idea of self-evident moral principles and basic goods fits with Jefferson's language in the Declaration: "We hold these truths to be self-evident. . . ."

A standard criticism of this idea would question whether any truths are self-evident in this way. And returning to Hume's problem of deriving an ought from an is, we can still ask (as G. E. Moore did) how we make the leap from fact to value. When we know something to be a fact, that things exist in a certain way, it still remains an open question whether this fact is good. One response for the natural law theory is to state that nature is **teleological**, that it has a certain directedness. The Thomistic approach grounds this directedness in God. But it is possible to develop this idea from a nontheistic point of view. In Aristotle's terms, we could say that things move or develop toward some natural goal, their final purpose. If we were going to defend natural law theory, we would have to be able to explain human nature in terms of its innate potentialities and the goals of human development. Yet from the time of the scientific revolution of the seventeenth century, such final purposes have become suspect. One could not always observe nature's directedness, and it came to be associated with discredited notions of nonobservable spirits directing things from within. If natural law theory does depend on there being purposes in nature, it must be able to explain where these purposes come from and how we can know what they are.

Consider one possible explanation of the source of whatever purposes there might be in nature.

Christian philosophers have long maintained that nature manifests God's plan for the universe. For Aristotle, however, the universe is eternal; it always existed and was not created by God. His concept of God was that of a most perfect being toward which the universe is in some way directed. According to Aristotle, there is an order in nature, but it did not come from the mind of God. For Christian philosophers such as Augustine and Thomas Aquinas, however, nature has the order it does is because the universe was created after a divine plan. Nature not only is intelligible but also exists for a purpose that was built into it. Some natural law theorists follow Aquinas on this, whereas others either follow Aristotle or abstain from judgments about the source of the order in nature. But can we conceive of an order in nature without a divine orderer? This depends on what we mean by order in nature. If it is taken in the sense of a plan, then this implies that it has an author. However, natural beings may simply develop in certain ways as a result of chance or evolutionary adaptation, while, in reality, there is no plan.

Evolutionary theory thus presents a challenge to natural law theory. If the way that things have come to be is the result of many chance variations, then there are no purposes, plans, or preordained functions in nature. The biological and anthropological sciences tend to undermine the idea that there is a universal human nature, since individuals and species vary and change over time. If we wanted to defend natural law theory in the context of contemporary biology, we would have to find natural bases and norms for behavior. One such Darwinian version of natural law has been defended by Larry Arnhart, who argues that human beings have a "natural moral sense" and that "modern Darwinian biology supports this understanding of the ethical and social nature of human beings by showing how it could have arisen by natural selection through evolutionary history."[16]

NATURAL RIGHTS

As we saw at the beginning of this chapter, the idea that moral requirements may be grounded in human nature is central to the theory of natural rights. John Locke provided a theory of natural rights that Thomas Jefferson drew on in the Declaration of Independence. According to Locke, certain things are essential for us as persons. Among these are life itself, as well as liberty and the ability to pursue those things that bring happiness. These are said to be rights not because they are granted by some state, but because of the fact that they are important for us as human beings or persons. They are thus moral rights first, though they may need to be enforced by societal institutions and laws.

A central feature of the Declaration's statement of our inalienable rights is the idea that these rights are self-evidently true. These rights are supposed to be known by the light of reason with as much clarity as the truths of mathematics. One apparent problem for natural rights claims is that not everyone agrees about rights. We've already mentioned the problems of slavery and the unequal treatment of women. For centuries of U.S. history, it was not self-evidently true to a majority of citizens that Africans and women were entitled to equal rights. In response to this problem, defenders of natural rights will argue that experience and education are required to show us what is true. No one is born knowing the truths of mathematics or ethics—and people can be mistaken about these truths. We learn these things over time. Indeed, cultures and traditions develop (even the traditions of mathematics). John Finnis, for example, explains self-evident truth as follows: "The important thing about a self-evident proposition is that people (with the relevant experience and understanding of terms) *assent* to it without needing the proof of argument."[17] Thus, in this view, Jefferson might mean that people with relevant experience and understanding will agree that we have the inalienable rights he enumerates in the Declaration (although such agreement continues to be a problem in our diverse, pluralistic culture).

Throughout the eighteenth century, political philosophers often referred to the laws of nature in discussions of natural rights. For example, Voltaire wrote that morality has a universal source. It is the "natural law...which nature teaches all men" what they should do.[18] The Declaration of Independence was influenced by the writings of jurists and philosophers who believed that a moral law is built into nature. Thus, in the first section, it asserts that the colonists were called on "to assume among the powers of the earth, the separate and equal station, to which the Laws of Nature and of Nature's God entitle them."[19]

Today, various international codes of human rights, such as the United Nations' Universal Declaration of Human Rights and the Geneva Conventions' principles for the conduct of war, contain elements of a natural rights tradition. These attempt to specify rights that all people have simply by virtue of their being human, regardless of their country of origin, race, or religion.

EVALUATING NATURAL RIGHTS THEORY

A famous criticism of natural rights comes from the utilitarian philosopher Jeremy Bentham, "Natural rights is simple nonsense: natural and imprescriptible rights, rhetorical nonsense—nonsense upon stilts."[20] Bentham thought that there were no rights outside of the legal and political system. Bentham worried that the idea of natural rights was a perversion of language—since there were no "rights" in nature. Bentham also worried that when people made declarations about the "rights of man" (as happened during the French Revolution), this only invited destructive revolutions and anarchy. While Locke, Jefferson, and Hobbes used the idea of natural rights to argue that states were founded on an underlying social contract (which we also discussed in Chapter 4), Bentham thought that the social contract was also a fiction. According to Bentham, governments develop through a long history involving habit and force. And Bentham thought that the ethical goal was to make sure that the legal system pointed in the direction of general happiness—not to postulate rights, which could lead to revolution against the legal system.

One problem for a natural rights theory is that not everyone agrees on what human nature requires or

which natural rights are central. In the UN's 1948 Universal Declaration of Human Rights, the list of rights includes welfare rights and rights to food, clothing, shelter, and basic security. Just what kinds of things can we validly claim as human rights? Freedom of speech? Freedom of assembly? Housing? Clean air? Friends? Work? Income? Many of these are listed in a range of treaties and other documents that nations have adopted. However, an account of human rights requires more than lists. A rationale for what constitutes a human right is necessary in order to determine which rights should be protected or promoted. This is also something that a natural rights theory should help provide. Some contemporary philosophers argue that the basic rights that society ought to protect are not welfare rights, such as rights to food, clothing, and shelter, but only liberty rights, such as the right not to be interfered with in our daily lives.[21] (See further discussion of negative and positive rights in the section on socialism in Chapter 14.) How are such differences to be settled?

As a further example of the problem of differences of opinion about the content of rights claims, consider the issue of equality for women (which we discuss further in Chapter 9). Does the concept of rights apply equally to men and to women? Women have historically not been given equal rights with men. In the United States, women were not all granted the right to vote until 1920, as some argued that they were by nature not fully rational or that they were closer in nature to animals than men. The women of Kuwait only gained the right to vote in 2005. Are our rights really self-evident, if people continue to disagree about them?

A theory of human rights should be connected to a theory of human nature, as discussed previously in relation to natural law. A significant problem arises, however, in terms of human beings who are not "natural" or "normal," and with regard to nonhuman animals. Do cognitively disabled humans or human fetuses have the same rights as adult human beings? Do nonhuman animals—especially those with advanced cognitive capacities, such as chimpanzees—have rights? These questions will return in our discussions of abortion and animal welfare in Chapters 11 and 17. But it is important to note here that considerations of rights raise complex questions about what sorts of creatures possess these rights. An account of rights that focuses on human nature will have to be careful to consider how human nature is expressed in fetuses and in disabled people. And if the concept of rights is to be restricted only to human beings, the defender of the concept of rights will have to explain the importance of the distinction between humans and our nonhuman relatives.

Finally, we should note that not all discussions of human rights are focused on human nature. John Stuart Mill argued that rights were related to general utility. "To have a right, then, is, I conceive, to have something which society ought to defend me in the possession of. If the objector goes on to ask, why it ought? I can give him no other reason than general utility."[22] For Mill, rights language provides a strong assertion of those values that promote the greatest happiness for the greatest number. Another example is found in the writings of Walter Lippmann, one of the most influential political commentators of the twentieth century, who held a rather utilitarian view that we ought to agree that there are certain rights because these provide the basis for a democratic society, and it is precisely such a society that works best. It is not that we can prove that such rights as freedom of speech or assembly exist; we simply accept them for pragmatic reasons because they provide the basis for democracy.[23]

The notion of rights can be and has been discussed in many different contexts. Among those treated in this book are issues of animal rights (Chapter 17), economic rights (Chapter 14), fetal rights (Chapter 11), women's rights (Chapter 9), equal rights and discrimination (Chapter 13), and war crimes and universal human rights (Chapter 19).

IS THERE A HUMAN NATURE?

Natural law and the idea of natural human rights presume that there is a common core to the human experience—that we are endowed with basic capacities, that we share common purposes, and that we value and enjoy a common set of intrinsic goods. In short, natural law and human rights rest upon an objective account of human nature. One way of putting this is to say that human nature is discovered by us through the use of reason—and that human nature is not created by us or constructed by society. Not all philosophers believe, however, that there is such a thing as human nature. In the twentieth century, existentialists such as Jean-Paul Sartre argued that there was no essential human nature. As Sartre puts it, "existence precedes essence," which means that through the course of our lives we create our own nature or essence. More recent authors—who are often described as "postmodernists"—have made this argument in even stronger terms. Richard Rorty put the criticism of human nature this way:

> There is nothing deep inside each of us, no common human nature, no built-in human solidarity, to use as a moral reference point. There is nothing to people except what has been socialized into them…. Simply by being human we do not have a common bond. For all we share with all other humans is the same thing we share with all other animals—the ability to feel pain.[24]

This skepticism about human nature might point toward a broader conception of what matters morally—toward solidarity with animals and toward inclusion of disabled humans. But from the standpoint of natural law, such a denial of a common human nature will look like the worst form of relativism. As Craig Boyd has argued in defense of natural law and against the sorts of criticism made by people like Sartre and Rorty, "Natural law requires, as a presupposition, that human beings have enduring, identifiable natures, which in turn requires some kind of realism."[25] As you reflect upon natural law ethics, one of the most fundamental questions is whether there is an enduring and identifiable human nature or whether the complexity and changeable history of the human experience undermines the very idea of a shared human nature.

The reading selections here from Thomas Aquinas and John Locke include discussions of the grounding of morality and rights in human nature. First, Aquinas explains how natural law is grounded in logical principles and an account of our natural inclinations. Then John Locke explains how natural law and natural rights are created by a benevolent God.

NOTES

1. Thomas Jefferson, "The Declaration of Independence," in *Basic Writings of Thomas Jefferson*, ed. Philip S. Foner (New York: Wiley, 1944), p. 551.

2. John Locke, *Two Treatises of Government* (London, 1690), ed. Peter Laslett (Cambridge: Cambridge University Press, 1960).

3. The Guantanamo Docket at *New York Times*, http://projects.nytimes.com/guantanamo/detainees

4. "Is Force-Feeding Torture?" *New York Times*, May 31, 2013, http://www.nytimes.com/2013/06/01/opinion/nocera-is-force-feeding-torture.html

5. Henry David Thoreau, "Civil Disobedience," in *Miscellanies* (Boston: Houghton Mifflin, 1983), pp. 136–37.

6. Cicero, *Republic*, in *Cicero's Tusculan Disputations. Also, Treatises on the Nature of the Gods, and on the Commonwealth*, bk. 3 at 22 (Project Gutenberg), http://www.gutenberg.org/files/14988/14988-h/14988-h.htm

7. Thomas Aquinas, *Summa Theologica*, in *Basic Writings of Saint Thomas Aquinas*, ed. Anton Pegis (New York: Random House, 1948).

8. Aquinas, *Summa Theologica*, Q.91 a.4. Aquinas is quoting Cicero's *Rhetoric*.

9. This is an incomplete presentation of the moral philosophy of Thomas Aquinas. We should also note that he was as much a theologian as a philosopher, if not more so. True and complete happiness, he believed, would be achieved only in knowledge or contemplation of God.

10. Hugo Grotius, *On the Rights of War and Peace* (Cambridge: Cambridge University Press, 1854), p. xxvii.

11. Aristotle, *Politics*, Chapters 5, 6.

12. Thomas Hobbes, *Leviathan*, ed. Michael Oakeshott (New York: Oxford University Press, 1962).

13. Henry Veatch, "Natural Law: Dead or Alive?" at Liberty Fund, http://oll.libertyfund.org/index.php?Itemid=259&id=168&option=com_content&task=view#anchor249499 (originally published 1978).

14. Ralph M. McInerny, *Ethica Thomistica* (Washington, DC: Catholic University of America Press, 1997), p. 56.

15. Germain Grisez, Joseph Boyle, and John Finnis, "Practical Principles, Moral Truth, and Ultimate Ends," *American Journal of Jurisprudence* 32 (1987), p. 106.

16. Larry Arnhart, *Darwinian Natural Right* (Albany: State University of New York Press, 1998), p. 7.

17. John Finnis, *Natural Law and Natural Rights* (Oxford: Oxford University Press, 2011), p. 31.

18. Voltaire, *Ouevres*, XXV, p. 39; XI, p. 443, quoted in Carl L. Becker, *The Heavenly City of the Eighteenth-Century Philosophers* (New Haven, CT: Yale University Press, 2003), p. 52; Becker's translation.

19. Thomas Jefferson, Declaration of Independence.

20. Jeremy Bentham, *Anarchical Fallacies*, in *The Works of Jeremy Bentham* (Edinburgh: William Tait, 1843), p. 501.

21. On negative or liberty rights, see, for example, the work of Robert Nozick, *State, Anarchy and Utopia* (New York: Basic Books, 1974). See further discussion on welfare and liberty rights in Chapter 14 of this book, "Economic Justice."

22. John Stuart Mill, *Utilitarianism*, in Mill, *On Liberty and Utilitarianism* (New York: Random House, 1993), p. 222.

23. The term *pragmatic* concerns what "works." Thus, to accept something on pragmatic grounds means to accept it because it works for us in some way. For Walter Lippmann's views, see *Essays in the Public Philosophy* (Boston: Little, Brown, 1955).

24. Richard Rorty, *Contingency, Irony, Solidarity* (Cambridge: Cambridge University Press, 1989), p. 175.

25. Craig Boyd, *A Shared Morality: A Narrative Defense of Natural Law Ethics* (Grand Rapids, MI: Brazos Press, 2007), p. 183.

READING

On Natural Law

THOMAS AQUINAS

MindTap®   For more chapter resources and activities, go to MindTap.

Study Questions

As you read the excerpt, please consider the following questions:
1. How does one determine whether something is good or evil, according to Aquinas? Give some of his examples.
2. What is the natural function of the human as human? How is this related to natural law? To virtue?
3. How does Aquinas believe that we should decide which laws are just?

WHETHER NATURAL LAW CONTAINS MANY PRECEPTS OR ONLY ONE

In the human context, the precepts of natural law relate to activities in a way similar to first principles in demonstrations. But there are many indemonstrable first principles. Therefore there are many precepts of natural law.

As was previously stated, precepts of natural law relate to practical reason just as the first principles of demonstration relate to speculative reason, both being self-evident. However, something is said to be self-evident in two ways: one intrinsically self-evident, the other evident to us. A particular proposition is said to be intrinsically self-evident when the predicate is implicit in the subject, although this proposition would not be self-evident to someone ignorant of the definition of the subject. For instance, this proposition "man is rational" is self-evident by its very nature since saying "human" entails saying "rational." Nevertheless this proposition is not self-evident to one who does not know what a man is....

[Now]that which is primary in apprehension is being, the understanding of which is included in anything whatsoever that is apprehended. Accordingly, the first indemonstrable principle is that one cannot simultaneously affirm and deny something. This is founded in the understanding of being and non-being and in this principle all others are founded, as stated in *Metaphysics IV*. Just as being is the first thing that falls under simple apprehension,

so also the good is the first thing that falls under the apprehension of practical reason which is ordered to action. Every agent acts for an end, which is understood as a good. Accordingly, the first principle of practical reason is the one based on the concept of the good: Good is what everything desires. This, accordingly, is the first principle of law: Good is to be done and evil avoided. All the other precepts of natural law are based on this. All concern what is to be done or avoided, because practical reason naturally apprehends what is the human good.

Good has the nature of an end while evil has a contrary nature. Accordingly, every thing for which a man has a natural inclination is naturally apprehended as a good and consequently something to be pursued, while anything contrary to this is to be avoided as evil. Therefore the ordering of the precepts of natural law stems from the order of natural inclinations. In the first place, there is the inclination of man towards natural good, an inclination shared by all substances inasmuch as they naturally desire self-preservation. The consequence of this inclination is that whatever preserves human life and avoids obstacles is a matter of natural law. Secondly, there is in man a more specialized inclination following the natural bent he shares with other animals. Accordingly these things are said to pertain to

From Thomas Aquinas, *Summa Theologica*, (1265–1272), trans. Edward MacKinnon.

natural law that "nature has taught to all animals," such as the mating of male and female, education of children, and similar things. Thirdly, there is in man an inclination toward good based on reason, something proper only to man. Thus man has a natural inclination to know the truth about God, and that he should live in society. On this ground, those things that stem from this inclination are also a matter of natural law. Thus, man should overcome ignorance and should not offend fellow members of society, and similar considerations.

WHETHER ALL ACTS OF VIRTUE ARE PRESCRIBED BY NATURAL LAW

... All those things to which man is inclined by nature pertain to natural law. Everything naturally inclines to operations that are appropriate to its form, as fire toward heating. Since a rational soul is the proper form of humans the natural inclination of a man is to act according to reason. And this is acting virtuously. In this respect, all virtuous acts pertain to natural law. Each person's reason naturally tells him to act virtuously. However, if we speak of virtuous acts in themselves, or according to their proper species, then not all virtuous acts are matters of natural law. For many things accord with virtue, though nature lacks an initial inclination. It is through rational inquisition that men come to know which things conduce to living well.

WHETHER THERE IS ONE NATURAL LAW FOR ALL

As was said previously, those things towards which man is naturally inclined pertain to natural law. Among such things it is distinctively human for a man to act in accord with reason. Reason inclines us to proceed from the common to the particular (as shown in *Physics I*). In this regard there is a difference between speculative and practical reason. Speculative reason is concerned in the first instance with things that are necessary, or could not be otherwise. Thus truth is easily found in proper conclusions just as in common principles. But practical reason is concerned with contingent matters involving human activity. Therefore, if there is some necessity in common principles, there is increasing error the further we descend

to particular conclusions. In speculative reason, there is the same degree of truth in principles and conclusions, although the truth of the conclusion may not be as well known to many as the principles are, for they are common conceptions. In activities, however, there is not the same degree of truth or practical rectitude, among all people concerning conclusions, but only concerning principles. Even those people who share the same rectitude concerning conclusions do not share the same knowledge.... With regard to the proper conclusions of practical reason, all do not share the same truth or rectitude. Even those that do share equal truth are not equally known. For everyone, it is right and true to act in accord with reason. From this principle follows a quasi-proper conclusion, that debts should be paid. This is true as a general rule. However, it may happen to be harmful in a particular case, and consequently unreasonable to give goods back, if for example someone is intending to attack the homeland. Thus, uncertainty increases the more we descend to particulars. Thus if it is claimed that goods are to be restored with certain precautions, or under certain conditions, then the more detailed the conditions are, the more uncertainty increases, even to the degree that it is not clear whether or not they should be restored.

Accordingly, we claim that first principles of natural law are the same for all, but in rectitude and knowledge. However, the quasi conclusions from these principles are for the most part the same for all both in rectitude and knowledge, though in a few cases there can be a deficit both with respect to rectitude because of some particular impediments (just as things naturally generated and corrupted are deficient in a few cases because of obstacles) and there can also be a deficit in knowledge. The reason for this is that some people have their reason perverted by passion, which may be due to bad customs or to a defective natural disposition....

WHETHER EVERY LAW FASHIONED BY HUMANS IS DERIVED FROM NATURAL LAW

But it should be recognized that something can be deviant from natural law in two ways. The first is as a conclusion from principles; the other as a determination of some common generalities. The first mode is similar to the practice of the sciences, where conclusions are produced by deduction from principles. The second mode, however, is more like what occurs in the arts, where common forms are tailored to special cases. A carpenter, for example, must determine the common form of a home to be this or that particular shape. Therefore, some things are derived from the common principle of natural law in the form of conclusions. Thus the prohibition of murder is derived from the general principle that evil should not be done. Other things, however, have the form of a determination. Natural law requires punishment for the evildoer, but whether he receives this or that penalty is a particular determination of natural law. Both forms, accordingly, are found in human law. However, determinations of the first mode are not only contained in human law, but they also have force through natural law. The second mode, however, derive their force only from human law....

In every being that is for an end it is necessary that its form has a determinate proportionality to the end, as the form of a saw is geared towards cutting as is clear in *Physics II*. Anything that is ruled and measured should have a form proportioned to its ruler and measure. Now human law has both, because it is something ordered to an end; and it has a rule or measure regulated or measured by a higher measure, which is both divine law and the law of nature, as previously explained. The end of human law is the well-being of humans... accordingly,... the first condition of law posits three things: That it accords with religion, inasmuch as it is proportioned to divine law; that it fosters discipline, inasmuch as it is proportional to natural law; and that it advances well-being inasmuch as it is proportional to human needs.

READING

Second Treatise of Civil Government

JOHN LOCKE

MindTap° For more chapter resources and activities, go to MindTap.

Study Questions

As you read the excerpt, please consider the following questions:
1. What two things characterize human beings in their natural state, according to Locke?
2. Why, according to Locke, do we need civil government?
3. According to Locke, was there ever really an existing state of nature as he describes it?

OF THE STATE OF NATURE

To understand political power aright, and derive it from its original, we must consider what estate all men are naturally in, and that is, a state of perfect freedom to order their actions, and dispose of their possessions and persons as they think fit, within the bounds of the law of Nature, without asking leave or depending upon the will of any other man.

A state also of equality, wherein all the power and jurisdiction is reciprocal, no one having more than another, there being nothing more evident than that creatures of the same species and rank, promiscuously born to all the same advantages of Nature,

From John Locke, *Second Treatise of Civil Government* (London: Routledge and Sons, 1887).

and the use of the same faculties, should also be equal one amongst another, without subordination or subjection, unless the lord and master of them all should, by a manifest declaration of his will, set one above another, and confer on him, by an evident and clear appointment, an undoubted right to dominion and sovereignty....

But though this be a state of liberty, yet it is not a state of license; though man in that state have an uncontrollable liberty to dispose of his person or possessions, yet he has not liberty to destroy himself, or so much as any creature in his possession, but where some nobler use than its bare preservation calls for it. The state of Nature has a law of Nature to govern it, which obliges every one, and reason, which is that law, teaches all mankind who will but consult it, that being all equal and independent, no one ought to harm another in his life, health, liberty or possessions; for men being all the workmanship of one omnipotent and infinitely wise Maker; all the servants of one sovereign Master, sent into the world by His order and about His business; they are His property, whose workmanship they are made to last during His, not one another's pleasure. And, being furnished with like faculties, sharing all in one community of Nature, there cannot be supposed any such subordination among us that may authorize us to destroy one another, as if we were made for one another's uses, as the inferior ranks of creatures are for ours. Every one as he is bound to preserve himself, and not to quit his station wilfully, so by the like reason, when his own preservation comes not in competition, ought he as much as he can to preserve the rest of mankind, and not unless it be to do justice on an offender, take away, or impair the life, or what tends to the preservation of the life, the liberty, health, limb, or goods of another.

And that all men may be restrained from invading other's rights, and from doing hurt to one another, and the law of Nature be observed, which willeth the peace and preservation of all mankind, the execution of the law of Nature is in that state put into every man's hands, whereby every one has a right to punish the transgressors of that law to such a degree as may hinder its violation. For the law of Nature would, as all other laws that concern men in this world, be in vain if there were nobody that in the state of Nature had a power to execute that law, and thereby preserve the innocent and restrain offenders; and if any one in the state of Nature may punish another for any evil he has done, every one may do so. For in that state of perfect equality, where naturally there is no superiority or jurisdiction of one over another, what any may do in prosecution of that law, every one must needs have a right to do.

And thus, in the state of Nature, one man comes by a power over another, but yet no absolute or arbitrary power to use a criminal when he has got him in his hands, according to the passionate heats, or boundless extravagancy of his own will, but only to retribute to him so far as calm reason and conscience dictate, what is proportionate to his transgression, which is so much as may serve for reparation and restraint. For these two are the only reasons why one man may lawfully do harm to another, which is that we call punishment. In transgressing the law of Nature, the offender declares himself to live by another rule than that of reason and common equity, which is that measure God has set to the actions of men for their mutual security, and so he becomes dangerous to mankind; the tie which is to secure them from injury and violence being slighted and broken by him, which being a trespass against the whole species, and the peace and safety of it, provided for by the law of Nature, every man upon this score, by the right he hath to preserve mankind in general, may restrain, or where it is necessary, destroy things noxious to them, and so may bring such evil on any one who hath transgressed that law, as may make him repent the doing of it, and thereby deter him, and, by his example, others from doing the like mischief. And in this case, and upon this ground, every man hath a right to punish the offender, and be executioner of the law of Nature....

From these two distinct rights (the one of punishing the crime, for restraint and preventing the like offence, which right of punishing is in everybody, the other of taking reparation, which belongs only to the injured party) comes it to pass that the magistrate, who by being magistrate hath the common right of punishing put into his hands, can often, where the public good demands not the execution of the law, remit the punishment of criminal offences by his own authority, but yet cannot remit the satisfaction due to any private man for the damage he has received. That he who hath suffered the damage has a right to demand in his own name, and he alone can remit. The damnified person has this power of appropriating to himself the goods or service of the offender by right of self-preservation, as every man has a power to punish the crime to prevent its being committed again, by the right he has of preserving all mankind, and doing all reasonable things he can in order to that end. And thus it is that every man in the state of Nature has a power to kill a murderer, both to deter others from doing the like injury (which no reparation can compensate) by the example of the punishment that attends it from everybody, and also to secure men from the attempts of a criminal who, having renounced reason, the common rule and measure God hath given to mankind, hath, by the unjust violence and slaughter he hath committed upon one, declared war against all mankind, and therefore may be destroyed as a lion or a tiger, one of those wild savage beasts with whom men can have no society nor security. And upon this is grounded that great law of Nature, "Whoso sheddeth man's blood by man shall his blood be shed." And Cain was so fully convinced that every one had a right to destroy such a criminal, that, after the murder of his brother, he cried out, "Every one that findeth me shall slay me," so plain was it writ in the hearts of all mankind.

By the same reason may a man in the state of Nature punish the lesser breaches of that law, it will, perhaps, be demanded, with death? I answer: Each transgression may be punished to that degree, and with so much severity, as will suffice to make it an ill bargain to the offender, give him cause to repent, and terrify others from doing the like. Every offence that can be committed in the state of Nature may, in the state of Nature, be also punished equally, and as far forth, as it may, in a commonwealth. For though

it would be beside my present purpose to enter here into the particulars of the law of Nature, or its measures of punishment; yet it is certain there is such a law, and that too as intelligible and plain to a rational creature and a studier of that law as the positive laws of commonwealths, nay, possibly plainer; as much as reason is easier to be understood than the fancies and intricate contrivances of men, following contrary and hidden interests put into words; for truly so are apart of the municipal laws of countries, which are only so far right as they are founded on the law of Nature, by which they are to be regulated and interpreted.

To this strange doctrine—viz., That in the state of Nature every one has the executive power of the law of Nature, I doubt not but it will be objected that it is unreasonable for men to be judges in their own cases, that self-love will make men partial to themselves and their friends; and, on the other side, ill-nature, passion, and revenge will carry them too far in punishing others, and hence nothing but confusion and disorder will follow, and that therefore God hath certainly appointed government to restrain the partiality and violence of men. I easily grant that civil government is the proper remedy for the inconveniencies of the state of Nature, which must certainly be great where men may be judges in their own case, since it is easy to be imagined that he who was so unjust as to do his brother an injury will scarce be so just as to condemn himself for it. But I shall desire those who make this objection to remember that absolute monarchs are but men; and if government is to be the remedy of those evils which necessarily follow from men being judges in their own cases, and the state of Nature is therefore not to be endured, I desire to know what kind of government that is, and how much better it is than the state of Nature, where one man commanding a multitude has the liberty to be judge in his own case, and may do to all his subjects whatever he pleases without the least question or control of those who execute his pleasure? and in whatsoever he doth, whether led by reason, mistake, or passion, must be submitted to? which men in the state of Nature are not bound to do one to another. And if he that judges, judges amiss in his own or any other case, he is answerable for it to the rest of mankind.

It is often asked as a mighty objection, where are, or ever were, there any men in such a state of Nature? To which it may suffice as an answer at present, that since all princes and rulers of "independent" governments all through the world are in a state of Nature, it is plain the world never was, nor never will be, without numbers of men in that state. I have named all governors of "independent" communities, whether they are, or are not, in league with others; for it is not every compact that puts an end to the state of Nature between men, but only this one of agreeing together mutually to enter into one community, and make one body politic; other promises and compacts men may make one with another, and yet still be in the state of Nature. The promises and bargains for truck, &c., between the two men in Soldania, or between a Swiss and an Indian, in the woods of America, are binding to them, though they are perfectly in a state of Nature in reference to one another for truth, and keeping of faith belongs to men as men, and not as members of society. . . .

REVIEW EXERCISES

1. Give a basic definition of natural law theory.
2. What is the difference between the scientific laws of nature and the natural law?
3. In what way is natural law theory teleological?
4. What specific natural or human species capacities are singled out by natural law theorists? How do these determine what we ought to do, according to the theory?
5. What is the difference between Aristotle and Aquinas on the theistic basis of natural law?
6. Explain one area of concern or criticism of natural law theory.
7. Describe the basis of rights according to natural rights theorists.
8. Give examples of what sorts of rights we are supposed to have according to natural law theory.
9. How do we know that we have natural rights?
10. Explain the criticism of natural law from the perspective of those who deny the idea of "human nature."

MindTap® For more chapter resources and activities, go to MindTap.

Virtue Ethics

iStockphoto.com/destiger-photo

Learning Outcomes

After reading this chapter, you should be able to:

- Explain how virtue ethics differs from other approaches to ethics.
- Describe some key virtues and how they are manifest in concrete situations.
- Explain how virtues are connected to an account of the functions or purposes of human life.
- Describe how *eudaimonia* functions in the theory of virtue.

- Identify some features of the diverse cultural approaches to virtue.
- Explain how the idea of the Golden Mean functions in virtue ethics.
- Provide an overview of Aristotle's moral philosophy.
- Defend your own thesis with regard to the value of virtue ethics.

MindTap° For more chapter resources and activities, go to MindTap.

Pat Tillman was a successful NFL player. He played safety for the Arizona Cardinals, earning hundreds of thousands of dollars. After the September 11 attacks in 2001, Tillman turned down a $3.6 million contract offer and enlisted in the Army. He qualified to become an Army Ranger. His unit served in Iraq and in Afghanistan, where he was killed, by accident, by members of his own platoon during a firefight. Tillman's death prompted a number of controversies. The Army initially informed Tillman's family and the public that he had been killed by enemy fire, in an apparent effort to preserve the image of Tillman as a war hero. (Among other awards, he posthumously received the Army's Silver Star for Valor.) A subsequent book about Tillman claimed that Tillman was not a supporter of the Iraq war and was critical of President George W. Bush.[1] Nonetheless, Tillman remains a model of virtue and courage. Senator John McCain used Tillman's story to explain the virtues of citizenship and patriotism in his book *Character Is Destiny*.[2] What is remarkable about Tillman is his willingness to sacrifice a lucrative football career for life and death as an Army Ranger. He seemed to embody virtues—such as courage, loyalty, self-sacrifice, and patriotism—that are often mourned as deficient or absent in contemporary society. Do you agree with this assessment? What role do such virtues play in your own moral life?

When thinking about virtue, it is useful to think about the people you admire. Whether it is a relative, a coworker, a friend, or some celebrity, it is helpful to consider the traits that make those people good. We usually admire people who are courageous, kind, honest, generous, loyal, diligent, temperate, fair, modest, and hospitable. Such traits of character are traditionally known as *virtues*.

VIRTUES AND EVERYDAY LIFE

The theories that we have treated so far in this text are concerned with how we determine the right action to take or policy to establish. The focus on virtue takes a different approach to morality. Rather than asking what we ought to *do*, virtue ethics asks how we ought to *be*. Virtue ethics is concerned with those traits of character, habits, tendencies, and dispositions that make a person good. When some or all of the traits mentioned above are unusually well developed in a person, that person may be regarded as a hero or even as a saint. One version of virtue ethics is focused on thinking about saints and heroes as paradigms or exemplars of human excellence.

In a well-known article on the topic, Susan Wolf described a moral saint as, "a person whose every action is as good as possible, that is, who is as morally worthy as can be."[3] But Wolf goes on to argue that moral saints are not especially happy, since the demands of saintly perfection might include self-sacrifice. At issue here is a definition of happiness. Virtue ethics tends to hold that happiness is something different from pleasure. Pat Tillman's life and death were not particularly pleasant—he suffered through Army Ranger training and then was killed at the age of twenty-seven. But perhaps there is something more important than pleasure. At any rate, even if it is difficult and unpleasant to become a hero or a saint, the virtue tradition maintains that people live better when they possess most or all of the virtues. People can also exhibit bad character traits. For example, they can be coward, dishonest, tactless, careless, boorish, stingy, vindictive, disloyal, lazy, or egotistical. Another word for these bad traits such as these is *vice*. An ethics focused on virtue encourages us to develop the good traits and

John Cordes/Icon SMI/ZUMA/Corbis

Pat Tillman is looked to as a model of virtue.

get rid of the bad ones, that is, to develop our virtues and eliminate our vices.

The ethical issues that are treated in the second half of this text are generally controversial social issues: the death penalty, abortion, and terrorism, for example. Virtue ethics seems more personal. It involves not so much asking which side of some social issue one should support as what kind of person one should be. Virtues can help us make good decisions in tough situations. But they also serve us on a daily basis. Virtues such as courage, loyalty, honesty, and fairness show up in our interactions with relatives, friends, and coworkers. We often think about virtues when we consider how our behavior serves as a good (or bad) model for our children, students, and colleagues.

Virtue ethics can be useful in thinking about the applied issues discussed in the second half of the text. Virtues depend, in part, on our roles and help us fulfill the requirements of our roles: so soldiers ought to be courageous and strong, while teachers ought to be patient and kind. Virtue ethics encourages us to consider the question of how a soldier's virtues might differ from those of a teacher. Some of the applied topics we will discuss have connections with questions about the virtues of various vocations and roles. In thinking about euthanasia and physician-assisted suicide, for example, issues arise regarding the proper virtues of health care providers. In thinking about the morality of abortion, we might think about proper virtues of parents and lawmakers, as well as doctors. In thinking about the morality of war, we consider the virtues we associate with military service.

There will be overlap among the virtues found in different vocations. But different roles require different character traits and habits. This reminds us that virtue ethics has a pluralistic aspect. There are many different virtues that can be emphasized and integrated in various ways in the life of an individual. Moreover, virtuous people tend to be responsive to the unique demands of various situations; they do the right thing, at the right time, in the right way, exhibiting a sort of "practical wisdom" that is sensitive to context. From the standpoint of utilitarianism or deontology, which wants clearly defined rules and principles for action, virtue ethics can seem imprecise and vague. But an asset of virtue ethics may be its sensitivity to context and its recognition of plurality in morals.

Although we probably do not use the term *virtuous* as frequently today as in times past, we still understand the essence of its meaning. A virtuous person is a morally good person, and virtues are good traits. Another word that is useful in understanding virtue is the word *excellence*. The virtues are those things that make us excellent; they allow us to manifest our highest potential. There is more than one thing that makes us excellent. Indeed, virtues are often described in the plural—as a list of qualities that lead to living well. Loyalty is a virtue, and so is honesty. A moral philosophy that concentrates on the notion of virtue is called a *virtue ethics*. For virtue ethics, the moral life is about developing good *character*. It is about determining the ideals for human life

and trying to embody these ideals in one's own life. The virtues are ways in which we embody these ideals. For example, if we consider honesty to be such an ideal, then we ought to try to become honest persons.

ARISTOTLE

Aristotle was born in 384 BCE in Stagira in northern Greece. His father was a physician for King Philip of Macedonia. Around age seventeen, he went to study at Plato's Academy in Athens. Aristotle traveled for several years and then for two or three years was the tutor to Alexander, Philip's young son who later became known as Alexander the Great. In 335 BCE, Aristotle returned to Athens and organized his own school, called the Lyceum. There, he taught and wrote almost until his death thirteen years later, in 322 BCE.[4] Aristotle is known not only for his moral theory, but also for writings in logic, biology, physics, metaphysics, art, and politics. The basic notions of his moral theory can be found in his *Nicomachean Ethics*, named for his son Nicomachus.[5]

As noted in Chapter 7, Aristotle was one of the earliest writers to ground morality in nature, and specifically in *human* nature. His theory of ethics and morality also stressed the notion of virtue. For Aristotle, virtue was an excellence of some sort. Our word *virtue* originally came from the Latin *vir* and referred to strength or manliness.[6] In Aristotle's Greek, the term for virtue was *arete*, a word that can also be translated as "excellence."

According to Aristotle, there are two basic types of virtue (or excellence): intellectual virtues and moral virtues. Intellectual virtues are excellences of mind, such as the ability to understand and reason and judge well. Moral virtues, on the other hand, dispose us to act well. These virtues are learned by repetition. For instance, by practicing courage or honesty, we become more courageous and honest. Just as repetition in playing a musical instrument makes playing easier, repeated acts of honesty make it easier to be honest. The person who has the virtue of honesty finds it easier to be honest than the person who does not have the virtue. It becomes habitual or second nature to him or her. The same thing applies to the opposite of virtue, namely, vice.

The person who lies and lies again finds that lying is easier and telling the truth is more difficult. One can have bad moral habits (vices) as well as good ones (virtues). Just like other bad habits, bad moral habits are difficult to change or break. And like other good habits, good moral habits take practice to develop.

Virtue as a Mean

Aristotle's philosophy outlines a variety of particular virtues including courage, temperance, justice, pride, and magnanimity. However, Aristotle also provides a unifying framework for understanding virtue in general, as a mean between extremes. This idea is occasionally known as the **Golden Mean** (and should not be confused with the Golden Rule, which we've discussed in previous chapters). By saying that virtue is a *mean*, we are using the word with reference to how it is used in mathematics, where the *mean* is the average. (The term *mean* here should also not be confused with the idea of using someone as a *means*, as we discussed in Chapter 6.)

To better understand the idea that virtue is a mean, take the following example. The virtue of courage can be understood as a mean or middle between the two extremes of deficiency and excess. The virtue of courage has to do with fear. When facing danger or challenges, we should have neither too much fear—which makes us unable to act—nor too little fear—which makes us take reckless or foolish risks. Too little fear leaves us "foolhardy"; too much fear is called "cowardice." The virtue of courage is having just the right amount of fear, depending on what is appropriate for us as individuals and for the circumstances we face. So, too, the other virtues can be seen as means between extremes (as indicated in the following table).

Different authors have offered different lists of virtues and corresponding vices. For the Greek tradition, following Plato, there were four basic or **cardinal virtues**: prudence (or wisdom), justice, temperance, and courage. Questions arise about which traits count as virtues and how these virtues are related to corresponding vices. For example, we might want to count loyalty and honesty as virtues. If loyalty is a virtue, then is it also a middle between two extremes? Can there be such a thing as too little or too much loyalty? What about honesty? Too much honesty might be seen as undisciplined openness, and too little as deceitfulness.

Not all virtues may be rightly thought of as means between extremes. For example, if justice is a virtue, then could there be such a thing as being too just? It is important to note that virtue ethics still maintains that some things are simply wrong and not amenable to explanation in virtue terminology. For example, murder is wrong; there is no right time for murder or right amount of murder.

Nature, Human Nature, and the Human Good

Aristotle was a close observer of nature. In fact, in his writings, he mentions some five hundred different kinds of animals.[7] He noticed that seeds of the same sort always grew to the same mature form. He opened developing eggs of various species and noticed that these organisms manifested a pattern in their development even before birth. Tadpoles, he might have said, always follow the same path and become frogs, not turtles. So also with other living things. Acorns always become oak trees, not elms. He concluded that there was an order in nature. It was as if natural beings, such as plants and animals, had a principle of order within them that directed

	Deficit (Too Little)	Virtue (the Mean)	Excess (Too Much)
Fear	Foolhardiness	Courage	Cowardice
Giving	Illiberality	Liberality	Prodigality
Self-Regard	Humility	Pride	Vanity
Pleasures	(No Name Given)	Temperance	Profligacy

them toward their goal—their mature final form. This view can be called a *teleological* view, from the Greek word for "goal," *telos*, because of its emphasis on a goal embedded in natural things. It was from this conclusion that Aristotle developed his notion of the good. You might also notice that the idea of a natural goal, purpose, or function showed up in the discussion of natural law (in Chapter 7).

According to Aristotle, "the good is that at which all things aim." Good things are things that fulfill some purpose, end, or goal. Thus, the good of the shipbuilder is to build ships. The good of the lyre player is to play well. The traits that allow for good shipbuilding or lyre-playing will be somewhat different. But good shipbuilders and good lyre players will share certain virtues, such as intelligence and creativity. Aristotle asks whether there is anything that is the good of the human being—not as shipbuilder or lyre player, but simply as human. To answer this question, we must first think about what it is to be human. According to Aristotle, natural beings come in kinds or species. From their species flow their essential characteristics and certain key tendencies or capacities. For example, a squirrel is a kind of animal that is, first of all, a living being. It develops from a young to a mature form. It is a mammal and therefore has other characteristics of mammals. It is bushy-tailed, can run along telephone wires, and gathers and stores nuts for its food. From the characteristics that define a squirrel, we also can know what a *good* squirrel is. A good specimen of a squirrel is one that is effective, successful, and functions well. It follows the pattern of development and growth it has by nature. A good squirrel does, in fact, have a bushy tail and good balance, and knows how to find and store its food. It would be a bad example of a squirrel if it had no balance, couldn't find its food, or had no fur and was sickly. It would have been better for the squirrel if its inherent natural tendencies to grow and develop and live as a healthy squirrel had been realized.

Aristotle thought of human beings as natural beings with a specific human nature. Human beings have certain specific characteristics and abilities that we share as humans. Unlike squirrels

and acorns, human beings can choose to act in the service of their good or act against it. But just what is their good? Aristotle recognized that a good eye is a healthy eye that sees well. A good horse is a well-functioning horse, one that is healthy and able to run and do what horses do. What about human beings? Is there something comparable for the human being as human? Is there some good for humans as humans?

Just as we can tell what the good squirrel is from its own characteristics and abilities as a squirrel, the same should be true for the human being. For human beings to function well or flourish, they should perfect their human capacities. If they do this, they will be functioning well as human beings. They will also be happy, for a being is happy to the extent that it is functioning well. Aristotle believed that the ultimate good of humans is happiness, blessedness, or prosperity. The Greek word for this sort of happiness is **eudaimonia**. *Eudaimonia* is not to be confused with pleasure. Indeed, the virtues are often at odds with pleasure. A coward who is afraid of danger is reluctant to experience pain. And a courageous person may have to forgo pleasure and submit to pain—including the pain of being killed. Aristotle warned that pleasure can distract us from what is good. Thus, Aristotle's account of *eudaimonia* aims at a kind of happiness that is deeper and longer lasting than mere pleasure. The term *eudaimonia* gives us a clue about this. The *eu-* prefix means "good"; and *daimonia* is related to the Greek word for "spirit" or "soul." Thus, Aristotle's idea is that virtue produces the happiness of having a good soul or spirit, which fulfills essential human functions or purposes.

Aristotle is thus interested in the question of what our human functions or purposes might be. Human beings have much in common with lower forms of beings. For example, we are living, just as plants are. Thus, we take in material from outside us for nourishment, and we grow from an immature to a mature form. We have senses of sight, hearing, and so forth, as do the higher animals. We are social animals as well, who must live in groups together with other human beings. Since human beings have various functions or purposes, there are various types of virtue. For example, the virtues of social life help us fulfill our function as social beings. The moral or social virtues would include honesty, loyalty, and generosity.

But is there anything unique to humans, an essentially human function or purpose? Aristotle believed that it is our "rational element" that is peculiar to us. The good for humans, then, is living in accord with this rational element. Our rational element has two different functions: one is to know, and the other is to guide choice and action. We must develop our ability to know the world and the truth. We must also choose wisely. In doing this, we will be functioning well, specifically as humans. Thus, in addition to social or moral virtues, there are also intellectual virtues, which help us fulfill our function as intelligent animals. According to Aristotle, these virtues include practical knowledge, scientific knowledge, and practical wisdom. It is not surprising that Aristotle—who was a philosopher and a student of Plato—thought that the intellectual virtues were more important than the other virtues, since they help us fulfill our uniquely human capacities.

CROSS-CULTURAL AND CONTEMPORARY VIRTUE ETHICS

Versions of virtue ethics can also be found in other traditions. The Confucian tradition in China is often described as a virtue tradition. This tradition traces its roots back to Confucius (551–479 BCE), a figure whose role in Chinese philosophy was similar to the role Socrates played in Greek philosophy—as founding character and touchstone for later authors who want to reflect upon virtue and wisdom. Unlike Socrates, however, who was something of a rough-mannered outsider to the elite social scene of Athens, Confucius was viewed as a model of courtly gentility and decorum. The Confucian tradition emphasizes two main virtues, *jen* (or *ren*) and *li*. *Jen* is often translated as "humaneness" or "compassion." *Li* is often translated as "propriety," "manners," or "culture." Confucian ethics aims toward a synthesis of the virtues oriented around compassion and propriety. In the *Analects* of Confucius, this is explained

in various ways. Consider the following saying attributed to Confucius:

> A youth, when at home, should be filial, and, abroad, respectful to his elders. He should be earnest and truthful. He should overflow in love to all, and cultivate the friendship of the good. When he has time and opportunity, after the performance of these things, he should employ them in polite studies.[8]

Confucius advises young people to be polite and respectful, earnest and truthful, and to overflow with love. Similar advice holds for others who are at different stages of life's journey. Confucius also holds that there are specific virtues for those inhabiting different roles: for fathers, brothers, sons, and government officials. As is true of most of the other traditions of the ancient world, the primary focus here is on male roles; women's roles were defined in subordination to the male.

Other traditions emphasize different forms of virtue. Hinduism emphasizes five basic moral virtues or *yamas*: nonviolence (*ahimsa*), truthfulness, honesty, chastity, and freedom from greed.[9] Hinduism also includes mental virtues to be perfected in meditation and yogic practice: calmness, self-control, self-settledness, forbearance, faith, and complete concentration, as well as the hunger for spiritual liberation.[10] Buddhism shares with Hinduism an emphasis on both intellectual and moral virtues. The "noble eightfold path" of Buddhism includes moral virtues such as right speech, right action, and right livelihood, as well as intellectual virtues of understanding and mindfulness.[11] Christian virtue ethics includes similar moral virtues, as well as what Thomas Aquinas called the "theological virtues." In the Christian tradition, the four cardinal moral virtues are prudence, justice, temperance, and fortitude, while the three theological virtues are faith, hope, and love. It is easy to see that there is overlap among these different traditions in terms of the virtues required for a good life, despite some clear differences. The common thread that links them as traditions of *virtue ethics* is the idea that habits and character traits matter, along with sustained philosophical reflection on the reasons that these habits and character traits matter.

Statue of Confucius in Shanghai, China.

iStockphoto.com/destiger-photo

Various contemporary moral philosophers have also stressed the importance of virtue.[12] For example, Philippa Foot has developed a contemporary version of virtue ethics. She believes that the virtues are "in some general way, beneficial. Human beings do not get on well without them."[13] According to Foot, virtues provide benefits both to the virtuous person and to his or her community, just as vices harm both the self and the community. Think of courage, temperance, and wisdom, for example, and ask yourself how persons having these virtues might benefit others as well as themselves. Some virtues such as charity, however, seem to benefit mostly others. But this makes sense for social virtues, which help us fulfill our function as social beings. However, there is an open question about which beneficial character traits are to be thought of as moral virtues and which are not. Wit or powers of concentration benefit us, but we would probably not consider them to be *moral* virtues.

Foot also asks whether virtue is best seen in the intention that guides an action or in the execution of an action. Think of generosity. Does the person who intends to be generous—but who cannot seem to do what helps others—really possess the virtue of generosity? Or rather, is it the person who actually does help who has the virtue? Foot believes that virtue is also something we must choose to develop and work at personifying. Furthermore, following Aristotle, Foot argues that the virtues are *corrective*. They help us be and do things that are difficult for us. For example, courage helps us overcome natural fear. Temperance helps us control our desires. Since people differ in their natural inclinations, they also differ in what virtues would be most helpful for them to develop. Foot's view is just one example of how the notion of virtue continues to be discussed by moral philosophers.

EVALUATING VIRTUE ETHICS

One question that has been raised for virtue ethics concerns how we determine which traits are virtues, and whether they are so in all circumstances. Are there any universally valuable traits? Wherever friendship exists, loyalty would seem necessary, although the form it might take would vary according to time and place. Honesty also seems necessary for good human relations. We might also start with Aristotle's own list of virtues, which reflected what were considered the primary civic virtues of his day. But Aristotle's society included slavery and gender hierarchy. One wonders whether it makes sense to speak of virtuous slave-masters or whether the submissive traits of women in patriarchal cultures are really virtuous. Similar problems occur as we consider differences among civilizations. Are the virtues of Confucian culture the same (or better or worse) than the virtues of Muslim, Christian, or Hindu cultures?

Contemporary moral philosopher Alasdair MacIntyre believes that virtues depend at least partly on the practices of a culture or society. A warlike society will value heroic virtues, whereas a peaceful and prosperous society might think of generosity as a particularly important virtue.[14] However, these must also be virtues specific to human beings as humans, for otherwise one could not speak of "human excellences." But this is just the problem. What is it to live a full human life? Can one specify this apart from what it is to live such a life in a particular society or as a particular person? The problem here is not only how we know what excellences are human excellences, but also whether there are any such traits that are ideal for all persons, despite differences in gender, social roles, and physical and mental capacities.

A further problem with regard to virtue is the question of the degree of effort and discipline required to be virtuous. Who manifests the virtue of courage the most—the person who, as Foot puts it, "wants to run away but does not or the one who does not even want to run away?"[15] We generally believe that we ought to be rewarded for our moral efforts, and thus, the person who wants to run away but does not seem more praiseworthy. On the other hand, possession of the virtue of courage is supposed to make it easier to be brave. Part of Foot's own answer to this dilemma involves the distinction between those fears for which we are in some way responsible and those that we cannot help. Thus, a woman who feels like running away because she has contributed by her own choices to being afraid is not the more virtuous person. Foot also addresses the question of whether someone who does something morally wrong—say, robs a bank or commits a murder—and does so courageously, demonstrates the virtue of courage.

We can also ask whether virtue ethics is really a distinct type of ethics. Consider two of the other theories we have discussed: utilitarianism (Chapter 5) and deontology (Chapter 6). The concept of virtue is not foreign to Mill or Kant. However, for both of them, it is secondary. Their moral theories tell us how we ought to decide what to *do*. Doing the right thing—and with Kant, for the right reason—is primary. However, if the development of certain habits of action or tendencies to act in a certain way will enable us to do good more easily, then they would surely be recognized by these philosophers as good. Utilitarians would encourage the development of those virtues that would be conducive to the maximization of happiness. If temperance in eating and drinking will help us avoid the suffering that can come from illness and drunkenness, then this virtue ought to be encouraged and developed in the young. So also with other virtues. According to a Kantian, we should develop habits and virtues that would make it more likely that we act fairly (according to universalizable maxims) and treat people as ends rather than simply as means.

When evaluating the virtue ethics tradition developed by Aristotle, we should also consider a more specific criticism of it introduced by Kant. Kant argues that Aristotle's notion of virtue as a mean between two vices—the Golden Mean—is simply false. Kant writes that, "it is incorrect to define any virtue or vice in terms of mere degree," which "proves the uselessness of the Aristotelian principles that virtue consists in the middle way between two vices."[16] Kant rejects the idea that there is a gradation of behaviors or dispositions from one extreme (or vice) to the other with virtue in the middle. Rather, for Kant, some things are praiseworthy and others are wrong, and do not vary by degrees on a continuum. Kant suggests that the Aristotelian idea of the Golden Mean simply confuses us and distracts us from thinking about why a given virtue is good. Bearing this argument in mind, it is worth considering whether the idea of virtue as a mean between vices really makes sense of the way we ordinarily understand virtues such as courage and vices like cowardice. Is this idea genuinely helpful to us in identifying the nature of virtue?

In virtue ethics, the primary goal is to be a good person. Now, a critic of virtue ethics might argue that *being* good is only a function of being *inclined* to do good. However, ethics appears to require not only a habitual inclination toward good deeds, but also actually doing good. Is what matters the deed or the inclination to carry it out? If what really matters is the actions and deeds, then virtue is simply one aspect of an action-oriented moral philosophy such as consequentialism. However, virtue ethics does have a somewhat different emphasis. It is an ethics whose goal is to determine what is essential to being a well-functioning or flourishing human person. Virtue ethics stresses an ideal for humans or persons. As an ethics of ideals or excellences, it is an optimistic and positive type of ethics. One problem that virtue ethics may face is what to say about those of us who do not meet the ideal. If we fall short of the virtuous model, does this make us bad or vicious? As with all moral theories, many questions concerning virtue remain to engage and puzzle us.

The reading selection for this chapter is from Aristotle's *The Nicomachean Ethics*. In this piece, Aristotle explains what virtue is, how it is related to human functioning, and how it is a mean between extremes.

NOTES

1. Jon Krakauer, *Where Men Win Glory* (New York: Doubleday, 2009).
2. John McCain, *Character Is Destiny* (New York: Random House, 2007).
3. Susan Wolf, "Moral Saints," *The Journal of Philosophy* 89, no. 8 (August 1982), p. 419.
4. W. T. Jones, *A History of Western Philosophy: The Classical Mind*, 2nd ed. (New York: Harcourt, Brace & World, 1969), pp. 214–16.
5. This was asserted by the neo-Platonist Porphyry (ca. 232 CE). However, others believe that the work got its name because it was edited by Nicomachus. See Alasdair MacIntyre, *After Virtue* (Notre Dame, IN: Notre Dame University Press, 1984), p. 147.
6. Milton Gonsalves, *Fagothy's Right and Reason*, 9th ed. (Columbus, OH: Merrill, 1989), p. 201.
7. W. T. Jones, *A History of Western Philosophy*, p. 233.
8. Confucius, *Analects*, in *The Chinese Classics—Volume 1: Confucian Analects*, bk. 1, Chapter 6, trans. James Legge (Project Gutenberg), http://www.gutenberg.org/files/4094/4094-h/4094-h.htm (accessed July 21, 2016).
9. Sunil Sehgal, ed., *Encyclopedia of Hinduism* (New Delhi: Sarup and Sons, 1999), p. 2:364.
10. Vensus A. George, *Paths to the Divine: Ancient and Indian* (Washington, DC: CRVP Press, 2008), p. 205.
11. Peter Harvey, *Buddhism: Teachings, History and Practices* (Cambridge: Cambridge University Press, 1990), pp. 68–69.
12. See, for example, the collection of articles in Christina Hoff Sommers, *Vice and Virtue in Everyday Life* (New York: Harcourt Brace Jovanovich, 1985).
13. Philippa Foot, *Virtues and Vices* (Oxford: Oxford University Press, 2002).
14. Alasdair MacIntyre, "The Virtue in Heroic Societies" and "The Virtues at Athens," in *After Virtue* (Notre Dame, IN: Notre Dame University Press, 1984), pp. 121–45.
15. Foot, *Virtues and Vices*, p. 10.
16. Kant, "Doctrine of Virtue," in *Metaphysics of Morals*, trans. Mary Gregor (Cambridge: Cambridge University Press, 1996), pp. 184–85.

READING

The Nicomachean Ethics

ARISTOTLE

MindTap°   For more chapter resources and activities, go to MindTap.

Study Questions

As you read the excerpt, please consider the following questions:
1. What is virtue, and how do we acquire it?
2. How is virtue a mean? Explain this by using some of Aristotle's examples.
3. Why is it so difficult to be virtuous?

THE NATURE OF THE GOOD*

Every art and every scientific inquiry, and similarly every action and purpose, may be said to aim at some good. Hence the good has been well defined as that at which all things aim. But it is clear that there is a difference in the ends; for the ends are sometimes activities, and sometimes results beyond the mere activities. Also, where there are certain ends beyond the actions, the results are naturally superior to the activities.

As there are various actions, arts, and sciences, it follows that the ends are also various. Thus health is the end of medicine, a vessel of shipbuilding, victory of strategy, and wealth of domestic economy. It often happens that there are a number of such arts or sciences which fall under a single faculty, as the art of making bridles, and all such other arts as make the instruments of horsemanship, under horsemanship, and this again as well as every military action under strategy, and in the same way other arts or sciences under other faculties. But in all these cases the ends of the architectonic arts or sciences, whatever they may be, are more desirable than those of the subordinate arts or sciences, as it is for the sake of the former that the latter are themselves sought after. It makes no difference to the argument whether the activities themselves are the ends of the actions, or something else beyond the activities as in the above mentioned sciences.

If it is true that in the sphere of action there is an end which we wish for its own sake, and for the sake of which we wish everything else, and that we do not desire all things for the sake of something else (for, if that is so, the process will go on ad infinitum, and our desire will be idle and futile) it is clear that this will be the good or the supreme good. Does it not follow then that the knowledge of this supreme good is of great importance for the conduct of life, and that, if we know it, we shall be like archers who

have a mark at which to aim, we shall have a better chance of attaining what we want? But, if this is the case, we must endeavour to comprehend, at least in outline, its nature, and the science or faculty to which it belongs....

HAPPINESS: LIVING AND DOING WELL

As every knowledge and moral purpose aspires to some good, what is in our view the good at which the political science aims, and what is the highest of all practical goods? As to its name there is, I may say, a general agreement. The masses and the cultured classes agree in calling it happiness, and conceive that "to live well" or "to do well" is the same thing as "to be happy." But as to the nature of happiness they do not agree, nor do the masses give the same account of it as the philosophers. The former define it as something visible and palpable, e.g. pleasure, wealth, or honour; different people give different definitions of it, and often the same person gives different definitions at different times; for when a person has been ill, it is health, when he is poor, it is wealth, and, if he is conscious of his own ignorance, he envies people who use grand language above his own comprehension. Some philosophers[1] on the other hand have held that, besides these various goods, there is an absolute good which is the cause of goodness in them all....

THE FUNCTION OF A PERSON

Perhaps, however, it seems a truth which is generally admitted, that happiness is the supreme good; what is wanted is to define its nature a little more clearly. The best way of arriving at such a definition will probably be to ascertain the function of Man. For, as with a flute-player, a statuary, or any artisan, or in fact anybody who has a definite function and action, his goodness, or excellence seems to lie in his function, so it would seem to be with Man, if indeed he has a definite function. Can it be said then that, while a carpenter and a cobbler have definite functions and actions, Man, unlike them, is naturally functionless? The reasonable view is that, as the eye, the hand, the foot, and similarly each several part of the body has a

---

From Aristotle, *The Nicomachean Ethics*, trans. J. E. C. Welldon (London: Macmillan, 1892), bks. 1 and 2.

*Headings added by the editor.

*Some notes omitted; the remaining notes renumbered.

definite function, so Man may be regarded as having a definite function apart from all these. What then, can this function be? It is not life; for life is apparently something which Man shares with the plants; and it is something peculiar to him that we are looking for. We must exclude therefore the life of nutrition and increase. There is next what may be called the life of sensation. But this too, is apparently shared by Man with horses, cattle, and all other animals. There remains what I may call the practical life of the rational part of Man's being. But the rational part is twofold; it is rational partly in the sense of being obedient to reason, and partly in the sense of possessing reason and intelligence. The practical life too may be conceived of in two ways,[2] viz., either as a moral state, or as a moral activity: but we must understand by it the life of activity, as this seems to be the truer form of the conception.

The function of Man then is an activity of soul in accordance with reason, or not independently of reason. Again the functions of a person of a certain kind, and of such a person who is good of his kind e.g. of a harpist and a good harpist, are in our view generically the same, and this view is true of people of all kinds without exception, the superior excellence being only an addition to the function; for it is the function of a harpist to play the harp, and of a good harpist to play the harp well. This being so, if we define the function of Man as a kind of life, and this life as an activity of soul, or a course of action in conformity with reason, if the function of a good man is such activity or action of a good and noble kind, and if everything is successfully performed when it is performed in accordance with its proper excellence, it follows that the good of Man is an activity of soul in accordance with virtue or, if there are more virtues than one, in accordance with the best and most complete virtue. But it is necessary to add the words "in a complete life." For as one swallow or one day does not make a spring, so one day or a short time does not make a fortunate or happy man....

VIRTUE

Virtue or excellence being twofold, partly intellectual and partly moral, intellectual virtue is both originated and fostered mainly by teaching; it therefore demands experience and time. Moral[3] virtue on the other hand is the outcome of habit.... From this fact it is clear that no moral virtue is implanted in us by nature; a law of nature cannot be altered by habituation. Thus a stone naturally tends to fall downwards, and it cannot be habituated or trained to rise upwards, even if we were to habituate it by throwing it upwards ten thousand times; nor again can fire be trained to sink downwards, nor anything else that follows one natural law be habituated or trained to follow another. It is neither by nature then nor in defiance of nature that virtues are implanted in us. Nature gives us the capacity of receiving them, and that capacity is perfected by habit.

Again, if we take the various natural powers which belong to us, we first acquire the proper faculties and afterwards display the activities. It is clearly so with the senses. It was not by seeing frequently or hearing frequently that we acquired the senses of seeing or hearing; on the contrary it was because we possessed the senses that we made use of them, not by making use of them that we obtained them. But the virtues we acquire by first exercising them, as is the case with all the arts, for it is by doing what we ought to do when we have learnt the arts that we learn the arts themselves; we become e.g. builders by building and harpists by playing the harp. Similarly it is by doing just acts that we become just, by doing temperate acts that we become temperate, by doing courageous acts that we become courageous. The experience of states is a witness to this truth, for it is by training the habits that legislators make the citizens good. This is the object which all legislators have at heart; if a legislator does not succeed in it, he fails of his purpose, and it constitutes the distinction between a good polity and a bad one.

Again, the causes and means by which any virtue is produced and by which it is destroyed are the same; and it is equally so with any art; for it is by playing the harp that both good and bad harpists are produced and the case of builders and all other artisans is similar, as it is by building well that they will be good builders and by building badly that they will be bad builders. If it were not so, there would be no need of anybody to teach them; they would all be born good or bad in their several trades. The case of the virtues is the same. It is by acting in such transactions as take place between man and man that we become either just or unjust. It is by acting in the face of danger and by habituating ourselves to fear or courage that we become either cowardly or courageous. It is much the same with our desires and angry passions. Some people become temperate and gentle, others become licentious and passionate, according as they conduct themselves in one way or another way in particular circumstances. In a word moral states are the results of activities corresponding to the moral states themselves. It is our duty therefore to give a certain character to the activities, as the moral states depend upon the differences of the activities. Accordingly the difference between one training of the habits and another from early days is not a light matter, but is serious or rather all-important.

DEFICIENCY AND EXCESS

The first point to be observed then is that in such matters as we are considering deficiency and excess are equally fatal. It is so, as we observe, in regard to health and strength; for we must judge of what we cannot see by the evidence of what we do see. Excess or deficiency of gymnastic exercise is fatal to strength. Similarly an excess or deficiency of meat and drink is fatal to health, whereas a suitable amount produces, augments and sustains it. It is the same then with temperance, courage, and the other virtues. A person who avoids and is afraid of everything and faces nothing becomes a coward; a person who is not afraid of anything but is ready to face everything becomes foolhardy. Similarly he who enjoys every pleasure and never abstains from any pleasure is licentious; he who eschews all pleasures like a boor is an insensible sort of person. For temperance and courage are destroyed by excess and deficiency but preserved by the mean state.

Again, not only are the causes and the agencies of production, increase and destruction in the moral states the same, but the sphere of their activity will be proved to be the same also. It is so in other instances which are more conspicuous, e.g. in strength; for strength is produced by taking a great deal of food and undergoing a great deal of labour, and it is the strong man who is able to take most food and to undergo most labour. The same is the case with the virtues. It is by abstinence from pleasures that we become temperate, and, when we have become temperate, we are best able to abstain from them. So too with courage; it is by habituating ourselves to despise and face alarms that we become courageous, and, when we have become courageous, we shall be best able to face them.

THE NATURE OF VIRTUE

We have next to consider the nature of virtue.

Now, as the qualities of the soul are three, viz. emotions, faculties and moral states, it follows that virtue must be one of the three. By the emotions I mean desire, anger, fear, courage, envy, joy, love, hatred, regret, emulation, pity, in a word whatever is attended by pleasure or pain. I call those faculties in respect of which we are said to be capable of experiencing these emotions, e.g. capable of getting angry or being pained or feeling pity. And I call those moral states in respect of which we are well or ill-disposed towards the emotions, ill-disposed e.g. towards the passion of anger, if our anger be too violent or too feeble, and well-disposed, if it be duly moderated, and similarly towards the other emotions.

Now neither the virtues nor the vices are emotions; for we are not called good or evil in respect of our emotions but in respect of our virtues or vices. Again, we are not praised or blamed in respect of our emotions; a person is not praised for being afraid or being angry, nor blamed for being angry in an absolute sense, but only for being angry in a certain way; but we are praised or blamed in respect of our virtues or vices. Again, whereas we are angry or afraid without deliberate purpose, the virtues are in some sense deliberate purposes, or do not exist in the absence of deliberate purpose. It may be added that while we are said to be moved in respect of our emotions, in respect of our virtues or vices we are not said to be moved but to have a certain disposition.

These reasons also prove that the virtues are not faculties. For we are not called either good or bad, nor are we praised or blamed, as having an abstract capacity for emotion. Also while Nature gives us our faculties, it is not Nature that makes us good or bad, but this is a point which we have already discussed. If then the virtues are neither emotions nor faculties, it remains that they must be moral states.

The nature of virtue has been now generically described. But it is not enough to state merely that virtue is a moral state, we must also describe the character of that moral state.

It must be laid down then that every virtue or excellence has the effect of producing a good condition of that of which it is a virtue or excellence, and of enabling it to perform its function well. Thus the excellence of the eye makes the eye good and its function good, as it is by the excellence of the eye that we see well. Similarly, the excellence of the horse makes a horse excellent and good at racing, at carrying its rider and at facing the enemy.

If then this is universally true, the virtue or excellence of man will be such a moral state as makes a man good and able to perform his proper function well. We have already explained how this will be the case, but another way of making it clear will be to study the nature or character of this virtue.

VIRTUE AS A MEAN

Now in everything, whether it be continuous or discrete, it is possible to take a greater, a smaller, or an equal amount, and this either absolutely or in relation to ourselves, the equal being a mean between excess and deficiency. By the mean in respect of the thing itself, or the absolute mean, I understand that which is equally distinct from both extremes; and this is one and the same thing for everybody. By the mean considered relatively to ourselves I understand that which is neither too much nor too little; but this is not one thing, nor is it the same for everybody. Thus if 10 be too much and 2 too little we take 6 as a mean in respect of the thing itself; for 6 is as much greater than 2 as it is less than 10, and this is a mean in arithmetical proportion. But the mean considered relatively to ourselves must not be

ascertained in this way. It does not follow that if 10 pounds of meat be too much and 2 be too little for a man to eat, a trainer will order him 6 pounds, as this may itself be too much or too little for the person who is to take it; it will be too little e.g. for Milo,[4] but too much for a beginner in gymnastics. It will be the same with running and wrestling; the right amount will vary with the individual. This being so, everybody who understands his business avoids alike excess and deficiency; he seeks and chooses the mean, not the absolute mean, but the mean considered relatively to ourselves.

Every science then performs its function well, if it regards the mean and refers the works which it produces to the mean. This is the reason why it is usually said of successful works that it is impossible to take anything from them or to add anything to them, which implies that excess or deficiency is fatal to excellence but that the mean state ensures it. Good . . . artists too, as we say, have an eye to the mean in their works. But virtue, like Nature herself, is more accurate and better than any art; virtue therefore will aim at the mean;—I speak of moral virtue, as it is moral virtue which is concerned with emotions and actions, and it is these which admit of excess and deficiency and the mean. Thus it is possible to go too far, or not to go far enough, in respect of fear, courage, desire, anger, pity, and pleasure and pain generally, and the excess and the deficiency are alike wrong; but to experience these emotions at the right times and on the right occasions and towards the right persons and for the right causes and in the right manner is the mean or the supreme good, which is characteristic of virtue. Similarly there may be excess, deficiency, or the mean, in regard to actions. But virtue is concerned with emotions and actions, and here excess is an error and deficiency a fault, whereas the mean is successful and laudable, and success and merit are both characteristics of virtue.

It appears then that virtue is a mean state, so far at least as it aims at the mean. Again, there are many different ways of going wrong; for evil is in its nature infinite, to use the Pythagorean[5] figure, but good is finite. But there is only one possible way of going right. Accordingly the former is easy and the latter difficult; it is easy to miss the mark but difficult to hit it. This again is a reason why excess and deficiency are characteristics of vice and the mean state a characteristic of virtue.

"For good is simple, evil manifold."[6]

Virtue then is a state of deliberate moral purpose consisting in a mean that is relative to ourselves, the mean being determined... by reason, or as a prudent man would determine it.

It is a mean state *firstly as lying* between two vices, the vice of excess on the one hand, and the vice of deficiency on the other, and secondly because, whereas the vices either fall short of or go beyond what is proper in the emotions and actions, virtue not only discovers but embraces that mean.

Accordingly, virtue, if regarded in its essence or theoretical conception, is a mean state, but, if regarded from the point of view of the highest good, or of excellence, it is an extreme.

But it is not every action or every emotion that admits of a mean state. There are some whose very name implies wickedness, as e.g. malice, shamelessness, and envy, among emotions, or adultery, theft, and murder, among actions. All these, and others like them, are censured as being intrinsically wicked, not merely the excesses or deficiencies of them. It is never possible then to be right in respect of them; they are always sinful.

Right or wrong in such actions as adultery does not depend on our committing them with the right person, at the right time or in the right manner; on the contrary it is sinful to do anything of the kind at all. It would be equally wrong then to suppose that there can be a mean state or an excess or deficiency in unjust, cowardly, or licentious conduct; for, if it were so, there would be a mean state of an excess or of a deficiency, an excess of an excess and a deficiency of a deficiency. But as in temperance and courage there can be no excess or deficiency because the mean is, in a sense, an extreme, so too in these cases there cannot be a mean or an excess or deficiency, but, however the acts may be done, they are wrong. For it is a general rule that an excess or deficiency does not admit of a mean state, nor a mean state of an excess or deficiency.

But it is not enough to lay down this as a general rule; it is necessary to apply it to particular cases, as in reasonings upon actions, general statements, although they are broader..., are less exact than particular statements. For all action refers to particulars, and it is essential that our theories should harmonize with the particular cases to which they apply.

SOME VIRTUES

We must take particular virtues then from the catalogue[7] *of virtues*.

In regard to feelings of fear and confidence, courage is a mean state. On the side of excess, he whose fearlessness is excessive has no name, as often happens, but he whose confidence is excessive is foolhardy, while he whose timidity is excessive and whose confidence is deficient is a coward.

In respect of pleasures and pains, although not indeed of all pleasures and pains, and to a less extent in respect of pains than of pleasures, the mean state is temperance..., the excess is licentiousness. We never find people who are deficient in regard to pleasures; accordingly such people again have not received a name, but we may call them insensible.

As regards the giving and taking of money, the mean state is liberality, the excess and deficiency are prodigality and illiberality. Here the excess and deficiency take opposite forms; for while the prodigal man is excessive in spending and deficient in taking, the illiberal man is excessive in taking and deficient in spending.

(For the present we are giving only a rough and summary account *of the virtues*, and that is sufficient for our purpose; we will hereafter determine their character more exactly.[8])

In respect of money there are other dispositions as well. There is the mean state which is magnificence; for the magnificent man, as having to do with large sums of money, differs from the liberal man who has to do only with small sums; and the excess corresponding to it is bad taste or vulgarity, the deficiency is meanness. These are different from the excess and deficiency of liberality; what the difference is will be explained hereafter.

In respect of honour and dishonour the mean state is highmindedness, the excess is what is called vanity, the deficiency littlemindedness. Corresponding to liberality, which, as we said, differs from magnificence as having to do *not with great but* with small sums of money, there is a moral state which has to do with petty honour and is related to highmindedness which has to do with great honour; for it is possible to aspire to honour in the right way, or in a way which is excessive or insufficient, and if a person's aspirations are excessive, he is called ambitious, if they are deficient, he is called unambitious, while if they are between the two, he has no name. The dispositions too are nameless, except that the disposition of the ambitious person is called ambition. The consequence is that the extremes lay claim to the mean or intermediate place. We ourselves speak of one who observes the mean sometimes as ambitious, and at other times as unambitious; we sometimes praise an ambitious, and at other times an unambitious person. The reason for our doing so will be stated in due course, but let us now discuss the other virtues in accordance with the method which we have followed hitherto.

Anger, like other emotions, has its excess, its deficiency, and its mean state. It may be said that they have no names, but as we call one who observes the mean gentle, we will call the mean state gentleness. Among the extremes, if a person errs on the side of excess, he may be called passionate and his vice passionateness, if on that of deficiency, he may be called impassive and his deficiency impassivity.

There are also three other mean states with a certain resemblance to each other, and yet with a difference. For while they are all concerned with intercourse in speech and action, they are different in that one of them is concerned with truth in such intercourse, and the others with pleasantness, one with pleasantness in amusement and the other with pleasantness in the various circumstances of life. We must therefore discuss these states in order to make it clear that in all cases it is the mean state which is an object of praise, and the extremes are neither right nor laudable but censurable. It is true that these mean and extreme states are generally nameless,

but we must do our best here as elsewhere to give them a name, so that our argument may be clear and easy to follow....

WHY IT IS SO DIFFICULT TO BE VIRTUOUS

That is the reason why it is so hard to be virtuous; for it is always hard work to find the mean in anything, e.g. it is not everybody, but only a man of science, who can find the mean or centre[9] of a circle. So too anybody can get angry—that is an easy matter—and anybody can give or spend money, but to give it to the right persons, to give the right amount of it and to give it at the right time and for the right cause and in the right way, this is not what anybody can do, nor is it easy. That is the reason why it is rare and laudable and noble to do well. Accordingly one who aims at the mean must begin by departing from that extreme which is the more contrary to the mean; he must act in the spirit of Calypso's[10] advice,

"Far from this smoke and swell keep thou thy bark,"

for of the two extremes one is more sinful than the other. As it is difficult then to hit the mean exactly, we must take the second best course,[11] as the saying is, and choose the lesser of two evils, and this we shall best do in the way that we have described, *i.e. by steering clear of the evil which is further from the mean*. We must also observe the things to which we are ourselves particularly prone, as different natures have different inclinations, and we may ascertain what these are by a consideration of our feelings of pleasure and pain. And then we must drag ourselves in the direction opposite to them; for it is by removing ourselves as far as possible from what is wrong that we shall arrive at the mean, as we do when we pull a crooked stick straight.

But in all cases we must especially be on our guard against what is pleasant and against pleasure, as we are not impartial judges of pleasure. Hence our attitude towards pleasure must be like that of the elders of the people in the Iliad towards Helen, and we must never be afraid of applying the words they use; for if we dismiss pleasure as they dismissed Helen, we shall be less likely to go wrong. It is by action of this kind, to put it summarily, that we shall best succeed in hitting the mean.

NOTES

1. Aristotle is thinking of the Platonic "ideas."
2. In other words life may be taken to mean either the mere possession of certain faculties or their active exercise.
3. The student of Aristotle must familiarize himself with the conception of intellectual as well as of moral virtues, although it is not the rule in modern philosophy to speak of the "virtues" of the intellect.
4. The famous Crotoniate wrestler.
5. The Pythagoreans, starting from the mystical significance of number, took the opposite principles of "the finite"...and "the infinite"...to represent good and evil.
6. A line—perhaps Pythagorean—of unknown authorship.
7. It would seem that a catalogue of virtues...must have been recognized in the Aristotelian school. Cp. *Eud. Eth.* ii. Chapter 3.
8. I have placed this sentence in a parenthesis, as it interrupts the argument respecting the right use of money.
9. Aristotle does not seem to be aware that the centre...of a circle is not really comparable to the mean...between the vices.
10. *Odyssey*, pp. xii, 219, and 200; but it is Odysseus who speaks there, and the advice has been given him not by Calypso but by Circe (ibid. pp. 101–110).
11. The Greek proverb means properly "we must take to the oars, if sailing is impossible."

REVIEW EXERCISES

1. What is the basic difference between virtue ethics and other types of ethics we have studied?
2. According to Aristotle, what is the difference between intellectual and moral virtue?
3. Explain the importance of character and habits in evaluating the morality of a human life.
4. Give a list of some virtues and related vices; explain how these virtues contribute to *eudaimonia*.
5. According to Aristotle, how is virtue a mean between extremes? Give some examples.
6. Are there virtues that are excellences for all human beings, or are virtues dependent upon our roles or our culture?
7. Who most exemplifies the virtue of courage—the person who finds it difficult to be brave or the person who finds it easy to be courageous?

MindTap® For more chapter resources and activities, go to MindTap.

Feminist Thought and the Ethics of Care

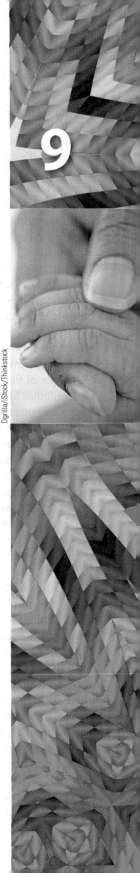

9

Learning Outcomes

After reading this chapter, you should be able to:

- Describe the importance of feminist thought for ethical inquiry.
- Explain some of the problems confronting women around the world.
- Explain feminist criticisms of traditional views about ethics and moral development.
- Identify the arguments of key feminist authors, including Carol Gilligan, Nel Noddings, Sarah Ruddick, Martha Nussbaum, Judith Butler, and Annette Baier.
- Describe the essential features of the ethics of care.
- Explain the difference between feminine ethics and feminist ethics.
- Distinguish between the several versions or "waves" of feminism.
- Defend your own ideas about the importance of feminist ethics and the ethics of care.

MindTap®   For more chapter resources and activities, go to MindTap.

In Pakistan in October 2012, a fifteen-year-old schoolgirl, Malala Yousafzai, was shot in the head by Taliban assassins as she waited for a bus. The Taliban targeted Malala because she had spoken out in defense of the right of girls to attend school. Malala recovered from her wounds and has gone on to become an international advocate for the rights of girls and women. In 2014, Malala became the youngest person ever to receive the Nobel Peace Prize. When asked if she was a feminist, she responded, "I'm a feminist" and said that we all should be feminists because "feminism is another word for equality."[1] Her case is an indication of the inequality and oppression that still afflict women throughout the world.

We like to imagine that violence against women is only a problem in other parts of the globe. But in the United States, there is still a significant amount of violence against women. According to data used by the White House in its "1 is 2 Many" campaign to reduce violence against women, one in five women will be sexually assaulted in college, one in nine teenage girls will be forced to have sex, and one in ten teens will be hurt on purpose by someone they are dating.[2] To combat the problem of sexual assault and date rape, the state of California enacted legislation in 2014 which requires "affirmative consent" for sex—popularly known as the "yes means yes" law. We will discuss this further in Chapter 12 in connection with sexual morality. But note that the issue of sex and sexuality is closely tied to the question of women's rights.

Some authors have also suggested that another insidious form of violence against women occurs through a cultural obsession with female beauty, which fuels the epidemic of eating disorders and the growing use of cosmetic surgery to "perfect" the female body.[3] Naomi Wolf links this to the rise of pornography; "the influence of pornography on women's sexual sense of self has now become so complete that it is almost impossible for younger women to distinguish the role pornography plays in creating their idea of how to be, look and move in sex from their own innate sense of sexual identity."[4] Some authors have argued that pornography is itself an example of violence against women, which in turn contributes to further violence against women.[5] It might be, however, that pornography is a celebration of sexuality, which empowers women. Pro-sex or sex-positive feminists such as Wendy McElroy argue that pornography benefits women both personally and politically. From McElroy's perspective, the point is to make sure that sex work is free of coercion, which respects women by affording them the freedom to choose as individuals to participate or not.[6] This dispute reminds us that feminism, like other approaches to moral theory, is subject to diverse interpretations.

While the charge about the degrading and violent aspects of pornography has been made by Western feminists, a similar argument against the general sexual objectification of women comes from defenders of traditional roles for women and rules of modesty. While this argument has been made in a variety of cultural contexts, the most prominent current discussion involves rules governing the use of veiling in Muslim cultures. Defenders of the veil, or *hijab*, argue that modest dress protects women from being publicly harassed or molested, often quoting a passage from the *Qur'an* (33:59), which states that modest dress for women will ensure that they are not abused. Similar ideas are found in other cultures and religious traditions, including

Women holding signs in support of Malala Yousafzai in 2012 in Islamabad, Pakistan.

in some ultra-Orthodox Jewish communities. Critics argue that women should be free from molestation regardless of how they dress. From this perspective, the problem is not what women wear or how they behave, but a male-dominated culture in which men seek to regulate and control women.

The problem of violence against women is a global issue. Nicholas Kristof and Sheryl WuDunn have chronicled the problem in their book (and documentary) *Half the Sky*. Across the world, rape and sex-slavery threaten the well-being of women. In some cases, women are denied access to medical care and resources simply because they are women. Female fetuses are aborted because of a cultural bias toward male offsprings. Girls' genitals are cut in a practice that some call ritual "circumcision" but critics call **female genital mutilation** or FGM. While cultural relativists might be reluctant to judge such cases (as discussed in Chapter 3), feminists focus on the harm that FGM causes to girls and women. Even worse than FGM is the fact that girls and women are often liable to be killed simply because of their gender. Kristof and WuDunn conclude,

> It appears that more girls have been killed in the last fifty years, precisely because they were girls, than men were killed in all the battles of the twentieth century. More girls are killed in this routine "gendercide" in any one decade than people were slaughtered in all the genocides of the twentieth century.[7]

A significant problem is "honor killing." In some cultures, when a woman has done something that the culture considers shameful, the male members of the family feel justified in killing her. In some places, rape is "punished" by killing the woman who has been raped or by forcing the rape victim to marry her rapist. A CBS News report from April 2012 concluded that at least 5,000 women are killed every year because of "honor."[8] In Pakistan, in 2011, nearly 1,000 women were murdered in this way. Some cases occur within the United States and Britain, including the murder in 2009 of Noor Almaleki by her own father in Peoria, Arizona, as reported on the CBS news program *48 Hours*.[9]

While the mainstream of Western culture now holds that women deserve to be treated equally, it is clear that we've still got a long way to go in terms of actualizing this idea internationally. Even within the United States, there is room for progress. In 2015, the World Economic Forum ranked the United States twenty-eighth in the world in terms of gender equality, calculated by measuring a variety of factors indicating economic opportunity, educational attainment, health outcomes, and political empowerment of women (as compared to men).[10] On the one hand, women do seem to be outperforming men academically. According to a report from the White House in 2014, "young women are more likely than young men to be college graduates or have a

graduate degree."[11] And yet, the report notes that there is a remaining "pay gap" in the United States, with women earning only "78 cents for every dollar earned by their male counterparts."

We might use the term *feminist* to describe those who are concerned about the well-being of women, while being critical of the unequal treatment and violence that afflict women. Feminist philosophers Sally Haslanger, Nancy Tuana, and Peg O'Connor define **feminism** as "an intellectual commitment and a political movement that seeks justice for women and the end of sexism in all forms."[12] Feminism shows up in ethical theory as a critique of traditional approaches to ethics, which are primarily focused on values such as autonomy, impartiality, and neutrality. While it is useful to invoke these values in criticizing women's oppression, some feminists worry that these sorts of values are themselves morally problematic. This criticism argues that values such as autonomy, impartiality, and neutrality are patriarchal values, distinctively stressed by male-dominant cultures, which downplay the importance of concrete caring relationships. Such caring relationships are typical of the private sphere and family life—those parts of life that are viewed as being feminine (as opposed to the masculine and patriarchal public sphere).

Debate about sex or gender differences in moral perspectives and moral reasoning was sparked by the work of psychologist Carol Gilligan.[13] She interviewed both male and female subjects about various moral dilemmas and found that the females she interviewed had a different view than the males of what was morally required of them. They used a different moral language to explain themselves, and their reasoning involved a different moral logic. Gilligan concluded that males and females have different kinds of ethics. The ensuing debate, which will be discussed here, has focused on whether there is a distinctively feminine morality. One significant question is whether the idea that there is a female approach to ethics helps or hinders the cause of reducing violence against women, and whether it helps or hinders the effort to promote liberty and equality for women.

GENDER IN MORAL REASONING AND THE ETHICS OF CARE

In Carol Gilligan's studies, conducted in the 1970s, a hypothetical situation was posed to two eleven-year-old children, Jake and Amy.[14] A man's wife was extremely ill and in danger of dying. A certain drug might save her life, but the man could not afford it, in part because the druggist had set an unreasonably high price for it. The question was whether the man should steal the drug? Jake answered by trying to figure out the relative value of the woman's life and the druggist's right to his property. He concluded that the man should steal the drug because he calculated that the woman's life was worth more. Amy was not so sure. She wondered what would happen to both the man and his wife if he stole the drug. "If he stole the drug, he might save his wife then, but if he did, he might have to go to jail, and then his wife might get sicker again."[15] She said that if the husband and wife talked about this, they might be able to think of some other way out of the dilemma.

One interesting thing about this case is the very different ways in which the two children tried to determine the right thing to do in this situation. The boy used a calculation in which he weighed and compared values from a neutral standpoint. The girl spoke about the possible effects of the proposed action on the two individuals and their relationship. Her method did not give the kind of definitive answer that is apparent in the boy's method. When researchers examined this and similar cases, they speculated that these differences in moral reasoning may be the result of sex or gender.[16]

Another representative example also seems to show a gender difference in moral reasoning.[17] In explaining how they would respond to a moral dilemma about maintaining one's moral principles in the light of peer or family pressure, two teen subjects responded quite differently. The case was one in which the religious views of each teen differed from those of their parents. The male said that he had a right to his own opinions, though he respected his parents' views. The female said that she was concerned about how her parents would react to her views. "I understand their fear of my new religious ideas." However, she added, "they really ought to listen to me and try to understand my beliefs."[18] Although the male and female subjects reached similar conclusions, they used different reasoning. They seemed to have two decidedly different orientations or perspectives. The male spoke in terms of an individual's right to his or her own opinions, while the female talked of the need for the particular people involved to talk with and come to understand one another. These and similar cases raise questions about whether a gender difference actually exists in the way people reason about moral matters.

Several contrasting pairs of terms are associated with or can be used to describe female and male ethical perspectives. These are listed in the following table:

Female Ethical Perspective	Male Ethical Perspective
Personal	Impersonal
Partial	Impartial
Private	Public
Natural	Contractual
Feeling	Reason
Compassionate	Fair
Concrete	Universal
Responsibility	Rights
Relationship	Individual
Solidarity	Autonomy

The various characteristics or values in this list may need explanation. First, consider the supposedly typical *female moral perspective*. The context for women's moral decision making is said to be one of *relatedness*. Women are supposedly more concerned about particular people and their relations and how they will be affected by some action. In this view, women's morality is highly personal. They are partial to their particular loved ones and think that one's primary moral responsibility is to these people. It is the private and personal natural relations of family and friends that are the model for other relations. Women stress the concrete experiences of this or that event and are concerned about the real harm that might befall a particular person or persons. The primary moral obligation is to prevent harm and to help people. Women are able to empathize with others and are concerned about how they might feel if certain things were to happen to them. They believe that moral problems can be solved by talking about them and by trying to understand others' perspectives. Caring and compassion are key virtues. The primary moral obligation is not to turn away from those in need.

Nel Noddings's work, *Caring: A Feminine Approach to Ethics and Moral Education*, provides a good example and further description of the ethics of care.[19] Noddings has spent her career defending and explaining her ideas about care ethics. This approach includes an account of how caring relationships are important from the standpoint of evolution—as a mother's care for her children promotes their survival and emotional and moral health. Indeed, Noddings maintains that we all have a natural desire to be cared for—and that we have the ability to provide care. This is true whether we are male or female, even though evolution and culture tend to make us think that care is more female than male. Noddings emphasizes that care is not a voluntary act of free and equal parties who enter into social contracts. Rather, we find ourselves already embedded in family and social contexts that create networks of care. These networks and relationships are not primarily governed by abstract rules; rather, they depend upon the needs and relations of the individuals. So, for Noddings, care is two-sided: it involves a complex interplay between the carer and the cared for. For Noddings, caring means listening attentively and seeing lovingly. It involves what she describes as motivational displacement, where the needs of the other overwhelm us, as in a mother's physical reaction to the crying of her infant child. Noddings thinks that the deep connections of care are psychologically and morally important for human flourishing and that society would be better if it promoted caring relationships through education and institutional design.

The supposedly typical *male moral perspective* contrasts sharply with a feminine ethics of care, such as we find in the work of Noddings. In this view, men take a more universal and impartial standpoint in reasoning about what is morally good and bad. Men are more inclined to talk in terms of fairness, justice, and rights. They ask about the overall effects of some action and whether the good effects, when all are considered, outweigh the bad. It is as though they think moral decisions ought to be made impersonally or from some unbiased and detached point of view. The moral realm would then, in many ways, be similar to the public domain of law and contract. The law must not be biased and must treat everyone equally. In this view, moral thinking involves a type of universalism that recognizes the equal moral worth of all persons, both in themselves and before the law. People ought to keep their promises because this is the just thing to do and helps create a reliable social order. Morality is a matter of doing one's duty, keeping one's agreements, and respecting other people's rights. Impartiality and respectfulness are key virtues. The primary obligation is not to act unfairly.

What are we to make of the view that two very different sets of characteristics describe male and female morality? In suggesting a difference between men's and women's morality, Carol Gilligan was taking aim at one of the dominant points of view about moral development, namely, that of the psychologist Lawrence Kohlberg.[20] According to Kohlberg, the highest stage of moral development is the stage in which an adult can be governed not by social pressure, but by personal moral principles and a sense of justice. Based on these principles, adults come to regard other people as moral equals and manifest an impartial and universal perspective. In his own research, Kohlberg found that women did not often reach this stage of development. He thus judged them to be morally underdeveloped or morally deficient. Of course, his conclusions were not totally surprising because he had used an all-male sample in working out his theory.[21] After deriving his principles from male subjects, he then used them to judge both male and female moral development.

Gilligan and Kohlberg were not the first psychologists to believe a difference existed between men's and women's morality. Sigmund Freud held that women "show less sense of justice than men, that they are less ready to submit to the great exigencies of life, that they are more often influenced in their judgments by feelings of affection or hostility. . . ."[22] According to Freud, women were morally inferior to men. Instead of being able to establish themselves as separate people living in society and adapting to its rules, girls remained in the home, attached to their mothers. Thus, girls developed a capacity for personal relations and intimacy while their male counterparts developed a sense of separateness and personal autonomy. The idea was that women base their morality on concerns about personal relations, while men base their morality on rules that can reconcile the separate competing individuals in society.[23] Believing that a focus on personal relations rather than a sense of justice was a lesser form of morality, Freud and others thought that women were morally inferior to men.

Is There a Gender Difference in Morality?

Several questions ought to be asked about the theory that women and men exhibit a different type of moral perspective and moral reasoning. First, is this contention true? Is it an empirical fact that men and women manifest a different type of moral thinking? Second, if it is a fact, then how are we to explain it? What may be the source or cause of this difference? Third, if there is a difference, is one type of moral thinking higher or more developed or better than the other? We might also wonder whether the attempt to distinguish between male and female forms of moral experience serves the feminist goal of helping women or whether it simply reiterates traditional gender stereotypes.

To determine whether there is, in fact, a difference between the moral language and logic of males and females, we need to rely on empirical surveys and studies. What do people find who have examined this supposed phenomena? We have already described some of the earlier findings of Carol Gilligan. Her conclusions in more recent studies have varied somewhat.[24] For example, her later research finds some variation in moral reasoning among both men and women. According to these findings, while both men and women sometimes think in terms of a justice perspective, few men think in terms of a care perspective. Being able to take one perspective rather than the other, she wrote, is much like being able to see the following well-known line drawing figure as a rabbit or as a duck. One's perspective affects how one sees the figure.

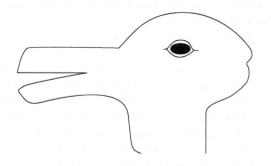

With regard to ethics, if one has a justice perspective, one will see that "the *self* as moral agent stands as the figure against a ground of social relationships, judging the conflicting claims of self and others against a standard of equality or equal respect." If one has a care perspective, then one will see that "the *relationship* becomes the figure, defining self and others. Within the context of relationship, the self as a moral agent perceives and responds to the perception of need."[25] In these more recent studies, Gilligan used "educationally advantaged North American adolescents and adults" and found that two-thirds had one or the other orientation as their primary focus. Still, she found sex differences in the results. "With one exception, all of the men who focused, focused on justice. The women divided, with roughly one-third focusing on justice and one-third on care" (the other third had a hybrid approach).[26] In this study, women did not always have the care perspective as their focus—but without the women in the study, the care focus would have been almost absent.

Other theorists are not so sure about what the data show. For example, Catherine Greeno and Eleanor Maccoby believe that any difference between men's and women's morality can be accounted for by social status and experience, rather than gender. Using other studies, they point out that in many cases, those who exhibit so-called feminine morality have been housewives and women who lack higher education. They found that career women showed types of moral reasoning similar to those of men.[27] The question of whether women do exhibit a unique type of moral language and logic will need to be decided by those who study the empirical data. And, of course, you can examine your own experience to see whether the males and females you know seem to reason differently when discussing moral issues.

The Source of Feminine Morality

At least three distinct types of explanation address a possible difference between masculine and feminine morality. One proposes differences in the psychosexual development of the two sexes; a second points to biological differences; and a third gives a social, cultural, or educational explanation.

We have already described something of the Freudian account of the effects of psychosexual development on male and female moral thinking. A few more points may be added. According to this view, males and females have different concepts of the self and their gender identities; this concept is influenced by their development in relation to their mothers and fathers. As they grow up, females develop a sense of being connected with their mothers, whereas males find themselves being different from their mothers. According to Nancy Chodorow, who amplifies Freud's theory, development of the self and one's sense of individuality depends on being able to separate oneself from others. Thus males, who tend to separate themselves from their mothers, come to have a sense of self as independent, whereas females do not develop the sense of separate selves and rather see themselves as attached or connected to others. From this developmental situation, males and females supposedly develop different senses of morality—males develop a morality associated with separation and autonomy, and females develop a morality with relationships and interdependence. According to traditional

views such as Kohlberg's (see earlier), mature moral thinking involves being able to be detached and see things from some impartial perspective. Judging from a care perspective means that one cannot judge dispassionately or without bias, and this was deemed to be a moral defect. However, as we have seen, this traditional view of care ethics has been criticized by feminists and others.

A second account of the source of differences in masculine and feminine morality is exemplified by the writings of Caroline Whitbeck, who locates it, at least in part, in women's and men's biology, that is, in the difference in their reproductive capacities and experiences. In pregnancy, labor, and childbirth, women experience certain feelings of dependency and contingency.[28] They do not have full control of their bodies. They experience weakness and pain. They feel themselves participating in "species life" at its most primitive level. Because of their own feelings during this time, they can sympathize more readily with the infant's or child's feelings of helplessness and dependency.

Some will claim that female caring and nurturing spring naturally from the intimate and sympathetic relation that mothers are supposed to have toward their children. A naturalistic explanation of this might maintain that there is some instinctive orientation toward nurturance in women that is ultimately a matter of biology and physiology. It might be, however, that culture and socialization also matter. Girls and women are taught to exhibit nurturing behaviors by a culture that expects them to be nurturers and caregivers. This points toward the idea that mothering is not only a biological phenomenon, but also a social and cultural one. Although some women bear children, it is not necessary that they rear them. Still, because they do give birth to and nurse infants, women have generally come to be the primary child rearers.

It is from the elements of so-called maternal practice that women's morality arises, according to this third view.[29] To Sara Ruddick, for example, maternal practice results in "maternal thinking," which is the "vocabulary and logic of connections" that arises from women "acting in response to demands of their children."[30] She believes that maternal thinking is not simply a kind of feeling that comes naturally to women, but a purposeful way of thinking and acting. It involves finding ways to preserve, develop, and promote one's children. Infants are extremely vulnerable and will not survive if they do not have the basics of food, clothing, and shelter. Children must be safeguarded from the many dangers of life. They need help in growing—physically, socially, and morally. Particular virtues are required for a mother to be able to satisfy the needs of her children. Among those described by Ruddick are humility (for one cannot do everything), cheerfulness combined with realism, and love and affection. Mothers also need to guard against certain negative traits and feelings, for example, feelings of hopelessness and possessiveness. According to this view, it is because they spend much of their lives mothering that women develop a morality consistent with this experience. And cultural norms tend to reinforce the value of care and nurturance for women. We praise caregiving women and celebrate mothering, while wondering about the femininity of women who don't exemplify the maternal virtues. Maternal morality stresses relationships and the virtues that are necessary for mothering. One does not necessarily have to be a biological mother, however, both to engage in mothering and develop maternal ethics, according to this viewpoint. Just because men and some women do not give birth does not mean that they cannot be parents and develop the outlook required for this practice. Until now, it has been a social phenomenon that maternal practice has been principally women's work.

Evaluating Gender-Specific Approaches to Morality

Many questions remain concerning these three explanations of gender differences in morality. Some are factual or empirical questions, for they ask whether something is or is not the case. Do women in fact think and act in the ways described above? Are they more likely to do so than men? Does giving birth or rearing children cause those involved in these practices to think in a certain way and to have a certain moral perspective? Much of what we

say here is quite speculative in that we are making guesses that cannot strictly be proved to be true. Nevertheless, there is a great deal of appeal and suggestiveness in the theory of the ethics of care. In particular, we should compare this type of morality with more traditional theories, such as utilitarianism and deontology, to see how different the perspectives are as exemplified by the theories.

Whether one way of judging morally is *better* than the other is also an open question. As we have seen, there has been a tradition of thought that says that the so-called feminine morality—an ethics of care focused on particular relations—is a lower-level morality. When we consider the sources of this tradition, we find many reasons to criticize it. Perhaps, on the contrary, it is the ethics of care that provides a better moral orientation. For example, instead of judging war in terms of whether the overall benefits outweigh the costs, we may do well to think about the particular people involved—for example, that every soldier is someone's daughter, son, sister, brother, mother, or father. Or perhaps the two orientations are complementary. Perhaps a justice orientation is the minimum that morality requires. We could then build on this minimum and, for example, temper justice with care and mercy. On the other hand, the care orientation may be the more basic one, and justice concerns could then be brought in to determine how best to care.

If specific female and male virtues parallel these ethical orientations, then another question arises. Would it not be possible and good for both men and women to develop both sets of virtues? If these virtues are described in a positive way—say, caring and not subservience—would they not be traits that all should strive to possess? These traits might be simply different aspects of the human personality, rather than the male or female personality. They would then be human virtues and human perspectives, rather than male or female virtues and perspectives. In this view, an ethics of fidelity, care, and sympathy would be just as important for human flourishing as an ethics of duty, justice, and acting on principle. While there would be certain moral virtues that all people should develop, other psychological traits could also vary according to temperament and choice. Individuals would be free to manifest, according to their own personalities, any combination of positive moral characteristics. These sets of characteristics and virtues would synthesize, in various ways, both stereotypical masculine and feminine traits.

FEMINIST THOUGHT

Not all feminist writers are supportive of the ethics of care. While most would agree that one can describe a particular type of morality that exhibits the characteristics said to belong to an ethics of care, these writers question whether all aspects of such an ethics of care are good. For example, care ethics seems to be based on relations between unequals. The mother–child relation is such a relation. The dependency in the relation goes only one way. One does all (or most of) the giving, and the other all (or most of) the receiving. This may tend to reinforce or promote a one-sided morality of self-sacrifice and subjugation. It may reinforce the view that women ought to be the ones who sacrifice and help and support others, chiefly children and men.

Other criticisms include the worry that care ethics tends to rest upon stereotypes about female and male behavior, which tend to reinforce male dominance. If we think that men are impartial while women are not, this may lead us to think twice about assigning women to positions of authority where impartiality is required. Furthermore, the hard distinction between the genders is problematic. And as we see in the case of transgender persons (which we will discuss in Chapter 12). Some women are not all that caring, and some men are quite caring. The differences may be described in terms such as masculine and feminine—but in reality, this gendered terminology does not map accurately onto actual differences among diverse individuals. Furthermore, these supposed differences may only be cultural differences. It might be the case in Western cultures that women are more caring and men are more impartial. But this may not be true in other cultures. Michael Slote, a prominent defender of care ethics, notes that in African cultures, both men and women exhibit caring behaviors; he also argues that "there are very strong elements of care thinking in both Confucian and Buddhist thought." Slote concludes that this shows that "the ethics of care can and should be regarded as a potential overall human morality, rather than as something just about, or at most only relevant to, women."[31]

We defined feminism at the outset of this chapter (following Haslanger, Tuana, and O'Connor) as a movement that seeks justice for women and an end to sexism in all forms. The history of feminism includes both those who are primarily concerned with promoting women's equality with men and those who want to raise the value of women's unique characteristics. However, the most well-known writers and activists of this movement have been those who have stressed women's rights and equality. Among the earliest examples is Mary Wollstonecraft, who wrote, in *A Vindication of the Rights of Women* (1792),[32] that women were not by nature weak and emotional, but that their social situation had in many ways made them so. It was society that taught women negative moral traits such as cunning and vanity, she insisted. The suffragettes who sought political equality and the right to vote followed in her footsteps. Many years later, Simone de Beauvoir's *The Second Sex* (1949) became a classic text for what has been called a "second wave" of feminists (the "first wave" being the nineteenth-century women's rights advocates).[33] According to de Beauvoir, women are a "second sex" because they are regarded always in terms of being an "other" to the primary male sex. In an existentialist vein, she stressed the need for women to be independent selves and free to establish their own goals and projects. Various other writers in the history of the women's movement stressed the importance of raising women's consciousness so that they might understand how women's experience is shaped by social and cultural norms. This involves helping women become aware of how certain social circumstances leave women with second-class status, while encouraging women to examine the various ways they have been oppressed and subordinated in their personal, professional, and political lives. The movement's aim was not only to raise consciousness, but also to act politically to bring about the equality of women. Thus, for example, they sought the passage of the Equal Rights Amendment to the U.S. Constitution. Although the Equal Rights Amendment passed through both houses of the U.S. Congress in 1972, it failed to receive enough support in the states in order to be ratified. The original Congressional authorization expired in 1982. Since 1982, members of the U.S. Congress have continued to reintroduce the Equal Rights Amendment at each new session of the Congress.

The so-called third wave of feminism (developing since the 1990s) has been more aware of the problem of diversity in dealing with women's issues. This includes the range of women's experiences in diverse cultures. Women's issues will be different in Pakistan, in Israel, and in the United States, depending upon religious, cultural, and even generational differences. Women in the Western world who are concerned with liberty and equality for women in the rest of the world have been more aware of the need to listen to women and appreciate their unique cultural situations. One prominent feminist who has been working on international women's issues is the philosopher Martha Nussbaum (whose work we touched upon in Chapter 3). Nussbaum reminds us that cultures are dynamic and internally complex. Nonetheless, Nussbaum thinks that it is still important to clarify abstract moral principles, provided that they are grounded in empirical reality. She explains that although feminist philosophy has often been "skeptical of universal moral normative approaches," feminism can make universal claims that "need not be insensitive to difference or imperialistic."[34] Nussbaum's own work dealing with gender issues in India exemplifies the approach she champions; criticism must be grounded in local practices and based upon the needs and interests of the women whose lives are characterized by the specifics of the local context.

Other recent feminist discussions point toward a further critique of abstract moral principles. These discussions are often concerned with the sheer complexity of gender terms and sexuality. One prominent author associated with third-wave feminism is Judith Butler, whose work is influenced by

AP Images/dapd/Thomas Lohnes

Feminist philosopher and queer theorist Judith Butler.

post-structuralist philosophy and what is often called *queer theory*—which is an approach that aims to deconstruct traditional norms for thinking about gender and sexuality. In her most influential book, *Gender Trouble*, Butler discusses such figures as hermaphrodites and drag queens in order to elucidate the ways in which gender norms are socially constructed and "performed," in an attempt to liberate gender and sexuality from strict social conventions. As might be expected, this approach has implications for sexual morality and the issue of transgender rights (as we'll discuss in Chapter 12).

Many of these forms of feminist moral thought may be said to advance a *feminist ethics*, distinguishable from an ethics of care (sometimes called *feminine ethics*, because of its focus on feminine virtues).[35] Writers who explore feminist ethics often focus on analyzing the causes of women's subordination and oppression and systematic violence against women. Feminist ethicists are also engaged in strategies for eliminating this violence and oppression. In this, they have an explicitly political orientation.

The political activist side of feminism may be directed at local and national issues, such as the Equal Rights Amendment mentioned previously. It might also have a global focus. At the international level, women have worked together to raise the status of women around the world and seek ways to better the conditions under which they live. International conferences have brought women together from all nations to discuss their problems and lend each other support. One initiative is the effort to provide small loans to women in impoverished areas (so-called microfinancing) so that women can stabilize their financial and family lives. Other focuses of activism include reproductive health, preventing violence against women, and educating women in an effort to equalize literacy rates and life prospects. Of course, such international and cross-cultural work requires sensitivity and awareness of the problems of cultural relativism and religious diversity.

Some feminists point out that traditional philosophy is among the causes of women's oppression. Traditional moral philosophy has not been favorable to women. It has tended to support the view that women should develop "women's virtues," such as modesty, humility, and subservience—which are often to the detriment of women. For example, Aristotle seems to have held that women are inferior to men not only because of certain biological phenomena having to do with heat in the body, but also because they lack certain elements of rationality. According to Aristotle, free adult males could rule over slaves, women, and children because of the weakness in their "deliberative" faculties. In the case of women, while they have such a faculty, Aristotle claims it is "without authority."[36] In *Emile*, Jean-Jacques Rousseau's work on the education of the young, the French philosopher advances a quite different type of ideal education for the protagonist Emile than for Emile's wife-to-be, Sophie. Because morality is different for men and women, the young of each sex ought to be trained in different virtues, according to Rousseau. Emile is to be trained in virtues such as justice and fortitude, while Sophie is to be taught to be docile and patient.[37] With this history of male-dominant moral philosophy in mind, it is easy to see why some feminists may be reluctant to affirm traditional notions about feminine virtues, since these are associated with a long history of the subordination of women.

Even contemporary moral philosophers have not given women and women's concerns their due,

according to many feminist writers. They have not been interested in matters of the home and domesticity. They have tended to ignore issues such as the "feminization of poverty," the use of reproductive technologies, sexual harassment, and violence against and sexual abuse of women. It is mainly with women writing on these topics in contemporary ethics that they have gained some respectability as topics of genuine philosophical interest. So also have the issues of female oppression and subordination become topics of wider philosophical interest.

EVALUATION OF FEMINIST THOUGHT AND THE ETHICS OF CARE

We have already pointed out some questions that have been raised about the ethics of care. As we have seen, some writers point out that care does not always come naturally to women, and not all women are good mothers or good nurturers. Moreover, men may also exhibit these characteristics, and some cultures emphasize care as a primary value for both men and women. However, supporters of the ethics of care may reply that their main concern is not the gender issue as much as the need to advance care in opposition to more traditional values, such as impartiality and universality.

In addition, many critics of care ethics contend that the promotion of so-called feminine traits may not be of benefit to women and may reinforce women's subservient position in society. Defenders of care ethics might respond that it is not such "feminine" virtues as obedience, self-sacrifice, silence, and service that define an ethics of care. Rather, such an ethics tells us from what perspective we are to judge morally, namely, from the perspective of specific persons in relation to each other, susceptible to particular harms and benefits.

Can an ethics of care free itself from the negative associations of traditional femininity? Can feminist ethicists support an ethics of care while also seeking to promote women's equality? It is clear, at least, that women cannot be restricted to traditionally subservient roles if they are to be treated equally and fairly in both the public realm and the realm of the home and family.

What these discussions have also suggested is that we can no longer maintain that one ethics exists for the home and the private realm (an ethics of care and relationships) and another ethics for work or the public realm (an ethics of justice and fairness and impartiality). "Neither the realm of domestic, personal life, nor that of non domestic, economic and political life, can be understood or interpreted in isolation from the other," writes feminist political philosopher Susan Moller Okin.[38] These two realms not only overlap, Okin argues, but also can and should exemplify the values and virtues of each other. Elements of altruism and concern for particular, concrete individuals have a place in the political as well as the domestic realm. Furthermore, when feminists say that "the personal is political," they mean that "what happens in the personal life, particularly in relations between the sexes, is not immune from the dynamic of *power*, which has typically been seen as a distinguishing feature of the political."[39] These relations should thus also be restrained by considerations of fairness and justice.

One further question arises about the ethics of care. While such an ethics describes an ideal context for ethical decision making, it does not tell us how we are to determine what will help or harm particular individuals. It does not in itself say what constitutes benefit or harm. It gives no rules for what we are to do in cases of conflict of interest, even among those to whom we are partial, or what to do when we cannot benefit all. It seems to give little definitive help for knowing what to do in cases where we must harm some to benefit others. Supporters of care ethics may respond that by setting the context for ethical decision making, an ethics of care has already done something valuable, for it thus provides a balance to the otherwise one-sided traditional ethics of the impersonal and universal. Perhaps this is a valuable minimum achievement. Or perhaps care ethics, with its emphasis on human connectedness, has an even more central role to play in today's ethical and political discussions. As Gilligan notes,

> By rendering a care perspective more coherent and making its terms explicit, moral theory may facilitate women's ability to speak about their experiences

and perceptions and may foster the ability of others to listen and to understand. At the same time, the evidence of care focus in women's moral thinking suggests that the study of women's development may provide a natural history of moral development in which care is ascendant, revealing the ways in which creating and sustaining responsive connection with others becomes or remains a central moral concern.[40]

Feminism and the ethics of care remain important focal points for moral theory. This chapter's reading selections include a brief excerpt from Nel Noddings, as well as longer essays by Annette Baier and Hilde Lindemann. Noddings is a key proponent of care ethics; the excerpt is from her book *Caring*, first published in 1984. Annette Baier's essay provides a critique of the traditional emphasis on justice that is derived from her reading of Carol Gilligan's account of moral development. Lindemann discusses the problem of power, male privilege, heterosexual norms, and a variety of other issues arising from a focus on gender. The feminist focus on power, inequality, and the importance of care connects with other areas of concern that will show up in later chapters of this book, including discrimination (Chapter 13), sexuality (Chapter 12), abortion (Chapter 11), and global justice (Chapter 20).

NOTES

1. "Malala Yousafzai tells Emma Watson: I'm a feminist thanks to you," *The Guardian* (November 5, 2015), http://www.theguardian.com/world/2015/nov/05/malala-yousafzai-tells-emma-watson-im-a-feminist-thanks-to-you (accessed February 8, 2016).
2. The White House, "1 is 2 Many," http://www.whitehouse.gov/1is2many (accessed July 21, 2016).
3. Naomi Wolf, *The Beauty Myth: How Images of Beauty Are Used against Women* (New York: Harper Perennial, 2002); Cressida J. Heyes and Meredith Jones, *Cosmetic Surgery: A Feminist Primer* (New York: Ashgate, 2009).
4. Naomi Wolf, *The Beauty Myth*, p. 5.
5. Most prominently, Andrea Dworkin, *Pornography: Men Possessing Women* (New York: Perigee Books, 1981).

6. Wendy McElroy, *XXX: A Woman's Right to Pornography* (New York: St. Martin's Press, 1995).

7. Nicholas D. Kristof and Sheryl WuDunn, *Half the Sky: Turning Oppression into Opportunity for Women Worldwide* (New York: Vintage, 2010), p. xvii.

8. http://www.cbsnews.com/news/honor-killing-under-growing-scrutiny-in-the-us/ (accessed July 21, 2016).

9. CBS, *48 Hours*, September 1, 2012.

10. World Economic Forum, *The Global Gender Gap Report 2015*, http://reports.weforum.org/global-gender-gap-report-2015/the-global-gender-gap-index-2015/ (accessed July 21, 2016).

11. The White House, *Women's Participation in Education and the Workforce* (October 2014), https://www.whitehouse.gov/sites/default/files/docs/womens_slides_final.pdf (accessed July 21, 2016).

12. Sally Haslanger, Nancy Tuana, and Peg O'Connor, "Topics in Feminism," *Stanford Encyclopedia of Philosophy* (2011), http://plato.stanford.edu/entries/feminism-topics/ (accessed July 21, 2016).

13. Carol Gilligan, "Concepts of the Self and of Morality," *Harvard Educational Review* (November 1977), pp. 481–517.

14. This is a summary of a question that was posed by researchers for Lawrence Kohlberg. In Carol Gilligan, *In a Different Voice* (Cambridge, MA: Harvard University Press, 1982), pp. 28, 173.

15. Ibid.

16. We use the term *sex* to refer to the biological male or female. The term *gender* includes psychological feminine and masculine traits as well as social roles assigned to the two sexes.

17. From Carol Gilligan, "Moral Orientation and Moral Development," in *Women and Moral Theory*, ed. Eva Kittay and Diana Meyers (Totowa, NJ: Rowman & Littlefield, 1987), p. 23.

18. Ibid.

19. Nel Noddings, *Caring: A Feminine Approach to Ethics and Moral Education* (Berkeley: University of California Press, 1984).

20. Lawrence Kohlberg, *The Psychology of Moral Development* (San Francisco: Harper & Row, 1984).

21. Gilligan, "Moral Orientation and Moral Development," p. 22.

22. Cited in Gilligan, "Moral Orientation and Moral Development."

23. See also Nancy Chodorow, *The Reproduction of Mothering* (Berkeley: University of California Press, 1978).

24. See, for example, Gilligan, "Adolescent Development Reconsidered," in *Mapping the Moral Domain*, ed. Carol Gilligan, Janie Victoria Ward, and Jill McLean Taylor (Cambridge, MA: Harvard University Press, 1988).

25. Gilligan, "Moral Orientation and Moral Development," pp. 22–23. Emphasis added.

26. Ibid., p. 25.

27. Catherine G. Greeno and Eleanor E. Maccoby, "How Different Is the Different Voice?" in "On *In a Different Voice*: An Interdisciplinary Forum," *Signs: Journal of Women in Culture and Society* 11, no. 2 (Winter 1986), pp. 211–20.

28. See, for example, Caroline Whitbeck, "The Maternal Instinct," in *Mothering: Essays in Feminist Theory*, ed. Joyce Treblicot (Totowa, NJ: Rowman & Allanheld, 1984).

29. See, for example, Sara Ruddick, *Maternal Thinking: Toward a Politics of Peace* (Boston: Beacon, 1989).

30. Ibid., p. 214.

31. Michael Slote, *The Ethics of Care and Empathy* (New York: Routledge, 2007), p. 9, footnote no. 7.

32. Mary Wollstonecraft, *A Vindication of the Rights of Women*, ed. Miriam Brody (London: Penguin, 1988).

33. Simone de Beauvoir, *The Second Sex*, trans. H. M. Parshley (New York: Knopf, 1953).

34. Martha C. Nussbaum, *Women and Human Development: The Capabilities Approach* (Cambridge: Cambridge University Press, 2001), p. 7.

35. This terminology is from Rosemary Tong's *Feminine and Feminist Ethics* (Belmont, CA: Wadsworth, 1993). As a source of this terminology, Tong also cites Betty A. Sichel, "Different Strains and Strands: Feminist Contributions to Ethical Theory," *Newsletter on Feminism* 90, no. 2 (Winter 1991), p. 90; and Susan Sherwin, *No Longer Patient: Feminist Ethics and Health Care* (Philadelphia: Temple University Press, 1992), p. 42.

36. Aristotle, *Politics*, as quoted in "Theories of Sex Difference," by Caroline Whitbeck in *Women and Moral Theory*, p. 35.
37. Jean-Jacques Rousseau, *Emile*, trans. Allan Bloom (New York: Basic Books, 1979). Also see Nancy Tuana, *Woman and the History of Philosophy* (New York: Paragon House, 1992).
38. Susan Moller Okin, "Gender, the Public and the Private," in *Political Theory Today*, ed. David Held (Stanford, CA: Stanford University Press, 1991), p. 77.
39. Ibid.
40. Gilligan, "Moral Orientation and Moral Development," p. 32.

READING

Caring

NEL NODDINGS

MindTap® For more chapter resources and activities, go to MindTap.

Study Questions

As you read the excerpt, please consider the following questions:
1. How does relatedness figure into ethics?
2. Is the caring approach to ethics that Noddings describes one that only women can enjoy?
3. How does caring connect with subjectivity in ethics and the idea of universality?

Ethical caring, the relation in which we do meet the other morally, will be described as arising out of natural caring—that relation in which we respond as one-caring out of love or natural inclination. The relation of natural caring will be identified as the human condition that we, consciously or unconsciously, perceive as "good." It is that condition toward which we long and strive, and it is our longing for caring—to be in that special relation—that provides the motivation for us to be moral. We want to be *moral* in order to remain in the caring relation and to enhance the ideal of ourselves as one-caring....

...In recognition of the feminine approach to meeting the other morally—our insistence on caring for the other—I shall want to preserve the uniqueness of human encounters. Since so much depends on the subjective experience of those involved in ethical encounters, conditions are rarely "sufficiently similar" for me to declare that you must do what I do. There is, however, a fundamental universality in our ethics, as there must be to escape relativism. The caring attitude, that attitude which expresses our earliest memories of being cared for and our growing store of memories of both caring and being cared for, is universally accessible. Since caring and the commitment to sustain it form the universal heart of the ethic, we must establish a convincing and comprehensive picture of caring at the outset.

Another outcome of our dependence on an ethical ideal is the emphasis upon moral education. Since we are dependent upon the strength and sensitivity of the ethical ideal—both our own and that of others—we must nurture that ideal in all of our educational encounters. I shall claim that we are dependent on each other even in the quest for personal goodness. How good *I* can be is partly a function of how *you*—the other—receive and respond to me.

Whatever virtue I exercise is completed, fulfilled, in you. The primary aim of all education must be nurturance of the ethical idea....

...I shall strike many contrasts between masculine and feminine approaches to ethics and education and, indeed, to living. These are not intended to divide men and women into opposing camps. They are meant, rather, to show how great the chasm is that already divides the masculine and feminine in each of us and to suggest that we enter a dialogue of genuine dialectical nature in order to achieve an

ultimate transcendence of the masculine and feminine in moral matters....

...When I look at my child—even one of my grown children—and recognize the fundamental relation in which we are each defined, I often experience a deep and overwhelming joy. It is the recognition of and longing for relatedness that form the foundation of our ethic, and the joy that accompanies fulfillment of our caring enhances our commitment to the ethical ideal that sustains us as one-caring.

READING

The Need for More Than Justice

ANNETTE BAIER

MindTap For more chapter resources and activities, go to MindTap.

Study Questions

As you read the excerpt, please consider the following questions:

1. Who are the challengers to the supremacy of justice as a social virtue, and in what way does Baier suggest that this is surprising?
2. How has the tradition of rights worked both against and for women?
3. According to Baier, what is wrong with the view that stresses relationships of equality?

In recent decades in North American social and moral philosophy, alongside the development and discussion of widely influential theories of justice, taken as Rawls takes it as the "first virtue of social institutions,"[1] there has been a counter-movement gathering strength, one coming from some interesting sources. For some of the most outspoken of the diverse group who have in a variety of ways been challenging the assumed supremacy of justice among the moral and social virtues are members of those sections of society whom one might have expected to be especially aware of the supreme importance of justice, namely, blacks and women. Those who have only recently won recognition of their equal rights, who have only recently seen the correction or partial correction of long-standing

racist and sexist injustices to their race and sex, are among the philosophers now suggesting that justice is only one virtue among many, and one that may need the presence of the others in order to deliver its own undenied value. Among these philosophers of the philosophical counterculture, as it were—but an increasingly large counterculture—I include Alasdair MacIntyre,[2] Michael Stocker,[3] Lawrence Blum,[4] Michael Slote,[5] Laurence Thomas,[6] Claudia Card,[7]

Annette Baier, "The Need for More Than Justice," *Canadian Journal of Philosophy*, supplementary vol. 13, ed. Marshal Hanen and Kai Nielsen (Calgary: University of Calgary Press, 1988), pp. 41–56. Copyright © Canadian Journal of Philosophy, reprinted by permission of Taylor & Francis Ltd, www.tandfonline.com on behalf of *Canadian Journal of Philosophy*.

Alison Jaggar,[8] Susan Wolf[9] and a whole group of men and women, myself included, who have been influenced by the writings of Harvard educational psychologist Carol Gilligan, whose book *In a Different Voice* (Harvard 1982; hereafter D.V.) caused a considerable stir both in the popular press and, more slowly, in the philosophical journals.[10]

Let me say quite clearly at this early point that there is little disagreement that justice is a social value of very great importance, and injustice an evil. Nor would those who have worked on theories of justice want to deny that other things matter besides justice. Rawls, for example, incorporates the value of freedom into his account of justice, so that denial of basic freedoms counts as injustice. Rawls also leaves room for a wider theory of right, of which the theory of justice is just a part. Still, he does claim that justice is the "first" virtue of social institutions, and it is only that claim about priority that I think has been challenged. It is easy to exaggerate the differences of view that exist, and I want to avoid that. The differences are as much in emphasis as in substance, or we can say that they are differences in tone of voice. But these differences do tend to make a difference in approaches to a wide range of topics not just in moral theory but in areas like medical ethics, where the discussion used to be conducted in terms of patients' rights, of informed consent, and so on, but now tends to get conducted in an enlarged moral vocabulary, which draws on what Gilligan calls the ethics of *care* as well as that of *justice*.

For "care" is the new buzz-word. It is not, as Shakespeare's Portia demanded, mercy that is to season justice, but a less authoritarian humanitarian supplement, a felt concern for the good of others and for community with them. The "cold jealous virtue of justice" (Hume) is found to be too cold, and it is "warmer" more communitarian virtues and social ideals that are being called in to supplement it. One might say that liberty and equality are being found inadequate without fraternity, except that "fraternity" will be quite the wrong word, if as Gilligan initially suggested, it is *women* who perceive this value most easily. ("Sorority" will do no better, since it is too exclusive, and English has no gender-neuter word for the mutual concern of siblings.) She has since modified this claim, allowing that there are two perspectives on moral and social issues that we all tend to alternate between, and which are not always easy to combine, one of them what she called the justice perspective, the other the care perspective. It is increasingly obvious that there are many male philosophical spokespersons for the care perspective (Laurence Thomas, Lawrence Blum, Michael Stocker) so that it cannot be the prerogative of women. Nevertheless Gilligan still wants to claim that women are most unlikely to take *only* the justice perspective, as some men are claimed to, at least until some mid-life crisis jolts them into "bifocal" moral vision (see D.V., Chapter 6).

Gilligan in her book did not offer any explanatory theory of why there should be any difference between female and male moral outlook, but she did tend to link the naturalness to women of the care perspective with their role as primary caretakers of young children, that is with their parental and specifically maternal role. . . . Later, both in "The Conquistador and the Dark Continent: Reflections on the Nature of Love" (*Daedalus* Summer 1984), and "The Origins of Morality in Early Childhood" (in press), she develops this explanation. She postulates two evils that any infant may become aware of, the evil of detachment or isolation from others whose love one needs, and the evil of relative powerlessness and weakness. Two dimensions of moral development are thereby set—one aimed at achieving satisfying community with others, the other aiming at autonomy or equality of power. The relative predominance of one over the other development will depend both upon the relative salience of the two evils in early childhood, and on early and later reinforcement or discouragement in attempts made to guard against these two evils. This provides the germs of a theory about *why*, given current customs of childrearing, it should be mainly women who are not content with only the moral outlook that she calls the justice perspective, necessary though that was and is seen by them to have been to their hard won liberation from sexist oppression. They, like the blacks, used the language of rights and justice to change their own social position, but nevertheless see limitations in that language, according to Gilligan's findings as a moral psychologist. She reports their discontent with the individualist more or less Kantian moral framework that dominates Western moral theory and which influenced moral psychologists such as Lawrence Kohlberg,[11] to whose conception of moral maturity she seeks an alternative. Since the target of Gilligan's criticism is the dominant Kantian tradition, and since that has been the target also of moral philosophers as diverse in their own views as Bernard Williams,[12] Alasdair MacIntyre, Philippa Foot,[13] Susan Wolf, Claudia Card, her book is of interest as much for its attempt to articulate an alternative to the Kantian justice perspective as for its implicit raising of the question of male bias in Western moral theory, especially liberal democratic theory. For whether the supposed blind spots of that outlook are due to male bias, or to nonparental bias, or to early traumas of powerlessness or to early resignation to "detachment" from others, we need first to be persuaded that they are blind spots before we will have any interest in their cause and cure. Is justice blind to important social values, or at least only one-eyed? What is it that comes into view from the "care perspective" that is not seen from the "justice perspective"?

Gilligan's position here is most easily described by contrasting it with that of Kohlberg, against which she developed it. Kohlberg, influenced by Piaget and the Kantian philosophical tradition as developed by John Rawls, developed a theory about typical moral development which saw it to progress from a pre conventional level, where what is seen to matter is pleasing or not offending parental authority-figures, through a conventional level in which the child tries to fit in with a group, such as a school community, and conform to its standards and rules, to a post conventional critical level, in which such conventional rules are subjected to tests, and where those tests are of a utilitarian, or, eventually, a Kantian sort—namely ones that require respect for each person's individual rational will, or autonomy, and conformity to any implicit social contract such wills are deemed to have made, or to any hypothetical

ones they would make if thinking clearly. What was found when Kohlberg's questionnaires (mostly by verbal response to verbally sketched moral dilemmas) were applied to female as well as male subjects, Gilligan reports, is that the girls and women not only scored generally lower than the boys and men, but tended to revert to the lower stage of the conventional level even after briefly (usually in adolescence) attaining the post conventional level. Piaget's finding that girls were deficient in "the legal sense" was confirmed.

These results led Gilligan to wonder if there might not be a quite different pattern of development to be discerned, at least in female subjects. She therefore conducted interviews designed to elicit not just how far advanced the subjects were towards an appreciation of the nature and importance of Kantian autonomy, but also to find out what the subjects themselves saw as progress or lack of it, what conceptions of moral maturity they came to possess by the time they were adults. She found that although the Kohlberg version of moral maturity as respect for fellow persons, and for their rights as equals (rights including that of free association), did seem shared by many young men, the women tended to speak in a different voice about morality itself and about moral maturity. To quote Gilligan, "Since the reality of interconnexion is experienced by women as given rather than freely contracted, they arrive at an understanding of life that reflects the limits of autonomy and control. As a result, women's development delineates the path not only to a less violent life but also to a maturity realized by interdependence and taking care" (D.V., 172). She writes that there is evidence that "women perceive and construe social reality differently from men, and that these differences center around experiences of attachment and separation...because women's sense of integrity appears to be intertwined with an ethics of care, so that to see themselves as women is to see themselves in a relationship of connexion, the major changes in women's lives would seem to involve changes in the understanding and activities of care" (D.V., 171). She contrasts this progressive understanding of care, from merely pleasing others to helping and nurturing, with the sort of progression that is involved in Kohlberg's stages, a progression in the understanding, not of mutual care, but of mutual respect, where this has its Kantian overtones of distance, even of some fear for the respected, and where personal autonomy and independence, rather than more satisfactory interdependence, are the paramount values.

This contrast, one cannot but feel, is one which Gilligan might have used the Marxist language of alienation to make. For the main complaint about the Kantian version of a society with its first virtue justice, construed as respect for equal rights to formal goods such as having contracts kept, due process, equal opportunity including opportunity to participate in political activities leading to policy and law-making, to basic liberties of speech, free association and assembly, religious worship, is that none of these goods do much to ensure that the people who have and mutually respect such rights will have any other relationships to one another than the minimal relationship needed to keep such a "civil society" going. They may well be lonely, driven to suicide, apathetic about their work and about participation in political processes, find their lives meaningless and have no wish to leave offspring to face the same meaningless existence. Their rights, and respect for rights, are quite compatible with very great misery, and misery whose causes are not just individual misfortunes and psychic sickness, but social and moral impoverishment....

Let me try to summarize the main differences, as I see them, between on the one hand Gilligan's version of moral maturity and the sort of social structures that would encourage, express and protect it, and on the other the orthodoxy she sees herself to be challenging. I shall from now on be giving my own interpretation of the significance of her challenges, not merely reporting them.[14] The most obvious point is the challenge to the individualism of the Western tradition, to the fairly entrenched belief in the possibility and desirability of each person pursuing his own good in his own way, constrained only by a minimal formal common good, namely a working legal apparatus that enforces contracts and protects individuals from undue interference by others. Gilligan reminds us that noninterference can, especially for the relatively powerless, such as the very young, amount to neglect, and even between equals can be isolating and alienating. On her less individualist version of individuality, it becomes defined by responses to dependency and to patterns of interconnexion, both chosen and unchosen. It is not something a person has, and which she then chooses relationships to suit, but something that develops out of a series of dependencies and interdependencies, and responses to them. This conception of individuality is not flatly at odds with, say, Rawls' Kantian one, but there is at least a difference of tone of voice between speaking as Rawls does of each of us having our own rational life plan, which a just society's moral traffic rules will allow us to follow, and which may or may not include close association with other persons, and speaking as Gilligan does of a satisfactory life as involving "progress of affiliative relationship" (D.V., 170) where "the concept of identity expands to include the experience of interconnexion" (D.V., 173). Rawls can allow that progress to Gilligan-style moral maturity may be a rational life plan, but not a moral constraint on every life-pattern. The trouble is that it will not do just to say "let this version of morality be an optional extra. Let us agree on the essential minimum, that is on justice and rights, and let whoever wants to go further and cultivate this more demanding ideal of responsibility and care." For, first, it cannot be satisfactorily cultivated without closer cooperation from others than respect for rights and justice will ensure, and, second, the encouragement of some to cultivate it while others do not could easily lead to exploitation of those who do. It obviously *has* suited some in most societies well enough that others take on the responsibilities of care (for the sick, the helpless, the young) leaving them free to pursue their own less altruistic goods. Volunteer forces of those who accept an ethic of care, operating within a society where the power is exercised and the institutions designed, redesigned, or maintained by those who accept a less communal ethic of minimally constrained self-advancement, will not be the solution. The liberal individualists may be able to "tolerate" the more communally minded, if they keep the liberals' rules, but it is not so clear that the more communally minded can be content with just those rules, not be content to be tolerated and possibly exploited.

For the moral tradition which developed the concept of rights, autonomy and justice is the same tradition that provided "justifications" of the oppression of those whom the primary right-holders depended on to do the sort of work they themselves preferred not to do. The domestic work was left to women and slaves, and the liberal morality for right-holders was surreptitiously supplemented by a different set of demands made on domestic workers. As long as women could be got to assume responsibility for the care of home and children, and to train their children to continue the sexist system, the liberal morality could continue to be the official morality, by turning its eyes away from the contribution made by those it excluded. The long unnoticed moral proletariat were the domestic workers, mostly female. Rights have usually been for the privileged. Talking about laws, and the rights those laws recognize and protect, does not in itself ensure that the group of legislators and rights-holders will not be restricted to some elite. Bills of rights have usually been proclamations of the rights of some in-group, barons, landowners, males, whites, non foreigners. The "justice perspective," and the legal sense that goes with it, are shadowed by their patriarchal past. What did Kant, the great prophet of autonomy, say in his moral theory about women? He said they were incapable of legislation, not fit to vote, that they needed the guidance of more "rational" males.[15] Autonomy was not for them, only for first class, really rational, persons. It is ironic that Gilligan's original findings in a way confirm Kant's views—it seems that autonomy really may not be for women. Many of them reject that ideal (D.V., 48), and have been found not as good at making rules as are men. But where Kant concludes—"so much the worse for women," we can conclude—"so much the worse for the male fixation on the special skill of drafting legislation, for the bureaucratic

mentality of rule worship, and for the male exaggeration of the importance of independence over mutual interdependence."

It is however also true that the moral theories that made the concept of a person's rights central were not just the instruments for excluding some persons, but also the instruments used by those who demanded that more and more persons be included in the favored group. Abolitionists, reformers, women, used the language of rights to assert their claims to inclusion in the group of full members of a community. The tradition of liberal moral theory has in fact developed so as to include the women it had for so long excluded, to include the poor as well as rich, blacks and whites, and so on. Women like Mary Wollstonecraft used the male moral theories to good purpose. So we should not be wholly ungrateful for those male moral theories, for all their objectionable earlier content. They were undoubtedly patriarchal, but they also contained the seeds of the challenge, or antidote, to this patriarchal poison.

But when we transcend the values of the Kantians, we should not forget the facts of history—that those values were the values of the oppressors of women. The Christian church, whose version of the moral law Aquinas codified, in his very legalistic moral theory, still insists on the maleness of the God it worships, and jealously reserves for males all the most powerful positions in its hierarchy. Its patriarchical prejudice is open and avowed. In the secular moral theories of men, the sexist patriarchal prejudice is today often less open, not as blatant as it is in Aquinas, in the later natural law tradition, and in Kant..., but is often still there. No moral theorist today would say that women are unfit to vote, to make laws, or to rule a nation without powerful male advisors (as most queens had), but the old doctrines die hard.... Traces of the old patriarchal poison still remain in even the best contemporary moral theorizing. Few may actually say that women's place is in the home, but there is much muttering, when unemployment figures rise, about how the relatively recent flood of women into the workforce complicates the problem, as if it would be a good thing if women just went back home whenever unemployment rises, to leave the available jobs for the men. We still do not really have a wide acceptance of the equal right of women to employment outside the home. Nor do we have wide acceptance of the equal duty of men to perform those domestic tasks which in no way depend on special female anatomy, namely cooking, cleaning, and the care of weaned children. All sorts of stories (maybe true stories), about children's need for one "primary" parent, who must be the mother if the mother breast feeds the child, shore up the unequal division of domestic responsibility between mothers and fathers, wives and husbands. If we are really to transvalue the values of our patriarchal past, we need to rethink all of those assumptions, really test those psychological theories. And how will men ever develop an understanding of the "ethics of care" if they continue to be shielded or kept from that experience of caring for a dependent child, which complements the experience we all have had of being cared for as dependent children? These experiences form the natural background for the development of moral maturity as Gilligan's women.

Exploitation aside, why would women, once liberated, not be content to have their version of morality merely tolerated? Why should they not see themselves as voluntarily, for their own reasons, taking on more than the liberal rules demand, while having no quarrel with the content of those rules themselves, nor with their remaining the only ones that are expected to be generally obeyed? To see why, we need to move on to three more differences between the Kantian liberals (usually contractarians) and their critics. These concern the relative weight put on relationships between equals, and the relative weight put on freedom of choice, and on the authority of intellect over emotions. It is a typical feature of the dominant moral theories and traditions...that relationships between equals or those who are deemed equal in some important sense, have been the relations that morality is concerned primarily to regulate. Relationships between those who are clearly unequal in power, such as parents and children, earlier and later generations in relation

to one another, states and citizens, doctors and patients, the well and the ill, large states and small states, have had to be shunted to the bottom of the agenda, and then dealt with by some sort of "promotion" of the weaker so that an appearance of virtual equality is achieved. Citizens collectively become equal to states, children are treated as adults-to-be, the ill and dying are treated as continuers of their earlier more potent selves, so that their "rights" could be seen as the rights of equals. This pretense of an equality that is in fact absent may often lead to desirable protection of the weaker, or more dependent. But it somewhat masks the question of what our moral relationships are to those who are our superiors or our inferiors in power. A more realistic acceptance of the fact that we begin as helpless children, that at almost every point of our lives we deal with both the more and the less helpless, that equality of power and interdependency, between two persons or groups, is rare and hard to recognize when it does occur, might lead us to a more direct approach to questions concerning the design of institutions structuring these relationships between unequals (families, schools, hospitals, armies) and of the morality of our dealings with the more and the less powerful....

The recognition of the importance for all parties of relations between those who are and cannot but be unequal, both these relations in themselves and for their effect on personality formation and so on other relationships, goes along with a recognition of the plain fact that not all morally important relationships can or should be freely chosen. So far I have discussed three reasons women have not to be content to pursue their own values within the framework of the liberal morality. The first was its dubious record. The second was its inattention to relations of inequality or its pretense of equality. The third reason is its exaggeration of the scope of choice, or its inattention to unchosen relations. Showing up the partial myth of equality among actual members of a community, and of the undesirability of trying to pretend that we are treating all of them as equals, tends to go along with an exposure of the companion myth that moral obligations arise from freely *chosen* associations between such equals. Vulnerable future generations do not choose their dependence on earlier generations. The unequal infant does not choose its place in a family or nation, nor is it treated as free to do as it likes until some association is freely entered into. Nor do its parents always choose their parental role, or freely assume their parental responsibilities any more than we choose our power to affect the conditions in which later generations will live. Gilligan's attention to the version of morality and moral maturity found in women, many of whom had faced a choice of whether or not to have an abortion, and who had at some point become mothers, is attention to the perceived inadequacy of the language of rights to help in such choices or to guide them in their parental role. It would not be much of an exaggeration to call the Gilligan "different voice" the voice of the potential parents. The emphasis on care goes with a recognition of the often unchosen nature of the responsibilities of those who give care, both of children who care for their aged or infirm parents, and of parents who care for the children they in fact have. Contract soon ceases to seem the paradigm source of moral obligation once we attend to parental responsibility, and justice as a virtue of social institutions will come to seem at best only first equal with the virtue, whatever its name, that ensures that each new generation is made appropriately welcome and prepared for their adult lives.

...The fourth feature of the Gilligan challenge to liberal orthodoxy is a challenge to its typical *rationalism*, or intellectualism, to its assumption that we need not worry what passions persons have, as long as their rational wills can control them. This Kantian picture of a controlling reason dictating to possibly unruly passions also tends to seem less useful when we are led to consider what sort of person we need to fill the role of parent, or indeed want in any close relationship. It might be important for father figures to have rational control over their violent urges to beat to death the children whose screams enrage them, but more than control of such nasty passions seems needed in the mother or primary parent, or parent-substitute, by most psychological theories.

They need to love their children, not just to control their irritation. So the emphasis in Kantian theories on rational control of emotions, rather than on cultivating desirable forms of emotion, is challenged by Gilligan, along with the challenge to the assumption of the centrality of autonomy, or relations between equals, and of freely chosen relations....

It is clear, I think, that the best moral theory has to be a cooperative product of women and men, has to harmonize justice and care. The morality it theorizes about is after all for all persons, for men and for women, and will need their combined insights. As Gilligan said (D.V., 174), what we need now is a "marriage" of the old male and the newly articulated female insights. If she is right about the special moral aptitudes of women, it will most likely be the women who propose the marriage, since they are the ones with more natural empathy, with the better diplomatic skills, the ones more likely to shoulder responsibility and take moral initiative, and the ones who find it easiest to empathize and care about how the other party feels. Then, once there is this union of male and female moral wisdom, we maybe can teach each other the moral skills each gender currently lacks, so that the gender difference in moral outlook that Gilligan found will slowly become less marked.

NOTES

1. John Rawls, *A Theory of Justice* (Harvard University Press).
2. Alasdair MacIntyre, *After Virtue* (Notre Dame: Notre Dame University Press).
3. Michael Stocker, "The Schizophrenia of Modern Ethical Theories," *Journal of Philosophy, 73* (14), pp. 453–466; and "Agent and Other: Against Ethical Universalism," *Australasian Journal of Philosophy, 54*, pp. 206–220.
4. Lawrence Blum, *Friendship, Altruism and Morality* (London: Routledge & Kegan Paul, 1980).
5. Michael Slote, *Goods and Virtues* (Oxford: Oxford University Press 1983).
6. Laurence Thomas, "Love and Morality," in James Fetzer (Ed.), *Epistemology and Sociobiology* (1985); and "Justice, Happiness and Self

Knowledge," *Canadian Journal of Philosophy* (March 1986). Also "Beliefs and the Motivation to be Just," *American Philosophical Quarterly*, 22 (4), pp. 347–352.

7. Claudia Card, "On Mercy," *Philosophical Review*, *81: 2*, p. 1; and "Gender and Moral Luck," forthcoming.

8. Alison Jaggar, *Feminist Politics and Human Nature* (Lanham, MD: Rowman and Littlefield, 1983).

9. Susan Wolf, "Moral Saints," *Journal of Philosophy*, *79* (August 1982), pp. 419–439.

10. For a helpful survey article see Owen Flanagan and Kathryn Jackson, "Justice, Care & Gender: The Kohlberg-Gilligan Debate Revisited," *Ethics, 97*, 3 (April 1987), pp. 622–637.

11. Lawrence Kohlberg, *Essays in Moral Development*, vols. I & II (New York: Harper & Row, 1981, 1984).

12. Bernard Williams, *Ethics and the Limits of Philosophy* (Cambridge: Cambridge University Press 1985).

13. Philippa Foot, *Virtues and Vices* (Berkeley: University of California Press, 1978).

14. I have previously written about the significance of her findings for moral philosophy in "What Do Women Want in a Moral Theory?" *Nous, 19* (March 1985); "Trust and Antitrust," *Ethics, 96* (1986); and in "Hume the Women's Moral Theorist?" in *Women and Moral Theory*, Kittay and Meyers (Eds.).

READING

What Is Feminist Ethics?

HILDE LINDEMANN

MindTap® For more chapter resources and activities, go to MindTap.

Study Questions

As you read the excerpt, please consider the following questions:

1. What does Lindemann mean when she claims that feminism is about power and that gender is a power relation?
2. Why, according to Lindemann, are feminists concerned with *describing* inequalities of power, including inequalities that show up in all kinds of social relations—from racial relations to parent-child relations?
3. How does Lindemann explain the meaning and importance of the idea that the personal is political?

WHAT IS FEMINISM?

What, then, is feminism? As a social and political movement with a long, intermittent history, feminism has repeatedly come into public awareness, generated change, and then disappeared again. As an eclectic body of theory, feminism entered colleges and universities in the early 1970s as a part of the women's studies movement, contributing to scholarship in every academic discipline, though probably most heavily in the arts, social sciences, literature, and the humanities in general. Feminist ethics is a part of the body of theory that is being developed primarily in colleges and universities.

Many people in the United States think of feminism as a movement that aims to make women the social equals of men, and this impression has been reinforced by references to feminism and feminists in the newspapers, on television, and in the movies. But bell hooks has pointed out in *Feminist Theory from Margin to Center* (1984, 18–19) that this way of defining feminism raises some serious problems. Which men do women want to be equal to? Women who are socially well off wouldn't get much

Hilde Lindemann, Invitation to Feminist Ethics, The McGraw-Hill Companies, 2006, pp. 2–3, 6–16.c.

advantage from being the equals of the men who are poor and lower class, particularly if they aren't white. Hooks's point is that there are no women and men in the abstract. They are poor, black, young, Latino/a, old, gay, able- bodied, upper class, down on their luck, Native American, straight, and all the rest of it. When a woman doesn't think about this, it's probably because she doesn't have to. And that's usually a sign that her own social position is privileged. In fact, privilege often means that there's something uncomfortable going on that others have to pay attention to but you don't. So, when hooks asks which men women want to be equal to, she's reminding us that there's an unconscious presumption of privilege built right in to this sort of demand for equality.

There's a second problem with the equality definition. Even if we could figure out which men are the ones to whom women should be equal, that way of putting it suggests that the point of feminism is somehow to get women to measure up to what (at least some) men already are. Men remain the point of reference; theirs are the lives that women would naturally want. If the first problem with the equality definition is "Equal to *which* men?" the second problem could be put as "Why equal to any men?" Reforming a system in which men are the point of reference by allowing women to perform as their equals "forces women to focus on men and address men's conceptions of women rather than creating and developing women's values about themselves," as Sarah Lucia Hoagland puts it in *Lesbian Ethics* (1988, 57). For that reason, Hoagland and some other feminists believe that feminism is first and foremost about women.

But characterizing feminism as about women has its problems too. What, after all, is a woman? In her 1949 book, *The Second Sex*, the French feminist philosopher Simone de Beauvoir famously observed, "One is not born, but becomes a woman. No biological, psychological, or economic fate determines the figure that the human female presents in society: it is civilization as a whole that produces this creature, intermediate between male and eunuch, which is described as feminine" (Beauvoir 1949, 301). Her point is that while plenty of human beings are born female, "woman" is not a natural fact about them—it's a social invention. According to that invention, which is widespread in "civilization as a whole," man represents the positive, typical human being, while woman represents only the negative, the not-man. She is the Other against whom man defines himself—he is all the things that she is not. And she exists only in relation to him. In a later essay called "One Is Not Born a Woman," the lesbian author and theorist Monique Wittig (1981, 49) adds that because women belong to men sexually as well as in every other way, women are necessarily heterosexual. For that reason, she argued, lesbians aren't women.

But, you are probably thinking, everybody knows what a woman is, and lesbians certainly *are* women. And you're right. These French feminists aren't denying that there's a perfectly ordinary use of the word *woman* by which it means exactly what you think it means. But they're explaining what this comes down to, if you look at it from a particular point of view. Their answer to the question "What is a woman?" is that women are different from men. But they don't mean this as a trite observation. They're saying that "woman" refers to *nothing but* difference from men, so that apart from men, women aren't anything. "Man" is the positive term, "woman" is the negative one, just like "light" is the positive term and "dark" is nothing but the absence of light.

A later generation of feminists have agreed with Beauvoir and Wittig that women are different from men, but rather than seeing that difference as simply negative, they put it in positive terms, affirming feminine qualities as a source of personal strength and pride. For example, the philosopher Virginia Held thinks that women's moral experience as mothers, attentively nurturing their children, may serve as a better model for social relations than the contract model that the free market provides. The poet Adrienne Rich celebrated women's passionate nature (as opposed, in stereotype, to the rational nature of men), regarding the emotions as morally valuable rather than as signs of weakness.

But defining feminism as about the positive differences between men and women creates yet another set of problems. In her 1987 *Feminism Unmodified*, the feminist legal theorist Catharine A. MacKinnon points out that this kind of difference, as such, is a symmetrical relationship: If I am different from you, then you are different from me in exactly the same respects and to exactly the same degree. "Men's differences from women are equal to women's differences from men," she writes. "There is an *equality* there. Yet the sexes are not socially equal" (MacKinnon 1987, 37). No amount of attention to the differences between men and women explains why men, as a group, are more socially powerful, valued, advantaged, or free than women. For that, you have to see differences as counting in certain ways, and certain differences being created precisely because they give men *power* over women.

Although feminists disagree about this, my own view is that feminism isn't—at least not directly— about equality, and it isn't about women, and it isn't about difference. It's about power. Specifically, it's about the social pattern, widespread across cultures and history, that distributes power asymmetrically to favor men over women. This asymmetry has been given many names, including the subjugation of women, sexism, male dominance, patriarchy, systemic misogyny, phallocracy, and the oppression of women. A number of feminist theorists simply call it gender, and...I will too.

WHAT IS GENDER?

Most people think their gender is a natural fact about them, like their hair and eye color: "Jones is 5 foot 8, has red hair, and is a man." But gender is a *norm*, not a fact. It's a prescription for how people are supposed to act; what they must or must not wear; how they're supposed to sit, walk, or stand; what kind of person they're supposed to marry; what sorts of things they're supposed to be interested in or good at; and what they're entitled to. And because it's an *effective* norm, it creates the differences between men and women in these areas.

Gender doesn't just tell women to behave one way and men another, though. It's a *power* relation, so it tells men that they're entitled to things that women aren't supposed to have, and it tells women that they are supposed to defer to men and serve them. It says, for example, that men are supposed to occupy positions of religious authority and women are supposed to run the church suppers. It says that mothers are supposed to take care of their children but fathers have more important things to do. And it says that the things associated with femininity are supposed to take a back seat to the things that are coded masculine. Think of the many tax dollars allocated to the military as compared with the few tax dollars allocated to the arts. Think about how kindergarten teachers are paid as compared to how stockbrokers are paid. And think about how many presidents of the United States have been women. Gender operates through social institutions (like marriage and the law) and practices (like education and medicine) by disproportionately conferring entitlements and the control of resources on men, while disproportionately assigning women to subordinate positions in the service of men's interests.

To make this power relation seem perfectly natural—like the fact that plants grow up instead of down, or that human beings grow old and die— gender constructs its norms for behavior around what is supposed to be the natural biological distinction between the sexes. According to this distinction, people who have penises and testicles, XY chromosomes, and beards as adults belong to the male sex, while people who have clitorises and ovaries, XX chromosomes, and breasts as adults belong to the female sex, and those are the only sexes there are. Gender, then, is the complicated set of cultural meanings that are constructed around the two sexes. Your sex is either male or female, and your gender—either masculine, or feminine—corresponds socially to your sex.

As a matter of fact, though, sex isn't quite so simple. Some people with XY chromosomes don't have penises and never develop beards, because they don't have the receptors that allow them to make use of the male hormones that their testicles produce. Are they male or female? Other people have ambiguous genitals or internal reproductive structures that don't correspond in the usual manner to their external genitalia. How should we classify them? People with Turner's syndrome have XO chromosomes instead of XX. People with Klinefelter's syndrome have three sex chromosomes: XXY, Nature is a good bit looser in its categories than the simple male/female distinction acknowledges. Most human beings can certainly be classified as one sex or the other, but a considerable number of them fall somewhere in between.

The powerful norm of gender doesn't acknowledge the existence of the in-betweens, though. When, for example, have you ever filled out an application for a job or a driver's license or a passport that gave you a choice other than M or F? Instead, by basing its distinction between masculine and feminine on the existence of two and only two sexes, gender makes the inequality of power between men and women appear natural and therefore legitimate.

Gender, then, is about power. But it's not about the power of just one group over another. Gender always interacts with other social markers—such as race, class, level of education, sexual orientation, age, religion, physical and mental health, and ethnicity—to distribute power unevenly among women positioned differently in the various social orders, and it does the same to men. A man's social status, for example, can have a great deal to do with the extent to which he's even perceived as a man. There's a wonderful passage in the English travel writer Frances Trollope's *Domestic Manners of the Americans* (1831), in which she describes the exaggerated delicacy of middle-class young ladies she met in Kentucky and Ohio. They wouldn't dream of sitting in a chair that was still warm from contact with a gentleman's bottom, but thought nothing of getting laced into their corsets in front of a male house slave. The slave, it's clear, didn't count as a man—not in the relevant sense, anyway. Gender is the force that makes it matter whether you are male or female, but it always works hand in glove with all the other things about you that matter at the same

time. It's one power relation intertwined with others in a complex social system that distinguishes your betters from your inferiors in all kinds of ways and for all kinds of purposes.

POWER AND MORALITY

If feminism is about gender, and gender is the name for a social system that distributes power unequally between men and women, then you'd expect feminist ethicists to try to *understand, criticize*, and *correct* how gender operates within our moral beliefs and practices. And they do just that. In the first place, they challenge, on moral grounds, the powers men have over women, and they claim for women, again on moral grounds, the powers that gender denies them. As the moral reasons for opposing gender are similar to the moral reasons for opposing power systems based on social markers other than gender, feminist ethicists also offer moral arguments against systems based on class, race, physical or mental ability, sexuality, and age. And because all these systems, including gender, are powerful enough to *conceal* many of the forces that keep them in place, it's often necessary to make the forces visible by explicitly identifying—and condemning—the various ugly ways they allow some people to treat others. This is a central task for feminist ethics.

Feminist ethicists also produce theory about the moral meaning of various kinds of *legitimate* relations of unequal power, including relationships of dependency and vulnerability, relationships of trust, and relationships based on something other than choice. Parent-child relationships, for example, are necessarily unequal and for the most part unchosen. Parents can't help having power over their children, and while they may have chosen to have children, most don't choose to have the particular children they do, nor do children choose their parents. This raises questions about the responsible use of parental power and the nature of involuntary obligations, and these are topics for feminist ethics. Similarly, when you trust someone, that person has power over you. Whom should you trust, for what purposes, and when is trust not warranted? What's involved in being trustworthy, and what must be done to repair breaches of trust? These too are questions for feminist ethics.

Third, feminist ethicists look at the various forms of power that are required for morality to operate properly at all. How do we learn right from wrong in the first place? We usually learn it from our parents, whose power to permit and forbid, praise and punish, is essential to our moral training. For whom or what are we ethically responsible? Often this depends on the kind of power we have over the person or thing in question. If, for instance, someone is particularly vulnerable to harm because of something I've done, I might well have special duties toward that person. Powerful social institutions—medicine, religion, government, and the market, to take just a few examples—typically dictate what is morally required of us and to whom we are morally answerable. Relations of power set the terms for who must answer to whom, who has authority over whom, and who gets excused from certain kinds of accountability to whom. But because so many of these power relations are illegitimate, in that they're instances of gender, racism, or other kinds of bigotry, figuring out which ones are morally justified is a task for feminist ethics.

DESCRIPTION AND PRESCRIPTION

So far it sounds as if feminist ethics devotes considerable attention to *description*—as if feminist ethicists were like poets or painters who want to show you something about reality that you might otherwise have missed. And indeed, many feminist ethicists emphasize the importance of understanding how social power actually works, rather than concentrating solely on how it ought to work. But why, you might ask, should ethicists worry about how power operates within societies? Isn't it up to sociologists and political scientists to describe how things *are*, while ethicists concentrate on how things *ought* to be?

As the philosopher Margaret Urban Walker has pointed out in *Moral Contexts*, there is a tradition in Western philosophy, going all the way back to Plato, to the effect that morality is something ideal

and that ethics, being the study of morality, properly examines only that ideal. According to this tradition, notions of right and wrong as they are found in the world are unreliable and shadowy manifestations of something lying outside of human experience—something to which we ought to aspire but can't hope to reach. Plato's Idea of the Good, in fact, is precisely not of this earth, and only the gods could truly know it. Christian ethics incorporates Platonism into its insistence that earthly existence is fraught with sin and error and that heaven is our real home. Kant too insists that moral judgments transcend the histories and circumstances of people's actual lives, and most moral philosophers of the twentieth century have likewise shown little interest in how people really live and what it's like for them to live that way. "They think," remarks Walker (2001), "that there is little to be learned from what is about what ought to be" (3).

. . . If you don't know how things are, your prescriptions for how things ought to be won't have much practical effect. Imagine trying to sail a ship without knowing anything about the tides or where the hidden rocks and shoals lie. You might have a very fine idea of where you are trying to go, but if you don't know the waters, at best you are likely to go off course, and at worst you'll end up going down with all your shipmates. If, as many feminists have noted, a crucial fact about human selves is that they are always embedded in a vast web of relationships, then the forces at play within those relationships must be understood. It's knowing how people are situated with respect to these forces, what they are going through as they are subjected to them, and what life is like in the face of them, that lets us decide which of the forces are morally justified. Careful description of how things are is a crucial part of feminist methodology, because the power that puts certain groups of people at risk of physical harm, denies them full access to the good things their society has to offer, or treats them as if they were useful only for often people's purposes is often hidden and hard to see. If this power isn't seen, it's likely to remain in place, doing untold amounts of damage to great numbers of people.

All the same, feminist ethics is *normative* as well as descriptive. It's fundamentally about how things ought to be, while description plays the crucial but secondary role of helping us to figure that out. Normative language is the language of "ought" instead of "is," the language of "worth" and "value," "right" and "wrong," "good" and "bad." Feminist ethicists differ on a number of normative issues, but as the philosopher Alison Jaggar (1991) has famously put it, they all share two moral commitments: "that the subordination of women is morally wrong and that the moral experience of women is worthy of respect" (95). The first commitment—that women's interests ought not systematically to be set in the service of men's—can be understood as a moral challenge to power under the guise of gender. The second commitment—that women's experience must be taken seriously—can be understood as a call to acknowledge how that power operates. These twin commitments are the two normative legs on which any feminist ethics stands.

MORALITY AND POLITICS

If the idealization of morality goes back over two thousand years in Western thought, a newer tradition, only a couple of centuries old, has split off morality from politics. According to this tradition, which can be traced to Kant and some other Enlightenment philosophers, morality concerns the relations between persons, whereas politics concerns the relations among nation-states, or between a state and its citizens. So, as Iris Marion Young (1990) puts it, ethicists have tended to focus on intentional actions by individual persons, conceiving of moral life as "conscious, deliberate, a rational weighing of alternatives," whereas political philosophers have focused on impersonal governmental systems, studying "laws, policies, the large-scale distribution of social goods, countable quantities like votes and taxes" (149).

For feminists, though, the line between ethics and political theory isn't quite so bright as this tradition makes out. It's not always easy to tell where feminist ethics leaves off and feminist political theory begins. There are two reasons for this. In the

first place, while ethics certainly concerns personal behavior, there is a long-standing insistence on the part of feminists that the personal *is* political. In a 1970 essay called "The Personal Is Political," the political activist Carol Hanisch observed that "personal problems are political problems. There are no personal solutions at this time" (204–205). What Hanisch meant is that even the most private areas of everyday life, including such intensely personal areas as sex, can function to maintain abusive power systems like gender. If a heterosexual woman believes, for example, that contraception is primarily her responsibility because she'll have to take care of the baby if she gets pregnant, she is propping up a system that lets men evade responsibility not only for pregnancy, but for their own offspring as well. Conversely, while unjust social arrangements such as gender and race invade every aspect of people's personal lives, "there are no personal solutions," either when Hanisch wrote those words or now, because to shift dominant understandings of how certain groups may be treated, and what other groups are entitled to expect of them, requires concerted political action, not just personal good intentions.

The second reason why it's hard to separate feminist ethics from feminist politics is that feminists typically subject the ethical theory they produce to critical political scrutiny, not only to keep untoward political biases out, but also to make sure that the work accurately reflects their feminist politics. Many nonfeminist ethicists, on the other hand, don't acknowledge that their work reflects their politics, because they don't think it should. Their aim, by and large, has been to develop ideal moral theory that applies to all people, regardless of their social position or experience of life, and to do that objectively, without favoritism, which requires them to leave their own personal politics behind. The trouble, though, is that they aren't really leaving their own personal politics behind. They're merely refusing to notice that their politics is inevitably built right in to their theories. (This is an instance of Lindemann's ad hoc rule Number 22: Just because you think you are doing something doesn't mean you're actually doing it.) Feminists, by contrast, are generally skeptical of the idealism nonfeminists favor, and they're equally doubtful that objectivity can be achieved by stripping away what's distinctive about people's experiences or commitments. Believing that it's no

wiser to shed one's political allegiances in the service of ethics than it would be to shed one's moral allegiances, feminists prefer to be transparent about their politics as a way of keeping their ethics intellectually honest.

REVIEW EXERCISES

1. What sorts of issues are feminists concerned with, and how does feminism help to identify and propose remedies for these issues?
2. Identify and explain the supposed differences between male and female ethical perspectives.
3. Contrast the research findings of Carol Gilligan and Lawrence Kohlberg on male and female moral development.
4. According to Freud, why were women supposed to be morally deficient?
5. What are the basic features of the ethics of care?
6. How does Gilligan's duck and rabbit example help explain the difference between the two moral perspectives?

7. Describe the psychosexual development explanation of female and male moral perspectives.
8. Summarize Caroline Whitbeck's biological explanation of the difference between female and male moral perspectives.
9. How has the difference been explained in terms of "maternal thinking"?
10. Describe the basic issues involved in trying to decide whether one type of moral perspective is better than another.
11. Describe some of the history and characteristics of feminist thought, including the so-called waves of feminism.

MindTap· For more chapter resources and activities, go to MindTap.

Euthanasia

Learning Outcomes

After reading this chapter, you should be able to:

- Describe the differences among the various forms of euthanasia: active, passive, voluntary, nonvoluntary, and involuntary.
- Evaluate disputes over criteria for determining death.
- Explain key cases and examples of euthanasia and other end-of-life decisions.
- Explain the importance of advance directives and living wills.

- Identify the difference between ordinary and extraordinary medical interventions.
- Evaluate moral arguments about suicide and killing, including both consequentialist and non-consequentialist arguments.
- Differentiate between killing and letting die.
- Apply the principle of double effect.
- Defend your own ideas about the ethics of euthanasia.

MindTap®   For more chapter resources and activities, go to MindTap.

In 2015, California legalized physician-assisted suicide, joining a handful of other states where physicians are permitted to prescribe lethal medication for terminally ill patients. In 2016, as the California law took effect, Canada also legalized assisted suicide. The model for most of this legislation is the physician-assisted suicide law in Oregon, which holds that a doctor may prescribe lethal medication to a patient who has fewer than six months to live, according to the judgment of two independent doctors. The patient must be competent; must have a clear and continuing request, made orally and in writing; and must be able to take the drug without assistance. In the United States, physician-assisted suicide legislation has been subject to referenda and has been litigated in the courts. This practice was not legal in the United States a generation ago, but it is slowly becoming accepted. In Europe, active euthanasia— where instead of simply prescribing lethal medication, the doctor administers the lethal injection—is legal in the Netherlands, Belgium, and Luxembourg. Active euthanasia is not legal in the United States.

In California, assisted suicide legislation was propelled into the limelight by the case of Brittany Maynard, a young woman with brain cancer, who moved from California to Oregon to avail herself of Oregon's assisted suicide process. She killed herself in November 2014 at the age of 29. Brittany's case raised awareness and provoked controversy. An ethicist at the Vatican, Ignacio Carrasco de Paula, claimed that the act was reprehensible; Brittany Maynard's mother claimed that sort of condemnation was "more than a slap in the face."[1] Brittany's case and the attention it generated led to the passage of California's assisted suicide law in 2015.

Since the state of Oregon legalized physician-assisted suicide, the state has kept detailed records. According to the state of Oregon, a slowly growing number of patients in Oregon obtain lethal prescriptions and take them. According to data published in February of 2016, in the eighteen years that assisted suicide has been legal in Oregon, 1,545 people have obtained lethal prescriptions and 991 patients have died as a result of these prescriptions.[2] In 2015, there were 218 prescription recipients, resulting in 132 deaths. Of those who completed suicide: 78 percent of these assisted suicides were 65 years old or older, with a median age of 73. Most were white (93.1 percent), well educated (43.1 percent had at least a baccalaureate degree), and had cancer (72 percent). This data—and the case of Brittany Maynard—points toward the ethical question of whether access to assisted suicide is fairly distributed. Affluent people may have better access to the procedure than the poor or disenfranchised. In some states, assisted suicide remains illegal. And some people remain adamantly opposed to the practice.

In the Netherlands, euthanasia has been legal since 2002, when the Termination of Life on Request and Assisted Suicide (Review Procedures) Act took effect. The law in the Netherlands stipulates that physicians must exercise "due care" in assisting in suicide or when terminating life on request. According to the law, "due care" means that the physician

- holds the conviction that the request by the patient was voluntary and well considered.
- holds the conviction that the patient's suffering was lasting and unbearable.
- has informed the patient about the situation and about its prospects.
- holds the conviction, along with the patient, that there was no other reasonable solution for the situation.

- has consulted at least one other, independent physician who has seen the patient and has given his or her written opinion on the requirements of due care.
- has terminated a life or assisted in a suicide with due care.[3]

This law applies only to adults; euthanasia for children is not legally permitted. However, there are some doctors who have argued in favor of euthanasia for infants when they suffer from "unbearable and hopeless pain" and when their parents agree in consultation with doctors.[4] A protocol has been proposed for dealing with infant euthanasia, the Groningen Protocol. Although infant euthanasia remains a legal gray area in the Netherlands, adult euthanasia is regulated, and detailed records of the practice exist. The government was notified in 2014 that 242 individuals were assisted with suicide and 5,033 were actively euthanized—with 31 other cases involving a combination of assisted suicide and active euthanasia.[5] Most of these cases (3,888) involved patients with cancer, while 81 were for dementia and 41 were for psychiatric disorders. The issue of euthanasia for dementia and psychiatric disorders is especially controversial, as the mental competency of those requesting death is up for debate. Is mental illness a sufficient cause for suicide or a euthanasia request? The report indicates that the number of cases has increased yearly for the past five years. In 2010, there were 3,136 total notifications of euthanasia or assisted suicide; in 2014 that number increased to 5,306, which is an increase of nearly 70 percent.

In Belgium, a euthanasia law became effective on January 1, 2002. The Belgian law differs somewhat from the Dutch law in two ways. First, it allows **advance directives**—documents by which patients dictate health care decisions in advance of treatment in case they are incapacitated. Second, it promotes "the development of palliative care."[6] (**Palliative care** focuses on pain management and alleviating the symptoms of disease.) Euthanasia may seem like a radical remedy for pain management, but the idea is that the euthanasia discussion helps focus attention on patient autonomy and solutions for pain management.

European opinion and law about euthanasia remain divided. With its own history of Nazis gassing some 100,000 people who were deemed physically or mentally handicapped, Germany has criticized Dutch approval of the practice as a dangerous breaching of a dike.[7] Still, 80 percent of Dutch citizens support the law as the best way to allow people to control their own lives. Assisted suicide is also legal in Switzerland, and people from countries where it is illegal often go to Switzerland to commit suicide, a controversial practice that has been described as "suicide tourism." A March 2010 episode of PBS's *Frontline* featured the story of Craig Ewert, an American who was diagnosed with ALS (Lou Gehrig's disease) and who traveled to Switzerland to end his life. Ewert explained, "If I go through with it, I die, as I must at some point. If I don't go through with it, my choice is essentially to suffer and to inflict suffering on my family and then die—possibly in a way that is considerably more stressful and painful than this way. So I've got death, and I've got suffering and death. You know, this makes a whole lot of sense to me."[8]

Several questions suggest themselves regarding this matter. One is about the terminology we are supposed to use with regard to these sorts of cases. The title of this chapter is **euthanasia**, which is a word meaning "good death" (the Greek *eu* means "good"; the Greek *thanatos* means "death"). Death is usually not considered to be a good thing. But is there such a thing as a good death? Is a good death one that comes suddenly or after some time to think about and prepare for it? Is it one that takes place at home and in familiar surroundings or one that occurs in a medical facility? Is it one that we know is coming and over which we have control or one that comes on us without notice? What about our obligations to our family and loved ones? And what about the physician's obligation: Is it to "do no harm" and defend life, to fulfill patient requests for help in dying, or to allow death in order to prevent suffering? Under what conditions should euthanasia be permitted—for consenting adults, for the disabled who cannot provide consent, for children and infants? And what methods of euthanasia are appropriate?

Euthanasia has been a controversial topic for decades. The discussion of euthanasia involves issues of patient rights, life and death, the proper function of doctors, the ethics of suicide, and the overlap between law and morality. This chapter addresses each of these issues.

EUTHANASIA FOR INFANTS AND THE DISABLED

Death is usually thought of as a bad thing. But could it be that in some cases death is a mercy? Consider the case of an infant, Sanne, who was born with a severe form of Hallopeau-Siemens syndrome.[9] The disease caused the infant's skin to blister and peel, leaving painful scar tissue in its place. The prognosis was for a life of suffering until the child would eventually die of skin cancer before reaching her teenage years. The hospital refused to allow the infant to be euthanized, and Sanne eventually died of pneumonia. In such a case, would it be more humane to actively end the infant's life?

Modern medicine has made great strides in the treatment of newborn and premature infants. According to one recent study in the UK, "overall survival among those born between 22 and 25 weeks rose from 40 percent in 1995 to 53 percent in 2006."[10] However, while newborn survival is better, premature infants still tend to struggle with complications and disability. That same study also noted, "the proportion of such infants who experience severe disability as a result has not changed. That stood at 18 percent in 1995 and was 19 percent in 2006." In the United States, according to the Centers for Disease Control and Prevention,

> Each year, preterm birth affects nearly 500,000 babies—that's 1 of every 8 infants born in the United States. Preterm birth is the birth of an infant prior to 37 weeks gestation. It is the most frequent cause of infant death, the leading cause of long-term neurological disabilities in children, and costs the U.S. health care system more than $26 billion each year.[11]

One obvious remedy for this situation is finding ways to decrease preterm birth through better prenatal care. Another remedy would be expanding social resources to support preterm infants and their families, especially those with severe disabilities.

Despite the progress in care for preterm infants, some seriously ill newborns do not fare well. Some have severe defects and cannot survive for long, while others will live but with serious impairments. Thus, improvements in medicine that have enabled us to save the lives of newborns have also given us new life-and-death decisions to make.

One issue to consider here is the patient's quality of life. Parents who consider letting severely disabled infants die struggle with questions about the quality of life their child is likely to have. A further utilitarian consideration is the impact that expensive and possibly futile health care might have on the rest of the family. An influential utilitarian philosopher, Peter Singer, has argued that it is possible to imagine killing a disabled newborn and "replacing" it with another healthy baby in a subsequent pregnancy to achieve a net outcome of happiness. Singer notes that we allow women to abort disabled fetuses, and he sees very little difference between abortion and euthanasia for infants. Singer argues that, "killing a disabled infant is not morally equivalent to killing a person. Very often it is not wrong at all."[12] One of Singer's points is that disabled infants lack the sort of mental capacity that would give them moral status as "persons" who have a right to life. We will return to the issue of moral status in Chapter 11 on abortion.

Singer's approach has prompted criticism and protest. Some donors—including former presidential candidate Steve Forbes—threatened to withdraw funding from Princeton University when Princeton hired Singer to teach ethics.[13] Disability rights advocates have been especially critical of Singer. Harriet McBryde Johnson argues that Singer is advocating genocide against the disabled. She explains that the problem is Singer's "unexamined assumption that disabled people are inherently 'worse off,' that we 'suffer,' that we have lesser 'prospects of a happy life.' Because of this all-too-common prejudice, and his rare courage in taking it to its logical conclusion, catastrophe looms."[14]

Those who advocate euthanasia for infants often focus on the question of the well-being of the infant, arguing that the lives of some disabled infants are miserable and hopeless. As indicated earlier, in the Netherlands there is a quasi-legal protocol for considering active euthanasia for newborns—the Groningen Protocol. That protocol focuses on infants with a hopeless prognosis and extremely poor quality of life. This latter designation specifically includes "severe cases of spina bifida," a birth defect in which the spinal column does not fully close in development; the most serious cases result in death or, if treated, may leave the person with "muscle weakness or paralysis below the area of the spine where the incomplete closure (or cleft) occurs, loss of sensation below the cleft, and loss of bowel and bladder control."[15] In some cases, spinal fluid builds up and can cause learning problems. In cases such as this, it is not clear whether medical assistance is in the infant's best interest. However, people have survived spina bifida and been able to enjoy life and contribute to their communities.[16] The question of quality of life and disability points toward a variety of issues including the kinds of functions that we view as normal and healthy. It also points toward reflection on how we view suffering, caregiving, and dependency. The care-ethics standpoint (which we discussed in Chapter 9) acknowledges the importance of caregiving and dependency. Indeed, we are all dependent for the first few years of life; and there will be moments of dependency in our future, in illness and old age. What value do we place upon care and dependency? Other approaches to ethics—including especially the Kantian approach—emphasize autonomy. As we shall see, autonomy is a central question for discussions of end -of -life care, assisted suicide, and euthanasia.

One significant problem here is whether we can accurately predict or judge the quality of an individual's life. Several authors have pointed out that it is difficult for those of us with normal function to judge the quality of life of the disabled. Those in the disability rights movement will also argue, as Tom Shakespeare does, that judgments about quality of life depend on social context; in nurturing societies, with ample resources to support people with different abilities, some "impairments" may not be "disabling."[17] Shakespeare emphasizes that the primary focus should be on providing adequate health care—and not so much on the question of euthanasia.

Even with better health care and social supports, there do seem to be truly hopeless cases, such as that of the infant Sanne mentioned previously. Even skeptics about making such quality-of-life judgments, such as John Robertson—a professor of law and ethics—admit that there may be obvious cases, "a deformed, retarded, institutionalized child, or one with incessant unmanageable pain, where continued life is itself torture. But these cases are few."[18] In many other cases, it is not clear what counts as suffering or hopelessness. Cases such as that discussed by James Rachels at the end of this chapter, in which an infant born with Down syndrome was left untreated and died, have drawn intense criticism. Down syndrome (also called trisomy 21) is a genetic anomaly that causes mental retardation and sometimes physical problems as well. In the case discussed by Rachels, the child had a reparable but life-threatening blockage between the stomach and the small intestines. The parents refused permission for surgery to repair the problem, and the doctors followed their wishes and let the infant die. Critics protested that this surgery was simple and effective, and the infant, although developmentally disabled, could have led a generally happy life.

Choosing not to treat in such cases has been interpreted as not using what would be considered ordinary means of life support—ordinary because the benefits to the patient would outweigh any burdens. Such cases have been criticized for their "buck-passing"—that is, shifting responsibility for the death to nature, as though in this situation, but not elsewhere in medicine, we should "let nature take its course."[19]

Two different moral questions can be raised about such cases. The first asks: who would be the best to decide whether to provide or deny certain treatments? The second asks: what are the reasons to provide or deny care? Some people insist that the primary decision makers should be the parents because they are not only the most likely to have the infant's best interests at heart, but also the ones most likely to provide care for the child. Needless to say, we can imagine situations in which the parents would not be the most objective judges. They might be fearful, disappointed about the child's health conditions, or in disagreement about the best course of action. A 1983 presidential commission that was established to review medical ethics problems concluded that parents ought to make decisions for their seriously ill newborns, except in cases of decision-making incapacity, an unresolvable difference between parents, or a choice that is clearly not in the infant's best interests. (According to this commission, if a treatment is futile, it is not advised.) While the commission gives priority to parental decision making, it also sets forth a more general and objective standard for surrogate decision making,

> Permanent handicaps justify a decision not to provide life-sustaining treatment only when they are so severe that continued existence would not be a net benefit to the infant. Though inevitably somewhat subjective and imprecise in actual application, the concept of "benefit" excludes honoring idiosyncratic views that might be allowed if a person were deciding about his or her own treatment. Rather, net benefit is absent only if the burdens imposed on the patient by the disability or its treatment would lead a competent decision maker to choose to forgo the treatment. As in all surrogate decision making, the surrogate is obligated to try to evaluate benefits and burdens from the infant's own perspective.[20]

Criteria for Death

This last claim points toward the problem of trying to adopt the standpoint of one who is suffering and whose death we are contemplating. This issue came up in the past decade in the controversial case of Terri Schiavo, a severely brain-damaged woman who was allowed to die in 2005 after more than a decade of being kept alive by a feeding tube. Schiavo was twenty-six years old when she suffered a cardiac arrest on the morning of February

25, 1990. Her husband, Michael Schiavo, called 911. Emergency personnel arrived and resuscitated her. However, Schiavo's brain had been deprived of oxygen for some time, and she remained in a **persistent vegetative state (or PVS)** for the next fifteen years. A persistent vegetative state is often defined as one of "unconscious wakefulness" that lasts for more than a few weeks. A person in this state has lost all cerebral cortex function but retains a basic level of brain stem function. In contrast, someone who is not totally brain dead but who is in a coma is unconscious but "asleep." His or her brain stem functions poorly, and thus this person does not live as long as someone in a persistent vegetative state.[21]

Schiavo's case was contentious because of the difficulty in determining what was in her best interests and what she would have wanted for herself. The legal dispute involved the question of whether Schiavo's parents could prevent her husband—who had been appointed her legal guardian—from removing her feeding tube. Her husband claimed Schiavo would not want to be kept alive artificially with minimal chance of recovery, and in fact had expressed such wishes orally before her cardiac arrest. Her parents disagreed, claiming that Schiavo's Catholic faith prohibited this sort of euthanasia. Over the ensuing years, Schiavo's parents repeatedly challenged Michael Schiavo's guardianship in court and were repeatedly denied—with Schiavo's feeding tube being removed and reinserted on multiple occasions. The legal battle surrounding Schiavo's care would eventually involve the Florida legislature and courts, as well as the U.S. Congress, which passed controversial legislation in 2005 to intervene in the case. Ultimately, Schiavo's case was fast-tracked to the U.S. Supreme Court. The Court refused to intervene and Schiavo's tube was removed.

Terri Schiavo died on March 31, 2005, at age 41. An autopsy later revealed that her brain had shrunk to half its normal size, and thus that she had not been conscious or aware. Some had claimed over the years that Schiavo seemed to follow their motions and respond to their voices. However, we know from her autopsy as well as earlier brain scans

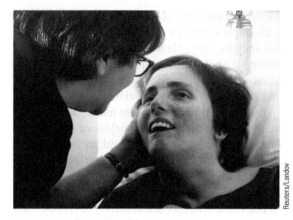

This photograph of Terri Schiavo was used to support the argument for keeping her on life support.

that she had no conscious function and that these were autonomic or reflexive responses. Even though her body might have continued its basic functions for decades, the medical evidence strongly suggests that Schiavo's consciousness permanently ceased in 1990.

The Schiavo case points to one of the problems of thinking about death and euthanasia. When does "death" occur?

Years ago, the *New York Times* reported on the case of a judge who was presiding over a similarly disputed medical situation. The dispute concerned whether a woman's respirator could be disconnected. The judge was reported to have said, "This lady is dead, and has been dead, and they are keeping her alive artificially."[22] Did the judge believe that the woman was alive or dead? She could not be both. He said that she was dead but also that she was being kept alive by machines. If the woman was really dead, then machines might have been keeping some of her bodily functions going, but could not have been keeping her *alive.* Perhaps the judge meant that, given her condition, she should be allowed to die. If so, then he should not have said she was dead. It is clear that we confuse questions about whether someone is dead or ought to be considered dead with other questions about whether it is permissible to do things that might hasten death.

We need not believe that an individual is dead in order to think it justifiable to disconnect a respirator and let him or her die. In fact, only if someone is not dead can we then sensibly ask whether we may let that person die. It seems useful here to consider here *how* we determine whether someone is dead, so as to distinguish this issue from other issues more properly related to euthanasia.

Throughout history, people have used various means to determine whether a human being is dead, and those means were a function of what they believed to be essential aspects of life. For example, if spirit was thought of as essential and was equated with a kind of thin air or breath, then the presence or absence of this "life breath" would indicate whether a person was living. When heart function was regarded as the key element of life, and the heart was thought to be like a furnace, then people would feel the body to see if it was warm in order to know whether the person was still living. Even today, with our better understanding of the function of the heart, other organs, and organ systems, we have great difficulty with this issue. One reason for this is that we now can use various machines to perform certain bodily functions, such as respiration and blood circulation. Sometimes this is a temporary measure, such as during a surgery. However, in other cases, the person may have lost significant brain function. In this latter sort of case, it is important to know whether the person is to be considered alive or dead.

Determining a precise condition and test for death became even more problematic in the past half-century, with the advent of heart transplants. Surgeons could not take a heart for transplant from someone who was considered living, only from someone who had been declared dead. Was an individual whose heart function was being artificially maintained but who had no brain function considered living or dead? We still debate this today. As transplantation science and life-support technologies were developing in the 1960s and 1970s, some courts had difficulty in figuring out how to apply brain death criteria. In some cases, defendants who were accused of murder attempted to argue that since the victim's heart was still beating after an initial assault, the assailant did not actually kill the victim—but that a subsequent transplant procedure or removal from life-support did. Since the 1980s, the courts have clarified that brain death is the appropriate criteria for use in such cases.[23]

In 1968, an ad hoc committee of the Harvard Medical School was set up to establish criteria for determining when a person should be declared dead. This committee determined that someone should be considered dead if he or she has permanently lost all detectable brain function. This meant that if there was some nonconscious brain function, for example, or if the condition was temporary, then the individual would not be considered dead. Thus, various tests of reflexes and responsiveness were required to determine whether an individual had sustained a permanent and total loss of all brain function.[24] This condition is now known as **whole brain death** and is the primary criterion used for the legal determination of death. This is true even when other secondary criteria or tests, such as loss of pulse, are used.

Whole brain death is distinguished from other conditions such as persistent vegetative states. In PVS, the individual has lost all cerebral cortex function but has retained some good brain stem function. Many nonconscious functions that are based in that area of the brain—respiratory and heart rate, facial reflexes and muscle control, and gag reflex and swallowing abilities—continue. Yet the individual in a permanent or persistent vegetative state has lost all conscious function. One reason for this condition is that the rate of oxygen used by the cerebral cortex is much higher than that of the brain stem, so these cells die much more quickly if deprived of oxygen for some time. The result is that the individual in this state will never regain consciousness but can often breathe naturally and needs no artificial aid to maintain circulation. Such an individual does not feel pain because he or she cannot interpret it as such. Because the gag reflex is good, individuals in this condition can clear their airways and thus may live for many years. They go through wake and sleep cycles in which they have their eyes open and then closed.

If we use whole brain death criteria to determine whether someone is dead, then neither a person in a persistent vegetative state nor a person in a coma is dead. In these cases, euthanasia questions about whether to let them die can be raised. On the other hand, if someone is dead by whole brain death criteria, then disconnecting equipment is not any form of euthanasia. We cannot let someone die who is already dead.

TYPES OF EUTHANASIA

If you were approached by a pollster who asked whether you supported euthanasia, you would do well first to ask what he or she meant and to what kind of euthanasia he or she was referring. It is important to distinguish what is called passive euthanasia from what is called active euthanasia. **Passive euthanasia** refers to withholding or withdrawing treatment and letting a patient die. Thus, passive euthanasia can also be described as "letting die" or "allowing to die." Sometimes this is referred to as "letting nature take its course." This might include either withdrawing care (as in removing a feeding tube) or withholding care (as in not prescribing antibiotics to cure an infection). **Active euthanasia** refers to more active intervention that aims to bring about the death of a person—a lethal injection, for example. **Physician-assisted suicide** is yet another thing—as the physician merely prescribes the lethal medication without administering it himself or herself. A further set of concepts focuses on whether euthanasia is given to those who request it and consent to it or not. **Voluntary euthanasia** implies that the patient consents. **Nonvoluntary euthanasia** describes euthanasia for those who are unable to give consent (infants or those with severe brain damage). **Involuntary euthanasia** implies that the killing is done in violation of the patient's will. There is no moral justification for involuntary euthanasia, which can also be called murder.

Active and Passive Euthanasia

Passive euthanasia is now a common practice and is not prohibited by law. Often, patients will decide

Passive euthanasia: Stopping (or not starting) some treatment, which allows the person to die. The person's condition causes his or her death.
Active euthanasia: Doing something such as administering a lethal drug or using other means that cause the person's death.
Voluntary euthanasia: Causing death with the patient's consent, knowingly and freely given.
Involuntary euthanasia: Causing death in violation of the patient's consent.
Nonvoluntary euthanasia: Causing the death of a patient who is unable to consent.
Physician-assisted suicide: Suicide that results from a physician's prescription of lethal medication.

in advance whether they want to be allowed to die from the progress of a fatal disease or from medical complications after surgery. Since the 1990s, with the passage of the Patient Self-Determination Act (PSDA) and through related case law, it has been acknowledged that patients have a right to refuse treatment. In these cases, the decision is made voluntarily. More controversial cases occur when the patient has not consented in advance and is unable to provide consent (or, as in the Schiavo case, there is a dispute about what the patient would have wanted). In such cases, next of kin are consulted in order to decide what the patient would have wanted in terms of treatment.

Legal precedents dealing with passive euthanasia were established in the cases of Karen Quinlan and Nancy Cruzan.[25] In Quinlan's case, the issue was whether a respirator that was keeping her alive could be disconnected. For some still unknown reason (some say it was a combination of prescription drugs and alcohol), she had gone into a coma in 1975. When doctors assured her parents that she would not recover, they sought permission to retain legal guardianship (since by then she was twenty-one years old) and have her respirator disconnected.

After several court hearings and final approval by the Supreme Court of the state of New Jersey, the Quinlans were finally permitted to disconnect her respirator. Although they expected she would die shortly after her respirator was removed, she continued to live in this comatose state for ten more years. One basic reason given by the court for its opinion in this case was that Quinlan did not lose her right of privacy by becoming incompetent and that her guardians could thus refuse unwanted and useless interventions by others to keep her alive. None of the various state interests or social concerns that might override this right were found to be relevant in her case.

Nancy Cruzan was twenty-five years old in 1983 when an accident left her in a persistent vegetative state until her death eight years later. In her case, the issue brought to the courts was whether a feeding tube that was providing her with food and water could be withdrawn. This case eventually reached the U.S. Supreme Court, which ruled that such lifesaving procedures could be withdrawn or withheld, but only if there was "clear and convincing evidence" that Cruzan would have wanted that herself. Eventually, such evidence was brought forward. Her feeding tube was removed, and she was allowed to die.

In contrast to the cases described above, active euthanasia involves taking a step that directly brings about a person's death. In the past, it was called "mercy killing." Drugs are the most common means. Rather than letting a person die, these means are used to actually kill the person. This is generally regarded as much more problematic.

In the United States, active euthanasia is legally prohibited. However, as we've noted, in the Netherlands and elsewhere, active euthanasia is permitted. The Netherlands has a historical tradition of tolerance and freedom going back centuries, as evidenced by its provision of refuge for religious minorities and such controversial philosophers as Descartes and Spinoza.[26] The Netherlands also allows for legalized prostitution and drug usage. Legalized active euthanasia in the Netherlands is not without its critics—some of whom worry that

active euthanasia is the first step on a slippery slope toward killing people who do not want to be killed. Critics also worry that this practice opens the door to killing those who feel they have become a financial burden on their families or who merely fear future suffering. One example of this occurred in 2012, when twin brothers Marc and Eddy Verbessem requested euthanasia in Belgium.[27] The twins were born deaf. They feared that they were going blind and suffered from other medical problems. They decided that rather than become incapacitated and dependent, and unable to see each other, they would rather die. In December 2012, their lives were ended at a hospital in Brussels. This case was unique, not only because it was a "double euthanasia," but also because the forty-five-year-old brothers were not terminally ill.

Voluntary, Nonvoluntary, and Involuntary Euthanasia

The laws in Belgium and the Netherlands require that the patient request euthanasia. These laws primarily focus on regulating *voluntary* euthanasia. Euthanasia laws—even in the United States—do allow for *nonvoluntary* passive euthanasia, which occurs, for example, when a feeding tube is removed from a patient in a persistent vegetative state. Clearly, someone like Terri Schiavo could not voluntarily request to be allowed to die, which makes her death a case of nonvoluntary passive euthanasia. There is some fear, however, that that the legalization of euthanasia might create a slippery slope from voluntary euthanasia toward involuntary euthanasia—that is, toward letting people die or actively killing them against their will.

In 2012, Senator Rick Santorum, who was campaigning for president, stoked the fear of involuntary euthanasia by claiming that "half of the people who are euthanized—ten percent of all deaths in the Netherlands—half of those people are euthanized involuntarily at hospitals because they are older and sick."[28] It would be frightening if 10 percent of deaths and half of all euthanasia cases were involuntary. However, it turns out that the data are not so frightening; and Santorum's alarmism was widely repudiated. The *New England Journal of Medicine* published an investigation of Dutch euthanasia practices in 2007, which indicated that only 0.4 percent of deaths "were the result of the ending of life without an explicit request by the patient."[29] This indicates that these were cases of nonvoluntary euthanasia, not involuntary euthanasia. We might still worry that even one involuntary case is too many. But it appears that the worry about a slippery slope is exaggerated.

Of course, one reason we might worry about a slippery slope toward involuntary euthanasia involves the high cost of health care at the end of life. Some entities can benefit from the death of a patient: family members who worry about losing an inheritance or paying for medical bills or insurance companies that have related financial concerns. (Also, in the case of young patients, there is concern about pressures with regard to organ donation.) It is possible to imagine a utilitarian argument that attempts to justify involuntary euthanasia. However, most serious discussions of euthanasia will insist that patient consent remains essential. Indeed, one might also argue that euthanasia should be for the sake of the one dying—and not for the sake of others (insurance companies, organ recipients, or heirs and family members).

In some circumstances, others must make decisions for a patient because the patient is incapable of doing so. This is true of infants and small children, and patients in comas or permanent vegetative states. It is also true of people who are only minimally competent, as in cases of senility or certain psychiatric disorders. Deciding who is sufficiently competent to make decisions for themselves is clear in many but not all cases. For example, what should we say of the mental competence of an eighty-year-old man who refuses an effective surgery that would save his life and, at the same time, says he does not want to die? Is such a person being rational?

ADVANCE DIRECTIVES

In some cases, when a patient is not able to express his or her wishes, we can attempt to infer what the person would want. For example, we can rely on past personality or statements the person has made. Perhaps the person commented to friends or relatives as to what he or she would want in specific medical situations.

In other cases, a person might have left a written expression of his or her wishes in an advance medical directive. One form of advance directive is a **living will**. The living will may specify that one does not want extraordinary measures used to prolong life if one is dying and unable to communicate. However, such a specification leaves it up to the physician—who may be a stranger—to determine what is extraordinary. Another directive is called a **durable power of attorney**. In this case, the patient appoints someone close to him or her who knows what he or she wants under certain conditions if he or she is dying and unable to communicate. Patients are generally advised to have one or two alternate appointees for durable powers of attorney.

The person with durable power of attorney need not be a lawyer but serves as the patient's legal representative to make medical decisions for him or her in the event of incapacitation. The form for durable power of attorney also provides for individualized expressions in writing about what a patient would want done or not done under certain conditions. The appointed person will also be the only one able to give permission for "do not resuscitate" (DNR) orders, or orders not to revive the patient under certain conditions. DNR orders can be controversial, particularly in cases in which a patient's family requests that physicians take all possible measures to save the patient. This causes conflict, especially if the physician believes that resuscitation attempts will be futile or even make the patient worse off.[30] At the very least, however, these directives have moral force as expressions of patients' wishes. They also have legal force in those states that have recognized them.[31] There is some dispute about whether advance directives are effective. One study published in 2010 maintains that advance directives are usually followed.[32] However, an editorial accompanying that study in the *New England Journal of Medicine* indicates that there are important limitations—including the impossibility of imagining all health care options in advance and the fact that our preferences may change.[33]

Living wills and durable powers of attorney can, if enforced, give people some added control over what happens to them in their last days. To further ensure this, Congress passed the Patient Self-Determination Act, which went into effect in December of 1991. This act requires that health care institutions that participate in the Medicare and Medicaid programs have written policies for providing individuals in their care with information about and access to advance directives, such as living wills.

Physician-Assisted Suicide

In 2014, there were 42,773 suicides in the United States, which is approximately 1.6 percent of all deaths. Of those suicides, 7,693 were older than 65 (and 5,079 were between the ages of 15 and 24); 33,113 males committed suicide compared to only 9,660 females. It is estimated that there are twenty-five nonfatal attempts for every actual suicide.[34]

There are a number of ethical issues related to suicide. Immanuel Kant famously condemned suicide in the *Fundamental Principles of the Metaphysic of Morals* (see Chapter 6). He held that it violated the categorical imperative, since the maxim of suicide was not universalizable. If the maxim of suicide were universalized, we'd end up saying that everyone should kill themselves, which Kant rejects as an impossible law of nature. Furthermore, if one commits suicide out of a self-interested motive (say to avoid misfortune), then there is a contradiction. Self-interest—what Kant calls self-love—contradicts itself when it leads to the killing of the self. Kant also held that suicide was disrespectful of personhood, in violation of the second form of the categorical imperative (as discussed in Chapter 6). The problem is that if a person destroys himself or herself in order to escape painful circumstances, he or she uses his or her own life as a means to an end. Western religious traditions also tend to condemn suicide. For example, Catholic moral teachings are radically pro-life, which means that they are opposed to suicide, euthanasia, and abortion. From

this standpoint, suicide is wrong because it is anti-life and violates the dignity and worth of the human person. Pope John Paul II claims, for example, that suicide is immoral because it is a "rejection of God's absolute sovereignty over life and death."[35]

Just as questions can be raised about whether suicide is ever morally acceptable, so also can questions be raised about whether it is morally permissible for physicians (or others for that matter) to help someone commit suicide. Physician-assisted suicide also poses problems for doctors who take the Hippocratic Oath to "do no harm." In some ways, it looks like active euthanasia. Whereas in passive euthanasia, the doctor refrains from trying to do what saves or prolongs life; in active euthanasia, the doctor acts to bring about the death by some cause or means. However, the causation by the doctor in physician-assisted suicide (i.e., the prescription of potentially lethal medication) is not immediate or direct, but rather takes place through the action of the patient.

One well-known advocate and practitioner of physician-assisted suicide was Dr. Jack Kevorkian. For several years, he helped people who wanted to die by providing them with the means to kill themselves. His first method was a "suicide machine" that consisted of a metal pole to which bottles of three solutions were attached. First, a simple saline solution flowed through an intravenous needle that had been inserted into the patient's vein. The patient then flipped a switch that started a flow of an anesthetic, thiopental, which caused the patient to become unconscious. After sixty seconds, a solution of potassium chloride followed, causing death within minutes by heart seizure. In a later version of the machine, carbon monoxide was used. When a patient pushed a control switch, carbon monoxide flowed through a tube to a bag placed over the patient's head.[36]

For eight years, starting in 1990, Kevorkian assisted more than 100 suicides, almost all of them in Michigan. To prevent these incidents from taking place in their state, Michigan legislators passed a law in 1993 against assisting a suicide. However, the law was struck down in the courts. Kevorkian was brought to trial in three separate cases, but juries found him not guilty in each case. However, in November 1998, he himself administered a lethal injection to a fifty-two-year-old man who was suffering from Lou Gehrig's disease. He also provided the news media with a videotape of the injection and death. It was aired on CBS's *60 Minutes* on November 22, 1998. This was no longer a case of suicide, and after a brief trial, on April 13, 1999, Kevorkian was convicted of second-degree murder and sentenced to serve a 10- to 25-year prison term in a Michigan prison. He was paroled in 2007 and died in 2011.

Many families of people he helped to die speak highly of Dr. Kevorkian. In addition, Dr. Kevorkian's patients can be seen pleading to be allowed to die in the videotapes he made of them before their deaths. His critics have a different view, however. They say that at least some of the people who wanted to die might not have done so if they had received better medical care—if their pain were adequately treated, for example. Some of the people were not terminally ill. One was in the early stages of Alzheimer's disease, and another had multiple sclerosis. The primary physician of another patient who claimed to have multiple sclerosis said the patient showed no evidence of this or any other disease; the patient had a history of depression, however. Another patient was determined by the medical examiner to have no trace of an earlier diagnosed cancer.[37] In still another case, a woman had what has come to be called "chronic fatigue syndrome" and a history of abuse by her husband.

Some critics have pointed out that Kevorkian's patients were predominantly women, who may have been worried about the impact of their diseases on others as much as the difficulty of the diseases themselves. In fact, according to data on suicide cited above, three times as many women as men attempt suicide, though men succeed three times more often than women.[38] Some suggest that women's suicide attempts are more of a cry for help than an actual desire to die. The choice of assisted suicide may also appear to women as a requirement of feminine virtues of care and service toward the family (as discussed in Chapter 9). However, the data

on assisted suicide in Oregon, for example, do not indicate a gender gap in assisted suicide; in 2015, 56 men and 76 women were assisted in committing suicide—and an approximate 50–50 gender split is common for the past decade of record keeping on the issue[39]

The American Medical Association continues to oppose physician-assisted suicide. The Hippocratic Oath contains the following claim: "I will neither give a deadly drug to anybody if asked for it, nor will I make a suggestion to this effect." This statement goes on to say that a physician should not provide abortion to women. Indeed, many people see a connection between the ethics of abortion and the ethics of euthanasia and suicide. They argue that a consistently pro-life position is opposed to all of these things (along with the death penalty and war, in most cases). But the medical profession does not have the same problem with abortion as it does with physician-assisted suicide. The American Medical Association continues to reject physician-assisted suicide as unethical. The organization's position on physician-assisted suicide states

> It is understandable, though tragic, that some patients in extreme duress—such as those suffering from a terminal, painful, debilitating illness—may come to decide that death is preferable to life. However, allowing physicians to participate in assisted suicide would cause more harm than good. Physician-assisted suicide is fundamentally incompatible with the physician's role as healer, would be difficult or impossible to control, and would pose serious societal risks.[40]

Legal scholars and philosophers have long seen a connection between the ethics of euthanasia and abortion. Some of the arguments that have been used to support physician-assisted suicide make use of the passive euthanasia decisions discussed above (Quinlan and Cruzan), as well as the legal reasoning that has been used to defend abortion. When cases involving physician-assisted suicide reached the Supreme Court in 1997, a group of well-known philosophers made arguments in favor of the practice in an amicus curiae known as "The Philosopher's Brief." (The group included many prominent philosophers who appear in this book, including Judith Jarvis Thomson, Robert Nozick, Thomas Nagel, and John Rawls.) These philosophers conclude

> Certain decisions are momentous in their impact on the character of a person's life—decisions about religious faith, political and moral allegiance, marriage, procreation, and death, for example. Such deeply personal decisions pose controversial questions about how and why human life has value. In a free society, individuals must be allowed to make those decisions for themselves, out of their own faith, conscience, and convictions.[41]

Despite such arguments, the U.S. Supreme Court decided in 1997 that there is no constitutional right to assisted suicide. However, individual states have not been prohibited from allowing the practice, and in 2006, the Court struck down an attempt by the Bush administration to invalidate the Oregon Death with Dignity Law through the use of federal drug laws. This opened the door to the legalization of physician-assisted suicide in other states, as noted previously.

Pain Medication and Palliative Sedation

A different practice that may be confused with active euthanasia but ought to be distinguished from it is giving pain medication to gravely ill and dying patients. In some cases, the amount of pain medication given can also be a contributing factor in bringing about death. This is known as **terminal sedation** or **palliative sedation**. To call it terminal sedation implies that the use of sedation aims at the termination of life; to call it palliative sedation implies that the sedation is intended as palliative (relieving or soothing) care. Palliative sedation can also hasten death when it is combined with other practices, such as cutting off food and water or withdrawing other medications. Various forms of palliative care, pain management, and passive euthanasia are now standard practices in hospice care (a *hospice* is a nursing facility that provides care for the dying). However, the intentional use of pain medication to end life remains controversial.[42] One notorious case involved the

possibility that terminal sedation was used to end the lives of patients after Hurricane Katrina in New Orleans.[43]

Physicians are often hesitant to administer sufficient pain medication to severely ill patients because they fear that the medication will actually cause their deaths. They fear that this would be considered comparable to mercy killing (or active euthanasia), which is legally impermissible. (The fact that they might cause addiction in their patients is another reason why some doctors hesitate to give narcotics for pain relief. This seems hardly a reasonable objection, especially if the patient is dying!) The **principle of double effect** may help justify physicians' use of terminal sedation. According to the principle of double effect, it is morally wrong to intend to do something bad as a means to an end; it is acceptable, however, to do something morally permissible for the purpose of achieving some good, while knowing that it also may have a bad secondary effect.

The following diagram may be used to help understand the essence of this principle. It shows a morally permissible act with two effects: one intended main effect and one unintended side effect.

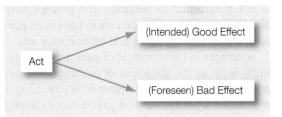

According to the principle of double effect, it may be morally permissible to administer a drug with the intention of relieving pain (a good effect), even though we know or foresee that our action also may have a bad effect (weakening the person and risking his death). Certain conditions must be met, however, for this to be permissible. First, the act itself must be morally permissible. One cannot do what is wrong to bring about a good end. Second, the person who acts must intend to bring about the good end rather than the harmful result. Third, the good results must outweigh the bad ones.

The idea behind the double effect principle is that there is a moral difference between intending to kill someone and intending to relieve pain. There is a moral difference between intending that someone die by means of one's actions (giving a drug overdose) and foreseeing that they will die because of one's actions (giving medication to relieve pain). Doing the latter is not, strictly speaking, active euthanasia. Active euthanasia would be the intentional giving of a drug with the purpose of bringing about a person's death. The difference is seen in the case of the conscientious dentist who foresees that he or she might cause a patient pain and the sadistic dentist who seeks to produce pain in a patient.

The principle of double effect continues to be an object of debate.[44] In real-world medical situations, it may be difficult to assess people's intentions—whether, for example, a patient requests an increased dose of pain medication just to relieve pain or actually bring about his or her own death. People may also have mixed or hidden motives for their actions. Nevertheless, trying to satisfy the principle of double effect can be useful for doctors, allowing them to give their patients sufficient pain medication without fear of being prosecuted for homicide. This principle may also help those who want patients to have good pain relief but are morally opposed to active euthanasia.

Advances in the treatment of pain may increasingly separate the questions of palliative and terminal sedation. New developments in pain control may make it possible to treat pain without causing death, thereby keeping this issue separate from that of active euthanasia—although pain management at the end of life remains a complicated and delicate task. Doctors and nurses are also increasingly aware of the need for a comprehensive approach to pain management. Nonetheless, it remains important to distinguish between pain management and the intention to end life. The American Nurses Association explains

> While nurses should make every effort to provide aggressive pain control and symptom relief for patients at the end of life, it is never ethically permissible for a nurse to act by omission or commission, including, but not limited to medication administration, with the intention of ending a patient's life.[45]

Ordinary and Extraordinary Measures

Philosophers have sometimes labeled those measures that are ineffective or excessively burdensome as *extraordinary*. They are often called *heroic* in the medical setting, in the sense that such extraordinary measures can be burdensome and go above and beyond what is likely to benefit the patient. A person's hospital medical chart might have the phrase *no heroics* on it, indicating that no such measures are to be used. There are other cases in which what is refused would actually be effective for curing or ameliorating a life-threatening condition. These measures are called *ordinary*—not because they are common but because they promise reasonable hope of benefit. With ordinary measures, the chances that the treatment will help are good, and the expected results are also good. And yet decisions are sometimes made not to use these measures and to instead let the person die.

Critics have complained that the idea of what is heroic or extraordinary is vague. One difficulty with determining whether a treatment would be considered ordinary or extraordinary is in making an objective evaluation of the benefits and burdens. It would be easier to do this if there were such a thing as an objective minimum standard for a patient's quality of life. Any measure that would not restore a person to at least that standard could then be considered extraordinary. However, if we were to set this standard very high, using it might also wrongly imply that the lives of disabled persons are of little or no benefit to them.

What would be considered an ordinary measure in the case of one person may be considered extraordinary in the case of another; a measure may effectively treat one person's condition, but another person would die shortly even if the measure were used (a blood transfusion, for example). Furthermore, the terminology can be misleading because many of the medical tools that used to be considered experimental and risky (such as antibiotics and respirators) are now common and largely beneficial. In many cases, such tools are now considered ordinary, whereas they once could have been considered extraordinary. (Here the word *ordinary* refers to proven benefit over time, rather than commonness. You will find use of the term *extraordinary* in the quote from the American Medical Association in the article by James Rachels at the end of this chapter. When reading that article, you also might consider whether one reason the cases of Smith and Jones are morally similar is because what was withheld from the child was an "ordinary" means of life support.)

The basic difference between ordinary and extraordinary measures of life support, then, is as follows:

Ordinary measures: Measures or treatments with reasonable hope of benefit, or the benefits outweigh the burdens to the patient

Extraordinary measures: Measures or treatments with no reasonable hope of benefit, or the burdens outweigh the benefits to the patient

---

One question that arises in relation to ordinary and extraordinary measures is how to view the withholding or withdrawing of artificial nutrition, as in the Terri Schiavo case discussed previously. It is instructive to remember that Schiavo's family was Catholic and that Catholic theology provides much of the intellectual basis for the distinctions between ordinary and extraordinary measures. Although we introduced the definitions above in the context of euthanasia, the key to the difference between ordinary and extraordinary is whether any medical measure that is withheld or withdrawn offers "a reasonable hope of benefit."[46] Although the U.S. Catholic medical guidelines assert that "a person may forgo extraordinary or disproportionate means of preserving life . . . there should be a presumption in favor of providing nutrition and hydration to all patients, including patients who require medically assisted nutrition and hydration, as long as this is of sufficient benefit to outweigh the burdens involved to the patient."[47] In other words, in some cases, this form of medical intervention would be deemed of insufficient benefit to a patient—for example, if it did not promise to return him or her to a conscious state. In Schiavo's case, Schiavo parents argued that the potential benefits of artificial nutrition outweighed the burdens; her husband and the medical community concluded that no benefits (such as restored consciousness) were possible.

Combining the Types of Euthanasia

We have noted the differences between various types of euthanasia: voluntary and nonvoluntary (we will ignore involuntary euthanasia, assuming it to be immoral), active and passive, and (if passive) the withholding of ordinary and extraordinary measures. Combining the types of euthanasia gives six forms, as illustrated below.

There are three types of voluntary euthanasia.

1. Voluntary active euthanasia: The person who is dying says, "Give me the fatal dose."
2. Voluntary passive euthanasia, withholding ordinary measures: The person says, "Don't use life-saving or life-prolonging medical measures even though the likely results of using them would be good and the costs or burdens minimal, because I want to die."
3. Voluntary passive euthanasia, withholding extraordinary measures: The person says, "Don't use those medical measures because the chances of benefit in terms of saving or extending my life would be small, the burdens too great, or both."

Likewise, there are three types of nonvoluntary euthanasia.

4. Nonvoluntary active euthanasia: Others decide to give the person a fatal drug overdose.
5. Nonvoluntary passive euthanasia, withholding ordinary measures: Others decide not to use life-saving or life-prolonging medical measures even though the likely results of using them would be good and the costs or burdens minimal.
6. Nonvoluntary passive euthanasia, withholding extraordinary measures: Others decide not to use those medical measures because the chances of benefit—saving or extending life—are small, the burdens are too great, or both.

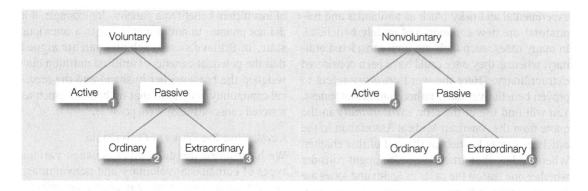

So far, we have attempted only to classify types of euthanasia. Our purpose has been to describe the various possible types so that we will then be better able to make appropriate distinctions in our moral judgments about these cases.

MAKING MORAL JUDGMENTS ABOUT EUTHANASIA

Before we consider the moral arguments about euthanasia, we should first distinguish moral judgments from assertions about what the law should or should not be on this matter. Although we may sometimes have moral reasons for what we say the law should or should not do, the two areas are distinct. There are many things that are moral matters that ought not to be legislated or made subject to law and legal punishment. Not everything that is immoral ought to be illegal. For example, lying is only sometimes illegal. In our thinking about euthanasia, we should keep this distinction in mind. On the one hand, in some cases we might say that a person acted badly, though understandably, in giving up too easily on life. Yet we also may believe that the law should not force some action here if the person knows what he or she is doing, and the person's action does not seriously harm others. On the other hand, a person's request to end his or her life might be reasonable given his or her circumstances, but there might also be social reasons why the law should not permit it. These reasons might be related to the possible harmful effects of some practice on other persons or on the practice of medicine. Just

because some action (for example, euthanasia) might be morally permissible does not necessarily mean that it ought to be legally permissible.

One way to get a handle on what to think about the morality of euthanasia is to look at its various types. We can then ask ourselves whether euthanasia of a certain type is morally justifiable. One way to help us answer these questions is to use the distinction introduced earlier between consequentialist theories (such as utilitarianism) and non-consequentialist theories (such as Kant's moral theory or natural law theory). If you think that it is the consequences, rather than the nature of actions themselves, that matter morally, then you can focus on those considerations. If, instead, you think that we should judge whether some action is right or wrong in itself for some reason, then you can focus on those considerations.

The Moral Significance of Voluntariness

Today, an individual's right over his or her own life is highly valued. And yet, the commonsense moral view is that there are limits to this right. It is limited, for example, when it conflicts with the interests or rights of others. Under what conditions and for what reasons should a person's own wishes prevail in euthanasia matters? How important is voluntary consent?

Consequentialist Considerations From your study of utilitarianism, you know that utilitarians focus moral judgment on the consequences of our actions or rules. From this perspective, voluntariness matters morally only to the extent that it affects human happiness and welfare. Respecting people's own choices about how they will die surely would have some beneficial consequences. For example, when people know that they will be allowed to make decisions about their own lives and not be forced into things against their will, then they may gain a certain peace of mind. Thus, many of the persons who have used Oregon's assisted suicide law reported that they did so because they did not want to be dependent and felt better having control over their lives. Moreover, those dying may be the best people to make good decisions about things that primarily affect them. These are good consequentialist reasons to respect a person's wishes in euthanasia cases.

Of course, it is not only the person who is dying who is affected by these decisions. Thus, it can be argued that the effects on others—on their feelings, for example—are also relevant. Moreover, individual decisions are not always wise and do not always work for the greatest benefit of the person making them, or for that of others. For example, critics of euthanasia worry that people who are ill or disabled might refuse certain lifesaving treatments because they lack money or do not know about services and supports available to them. On consequentialist grounds, we should do what, in fact, is most likely to bring about the greatest happiness, not only for ourselves but also for all those affected by our actions. It does not in itself matter who makes the judgment. But it does matter insofar as one person, rather than another, is more likely to make a better judgment—one that would have better consequences overall, including consequences to the individual.

Rule utilitarians will also tell us that we ought to consider which policies and practices would maximize happiness. (It is here that morality comes closer to concerns about what the law should be.) Would a policy that universally follows individual requests about dying be most likely to maximize happiness? Or would a policy that gives no special weight to individual desires, but that directs us to do whatever some panel decides, be more likely to have the best outcome? Or would some moderate policy be best, such as one that gives special but not absolute weight to what a person wants? An example of such a policy might place a substantial burden of proof on proposals that would deny a dying person's wishes.

Non-consequentialist Considerations To appeal to the value of personal autonomy in euthanasia decisions is to appeal to a non-consequentialist reason or moral norm. The idea is that autonomy is a good in itself and therefore carries heavy moral weight. We like to think of ourselves, at least ideally, as masters of our own fate. According to Kant, autonomy makes morality possible. His famous phrase "an ought implies a can" indicates that if and only if we can or are free to act in certain ways can we be commanded to do so. According to a Kantian deontological position, persons are unique in being able to choose freely, and this capacity for choice ought to be respected.

However, in many euthanasia cases, a person's mental competence and thus autonomy is compromised by fear, lack of understanding, dependency, and hopelessness. Illness and dependency can make a person more subject to undue influence or coercion. Moreover, patients with terminal illnesses can become depressed and despondent. One study of terminally ill patients who consider suicide concluded, "Depression and hopelessness are the strongest predictors of desire for hastened death."[48] It might make sense for people with terminal illness to be depressed and to feel hopeless. But it might also be that it is possible to treat the depression along with pain in order to provide patients with more autonomy as they confront the end of life.

The issues of depression, dependency, and hopelessness point toward some of the problems for thinking about the importance of autonomy. **Autonomy** literally means self-rule. But how often are we fully clear about who we are and what we want to be? Is the self whose decisions are to be respected the current self or one's ideal or authentic self? In cases of dementia or mental illness, should the person's current wishes outweigh the wishes the person expressed before he became demented or mentally ill? These issues of selfhood and personal identity are crucial to euthanasia arguments that focus on autonomy and personal decision making. It is also the case that they take us beyond ethics itself into philosophical notions of the self and freedom as well as into empirical psychology.

Although we have concentrated on pointing out the kinds of things that would be morally relevant from both consequentialist and non-consequentialist points of view, the issues also may be analyzed from the perspective of an ethics of care. One would suppose that from this perspective both matters that relate to benefits and harms and those that relate to a person's autonomy would be relevant.

Active versus Passive Euthanasia

The distinction between active and passive euthanasia is a conceptual distinction, a matter of classification. Giving patients lethal drugs to end their lives is classified as active euthanasia. Stopping or not starting some life-lengthening treatment, knowing that a patient will die, is classified as passive euthanasia. For example, either not starting a respirator or disconnecting it is generally considered passive euthanasia because it is a matter of not providing life-prolonging aid for the person. In this case, the person's illness or weakness is the cause of death if he or she dies. That passive euthanasia does not directly cause a patient's death tells us nothing about whether the practice is justified or unjustified.

Outline of Moral Approaches to Voluntary Euthanasia and Physician Assisted Suicide

	Pro-Euthanasia	Moderate	Anti-Euthanasia
Thesis	Patients should be free to choose death	Stringent limits on euthanasia and assisted suicide	Death should not be chosen or intended
Corollaries and Implications	Death with dignity involves respecting a patient's choices, including desire for death; active euthanasia may be more humane than passive; involuntary euthanasia remains wrong	Restricted to patients with terminal illness and mental competence; voluntary euthanasia is more restricted than assisted suicide	Pain management and dignified treatment options are primary; worries about slippery slopes toward involuntary euthanasia
Connections with Moral Theory	Autonomy of the patient as key; consequentialists may view death as better than suffering	Respect for autonomy; but consequentialists worry about slippery slopes and implications for medical ethics	Killing is fundamentally wrong (e.g., Kant's argument about suicide); consequentialists may worry about miracle cures, slippery slopes, and implications for the vulnerable and disabled
Relevant authors/ examples	James Rachels	Physician-assisted suicide legislation in U.S. states	J. Gay-Williams

Let's pose the moral question about active and passive euthanasia like this: Is there any moral difference between them? Is active euthanasia more morally problematic than passive euthanasia? Or are they on a moral par such that if passive euthanasia is morally permissible in a particular case, then so is active euthanasia? Is physician-assisted suicide (in which a physician only provides the means of death to the person) any more or less problematic than cases in which the physician actually administers the drug or uses other means to bring about death?

Consequentialist Concerns   Again, if we take the perspective of the consequentialist or act utilitarian, for example, we should be concerned about our actions only in terms of their consequences. The means by which the results come about do not matter in themselves. They matter only if they make a difference in the result. Generally, then, if a person's death is the *best outcome* in a difficult situation, it would not matter whether it came about through the administration of a lethal drug dose or from the discontinuance of some lifesaving treatment. Now, if one or the other means did make a difference in a person's experience (of pain or suffering), then this would count in favor of or against that method.

A rule utilitarian would be concerned about the overall results or consequences of practices and policies. Which would be the best policy: one that allows those who are involved to choose active euthanasia, one that requires active euthanasia in certain cases, one that permits it only in rare cases, or one that prohibits it and attaches legal penalties to it? Which policy would make more people happy and fewer people unhappy? One that prohibited active euthanasia would frustrate those who wished to use it, but it would prevent some abuses that might follow if it were permitted. Essential to this perspective are predictions about how a policy would work. Some people are concerned, in particular, about the effects of physician participation in the practice of euthanasia. It may have the positive results of being under the control of a profession known for its ethical concerns. Or it may have negative effects such as the lessening of patient trust in physicians. The

disability advocacy group called Not Dead Yet has voiced its concerns about physician-assisted suicide and the plight of the disabled.[49] Its members argue that legalized physician-assisted suicide may make people more inclined to think the lives of the disabled are not worth living and that there might be pressure on them to commit suicide. Instead of legalizing assisted suicide, critics argue, we should emphasize universal access to health care, better pain management, and better social work to deal with the concerns of the aged and disabled.

Even those who support physician-assisted suicide and, in some cases, active euthanasia worry about whether these practices would be open to abuse. The argument that there would be abuse has been given various names, depending on the particular metaphor of choice: the "domino effect," "slippery slope," "wedge," or "camel's nose" argument. The idea is that if we permit active euthanasia in a few reasonable cases, then we may approve it in more and more cases until we are approving it in cases in which it is clearly unreasonable. In other words, if we permit euthanasia when a person is soon dying, in unrelievable pain, and has requested that his or her life be ended, then we will eventually permit it when a person is not dying or has not requested to be killed. Evidence about involuntary euthanasia in the Netherlands, as cited above, may or may not be relevant in the United States or elsewhere. But we may still ask: would we slide down the slope to involuntary euthanasia or other morally unacceptable results? Is there something about us that would cause us to slide? Would we be so weak of mind that we could not see the difference between these cases? Would we be weak of will, not wanting to care for people whose care is costly and burdensome? This is an empirical and predictive matter. To know the force of the argument, we would need to show evidence about the likelihood of sliding down such a slippery slope.

Non-consequentialist Concerns   Many arguments and concerns about active and passive euthanasia are not based on appeals to good or bad results or consequences. Arguments about the right to die or to make one's own decisions about dying are non-consequentialist arguments. On the one hand, some people argue that respecting personal autonomy is so important that it should override any concerns about bad results. Thus, we might conclude that people ought to be allowed to end their lives when they choose as an expression of their autonomy, and that this choice should be respected regardless of the consequences to others or even mistakes about their own cases.

On the other hand, some people believe that there is a significant moral difference between killing another person or killing themselves and letting a person die. Killing people, except in self-defense, is morally wrong, according to this view. Just why it is thought wrong is another matter. Some people rely on reasons like those advanced by natural law, citing the innate drive toward living as a good in itself, however compromised—a good that should not be suppressed. Kant uses reasoning similar to this in his argument against suicide. He argues that making a case for ending life based on a concern for life is inherently contradictory and a violation of the categorical imperative. Some people use religious reasons to argue against any form of suicide, such as the belief that life-and-death decisions are for God and not ourselves to make. Some people use reasons that rely on concerns about the gravity of ending a life directly and intentionally, and claim that in doing so, we ally ourselves with what is at best a necessary evil.

We each need to consider what role consequentialist and non-consequentialist or deontological reasons play in our own views about the morality of active and passive euthanasia. If consequentialist arguments (either egoistic or utilitarian) have primacy, then one's argument for or against active euthanasia will depend on empirical judgments about the predicted consequences. If deontological reasons have primacy, then these reasons must be evaluated. Is the principle of respecting patient autonomy more important, for example, than prohibitions against killing? This text does not intend to answer these questions for the student, but it does assume that a good start can be made in answering

them if one is able to know whether an argument is based on egoistic, utilitarian, or deontological considerations.

In the readings in this chapter, J. Gay-Williams and James Rachels address euthanasia from a variety of perspectives. Gay-Williams discusses the natural instinct to live, while also considering different types of euthanasia, and generally arguing against euthanasia. Rachels considers euthanasia for disabled infants, while asking whether there is a moral difference between passive and active euthanasia. Rachels concludes that if the motive is morally appropriate, active euthanasia is not morally worse than passive euthanasia.

> MindTap® For more chapter resources and activities, go to MindTap.

NOTES

1. "Vatican Official Calls Assisted Suicide of U.S. Woman 'Reprehensible,'" *CBS News*, November 4, 2014, http://www.cbsnews.com/news/brittany-maynards-assisted-suicide-condemned-by-vatican-official/ (accessed March 28, 2016).
2. Oregon Public Health Division, *Oregon Death with Dignity Act: 2015 Data Summary*, February 4, 2016, https://public.health.oregon.gov/ProviderPartnerResources/EvaluationResearch/DeathwithDignityAct/Documents/year18.pdf (accessed March 28, 2016)
3. *Termination of Life on Request and Assisted Suicide (Review Procedures) Act* in *Death and Dying: A Reader*, ed. Thomas A. Shannon (Rowman & Littlefield, 2004), p. 122.
4. Eduard Verhagen and Pieter J. J. Sauer, "The Groningen Protocol—Euthanasia in Severely Ill Newborns," *New England Journal of Medicine* 352 (March 10, 2005), pp. 959–62.
5. Regional Euthanasia Review Committees, *Annual Report 2014*, August 2012, https://www.rijksoverheid.nl/documenten/jaarverslagen/2015/08/01/regionale-toetsingscommissies-euthanasie-jaarverslag-2014 (accessed April 8, 2016).

6. Richard H. Nicholson, "Death Is the Remedy?" *Hastings Center Report* 32, No. 1 (January–February 2002), p. 9.

7. *The New York Times*, April 12, 2001, p. A6.

8. "The Suicide Tourist," PBS's *Frontline*, March 2, 2010, http://www.pbs.org/wgbh/pages/frontline/ suicidetourist/ (accessed March 28, 2016).

9. Jim Holt, "Euthanasia for Babies?" *New York Times Magazine*, July 10, 2005, http://travel.nytimes.com/ 2005/07/10/magazine/10WWLN.html?pagewanted=all (accessed March 28, 2016).

10. Denis Campbell, "Premature Babies Study Shows Survival Rates on Rise," *The Guardian*, December 4, 2012, http://www.guardian.co.uk/society/2012/ dec/05/survival-rates-premature-babies-rise (accessed March 28, 2016).

11. "Preterm Birth," Centers for Disease Control and Prevention, http://www.cdc.gov/reproductivehealth/ maternalinfanthealth/PretermBirth.htm (accessed March 28, 2016).

12. Peter Singer, *Practical Ethics*, 3rd ed. (Cambridge: Cambridge University Press, 2011), p. 167.

13. Debra Galant, "Peter Singer Settles In, and Princeton Looks Deeper; Furor over the Philosopher Fades Though Some Discomfort Lingers," *The New York Times*, March 5, 2000, http://www.nytimes .com/2000/03/05/nyregion/peter-singer-settles- princeton-looks-deeper-furor-over-philosopher- fades-though.html? pagewanted=all&src=pm (accessed March 28, 2016).

14. Harriet McBryde Johnson, "Unspeakable Conversa- tions," *New York Times Magazine*, February 16, 2003, http://www.nytimes.com/2003/02/16/magazine/ unspeakable-conversations.html?pagewanted= all&src=pm (accessed March 28, 2016).

15. Spina bifida fact sheet, National Dissemination Center for Children with Disabilities, http://nichcy.org/disability/ specific/spinabifida (accessed March 28, 2016).

16. John Schwartz, "When Torment Is Baby's Destiny, Euthanasia Is Defended," *The New York Times*, March 10, 2005, p. A3.

17. Tom Shakespeare, *Disability Rights and Wrongs* (New York: Routledge, 2006), Chapter 8.

18. John A. Robertson, "Involuntary Euthanasia of Defective Newborns: A Legal Analysis," *Stanford Law Review* 27, no. 2 (January 1975), p. 255.

19. From a comment made by a reviewer of this text, Robert P. Tucker of Florida Southern College, who has had hospital experience in this regard.

20. *The President's Commission Report*, reprinted in *Source Book of Bioethics*, ed. Albert R. Jonsen, Robert M. Veatch, and LeRoy Walters (Washington, D.C.: Georgetown University Press, 1998), pp. 192–93. For a perspective from a disabled person, see Harriett McBryde Johnson, "Unspeakable Conversations," *New York Times Magazine*, February 16, 2003, http://www .nytimes.com/2003/02/16/magazine/unspeakable- conversations.html?pagewanted=all&src=pm (accessed March 28, 2016). I thank Jennifer MacKinnon for this reference.

21. Two types of cases are to be distinguished from both persistent vegetative state and coma. One is called *locked-in syndrome*, in which a person may be conscious but unable to respond. The other is *dementia*, or senility, in which the content of con- sciousness is impaired, as in Alzheimer's disease. Neither the person in a persistent vegetative state or coma nor the person with locked-in syndrome or dementia is considered dead by whole brain death criteria. We may say the person's life has a dimin- ished value, but he or she is not legally dead. How- ever, some people argue that because the ability to think is what makes us persons, when someone loses this ability, as in the case of PVS, we ought to consider the person dead. Newborns with little or no upper brain or brain function also then and for the same reason could be considered dead. How- ever, these are living, breathing beings, and it would be difficult to think of them as dead in the sense that we would bury them as they are. Rather than declare them dead, as some people have argued, others believe that it would be more practi- cal and reasonable to judge these cases in terms of the kind of life they are living and to ask whether it would be morally permissible to bring about their deaths or allow them to die.

22. "Life-Support Ended, A Woman Dies," *The New York Times*, December 5, 1976.

23. Robert Miller, *Problems in Health Care Law* 9th ed. (Sudbury, MA: Jones and Bartlett Publishers), p. 768 ff.

24. Ad Hoc Committee of the Harvard Medical School to Examine the Definition of Brain Death, "A Definition of Irreversible Coma," *Journal of the American Medical Association* 205 (1968), p. 377.

25. See *In re Quinlan*, 70 N.J. 10, 335 A. 2d 647 (1976); and *Cruzan v. Director, Missouri Department of Health*, United States Supreme Court, 110 S. Ct. 2841 (1990).

26. Herbert Hendin, "The Dutch Experience," *Issues in Law & Medicine* 17, No. 3 (Spring 2002), pp. 223–47.

27. Bruno Waterfield, "Euthanasia Twins 'Had Nothing to Live For,'" *Telegraph*, January 14, 2013, http://www.telegraph.co.uk/news/worldnews/europe/belgium/9801251/Euthanasia-twins-had-nothing-to-live-for.html (accessed March 28, 2016).

28. Glenn Kessler, "Euthanasia in the Netherlands: Rick Santorum's Bogus Statistics," *The Washington Post*, February 22, 2012, http://www.washingtonpost.com/blogs/fact-checker/post/euthanasia-in-the-netherlands-rick-santorums-bogus-statistics/2012/02/21/gIQAJaRbSR_blog.html (accessed March 28, 2016).

29. "End-of-Life Practices in the Netherlands under the Euthanasia Act," *New England Journal of Medicine* (May 10, 2007), quotation from "Results" section at http://www.nejm.org/doi/full/10.1056/NEJMsa071143 (accessed March 28, 2016).

30. Jan Hoffman, "The Last Word on the Last Breath" *The New York Times*, October 10, 2006, http://www.nytimes.com/2006/10/10/health/10dnr.html?pagewanted=all (accessed March 28, 2016).

31. However, what is requested in these documents may or may not be followed, depending on the circumstances and on what is requested. Medical staff may decide not to stop lifesaving treatments for a person who is not otherwise dying, even if she has stated this in writing. Staff members also may decide not to do certain things that they consider not medically appropriate or not legally permissible, even though these things have been requested in writing.

32. Maria J. Silveira, Scott Y. H. Kim, and Kenneth M. Langa, "Advance Directives and Outcomes of Surrogate Decision Making before Death," *New England Journal of Medicine* 362 (2010), pp. 1211–18.

33. Muriel R. Gillick, "Reversing the Code Status of Advance Directives?" *New England Journal of Medicine* 362 (2010), pp. 1239–40.

34. USA Suicide: 2014 Official Final Data, http://www.suicidology.org/Portals/14/docs/Resources/FactSheets/2014/2014datapgsv1b.pdf (accessed February 16, 2016).

35. Pope John Paul II, *Evangelium Vitae* (1995), para. 66, http://www.vatican.va/holy_father/john_paul_ii/encyclicals/documents/hf_jp-ii_enc_25031995_evangelium-vitae_en.html (accessed March 28, 2016).

36. *New York Times*, December 4, 1990, describes the first publicized case in which Dr. Kevorkian's "suicide machine" was used, and the other two cases can be found, for example, in the *San Francisco Chronicle*, October 29, 1991.

37. Stephanie Gutmann, "Death and the Maiden," *The New Republic*, June 24, 1996, pp. 20–28.

38. USA Suicide: 2014 Official Final Data, http://www.suicidology.org/Portals/14/docs/Resources/FactSheets/2014/2014datapgsv1b.pdf (accessed February 16, 2016).

39. Oregon Public Health Division, *Oregon Death with Dignity Act: 2015 Data Summary*, February 4, 2016, https://public.health.oregon.gov/ProviderPartnerResources/EvaluationResearch/DeathwithDignityAct/Documents/year18.pdf (accessed March 28, 2016).

40. "Opinion 2.211—Physician-Assisted Suicide," American Medical Association, issued June 1994, https://www.ama-assn.org/ama/pub/physician-resources/medical-ethics/code-medical-ethics/opinion2211.page (accessed March 28, 2016).

41. "Assisted Suicide: The Philosophers' Brief," *New York Review of Books*, March 27, 1997.

42. See "When Is Sedation Really Euthanasia?" *Time*, March 21, 2008; and Molly L. Olsen, Keith M. Swetz, and Paul S. Mueller, "Ethical Decision Making with End-of-Life Care: Palliative Sedation and Withholding or Withdrawing Life-Sustaining Treatments," *Mayo Clinic Proceedings* 85, No. 10 (October 2010), pp. 949–54.

43. Denise Grady, "Medical and Ethical Questions Raised on Deaths of Critically Ill Patients," *The New York Times*, July 20, 2006, http://www.nytimes.com/2006/07/20/health/20ethics.html?_r=0 (accessed March 28, 2016).

44. See, for example, Warren S. Quinn, "Actions, Intentions, and Consequences: The Doctrine of Double Effect," *Philosophy and Public Affairs* 18, No. 4 (Fall 1989), pp. 334–51.

45. American Nurses Association, *Position Statement*, "Registered Nurses' Roles and Responsibilities in Providing Expert Care and Counseling at the End of Life," June 14, 2010, http://www.nursingworld.org/MainMenuCategories/EthicsStandards/Ethics-Position-Statements/etpain14426.pdf (accessed March 28, 2016).

46. Directives 56 and 57 of the *Ethical and Religious Directives for Catholic Health Care Services*, approved by the U.S. bishops in 1995 and

approved by the Vatican. See James Keenan, S. J., "A 400-Year-Old Logic," *Boston College Magazine*, Spring 2005, pp. 41–42.

47. Ibid.

48. William Breitbart, Barry Rosenfeld, Hayley Pessin, Monique Kaim, Julie Funesti-Esch, Michele Galietta, Christian J. Nelson, and Robert Brescia, "Depression, Hopelessness, and Desire for Hastened Death in Terminally Ill Patients with Cancer," *Journal of the American Medical Association* 284, no. 22 (2000), pp. 2907–11.

49. Not Dead Yet, http://www.notdeadyet.org/ (accessed March 28, 2016).

READING

The Wrongfulness of Euthanasia

J. GAY-WILLIAMS

MindTap For more chapter resources and activities, go to MindTap.

Study Questions

As you read the excerpt, please consider the following questions:

1. What is Gay-Williams's definition of euthanasia? Why does he believe that it is misleading to speak of "passive euthanasia"?
2. How does he believe that euthanasia acts against our nature?
3. How could euthanasia have a corrupting influence and lead to a "slippery slope"?

My impression is that euthanasia—the idea, if not the practice—is slowly gaining acceptance within our society. Cynics might attribute this to an increasing tendency to devalue human life, but I do not believe this is the major factor. The acceptance is much more likely to be the result of unthinking sympathy and benevolence. Well-publicized, tragic stories like that of Karen Quinlan elicit from us deep feelings of compassion. We think to ourselves, "She and her family would be better off if she were dead." It is an easy step from this very human response to the view that if someone (and others) would be better off dead, then it must be all right to kill that person.[1] Although I respect the compassion that leads to this conclusion, I believe the conclusion is wrong. I want to show that euthanasia is wrong. It is inherently

wrong, but it is also wrongly judged from the standpoints of self-interest and of practical effects.

Before presenting my arguments to support this claim, it would be well to define "euthanasia." An essential aspect of euthanasia is that it involves taking a human life, either one's own or that of another. Also, the person whose life is taken must be someone who is believed to be suffering from some disease or injury from which recovery cannot reasonably be expected. Finally, the action must be deliberate and intentional. Thus, euthanasia is intentionally taking the

J. Gay-Williams, "The Wrongfulness of Euthanasia," from *Intervention and Reflection: Basic Issues in Medical Ethics* 7th ed. (Belmont, CA: Thomson/Wadsworth, 2004). Reprinted by permission of University of Missouri.

life of a presumably hopeless person. Whether the life is one's own or that of another, the taking of it is still euthanasia.

It is important to be clear about the deliberate and intentional aspect of the killing. If a hopeless person is given an injection of the wrong drug by mistake and this causes his death, this is wrongful killing but not euthanasia. The killing cannot be the result of accident. Furthermore, if the person is given an injection of a drug that is believed to be necessary to treat his disease or better his condition and the person dies as a result, then this is neither wrongful killing nor euthanasia. The intention was to make the patient well, not kill him. Similarly, when a patient's condition is such that it is not reasonable to hope that any medical procedures or treatments will save his life, a failure to implement the procedures or treatments is not euthanasia. If the person dies, this will be as a result of his injuries or disease and not because of his failure to receive treatment.

The failure to continue treatment after it has been realized that the patient has little chance of benefitting from it has been characterized by some as "passive euthanasia." This phrase is misleading and mistaken.[2] In such cases, the person involved is not killed (the first essential aspect of euthanasia), nor is the death of the person intended by the withholding of additional treatment (the third essential aspect of euthanasia). The aim may be to spare the person additional and unjustifiable pain, to save him from the indignities of hopeless manipulations, and to avoid increasing the financial and emotional burden on his family. When I buy a pencil it is so that I can use it to write, not to contribute to an increase in the gross national product. This may be the unintended consequence of my action, but it is not the aim of my action. So it is with failing to continue the treatment of a dying person. I intend his death no more than I intend to reduce the GNP by not using medical supplies. His is an unintended dying, and so-called "passive euthanasia" is not euthanasia at all.

1. THE ARGUMENT FROM NATURE

Every human being has a natural inclination to continue living. Our reflexes and responses fit us to fight attackers, flee wild animals, and dodge out of the way of trucks. In our daily lives we exercise the caution and care necessary to protect ourselves. Our bodies are similarly structured for survival right down to the molecular level. When we are cut, our capillaries seal shut, our blood clots, and fibrinogen is produced to start the process of healing the wound. When we are invaded by bacteria, antibodies are produced to fight against the alien organisms, and their remains are swept out of the body by special cells designed for clean-up work.

Euthanasia does violence to this natural goal of survival. It is literally acting against nature because all the processes of nature are bent toward the end of bodily survival. Euthanasia defeats these subtle mechanisms in a way that, in a particular case, disease and injury might not.

It is possible, but not necessary, to make an appeal to revealed religion in this connection.[3] Man as trustee of his body acts against God, its rightful possessor, when he takes his own life. He also violates the commandment to hold life sacred and never to take it without just and compelling cause. But since this appeal will persuade only those who are prepared to accept that religion has access to revealed truths, I shall not employ this line of argument.

It is enough, I believe, to recognize that the organization of the human body and our patterns of behavioral responses make the continuation of life a natural goal. By reason alone, then, we can recognize that euthanasia sets us against our own nature.[4] Furthermore, in doing so, euthanasia does violence to our dignity. Our dignity comes from seeking our ends. When one of our goals is survival, and actions are taken that eliminate that goal, then our natural dignity suffers. Unlike animals, we are conscious through reason of our nature and our ends. Euthanasia involves acting as if this dual nature—inclination toward survival and awareness of this as an end—did not exist. Thus, euthanasia denies our basic human character and requires that we regard ourselves or others as something less than fully human.

2. THE ARGUMENT FROM SELF-INTEREST

The above arguments are, I believe, sufficient to show that euthanasia is inherently wrong. But there are reasons for considering it wrong when judged by standards other than reason. Because death is final and irreversible, euthanasia contains within it the possibility that we will work against our own interest if we practice it or allow it to be practiced on us.

Contemporary medicine has high standards of excellence and a proven record of accomplishment, but it does not possess perfect and complete knowledge. A mistaken diagnosis is possible, and so is a mistaken prognosis. Consequently, we may believe that we are dying of a disease when, as a matter of fact, we may not be. We may think that we have no hope of recovery when, as a matter of fact, our chances are quite good. In such circumstances, if euthanasia were permitted, we would die needlessly. Death is final and the chance of error too great to approve the practice of euthanasia.

Also, there is always the possibility that an experimental procedure or a hitherto untried technique will pull us through. We should at least keep this option open, but euthanasia closes it off. Furthermore, spontaneous remission does occur in many cases. For no apparent reason, a patient simply recovers when those all around him, including his physicians, expected him to die. Euthanasia would just guarantee their expectations and leave no room for the "miraculous" recoveries that frequently occur.

Finally, knowing that we can take our life at any time (or ask another to take it) might well incline us to give up too easily. The will to live is strong in all of us, but it can be weakened by pain and suffering and feelings of hopelessness. If during a bad time we allow ourselves to be killed, we never have a chance to reconsider. Recovery from a serious illness requires that we fight for it, and anything that weakens our determination by suggesting that there is an easy way out is ultimately against our own interest. Also, we may be inclined toward euthanasia because of our concern for others. If we see our sickness and suffering as an emotional and financial burden on our family, we may feel that to leave our life is to make their lives easier.[5] The very presence of the possibility of euthanasia may keep us from surviving when we might.3.

3. THE ARGUMENT FROM PRACTICAL EFFECTS

Doctors and nurses are, for the most part, totally committed to saving lives. A life lost is, for them, almost a personal failure, an insult to their skills and knowledge. Euthanasia as a practice might well alter this. It could have a corrupting influence so that in any case that is severe doctors and nurses might not try hard enough to save the patient. They might decide that the patient would simply be "better off dead" and take the steps necessary to make that come about. This attitude could then carry over to their dealings with patients less seriously ill. The result would be an overall decline in the quality of medical care.

Finally, euthanasia as a policy is a slippery slope. A person apparently hopelessly ill may be allowed to take his own life. Then he may be permitted to deputize others to do it for him should he no longer be able to act. The judgment of others then becomes the ruling factor. Already at this point euthanasia is not personal and voluntary, for others are acting "on behalf of" the patient as they see fit. This may well incline them to act on behalf of other patients who have not authorized them to exercise their judgment. It is only a short step, then, from voluntary euthanasia (self-inflicted or authorized), to directed euthanasia administered to a patient who has given no authorization, to involuntary euthanasia conducted as part of a social policy.[6] Recently many psychiatrists and sociologists have argued that we define as "mental illness" those forms of behavior that we disapprove of.[7] This gives us license then to lock up those who display the behavior. The category of the "hopelessly ill" provides the possibility of even worse abuse.

Embedded in a social policy, it would give society or its representatives the authority to eliminate all those who might be considered too "ill" to function normally any longer. The dangers of euthanasia are too great to all to run the risk of approving it in any form. The first slippery step may well lead to a serious and harmful fall.

I hope that I have succeeded in showing why the benevolence that inclines us to give approval of euthanasia is misplaced. Euthanasia is inherently wrong because it violates the nature and dignity of human beings. But even those who are not convinced by this must be persuaded that the potential personal and social dangers inherent in euthanasia are sufficient to forbid our approving it either as a personal practice or as a public policy.

Suffering is surely a terrible thing, and we have a clear duty to comfort those in need and to ease their suffering when we can. But suffering is also a natural part of life with values for the individual and for others that we should not overlook. We may legitimately seek for others and for ourselves an easeful death, as Arthur Dyck has pointed out.[8] Euthanasia, however, is not just an easeful death. It is a wrongful death. Euthanasia is not just dying. It is killing.

NOTES

1. For a sophisticated defense of this position see Philippa Foot, "Euthanasia," *Philosophy and Public Affairs*, vol. 6 (1977), pp. 85–112. Foot does not endorse the radical conclusion that euthanasia, voluntary and involuntary, is always right.

2. James Rachels rejects the distinction between active and passive euthanasia as morally irrelevant in his "Active and Passive Euthanasia," *New England Journal of Medicine*, vol. 292, pp. 78–80. But see the criticism by Foot, pp. 100–103.

3. For a defense of this view see J. V. Sullivan, "The Immorality of Euthanasia," in *Beneficent Euthanasia*, ed. Marvin Kohl (Buffalo, NY: Prometheus Books, 1975), pp. 34–44.

4. This point is made by Ray V. McIntyre in "Voluntary Euthanasia: The Ultimate Perversion," *Medical Counterpoint*, vol. 2, pp. 26–29.

5. See McIntyre, p. 28.

6. See Sullivan, "Immorality of Euthanasia," pp. 34–44, for a fuller argument in support of this view.

7. See, for example, Thomas S. Szasz, *The Myth of Mental Illness*, rev. ed. (New York: Harper & Row, 1974).

8. Arthur Dyck, "Beneficent Euthanasia and Benemortasia," in Kohl, op. cit., pp. 117–129.

READING

Active and Passive Euthanasia

JAMES RACHELS

MindTap® For more chapter resources and activities, go to MindTap.

Study Questions

As you read the excerpt, please consider the following questions:
1. Why does Rachels believe that letting a person die is sometimes worse than bringing about the person's death, such as through a lethal injection?
2. What is the example of Smith and Jones and their cousin supposed to show?
3. Why does he believe that we usually think that killing is worse than letting die?

The distinction between active and passive euthanasia is thought to be crucial for medical ethics. The idea is that it is permissible, at least in some cases, to withhold treatment and allow a patient to die, but it is never permissible to take any direct action designed to kill the patient. This doctrine seems to be accepted by most doctors, and it is endorsed in a statement adopted by the House of

James Rachels, "Active and Passive Euthanasia" *The New England Journal of Medicine* 292, no. 2, (January 9, 1975). Reprinted by permission.

Delegates of the American Medical Association on December 4, 1973:

> The intentional termination of the life of one human being by another—mercy killing—is contrary to that for which the medical profession stands and is contrary to the policy of the American Medical Association.
> The cessation of the employment of extraordinary means to prolong the life of the body when there is irrefutable evidence that biological death is imminent is the decision of the patient and/or his immediate family. The advice and judgment of the physician should be freely available to the patient and/or his immediate family.

However, a strong case can be made against this doctrine. In what follows I will set out some of the relevant arguments, and urge doctors to reconsider their views on this matter.

To begin with a familiar type of situation, a patient who is dying of incurable cancer of the throat is in terrible pain, which can no longer be satisfactorily alleviated. He is certain to die within a few days, even if present treatment is continued, but he does not want to go on living for those days since the pain is unbearable. So he asks the doctor for an end to it, and his family joins in the request.

Suppose, the doctor agrees to withhold treatment, as the conventional doctrine says he may. The justification for his doing so is that the patient is in terrible agony, and since he is going to die anyway, it would be wrong to prolong his suffering needlessly. But now notice this. If one simply withholds treatment, it may take the patient longer to die, and so he may suffer more than he would if more direct action were taken and a lethal injection given. This fact provides strong reason for thinking that, once the initial decision not to prolong his agony has been made, active euthanasia is actually preferable to passive euthanasia, rather than the reverse. To say otherwise is to endorse the option that leads to more suffering rather than less, and is contrary to the humanitarian impulse that prompts the decision not to prolong his life in the first place.

Part of my point is that the process of being "allowed to die" can be relatively slow and painful, whereas being given a lethal injection is relatively quick and painless. Let me give a different sort of example. In the United States about one in 600 babies is born with Down's syndrome. Most of these babies are otherwise healthy, that is, with only the usual pediatric care, they will proceed to an otherwise normal infancy. Some, however, are born with congenital defects such as intestinal obstructions that require operations if they are to live. Sometimes, the parents and the doctor will decide not to operate, and let the infant die. Anthony Shaw describes what happens then,

> ... When surgery is denied [the doctor] must try to keep the infant from suffering while natural forces sap the baby's life away. As a surgeon whose natural inclination is to use the scalpel to fight off death, standing by and watching a salvageable baby die is the most emotionally exhausting experience I know. It is easy at a conference, in a theoretical discussion, to decide that such infants should be allowed to die. It is altogether different to stand in the nursery and watch as dehydration and infection wither a tiny being over hours and days. This is a terrible ordeal for me and the hospital staff—much more so than for the parents who never set foot in the nursery.[1]

I can understand why some people are opposed to all euthanasia, and insist that such infants must be allowed to live. I think I can also understand why other people favor destroying these babies quickly and painlessly. But why should anyone favor letting "dehydration and infection wither a tiny being over hours and days"? The doctrine that says that a baby may be allowed to dehydrate and wither, but may not be given an injection that would end its life without suffering, seems so patently cruel as to require no further refutation. The strong language is not intended to offend, but only to put the point in the clearest possible way.

My second argument is that the conventional doctrine leads to decisions concerning life and death made on irrelevant grounds.

Consider again the case of the infants with Down's syndrome who need operations for congenital defects unrelated to the syndrome to live. Sometimes, there is no operation, and the baby dies, but when there is no such defect, the baby lives on. Now, an operation such as that to remove an intestinal obstruction is not prohibitively difficult.

The reason why such operations are not performed in these cases is, clearly, that the child has Down's syndrome and the parents and doctor judge that because of that fact it is better for the child to die.

But notice that this situation is absurd, no matter what view one takes of the lives and potentials of such babies. If the life of such an infant is worth preserving, what does it matter if it needs a simple operation? Or, if one thinks it better that such a baby should not live on, what difference does it make that it happens to have an unobstructed intestinal tract? In either case, the matter of life and death is being decided on irrelevant grounds. It is the Down's syndrome, and not the intestines, that is the issue. The matter should be decided, if at all, on that basis, and not be allowed to depend on the essentially irrelevant question of whether the intestinal tract is blocked.

What makes this situation possible, of course, is the idea that when there is an intestinal blockage, one can "let the baby die," but when there is no such defect there is nothing that can be done, for one must not "kill" it. The fact that this idea leads to such results as deciding life or death on irrelevant grounds is another good reason why the doctrine should be rejected.

One reason why so many people think that there is an important moral difference between active and passive euthanasia is that they think killing someone is morally worse than letting someone die. But is it? Is killing, in itself, worse than letting die? To investigate this issue, two cases may be considered that are exactly alike except that one involves killing whereas the other involves letting someone die. Then, it can be asked whether this difference makes any difference to the moral assessments. It is important that the cases be exactly alike, except for this one difference, since otherwise one cannot be confident that it is this difference and not some other that accounts for any variation in the assessments of the two cases. So, let us consider this pair of cases:

In the first, Smith stands to gain a large inheritance if anything should happen to his six-year-old cousin. One evening while the child is taking his bath, Smith sneaks into the bathroom and drowns the child, and then arranges things so that it will look like an accident.

In the second, Jones also stands to gain if anything should happen to his six-year-old cousin. Like Smith, Jones sneaks in planning to drown the child in his bath. However, just as he enters the bathroom Jones sees the child slip and hit his head, and fall face down in the water. Jones is delighted; he stands by, ready to push the child's head back under if it is necessary, but it is not necessary. With only a little thrashing about, the child drowns all by himself, "accidentally," as Jones watches and does nothing.

Now Smith killed the child, whereas Jones "merely" let the child die. That is the only difference between them. Did either man behave better, from a moral point of view? If the difference between killing and letting die were in itself a morally important matter, one should say that Jones's behavior was less reprehensible than Smith's. But does one really want to say that? I think not. In the first place, both men acted from the same motive, personal gain, and both had exactly the same end in view when they acted. It may be inferred from Smith's conduct that he is a bad man, although that judgment may be withdrawn or modified if certain further facts are learned about him—for example, that he is mentally deranged. But would not the very same thing be inferred about Jones from his conduct? And would not the same further considerations also be relevant to any modification of this judgment? Moreover, suppose Jones pleaded, in his own defense, "After all, I didn't do anything except stand there and watch the child drown. I didn't kill him; I only let him die." Again, if letting die were in itself less bad than killing, this defense should have at least some weight. But it does not. Such a "defense" can only be regarded as a grotesque perversion of moral reasoning. Morally speaking, it is no defense at all.

Now, it may be pointed out, quite properly, that the cases of euthanasia with which doctors are concerned are not like this at all. They do not involve personal gain or the destruction of normal healthy children. Doctors are concerned only with cases in which the patient's life is of no further use to him, or in which the patient's life has become or will soon become a terrible burden. However, the point is the same in these cases: the bare difference between killing and letting die does not, in itself, make a moral difference. If a doctor lets a patient die, for humane reasons, he is in the same moral position as if he had given the patient a lethal injection for humane reasons. If his decision was wrong—if, for example, the patient's illness was in fact curable—the decision would be equally regrettable no matter which method was used to carry it out. And if the doctor's decision was the right one, the method used is not in itself important.

The AMA policy statement isolates the crucial issue very well; the crucial issue is "the intentional termination of the life of one human being by another." But after identifying this issue, and forbidding "mercy killing," the statement goes on to deny that the cessation of treatment is the intentional termination of a life. This is where the mistake comes in, for what is the cessation of treatment, in these circumstances, if it is not "the intentional termination of the life of one human being by another?" Of course it is exactly that, and if it were not, there would be no point to it.

Many people will find this judgment hard to accept. One reason, I think, is that it is very easy to conflate the question of whether killing is, in itself, worse than letting die, with the very different question of whether most actual cases of killing are more reprehensible than most actual cases of letting die. Most actual cases of killing are clearly terrible (think, for example, of all the murders reported in the newspapers), and one hears of such cases every day. On the other hand, one hardly ever hears of a case of letting die, except for the actions of doctors who are motivated by humanitarian reasons. So one learns to think of killing in a much worse light than of letting die. But this does not mean that there is something about killing that makes it in itself worse than letting die, for it is not the bare difference between killing and letting die that makes the difference in these cases. Rather, the other factors—the murderer's motive of personal gain, for example, contrasted with the doctor's humanitarian motivation—account for different reactions to the different cases.

I have argued that killing is not in itself any worse than letting die; if my contention is right, it follows that active euthanasia is not any worse than passive euthanasia. What arguments can be given on the other side? The most common, I believe, is the following:

The important difference between active and passive euthanasia is that, in passive euthanasia, the doctor does not do anything to bring about the patient's death. The doctor does nothing, and the patient dies of whatever ills already afflict him. In active euthanasia, however, the doctor does something to bring about the patient's death: he kills him. The doctor who gives the patient with cancer a lethal injection has himself caused his patient's death; whereas if he merely ceases treatment, the cancer is the cause of the death.

A number of points need to be made here. The first is that it is not exactly correct to say that in passive euthanasia the doctor does nothing, for he does do one thing that is very important; he lets the patient die. "Letting someone die" is certainly different, in some respects, from other types of action—mainly in that it is a kind of action that one may perform by way of not performing certain other actions. For example, one may let a patient die by way of not giving medication, just as one may insult someone by way of not shaking his hand. But for any purpose of moral assessment, it is a type of action nonetheless. The decision to let a patient die is subject to moral appraisal in the same way that a decision to kill him would be subject to moral appraisal; it may be assessed as wise or unwise, compassionate or sadistic, right or wrong. If a doctor deliberately let a patient die who was suffering from a routinely curable illness, the doctor would certainly be to blame for what he had done, just as he would be to blame if he had needlessly killed the patient. Charges against him would then be appropriate. If so, it would be no defense at all for him to insist that he didn't "do anything." He would have done something very serious indeed, for he let his patient die.

Fixing the cause of death may be very important from a legal point of view, for it may determine whether criminal charges are brought against the doctor. But I do not think that this notion can be used to show a moral difference between active and passive euthanasia. The reason why it is considered bad to be the cause of someone's death is that death is regarded as a great evil—and so it is. However, if it has been decided that euthanasia—even passive euthanasia—is desirable in a given case, it has also been decided that in this instance death is no greater an evil than the patient's continued existence. And if this is true, the usual reason for not wanting to be the cause of someone's death simply does not apply.

Finally, doctors may think that all of this is only of academic interest—the sort of thing that philosophers may worry about but that has no practical bearing on their own work. After all, doctors must be concerned about the legal consequences of what they do, and active euthanasia is clearly forbidden by the law. But even so, doctors should also be concerned with the fact that the law is forcing upon them a moral doctrine that may well be indefensible, and has a considerable effect on their practices. Of course, most doctors are not now in the position of being coerced in this matter, for they do not regard themselves as merely going along with what the law requires. Rather, in statements such as the AMA policy statement that I have quoted, they are endorsing this doctrine as a central point of medical ethics. In that statement, active euthanasia is condemned not merely as illegal but as "contrary to that for which the medical profession stands," whereas passive euthanasia is approved. However, the preceding considerations suggest that there is really no moral difference between the two, considered in themselves (there may be important moral differences in some cases in their consequences, but, as I pointed out, these differences may make active euthanasia, and not passive euthanasia, the morally preferable option). So whereas doctors may have to discriminate between active and passive euthanasia to satisfy the law, they should not do any more than that. In particular, they should not give the distinction any added authority and weight by writing it into official statements of medical ethics.

NOTES

1. A. Shaw, "Doctor, Do We Have a Choice?" *The New York Times Magazine*, January 30, 1972, p. 54.

REVIEW EXERCISES

1. What is the difference between "whole brain death" and "persistent vegetative state?"
2. If a person has whole brain death, then what kind of euthanasia is possible? Explain.
3. What is the difference between active and passive euthanasia? Is physician-assisted suicide more like active or passive euthanasia? How so?
4. Where do advance directives such as living wills and durable powers of attorney fit into the distinction between voluntary and nonvoluntary euthanasia?
5. What is the difference between ordinary and extraordinary measures of life support? If some measure of life support were common and inexpensive, would this necessarily make it an ordinary means of life support? Explain.

6. Label the following as examples of voluntary or nonvoluntary and active or passive euthanasia; if passive, are the measures described more likely to be considered ordinary or extraordinary measures of life support?
   a. A person who is dying asks to be given a fatal drug dose to bring about his death.
   b. A dying patient asks that no more chemotherapy be administered because it is doing nothing but prolonging her time until death, which is inevitable in a short time anyway.
   c. Parents of a newborn whose condition involves moderate retardation refuse permission for a simple surgery that would repair a physical anomaly inconsistent with continued life, and they let the infant die.

d. A husband gives his wife a lethal overdose of her pain medicine because he does not want to see her suffer anymore.

e. Doctors decide not to try to start an artificial feeding mechanism for their patient because they believe that it will be futile, that is, ineffective given the condition of their patient.

7. List the consequentialist concerns that could be given in arguing about whether the actions proposed in three of the scenarios in Question 6 are justified.

8. What non-consequentialist concerns could be given in arguing about these same three scenarios?

DISCUSSION CASES

1. Respirator Removal. Jim is an active person. He is a lawyer by profession. When he was forty-four years old, a routine physical revealed that he had a tumor on his right lung. After surgery to remove that lung, he returned to a normal life. However, four years later, a cancerous tumor is found in his other lung. He knows he has only months to live. Then comes the last hospitalization. He is on a respirator. It is extremely uncomfortable for him, and he is frustrated by not being able to talk because of the tubes. After some thought, he decides that he does not want to live out his last few weeks like this and asks to have the respirator removed. Because he is no longer able to breathe on his own, he knows this means he will die shortly after it is removed.

Do Jim or the doctors who remove the respirator and then watch Jim die as a result do anything wrong? Why or why not? Would there be any difference between this case and that of a person such as Terri Schiavo, who was in a persistent vegetative state, was not able to express her current wishes, and had left no written request? Would there be a difference in cases such as hers between removing a respirator (which she was not using) and removing a feeding tube? How would you tell whether a respirator or a feeding tube would be considered an ordinary or extraordinary means of life support? What would be the significance of these labels in each case?

2. Pill Overdose. Mary Jones has a severe case of cerebral palsy. She has spent twenty-eight years of life trying to cope with the varying disabilities it caused. She can get around somewhat in her motorized wheelchair. An aide feeds her and takes care of her small apartment. She went to junior college and earned a degree in sociology. She also has a mechanism whereby she can type on a computer. However, she has lately become weary with life. She sees no improvement ahead and wants to die. She has been receiving pain pills from her doctor. Now, she asks for several weeks' worth of prescriptions so that she will not have to return for more so often. Her doctor suspects that she might be suicidal.

Should Mary Jones's doctor continue giving her the pills? Why or why not? Would she be assisting in Mary's suicide if she did? Should Mary have a right to end her life if she chooses? Why or why not? Should her physician actually be able to administer some death-causing drug and not just provide the pills? Why or why not?

3. Teen Euthanasia. Thirteen-year-old Samantha is in the last stages of cancer. She says she doesn't want any further treatment because she thinks that it is not going to make her well. Her parents want the doctors to try a new experimental therapy for which there is some hope. If they cannot convince Samantha to undergo this experimental procedure, should the doctors sedate Samantha and go ahead with it anyway, or should they do what she asks and let her die? Do you think that the doctors should be allowed to end her life with a fatal dose of a drug if that is what she wishes, even though her parents object and they are still her legal guardians?

4. Baby John Doe. Sarah and Mike's baby boy was born with a defect called spina bifida, which involves an opening in the spine. In his case, it is of the more severe kind in which the spinal cord also protrudes through the hole. The opening is moderately high in the spine, and thus they are told that his neurological control below that level will be affected. He will have no bowel and bladder control and will not be able to walk unassisted. The cerebral spinal fluid has already started to back up into the cavity surrounding his brain, and his head is swelling. Doctors advise that they could have a shunt put in place to drain this fluid and prevent pressure on the brain. They could also have the spinal opening repaired. If they do not do so, however, the baby will probably die from an infection. Sarah and Mike are afraid of raising such a child and worry that he would have an extremely difficult life. In a few cases, however, children with this anomaly who do not have the surgery do not die, and then they are worse off than if the operation were performed. What should Sarah and Mike do? Why?

MindTap® For more chapter resources and activities, go to MindTap.

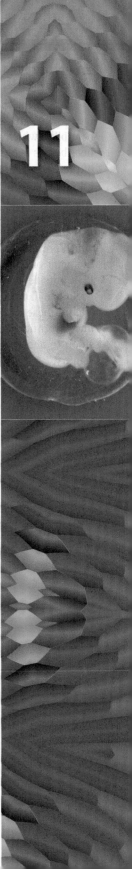

Carolina Biological/Visuals Unlimited/Corbis

Abortion

Learning Outcomes

After reading this chapter, you should be able to:

- Describe different stages of fetal development and various forms of abortion.

- Differentiate among various ways of approaching the moral status of the fetus.

- Explain how abortion relates to women's rights.

- Describe the importance of attempts at regulating abortion, including parental consent laws and laws requiring the use of ultrasound technology.

- Evaluate moral arguments about abortion, including both consequentialist and non-consequentialist arguments.

- Apply moral reasoning to a variety of issues related to abortion, including considerations of fetal abnormality, rape, risky pregnancies, and birth control.

- Defend your own ideas about the ethics of abortion.

MindTap° For more chapter resources and activities, go to MindTap.

Abortion has been legal in the United States since 1973, when the U.S. Supreme Court's *Roe v. Wade* decision prohibited states from banning the procedure before the last three months of pregnancy. Rooted in the concept of a woman's "right to privacy," the *Roe* decision was often seen as the culmination of a growing societal concern for women's equality and autonomy. In fact, in the 1970s, many people assumed that the abortion issue was settled and that Americans would never return to the days of "back alley" abortions—the illegal and unsafe procedures that had become notorious in states prohibiting abortion. But far from settling the abortion issue, the years since *Roe v. Wade* have witnessed the growth of a vehement political and religious movement opposed to abortion and a countermovement in support of women's reproductive rights. Today, Americans continue to carry on a highly emotional and sometimes violent debate over the morality and legality of abortion.

Public opinion about the morality of abortion has fluctuated over time. A solid majority of Americans is opposed to overturning *Roe v. Wade*. But, in general, we are evenly divided when asked to describe ourselves as either pro-choice or pro-life.[1] Reflecting this divided opinion about the morality of abortion, a number of state governments have taken action in recent years to restrict abortion access and to establish the "personhood" and legal rights of the fetus. Legislative efforts have included fetal heartbeat bills, which seek to ban abortion once a fetal heartbeat is detected (often at around twelve weeks of pregnancy), and regulations that make it difficult for abortion clinics to operate. Such laws appear to violate the legal framework for abortion that was established in Supreme Court decisions such as *Roe v. Wade* and *Casey v. Planned Parenthood* (1992)—which prohibits states from banning abortion before the point of fetal viability. (A fetus's ability to survive outside the womb is generally considered to begin late in the second trimester of pregnancy.) But even if these new abortion restrictions are declared unconstitutional, they exemplify the fierce opposition to abortion that exists in many parts of the country.

In addition to legislative efforts, abortion opponents employ a range of strategies. Take, for example, "crisis pregnancy centers," which often advertise on billboards, suggesting that "pregnant and scared" women should visit their offices for help. Rather than offering medical services (such as abortion), these centers often focus on counseling women *against* terminating their pregnancies—presenting them with baby booties, congratulatory "You're a mom!" cards, and tiny rubber fetuses. Such centers have been criticized for providing inaccurate information about links between abortion and breast cancer, infertility, and suicide.[2] While pro-choice groups argue that these centers take advantage of women at emotionally difficult moments, abortion opponents see them as laudable outposts in a grassroots battle against legalized mass murder.

The high-stakes abortion issue—which abortion opponents frequently compare to slavery and the Holocaust—has produced violent protest. A number of people associated with abortion clinics—doctors, clinic staff, security guards, and others—have been murdered by antiabortionists. In 2009, a Kansas physician named George Tiller was shot and killed in his church during a service by Scott Roeder, a vehement antiabortion activist. Dr. Tiller was known to perform late-term abortions; he had been the subject of previous threats and assassination attempts. Scott Roeder explained that he killed Tiller in order to prevent more babies from being killed.[3] Another militant abortion opponent, Eric Rudolph,

Pro-choice and pro-life protesters confront each other at a demonstration.

Shawn Thew/EPA/Corbis

was sentenced to life in prison for the 1998 bombing of an Alabama women's health care clinic that also performed abortions. This bomb killed an off-duty police officer and seriously injured and blinded the director of nursing at the clinic. Rudolph has insisted that he was justified in attacking those involved in abortion, which he considers murder. A more recent case occurred in Colorado Springs in November 2015, when Robert L. Dear stormed into a Planned Parenthood clinic, killing three and wounding nine others—including police responders. Dear defended his actions in court by declaring himself a "warrior for the babies." The clinic reopened in early 2016.[4]

While some abortion opponents have resorted to violence, most abortion opponents disagree with the tactics of the movement's more militant individuals and groups. They believe that these tactics and the murders of physicians have hurt their cause. They preach nonviolence and urge respect for all persons, including the unborn.[5] Nevertheless, some abortion foes feel justified in applying intense pressure on individuals involved in abortions, whom they view as murderers. Activists have distributed "Wanted" posters, featuring photos of abortion providers along with their names, addresses, telephone numbers—and sometimes even information about their children and other family members. Abortion opponents also demonstrate outside family planning clinics that provide abortions and forcefully try to persuade female visitors not to go inside. Supporters of abortion rights have responded by seeking legal injunctions to keep protesters from blocking clinic entrances and by engaging volunteers to escort patients through the protests.

As these examples demonstrate, abortion is an issue about which people have extremely strong opinions. Expressions of these opinions are often highly emotionally charged. For those opposed to abortion, the practice constitutes nothing less than the murder of more than a million innocent children each year in the United States. For abortion rights supporters, the practice is a crucial component in women's ability to control their own bodies and exercise their rights to autonomy and equality under the law. Abortion touches on some of the most intimate and powerful aspects of our lives. Some people's views about abortion are based on religious beliefs, but this is not always the case.

To complicate matters further, there may be a difference between what we think about the morality of abortion and what we think about the law regulating abortion. In fact, one could hold that the law ought to allow abortion and still believe that abortion is morally objectionable. In addition, the language that is used in the debate over abortion often begs important questions: "pro-life" and "pro-choice" labels do not tell us what counts as "life" or whether there are moral limits to our choices. While it is possible to schematize moral views of abortion, it is important to note that any schematic representation of abortion views leaves out a variety of complex questions—about moral theory in general, about the law and its limits, and about the moral status of the fetus and the rights of women.

What we say about the morality of abortion depends on several issues. Some are strictly ethical matters and involve basic ethical perspectives, such as the nature and basis of moral rights. Others are factual matters about what happens at different stages of fetal development and about consequences that follow from certain actions given particular social conditions. Others still are conceptual matters, such as the meaning of terms such as *abortion*, *personhood*, or even *human*. We begin our analysis with certain factual matters about the stages of fetal development and contemporary methods of abortion.

STAGES OF FETAL DEVELOPMENT

The scientific stages of fetal development are important for our analysis because many ethical discussions about abortion take into account such factors as the fetus's heartbeat, its ability to feel pain, and its ability to survive outside the womb. The scientific labels given to the different stages of fetal development do not, in themselves, help us reach ethical conclusions. But they provide a standard framework for any discussion of human development. In fact, the terms used to describe human fetal development

Outline of Moral Approaches to Abortion

	Radical Pro-Choice	Moderate Choice	Pro-Life
Thesis	Mother is free to dispose of the fetus as she wishes	Early abortion is permissible; but late-term abortions are morally problematic	Abortion is prohibited, with possible exceptions for cases of rape, incest, or threat to the mother's health
Corollaries and Implications	Fetus is not a person	Moral status of the fetus may change during the course of a pregnancy	Fetus is a person; "life begins at conception"
Connections with Moral Theory	Emphasis on the mother's right to her own body and freedom to control her reproductive life; consequentialist focus on benefits of abortion and harms of continued pregnancy	Conflict of rights between the mother's right to choose and the fetus's developing right to life; judgments about consequences may depend on the stage of pregnancy	Focus on the fetus's right to life; may celebrate the benefits of family life or appeal to natural law ideas about reproduction and pregnancy
Relevant authors	Mary Anne Warren	Judith Jarvis Thomson	Don Marquis

are used throughout the biological sciences and pertain to most, if not all, vertebrates.

Conception occurs when an egg is fertilized by a sperm. This produces a *zygote*—which simply means "joining together"—a single cell that begins to divide and move through the fallopian tube. When the ball of cells reaches the uterus seven to ten days after fertilization, it is called a *blastocyst*. (A *blastula* is a fluid-filled cavity surrounded by a single layer of cells.) From the second to eighth week of gestation, the developing organism is called an *embryo*, as is any mammal at this early stage of primitive tissue and organ development. From then until birth, it is called a *fetus*, which means "young unborn." It is common in philosophical discussions of abortion to use the term *fetus* for all stages of prenatal development, but use of this term does not imply anything about value or status. We can single out the following stages of fetal development (times are approximate).

- **Day 1**: Fertilization—An ovum, or egg (twenty-three chromosomes), is penetrated by sperm (twenty-three chromosomes), and one cell is formed that contains forty-six chromosomes.
- **Days 2–3**: The fertilized ovum passes through the fallopian tube as cell division increases.
- **Days 7–10**: The blastocyst reaches the uterus; it has now become a "ball of cells."
- **Week 2**: The developing embryo becomes embedded in the uterine wall.
- **Weeks 2–8**: Organ systems such as the brain, spinal cord, heart, and digestive tube—and certain structural features such as arm and leg buds—begin and then continue to develop. (The photo that opens this chapter is of an embryo 40 days after conception.)
- **Weeks 12–16**: *Quickening* occurs, which means that the mother can begin to feel the fetus's movements; the fetus is approximately 5½ inches long.

- **Weeks 20–26**: Fetal brain development makes it possible that fetuses could feel pain. While there is controversy about exactly when this level of brain development takes place, the consensus is that neuronal activity and neural pathways are not sufficiently established to allow for the experience of pain prior to twenty weeks.[6]
- **Weeks 20–28**: The process of viability takes place, and the fetus is able to live apart from its mother, depending on its size and lung development.
- **Week 40**: Birth.

All changes during fetal development occur gradually. Even conception takes some time as the sperm penetrates the egg and together they come to form one cell. Any of these stages may or may not be morally relevant, as we shall consider shortly.

METHODS OF ABORTION

The historical record suggests that humans have had access to various methods of abortion for millennia. As early as 1550 BCE, the Egyptians recommended inserting pieces of papyrus into the cervix to stimulate an abortion.[7] Plato recognized that midwives could cause a miscarriage with "drugs and incantations," and in the *Republic*, he indicates that abortion and infanticide might be useful methods of creating eugenic outcomes.[8] The Hippocratic Oath of the fourth century BCE forbids giving a woman a pessary (a vaginal suppository) to produce abortion.[9] Ancient methods of inducing abortion included shaking women and inserting foreign objects into the vagina in the hope of causing infection. The first law forbidding abortion was promulgated by the Roman Emperor Caracalla in 211 CE; Christian authors at the time, such as Tertullian, also condemned abortion.[10]

When we speak of abortion today, we mean induced abortion performed by trained doctors. This is to be distinguished from spontaneous abortion, or what we generally call *miscarriage*. Among current methods of inducing abortion are the following:

- **Morning-after pill**: This chemical compound, which the Food and Drug Administration refers to as Plan B, is considered by some to be related to abortion because it prevents the blastocyst from embedding in the uterine wall. The intrauterine device—IUD—and some contraceptive pills operate in a similar way, causing the fertilized egg to be expelled by making the uterine wall inhospitable. Since August 2006, the Plan B pill has been available over the counter for customers eighteen years of age and older. Not everyone agrees that the use of Plan B and the IUD count as abortion, since they *prevent* pregnancy rather than terminate it.
- **RU486 (mifepristone)**: This prescription drug used in combination with other prostaglandin drugs, such as misoprostol, induces uterine contractions and expulsion of the embryo. It must be used within sixty-three days of a missed menstrual period. Although there has been some concern about its safety, since the drug was approved for use in the United States, millions of women have safely used it to end their pregnancies.[11]
- **Uterine or vacuum aspiration**: In this procedure, the cervix (the opening of the uterus) is dilated, and the uterine contents are removed by suction tube.
- **Dilation and curettage (D&C)**: This procedure also dilates the cervix so that the uterus can be scraped with a spoon-shaped curette. This method is similar to the vacuum method except that it is performed somewhat later and requires that the fetus be dismembered and then removed.
- **Saline solution**: A solution of salt and water is used to replace amniotic fluid and thus effect a miscarriage.
- **Prostaglandin drugs**: These pharmaceuticals induce early labor and may be used in combination with RU-486, as mentioned previously.
- **Hysterotomy**: This uncommon procedure is similar to a cesarean section but is used for later-term abortions.
- **Dilation and extraction (D&X) or intact D&X or "partial birth abortion"**: In this uncommon second- and third-trimester procedure, forceps are used to deliver the torso of the fetus, its skull is punctured and the cranial contents suctioned out, and then delivery is completed.

In recent years, there have been around one million abortions performed annually in the United States, with the abortion rate slowly declining from a high in the 1980s. According to the Guttmacher Institute, each year approximately two out of every hundred women aged fifteen to forty-four have an abortion. Half have had at least one previous abortion. Eighteen percent of women obtaining abortions are teenagers younger than twenty. Women in their twenties account for more than 50 percent of abortions.[12] African American women are five times as likely as white women to have an abortion, and Hispanic women are twice as likely as whites to have the procedure.[13] One cause of this higher rate may be cuts to family planning funding in recent years, resulting in, among other things, reduced contraceptive use, especially among poor women.[14] *New York Times* columnist Nicholas Kristof argues, "The cost of birth control is one reason poor women are more than three times as likely to end up pregnant unintentionally as middle-class women."[15] Indeed, 42 percent of women who have abortions have incomes below the federal poverty line. In terms of claimed religious affiliation, 37 percent are Protestant and 28 percent are Catholic.[16] A 2004 study reported that among the reasons that women cite for choosing an abortion are the following:

- Having a child would dramatically change their lives, their ability to continue with school or work, or their ability to care for others (74 percent).
- They could not afford children (73 percent).
- They did not want to become single mothers (48 percent).
- They were finished having children (38 percent).
- Health problems of either fetus or mother (12 percent).[17]

Around the world, abortion is permitted without restriction as to reason in fifty-six countries (39 percent of the world's population) and is completely illegal in thirty-two countries, with no exception for rape or to save the life of the woman (6 percent of the world's population).[18] Thirty-six countries allow abortion only to save the life of the mother or in exceptional cases, such as when the woman has been raped or there is fetal impairment (21 percent of the world's population).[19] There are more than 40 million abortions performed each year around the world. Of these, 21.6 million are deemed unsafe—the vast majority in countries where abortion is illegal or highly restricted. According to the World Health Organization, "deaths due to unsafe abortion remain close to 13 percent of all maternal deaths," with forty-seven thousand women dying each year from complications of unsafe abortions.[20]

In China, abortion has been used as a means of population control in tandem with a general policy of encouraging one child per family. While this policy has recently (2015) been relaxed, in some cases, women were forced to have abortions when they could not pay the fine for having more than one child.[21] This has resulted in a strange demographic phenomenon because of Chinese parents' preferences for boys (who are expected to financially support their parents in old age). According to a study published in 2009, the ratio of boys to girls in China was 120 to 100. (Among families' second births—which were often permitted only if the first child was a girl—the ratio is 143 to 100.[22]) This means that for children under twenty, there were thirty-two million more boys than girls. Since the widespread availability of ultrasound scanners in the 1990s, many potential parents have chosen to terminate their pregnancies if the fetus was female. This practice was less prevalent in larger cities, where women have a higher status.[23]

Similar problems have occurred in India, where the ratio of boys to girls is 1,000 to 914.[24] And a recent report indicates that immigrant communities in Europe and the United Kingdom also practice **sex-selective abortion**.[25] This practice—in which parents choose to terminate a pregnancy based solely on the fetus's sex—is illegal in some countries. There is currently no such restriction on a national level in the United States, although American lawmakers have considered bills that would ban the practice (for example, the Prenatal Nondiscrimination Act).[26] Eight American states have bans on sex-selective abortion. States have considered outlawing sex-selective abortion, abortions based on race, and abortions based on genetic abnormalities in the fetus, such as Down Syndrome.[27] Like many of the other recent state-level abortion bills, the ultimate constitutional status of this legislation remains unclear.

ABORTION AND THE LAW

Much of the contemporary debate about abortion is concerned with whether the law ought to permit abortion and, if so, what, if any, legal regulations ought to be placed on it. The relationship between morality and the law is often ignored in these debates. Sometimes, it is assumed that if abortion is immoral, it ought to be illegal just for that reason, or if it is morally permissible, it therefore ought to be legally permissible. As noted in Chapter 10 on euthanasia, this equivalence between morality and the law is questionable. We can think of actions that are possibly immoral but that we would not want to be legally prohibited. For example, I may wrongly waste my talents, but I would not want the law to force me to develop and use them. However, many of our laws, such as civil rights laws, are grounded in moral reasons. The profound questions about what the law should and should not do are bound up with an entire philosophy of law. Because this is an ethics text, we will not be able to explore such questions here. Nevertheless, as we review the constitutional and legislative status of abortion (primarily in the United States), we should pay close attention to the moral reasons claimed for various positions in the debate and the appeals made to rights and other moral values.

It may be surprising to discover that abortion was not always prohibited or condemned by many of the authorities that are now most emphatically opposed to it, including the Roman Catholic Church. Following the teachings of Augustine and Aquinas, the Church held that the fetus was not human until sometime after conception when the matter was suitable for the reception of a human soul.[28] For example, the Church fathers held that the soul did not enter the fetus until forty days of gestation for males and eighty or ninety days for females, a calculation

that they based upon ideas found in Aristotle and in the Bible—a point that was noted in a footnote to the *Roe v. Wade* decision.[29] It was not until 1869 that Pope Pius IX decreed that the embryo's soul was present from conception, declaring abortion to be a sin.[30] Indeed, for much of Western history and in British Common Law, abortion before the quickening of the fetus (at twelve to sixteen weeks) was legal and not considered immoral.[31] Nor was it always illegal in the United States before the 1970s. As U.S. Supreme Court Justice Blackmun notes in the *Roe v. Wade* opinion, "At the time of the adoption of our Constitution, and throughout the major portion of the 19th century, abortion was viewed with less disfavor than under most American statutes currently in effect."[32]

In the first half of the twentieth century, most U.S. states passed laws regulating or making abortion illegal, except in certain cases such as a pregnancy resulting from rape or incest or when the pregnant woman's life or health was threatened. However, women continued to have abortions illegally and under dangerous conditions. (The most notorious of these "back alley" abortion methods involved the use of a coat hanger to scrape the uterine lining, which became a symbol used by the movement to legalize abortion.) In the early 1970s, a pregnant woman from Texas, who was given the fictitious name Jane Roe, challenged the state's abortion law, which allowed the procedure only to save the life of the mother. This case, which became known as *Roe v. Wade*, made its way to the U.S. Supreme Court, which ruled in favor of Jane Roe in 1973. In the majority opinion, the Court concluded that no state may ban abortion before the time of fetal viability based on a fundamental "right to privacy" grounded in the Constitution, chiefly in the liberty and due process clauses of the Fourteenth Amendment. The term *privacy* here does not refer to matters that must be kept secret or to what goes on in one's own home, but to a basic liberty, a freedom from restraint in decisions about how to live and enjoy one's life.[33]

However, the Court noted that the state did have some interest in protecting maternal health as well as what it called the "potential life" of the fetus. (Note that the phrase is not especially illuminating because most people do not deny that the fetus is actually alive.) In the case of maternal health, this interest becomes "compelling" only after the first *trimester* (or third month) of pregnancy and allows for some degree of health-related regulation. In the case of the fetus's "potential life," the right to privacy was said not to be absolute but limited, due to state or social interests that become compelling at the point of fetal viability. The ruling was thus based on the trimester formula and concluded that:

1. from approximately the end of the first trimester, state laws could regulate the medical safety of abortion procedures;
2. before the time of viability, about the end of the second trimester (the sixth month), the abortion decision should be left up to the pregnant woman and her doctor; and
3. from the time of viability on, states could prohibit abortion except in those cases in which the continued pregnancy would endanger the life or health of the pregnant woman.[34]

While the trimester formula is considered to be a rough guide to the legal status of abortion, the U.S. Supreme Court has handed down several other abortion-related decisions that have altered this original formulation. Most important, in *Casey v. Planned Parenthood* (1992), the Court rejected the trimester formula and simply maintained that states could not ban abortion before the point of viability. (Advances in medical science had already shifted the point at which fetal viability was possible.) It also reiterated the state's compelling interest in protecting life after the point of viability. Nonetheless, the Court affirmed the basic decision in *Roe v. Wade*. Citing the importance of a legal precedent on which citizens have come to depend and the absence of significant factual or legal developments, the Court again ruled in favor of a constitutional right to privacy and abortion. The majority opinion also commented on the essential relationship of abortion rights to the "capacity of women to act in society and to make reproductive decisions" and

upheld those rights as a matter of liberty and "personal autonomy." While the Court concluded that states could impose such restrictions as twenty-four-hour waiting periods and parental or state consent requirements (for minors seeking abortions), they must not place an *undue burden* on women in the exercise of their constitutional right to privacy. This means that state laws may not create "substantial obstacles" for women who seek to have abortions, such as the requirement that they first get consent from their spouses—a regulation the Court rejected.[35]

Since 1992, many abortion-related legal decisions have involved the *undue burden* standard. In 2007, in *Gonzalez v. Carhart*, the U.S. Supreme Court upheld, by a vote of five to four, a federal law banning so-called "partial birth abortion" or "intact dilation and extraction." It held that this law did not impose "an undue burden on women's exercise of their right to end a pregnancy." The majority opinion concluded that there were alternatives to this procedure and that the law enacted by Congress reflected the government's "legitimate, substantial interest in preserving and promoting fetal life."[36] The decision raised controversy, however, because the law it upheld allowed exceptions to protect a woman's life, but not her health. Some physicians and other critics of the measure argued that the procedure is "often the safest to use late in the pregnancy because it minimizes the chances of injury to the uterus" and was thus deemed appropriate for certain cases by the American College of Obstetricians and Gynecologists.[37] Other critics have challenged parental consent laws as placing an undue burden on minors seeking abortions (especially in cases of incest) and pointed to the Court's ruling in *Planned Parenthood of Kansas City v. Ashcroft* (1983) that such laws must offer a "judicial alternative" whereby a judge can overrule parental refusals.[38]

As we noted at the beginning of this chapter, the past decade has witnessed an increasing number of legal efforts to restrict abortion based on a number of different criteria. In 2010, for example, the governor of Nebraska signed into law a statute "banning most abortions 20 weeks after conception or later on the theory that a fetus by that stage in pregnancy has the capacity to feel pain."[39] An increasing number of state legislatures and referenda have also sought to establish full legal "personhood" beginning at conception. Other states are in the process of enacting fetal "heartbeat" laws, some of which would require that women seeking abortions undergo transvaginal ultrasounds to detect fetal heartbeat. This last requirement has generated a particularly intense controversy. Antiabortion advocates support the requirement based on their belief that if a woman views the fetus on an ultrasound, she will mostly likely decide against abortion; while women's rights advocates have called state-mandated transvaginal ultrasounds a form of "medical rape."[40] Meanwhile, the evidence appears to show that there is very little correlation between ultrasound viewing and women's choice to abort.[41]

Questions have also been raised about the new "feticide" laws now enacted in more than half of U.S. states. These are laws that make it a crime to cause harm to a fetus. Thus, someone who attacks a pregnant woman and kills the fetus that she wanted to carry to term can be found guilty of murder or manslaughter. States differ in how they classify the crime, whether as "feticide" or under general manslaughter or murder laws. It may seem contradictory that a woman can end a fetus's life through abortion but a third party who kills a fetus she wanted may be guilty of murder. Some have said that the difference is between a person who exercises a "reproductive choice" and another person who does not. Further questions are raised by state laws that seek to protect fetal life from harmful actions of the pregnant woman herself, such as ingesting drugs or alcohol. She could be punished if her fetus is born harmed, but not if she aborts the fetus. And in some jurisdictions, the state can commit a pregnant woman who has drug or alcohol problems with the goal of defending the health of the unborn child. For example, a law in Wisconsin states that "unborn children have certain basic needs which must be provided for, including the need to develop physically to their potential and the need to be free from physical harm due to the habitual lack of self-control

of their expectant mothers in the use of alcohol beverages, controlled substances or controlled substance analogs, exhibited to a severe degree."[42] Should a state be able to prevent a mother from continuing drug use during pregnancy by having her committed, against her will, to a rehab facility? Many abortion rights supporters see such policies as withholding from women the rights of autonomy and personal liberty that are granted to men. Those who condemn abortion, on the other hand, typically support these measures.

In recent years, abortion opponents have worked to find other legal ways to restrict access to abortion. Consider what happened in Wichita, Kansas, after Dr. George Tiller was murdered. His clinic, the state's only abortion clinic outside of Kansas City, closed after his death in 2009. In 2013, a former employee attempted to reopen the clinic but faced legal challenges and local lobbying efforts, including attempts to change zoning and taxation rules.[43] The clinic reopened. But throughout the country, abortion providers and clinics are facing similar legal challenges and restrictions, effectively blocking access to abortion in large portions of many states. For example, laws in some states require doctors to have admitting privileges at local hospitals, which frequently refuse them to avoid controversy. Other laws require abortion clinics to adhere to architectural standards that apply to hospitals. And in some states insurance plans are prohibited from paying for abortion. A Bloomberg report from 2016 summarized the impact of this piecemeal approach to abortion regulation, concluding that "since 2011, at least 162 abortion providers have shut or stopped offering the procedure, while just 21 opened. At no time since before 1973, when the U.S. Supreme Court legalized abortion, has a woman's ability to terminate a pregnancy been more dependent on her zip code or financial resources to travel."[44]

Recent Supreme Court decisions on abortion have not been unanimous. This indicates the difficulty of balancing concerns for the various moral values involved. In doing so, however, these decisions have made neither side in the abortion debate particularly happy. On the one hand, they stress the values of privacy, liberty, and equal opportunity; on the other hand, they conclude that some recognition ought to be given to the origins of human life. Because these are moral values reflected in the law, some of the issues surrounding the morality of abortion will be relevant to what we think the law should or should not do. In what follows, however, we will concentrate on the underlying moral issues that typically frame the abortion debate.

ABORTION: THE MORAL QUESTION

Although many people have argued that abortion is a private decision that ought not to be a matter of law, it is much more difficult to make the case that abortion is not a moral matter at all. After all, abortion involves questions about rights, happiness, and well-being, as well as the status and value of human life. If these things are morally relevant, then abortion is a moral matter. This is not to say that abortion is good, bad, or neutral, but simply that it is morally important.

The moral status of abortion also may have relevance for how we approach fetal research. For example, promising studies have shown that embryonic stem cells (taken from human blastocysts) as well as tissue from aborted fetuses might be used for treatments for diseases, such as Parkinson's disease, and to regenerate damaged organs and tissues. These issues are discussed further in Chapter 18.

In considering the morality of abortion, we can distinguish two types of arguments both for and against abortion: (1) arguments for which the moral status of the fetus is irrelevant, and (2) arguments for which it is relevant. One might suppose that all arguments regarding abortion hinge on the moral status of the fetus, but this is not the case. As we will see, when we use the phrase "moral status of the fetus," we refer to questions about whether the fetus is a human being or a person and whether the fetus has inherent value or any rights, including a right to life. We look first at arguments that do not concern themselves with these questions. As you examine these arguments, you may find that one or another seems more valid or reasonable to you.

ARGUMENTS THAT DO NOT DEPEND ON THE MORAL STATUS OF THE FETUS

First, we will consider arguments for which the moral status of the fetus is irrelevant. These arguments are typically either based on utilitarian reasoning or on claims about the rights of persons.

Utilitarian Reasoning

Many arguments that focus on something other than the moral status of the fetus are consequentialist in nature and broadly utilitarian. Arguments for abortion often cite the bad consequences that may result from a continued pregnancy—for example, the loss of a job or other opportunities for the pregnant woman, the suffering of the future child, the burden of caring for the child under difficult circumstances, and so on. Some utilitarian arguments against abortion also cite the loss of potential happiness and future social contributions of the being who is aborted.

According to act utilitarian reasoning, each case or action stands on its own, so to speak. Its own consequences determine whether it is good or bad, better or worse than other alternatives. Act utilitarians believe that the people making the abortion decision must consider the likely consequences of the alternative actions—in other words, having or not having an abortion (as well as such considerations as where and when these events might occur). Among the kinds of consequences to consider are health risks and benefits, positive or negative mental or psychological consequences, and financial and social results of the alternative choices. For example, a pregnant woman should consider questions such as these: What would be the effect on her of having the child versus ending the pregnancy? What are the consequences to any others affected? Would the child, if born, be likely to have a happy or unhappy life, and how would one determine this? How would an abortion or the child's birth affect her family, other children, the father, the grandparents, and so on?

Notice that the issue of whether the fetus (in the sense we are using it here) is a person or a human being is not among the things to consider when arguing from this type of consequentialist perspective. Abortion at a later stage of pregnancy might have different effects on people than at an earlier stage, and it might also have different effects on the fetus in terms of whether it might experience pain. It is the effects on the mother, the fetus, the potential child, and others that count in utilitarian thinking, not the moral status of the fetus (what kind of value it has) or its ontological status (i.e., what kind of being we say it is). Also notice that on utilitarian or consequentialist grounds, abortion sometimes would be permissible (the morally right thing to do) and sometimes not; it would depend on the consequences of the various sorts noted earlier. Moral judgments about abortion will be better or worse, according to this view, depending on the adequacy of the prediction of consequences.

Critics of utilitarian reasoning generally object to its seeming disregard of rights. They may point out that if we do not take the right to life seriously, then utilitarian reasoning may condone the taking of any life if the overall consequences of doing so are good. A utilitarian may respond by appealing to the idea of rule utilitarianism. A rule utilitarian must consider which practice regarding abortion would be best. Would the rule "No one should have an abortion" be likely to maximize happiness? Would the rule "No one should have an abortion unless the pregnancy threatens the mother's health or well-being" have better consequences overall? What about a rule that says "Persons who are in situations x, y, or z should be allowed to have abortions"? How would easy access to abortion affect our regard for the very young? How would the practice of abortion when the fetus has certain abnormalities affect our treatment of the physically or mentally disabled, in general? How would a restrictive abortion policy affect women's health as well as their ability to participate as equal human beings, enjoying jobs and other opportunities? Whichever practice or rule is likely to have the better net result—that is, more good consequences and fewer bad ones—is the best practice or rule to follow.

In any case, some critics of the utilitarian approach would argue that the moral status of the fetus, such as whether it is the kind of being that has a right to life, is, in fact, essential to moral decisions about abortion. Others would insist that we address the matter of the rights of the pregnant woman (or others) and the problem of conflicts of rights.

Some Rights Arguments

Some arguments about abortion consider the rights of persons but still maintain that the moral status of the fetus is irrelevant. It is irrelevant in the sense that whether or not we think of the fetus as a person with full moral rights is not crucial for decisions about the morality of abortion. An influential article on abortion by Judith Jarvis Thomson—an excerpt of which appears at the end of this chapter—presents such an argument. Thomson assumes, for the purpose of argument, that the fetus is a person from early on in pregnancy. But her conclusion is that abortion is still justified, even if the fetus is a person with a right to life (and she assumes it is also permissible if the fetus is not a person).[45] This is why the argument does not turn on what we say about the moral status of the fetus.

The question Thomson poses is whether the pregnant woman has an obligation to sustain the life of the fetus by providing it with the use of her body. To have us think about this, she asks us to consider an imaginary scenario. Suppose, she says, that you wake up one morning and find yourself attached through various medical tubes and devices to a famous violinist. You find out that during the night, you have been kidnapped and "hooked up" to this violinist by a group of classical music enthusiasts. The violinist has severe kidney problems, and the only way that his life can be saved is through being so attached to another person—so that the other person's kidneys will do the work of purifying his blood for some fixed period of months, until his own kidneys have recovered. The question Thomson poses is this: Would you be morally permitted or justified in "unplugging" the violinist, even though doing so would result in his death? Thomson argues that you would be justified, in particular because you have not consented to devote your body and your time to saving the violinist's life. She goes on to argue that this example has an analogy to abortion, most obviously in cases of pregnancy due to rape.

However, Thomson means her argument to apply more widely, and she uses other analogies to help make her point. One would only have a responsibility to save the violinist (or nurture the fetus) if one had agreed to do so. The consent that Thomson has in mind is a deliberate and planned choice. She argues that although it would be generous of you to save the life of the violinist (or the fetus), you are not obligated to do so. Her point is that no one has a right to use your body, even to save his or her own life, unless you give him or her that right. Such views are consistent with a position that insists that women are persons and have the same right to bodily integrity as men do. As persons, they ought not to be used against their will for whatever purposes by others, even noble purposes such as the nurturing of children. Critics of this argument point out that it may apply at most to abortion in cases of rape, for in some other cases, one might be said to implicitly consent to a pregnancy if one did what one knew might result in it. One response to this is that we do not always consider a person to have consented to chance consequences of their actions. Thomson argues that, in the end, it is the woman's right to choose whether to allow her body to be used or not—in the case of rape or in other cases of accidental pregnancy.

MindTap® For more chapter resources and activities, go to MindTap.

Rights-based and utilitarian arguments are examples of positions on abortion that do not depend on what we say about the moral status of the fetus, but other arguments hold this issue to be crucial. Some arguments for the moral permissibility of abortion as well as some against it rely, in crucial ways, on what is said about the fetus. We next consider some of these arguments.

ARGUMENTS THAT DEPEND ON THE MORAL STATUS OF THE FETUS

Abortion arguments that emphasize the moral status of the fetus are concerned with a broad range of ethical issues. They ask such questions as: Is the fetus a human being? A person? Alive? For the moment, let us focus not on these terms and what they might mean, but on an even more fundamental question, namely, what kind of value or moral status does the developing fetus have? Does it have a different moral status in various stages of development? If so, when does the status change, and why? (Further questions may include how to weigh its value or rights in comparison to other values or the rights of others.) At bottom, these questions point toward the ontological and moral status of the fetus. **Ontology** means "theory of being," so the ontological question asks what sort of being the fetus is (whether it is merely a part of its mother or whether it is a unique and distinct being and so on). The ontological question is connected to the moral question of the moral status of the being. What we want to know is both what kind of a being the fetus is and what sort of value that kind of being has.

To begin to answer these questions, we will examine an initial approach to the value of the fetus and call it "Method I," to distinguish it from a broader approach we will term "Method II." Briefly put, Method I focuses on the characteristics of the fetus and asks when it has characteristics sufficiently significant to classify it as a person, who is worthy of our moral concern. Method II asks a more general question. It asks us to think about what kind of beings of any sort, human or nonhuman, have some special moral status or rights, such as a right to life.

Method I

In using this method, we focus on fetal development and ask three things about each potentially significant stage: (1) *What* is present? (2) *When* is this present (at what stage)? and (3) *Why* is this significant—in other words, why does this confer a special moral status, if it does? By "special moral status," we might mean various things. Among the most important would be a status such that the fetus would be thought to have something like a right to life. If this were the case, then abortion would become morally problematic.[46]

In the following sections, we will apply Method I to the various stages of fetal development and see what the arguments would look like. In each case, we will consider the arguments for the position and then some criticisms of these arguments.

Conception or Fertilization Conception, or the stage at which the sperm penetrates and fertilizes the ovum, is the time at which many opponents of abortion say that the fetus has full moral status. The reason usually given for this claim is that at conception the fetus receives its full genetic makeup, from the combination of sperm and egg.[47] The argument for taking this stage as morally significant appears to be based on an ontological argument that goes something like this: If the being that is born at the end of a pregnancy is a human being or person, and if there is no substantial change in its constitution from its initial form, then it is the same being all the way through the stages of development. Otherwise, we would be implying that different beings are succeeding one another during this process.

Critics of this position often point out that although fetal development is continuous, the bare genetic material present at conception is not enough to constitute a person at that point. In this early stage, the cells are *totipotent*, which means they can become skin cells, heart cells, or many other types of cells.[48] There is no structure or differentiation at this point of development, nothing that resembles a person in this initial form. The fertilized egg is not even clearly an individual. For example, consider what happens in the case of identical twinning. Before implantation, identical twins are formed by the splitting of cells in the early embryo. Each resulting twin has the same genetic makeup. Now, what are we to think of the original embryo? Suppose we assume that its conception created an individual being or person, and we name him John.

The twins that develop from the original embryo and are later born, we name Jim and Joe. But what happened to John, if there was a John? Jim and Joe are two new individuals, genetically alike as twins, but also two different people. Is there a little of John in each of them? Or does the fact that there are two individuals after twinning mean that there was not any individual there before that time—that John never existed? Those who support conception as the crucial time at which we have a being with full moral status and rights must explain how there can be an individual at conception, at least in the case of identical twinning.

Brain Development Another possible stage at which a fetus might attain new moral status is that point at which the brain is sufficiently developed. The idea is reasonable given that the human brain is the locus of consciousness, language, and communication, and it is what makes us crucially different from other animals. Moreover, we now use the cessation of brain function as the determinant of death. Why should we not use the beginning of brain function as the beginning of an individual's life? We can detect brain activity between the sixth and eighth weeks of fetal development, which makes that point the significant time period for this argument.

Critics of the argument point out that brain activity develops gradually, and we cannot identify any single point during fetal development that presents an entirely unique or qualitative change in brain activity. Of course, this may be only a practical problem. We might be satisfied with an approximation, rather than a determinate time. Other questions about the type of brain function also might be raised. At six to eight weeks, the brain is quite simple; only much later do those parts develop that are the basis of conscious function. Early in pregnancy, the brain is arguably not significantly different from other animal brains in structure or function. And as mentioned previously, most experts maintain that neuronal development is not advanced enough to speak of the fetus as feeling pain until somewhere between twenty and twenty-six weeks of development.

Quickening Usually, the pregnant woman can feel the fetus kick or move in approximately the fourth month of fetal development. This is what is meant by *quickening*. In prescientific eras, people believed that there was no fetal movement before this time—and if this were so, it would then constitute a persuasive reason to consider this stage as crucial. While contemporary science can detect movement before this stage, one might still focus on quickening as the start of self-initiated movement in the fetus, arising from a new level of brain development. This would constitute a better reason for identifying quickening as the beginning of a new moral status or right to life because the fetus would now be moving about on its own. As we saw previously, for much of Western history, civil and religious authorities prohibited abortion only after this stage.

Critics of this position may make the same argument about quickening as was made with regard to brain development, namely, that there is no dramatic break in the development of the fetus's ability to move. Moreover, they might also point out that other animals and even plants move on their own, and this does not give them special moral status or a right to life. Furthermore, those who argue for animal rights usually do so because of their *sentience*—that is, their ability to feel pleasure and pain—and not their ability to move.

Viability Viability is possible at approximately the twenty-fourth week of fetal development and means that the fetus is at least potentially capable of existing apart from the mother. Its organs and organ systems are sufficiently developed that it may have the capacity to function on its own. The last of these systems to be functionally complete is the respiratory system, which often causes fatal problems for fetuses delivered before six months. During previous stages of fetal development, the fetus "breathes" amniotic fluid. Before twenty-three or twenty-four weeks of gestation, "capillaries have not yet moved close enough to the air sacs to carry gases to and from the lung."[49] A lubricant, called surfactant, can be administered to assist the lungs' capacity to breathe air, but even then, the chance of survival is slim.

As we can see, one practical problem with using viability as a moral criterion is its variability. When *Roe v. Wade* took effect, the point of viability for a premature infant was considered to be approximately twenty-six weeks; the estimation has since been shortened by a couple of weeks. At twenty-three or twenty-four weeks, a "micropreemie" weighs slightly less than a pound. Its viability is also a function of this weight and the mother's socioeconomic status; if she's poor, then the chances are that her nutrition is poor, which has negative effects on the fetus. The degree of prematurity at different stages of pregnancy also varies by sex and race: girls are approximately one week ahead of boys in development, and blacks are approximately one week ahead of whites.[50]

Why is the stage of viability singled out as the stage at which the fetus may take on a new moral status? Some answer that it is the potential for life independent of the mother that forms the basis of the new status. However, if the fetus were delivered at this stage and left on its own, no infant would be able to survive. Perhaps the notion of separate existence is a better basis for viability as a moral criterion. The idea would be that the fetus is more clearly distinct from the mother at this point in pregnancy. Or perhaps the notion of completeness is what is intended. Although the fetus is not fully formed at viability because much development takes place after birth, the argument might be made that the viable fetus is sufficiently complete, enabling us to think of it as an entirely new being.

Critics of the viability criterion may point again to the gradual nature of development and the seeming arbitrariness of picking out one stage of completeness as crucially different from the others. They also can point out that even if it were delivered at the point of viability, the fetus would still be dependent on others (and on an array of sophisticated medical technologies) for its survival. They can also question the whole notion of making moral status a function of independence. We are all dependent on one another, and those who are more independent (e.g., because they can live apart from others) have no greater value than those who are more dependent. Even someone dependent on medical machines is not, for this reason, less human, they might argue. Furthermore, a viable unborn fetus is still, in fact, dependent on its mother and does not have an existence separate from her. Birth, on these terms, would be a better stage to pick than viability, these critics might argue, if it is separateness and independence that are crucial.

Each point in fetal development may provide a reasonable basis for concluding something about the moral status of the fetus. However, as we can clearly see, none are problem free. In any case, the whole idea of grounding moral status and rights on the possession of certain characteristics also may be called into question. Instead, we may want to consider a more general approach to this problem by looking at a second method.

Method II

If the status of the fetus is crucial to arguments about the morality of abortion, then we may want to compare those arguments with more general arguments made with regard to beings other than human fetuses. For example, why do we believe that people generally have rights? Are we significantly different from other animals, such that we have unique moral status simply because we are human beings? Or is the crucial determinant of that special moral status the ability to reason, imagine, use language, or something else? If so, then if there were other intelligent beings in the universe, would they have the same moral status as we do, even if they were not members of our species? And what of human beings who do not have the capacity for reasoning, imagination, and communication?

Take, for example, the case of a newborn with anencephaly—that is, without a developed upper brain and thus with no chance of consciousness or thought. In fact, such an infant does not usually live for long. But it is a human being biologically and not a member of some other species. Or take the case of a person in a permanent vegetative state. There is no doubt that the person is still human in the biological sense, but does this person lack human rights because he or she lacks some mental qualities that are the basis for rights?

Finally, perhaps it is not actual ability to think or communicate, but the *potential* for the development of such characteristics that grounds special moral worth and rights. A normal fetus would have this potentiality, whereas a two-year-old dog would not. Of course, this depends on the level or type of thinking that is seen to be crucial because dogs do have some type of mental capacity and some ability to communicate.

Distinguishing among the different criteria discussed above, we might arrive at something like the following positions. Each gives an answer to this question: What kind of beings have special moral status, which may include something like a right to life?[51]

Being Human   According to one point of view, it is being human that counts—being a member of the human species. Now, using this criterion, we might note that human fetuses are members of the human species and conclude that they have equal moral status with all other human beings. The argument for this position might include something about the moral advance we make when we recognize that all humans have equal moral worth. This has not always been the case, for example, when children or women were treated more like property than as human beings with equal and full moral status, or when African American slaves were deemed in the U.S. Constitution to be three-fifths of a person.

Critics of this position may point out that unfertilized eggs and sperm, not to mention organs such as gallbladders and appendices, are also biologically human. But no one argues that they deserve equal moral status with human persons. Questions can also be raised about why only members of the human species are included here. If some other species of being were sufficiently like us in the relevant respects, then should they not be considered to have the same worth as members of our own species? In considering this possibility, we may be better able to decide whether it is membership in a species or something else that grounds moral worth. (See further discussion in Chapter 17.)

Being Like Human Beings Suppose that moral status (or personhood) depends on being a member of any species whose members have certain significant characteristics like human beings. But what characteristics are significant enough to ground high moral value and status, including rights? For example, consider the abilities to communicate, reason, and plan. Depending on how high a level of communicating, reasoning, and planning is required, perhaps other animals would qualify for the high moral status envisioned. For instance, some chimpanzees and gorillas appear to be able to communicate through sign language. If there were beings elsewhere in the universe who were members of a different species but who could communicate, reason, and plan, then according to this criterion, they too would have the same moral worth as humans. If a lower level of ability were used, then members of other animal species would also qualify. It is important to aim for some kind of consistency here in thinking about the moral standing of fetuses and nonhuman animals. It is useful to clarify our thinking about animals by considering what we think about fetuses and vice versa. We might also want to test our intuitions by considering what we think about cognitively disabled humans or those with brain injuries. But those who want to emphasize species-belonging as the primary criterion for personhood will not be persuaded by arguments that focus on cognitive capacities.

These first two criteria are alike in that it is membership in a species that is the determinant of one's moral status. If any humans have this status, then they all do. If chimpanzees or Martians have this status, then all members of their species also have this status. It does not matter what the individual member of the species is like or what individual capacities she or he possesses. On the other hand, perhaps it is not what species you belong to but what individual characteristics you possess that forms the basis of the special moral status. If this were the case, then there would be at least three other possible positions about the basis of this moral status. These are as follows:

Potentiality *Potentiality* literally means "power." According to this criterion, all beings that have the power to develop certain key characteristics have full moral worth. Thus, if a particular fetus had the potential for developing the requisite mental capacities, then this fetus would have full moral status. However, any fetus or other human being that does not have this potential (anencephalic infants or those in a permanent vegetative state, for example) does not have this status.

Some critics of abortion argue that abortion is wrong because it prevents a being (the fetus) from actualizing its potential. One version of this argument has been articulated by the philosopher Don Marquis, who we will read at the end of this chapter. Marquis argues that it is seriously wrong to kill children and infants because we presume that children and infants have "futures of value."[52] According to Marquis, abortion is wrong for a similar reason, which is that it deprives the fetus from obtaining the future good it would have if it were left alone and allowed to be born. Marquis concludes, "The future of a standard fetus includes a set of experiences, projects, activities, and such which are identical with the futures of adult human beings and are identical with the futures of young children."[53] To kill the fetus is to deprive the fetus of those goods that it potentially could have enjoyed.

Yet how important is potential and what, in fact, is it? If a fetus is aborted and it is unaware that it even had the potential to develop into a person with a future of value, how has it been deprived of anything? Is it possible to deprive you of something if you are not aware or conscious? Potentiality appears to be vague and undefined. Suppose that one had the potential to become a famous star or hold high political office. Would one then deserve the same respect and powers of an actual star or legislator? Consider the following fictitious story described by philosopher Michael Tooley.[54] Suppose that we have a kitten that will grow into a mature cat if left alone. We also have a serum that if injected into the kitten will make it grow into a human being. Tooley suggests that there is no reason to allow the kitten to develop into a human being, since although it has the potential to develop into a human being (after being injected by this magic serum), it is not yet actually a human being. Tooley concludes, "If it is seriously wrong to kill something, the reason cannot be that the thing will later acquire properties that in themselves provide something with a right to life. . . . if it is wrong to kill a human fetus, it cannot be because of its potentialities."[55] Tooley's point is that those potentialities are merely that—potentialities—and so are not yet actual.

Taking Tooley's story a bit further, we might wonder if there is an obligation to inject the kitten with the serum, since the serum possesses the potentiality to cause the kitten to develop into a human being. But the same argument applies. This points toward a consideration of contraception. Is contraception wrong because it somehow prevents the potentiality contained in the sperm and egg from actualizing itself? Marquis responds to this question by maintaining that there is a qualitative difference between contraception and abortion. Prior to fertilization, there is no actual thing—only a net of probabilities. We don't know, for example, which of the millions of sperm will fertilize the egg. And so, no definite subject is deprived of its potentiality through contraception. But, according to Marquis, once the fetus is developing in the womb, there is a definite set of potentialities that now are worthy of moral consideration.

Actuality At the other end of the spectrum is the view according to which simple "potentiality" for developing certain characteristics counts for nothing (or at least does not give one the kind of moral status about which we are concerned). Only the actual possession of the requisite characteristics is sufficient for full moral status. Again, it makes a significant difference to one's position here whether the characteristics are high level or low level. For example, if a rather high level of reasoning is required before an individual has the requisite moral status, then newborns probably would not be included, as well as many others. The claim that even newborns

lack the high-level capacities relevant to full moral status is defended by the philosopher Mary Anne Warren, whose argument is included at the end of this chapter.[56] According to this view, although the fetus, newborn infant, and extremely young child are human beings biologically, they are not yet persons or beings with the requisite moral status. They are not yet members of the moral community. There may be good reasons to treat them well and with respect, but it is not because they are persons with rights.

Evolving Value Finally, let us consider a position that is intermediate between the last two positions. Its underlying idea is that potential counts, but not as much as actual possession of the significant characteristics. Furthermore, as the potential is gradually realized, the moral status of the being also grows. This position also could be described in terms of competing interests and claims. The stronger the claim, the more it should prevail.

In applying this criterion to fetal development, the conclusion would be that the early-term fetus has less moral value or moral status than the late-term fetus. Such an approach would parallel the idea, found in the law, that the state can regulate late-term abortions, but not early-term abortion. Less of a claim or interest on the part of others is needed to override the early-term fetus's claim to consideration. Moderately serious interests of the pregnant woman or of society could override the interests or claims of the early-term fetus, but it would take more serious interests to override the claims of the late-term fetus. In the end, according to this view, when potentiality is sufficiently actualized, the fetus or infant has as much right as any other person.

We might note a variant view held by some feminists. Most feminists support a woman's legal right to abortion, but not all are happy with the rationale for it provided in *Roe v. Wade*.[57] For example, some worry that the "right to privacy" could be interpreted in ways that are detrimental to women. If this right is taken to imply that everything done in the privacy of one's home is out of the law's reach, then this might seem to suggest that the subordination or abuse of women and children is merely "domestic" and not a matter of public concern.

Some feminists also have misgivings about denying the moral status of the fetus, viewing the focus on moral status and individual rights as the product of a male-dominant worldview. Such a worldview is taken to approach individuals as distinct atomic beings who are separated from one another and whose conflicts are best described as conflicts of rights. Feminists such as Catharine A. MacKinnon point out that, from the standpoint of women, things may be more complicated:

> So long as it gestates in utero, the fetus is defined by its relation to the pregnant woman. More than a body part but less than a person, where it is, is largely what it is. From the standpoint of the pregnant woman, it is both me and not me. It "is" the pregnant woman in the sense that it is in her and of her and is hers more than anyone's. It "is not" her in the sense that she is not all that is there. In a legal system that views the individual as a unitary self, and that self as a bundle of rights, it is no wonder that the pregnant woman has eluded legal grasp, and her fetus with her.[58]

This approach recognizes that abortion is morally problematic precisely because of the ontological and moral question of motherhood—which is a circumstance in which one being gives birth to another. According to this approach, the loss of an early form of human life is a significant loss, which is indicated by the seriousness with which most women treat miscarriages. However, this is not to imply that the fetus has full moral status and rights.

Another approach along these lines is associated with the work of philosopher Rosalind Hursthouse, who uses virtue ethics to consider the topic of abortion. Hursthouse is critical of those who have abortions for frivolous reasons, but she argues that there may be a number of virtuous reasons that a woman could choose to have an abortion.[59] One reason might be that the mother is concerned for the well-being of her other children when an unexpected pregnancy occurs. Or perhaps a mother wants to prevent possible suffering for a fetus that would suffer from severe disability.

If the fetus does not have the requisite moral status, then abortion is probably morally permissible. If it is considered to be a person, then abortion is morally problematic. If the fetus is said to have a somewhat in-between status, then the conclusion about abortion may be mixed or vary depending on stages of development or other factors. Again, these are positions that put the whole weight of the moral judgment about abortion on the status of the fetus.

As the utilitarian and rights-based arguments exemplified, however, there are other considerations about what counts in thinking about the morality of abortion. For example, we might be concerned, as Hursthouse is, about whether a mother aborts for serious reasons or whether she does so for frivolous reasons. Along these lines, some will argue that abortion should not be used as birth control. But such a claim holds weight only if we believe that there is something wrong with abortion to begin with, perhaps because of a claim about the moral status of the fetus. Finally, remember that not everything that we consider immoral can (or should) be made illegal. Thus, even if abortion were in some case thought to be immoral, one would need to give further reasons about the purpose of law to conclude that it also ought to be illegal. At the same time, we must ask if the only reason to make something illegal is if it is immoral. There may be cases when we want to permit people the liberty to choose for themselves about morally controversial issues. This seems to be the status quo for the moment in the United States, where even some of those who think that abortion is morally wrong agree that women should be permitted to make decisions about abortion based upon their own conception of morality. This conclusion points toward a broader conversation about the importance of liberty, tolerance, and individual conscience.

In the readings in this chapter, we begin with a short excerpt from Judith Jarvis Thomson's article published in 1971, before the U.S. Supreme Court guaranteed abortion rights across the United States. Thomson's basic argument is in defense of abortion rights for women, even if we grant that a fetus is a person. Her argument is outlined above. The next essay is from Don Marquis, who provides an argument against abortion that focuses on the potential of the fetus to experience significant goods in its future. Finally, Mary Anne Warren's argument provides a response that focuses on the criteria for personhood. Finally, we have recent article by Bertha Alvarez Manninen that looks at abortion from the vantage point of care ethics, virtue ethics, and from the psychological perspective of women.

NOTES

1. Gallup Poll data on public opinion regarding morality of abortion, http://www.gallup.com/poll/183434/americans-choose-pro-choice-first-time-seven-years.aspx; Gallup Poll data on public opinion regarding Roe v. Wade: http://www.gallup.com/poll/160058/majority-americans-support-roe-wade-decision.aspx (accessed February 25, 2016).

2. In fact, the National Cancer Institute, in a 2003 study, found no increased risk of breast cancer associated with abortion. Other studies note that "fewer than 0.3% of patients experience a complication serious enough to require hospitalization." Abortion, rather, is said to be "one of the most common surgical procedures" and especially in the first trimester is "extremely safe." (*Time*, February 26, 2007, p. 28).

3. David Barstow, "An Abortion Battle, Fought to the Death," *New York Times*, July 25, 2009, http://www.nytimes.com/2009/07/26/us/26tiller.html?pagewanted=all&_r=0 (accessed April 23, 2013).

4. "With emotions high, Colorado Planned Parenthood clinic reopens after gunman's attack" *Los Angeles Times*, February 15, 2016, http://www.latimes.com/nation/la-na-planned-parenthood-reopen-20160215-story.html (accessed February 25, 2016).

5. Based on a report in the *New York Times*, March 7, 1993, p. B3, and March 11, 1993, p. A1. Also see Jennifer Gonnerman, "The Terrorist Campaign against Abortion," *Village Voice*, November 3–9, 1998, www.villagevoice.com/features/9845/abortion.shtml

6. Bonnie Steinbock, *Life Before Birth: The Moral and Legal Status of Embryos and Fetuses, Second Edition* (Oxford: Oxford University Press, 2011),

pp. 46–50. Also see American Congress of Obstetricians and Gynecologists, *ACOG Statement on HR 3803*, June 18, 2012, http://www.acog.org/~/media/Departments/Government%20Relations%20and%20Outreach/20120618DCAborStmnt.pdf?dmc=1&ts=20120915T2120559712 (accessed April 23, 2013).

7. Joyce Salisbury, *Women in the Ancient World* (Santa Barbara, CA: ABC-CLIO, 2001), p. 1.

8. Plato, "Theatetus," 149d and Plato, "Republic," 461c both in *Plato: Collected Dialogues*, ed. Edith Hamilton and Huntington Cairns (Princeton: Bollingen, 1961).

9. Hippocrates, "The Oath" (Internet Classics Archive: http://classics.mit.edu//Hippocrates/hippooath.html)

10. Salisbury, *Women in the Ancient World*, p. 2.

11. "Facts about Mifepristone (RU-486)," National Abortion Federation, http://www.prochoice.org/about_abortion/facts/facts_mifepristone.html (accessed April 23, 2013).

12. "Facts on Induced Abortion in the United States," Guttmacher Institute, July 2014, https://www.guttmacher.org/fact-sheet/induced-abortion-united-states (accessed July 21, 2016).

13. "Abortion and Women of Color: The Bigger Picture," *Guttmacher Policy Review* 11, No. 3 (Summer 2008), http://www.guttmacher.org/pubs/gpr/11/3/gpr110302.html (accessed April 23, 2013).

14. *New York Times*, May 5, 2006, p. A19.

15. Nicholas D. Kristof, "Beyond Pelvic Politics," *New York Times*, February 11, 2012, http://www.nytimes.com/2012/02/12/opinion/sunday/kristof-beyond-pelvic-politics.html (accessed April 23, 2013).

16. "Facts on Induced Abortion in the United States," Guttmacher Institute, http://www.guttmacher.org/pubs/fb_induced_abortion.html

17. "Reasons U.S. Women Have Abortions: Quantitative and Qualitative Perspectives" *Perspectives on Sexual and Reproductive Health* 37: 3 (September 2005), http://www.guttmacher.org/pubs/journals/3711005.pdf (accessed July 27, 2013).

18. Guttmacher Institute, *Abortion Worldwide: A Decade of Uneven Progress* (2009), http://www.guttmacher.org/pubs/Abortion-Worldwide.pdf (accessed February 22, 2016).

19. Singh S et al., *Abortion Worldwide: A Decade of Uneven Progress* (New York: Guttmacher Institute, 2009), http://www.guttmacher.org/pubs/Abortion-Worldwide.pdf (accessed July 27, 2013).

20. "Expanding Access to Medical Abortion in Developing Countries," World Health Organization, http://www.who.int/reproductivehealth/topics/unsafe_abortion/en/index.html; also see http://www.who.int/reproductivehealth/topics/unsafe_abortion/magnitude/en/index.html (accessed July 21, 2016).

21. Frank Langfitt, "After a Forced Abortion, a Roaring Debate in China," NPR's *All Things Considered*, July 5, 2012, http://www.npr.org/2012/07/05/156211106/after-a-forced-abortion-a-roaring-debate-in-china (accessed February 15, 2013).

22. Wei Xing Zhu, Li Lu, and Therese Hesketh, "China's Excess Males, Sex Selective Abortion, and One Child Policy: Analysis of Data from 2005 National Intercensus Survey," *British Medical Journal* (April 9, 2009), p. 388, http://dx.doi.org/10.1136/bmj.b1211 (accessed February 15, 2013).

23. Stanley K. Henshaw, Sushelela Singh, and Taylor Haas, "Recent Trends in Abortion Rates Worldwide," *Family Planning Perspectives* 25, No. 1 (March 1999).

24. Sneha Barol, "A Problem-and-Solution Mismatch: Son Preference and Sex-Selective Abortion Bans," *Guttmacher Policy Review* 15, No. 2 (Spring 2012), http://www.guttmacher.org/pubs/gpr/15/2/gpr150218.html (accessed February 15, 2013).

25. Rowena Mason, "The Abortion of Unwanted Girls Taking Place in the UK," *Telegraph*, January 10, 2013, http://www.telegraph.co.uk/news/uknews/crime/9794577/The-abortion-of-unwanted-girls-taking-place-in-the-UK.html (accessed February 15, 2013).

26. Ed O'Keefe, "Bill Banning 'Sex-Selective Abortions' Fails in the House," *Washington Post*, May 31, 2012, http://www.washingtonpost.com/blogs/2chambers/post/bill-banning-sex-selective-abortions-fails-in-the-house/2012/05/31/gJQAgCYn4U_blog.html (accessed February 15, 2013).

27. *Replacing Myths with Facts: Sex Selective Abortion Laws in the United States* (University of Chicago Law School, 2014), https://napawf.org/wp-content/uploads/2014/06/Replacing-Myths-with-Facts-final.pdf (accessed February 24, 2016). And also "Abortion Bans in Cases of Sex or Race Selection or Genetic Anomaly" (February 1, 2016), http://www.guttmacher.org/statecenter/spibs/spib_SRSGAAB.pdf (accessed February 24, 2016).

28. See John Noonan, *The Morality of Abortion* (Cambridge, MA: Harvard University Press, 1970), p. 18ff.

29. Associate Justice Harry A. Blackmun, majority opinion in Roe v. Wade, 410 U.S. 113 (1973), footnote 22.

30. Dorothy E. McBride, *Abortion in the United States: A Reference Book* (Santa Barbara, CA: ABC-CLIO, 2008), p. 7.

31. "Historical Attitudes to Abortion," BBC Ethics Guide, http://www.bbc.co.uk/ethics/abortion/legal/history_1.shtml (accessed July 21, 2016).

32. Associate Justice Harry A. Blackmun, majority opinion in *Roe v. Wade*, 410 U.S. 113 (1973).

33. See comments about this interpretation in Ronald Dworkin, "Feminists and Abortion," *New York Review of Books*, No. 11 (June 10, 1993), pp. 27–29.

34. Blackmun, *Roe v. Wade*.

35. Justices O'Connor, Kennedy, and Souter, majority opinion in Planned Parenthood of Southeastern *Pennsylvania v. Casey*, 505 U.S. 833 (1992).

36. *Gonzalez v. Carhart*, 550 U.S. 124 (2007).

37. David Stout, "Supreme Court Upholds Ban on Abortion Procedure," *New York Times*, April 18, 2007, http://www.nytimes.com/2007/04/18/us/18cnd-scotus.html?_r=0 (accessed July 21, 2016).

38. *Planned Parenthood Assn. v. Ashcroft*, 462 U.S. 476 (1983).

39. *New York Times*, April 14, 2010, p. A15.

40. Kathy Lohr, "Virginia Governor Backs Down from Ultrasound Bill," NPR's *All Things Considered*, February 23, 2012, http://www.npr.org/2012/02/23/147297375/virginia-governor-backs-down-from-ultrasound-bill (accessed April 4, 2013).

41. "Ongoing Study Shows Ultrasounds Do Not Have Direct Impact on Abortion Decision," *American Independent*, February 6, 2012, http://americanindependent.com/210411/ongoing-study-shows-ultrasounds-do-not-have-direct-impact-on-abortion-decision (accessed March 8, 2013).

42. WIS. STAT. § 48.193 (2003); see Erin N. Linder, "Punishing Prenatal Alcohol Abuse: The Problems Inherent in Utilizing Civil Commitment to Address Addiction," *University of Illinois Law Review* 2005, No. 3.

43. "Four Years Later, Slain Abortion Doctor's Aide Steps into the Void," *New York Times*, February 13, 2013, http://www.nytimes.com/2013/02/14/us/kansas-abortion-practice-set-to-replace-tiller-clinic.html (accessed February 15, 2013).

44. "Abortion Clinics Are Closing at Record Pace" *Bloomberg*, February 24, 2016, http://www.bloomberg.com/news/articles/2016-02-24/abortion-clinics-are-closing-at-a-record-pace (accessed February 24, 2016).

45. Judith Jarvis Thomson, "A Defense of Abortion," *Philosophy and Public Affairs* 1, No. 1 (Fall 1971), pp. 47–66.

46. Note that if the fetus had no right to life, then this would not automatically make abortion problem free. See the comments in the last paragraph under "Method II."

47. In the prescientific era, many people held that the egg provided the entire substance and the sperm only gave it a charge or impetus to grow, or that the sperm was "the little man" and only needed a place to grow and obtain nourishment, which the egg provided. We now know about the contribution of both sperm and ovum to the zygote.

48. This issue has recently arisen with developments in stem cell research and cloning.

49. Sheryl Gay Stolberg, "Definition of Fetal Viability Is Focus of Debate in Senate," *New York Times*, May 15, 1997, p. A13.

50. Ibid.

51. Compare this discussion with similar discussions in Chapters 16 and 17 on the environment and animal rights. In particular, note the possible distinction between having moral value and having rights.

52. Don Marquis, "Why Abortion Is Immoral," *Journal of Philosophy* 86, No. 4 (1989), p. 191.

53. Ibid., p. 192.

54. This is taken from Michael Tooley's "Abortion and Infanticide," *Philosophy and Public Affairs* 2, No. 1 (1972), pp. 37–65.

55. Ibid., p. 62.

56. Mary Anne Warren in "On the Moral and Legal Status of Abortion," *Monist* 57, No. 1 (January 1973), pp. 43–61.

57. See the summary of these views in Dworkin, "Feminists and Abortion," op. cit.

58. Catharine A. MacKinnon, *Women's Lives—Men's Laws* (Cambridge, MA: Harvard University Press, 2005), p. 140.

59. See Rosalind Hursthouse, "Virtue Theory and Abortion," *Philosophy and Public Affairs* 20, No. 3 (1991).

READING

A Defense of Abortion

JUDITH JARVIS THOMSON

MindTap°   For more chapter resources and activities, go to MindTap.

Study Questions

As you read the excerpt, please consider the following questions:

1. Why does Thomson suggest that abortion is not murder?
2. Why does Thomson say that "a sick and desperately frightened fourteen-year-old schoolgirl, pregnant due to rape, may of course choose abortion"?
3. What is the moral difference between a woman's right to end her pregnancy and a woman's desire to secure the death of her fetus?

If directly killing an innocent person is murder, and thus is impermissible, then the mother's directly killing the innocent person inside her is murder, and thus is impermissible. But it cannot seriously be thought to be murder if the mother performs an abortion on herself to save her life. It cannot seriously be said that she *must* refrain, that she *must* sit passively by and wait for her death....

Nobody is morally *required* to make large sacrifices, of health, of all other interests and concerns, of all other duties and commitments, for nine years, or even for nine months, in order to keep another person alive....

If a set of parents do not try to prevent pregnancy, do not obtain an abortion, but rather take it home with them, then they have assumed responsibility for it, they have given it rights, and they cannot *now* withdraw support from it at the cost of its life because they now find it difficult to go on providing for it. But if they have taken all reasonable precautions against having a child, they do not simply by virtue of their biological relationship to the child who comes into existence have a special responsibility for it. They may wish to assume responsibility for it, or they may not wish to. And I am suggesting that if assuming responsibility for it would require large sacrifices, then they may refuse.... While I do argue that abortion is not impermissible, I do not argue that it is always permissible. There may well be cases in which carrying the child to term required only Minimally Decent Samaritanism of the mother, and this is a standard we must not fall below. I am inclined to think it a merit of my account precisely that it does *not* give a general yes or a general no. It allows for and supports our sense that, for example, a sick and desperately frightened fourteen-year-old schoolgirl, pregnant due to rape, may *of course* choose abortion, and that any law which rules this out is an insane law. And it also allows for and supports our sense that in other cases resort to abortion is even positively indecent. It would be indecent in the woman to request an abortion, and indecent in a doctor to perform it, if she is in her seventh month, and wants the abortion just to avoid the nuisance of postponing a trip abroad....

Secondly, while I am arguing for the permissibility of abortion in some cases, I am not arguing for the right to secure the death of the unborn child. It is easy to confuse these two things in that up to a certain point in the life of the fetus it is not able to survive outside the mother's body; hence removing it from her body guarantees its death. But they are importantly different....

Judith Jarvis Thomson, "A Defense of Abortion," *Philosophy & Public Affairs* 1, No. 1 (Fall 1971), pp. 47–66. Copyright © 1971 Wiley Periodicals, Inc.

READING

Why Abortion Is Immoral

DON MARQUIS

MindTap® For more chapter resources and activities, go to MindTap.

Study Questions

As you read the excerpt, please consider the following questions:
1. What is it that makes killing a person wrong?
2. Why does Marquis believe that this also makes killing a fetus wrong?
3. Why does it not follow, according to Marquis, that contraception is wrong?

The view that abortion is, with rare exceptions, seriously immoral has received little support in the recent philosophical literature. No doubt most philosophers affiliated with secular institutions of higher education believe that the anti abortion position is either a symptom of irrational religious dogma or a conclusion generated by seriously confused philosophical argument. The purpose of this essay is to undermine this general belief. This essay sets out an argument that purports to show, as well as any argument in ethics can show, that abortion is, except possibly in rare cases, seriously immoral, that it is in the same moral category as killing an innocent adult human being.

The argument is based on a major assumption. Many of the most insightful and careful writers on the ethics of abortion—such as Joel Feinberg, Michael Tooley, Mary Anne Warren, H. Tristram Engelhardt, Jr., L. W. Sumner, John T. Noonan, Jr., and Philip Devine[1]—believe that whether or not abortion is morally permissible stands or falls on whether or not a fetus is the sort of being whose life it is seriously wrong to end. The argument of this essay will assume, but not argue, that they are correct.

Also, this essay will neglect issues of great importance to a complete ethics of abortion. Some anti abortionists will allow that certain abortions, such as abortion before implantation or abortion when the life of a woman is threatened by a pregnancy or abortion after rape, may be morally permissible. This essay will not explore the casuistry of these hard cases. The purpose of this essay is to develop a general argument for the claim that the overwhelming majority of deliberate abortions are seriously immoral.

I

A sketch of standard anti abortion and pro choice arguments exhibits how those arguments possess certain symmetries that explain why partisans of those positions are so convinced of the correctness of their own positions, why they are not successful in convincing their opponents, and why, to others, this issue seems to be unresolvable. An analysis of the nature of this standoff suggests a strategy for surmounting it.

Consider the way a typical anti abortionist argues. She will argue or assert that life is present from the moment of conception or that fetuses look like babies or that fetuses possess a characteristic such as a genetic code that is both necessary and sufficient for being human. Anti abortionists seem to believe that: (1) the truth of all of these claims is quite obvious, and (2) establishing any of these claims is sufficient to show that abortion is morally akin to murder.

A standard pro choice strategy exhibits similarities. The pro choicer will argue or assert that fetuses are not persons or that fetuses are not rational agents or that fetuses are not social beings. Pro choicers seem to believe that: (1) the truth of any of these claims is quite obvious, and (2) establishing any of these claims is sufficient to show that an abortion is not a wrongful killing.

In fact, both the pro choice and the anti abortion claims do seem to be true, although the "it looks like a baby" claim is more difficult to establish the earlier the pregnancy. We seem to have a standoff. How can it be resolved?

As everyone who has taken a bit of logic knows, if any of these arguments concerning abortion is a good argument, it requires not only some claim characterizing fetuses, but also some general moral principle that ties a characteristic of fetuses to having or not having the right to life or to some other moral characteristic that will generate the obligation or the lack of obligation not to end the life of a fetus. Accordingly, the arguments of the anti abortionist and the pro choicer need a bit of filling in to be regarded as adequate.

Note what each partisan will say. The anti abortionist will claim that her position is supported by such generally accepted moral principles as "It is always prima facie seriously wrong to take a human life" or "It is always prima facie seriously wrong to end the life of a baby." Since these are generally accepted moral principles, her position is certainly not obviously wrong. The pro choicer will claim that

Don Marquis, "Why Abortion is Immoral," *The Journal of Philosophy*, vol. LXXXVI, no. 4 (April 1989), pp. 183–195, 200–202. Reprinted by permission from the *Journal of Philosophy*.

her position is supported by such plausible moral principles as "Being a person is what gives an individual intrinsic moral worth" or "It is only seriously prima facie wrong to take the life of a member of the human community." Since these are generally accepted moral principles, the pro choice position is certainly not obviously wrong. Unfortunately, we have again arrived at a standoff.

Now, how might one deal with this standoff? The standard approach is to try to show how the moral principles of one's opponent lose their plausibility under analysis. It is easy to see how this is possible. On the one hand, the anti abortionist will defend a moral principle concerning the wrongness of killing which tends to be broad in scope in order that even fetuses at an early stage of pregnancy will fall under it. The problem with broad principles is that they often embrace too much. In this particular instance, the principle "It is always prima facie wrong to take a human life" seems to entail that it is wrong to end the existence of a living human cancer-cell culture, on the grounds that the culture is both living and human. Therefore, it seems that the anti abortionist's favored principle is too broad.

On the other hand, the pro choicer wants to find a moral principle concerning the wrongness of killing which tends to be narrow in scope in order that fetuses will *not* fall under it. The problem with narrow principles is that they often do not embrace enough. Hence, the needed principles such as "It is prima facie seriously wrong to kill only persons" or "It is prima facie wrong to kill only rational agents" do not explain why it is wrong to kill infants or young children or the severely retarded or even perhaps the severely mentally ill. Therefore, we seem again to have a standoff. The anti abortionist charges, not unreasonably, that pro choice principles concerning killing are too narrow to be acceptable; the pro choicer charges, not unreasonably, that anti abortionist principles concerning killing are too broad to be acceptable.

Attempts by both sides to patch up the difficulties in their positions run into further difficulties. The anti abortionist will try to remove the problem in her position by reformulating her principle concerning killing in terms of human beings. Now we end up with: "It is always prima facie seriously wrong to end the life of a human being." This principle has the advantage of avoiding the problem of the human cancer-cell culture counterexample. But this advantage is purchased at a high price. For although it is clear that a fetus is both human and alive, it is not at all clear that a fetus is a human *being*. There is at least something to be said for the view that something becomes a human being only after a process of development, and that therefore first trimester fetuses and perhaps all fetuses are not yet human beings. Hence, the anti abortionist, by this move, has merely exchanged one problem for another.[2]

The pro choicer fares no better. She may attempt to find reasons why killing infants, young children, and the severely retarded is wrong which are independent of her major principle that is supposed to explain the wrongness of taking human life, but which will not also make abortion immoral. This is no easy task. Appeals to social utility will seem satisfactory only to those who resolve not to think of the enormous difficulties with a utilitarian account of the wrongness of killing and the significant social costs of preserving the lives of the unproductive.[3] A pro choice strategy that extends the definition of "person" to infants or even to young children seems just as arbitrary as an anti abortion strategy that extends the definition of "human being" to fetuses. Again, we find symmetries in the two positions and we arrive at a standoff.

There are even further problems that reflect symmetries in the two positions. In addition to counterexample problems, or the arbitrary application problems that can be exchanged for them, the standard anti abortionist principle "It is prima facie seriously wrong to kill a human being," or one of its variants, can be objected to on the grounds of ambiguity. If "human being" is taken to be a *biological* category, then the anti abortionist is left with the problem of explaining why a merely biological category should make a moral difference. Why, it is asked, is it any more reasonable to base a moral conclusion on the number of chromosomes in one's cells than on the color of one's skin?[4] If "human being," on the other hand, is taken to be a *moral* category, then the claim that a fetus is a human being cannot be taken to be a premise in the anti abortion argument, for it is precisely what needs to be established. Hence, either the anti abortionist's main category is a morally irrelevant, merely biological category, or it is of no use to the anti abortionist in establishing (noncircularly, of course) that abortion is wrong.

Although this problem with the anti abortionist position is often noticed, it is less often noticed that the pro choice position suffers from an analogous problem. The principle "Only persons have the right to life" also suffers from an ambiguity. The term "person" is typically defined in terms of psychological characteristics, although there will certainly be disagreement concerning which characteristics are most important. Supposing that this matter can be settled, the pro choicer is left with the problem of explaining why *psychological* characteristics should make a *moral* difference. If the pro choicer should attempt to deal with this problem by claiming that an explanation is not necessary, that in fact we do treat such a cluster of psychological properties as having moral significance, the sharp-witted anti abortionist should have a ready response. We do treat being both living and human as having moral significance. If it is legitimate for the pro choicer to demand that the anti abortionist provide an explanation of the connection between the biological character of being a human being and the wrongness of being killed (even though people accept this connection), then it is legitimate for the anti abortionist to demand that the pro choicer provide an explanation of the connection between psychological criteria for being a person and the wrongness of being killed (even though that connection is accepted).[5]

Feinberg has attempted to meet this objection (he calls psychological personhood "commonsense personhood"):

> The characteristics that confer commonsense personhood are not arbitrary bases for rights and duties, such as race, sex or species membership; rather they are traits that make sense out of rights and duties and without which those moral attributes would have no point or function. It is because people are

conscious; have a sense of their personal identities; have plans, goals, and projects; experience emotions; are liable to pains, anxieties, and frustrations; can reason and bargain, and so on—it is because of these attributes that people have values and interests, desires and expectations of their own, including a stake in their own futures, and a personal well-being of a sort we cannot ascribe to unconscious or nonrational beings. Because of their developed capacities they can assume duties and responsibilities and can have and make claims on one another. Only because of their sense of self, their life plans, their value hierarchies, and their stakes in their own futures can they be ascribed fundamental rights. There is nothing arbitrary about these linkages (op. cit., p. 270).

The plausible aspects of this attempt should not be taken to obscure its implausible features. There is a great deal to be said for the view that being a psychological person under some description is a necessary condition for having duties. One cannot have a duty unless one is capable of behaving morally, and a being's capability of behaving morally will require having a certain psychology. It is far from obvious, however, that having rights entails consciousness or rationality, as Feinberg suggests. We speak of the rights of the severely retarded or the severely mentally ill, yet some of these persons are not rational. We speak of the rights of the temporarily unconscious. The New Jersey Supreme Court based their decision in the Quinlan case on Karen Ann Quinlan's right to privacy, and she was known to be permanently unconscious at that time. Hence, Feinberg's claim that having rights entails being conscious is, on its face, obviously false.

Of course, it might not make sense to attribute rights to a being that would never in its natural history have certain psychological traits. This modest connection between psychological personhood and moral personhood will create a place for Karen Ann Quinlan and the temporarily unconscious. But then it makes a place for fetuses also. Hence, it does not serve Feinberg's pro choice purposes. Accordingly, it seems that the pro choicer will have as much difficulty bridging the gap between psychological personhood and personhood in the moral sense as the anti abortionist has bridging the gap between being a biological human being and being a human being in the moral sense.

Furthermore, the pro choicer cannot any more escape her problem by making person a purely moral category than the anti abortionist could escape by the analogous move. For if person is a moral category, then the pro choicer is left without the resources for establishing (noncircularly, of course) the claim that a fetus is not a person, which is an essential premise in her argument. Again, we have both a symmetry and a standoff between pro choice and anti abortion views.

Passions in the abortion debate run high. There are both plausibilities and difficulties with the standard positions. Accordingly, it is hardly surprising that partisans of either side embrace with fervor the moral generalizations that support the conclusions they preanalytically favor, and reject with disdain the moral generalizations of their opponents as being subject to inescapable difficulties. It is easy to believe that the counterexamples to one's own moral principles are merely temporary difficulties that will dissolve in the wake of further philosophical research, and that the counterexamples to the principles of one's opponents are as straightforward as the contradiction between A and O propositions in traditional logic. This might suggest to an impartial observer (if there are any) that the abortion issue is unresolvable.

There is a way out of this apparent dialectical quandary. The moral generalizations of both sides are not quite correct. The generalizations hold for the most part, for the usual cases. This suggests that they are all *accidental* generalizations, that the moral claims made by those on both sides of the dispute do not touch on the *essence* of the matter.

This use of the distinction between essence and accident is not meant to invoke obscure metaphysical categories. Rather, it is intended to reflect the rather atheoretical nature of the abortion discussion. If the generalization a partisan in the abortion dispute adopts were derived from the reason why ending the life of a human being is wrong, then there could not be exceptions to that generalization unless some special case obtains in which there are even

more powerful countervailing reasons. Such generalizations would not be merely accidental generalizations; they would point to, or be based upon, the essence of the wrongness of killing, what it is that makes killing wrong. All this suggests that a necessary condition of resolving the abortion controversy is a more theoretical account of the wrongness of killing. After all, if we merely believe, but do not understand, why killing adult human beings such as ourselves is wrong, how could we conceivably show that abortion is either immoral or permissible?

II

In order to develop such an account, we can start from the following unproblematic assumption concerning our own case; it is wrong to kill *us*. Why is it wrong? Some answers can be easily eliminated. It might be said that what makes killing us wrong is that a killing brutalizes the one who kills. But the brutalization consists of being inured to the performance of an act that is hideously immoral; hence, the brutalization does not explain the immorality. It might be said that what makes killing us wrong is the great loss others would experience due to our absence. Although such hubris is understandable, such an explanation does not account for the wrongness of killing hermits, or those whose lives are relatively independent and whose friends find it easy to make new friends.

A more obvious answer is better. What primarily makes killing wrong is neither its effect on the murderer nor its effect on the victim's friends and relatives, but its effect on the victim. The loss of one's life is one of the greatest losses one can suffer. The loss of one's life deprives one of all the experiences, activities, projects, and enjoyments that would otherwise have constituted one's future. Therefore, killing someone is wrong, primarily because the killing inflicts (one of) the greatest possible losses on the victim. To describe this as the loss of life can be misleading, however. The change in my biological state does not by itself make killing me wrong. The effect of the loss of my biological life is the loss to me of all those activities, projects, experiences, and enjoyments which would otherwise have constituted my future personal life. These activities, projects, experiences, and enjoyments are either valuable for their own sakes or are means to something else that is valuable for its own sake. Some parts of my future are not valued by me now, but will come to be valued by me as I grow older and as my values and capacities change. When I am killed, I am deprived both of what I now value which would have been part of my future personal life, but also what I would come to value. Therefore, when I die, I am deprived of all of the value of my future. Inflicting this loss on me is ultimately what makes killing me wrong. This being the case, it would seem that what makes killing any adult human being prima facie seriously wrong is the loss of his or her future.[6]

How should this rudimentary theory of the wrongness of killing be evaluated? It cannot be faulted for deriving an "ought" from an "is," for it does not. The analysis assumes that killing me (or you, reader) is prima facie seriously wrong. The point of the analysis is to establish which natural property ultimately explains the wrongness of the killing, given that it is wrong. A natural property will ultimately explain the wrongness of killing, only if: (1) the explanation fits with our intuitions about the matter, and (2) there is no other natural property that provides the basis for a better explanation of the wrongness of killing. This analysis rests on the intuition that what makes killing a particular human or animal wrong is what it does to that particular human or animal. What makes killing wrong is some natural effect or other of the killing. Some would deny this. For instance, a divine-command theorist in ethics would deny it. Surely this denial is, however, one of those features of divine-command theory which renders it so implausible.

The claim that what makes killing wrong is the loss of the victim's future is directly supported by two considerations. In the first place, this theory explains why we regard killing as one of the worst of crimes. Killing is especially wrong, because it deprives the victim of more than perhaps any other crime. In the second place, people with AIDS or cancer who know they are dying believe, of course, that dying is a very bad thing for them. They believe that the loss of a future to them that they would otherwise have experienced is what makes their premature death a very bad thing for them. A better theory of the wrongness of killing would require a different natural property associated with killing which better fits with the attitudes of the dying. What could it be?

The view that what makes killing wrong is the loss to the victim of the value of the victim's future gains additional support when some of its implications are examined. In the first place, it is incompatible with the view that it is wrong to kill only beings who are biologically human. It is possible that there exists a different species from another planet whose members have a future like ours. Since having a future like that is what makes killing someone wrong, this theory entails that it would be wrong to kill members of such a species. Hence, this theory is opposed to the claim that only life that is biologically human has great moral worth, a claim which many anti abortionists have seemed to adopt. This opposition, which this theory has in common with personhood theories, seems to be a merit of the theory.

In the second place, the claim that the loss of one's future is the wrong-making feature of one's being killed entails the possibility that the futures of some actual nonhuman mammals on our own planet are sufficiently like ours that it is seriously wrong to kill them also. Whether some animals do have the same right to life as human beings depends on adding to the account of just what it is about my future or the futures of other adult human beings which makes it wrong to kill us. No such additional account will be offered in this essay. Undoubtedly, the provision of such an account would be a very difficult matter. Undoubtedly, any such account would be quite controversial. Hence, it surely should not reflect badly on this sketch of an elementary theory of the wrongness of killing that it is indeterminate with respect to some very difficult issues regarding animal rights.

In the third place, the claim that the loss of one's future is the wrong-making feature of one's being killed does not entail, as sanctity-of-human-life theories do, that active euthanasia is wrong. Persons who are severely and incurably ill, who face a future of pain and despair, and who wish to die will not have suffered a loss if they are killed. It is, strictly speaking, the value of a human's future which makes killing wrong in this theory. This being so, killing does not necessarily wrong some persons who are sick and dying. Of course, there may be other reasons for a prohibition of active euthanasia, but that is another matter. Sanctity-of-human-life theories seem to hold that active euthanasia is seriously wrong even in an individual case where there seems to be good reason for it independently of public policy considerations. This consequence is most implausible, and it is a plus for the claim that the loss of a future of value is what makes killing wrong that it does not share this consequence.

In the fourth place, the account of the wrongness of killing defended in this essay does straightforwardly entail that it is prima facie seriously wrong to kill children and infants, for we do presume that they have futures of value. Since we do believe that it is wrong to kill defenseless little babies, it is important that a theory of the wrongness of killing easily account for this. Personhood theories of the wrongness of killing, on the other hand, cannot straightforwardly account for the wrongness of killing infants and young children.[7] Hence, such theories must add special ad hoc accounts of the wrongness of killing the young. The plausibility of such ad hoc theories seems to be a function of how desperately one wants such theories to work. The claim that the primary wrong-making feature of a killing is the loss to the victim of the value of its future accounts for the wrongness of killing young children and infants directly; it makes the wrongness of such acts as obvious as we actually think it is. This is a further merit of this theory. Accordingly, it seems that this value of a future-like-ours theory of the wrongness of killing shares strengths of both sanctity-of-life and personhood accounts while avoiding weaknesses of both. In addition, it meshes with a central intuition concerning what makes killing wrong.

The claim that the primary wrong-making feature of a killing is the loss to the victim of the value of

its future has obvious consequences for the ethics of abortion. The future of a standard fetus includes a set of experiences, projects, activities, and such which are identical with the futures of adult human beings and are identical with the futures of young children. Since the reason that is sufficient to explain why it is wrong to kill human beings after the time of birth is a reason that also applies to fetuses, it follows that abortion is prima facie seriously morally wrong.

This argument does not rely on the invalid inference that, since it is wrong to kill persons, it is wrong to kill potential persons also. The category that is morally central to this analysis is the category of having a valuable future like ours; it is not the category of personhood. The argument to the conclusion that abortion is prima facie seriously morally wrong proceeded independently of the notion of person or potential person or any equivalent. Someone may wish to start with this analysis in terms of the value of a human future, conclude that abortion is, except perhaps in rare circumstances, seriously morally wrong, infer that fetuses have the right to life, and then call fetuses "persons" as a result of their having the right to life. Clearly, in this case, the category of person is being used to state the *conclusion* of the analysis rather than to generate the *argument* of the analysis.

The structure of this anti abortion argument can be both illuminated and defended by comparing it to what appears to be the best argument for the wrongness of the wanton infliction of pain on animals. This latter argument is based on the assumption that it is prima facie wrong to inflict pain on me (or you, reader). What is the natural property associated with the infliction of pain which makes such infliction wrong? The obvious answer seems to be that the infliction of pain causes suffering and that suffering is a misfortune. The suffering caused by the infliction of pain is what makes the wanton infliction of pain on me wrong. The wanton infliction of pain on other adult humans causes suffering. The wanton infliction of pain on animals causes suffering. Since causing suffering is what makes the wanton infliction of pain wrong and since the wanton infliction of pain on animals causes suffering, it follows that the wanton infliction of pain on animals is wrong.

This argument for the wrongness of the wanton infliction of pain on animals shares a number of structural features with the argument for the serious prima facie wrongness of abortion. Both arguments start with an obvious assumption concerning what it is wrong to do to me (or you, reader). Both then look for the characteristic or the consequence of the wrong action which makes the action wrong. Both recognize that the wrong-making feature of these immoral actions is a property of actions sometimes directed at individuals other than postnatal human beings. If the structure of the argument for the wrongness of the wanton infliction of pain on animals is sound, then the structure of the argument for the prima facie serious wrongness of abortion is also sound, for the structure of the two arguments is the same. The structure common to both is the key to the explanation of how the wrongness of abortion can be demonstrated without recourse to the category of person. In neither argument is that category crucial.

This defense of an argument for the wrongness of abortion in terms of a structurally similar argument for the wrongness of the wanton infliction of pain on animals succeeds only if the account regarding animals is the correct account. Is it? In the first place, it seems plausible. In the second place, its major competition is Kant's account. Kant believed that we do not have direct duties to animals at all, because they are not persons. Hence, Kant had to explain and justify the wrongness of inflicting pain on animals on the grounds that "he who is hard in his dealings with animals becomes hard also in his dealing with men."[8] The problem with Kant's account is that there seems to be no reason for accepting this latter claim unless Kant's account is rejected. If the alternative to Kant's account is accepted, then it is easy to understand why someone who is indifferent to inflicting pain on animals is also indifferent to inflicting pain on humans, for one is indifferent to what makes inflicting pain wrong in both cases. But, if Kant's account is accepted, there is no intelligible reason why one

who is hard in his dealings with animals (or crabgrass or stones) should also be hard in his dealings with men. After all, men are persons: animals are no more persons than crabgrass or stones. Persons are Kant's crucial moral category. Why, in short, should a Kantian accept the basic claim in Kant's argument?

Hence, Kant's argument for the wrongness of inflicting pain on animals rests on a claim that, in a world of Kantian moral agents, is demonstrably false. Therefore, the alternative analysis, being more plausible anyway, should be accepted. Since this alternative analysis has the same structure as the anti abortion argument being defended here, we have further support for the argument for the immorality of abortion being defended in this essay.

Of course, this value of a future-like-ours argument, if sound, shows only that abortion is prima facie wrong, not that it is wrong in any and all circumstances. Since the loss of the future to a standard fetus, if killed, is, however, at least as great a loss as the loss of the future to a standard adult human being who is killed, abortion, like ordinary killing, could be justified only by the most compelling reasons. The loss of one's life is almost the greatest misfortune that can happen to one. Presumably abortion could be justified in some circumstances, only if the loss consequent on failing to abort would be at least as great. Accordingly, morally permissible abortions will be rare indeed unless, perhaps, they occur so early in pregnancy that a fetus is not yet definitely an individual. Hence, this argument should be taken as showing that abortion is presumptively very seriously wrong, where the presumption is very strong—as strong as the presumption that killing another adult human being is wrong. . . .

V

In this essay, it has been argued that the correct ethic of the wrongness of killing can be extended to fetal life and used to show that there is a strong presumption that any abortion is morally impermissible. If the ethic of killing adopted here entails, however, that contraception is also seriously immoral, then there would appear to be a difficulty with the analysis of this essay.

But this analysis does not entail that contraception is wrong. Of course, contraception prevents the actualization of a possible future of value. Hence, it follows from the claim that futures of value should be maximized that contraception is prima facie immoral. This obligation to maximize does not exist, however; furthermore, nothing in the ethics of killing in this paper entails that it does. The ethics of killing in this essay would entail that contraception is wrong only if something were denied a human future of value by contraception. Nothing at all is denied such a future by contraception, however.

Candidates for a subject of harm by contraception fall into four categories: (1) some sperm or other, (2) some ovum or other, (3) a sperm and an ovum separately, and (4) a sperm and an ovum together. Assigning the harm to some sperm is utterly arbitrary, for no reason can be given for making a sperm the subject of harm rather than an ovum. Assigning the harm to some ovum is utterly arbitrary, for no reason can be given for making an ovum the subject of harm rather than a sperm. One might attempt to avoid these problems by insisting that contraception deprives both the sperm and the ovum separately of a valuable future like ours. On this alternative, too many futures are lost. Contraception was supposed to be wrong, because it deprives us of one future of value, not two. One might attempt to avoid this problem by holding that contraception deprives the combination of sperm and ovum of a valuable future like ours. But here the definite article misleads. At the time of contraception, there are hundreds of millions of sperm, one (released) ovum and millions of possible combinations of all of these. There is no actual combination at all. Is the subject of the loss to be a merely possible combination? Which one? This alternative does not yield an actual subject of harm either. Accordingly, the immorality of contraception is not entailed by the loss of a future-like-ours argument simply because there is no non-arbitrarily identifiable subject of the loss in the case of contraception.

VI

The purpose of this essay has been to set out an argument for the serious presumptive wrongness of abortion subject to the assumption that the moral permissibility of abortion stands or falls on the moral status of the fetus. Since a fetus possesses a property, the possession of which in adult human beings is sufficient to make killing an adult human being wrong, abortion is wrong. This way of dealing with the problem of abortion seems superior to other approaches to the ethics of abortion, because it rests on an ethics of killing which is close to self-evident, because the crucial morally relevant property clearly applies to fetuses, and because the argument avoids the usual equivocations on "human life," "human being," or "person." The argument rests neither on religious claims nor on Papal dogma. It is not subject to the objection of "speciesism." Its soundness is compatible with the moral permissibility of euthanasia and contraception. It deals with our intuitions concerning young children.

Finally, this analysis can be viewed as resolving a standard problem—indeed, *the* standard problem—concerning the ethics of abortion. Clearly, it is wrong to kill adult human beings. Clearly, it is not wrong to end the life of some arbitrarily chosen single human cell. Fetuses seem to be like arbitrarily chosen human cells in some respects and like adult humans in other respects. The problem of the ethics of abortion is the problem of determining the fetal property that settles this moral controversy. The thesis of this essay is that the problem of the ethics of abortion, so understood, is solvable.

NOTES

1. Feinberg, "Abortion," in *Matters of Life and Death: New Introductory Essays in Moral Philosophy*, Tom Regan, ed. (New York: Random House, 1986), 256–93; Tooley, "Abortion and Infanticide," *Philosophy and Public Affairs*, II, 1 (1972):37–65, Tooley, *Abortion and Infanticide* (New York: Oxford, 1984); Warren, "On the Moral and Legal Status of Abortion," *The Monist*, LVII, 1 (1973): 43–61; Engelhardt, "The Ontology of Abortion,"

Ethics, LXXXIV, 3 (1974):217–234; Sumner, *Abortion and Moral Theory* (Princeton: University Press, 1981); Noonan, "An Almost Absolute Value in History," in *The Morality of Abortion: Legal and Historical Perspectives*, Noonan, ed. (Cambridge: Harvard, 1970); and Devine, *The Ethics of Homicide* (Ithaca: Cornell, 1978).

2. For interesting discussions of this issue, see Warren Quinn, "Abortion: Identity and Loss," *Philosophy and Public Affairs*, XIII, 1 (1984):24–54; and Lawrence C. Becker, "Human Being: The Boundaries of the Concept," *Philosophy and Public Affairs*, IV, 4 (1975):334–59.

3. For example, see my "Ethics and the Elderly: Some Problems," in Stuart Spicker, Kathleen Woodward, and David Van Tassel, eds., *Aging and the Elderly:*

Humanistic Perspectives in Gerontology (Atlantic Highlands, NJ: Humanities, 1978), 341–55.

4. See Warren, op. cit., and Tooley, "Abortion and Infanticide."

5. This seems to be the fatal flaw in Warren's treatment of this issue.

6. I have been most influenced on this matter by Jonathan Glover, *Causing Death and Saving Lives* (New York: Penguin, 1977), Chapter 3; and Robert Young, "What Is So Wrong with Killing People?" *Philosophy*, LIV, 210 (1979):515–28.

7. Feinberg, Tooley, Warren, and Engelhardt have all dealt with this problem.

8. "Duties to Animals and Spirits," in *Lectures on Ethics*, Louis Infeld, trans. (New York: Harper, 1963), 239.

READING

The Value of Choice and the Choice to Value: Expanding the Discussion About Fetal Life within Prochoice Advocacy

BERTHA ALVAREZ MANNINEN

MindTap® For more chapter resources and activities, go to MindTap.

Study Questions for Manninen

As you read the excerpt, please consider the following questions:

1. How does Manninen's account deal with the difference between the legality and morality of abortion as well as the difference between prochoice, antichoice, prolife, and proabortion positions?
2. How does Manninen explain the difference between rights-based discussions such as Thomson's and those that focus on virtues such as care and vices such as callousness?
3. What are the two ways that Manninen suggests we reduce the abortion rate; and how do those concerns relate to larger feminist and social justice concerns?

In 2005, prochoice advocate Frances Kissling, the former president of Catholics for a Free Choice, challenged prochoice advocates to begin viewing the fetus as a being with some degree of intrinsic worth. To refuse to do so, she argued, paints a picture of prochoice advocacy as hardened or callous toward fetal life.

> I am deeply struck by the number of thoughtful, progressive people who have been turned off to the prochoice movement by the lack of adequate

and clear expressions of respect for fetal life....There is a strong distaste of the prochoice community in many facets of society because of the inability or unwillingness to acknowledge one iota of value in fetal life. (Kissling 2005)

Kissling seems to conclude that there is something intrinsic about prochoice advocacy that results in a "hardening of the heart" in regard to fetal life, and her evidence for this is that many individuals, including those who are sympathetic to the view that women possess abortion rights, *perceive* prochoice advocates in this way. This conclusion, of course, does not follow—we cannot conclude that belief x is intrinsic to position y simply because many individuals believe that it is. However, Kissling's conclusion is one that is shared by many individuals, including many young women who make up the new generation of abortion rights supporters.

Consider the words of Heidi, a young woman who obtained an abortion and, while supporting abortion choice for other women, is hesitant to self-identify as a prochoice advocate:

> Heidi also feels alienation from reproductive rights activists, whom she feels treat abortion too casually. She says, "I find myself not being a great supporter of the pro-choice movement. When I ask myself why that is, since I believe in the right to choose, what comes back as my answer is that it is something you are killing." Heidi laments that so much of the pro-choice side "tries to pretend that's not true." (Kushner 1997, 148)

Even though Heidi shared the core belief of the prochoice movement that women have a right to decide whether they will continue a pregnancy, she did not want to be labeled "prochoice" because she did not want to be associated with views that she regarded as intrinsic to the position: that the taking of fetal life is of little or no consequence.

A recent article in *Newsweek* entitled "Remember Roe!" tells about how women of the post-*Roe* generation have become lax in defending abortion rights, mostly because they take them for granted. Young members of NARAL Pro-Choice America don't "view abortion as an imperiled right in need of defenders." Moreover, "young voters flat-out disapproved of a woman's abortion, called her actions immoral, yet maintained that the government had absolutely no right to intervene" (Kliff 2010). Another poll finds that although 52% of young

people agree that abortion should remain legal in all or most cases, "legalities aside, 59% believe abortion is morally wrong." One telling finding is that "[f]or millennials, three-quarters said they identified with the term prochoice, while 65% said they could also be described as pro-life" (Rovner 2011). In other words, the younger generation holds complex and nuanced views regarding abortion; although most of them support keeping abortion legal, they also recognize that there is a moral dimension to abortion that expands beyond the issue of legalities. According to one young prochoice woman: "I only get mad when [a friend] tries telling me, 'It is nothing, oh well, it is just an abortion.' It wasn't the abortion itself that seemed to trouble the woman; rather, it was her friend's nonchalance. 'Even if it was like nothing,' the woman told NARAL, 'it was something'" (Kliff 2010).

What we can conclude from all this is that a stereotype of prochoice advocacy exists that paints abortion rights supporters as callous toward fetal life and unwilling to acknowledge the moral ambiguities of abortion. Antichoice advocates have seized upon this stereotype, and have used it to advance their cause. As Kathleen McDonnell notes:

> Abortion rights, and, indeed, feminism itself had come to be identified in the popular mind with an anti-family, anti-child mentality that had little respect for traditional values and cultural traditions. The opponents of feminism and abortion attempted to capitalize on this: feminists, they said, see children as mere inconveniences, obstacles to career fulfillment; pro-abortionists, they said, have no respect for the value of life and, even worse, want to impose their lack of values on the rest of society. (McDonnell 1984, 68)

Francke's and Little's respective citations illustrate that this view of prochoice advocacy is indeed a stereotype—there are prochoice feminists, academics, and even women who themselves have obtained abortions who deeply grapple with the moral ambiguity of abortion. From where, then, does this pervasive stereotype come? To be sure, there are prochoice advocates who do not regard abortion as a moral issue, and who disagree that fetal life is valuable and worthy of some degree of protection. But given that there *is* disagreement among prochoice advocates concerning this issue, why isn't this disagreement more showcased, and why has the pendulum swung in favor of representing prochoice advocacy in the spirit of Warren, rather than in the spirit of Francke or Little? Much of it can be attributed to the pervasive distortion of the prochoice view from the rhetoric of some antichoice advocates themselves. But prochoice supporters are also to blame, for we have allowed this misrepresentation of our position to go largely unchecked.

Reading about the experiences of women who obtain abortions reveals that regarding the fetus as a subject of little value does not reflect the phenomenology of pregnancy or abortion for many women. Consider these two examples:

> The whole handling of the abortion issue is wrong. You don't toss [the fetus] in the garbage. I mean, I've had an abortion, it was an incredibly painful experience. I didn't toss it in the garbage. And I find it really distressing to hear it referred to in that way. (Cannold 1998, 36)

> I desperately wanted a feminist article, pamphlet, speech, *anything* that would let me have both the abortion and my own ambivalence....I wanted to *deal* with the moral balance sheet of abortion, not to have to deny that one existed for me. Instead people kept telling me I was misguided, brainwashed by the patriarchy. They patiently explained that the fetus was just a bunch of cells. (Van Gelder 1978, 66–67)

This last citation reveals a need many women have that it seems the prochoice community is failing to meet. When prochoice supporters dismiss fetal life as being no more valuable than a "clump of cells," we do a disservice to the many women who obtain abortions but who, nevertheless, feel quite strongly that there is a moral dimension to their action that they wish to openly discuss. Even in the immediate aftermath of an abortion, a woman can feel some degree of sadness. Bobbie Jeanne Kennedy, an abortion nurse, writes about dealing with the emotional reactions of postabortive women. She tells the story

of a woman who "reached out her beautifully delicate young hand, gently touched the cheek of her newly aborted tiny fetus and said 'I'm sorry, baby'" (Kennedy 1988, 1067). Another woman obtained an abortion after her fetus was diagnosed with a deformity: "The woman said: 'I don't want to deny that this baby existed.' She gave it a name, had a funeral for it, and buried it in the family plot alongside her grandmother" (1068). Discussing this moral dimension does not entail regretting the abortion, or even feeling that the choice to abort in a particular circumstance is wrong. Also, the reactions of the above-cited women should not be taken as evidence for what some antichoice advocates call "Post-Abortion Syndrome," a kind of posttraumatic stress disorder that they argue is intrinsic to abortion choice (see, for example, Reardon 1987). There is no evidence such a condition exists; although some women (but certainly not all) may feel sadness in the aftermath of an abortion, *emotions* of sadness are not equivalent to a clinical or pathological *disease*.[2] What these women pine for is acknowledgment of their emotions, and they desire to ground their abortion decision not via a dismissal of the worth of fetal life, but, rather, by acknowledging its value and still defending abortion rights through this lens. As is illustrated in "Remember *Roe*!" and in Heidi's comment, it is the perception of prochoice advocates as having "hardened hearts" that has resulted in some women turning their backs on the prochoice movement. Indeed, as a result of her conversation with the younger members of NARAL, pollster Anna Greenberg has concluded that the prochoice community needs to start "an open discussion about the moral, ethical, and emotional complexity of abortion that would be more likely to resonate with young Americans" (Kliff 2010).

Most antichoice advocates also hold a highly negative view of prochoice advocacy. Writing about the experiences and activities of antichoice advocates, Carol J. C. Maxwell reports the following words from an interviewee: "I think that we do not value people and we do not value ourselves....That's part of why we have all these women killing their kids" (Maxwell 2002, 141). Similarly, some maintain that women who abort must think it permissible to kill anyone who is unwanted (98). According to Faye Ginsburg in her book *Contested Lives,* antichoice women regard women who abort as callous, materialistic, and uncaring (Ginsburg 1998 185). Many antichoice supporters take these views and use them to gain political influence for restrictive abortion laws. For example, Kristi Burton, sponsor of 2008's Personhood Amendment in Colorado (which, had it passed, would have granted embryos and fetuses the legal status of persons from fertilization), argued in favor of passing the amendment by stating that abortion rights have resulted in the cheapening of the value of life, and that it is only through granting fetuses the status of persons that society can "restore the dignity and respect unborn children have lost" (Ertelt 2008). For all these reasons, in the general reluctance to openly discuss abortion as a hard moral question, or acknowledge the value of fetal life, the prochoice position has suffered. As McDonnell writes:

> the feminist tendency has been to sidestep the entire moral discussion of abortion, either because we didn't see it as relevant to our concerns or because, though we may have been uncomfortable with the "clump of tissue" argument, we couldn't see anything else that didn't pose a threat to our basic position that women must control their own bodies. Consequently, we have largely abdicated any role in the moral discussion of abortion, and Right-to-Life ideology has filled the vacuum. (McDonnell 1984, 47)

There are two interconnected reasons, then, why prochoice feminists should strive to move away from Warren-like views regarding the value of fetal life.[3] First, because many pregnant women *do* view fetal life as valuable, even though some may nevertheless opt for abortion, regarding fetal life in a disparaging manner is insensitive to their views and alienates them from the prochoice community. Second, the younger prochoice generation is hungry for a discussion of the moral complexities of abortion, one that includes a discussion of the moral value of the fetus that moves beyond regarding it as

mere "tissue." The prochoice community must work toward satiating this hunger.

MEETING KISSLING'S CHALLENGE

In this section I will outline three ways prochoice advocates can meet Kissling's challenge by doing more to acknowledge the moral complexities, and at times ambiguities, of abortion. Weaving these suggestions into prochoice ideology can help soften the view of prochoice advocacy as necessarily callous toward fetal life, and to respect the women who regard abortion as a choice they indeed ought to possess, but one that carries with it serious moral dimensions. This, in turn, will allow us to begin the conversation in which it seems the younger generation of prochoice supporters is eager to partake.

Abortion, Decency, and Virtue

In Judith Jarvis Thomson's "A Defense of Abortion," she argues that, in terms of maintaining a pro-abortion-rights stance, it matters not whether the fetus is regarded as a person with rights equal to that of any extra-uterine person. Because no person's right to life entails that another person can be compelled to use her body for continued sustenance, the fetus cannot be given this right over the woman either. Thomson's argument is regarded as a seminal defense of abortion rights, but it has also been met with much criticism (see, for example, Wilcox 1989; Beckwith 1992; and Kaczor 2011, among many others). Yet although she spends the bulk of her essay arguing in favor of abortion rights, there is one aspect of her argument that is often overlooked. Although she argues that abortions are never unjust, she does argue that there are some abortions that are *indecent.* Although she never defines what she means by an "indecent" abortion, she does give an example of what such an abortion would look like: "It would be indecent in the woman to request an abortion, and indecent in a doctor to perform it, if she is in her seventh month, and wants the abortion just to avoid the nuisance of postponing a trip abroad" (Thomson 1971, 65). She also lumps "indecency" together with other displays of nonvirtuous character traits, such as self-centeredness and callousness (61). Therefore, Thomson seems to be arguing that although a woman is always within her moral rights to obtain an abortion, some reasons for doing so do not reflect a good character.

Rosalind Hursthouse develops this position in her article "Virtue Theory and Abortion." She argues that, from a virtue ethics perspective, although it may be the case that women possess a right to abort, this does not exhaust the moral dimensions of the matter. According to Hursthouse, we must ask the further, complex, question: are women using their abortion rights *well*?

> [I]n exercising a moral right I can do something cruel or callous, or selfish, light-minded, self-righteous, stupid, inconsiderate, disloyal, dishonest—that is, act viciously. Love and friendship do not survive their parties' constantly insisting on their rights, nor do people live well when they think that getting what they have a right to is of preeminent importance; they harm others, and they harm themselves. (Hursthouse 1991, 235)

Hursthouse spends the rest of her article detailing the difference between a vicious and a nonvicious/virtuous abortion. Because of her adherence to virtue theory, this will be determined largely by whether the woman in question was manifesting a virtuous or vicious character when coming to her decision to abort. As an example of an abortion that would betray a less-than-virtuous character, Hursthouse cites aborting for the sake of avoiding one's responsibilities in exchange for "'having a good time,' or for the pursuit of some false vision of ideals of freedom or self-realization" (242). Hursthouse also offers a criticism of Warren's disparaging view of fetal life.

> The fact that the premature termination of a pregnancy is, in some sense, the cutting off of a new human life, and thereby, like the procreation of a new human life, connects with all our thoughts about human life and death, parenthood, and family relationships, must make it a serious matter. To disregard this fact about it, to think of abortion as nothing but the killing of something that does not matter, or as nothing but the exercise of some right or rights one has, or as the incidental means to some

> desirable states of affairs, is to do something callous and light-minded, the sort of thing that no virtuous or wise person would do. (237–38)

Yet she also argues that some abortions do not reflect a vicious character; that, indeed, some abortions can be obtained for reasons that manifest virtues such as responsibility and care.

> Consider, for instance, a woman who has already had several children and fears that to have another will seriously affect her capacity to be a good mother to the ones she has—she does not show a lack of appreciation of the intrinsic value of being a parent by opting for abortion. Nor does a woman who has been a good mother and is approaching the age at which she may be looking forward to being a good grandmother. Nor does a woman who discovers that her pregnancy may well kill her. Nor, necessarily, does a woman who has decided to lead a life centered around some other worthwhile activity or activities with which mother-hood would compete...(241)

Hursthouse is not arguing, then, that women should not have a right to an abortion. Rather, what she is maintaining is that we extend the conversation beyond the question of rights. With all our rights there are responsible and irresponsible, callous and caring, ways of exercising them. Although some prochoice advocates may recoil at the thought of subjecting the abortion right to this analysis, it seems that, in light of the abovementioned desire to have this conversation by prochoice supporters themselves, we have come to a point where it is essential to start doing so.

Leslie Cannold's research, featured in her book *The Abortion Myth*, illustrates that there are many prochoice women who already make judgments about particular abortion decisions in a manner similar to that of Hursthouse and Thomson.

> Almost all the women I interviewed saw the abortion issue as revolving around the pregnant woman's decision-making process. An abortion decision that did not reflect a woman's "feelings" and "love" for her could-be child and other significant people in her life, and that was not motivated by care and protective concern for all those she loves, was just plain wrong. (Cannold 1998, xix–xx)

In her interviews with the young women who support abortion choice, Cannold notes that they were eager to move beyond the discussion of abortion *qua* rights and more toward discussion of the morality of individual abortion choices; a "morally right" abortion is one that displays certain virtues: responsibility, caring, compassion, and respect for fetal life (17). As an illustration of this, Cannold asks many of the women to give their thoughts on what is known as "abortion doping": the rumored practice among olympian female runners to deliberately become pregnant in order to abort right before a competition; the added hormones produced by the recently terminated pregnancy are said to enhance performance. According to Cannold, the "vast majority of women found the idea of using pregnancy as a means to another end completely repugnant." one prochoice woman, Carey, chastised anyone who participated in abortion doping for failing to "'honor' pregnancy as 'the phenomenal creation of life'" (91). Another prochoice woman, Frances, maintained that what's wrong about abortion doping is that it leaves out "the 'emotional' and 'spiritual' aspects of the pregnancy..." (91). Notice that what is being judged is not the act of abortion itself, but rather the *motivations* for the abortion, or what *traits of character* were being expressed by women who engage in abortion doping. Whereas an abortion obtained for reasons having to do with caring for dependents, out of respect for the value of motherhood (and perhaps being honest about one's inability to fulfill the requirements of motherhood to a particular fetus at a particular time), and even out of love for the fetus, would be considered acceptable, aborting for reasons such as abortion doping, or for the sake of "having a good time" would be considered morally repugnant. These women never contested the *right* to an abortion, but the *reasons* for which one exercises that right can be subject to moral scrutiny.

From this we can conclude that the newer generation of prochoice women are already having these discussions among themselves, and that, in general, the prochoice community must keep up with these women by taking up the discussion as an important aspect of prochoice ideology. The new questions that need to be asked are: "Are there irresponsible pregnancies? Which reasons for having an abortion are bad ones? Even if women have a right to choose abortion, is it always right for them to do so? Why, after all this time, have these questions never been answered, and so rarely been asked?" (Cannold 1998, 17). Even NARAL President Nancy Keenan has noticed the need to engage in this discussion: "our reluctance to address the moral complexity of this debate is no longer serving our cause or our country well. In our silence, we have ceded moral ground" (Kliff 2010).

No doubt some antichoice advocates will attempt to usurp the discussion as evidence that even prochoice advocates recognize the moral wrongness of abortion, but this is why it is critical that prochoice advocates have this discussion on *their* own terms. Moreover, acknowledging that there is a moral dimension to abortion beyond the subject of rights recognizes what so many pro- and antichoice women already believe: that fetal life has value, and that, therefore, there has to be a framework for determining what constitutes a morally acceptable reason for taking that life. This, of course, needs much more development than I can provide here, but expanding upon Hursthouse's use of virtue ethics provides a promising way.

Caring for Women Who Grieve

As mentioned above, the evidence strongly suggests that there is no such thing as Post-Abortion Syndrome. Most women typically handle their decision to abort well; there is even evidence that some women who choose abortion see it as an overall positive life experience (see, for example, Zabin et al. 1989 and Warren et al. 2010). However, there are women who do experience postabortion maladjustment. Some risk factors include events that occur after the abortion, perceived lack of support for the abortion decision, ambivalence concerning the decision to abort, compromised coping capacities in general, quality of relationship with male partner, and feeling coerced into the abortion (see, for example, Adler et al. 1990; Major and Cozzarelli 1992; Major et al. 1997). Moreover, many women who experience psychiatric disorders after an abortion likely suffered from psychiatric disorders before the abortion as well (Major et al. 2008, 89). Consequently, it is "likely that psychological maladjustment occurring subsequent to an abortion frequently is misattributed to the abortion experience, whereas it may be more indicative of adjustment problems present prior to pregnancy" (Major and Cozzarelli 1992, 136).[4] However, this is not to say that there aren't women who feel some degree of sadness, sorrow, or feelings of loss after an abortion, for "[a] bortion is an experience often hallmarked by ambivalence, and a mix of positive and negative emotions is to be expected" (Major et al. 2008, 885).

Ambivalent postabortion feelings are sometimes not taken very seriously, even by members of the prochoice community. In her book, Cannold writes about the reaction of a prochoice colleague when she shared her research findings that many women who abort do indeed regard the fetus as a valuable entity worthy of respect: "When I pointed out to him how women's views and experiences repeatedly contradicted established moral thought on abortion he replied: 'Well, who cares what women think? That they think it doesn't make it right'" (Cannold 1998, xxxi). Consider Heather's experiences after her abortion; she writes that she felt "angry at the feminist movement, which I am whole-heartedly a part of. I didn't expect such an emotional experience. . . . I felt betrayed that abortion was made to look like an easy decision, and it wasn't for me. I had carefully weighed it all out. It was still the right decision at the time. But I still had to cry, to grieve the loss of this potential child, and the loss of my pregnant state" (Banoit 1983, 21). Another woman, Naomi, writes that "[t]he women I talked to weren't all that supportive of my feelings. In fact some of them were cruel, telling me not to be so upset. After all, I had chosen this" (20). Another woman is hesitant to express sadness over an abortion precisely because she fears being regarded as traitorous to the feminist movement: "[t]here seemed to be this unspoken rule that a good feminist isn't supposed to grieve" (McDonnell 1984, 34). When Ava Torre-Bueno, a head counselor at San Diego's Planned Parenthood

for twenty years, tried to get Planned Parenthood to help market her book *Peace After Abortion,* she was denounced by the director as being a "dupe of the antis" (Bazelon 2007). Torre-Bueno is an ardent prochoice advocate who firmly maintains that there is no such condition as Post-Abortion Syndrome (Torre-Bueno 1997, 78). Nevertheless, she legitimizes postabortion grief (4–7) and argues that the prochoice community should as well: "what you hear in the movement is 'Let's not make noise about this' and 'Most women are fine, I'm sure you will be too.' And that is unfair" (Bazelon 2007).

What can prochoice advocates do to support these women? One pivotal step is to ensure excellent pre-abortion counseling that would be sensitive to the abovementioned markers for postabortion maladjustment. One example of stellar pre-abortion counseling can be found in Dr. Susan Wicklund's book *This Common Secret,* which chronicles her decades-long experiences as an abortion provider. In her practice, she offers extensive pre-abortion counseling, where she insists on ensuring that the woman is acting out of her own volition. If there seems to be any hesitation regarding the extent to which a woman is certain of her decision to abort, Wicklund refuses to perform the procedure. In one example, she sends a prospective patient away twice because of her ambivalence, performing the abortion only after she is sure that her uncertainty has abated. The patient thanks Wicklund for her patience, admitting to her that "I'd have been a wreck if you had done the abortion the first time I came in" (Wicklund and Kesselheim 2007, 100).

Counseling sessions at Wicklund's practice often last hours before the abortion is performed to ensure the woman's emotional stability and, most important, to make certain that the decision to abort is entirely autonomous (Wicklund and Kesselheim 2007, 98). Her methods are the epitome of what prochoice philosophy ought to be. Despite what some antichoice advocates may believe, being prochoice is not about pushing or touting abortion as the best option for all women facing an unplanned pregnancy. Being prochoice is about three things: one, ensuring that women have access to safe and legal abortion *if they so choose*; two, ensuring that a woman's choice to abort really is a genuine choice of her own accord and free will; and three, respecting and supporting *any* choice that a woman makes in regard to her pregnancy, whether that be abortion, adoption, or parenting.

Excellent pre-abortion counseling must be accompanied by excellent postabortion counseling as well. Rachel Needle and Lenore Walker's book *Abortion Counseling* illustrates effective postabortion counseling techniques. one case study involves a woman, Laura, who felt sadness, loss, and guilt after her abortion. Her counselor writes:

> The most important thing for me to do when Laura came back to my office was to be empathic and allow her to express her feelings of guilt and sadness. I gave Laura permission to cry. We then began to explore her decision to have an abortion. Laura had a long list of reasons why having the abortion was the right thing for her to do. I reinforced her decision, by reflecting back her reasons that helped her make the decision to terminate the pregnancy Being empathic, listening, and helping Laura reflect on her decision proved helpful to her. (Needle and Walker 2008, 134)

Similar examples abound throughout the book, but the common denominator is that, in all cases where women express postabortion grief or sorrow, the therapist creates a "safe, compassionate, non-judgmental and trusting environment" (Needle and Walker 2008, 135) for the patient. One important thing to note is how the use of dismissive language to refer to the fetus may have an adverse affect on a woman's postabortion coping abilities. Torre-Bueno notes that one of her patients had lingering sorrow after an abortion partly because "[s]he couldn't grieve for them earlier because she had no one to support her in thinking of them as babies or children she had lost" (Torre-Bueno 1997, 23). The employees at another abortion clinic justify their use of the term "baby" to describe fetuses given similar concerns: "if the woman who is choosing abortion experiences this as a baby, how are we helping her deal with her decision if we tell her she is wrong?" (Ludlow 2008, 43).

Finally, postabortion counseling services should provide, for the women who desire them, postabortion rituals designed to help women deal with any negative feelings they may be experiencing. Torre-Bueno's book describes many different kinds of postabortion rituals, some as simple as "lighting candles on the anniversary of your abortion, or the date you would have delivered if you hadn't had the abortion" as a way of working through grief (Torre-Bueno 1997, 23). A prochoice grieving ritual should affirm the validity of a woman's decision to abort, both by acknowledging the reasons she aborted as well as the difficulties she may have experienced in reaching that decision. Moreover, the ritual should serve as an open forum to allow women to express any and all emotions that come with her abortion, from sorrow to relief or any feelings in between, and allow her an opportunity to say goodbye to the fetus.[5] Finally, the ritual should acknowledge that fetal death is of some consequence; that the very reason a ritual is desired, and that abortion can be painful, is because the destruction of fetal life is so very unlike the destruction of any other part of a woman's body. Prochoice advocates consistently (and correctly) argue that abortion is never an easy decision for women, that they typically make the decision carefully and responsibly. The likely reason for this is that women who abort typically understand the significance of their decision precisely because they understand that aborting a fetus is *not* like removing any other organic material from one's body. That is, women do not typically experience pregnancy and abortion as a form of "disembodiment, of separation of woman from fetus, of mother from child. These are the experiences that speak to the complexity of abortion as it is lived by women rather than as it is expounded by activists" (Ludlow 2008, 44).

Reducing Abortions

Although prochoice advocates need to continue fighting for a woman's right to safe and legal abortion, they should also make it an important part of prochoice advocacy that abortion is a right that is exercised with less frequency. Adopting this secondary goal helps to draw a distinction between being "prochoice" and being "proabortion"; a distinction that is often collapsed. The term "proabortion" denotes someone who encourages abortion, who celebrates abortion, who desires to see women choose abortion over other options. I know of no prochoice advocate who meets this definition.

There are, essentially, two ways to reduce abortion rates: one, via the prevention of unplanned pregnancies and two, via changing certain aspects of society so that women aren't coerced into choosing abortion because they fear having a child will force them to compromise other worthwhile goals. Achieving the first goal is rather straightforward— various studies have confirmed that an essential component to reducing unplanned pregnancies is to increase access to effective contraception, in addition to comprehensive sex education that ensures its correct and consistent use (see, for example, Bongaarts and Westoff 2000; Deschner and Cohen 2003). The second part of the abortion-reducing equation is more difficult to achieve. The reality facing single young women if they decide to bring an unplanned pregnancy to term is stark enough to understand why so many decide to abort. Women who live below the poverty line are about four times as likely to obtain an abortion when compared to women who live 300% above the poverty level (Jones, Darroch, and Henshaw 2002). On average, single women have higher poverty rates than single men, a phenomenon described by Diana Pearce as "the feminization of poverty" (Pearce 1978, 28–36; see also Casper, McLanahan, and Garfinkel 1994; Pressman 2002).

Children born to unwed teenage mothers, and the mothers themselves, face a host of difficulties, including an increased risk of failure in school, of poverty, and even of incidences of physical and mental illness (American Academy of Child and Adolescent Psychiatry 2004). One of the most prevalent reasons women choose abortion is financial difficulty (see, for example, Finer et al. 2005; Jones, Finer, and Singh 2008). This should concern prochoice advocates because aborting for such reasons compromises genuine choice. As McDonnell writes:

> If poverty is the reason she is terminating the pregnancy, if in fact she wants the child but cannot afford to have it, she is actually being coerced into an abortion. She does not, in fact, have a choice at all Feminists should make our position clear that when we talk about the "right to choose," we are not talking about women having abortions solely because they can't afford the child. Obviously, if we are going to work for choice in our reproductive lives, we also have to work to bring about the conditions—social, economic, cultural—that will make it a real possibility. (McDonnell 1984, 71)

Tellingly, the countries with the fewest incidences of abortion are the ones that have implemented comprehensive sex education programs and access to contraception, in addition to offering social support programs that provide a financial safety net for their citizens and residents. The Netherlands, for example, has one of the lowest rates of abortion in the world (7 for every 1,000 women). It also provides

> a range of what sociologists call "social" and what reproductive health advocates call "human" rights: the right to housing, healthcare, and a minimum income. Not only do such rights ensure access, if need be, to free contraceptive and abortion services, government support makes coming of age less perilous for both teenagers and parents. This might make the prospect of sex derailing a child less haunting. Ironically, the very lack of such rights and high rates of childhood poverty in the U.S. contribute to high rates of births among teenagers. Without adequate support systems or education and job opportunities, young people are simply more likely to start parenthood early in life. (Schalet 2010, 20)

There is evidence that providing assistance in the form of financial help, childcare services, and medical services results in decreased abortion rates (Reid 2010). In addition to providing postnatal medical support, which eases the economic hardship that comes with raising a child, easy access to medical care means easy access to effective contraception, which, in turn, reduces the need to seek abortions in the first place. Joseph Wright, writing on behalf of the group Catholics in Alliance for the Common Good, issued a report on the various studies that illustrate the socioeconomic factors that influence many women's decision to abort. Because he represents a Catholic organization, Wright makes it clear that he is in favor of restrictive abortion laws; however, he also argues that, if the goal is to reduce abortion, criminalizing it without offering concurrent social support will be ineffective. Rather, a genuine effort to reduce abortions would include implementing social policies that would offer prenatal and postnatal care, nutritional care for both mother and child, as well as pediatric care for the child, quality and affordable childcare so that young parents can either complete their education or obtain full-time work, and support for victims of sexual and physical abuse (Wright 2008).

In reference to the impact financial assistance has on the decision to abort, Wright notes that "[i]n states where families typically have higher incomes, there may be less economic pressure to end a pregnancy through abortion because the cost of caring for a child constitutes a smaller share of the typical family's income" (Wright 2008). In reference to the correlation between increased financial assistance to poor families and reduced abortion rates, Wright reports that an increase of $100 per person in the form of child-centered welfare "was correlated with a decrease in the abortion rate of about 20%...approximately 195,000 abortions per year" (Wright 2008). Increasing poverty by 3.8% increased the rate of abortion by 10% (90,000 more abortions per year). In terms of employment, increasing male employment by 4% is correlated with a 21% drop in abortion rates, whereas increasing female employment by 4% is correlated with a 17% increase in abortion rates. Wright argues this increase may be related to a lack of affordable and quality childcare (Wright 2008). What seems to be effective in reducing abortion rates is not simply criminalizing abortions (research illustrates that countries with restrictive abortion laws nevertheless have high incidences of abortion) (Deschner and Cohen 2003, 7). Rather, what is effective is support for families once the infant is born: commitment to nutritional and health care, quality childcare, and access to education or work programs designed to help single mothers overcome poverty.

For those whose political theory regards the state as having an important role in social welfare, advocating for this particular instance of social welfare should be regarded as a core component of their position on abortion.[6] In addition to fostering genuine choice, this helps meet Kissling's challenge because it illustrates that not even prochoice advocates see abortion as an innocuous action; rather, that they see it as a choice that, ideally, fewer and fewer women would have to make. Of course, this will not eliminate abortions—contraception will occasionally fail, even with perfect use, and some women simply do not want to be mothers, neither at the time of their unplanned pregnancy nor ever. Moreover, as long as sexual violence exists against women, abortion access is needed for the women who cannot bring themselves to gestate after being victimized.

WHY ENDORSING ABORTION RIGHTS AND FETAL VALUE ARE NOT MUTUALLY EXCLUSIVE

If successful, Thomson's argument illustrates that granting fetuses the status of persons is not sufficient for justifying a ban on abortion. Even if we grant the fetus all the rights of any extra-uterine person, this does not entail that abortions are impermissible, since no extra-uterine person has a right to use the body of another for sustenance. But Thomson's argument may serve a secondary function as well: if successful, it allows us to simultaneously express respect for fetal life while maintaining that women have a right to an abortion. As much as we can feel for the life of patients in need of organ transplants, we cannot force otherwise healthy persons to donate nonvital organs to save the sick. This does not mean that the lives of these patients have no value; rather what it means is that no matter how valuable they are, this value cannot be used as grounds to infringe upon the rights of other persons. Similarly, we can argue that being prochoice need not entail a wanton disregard of fetal life, but, rather, an acknowledgment that, like all persons, pregnant women have a right to decide if they want to use their bodies to sustain another.

Even if Thomson's argument is rejected, however, there are other avenues open to those who wish to simultaneously endorse abortion rights and respect for fetal life. As mentioned above, we can appeal to Hursthouse's use of virtue ethics to distinguish between supporting a right to x, without always endorsing how that right is exercised. Drawing this distinction allows one to argue that there are really *two* pertinent questions in abortion rights discourse: 1. Do women have a right to obtain abortions? 2. Are all exercises of this right virtuous ones? one can answer the first question in the affirmative, while admitting that in some cases the second can be answered in the negative. The reason we may sometimes frown upon certain justifications for obtaining an abortion is that it does involve the death of a being that has moral value, and the death of that being should be regarded with respect rather than flippancy (the latter, for example, is certainly the way the death of the fetus is regarded in cases of abortion doping).

A third way is to deny that human fetuses are persons who have interests, and therefore are not rights-bearers (so that killing them does not violate a right to life), but still maintain that they are valuable beings in virtue of their status as nascent human life. A way to understand this perspective is to consider our treatment of nonhuman animals; although they are not typically considered persons with a right to life (euthanizing an animal, for example, is not considered homicide), many would agree that they should be treated humanely and with respect in virtue of their sentient nature, and that they should not be unjustifiably or wantonly killed, even if, ultimately, their deaths are not tantamount to murder. Similarly, one can argue, because embryos and early fetuses lack certain morally relevant traits (for example, embryos and early fetuses are nonsentient and lack the capacity for conscious awareness), killing them is not tantamount to murder. Yet because they are living members of the species *Homo sapiens* and because they are potential persons, they possess morally relevant traits that render them worthy of some degree of respect, and their deaths

ought not to be taken lightly. This, for example, is the position of Ronald Dworkin, who spends most of his book *Life's Dominion* defending the right to an abortion on the grounds that early to mid-term fetuses lack interests due to their lack of sentience and consciousness. Nevertheless, he still regards an abortion as "a waste of a human life and is, therefore, in itself, a bad thing to happen, a shame" (Dworkin 1993, 84). In other words, one can simultaneously deny that fetuses possesses moral status and rights equal to those of persons (because they lack certain morally relevant traits), but also deny that they are completely devoid of value altogether (because they possess other morally relevant traits).

These are brief sketches of possible ways a prochoice advocate can simultaneously endorse abortion rights and embrace the value of fetal life. All deserve more elaboration than I can offer here, and none are devoid of difficulties. What I want to show is that we do not have to completely erase the fetus from moral consideration in order to defend abortion rights. The stereotype that prochoice advocacy inevitably entails the dehumanization of the fetus does not advance the prochoice position in the eyes of American society. Prochoice advocates must do more to combat this stereotype, and we must do more to broaden our arguments in favor of abortion rights in a way that is open to respecting fetal life. Given the constant onslaught of restrictive abortion laws, prochoice advocacy cannot afford to be reduced or erased from public discourse. Fetal life matters to many women, including women who abort and who defend the right to abortion. Prochoice discourse could become stronger if we "embraced discussion and images of the fetus and honest stories of the full range—from joy to grief—of women's relationships to their fetuses and emotional responses to abortion" (Ludlow 2008, 46).

To trivialize fetal life is to dismiss the phenomenology of pregnancy and abortions for many women. It is to be dismissive not just of nascent human life, but of the very women whose rights we fight so vehemently to defend and whose support we may stand to lose.

NOTES*

Many thanks to Nina Anton, Jackie Gately (Arizona State University), Kate Padgett Walsh (Iowa State University), and Michelle Beer (Florida International University), for their help with earlier drafts and incarnations of this paper. Also, thank you to Ann Cudd, Asia Ferrin, and to the anonymous *Hypatia* reviewers for all their comments, suggestions, and patience. Finally, as always, thank you to my husband Tuomas Manninen and our daughter Michelle for their support and love.

I would like to dedicate this paper to Professors Jack and Melissa Mulder (Hope College). Although we share differing views on abortion, they have helped me realize the need that exists for prochoice and prolife advocates to dialogue about the difficult issues that are present on both sides of the abortion debate, and the need that exists to take each other's concerns more seriously.

2. Some examples of studies that conclude there is no such condition as Post-Abortion Syndrome: Buckels 1982; Adler et al. 1990; Dagg 1991; Stotland 1991; Major and Cozzarelli 1992; Wilmouth et al. 1992; Gilchrist et al. 1995; Major et al. 2000; Needle and Walker 2008; Major et al. 2009; and Munk-Olsen et al. 2011.

3. It should be noted that Warren later softened her view regarding the moral status of the fetus, and was willing to grant it some degree of moral status after the fetus has acquired sentience. However, until her death she still held to a generally prochoice position. See Warren 1997 for her updated arguments.

4. One noteworthy consequence of these predictors of abortion maladjustment is that parental and spousal notification laws may serve to work against a woman's mental well-being. If a woman perceives her parents or partner as being supportive of her decision to abort, she will likely voluntarily inform them of her decision. A woman who typically refuses to reveal this information to her parents or partner does so because she likely feels they will be unsupportive, or that they will attempt to thwart the abortion. Consequently, laws that require her to do so will likely put her in a situation of perceived lack of support, which, in turn, may serve to retard her postabortion emotional adjustment.

5. I should emphasize here that I am not condemning women who fail to grieve after an abortion. Women who grieve should be allowed to do so, but that is not to say that women *must* grieve, or that they are morally remiss if they fail to do so. In 2000, a post-abortion telephone counseling service called "Exhale" opened its doors for any woman, partners, family, or friends who wish to talk about any difficulties they are facing after an abortion. Their mission statement reads: "Exhale creates a social climate where each person's unique experience with abortion is supported, respected and free from stigma." Although founded by women who have procured abortions, Exhale counselors do not describe themselves as either "prochoice" or "prolife," but, rather, "provoice." The popularity of Exhale points to a need for their services, and prochoice advocates should make it a priority, as an essential aspect of prochoice advocacy, to help meet the needs of these women.

6. Thank you to my anonymous *Hypatia* reviewer for this wording.

REFERENCES

Adler, Nancy, Henry P. David, Brenda Major, Susan Roth, Nancy Russo, and Gail Wyatt. 1990. Psychological responses after abortion. *Science* 248 (4951): 41–44.

American Academy of Child and Adolescent Psychiatry. 2004. When children have children. http://www.aacap.org/cs/root/facts_for_families/when_children_have_children (accessed November 12, 2011).

Banoit, Cecilia. 1983. The right to grieve: Two women talk about their abortions. *Health- sharing: A Woman's Health Quarterly* 5 (1): 19–26.

Bazelon, Emily. 2007. Is there a post-abortion syndrome? *The New York Times,* January 21. http://www.nytimes.com/2007/01/21/magazine/21abortion.t.html?_r=1&pagewanted=print (accessed November 12, 2011).

---

*The numbers correspond to the original excerpt.

Beckwith, Francis. 1992. Personal bodily rights, abortion, and unplugging the violinist. *International Philosophical Quarterly* 32 (1): 105–18.

Bongaarts, John, and Charles Westoff. 2000. The potential role of contraception in reducing abortion. *Studies in Family Planning* 31 (3): 193–202.

Buckels, Nancy. 1982. Abortion: A technique for working through grief. *Journal of American College Health Association* 30 (4): 18–19.

Cannold, Leslie. 1998. *The abortion myth: Feminism, morality, and the hard choices women make.* Hanover, N.H.: Wesleyan University Press.

Casper, Lynn, Sara S. McLanahan, and Irwin Garfinkel. 1994. The gender-poverty gap: What we can learn from other countries. *American Sociological Review* 59 (4): 594–605.

Dagg, Paul K. B.. 1991. The psychological sequelae of therapeutic abortions—denied and completed. *American Journal of Psychiatry* 148 (5): 578–85.

Deschner, Amy, and Susan Cohen. 2003. Contraceptive use is key to reducing abortion worldwide. *The Guttmacher Report on Public Policy* 6 (4): 7–10.

Dworkin, Ronald. 1993. *Life's dominion: Argument about abortion, euthanasia, and individual freedom.* New York: Random House.

Ertelt, Steven. 2008. Colorado Abortion-Personhood Amendment Gets OK from Top Pro-Life Group. http://www.lifenews.com/2008/08/06/state-3430/ (accessed March 20, 2012).

Francke, Linda. 1978. *The ambivalence of abortion.* New York: Random House.

Finer, Lawrence B., Lori F. Finer, Lindsay Frohwirth, A. Dauphinee, Sushella Singh, and Ann M. Moore. 2005. Reasons U.S. women have abortions: Quantitative and qualitative perspectives. *Perspectives on Sexual and Reproductive Health* 37 (3): 110–18.

Gilchrist, A. C., P. C. Hannaford, P. Frank, and C. R. Kay. 1995. Termination of pregnancy and psychiatric morbidity. *British Journal of Psychiatry* 167 (2): 243–48.

Ginsburg, Faye. 1998. *Contested lives: The abortion debate in an American community.* Los Angeles: University of California Press.

Hursthouse, Rosalind. 1991. Virtue theory and abortion. *Philosophy and Public Affairs* 20 (3): 223–46.

Jones, Rachel, Lawrence B. Finer, and Susheela Singh. 2008. Characteristics of U.S. abortion patients. http://www.guttmacher.org/pubs/US-Abortion-Patients.pdf (accessed November 21, 2011).

Jones, Rachel, Jacqueline Darroch, and Stanley K. Henshaw. 2002. Patterns in the socioeconomic characteristics of women obtaining abortion in 2000–2001. *Perspectives on Sexual and Reproductive Health* 34 (5): 226–35.

Kaczor, Christopher. 2011. *The ethics of abortion: Women's rights, human life, and the question of justice.* New York: Routledge.

Kennedy, Bobbie Jeanne. 1988. I'm sorry baby. *American Journal of Nursing* 88 (8): 1067–69.

Kissling, Frances. 2005. Is there life after *Roe*?: How to think about the fetus. *Conscience: The News Journal of Catholic Opinion.* http://www.catholicsforchoice.org/conscience/archives/c2004win_lifeafterroe.asp (accessed January 5, 2012).

Kliff, Sarah. 2010. Remember Roe! How can the next generation defend abortion rights when they don't think abortion rights need defending? *Newsweek*, April 29.

Kushner, Eve. 1997. *Experiencing abortion: A weaving of women's words.* New York: Harrington Park Press.

Little, Margaret olivia. 2002. The morality of abortion. In *Ethical issues in modern medicine*, ed. Bonnie Steinbock, John Arras and Alex John London. New York: McGraw Hill.

Ludlow, Jeannie. 2008. Sometimes, it's a child and a choice: Toward an embodied abortion praxis. *Feminism Formations* 20 (1): 26–50.

Major, Brenda, and Catherine Cozzarelli. 1992. Psychosocial predictors of adjustment to abortion. *Journal of Social Issues* 48 (3): 121–42.

Major, Brenda, Josephine Zubek, M. Lynne Cooper, Catherine Cozzarelli, and Caroline Richards. 1997. Mixed messages: Implications of social conflict and social support within close relationships for adjustment to a stressful life event. *Journal of Personality and Social Psychology* 72 (6): 1349–63.

Major, Brenda, Mark Appelbaum, Linda Beckman, Mary Ann Dutton, Nancy Felipe Russo, and Carolyn West. 2009. Abortion and mental health—evaluating the evidence. *American Psychologist* 64 (9): 863–90.

Major, Brenda, Catherine Cozzarelli, M. Lynne Cooper, Josephine Zubek, Caroline Richards, Michael Wilhite, and Richard Gramzow. 2000. Psychological response of women after first-trimester abortion. *Archives of General Psychiatry* 57: 777–78.

Major, Brenda, Mark Applebaum, Linda Beckman, Mary Ann Dutton, Nancy Felipe Russo, and Carolyn West. 2008. Report of the APA task force on mental health and abortion. http://www.apa.org/pi/wpo/mental-health-abortion-report.pdf (accessed November 21, 2011).

Maxwell, Carol. 2002. *Pro-life activists in America.* New York: Cambridge University Press.

McDonagh, Eileen. 1996. *Breaking the abortion deadlock: From choice to consent.* New York: oxford University Press.

McDonnell, Kathleen. 1984. *Not an easy choice: A feminist re-examines abortion.* Toronto: The Women's Press.

Munk-Olsen, Trine, Thomas Munk Laursen, Carsten B. Pedersen, Øjvind Lidegaard, and Preben Bo Mortensen. 2011. Induced first-trimester abortion and risk of mental disorder. *New England Journal of Medicine* 364 (4): 332–38.

Needle, Rachel, and Lenore Walker. 2008. *Abortion counseling: A clinician s guide to psychology, legislation, politics, and competency.* New York: Springer Publishing Company.

Pearce, Diana. 1978. The feminization of poverty: Women, work, and welfare. *Urban and Social Change Review* 11 (1-2): 28–36.

Poppema, Suzanne. 1996. *Why I am an abortion doctor.* New York: Prometheus Books.

Pressman, Steven. 2002. Explaining the gender poverty gap in developed and transitional economies. *Journal of Economic Issues* 36 (1): 17–40.

Reardon, David. 1987. *Aborted women: Silent no more.* Westchester, Ill.: Crossway Books.

Reid, T. R. 2010. Universal healthcare tends to cut abortion rate. *The Washington Post,* March 14. http://www.washingtonpost.com/wpdyn/content/article/2010/03/12/AR2010031202287.html (accessed November 12, 2011).

Rovner, Julie 2011. Poll: Generation Y divided on abortion, like their parents. http://www.npr.org/blogs/health/2011/06/09/137079714/poll-generation-y-supports-gay-mar-riage-but-is-divided-on-abortion?sc=fb&cc=fp (accessed November 21, 2011).

Schalet, Amy. 2010. Sex, love, and autonomy in the teenage sleepover. *Contexts* 9 (3): 16–21.

Stotland, Nada, ed. 1991. *Psychiatric aspects of abortion.* Washington, D.C.: American Psychiatric Press.

Thomson, Judith Jarvis. 1971. A defense of abortion. *Philosophy and Public Affairs* 1 (1): 47–66.

Torre-Bueno, Ava. 1997. *Peace after abortion.* San Diego: Pimpernel Press.

Van Gelder, Linsy. 1978. Cracking the women's movement protection game. Ms. *Magazine,* December.

Warren, Jocelyn T., S. Marie Harvey, and Jillian T. Henderson. 2010. Do depression and low self-esteem follow abortion among adolescents? *Evidence from a national study. Perspectives on Sexual and Reproductive Health* 42 (4): 230–35.

Warren, Mary Anne. 1973. On the moral and legal status of abortion. *The Monist* 57 (1): 43–61.

———. 1997. *Moral status: Obligations to persons and other living things.* New York: Oxford University Press.

Wicklund, Sue, and Alan Kesselheim. 2007. *This common secret: My journey as an abortion doctor.* New York: Perseus Books.

Wilcox, John. 1989. Nature as demonic in Thomson's defense of abortion. *New Scholasticism* 63 (4): 463–84.

Wilmouth, Gregory, Martin de Alteriis, and Danielle Bussell. 1992. Prevalence of psychological risks following legal abortion in the U.S.: Limits of the evidence. *Journal of Social Issues* 48 (3): 37–66.

Wright, Joseph. 2008. Reducing abortion in America: The effect of socioeconomic factors. http://www.catholicsinalliance.org/files/CACG_Final.pdf (accessed November 12, 2011).

Zabin, L. S., M. B. Hirsch, and M. R. Emerson. 1989. When urban adolescents choose abortion: Effects on education, psychological status, and subsequent pregnancy. *Family Planning Perspective* 21 (6): 248–55.

REVIEW EXERCISES

1. Outline the various stages of fetal development.
2. Explain the conclusions of *Roe v. Wade* and *Planned Parenthood v. Casey*.
3. Give a utilitarian argument for abortion. Give one against abortion. Are these act or rule utilitarian arguments? Explain.
4. Describe how Thomson uses the violinist analogy to make an argument about the moral permissibility of abortion.
5. Use Method I to make one argument for and one against abortion.
6. Which of the positions under Method II does each of the following statements exemplify?
   a. Because this fetus has all the potential to develop the abilities of a person, it has all the rights of a person.
   b. Only when a being can think and communicate does it have full moral status. Because a fetus does not have these abilities, it has neither moral rights nor claims.
   c. If a fetus is a human being, then it has full moral status and rights.
   d. Its capacity to feel pain gives a being full moral status. The fetus has this capacity beginning in the fifth or sixth month, and so abortion is not morally justifiable beyond that stage.
   e. Early-term fetuses do not have as much moral significance as later-term fetuses because their potential is not as fully realized as it is later.

DISCUSSION CASES

1. **Abortion for Sex Selection.** The sex of a child can now be determined before birth. In the waiting room of a local women's clinic, June has started a conversation with another woman, Ann. She finds out that each woman is there for an amniocentesis to determine the sex of her fetus. June reveals that she wants to know the sex because her husband and his family really want a boy. Because they plan to have only one child, they plan to end this pregnancy if it is a girl and try again. Ann tells her that her reason is different. She is a genetic carrier of a particular kind of muscular dystrophy. Duchenne muscular dystrophy is a sex-linked disease that is inherited through the mother. Only males develop the disease, and each male child has a 50 percent chance of having it. The disease causes muscle weakness and often some mental retardation. It also causes death through respiratory failure, usually in early adulthood. Ann does not want to risk having such a child, and this abnormality cannot yet be determined through prenatal testing. Thus, if the prenatal diagnosis reveals that her fetus is male, she plans to end this pregnancy.

   Is Ann justified in her plan to abort a male fetus? Is June justified? Should there be laws regulating sex-selective abortion?

2. **Father's Consent to Abortion.** Jim and Sue have been planning to have a child for two years. Finally, Sue becomes pregnant. However, their marriage has been a rough one, and by the time she is in her third month of pregnancy, they have decided to divorce. At this point, both parents are ambivalent about the pregnancy. They had both wanted the child, but now things are different. Sue finally decides that she does not want to raise a child alone and does not want to raise Jim's child. She wants to get on with her life. However, Jim has long wanted a child, and he argues that the developing fetus is partly his own because he has provided half of its genetic makeup. He does not want Sue to end the pregnancy. He wants to keep and raise the child.

   Do you think that Jim has any moral rights in this case or should the decision be strictly Sue's? Why or why not?

3. **Parental Consent to Abortion.** Judy is a high school sophomore and fifteen years old. She recently became sexually active with her boyfriend. She does not want to tell him that she is now pregnant, and she does not feel that she can talk to her parents. They have been quite strict with her and would condemn her recent behavior. They also oppose abortion. Judy would simply like to end this pregnancy and start over with her life. However, minors in her state must get parental consent for an abortion; it is viewed as a medical procedure like any other, and parents must consent to other medical procedures for their children.

   What should Judy do? Do you agree that states should require parental consent for abortion for minors? Why or why not?

4. **Pregnant Woman Detained.** In 1995, a woman who was pregnant and refused to discontinue her use of cocaine was reported by her obstetrician to child-abuse authorities.[1] They obtained an order from the juvenile court to take custody of the unborn child, which, in this case, involved detaining the mother against her will. The court maintained that in order to protect the fetus, it had to detain the mother. The mother gave birth while in a drug treatment center. She sued the state for detaining her illegally. The case was settled after the child was born, with the court finding that the state acted wrongly in taking protective custody of the fetus while it was still in the womb. As a result of these sorts of cases, state legislatures have passed laws such as the Wisconsin law mentioned above, which define fetuses more clearly as children deserving protection.[2]

   If the fetus is regarded as a child who is being abused, then is it reasonable, in your view, to detain the mother? If the fetus is thus viewed as a person, should it have access to other rights and privileges? Would it also be reasonable for a pregnant woman to be able to use a car-pool lane by counting her fetus as a second person in the car? If a pregnant woman is killed, resulting in the death of the fetus, does that count as one murder or two?

NOTES

1. "Detention of Pregnant Woman for Drug Use Is Struck Down," *New York Times*, April 23, 1997, http://www.nytimes.com/1997/04/23/us/detention-of-pregnant-woman-for-drug-use-is-struck-down.html (accessed May 13, 2013).

2. Robert D. Miller, *Problems in Health Care Law* (Sudbury, MA: Jones & Bartlett, 2006), p. 395.

MindTap   For more chapter resources and activities, go to MindTap.

12

Sexual Morality

Learning Outcomes

After reading this chapter, you should be able to:

- Summarize disputes about same-sex marriage and other topics in sexual morality.

- Explain key cases and examples, including recent developments.

- Explain the importance of autonomy and consent in thinking about sexual morality.

- Evaluate moral arguments about sexual ethics including both consequentialist and non-consequentialist arguments.

- Understand and criticize natural law approaches to sexual morality.

- Defend your own ideas about sexual ethics.

MindTap For more chapter resources and activities, go to MindTap.

In 2015, the United States Supreme Court ruled that same-sex marriages should be legally recognized in all states. The Court concluded in its landmark *Obergefell v. Hodges* decision, "same-sex couples may exercise the fundamental right to marry in all States . . . there is no lawful basis for a State to refuse to recognize a lawful same-sex marriage performed in another State on the ground of its same-sex character."[1] This decision concluded a decades-long debate that had raged across the country regarding the legality of same-sex marriage. The moral question remains open, however. Soon after the *Obergefell* decision was reached, a county clerk in Kentucky, Kim Davis, refused to issue a marriage licenses. She stated, "To issue a marriage license which conflicts with God's definition of marriage, with my name affixed to the certificate, would violate my conscience."[2] Davis was jailed as a result of her refusal. For some, Davis is a hero. For others, Davis's moral and religious objection to same-sex marriage is old-fashioned and intolerant.

Some may think that the same-sex marriage issue is merely a matter of civil rights, more properly discussed in Chapter 13 on equality and discrimination. They might point out that interracial marriage was once viewed as a "moral" issue, while today it is viewed almost exclusively as a question of civil rights. But underlying many of the arguments against same-sex marriage is a moral claim about the proper form of sexual relationships. It has only been since 2003 that the Supreme Court (in its decision in *Lawrence v. Texas*) declared that laws against sodomy are unconstitutional—*sodomy* is usually taken to include any form of homosexual sex, as well as oral and anal sex between heterosexual couples. The late Supreme Court Justice Antonin Scalia, who died in 2016, explained the thinking of those who want to avoid homosexuals in his dissent in the *Lawrence v. Texas* decision: "Many Americans do not want persons who openly engage in homosexual conduct as partners in their business, as scoutmasters for their children, as teachers in their children's schools, or as boarders in their home. They view this as protecting themselves and their families from a lifestyle that they believe to be immoral and destructive."[3] The claim that homosexuality is immoral and destructive points beyond the question of civil rights toward a deeper moral analysis of sexual morality.

The evolution of Americans' perspectives on same-sex marriage has ranged across several decades. The federal Defense of Marriage Act was passed in 1996 and signed into law by President Bill Clinton. The Act is intended to "define and protect the institution of marriage" and defines marriage as follows: "The word 'marriage' means only a legal union between one man and one woman as husband and wife, and the word 'spouse' refers only to a person of the opposite sex who is a husband or a wife."[4] The law stipulated that states do not have to recognize marriages between homosexual couples or provide these couples with the federal benefits accorded to couples in heterosexual marriages.

There are some 1,100 benefits that do not extend to same-sex partners, including eligibility to file joint income taxes, to inherit Social Security benefits, and to defer estate taxes by passing property on to surviving spouses.[5] In June 2013, the Supreme Court ruled, in *United States v. Windsor*, that part of the Defense of Marriage Act was unconstitutional. The Court concluded, "DOMA instructs all federal officials, and indeed all persons with whom same-sex couples interact, including their own children, that their marriage is less worthy than the marriages of others." The Court ruled that by "treating those persons as living in marriages less respected than others" the law violated citizens due process rights.[6] During the course of the past two decades, homosexuals have gradually been granted legal rights and equal opportunities, culminating in the *Obergefell* decision of 2015. In 2011, for example, homosexuals were allowed to openly serve in the military; in 2013, the Pentagon extended medical and other benefits to the partners of gay soldiers.[7]

While the United States has been debating the issue, other countries have also legalized same-sex marriage. According to research published in 2015, nearly two dozen countries permit same-sex marriage, primarily in Western Europe and the

Tori (Left) and Kate Kuykendall with their five-month-old daughter, Zadie, celebrate their civil marriage ceremony in West Hollywood, California.

Rob Melnychuk/Digital Vision/Getty Images

Americas.[8] While the legal tides appear to be rapidly turning in favor of same-sex marriage in some parts of the world, homosexuality and legal recognition of homosexual relationships are fiercely contested in other parts of the world. In 75 countries (mostly in Africa and the Middle East), homosexuality is illegal. In some countries, homosexuality is punishable by death, including in Iran, Mauritania, Saudi Arabia, Sudan, and Yemen.[9] And violence against homosexual people continues to be a problem. In June of 2016, a mass murderer opened fire in a gay nightclub in Orlando, killing 49 people in the worst atrocity committed against homosexual people in the history of the United States.

While some may think that discussions of sexual ethics are of minor importance since sex is a private matter, the fact that some people are liable to be killed because of their sexual orientation indicates the importance of the discussion and the depth of the dispute about sexual ethics.

CURRENT ISSUES

The issue of homosexuality and same-sex marriage is one example of the sorts of ethical issues that arise with regard to sex and sexuality. Some of these issues may overlap with considerations found in other chapters. Sexual relations produce offspring, which may point toward discussions of contraception and abortion (as we discuss in Chapter 11), as well as discussions of the use of biotechnologies including in vitro fertilization and genetic testing (as discussed in Chapter 18). Questions about sexuality are connected to issues related to gender identity, women's rights, and issues related to male dominance (as discussed in Chapter 9). A thorough examination of sexual morality would include considerations of a range of issues including honor crimes, genital mutilation, sex trafficking, prostitution, pornography, polygamy, and so on.

For example, consider the issue of transgender transitions and non-traditional gender and sexual identities. In the summer of 2015, just as the Supreme Court was ruling on the *Obergefell* case, Caitlyn Jenner publicly announced that her transition from the male Bruce to the transgender woman Caitlyn was complete. Suddenly, a range of issues related to gender and sexual identity came into public focus. The now

well-known acronym **LGBT** stands for "Lesbian, Gay, Bisexual, and Transgender" (some add other letters and identities here including Queer, Questioning, Intersex, Pansexual, Asexual, and so on). And new terms entered the public vocabulary, including the term **cisgender**, which is more or less the opposite of transgender. Cisgender individuals feel at home in traditional gender identities, while transgender individuals do not feel so at home. Discussions of the ethics of gender overlap somewhat with discussions of feminist concerns (as discussed in Chapter 9). The question of sex or gender-reassignment surgeries and other procedures also overlap with issues in biotechnology (see Chapter 18). But they also connect with questions of sexual ethics. For example, one basic question is whether we should be free to choose or change our gender—or whether obedience to the natural law should lead us to conform to supposed natural gender and sexual categories.

While homosexuality and transgender issues have been in the public eye lately, one important basic moral idea has to do with consent and autonomy. Most would agree that rape is wrong—because it violates the autonomy of the victim. But what about sexual acts that are freely consented to: masturbation, anal or oral sex, sex with multiple partners, and so on—are those actions somehow intrinsically wrong, or should consenting adults be permitted to do whatever they want with their own bodies? A related question is whether the law should regulate these practices, or whether the law should leave individuals alone to pursue their own sexual gratification and sexual relationships.

With regard to consent, there has been a renewed public focus on the importance of obtaining affirmative consent for sexual relations. In California, for example, in 2014, a law was passed which requires "affirmative consent" for sexual relations. One intent of the so-called "yes means yes" law was to rule out sexual relations that happened, for example, when someone was drunk or otherwise unable to consent. Defenders of the legislation worried that in some cases "no means no" was not enough. And behind this was a concern about an epidemic in sexual assaults and rapes on college campuses. One bit of data is important to note with regard to unwanted sexual activity.

The Center for Disease Control report from 2011 notes that "among females aged 18–24 whose first sex was before age 20, 11% "didn't really want it to happen at the time," 48% had mixed feelings." Only 41% "really wanted it to happen at the time."[10] The standard of "yes means yes" rules out indifference, ignorance, and mixed feeling. If someone doesn't say no, that's not enough; consensual sex requires a positive affirmation—and if you don't know whether your partner says "yes," you are obligated to ask.

It is clear that there are a variety of ways that human beings engage in sexual activity. Recent CDC data on sexuality offer some details about sexuality in the United States.[11] For example, only about half of teenagers 15–19 years old have had sex at least once. This is a decline from previous decades. And the data indicate that teenagers are more responsible than they have been in previous generations, using birth control and condoms during sexual encounters.[12] The good news is that teen pregnancy rates have been declining in recent years. In 2011, teen birth rates fell to an historic low of only 31.3 per 1,000 women. That rate represents a 49 percent drop from the high teen birth rate of 61.8 per 1,000 in 1991.[13] Teen sex is more consensual and teen pregnancy rates are declining, even though American teen pregnancy rates are higher than in European countries.[14]

In the United States, adult sexual activity is varied, as reported by the Centers for Disease Control.[15] More than 80 percent of adults aged 18–44 report that they have engaged in oral sex. 35 percent of women and 42 percent of men report that they have had anal sex. 17 percent of women and 6 percent of men report having engaged in same-sex sexual contact. More than 92 percent of women and 95 percent of men identify as heterosexual or straight. 1.3 percent of women and 1.9 percent of men identified as homosexual, gay, or lesbian, and 5 percent of women and 2 percent of men identified as bisexual.

Sexual activity is not risk free. The CDC estimates that there are 19 million new cases of sexually transmitted infections every year, including 50,000 new cases of HIV. More than one million Americans are currently living with HIV. The good news is that HIV infections and deaths are declining—which is a worldwide trend.[16] But more work still needs to be done to prevent sexually transmitted disease—including common sense use of condoms for protection. But some argue that condom use—and contraception in general—is immoral. For example, the Catholic Church has been opposed to condom use on moral grounds—and condemned by some for this. But in recent years, the Church has softened its position. In 2010, Pope Benedict XVI hinted that condom use might be a sort of lesser evil, since it would prevent sexually transmitted disease.[17]

Sexually transmitted diseases raise a number of ethical issues. Lying or concealing one's STD status from sexual partners is generally considered to be a violation of moral standards, although ethicists disagree about when in a romantic relationship this information must be disclosed. One could also argue that risky sexual behavior is not only dangerous for the individuals involved but also for society. From a utilitarian perspective that is concerned with public health—including the costs of sexually transmitted diseases—it is important to work to reduce the incidence of such diseases. One conservative strategy is to minimize casual sexual encounters and encourage monogamous sex within the confines of marriage. A more liberal strategy is to find ways to increase usage of condoms, especially among sex workers and others who are at an increased risk of contracting and transmitting disease. One interesting related case is the effort to require adult film stars to use condoms. Proponents of such regulation argue that this models appropriate sexual behavior and prevents disease in an era when pornography is more readily available. Opponents will argue that when adults engage in sexual activity in the pornography industry, it is up to them to make their own decisions about protection against disease.

This brings us to a discussion of pornography. In the Internet age, pornography is easily found, even stumbled upon. Defenders of pornography will argue that it provides an outlet for sexual desire and a source of sexual stimulation which can enhance sexual relations, and that as long as it is consensual, there is no harm done. On the other hand, opponents of pornography will argue that pornography represents a general loosening of sexual mores in our culture. Opponents may also argue that pornography has a negative impact on gender relations because pornography tends to objectify women (see further discussion in Chapter 9). Opponents will also argue that pornography can undermine healthy sexual relations, especially when men expect women to behave and respond as they do in pornography or when pornography helps create sex-addiction and unhealthy attitudes toward sex. Opponents will also argue that pornography can be produced as a result of coercion and sex-trafficking, which is linked to illegal prostitution and rape. Other problems include: child pornography, in which images of underage minors are exchanged; so-called "revenge pornography," where people post pornographic images of former partners; and the emerging problem of "sexting." **Sexting** involves trading explicit photos via email or through text messages. While sexting between consenting adults might seem to be morally unproblematic, sexting has become a problem in high schools. Minors who exchange sexually explicit pictures are actually engaging in the exchange of child pornography. Although the legal system and disciplinary systems in the schools have tried to find a way to deal with high school sexting that does not result in labeling experimenting teens as child pornographers and sex offenders, this issue points toward the problem of sexual morality and pornography in the era of smart phones and social media.

> MindTap   For more chapter resources and activities, go to MindTap.

In addition to its impact on physical health, sexuality can also affect emotional and psychological health. A 2007 study that explored teens' post-sex emotions found that many first-time experiences resulted in guilt or feeling manipulated, with girls more often reporting this than boys. Of the teens who had engaged in oral sex, 41 percent "said they felt bad about themselves later" and "nearly 20 percent felt guilty, and 25 percent felt used," while the figures were 42 percent and 38 percent for sexual intercourse.[18] It's not just teens who report mixed feelings about sexual experiences and their outcomes. The CDC found that that 13.8 percent of all pregnancies were "unwanted at the time of conception."[19]

One solution to unwanted pregnancy and sexually transmitted disease is better sex education. But in the United States, sex education is a contested area. Some want to promote abstinence and discourage sexual activity among teenagers and outside of marriage. Others maintain that the key is to teach sexual health, including information about condoms—which prevent STDs—and other forms of birth control. Studies do not clearly indicate whether any single approach to sex education has any significant impact on the subsequent sexual behavior of students.[20] But some studies do indicate that comprehensive sex education may help reduce teen pregnancies without increasing levels of sexual intercourse or sexually transmitted disease.[21] Sexual education curricula pose ethical challenges. Proponents of comprehensive sex education want to empower students to make informed choices about sexuality, without imposing moral values on students. But proponents of abstinence-only sex education maintain that teenagers are too young to be engaging in sexual acts, which they believe should take place only within marriages. Defenders of abstinence-only sex education also worry that when sexual practices are discussed with children, this discussion can stimulate unhealthy interest in having sex. Opponents of abstinence-only sex education complain that abstinence programs sneak religious ideas about marriage and sexuality into the classroom, while proponents of abstinence maintain that their primary concern is student health.[22]

While teen pregnancy has declined, the overall rate of births outside of marriage is rising. More than half of births to women under age 30 occur outside of marriage.[23] In addition, the incidence of *cohabitation*, or living with one's partner before marriage, has increased dramatically in recent years, nearly tripling between 1990 and 2000.[24] As of May 2009, there were more than five million cohabiting couples in the United States. Further, "the majority of cohabitants either break up or marry within five years."[25] This rise in cohabitation comes at a time when Americans are delaying marriage until later in life. Those who marry after age twenty-five are less likely to divorce than those who marry in their teens. It is often assumed that cohabiting couples who marry are more likely to divorce than those who did not live together before marriage, and there is some evidence for this.[26] "Couples who live together before they get married are less likely to stay married," a recent study has found.[27] However, this may also be because of the type of people who cohabitate, being more liberal and less religious, for example. If they are engaged or committed or their relationship is based on love, then they are no less likely to later divorce.[28]

Almost everywhere in the world, different sexual standards apply to men and to women. In many traditional societies, women's sexuality is viewed as unclean or sinful and in need of control or suppression. In some Arab countries, women are not allowed to appear in public without special clothing to preserve their "modesty" or without the presence of a male relative. Many religious traditions, including Orthodox Judaism, prohibit men from coming into contact with women while they are menstruating and require rituals to "cleanse" women after menstruation.

A particularly extreme example of societal control of women's sexuality is that of **female genital mutilation** (FGM), or so-called female circumcision. Although many countries have outlawed it, the practice persists in more than twenty-eight African countries and several countries in Asia and the Middle East, as well as some immigrant communities in the West.[29] According to the World Health Organization, 140 million girls and women are living with the consequences of FGM, while more than three million girls have this done to them every year (that's more than eight thousand girls per day).[30] FGM can involve different degrees of severity—from excision of the skin surrounding the clitoris, to removal of all or part of the clitoris and some of the surrounding tissues, to stitching the labia together so that only a small opening remains. Among the cultural and parental reasons given for these practices are to enable families to exercise control over reproduction, to keep women virgins until marriage, and to reduce or eliminate female sexual pleasure.[31] The procedure is usually done without even a local

anesthetic and often performed with unclean and crude instruments. If the labia have been stitched together, a reverse cutting is frequently necessary before intercourse can take place—this subsequent procedure can also be quite painful. In addition, FGM can cause problems in childbirth.[32] In fact, the more extensive forms of this procedure raise "by more than 50 percent the likelihood that the woman or her baby will die."[33] The World Health Organization explains, "the FGM procedure that seals or narrows a vaginal opening needs to be cut open later to allow for sexual intercourse and childbirth. Sometimes it is stitched again several times, including after childbirth, hence the woman goes through repeated opening and closing procedures, further increasing both immediate and long-term risks."[34]

The 1996 U.S. Federal Criminalization of Female Genital Mutilation Act prohibited this practice for women under eighteen years of age. Human rights groups have lobbied internationally for an end to this practice, which in some countries is "routinely forced on girls as young as four or five years old, and . . . sustained through social coercion."[35] In Africa, between 60 and 90 percent of all women and girls in certain countries undergo the procedure, even in countries where it is illegal. Many Muslim critics argue that there is no basis for this practice in the *Qur'an*; in fact, they note that this holy book commands parents to protect their children from harm and regards people's anatomy as part of God's creation.[36] Despite the fact that FGM is already illegal in this country, the practice persists in some immigrant communities, and parents have been known to take their daughters to other countries for this procedure. In early 2013, President Obama signed the Transport for Female Genital Mutilation Act, which amended the 1996 law by making it a crime to take girls from the United States to foreign countries for the purpose of mutilating their genitals. This followed closely a United Nations General Assembly resolution that called for a global ban against the practice of FGM. According to the UN Women website, "the FGM resolution urges countries to condemn all harmful practices that affect women and girls, in particular female genital mutilations, and to take all necessary measures, including enforcing legislation, awareness-raising and allocating sufficient resources to protect women and girls from this form of violence."[37]

A central idea in the move to eliminate female genital mutilation is the idea that women as well as men have a right to benefit from sexual pleasure and that individuals have a right to control their own anatomy. According to the World Health Organization, one significant motivation behind the practice appears to be the desire to control female sexuality. One common theme in cultures that practice FGM is an effort to minimize women's sexual urges, which would "thereby increase their ability to remain a virgin prior to marriage, and to remain faithful and not too demanding within marriage."[38] The issue of controlling female sexuality is obviously connected to feminist concerns (as discussed in Chapter 9).

Attempts to exercise control over female sexuality is also closely connected to the problem of rape. At one point, rape was rationalized as being the result of uncontrollable male lust. But starting in the 1970s, feminists such as Susan Brownmiller began pushing society to recognize that rape is "not a crime of irrational, impulsive, uncontrollable lust, but is a deliberate, hostile, violent act of degradation and possession on the part of a would-be conqueror."[39] While it is important to recognize that rape is a crime of violence and domination, it also has an unmistakably sexual element. Reliable statistics on the incidence of rape are difficult to establish. One reason is underreporting. Another reason is the incidence of acquaintance rape. Two-thirds of rapes are committed by someone known to the victim.[40] One form of this is so-called "date rape," a form of sexual assault that is particularly prevalent among young adults of college age. While there are problems with regard to the way that data on rape and sexual assault are collected, one estimate, from the Rape, Abuse & Incest National Network, is that every two minutes someone in the United States is sexually assaulted. In raw numbers, that means that more than two hundred thousand people are sexually assaulted in the United States every year. These numbers remain high despite the fact that

sexual assault has fallen by more than 60 percent in recent years.[41] Rape is clearly wrong according to many different ethical standards. In most places, it is illegal. But in many parts of the world, women are still blamed (to varying degrees) for being victims of rape. As we mentioned in our discussion of honor crimes in Chapter 9, in some cultures, rape victims are forced to marry their rapists or are even killed by family members for bringing shame on the family.

Rape can happen within the family. In most cases, incest is a form of rape because it involves minors who cannot consent to sexual acts. And since the 1970s, European countries and individual states in the United States have recognized that women can be raped by their husbands. It wasn't until 1993 that all states in the United States criminalized spousal rape.[42] But married women in other parts of the world are not protected by marital rape laws. There is no law against raping one's wife in India, China, Afghanistan, Pakistan, or Saudi Arabia.[43]

Another issue of profound moral concern is **sex trafficking**, which generally involves women and girls being coerced into the sex trade both in the United States and abroad. Sex trafficking is a subset of human trafficking, which involves the transport and captivity of individuals across international borders for a variety of illegal purposes. According to a 2012 report by the United Nations Office on Drugs and Crime, "trafficking for the purpose of sexual exploitation accounts for 58 percent of all trafficking cases detected globally."[44] The FBI states that, "human sex trafficking is the most common form of modern-day slavery. Estimates place the number of domestic and international victims in the millions, mostly females and children enslaved in the commercial sex industry for little or no money."[45] The report continues,

> The average age at which girls first become victims of prostitution is 12 to 14. It is not only the girls on the streets who are affected; boys and transgender youth enter into prostitution between the ages of 11 and 13 on average....These women and young girls are sold to traffickers, locked up in rooms or brothels for weeks or months, drugged, terrorized, and raped repeatedly. These continual abuses make it easier for

the traffickers to control their victims. The captives are so afraid and intimidated that they rarely speak out against their traffickers, even when faced with an opportunity to escape.

The bleak and brutal reality of the sex trade throws a moral wrench in the arguments of those who would defend consensual prostitution as a victimless crime. (It also raises questions about pornography, some of which clearly involves victims of sex trafficking.) It might be that some sex transactions are consensual and mutually beneficial both for the prostitute and for the customer. But in many cases, there is coercion and exploitation. One proposal to solve this problem is to legalize prostitution to encourage healthy and noncoercive sexual exchanges. In the state of Nevada, some counties allow highly regulated brothels to operate legally. And in some countries, such as the Netherlands, prostitution is legal. In other countries, such as Thailand and Belgium, prostitution is nominally illegal—but, in practice, it is tolerated. It remains an open question whether legal sex trades prevent or reduce sex crimes and abuse.

Sex trafficking, rape, and FGM clearly raise serious moral issues about human autonomy, agency, and rights to bodily integrity. Some ethicists would argue that it is these ethical standards that should be the focus of what we call "sexual morality"—rather than any judgments we make about the sexual preferences and practices between consenting adults. They would further argue that we make too much of the morality of sexual behavior and often talk about it as the only moral issue. When we hear expressions such as "Doesn't he have any morals?" or "She has loose morals," the speakers are often referring to the person's sexual morals. But many other moral issues are arguably more important than sexual behavior between consenting adults.

Some people may even be inclined to say that one's sexual behavior is not a moral matter at all. Is it not a private matter and too personal and individual to be a moral matter? To hold that it is not a moral matter, however, would seem to imply that our sexual lives are morally insignificant. Or it might imply that something has to be public or universal

in order to have moral significance. However, most of us would not want to hold that personal matters cannot be moral matters. Furthermore, consider that sexual behavior lends itself to valuable experiences—those of personal relations, pleasure, fruitfulness and descendants, and self-esteem and enhancement. It also involves unusual opportunities for cruelty, deceit, unfairness, and selfishness. Because these are moral matters, sexual behavior must have moral significance.

CONCEPTUAL PROBLEMS: WHAT IS AND IS NOT SEXUAL

Discussions of sexual morality are likely to benefit from a more intensive analysis of sexuality itself. Just what are we talking about when we speak of sexual pleasure, sexual desire, or sexual activity? Consider the meaning of the qualifier *sexual*. Suppose we said that behavior is sexual when it involves "pleasurable bodily contact with another." Will this do? This definition is quite broad. It includes passionate caresses and kisses as well as sexual intercourse. But it would not include activity that does not involve another individual, such as masturbation or looking at pornography. It would also exclude erotic dancing, phone sex, and "sexting" because these activities do not involve physical contact with another. So the definition seems to be too narrow.

However, this definition is also too broad. It covers too much. Not all kisses or caresses are sexual, even though they are physical and can be pleasurable. And the contact sport of football is supposedly pleasurable for those who play it, but presumably not in a sexual way. It seems reasonable to think of sexual pleasure as pleasure that involves our so-called erogenous zones—those areas of the body that are sexually sensitive. Could we then say that sexuality is necessarily bodily in nature? To answer this question, try the following thought experiment. Suppose we did not have bodies—in other words, suppose we were ghosts or spirits of some sort. Would we then be sexual beings? Could we experience sexual desire, for example? If we did, it would surely be different from that which we now experience.

Moreover, it is not just that our own bodily existence seems required for us to experience sexual desire, but sexual desire for another would seem most properly to be for the embodied other. It cannot be simply the body of another that is desirable—or dead bodies generally would be sexually stimulating. It is an embodied person who is the normal object of sexual desire. This is not to say that bodily touching is necessary, as is clear from the fact that dancing can be sexy and phone sex can be heated. Finally, if the body is so important for sexuality, we also can wonder whether there are any significant differences between male and female sexuality in addition to, and based on, genital and reproductive differences.

Let us also note one more conceptual puzzle. Many people refer to sexual intercourse as *making love*. Some people argue that sexual intercourse should be accompanied by or be an expression of love, while others do not believe that this is necessary. Perhaps we would do best to consult the poets about the meaning of love. But let us briefly consider what you would regard as the difference between being in love (or falling in love) and loving someone. To *be in love* seems to suggest passivity. Similarly, to *fall in love* seems to be something that happens to a person. Supposedly, one has little control over one's feelings and even some thoughts in such a state. One cannot get the other person out of one's mind. We say one is *head over heels in love* or *madly in love*; one has *fallen passionately in love*. Yet compare these notions to those of *loving someone*. This is not necessarily a sexual feeling, and we often say we love our relatives and friends. Many people would say that to genuinely love someone in this way is to be actively directed to that person's good. We want the best for him or her. In his essay on friendship in *The Nicomachean Ethics*, Aristotle wrote that true friendship is different from that which is based on the usefulness of the friend or the pleasure one obtains from being with the friend. The true friend cares about his or her friend for the friend's own sake. According to Aristotle, "Those who wish well to their friends for their sake are most truly friends."[46] This kind of friendship is less common,

he believed, though more lasting. For Aristotle and the Greeks of his time, true friendship was more or less reserved for men. One contribution an ethics of care makes to this discussion is the importance to all of friendship and loving care. Moreover, we need not be in love with someone to love them. We can love our friends, parents, or children, and yet, we are not in love with them. So when considering what sex has to do with love, we would do well to consider the kind of love that is intended. We might also do well to ponder what happens when sexual feelings are joined with friendship.

RELEVANT FACTUAL MATTERS

In addition to conceptual clarification, certain factual matters may also be relevant to what we say about matters of sexual morality. For example, would it not be morally significant to know the effects of celibacy or of restraining sexual urges? It is well known that Freud thought that if we repressed our sexual desires, we would become either neurotic or artists! Art, he argues, provides an emotionally expressive outlet for repressed sexual feelings. Freudian theory about both sexual repression and the basis of art still has supporters—for example, Camille Paglia is a social critic and theorist of sexuality who credits Freud with inventing "modern sex analysis."[47] It also has not gone unchallenged. Knowing what the likely effects of sexual promiscuity would be, both psychologically and physically, might also be useful for thinking about sexual morality. Does separating sex and bodily pleasure from other aspects of oneself have any effect on one's ability to have a psychologically healthy and fulfilling sexual experience? Furthermore, factual matters such as the likelihood of contracting a disease, such as AIDS, would be important for what we say about the moral character of some sexual encounters. Our conclusions about many factual or empirical matters would seem to influence greatly what we say about sexual morality—that is, the morality of sex, just like the morality of other human activities, is at least sometimes determined by the benefits and harms that result from it.

SEXUAL MORALITY AND ETHICAL THEORIES

Factual matters may be relevant only if we are judging the morality of actions on the basis of their consequences. If, instead, we adopt a non-consequentialist moral theory such as Kant's, then our concerns will not be about the consequences of sexual behavior but about whether we are cherishing or using people, for example, or being fair or unfair. If we adopt a natural law position, our concerns will again be significantly different, or at least based on different reasons. We will want to know whether certain sexual behavior fits or is befitting of human nature.

In fact, the moral theory that we hold will even determine how we pose the moral questions about sex. For example, if we are guided by a consequentialist moral theory such as utilitarianism, then we will be likely to pose moral questions in terms of good or bad, better or worse outcomes of sexual behavior. If we are governed by deontological principles, then our questions will more likely be in terms of right or wrong, justifiable or unjustifiable sexual behavior. And if we judge from a natural law basis, then we will want to know whether a particular sexual behavior is natural or unnatural, proper or improper, or even perverted. Let us consider each of these three ways of posing moral questions about sexual matters and see some of the probable considerations appropriate to each type of reasoning.

Consequentialist or Utilitarian Considerations

If we were to take a consequentialist point of view—say, that of an act utilitarian—we would judge our actions or make our decisions about how to behave sexually one at a time. In each case, we would consider our alternatives and their likely consequences for all who would be affected by them. In each case, we would consider who would benefit or suffer, as well as the type of benefit or suffering. In sexual relations, we would probably want to consider physical, psychological, and social consequences. Considerations such as these are necessary for arguments that are consequentialist in nature. According to this perspective, the sexual practice or relation that has better consequences than other possibilities is the preferred one. Any practice in which the bad consequences outweigh the good consequences would be morally problematic.

Among the negative consequences to be avoided are physical harms, including sexually transmitted diseases. Psychic harms are no less real. There is the embarrassment caused by sexual rejection or the trauma of rape. Also to be considered are possible feelings of disappointment and foolishness for having false hopes or of being deceived or used. Pregnancy, although regarded in some circumstances as a good or a benefit, may in other circumstances be unwanted and involve significant suffering. Some people might include as a negative consequence the effects on the family of certain sexual practices. Incest could create harms and dysfunction within the family. And adultery is generally seen to undermine marriages, although some couples in "open marriages" (with a mutual agreement to have sexual partners outside of the marriage) would disagree. Opponents of same-sex marriage go further, arguing that same-sex marriage undermines the institution of marriage. By contrast, many maintain that there is no evidence that same-sex marriage would have any impact whatsoever on straight marriages. And same-sex couples claim the right to marry in order to strengthen and benefit their families. In consequentialist reasoning, all of the consequences count, and short-term benefit or pleasure may be outweighed by long-term suffering or pain. However, the pain caused to one person also can be outweighed by the pleasure given to another or others, which is a major problem for this type of moral theory.

Many positive consequences or benefits also may come from sexual relations or activity. First of all, there is sexual pleasure itself. Furthermore, we may benefit both physically and psychologically from having this outlet for sexual urges and desires. It is relaxing. It enables us to appreciate other sensual things and to be more passionate and perhaps even more compassionate. It may enhance our perceptions of the world. Colors can be brighter and individual differences more noticeable. For many people, intimate sexual relations supposedly improve personal relations by breaking down barriers. However, many would argue that this is likely to be so only where a good relationship already exists between the persons involved.

What about sex in the context of marriage and children? The future happiness or unhappiness of potential children must play a role in consequentialist considerations. The increased availability of contraception now makes it easier to control these consequences, so offspring that result from sexual relations are presumably (but not necessarily) more likely to be wanted and well cared for. Abortion and its consequences also may play a role in determining whether a particular sexual relation is good from this perspective.

Finally, consequentialist thinking has room for judging not only what is good and bad, or better and worse, but also what is best and worst. On utilitarian grounds, the most pleasurable and most productive of overall happiness is the best. If one cannot have the ideal best, however, then one should choose the best that is available, provided that this choice does not negatively affect one's ability to have the best or cause problems in other aspects of one's life. It is consistent with a consequentialist perspective to judge sexual behavior not in terms of what we must avoid to do right, but in terms of what we should hope and aim for as the best. Nevertheless, in classical utilitarianism, the ideal is always to be thought of in terms of happiness or pleasure.

It is important to note, in this regard, that although the utilitarian philosopher John Stuart Mill was a proponent of liberty, he was also a defender of sexual equality. This helps explain why Mill was opposed to prostitution.

> Of all modes of sexual indulgence, consistent with the personal freedom and safety of women, I regard prostitution as the very worst; not only on account of the wretched women whose whole existence it sacrifices, but because no other is anything like so corrupting to the men. In no other is there the same total absence of even a temporary gleam of affection and tenderness; in no other is the woman to the man so completely a mere thing used simply as a means, for a purpose which to herself must be disgusting.[48]

Mill's point is that appropriate sexual relations should be mutual and equal. To use another as a means for sexual gratification may produce pleasure. But from a utilitarian perspective, this produces more unhappiness on balance, since it corrupts the men involved and degrades the women.

A rival utilitarian argument was made by Jeremy Bentham. Bentham held that although prostitution was shameful, it was better to legalize it than to make it illegal. Bentham thought that illegal prostitution increased the corrupting effect of prostitution on the prostitute, driving prostitutes to excessive use of "intoxicating liquors, that they may find in them a momentary oblivion of their misery," which also renders them "insensible to the restraint of shame."[49] A utilitarian might argue in a similar way that if prostitution were legalized and regulated, it might provide happiness for both the women and men involved. The customers would obtain sexual pleasure, the prostitutes would be able to capitalize on the transaction, state regulation would ensure healthy and safe sex, and the state could tax the transaction. But opponents of this idea, such as Carol Pateman, argue that there is something wrong with the idea that men could pay to use women's bodies in this way.[50]

Non-consequentialist or Deontological Considerations

The idea that it is simply wrong to use another person's body for sexual pleasure is a deontological one. Discussions of what is corrupting and degrading also point toward non-consequentialist concerns. Non-consequentialist moral theories, such as that of Kant, would direct us to judge sexual actions, as well as other actions, quite differently from consequentialist theories. Although the Golden Rule is not strictly the same thing as the categorical imperative, there are similarities between these two moral principles. According to both, as a person in a sexual relation, I should do only what would seem acceptable no matter whose shoes I were in or from whose perspective I judged. In the case of a couple, each person should consider what the sexual relation would look like from the other's point of view, and each should proceed only if a contemplated action or relation is also acceptable from that other viewpoint. This looks like a position regarding sexual relations according to which anything is permissible sexually as long as it is agreed to by the participants.

In one interpretation of Kantian sexual ethics—which focuses on respect for persons—consent and autonomy are the key factors to be considered. However, it is important to note that Kant's own views of sexual ethics are not exclusively focused on consent. Instead, he brings in considerations of the function and natural purpose of sex. In fact, he views the purpose of sexuality as the preservation of the species and condemns homosexuality, masturbation, and sex with animals on these grounds.[51]

We will turn to the natural law argument in the next section. But let's first further examine the Kantian emphasis on consent and respect for autonomy. The primary concern would be whether mutual consent to any given sexual act is real. For example, we would want to know whether the participants are fully informed and aware of what is involved. Lying would certainly be morally objectionable. So also would other forms of deceit and failure to inform. Not telling someone that one is married or that one has a communicable disease could also be forms of objectionable deceit, in particular when this information, if known, would make a difference to the other person's willingness to participate.

In addition, any sexual relation would have to be freely entered into. Any form of coercion would be morally objectionable on Kantian grounds. This is one of the strongest reasons for prohibiting sex with children, namely, that they cannot fully consent to it. They have neither the experience nor understanding of it, and they are not independent enough to resist pressure or coercion. As with deceit, what counts as coercion is not always easy to say, both in general and in any concrete case. Certainly, physically forcing a person to engage in sexual intercourse against his or her will is coercion. We call it rape. However, some forms of "persuasion"

may also be coercive. Threats to do what is harmful are coercive. For example, threatening to demote an employee or deny him or her a promotion if he or she does not engage in a sexual relation can be coercive. But subtler forms of coercion also exist, including implied threats to withhold one's affection from the other or to break off a relationship. Perhaps even some offers or bribes are coercive, especially when what is promised is not only desirable, but also something that one does not have and cannot get along without. Saying "I know that you are starving, and I will feed you if you have sex with me" is surely coercive.

Natural Law Considerations

Natural law theories (as described in Chapter 7) hold that morality is grounded in human nature. That is good which furthers human nature or is fitting for it, and that is bad or morally objectionable which frustrates or violates or is inconsistent with human nature. How would such a theory be used to make moral judgments about sexual behavior? Obviously, the key is the description of human nature.

In any use of human nature as a basis for determining what is good, a key issue will be describing that nature. To see how crucial this is, suppose that we examine a version of natural law theory that stresses the biological aspects of human nature. How would this require us to think about sexual morality? It would probably require us to note that an essential aspect of human nature is the orientation of the genital and reproductive system toward reproducing young. The very nature of heterosexual sexual intercourse (unless changed by accident or human intervention by sterilization or contraception) is to release male sperm into a female vagina and uterus. The sperm naturally tend to seek and penetrate an egg, fertilizing it and forming with the egg the beginning of a fetus, which develops naturally into a young member of the species. In this version of natural law theory, that which interferes with or seeks deliberately to frustrate this natural purpose of sexual intercourse as oriented toward reproduction would be morally objectionable. Thus, contraception, masturbation, and homosexual sexual relations would be contrary to nature. Further arguments would be needed for natural law theories that claim that sexual relations should take place only in marriage. These arguments would possibly have to do with the relation of sex and commitment, with the biological relation of the child to the parents, and with the necessary or best setting for the raising of children.

We could also envision other nature-focused arguments about sexual morality that are based on somewhat different notions of human nature. For example, we could argue that the natural purpose of sexual relations is pleasure because nature has so constructed the nerve components of the genital system. Furthermore, the intimacy and naturally uniting aspect of sexual intercourse may provide a basis for arguing that this is its natural tendency—to unite people, to express their unity, or to bring them

closer together. This account of the function of sex would not necessarily rule out homosexual relations.

To believe that there is such a thing as sexual behavior that is consistent with human nature—or natural—also implies that there can be sexual behavior that is inconsistent with human nature or unnatural. Sometimes the term *perverted* has been used synonymously with *unnatural*. Thus, in the context of a discussion or analysis of natural law views about sexual morality, we also can consider the question of whether there is such a thing as sexual perversion. This is not to say that notions of sexual perversion are limited to natural law theory, however. *Perversion* literally means "turned against" or "away from" something—usually away from some norm. Perverted sexual behavior would then be sexual behavior that departs from some norm for such behavior. "That's not normal," we

Outline of Moral Approaches to Sexual Relations

	Liberal	Moderate	Conservative
Thesis	Sexual relations ought to be free and open	There are reasons to limit and regulate sexual behavior	Sexual relations ought to be subject to strict regulation
Corollaries and Implications	Same-sex marriage should be permitted; pornography, prostitution, and freely adopted sexual identity should be permitted—with limits based upon consent	Sexual relations and identities should be limited by social concerns, including regulating disease, protecting the rights of women, minimizing unwanted pregnancy, and so on	Sexual relations ought to conform to traditional heterosexual norms, including limiting sexual relations within traditional marriages
Connections with Moral Theory	Libertarian freedom based upon respect for autonomy; consequentialist focus on producing happiness for people to explore sexual experience and sexual identities	Respect for individual liberty balanced with need to minimize harms; utilitarian concern for the well-being of women and others who may be exploited	Natural law basis for traditional gender identities and sexual norms; consequentialist focus on maintaining social stability and traditional values
Relevant Authors	John Corvino	Jeremy Bentham; John Stuart Mill	John Finnis; Immanuel Kant

say. By norm, here, we mean not just the usual type of behavior, for this depends on what people do. Rather, by norm or normal, we mean what coincides with a moral standard.

To consider whether there is a natural type of sexual behavior or desire, we might compare it with another appetite, namely, the appetite of hunger, whose natural object we might say is food. If a person were to eat pictures of food instead of food, this would generally be considered abnormal. Would we also say that a person who was satisfied with pictures of a sexually attractive person and used them as a substitute for a real person was in some sense abnormal or acting abnormally? This depends on whether there is such a thing as a normal sex drive and what its natural object would be. People have used the notion of normal sex drive and desire to say that things such as shoe fetishism (being sexually excited by shoes) and desire for sex with animals or dead bodies are abnormal. One suggestion is that the object of normal sexual desire is another individual, and the desire is not just for the other but for the other's mutual and embodied response.

These notions of perverted versus normal sexual desire and behavior can belong in some loose way to a tradition that considers human nature as a moral norm. Like the utilitarian and Kantian moral traditions, natural law theory has its own way of judging sexual and other types of behavior. These three ways of judging sexual behavior are not necessarily incompatible with one another, however. We might find that some forms of sexual behavior are not only ill-fitted for human nature, but also involve using another as a thing rather than treating her or him as a person, and that such behavior also has bad consequences. Or we may find that what is most fitting for human nature is also what has the best consequences and treats persons with the respect that is due to them. The more difficult cases will be those in which no harm comes to persons from a sexual relation, but they have nevertheless been used. No less difficult will be cases in which knowing consent is present, but it is for activities that seem ill-fitted for human nature or do not promise happiness, pleasure, or other benefits.

SAME-SEX MARRIAGE

We can further explore the moral theories we have just discussed by attempting to apply them to the issue with which we began this chapter: same-sex marriage. When making moral judgments about homosexuality and same-sex marriage, the same considerations can be used as for sexual morality generally: consequentialist and non-consequentialist considerations, as well as naturalness. Some issues are conceptual, such as what is meant by *homosexual* as opposed to *heterosexual* and *bisexual*. And there is a deep and contested empirical question of whether one's gender or sexual identity is a naturally given fact of life or whether it is a matter of individual choice. Some opponents of same-sex marriage will claim that sexuality is a matter of choice and that individuals simply ought to choose traditional heterosexual relationships. In opposition to this, some proponents of same-sex marriage will claim that individuals should be free to choose to marry whomever they want. Other defenders of same-sex marriage will argue that since homosexual attraction is not a matter of choice but, rather, a natural disposition over which individuals have no control, homosexuals should be free to engage in relationships that are natural and rewarding for them.

From a consequentialist point of view, there is nothing in the nature of sex itself that requires that it be heterosexual or for reproductive purposes. In this view, the sexual activity that produces the most happiness for the people involved is the best, regardless of the gender of the parties involved and whether or not they intend to produce children. Some have argued against same-sex marriage and homosexuality in general on the grounds that such relationships and sexual behavior produce more bad consequences than good ones—that they undermine the traditional family, de-couple marriage from reproduction, and deprive children of a stable family environment. As with many other controversial topics, the empirical evidence supporting such consequentialist claims is disputed. One widely discussed recent study by sociologist Mark Regnerus has been cited by conservatives who claim that it shows that children raised by homosexual couples fare poorly.[52] This study was cited by the U.S. Conference of Catholic Bishops in its friend-of-the-court brief filed in the *Hollingsworth v. Perry* case, which legalized same-sex marriage in California in 2013. The bishops appealed to the Regnerus study in arguing that heterosexual marriages created the "optimal environment" for raising children.[53] On the other side, sociologists have criticized the Regnerus study's conclusions as well as its source of funding (the study was supported by funding from conservative, "family values" sources).[54] The American Sociological Association concluded, in its friend-of-the-court brief for the *Hollingsworth v. Perry* case, that the "scholarly consensus is clear: children of same-sex parents fare just as well as children of opposite-sex parents."[55]

While it is true that traditional heterosexual marriage has declined as a social value—with more divorce and more people cohabiting outside of marriage—there is no evidence that same-sex marriage is the cause of these phenomena. Rather, the general decline in marriage is better described in terms of a variety of causal factors, including the decline of religious traditionalism, changing sexual mores, the liberation of women, and larger economic forces.[56] Proponents of same-sex marriage have also pointed out that if the true moral purpose of marriage is reproduction, then we should ban infertile heterosexual couples from marrying, as well as older couples and couples who desire to remain childless.

The social context may also make a difference to consequentialist viewpoints on homosexuality. Social acceptability or stigma will make a difference in whether people can be happy in certain kinds of relationships. Greater social acceptance of homosexuality—along with legalization of same-sex marriage—might produce more happiness for homosexuals. Moreover, if same-sex marriage were legalized throughout the country, then the full benefits of marriage would be extended to homosexuals, including benefits for married couples that are obtained through tax policy, insurance coverage, and inheritance law.

Non-consequentialist considerations also apply to discussions about homosexuality and same-sex marriage. One of the most common non-consequentialist arguments against homosexual sex is that it is unnatural, that it goes against nature. Many gay men and lesbians respond to such arguments by emphasizing that their same-sex attractions are profoundly "natural" and were present from childhood. They also point to the occurrence of same gender sexual behavior in the natural world.

According to traditional natural law theory, although we differ individually in many ways, people share a common human nature. I may have individual inclinations or things may be natural to me that are not natural to you, simply because of our differing talents, psychic traits, and other unique characteristics. Natural law theory tells us that certain things are right or wrong not because they further or frustrate our individual inclinations, but because they promote or work against our species' inclinations and aspects of our common human nature. Arguments about homosexuality that appeal to traditional natural law theory may need to determine whether homosexuality is consistent with common human nature or simply present in some individual natures.

Thus, the argument that gay men or lesbian women find relating sexually to members of their own sex "natural" to them as individuals may or may not work as part of a natural law argument that supports that behavior. However, if one takes a broader view of sexuality in its passionate, emotional, and social aspects, then one could make a reasonable argument based on natural law that homosexuality is but one expression of a common human sexuality. Historically, natural law arguments have not gone this way. But this is not to say that such an argument could not be reasonably put forth.

Natural law arguments against homosexuality and same-sex marriage have often traditionally been grounded in religious viewpoints on sexuality and the sanctity of heterosexual marriage. For example, many Christians and Jews who denounce homosexuality do so on the basis of Old Testament Bible verses such as Deuteronomy 23:17–18, Leviticus 18:22, and Leviticus 20:13. The apostle Paul also condemns it in the New Testament: 1 Corinthians 6:9–10 and Timothy 1:9–10 and in Romans 1:26–27.[57] One problem for such scripturally based arguments is that these sacred texts are based upon ancient social mores, which include values that we might find objectionable today such as the subordination of women. The Old Testament appears to permit polygamy. And the New Testament prohibits divorce. If we reject same-sex marriage on biblical grounds, should we also reject divorce and permit polygamy? Some religions (Islam, for example, and Mormonism at one point in its history) do permit polygamous marriage, which is now illegal in the United States and other Western countries. (It is an open question of whether it is more natural for men to be polygamous or monogamous.) An explicitly religious foundation for marriage also runs afoul of secular principles (as discussed in Chapter 2), which aim to keep the legal system neutral with regard to religion.

As noted earlier, arguments about homosexuality and same-sex marriage may be more properly framed as civil rights issues, rather than moral issues per se. It may be helpful to put this issue in a larger context. For example, African Americans in the United States were not allowed to marry until after the Civil War, and mixed race couples could not do so everywhere in the United States until a Supreme Court decision in 1967. Since the early 2000s, various countries around the world and states in the United States have come to permit same-sex marriage. More widely available are so-called civil unions or domestic partnerships that grant many of the same legal benefits as married couples have.

While proponents of civil unions may think that this solves the question without extending the concept of marriage in a way that includes same-sex marriages, the current debate about same-sex marriage points beyond the legal issue of how domestic partners might share social benefits. The larger question is whether homosexual relationships deserve to be considered as the same kind of loving and sexual relationship as heterosexual relationships. The Defense of Marriage Act of 1996, which we mentioned at the outset of this chapter, was described in a report to Congress as focused on the

moral question of homosexuality: "Civil laws that permit only heterosexual marriage reflect and honor a collective moral judgment about human sexuality. This judgment entails both moral disapproval of homosexuality, moral conviction that heterosexuality better comports with traditional (especially Judeo-Christian) morality."[58] The 2013 Supreme Court ruling overturning the Defense of Marriage Act (*U.S. v. Windsor*) rejects this institutional expression of moral disapproval of homosexuality.

Laws that address issues of civil rights, whether in this area or others, are often grounded in questions of morality. Nevertheless, morality is a distinct realm, and we may ask whether certain actions or practices are morally good or bad, apart from whether they ought to be regulated by law. So, in the realm of sexual matters, we can ask about the morality of certain actions or practices. Questions about sexual morality are obviously quite personal. Nevertheless, because this is one of the major drives and aspects of a fulfilling human life, it is important to think about what may be best and worst, and what may be right and wrong in these matters.

MindTap· For more chapter resources and activities, go to MindTap.

In this chapter's readings, the issue of sexual morality is discussed with a particular focus on homosexuality and same-sex marriage. The moral issues that arise in these essays can be applied in various ways to the other issues we've discussed here. We begin with an excerpt from the majority opinion of the U.S. Supreme Court's *Obergefell v. Hodges* decision, which legalized same-sex marriage in the United States. Following that is an essay by John Finnis, which presents an argument based in natural law tradition, which holds that homosexuality is wrong and that marriage is supposed to be heterosexual. Finnis is one of the most prominent contemporary defenders of the natural law tradition. Finally, we conclude with an excerpt from a book by John Corvino, which critically examines the claim that homosexuality is unnatural and the natural law arguments presented by theorists such as Finnis.

NOTES

1. U.S Supreme Court, *Obergefell v. Hodges*, Decided June 26, 2015.

2. "Kentucky Clerk Kim Davis on Gay Marriage Licenses" *Washington Post*, September 1, 2015, https://www.washingtonpost.com/news/acts-of-faith/wp/2015/09/01/kentucky-clerk-kim-davis-on-gay-marriage-licenses-it-is-a-heaven-or-hell-decision/ (accessed March 3, 2015).

3. Justice A. Scalia dissent, *Lawrence v. Texas* (02–102) 539 U.S. 558 (2003).

4. Defense of Marriage Act, http://www.gpo.gov/fdsys/pkg/BILLS-104hr3396enr/pdf/BILLS-104hr3396enr.pdf (accessed March 1, 2013).

5. Lindsay Wise, "In Federal Gay-Marriage Case, More Than 1,100 Benefits at Stake," *McClatchy News*, March 27, 2013, http://www.mcclatchydc.com/2013/03/27/187120/in-federal-gay-marriage-case-more.html#storylink=cpy (accessed April 25, 2013).

6. *United States v. Windsor* 570 U.S. ___ (2013), pp. 25–26.

7. Thom Shanker, "Partners of Gays in Service Are Granted Some Benefits," *New York Times*, February 11, 2013, http://www.nytimes.com/2013/02/12/us/partners-of-gay-military-personnel-are-granted-benefits.html (accessed March 1, 2013).

8. Pew Center, "Gay marriage Around the World," http://www.pewforum.org/2015/06/26/gay-marriage-around-the-world-2013/ (accessed February 29, 2016).

9. International Lesbian, Gay, Bisexual, Trans and Intersex Association: Carroll, A. & Itaborahy, L.P. *State Sponsored Homophobia 2015: A world survey of laws: criminalisation, protection and recognition of same-sex love* (Geneva; ILGA, May 2015).

10. CDC, "Teenagers in the United States: Sexual Activity, Contraceptive Use, and Childbearing, 2006–2010 National Survey of Family Growth" (October 2011), p. 7, http://www.cdc.gov/nchs/data/series/sr_23/sr23_031.pdf (accessed March 4, 2016).

11. "National Survey of Family Growth" (2005–2010), Centers for Disease Control and Prevention, http://www.cdc.gov/nchs/nsfg.htm (accessed July 21, 2016).

12. Centers for Disease Control, "Sexual Activity, Contraceptive Use, and Childbearing of Teenagers Aged 15–19 in the United States" (July 2015), http://www.cdc.gov/nchs/data/databriefs/db209.pdf (accessed March 4, 2016).

13. Brady E. Hamilton, Donna L. Hoyert, Joyce A. Martin, Donna M. Strobino, and Bernard Guyer, "Annual Summary of Vital Statistics: 2010–2011," *Pediatrics* (published online February 11, 2013), http://pediatrics.aappublications.org/content/early/2013/02/05/peds.2012-3769.abstract (accessed July 27, 2013).

14. Guttmacher Institute, "American Teens' Sexual and Reproductive Health" (May 2014), http://www.guttmacher.org/pubs/FB-ATSRH.html (accessed March 4, 2016).

15. "Sexual Behavior, Sexual Attraction, and Sexual Orientation Among Adults Aged 18–44 in the United States: Data From the 2011–2013 National Survey of Family Growth" (January 2016), http://www.cdc.gov/nchs/data/nhsr/nhsr088.pdf (accessed March 4, 2016).

16. "HIV infections and deaths still in decline" *The Economist*, July 14, 2015, http://www.economist.com/news/science-and-technology/21657647-virus-being-beaten-back-ever-faster-hiv-infections-and-deaths-still (accessed March 4, 2016).

17. "Pope signals shift away from Catholic church's prohibition of condoms" *The Guardian*, November 20, 2010, http://www.theguardian.com/world/2010/nov/20/pope-benedict-catholic-church-condoms (accessed March 4, 2016).

18. Ilene Lelchuk, "UCSF Explores Teens' Post-Sex Emotions," *San Francisco Chronicle*, February 15, 2007, http://www.sfgate.com/bayarea/article/SAN-FRANCISCO-UCSF-explores-teens-post-sex-2617439.php (accessed April 26, 2013).

19. "Key Statistics from the National Survey of Family Growth," Centers for Disease Control and Prevention, http://www.cdc.gov/nchs/nsfg/key_statistics.htm (accessed July 21, 2016).

20. "Under Obama Administration, Abstinence-Only Education Finds Surprising New Foothold," *Washington Post*, May 8, 2012, http://www.washingtonpost.com/blogs/wonkblog/post/under-obama-administration-abstinence-only-education-

finds-surprising-new-foothold/2012/05/08/
gIQA8fcwAU_blog.html (accessed March 1, 2013);
also see *Impacts of Four Title V, Section 510 Abstinence Education Program*, Mathematica Policy
Research for Department of Health and Human
Services (April 2007), http://www.mathematica-
mpr.com/publications/pdfs/impactabstinence.pdf
(accessed April 26, 2013).

21. "Sex Ed Can Help Prevent Teen Pregnancy,"
Washington Post, March 24, 2008, http://www
.washingtonpost.com/wp-dyn/content/article/
2008/03/24/AR2008032401515.html (accessed
March 1, 2013).

22. For abstinence sex education, see National Abstinence Education Association, http://www
.abstinenceassociation.org/index.html; for comprehensive sex education, see Advocates for Youth,
http://www.advocatesforyouth.org/index.php

23. Jason DeParle and Sabrina Tavernise, "For Women
Under 30, Most Births Occur Outside Marriage,"
New York Times, February 17, 2012, http://www
.nytimes.com/2012/02/18/us/for-women-under-
30-most-births-occur-outside-marriage.
html?pagewanted=all (accessed April 26, 2013).

24. Dennie Hughes, "Is It So Wrong to Live Together?"
USA Weekend, January 16–18, 2004, p. 12.

25. *Time*, May 25, 2009, pp. 57–58.

26. David Whitman, "Was It Good for Us?" *U.S. News
& World Report* 122, No. 19 (May 19, 1997), p. 56.

27. *New York Times*, March 3, 2010, p. A14.

28. Hughes, op. cit.

29. "Violence against Women," Amnesty International,
http://www.amnestyusa.org/our-work/issues/
women-s-rights/violence-against-women/
violence-against-women-information (accessed
April 26, 2013).

30. "Female Genital Mutilation Fact Sheet," World
Health Organization, updated February 2013,
http://www.who.int/mediacentre/factsheets/
fs241/en/ (accessed April 26, 2013).

31. James Ciment, "Senegal Outlaws Female Genital
Mutilation," *British Medical Journal* 3 (February 6,
1999), p. 348; and Joel E. Frader et al., "Female
Genital Mutilation," *Pediatrics* 102 (July 1998),
p. 153.

32. Ibid.

33. Elizabeth Rosenthal, "Genital Cutting Raises by
50% Likelihood Mothers or Their Newborns Will
Die, Study Finds," *New York Times*, June 2, 2006,
p. A10, http://www.nytimes.com/2006/06/02/
world/africa/02mutilation.html?_r=0 (accessed
May 12, 2013).

34. "Female Genital Mutilation Fact Sheet," World
Health Organization, http://www.who.int/media-
centre/factsheets/fs241/en/

35. Xiaorong Li, "Tolerating the Intolerable: The Case of
Female Genital Mutilation," *Philosophy and Public
Policy Quarterly* 21, No. 1 (Winter 2001), p. 4.

36. Ibid., p. 6.

37. "United Nations Bans Female Genital Mutilation,"
UN Women, December 20, 2012, http://www
.unwomen.org/2012/12/united-nations-bans-female-
genital-mutilation/ (accessed March 1, 2013).

38. "Female Genital Mutilation and Other Harmful
Practices," World Health Organization, http://www
.who.int/reproductivehealth/topics/fgm/fgm-
sexuality/en/ (accessed April 26, 2013).

39. Susan Brownmiller, *Against Our Will: Men,
Women, and Rape* (New York: Ballantine Books,
1993, originally published in 1975), p. 391.

40. "The Offenders" Rape, Abuse, & Incest National
Network, http://www.rainn.org/get-information/
statistics/sexual-assault-offenders (accessed
July 27, 2013).

41. "How Often Does Sexual Assault Occur?" Rape,
Abuse & Incest National Network (2010 data),
http://www.rainn.org/get-information/statistics/
frequency-of-sexual-assault (accessed March 1,
2013).

42. "Marital Rape," Rape, Abuse & Incest National
Network, http://www.rainn.org/public-policy/
sexual-assault-issues/marital-rape (accessed
April 26, 2013).

43. Preetika Rana, "Why India Still Allows Marital
Rape," *Wall Street Journal*, March 26, 2013,
http://blogs.wsj.com/indiarealtime/2013/03/26/
why-india-allows-men-to-rape-their-wives/
(accessed April 26, 2013).

44. UNODC, "Global Report on Trafficking in Persons"
(2012), p. 7, http://www.unodc.org/documents/
data-and-analysis/glotip/Trafficking_in_Persons_
2012_web.pdf (accessed March 1, 2013).

45. Amanda Walker-Rodriguez and Rodney Hill, "Human Sex Trafficking," FBI, March 2011, http://www.fbi.gov/stats-services/publications/law-enforcement-bulletin/march_2011/human_sex_trafficking (accessed March 1, 2013).

46. Aristotle, *The Nicomachean Ethics*, bk. 8, Chapter 4.

47. Camille Paglia, *Sex, Art, and American Culture* (New York: Vintage Books, 1992), p. 113.

48. John Stuart Mill, "Letter to Lord Amberly," February 2, 1870, in *The Collected Works of John Stuart Mill*, vol. 17, ed. Francis E. Mineka and Dwight N. Lindley (Toronto: University of Toronto Press, London: Routledge and Kegan Paul, 1972), p. 1525.

49. Jeremy Bentham, *Principles of Penal Law* in *Works of Jeremy Bentham* (Edinburgh: W. Tait, 1838), vol. 1, pt. 2, p. 546.

50. Carol Pateman, "What's Wrong with Prostitution?" Chapter 7 in *The Sexual Contract*, (Stanford, CA: Stanford University Press, 1988).

51. Kant, *Lectures on Ethics* (Indianapolis, IN: Hackett Publishing, 1981), pp. 169–71.

52. Mark Regnerus, "How Different Are the Adult Children of Parents Who Have Same-Sex Relationships? Findings from the New Family Structures Study," *Social Science Research* 41 (2012), p. 752.

53. "Brief Amicus Curiae of the United States Conference of Catholic Bishops in Support of Petitioners and Supporting Reversal"—re *Hollingsworth v. Perry*, January 29, 2013, http://www.usccb.org/about/general-counsel/amicus-briefs/upload/hollingsworth-v-perry.pdf (accessed April 26, 2013).

54. "Controversial Gay-Parenting Study Is Severely Flawed, Journal's Audit Finds," *Chronicle of Higher Education* (July 26, 2012).

55. "Brief of Amicus Curiae American Sociological Association in Support of Respondent Kristin M. Perry and Respondent Edith Schlain Windsor"—re *Hollingsworth v. Perry*, http://www.asanet.org/documents/ASA/pdfs/12-144_307_Amicus_%20(C_%20Gottlieb)_ASA_Same-Sex_Marriage.pdf (accessed April 26, 2013).

56. Derek Thompson, "The Decline of Marriage and the Rise of Unwed Mothers: An Economic Mystery," *Atlantic*, March 18, 2013, http://www.theatlantic.com/business/archive/2013/03/the-decline-of-marriage-and-the-rise-of-unwed-mothers-an-economic-mystery/274111/ (accessed April 26, 2013).

57. See Andrew Fiala, *What Would Jesus Really Do?* (Lanham, MD: Rowman & Littlefield, 2007), Chapter 9.

58. *Defense of Marriage Act*, http://www.gpo.gov/fdsys/pkg/CRPT-104hrpt664/pdf/CRPT-104hrpt664.pdf (accessed April 26, 2013).

READING

U.S. Supreme Court Decision June 26, 2015

OBERGEFELL V. HODGES

MindTap° For more chapter resources and activities, go to MindTap.

Study Questions

As you read the excerpt, please consider the following questions:

1. How does the Court situate homosexuality and same-sex marriage in the evolving sexual morality of the United States?
2. What basic rights are appealed to in the Court's decision?
3. What is the Court's view of the value of marriage to children and to the nation?

The history of marriage is one of both continuity and change. Changes, such as the decline of arranged marriages and the abandonment of the law of coverture, have worked deep transformations in the structure of marriage, affecting aspects of marriage once viewed as essential. These new insights have strengthened, not weakened, the institution. Changed understandings of marriage are characteristic of a Nation where new dimensions of freedom become apparent to new generations.

This dynamic can be seen in the Nation's experience with gay and lesbian rights. Well into the 20th century, many States condemned same-sex intimacy as immoral, and homosexuality was treated as an illness. Later in the century, cultural and political developments allowed same-sex couples to lead more open and public lives. Extensive public and private dialogue followed, along with shifts in public attitudes. Questions about the legal treatment of gays and lesbians soon reached the courts, where they could be discussed in the formal discourse of the law....

The fundamental liberties protected by the Fourteenth Amendment's Due Process Clause extend to certain personal choices central to individual dignity and autonomy, including intimate choices defining personal identity and beliefs.... Courts must exercise reasoned judgment in identifying interests of the person so fundamental that the State must accord them its respect. History and tradition guide and discipline the inquiry but do not set its outer boundaries. When new insight reveals discord between the Constitution's central protections and a received legal stricture, a claim to liberty must be addressed.

Applying these tenets, the Court has long held the right to marry is protected by the Constitution. For example, *Loving* v. *Virginia* invalidated bans on interracial unions, and *Turner* v. *Safley* held that prisoners could not be denied the right to marry....

Four principles and traditions demonstrate that the reasons marriage is fundamental under the Constitution apply with equal force to same-sex couples. The first premise of this Court's relevant precedents is that the right to personal choice regarding marriage is inherent in the concept of individual autonomy. This abiding connection between marriage and liberty is why *Loving* invalidated interracial marriage bans under the Due Process Clause. Decisions about marriage are among the most intimate that an individual can make.... This is true for all persons, whatever their sexual orientation.

A second principle in this Court's jurisprudence is that the right to marry is fundamental because it supports a two-person union unlike any other in its importance to the committed individuals. The intimate association protected by this right was central to *Griswold* v. *Connecticut*, which held the Constitution protects the right of married couples to use contraception.... Same-sex couples have the same right as opposite-sex couples to enjoy intimate association, a right extending beyond mere freedom from laws making same-sex intimacy a criminal offense.

A third basis for protecting the right to marry is that it safeguards children and families and thus draws meaning from related rights of childrearing, procreation, and education. Without the recognition, stability, and predictability marriage offers, children suffer the stigma of knowing their families are somehow lesser. They also suffer the significant material costs of being raised by unmarried parents, relegated to a more difficult and uncertain family life. The marriage laws at issue thus harm and humiliate the children of same-sex couples. This does not mean that the right to marry is less meaningful for those who do not or cannot have children. Precedent protects the right of a married couple not to procreate, so the right to marry cannot be conditioned on the capacity or commitment to procreate.

Finally, this Court's cases and the Nation's traditions make clear that marriage is a keystone of the Nation's social order. States have contributed to the fundamental character of marriage by placing it at the center of many facets of the legal and social order. There is no difference between same- and opposite-sex couples with respect to this principle, yet same-sex couples are denied the constellation

---

United States Supreme Court, *Obergefell v. Hodges*, 576 U.S.___ (2015).

of benefits that the States have linked to marriage and are consigned to an instability many opposite-sex couples would find intolerable. It is demeaning to lock same-sex couples out of a central institution of the Nation's society, for they too may aspire to the transcendent purposes of marriage. The limitation of marriage to opposite-sex couples may long have seemed natural and just, but its inconsistency with the central meaning of the fundamental right to marry is now manifest....

The challenged laws burden the liberty of same-sex couples, and they abridge central precepts of equality. The marriage laws at issue are in essence unequal: Same-sex couples are denied benefits afforded opposite-sex couples and are barred from exercising a fundamental right. Especially against a long history of disapproval of their relationships, this denial works a grave and continuing harm, serving to disrespect and subordinate gays and lesbians.

Finally, the First Amendment ensures that religions, those who adhere to religious doctrines, and others have protection as they seek to teach the principles that are so fulfilling and so central to their lives and faiths.

READING

Law, Morality, and "Sexual Orientation"

JOHN FINNIS

MindTap For more chapter resources and activities, go to MindTap.

Study Questions

As you read the excerpt, please consider the following questions:

1. Why does Finnis condemn all nonmarital intercourse, including homosexual relations, masturbation, and prostitution?
2. What is the purpose of marriage, according to Finnis? And why does Finnis claim that gay marriage is "a sham?"
3. Why does Finnis worry that gay marriage might lead to group marriages and revolving partnerships?

Let me begin by noticing a too little noticed fact. All three of the greatest Greek philosophers, Socrates, Plato and Aristotle, regarded homosexual *conduct* as intrinsically shameful, immoral, and indeed depraved or depraving. That is to say, all three rejected the linchpin of modern "gay" ideology and lifestyle.

Socrates is portrayed by Plato (and by Xenophon) as having strong homosexual (as well as heterosexual) inclinations or interest, and as promoting an ideal of homosexual romance between men and youths, but at the same time as utterly rejecting homosexual conduct....

What, then, about Plato? Well, the same Plato who in his Symposium wrote a famous celebration of *romantic and spiritual* man-boy erotic relationships, made very clear that all forms of sexual *conduct* outside heterosexual marriage are shameful, wrongful and harmful. This is particularly evident from his treatment of the matter in his last work, the *Laws*, but is also sufficiently clear in the *Republic* and the *Phaedrus*, and even in the *Symposium* itself. This is affirmed unequivocally both by Dover and by Vlastos, neither of whom favours these views of Plato. According to Vlastos, for example, Plato-

John Finnis, "Law, Morality, and Sexual Orientation" *Notre Dame Law Review*, 69 (1994), pp. 1049–76. Reprinted with permission. © Notre Dame Law Review, University of Notre Dame.

The publisher bears responsibility for any errors which have occurred in reprinting or editing.

saw anal intercourse as 'contrary to nature', (footnote: *Ph[ae]dr[us]* 251A1, *L[aws]* 636–7) a degradation not only of man's humanity, but even of his animality....[1]

It is for Plato, Vlastos adds, a type of act far more serious than any mere going "contrary to the rules".[2] As for Aristotle, there is widespread scholarly agreement that he rejected homosexual conduct. In fact, such conduct is frequently represented by Aristotle (in some cases directly and in other cases by a lecturer's hint) as intrinsically perverse, shameful and harmful both to the individuals involved and to society itself.[3]

Although the ideology of homosexual love (with its accompanying devaluation of women) continued to have philosophical defenders down to the end of classical Greek civilisation, there equally continued to be influential philosophical writers, wholly untouched by Judeao-Christian tradition, who taught that homosexual conduct is not only intrinsically shameful but also inconsistent with a proper recognition of the equality of women with men in intrinsic worth. (The ancients did not fail to note that Socrates' homoerotic orientation, for all its admirable chastity—abstention from homosexual conduct— went along with a neglect to treat his wife as an equal.)

At the heart of the Platonic-Aristotelian and later ancient philosophical rejections of all homosexual conduct, and thus of the modern "gay" ideology, are three fundamental theses: (1) The commitment of a man and woman to each other in the sexual union of marriage is intrinsically good and reasonable, and is incompatible with sexual relations outside marriage. (2) Homosexual acts are radically and peculiarly non-marital, and for that reason intrinsically unreasonable and unnatural. (3) Furthermore, according to Plato, if not Aristotle, homosexual acts have a special similarity to solitary masturbation,[4] and both types of radically non-marital act are manifestly unworthy of the human being and immoral.

II

Genital intercourse between spouses enables them to actualise and experience (and in that sense express) their marriage itself, as a single reality with two blessings (children and mutual affection).[5] Non-marital intercourse, especially *but not only* homosexual, has no such point and therefore is unacceptable.

Why cannot non-marital friendship be promoted and expressed by sexual acts? Why is the attempt to express affection by orgasmic non-marital sex the pursuit of an illusion? Why did Plato and Socrates, Xenophon, Aristotle, Musonius Rufus, and Plutarch, right at the heart of their reflections on the homo-erotic culture around them, make the very deliberate and careful judgment that homosexual conduct (and indeed all extra-marital sexual gratification) is radically incapable of participating in, actualising, the common good of friendship?

Implicit in the philosophical and common-sense rejection of extra-marital sex is the answer to these questions. The union of the reproductive organs of husband and wife really unites them biologically (and their biological reality is part of, not merely an instrument of, their *personal* reality); reproduction is *one* function and so, in respect of that function, the spouses are indeed one reality. So their union in a sexual act of the reproductive kind (whether or not actually reproductive or even capable of resulting in generation in this instance) can *actualise* and allow them to *experience* their *real common good*. That common good is precisely *their marriage* with the two goods, parenthood and friendship, which are the parts of its wholeness as an intelligible common good even if, independently of what the spouses will, their capacity for biological parenthood will not be fulfilled by that act of genital union. But the common good of friends who are not and cannot be married (for example, man and man, man and boy, woman and woman) has nothing to do with their having children by each other, and their reproductive organs cannot make them a biological (and therefore personal) unit.[6] So their sexual acts together cannot do what they may hope and imagine. Because their activation of one or even each of their reproductive organs cannot be an actualising and experiencing of the *marital* good—as marital intercourse (intercourse between spouses in a marital way) can, even between spouses who *happen* to be sterile—it can do no more than provide each partner with an individual gratification. For want of a *common good* that could be actualised and experienced *by and in this bodily union*, that conduct involves the partners in treating their bodies as instruments to be used in the service of their consciously experiencing selves; their choice to engage in such conduct thus dis-integrates each of them precisely as acting persons.[7]

Reality is known in judgment, not in emotion. In reality, whatever the generous hopes and dreams and thoughts of *giving* with which some same-sex partners may surround their 'sexual' acts, those acts cannot express or do more than is expressed or done if two strangers engage in such activity to give each other pleasure, or a prostitute pleasures a client to give him pleasure in return for money, or (say) a man masturbates to give himself pleasure and a fantasy of more human relationships after a gruelling day on the assembly line. This is, I believe, the substance of Plato's judgment—at that moment in the *Gorgias* 494–495 which is also decisive for the moral and political philosophical critique of hedonism[8] that there is no important distinction in essential moral worthlessness between solitary masturbation, being sodomized as a prostitute, and being sodomized for the pleasure of it. Sexual acts cannot *in reality* be self-giving unless they are acts by which a man and a woman actualize and experience sexually the real giving of themselves to each other—in biological, affective, and volitional union in mutual commitment, both open-ended and exclusive—which like Plato and Aristotle and most peoples we call *marriage*.

In short, sexual acts are not unitive in their significance unless they are marital (actualizing the all-level unity of marriage) and (since the common good of marriage has two aspects) they are not marital unless they have not only the generosity of acts of friendship but also the procreative significance, not necessarily of being intended to generate or capable in the circumstances of generating but at least of being, as human conduct, acts of the reproductive kind—actualizations, so far as the spouses then and there can, of the reproductive function in which they are biologically and thus personally one.

The ancient philosophers do not much discuss the case of sterile marriages, or the fact (well known to them) that for long periods of time (e.g., throughout pregnancy) the sexual acts of a married couple are naturally incapable of resulting in reproduction. They appear to take for granted what the subsequent Christian tradition certainly did, that such sterility does not render the conjugal sexual acts of the spouses non-marital. For: a husband and wife who unite their reproductive organs in an act of sexual intercourse which, so far as they then can make it, is of a kind suitable for generation, do function as a biological (and thus personal) unit and thus can be actualising and experiencing the two-in-one-flesh common good and reality of marriage, even when some biological condition happens to prevent that unity resulting in generation of a child. Their conduct thus differs radically from the acts of a husband and wife whose intercourse is masturbatory, for example sodomitic or by fellatio or coitus interruptus.[9] In law such acts do not consummate a marriage, because in reality (whatever the couple's illusions of intimacy and self-giving in such acts) they do not actualise the one-flesh, two-part marital good.

Does this account seek to "make moral judgments based on natural facts"?[10] Yes and no. No, in the sense that it does not seek to infer normative conclusions or theses from only non-normative (natural-fact) premises. Nor does it appeal to any norm of the form, "Respect natural facts or natural functions". But yes, it is to the realities of our constitution, intentions and circumstances that the argument applies the relevant practical reasons (especially that marriage and inner integrity are basic human goods) and moral principles (especially that one may never *intend* to destroy, damage, impede, or violate any basic human good, or prefer an illusory instantiation of a basic human good to a real instantiation of that or some other human good).

III

Societies such as classical Athens and contemporary England (and virtually every other) draw a distinction between behaviour found merely (perhaps extremely) offensive (such as eating excrement), and behavior to be repudiated as destructive of human character and relationships. Copulation of humans with animals is repudiated because it treats human sexual activity and satisfaction as something appropriately sought in a manner as divorced from the expressing of an intelligible common good as is the instinctive coupling of beasts—and so treats human bodily life, in one of its most intense activities, as appropriately lived as merely animal. The deliberate genital coupling of persons of the same sex is repudiated for a very similar reason. It is not simply that it is sterile and disposes the participants to an abdication of responsibility for the future of humankind. Nor is it simply that it cannot really actualise the mutual devotion which some homosexual persons hope to manifest and experience by it, and that it harms the personalities of its participants by its dis-integrative manipulation of different parts of their one personal reality. It is also that it treats human sexual capacities in a way which is deeply hostile to the self-understanding of those members of the community who are willing to commit themselves to real marriage in the understanding that its sexual joys are not mere instruments or accompaniments to, or mere compensations for, the accomplishment of marriage's responsibilities, but rather enable the spouses to *actualise and experience* their intelligent commitment to share in those responsibilities, in that genuine self-giving....

All who accept that homosexual acts can be a humanly appropriate use of sexual capacities must, if consistent, regard sexual capacities, organs and acts as instruments for gratifying the individual "self" who has them. Such an acceptance is commonly (and in my opinion rightly) judged to be an active threat to the stability of existing and future marriages; it makes nonsense, for example, of the view that adultery is inconsistent with conjugal love, in an important way and *intrinsically*—not merely because it may involve deception. A political community which judges that the stability and protective and educative generosity of family life are of fundamental importance to the whole community's present and future can rightly judge that it has compelling reasons for

judging that homosexual conduct—a "gay lifestyle"—is never a valid, humanly acceptable choice and form of life, in denying that same-sex partners are capable of marrying, and in doing whatever it *properly* can, as a community with uniquely wide but still subsidiary functions, to discourage such conduct.[11]

IV

The question of sex ethics which seems to have interested Aquinas far more than any other is: When must sex acts *between spouses*, even acts of intercourse of the generative kind, be regarded as seriously wrongful? His answer is, in effect: When such acts are de-personalised, and de-maritalised. That is to say, if I choose this act of intercourse with my spouse, not for the sake of pleasurably actualising and expressing our marital commitment, but *'solely* for pleasure', or *solely* for the sake of my health, or *solely* as a relief from temptations to masturbation or extra-marital sex, and *would be just as (or more!) willing* to be having intercourse with someone else—so that I am seeing in my spouse, in this act of intercourse, no more than I would see in a goodtime girl or a gigolo or another acquaintance or someone else's spouse—then my sex act with my spouse is *non-marital* and is in principle seriously wrong.[12] It is contrary to reason, and therefore contrary to nature.[13] It is contrary to reason because it is contrary to—disintegrated from—an intrinsic good to which we are directed by one of the first principles of practical reason (and therefore of natural law), a good which may therefore be called primary, fundamental, or basic: the good of marriage itself.[14]

Why are sex acts (seeking the orgasm of one or more of the parties) unreasonable unless marital? Implicit in Aquinas' often misunderstood[15] work is a rarely recognised train of thought, substantially as follows.

Marriage, in which a man and a woman would find their friendship and devotion to each other fulfilled in their procreation, nurture, protection, education and moral formation of their children,[16] is an intrinsic, basic human good. Sexual intercourse between the spouses, provided it is authentically marital, actualises and promotes the spouses' mutual commitment in marriage (their marital *fides*). But my sex act with my spouse will not be truly marital—and will not authentically actualise, and allow us in a non-illusory way to experience, our marriage—if I engage in it while I *would be willing* in some circumstance(s) to engage in a sex act of a non-marital kind—e.g. adultery, fornication, intentionally sterilised intercourse, solitary masturbation or mutual masturbation (e.g. sodomy), and so forth. To regard any of such types of sex act as morally acceptable is to regard one or more of them as something I might under some circumstances engage in, and this state of mind undermines the marital character of my sex acts with my spouse. In short, the complete *exclusion* of non-marital sex acts from the range of acceptable human options is a pre-condition for the truly marital character of any spouses' intercourse. Blindness or indifference to the inherent wrongness of non-marital sex acts renders non-marital the choosing and carrying out of even those actual sex acts which in all other respects are marital in kind.

Moreover, without the possibility of truly marital intercourse the good of marriage is seriously impaired. Any willingness to (counter-factually or actually) engage in non-marital sex radically undermines my marriage itself. For it disintegrates the intelligibility of my marriage; our sex acts no longer truly actualise and enable us authentically to experience our *marriage;* they are unhinged from the other aspects of our mutual commitment and project. And this unhinging or dis-integration threatens—runs contrary to—both of the goods inherent in the complex basic good of marriage:[17] not only the good of friendship and *fides* but also the good of procreation and of the children whose education etc. so depends on the context of a *good* marriage. *So* any kind of assent—even if conditional—to non-marital sex is unreasonable. (Indeed, all sexual immorality, including all willingness to treat it as a potentially acceptable option, is contrary to love-of-neighbour, i.e. of children).[18] *And so* it is immoral, *and* out of line with human nature (and, Aquinas adds, with God's intentions about human conduct).[19]

This line of thought may seem complex when spelled out on the page. But it is no more than the articulation of married people's common-sense appreciation of the offensiveness of adultery and of being treated by one's spouse as a mere object of sexual relief, sexual servicing, de-personalised sex—'he/she doesn't love me, he/she only wants me for my body (or: as a baby-maker)'.[20] The traditional sex ethic which, despite all backsliding, was fairly perspicuous to almost everyone until the acceptance by many people of divorce-for-remarriage and contraception began to obscure its coherence a few decades ago, is no more and no less than a drawing out of the implications of this same reasonable thought: the intending, giving, and/or receiving of pleasure in sex acts is reasonably respectful of and coherent with intelligible human goods *only* when those acts are fully expressive of and (so far as my willing goes) instantiations of the complex good of marriage. Acts of the kind that same-sex partners engage in (intended to culminate in orgasmic satisfaction by finger in vagina, penis in mouth, etc.) remain non-marital, and so unreasonable and wrong, when performed in like manner by a married couple.

Sexual acts which are marital are 'of the reproductive kind' because in willing such an act one wills sexual behaviour which is (a) the very same as causes generation (intended or unintended) in every case of human *sexual* reproduction, and (b) the very same as one would will if one were intending precisely sexual reproduction as a goal of a particular marital sexual act. This kind of act is a 'natural kind', in the morally relevant sense of 'natural', not (as Koppelman supposes) if and only if one is intending or attempting an *outcome*, viz. reproduction or procreation. Rather it is a distinct rational kind—and therefore in the morally relevant sense a natural kind—because (i) in engaging in it one is intending a *marital* act, (ii) its being of the reproductive kind is a necessary though not sufficient condition of it being marital, and (iii) marriage is a rational and natural kind of institution. One's reason for action—one's rational motive—is precisely the complex good of *marriage*.

For: marriage is rational and natural primarily because it is the institution which physically, biologically, emotionally, and in every other practical way is peculiarly apt to promote suitably the reproduction of the couple by the generation, nurture, and education of ultimately mature offspring. . . .

The reason why marriage involves the commitment to permanence and exclusiveness in the spouses' sexual union is that, as an institution or form of life, it is fundamentally shaped by its dynamism towards, appropriateness for, and fulfilment in, the generation, nurture, and education of children who each can only have two parents and who are fittingly the primary responsibility (and object of devotion) of *those two parents*. Apart from this orientation towards children, the institution of marriage, characterised by marital *fides* (faithfulness), would make little or no sense. Given this orientation, the marital form of life does make good sense, and the marital sexual acts which actualise, express, and enable the spouses to experience that form of life make good sense, too.

Moreover, a man and a woman *who can engage in precisely the marital acts with precisely the same behaviour and intentions*, but who have reason to believe that in their case those very same acts will never result in children, can still opt for this *form of life* as one that makes good sense. Given the bodily, emotional, intellectual, and volitional complementarities with which that combination of factors we call human evolution[21] has equipped us as men and women, such a commitment can be reasonable as a participation in the good of marriage in which these infertile spouses, if well-intentioned, would wish to have participated more fully than they can.[22] By their model of fidelity within a relationship involving acts of the reproductive kind, these infertile marriages are, moreover, strongly supportive of marriage as a valuable social institution.

But same-sex partners cannot engage in acts of the reproductive kind, i.e. in marital sexual intercourse. The permanent, exclusive commitment of marriage, which presupposes bodily union as the biological actuation of the multi-level (bodily, emotional, intellectual, and volitional) marital

relationship, makes no sense for them. Of course, two, three, four, five or any number of persons of the same sex can band together to raise a child or children. That may, in some circumstances, be a praiseworthy commitment. It has nothing to do with marriage. Koppelman and Macedo remain discreetly silent on the question why the same-sex 'marriage' they offer to defend is to be between two persons rather than three, four, five, or more, all engaging in sex acts 'faithfully' with each other. They are equally silent on the question why this group sex-partnership should remain constant in membership, rather than revolving like other partnerships.

The plain fact is that those who propound 'gay' ideology have no principled moral case to offer against (prudent and moderate) promiscuity, indeed the getting of orgasmic sexual pleasure in whatever friendly touch or welcoming orifice (human or otherwise) one may opportunely find it. In debate with opponents of their ideology, these proponents are fond of postulating an idealised (two-person, lifelong. . .) category of relationship—'gay marriage'—and of challenging their opponents to say how such a relationship differs from *marriage* at least where husband and wife know themselves to be infertile. As I have argued, the principal difference is very simple and fundamental: the artificially delimited (two-person, lifelong. . .) category named 'gay marriage' or 'same-sex marriage' corresponds to no intrinsic reason or set of reasons at all. It has few presentable counterparts in the real world outside the artifice of debate. *Marriage*, on the other hand, is the category of relationships, activities, satisfactions, and responsibilities which can be intelligently and reasonably chosen by a man and a woman, and adopted as their integral commitment, because the components of the category respond and correspond coherently to a complex of interlocking, complementary good reasons: the good of marriage. True and valid sexual morality is nothing more, and nothing less, than an unfolding of what is involved in understanding, promoting, and respecting that basic human good, and of the conditions for instantiating it in a real, non-illusory way—in the marital act.

NOTES

1. In the footnote, Vlastos complains that by *para physin*, "contrary to nature," Plato here and in BC836 meant something "far stronger" than the phrase "against the rules," which Dover had used in a 1966 article on *eros* and *nomos*. Sometime before the revised edition, Vlastos and Dover corresponded about this complaint, and Vlastos records a letter from Dover:

   What [Plato] did believe was that the act was "unnatural," in the sense "against the rules"; it was a morally ignorant exploitation of pleasure beyond what was "granted" (*kata physin apodedosthai*, [Lg] 636C4), the product of an *akrateia* ([636]C6) which can be aggravated by habituation and bad example. His comparison of homosexuality with incest ([*Laws* 837E8–838E1) is particularly revealing.

   And Vlastos immediately remarks that Dover's allusion to Plato's comparison of homosexuality with incest shows that Dover acknowledges the great force with which Plato is condemning what Vlastos called "anal intercourse" and Dover, loosely, "the act" and "homosexuality."

2. Anthony Price's valuable book, *Love and Friendship in Plato and Aristotle* at p. 89 firmly rejects Vlastos's theory that Socrates and Plato, though forbidding homosexual acts, accepted that lovers could nevertheless rightly engage in the sort of petting spoken of in *Phaedrus* 255e.

3. See *Nicomachean Ethics* VII,5:1148b29; *Politics* II,1:1262a33–39, together with the hints in II,6:1269b28 and II,7:1272a25. (See e.g.) Price, op. cit. p. 225, citing Plato, *Republic* 403b4–6 and Aristotle, *Politics* 1262a32–7.)

4. See Plato, *Gorgias* pp. 494–95, especially 494e1–5, 495b3.

5. The core of this argument can be clarified by comparing it with St. Augustine's treatment of marriage in his *De Bono Coniugali*. There the good of marital communion is presented primarily as an instrumental good, in the service of the procreation and education of children: see Finnis, 'Law, Morality, and "Sexual Orientation" *Notre Dame Law Review* 69 (1994) 1049 at 1064–65.

6. Steven Macedo, "The New Natural Lawyers," *The Harvard Crimson*, October 28, 1993, writes, "In effect, gays can have sex in a way that is open to procreation, and to new life. They can be, and many are, prepared to engage in the kind of loving relations that would result in procreation—were conditions different. Like sterile married couples, many would like nothing better." Here fantasy has taken leave of reality. Anal or oral intercourse, whether between spouses or between males, is no more a biological union "open to procreation" than is intercourse with a goat by a shepherd who fantasizes about breeding a faun; each "would" yield the desired mutant "were conditions different."

   Biological union between humans is the *inseminatory* union of male genital organ with female genital organ; in most circumstances it does not result in generation, but it is the behavior that unites biologically because it is the behavior which, as behavior, is suitable for generation. (See also fn. 32.)

7. For the whole argument, see Grisez, *Living a Christian Life*, pp. 634–39, 648–54, 662–4

8. *Gorgias* pp. 494–95, especially 494e1–5, 495b3.

9. Or deliberately contracepted, which I omit from the list in the text only because it would no doubt not now be accepted by secular civil law as preventing consummation a failure of understanding. See also footnote 35.

10. Macedo, loc. cit.

11. The criminal law upheld in *Bowers v Hardwick* seems to me unsound in principle. But there was a sound and important distinction of principle which the Supreme Court of the United States overlooked in moving from *Griswold* v. *Connecticut* 381 US 479 (1965) *(private use* of contraceptives by *spouses)* to *Eisenstadt* v. *Baird* 405US 438 (1970) *(public distribution* of contraceptives to *unmarried* people). (The law struck down in *Griswold* was the law forbidding use of contraceptives even by married persons; Griswold's conviction as an accessory to such use fell with the fall of the substantive law against the principals in such use. Very different, in principle, would have been a law directly forbidding Griswold's activities as a public promoter of

contraceptive information and supplies.) The truth and relevance of that distinction, and its high importance for the common good, would be overlooked again if laws criminalising private acts of sodomy between adults were to be struck down by the Court on any ground which would also constitutionally require the law to tolerate the advertising or marketing of homosexual services, the maintenance of places of resort for homosexual activity, or the promotion of homosexualist "lifestyles" via education and public media of communication, or to recognise homosexual "marriages" or permit the adoption of children by homosexually active people, and so forth.

12. See Aquinas, IV *Sent.* q. 26 q. 1 a. 4c (=*Summa Theologiae* Supp. q. 41 a. 4c); d. 31 q. 2 a. 2 (= Supp. q. 41 a. 5) ad 2 & ad 4; q. 2 a. 3c (= Supp. q. 49 a. 6c) & tit. & obj. 1; *Commentary on I Corinthians*, c.7 ad v. 6 [329]; *Summa Theologiae* II–II q. 154 a. 8 ad 2; *De Malo* q. 15 a. 1c. For a much fuller treatment of Aquinas' sex ethics, see Finnis, *Aquinas* (Oxford University Press, 1998). Chapter VII.2.

13. All extra-marital sex (and even conditional assent {consensus} to it) is contrary to nature *inasmuch as (and because)* it is contrary to reason's requirements, e.g., *De Malo.* q. 15 a. 1 ad 7.

14. See Aquinas, *Summa Theologiae* I–II q. 94 a. 2c. In his treatment of sex ethics, Aquinas usually refers to the good of marriage, insofar as it is always at stake in the spouses' sexual activity, as the good of *fides*, i.e., of *mutual commitment in marriage*. The literal translation of *fides* would be faith(fulness), but in English this suggests merely absence of infidelity (i.e., of sexual relations with other persons), whereas Aquinas explains (IV *Sent.* d. 31 q. 1 a. 2c & ad 3 (= Supp. q. 49 a. 2c & ad 3); *Commentary on I Cor.* c. 7.1 ad v. 2 [318]) that marital *fides* involves also, and primarily, a positive willingness to be maritally, including sexually, united (on a basis of mutuality and absolute equality in initiating or requesting intercourse.)

15. Thoroughly misunderstood and misrepresented in John T. Noonan, *Contraception* (Harvard U.P., 1965, 1986); John Boswell, *Christianity, Social Tolerance, and Homosexuality* (University of Chicago Press, 1980). Koppelman's view of Aquinas has (not unreasonably, but certainly unfortunately) been reliant upon these writers: see the longer version of his present essay; Koppelman, 'Is Marriage Inherently Heterosexual?', 42 *American Journal of Jurisprudence* (1997); and for a discussion of Noonan's and Boswell's misreadings, see Finnis, 'The Good of Marriage: Some Historical and Philosophical Observations', 42 *American Journal of Jurisprudence* 42 (1998), pp. 97–134.

16. The marriage of a couple who have reason to believe that they are incapable of generating children is considered, once the basic lines of the argument are in place, below.

17. Marriage is a complex but unified good inasmuch as its unitive goodness is inseparable from its procreative significance (even where procreation is *per accidens* impossible). Aquinas' train of thought sets out one way of understanding and acknowledging this inseparability.

18. See *De Malo* q. 15 a. 2 ad 4; IV *Sent.* d. 33 q. 1 a. 3 sol. 2 (= Supp. q. 65 a. 4c).

19. Koppelman says that for Aquinas homosexual acts are uniquely monstrous. That is an exaggeration; for Aquinas, bestiality is a worse type of surrender to unreasonable, dis integrated desire for pleasure, and rape and adultery are characteristically much worse in terms of injustice. Considered simply as sexually unreasonable, acts of sexual vice are, *other things being equal*, worse the more distant they are from the truly marital type of act: IV *Sent.* d. 41 a. 4 sol. 3c; see also *De Malo* q. 15 a. 1c. Aquinas seems to be correct in thinking that homosexual sex acts are a type particularly distant from the marital; they are between persons who *could never be married*. (Indeed, this seems to be part of the reason why the word 'gay' was co opted by the homosexual ideology.) A businessman copulating with a call-girl, though he is engaged in seriously wrongful sexual vice, can imagine himself being married to this woman, and engaging with her in behavior of the same kind as spouses at some time in the future. But men committing or contemplating sex acts (even buggery) with each other cannot *rationally* think of those acts as acts of the kind Aquinas (rightly) considers the reproductive and

marital kind. (See n. 14 and text near n. 38). Of course, in grading the gravity of *types* of sexual vice, Aquinas is not attempting to estimate the culpability of particular acts of particular persons, culpability which may sometimes be much diminished by passion that fetters freedom and/or by confusion of mind (e.g., ideology, fantasy) that obscures rational deliberation towards choice.

20. On regarding one's wife as a baby-maker, see Robert P. George and Gerard V. Bradley, 'Marriage and the Liberal Imagination', 84 *Georgetown Law Journal*, pp. 301–20 (1995) at 305 text and n. 19.

21. Koppelman (like Strauss) has not fully, or at all, come to grips with the radically teleological character of contemporary 'Darwinian' biology's account of the molecular-biological genetic primordia, fundaments, or engine of evolution. But that, like the half-truth of the 'disenchantment' of the universe, is an issue with no bearing on the present argument.

22. Those, however, who search out infertile spouses, choosing them *precisely for their infertility*, may well be manifesting the kind of contempt for the marital good which Philo Judaeus condemned in the rather confused passage from which Koppelman and Boswell quote some over-heated fragments.

READING

"It's Not Natural"

JOHN CORVINO

MindTap° For more chapter resources and activities, go to MindTap.

Study Questions

As you read the excerpt, please consider the following questions:

1. Why does Corvino think that "new natural law" (NNL) have mis-located the moral value of sex?
2. What is Corvino's criticism of the term "unnatural"?
3. What is Corvino's view of non-coital sex in general?

Consider the goods people usually associate with sex. "Organic bodily union" is generally not on the list. Procreation sometimes is, but neither the sterile heterosexual couple nor the homosexual couple can achieve procreation. There are others, however: the expression of a certain kind of affection, the building of intimacy, and shared pleasure, to name a few. The NNL [New Natural Law] theorists must either deny that these are genuine goods or else deny that non-coital sex can achieve them. Such denials fly in the face of common sense....

Consider a man who enjoys performing cunnilingus with his wife to express affection and experience mutual pleasure. He need not be choosing such an activity as a counterfeit version of coitus. He might choose it, rather, in order to please his wife, a result

that in turn pleases him. Such an act constitutes a genuine expression of affection, and it may facilitate each partner's emotional and physical well-being. It may be a special intimacy that they reserve only for each other, something that enhances the bond between them.... They are bodily persons expressing affection in a bodily way, and that real bodily experience, which they know to be intensely pleasurable, is what they choose.... They seek genuine personal interaction in the form of non-coital sex....

But what about various arousing activities that may, but need not, lead to male orgasm: kissing, stroking, licking, erotic massage, and so on? What

From John Corvino, *What's Wrong with Homosexuality?* (Oxford University Press, 2013), pp. 78–97.

about cuddling? In ordinary romantic life—for gays as well as straights—the line between the sexual and the nonsexual is typically not so sharp. There is no obvious point where one starts choosing gratification for its own sake, and it's hard to imagine that NNL would condemn *all* these activities unless they were followed by coitus. It would be interesting to see the NNL reasons—if there are any—for why gay *kissing* might be unnatural.

I conclude that the NNL theorists have mislocated the moral value of sex, and that even if there's something distinctively valuable about coitus (apart from its procreative potential), they have failed to show what it is, let alone that other forms of sex are positively bad. The very same things that make non-coital sex valuable for heterosexual

partners—expression of affection, experience of mutual pleasure, physical and emotional well-being, and so on—make it valuable for same-sex couples as well....

It is worth adding that any view that rests the wrongness of homosexual conduct on the wrongness of masturbation ought to face a severe burden of persuasion.... Like Aquinas, the NNL theorists label masturbation, contraception, and non-coital heterosexual sex unnatural for the very same reasons that they label homosexual sex unnatural: the failure to achieve a reproductive-type union....

"Unnatural" according to this view is simply a term of abuse, a fancy word for "disgusting," a way to mask visceral reactions as well-considered moral judgments. We can do better.

REVIEW EXERCISES

1. Distinguish conceptual from factual matters with regard to sexual morality. What is the difference between them?

2. What are some factual matters that would be relevant for consequentialist arguments regarding sexual behavior?

3. According to a Kantian type of morality, we ought to treat persons as persons. Deceit and coercion violate this requirement. In this view, what kinds of things regarding sexual morality would be morally objectionable?

4. How would a natural law theory be used to judge sexual behavior? Explain.

5. What is meant by the term *perversion*? How would this notion be used to determine whether there was something called "sexual perversion?"

6. How do arguments about homosexuality and same-sex marriage connect to claims about other forms of nonmarital sex, adultery, and even marital sex among sterile couples?

7. Is the move toward the legalization of same-sex marriage in some countries and states in the United States a good thing or a bad thing? Justify your response with specific references to the moral theories discussed in this chapter.

DISCUSSION CASES

1. **Date Rape.** Early one Sunday morning, Dalia opens her dorm room door and finds her friend Amy standing there, her eyes red from crying. Inside Dalia's room, Amy begins talking about what happened to her the night before. She had been at a large party in another dorm, drinking beer and dancing with a group of friends, until the party started winding down around 2:00 a.m. Then, a guy she'd been flirting with invited her back to his room down the hall from the party. She said goodbye to her friends and went with him. In his room, they had another beer and started making out. Amy tells Dalia that everything was fine until the guy pushed her down hard onto his bed and began pulling off her clothes. "It happened so fast," Amy said. "I was in shock and was scared because all of a sudden he was acting so rough. I just sort of let it happen, but it was awful." Amy begins to cry. "Did you tell him to stop?" Dalia asks. "I didn't say anything," Amy says. "But inside, I was screaming 'no.' I just lay there completely still until it was over."

"Are you saying he raped you?" Dalia asks. "I don't know," Amy says. "Maybe."

Do you think what happened to Amy was rape? Why or why not? What do you think is required for true consent to a sexual encounter?

2. **Defining Marriage.** Maria is opposed to the idea of same-sex marriage. In a recent conversation in the school cafeteria, Maria argues, "If homosexuals are allowed to marry, then why not allow polygamy or other kinds of marriages?" Richard is gay. He responds, "That's ridiculous. All we're asking is that our relationships be respected by society and the law. Nobody is asking to legalize polygamy. Even the Mormons have given up on polygamy." Maria replies, "I know the Mormon Church no longer officially approves of it. But there are still Mormons who live in polygamous families. What if some of those folks—or Muslims who live in the U.S.—want to legalize polygamy?" Richard thinks about it for a minute and then replies, "I still think you are comparing apples and oranges. Same-sex marriage is not at all like polygamous marriage. I'm talking about

marriage between two and only two committed partners, not marriage of multiple partners. You can legalize the one without legalizing the other. You think that there's a slippery slope here. But I deny it." Maria responds, "How can you draw the line once you open the door to nontraditional marriage?"

Is there a slippery slope here? Should we open marriage up to a variety of other arrangements? Is it possible to draw a clear line in this case? Please justify your response with specific reference to the philosophical concepts discussed in the chapter.

3. **Prostitution.** David's friends are arranging his bachelor party. They are making plans to go as a group to Las Vegas for one last weekend "out with the boys." One of David's friends, Steven, suggests that they pool their money and treat David to a night in one of Nevada's legal brothels. Another friend, Tom, is opposed to the idea. Tom says that prostitution is wrong. Tom thinks prostitution exploits women. Tom also thinks that David's fiancée, Monica, would be hurt if she ever found out about it. But Steven argues that prostitution is legal in Nevada and the women make good money doing what they do. Steven also says that David has already told him that he wants to go to a strip club as part of the bachelor party. "There's not much difference between a strip club and a brothel," Steven says. Tom responds, "But one is fantasy and the other is reality." Steven shakes his head. "It's all sex, man," he adds. Tom thinks about that for a moment. Then he says, "You know, maybe we shouldn't go to the strip club either. Monica wouldn't like it." Steven replies, "Well, this is David's party. And it all depends on what we tell Monica. Remember, what happens in Vegas stays in Vegas!"

Whose side are you on? Is there something wrong with prostitution? Is there a difference between visiting a strip club and visiting a prostitute? Would it make a difference if David and his friends were honest with Monica about their plans?

MindTap° For more chapter resources and activities, go to MindTap.

Equality and Discrimination

Learning Outcomes

After reading this chapter, you should be able to:

- Explain the concepts of race, racism, and institutional or structural racism.
- Evaluate the principle of equality.
- Analyze how consequentialist and non-consequentialist reasoning applies in discussions of discrimination and affirmative action.

- Provide an overview of the development of civil rights law in the United States.
- Defend a thesis about the ethics of racial profiling and affirmative action.

MindTap®   For more chapter resources and activities, go to MindTap.

In recent years, a movement known as "Black Lives Matter" has erupted onto the scene in response to a series of killings in which young black men have been shot by police or have died while in police custody. For example: Michael Brown in Ferguson, Missouri; Eric Garner in New York; Freddie Gray in Baltimore; and Tamir Rice—a 12-year-old—in Cleveland, Ohio. In the background of these highly publicized cases were other newsworthy cases in which black youth were killed by police, such as the killing of Oscar Grant in Oakland in 2009 (which became a popular film, *Fruitvale Station*) and the killing of Trayvon Martin, an unarmed 17-year-old, who was shot by George Zimmerman in 2012 in Florida. In the summer of 2016 as this text was going to press, other police shootings of unarmed black males occurred: Philando Castile in Minneapolis, Alton Sterling in Baton Rouge, and Charles Kinsey in Miami. In response to these killings and others, massive protests and civil unrest broke out in a number of American cities from St. Louis and Baltimore to Oakland and beyond. Adding to the outrage in the black community was the sense that those involved in these killings were not properly punished. George Zimmerman was acquitted in 2013, and the officers involved in other killings have been acquitted. Police brutality is a subject of concern, which might properly be addressed in Chapter 15 on punishment. But one of the prevailing concerns of the Black Lives Matter movement is inequality and discrimination. As the Black Lives Matter protests gathered steam, violence escalated. Police officers were ambushed and shot by individuals who claimed outrage over the black shootings. Three police officers were killed in Baton Rouge. Five were

Protestors, angry about the killing of black youth by police, have rallied under the banner of "Black Lives Matter."

killed in Dallas. For further discussion of violence, see Chapter 19.

Some have responded to the Black Lives Matter movement by arguing that "All Lives Matter" (a motto some counter-protestors have used when they have spoken up in defense of law enforcement). Other counter-protestors have claimed that "Blue Lives Matter," establishing their solidarity with the police. There is no doubt that the Black Lives Matter activists believe that all lives matter, but those activists maintain that our society contains racist discrimination in which black lives matter less than the lives of others. And they will point to institutional and systematic structures which create a world of unequal outcomes, including problems such as **implicit bias** (which causes people—the police included—to respond negatively to blacks or associate them with crime) and **racial profiling** (through which police engage in tactics that target people based upon racial identity). Defenders of police action will claim that the police must do a difficult and dangerous job and that most cops are not racist. Critics will argue that structural racism plagues the criminal justice system and police tactics.

Is it always wrong to use profiling if that helps us catch bad guys? And why, exactly, is it wrong to discriminate? To think seriously about these sorts of cases, we will have to define discrimination and profiling. We also need to understand the importance of the moral idea of equality.

DISCRIMINATION

A very basic definition of discrimination tells us that to discriminate is to distinguish between things, usually in ways that imply a judgment about what is better or worse. We say, for example, that someone has discriminating taste, which implies that she makes good judgments about what is good or bad (say with regard to food, wines, art, or music). As we shall see in the discussion of war (in Chapter 19), discrimination is viewed as a good thing in the ethics of war; we want soldiers and armies to discriminate between those who can legitimately be killed (soldiers) and those who ought not be killed (civilians). But in this chapter, we are primarily concerned with *unjust* discrimination. In this negative sense, **discrimination** is unjustified differential treatment, especially on the basis of characteristics such as race, ethnicity, gender, sexual orientation, or religion. The goal of eliminating unjustified discrimination is an established policy of our legal system, with a variety of civil rights laws focused on preventing and finding remedies for it. The Civil Rights Act of 1964 explicitly states that its goal is to "provide relief from discrimination" and to "prevent discrimination" in public and federally funded programs and institutions.[1] This idea has led to the development of explicit equal opportunity clauses that show up in policy statements and contracts for a variety of institutions. The Equal Employment Opportunity Commission (EEOC) explains its own antidiscrimination policy as follows:

> EEOC employees are protected by federal laws prohibiting discrimination on the basis of race, religion, color, sex (including pregnancy and gender identity), national origin, age, disability, family medical history, or genetic information. Moreover, consistent with Presidential Executive Orders and other laws designed to protect federal employees, we must vigilantly prevent discrimination based on sexual orientation, parental status, marital status, political affiliation, military service, or any other non-merit based factor.[2]

This statement provides an extensive list of factors that should not be considered as relevant to employment. Indeed, as the statement's conclusion implies, the only relevant consideration should be "merit."

Racial Discrimination

While each of the potentially discriminatory factors listed above is worthy of further consideration, in this section, we'll look more closely at the issue of *racial* discrimination as a paradigmatic example of the problem of discrimination. One might think, given the fact that the United States has elected an African American president, that racism is behind us. But while some imagine that we are entering a post-racial era, evidence suggests that we continue to deal with racism. The Black Lives Matter movement has pointed out that overt racism exists, and it has also directed our attention to structural racism. A poll conducted by the Associated Press in

October 2012 found that 51 percent of Americans were willing to express explicitly anti-black attitudes. This is up from 48 percent four years ago.[3] Discriminatory stereotypes about other racial and ethnic groups show up in other ways. For example, Asians are often viewed as a "model minority." But this stereotype implicitly condemns other minorities. And it ignores much. Viewing Asians as a "model minority" creates a stereotype that does not necessarily comport with the diverse range of people who are counted as "Asian."[4] Moreover, the "positive" stereotype of Asians as hardworking and brainy has created disadvantages for some Asians. One worry is that elite universities are trying to find ways to limit the number of Asians they admit.[5] Racial stereotypes—whether positive or negative—are based upon generalizations about groups. These generalizations treat different people in groups as if they were all alike. And they may foster divisive competition among groups and their members.

Race, Racialism, and Critical Race Theory   One significant philosophical problem in discussions of racial discrimination is the very idea of race, a category that attempts to identify similarities among diverse individuals. Some may deny that race and racial differences matter, arguing that supposed racial differences are merely skin deep and that we should look beyond race to a sort of "color-blind" equality of persons. Others will argue that in today's world, race still remains as a powerful concept with deep historical roots which helps to explain ongoing inequality and discrimination. A field of philosophical inquiry that considers the question of race is known as **critical race theory**. Critical race theorists ask about the ontological status of race and about the moral, social, and political import of race and racism. They begin their inquiry from a standpoint that takes the existence of racism, racial supremacy, and racial privilege as a fact of the matter in contemporary society.

Racial differences have often been held to be natural biological differences. Racial distinctions have been drawn based upon such factors as appearance, blood group, geographic location, and gene frequency. However, it is difficult to clearly define the sorts of biological differences that might create racial identity. It is also difficult to narrow down the number of races of human beings. Depending on which characteristics and criteria are employed, anthropologists have classified the human species into anywhere from six to eighty races.[6] Thus, any strictly biological definition of race is seriously flawed. One problem is that human populations have rarely been isolated in ways that would limit genetic intermingling. Indeed, even if we were able to isolate populations in this way, there would be substantial overlap among the supposedly different races, and individuals within a given racial or ethnic group show substantial genetic variation. Another problem with genetic accounts of race is that human populations across the globe do not vary that much from one another genetically. As one important study concludes, "the major stereotypes, all based on skin color, hair color and form, and facial traits, reflect superficial differences that are not confirmed by deeper analysis with more reliable genetic traits and whose origin dates from recent evolution mostly under the effect of climate and perhaps sexual selection."[7]

While we should be wary of reductive biological accounts of racial differences—especially those racial categories that are used to unjustly discriminate—we might want to consider a genetic basis of race for benevolent purposes. Genetic variations do have implications for human health. Different ethnic and racial groups may have different susceptibilities to disease. Thus, it is important to understand how medical treatments affect different racial types. Some scientific studies, for instance, have been designed to "catalogue and compare the genetics of people with African, Asian, and European ancestry."[8] It would be beneficial to understand how these differences affect susceptibility to diseases such as sickle-cell anemia, diabetes, and hypertension. One international project—the Haplotype (or HapMap) Project—seeks to determine why certain groups suffer differential rates of high blood pressure and heart attacks, for example, by finding genetic variants

or mutations that may be involved in these conditions. Such information might help scientists design tailor-made drugs or treatments for people in these groups.[9]

Nevertheless, the conceptual and scientific basis for race remains highly contested. For example, the philosopher Kwame Anthony Appiah maintains that the idea of firm and essential differences among the races is false. (See the excerpt from Appiah at the end of this chapter.) Appiah uses the term *racialism* to describe the problematic notion that there are firm distinctions among races. Appiah argues that the superficial characteristics that people use to distinguish among the races are merely skin deep and not tied to a deeper essential difference. Another problem for racialist views is that there is a long history of people marrying, having children, and raising families across so-called racial divides. In many cases, it is difficult for people to decide how they might identify themselves based upon old-fashioned racial categories. President Obama is a case in point; his mother was white and his father was Kenyan, and he identifies himself as an African American. Critics of racialism generally agree that race is a *social construct*. That is to say, racial categories are ideas made up for social purposes, which are not clearly grounded in hard and fast natural distinctions. Not everyone agrees with Appiah's deflationary analysis of the concept of race. For example, Lucius Outlaw Jr. argues that race is not merely a social construction. Outlaw points out that genetic differences exist, which help explain morphological difference, and that these differences are actually created in part by cultural practices (such as marriage and reproduction practices, which have often been racially exclusive). Building upon his interpretation of the work of W.E.B. Du Bois, Outlaw argues that the existence of cultural, historical, and biological groupings should not be denied or neglected.[10] Indeed, from this point of view, oppressed racial groups may benefit from affirming their own racial identity, which may help solidify social power in the struggle for equal treatment. From this standpoint, to deny the importance of race is to ignore the reality of struggles for equality in the world. Outlaw suggests, race "continues to be a major fulcrum of struggles over the distribution and exercise of power."[11]

Whether we think that race should be deconstructed and discarded as a mere social construct or whether we think that race remains as an important and useful concept, the ethical question is whether racial categories are used to make *unjust* discriminatory judgments, which are typically described as racist.

Racism It is generally understood that **racism** involves making race a significant factor in the judgment and treatment of persons. Racism sets people of one race apart from people of other races, leading to demarcations between "us" and "them" and the construction of unequal or hierarchical social conditions. Racism involves not only making distinctions and grouping people, but also denigration. It involves beliefs that all persons of a certain race are inferior to persons of other races in some way. Racism appears to be unjust to individuals not just because such generalizations are typically false, but also because individuals do not choose their own parents or racial heritage and cannot change their external appearance. Similarly, racists or racial supremacists who celebrate their own race take credit for something over which they have no control.

There is nothing inherently wrong with noting our physical differences. In the abstract, it would seem that believing that someone is shorter than another or less strong is not necessarily objectionable, especially if the belief is true. However, what makes racism wrong is that it involves making false judgments about people and their worth. It also involves power and oppression, for those groups that are devalued by racism are also likely to be treated accordingly, even by those who don't think of themselves as racist.

Racism is not exactly the same as prejudice. *Prejudice* is making judgments or forming beliefs before knowing the truth about something or someone. These prejudgments might accidentally be correct beliefs. However, the negative connotation of the term *prejudice* indicates that these beliefs or judgments are formed without adequate information and are also mistaken. Moreover, prejudice in this context also may be a matter of judging an individual on the basis of stereotypical characteristics of a group to which he or she belongs. There is often a problem here of false or hasty generalization (when we make judgments about all members of a group based upon a few we've encountered). Racism, although different from prejudice, may follow from prejudiced beliefs. Racism appears especially objectionable when it leads to unequal treatment and harmful behavior.

Structural Racism and Implicit Bias Racism is usually thought of in terms of the attitudes and behaviors of individuals. It is possible, however, for racism and other forms of oppression to occur at the level of institutions and social structures.[12] **Structural** or **institutional racism** occurs when social structures and institutions are set up in ways that are oppressive or produce unequal outcomes. It is more difficult to see institutional or structural oppression because we often take social structures for granted. Moreover, nonbiased individuals may be working within a system that produces racially biased outcomes. These individuals may not be racist themselves—even if the system or institution produces undeserved unequal outcomes.

Consider this issue in the context of education. Education is often thought of as the great equalizer and the hope of the less fortunate. However, educational outcomes are often strikingly unequal in the United States. Poorer schools in urban, minority neighborhoods typically have lower standardized test scores and lower graduation rates than affluent, largely white schools in the suburbs. The problem is not typically that teachers or administrators are racist. Rather, the problem may be that present (and past) institutions have been set up in ways that reinforce disparate outcomes.

These outcomes include a dropout rate for African American college students that is substantially higher than for white students. The six-year college graduation rates by race—as calculated in 2011—were white students (62 percent), Hispanic students (50 percent), and black and American Indian/Alaska Native students (39 percent each).[13] Black and Hispanic youth also drop out of high school at a higher rate than white youth. In 2010, the high school dropout rates were white (5.1 percent), Hispanic (8.0 percent), and black (15.1 percent).[14] These racially disparate outcomes are most likely not caused by racist teachers. Rather, they are the result of a variety of social structures.

One of these structures may be social class and income level. If we look at employment statistics, for example, we find racial disparities. In 2010, with the economy in recession, the black unemployment rate stood at 16 percent, Hispanic unemployment at 12.5 percent, Asian unemployment at 7.5 percent, and white unemployment at 8.7 percent.[15] According to 2011 data, white Americans have, on average, twenty-two times more wealth than blacks and fifteen times more wealth than Hispanics.[16] Such economic disparities have clear impacts on education. According to a special report by the *New York Times* in 2012, "Low-income students with above-average scores on eighth grade tests have a college graduation rate of 26 percent—lower than more affluent students with worse test scores. Thirty years ago, there was a 31 percentage point difference in the share of affluent and poor students who earned a college degree. Now the gap is 45 points."[17] It is difficult to disentangle the differences between race, class, and education in this sort of data. This is a reminder that there are a variety of social categories (including gender, religion, sexual orientation, etc.) that should concern us when we are thinking about equality and discrimination. Different people have access to different opportunities based upon racial, class, gender, and other differences.

One area in which such differences occur is standardized testing. Consider the correlation between ethnicity, race, and SAT scores. White students earned on average (in 2012) 527 on the verbal section, 536 on the mathematics section, and 515 on the writing section.[18] Black students earned 428 (verbal), 428 (math), and 417 (writing). Similar disparities exist for Hispanic and Native American students. Critics of the SAT say this and other standardized tests are culturally biased and rely on references and associations tied to a particular class or cultural background. Children of those who are fortunate enough to have good incomes and access to good schools will have an advantage over other children. They can afford to take expensive SAT preparation courses, for example. This has led one critic to claim, "The SAT is increasingly a wealth test, and it provides the highest scores for those who have the most opportunity in society."[19] This is not necessarily the fault of any of the parents or children involved. Rather, it is a feature of the structure of our institutions, which leave us with unequal outcomes. Those who seek to remedy institutional and structural disparities remind us that these institutions could be organized differently. We could devote greater funds to schools in minority neighborhoods so that students from those schools will have more opportunities to succeed later in life. Or colleges and universities could offer greater financial aid and other forms of assistance to poor students. Further, we could encourage employers to take positive steps ("affirmative action") to recruit and train poor and minority applicants.

Another potential source of institutional racism may be racial stereotyping that occurs in the media. A 2008 analysis by Travis Dixon, an expert on stereotypes in the media, concludes, "African Americans typically occupy roles as poor people, loud politicians, and criminals on network news."[20] There is evidence that these stereotypical depictions can taint people's judgments about individual African Americans. Dixon conducted a related study, in which he examined how attitudes about crime and race correspond to media viewing habits. He concludes that "exposure to Blacks' overrepresentation as criminals on local news programming was positively related to the perception of Blacks as violent."[21] This kind of research—and numerous other examples—supports the idea known as **implicit bias**. People who do not directly admit to having racist attitudes may still have biased attitudes toward members of different racial groups (as well as bias toward gender identity, sexual orientation, religion, disability, and so on). It is not that those of us who are implicitly biased (and there is a good chance that we all harbor implicit biases) are lying or denying our biases and prejudices. Rather, the biases are often unconscious, and well-meaning individuals may not be aware of their own racial (and other) biases.

Critics of structural racism argue that things could be different; news organizations could de-emphasize race in their coverage of crime stories and focus instead on economic issues, for example. And the more aware we are of our implicit biases, the better able we will be at correcting for biased and prejudicial outcomes. Those who are concerned with structural racism will argue that structural and institutional changes must be made to remedy the unequal outcomes that occur in society. It is not enough for individuals to overcome racist attitudes; the institutions must be changed and proactive remedies must be employed to respond to racially disparate outcomes. One example of this is affirmative action, which we discuss in more detail below.

Other Forms of Discrimination We have considered racism as one example of unjustified discrimination. Similar issues come up in consideration of other forms of discrimination. Consider gender discrimination, which we discussed in more detail in Chapter 9. At the end of that chapter, we noted that some philosophers, such as Judith Butler, argue that gender is a social construction—an argument that can be seen as similar to Appiah's claim that race is a social construction. Feminists also speak of structural or institutional gender discrimination, which occurs when institutions are set up in ways that unjustifiably harm women. For example, while the average income of women compared to that of men has improved over the years, in 2011 women still only earned 77 percent of what men earned.[22] This wage gap also has a racial element, with Hispanic and black women earning the least. One interpretation of the gender wage gap is that it is structural or institutional. Those who do so-called women's work—traditionally teaching, nursing, food service,

and so on—have historically been underpaid. As women move into less traditionally female jobs, perhaps the pay gap will be reduced. However, there is substantial evidence that women continue to make less than their male counterparts in various professions; for example, women who work as physicians, real estate agents, and stockbrokers make less than 70 percent of what their male counterparts make.[23]

Other forms of discrimination exist. Forty-three million Americans have one or more physical or mental disabilities. Substantial legal efforts have been made to remove barriers and expand opportunities for such individuals, most notably the Americans with Disabilities Act (ADA) of 1990. But disabled individuals are still disadvantaged in many areas. Although fewer disabled people are trapped in their homes or institutionalized, stereotypes and stigma remain. And social institutions are sometimes set up in ways that create structural and institutional impediments for the disabled. For example, many private businesses still provide no alternatives to steps and staircases for customers in wheelchairs. The architects and planners who designed buildings with such features were not necessarily bigoted against the disabled, but they did not consider how their designs caused systematic hardship. The ADA requires that new construction and remodeling include ramps, if necessary, to give disabled people greater access.

Age can also be grounds for unjust discrimination and stereotyping. Older workers are subjected to arbitrary age limits in employment, as, for example, when age alone, rather than judgments of individual job performance, is used to dismiss someone. Discrimination also occurs against lesbian, gay, bisexual, and transgender people (LGBT), a topic we discussed in Chapter 12. Religious minorities can also be discriminated against, most notoriously in the treatment of Jews throughout Europe, which culminated in the Nazi Holocaust of the 1930s and 1940s. The ideal of equal treatment and equal respect for all people regardless of race, ethnicity, sex, sexual orientation, national origin, and religion is an important goal, one that contemporary societies are still working to achieve.

THE PRINCIPLE OF EQUALITY

Racism, sexism, and other forms of discrimination are unfair and unjust. As we have seen, the racist, sexist, or homophobic individual treats people of a particular race, gender, or sexual orientation poorly simply because of these characteristics.

Yet perhaps we still have not gotten to the root of what is wrong with racism or sexism. Suppose that our views about members of a group are not based on prejudice, but on an objective factual assessment of that group. For example, if men differ from women in significant ways—and surely they do—then is this not a sufficient reason to treat them differently? A moral principle can be used to help us think about this issue. The **principle of equality** is the idea that we should treat equal things in equal ways and that we may treat different things in unequal ways. In analyzing this principle, we will be able to clarify whether or why discrimination is morally objectionable. The principle of equality can be formulated in various ways. Consider the following formulation:

It is unjust to treat people differently in ways that deny to some of them significant social benefits unless we can show that there is a difference between them that is relevant to the differential treatment.

To better understand the meaning of this principle, we can break it down into several different concerns.

Justice

The principle of equality is a principle of justice. It tells us that certain actions or practices that treat people unequally are unjust. For instance, consider our symbolic representations of justice. A statue of Lady Justice stands outside the U.S. Supreme Court building in Washington, D.C. where she is depicted as blindfolded and holding a scale in one hand. The idea here is that justice is blind—in other words, it is not biased. It does not favor one person over another on the basis of irrelevant characteristics. The same laws are supposed to apply to all. The scale suggests

that justice need not involve strict equality but must be proportional. It requires that treatment of persons be according to what is due to them on some grounds. Therefore, it requires that there be valid reasons for differential treatment.

Social Benefits and Harms

We are not required to justify treating people differently from others in every case. For example, I may give personal favors to my friends or family and not to others without having to give a reason. However, sometimes social policies and practices treat people differently in ways that harm some and benefit others. This harm can be obvious or it can be subtle. In addition, there is a difference between *primary* discrimination and *secondary* discrimination.[24] In primary discrimination, a person is singled out and directly penalized simply because he or she is a member of a particular group, as when denied school admissions or promotions just because of this characteristic. In secondary discrimination, criteria for benefit or harm are used that do not directly apply to members of particular groups and only indirectly affect them. Thus, the policy "last hired, first fired" is often likely to have a discriminatory effect. Such a policy may seem harmless but can actually have a harmful effect on certain groups—particularly if these groups, such as women or blacks, have traditionally been excluded from a particular profession. The principle of equality directs us to consider the ways that social benefits and harms are distributed.

Proof and Reality of Difference

The principle of equality states that we must show or prove that certain differences exist if we are to justify treating people differently. The principle can be stronger or weaker depending on the kind of proof of differences required by it. It is not acceptable to treat people differently on the basis of differences that we only think or suspect exist. For example, scientific studies of sex differences must be provided to show that certain sex differences actually exist, if we are to allow for differential treatment based on sex.

The principle of equality requires that we show or prove that actual differences exist between the people whom we would treat differently. Many sex differences are obvious, and others that are not obvious have been confirmed by empirical studies—such as differences in metabolic rate, strength and size, hearing acuity, shoulder structure, and disease susceptibility. However, it is unlikely that these differences would be relevant for any differential social treatment. More relevant would be differences such as certain types of intellectual ability, aggressiveness, or nurturing capacity.

We might look to scientific studies of sex differences to help us determine whether any such possibly relevant sex differences exist. For example, women have been found to do better on tests that measure verbal speed, and men have been found to do better at being able to imagine what an object would look like if it were rotated in three-dimensional space. Recent discoveries have shown that men and women use different parts of their brains to do the same tasks. For example, to recognize whether nonsense words rhyme, men use a tiny area in the front left side of the brain, whereas women use a comparable section of the right side.[25] Whether such differences have a wider significance for different types of intelligence is a matter of intense debate. So also are the studies of aggressiveness. Testosterone has been shown to increase size and strength, but whether it also makes males more aggressive than females is disputed. This dispute arises not only because of the difficulties we have in tracing physical causation, but also because of our uncertainty about just what we mean by aggressiveness.

Most studies that examine supposed male and female differences also look at males and females after they have been socialized. Thus, it is not surprising that they do find differences. Suppose that a study found that little girls play with dolls and make block houses, while little boys prefer trucks and use the blocks to build imaginary adventure settings. Would this necessarily mean that some innate difference causes this? If there were such differences and if they were innate, then this may be relevant to how we would structure education and some other aspects of society. We might prefer women for the job of nurse or early child care provider, for example.

We might provide women, but not men, with paid child care leave. However, if we cannot prove that these or any such characteristics come from nature rather than nurture, then we should be more careful about differential treatment. We should consider whether our social institutions perpetuate socially induced differences.

Relevant Differences

The principle of equality requires more than proving that innate or real differences exist between groups of people before we are justified in treating them differently. It also requires that the differences be relevant. For example, if it could be shown that women are by nature better at bricklaying than men, then this would be a "real" difference between them. Although we might then be justified in preferring women for bricklaying jobs, we would not be justified in using this difference to prefer women for the job of airline pilot. On the other hand, if men and women think differently and if certain jobs require these particular thinking skills, then according to the principle of equality we may well prefer those individuals with these skills for the jobs. We might also prefer different people for bona fide reasons, such as hiring men to model male swimsuits and women to model female swimsuits. What counts as a bona fide reason will depend on the context.

The relevance of a talent, characteristic, or skill to a job is not an easy matter to determine. For example, is upper body strength an essential skill for the job of firefighter or police officer? Try debating this one with a friend. In answering this question, it would be useful to determine what kinds of things firefighters usually have to do, what their equipment is like, and so forth. Similarly, with the job of police officer, we might ask how much physical strength is required and how important are other physical or psychological skills or traits. And is being an African American, Asian American, or female an essential qualification for a position as university teacher of courses in black studies, Asian studies, or women's studies? It may not be an essential qualification, but some people argue that one's identity does help qualify a person because she or he is more likely to understand the issues and problems with which such courses deal. Nevertheless, this view has not gone unchallenged.

In addition to determining which characteristics or skills are relevant to a particular position, we must be able to assess adequately whether particular persons possess these characteristics or skills. Designing such assessments presents a difficulty, as prejudice may play a role in designing or evaluating them. For instance, how do we know whether someone works well with people or has sufficient knowledge of the issues that ought to be treated in a women's studies course? This raises a broader issue. Should we always test or judge people as individuals, or is it ever permissible to judge an individual as a member of a particular group?

Challenges to the Principle

One significant problem for the principle of equality stems from the fact that those group differences that are both real and relevant to differential treatment are often, if not always, *average* differences. In other words, a characteristic may be typical of a group of people, but it may not belong to every member of the group. Consider height. Men are typically taller than women. Nevertheless, some women are taller than some men. Even if women were typically more nurturing than men, it would still be possible that some men would be more nurturing than some women. Thus, it would seem that we ought to consider what characteristics an individual has rather than what is typical of the group to which he or she belongs. This would only seem to be fair or just. But social life does occasionally require that we deal with individuals as members of groups, especially when making policies from a utilitarian perspective that aims to produce the greatest happiness for the greatest number of people. Critics will object, however, that individuals, rather than groups, ought to be the focal point of moral concern. Such an objection might be a Kantian one that holds that we ought to respect persons as ends in themselves and that to consider individuals merely as members of a group is an affront to their dignity.

Are we ever justified in treating someone differently because of his or her membership in a particular demographic and because of that group's typical characteristics—even if he or she does not possess them? We do this in some cases and presumably think it is just. Consider our treatment of people as members of an age group, say, for purposes of driving or voting. We have rules that require that a person must be at least fifteen years old to obtain a driver's permit or license. Of course, it is true that some individuals who are fourteen would be better drivers than some individuals who are eighteen. Yet we judge them on the basis of a group characteristic, rather than their individual abilities. Similarly, in the United States, we require that people be eighteen years of age before they can vote. However, some people who are younger than eighteen would be more intelligent voters than some who are older than eighteen.

Social policies about voting and driving are based on generalizations about age cohorts. Those who agree to the policies resulting from these generalizations most likely do so for utilitarian reasons; these policies tend to produce good outcomes for most of us. If a fourteen-year-old is well qualified to drive, then he or she only has to wait a year or two, depending on the laws in his or her state. This causes no great harm to him or her. Nor is any judgment made about his or her natural abilities. Even those fifteen and older have to take a test on which they are judged as individuals, and not just as members of a group. Furthermore, suppose that we tried to judge people as individuals for the purposes of voting. We would need to develop a test of "intelligent voting ability." Can you imagine what political and social dynamite this testing would be? The cost to our democracy of instituting such a policy would be too great, whereas the cost to the individual of being judged as a member of an age group and having to wait a couple of years to vote is comparatively small. Thus, this practice does not seem unduly unfair.

However, if real and relevant sex differences existed, and if we treated all members of one sex alike on the basis of some typical group characteristic, rather than on the basis of their characteristics as individuals, then this would involve both significant costs and significant unfairness. It would be of great social cost to society not to consider applicants or candidates because of their sex; these individuals might otherwise make great contributions to society. In addition, those who are denied consideration could rightly complain that it was unfair to deny them a chance at a position for which they qualified, something that would also affect them their whole lives.

One significant recent example is the decision to allow women to serve in combat roles in the American military. Prior to this decision, the military careers of women were limited because of a "brass ceiling": high-level military jobs tend to go to soldiers with combat experience. Proponents of combat roles for women argue that now individual women will have the opportunity to be judged on merit and ability, and not merely on their membership in a group. As former Army Capt. Tanya L. Domi concludes, "With this momentous shift, America once again reaffirms its core values of equality and respect—values predicated upon a person's capabilities and demonstrated competence, not an immutable characteristic like gender. This is good for our military, and our country too."[26]

Another challenge to the principle of equality, or to its application, can be found in the debates over *preferential treatment* programs. Past discrimination may be a relevant difference between groups of people, which might justify differential treatment in order to remedy differences that have resulted from past injustice. Preferential treatments would be designed to benefit those who are members of groups that have been discriminated against in the past. The idea here is that being a member of a group is a sufficient reason to treat someone in a special way. Would we need to show that every member of that group was in some way harmed or affected by past discrimination? Some individual members of particular groups would not obviously have been harmed by past discrimination. However, we should also be aware of the complicated ways in which group or community membership affects

a person and the subtle ways in which he or she might thus be harmed.

A different problem for the principle concerns the problem of managing natural and cultural differences. Recall that over the past centuries, women have sought equality with men in the workplace, in education, and in public life generally. At the same time, they remain the primary child care providers in most families, which places them at an inevitable disadvantage in terms of advancement in many professions. As a result, some feminists have argued that the liberal notion of equality can be detrimental to women because it fails to take gender-specific circumstances into account. Perhaps differences between males and females in such areas as parental responsibilities would be relevant to the justness of requirements for professional advancement. Perhaps women should be treated differently in ways that allow them to fulfill the responsibilities of breastfeeding and child care. Other feminists point out that if men took an equal share of child care, such differential treatment would not be required, except with regard to such things as pregnancy and childbirth.

Issues of multiculturalism also could be raised with regard to the principle of equality. Americans live in a complex society in which there are many forms of cultural expression and heritage. To what extent should individuals' distinct cultural backgrounds and traditions be acknowledged and encouraged? Sometimes, respect for such cultural practices would lead to the condoning of gender inequality and discrimination.[27] The challenge raised here is a variety of the paradox of toleration (which we discussed in Chapter 2). Do those groups that deny the principle of equality deserve to be treated equally? Do groups who do not treat their own members equally deserve to be treated equally? The challenges to the principle of equality that we've mentioned here indicate that while the principle of equality is an important one, it is not always clear how it is to be applied in practice.

MindTap® For more chapter resources and activities, go to MindTap.

CURRENT ISSUES AND THE LAW

Civil rights laws enacted in the United States and other Western countries have proved to be powerful tools for reducing racial injustice and promoting equal treatment of citizens. When we speak of *civil rights*, we are referring primarily to rights that are granted by the government—they are rights of civil or political society, so-called rights of citizenship. Civil rights can be contrasted with the idea of natural rights or human rights, which we discussed in Chapter 7. Some may think that civil rights and human rights are synonymous. To understand the difference between civil rights and human rights, you might consider whether citizens should have different rights than noncitizens. Most civil societies do recognize a difference between the rights of citizens and the natural rights possessed by noncitizens. Civil rights are sometimes thought of as applications of or means for the protection of more basic human rights. As Thomas Paine explained, "every civil right grows out of a natural right; or in other words, is a natural right exchanged."[28] Thus, the right to vote may be understood as the result of certain democratic social and political arrangements. Such a right is ultimately based on some other claim about natural rights, such as the right to liberty or self-governance. In the United States, civil rights are thought to rest upon constitutional bases, such as the rights enumerated in the Bill of Rights (the first ten amendments to the Constitution, which were ratified in 1791).

From the founding of the United States onward, there were deep and often violent conflicts about which members of society should be granted civil rights—most notably with regard to the issue of slavery. African slaves had become an integral part of the American colonies' culture and economy long before the nation's independence from Britain. By the time the founding documents were written, slavery was so ingrained in America, particularly in the South, that its presence was officially affirmed in Article I of the Constitution. (Slaves were to be counted as three-fifths of a person for purposes of taxation and representation.) Thus, from the start, America's concept of civil rights for all "men" explicitly excluded several categories of people living in America (women were also excluded from many of these civil rights, including the right to vote).

In the nineteenth century, grassroots movements to abolish slavery developed in America, particularly among Northern religious constituencies. As the abolitionist movement gained political traction, a stark regional conflict arose between North and South, a struggle that culminated in the Civil War. In 1868, after the Civil War ended slavery in the United States, the Fourteenth Amendment to the Constitution was ratified. This amendment declares that no state may "deny to any person within its jurisdiction the equal protection of the law." The Fourteenth Amendment guaranteed full citizenship rights to adult males who were born or naturalized in the United States. (It was not until 1920 that women secured voting rights, with the ratification of the Nineteenth Amendment.) Although the Fourteenth Amendment established formal equality for males, the United States remained racially segregated after its passage due to a combination of laws known as "Jim Crow." The Jim Crow system in the American South included laws that restricted voting rights and others that kept blacks segregated from whites. A challenge to Jim Crow was mounted by Homer Plessy, a black man who sat in a white-only railroad car. After he was arrested, he sued in a case that made it to the U.S. Supreme Court. The Court ruled in *Plessy v. Ferguson* (1896) that it was acceptable for states to create a segregated system based on the idea of "separate but equal." But the "equality" affirmed by this ruling was in name only; accommodations and services for African Americans were invariably below the quality of those provided for white Americans. This legal system of segregation and discrimination continued largely unchallenged until the U.S. Supreme Court ruling *Brown v. Board of Education* (1954) overturned the idea that "separate but equal" schooling was justifiable. In 1955, Rosa Parks challenged the segregated bus system in Montgomery, Alabama, by sitting in a bus seat reserved for whites. This prompted a bus boycott in Montgomery led by a young Baptist minister named Martin Luther King Jr.

The 1960s ushered in a host of significant civil rights legislation. In an executive order in 1961, President John F. Kennedy instituted affirmative action in government hiring and in governmental contracts with the goal of encouraging "by positive measures" equal opportunity for all qualified persons.[29] These new hiring procedures increased the number of African Americans in the employ of the federal government.[30] In 1965, President Lyndon B. Johnson issued enforcement procedures such as goals and timetables for hiring women and underrepresented minorities. The Equal Pay Act of 1963 required that male and female employees receive equal pay for substantially equal work. The landmark Civil Rights Act of 1964 prohibited a range of discriminatory practices by private employers, employment agencies, and unions; it also prohibited, among other things, discriminatory voter registration requirements. In 1965, the Voting Rights Act prohibited states from creating restrictions on voting that would "abridge the right of any citizen to vote based on race or color."

While the 1960s saw a broad expansion of civil rights protections, more recent decades have witnessed a narrowing of their scope and legal foundations. Take, for instance, affirmative action laws. In the 1978 *Bakke v. U.C. Davis Medical School* decision, the Supreme Court forbade the use of racial quotas in school admissions but allowed some consideration of race in admissions decisions. This decision was challenged by the 1995 decision *Adarand v. Pena*, which held that any race-conscious federal program must serve a "compelling state interest" and must be "narrowly tailored" to achieve its goal. However, in 2003, a less rigid standard for acceptance of a race-conscious program was used by the Court in its decision regarding the affirmative action practices of the University of Michigan. In *Grutter v. Bollinger*, the Court upheld the university's law school policy, which considers an applicant's race as one factor among others such as test scores, talent, and grade-point average in admissions. The Court rejected the undergraduate school's more mechanical practice of automatically giving extra points to applicants with specific racial backgrounds. The Court also gave added support to earlier rulings that there was a "compelling state interest" in racial diversity in education.[31] In an affirmative action case involving an employer, the 1979 *Weber v. Kaiser Aluminum* decision, the Court permitted a company to remedy its past discriminatory practices by using race as a criterion for admission to special training programs. These programs were aimed at ensuring that a percentage of black persons equal to that in the local labor force could rise to managerial positions in the company.

In the 1990s, two significant pieces of civil rights legislation were passed: the Americans with Disabilities Act of 1990, which prohibited discrimination based upon disability and was discussed previously, and the Civil Rights Act of 1991. The latter required that businesses using employment practices with a discriminatory impact (even if unintentional) must show that the practices are business necessities; otherwise, these businesses must reform their practices to eliminate this impact.[32] Hiring quotas were forbidden except when required by court order for rectifying wrongful past or present discrimination. Sexual harassment was also noted as a form of discrimination.

Many of the most recent advances in civil rights law have involved issues of sex, gender, and sexual harassment. Today, two forms of sexual harassment are generally recognized. One promises employment rewards for sexual favors, and the other creates a "hostile work environment." Sexual harassment also includes harassment based on sexual orientation or gender identity; discrimination based on these categories is also illegal in some, but not all, areas in the United States. A case decided by the Equal Employment Opportunity Commission in 2012 (*Macy v. Department of Justice*) established that Title VII of the Civil Rights Act of 1964 extends to protect transgendered persons against discrimination.[33] Other recent developments include the passage in 2009 of the Lilly Ledbetter Fair Pay Act, which guarantees an employee's right to fair compensation without discrimination.[34] The law is named after a supervisor at a Goodyear tire plant who experienced systematic pay discrimination based on gender for nearly two decades.

These are just a few of the highlights of the past 150 years of civil rights laws. A more thorough discussion might involve laws and court decisions that concern housing, lending, and the busing of school students, as well as laws that have been designed to prevent discrimination on the basis of religion, age, and other characteristics.

Profiling

One basic issue that arises in the context of civil rights law is the problem of profiling. Profiling happens when law enforcement agencies treat individuals as suspects simply because of their race, ethnicity, religion, or other traits.

Profiling has sometimes been endorsed by law enforcement agencies as a useful tool for identifying criminals. One example of this is so-called stop-and-frisk policing, in which police stop individuals and search for contraband or illegal activity. Although not obviously a form of racial profiling, it turns out that stop and frisk policing is often differentially applied. Critics complain that profiling leads to unjustified harassment. For example, African Americans have for decades reported being stopped by traffic police simply because they were African Americans—for the supposed crime of "driving while black."[35] One analysis offered this data from traffic stops in Missouri in 2007:

> Blacks were 78 percent more likely than whites to be searched. Hispanics were 118 percent more likely than whites to be searched. Compared to searches of white drivers, contraband was found 25 percent less often among black drivers and 38 percent less often among Hispanic drivers.[36]

Police stopped black and Hispanic drivers more often but found contraband at a lower rate among these drivers. This makes one wonder whether profiling of this sort is really effective.

Profiling is often connected to drug enforcement practices, such as the federal Drug Enforcement Administration's Operation Pipeline drug interdiction project. According to critics, in the 1980s and 1990s, police agencies involved in Operation Pipeline used racial profiling in their effort to stop drug traffickers on the highways.[37] U.S. courts have tended to rule that racial profiling is illegal—under the Constitution's Fourth Amendment protection against unreasonable searches and seizures and the Fourteenth Amendment requirement of equal protection under the law. But the practice continues. In 2010, the ACLU and the NAACP filed a lawsuit against the state of Maryland, alleging that the state police practiced racial profiling and demanding that the state turn over internal documents—a request that was affirmed by the Maryland Supreme Court in 2013. Similar issues have arisen in New York City, where a widespread policy of stop-and-frisk policing has been criticized as relying heavily on racial profiling. According to ABC News, "While black and Hispanic residents make up only 23 percent and 29 percent of the city's population respectively, 84 percent of recorded stops are young men of color and only around 6 percent of stops lead to an arrest."[38]

Other recent events have raised concerns about profiling. In 2010, the governor of Arizona, Jan Brewer, signed into law Senate Bill 1070, which gave local police extensive power to enforce federal immigration law. The law was intended to discourage illegal immigration and its stated goal is to "discourage and deter the unlawful entry and presence of aliens and economic activity by persons unlawfully present in the United States."[39] The law authorized local police officers to stop people if they have a "reasonable suspicion" of their being unauthorized immigrants.[40] Police could demand that they show proof of citizenship without there being any indication of criminal activity. Other states, such as Alabama, Georgia, Indiana, South Carolina, and Utah, have modeled immigrations laws on the Arizona law. However, the Arizona law was soon legally contested, and parts of the law were overturned by the U.S. Supreme Court in 2012. Nevertheless, the Court allowed law enforcement to act on "reasonable suspicion" that a person is an unauthorized immigrant, a standard that critics say encourages profiling and discrimination. They argue that racial and ethnic characteristics are the only possible basis for a "reasonable suspicion" that a person is in the United States illegally. Some immigration advocates call such legal measures "Juan Crow" laws—recalling the Jim Crow laws of the twentieth century, which discriminated against African Americans.[41] They cite cases of harassment and wrongful detention such as that of Antonio Montejano. Montejano was stopped by the police on suspicion of shoplifting a $10 bottle of perfume. The shoplifting charge was dropped, but the police suspected him of being an illegal immigrant and held him on those grounds. He was incarcerated for four nights, until authorities confirmed that Montejano is in fact a U.S. citizen. Apparently, Montejano had triggered a positive identification in Homeland Security databases because he had been mistakenly deported in 1996. Montejano argues that he has been singled out for such treatment because "I look Mexican, 100 percent."[42]

A different type of profiling involves suspicions based on a person's religion. Since the September 11 terrorist attacks, there have been a number of cases in which American Muslims have been harassed and profiled. For example, consider the 2006 case of six imams (Muslim religious leaders) detained at the Minneapolis–Saint Paul airport while trying to return from an Islamic conference. Several passengers and a gate agent complained that the imams' behavior was suspicious. They said the imams had knelt and prayed loudly at the boarding gate and made anti-American comments. When the imams boarded their U.S. Airways flight, they sat in different places throughout the plane, and a couple of them asked for seat belt extenders with heavy buckles on the ends. In response to the reports of fellow passengers, security personnel asked the six imams to leave the plane before takeoff. When they refused, the police were called, and they were handcuffed and taken off the plane. After hours of questioning, they were allowed to take another flight.[43] The imams later said they had not acted suspiciously or even prayed loudly and that their only "crime" was being identifiable as Muslims. They sued the airline, the police authorities, and the passengers who had reported them to authorities, claiming that they had been discriminated against. Their lawsuit was settled in 2009 for an undisclosed amount. A similar case occurred in 2009 when a Muslim family from Alexandria, Virginia, was ordered off an AirTran flight and detained after other passengers overheard them discussing the safest place to sit on a plane. Despite the absence of evidence that the family meant any harm, the airline refused to let them purchase new tickets. After the story became public, AirTran apologized and offered to refund the family for the price of their replacement tickets on another airline.[44]

While many people condemn such incidents as unjustified discrimination, popular author Sam Harris has argued that security officials should use profiling at airports. He argues that it is a waste of security resources to try to be fair and randomly screen people, including grandmothers, who pose no threat. Harris calls the effort to avoid profiling "the tyranny of fairness." Harris writes, "Some semblance of fairness makes sense and, needless to say, everyone's bags should be screened, if only because it is possible to put a bomb in someone else's luggage. But the TSA has a finite amount of attention: Every moment spent frisking the Mormon Tabernacle Choir subtracts from the scrutiny paid to more likely threats."[45] Arguments of this sort are often subject to criticism from civil rights advocates. Not only does profiling unfairly generalize about group members, but it also can have negative consequences. Not all terrorists are Muslims; terrorists can also be Christians, Jews, or atheists. Furthermore, profiling Muslims may generate resentment and provoke backlash.

One of the problems of profiling is that it tends to focus on obvious and overt signs of racial, ethnic, or religious belonging and then involves sweeping generalizations about the behaviors of individuals who appear to fit those categories. Whether a policy counts as profiling and whether it always implies discrimination is a matter of some debate. For example, when decisions to stop motorists are made primarily or solely on the basis of race, this is surely discriminatory. However, in other cases in which race is just one of many factors in selecting targets of investigation, the question of discrimination is not so clear. This is the difference between "hard" and "soft" profiling. In the former case, race is the only factor used to single out someone, whereas in the latter it is just one of many factors. An example of the latter might be "questioning or detaining a person because of the confluence of a variety of factors—age (young), dress (hooded sweatshirt, baggy pants, etc.), time (late evening), geography (the person is walking through the 'wrong' neighborhood)—that include race (black)."[46] Sometimes it may be hard to tell what kind of profiling an example involves. Consider a New Jersey highway patrolman who pulls over a black driver in a Nissan Pathfinder because the police have intelligence that Jamaican drug rings favor this car as a means for their marijuana trade in the Northeast.[47] Is this an example of unjust discrimination or a reasonable procedure?

Hate Crimes

A more obvious expression of discrimination and bias can be found in hate crimes, which are defined as crimes accompanied or motivated by bias. The attack on the Sikh temple in Oak Creek, Wisconsin, in August 2012 was a sadly typical case. A white supremacist, motivated by racial hatred, opened fire at a Sikh temple, killing six.

The FBI defines a hate crime as a "criminal offense against a person or property motivated in whole or in part by an offender's bias against a race, religion, disability, ethnic origin or sexual orientation."[48] The legal focus on crimes that are motivated by bias became an issue in the 1980s, as Washington and Oregon passed legislation identifying this category of crime.[49] By 2009, the U.S. Congress passed the "Matthew Shepard and James Byrd, Jr. Hate Crimes Prevention Act." The two individuals named in this legislation were murdered by offenders who targeted them because of bias. Matthew Shepard was brutally beaten, tied to a fence, and left to die in 1998 in Laramie, Wyoming, where he was a university student. Shepard's assailants targeted him because he was gay. However, Wyoming did not have a hate crime law at the time. James Byrd Jr. was a black man who was murdered in 1998 in Jasper, Texas, by three white men who beat him, urinated on him, tied a chain around his legs, and dragged him

behind their truck until his arm and head were severed when his body hit a culvert. The murderers were white supremacists. Byrd's murder prompted the Texas legislature to pass hate crime legislation in 2001.

As a result of the federal Hate Crime Statistics Act of 1990, the Department of Justice keeps extensive data on hate crimes.[50] Recent data indicate that more than 6,200 hate crimes were reported in 2011, involving more than 7,600 victims.[51] Of those crimes,

- 46.9 percent were racially motivated.
- 20.8 percent resulted from sexual-orientation bias.
- 19.8 percent were motivated by religious bias.
- 11.6 percent stemmed from ethnicity/national origin bias.
- less than 1 percent (0.9) were prompted by disability bias.

While hate crimes occur in a variety of ways, they often focus on humiliating the victim. Consider, for example, a hate crime that occurred in Ohio in 2011 among the Amish. Some Amish men attacked other Amish people, holding them down and cutting off the women's hair and the men's beards. The beards and hair were a symbol of faith. The crime was motivated by religious reasons. And so, it was prosecuted as a hate crime.[52]

Just as there are special, more severe penalties for killing police officers, federal and state laws sometimes impose more severe penalties for crimes motivated by hatred. Critics of these policies respond that to do this is to punish people for the views they hold, and that no matter how objectionable hate crimes might be, such laws constitute a violation of free speech. The FBI makes it clear, however, that its hate crime prosecutions are focused on crimes such as murders, arsons, and assaults that are *accompanied by* bias—and not in prosecuting bias itself, which is protected by the First Amendment. As we have seen in other chapters, equality and nondiscrimination are ethical values that must be balanced against other values, such as the free speech and privacy rights of individuals.

Chapter 13

AFFIRMATIVE ACTION AND PREFERENTIAL TREATMENT

One recurrent question in discussions of equality and discrimination is whether it is ever justified to treat people in unequal ways as a remedy for past discrimination. This question is most frequently raised with regard to programs of affirmative action and preferential treatment. Affirmative action plans try to take active ("affirmative") steps to remedy past inequality. One way to do this is to give preferential consideration or treatment to members of groups that have been discriminated against in the past.

As noted previously, there are still stark disparities in American society, which many say are the legacy of past injustices. Some of these disparities will be outlined in economic terms in Chapter 14. And in Chapter 15, we discuss racial disparities in the criminal justice system. In terms of the general demographic of the United States (based on 2014 data), whites make up 77.4 percent of the population (non-Hispanic whites are 62.1 percent), Hispanics make up 17.4 percent (Hispanics can be of any race), blacks make up 13.2 percent, and Asian and Pacific Islanders make up just under 6 percent.[53] But consider that only thirteen African Americans have ever been a CEO of a Fortune 500 company.[54] Despite this, we are making progress toward more diversity and equality. The 114th Congress (resulting from the November 2014 elections) is the most diverse in history (out of 535 members): 96 racial minorities, and 104 women, which means about 20 percent are women and about 17 percent are nonwhite. The Congress is 92 percent Christian, which leaves about 5 percent Jewish members as well as two Muslim members, two Buddhist members, and one Hindu member. There are also, by the way, some openly LGBT members.[55]

Affirmative action comes in many forms. The idea suggested by the term is that to remedy certain injustices, we need to do more than follow the negative requirement "Don't discriminate" or "Stop discriminating." The basic argument given for doing something more is usually that merely ceasing discrimination will not or has not worked.

Psychological reasons may be cited, for example, that discrimination and prejudice are so ingrained in people that they cannot help discriminating and do not even recognize when they are being discriminatory or prejudiced. To illustrate this dynamic, the philosopher Robert Fullinwider asks us to imagine that we have been transported to a land of giants, where everything is made for folks their size. They might fail to see why smaller people like us might have difficulties, assuming instead that we are just inferior or incompetent.[56] Social and political reasons for affirmative action can also be given, such as evidence of structural or institutional racism (as we discussed previously). The only way to change things, the argument goes, is to do something more positive, which would change established patterns of discrimination.

But what are we to do? There are many possibilities. One is to make a greater positive effort to find qualified persons from underrepresented groups. Thus, in hiring, a company might place ads in minority newspapers. In college admissions, counselors might recruit more actively among disadvantaged minority groups. Once the pool is enlarged, then all in the pool are judged by the same criteria, and no special preferences are given on the basis of race or sex.

Other versions of affirmative action involve what have come to be known as *preferences*. In this approach, preference is given to minority group members or women who are as well qualified as other candidates—their membership in a disadvantaged group simply gives them an edge. Preference also may be given to underrepresented group members who are somewhat less well qualified than other applicants. In either case, it is clear that determining equality of qualifications is in itself a problem. One reason for this is that applicants are usually better qualified for some aspects of a given position and less well qualified for others. Another is the difficulty of deciding just what qualifications are necessary or important for a given position. Although those who support and those who oppose preferences often imply that determining requirements for a position is easy, it is not at all that simple.

Other forms of affirmative action also exist. For example, companies or institutions may establish goals and quotas to be achieved for increasing minority or female representation. *Goals* are usually thought of as ideals that we aim for but that we are not absolutely required to reach. Goals can be formulated in terms of percentages or numbers. *Quotas*, in contrast, are usually fixed percentages or numbers that an institution intends to actually reach. Thus, a university or professional school might set aside a fixed number of slots for its incoming first-year class for certain minority group members. The institution would fill these positions even if this meant admitting people with lesser overall scores or points in the assessment system.

In past decades, an effort was made to increase the representation of minority groups on college campuses. These efforts have been successful enough to prompt a backlash against race-based admissions processes. In its 1996 decision in *Hopwood v. Texas*, a three-judge panel of the U.S. Court of Appeals for the Fifth Circuit struck down an affirmative action program at the University of Texas law school. This program had accepted lower scores on the Law School Admission Test (LSAT) for black and Hispanic applicants. In a parallel development, Proposition 209 in California outlawed racial preferences in the public sector, and in 1995, the board of regents of the University of California (UC) system voted to ban race considerations in admissions. As we saw previously, the U.S. Supreme Court upheld the University of Michigan's graduate admissions program, in which race was one of several factors, but found unconstitutional the university's undergraduate admissions program, which gave a fixed number of additional points to minority applicants.

The *Hopwood* decision and others like it had negative impacts on minority enrollments in colleges and universities. In Texas, black college enrollment fell by 28 percent in the two years following *Hopwood*.[57] In California, between 1995 (when Prop. 209 passed) and 1998, minority enrollments at UC Berkeley and UCLA dropped by more than 50 percent. The numbers of minority students continue to

be low and fail to reflect California's rapidly changing demography.[58] Other analyses indicate that while these policies may have an adverse effect on minority enrollment at elite universities, this problem is not as pronounced for less selective schools. Moreover, there is some data to suggest that minority graduation rates are increasing.[59] Nonetheless, there is still concern about finding ways to increase minority enrollments. Some states have attempted to find other ways to help generate a diverse student body. In Texas, the legislature guaranteed a place in Texas's public universities to the top 10 percent of graduates from Texas high schools. The idea of this approach was to ensure that students from minority-serving high schools had a better chance at college admissions.

Most recently, the Supreme Court considered affirmative action in *Fisher v. University of Texas at Austin*, in which the plaintiff challenged the University of Texas's affirmative action policy. The plaintiff claimed that the state had achieved a sufficient level of diversity in the university and thus that the university no longer had a need to give extra consideration to applicants based upon race. It is a factual question as to whether affirmative action has been effective or not. The moral question of whether affirmative action is justified is another matter. At any rate, the Supreme Court's decision in *Fisher* was not decisive. A final ruling was made in June, 2016, when the Court affirmed race based admissions that aim to recruit a diverse student body.

In any discussion of affirmative action, it is important to specify exactly what kind of practice one favors or opposes. Let us examine the arguments for and against the various types of affirmative action in terms of the reasons given to support them. As in other chapters, these arguments can be divided into consequentialist and non-consequentialist approaches.

Consequentialist Considerations

Arguments both for and against various affirmative action programs have relied on consequentialist considerations for their justification. These considerations are broadly utilitarian in nature. The question

Outline of Moral Approaches to Affirmative Action

	Strong Affirmative Action	Moderate Affirmative Action	Opposed to Affirmative Action
Thesis	Positive steps should be taken to remedy past discrimination	Some affirmative action can be justified	Affirmative action is wrong
Corollaries and Implications	Past inequalities will only be overcome when disadvantaged groups are given extra advantages, including possibly fulfilling *quotas*	Need to balance merit, equality, and redress for disadvantage; diversity is viewed as an asset worthy of preference and special consideration	Non-discrimination is enough; affirmative action causes more unequal treatment and is a kind of *reverse discrimination*
Connections with Moral Theory	*Compensatory justice* requires redress for past injustice; consequentialist considerations aim to remedy lack of opportunity for members of historically disadvantaged groups	Respect for individual merit is balanced with social value of diversity; consequentialist concern for fixing past injustice and establishing more equitable social outcomes	*Merit* as the primary consideration is based upon respect for individual achievement; consequentialist concern that affirmative action increases racial tension and causes disrespectful *tokenism*

is whether affirmative action programs do more good than harm or more harm than good. People who argue in favor of these programs urge the following sorts of considerations: These programs benefit us all. We live in a multiracial society and benefit from mutual respect and harmony. We all bring diverse backgrounds to our employment and educational institutions, and we all benefit from the contributions of people who have a variety of diverse perspectives. Our law schools should reflect the full diversity of our society to help ensure that all people have access to adequate representation and protection under the law. Others argue that affirmative action is one way to break the vicious cycle of discrimination and inequality. Past discrimination has put women and some minority group members at a continuing disadvantage. Unless something is done, they will never be able to compete on an equal basis. Low family income leads to poorer education for

children, which leads to lower-paying jobs, which leads to low family income, and so on. Children need role models to look up to. They need to know that certain types of achievement and participation are possible for them. Otherwise, they will lack hope and opportunities to pursue success. Without affirmative action programs, supporters argue, things are not likely to change. Discrimination and its long-term effects are so entrenched that drastic measures are needed to overcome them.

Those who argue against affirmative action on consequentialist grounds usually maintain that the programs do not work or that they do more harm than good. They cite statistics to show that these programs have benefited middle-class African Americans, for example, but not the lower class. As Stephen Carter argues, "The most disadvantaged black people are not in a position to benefit from preferential admission."[60] Critics such as

Carter suggest that unless affirmative action admissions programs are accompanied by other aid, both financial and tutorial, they are often useless or wasted. Some critics point out that lawsuits filed under the 1964 Civil Rights Act have done more than affirmative action to increase the percentage of blacks in various white-collar positions.[61] Other consequentialist critics argue that there is a stigma attached to those who have been admitted or hired through affirmative action programs and that this can be debilitating for those so chosen. Some black neoconservatives even argue that quotas and racially weighted tests "have psychologically handicapped blacks by making them dependent on racial-preference programs rather than their own hard work."[62]

Those who oppose affirmative action programs also cite the increased racial tension that they believe results from these programs—in effect, a white male backlash against women and members of minority groups. Some of the same writers who support affirmative action for underrepresented minority groups and women have also made a case for giving special attention to economically disadvantaged students in college and university admissions.[63] They point out that elite universities have only a minuscule percentage of admissions from lower-income families, even when they have sizable minority enrollments. These thinkers argue that such class-based affirmative action is not only justified for reasons of fairness but also serves the purpose of increasing class diversity.

The key to evaluating these consequentialist arguments both for and against affirmative action is to examine the validity of their assessments and predictions. What, in fact, have affirmative action programs achieved? Have they achieved little because they benefit those who least need it and might have succeeded without them, or have they actually brought more disadvantaged students into the system and employees into better and higher-paying jobs, thus helping break a vicious cycle? Have affirmative action programs benefited society by increasing diversity in the workforce and

in various communities, or have they led only to increased racial tensions? These are difficult matters to assess. Here is another place where ethical judgments depend on empirical information drawn from the various sciences or other disciplines. The consequentialist argument for affirmative action programs will succeed if it can be shown that there is no better way to achieve the good the programs are designed to achieve and that the good done by these affirmative action programs outweighs any harm they cause. The consequentialist argument against affirmative action programs will succeed if it can be shown that there are better ways to achieve the same good ends or that the harm they create outweighs the good they help achieve.

Non-consequentialist Considerations

Not all arguments about affirmative action programs are based on appeals to consequences. Some arguments appeal to deontological considerations. For instance, some people argue for affirmative action programs on the grounds that they provide *compensatory justice*, a way of compensating for past wrongs done to members of certain groups. People have been harmed and wronged by past discrimination, and we now need to make up for that by benefiting them, by giving them preferential treatment. However, it can be difficult to assess how preferential treatment can right a past wrong. We may think of it as undoing the past harm done. But we find that it is often difficult to undo the harm. How does one really prevent or erase results such as the loss of self-esteem and confidence in the minority child who asks, "Mom, am I as good as that white kid?" or in the little girl who says, "I can't do that; I'm a girl"? This interpretation of making compensation then becomes a matter of producing good consequences or eliminating bad ones. It is a matter of trying to change the results of past wrongs. Thus, if we are to compensate for non-consequentialist reasons, then it must involve a different sense of righting a wrong—a sense of justice being done in itself, whether or not it makes any difference in the outcome.

Some non-consequentialist critics also argue against affirmative action on grounds of its injustice. They appeal to the principle of equality, arguing that race and sex are irrelevant characteristics that should not be recognized by government policy. Just as it was wrong in the past to use these characteristics to deny people equal chances, so it is also wrong in the present, even if it is used this time to their advantage. Race and sex are not differences that should count in treating people differently, they argue. Preferences for some also mean denial of benefits to others. For this reason, preferential treatment programs have sometimes been labeled *reverse discrimination*. Moreover, opponents of affirmative action criticize the use of compensatory justice arguments. In a valid application of compensatory justice, they argue, only those wronged should be compensated, and only those responsible for the wrong should be made to pay. They object to affirmative action programs that compensate people based on group membership and without establishing whether they themselves have been harmed by past discriminatory practices. Those who lose out in affirmative action programs, they argue, may not have ever been guilty of discrimination or may not have wronged anyone.

Consider the case of a group of white firefighters in New Haven, Connecticut, that went to the U.S. Supreme Court in 2009. That city administered a test to its firefighters to determine who would be promoted. When no black firefighters passed the test, the city simply dropped all of the results. Those white firefighters who had passed the test complained of reverse discrimination. By a 5–4 ruling, the Court agreed with them.[64]

The arguments for affirmative action based on considerations of justice will succeed only if those persons who make them also can make a case for the justice of the programs. They must show that such programs do in fact compensate those who have been wronged, even if they have been affected by discrimination in ways that are not immediately obvious. Supporters may also argue that those who lose out as a result of preferences are not badly harmed—they have other opportunities and are not demeaned by their loss. And though they have not intentionally wronged anyone, they have likely benefited from structures of discrimination.

Those who oppose affirmative action based on considerations of justice will succeed if they can effectively apply the principle of equality to their arguments. They may argue, for example, that affirmative action singles out some groups for special treatment in a way that is inconsistent with the idea of equality. But if they rely primarily on the harms done by continuing to use race or sex as grounds for differential treatment, then they will be appealing to a consequentialist consideration and must be judged on that basis.

This chapter has dealt with a range of issues collected together under the general rubric of equality and discrimination; racial profiling, racism, hate crimes, and affirmative action. The guiding principle is that we should treat people fairly and equally. While there is disagreement about how the principle of equality applies in these cases and about its moral basis, there is widespread agreement that equality matters.

In the first reading for this chapter, we have an excerpt from Iris Marion Young's essay "Five Faces of Oppression." Young's essay has been influential in helping to explain the idea of *institutional* or *structural oppression*. In the second excerpt, Kwame Anthony Appiah discusses *racialism* and *racism*. He argues that there are good reasons to be suspicious of what he calls *racialist* reasoning, which holds that racial difference are biologically grounded, and the *racist* ideas that often follow from it. He applies Kantian insights and argues that racism is wrong because it violates the ideal of universality. In the final reading of the chapter, we offer an excerpt from Naomi Zack's book, *White Privilege and Black Rights*. Zack outlines some of the problems that have given rise to the Black Lives Matter movement, while arguing that, at bottom, unequal treatment is a human rights violation.

NOTES

1. Preamble to the Civil Rights Act of 1964, http://www.ourdocuments.gov/doc.php?flash=true&doc=97&page=transcript (accessed April 11, 2013).

2. EEO Policy Statement, U.S. Equal Employment Opportunity Commission, January 31, 2011, http://www.eeoc.gov/eeoc/internal/eeo_policy_statement.cfm (accessed April 11, 2013).

3. "Racial Prejudice in US Worsened during Obama's First Term, Study Shows," *Guardian*, October 27, 2012, http://www.guardian.co.uk/world/2012/oct/27/racial-prejudice-worsened-obama (accessed March 24, 2013).

4. See Julianne Hing, "Asian Americans Respond to Pew: We're Not Your Model Minority," *Colorlines*, June 21, 2012, http://colorlines.com/archives/2012/06/pew_asian_american_study.html (accessed April 30, 2013); also see, "The Rise of Asian Americans," Pew Center Report, June 19, 2012, http://www.pewsocialtrends.org/2012/06/19/the-rise-of-asian-americans/ (accessed April 30, 2013).

5. Carolyn Chen, "Asians: Too Smart for Their Own Good?" *New York Times*, December 19, 2012, http://www.nytimes.com/2012/12/20/opinion/asians-too-smart-for-their-own-good.html?_r=0 (accessed April 30, 2013); also see "Fears of an Asian Quota in the Ivy League," *New York Times*, December 19, 2012, http://www.nytimes.com/roomfordebate/2012/12/19/fears-of-an-asian-quota-in-the-ivy-league/?ref=opinion (accessed April 30, 2013).

6. R. C. Lewontin, "Race: Temporary Views on Human Variation," *Encyclopedia Americana*, http://ea.grolier.com Also see R. C. Lewontin, *Human Diversity* (New York: W. H. Freeman, 1982).

7. L. Luigi Luca Cavalli-Sforza, Paolo Menozzi, and Alberto Piazza, *History and Geography of Human Genes* (Princeton, NJ: Princeton University Press, 1994), p. 19.

8. Carolyn Abraham, "Race," *Globe and Mail*, June 18, 2005, F1, F8.

9. See International HapMap Project, www.hapmap.org

10. Lucius Outlaw, Jr., "If Not Races, Then What? Toward a Revised Understanding of Bio-Social Groupings" *Graduate Faculty Philosophy Journal* 35: 1–2 (2014), pp. 275–296.

11. Lucius Outlaw, Jr., "Toward a Critical Theory of 'Race'" in Bernard Boxil, ed., *Race and Racism* (Oxford: Oxford University Press, 2001), p. 69.

12. See Sally Haslanger, "Oppressions: Racial and Other," in *Racism in Mind* (Ithaca, NY: Cornell University Press, 2004).

13. U.S. Department of Education, National Center for Education Statistics, 2012, *The Condition of Education 2011* (NCES 2012-045), http://nces.ed.gov/fastfacts/display.asp?id=40 (accessed March 22, 2013).

14. U.S. Department of Education, National Center for Education Statistics, 2012, *The Condition of Education 2012* (NCES 2012-045), http://nces.ed.gov/fastfacts/display.asp?id=16 (accessed March 22, 2013).

15. Bureau of Labor Statistics, U.S. Department of Labor, "Unemployment Rates by Race and Ethnicity, 2010," http://www.bls.gov/opub/ted/2011/ted_20111005.htm (accessed March 22, 2013).

16. Tami Luhby, "Worsening Wealth Inequality by Race," *CNN Money*, June 21, 2012, http://money.cnn.com/2012/06/21/news/economy/wealth-gap-race/index.htm (accessed March 23, 2013).

17. "Affluent Students Have an Advantage and the Gap Is Widening," *New York Times*, December 22, 2012, http://www.nytimes.com/interactive/2012/12/22/education/Affluent-Students-Have-an-Advantage-and-the-Gap-Is-Widening.html?_r=0 (accessed March 22, 2013).

18. Scott Jaschik, "SAT Scores Drop Again," *Inside Higher Ed*, September 25, 2012, http://www.insidehighered.com/news/2012/09/25/sat-scores-are-down-and-racial-gaps-remain (accessed March 22, 2013).

19. Scott Jaschik, "SAT Scores Down Again, Wealth Up Again," *Inside Higher Ed*, August 29, 2007, http://www.insidehighered.com/news/2007/08/29/sat#ixzz2Rzt6hJJ3 (accessed April 30, 2013).

20. T. L. Dixon, "Network News and Racial Beliefs: Exploring the Connection between National Television News Exposure and Stereotypical Perceptions of African Americans," *Journal of Communication* 58 (2008), pp. 321–37.

21. T. L. Dixon, "Crime News and Racialized Beliefs: Understanding the Relationship between Local News Viewing and Perceptions of African Americans and Crime," *Journal of Communication* 58 (2008), pp. 106–25.

22. "The Simple Truth about the Pay Gap" (2013), AAUW, http://www.aauw.org/resource/the-simple-truth-about-the-gender-pay-gap/ (accessed March 22, 2013).

23. Lam Thuy Vo, "The Jobs with the Biggest (and Smallest) Pay Gaps between Men and Women," NPR Planet Money, http://www.npr.org/blogs/money/2013/02/05/171196714/the-jobs-with-the-biggest-and-smallest-pay-gaps-between-men-and-women (accessed April 22, 2013).

24. See Mary Anne Warren, "Secondary Sexism and Quota Hiring," *Philosophy and Public Affairs* 6, no. 3 (Spring 1977), pp. 240–61.

25. Gina Kolata, "Men and Women Use Brain Differently, Study Discovers," *New York Times*, February 16, 1995, p. A8.

26. Tanya L. Domi, "Women in Combat: Policy Catches Up with Reality," *New York Times*, February 8, 2013, http://www.nytimes.com/2013/02/09/opinion/women-in-combat-policy-catches-up-with-reality.html?_r=0 (accessed May 1, 2013).

27. Susan Moller Okin, *Is Multiculturalism Bad for Women?*, ed. Joshua Cohen, Matthew Howard, and Martha C. Nussbaum (Princeton, NJ: Princeton University Press, 2000).

28. Thomas Paine, *Rights of Man* in *Thomas Paine: Collected Writings* (New York: Library of America, 1955, reprinted 2012), p. 465.

29. Executive Order 10925 (1961), http://www.eeoc.gov/eeoc/history/35th/thelaw/eo-10925.html (accessed May 13, 2013).

30. Bruce P. Lapenson, *Affirmative Action and the Meanings of Merit* (Lanham, MD: University Press of America, 2009), p. 3.

31. Linda Greenhouse, "University of Michigan Ruling Endorses the Value of Campus Diversity," *New York Times*, June 24, 2003, pp. A1, A25.

32. This aspect of the bill confirmed the "disparate impact" notion of the 1971 U.S. Supreme Court ruling in *Griggs v. Duke Power Company*, which required companies to revise their business practices that perpetuated past discrimination. This was weakened by the Court's 1989 ruling in *Wards Cove Packing Co. v. Antonio*, which, among other things, put the burden of proof on the employee to show that the company did not have a good reason for some discriminatory business practice.

33. *Equal Opportunity Employment Commission*, http://www.eeoc.gov/federal/otherprotections.cfm (accessed May 2, 2013).

34. http://www.lillyledbetter.com/

35. David A. Harris, "Driving While Black: Racial Profiling on Our Nation's Highways," *ACLU*, June 7, 1999, http://www.aclu.org/racial-justice/driving-while-black-racial-profiling-our-nations-highways (accessed March 21, 2013).

36. Donald Tomaskovic-Devey and Patricia Warren, "Explaining and Eliminating Racial Profiling," *American Sociological Association Contexts* (Spring 2009), http://contexts.org/articles/spring-2009/explaining-and-eliminating-racial-profiling/ (accessed March 21, 2013).

37. Harris, "Driving While Black."

38. Bill Weir and Nick Capote, "NYPD's Controversial Stop-and-Frisk Policy: Racial Profiling or 'Proactive Policing'?" ABC's *Nightline*, May 1, 2013, http://abcnews.go.com/US/nypds-controversial-stop-frisk-policy-racial-profiling-proactive/story?id=19084229#.UYLbtSvEo_s (accessed May 2, 2013).

39. SB 1070, http://www.azleg.gov/legtext/49leg/2r/bills/sb1070s.pdf (accessed March 21, 2013).

40. SB 1070, http://www.azleg.gov/legtext/49leg/2r/bills/sb1070s.pdf (accessed March 21, 2013).

41. Diane McWhorter, "The Strange Career of Juan Crow," *New York Times*, June 16, 2012, http://www.nytimes.com/2012/06/17/opinion/sunday/no-sweet-home-alabama.html (accessed March 21, 2013).

42. Julia Preston, "Immigration Crackdown Also Snares Americans," *New York Times*, December 13, 2011, http://www.nytimes.com/2011/12/14/us/measures-to-capture-illegal-aliens-nab-citizens.html?pagewanted=all (accessed April 11, 2013).

43. Libby Sander, "6 Imams Removed from Flight for Behavior Deemed Suspicious," *New York Times*, November 22, 2006, http://www.nytimes.com/

2006/11/22/us/22muslim.html?bl&ex=116451720
0&en=24531ca1fa7314e1&ei=5087%0A (accessed
April 23, 2013).

44. Amy Gardner, "9 Muslim Passengers Removed
from Jet," *Washington Post*, January 2, 2009,
http://www.washingtonpost.com/wp-dyn/content/
article/2009/01/01/AR2009010101932.
html?hpid=topnews (accessed April 11, 2013).
Also see Amy Gardner and Spencer S. Hsu, "Airline
Apologizes for Booting 9 Muslim Passengers from
Flight," *Washington Post*, January 3, 2009,
http://www.washingtonpost.com/wp-dyn/content/
article/2009/01/02/AR2009010201695.html
(accessed April 23, 2013).

45. Sam Harris, "In Defense of Profiling," Sam Harris
Blog, April 2012, http://www.samharris.org/blog/
item/in-defense-of-profiling (accessed March 19,
2013).

46. Randall Kennedy, "Suspect Policy," *New Republic*,
September 13 and 20, 1999, p. 35.

47. Heather MacDonald, "The Myth of Racial Profiling,"
City Journal 11, No. 2 (Spring 2001), http://www
.city-journal.org/html/11_2_the_myth.html

48. "Hate Crime—Overview," FBI, http://www.fbi.gov/
about-us/investigate/civilrights/hate_crimes/
overview (accessed March 21, 2013).

49. "Hate Crime," National Institute of Justice, http://
www.nij.gov/topics/crime/hate-crime/ (accessed
May 2, 2013).

50. Brian Levin, "The Long Arc of Justice: Race,
Violence and the Emergence of Hate Crime Law," in
Hate Crimes, ed. Barbara Perry (Westport, CT:
Greenwood Publishing, 2008), p. 1:8.

51. "Hate Crime Statistics, 2011," FBI, http://www.fbi
.gov/about-us/cjis/ucr/hate-crime/2011/narratives/
incidents-and-offenses (accessed March 21, 2013).

52. "Amish Beard Cutting Case," FBI, February 8,
2013, http://www.fbi.gov/news/stories/2013/
february/16-sentenced-in-amish-beard-cutting-case
(accessed March 21, 2013).

53. U.S. Census Quick Facts, http://www.census.gov/
quickfacts/table/PST045215/00

54. "African American CEO's of Fortune 500
Companies," *Black Entrepreneur*, April 7, 2012,
http://www.blackentrepreneurprofile.com/fortune-
500-ceos/ (accessed May 2, 2013).

55. Combining data from: Pew Forum, "Faith on the
Hill" January 5, 2015, http://www.pewforum.org/
2015/01/05/faith-on-the-hill/ (accessed March 5,
2016); *Washington Post*, "The new Congress is
80 percent white, 80 percent male and 92 percent
Christian" January 5, 2015, https://www
.washingtonpost.com/news/the-fix/wp/2015/01/
05/the-new-congress-is-80-percent-white-80-percent-
male-and-92-percent-christian/ (accessed March 5,
2016); and Ballotopedia, "114th Congress,"
https://ballotpedia.org/114th_United_States_
Congress (accessed March 5, 2016).

56. Robert K. Fullinwider, "Affirmative Action and
Fairness," *Report from the Institute for Philosophy
and Public Policy* 11, No. 1 (Winter 1991),
pp. 10–13.

57. John F. Kain, Daniel M. O'Brien, and Paul A.
Jargowsky, *Hopwood and the Top 10 Percent Law:
How They Have Affected the College Enrollment
Decisions of Texas High School Graduates*, Report
for the Texas Schools Project at the University of
Texas at Dallas, March 25, 2005, http://www
.utdallas.edu/research/tsp-erc/pdf/wp_kain_2005_
hopwood_top_10_percent.pdf.pdf (accessed May 2,
2013).

58. "Despite Diversity Efforts, UC Minority Enrollment
Down Since Prop. 209," California Watch,
February 24, 2013, http://californiawatch.org/
dailyreport/despite-diversity-efforts-uc-minority-
enrollment-down-prop-209-15031 (accessed
May 2, 2013).

59. Peter Arcidiacono, Esteban Aucejo, Patrick Coate,
and V. Joseph Hotz, "The Effects of Proposition 209
on College Enrollment and Graduation Rates in
California" (working paper, December 2011),
http://public.econ.duke.edu/~psarcidi/prop209.pdf
(accessed May 2, 2013).

60. Stephen Carter, *Reflections of an Affirmative Action
Baby* (New York: Basic Books, 1991).

61. Professor Jonathan Leonard, cited in the *San
Francisco Examiner*, September 29, 1991.

62. *Time*, May 27, 1991, p. 23.

63. Amy Argetsinger, "Princeton's Former President
Challenges 'Bastions of Privilege,'" *San Francisco
Chronicle*, April 17, 2004, p. A5.

64. *Ricci v. DeStefano*, 557 U.S.—(2009).

READING

Five Faces of Oppression

IRIS MARION YOUNG

MindTap®   For more chapter resources and activities, go to MindTap.

Study Questions

As you read the excerpt, please consider the following questions:
1. How does Young suggest that the idea of oppression has evolved?
2. How can oppression be unconscious, structural, and systematic, according to Young?
3. Why does Young's account still leave us with the idea of a privileged group who benefits from oppression?

One reason that many people would not use the term oppression to describe injustice in our society is that they do not understand the term in the same way as do new social movements. In its traditional usage, oppression means the exercise of tyranny by a ruling group. Thus many Americans would agree with radicals in applying the term oppression to the situation of Black South Africans under apartheid. Oppression also traditionally carries a strong connotation of conquest and colonial domination....

In dominant political discourse it is not legitimate to use the term oppression to describe our society, because oppression is the evil perpetrated by the Others.

New left social movements of the 1960s and 1970s, however, shifted the meaning of the concept of oppression. In its new usage oppression designates the disadvantage and injustice some people suffer not because a tyrannical power coerces them, but because of the everyday practices of a well-intentioned liberal society. In this new left usage, the tyranny of a ruling group over another as in South Africa, must certainly be called oppressive. But oppression also refers to systemic constraints on groups that are not necessarily the result of the intentions of a tyrant. Oppression in this sense is structural, rather than the result of a few people's choices or policies. Its causes are embedded in unquestioned norms, habits, and symbols, in the assumptions underlying institutional rules and the collective consequences of following those rules....In this extended structural sense oppression refers to the vast and deep injustices some groups suffer as a consequence of often unconscious assumptions and reactions of well-meaning people in ordinary interactions, media and cultural stereotypes, and structural features of bureaucratic hierarchies and market mechanisms—in short the normal processes of everyday life. We cannot eliminate this structural oppression by getting rid of the rulers or making some new laws, because oppressions are systematically reproduced in major economic, political, and cultural institutions.

The systemic character of oppression implies that an oppressed group need not have a correlate oppressing group. While structural oppression involves relations among groups, these relations do not always fit the paradigm of conscious and intentional oppression of one group by another....

The conscious actions of many individuals daily contribute to maintaining and reproducing oppression, but those people are usually simply doing their jobs or living their lives, and do not understand themselves as agents of oppression.

I do not mean to suggest that within a system of oppression individual persons do not intentionally harm others in oppressed groups. The raped woman, the beaten Black youth, the locked-out worker, the gay man harassed on the street are victims of intentional actions by identifiable agents. I also do not mean to deny that specific groups are beneficiaries of the oppression of other groups, and thus have an interest in their continued oppression. Indeed, for every oppressed group there is a group that is privileged in relation to that group.

Iris Marion Young, *Justice and the Politics of Difference* (Princeton, NJ Princeton University Press, 1990), pp. 40–42.

READING

Racisms

KWAME ANTHONY APPIAH

MindTap® For more chapter resources and activities, go to MindTap.

Study Questions

As you read the excerpt, please consider the following questions:
1. What does Appiah mean when he says that racists have a cognitive incapacity?
2. According to Appiah, why is racism based upon false or mistaken racialist ideas?
3. How does Appiah employ Kantian moral ideas in his critique of racism?

Racialism is not, in itself, a doctrine that must be dangerous, even if the racial essence is thought to entail moral and intellectual dispositions. Provided positive moral qualities are distributed across the races, each can be respected, can have its "separate but equal" place....I believe—and I have argued elsewhere—that racialism is false; but by itself, it seems to be a cognitive rather than a moral problem....

Racialism is, however, a presupposition of other doctrines that have been called "racism," and these other doctrines have been, in the last few centuries, the basis of a great deal of human suffering and the source of a great deal of moral error.

One such doctrine we might call "extrinsic racism": extrinsic racists make moral distinctions between members of different races because they believe that the racial essence entails certain morally relevant qualities. The basis for the extrinsic racists' discrimination between people is their belief that members of different races differ in respects that *warrant* the differential treatment, respects—such as honesty or courage or intelligence—that are uncontroversially held (at least in most contemporary cultures) to be acceptable as a basis for treating people differently. Evidence that there are no such differences in morally relevant characteristics—that Negroes do not necessarily lack intellectual capacities, that Jews are not especially avaricious—should thus lead people out of their racism if it is purely extrinsic. As we know, such evidence often fails to change an extrinsic racist's attitudes substantially...if the racist is sincere—what

we have is no longer a false doctrine but a cognitive incapacity....

This cognitive incapacity is not, of course, a rare one. Many of us are unable to give up beliefs that play a part in justifying the special advantages we gain (or hope to gain) from our positions in the social order—in particular, beliefs about the positive characters of the class of people who share that position. Many people who express extrinsic racist beliefs—many white South Africans, for example—are beneficiaries of social orders that deliver advantages to them by virtue of their "race," so that their disinclination to accept evidence that would deprive them of a justification for those advantages is just an instance of this general phenomenon....

But even if racialism were true, both forms of theoretical racism would be incorrect. Extrinsic racism is false because the genes that account for the gross morphological differences that underlie our standard racial categories are not linked to those genes that determine, to whatever degree such matters are determined genetically, our moral and intellectual characters. Intrinsic racism is mistaken because it breaches the Kantian imperative to make moral distinctions only on morally relevant grounds—granted that there is no reason to believe that race, *in se*, is morally relevant, and also no reason to suppose that races are like families in providing a sphere of ethical life that legitimately escapes the demands of a universalizing morality.

Kwame Anthony Appiah, "Racisms," in *Anatomy of Racism*, ed. David Goldberg (Minneapolis, MN: University of Minnesota Press, 1990).

READING

White Privilege, Black Rights

NAOMI ZACK

> **MindTap** For more chapter resources and activities, go to MindTap.

Study Questions

As you read the excerpt, please consider the following questions:
1. How does Zack contrast the problems of implicit racism and more overt violations of human rights?
2. How does Zack explain the need for criticism of police violence directed against young black men?
3. What does Zack mean when she suggests that the issue of unpunished killings of black youth is a symbol of overall social injustice?

Trayvon Martin, Michael Brown, Eric Gamer, Tamir Rice, and many others. *"Hands up, don't shoot, Black Lives Matter, I can't breathe, I can't breathe, I can't breathe...I can't breathe."* If you work in philosophy of race and are black or have black ancestry—I am multiracial—and if your personal sensitivity is greater than that of a plant, then the past two years have been painful and shameful to live through. There seems to be something drastically wrong about a justice system that allows police to kill unarmed young black men with impunity, with American elites of all races, who feel sorry for the misfortunes of our already disadvantaged but cannot do anything to help them, with academic whites who have created a discourse about their privilege, and with all those who are apathetic in the face of black tragedy in our time. I wrote this book quickly and with a sense of urgency, in November and December 2014, while interrupting work on a longer and more theoretical project (*Applicative Justice: A Pragmatic Theory for Correcting Injustice*) that will eventually provide more comprehensive underpinnings for this work. In other words, I had to stop philosophizing for a minute, to think about reality.

This book focuses on one specific problem: police killings of unarmed young black men that are not legally punished. The writing also had two specific promptings. First I was inspired by responses to my November 5, 2014 *NY Times* Stone interview by George Yancy, "What "White Privilege' Really Means."[1] The liveliest hostile reader commentary (and maybe, also, 1274 'likes' on the *NY Times* Facebook page for November 6[2]) focused on this: *"Not fearing that the police will kill your child for no reason isn't a privilege. It's a right."*

My second inspiration was the heated argument between former New York City Mayor Rudolf Giuliani and Georgetown University Professor Michael Eric Dyson on *Meet the Press* on November 24, 2014. The moderator introduced the claim that white police officers do not racially reflect the population of black communities. Giuliani said it was more important to talk about the fact that 93 percent of blacks who are killed, are killed by other blacks. Dyson said that black-on-black crime was a "false equivalency" to white police officers shooting blacks, because blacks were punished for killing other blacks and white police officers were not. Giuliani said, "White police officers wouldn't be there if you weren't killing each other 70 percent of the time." Dyson replied that Giuliani had a white supremacist mindset.[3]

The same 93 percent figure was trotted out in comments (mostly from Internet 'trolls') about what I said in the *NY Times* interview. It is completely irrelevant to the discussion of racial profiling and the impunity enjoyed by white police officers who kill blacks in 'stop and frisks' or while attempting to

Naomi Zack, *White Privilege and Black Rights: The Injustice of U.S. Police Racial Profiling and Homicide* (Lanham, MD: Rowman and Littlefield, 2015).

perform stop and frisks.[4] The reason acquittals and failures to indict ignite such strong public protest is that the police are presumed to *protect* members of the communities in which they serve. These ruptures between police and communities undermine trust in government, as well as the constitutional legitimacy of government as represented by such police action and its prosecutorial and juridical blessings. Distrust of government is an unfortunate trend now shared by both extremes of the political spectrum. Tea Party Republicans distrust government because they fear it gives too much to the undeserving. Radicals to the left distrust government because they view it as crushing, when it is not ignoring, the rights of the disadvantaged, especially poor nonwhites, and especially poor blacks. Indeed, a strong case can be made for negative *black male exceptionalism*, not only throughout U.S. history, but in present conditions of police racial profiling and homicide.[5]

Moreover, to bring up the 93 percent statistic when the subject is white police officer homicide following racial profiling is a distraction back to the mode of discourse preferred by those who insist that American society is not racist against blacks. That mode of discourse seeks to find ways to blame victims and hold them responsible for their own misfortune and disadvantage. The reasoning that could be implicit in Giuliani's remarks is that if blacks can be blamed for most of the death rate of young black males, then homicides against blacks committed by white police officers are less blameworthy, by comparison. However, blame is a moral assessment that is not a matter of numbers alone. American citizens have constitutional rights that are at stake in these cases of police homicide. The Fourth Amendment is supposed to protect against arbitrary searches and seizures. The Fourteenth Amendment is supposed to guarantee equal protection under the law and in actions of government officials. Police racial profiling violates both amendments, first by arbitrary stops and searches, and second by disproportionate use of those methods against blacks. The police have a special duty, stated in their oaths, to "uphold the Constitution." That is the issue missed by Giuliani and many others.

Contemporary academic discussion of social justice has now shifted to the discourse of white privilege. I think this is a mistake, insofar as privileges are extra perks and more is at stake in recent police killings of unarmed black men than denial of perks. I hope we have not sunk so low in American society that plain, simple, justice according to the Constitution must be regarded as a perk. Police killings that rest in impunity when grand juries do not indict and trial juries do not convict, violate ultimate, nonnegotiable rights.

About two thirds through the writing of this manuscript, on December 17, 2014, I attended a very timely event at the University of Oregon. Yvette M. Alex-Assensoh, Vice President for Equity and Inclusion, organized "'I Can't Breathe': A Conversation Starter about Racism, Justice, and Love." A diverse group of administrators, staff, faculty, students, community representatives, faith-based representatives, campus police, and city police assembled to discuss the effects on their lives of the recent killings that have not been followed by jury convictions or grand jury indictments, and how a university community might respond.

We sat at round tables of six or eight people, beginning with one-on-one discussions, expanding to full table discussions, and then summarizing to the rest of room. At my table, a young woman of color commented on responses to recent police killings on social media. She reflected that those who were nonwhite among her friends and relations showed engaged responses on their Facebook pages, while her white friends and relations seemed unaware of these events and posted nothing about them. A young white woman at the table talked about the silence on our campus about these incidents. African Americans are under-represented at all levels at the University of Oregon, perhaps reflecting the racial demographics of Oregon itself, which in 2013 had only 2 percent blacks in its population, compared to 13.2 percent for the United States overall.[6] (Oregon's racial statistics may be related to a nineteenth century history of the exclusion of blacks by law, and race-restrictive real estate covenants, which were not fully corrected until 1968.[7])

I was led to wonder if reactions to public trauma depend on the race of those observing and responding. Have we re-inscribed old-fashioned segregation into social media, so that blacks care when terrible things happen to black youth, but whites are unmoved? Is our collective sense of justice dead? I hope not. The great masses of people of all races and ethnicities go about their daily lives, working, socializing, falling in love, ending romantic relationships, raising families, getting sick, and worrying about money. In all of this, most are fully enmeshed in what D. H. Lawrence called the lesser day of ordinary life that can crack "like some great blue bubble" so that we seem to see "through the fissures the deeper blue of that other Greater Day where [moves] the other sun shaking its dark blue wings."[8]

The Greater Day for race in our time is not a matter of what race a person is, but a matter of justice for persons of all races. Justice is not based on common early homo sapiens African ancestry, an immigrant melting pot, or equal opportunities for material success. Justice is a matter of human rights and human dignity. Fortunately, we have a Constitution that names and supports protection for such rights. But unfortunately, that constitution has been interpreted by U.S. Supreme Court judges in ways that ignore both individual and institutional racism. Failure to recognize and support constitutional rights is unjust. People can come together in response to injustice and share the simple, common aspiration that those who are innocent will be left alone by the government as represented by the police and those who are guilty, including the police, will be punished. That aspiration is an attainable goal which we can reach by understanding the nature of the injustices now committed. The focus of this book is very narrow—How do the injustices of the police killing of innocent young African American men work? Why are such homicides not punished? What can be done about this?

In *The Souls of Black Folk*, W. E. B. Du Bois predicted in 1903 that "The problem of the twentieth century is the problem of the color-line—the relation of the darker to the lighter races of men in Asia and Africa, in America and the islands of the sea."[9]

More than a century later, it is evident that the color line has blurred in a number of ways: the U.S. Civil Rights Movement has yielded formal equality; the "darker races of men in Asia and Africa. . . . and in the islands of the sea" are viewed not in racial terms but in terms of economic development and military capability and threat (which may be as bad, but it is something different); it is well understood by intellectuals in the humanities that much of older definitions of race were based on myths and stereotypes; there is a consensus in the physical biological sciences that racial kinds are not real natural kinds, independently of social divisions: that are projected onto genetic and phenotypical taxonomies;[10] in the United States, where race was most drastically a matter of black and white, multiracial individuals are accorded some recognition and Latino/Hispanics, while officially an ethnicity, nonetheless are regarded as racially nonwhite, for the most part.

However, it is important to return to the black-white dichotomy in these early decades of the twenty-first century, not as a matter of racial identities, but as a matter of justice. Justice, or good enough approximations to justice, exists for white Americans, but not in the same ways for the rest. The starkest examples of injustice are evident in how black Americans are treated by the police. Yes, there is overt and implicit racism and bias, and yes, there are institutional structures, including the U.S. prison system, which make black Americans, especially young males, especially vulnerable. But the crucial issue at stake is application of the forms of justice that are stated in U.S. Constitutional Amendments and the Civil Rights legislation of the 1960s, to black Americans. To do that will require beginning with contemporary instances of race-based injustice that have fallen through the cracks in U.S. Supreme Court Opinions since 1968 and revisiting some of those opinions. This will be a long-term legal project. First, it is necessary to understand how the legal system now works unjustly and how a number of progressive academics, who should know better, have been politically anesthetizing themselves.

Overall, the present situation in New York City and beyond does not support optimism about an end to police racial profiling and homicide following stops and frisks, or their attempts. There are unlikely to be fast dramatic solutions to the underlying legal and social problems that have erupted into the recent events that prompted this book. Nevertheless, hope is a healthy attitude and violent response is not an option. No reasonable or sane voices in this ongoing crisis want more violence and that does speak positively to future solutions.

Recent U.S. Supreme Court opinions do not explicitly take racial bias into account, as the mental and emotional content of what may motivate individual police action. The Court's objective standards for what "a reasonable police officer" decides to do in what is perceived to be a dangerous situation, would inevitably defer to broad beliefs and attitudes within existing police culture. Policies of racial profiling that are based on racial proportions in the prison population, rather than crime rates in areas being patrolled, have not been thoroughly challenged in the courts. American police officers remain within their legal rights to both practice racial profiling and shoot to kill while attempting stops and frisks, in the absence of probable cause. Indictments and guilty verdicts for police homicide of unarmed suspects are constrained by very broad police discretion and criminal laws that were designed for civilians and are preempted by that discretion. Definitive legal solutions to these problems are in need of new, brilliant, and dedicated lawyering, which will take years to succeed, and more years to effectively apply.

Applicative justice requires that the legal treatment of American blacks be brought on a par with that of American whites, beyond written law, into real life practice. Simply reiterating how whites are "privileged" is not an effective response on the part of concerned academics, because it merely reinscribes their white privileges into new white identities. Perceptions of current injustice rest on basic human rights that people value intuitively and call for in anguished protests and demonstrations, but without understanding how the American legal system fails to protect the rights of black Americans. It may be possible to improve the situation by correcting specific comparative injustices,

before the relevant interpretations of constitutional law change, or even if they never do change. Institutional and government practices go far beyond what is formally written, into real life. Such practices can mirror formal law, be less just than it describes, or more just.

Many responsible and compassionate leaders and officials feel that they should do something, offer some reassurance to the disillusioned, some balm to the bereaved. When part of the population perceives injustice in specific harm or death to some of its; members, it is essential that responsible leadership in all areas of public life offer consolation. Present blame, violent reaction, and protests and demonstrations have bypassed or denied the need for what should be a period of official nationwide (if not formally "national") mourning. The killing of innocent young people—Tamir Rice was a twelve-year-old child!—by government officials is a national concern, even if it is not acknowledged. It is a national concern because whites and nonwhites together make up the nation in which such events now occur and they draw their individual and collective identities from being members of that nation. Such sudden and unjust loss of life should be publically shared, during time respectfully set aside for sadness. It calls not only for black armbands, but for public memorials, communal prayer or meditation, and designated *silence*. Reactions of this nature should be immediate, but it is just as important that permanent public memorials be planned in honor of those killed, so that people do not forget wrongful deaths.[3]

After sadness and silence, immediate practical remedies should be designed for institutional and social change out of concern for the well-being of over 90 percent of the black population who are not criminals. Racial profiling or fear and suspicion is not primarily a moral matter for whites in terms of their moral virtues or vices, but an offense to blacks, as individual human beings. As Judge Shira Scheindlin stated, "No one should live in fear of being stopped whenever he leaves his home to go about the activities of daily life." So long as police racial profiling continues, concerned educators and other leaders of societal institutions can continue to host conversations for those who are not directly affected by it, to consider what it is like to live in such fear, for one's children and grandchildren, as well as oneself.[4]

Americans are not about to abandon their ideals concerning the police. Police officers, like military personnel, remain enshrined as sources of protection, heroism, and the kind of discipline that administers public order. It is not accidental that Wikipedia prefaces its 2014 alphabetical list of over five hundred police shows with, "Dramas involving police procedural work, and private detectives, secret agents, and the justice system have been a mainstay of broadcast television since the early days of broadcasting."[5] As popular entertainment, police television shows, movies, and fiction are usually morality plays, narratives of good triumphing over bad. People watch them as food for moral aspirations and the expression of shared intuitions about justice and glory. No matter how long it will take to bring the treatment by police of innocent young blacks on a par with their treatment of innocent young whites, no matter how difficult and bitter that struggle may be, police officers, like military personnel, will remain enshrined as sources of protection, heroism, and the kind of discipline that administers public order. But that doesn't mean they should not be recognized to have the same frailties of others, in beliefs and motivations that derive from antiblack cultural norms and myths, or that there are not ways in which they can become better, in how they regard and treat people of color, in their roles as first responders.

Not only are police officers first responders to crime, but they represent the entire legal and criminal justice system to members of the public in public places. For society to be orderly, it is essential that members of the public, especially young people, and especially young people who are not white, have good reason to believe that police officers will deal with them fairly. To criticize police practices is not the same thing as saying that all American police officers are bad people. In a democratic society, it must be possible for everyone in a position of power to accept criticism and be open to the possibility of change. Local police departments often create the impression of not distinguishing between being blameworthy and accepting responsibility. Blame is accusatory and may be avoided as dishonorable, whereas the acceptance of responsibility allows for future growth and honor. By the same token, just as it is not necessary "to burn the whole house down in order to get rid of the mice," neither is it necessary to rebuild the entire house in order to refurbish a damaged part. What many critics may correctly perceive as society-wide and historically deep antiblack racism in the United States does not have to be thoroughly corrected before the immediate issue of police killings of unarmed young black men can be addressed. The immaturity of some armed young police officers and their lack of experience in interacting with members of the communities they serve can be addressed by police administrators and supervisors, who have as much at stake in the public's trust of them, as the public does. The American police, as a professional community, appear to know this. Not one of the officers responsible for the death of innocent victims in the high profile cases has been lauded or honored by his peers. Most have resigned or been dismissed and that is an indication of responsiveness within police ranks, even if it is not part of their culture to readily and publicly admit wrongdoing.

The way that the Broken Window Policy has been implemented in major U.S. cities has failed to serve many members of communities it was deigned to support, as totalities. Former New York City mayor Giuliani has reportedly brought attention to the fact that 93 percent of black homicide victims are killed by other blacks. While that fact is irrelevant to the issue of recent killings of unarmed young black men by young white police officers performing or attempting to perform stop and frisks, it is a major social problem. To the extent that it is a responsibility of the police to address, and it is insofar as their charge is to detect and prevent serious crime, it should be remembered and emphasized that stop and frisk policies were originally designed to be part of a much wider program that included *community policing*. The core idea in community policing is that members of police departments interact with members of high crime communities, to build community and prevent crime.[6] The importance of that idea lies in its ability to diffuse perceptions on the part of the public within and from these communities that the police are pitted against them as an occupying force. By the same token, attitudes on the part of the police that the prevention and detection of crime always or usually requires direct combat with criminals and suspects, require reexamination.

As offensive as stop and frisk policies are to those caught in their nets, the numbers of deadly escalations of attempts to stop and frisk can be considered against bigger numbers. As noted earlier, from 2002–2012, over 4.4 million stops and frisks were performed in New York City. At a rate of about 50 percent black suspects, this would amount to 220,000 stops of black suspects a year. Compared to nationwide estimates of 136–200 killings of blacks by police on a yearly basis, the odds of death for a black person from a police stop and frisk based on the New York City statistics would be at most near 1 in 1,000 each year. The odds are likely better on a national level, because New York City has a disproportionately large black population. Still, the odds of a black person being killed by a police officer are significantly higher than the likelihood of being killed in a car crash, which is 1 in 6,500 a year.[7]

Communities of color react to killings of unarmed young black men, symbolically and iconographically, as they should, because even one unjust race-related event creates an atmosphere of race-related injustice. Each unpunished killing is treated as a symbol of overall social injustice to whole communities of people of color. Attempts to suppress nonviolent expressions of outrage are disturbing insofar as they fail to respect human sensibilities and encroach on First Amendment rights. But on the other side, American police have been behaving within the law concerning stop and frisk polices and the use of deadly force. If judges and legislatures change the law, there is every reason to believe that American police will behave in accordance with new regulations, policies, and laws. Until then, because police officers have such important roles in American society and culture, their full understanding of black innocence, black crime, and black poverty is a worthy goal for all concerned individuals and groups.[8]

Ian Ayres and Daniel Markovits suggested in a December 25, 2014, opinion piece in the *Washington Post* that before racially profiled encounters with police can escalate into homicide, in the absence of probable cause for a serious crime, there ought to be rules of engagement for police encounters. Ayres and Markovits propose that officers issue warnings to stop, and then secure warrants for arrests if they are not obeyed. Such measures would check the present situation, where police homicides for attempted stops regarding minor misdemeanors can result in far more drastic punishment than convictions for minor crimes would.[9]

What about the responses of prosecutors, juries, and grand juries to cases of police homicide involving unarmed black victims? Joshua Deahl, writing for *Bloomberg View* cites the Cato Institute's National Police Misconduct Reporting Project's documentation of 4,861 unique reports of misconduct in 2010, including 127 fatalities. In almost all U.S. jurisdictions, police and prosecutors are on the same legal team in their jurisdictions. Deahl reasons that federal prosecution is not a solution because it would require difficult-to-apply charges of civil rights violations based on victims' race or ethnicity. To achieve some distance from the police-prosecutor team loyalty, Deahl proposes permanent special prosecutors, who would be less costly to maintain than ad hoc special prosecutors.[10]

An especially poignant case of police homicide by a white officer against a black suspect involved Jonathan Ferrell, twenty-four, a former Florida A&M football player, who sought help after a car crash. He knocked on the door of the home of a woman who was alone with her infant child and she called 911. When police arrived, Ferrell approached them and was first tasered and then shot dead by Officer Randall Kerrick, age twenty-seven. The Charlotte-Mecklenburg Police Department called the shooting unlawful, but a first grand jury did not indict. A week later, a second grand jury, from which the district attorney had recused himself, did indict Kerrick for voluntary manslaughter.[11]

Cultures change in small unnoticed ways over varied periods of time and then they can change overnight. Violence will not improve the present situation. Apathy and civic incivility add to personal stress and tensions based on racial identities. Peaceful protest and assembly is still protected under the First Amendment. Living with this crisis requires concern, restraint, civility, and moral appeal to basic human rights that fall through the cracks of present U.S. law.

NOTES

1. George Yancy and Naomi Zack, "What 'White Privilege' Really Means." The Stone, Opinionator, *NY Times*, November 5, 2014, Http://opinionator .blogs.nytimes.com/2014/11/05/what-white-privilege-really-means/#more-154773

2. George Yancy and Naomi Zack, "What 'White Privilege' Really Means." The Stone, Opinionator, November 5, 2014, *The New York Times*, Posts, November 6, 2014, Facebook, https://www.facebook .com/nytimes/posts/10150482504744999

3. "Giuliani and Dyson Argue over Violence in Black Communities," *Meet the Press*, NBC, Nov. 24, 2014. http://www.nbcnews.com/storyline/michael-brown-shooting/giuliani-dyson-argue-over-violence-black-communities-n254431. For a transcript see, http://www.realclearpolitics.com/video/2014/11/23/fireworks_giuliani_vs_michael_eric_dyson_white_police_officers_wont_be_there_if_you_werent_killing_each_other_70_of_the_time .html

4. For discussion of the importance of how early on in a chain of criminal justice such homicides have occurred, and a specific suggestion to correct that with a change in police procedure, see: Ian Ayres and Daniel Markovits, "Ending Excessive Police Force Starts with New Rules of Engagement," *The Washington Post*, December 25, 2014, http://www.washingtonpost.com/opinions/ending-excessive-police-force-starts-with-new-rules-of-engagement/2014/12/25/7fa379c0-8ale-lle4-a085-34e9b9f09a58_story.html

5. Thanks to Yvette Alex-Assensoh for making this point after reading the manuscript.

6. Oregon, State and County Quickfacts, U.S. Census, http://quickfacts.census.gov/qfd/states/41000.html

7. See: Blackpast.Org. "The Black Laws of Oregon, 1844–1857," http://www.blackpast.org/perspectives/black-laws-oregon-1844-1857 "NAREB (National Association of Real Estate Brokers) Code of Ethics, "The Oregon History Project," http://www.ohs.org/education/oregonhistory/historical_records/dspDocument.cfm?doc_ID=C62459FE-B688-7AC7-1F037E830F143F40

8. The distinction between the lesser day of ordinary life and the Greater Day goes back to Ovid's *Fasti*, through the medieval *Book of Days* and the nineteenth century version by Robert Chambers. The passage is from Lawrence's, "The Flying Fish." See: Keith Sagar, *The Art of D.H. Lawrence*, New York, NY: Cambridge University Press, 1996, pp. 205–230, quote from p. 206.

9. W. E. B. Du Bois, *The Souls of Black Folk*, New York, NY: New American Library, 1903, p. 19.

10. On the lack of independent scientific foundation for social racial categories, see: Albert Atkin, *The Philosophy of Race*, Oxford, UK: Acumen, 2012; Nina G. Jablonski, *Living Color: The Biological and Social Meaning of Skin Color*, Oakland, CA: University of California Press, 2012. John Relethford, *The Human Species: An Introduction to Biological Anthropology*, McGraw Hill, 2009–2012; Naomi Zack, *Philosophy of Science and Race*, New York, NY: Routledge, 2002.

CONCLUSION*

3. On the subject of the importance of public memorials and collective remembering for harms done to African Americans, see, Al Frankowski, *Post-Racial Violence, Mourning, and the Limits of Memorialization*, Lanham, MD: Lexington Books, forthcoming.

4. Marc Santora, "Mayor de Blasio Calls for Suspension of Protests," *NY Times*, December 22, 2014. http://www.nytimes.com/2014/12/23/nyregion/mayor-bill-de-blasio-nypd-officers-shooting.html; Patrick Lynch's vulgar political rhetoric is directly quoted in Tina Moore, Rocco

---

*The note numbers correspond to the original excerpt.

Parascandola, and Thomas Tracy, "Patrolmen's Benevolent Association President Patrick Lynch blasts de Blasio, says he is 'running a f—ing revolution'" *New York Daily News*, December 18, 2014. http://www.nydailynews.com/news/politics/pba-president-blasts-de-blasio-ruris-revolution-article-1.2050551; For argument about the harms of racial profiling, see Annabelle Lever, "Why Racial Profiling is Hard to Justify: A Response to Risse and Zeckhauser," *Philosophy and Public Affairs*, 33(1), 2005: 94–110.

5. "List of Police Television Drama," *Wikipedia*, http://en.wikipedia.org/wiki/List_of_police_television_dramas

6. Carlos Fields, "Award-Winning Community Policing Strategies, 1999–2006, A Report for the International Association of Chiefs of Police," Community Policing Committee, U.S. Department of Justice, COPS Office Community Policing, http://ric-zai-inc.com/Pubhcations/cops-w0451-pub.pdf

7. Ronald Bailey, "Don't Be Terrorized," *Reason.Com*, August 11, 2006. http://reason.com/archives/2006/08/11/dont-be-terrorized

8. Thanks to Kwandwo Assensoh for stressing this point in relation to general ways in which those who are motivated by ideologies may not fully understand their own actions.

9. Ian Ayres and Daniel Markovits, "Ending Excessive Police Force Starts With New Rules of Engagement," *Washington Post*, December 25, 2014, http://www.washingtonpost.com/opinions/ending-excessive-police-force-starts-with-new-rules-of-engagement/2014/12/25/7fa379c0-8ale-lle4-a085-34e9b9f09a58_story.html.

10. Joshua Daehl, "Police Killings Call for New Kind of Prosecutor," *Bloomberg View*, December 4, 2014, http://www.bloombergview.com/articles/2014-12-04/police-kilings-call-for-new-kind-of-prosecutor

11. "Jonathan Ferrell Killed: Man Shot in North Carolina Was A Former FAMU Football Player," AP, November 13, 2013. *Huffington Post, Crime*, http://www.huffingtonpost.com/2013/09/15/jonathanferrell-killed_n_3931282.html; Eliott C. McLaughlin, "2nd grand jury indicts officer in shooting of ex-FAMU football player," *CNN*, January 28, 2014. http://www.cnn.com/2014/01/27/us/north-carolina-police-shooting/

REVIEW EXERCISES

1. Summarize the history of civil rights law, including recent affirmative action decisions. Have we made progress in actualizing the principle of equality in the law? Why or why not?

2. Should racial, gender, or other differences ever be relevant to making decisions about qualified candidates for jobs or educational opportunities? Please support your answer with reference to concepts discussed in the chapter.

3. Explain the principle of equality. How is this principle related to other moral principles we've discussed in other chapters?

4. Evaluate the ethics of racial profiling and hate crime legislation. Are these useful legal tools?

5. What is "affirmative action," and why does it have this name? Explain different types of affirmative action. Which of them involve or may involve giving preferential treatment?

6. Summarize the consequentialist arguments for and against affirmative action.

7. Summarize the non-consequentialist arguments for and against affirmative action.

DISCUSSION CASES

1. **Women in Combat**. Denise and Edward are debating the new plan to allow women to officially serve in combat in the military. Denise is opposed to the idea. She says, "I think that fighting is men's work. Men are stronger and more aggressive. They're just better at fighting. Plus, it just seems better to leave women behind the lines to care for the wounded and take care of logistics." Edward can't believe that Denise is saying this. "You're kidding, right? I thought you were a feminist, in favor of equality for women. I mean, if men are asked to fight and die for their country, it's only fair to ask women to do that too." Denise says, "Yes, I know that equality matters. But in this case, there are some big differences between men and women—especially their upper body strength—that are relevant to what kinds of jobs they should have." Edward responds, "But not all men are stronger or more aggressive than all women. There are lots of women who are stronger than me." "Yes," Denise answers. "But we need a general policy that creates the best fighting unit. I'm worried that allowing women into combat will have bad results." Edward shakes his head. "I doubt it," he says. "And besides, it's only fair to give women a chance to prove themselves in combat."

   Which side are you on? Should women be allowed into combat? Why or why not?

2. **Campus Diversity**. During the past couple of decades, colleges and universities have tried to increase their numbers of minority students by various forms of affirmative action. At Campus X, this has led to controversy and discord. Some students criticize as unfair the policy of accepting students with lower SAT and other scores just because of their race or minority status. Others believe that the diversity that results from such policies is good for everyone because it is reflected in the broader society and a university should prepare people to participate in our diverse culture. Still, there is some question even among members of this group as to how well different ethnic groups relate on campus. Furthermore, a different type of problem has recently surfaced. Because Asian Americans are represented on campus in numbers greater than

their percentage of the population, Campus X may restrict the percentage of Asians they will accept even when their scores are higher than others. Campus X is also considering eliminating its affirmative action program entirely, which alarms some students. They point to declining numbers of minorities at certain medical and law schools that have done away with their affirmative action programs.

   Do you think that diversity ought to be a goal of campus admissions? Or do you believe that only academic qualifications ought to count? Do you think limiting the university enrollment of overrepresented groups (such as Asians and whites) based on their percentage of the overall population would be justified? Why or why not?

3. **Profiling**. Daniel and Ezra were both recently stopped and frisked by the cops while walking down the street in New York City. Daniel is African American. Ezra is an immigrant from Israel. Daniel feels that stop-and-frisk policing is blatantly racist. "The cops just target people of color, looking for an excuse to hassle us," he says. "I've got no reason to fear the police. I've done nothing wrong. But it makes me mad." Ezra is a bit more sympathetic to stop-and-frisk policing. In Israel, people's bags are searched when they go to the corner store. Ezra says, "I'm not worried about it. The cops know something about who is likely to commit a crime. They're not searching old ladies. That would be a waste of time. There are bad guys out there. And I want the cops to catch them. If I fit the profile somewhat, it's worth the hassle. It actually makes me feel safer to know that they are targeting their searches." Daniel replies, "Yeah, but this is America, not the Middle East!"

   Is it racist and discriminatory to target certain people for searches? Would it make you feel safer to know that the police were targeting people in this way? Should equal treatment be sacrificed in the name of public safety?

MindTap® For more chapter resources and activities, go to MindTap.

14

Economic Justice

Learning Outcomes

After reading this chapter, you should be able to:

- Describe the problem of economic inequality.
- Explain the concept of social justice from both utilitarian and deontological points of view.
- Describe why charity might be considered supererogatory.
- Identify differences between capitalism and socialism.
- Explain libertarian and liberal ideas about distributive justice.
- Describe the difference between procedural and end-state ideas about justice.
- Recount John Rawls's theory of justice.
- Defend a thesis about economic justice.

MindTap® For more chapter resources and activities, go to MindTap.

In Fall 2011, people took to the streets in massive numbers across the globe, protesting economic inequality. The protests, which began under the name "Occupy Wall Street," grew out of frustration with practices in the financial sector that contributed to the global recession that began in 2007. Occupy encampments were set up in cities across the country, as protesters showed up with tents and sleeping bags in city parks, outside of city halls, and in public places from San Francisco to Washington, D.C. The movement identified itself with the slogan, "We are the 99 percent," which was meant to highlight the economic gap between the vast majority of people (the 99 percent) and the wealthiest (top 1 percent). Since 2007, income inequality has continued to grow. In 2015, Americans in the top 1 percent earned about 38 times as much as those in the bottom 90 percent. And those in the top 0.1 percent earned, on average, 184 times what the average worker in the bottom 90 percent earned.[1] One of the explanations for the growing wealth disparity is that while incomes have increased for the wealthy, they are also paying less in taxes. Since the 1970s, tax rates on the rich have fallen dramatically in the United States. In 2013, the top 1 percent—those earning more than $1.4 million—paid an effective tax rate of 35.5 percent; this was a slight increase from the previous decade.[2] But in 1960, that same group—the top 1 percent of earners—would have paid an effective tax rate of more than 50 percent.[3] The Occupy Movement and the global recession that began in 2007 brought the issue of economic justice into the forefront of people's consciousness, with many arguing that government had a greater role to play in ensuring economic fairness and a basic level of security for all members of society.

The Occupy Movement arose in contrast to the Tea Party—a conservative grassroots movement concerned about rising national debt and government overreach in areas such as health care and taxation. Rather than focusing on inequality, the Tea Party emphasized the importance of liberty and the free market and viewed government as a threat to both. Those who support this approach might argue, for example, that as a matter of equality and fairness, tax rates should be the same for the poor and the wealthy. The same issues have played out in recent campaigns in the United States. Senator Bernie Sanders ran for president as a Democrat in 2016 as a self-declared democratic socialist, vowing to raise taxes on the wealthy. And on the Republican side, candidates advocated for a flat tax, while billionaire businessman Donald Trump promised to make America great again. Some Americans continue to worry that the global economy is making life difficult for working the working class.

The growth of the Tea Party and Occupy movements and the Sanders and Trump campaigns reflect a serious debate in the United States and beyond about the state of the economy, the morality of capitalism, and the problem of economic justice. In classrooms, in the media, and around dinner tables, Americans can still be heard having conversations much like the following debate between Betty (a business major) and Phil (a philosophy major).

Betty: I think that people have a right to make and keep as much money as they can as long as they do not infringe on others' rights. We shouldn't be taxing the rich to give to the poor.

Phil: Is it fair that some people are born with a silver spoon in their mouths and others are not? Society should ensure that everyone has an equal opportunity to succeed. Right now it seems like the deck is stacked against the working and middle classes, which are 99 percent of the population.

Betty: But how could we guarantee that the poor will not waste what we give them? In any case, it is just not right to take the money of those who have worked hard for it and redistribute it. The top 1 percent earned their money and deserve to keep it.

Poverty and economic inequality are concerns of social justice.

Morgan Hill/Alamy Stock Photo

Phil: Have they really earned it? A lot of rich people inherit money and other benefits from their parents, including access to good schools, connections, and other opportunities. Even if they didn't, they probably benefited from public goods paid for by taxes, such as interstate highways, the Internet, and public schools.

Betty: In any case, if we take away what people have earned, whether they deserve it or not, they will have no incentive to work. Profits are what make the economy of a nation grow.

Phil: And why is that so? Are you saying that the only reason people work is for their own self-interest? And do you really think self-interest alone can produce a just society, as Adam Smith and his "invisible hand" would have it? Capitalism sometimes creates inequalities that are unjust; governments should correct for this.

Betty: A just society doesn't mean that everyone has to have equal amounts of wealth. If justice is fairness, as some of your philosophers say, it is only fair, and therefore just, that people get out of the system what they put into it. And, besides, there are other values. We value freedom, too, don't we? People ought to be free to work and keep what they earn.

Phil: Freedom? What freedom is there for the little guy when the economy collapses as a result of the greed and corruption of the corporate elites? It's the little guy whose house is taken away in foreclosure and who loses his job. While most people's real wages have stagnated for decades, the incomes of the top 1 percent have continued to increase.

Betty: Well, that's the way capitalism works. People take risks with their money, buying houses or investing in businesses. Sometimes they lose big bucks, the market turns downward—maybe they lose a house or a business. But in the long run, this shock to the system increases productivity, as people have to respond creatively to the demands of the market.

Phil: But it's not a level playing field; not everyone can afford to take risks with their money. Unrestrained capitalism helps rich people get richer but gives poor people few opportunities to get ahead.

While your 1 percent is responding "creatively" to the market crash, the 99 percent is just trying to pay for their kids' college education or save for retirement.

Betty: You sound like a socialist. But you can't be serious about thinking that the government should control large sectors of the economy, as they do in Cuba, or that we should be taxed to the hilt like they are in Europe.

Phil: Well, the average worker does pretty well in Europe and has to pay far less for things like health care and retirement. From a utilitarian perspective, some degree of socialism isn't so bad.

Betty: But socialism limits the freedom of the individual. It is disrespectful of the right of individuals to earn as much as they can.

Phil: At least we can agree on one thing, that something ought to be done about corporate misdeeds. We need good ethics to prevail in the corporate boardroom.

Betty: Agreed. Corruption doesn't produce good outcomes in the long run. If there is not sufficient transparency in corporate business practices, then investors will not be able to make wise decisions and inefficiency will harm the system.

The issues touched on in this conversation belong to a group of issues that fall under the topic of *economic justice*. This includes other issues as well. For example, do people have a right to a job and good wages? Is welfare aid to the poor a matter of charity or justice? Is it fair to tax the rich more heavily than the middle class? And what should the role of the government be in terms of controlling the economy and regulating business practices?

ECONOMIC INEQUALITY

In the United States, in 2014 (the last year for which data was available), 46.7 million people—nearly 15 percent of the population—lived in poverty. For children under age eighteen, the poverty rate was higher: 21.1 percent of children (more than one in five) live in poverty.[4] According to the Census Bureau, these numbers have remained about the same for several years. The Census's poverty threshold varies according to family size. But, for example, in 2014 the poverty threshold for a family of five was $28,960.[5] The median household income in the United States between 2010 and 2014 was $53,482.[6] The richest American, Bill Gates, had a net worth of $75 billion.[7]

These statistics point toward the problem of income inequality. In March 2007, Alan Greenspan, the former chairman of the Federal Reserve, noted, "Income inequality is where the capitalist system is most vulnerable. You can't have the capitalist system if an increasing number of people think it is unjust."[8] By the end of 2007, the global economy was afflicted by a financial crisis that stemmed, in part, from the bursting of a speculative housing bubble. Large numbers of people lost their homes, and still more lost home equity. The banking and financial sector experienced a massive shock. Many wondered about the causes of this catastrophe. Some blamed banks for making bad loans. Others blamed the financial industry for creating exotic financial instruments, which allowed some investors to profit at the expense of homeowners and others. And some blamed unscrupulous financiers such as Bernie Madoff, who ran an elaborate Ponzi scheme—a pyramid scheme that takes money from new investors and uses it to pay previous investors in an ever-growing cycle of debt. Eventually, the crisis caused several important financial firms to collapse. Lehman Brothers—the fourth largest investment bank in the country—declared bankruptcy. The U.S. government stepped in and bailed out several other large banking and financial concerns, insurance companies, and auto manufacturers.

As a result of the economic meltdown, cities suffered, with some, including Stockton and San Bernardino in California, collapsing into bankruptcy. States suffered economic problems as tax revenues fell. As they struggled to respond, the states borrowed and cut—laying off state workers and accumulating debt. At the same time, the federal government struggled to balance its books. At the end of 2015, the national debt was estimated to be above $18 trillion. The rising debt has prompted intense political squabbling and last-minute budget deals, as politicians and economists struggle to find some way to manage the economy. Worse debt obligations have wreaked havoc in other countries—Greece, Italy, Spain, and other European countries faced economic turmoil in recent years as a private and public debt crisis swept through Europe. In these countries, pensions have vanished and unemployment rates have hovered around 20 percent for several years.

Meanwhile, the richest among us are doing very well, especially in the United States. We cited some data on income inequality at the outset of this chapter. A few other data points can help to frame this discussion. The twenty wealthiest people in the United States now own more wealth than the bottom half of the American population: in other words, twenty people own more wealth than the combined wealth of 152 million other people. And the combined wealth of the *Forbes* list of the four hundred richest people is larger than the combined wealth of the bottom 61 percent of the U.S. population: in other words, four hundred Americans own more wealth than 194 million other Americans.[9] Another measure of economic disparity is the difference between the amount of money the average worker makes and the compensation of corporate CEOs. CEO compensation continues to rise. *Forbes* reports that CEOs earn more than ten times what they earned three decades ago, while the average worker's earnings have only increased by 10 percent. Top CEOs now earn more than three hundred times more than an average worker.[10] *Payscale.com*, which monitors salary data, reports that at least one company has a CEO to average employee ratio of 422:1 (the CEO of CVS earned over $12 million, while the average employee earned only $28,700.[11] CEO compensation makes occasional headlines. Google's CEO, Sundar Pichai, received $199 million in a compensation deal in 2016 that made him one of the highest paid executives on the planet.[12]

These disparities in wealth might not matter all that much if it were possible for each of us to do better through hard work and natural talent. Modern social life is no longer bound by traditional class distinctions and there are no legal barriers to social and economic advancement. However, in reality, social mobility is not as easy as we might think. One analysis concludes that roughly half of Americans remain in the same social strata into which they are born. And movement from bottom to top is difficult. If you were born in the bottom 20 percent, you have a 5 percent chance of making it into the top 20 percent; and those who were born into the top 20 percent have a similar one in twenty chance of falling into the bottom 20 percent.[13]

Other interesting facts help describe economic inequality. In Chapter 13, we noted that white Americans have twenty-two times more wealth than blacks and fifteen times more wealth than Hispanics.[14] We also discussed the difference between male and female income. While the economic prospects of women are improving, there is still work to be done. According to a report from *Time* magazine in 2012, a growing number of women outearn their husbands.[15] Women are also doing better in terms of educational attainment, which may factor into improved economic prospects in the future.[16] Some have pointed out that the gender income gap may be, in part, a result of the fact that more women leave work to care for children and elderly parents, and they are more likely to work part time. It should be noted, though, that women experience a variety of social and economic pressures that men do not—including the gender pay gap—that may push them to put caregiving ahead of their careers. Even after factoring out differences between men and women in educational attainment, work experience, occupation, career interruptions, part-time status, and overtime worked, the gender wage gap is still between 4.8 and 7.1 percent.[17] (This remaining gap is attributable to simple gender discrimination.) In 2016, the U.S. Department of Labor reported that a typical woman working full-time earns 21 percent less than a similarly employed man; they also report that black non-Hispanic women earn 60 percent less than white non-Hispanic men and that Hispanic women earned 55 percent less.[18]

One explanation of general income inequality is that it reflects differences in employees' value to their employers. So in this theory, if a woman (or a man) takes time off to raise a family, she or he will earn less as a result of missing out on training and experience that would have occurred during the absence. But does a similar argument work to explain the gross disparities in income between CEOs and average workers or between the top 1 percent and the rest of us? Are CEOs justified in earning hundreds of times more than the average worker? One justification of those sorts of disparities would focus on the skills, intelligence, effort, and experience of CEOs and other top earners. Maybe the CEO is simply a better worker than the average employee. Another justification of wage disparities focuses on the need to allow the free market to determine compensation—people should be free to negotiate and earn whatever the market will pay them.

A critic might point in another direction, toward the sorts of burdens faced by those on the low end of the economic pyramid. Is it fair that the poor and unemployed have reduced opportunities and decreased life prospects? One problem for the unemployed is that even if they are willing to work, they often cannot find a job. The problem for the working poor is that even though they do work, they cannot earn a decent living. One factor to consider is the issue of the difference between the minimum wage and a living wage. The **minimum wage** is the minimum hourly wage an employer can pay its employees, a standard that is set by federal and state governments. In the United States, in 2016, the federal minimum wage was set at $7.25 per hour. (In some places, it is higher. For example, it is $10.00 per hour in California and Massachusetts and $11.50 in the District of Columbia).[19] By contrast, a **living wage** is calculated based upon the cost of living in a given region, factoring in things like rent, food, transportation, and child care. Living wage calculations vary from place to place. In New York City, the living wage is calculated at $14.30 an hour for a single adult and $27.44 an hour for an adult with one child. In Los Angeles, California, the living wage is $12.82 an hour for a single adult and $26.10 an hour for an adult with one child. In a small town like Green Bay, Wisconsin, the living wage is $9.67 an hour for a single adult and $21.83 an hour for an adult with one child.[20] In each of these cases, the living wage is above the federal minimum wage. And in each of these places, a working mother with one child would be unable to provide for herself and her child by working at a minimum wage job. This helps explain why nearly 15 percent of Americans (46.7 million people) were living in poverty in 2014 and why one in five American children (21.1 percent) was living in poverty.[21] In 2014, the poverty threshold was set at $24,230 for a family of four. According to the U.S. Census Bureau data from 2014, 6.2 percent of married couples lived in poverty, and 30.6 percent of families with a female householder lived in poverty, while 15.7 percent of families with a male householder lived in poverty.[22] The question of fairness and justice arises here: is it fair to impoverished children that, through no fault of their own, they grow up in poverty?

Poverty, Education, and Health Care

And why does poverty matter? One reason is that income disparities lead to disparate outcomes in terms of life prospects. The poor suffer from a variety of problems, many of which also become problems for society as a whole. One significant problem is the educational achievement gap between poor and wealthier children. Children from poor families do worse in school. The gap in standardized test scores between affluent and low-income students has grown by 40 percent since the 1960s. A similar income gap shows up in terms of college completion—with fewer poor kids completing college. This has a lifelong impact, as college completion is correlated with better prospects for future income.[23]

Income inequities are matched by inequities in health care. Although genes and lifestyle certainly play their roles in a person's health, poverty does as well. Poor people are more likely to be obese and to suffer from diabetes and heart disease than those who are economically better off. Low-income families also tend to be uninsured and to defer preventive medical and dental care. Children in low-income families are more prone to asthma, lead poisoning, anemia, and other ailments that create cognitive and behavioral problems. They are more likely to live in

neighborhoods that are unsafe. They are more likely to lack access to books and computers.

One recent study concludes, "poverty, low levels of education, poor social support and other social factors contribute about as many deaths in the U.S. as such familiar causes as heart attacks, strokes and lung cancer."[24] Such health disparities between the rich and poor are even starker outside the developed world (we will look at the issue of global poverty in more detail in Chapter 20).

One pressing issue in the United States is the high cost of health care and health insurance. A family's savings can be wiped out by a major health problem if the family lacks health insurance. A recent Harvard study found that seven hundred thousand Americans go bankrupt every year due to medical bills. (Medical bankruptcy is unheard of in almost all other developed nations.)[25] One of the goals of the Affordable Care Act, passed in 2010, was to expand health insurance coverage to many of the tens of millions of uninsured, mostly low-income Americans. One of the mechanisms to accomplish this is to expand Medicaid to allow the working poor to obtain coverage through the program. The Affordable Care Act includes coverage for preventive care such as blood pressure, diabetes, and cholesterol tests. It also covers prenatal care and well visits and checkups for children. And it covers routine health care for women, including mammograms. Another of the goals of the Affordable Care Act was to address health care inequities related to income level and employment—those in lower-income jobs tend to lack health care benefits while people in high-paying jobs tend to be offered generous health care benefits. While there is more to be said about how the Affordable Care Act is going to be implemented, the overarching goal of the act is to make health care more accessible. By 2022, the law will provide health insurance to thirty-three million Americans who would otherwise be uninsured.[26] Defenders of the law argue that it is providing access to the basic good of health care.

Opponents of the act criticize it as "socialized medicine." They argue that the government should not heavily regulate, much less provide, health insurance because this interferes with the free market. According to the conservative Heritage Foundation, which opposes the Affordable Care Act and is calling for its repeal, the solution is "market-based health care that gives people better choices and allows them to take account of the price and value of health care."[27]

The conservative approach is premised on the idea that government should stay out of the health care business, allowing individuals to make their own choices about insurance coverage. From this perspective, health care, like other businesses, should be left alone so that free markets might work to regulate prices and basic services. In this view, health care is a commodity, like others, to be bought and sold in an open market, where the laws of supply and demand would operate freely. Some unfortunate people may end up with bad outcomes in such a system—losing their savings to pay for health care or being denied health care—but this is part of the risk of a free-market society. Some conservatives even suggest that emergency medical care (currently guaranteed by law in the United States, regardless of one's ability to pay) should also be subject to market forces, allowing hospitals to turn away indigent or uninsured dying patients.

The conservative idea is that the market will provide the best outcome for the greater number of people. Some conservatives also worry that government regulation of health care may result in "rationing," with the government denying coverage for certain expensive treatments. But liberals will reply that the market also "rations" health care in other ways, namely, by price and ability to pay.[28] Furthermore, liberals will argue that health care is a basic right that should be guaranteed by the government and not subject to market forces. From this perspective, health care is not simply a commodity to be bought and sold; rather, justice requires that individuals be provided with basic health care—even if they cannot afford it. While other nations do stipulate that health care is a basic right, in the United States, there is no civil right to health care (see Chapter 13 for a discussion of civil rights).[29] The Constitution does not guarantee a right to health care. However, some will argue that there is a basic human right to health care, as well as a right to a living wage, a right to education, and so on.

CONCEPTIONS OF SOCIAL JUSTICE

As we saw in the previous section, there is a fundamental dispute between those who focus on the fairness of social institutions in terms of their outcomes and those who advocate the importance of individual choice and the free market. The first concern—for the impact that social arrangements have on people—is often called **social justice** (as distinguished, for example, from criminal justice). The idea of social justice has roots in the natural law tradition of Thomas Aquinas, as developed by the Catholic tradition (which we discussed in Chapter 7). Thomas Massaro, a Jesuit scholar of social justice, explains that the notion of social justice boils down to "the goal of achieving a right ordering of society. A just social order is one that ensures that all people have fair and equitable opportunities to live decent lives free of inordinate burdens and deprivation."[30] The social justice idea has been advocated recently by the Roman Catholic Pope Francis, an outspoken critic of consumer society and unbridled capitalism that neglects the needy (see the excerpt from Pope Francis at the end of this chapter).

Social justice is often focused on distributions of goods among people in society, with an emphasis on minimizing inequalities across social classes. While the social justice idea has roots in Christian natural law ethics, it can also be grounded in utilitarianism. For example, John Stuart Mill was particularly interested in the question of economic justice. Mill thought that the vast majority of workers were "slaves to toil in which they have no interest, and therefore feel no interest—drudging from early morning till late at night for bare necessaries, and with all the intellectual and moral deficiencies which that implies."[31] As a utilitarian, Mill was interested in finding ways to alleviate drudgery and poverty, while producing the greatest happiness for the greatest number.

We should also note that Mill was opposed to slavery, which was legal in the United States during most of his life. Not only did he reject the notion that whites should have despotic power over blacks, but he also rejected the idea that individuals should be reduced to mere working machines. He saw no value in "work for work's sake" and he thought that human happiness required leisure. Mill concluded, "To reduce very greatly the quantity of work required to carry on existence, is as needful as to distribute it more equally."[32] He also thought that the economy was unjust insofar as it did not connect hard work with profit. From Mill's perspective, the problem is that the rich are born into wealth and leisure, while the poor are born into a life of poverty and hard work. This runs counter to the idea that there should be a connection between success and merit. As Mill explains, "The very idea of distributive justice, or of any proportionality between success and merit, or between success and exertion, is in the present state of society so manifestly chimerical as to be relegated to the regions of romance."[33] Mill means that there is no justice in an economy in which those who work hard remain poor, while the rich don't work. Mill wanted to find a way to help the poor without producing dependence upon that help. As he explained it, the goal is to "give the greatest amount of needful help, with the smallest encouragement to undue reliance on it."[34] From the utilitarian standpoint, the challenge is to figure out how best to regulate the economy in a way that produces encouragement for hard work, while also preventing the impoverished, unemployed, and working poor from falling through the cracks.

Concern for social justice is sometimes connected with claims about the value of equality itself, as well with claims about the value of human rights, human dignity, and solidarity among people. There are disagreements about the exact definition of these terms, even among those who are concerned with social justice. For example, equality may be defined as *substantial equality*, meaning that individuals should have exactly the same access to and amount of substantial goods. Or equality can be defined as *equality of opportunity*, meaning that individuals should have an equal chance to obtain goods. In either case, the pursuit of equality can lead to a conflict with other values, such as liberty. For example,

to ensure equality, we may have to violate the liberty of those who possess certain goods so that we might redistribute those goods among others (as we do to some extent in a system of taxation that redistributes private property for social welfare purposes). Some conceptions of justice do emphasize liberty as the central value, as Mill himself did in his work, *On Liberty*. The trick, for a utilitarian like Mill, is to find a way to balance liberty and the need for distributive or social justice.

The deontological theory of Immanuel Kant provides another source for thinking about human dignity and respect for autonomy. Kant is opposed to using individuals as a means to an end, and some would argue that to take a part of someone's income through taxation and redistribute it to others is a form of using that person as a means. But Kant also thought that charity and beneficence were important values. In the *Foundations of the Metaphysics of Morals* (excerpted in Chapter 6), Kant indicates that those who don't want to help the needy end up contradicting themselves, since they would expect others to help them if they were in need. In his *Lectures on Ethics*, Kant indicates that one reason to give to the needy is out of a sense that the social structure is unjust:

> In giving to an unfortunate man we do not give him a gratuity but only help to return to him that of which the general injustice of our system has deprived him. For if none of us drew to himself a greater share of the world's wealth than his neighbor, there would be no rich and no poor. Even charity therefore is an act of duty imposed upon us by the rights of others and the debt we owe to them.[35]

Accounts of justice that emphasize liberty are often grounded in a natural law approach to ethics with roots in the work of John Locke (excerpted in Chapter 7). Locke's emphasis on a natural right to property is a fundamental starting point for those who want to defend a free-market economy. Other philosophers who focus on liberty connect their ideas to those of Ayn Rand (mentioned in our discussion of egoism in Chapter 4—see the excerpt at the end of this chapter). Tibor Machan, a contemporary libertarian author who builds upon Rand's ideas, stresses the idea that individual human beings "possess free will and need to guide their own lives to achieve excellence or to flourish."[36] Machan contrasts his theory of justice with other views of justice that require fairness, order, harmony, or social welfare. From Machan's libertarian point of view, the economy should be left alone so that individuals are free to create, trade, and earn whatever nature and the market allow them to. From this standpoint, charity is acceptable—but as the free choice of an individual to help others in need and not as an obligation of justice.

We can see from the philosophies of social justice discussed previously that we should distinguish justice from certain other moral notions. For example, justice is not the same as charity. It is one thing to say that a community, like a family, should help its poorer members when they are in need, out of concern for their welfare. But is helping people in need ever a matter of justice? If we say that it is, then we imply that it is not morally optional. Justice is often defined as giving people what is rightly due. Charity gives above and beyond the requirements of justice. Ethicists use the term **supererogatory** to describe actions that go above and beyond the call of duty. The word *supererogatory* comes from Latin roots, which can be translated to mean "paying more than is due" or "payment in addition." There is nothing unjust about giving charity. But we usually think that charity is not required by justice, it is supererogatory. Furthermore, justice is not the only relevant moral issue in economic matters. Efficiency and liberty are also moral values that play a role in discussions on ethics and economics. When we say that a particular economic system is *efficient*, we generally mean that it produces a maximum amount of desired goods and services, or the most value for the least cost. Thus, some people say that a pure free-market economy is a good economic system, based on the claim that it is the most efficient, the one best able to create wealth. But it is quite another question whether such a system is also a *just* system or if it enhances liberty. If we could have the most efficient and perhaps even the most just economic system

in the world, then would it be worth it if we were not also free to make our own decisions about many things, including how to earn a living?

Sorting out the relationship among these values is one of the primary goals of social justice philosophies. Such philosophies are often primarily concerned with the issue of **distributive justice**, which involves how the benefits and burdens of society are allocated—for example, who and how many people have what percentage of the goods or wealth in a society. Thus, suppose that in some society, 5 percent of the people possessed 90 percent of the wealth, and the other 95 percent of the people possessed only 10 percent of the wealth. Asking whether this arrangement would be just raises a question of distributive justice. Now, how would we go about answering this question? It does seem that this particular distribution of wealth is quite unbalanced. But must a distribution be equal for it to be just? To answer this question, we can examine two quite different ways of approaching distributive justice. One is what we can call a *process view*, and the other is an *end-state view*.

Process Distributive Justice

According to some philosophers, any economic distribution (or any system that allows a particular economic distribution) is just if the process by which it comes about is itself just. Some call this **procedural justice**. For example, if the wealthiest 5 percent of the people got their 90 percent of the wealth fairly—they competed for jobs, they were honest, they did not take what was not theirs—then what they earned would be rightly theirs. In contrast, if the wealthy obtained their wealth through force or fraud, then their having such wealth would be unfair because they took it unfairly. Indeed, we might suspect that because talent is more evenly distributed, there is something suspicious about this uneven distribution of wealth. But there would be nothing unfair or unjust about the uneven distribution in itself. Some people are wealthy because of good luck and inheritance, and others are poor because of bad economic luck. However, in this view, those with money they get through luck or inheritance are not being unjust in keeping it even when others are poor. (See the reading selection by Robert Nozick, which appears at the end of this chapter, for an example of elements of this view.)

End-State Distributive Justice

Other philosophers believe that the process by which people attain wealth is not the only consideration relevant to determining the justice of an economic distribution. They believe that we also should look at the way things turn out, the end state, or the resulting distribution of wealth in a society, and ask about its fairness. Suppose that, through inheritance, a small minority of lucky people came to possess 95 percent of society's wealth. Would it be fair for them to have so much wealth when others in the society are extremely poor? How would we usually judge whether such an arrangement is fair? We would look to see if there is some good reason why the wealthy are wealthy. Did they work hard for it? Did they make important social contributions? These might be nonarbitrary or good reasons for the wealthy to possess their wealth rightly or justly. However, if they are wealthy while others are poor because they, unlike the others, were born of a certain favored race, sex, eye color, or height, then we might be inclined to say that it is not fair for them to have more. What reasons, then, justify differences in wealth?

Several different views exist on this issue. Radical egalitarians deny that there is any good reason why some people should possess greater wealth than others. Their reasons for this view vary. They might stress that human beings are essentially alike as human and that this is more important than any differentiating factors about them, including their talents and what they do with them. They might argue that society is an agreement for the mutual advancement of all and should treat each of its members as free and equal citizens. Or they might use religious or semireligious reasons, such as the idea that the Earth is given to all of us equally and thus, we each have an equal right to the goods derived from it. However, even egalitarians must decide what it is that they believe should be equal.

For example, should there be equality of wealth and income or equality of satisfaction or welfare? These are not the same. Some people have little wealth or income but nevertheless are quite satisfied, while others who have great wealth or income are quite dissatisfied. Some have champagne tastes, and others are satisfied with beer!

On the other hand, at least some basic differences between people should make a difference in what distribution of goods is thought to be just. For example, some people simply have different needs than others. People are not identical physically, and some of us need more food and different kinds of health care than others. Karl Marx's phrase, "To each according to his need" captures something of this variant of egalitarianism.[37] Nevertheless, it is puzzling why only this particular differentiating factor—need—should justify differences in wealth. In fact, we generally would tend to pick out others as well—differences in merit, achievement, effort, or contribution.

Suppose, for example, that Jim uses his talent and education and produces a new electronic device that allows people to transfer their thoughts to a computer directly. This device would alleviate the need to type or write the thoughts—at least, initially. Surely, people would value this device, and Jim would probably make a great deal of money from his invention. Wouldn't Jim *merit*, or have a right to, this money? Wouldn't it be fair that he has this money and others who didn't come up with such a device have less? It would seem so. But let's think about why. Is it because Jim has an innate or *native talent* that others do not have? Then, through no fault of their own, those who happen to lack the talent would have less. It is a matter of arbitrary luck that Jim was born with this talent and thus became wealthy.

But perhaps Jim's wealth stems not only from his talent, but also from his use of it. He put a great deal of *effort* into cultivating his talent. He studied electronics and brain anatomy and spent years working on the invention in his garage. His own effort, time, and study were his own contribution. Would this be a good reason to say that he deserved the wealth that he earned from it? This might seem reasonable, if we did not also know that his motivation and work ethic might also have been, in some ways, gifts of his circumstances and family upbringing. Furthermore, effort alone would not seem to be a good reason for monetary reward, or else John, who takes three weeks to make a pair of shoes, should be paid more than Jeff, who can make equally good ones in three hours. Similarly, a student would not be justified in demanding an A simply because he or she spent a lot of time and effort studying for a test—when his or her performance actually merited a B.

Finally, perhaps Jim should have the rewards of his invention because of the nature of his *contribution*, because of the product he made and its value to people. Again, this argument seems at first reasonable, and yet, there are also fairness problems here. Suppose that he had produced this invention before computers became affordable for most consumers. The invention would be wonderful but not valued by people because they could not use it. Or suppose that others at the same time produced similar inventions. Then, this happenstance would also lessen the value of the product and its monetary reward. Jim could rightly say that it was unfair that he did not reap a great reward from his invention just because he happened to be born at the wrong time or finished his invention a little late. This may be just bad luck. But is it also unfair? Furthermore, it is often difficult to know how to value particular contributions to a jointly produced product or result. How do we measure and compare the value of the contributions of the person with the idea, the investors, the product developers, and so forth, so that we can know what portion of the profits are rightly due to them? Marxists are well known for their claim that the people who own the factories or have put up the money for a venture profit from the workers' labor unfairly or out of proportion to their own contributions.

This mention of Marx and Marxism reminds us that there is no consensus about what counts as a fair distribution of wealth. Revolutions and wars have been fought in the name of various ideas of economic justice.

Equal Opportunity

Another viewpoint on distributive justice does not fit easily into either the process or end-state categories. In this view, the key to whether an unequal distribution of wealth in a society is just is whether people have a fair chance to attain positions of greater income or wealth. That is, equality of wealth is not required, only equal opportunity to attain it. (We discussed equal opportunity in connection to civil rights and nondiscrimination in Chapter 13.) We might see the notion of equal opportunity as symbolized by the Statue of Liberty in New York Harbor. The statue sits on Liberty Island, where, historically, new immigrants to the United States were processed. It represents the idea that in the United States, all people have a chance to make a good life for themselves provided they work hard. But just what is involved in the notion of equal opportunity, and is it a realizable goal or ideal? Literally, it involves both opportunities and some sort of equality of chances to attain them. An *opportunity* is a chance to attain some benefit or goods. People have equal chances to attain these goods, first of all, when there are no barriers to prevent them from attaining them. Opportunities can still be said to be equal if barriers exist as long as they affect everyone equally. Clearly, if racism, sexism, or other forms of prejudice prevent some people from having the same chances as others to attain valued goals or positions in a society, then there is not equal opportunity. For example, if women have twice the family responsibilities as men, then do they really have an equal opportunity to compete professionally? Our discussion of the gender pay gap previously shows how opportunities that are supposed to be equal by law or policy may, in fact, be rendered unequal by social practices.

According to James Fishkin, an expert on political theory, if there is equal opportunity in my society, "I should not be able to enter a hospital ward of healthy newborn babies and, on the basis of class, race, sex, or other arbitrary native characteristics, predict the eventual positions in society of those children."[38] However, knowing what we do about families, education, and the real-life prospects of children, we know how difficult this ideal would be to realize. In reality, children do not start life with equal chances. Advantaged families give many educational, motivational, and experiential benefits to their children that disadvantaged families cannot, and this makes their opportunities effectively unequal. Schooling greatly affects equal opportunity, and money spent for a school—teachers, facilities, and books—can make a big difference in the kind of education provided. However, funding per pupil on schooling in the United States varies considerably according to locale.[39] And affluent parents can supplement public schooling with private tutors, educational summer camps, music lessons, and other educational opportunities. Is it fair that some kids have these opportunities while others do not?

One version of equal opportunity is the *starting-gate theory*, which assumes that if people had equal starts in life, then they would have equal chances. The philosopher Bernard Williams provides a famous example of such a theory. In his imaginary society, a class of skillful warriors has for generations held all of the highest positions and passed them on to their offspring. At some point, the warriors decide to let all people compete for membership in their class. The children of the warrior class are much stronger and better nourished than the other children who, not surprisingly, fail to gain entrance to the warrior class. Would these other children have had effective equality of opportunity to gain entrance to the warrior class and its benefits? Even if the competition was formally fair, the outside children were handicapped and had no real chance of winning. But how could initial starting points then be equalized? Perhaps by providing special aids or help to the other children to prepare them for the competition. Applying this example to our real-world situation would mean that a society should give special aid to the children of disadvantaged families if it wants to ensure equal opportunity.[40] According to James Fishkin, however, to do this effectively would require serious infringements on family autonomy. For it would mean not only helping disadvantaged children, but also preventing wealthier parents from giving special advantages to their children.

Moreover, people have different natural talents and abilities, and those who have abilities that are more socially valued will likely have greater opportunities. Does this mean, then, that the idea of equal opportunity is unrealizable? It may only mean that our efforts to increase equality of opportunity must be balanced with the pursuit of other values, such as family autonomy and efficiency.

Still, some philosophers have other questions about the ideal of equal opportunity. They argue that the whole emphasis on equality is misplaced and distracts us from what is really important. The philosopher Harry Frankfurt claims that rather than focusing on the fact that some have more than others, it would be better to focus on whether people have enough. We care not that one billionaire makes a few million more than another, but rather, that everyone should have sufficient means to pursue their aspirations. Frankfurt calls his position the "doctrine of sufficiency," in contrast to theories that make equality, in itself, the primary goal.[41]

Although the doctrine of equal opportunity is appealing because it implies equal rewards for equal performance and doors open to all, some thinkers object to the notion of meritocracy on which it is based. According to John Schaar, the equal opportunity ideal is based on notions of a natural aristocracy.[42] Those of us who do not have the natural talent of an Einstein, a Steve Jobs, or a LeBron James will not have the same chances to succeed and prosper as those who do have such talents. We can enter the race, but we delude ourselves if we think that we have a real chance to win it. Schaar believes that stress on equal opportunity thus contributes to the gap between rich and poor. He also argues that emphasis on equal opportunity threatens the foundations of equality and democracy. Based, as it is, on the notion of a marketplace in which we, as atomic individuals, compete against our fellows, it threatens human solidarity. It does so even more if it is accompanied by a tendency to think that those who win are in some way more valuable as persons.[43]

Other philosophers argue that justice demands that people should not be penalized for things over which they have no control. Thus, it would seem unjust or unfair for people to suffer who, through no fault of their own, cannot compete or cannot compete well in the market, for example, the physically or mentally ill, or the physically or mentally handicapped.[44] Here, we return to the idea that matters of luck may be seen as morally arbitrary and should not be reflected in a just distribution of society's benefits and burdens.

POLITICAL AND ECONOMIC THEORIES

Within discussions of economic justice, people often make use of specific economic and political terms and theories—including *libertarianism, capitalism, socialism, liberalism,* and *communitarianism.* To more fully understand the central issues of economic justice, it will be helpful to take a closer look at these terms and theories, to distinguish them from each other and to determine how each relates to different conceptions of justice. Some of the theories—capitalism and socialism, for example—can be differentiated from one another not only by basic definitions, but also by the different emphases they place on the values of liberty, efficiency, and justice. They are further differentiated by how they favor or disfavor process or end-state views of distributive justice. A brief discussion of each will help elucidate these values and views of distributive justice.

Libertarianism

Libertarianism is a political theory about both the role of government and the importance of liberty in human life. Libertarians such as Tibor Machan (whom we mentioned previously) and Ayn Rand (see Chapter 4) believe that we are free when we are not constrained or restrained by other people. Sometimes, this type of liberty is referred to as a basic right to noninterference. Thus, if you stand in the doorway and block my exit, you are violating my liberty to go where I wish. However, if I fall and break my leg and am unable to leave, then my liberty rights are violated by no one. The doorway is open and unblocked, and I am free to go out. I cannot go out simply because of my injury.

According to libertarianism, government has a minimal function that is primarily administrative. It should provide an orderly civic space in which people can go about their business. It does have an obligation to ensure that people's liberty rights are not violated, that people do not block doorways (or freeways, for that matter). However, government has no obligation to see that my broken leg is repaired so that I can walk where I please. In particular, it has no business taxing you to pay for my leg repair or any other good that I (or you) might like to have or even need. Such needs can be addressed by charities, but they are not matters of social justice or obligation.

Libertarians would be more likely to support a process view of distributive justice than an end-state view. Any economic arrangement would be just so long as it resulted from a fair process of competition, and so long as people did not take what is not theirs or get their wealth by fraudulent or coercive means. However, libertarians do not believe that governments should be concerned with end-state considerations. They should not try to even out any imbalance between rich and poor that might result from a fair process. They should not be involved in any redistribution of wealth. This includes potential redistributions from social insurance arrangements such as Social Security, Medicare, and Medicaid.

The reading at the end of this chapter by Robert Nozick illustrates many aspects of the libertarian theory. For example, he argues that people ought to be free to exchange or transfer to others what they have acquired by just means. Nozick's theory of justice is not focused on end-states. He refers to end-state concerns as "patterned" or "current time-slice principles of justice." For Nozick, the goal should not be to establish a pattern of distribution, since that pattern would hold good only for a limited slice of time. If individuals were free to trade and create, then the pattern would be disrupted. To ensure that the distributive pattern would continue to hold, the state would have to employ coercive measures to enforce the ideal pattern. Those coercive measures would violate the liberty of individuals to create, to trade, and to acquire surpluses that create inequalities. Following other libertarians, Nozick thinks of taxation of earnings to achieve even desirable public goods as "on a par with forced labor." You can reflect further on these views as you study this selection.

Ultimately, libertarianism is a theory about the importance of liberty, of rights to noninterference by others, and of the proper role of government. Libertarians also have generally supported capitalist free-market economies, so brief comments about this type of economic system and its supporting values are appropriate here.

Capitalism

Capitalism is an economic system in which individuals or business corporations (not the government or community) own and control much or most of the country's capital. *Capital* is the wealth or raw materials, factories, and other means that are used to produce more wealth. Capitalism is also usually associated with a free-enterprise system, an economic system that allows people freedom to set prices and determine production, and to make their own choices about how to earn and spend their incomes. A more extreme version of free enterprise is often called a **laissez-faire** economic system. *Laissez-faire* means "leave alone" or "let be"; in laissez-faire capitalism, the government is supposed to leave the economy and markets alone, without regulation or other interference. It generally assumes that people are motivated by profit and engage in competition, and that value is a function of supply and demand. Proponents of laissez-faire capitalism take a range of positions—with some arguing that the government should keep its hands entirely off the economy and others accepting various minimal forms of governmental regulation.

Certain philosophical values and beliefs also undergird capitalism. Among these can be a libertarian philosophy that stresses the importance of liberty and limited government. Certain beliefs about the nature of human motivation also are often implicit, for example, that people are motivated by rational self-interest. Some people argue that capitalism and a free-market economy constitute the best economic system because it is the most efficient one, producing greater wealth for more people than any other system. People produce more and better, they say, when there is something in it for them or their families, or when what they are working for is their own profit. Moreover, producers will usually make only what consumers want, and they know what consumers want by what they are willing to buy. So if people make mousetraps and mind-reading computers that consumers want, they will be rewarded by people buying their products. Exemplifying this outlook is economist Milton Friedman, who maintained that the one and only "social responsibility" of a business is "to use its resources and engage in activities designed to increase profits."[45] Friedman warned that it was "subversive" to claim that corporations have any other form of responsibility than profit making. "Few trends could so thoroughly undermine the very foundations of our free society as the acceptance by corporate officials of a social responsibility other than to make as much money for their stockholders as possible."[46] Libertarians and other supporters of capitalism stress process views of justice. They generally agree that people deserve what they earn through natural talent and hard work.

Socialism

Socialism is an economic system, a political movement, and a social theory. Socialists tend to hold that the economy should be deliberately structured so that the results benefit most people. This way of describing socialism suggests its overlap with utilitarianism. Indeed, it is not surprising that John Stuart Mill was sympathetic to socialism (as might be inferred from some of Mill's comments discussed previously).[47] In contemporary societies, socialism often involves some degree of public management and ownership of goods and services such as education, health care, utilities, or (more rarely) industry and natural resources.

Communism, which can be considered an extreme version of socialism, calls for public ownership of all means of production, radical equality, and the abolition of social classes. Communism is most closely associated with the ideas of the philosopher Karl Marx, who called for a revolution of the working class (what he called *the proletariat*) against the ruling upper class of capitalists (what he called *the bourgeoisie*).

Socialists criticize capitalism for its unpredictable business cycles, which often produce unemployment and poverty. They argue that it inevitably generates conflicts between workers and the owners of the means of production. Rather than allow the few to profit, often at the expense of the many, socialism holds that the government should engage in planning and adjust production to the needs of all of the people. Justice is stressed over efficiency, but central planning is thought to contribute to efficiency as well as justice. Generally, socialism is concerned with end-state justice and is egalitarian in orientation, while making allowances for obvious differences among people in terms of their different needs. Socialism can also be seen to emphasize the value of a certain form of liberty. But in contrast to libertarianism, socialism holds that it is not just external constraints, such as laws, that can limit people's liberty. Socialists tend to think that liberty actually requires freedom from such "internal" constraints as lack of food, education, or health care. Socialists believe that the government has an obligation to address these needs.

As with all labels, the term socialism simplifies. Thus, there are also different kinds or levels of socialism. Some are highly centralized and rely on a command economy, where the state determines prices and wages. Others stress the need for the government to cushion the economy in times of recession, for example, by manipulating interest rates and monetary policy. Most contemporary societies are, in fact, hybrids of socialism and capitalism. For example, in the United States, most K–12 education is socialized, along with police and fire services and such programs as Medicare and Social Security. In various European countries, such services as health insurance, health care, and higher education may be publicly managed or provided.

One key distinction between a libertarian and a socialist conception of justice is that the former recognizes only negative rights and the latter stresses positive rights. **Negative rights** are rights not to be harmed in some way. Because libertarians take liberty as a primary value, they stress the negative right of people not to have their liberty restricted by others. These are rights of noninterference. In the economic arena, libertarians support economic liberties that create wealth, and they believe that people should be able to dispose of their wealth as they choose. For the libertarian, the government's role is to protect negative rights, not positive rights. Contrary to this view, socialists believe that the government should not only protect people's negative rights not to be interfered with, but also attend to their positive rights to basic necessities. Consequently, a right to life must not only involve a right not to be killed, but also a right to what is necessary to live, namely, food, clothing, and shelter. **Positive rights** to be helped or benefited are sometimes called "welfare rights." Those who favor such a concept of rights may ask what a right to life would amount to if one did not have the means to live. Positive economic rights are often defined as rights to basic economic subsistence. Those who favor positive rights would allow for a variety of ways to provide for them, from direct public grants to incentives of various sorts.

None of these systems is problem free. Socialism, at least in recent times, often has not lived up to the ideals of its supporters. Central planning systems have often failed as societies become more complex and participate in international economic systems. Communist societies have tended to become authoritarian, in part, because it is difficult to get universal voluntary consent to centrally controlled plans for production and other policies. Basic necessities may be provided for all, but their quality has often turned out to be low.

Capitalism and a free-market economy also are open to moral criticism. Many people, through no fault of their own, cannot or do not compete well and fall through the cracks. Unemployment is a natural part of the system, but it is also debilitating for the unemployed worker. When unemployment is high and labor markets are tight, as they have been in recent years, employers can make ever-increasing demands on their employees, knowing that they can always be replaced by someone who will be grateful for a job. While this means that recessions and high unemployment help to increase productivity, the cost of increased productivity is felt in the lives of laborers. As productivity increases, those at the top profit, while those at the bottom suffer. As the economy has worked to recover from the "Great Recession," corporate profits have soared, while unemployment has remained high.[48] From a social justice standpoint, what matters most is the dignity and well-being of working people, not the profits of those at the top of the corporate ladder.

Libertarianism has been criticized for failing to notice that society provides the means by which individuals seek their own good, for example, by means of transportation and communication. It often fails to notice that state action is needed to protect liberty rights and rights to security, property, and litigation. It has also been criticized for rejecting popular social welfare programs such as publicly funded compulsory primary education.[49] Libertarians have been accused of ignoring the effects that individuals' initial life circumstances have on their fair chances to compete for society's goods.

Let us consider whether a hybrid political and economic system might be better, one that combines aspects of libertarianism, capitalism, and socialism. The most accurate term for such a system is *modern liberalism,* even though the term *liberalism* has meant many things to many people. One reason for using this name is that it is typically applied to the views of one philosopher whose work exemplified it and whose philosophy we shall also discuss here: John Rawls.

MindTap® For more chapter resources and activities, go to MindTap.

Modern Liberalism

Suppose we were to attempt to combine the positive elements of libertarianism, capitalism, and socialism. What would we pull from each? Liberty, or the ability to be free from unjust constraint by others, the

primary value stressed by libertarianism, would be one value to preserve. However, we may want to support a fuller notion of liberty that also recognizes the power of internal constraints. We also might want to recognize both positive and negative rights and hold that government ought to play some role in supporting the former as well as the latter. Stress on this combination of elements characterizes modern liberalism.

In a draft version of the American Declaration of Independence, Thomas Jefferson wrote of the inalienable rights to life, liberty, and happiness, and concluded that, "in order to *secure these ends* governments are instituted among men." In Jefferson's final draft, the phrase is "in order to *secure these rights* governments are instituted among men."[50] In some ways, these two accounts of the purpose of government parallel the two major approaches to determining when a distribution of wealth is just: the end-state view with its stress on positive rights ("to secure these ends") and the process view with its stress on negative rights of noninterference ("to secure these rights"). Liberalism features a mixture of these two conceptions of rights.

Modern liberalism also generally seeks to promote an economic system that is efficient as well as just. Thus, it usually allows capitalist incentives and inequalities of wealth. However, since it values positive as well as negative rights, modern liberalism is also concerned about the least advantaged members of the society. In this view, companies and corporations are generally regarded as guests in society, because government allows their creation and protects them from certain liabilities, with the understanding that they will contribute to the good of all. Accordingly, they are thought to owe something in return to the community—as a matter of justice—and have responsibilities beyond their own best interest. Modern liberalism also points out that the economic productivity and efficiency of a society depend on human development and communication and transportation systems. Thus, public investment in education, health, roads, technology, and research and development provides a crucial foundation for the private economy.[51]

John Rawls's Theory of Justice

The most widely discussed work of political philosophy of the past four decades is John Rawls's 1971 book, *A Theory of Justice*, which lays out a moral justification for a modern liberal state.[52] According to Rawls, justice is the first virtue of social institutions, just as truth is the first virtue of scientific systems. It is most important for scientific systems to be true or well supported. They may be elegant or interesting or in line with our other beliefs, but that is not the primary requirement for their acceptance. Something similar would be the case for social and economic institutions with regard to justice. We would want them to be efficient, but what is the point of efficiency if the overall society is unjust? Among the fundamental questions Rawls raises are: what is justice, and how do we know whether an economic system is just? Rawls sought to develop a set of principles or guidelines that we could apply to our institutions, enabling us to judge whether they are just or unjust. To do so, he uses a famous thought experiment, which he calls the *original position,* designed to produce basic principles of justice.

Rawls asks us to consider what rational individuals would agree upon if they came together to form a society for their mutual benefit. Rawls argues that the principles these rational individuals would select to guide their society can be taken as basic principles of justice, provided that the decision procedure was genuinely fair. In other words, we must first ensure that these individuals are so situated that they can choose fairly. We can then ask what principles of justice they would be likely to accept.

But what makes a choice or a choice situation fair, and what would make it unfair? One obvious answer is that a fair decision should be free from *bias*; it should prevent individuals from being able to "rig the system" in their favor or "stack the deck" to benefit people like them. The way to avoid bias is for people to ignore or forget their own particular situation so that their judgments might be free from bias. To eliminate such bias, then, Rawls argues that people in the original position must not be able to know biasing information about themselves. They must not know their age, sex, race, talents, education, social and economic status, religion, political views, and so on. A truly fair choice can thus be made only from behind what he calls a *veil of ignorance.*

With this basic requirement of fairness established, we can then try to determine what principles of justice our would-be citizens might select. Rawls takes pains to emphasize that we need not think of these people as altruistic or selfless. Indeed, they are assumed to want what most people want of the basic goods of life. And they want the means to be able to pursue their own conceptions of a good life (whatever those may be), free from unnecessary interference. Based on these simple motives, and assuming that our citizens make a rational choice (rather than one out of spite or envy), then what basic principles would they select? Rawls argues that we can determine that they would choose two fundamental principles in particular. The first has to do with their political liberties, and the second concerns economic arrangements:

1. Each person is to have an equal right to the most extensive total system of equal basic liberties compatible with a similar system of liberty for all.
2. Social and economic inequalities are to be arranged so that they are:
   a. to the greatest benefit of the least advantaged..., and
   b. attached to offices and positions open to all under conditions of fair equality of opportunity.[53]

Much of *A Theory of Justice* is devoted to explaining why individuals would in fact choose these two principles for their society, if they didn't know their identities or position in that society. But the basic reasoning for each principle is fairly simple. Rawls believes that such individuals, seeking liberty to pursue their own conceptions of the good life (but not knowing what they are), would require that there be *equality of liberties*—that is, they would not be willing to be the people who had less freedom than others. They would want as much say about matters in their society that affect them as any other people, no matter what their personal characteristics or conceptions of life happen to be. This reflects the importance of liberty to all people as people, no matter who they are.

When it comes to society's goods, however, Rawls argues that the would-be citizens would accept a society with *unequal shares* of wealth and other goods, provided certain conditions were met. They would accept that some would be richer and some poorer, provided that the not-so-rich are better off than they otherwise would be if all had equal amounts of wealth. Since each individual could turn out to be the poorest member of the society, this principle makes sense as a kind of insurance against the worst outcome.

You can test yourself to see if your choices coincide with Rawls's claim for the acceptance of unequal shares. The following table shows the average yearly income at three different wealth levels (high, medium, and low) in three societies (A, B, and C). Assume that you have no information about which income group you will end up in, or about your relative odds of ending up in one rather than another. Under these circumstances, to which society would you want to belong?

If you chose Society A—perhaps because you think it would be great to earn $200,000 a year—then you are taking an irrational risk, according to Rawls. For you do not know (under the veil of

Wealth Levels	Society A	Society B	Society C
High income	$200,000	$70,000	$20,000
Medium income	$70,000	$40,000	$20,000
Low income	$15,000	$30,000	$20,000

ignorance) what your chances are of being in any of the three positions in the society. For example, you do not know whether your chances of being in the highest income group are near zero or whether your chances of being in the lowest income group are greater than 50 percent. Your best bet, when you do not know what your chances are, is to choose Society B. In this society, no matter what group you are in, you will do better than you would in any position

in completely egalitarian Society C. And even if you were in the lowest income group in Society B, you would be better off than you would be in the lowest groups of either A or C. Choosing Society B for these reasons is often called a *maximin* strategy; in choosing under conditions of uncertainty, you select that option with the best worst or minimum position.

The maximin approach has clear relevance to Rawls's principles of justice and his argument that they would be selected in the original position. Remember that to avoid bias, people in the original position must choose principles for their society in ignorance of the basic facts about who they are. They do not know the economic or social position they will occupy—and they know that they might end up in the group that is worst off. Thus, Rawls argues that rational self-interest will demand that they look out for the bottom position in society. If economic inequalities (some people being richer than others) would produce a better situation for the worst off than equal shares would, then it would be selected as a principle. For it ensures the best possible life for the individuals in the lowest group, which they know could be themselves. This is the rationale for the first part of Rawls's second principle of justice, which says that economic inequalities should be arranged to the benefit of the least advantaged.

Rawls also provides a corollary argument for his maximin principle, one that does not depend on the idea of the original position. Here, he examines "accidents of natural and social circumstance," the random facts of where one is born and what capacities one is born with—which he says are neither just nor unjust, but *morally arbitrary*. If some are born into unfortunate circumstances, it is through no fault of their own but merely because of the arbitrary circumstances of their birth. Similarly, "No one deserves his greater natural capacity nor merits a more favorable starting place in society."[54] While society cannot eliminate these different starting places, a just society should not blindly accept such morally arbitrary facts—as does the warrior aristocracy imagined by Bernard Williams described previously. Rawls maintains that in a just society, those who have been favored by nature may be permitted to gain from their good fortune "only on terms that improve the situation of those who have lost out."[55] Again, the idea is that economic inequalities can be allowed by justice, but only if these inequalities work to the benefit of society's least fortunate members.

The second part of Rawls's second principle concerns equal opportunity. If inequality of income and wealth are to be considered just, then society's institutions must provide an equal opportunity for those with the relevant interests, talents, and ambition to attain positions of wealth, power, and prestige. For Rawls, social class distinctions should not prevent social mobility. As he explains, the point is not merely to guarantee *formal* equality and nondiscrimination, but to guarantee that everyone should have a fair chance at gaining access to social goods. "The expectations of those with the same abilities and aspirations should not be affected by their social class."[56] Rawls's primary concern is to limit the impact of social class. But the idea of fair equality of

opportunity can also apply to racial and gender disparities (such as we discussed in Chapter 13).

Rawls's two principles would most likely be accepted by people who are brought up in modern democratic and liberal societies. But modern democratic societies are also pluralistic—that is, their people will have many different and irreconcilable sets of moral and religious beliefs. Rawls admits that pluralism is a problem in his later works.[57] He acknowledges that in modern societies, people have sharply different moral and religious views; there is irremediable and irreducible pluralism. Thus, the only way that citizens can agree is by thinking of themselves as persons who want whatever persons in general would want and who do not bias the rules of society in their own favor based on their particular characteristics. But such an approach may not satisfy all those with diverse points of view on culture, religion, economics, and justice; for example, libertarians and communists may not agree with

Outline of Moral Approaches to Theories of Economic Justice

	Socialism	Liberalism	Libertarianism
Thesis	Equality is a primary value	Liberty and equality are values that ought to be balanced	Liberty is a primary value
Corollaries and Implications	Economic inequality should be moderated through centralized redistributions of wealth	Two principles of justice aim to balance liberty and equality, with the state playing a role in distributive justice	Capitalist property relations and market exchanges produce innovation and wealth; liberty upsets patterned distributions
Connections with Moral Theory	Utilitarian concern for greatest happiness for the greatest number; natural law concern for social justice; focus on "positive" rights	Ideal social contract under a veil of ignorance, based upon intuitions about fairness; utilitarian concern for balancing liberty with welfare	Autonomy is a key value, including respect for property rights, which is considered as a "negative" right
Relevant Authors/ Examples	John Stuart Mill; Pope Francis	John Rawls	Robert Nozick; Ayn Rand

the procedures Rawls uses to derive his basic principles of justice. This substantial problem points back toward the issues of pluralism and relativism, which we discussed in Chapters 2 and 3.

The issues and perspectives discussed in this section are summarized in the table above, which outlines a range of positions from socialism to libertarianism.

Communitarianism

The issue of pluralism reminds us that there are other possible views of economic justice. Some might defend traditional class structures based upon religious or cultural claims about caste. Others might argue in favor of radical egalitarianism that requires a kind of communal pooling of assets. And others may maintain, as egoists do, that in the dog-eat-dog world of economics, it is every man for himself.

While Rawls's version of economic liberalism is based on the notion of rational beings applying a maximin strategy to the problem of economic justice, not everyone agrees with this strategy. One line of substantial criticism of Rawls's notion of rationality and his vision of economic justice has been offered by communitarian philosophers. Communitarians generally reject Rawls's idea that justice should be understood as a maximin strategy developed from within the original position. They also think that liberals like Rawls smuggle in claims about rationality and about social justice when they make claims about how rational persons would think about justice. Some communitarian writers object to what they believe are the individualistic elements in Rawls's theory. For example, Rawls asks us to imagine thinking about social justice as individuals under a veil of ignorance, rather than as members of families, who have substantial obligations to the welfare of our family members.

Communitarians, in general, tend to believe that people are by nature social and naturally belong to communities. They often invoke Aristotle and Aquinas as sources, who each claimed that human beings are naturally social beings. Communitarians do not generally accept the idea that individuals are rational choosers who could consistently apply the maximin theory of rationality that Rawls advocates. They stress the importance of belonging to families, cities, nations, religious communities, neighborhood associations, political parties, and groups supporting particular causes. The communitarian view of social justice may depend upon the views of the groups to which they belong, as a matter of tradition and culture. But, in general, communitarian ideas emphasize concrete social relations instead of abstract principles of distributive justice. One explanation can be found in the "Responsive Communitarian Platform," which asserts, "At the heart of the communitarian understanding of social justice is the idea of reciprocity: each member of the community owes something to all the rest and the community owes something to each of its members. Justice requires responsible individuals in a responsive community."[58]

There is some connection between communitarian ideas of social justice and the ideas of care ethics (as discussed in Chapter 9). But the communitarian approach is more focused on economic issues, including the problem of economic inequality. Amitai Etzioni, one of the authors of the aforementioned "Responsive Communitarian Platform" and an important proponent of communitarianism, explains that inequality creates a serious social problem. "If some members of a community are increasingly distanced from the standard of living of most other members, they will lose contact with the rest of the community. The more those in charge of private and public institutions lead lives of hyperaffluence…the less in touch they are with other community members."[59]

Rawls might permit economic inequalities so long as they benefit the least advantaged and so long as there is fair opportunity for advancement. Nozick and the libertarians would not see economic inequality as a problem, so long as it results from a free marketplace in which individual talent and ambition were rewarded. But the communitarian critique worries that the fabric of community becomes frayed when there is too much inequality. A version of communitarianism can be derived from Catholic social justice teachings, which views economics as "the art of achieving a fitting management of our common home," as the Roman Catholic Pope Francis has explained (in the excerpt at the end of this chapter).

A problem for communitarianism is that it can sometimes seem to resemble a kind of cultural relativism that claims that the values of any community are as good as the values of any other. Some communitarian authors do appear to affirm a version of cultural relativism. However, Etzioni focuses on basic features of human communities and human functions, such as the need for solidarity and a sense of connection within a community. The idea of basic human function is also central to the work of Amartya Sen, a Nobel Prize–winning economist. Sen rejects relativism, but he is also critical of Rawls's abstract approach to distributive justice. Sen's idea is that concerns about economic equality should focus on human functions and capabilities—what people can actually do with their resources—and not merely on the abstract idea of income equality.[60] (Sen's account is connected with Martha Nussbaum's ideas about human capabilities as discussed in Chapter 3.) The point of this sort of criticism is that there are a variety of concerns that we ought to attend to when thinking about equality including family structure, age, ability (or disability), gender roles, cultural practices, traditions, and so on. A concern for equality requires us to account for the complexity of human life in all of its richness.

This chapter has considered the complicated issues of economic justice, social justice, and political philosophy. One basic question of this chapter is whether one should egoistically pursue one's own self-interest and maximize profit or whether there are ethical constraints to profit, such as a worry about inequality or equality of opportunity. There is much more to be said about the limits of political power and the proper relation between the state and the economy. To better evaluate the theories we've examined here, we would also need further empirical study of the efficiency of various forms of economic organization. And there are vexing psychological and sociological problems that remain to be considered, such as how best to help those in poverty and

the unemployed without disempowering or denigrating them. These issues remind us that questions of justice also need to be informed by practical information from empirical fields of study.

The readings in this chapter are selections from John Rawls's *A Theory of Justice* and Robert Nozick's *Anarchy, State, and Utopia*. Rawls is a proponent of modern liberalism, while Nozick's entitlement theory of justice is most closely related to libertarian theory. Rawls was one of the most prominent moral and political philosophers of the twentieth century, and Nozick was an influential colleague of Rawls's at Harvard. *Anarchy, State, and Utopia*, first published in 1974, is in part a response to Rawls's *A Theory of Justice*, which was first published in 1971. The other two readings are from Ayn Rand—whose defense of egoism and capitalism was explained in this chapter (and in Chapter 4)—and from the Roman Catholic Pope Francis—whose critique of global capitalism, *Evangelii Gaudium* (which can be translated as *The Joy of the Gospel*), was published in 2013.

NOTES

1. "Income Inequality," *Inequality.org* (A Project of the Institute for Policy Studies), http://inequality.org/income-inequality/ (accessed March 9, 2016).
2. "Wealthy's Tax Bill Will Hit 30-Year High in 2013," *CNBC*, March 4, 2013, http://www.cnbc.com/id/100518058 (accessed March 9, 2016).
3. *Economic Report of the President* (Washington, D.C.: Government Printing Office, 2010), p. 154, http://www.whitehouse.gov/sites/default/files/microsites/economic-report-president.pdf (accessed March 9, 2016).
4. U.S. Census Bureau, "2014 Highlights," https://www.census.gov/hhes/www/poverty/about/overview/index.html (accessed March 9, 2016).
5. U.S. Census Bureau, "How the Census Bureau Measures Poverty," https://www.census.gov/hhes/www/poverty/about/overview/measure.html (accessed March 9, 2016).
6. U.S. Census Bureau, "QuickFacts: What's New & FAQs," http://www.census.gov/quickfacts/table/PST045215/00 (accessed March 9, 2016).

7. "The World's Billionaires," *Forbes*, March 1, 2016, http://www.forbes.com/billionaires/ (accessed March 9, 2016).

8. Martin Crutsinger, "Greenspan Talk Doesn't Roil Markets," *The Washington Post*, March 13, 2007, http://www.washingtonpost.com/wp-dyn/content/article/2007/03/13/AR2007031300744.html (accessed March 9, 2016).

9. Chuck Collins and Josh Hoxie, "Billionaire Bonanza: The Forbes 400 and the Rest of Us," Institute for Policy Studies, December 1, 2015, http://www.ips-dc.org/billionaire-bonanza/ (accessed March 9, 2016).

10. Susan Adams, "CEO Pay Continues to Rise," *Forbes*, June 30, 2015, http://www.forbes.com/sites/susanadams/2015/06/30/ceo-pay-continues-to-rise-widening-wealth-gap-cubicle-dweller-pay-barely-budges/#6d063dc45d86 (accessed March 9, 2016).

11. "CEO to Worker Pay Ratio Top 5," *Payscale.com*, http://www.payscale.com/data-packages/ceo-income/top-5 (accessed March 9, 2016).

12. Anders Melin and Caleb Melby, "Google CEO Pichai Receives record $199 million Stock Grant," *Bloomberg*, February 8, 2016, http://www.bloomberg.com/news/articles/2016-02-08/google-ceo-pichai-receives-record-199-million-stock-grant (accessed March 9, 2016).

13. Eric Zuesse, "Why Social Mobility in the United States Is a Total Myth," *Business Insider*, March 18, 2013, http://www.businessinsider.com/social-mobility-is-a-myth-in-the-us-2013-3 (accessed May 9, 2016).

14. Tami Luhby, "Worsening Wealth Inequality by Race," *CNN Money*, June 21, 2012, http://money.cnn.com/2012/06/21/news/economy/wealth-gap-race/index.htm (accessed March 9, 2016).

15. Liza Mundy, "Women, Money, and Power," *Time*, March 26, 2012, http://www.time.com/time/magazine/article/0,9171,2109140,00.html (accessed March 9, 2016).

16. "Women Make Significant Gains in the Workplace and Educational Attainment, but Lag in Pay," Pew Research Center, March 8, 2013, http://www.pewresearch.org/daily-number/women-make-significant-gains-in-the-workplace-and-educational-attainment-but-lag-in-pay/ (accessed March 9, 2016).

17. *An Analysis of Reasons for the Disparity in Wages between Men and Women*, report prepared for U.S. Department of Labor (January 2009), http://www.consad.com/content/reports/Genderpercent20Wagepercent20Gappercent20Finalpercent20Report.pdf (accessed March 9, 2016).

18. Secretary Tom Perez, Jenny R. Yang, and Valerie Jarrett, "Better Data Equals Greater Pay Equality," U.S. Department of Labor, January 29, 2016, https://blog.dol.gov/2016/01/29/better-data-equals-greater-pay-equality/ (accessed March 15, 2016).

19. "What's the Minimum Wage in Your State?" *RaisetheMinimumWage.com* (A Project of the National Employment Law Project), http://www.raisetheminimumwage.com/pages/minimum-wage-state (accessed March 15, 2016).

20. See the Living Wage Calculator, http://livingwage.mit.edu/ (accessed March 15, 2016).

21. U.S. Census Bureau, "Income and Poverty in the United States: 2014 – Highlights," https://www.census.gov/hhes/www/poverty/data/incpovhlth/2014/highlights.html (accessed March 15, 2016).

22. U.S. Census Bureau, "Income, Poverty and Health Insurance Coverage in the United States: 2014," https://www.census.gov/newsroom/press-releases/2015/cb15-157.html (accessed March 15, 2016).

23. Sabrina Tavernise, "Education Gap Grows between Rich and Poor, Studies Say," *New York Times*, February 9, 2012, http://www.nytimes.com/2012/02/10/education/education-gap-grows-between-rich-and-poor-studies-show.html?pagewanted=all&_r=0 (accessed March 15, 2016).

24. "How Many U.S. Deaths are Caused by Poverty, Lack of Education, and Other Social Factors?" https://www.mailman.columbia.edu/public-health-now/news/how-many-us-deaths-are-caused-poverty-lack-education-and-other-social-factors (accessed May 9, 2016); this conclusion is based on data from Sandro Galea, Melissa Tracy, Katherine J. Hoggatt, Charles DiMaggio, and Adam Karpati, "Estimated Deaths Attributable to Social

Factors in the United States," *American Journal of Public Health* 11, No. 8 (2011), pp. 1456–65.

25. David Himmelstein et al., "MarketWatch: Illness and Injury as Contributors to Bankruptcy," *Health Affairs* Web Exclusive, February 2, 2005, W5–62. As cited in T. R. Reid, *The Healing of America: A Global Quest for Better, Cheaper, and Fairer Health Care* (New York: Penguin, 2009).

26. Ezra Klein, "11 Facts about the Affordable Care Act," *The Washington Post*, June 24, 2012, http://www.washingtonpost.com/blogs/wonkblog/wp/2012/06/24/11-facts-about-the-affordable-care-act/ (accessed March 15, 2016).

27. Nina Owcharenko, "Repealing Obamacare and Getting Health Care Right," *The Heritage Foundation*, November 9, 2010, http://www.heritage.org/research/reports/2010/11/repealing-obamacare-and-getting-health-care-right (accessed March 15, 2016).

28. Beatrix Hoffman, *Health Care for Some: Rights and Rationing in the United States Since 1930* (Chicago: University of Chicago Press, 2012).

29. Ibid.

30. Thomas Massaro, *Living Justice: Catholic Social Teaching in Action*, 2nd classroom ed., (Lanham, MD: Rowman & Littlefield, 2011), p. 2.

31. John Stuart Mill, *Principles of Political Economy with some of their Applications to Social Philosophy*, ed. William J. Ashley (originally published 1909; from Library of Economics and Liberty), bk. 2, Chapter 13, sec. 2, http://www.econlib.org/library/Mill/mlP26.html (accessed March 15, 2016).

32. John Stuart Mill, "The Negro Question" (1850) in *The Collected Works of John Stuart Mill, Volume XXI - Essays on Equality, Law, and Education*, ed. John M. Robson (Toronto: University of Toronto Press, London: Routledge and Kegan Paul, 1984), http://oll.libertyfund.org/title/255/21657 (accessed March 15, 2016).

33. John Stuart Mill, *Chapters on Socialism* (1879) in *The Collected Works of John Stuart Mill, Volume V - Essays on Economics and Society Part II*, ed. John M. Robson (Toronto: University of Toronto Press, London: Routledge and Kegan Paul, 1967), http://oll.libertyfund.org/title/232/16747 (accessed March 15, 2016).

34. John Stuart Mill, *Principles of Political Economy*, bk. 5, Chapter 11, sec. 44.

35. Immanuel Kant, *Lectures on Ethics* (Indianapolis, IN: Hackett, 1981), p. 194.

36. Tibor R. Machan, "Libertarian Justice: A Natural Rights Approach" in Tibor R. Machan, ed., *Liberty and Justice* (Stanford, CA: Hoover Institution Press, 2006), p. 111.

37. We associate the saying "From each according to his ability, to each according to his need" with Karl Marx, but it actually originated with the "early French socialists of the Utopian school, and was officially adopted by German socialists in the Gotha Program of 1875." Nicholas Rescher, *Distributive Justice* (Indianapolis, IN: Bobbs-Merrill, 1966), pp. 73–83.

38. James Fishkin, *Justice, Equal Opportunity, and the Family* (New Haven, CT: Yale University Press, 1983), p. 4.

39. See "D.C. Leads Nation as U.S. per Pupil Tops $10,600, Census Bureau Reports," U.S. Census Bureau, June 21, 2012, http://www.census.gov/newsroom/releases/archives/finance_insurance_real_estate/cb12-113.html (accessed March 15, 2016); or "California School District Spending and Test Scores," California Watch, June 2, 2011, http://schoolspending.apps.cironline.org/ (accessed March 15, 2016).

40. Bernard Williams, "The Idea of Equality," in *Philosophy, Politics and Society* (second series), ed. Peter Laslett and W. G. Runciman (Oxford: Basil Blackwell, 1962), pp. 110–31.

41. Harry Frankfurt, "Equality as a Moral Ideal," *Ethics* 98 (1987), pp. 21–43.

42. John H. Schaar, "Equality of Opportunity, and Beyond," in *NOMO SIX: Equality*, ed. J. Chapman and R. Pennock (New York: Atherton Press, 1967).

43. Ibid.

44. See Thomas Nagel, "Justice," in *What Does It All Mean: A Very Short Introduction to Philosophy* (New York: Oxford University Press, 1987), pp. 76–86.

45. Milton Friedman, *Capitalism and Freedom* (Chicago: University of Chicago Press, 1982), p. 133.

46. Milton Friedman, *Capitalism and Freedom* (Chicago: University of Chicago Press, 1982), p. 133.

47. Stephen Nathanson, "John Stuart Mill on Economic Justice and the Alleviation of Poverty," *Journal of Social Philosophy* 43, No. 2 (Summer 2012), pp. 161–76.

48. Nelson D. Schwartz, "Recovery in U.S. Is Lifting Profits, but Not Adding Jobs," *New York Times*, March 3, 2013, http://www.nytimes.com/2013/03/04/business/economy/corporate-profits-soar-as-worker-income-limps.html?pagewanted=all (accessed March 15, 2016).

49. Stephen Holmes, "Welfare and the Liberal Conscience," *Report from the Institute for Philosophy and Public Policy* 15, No. 1 (Winter 1995), pp. 1–6.

50. Morton White, *The Philosophy of the American Revolution* (New York: Oxford University Press, 1978), p. 161. Italics added by White and editors.

51. Robert B. Reich, "The Other Surplus Option," *New York Times*, http://www.nytimes.com/1999/08/11/opinion/the-other-surplus-option.html (accessed May 9, 2016).

52. John Rawls, *A Theory of Justice* (Cambridge, MA: Harvard University Press, 1971).

53. Ibid., p. 302.

54. Ibid., pp. 100–03.

55. Ibid.

56. Ibid., p. 73.

57. John Rawls, *Political Liberalism* (New York: Columbia University Press, 1993).

58. Amitai Etzioni and Rothschild Volmert, *The Communitarian Reader: Beyond the Essentials* (Lanham, MD: Rowman & Littlefield, 2004), p. 21.

59. Amitai Etzioni, *Next: The Road to the Good Society* (New York: Basic Books, 2001), p. 101.

60. Amartya Sen, *Development as Freedom* (Oxford: Oxford University Press, 1999).

READING

Justice as Fairness

JOHN RAWLS

MindTap® For more chapter resources and activities, go to MindTap.

Study Questions

As you read the excerpt, please consider the following questions:

1. Why does Rawls think it is useful to imagine justice from behind a "veil of ignorance"?
2. What are the two basic principles of justice that Rawls describes—and how or why would they be chosen under the veil of ignorance?
3. How and why is equality a significant concern for Rawls?

In justice as fairness the original position of equality corresponds to the state of nature in the traditional theory of the social contract. This original position is not, of course, thought of as an actual historical state of affairs, much less as a primitive condition of culture. It is understood as a purely hypothetical situation characterized so as to lead to a certain conception of justice. Among the essential features of this situation is that no one knows his place in society, his class position or social status, nor does any one know his fortune in the distribution of natural assets and abilities, his intelligence, strength, and the like. I shall even assume that the parties do not know their conceptions of the good or their special psychological propensities. The

From John Rawls, *A Theory of Justice* (Cambridge, MA: Belknap Press of Harvard, 1971, 1999) Copyright © 1971, 1999.

principles of justice are chosen behind a veil of ignorance. This ensures that no one is advantaged or disadvantaged in the choice of principles by the outcome of natural chance or the contingency of social circumstances. Since all are similarly situated and no one is able to design principles to favor his particular condition, the principles of justice are the result of a fair agreement or bargain. For given the circumstances of the original position, the symmetry of everyone's relations to each other, this initial situation is fair between individuals as moral persons...

...The persons in the initial situation would choose two rather different principles: the first requires equality in the assignment of basic rights and duties, while the second holds that social and economic inequalities, for example inequalities of wealth and authority, are just only if they result in compensating benefits for everyone, and in particular for the least advantaged members of society. These principles rule out justifying institutions on the grounds that the hardships of some are offset by a greater good in the aggregate. It may be expedient but it is not just that some should have less in order that others may prosper. But there is no injustice in the greater benefits earned by a few provided that the situation of persons not so fortunate is thereby improved....

I shall now state in a provisional form the two principles of justice that I believe would be chosen in the original position....

First: each person is to have an equal right to the most extensive basic liberty compatible with a similar liberty for others.

Second: social and economic inequalities are to be arranged so that they are both: (a) reasonably expected to be to everyone's advantage, and (b) attached to positions and offices open to all....

...The two principles...are a special case of a more general conception of justice that can be expressed as follows:

All social values—liberty and opportunity, income and wealth, and the bases of self-respect—are to be distributed equally unless an unequal distribution of any, or all, of these values is to everyone's advantage.

READING

Distributive Justice

ROBERT NOZICK

MindTap® For more chapter resources and activities, go to MindTap.

Study Questions

As you read the excerpt, please consider the following questions:

1. According to Nozick, why can the term *distributive justice* be misleading; why is the focus on "distribution" misleading?
2. How is Nozick's focus on entitlement different from the focus on "patterns" of distribution?
3. How do patterned systems of distributive justice lead to "continuous interference" in the life and liberty of people?

...We are not in the position of children who have been given portions of pie by someone who now makes last minute adjustments to rectify careless cutting. There is no *central* distribution, no person or group entitled to control all the resources, jointly deciding how they are to be doled out. What each person gets, he gets from others who give to him in exchange for something, or as a gift. In a free society,

From Robert Nozick, "Distributive Justice," in *Anarchy, State, and Utopia* (New York: Basic Books, 1977) pp. 149–157, 161–163, 167–169. Copyright © 1977 Basic Books, Inc.

diverse persons control different resources, and new holdings arise out of the voluntary exchanges and actions of persons. There is no more a distributing or distribution of shares than there is a distributing of mates in a society in which persons choose whom they shall marry. The total result is the product of many individual decisions which the different individuals involved are entitled to make. . . .

The general outlines of the theory of justice in holdings are that the holdings of a person are just if he is entitled to them by the principles of justice in acquisition and transfer, or by the principle of rectification of injustice (as specified by the first two principles). If each person's holdings are just, then the total set (distribution) of holdings is just. . . .

Almost every suggested principle of distributive justice is patterned; to each according to his moral merit, or needs, or marginal product, or how hard he tries, or the weighted sum of the foregoing, and so on. The principle of entitlement we have sketched is *not* patterned. There is no one natural dimension or weighted sum or combination of a small number of natural dimensions that yields the distributions generated in accordance with the principle of

entitlement. The set of holdings that results when some persons receive their marginal products, others win at gambling, others receive a share of their mate's income, others receive gifts from foundations, others receive interest on loans, others receive gifts from admirers, others receive returns on investment, others make for themselves much of what they have, others find things, and so on, will not be patterned. . . .

. . . No end-state principle or distributional patterned principle of justice can be continuously realized without continuous interference with people's lives. Any favored pattern would be transformed into one unfavored by the principle, by people choosing to act in various ways; for example, by people exchanging goods and services with other people, or giving things to other people, things the transferrers are entitled to under the favored distributional pattern. To maintain a pattern one must either continually interfere to stop people from transferring resources as they wish to, or continually (or periodically) interfere to take from some persons resources that others for some reason chose to transfer to them.

READING

Capitalism: The Unknown Ideal

AYN RAND

MindTap®   For more chapter resources and activities, go to MindTap.

Study Questions

As you read the excerpt, please consider the following questions:
1. What is the virtue of capitalism, as Rand describes it?
2. What is Rand's opinion of sacrifices made for the common good?
3. What is the basic right upon which capitalism and its success is grounded, according to Rand?

The magnificent progress achieved by capitalism in a brief span of time, the spectacular improvement in the conditions of man's existence on earth, is a matter of historical record. It is not to be hidden, evaded, or explained away by all the propaganda of capitalism's enemies. But what needs special

emphasis is the fact that this progress was achieved by non-sacrificial means.

Progress cannot be achieved by forced privations, by squeezing a "social surplus" out of starving

Ayn Rand, *Capitalism: The Unknown Ideal* (Signet 1967), pp. 21–23.

victims. Progress can come only out of individual surplus, i.e., from the work, the energy, the creative over-abundance of those men whose ability produces more than their personal consumption requires, those who are intellectually and financially able to seek the new, to improve on the known, to move forward. In a capitalist society, where such men are free to function and to take their own risks, progress is not a matter of sacrificing to some distant future, it is part of the living present, it is the normal and natural, it is achieved as and while men live—and enjoy—their lives.

. . . .

America's abundance was not created by public sacrifices to "the common good," but by the productive genius of free men who pursued their own personal interests and the making of their own private fortunes. They did not starve the people to pay for America's industrialization. They gave the people better jobs, higher wages, and cheaper goods with every new machine they invented, with every scientific discovery or technological advance—and thus the whole country was moving forward and profiting, not suffering, every step of the way.

Do not, however, make the error of reversing cause and effect: the good of the country was made possible precisely by the fact that it was not forced on anyone as a moral goal or duty; it was merely an effect; the cause was a man's right to pursue his own good. It is this right—not its consequences—that represents the moral justification of capitalism.

. . . .

While altruism seeks to rob intelligence of its rewards, by asserting that the moral duty of the competent is to serve the incompetent and sacrifice themselves to anyone's need—the tribal premise goes a step further: it denies the existence of intelligence and of its role in the production of wealth.

It is morally obscene to regard wealth as an anonymous, tribal product and to talk about "redistributing" it. The view that wealth is the result of some undifferentiated, collective process, that we all did something and it's impossible to tell who did what, therefore some sort of equalitarian "distribution" is necessary—might have been appropriate in a primordial jungle with a savage horde moving boulders by crude physical labor (though even there someone had to initiate and organize the moving). To hold that view in an industrial society—where individual achievements are a matter of public record—is so crass an evasion that even to give it the benefit of the doubt is an obscenity.

READING

Evangelii Gaudium

POPE FRANCIS

MindTap° For more chapter resources and activities, go to MindTap.

Study Questions

As you read the excerpt, please consider the following questions:

1. How and why does Pope Francis criticize the economy of "exclusion and inequality"?
2. What is Pope Francis's opinion of consumerism and our obsession with money?
3. Given that Pope Francis is a religious figure who appeals to religious sources, can his argument make sense to non-religious people or to people from different religious traditions?

52. In our time humanity is experiencing a turning-point in its history, as we can see from the advances being made in so many fields. We can only praise

http://w2.vatican.va/content/francesco/en/apost_exhortations/documents/papa-francesco_esortazione-ap_20131124_evangelii-gaudium.html the steps being taken to improve people's welfare in areas such as health care, education and communications. At the same time we have to remember that the majority of our contemporaries are barely living from day to day, with dire consequences. A number of diseases are spreading. The hearts of many people are gripped by fear and desperation, even in the so-called rich countries. The joy of living frequently fades, lack of respect for others and violence are on the rise, and inequality is increasingly evident. It is a struggle to live and, often, to live with precious little dignity. This epochal change has been set in motion by the enormous qualitative, quantitative, rapid and cumulative advances occurring in the sciences and in technology, and by their instant application in different areas of nature and of life. We are in an age of knowledge and information, which has led to new and often anonymous kinds of power.

53. Just as the commandment "Thou shalt not kill" sets a clear limit in order to safeguard the value of human life, today we also have to say "thou shalt not" to an economy of exclusion and inequality. Such an economy kills. How can it be that it is not a news item when an elderly homeless person dies of exposure, but it is news when the stock market loses two points? This is a case of exclusion. Can we continue to stand by when food is thrown away while people are starving? This is a case of inequality. Today everything comes under the laws of competition and the survival of the fittest, where the powerful feed upon the powerless. As a consequence, masses of people find themselves excluded and marginalized: without work, without possibilities, without any means of escape.

Human beings are themselves considered consumer goods to be used and then discarded. We have created a "throw away" culture which is now spreading. It is no longer simply about exploitation and oppression, but something new. Exclusion ultimately has to do with what it means to be a part of the society in which we live; those excluded are no longer society's underside or its fringes or its disenfranchised—they are no longer even a part of it. The excluded are not the "exploited" but the outcast, the "leftovers".

54. In this context, some people continue to defend trickle-down theories which assume that economic growth, encouraged by a free market, will inevitably succeed in bringing about greater justice and inclusiveness in the world. This opinion, which has never been confirmed by the facts, expresses a crude and naïve trust in the goodness of those wielding economic power and in the sacralized workings of the prevailing economic system. Meanwhile, the excluded are still waiting. To sustain a lifestyle which excludes others, or to sustain enthusiasm for that selfish ideal, a globalization of indifference has developed. Almost without being aware of it, we end up being incapable of feeling compassion at the outcry of the poor, weeping for other people's pain, and feeling a need to help them, as though all this were someone else's responsibility and not our own. The culture of prosperity deadens us; we are thrilled if the market offers us something new to purchase. In the meantime all those lives stunted for lack of opportunity seem a mere spectacle; they fail to move us.

55. One cause of this situation is found in our relationship with money, since we calmly accept its dominion over ourselves and our societies. The current financial crisis can make us overlook the fact that it originated in a profound human crisis: the denial of the primacy of the human person! We have created new idols. The worship of the ancient golden calf (cf. Ex 32:1-35) has returned in a new and ruthless guise in the idolatry of money and the dictatorship of an impersonal economy lacking a truly human purpose. The worldwide crisis affecting finance and the economy lays bare their imbalances and, above all, their lack of real concern for human beings; man is reduced to one of his needs alone: consumption.

56. While the earnings of a minority are growing exponentially, so too is the gap separating the majority from the prosperity enjoyed by those happy few. This imbalance is the result of ideologies which defend the absolute autonomy of the marketplace and financial speculation. Consequently, they reject the right of states, charged with vigilance for the common good, to exercise any form of control. A

new tyranny is thus born, invisible and often virtual, which unilaterally and relentlessly imposes its own laws and rules. Debt and the accumulation of interest also make it difficult for countries to realize the potential of their own economies and keep citizens from enjoying their real purchasing power. To all this we can add widespread corruption and self-serving tax evasion, which have taken on worldwide dimensions. The thirst for power and possessions knows no limits. In this system, which tends to devour everything which stands in the way of increased profits, whatever is fragile, like the environment, is defenseless before the interests of a deified market, which become the only rule.

....

58. A financial reform open to such ethical considerations would require a vigorous change of approach on the part of political leaders. I urge them to face this challenge with determination and an eye to the future, while not ignoring, of course, the specifics of each case. Money must serve, not rule! The Pope loves everyone, rich and poor alike, but he is obliged in the name of Christ to remind all that the rich must help, respect and promote the poor. I exhort you to generous solidarity and to the return of economics and finance to an ethical approach which favours human beings.

....

60. Today's economic mechanisms promote inordinate consumption, yet it is evident that unbridled consumerism combined with inequality proves doubly damaging to the social fabric. Inequality eventually engenders a violence which recourse to arms cannot and never will be able to resolve. It serves only to offer false hopes to those clamouring for heightened security, even though nowadays we know that weapons and violence, rather than providing solutions, create new and more serious conflicts. Some simply content themselves with blaming the poor and the poorer countries themselves for their troubles; indulging in unwarranted generalizations, they claim that the solution is an "education" that would tranquilize them, making them tame and harmless. All this becomes even more exasperating for the marginalized in the light of the

widespread and deeply rooted corruption found in many countries—in their governments, businesses and institutions—whatever the political ideology of their leaders.

....

202. The need to resolve the structural causes of poverty cannot be delayed, not only for the pragmatic reason of its urgency for the good order of society, but because society needs to be cured of a sickness which is weakening and frustrating it, and which can only lead to new crises. Welfare projects, which meet certain urgent needs, should be considered merely temporary responses. As long as the problems of the poor are not radically resolved by rejecting the absolute autonomy of markets and financial speculation and by attacking the structural causes of inequality,[1] no solution will be found for the world's problems or, for that matter, to any problems. Inequality is the root of social ills.

203. The dignity of each human person and the pursuit of the common good are concerns which ought to shape all economic policies. At times, however, they seem to be a mere addendum imported from without in order to fill out a political discourse lacking in perspectives or plans for true and integral development. How many words prove irksome to this system! It is irksome when the question of ethics is raised, when global solidarity is invoked, when the distribution of goods is mentioned, when reference is made to protecting labour and defending the dignity of the powerless, when allusion is made to a God who demands a commitment to justice. At other times these issues are exploited by a rhetoric which cheapens them. Casual indifference in the face of such questions empties our lives and our words of all meaning. Business is a vocation, and a noble vocation, provided that those engaged in it see themselves challenged by a greater meaning in life; this will enable them truly to serve the common good by striving to increase the goods of this world and to make them more accessible to all.

204. We can no longer trust in the unseen forces and the invisible hand of the market. Growth in justice requires more than economic growth, while presupposing such growth: it requires decisions,

programmes, mechanisms and processes specifically geared to a better distribution of income, the creation of sources of employment and an integral promotion of the poor which goes beyond a simple welfare mentality. I am far from proposing an irresponsible populism, but the economy can no longer turn to remedies that are a new poison, such as attempting to increase profits by reducing the work force and thereby adding to the ranks of the excluded.

. . . .

206. Economy, as the very word indicates, should be the art of achieving a fitting management of our common home, which is the world as a whole. Each meaningful economic decision made in one part of the world has repercussions everywhere else; consequently, no government can act without regard for shared responsibility. Indeed, it is becoming increasingly difficult to find local solutions for enormous global problems which overwhelm local politics with difficulties to resolve. If we really want to achieve a healthy world economy, what is needed at this juncture of history is a more efficient way of interacting which, with due regard for the sovereignty of each nation, ensures the economic well-being of all countries, not just of a few.

NOTES

1. This implies a commitment to "eliminate the structural causes of global economic dysfunction": Benedict XVI, *Address to the Diplomatic Corps* (8 January 2007): AAS 99 (2007), p. 73.

REVIEW EXERCISES

1. Consider the morality of the sorts of economic inequalities discussed in this chapter; are they justifiable?
2. What is the difference between a process view of distributive justice and an end-state view?
3. Discuss the meaning and problems associated with using the end-state view criteria of merit, achievement, effort, and contribution.
4. What is the literal meaning of *equal opportunity*? What criterion does James Fishkin use for judging whether it exists? What is Bernard Williams's "starting-gate theory" of equal opportunity?
5. Describe some problems raised by philosophers Frankfurt and Schaar regarding equal opportunity.
6. Summarize the libertarian position on liberty and the role of government.
7. What are the basic differences between capitalism and socialism as social and economic theories?
8. What is Rawls's *original position*, and what role does it play in his derivation of principles of justice?
9. What is Rawls's "maximin" principle, and how is it related to his second principle of justice?
10. How does communitarianism differ from liberalism?

DISCUSSION CASES

1. **The Homeless.** Joe was laid off two years ago from the auto repair company where he had worked for fifteen years. For the first year, he tried to get another job. He read the want ads and left applications at local employment agencies. After that, he gave up. He had little savings and soon had no money for rent. He has been homeless now for a year. He will not live in the shelters because they are crowded, noisy, and unsafe. As time goes by, he has less and less chance of getting back to where he was before. When he can, he drinks to forget the past and escape from the present. Other people he meets on the streets are developmentally disabled or psychologically disturbed. He realizes that the city offers some things to try to help people like him, but there is little money and the number of homeless people seem to be growing. Does society have any responsibility to do anything for people like Joe? Why or why not? What ethical principles might be relevant to this situation?

2. **Rights to Keep What One Earns.** Gene and his coworkers have been talking over lunch about how their taxes have continued to rise. Some complain that the harder they work, the less they are making. Others are upset because their taxes are going to pay for things that they do not believe the government should support with their tax dollars—the arts, for example. "Why should we support museums or arts programs in public schools when we don't use these services?" they ask. They argue these should be matters for charity. They also complain that they work hard but that their income is being used to take care of others who could work but do not.

   Are they right? Why or why not?

3. **Inequality.** Stephanie and Peyton are working the midnight shift at a fast-food restaurant, where they make slightly above the national minimum wage. Business is slow, and they begin discussing income inequality after a Mercedes SUV full of college-aged kids comes through the drive-thru for burgers and shakes. Stephanie believes that the growing disparity between the rich and the poor is wrong: "It's just not fair that people like us are poor and often out of work, while millionaires and their kids are living large." Peyton is not so sure. "Well, millionaires work hard for their money. They deserve to enjoy the fruit of their labors." Stephanie says, "But we work hard too. I could work forever at this minimum wage job and never get ahead. Most rich people start out with an advantage, go to a good college, and then get richer. And that's not fair." Peyton responds, "It may not be fair, but capitalism is the only system that works, and everyone deserves a chance to get rich. Would you prefer a communist system where nobody has that chance?" Stephanie shrugs. "Maybe not communism," she replies. "But I say we should tax the rich more heavily and use that money to reduce the burden on the poor and unemployed." Peyton shakes his head. "Do that and you'll ruin our country."

   Whose side are you on? Do you agree with Stephanie or with Peyton? Is there a third alternative? Explain your answer with specific concepts discussed in this chapter.

MindTap® **For more chapter resources and activities, go to MindTap.**

Punishment and the Death Penalty

Lou Oates/iStock/Thinkstock

Learning Outcomes

After reading this chapter, you should be able to:

- Cite incarceration rates and execution practices in the United States and elsewhere.
- Describe the problem of racial disparities in the punishment system.
- Explain key terms such as *deterrence*, *prevention*, *retributive justice*, and *restorative justice*.
- Evaluate moral arguments about punishment, prison, and the death penalty.

- Apply consequentialist and non-consequentialist arguments to the issue of punishment.
- Differentiate between legal punishment and other forms of punishment.
- Apply the ideas about the death penalty described by Mill and Kant.
- Defend your own ideas about punishment and the death penalty.

MindTap® For more chapter resources and activities, go to MindTap.

In the past half-century, the incarceration rate in the United States has increased by a factor of seven.[1] In the United States, many people are in jails, prisons, and under correctional supervision. According to the U.S. Bureau of Justice Statistics, at the end of 2014 (the most recent year for which complete data were available), over 2.2 million people were incarcerated (in federal and state prisons and local jails)—the prison population (for individuals *sentenced* and not simply held until trial) was about 1.5 million. Including probation and parole, correctional authorities supervised about 6.8 million offenders as of year-end 2014, which was down slightly from a high of almost 7 million in 2011.[2] This means that more than 2 percent of the U.S. population is under some form of correctional supervision (including probation and alternatives to incarceration). In raw numbers, the United States has the world's largest prison population. Of the 10.35 million people in prisons and jails around the world, about 20 percent of them are in American prisons.[3]

In more recent years, there has been a slow decline in incarceration rates, due in part to budget pressures on state governments and also due to political pressure to reduce the prison population in light of these startling statistics. But the problem of "mass incarceration" remains a significant one, including racial disparities in incarceration rates. According to the Bureau of Justice Statistics, in 2014, nearly 3 percent of black males were in prison and 1 percent of Hispanic males were in prison (compared to 0.5 percent for non-Hispanic white males).[4] Of those incarcerated, 37 percent were black males; 32 percent were white males; and 22 percent were Hispanic males. Critics have argued that there is something wrong with a society that locks away so many people, many of them people of color.

The public is concerned about crime. Every day, it seems, we hear stories of horrible violence. School shootings, kidnappings, rapes, and other violent crimes flood the headlines. Horrendous crimes have occurred at Columbine, in Colorado; at Virginia Tech; in Newtown, Connecticut; at the Boston Marathon; in San Bernardino, California; in Orlando, Florida and elsewhere. In many cases, the perpetrators of mass atrocity have wound up dead—either killing themselves or being killed by police. If mass murderers are captured alive, is it appropriate to sentence them to death? We tend to assume that police, in the heat of the moment, are entitled to kill dangerous criminals, without a trial, in order to protect themselves or the general public. But can that justification of lethal violence be extended to a justification of the death penalty, which is carried out after a legal trial and subsequent appeals long after the original crime occurred? More and more states are moving to abolish the death penalty. But would the death penalty be justifiable in cases of mass murder or terrorism?

While horrific crimes can make us feel insecure, the good news is that crime, in general, is down in the United States. The murder rate has fallen from 8 per 100,000 in 1995 to 4.5 per 100,000 in 2014.[5] In New York City, the home of more than eight million people, there have even been days in recent years when no one at all has been murdered.[6] Some American cities still have significant crime problems, but nationwide, there is a general downward trend in violent crime. There is also a trend toward less violent forms of punishment. Although American authorities used torture on suspects in the "war on terrorism" following September 11, the Supreme Court has restricted the use of the death penalty (for example, it has forbidden the practice when the convicted is mentally retarded or a minor at the time

the crime was committed), and some states have abolished capital punishment altogether. As of early 2016, nineteen states have eliminated capital punishment, including Nebraska, which abolished the death penalty in 2015.[7]

So why is crime down? Experts debate the reasons for this. It may have something to do with economics and opportunities. Or it may have something to do with our massive prison system and the huge numbers of people incarcerated in it. It may have to do with the epidemiology of drug addiction. Or it may have to do with aggressive policing—for example, the use of "stop-and-frisk" techniques. On the other hand, it may have to do with more engaged community policing and grassroots neighborhood activism. Perhaps it has to do with the success of social welfare programs, which provide hope, opportunities, and alternatives to crime and violence. At least one expert, economist Steven Levitt, has claimed that the decline in crime may have something to do with the legalization of abortion, which prevents the birth of unwanted children.[8] A more recent theory is that the decrease in crime may be a result of decreasing levels of lead in the atmosphere. According to this view, the lead produced by old-fashioned leaded gasoline—which causes neurological and behavioral problems—may have produced the rise in violence and deviance that peaked in the 1990s.[9]

Some worry that as we get soft on crime, rates will rise. It could be that rates declined in past decades because so many people are already in prison. Prison reform movements and the use of alternatives to incarceration may impact future crime rates. Some argue that recent data indicating an upswing in crime can be chalked up to sentencing reform and a general tendency toward a lenient crime policy.[10]

This discussion makes use of a basic utilitarian approach to punishment. For utilitarians, punishment prevents crime. Some defend the death penalty, for example, by claiming that capital punishment has a strong deterrent effect. Others defend long prison sentences by arguing that this increases public safety by keeping criminals off the street. But utilitarian reasoning can reach different conclusions—if the death penalty does not deter crime, or if there are equally useful (and cheaper) alternatives to incarceration. A different approach focuses on deontological or natural law claims about the demand for retributive justice and retaliation. The thinking is that maybe murderers simply deserve to be executed, and thieves and rapists deserve long prison sentences. The question of "desert" is quite different from the question of what works. This chapter will consider justifications for punishment such as these.

Moral questions abound with regard to punishment. How do we determine appropriate sentences for criminals, converting such disparate crimes as shoplifting, selling drugs, and murder into the common currency of months and years in prison? And while some argue against the death penalty in favor of life imprisonment without the possibility of parole, we may wonder whether it remains useful to keep seventy-year-olds in prison for crimes committed half a century ago. We might also wonder why taxpayer dollars should be used to keep people in prison, feeding and housing them for decades, while the victims of crime have to fend for themselves and pay their bills just like anyone else. Other moral questions might focus on the conditions in prison—for example, whether it is cruel to use solitary confinement in supermax facilities as a way to control the worst criminals. We might also be concerned about the impact of prison or the death penalty on the families and communities of those who are imprisoned or executed. Further, we may consider whether there are ways to rehabilitate criminals and restore communities that are broken by crime.

THE NATURE OF LEGAL PUNISHMENT

To know what to think about the ethics of prison and the death penalty, we need to first examine some of the reasons that have been given for the practice of legal punishment. Our focus is not *any* sort of punishment, but rather, only legal punishment. Eight-year-old Jimmy's parents can punish him with no TV for a week for a failing grade, and I can punish myself for a caloric indulgence by spending twice as much time at the gym—but these punishments

are not legal. Legal punishment, in common with parental and self-punishment, is designed to "hurt"; if something is gladly accepted or enjoyed, then it is not really punishment. The most visible form of legal criminal punishment is imprisonment. Other forms include fines and court-mandated community service.

However, legal punishment is distinct from other forms of punishment in several respects. Legal punishment must follow legal rules of some sort. It is authorized by a legal entity and follows a set of rules that establish who is to be punished, how, and by how much. Lynching is not a legal punishment since it is carried out by a mob and not by a constituted authority. Furthermore, to be punished within the legal system, you must first commit the crime or be suspected of it. Whatever we say about the justification of detaining people before they commit (or we think they will commit) a crime, it is not punishment. Punishment of any sort presumes someone has done something to merit the penalty. In the case of legal punishment, it is a penalty for doing what the law forbids. Criminal law, by its very nature, must have some sanction, some threat attached to breaking it, or else it loses its force. Without such force, it may be a request, but it is not law.

Thus, we can say that legal punishment is the state's infliction of harm or pain on those who break the law, according to a set of legally established rules. But is such a practice justified? What gives a society the right to inflict the pain of punishment on any of its members? In asking this, we are asking a moral and not just a legal question. Is legal punishment of any sort morally justifiable? If so, why?

Traditional approaches to the justification of punishment focus on **deterrence** and prevention, or the idea of **retributive justice** and just deserts. When we say a punishment *deters*, we mean that it prevents other crimes in the future. When we speak of *retribution*, we mean making wrongdoers somehow pay for the crimes they have committed. But it is important to note that an alternative to these approaches can be found in the ideas of rehabilitation, crime prevention, and restorative justice. These approaches aim to transform the social situation in ways that minimize the need for punishment. While restorative justice is an important idea, it is not exactly "punishment," but rather an alternative to punishment. The traditional justifications for punishment focus either on utilitarian concerns about preventing and deterring crime, or on natural law or deontological ideas about the need for just retribution. We will turn to utilitarian arguments first.

THE DETERRENCE ARGUMENT

One answer to the question of whether legal punishment is morally justifiable is, "Yes, if (and only if) the punishment could be fashioned to prevent or deter crime." The general idea involved in this first rationale for legal punishment is related to both the nature of law and its purpose. For a criminal law to be a law, and not just a request, sanctions must be attached to it. It must have force behind it. Further, law has many possible purposes, and one purpose is to prevent people from harming others. Since our laws presumably are directed to achieving some good, penalties for breaking these laws should help ensure that the good intended by the laws will be achieved. Of course, not all laws are good laws. However, the idea is that we want not only to have good laws, but also to have them enforced in ways that make them effective.

The purpose of legal punishment, according to this reasoning, is to prevent people from breaking the law, deter them from doing so, or both. As such, this is a forward-looking, consequentialist rationale. In terms of prevention, crime is prevented when would-be or actual criminals are arrested and held somewhere so that they cannot do social damage. We also can prevent crime by other means such as increased street lighting, more police officers, and so on. In terms of deterrence, we deter crime by holding out a punishment as a threat, which persuades would-be criminals not to break the law. If a punishment works as a deterrent, then it works in a particular way through the would-be lawbreaker's thinking and decision-making processes. One considers the possibility of being punished for doing some contemplated action and concludes that the gain achieved from the act is not worth the price to be paid, namely, the punishment. Then, one acts accordingly.

If deterrence works as described above, we can readily identify certain circumstances in which it is not likely to succeed in preventing crime. For instance, deterrence is not likely to prevent crimes of passion, in which people are overcome by strong emotions. They are not in the mood to calculate the risks and benefits of what they're about to do and unlikely to stop themselves from continuing to act as they will. The threat of punishment is also not likely to work in cases in which people *do* calculate the risks and the benefits and decide the benefits are greater than the risks. These would be cases in which the risks of being caught and punished are perceived as small, and the reward or benefit is perceived as great. The benefit could be financial, status-oriented, or even the reward of having done what one believed to be right as in acts of civil disobedience or in support of any cause, whether actually good or bad. Although punishment does not deter in some cases, in others, presumably, it does. A system of legal punishment is worthwhile if it works for the great majority, even if not for all, and if bad consequences do not outweigh good ones.

The deterrence rationale for legal punishment raises a more general issue about any utilitarian perspective on punishment, which relies on weighing costs and benefits. In this view, punishment is *externally related* to lawbreaking. In other words, it is not essential. If something else works better than punishment, then that other means ought to be used, either as a substitution for punishment or in addition to it. Some people argue that punishment itself does not work, but might only be effective when combined with rehabilitation, psychological counseling, and perhaps even job training or placement. However, if a punishment system is not working, then, in this view, it is not morally justifiable, for the whole idea is not to punish for punishment's sake but to achieve the goal of law enforcement. On utilitarian grounds, pain is never good in itself. Thus, if punishment involves suffering, it must be justified. The suffering must be outweighed by the good to be achieved by it.

One problem is that if deterrence is the sole ground of legal punishment, we might seem to be justified in using extreme measures to achieve the desired deterrent effect—if these measures work better than less extreme ones. Suppose that a community has a particularly vexing problem with graffiti. To get rid of the problem, suppose the community decides to institute a program in which it randomly picks up members of particular gangs believed to be responsible for the graffiti and punishes these individuals with floggings in the public square. Or suppose that cutting off their hands would work better! We would surely have serious moral objections to this program. One objection would be that these particular individuals may not have been responsible for the graffiti; they were just picked because of their gang affiliation. Another objection would be that the punishment seems out of proportion to the offense. However, on deterrence grounds, there would be nothing essentially wrong with such punishments. What is crucial for the deterrence argument is whether the punishment worked or worked better than alternative forms, not whether the individual is guilty or the punishment fits the crime.

Another version of the deterrence argument that we might evaluate has to do with how deterrence is supposed to work. According to this view, legal punishment is part of a system of social moral education. A society has a particular set of values, and one way to instill those values in its members from their youth is to establish punishments for those who undermine them. If private property is valued, then society should punish those who damage or take others' property. These punishments would act as deterrents, helping individuals to internalize social values and giving them internal prohibitions against violating those values. Key to evaluating this view is determining whether punishment actually works in this fashion. What does punishment teach us? Does it help us internalize values, and does it motivate us? The way the system is administered also can send a message, and in some cases, it might be the wrong message. For example, if legal punishment is not applied fairly or equally, what might people learn?

THE RETRIBUTIVIST ARGUMENT

The second primary rationale for legal punishment is retribution. In the retributivist view, legal punishment is intended to make those who are responsible for a crime pay for it. As such, it is a backward-looking argument because it is based on past actions. This idea can be understood from a natural law or deontological perspective. The natural law approach maintains that it is only fair or right for a criminal to pay for what he or she has damaged, and as Locke suggests in his *Second Treatise on Government* (discussed in Chapter 7), there is a natural right to repayment. A retributivist might say that when someone harms another, it is only just or fair that he or she suffer similarly or proportionately to the harm or pain he or she caused the other person. Or we might say that a criminal deserves to suffer because he or she made his or her victim suffer; the punishment is deserved as fair recompense. In this view, punishment is *internally related* to the wrongful conduct. In a sense, the punishment "fits the crime." From the retributivist standpoint, one cannot say that if something else works better than punishment, then that is what ought to be done. The concern here is not what works but, rather, what is right. Indeed, retributivists might also maintain that punishment is required as a matter of duty; from a deontological standpoint, we ought to punish people who do wrong because they *deserve* to be punished. From this perspective, it would be wrong not to punish criminals, since failing to punish them would give them less than what they deserve.

This approach is based on a somewhat abstract notion of justice. We punish to right a wrong or restore some original state, or to reset the scales of justice. However, in many cases, we cannot really undo the suffering of the victim by making the perpetrator suffer. One can pay back stolen money or return stolen property. But even in these cases, there are other harms that cannot be undone, such as the victim's lost sense of privacy or security. Thus, the erasing, undoing, or righting of the wrong is of some other abstract or metaphysical type. It may be difficult to explain, but supporters of this rationale for punishment believe that we do have some intuitive sense of what we mean when we say "justice was done."

According to the retributivist view, payment must be made in some way that is equivalent to the crime or harm done. Philosophers distinguish two senses of equivalency: an *egalitarian* sense and a *proportional* sense. With egalitarian equivalency, one is required to pay back something identical or almost identical to what was taken. If you make someone suffer for two days, then you should suffer for two days. It would also mean that if you caused someone's arm to be amputated, then your arm should be cut off as well. This version of retributivism is often given the label *lex talionis*. Translated, it means the "law of the talon" (as among birds of prey). We also call egalitarian equivalency the "law of the jungle" or taking "an eye for an eye."

Proportional equivalency holds that what is required by punishment is not something more or less identical to the harm done or pain caused, but something proportional. In this version, we can think of harms or wrongs as matters of degree, namely, of bad, worse, and worst. Punishments are also scaled from the minimal to the most severe. In this view, punishment must be proportional to the degree of the seriousness of the crime.

Obviously, there are serious problems, both practical and moral, with the *lex talionis* version of the retributivist view. In some cases—for example, in the case of multiple murders—it is not possible to deliver something equal to the harm done, for one cannot kill the murderer more than once. Presumably, we would also have some moral problems with torturing a torturer or raping a rapist.

We should notice that the retributivist justification of legal punishment responds to two major problems with the deterrence argument, namely that deterrence-focused punishments need not punish actual criminals or be proportional to crimes. By contrast, if retributivist punishments are to be just, they must fit both the perpetrators and the crimes.

First, only those who are responsible for a crime should be punished: guilt must be proved, and we should not single out likely suspects or representatives of a group to make examples of them or use them to intimidate other group members, as in our graffiti example. It is also important that the punishment fit the person in terms of the degree of his or her responsibility. This requirement would address concerns we have about differentiating between criminals and their accomplices and also about the mental state of a criminal. Diminished mental capacity, mitigating circumstances, and duress—which lessen a person's responsibility—are significant elements of the U.S. criminal punishment system.

Second, it is essential in the retributivist view that the punishment fit the crime. Defacing property is not a major wrong or harm and thus should not be punished with amputation of the perpetrator's hand, however well that might work to deter graffiti. Thus, this view requires that we have a sense of what is more or less serious among crimes and also among punishments so that they can be well matched.

It is because the punishment should fit the crime that many people argue against the "three-strikes" laws that several states have passed. These laws mandate life imprisonment for anyone with two previous convictions for serious crimes who is then found guilty of a third felony. In California in 2012, voters overturned the state's three-strikes law. Opponents had noted that in some cases the third "strike" was merely petty theft—a felony charge for anyone who had already served a prison sentence for theft. A life sentence looks quite out of proportion to such infractions. On the other side, however, consequentialists might support three-strikes laws, arguing that it is better for all of us when people who have a history of lawbreaking are removed from society and prevented from continuing in such behavior.

As with the deterrence argument, one might raise objections against the retributivist argument. We have already referred to one: that punishing the perpetrator does not concretely undo the wrong done to the victim. Those who defend retributivism would have to explain in what sense the balance is restored or the wrong righted by punishment. However, the retributivist would not have any problem with those who point out that a particular form of punishment does not work. According to a retributivist, this is not the primary reason to punish. A perpetrator should be punished as a way of achieving satisfaction or restitution, even if it does the perpetrator or others no good.

A more common objection to the retributivist view is that it amounts to condoning revenge. To know whether or not this is true, we would have to clarify what we mean by *revenge*. Suppose we mean that particular people—say a victim or his or her family—will get a sense of satisfaction in seeing the wrongdoer punished. This sense of satisfaction is merely contingent and psychological—a matter of feelings. We may not want a system of legal punishment to be used to satisfy merely personal feelings of vengeance or resentment. But the retributivist view is not about our feelings. Indeed, if we have a duty to punish on retributivist grounds, we ought to carry out the punishment, even if we do not feel inclined to do so (perhaps because we are squeamish about carrying out a particular punishment). Retributive justice requires that justice be done, whether or not people feel good about it. However, some may question whether any type of justice exists that is not a matter of providing emotional satisfaction to victims or others who are enraged by a wrong done to them.

Finally, we can wonder whether the retributivist view provides a good basis for a system of legal punishment. Is the primary purpose of such a system to see that justice is done? Do we not have a system of legal punishment to ensure social order and safety? If so, then it would seem that the deterrence argument is the best reason for having any system of legal punishment.

One solution to the problem of whether to use deterrence or retribution to justify legal punishment is to use both.[11] In designing such a hybrid system, we could retain consequentialist reasons for having a legal punishment system, and consider first what works best to deter and prevent crimes. However, we could also use retributivist standards to determine who is punished (only those who are guilty and only to the extent that they are guilty) and by how much (the punishment fitting the crime). In fashioning the punishment system, however, there may be times when we need to determine which rationale takes precedence. For example, in setting requirements for conviction of guilt, we may need to know how bad it is to punish an innocent person. We may decide to give precedence to the retributivist rationale and then make the requirements for conviction of guilt very strenuous, requiring unanimous jury verdicts and guilt beyond a reasonable doubt. In doing so, we also let some guilty people go free and thus run the risk of lessening the deterrent effect of the punishment system. Or we may decide to give precedence to the deterrence rationale. Thus, we may weaken the requirements for conviction so that we may catch and punish a greater number of guilty people. In doing so, however, we run the risk of also punishing a greater number of innocent persons.

PUNISHMENT AND RESPONSIBILITY

A key element of our legal punishment system and practice is the link between punishment and responsibility. The retributivist believes responsibility is essential for punishment, and thus, it is unjust to punish those who are not responsible for a crime. This concept can also be supported on deterrence grounds; it probably would work better to punish only those who are responsible for crimes, since this focuses punishment in a way that encourages obedience to the law.

Our legal system allows for defenses that appeal to the question of responsibility. For example, under the defense of *duress*, we would probably say a person was not responsible if he or she were forced to commit a crime, either physically forced or under threat to life. He or she may have committed the crime, but that is not enough to prove that he or she was responsible. (We do not have a system of strict liability, in which the only issue is whether or not you actually did or caused something.)

One of the most problematic defenses in our criminal justice system may well be the insanity defense. It involves a plea and a finding of "not guilty by reason of insanity," or something similar such as "mental defect." Another verdict available in some jurisdictions is that the defendant is "guilty but mentally ill." The difference between these two ways of conceiving crime, guilt, and mental illness is significant. Is someone *guilty but mentally ill* or is he or she *not guilty* because of his or her mental illness? This points toward a deep question about responsibility and guilt. We presume that people ought to know the difference between right and wrong in order to be held responsible for their actions, and that a responsible person has the capacity to control his or her own behavior. There have been a variety of standards for describing responsibility and guilt, and their connection with mental competence. One significant event in the evolution of these standards in the United States was the trial of John Hinckley Jr., who shot President Ronald Reagan and two other individuals in 1981. Hinckley was found not guilty by reason of insanity and confined to a hospital. In response, there was a backlash against the insanity defense, with some states—Idaho, Montana, and Utah—abolishing it altogether. States that retain some version of the insanity defense have different standards for determining mental illness. One common standard has roots in nineteenth-century England, with the *M'Naghten Rule* (1843). According to this rule, people are not responsible for their actions if they did not know what they were doing or did not know that it was wrong. This is often referred to as the "right from wrong test." Since that time, other attempts have been made to list the conditions under which people should not be held responsible for their actions. One example is the "irresistible impulse test." The idea underlying this test for insanity is that sometimes persons are not able to control their conduct and thus act through no fault of their own. The moral question of responsibility and guilt rests upon our capacity to understand right from wrong and the ability to control our own behavior.

Common criticisms of the insanity defense concern our ability to determine whether someone is mentally insane or incompetent. Can't someone feign this? How do psychiatrists or other experts determine whether a person knows what he or she is doing? Even if we could diagnose these conditions with absolute certainty, a more basic question would still remain, namely, would the conditions diminish or take away responsibility? If so, then would punishment be appropriate? In the extreme case in

which a person has a serious brain condition that prevents normal mental function, we assume that this would excuse him or her from full responsibility. However, he or she may be dangerous, and this may be another reason to detain as well as treat him or her.

Some people have criticized the entire notion of mental illness, especially as it is used in criminal proceedings. For example, it may result in indeterminate sentences for minor crimes because one must remain in custody in a criminal mental institution until sane. One longtime critic of the penal system, Thomas Szasz, holds that we have sometimes used the diagnosis of mental illness to categorize and stigmatize people who are simply different.[12] He finds this diagnosis often to be a dangerous form of social control. Another significant concern here is indefinite civil commitment for sex offenders. In some states in the United States, sexual predators who continue to report having violent sexual thoughts can be detained indefinitely out of suspicion that they will commit a crime.[13] But does it make sense to confine people for their thoughts when they have not yet committed a crime?

Some of us tend to look at heinous crimes and say, "No sane person could have done that!" Or we might say that a certain crime was "sick." We use the horror of the crime, its serious wrongness, to conclude that the person committing it must be mentally diseased. One problem with this conclusion is that it implies that the person is not responsible, since mental competence is a requirement for criminal liability. Are we then implying that people who do evil things are not responsible for what they do? If so, then perhaps they should not be punished. The connection between punishment and responsibility is not only central to our system of legal punishment, but it is also an important element of the morality of legal punishment.

Underlying this discussion of responsibility is a metaphysical account of free will. We hold people responsible for things that they freely choose to do. But, of course, there are deep questions here. Are we really free? Or are our actions determined by genetics, by social context, and by the laws of physics? If our actions are entirely determined, then we are not entirely responsible for what we do (in the sense that we could not have done otherwise). If we are not free, then it would seem that punishment as such (at least in the retributive sense of giving someone what was due to them) would never be appropriate. Our legal system normally assumes that we have free will and treats criminals accordingly. But social context and physiological factors can mitigate responsibility and guilt.

Advocates of rehabilitation and alternatives to punishment often focus on the issue of social context, arguing that instead of seeking retribution, we should work to change the social conditions that cause crime. From a consequentialist perspective, if drug-treatment programs or job-training programs in prison would help reduce crime, then those programs would be morally recommended. From a non-consequentialist perspective, there might also be grounds for promoting such programs. One might want to consider whether persons ought to be given a second chance in light of the fact that, given certain circumstances, they might not have been fully responsible for their crimes. On the other hand, those who argue from a consequentialist perspective might point out that in certain kinds of cases—say, with sexual predators—there is not much likelihood of reform. Similarly, from a non-consequentialist perspective, some might argue that given the severity of certain crimes, persons deserve the strictest and most severe punishment, not a second chance.

PRISONS

We mentioned at the outset of this chapter that U.S. crime rates have fallen in recent years. Although it is difficult to establish any single reason that crime is down, one fact may be that more people are in prison. If deterrence is one of the primary purposes of punishment, we might conclude that the prison system is doing a good job. However, the U.S. incarceration system has generated serious charges of injustice and inefficiency. One concern is the cost and extent of the American prison system. Another worry is racial and other disparities in rates of

incarceration, as we also mentioned previously. Still others argue that rehabilitation or restorative justice could provide a more effective and humane alternative to prison. Some have argued for prison reform and for finding alternatives to incarceration. Others have strongly criticized what they call "the prison industrial complex" (which includes the so-called school to prison pipeline and the way that prison funding is tightly woven into state budgets). The most radical suggestions aim at **decarceration**, the idea of eliminating prison as a form of punishment (or at least radically reducing the use of prisons).

The number of people incarcerated in the United States dwarfs that of other countries, amounting to about 20 percent of the world's entire prison population. The World Prison Brief estimates that the United States has an incarceration rate of 698 per 100,000 people (based on 2013 data). This has declined from a peak of more than 750 per 100,000 in 2008.[14] But the U.S. incarceration rate is substantially higher than other countries with large prison populations. China comes in second in terms of prison population—but China has a relatively modest incarceration rate, given the country's size, of 118 per 100,000. Russia ranks third in prison population, with an incarceration rate of 442 per 100,000. In the United States, there are also racial disparities in rates of incarceration, as mentioned previously. The Bureau of Justice Statistics summarized some of the 2014 data on race as follows:

Imprisonment rates for black males were 3.8 to 10.5 times greater for each age group than white males and 1.4 to 3.1 times greater than rates for Hispanic males. The largest disparity between white and black male prisoners occurred among inmates ages 18 to 19. Black males (1,072 prisoners per 100,000 black male residents ages 18 to 19) were more than ten times likelier to be in state or federal prison than whites (102 per 100,000).[15]

There are various reasons for the high rate of incarceration in the United States. The causes most often cited are mandatory sentences for drug crimes, an increase in the number of so-called three-strikes violations, and truth-in-sentencing laws that lessen the number of prisoners released early.[16]

Also mentioned are democratically elected judges, as they may "yield to populist demands for tough justice."[17] There is also the issue of gun ownership and the easy availability of guns. Some claim that gun ownership could decrease crime by empowering citizens to defend themselves, while others claim that the high number of guns available in the United States exacerbates the problem of crime. While some see high incarceration rates as a justifiable response to the threat of violent crime, critics argue that the prison system reinforces a legacy of racial and class division in the United States.

Although many prisoners are incarcerated for having committed violent crimes, more than half are nonviolent, mostly drug-related, offenders. Moreover, it is estimated that some 16 percent of the prison population suffers from mental illness.[18] A report on prisons from 2006 warned that the experience of prisoners is too often marked by "rape, gang violence, abuse by officers, infectious disease, and never-ending solitary confinement."[19] In 2013, Human Rights Watch concluded that the American prison system was suffering from problems caused by "massive overincarceration" resulting from harsh sentencing practices that were "contrary to international law." Problems include a growing population of elderly prisoners, the incarceration of children in adult facilities, and the use of solitary confinement.[20]

The average annual cost to incarcerate an inmate in the United States in 2014 was about $31,000.[21] In some states—New York, Washington, and Connecticut—the cost is estimated at $50,000 to $60,000 per inmate.[22] When multiplied by the nearly seven million inmates in the United States, the total annual cost of our prison system is staggering. Out of all states, California has the highest overall expenditure on prisons. With a prison population of more than 167,000 and a cost per inmate of $47,421, the total annual cost in California is more than $7.9 billion. In 2011, the amount of money California spent on prisons exceeded the amount it spent on higher education.[23] This prompted former Gov. Arnold Schwarzenegger to opine, "the priorities have become out of whack over the years.... What does it say about any state that focuses more on

prison uniforms than on caps and gowns?"[24] The comparison serves as a reminder that budget priorities reflect ethical judgments. Are we spending too much on prisons? And is this spending working? We noted that crime is down. But recidivism rates for ex-cons remain high—one study from 2005 found recidivism rates between 67 and 75 percent.[25] Such seemingly conflicting facts further complicate cost-benefit analyses of the U.S. prison system.

Race

Other ethical concerns arise from the stark racial disparities in the criminal justice system. As we have seen, black and Hispanic males are imprisoned at dramatically higher rates than white non-Hispanic males. As stated at the outset of this chapter, in 2014, nearly 3 percent of black males were in prison and 1 percent of Hispanic males were in prison (compared to 0.5 percent for non-Hispanic white males).[26] Of those incarcerated, 37 percent were black males, 32 percent were white males, and 22 percent were Hispanic males. One issue here is that a disproportionate number of blacks and Hispanics are sentenced to prison on drug charges.[27] Furthermore, while all high school dropouts are at greater risk for being in prison, a 2007 report concluded that "by the time they reach their mid-thirties, a full 60 percent of black high-school dropouts are now prisoners or ex-cons."[28]

A widely quoted statistic holds that one in three black males will serve time in prison. That statistic is based on data from 2001. Prison rates have changed since then. A *Washington Post* report from 2015 suggested that the rate may have declined to 1 in 4.[29] But whether 30 percent or merely 25 percent of blacks serve time, these numbers are still significant.

There are political implications to the racial disparities in incarceration rates. For example, given that many states do not allow ex-felons to vote and that a high percentage of blacks vote Democratic, conviction and incarceration rates can have an impact on election outcomes. According to one estimate, and using conservative figures on voting, if ex-felons had been able to vote in the 2000 presidential election, Al Gore would have carried the state of Florida by 30,000 votes and, thus, would have won the Electoral College and the presidency.[30] Prison also tends to produce social stigma and disadvantage for ex-convicts and their families. Michelle Alexander, a civil rights advocate and law professor, suggests that these social costs have a racial complexion that has contributed to the creation of a new "Jim Crow" system. Alexander explains, "the criminalization and demonization of black men has turned the black community against itself, unraveling community and family relationships, decimating networks of support, and intensifying the shame and self-hate experienced by the current pariah caste."[31] (You can read an excerpt from Alexander's essay at the end of this chapter.)

Racial disparities in imprisonment are also linked to disparities in social class. Affluent people get better lawyers, while poor people are more likely to take a plea bargain, resulting in incarceration.[32] Some sociologists have noted that incarceration fosters social stratification, with imprisonment helping to define the experience of those in the so-called "underclass." Incarceration disrupts families. And it pushes convicts out of the labor market, depresses their wages, and undermines their long-term life prospects.[33] Although it is illegal to discriminate against ex-convicts, employers remain wary of hiring those with prison records.[34] From a perspective that takes equality and social justice concerns seriously (as discussed, for example, in Chapter 13), racial disparities in incarceration are a cause for further reflection.

Restoration and Rehabilitation

These sorts of issues have led some authors—such as Angela Davis, whom we will read at the end of this chapter—to argue that the current system of mass incarceration ought to be abolished. Davis is concerned with the way that racial, gender, and economic inequities show up in the prison system. She suggests that the prison system ought to be replaced with a system that is focused on principles of reparation, restoration, and rehabilitation, rather than on principles of retributive justice.

Related ideas have been defended by the U.S. Conference of Catholic Bishops, which maintains that the human dignity of crime victims and perpetrators should both be respected. The bishops note that "the status quo is not really working—victims are often ignored, offenders are often not rehabilitated, and many communities have lost their sense of security."[35] While not advocating for the abolition of prisons, the bishops emphasize "responsibility, rehabilitation, and restoration." They conclude,

> We respect the humanity and promote the human dignity of both victims and offenders. We believe society must protect its citizens from violence and crime and hold accountable those who break the law. These same principles lead us to advocate for rehabilitation and treatment for offenders, for, like victims, their lives reflect that same dignity. Both victims and perpetrators of crime are children of God.[36]

Such perspectives draw on the idea of **restorative justice**, which seeks to heal the wounds caused by crime, while finding a way to allow criminals to take responsibility, make amends, and restore the community that they have broken. Proponents of restorative justice admit that it is not appropriate for all crimes, especially in situations where offenders are unable or unwilling to take responsibility or make amends. But proponents argue that restorative justice can produce better outcomes for both victims and offenders, while also reducing recidivism.[37] Interest has been growing in restorative justice programs as ways of dealing with bullying and other forms of misbehavior in schools. Restorative justice programs have been developed for school systems in cities such as in Oakland, California, in which the goal is to build community and defuse conflict among students whose lives are impacted by violence.[38]

Restorative justice points toward a broader conception of social justice that aims to alter social conditions so that crime is prevented and its harms are minimized. The move toward restorative justice and away from prisons is often connected with religious groups that have a historical commitment to pacifism, such as the Quakers and the Mennonites.[39]

Key values in this approach include mercy and for-giveness, as well as justice.[40]

The most famous example of restorative justice is the "truth and reconciliation" process that occurred in the 1990s in South Africa. South Africa had suffered for decades under the racist system of apartheid that bred violence and resentment. The truth and reconciliation process allowed offenders to apply for amnesty from prosecution in exchange for honest testimony and public scrutiny. In the six-year period during which the Truth and Reconciliation Committee did its work, 22,000 victim statements were taken and 7,000 perpetrators applied for amnesty; 849 people were granted amnesty, while thousands of others were not.[41] The process was contentious, but it is generally regarded as a successful model. Archbishop Desmond Tutu explained in his foreword to the South African Truth and Reconciliation Committee report, "We believe, however, that there is another kind of justice—a restorative justice which is concerned not so much with punishment as with correcting imbalances, restoring broken relationships—with healing, harmony and reconciliation."[42] While rehabilitation and restorative justice sound like noble ideas, they appear to run counter to the demand for retributive justice. And from a utilitarian perspective, one might wonder whether those ideas are useful for deterring and preventing crime.

THE DEATH PENALTY

One of the most contentious issues for any philosophical conception of legal punishment—whether focused on retribution, deterrence, or some other value—is capital punishment. While the vast majority of developed nations (the United States being a notable exception) have abolished the death penalty, this most extreme form of punishment raises profound moral questions about the nature of punishment itself. Retributivists might be seen to favor capital punishment for murderers as an application of *lex talionis*, but it is hard to see how the death of another person "makes up for" the loss of the victim. Consequentialists may argue that the death penalty deters people from committing murder, but scholars continue to debate the actual deterrent effect of the death penalty.

The outrage, harm, and injustice of murder seem to call for the harshest of punishments, which may be why murder remains one of the only crimes punishable by death (at least in some states within the United States). However, we should note that advocates of restorative justice are often opposed to the death penalty. The U.S. Conference of Catholic Bishops also rejects the death penalty as part of a broader theological and philosophical commitment to a "culture of life." But retributivist advocates of the death penalty argue that for murder, the only acceptable punishment is death. The murder victim cannot be restored to life, and it also seems unlikely that the murderer can make amends for his or her crime in the same way that a thief can. Moreover, for some unrepentant predatory criminals—such as those who continue to murder while in prison—execution may be viewed as the only solution. Although the death penalty was once widely used for a variety of crimes, most people now view the death penalty as an extraordinary sort of punishment that requires extra justification. Ethicist Lloyd Steffen argues on natural law grounds (in the article at the end of this chapter) that we ought to preserve life and not kill people, and that the state ordinarily ought not kill its own citizens. Thus, he maintains that the death penalty requires special justification and that it may no longer be justifiable in contemporary social and political circumstances.

> MindTap® For more chapter resources and activities, go to MindTap.

Legal Issues

According to Amnesty International, as of July 2015, 140 countries have abolished the death penalty either outright—by law—or in practice.[43] The global leader in death sentences is China, where the number of suspected executions annually is estimated to be in the thousands (but data on Chinese executions are not officially published by the Chinese government). After China, the largest numbers of executions in 2014 (according to official reports) occurred in Iran (289), Saudi Arabia (90), Iraq (61), the United States (35), Sudan (23), and Yemen (22). (Amnesty International notes that the numbers may be higher in some countries, which conceal or underreport executions.)

Capital punishment has a long history in the United States, but by the 1960s, a majority of Americans had come to oppose it.[44] In 1972, the U.S. Supreme Court case *Furman v. Georgia* ushered in a brief moratorium on the death penalty, as the Court found that its imposition had become too "arbitrary and capricious" and thus violated the Constitution's ban on cruel and unusual punishment. That ruling also invalidated the use of the death penalty as punishment for the crime of rape. By 1976, however, the country's mood had again begun to change, and states had established less arbitrary sentencing guidelines. That year, the High Court ruled in *Gregg v. Georgia* that the death penalty does not violate the Eighth Amendment's ban on cruel and unusual punishment. The Court argued that the death penalty is justifiable on both retributivist and deterrence grounds. The Court concluded that the death

penalty could be "an expression of the community's belief that certain crimes are themselves so grievous an affront to humanity that the only adequate response may be the penalty of death."[45] The Court acknowledged that there was no conclusive empirical evidence about the deterrent effect of the death penalty—but the Court also held that it was reasonable to suspect that it might deter.

One recent ruling returned to the question of whether the death penalty is cruel and unusual punishment. In 2014, federal judge Cormac Carney ruled that the death penalty in California was indeed cruel and unusual because it was so rarely applied. California has the nation's largest death row population (743 convicts on death row as of January 2016), but the last person California executed was Clarence Ray Allen, in 2006. One reason that California executes so few convicts is that there is ongoing resistance to the death penalty, including legal challenges and difficulty obtaining the drugs for lethal injection. Judge Carney argued that since California exercised the death penalty so infrequently, an execution would be the result of arbitrary factors; he concluded that arbitrary executions serve neither a retributive nor a

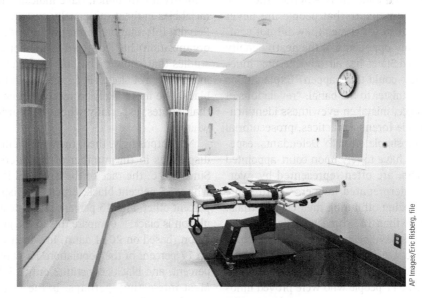

The lethal injection chamber at California's San Quentin Prison.

AP Images/Eric Risberg, file

deterrent purpose. Carney's decision was overturned by the Ninth Circuit Court of Appeals in 2015.[46]

Public support for the death penalty has varied in the decades since. According to the Pew Center for the People and the Press, "In 1996, 78 percent favored capital punishment for people convicted of murder. Support for the death penalty subsequently declined, falling to 66 percent in 2001 and 62 percent in late 2005. Since then, support has mostly remained in the low-to-mid-1960s, though it dipped slightly (to 58 percent) in October 2011."[47]

Currently, nineteen states and the District of Columbia do not have the death penalty. While there seems to be a trend toward the abolition of the death penalty, there are countervailing forces. In 2012, however, voters in California rejected a referendum (Proposition 34) that would have abolished the death penalty. As of early 2016, there have been 1,430 executions in the United States since the death penalty was reinstated in 1976.[48] The largest number of executions has occurred in Texas (with 535 executions as of early 2016), Oklahoma (with 112), and Virginia (with 111).[49]

Exonerations

One issue of grave concern is whether the U.S. justice system can ensure that people are never wrongfully executed for crimes they did not commit. Indeed, many opponents of the death penalty believe the United States has already executed innocent people. How could this happen? Explanations range from the sinister to the banal: "revelations of withheld evidence, mistaken eyewitness identification, questionable forensic practices, prosecutorial misconduct, and simple error."[50] Defendants, especially those who have to rely upon court-appointed public defenders, are often represented by overworked and underprepared lawyers—with some even cited for dozing off during their clients' trials. Since 1973, more than 156 convicts on death row in the United States have been exonerated.[51] According to the Innocence Project, a national organization that works to exonerate the wrongly convicted, there have been 341 people who were proved innocent of a variety of crimes since 1989 by the use

of DNA technology, including 18 people on death row.[52] Among those exonerated, the average prison time served is 14 years.[53]

Such revelations of innocence have raised doubts about the death penalty for some political leaders who once supported it. In January 2000, the governor of Illinois, George Ryan, ordered that all executions in his state be halted—after Northwestern University journalism students reviewed cases and proved the innocence of several inmates, including one who was within forty-eight hours of his scheduled execution. "Until I can be sure with moral certainty," Ryan said, "that no innocent man or woman is facing a lethal injection, no one will meet that fate."[54] Because of these concerns and after a review of the cases, Ryan—in one of his last acts as governor in 2003—pardoned four inmates and commuted the death sentences of the remaining 167 on death row. Illinois officially abolished the death penalty in 2011.

Racial Bias and Fairness

Another issue that raises concerns about the death penalty is the evidence of racial bias in death penalty sentencing. A number or sources, including Amnesty International, have indicated that there is racial bias in the death penalty system.[55] The Death Penalty Information Center (an anti-death penalty organization) has collected a number of empirical studies that show racial bias in the death penalty in a number of states. For example, in many states, blacks are more likely to receive a death sentence than whites, especially when the murder victim is white.[56]

Not surprisingly, then, there are significant racial disparities in the number of prisoners executed. Since 1976, the race of the executed is 56 percent white, 35 percent black, 8 percent Hispanic, and 2 percent other; and 43 percent of the death row population is black.[57] Compare this to the general population (based on 2014 data), in which whites make up 77 percent of the population, Hispanics are 17.4 percent, and blacks constitute only 13.2 percent.[58] Most interesting, perhaps, is the fact that cases resulting in death sentences for interracial murders are quite skewed. Thirty-one whites have been executed for murdering a black victim, but 296 blacks have been executed for killing a white victim.[59] There are also racial issues in the makeup of juries. According to a 2003 report from Amnesty International, "At least one in five of the African Americans executed since 1977 had been convicted by all white juries, in cases which displayed a pattern of prosecutors dismissing prospective black jurors during jury selection."[60]

Other issues related to the death penalty have recently gained public attention, for example, whether mentally retarded persons or juveniles should be executed. In June 2002, in *Atkins v. Virginia*, the U.S. Supreme Court ruled that mentally retarded defendants should not be subject to the death penalty. Obviously, one practical problem is how to determine when someone is retarded and what degree of mental retardation should exempt a person from the death penalty. In Georgia, for example, the defense has to determine beyond a reasonable doubt that a convict is mentally retarded. This standard is quite strict, requiring substantial proof of disability. Consider the case of Warren Lee Hill, a convicted Georgia murderer with an IQ of 70. (Those with IQs below 70 are generally regarded to be intellectually disabled.) Hill was scheduled to be executed in February 2013, but the execution was stayed hours before it was scheduled to allow courts to review the issue of Hill's mental capacity. Hill's execution was subject to ongoing legal challenges.[61] Hill's lawyers hoped that a 2014 Supreme Court ruling might save him. That decision, *Hall v. Florida* ruled that IQ alone was not sufficient to prove intellectual disability. Unfortunately for Hill, the ruling did not change the outcome. Hill was executed by the state of Georgia in 2015. Related to the question of mental capacity is the issue of executing juveniles. In March 2005, the U.S. Supreme Court ruled (in *Roper v. Simmons*) that it was cruel and unusual punishment, forbidden by the Constitution, to execute those who were under age eighteen when they committed their crimes. (A growing body of biological and psychological evidence suggests that adolescents "lack mature judgment and a full appreciation

of the consequences of their actions."[62]) Until this ruling, the United States had been the only remaining country in the world that executed juveniles, as Justice Kennedy explained in the Court's majority decision.

Racial disparities in executions, as well as executions of juveniles and the mentally disabled, raise serious questions about the fairness of the death penalty and its application. These cases remind us that concepts such as criminal responsibility and appropriate punishment are complex and highly disputed issues, and are all the more so when the punishment being considered is death.

Costs

Death penalty cases are expensive, both in terms of court costs and prison costs. While costs vary from state to state, one analysis from the Death Penalty Information Center in 2009 concludes that, "for a single trial, the state may pay $1 million more than for a non-death penalty trial. But only one in every three capital trials result in a death sentence, so the true cost of that death sentence is $3 million. Further down the road, only one in ten of the death sentences handed down may result in an execution. Hence the cost to the state to reach that one execution is $30 million."[63]

The costs of death row are also inordinate. The California Innocence Project estimated in 2012 that it costs $175,000 per year to house a death row inmate, compared to about $47,000 per year for an inmate not on death row. This means that $177 million per year is spent housing the more than 700 inmates on death row in California.[64] This is especially stunning considering that only thirteen California inmates have been executed since 1978. Opponents of the death penalty often cite the high cost as an argument against capital punishment. Proponents argue that costs could be controlled by speeding up the trial and appeals process. But a central reason for the lengthy trials and appeals is to ensure that innocent people are not executed.

The controversies surrounding the death penalty point to deeper philosophical questions about its justification. Generally, the same two arguments regarding legal punishment—deterrence and retribution—are used in arguments about the death penalty. We will return now to these rationales and see what considerations would be relevant to arguments for and against the death penalty.

Deterrence Considerations

Utilitarian philosopher John Stuart Mill defended the death penalty by arguing that it was the least cruel punishment that works to deter murder.[65] Mill pointed out that there were punishments worse than death—torture, for example. However, Mill argued (see his speech at the end of this chapter) that people fear death, even though a quick and painless death is not nearly as bad as a life of torture. For a utilitarian such as Mill, the death penalty works to minimize pain (for the convict), while promoting the greatest happiness (by deterring murder).

But is the death penalty a deterrent? Does it prevent people from committing certain capital crimes? Consider first the issue of prevention. One would think that at least there is certainty here. If you execute someone, then that person will not commit any future crime—including murders—because he or she will be dead. However, on a stricter interpretation of the term *prevent,* this may not necessarily be so.[66] When we execute a convicted murderer, do we really prevent that person from committing any further murders? The answer is, "Maybe." If that person would have committed another murder, then we have prevented him or her from doing so. If that person would not have committed another murder, then we would not have prevented him or her from doing so. In general, by executing all convicted murderers we would, strictly speaking, have prevented some of them (those who would have killed again) but not others (those who would not have killed again) from doing so. How many murders would we have prevented? It is difficult to tell. Those who support the death penalty may insist that it will have been worth it, no matter how small the number of murders prevented, because the people executed are convicted murderers anyway.

By contrast, what do we make of arguments for the death penalty that claim it deters those who

have not already committed murder? If the death penalty deters would-be murderers from committing their crimes, then it is worth it, according to this rationale. Granted, it will not deter those who kill out of passion or those who determine the crime is worth the risk of punishment, but presumably it would deter others. How can we determine if the death penalty really is an effective deterrent? First, we can consider our intuitions about the value of our own lives—that we would not do what would result in our own death. Threats of being executed would deter us, and thus, we think, they also would deter others. More likely, however, reasons other than fear of the death penalty restrain most of us from committing murder.

We might also gauge the death penalty's deterrent effect by examining empirical evidence. For example, we could compare two jurisdictions, say, two states. One has the death penalty, and one does not. If we find that in the state with the death penalty there are fewer murders than in the state without the death penalty, can we assume that the death penalty has made the difference and is thus a deterrent? Not necessarily. Perhaps it was something else about the state with the death penalty that accounted for the lesser incidence of murder. For example, the lower homicide rate could be the result of good economic conditions or a culture that has strong families or religious institutions. Something similar could be true of the state with a higher incidence of homicide. In this case, the cause could be high unemployment, high rates of drug and alcohol abuse, and other social problems. So, also, if there were a change in one jurisdiction from no death penalty to death penalty (or the opposite), and the statistics regarding homicides also changed, then we might conclude that the causal factor was the change in the death penalty status. But again, this is not necessarily so. For example, the murder rate in Canada actually declined after that country abolished the death penalty in 1976.[67] Other studies have found no correlation between having, instituting, or abolishing the death penalty and the rate of homicide.[68] For example, statistics show that states without the death penalty and with similar demographic profiles do not differ in homicide rates from states with the death penalty. Moreover, since 1976, homicide rates in states that instituted the death penalty have not declined more than in states that did not institute the death penalty. And homicide rates in states with the death penalty have been found to be higher than states without it.[69] But some studies still maintain that executions have a deterrent effect. A 2007 article in the *Wall Street Journal* claimed that "Capital Punishment Works." The authors charted execution rates and murder rates for the twenty-six-year period from 1979 through 2004. The data indicate that as execution rates increase, murder rates decline. They conclude, "each execution carried out is correlated with about 74 fewer murders the following year."[70] These results—and others like them from recent studies—have been criticized by economists and statisticians who maintain that any deterrent effect, if there is one, is "too fragile to be certain."[71] One problem is that there are very few executions and these occur in a few states. It is difficult to draw general conclusions about a causal relation between execution rates and murder rates from the sorts of correlations mentioned here. The National Academy of Sciences concluded in 2012, "research to date on the effect of capital punishment on homicide is not informative about whether capital punishment decreases, increases, or has no effect on homicide rates."[72]

To make a good argument for the death penalty on utilitarian grounds, a proponent would have to show that it works to deter crime. In addition, the proponent may have to show that the death penalty works better than alternatives—for example, life in prison without the possibility of parole or community-based crime prevention efforts. If we have the death penalty and it does not provide an effective deterrent, then we will have executed people for no good purpose. If we do not have the death penalty and it would have been an effective deterrent, then we risk the lives of innocent victims who otherwise would have been saved. Because this is the worse alternative, some argue, we ought to retain the death penalty. But because the deterrence argument broadly construed is a consequentialist

argument, using it also should require thinking more generally of costs and benefits. Here, the higher cost of execution could be compared to the lower cost of life imprisonment.

Retributivist Considerations

Immanuel Kant defended the death penalty on retributivist grounds. He argues, "undeserved evil which any one commits on another, is to be regarded as perpetrated on himself."[73] This principle has obvious connections with Kant's idea that the categorical imperative requires that we view our maxims as universal moral laws (as discussed in Chapter 6). Kant advocates a type of retaliation, which demands like for like or life for life. Kant maintains that the death penalty is justified because it treats a murderer as a rational being, giving him or her what he or she deserves according to this basic principle of retributive justice. Kant also maintains that we should respect the human dignity of a prisoner awaiting execution and not torture or abuse him or her.

As we have already noted, according to the retributivist argument for legal punishment, we ought to punish people to make them pay for the wrong or harm they have done. Those who argue for the death penalty on retributivist grounds must show that it is a fitting punishment and the only or most fitting punishment for certain crimes and criminals. This is not necessarily an argument based on revenge—that the punishment of the wrongdoer gives others satisfaction. It appeals, rather, to a sense of justice and an abstract righting of wrongs done. Again, there are two different versions of the retributive principle: egalitarian (or *lex talionis*) and proportional. The egalitarian version says that the punishment should equal the crime. An argument for the death penalty would attempt to show that the only fitting punishment for someone who takes a life is that his or her own life be taken in return. In this view, the value of a life is not equivalent to anything else. Thus, even life in prison is not sufficient payment for taking a life, though it would also seem that the only crime deserving of the death penalty would be murder. Note that homicide is not the only crime for which we have assigned the death penalty. We have also done so for treason and, at times, for rape. Moreover, only some types of murder are thought by proponents of the death penalty to call for this form of punishment. And as noted in the critique of the lex talionis view previously, strict equality of punishment would be not only impractical in some cases, but also morally problematic.

Perhaps a more acceptable argument could be made on grounds of proportionality. In this view, death is the only fitting punishment for certain crimes. These are worse than all others and should receive the worst or most severe punishment. Surely, some say, death is a worse punishment than life in prison. However, others argue that spending one's life in prison is worse. This form of the retributivist principle would not require that the worst crimes receive the worst possible punishment. It only requires that, of the range of acceptable punishments, the worst crimes receive the top punishment on the list. Death by prolonged torture might be the worst punishment, but we probably would not put that at the top of our list. So, also, the death penalty could be—but need not be—included on that list.

Using the retributivist rationale, one would need to determine the most serious crimes. Can these be specified and a good reason given as to why they are the worst crimes? Multiple murders would be worse than single ones, presumably. Murder with torture or of certain people also might be found to be among the worst crimes. What about treason? What about huge monetary swindles that cost thousands of people their life savings? We rate degrees of murder, distinguishing murder in the first degree from murder in the second degree. The first is worse because the person not only deliberately intended to kill the victim, but also did so out of malice. These crimes are distinguished from manslaughter (both voluntary and involuntary), which is also killing. Supposedly, the idea is that the kind of personal and moral involvement makes a difference. The more the person planned with intention and deliberateness, the more truly the person owned the act. The more malicious crime is also thought to be worse. Critics of the death penalty sometimes argue that such

rational distinctions are perhaps impossible to make in practice. However, unless it is impossible in principle or by its very nature, supporters could continue to try to refine the current distinctions.

Mercy and Restorative Justice

Opponents of the death penalty often argue against it on deterrent grounds, maintaining that if it does not work to deter crime (or if some other punishment works better), it causes unnecessary and unjustifiable pain. For example, utilitarian philosopher Jeremy Bentham opposed the death penalty by arguing that life imprisonment would work better. Others argue against the death penalty while acknowledging the retributivist argument in favor of capital punishment. Philosopher Jeffrey Reiman maintains that the death penalty represents a sort of maximal amount of retribution that can be justified. We can execute a murderer, for example, but we cannot kill his or her family. Reiman further suggests that there are circumstances in which it is morally permissible to give criminals less than the maximum punishment, so long as we attend to the needs and interests of the victims of crime.[74] In other words, we could execute murderers, but there may be good reasons for not doing so. Among the reasons for not executing may be upholding other values, such as mercy. Along these lines, Pope John Paul II argued that while the death penalty could be justified in cases where it was absolutely necessary to protect society, in a world with a modern prison system, the death penalty was no longer necessary.[75] The U.S. Conference of Catholic Bishops explains that while the death penalty can be justified, there is a higher road that involves the value of mercy.[76]

Indeed, the relatively greater value of mercy is often a central claim for religious opponents of the death penalty. Such opposition to capital punishment is often connected with a broader commitment to nonviolence and pacifism (see Chapter 19), one that sees little purpose in responding to violence with violence. "An eye for an eye leaves the whole world blind" is a sentiment that is frequently attributed to Mohandas Gandhi. In the Christian tradition, the value of mercy is connected to other values such as forgiveness and compassion.[77] The Catholic Church is opposed to the death penalty on these grounds, holding that mercy is an important value and that the death penalty is simply not the best way for murder victims to find closure.[78]

The idea of finding closure is connected with arguments in favor of restorative justice. While it is certainly not possible to restore a murder victim to life, it may be possible to imagine responses to murder that do not involve the desire for retribution. Consider, for example, the response to a 2006 school shooting in an Amish community in Nickel Mines, Pennsylvania. (Ten Amish children were shot and five killed by a local milk truck driver who was not Amish.) The community gathered together after these murders and offered forgiveness to the murderer (who had committed suicide) and his family.[79] Afterward, the mother of the murderer recalled how the Amish community's forgiving attitude helped her heal and recover from the horror of knowing that her son was a mass murderer.[80] Another example comes from Tallahassee, Florida. Ann Grosmaire, a nineteen-year-old college student, was shot and killed by her boyfriend, Conor McBride, in 2010. Despite their grief and the horrific nature of the crime, the Grosmaire family reached out to Conor's family. Citing their Christian faith and a belief that Ann would want them to forgive Conor, the Grosmaires worked with the prosecutor to implement a version of restorative justice. A conference was held in which Conor confessed his crime to Ann's family, and Ann's family explained the depth of the loss that they had experienced. Conor

Outline of Moral Approaches to the Death Penalty

	Death Penalty Abolition	Moderate	Death Penalty Retention
Thesis	Abolish the death penalty	Employ the death penalty for a limited number of crimes	Keep the death penalty
Corollaries and Implications	Replace the death penalty with life imprisonment	List of crimes deserving death might include special circumstances, mass/serial murder, treason, etc., with high burden of proof	Death penalty for ordinary murder and perhaps for other crimes
Connections with Moral Theory	Restorative justice, forgiveness, and mercy (natural law, care ethics, virtue ethics); consequentialist claim that the death penalty does not deter or that life imprisonment is a sufficient deterrent	Natural law and deontological justification of the death penalty moderated by mercy and desire to protect the innocent; consequentialist concern for costs of death penalty administration	Retributive justice (natural law, deontology) concern for retaliation or lex talionis; consequentialist focus on deterrence and prevention
Relevant authors/ examples	Lloyd Steffen (abolition in practice)	Lloyd Steffen (justification of the death penalty in exceptional circumstances)	John Stuart Mill, Immanuel Kant

was eventually sentenced to twenty years in prison. Kate Grosmaire, Ann's mother, later explained that forgiveness had a positive effect on her. "Forgiveness for me was self-preservation," she said. But she also noted that forgiveness is a difficult and ongoing process, "Forgiving Conor doesn't change the fact that Ann is not with us. My daughter was shot, and she died. I walk by her empty bedroom at least twice a day."[81] While proponents of restorative justice argue that the message of forgiveness and mercy provides an important addition to discussions of the death penalty, retributivists will argue that mercy and forgiveness give people less than what they deserve.

Humane Executions

Other concerns with regard to the death penalty are often about the nature of political power. Should the state have the power to kill people? As mentioned previously, most Western nations no longer have a death penalty. One reason may be that liberal-democratic polities want to limit the power of the state. Others may argue, as Reiman suggests, that killing is uncivilized, brutalizing, degrading, barbarous, and dehumanizing. This sort of argument may be grounded in a kind of visceral repugnance about the act of killing. But it also appeals to the constitutional prohibition on cruel and unusual punishment. Is the death penalty inherently cruel or inhumane? Or is it possible to humanely execute criminals?

Contemporary methods of execution can sometimes appear to cause suffering. Depending on the form of execution, the person put to death may gasp for air, strain, or shake uncontrollably. With some methods, the eyes bulge, the blood vessels expand, and sometimes more than one try is needed to complete the job. In 1999, for example, 344-pound Allen Lee Davis was executed in Florida's electric chair. The execution caused blood to appear on Davis's face and shirt, which some believed demonstrated that he had suffered greatly. Others said it was simply a nosebleed.[82] Nevertheless, in 2000, the Florida legislature voted to use lethal injections instead of the electric chair in future executions.

Just as the electric chair was thought to be more humane than earlier execution methods when Thomas Edison invented it in 1888, so now, death by lethal injection has generally taken the place of electrocution and other earlier methods. The last death by gas chamber was in 1999 in Arizona, and the last death by hanging was in 1996 in Delaware. In June 2010, Ronnie Lee Gardner was executed by firing squad in Utah, but this was at his own request. Though there has been a move toward lethal injections as other methods of execution have been criticized, one of the current debates regarding the death penalty is whether lethal injection, itself, is humane.

Three chemicals are used in a lethal injection, which is administered via an IV. First, an ultrashort-acting barbiturate, usually sodium thiopental, is given. This causes the inmate to become unconscious. Next, a muscle relaxant, either pancuronium bromide or a similar drug, is given to cause paralysis of the muscles, including those responsible for breathing. Finally, potassium chloride, which causes cardiac arrest, is given. If all goes as expected, the inmate loses consciousness and does not experience any pain as death takes place. The entire process can take as little as ten minutes or much longer. Some of the delay is caused by the difficulty the technicians sometimes have in finding an acceptable vein to use. For example, there have been cases of drug users whose veins were not in good condition or who had to help the technician find a good vein. It is also possible that the condemned person may remain conscious or partially conscious and experience acute pain or the feeling of suffocation but cannot communicate this because of the inability to move caused by the second chemical. Technicians can be more or less capable of giving the drugs correctly and in sufficient quantity. Doctors would be more capable but are prohibited by their code of ethics from taking part in executions in this way.[83] There have been at least forty-three cases of botched executions recorded since 1976. These include instances in which IVs were not administered properly, prolonging the execution process; those in which the initial administration of gas or electricity failed to kill; and those in which the bodies of the condemned caught fire during electrocutions.[84] In recent years, several states suspended lethal injection out of the concern that the practice was not humane.[85] Meanwhile, American prisons have had difficulty obtaining lethal drugs since European manufacturers oppose their use in executions and have refused to sell them to American prisons.[86] Clearly, both opponents and supporters of the death penalty may find evidence for their positions in the various descriptions of lethal injection as a more or less humane method of execution.

The concern about lethal injection is related to a range of questions about the meaning of the death penalty and what it symbolizes. For example, some who favor more violent forms of execution argue that those who spill blood must have their own blood spilled. In this view, a firing squad may be more appropriate than lethal injection. Nevertheless, Americans tend to view beheading, such as happens in Saudi Arabia and elsewhere, as a barbaric way to execute a criminal. Consider, further, the question of whether a condemned prisoner should have the right to choose his or her own means of execution. Is it morally appropriate to give a criminal that choice? As noted, the Utah execution by firing squad in 2010 was selected by the condemned man himself; not long ago, a convicted murderer in Oregon asked to be hanged.[87] A further question in terms of the symbolic value of executions is whether they should be held in public or videotaped for purposes of information and instruction. We might consider the potential deterrent power of public executions. But we may also think that executions are no longer held in public for good reasons. Is it because we are ashamed of them? Do we think it is cruel or inhumane to display an executed person's body in public as a warning to others? Or are we simply trying to keep the proceedings dignified, while avoiding the use of the executed criminal's death as a means (in a way that Kant would find immoral)? When we ask questions such as these, our views on the death penalty and our reasons for supporting or opposing

it will be put to the test, which is probably not a bad thing.

As you can see from the discussions in this chapter, legal punishment and the death penalty are complex issues. The readings for this chapter will take us deeper into these issues. First, we'll read an excerpt from Michelle Alexander's critique of prisons, *The New Jim Crow*. Alexander's analysis of racial disparities in the system, which was first published in 2010, has been widely influential and often cited by proponents of prison reform, decarceration, and alternatives to incarceration. Next, we'll read an excerpt from the radical author, social theorist, and political activist Angela Y. Davis. Drawing on her critiques of racism, sexism, and economic inequality, Davis uses this essay to challenge the idea that prisons are necessary features of the social landscape. Her argument builds upon the insights of the French philosopher and social theorist Michel Foucault, who viewed prisons as mechanisms of social and political control. Next, we'll read an excerpt from John Stuart Mill's 1868 defense of capital punishment, delivered when he was serving as a member of parliament. Mill's defense is based on utilitarian reasoning (see Chapter 5). The last selection is from Lloyd Steffen, a religious studies scholar and university chaplain at Lehigh University. Drawing on natural law ethics, Steffen maintains that there is a common set of moral agreements that can allow us to reach consensus on issues such as the death penalty. His theory of just execution is derived from the idea of justified war (which we discuss in more detail in Chapter 19).

NOTES

1. Todd R. Clear, Michael D. Reisig, and George F. Cole, eds., *American Corrections* (Stamford, CT: Cengage Learning, 2012), Chapter 18.

2. Bureau of Justice Statistics, "Total Correctional Population," accessed March 16, 2016, http://www.bjs.gov/index.cfm?ty=kfdetail&iid=487; also see E. Ann Carson, Ph.D, "Prisoners in 2014," U.S. Department of Justice, September 2015, accessed

March 16, 2016, http://www.bjs.gov/content/pub/pdf/p14.pdf; and Danielle Kaeble, Lauren Glaze, Anastasios Tsoutis, and Todd Minton, "Correctional Populations in the United States, 2014," U.S. Department of Justice, Revised January 21, 2016, accessed March 16, 2016, http://www.bjs.gov/content/pub/pdf/cpus14.pdf

3. Institute for Criminal Policy Research, "World Prison Brief," accessed March 16, 2016, http://www.prisonstudies.org/

4. Bureau of Justice Statistics, "Prisoners in 2014," September 2015, accessed March 16, 2016, http://www.bjs.gov/content/pub/pdf/p14_Summary.pdf

5. Combining data from FBI, "Crime in the United States (2014), accessed March 16, 2016, https://www.fbi.gov/about-us/cjis/ucr/crime-in-the-u.s/2014/crime-in-the-u.s.-2014/tables/table-4 and United Nations Office on Drugs and Crime, "Intentional Homicide, Count and Rate per 100,000 Population (1995–2011)," accessed March 24, 2016, http://www.unodc.org/unodc/en/data-and-analysis/homicide.html

6. Chris Francescani, "Violent Crime Takes a Holiday in New York City," *Reuters,* November 28, 2012, accessed March 24, 2016, http://www.reuters.com/article/2012/11/28/us-usa-newyork-crime-idUSBRE8AR18S20121128

7. Death Penalty Information Center, accessed March 15, 2016, www.deathpenaltyinfo.org

8. Steven D. Levitt, "Understanding Why Crime Fell in the 1990s: Four Factors That Explain the Decline and Six That Do Not," *Journal of Economic Perspectives* 18, No. 1 (2004), pp. 163–90.

9. Kevin Drum, "America's Real Criminal Element: Lead," *Mother Jones,* January/February 2013, accessed March 24, 2016, http://www.motherjones.com/environment/2013/01/lead-crime-link-gasoline

10. David Frum, "The Coming Democratic Crack-Up" *The Atlantic,* September 21, 2015, accessed March 16, 2016, http://www.theatlantic.com/politics/archive/2015/09/the-democrats-looming-dilemma/406426/

11. See Richard Brandt, *Ethical Theory* (Englewood Cliffs, NJ: Prentice Hall, 1959).

12. Thomas Szasz, *The Myth of Mental Illness* (New York: Harper & Row, 1961).

13. Rachel Aviv, "The Science of Sex Abuse," *The New Yorker,* January 14, 2013, accessed March 24, 2016, http://www.newyorker.com/magazine/2013/01/14/the-science-of-sex-abuse

14. Institute for Criminal Policy Research, "World Prison Brief: Highest to Lowest—Prison Population Total," accessed March 16, 2016, http://www.prisonstudies.org/highest-to-lowest/prison-population-total?field_region_taxonomy_tid=All

15. E. Ann Carson, Ph.D., "Prisoners in 2014," U.S. Department of Justice, September 2015, p. 15, accessed March 16, 2016, http://www.bjs.gov/content/pub/pdf/p14.pdf

16. Jim Webb, "Why We Must Fix Our Prisons," *San Francisco Chronicle,* March 29, 2009, p. 4; also see Associated Press, "Nation's Inmate Population Increased 2.3 Percent Last Year," *The New York Times,* April 25, 2005, p. A14.

17. "U.S. Inmate Count Far Exceeds Those of Other Nations," *The New York Times,* April 23, 2008, pp. A1, A14.

18. Jason DeParle, "The American Prison Nightmare," *New York Review of Books,* April 12, 2007, pp. 33, 36, accessed March 24, 2016, http://www.nybooks.com/articles/2007/04/12/the-american-prison-nightmare/

19. John J. Gibbons and Nicholas de B. Katzenbach, *Confronting Confinement* (New York: Vera Institute of Justice, 2006), p. iii.

20. "US: Injustices Filling the Prisons," Human Rights Watch, January 31, 2013, accessed March 24, 2016, http://www.hrw.org/news/2013/01/31/us-injustices-filling-prisons

21. Prisons Bureau, "Annual Determination of Average Cost of Incarceration" Federal Register, March 9, 2015, accessed March 17, 2016, https://www.federalregister.gov/articles/2015/03/09/2015-05437/annual-determination-of-average-cost-of-incarceration

22. Christian Henrichson and Ruth Delaney, *The Price of Prisons: What Incarceration Costs Taxpayers,* Vera Institute of Justice, January 2012, updated July 20, 2012, accessed March 24, 2016, http://www.vera.org/sites/default/files/resources/

downloads/Price_of_Prisons_updated_version_072512.pdf

23. Prerna Anand, "Winners and Losers: Corrections and Higher Education in California," *California Common Sense,* September 5, 2012, accessed March 24, 2016, http://www.cacs.org/ca/article/44

24. Jennifer Steinhauer, "Schwarzenegger Seeks Shift from Prisons to Schools," *The New York Times,* January 6, 2010, accessed March 24, 2016, http://www.nytimes.com/2010/01/07/us/07calif.html

25. National Institute of Justice, "Recidivism," accessed March 17, 2016, http://www.nij.gov/topics/corrections/recidivism/pages/welcome.aspx

26. Bureau of Justice Statistics, "Prisoners in 2014," September 2015, accessed March 16, 2016, http://www.bjs.gov/content/pub/pdf/p14_Summary.pdf

27. Jim Webb, "Why We Must Fix Our Prisons," *San Francisco Chronicle*, March 29, 2009, p. 5, accessed May 9, 2016, http://parade.com/104227/senatorjimwebb/why-we-must-fix-our-prisons/

28. Jason DeParle, "The American Prison Nightmare," *New York Review of Books*, April 12, 2007, pp. 33, 36, accessed March 24, 2016, http://www.nybooks.com/articles/2007/04/12/the-american-prison-nightmare/

29. Glenn Kessler, "The Stale Statistic that One in Three Black Males 'Born Today' Will End Up in Jail" *The Washington Post*, June 16, 2015, accessed March 17, 2016, https://www.washingtonpost.com/news/fact-checker/wp/2015/06/16/the-stale-statistic-that-one-in-three-black-males-has-a-chance-of-ending-up-in-jail/

30. Jason DeParle, "The American Prison Nightmare," *New York Review of Books*, April 12, 2007, pp. 33, 36, accessed March 24, 2016, http://www.nybooks.com/articles/2007/04/12/the-american-prison-nightmare/

31. Michelle Alexander, *The New Jim Crow: Mass Incarceration in the Age of Colorblindness* (New York: The New Press, 2010), p. 17.

32. John H. Langbein interview, *Frontline*, PBS, January 16, 2004, accessed March 24, 2016, http://www.pbs.org/wgbh/pages/frontline/shows/plea/interviews/langbein.html

33. Sara Wakefield and Christopher Uggen, "Incarceration and Stratification," *Annual Review of Sociology* 36 (2010), pp. 387–406.

34. Stan Alcorn, "'Check Yes Or No': The Hurdles of Job Hunting with a Criminal Past," NPR's *All Things Considered*, January 31, 2013, accessed March 24, 2016, http://www.npr.org/2013/01/31/170766202/-check-yes-or-no-the-hurdles-of-employment-with-criminal-past

35. "Responsibility, Rehabilitation, and Restoration: A Catholic Perspective on Crime and Criminal Justice" (2000), U.S. Conference of Catholic Bishops, accessed May 9, 2016, http://www.usccb.org/issues-and-action/human-life-and-dignity/criminal-justice-restorative-justice/crime-and-criminal-justice.cfm.

36. Ibid.

37. Hennessey Haynes, "Reoffending and Restorative Justice," in *Handbook of Restorative Justice*, eds. Gerry Johnstone and Daniel Van Ness (London: Willan Publishing, 2007), p. 432 ff.

38. Patricia Leigh Brown, "Opening Up, Students Transform a Vicious Circle," *The New York Times*, April 4, 2013, accessed March 24, 2016, http://www.nytimes.com/2013/04/04/education/restorative-justice-programs-take-root-in-schools.html?pagewanted=all

39. See Laura Magnani and Harmon L. Wray, *Beyond Prisons: A New Interfaith Paradigm for Our Failed Prison System* (Minneapolis, MN: Fortress Press, 2006).

40. See Trudy Conway, David McCarthy, and Vicki Schieber, eds., *Where Justice and Mercy Meet* (Collegeville, MN: Liturgical Press, 2013).

41. Lyn S. Graybill, *Truth and Reconciliation in South Africa* (London: Lynne Rienner Publishing, 2002), p. 8; "Truth and Reconciliation Commission (TRC)," South African History Online, accessed March 24, 2016, http://www.sahistory.org.za/topic/truth-and-reconciliation-commission-trc

42. *Truth and Reconciliation Commission of South Africa Report* (1998), Vol. 1, para. 36, p. 9, accessed May 9, 2016, http://www.justice.gov.za/trc/report/

43. Amnesty International, "Death Sentences and Executions in 2014", April 1, 2015, accessed

March 17, 2016, https://www.amnesty.org/en/documents/act50/0001/2015/en/

44. "Introduction to the Death Penalty," Death Penalty Information Center, accessed May 9, 2016, http://www.deathpenaltyinfo.org/part-i-history-death-penalty

45. Gregg v. Georgia, 428 U.S. 153 (1976) at III.c.

46. Maura Dolan and Joseph Serna, "Federal Appeals Court Upholds California's Death Penalty," *Los Angeles Times*, November 12, 2015, accessed March 17, 2016, http://www.latimes.com/local/lanow/la-me-ln-court-upholds-california-death-penalty-20151112-story.html

47. "Continued Majority Support for Death Penalty," Pew Research Center, January 6, 2012, accessed March 24, 2016, http://www.people-press.org/2012/01/06/continued-majority-support-for-death-penalty/

48. Death Penalty Information Center, "Facts about the Death Penalty," Updated March 23, 2016, accessed March 24, 2016, http://www.deathpenaltyinfo.org/documents/FactSheet.pdf

49. Ibid.

50. Mike Farrell, "Death Penalty Thrives in Climate of Fear," *San Francisco Chronicle*, February 24, 2002, p. D3.

51. Death Penalty Information Center, "Facts about the Death Penalty," Updated March 23, 2016, accessed March 24, 2016, http://www.deathpenaltyinfo.org/documents/FactSheet.pdf

52. Innocence Project, accessed May 9, 2016, http://www.innocenceproject.org/

53. Ibid.

54. Margaret Carlson, "Death, Be Not Proud," *Time*, February 21, 2000, p. 38, accessed May 9, 2016, http://content.time.com/time/magazine/article/0,9171,39180,00.html.

55. Amnesty International, "Death Penalty and Race," accessed March 25, 2016, http://www.amnestyusa.org/our-work/issues/death-penalty/us-death-penalty-facts/death-penalty-and-race

56. Death Penalty Information Center, "Research on the Death Penalty," accessed March 24, 2016, http://www.deathpenaltyinfo.org/research-death-penalty

57. Death Penalty Information Center, "Facts about the Death Penalty," Updated March 23, 2016, accessed March 24, 2016, http://www.deathpenaltyinfo.org/documents/FactSheet.pdf

58. U.S. Census Bureau, "Quick Facts," accessed March 24, 2016, http://www.census.gov/quickfacts/table/PST045215/00

59. Death Penalty Information Center, "Facts about the Death Penalty," Updated March 23, 2016, accessed March 24, 2016, http://www.deathpenaltyinfo.org/documents/FactSheet.pdf

60. Amnesty International, *Death by Discrimination: The Continuing Role of Race in Capital Cases*, April 2003, p. 2, accessed May 9, 2016, https://www.amnesty.org/en/documents/AMR51/046/2003/en/

61. Lincoln Caplan, "Disgracing 'the Quintessential System of Justice,' " *The New York Times*, April 26, 2013, accessed March 24, 2016, http://takingnote.blogs.nytimes.com/2013/04/26/disgracing-the-quintessential-system-of-justice/

62. See, for example, Claudia Wallis, "Too Young to Die," *Time*, March 14, 2005, p. 40, accessed May 9, 2016, http://content.time.com/time/magazine/article/0,9171,1034712,00.html

63. Richard C. Dieter, "Smart on Crime: Reconsidering the Death Penalty in a Time of Economic Crisis," Death Penalty Information Center, October 2009, accessed March 24, 2016, http://www.deathpenaltyinfo.org/documents/CostsRptFinal.pdf

64. Jeff Chinn, "Death Penalty Infographic," December 18, 2012, accessed March 24, 2016, http://californiainnocenceproject.org/blog/2012/12/18/death-penalty-infographic/

65. John Stuart Mill, "Speech in Defense of Capital Punishment," vol. 28 in *The Collected Works of John Stuart Mill*, eds. John M. Robson and Bruce L. Kinzer (Toronto: University of Toronto Press, 1988), pp. 305–10.

66. See Hugo Bedau, "Capital Punishment and Retributive Justice," in *Matters of Life and Death*, ed. Tom Regan (New York: Random House, 1980), pp. 148–82.

67. It dropped from 3.09 people per 100,000 residents in 1975 to 2.74 per 100,000 in 1983. "Amnesty International and the Death Penalty," Amnesty International USA, *Newsletter* (Spring 1987).

68. See Hugo Bedau, *The Death Penalty in America* (Chicago: Aldine, 1967), in particular Chapter 6, "The Question of Deterrence."

69. Death Penalty Information Center, "What's New," accessed March 24, 2016, www.deathpenaltyinfo. org; Raymond Bonner and Ford Fessenden, "States with No Death Penalty Share Lower Homicide Rates, *The New York Times*, September 22, 2000, accessed March 24, 2016, www.truthinjustice. org/922death.htm

70. Roy D. Adler and Michael Summers, "Capital Punishment Works," *The Wall Street Journal*, November 2, 2007, accessed May 9, 2016, http:// www.wsj.com/articles/SB119397079767680173

71. Gebhard Kirchgassner, "Econometric Estimates of Deterrence of the Death Penalty: Facts or Ideology?" *Kyklos* 64, No. 3 (August 2011), pp. 468–69.

72. Daniel S. Nagin and John V. Pepper, eds., *Deterrence and the Death Penalty* (Washington, D.C.: National Academies Press, 2012), p. 2.

73. Immanuel Kant, *The Philosophy of Law* (Edinburgh: T&T Clark, 1887), Part. 2, Sec. 49.E.

74. Jeffrey Reiman, "Justice, Civilization, and the Death Penalty," *Philosophy and Public Affairs* 14 (1985), pp. 119–34.

75. Pope John Paul II, *Evangelium Vitae*, Para. 56.

76. U.S. Conference of Catholic Bishops, *A Culture of Life and the Penalty of Death* (2005), accessed March 24, 2016, http://www.usccb.org/issues-and-action/human-life-and-dignity/death-penalty-capital-punishment/upload/penaltyofdeath.pdf

77. See Andrew Fiala, *What Would Jesus Really Do?* (Lanham, MD: Rowman & Littlefield, 2006), especially Chapter 8.

78. Vicki Schieber, Trudy D. Conway, and David Matzko McCarthy, *Where Justice and Mercy Meet: Catholic Opposition to the Death Penalty* (Collegeville, MN: Liturgical Press, 2013).

79. Donald Kraybill, Steven Nolt, and David Weaver-Zercher, *Amish Grace* (San Francisco, CA: John Wiley and Sons/Jossey-Boss, 2007). See Andrew Fiala, "Radical Forgiveness and Human Justice," *Heythrop Journal* 53, No. 3 (May 2012), pp. 494–506.

80. Associated Press, "Mother of Gunman Who Killed Five Amish Girls in 2006 Cares for Survivor of Son's Massacre" December 9, 2013, accessed May 9, 2016, http://www.nydailynews.com/news/national/mother-amish-killer-cares-survivor-son-massacre-article-1.1542337

81. Paul Tullis, "Can Forgiveness Play a Role in Criminal Justice?," *The New York Times,* January 4, 2013, accessed March 24, 2016, http://www .nytimes.com/2013/01/06/magazine/can-forgiveness-play-a-role-in-criminal-justice.html? pagewanted=all

82. "Uproar over Bloody Electrocution," *San Francisco Chronicle*, July 9, 1999, p. A7, accessed May 9, 2016, http://www.sfgate.com/news/article/Uproar-Over-Bloody-Electrocution-Florida-2919750.php; "An Execution Causes Bleeding," *The New York Times*, July 8, 1999, p. A10, accessed May 9, 2016, http://www.nytimes.com/1999/07/09/us/an-execution-causes-bleeding.html.

83. See Adam Liptak, "Critics Say Execution Drug May Hide Suffering," *The New York Times*, October 7, 2003, pp. A1, A18, accessed May 9, 2016, http://www.nytimes.com/2003/10/07/us/critics-say-execution-drug-may-hide-suffering.html? pagewanted=all.

84. Michael L. Radelet, "Some Examples of Post-Furman Botched Executions," Death Penalty Information Center, accessed March 24, 2016, http://www.deathpenaltyinfo.org/some-examples-post-furman-botched-executions

85. Reuters, "Drugs for Lethal Injection Aren't Reliable, Study Finds," *The New York Times*, April 24, 2007, accessed March 24, 2016, http://www.nytimes.com/2007/04/24/us/24injection.html?_r=0

86. Makiko Kitamura and Adi Narayan, "Europe Pushes to Keep Lethal Injection Drugs from U.S. Prisons," *Bloomberg Business Week*, February 7, 2013, accessed March 24, 2016, http://www .businessweek.com/articles/2013-02-07/europe-pushes-to-keep-lethal-injection-drugs-from-u-dot-s-dot-prisons

87. Thanks to Wendy Lee-Lampshire of Bloomsburg University, for sharing this fact.

READING

The New Jim Crow

MICHELLE ALEXANDER

MindTap° For more chapter resources and activities, go to MindTap.

Study Questions

As you read the excerpt, please consider the following questions:
1. How does Alexander explain the discriminatory outcome of the criminal justice system?
2. Why does Alexander use the term "Jim Crow" to describe the result of the criminal justice system?
3. What is the significance of Alexander's use of the term "mass incarceration"?

...America is still not an egalitarian democracy. The arguments and rationalizations that have been trotted out in support of racial exclusion and discrimination in its various forms have changed and evolved, but the outcome has remained largely the same. An extraordinary percentage of black men in the United States are legally barred from voting today, just as they have been throughout most of American history. They are also subject to legalized discrimination in employment, housing, education, public benefits, and jury service, just as their parents, grandparents, and great-grandparents once were.

What has changed since the collapse of Jim Crow has less to do with the basic structure of our society than with the language we use to justify it. In the era of colorblindness, it is no longer socially permissible to use race, explicitly, as a justification for discrimination, exclusion, and social contempt. So we don't. Rather than rely on race, we use our criminal justice system to label people of color "criminals" and then engage in all the practices we supposedly left behind. Today it is perfectly legal to discriminate against criminals in nearly all the ways that it was once legal to discriminate against African Americans. Once you're labeled a felon, the old forms of discrimination—employment discrimination, housing discrimination, denial of the right to vote, denial of educational opportunity, denial of food stamps and other public benefits, and exclusion from jury service—are suddenly legal. As a criminal, you have scarcely more rights, and arguably less respect, than

a black man living in Alabama at the height of Jim Crow. We have not ended racial caste in America; we have merely redesigned it.

....

When I began my work at the ACLU [American Civil Liberties Union], I assumed that the criminal justice system had problems of racial bias, much in the same way that all major institutions in our society are plagued with problems associated with conscious and unconscious bias. As a lawyer who had litigated numerous class-action employment-discrimination cases, I understood well the many ways in which racial stereotyping can permeate subjective decision-making processes at all levels of an organization, with devastating consequences. I was familiar with the challenges associated with reforming institutions in which racial stratification is thought to be normal—the natural consequence of differences in education, culture, motivation, and, some still believe, innate ability. While at the ACLU, I shifted my focus from employment discrimination to criminal justice reform and dedicated myself to the task of working with others to identify and eliminate racial bias whenever and wherever it reared its ugly head.

By the time I left the ACLU, I had come to suspect that I was wrong about the criminal justice system. It was not just another institution infected with racial

Michelle Alexander, *The New Jim Crow* (New York: The New Press, 2010), pp. 1–4.

bias but rather a different beast entirely. . . . I came to see that mass incarceration in the United States had, in fact, emerged as a stunningly comprehensive and well-disguised system of racialized social control that functions in a manner strikingly similar to Jim Crow.

Are Prisons Obsolete?

ANGELA Y. DAVIS

MindTap® For more chapter resources and activities, go to MindTap.

Study Questions

As you read the excerpt, please consider the following questions:
1. What does Davis mean by "the prison industrial complex?"
2. What does Davis think decarceration would look like?
3. What might Davis mean when she says that punishment does not necessarily follow from crime?

. . . If jails and prisons are to be abolished, then what will replace them? This is the puzzling question that often interrupts further consideration of the prospects for abolition.

It is true that if we focus myopically on the existing system . . . it is very hard to imagine a structurally similar system capable of handling such a vast population of lawbreakers. If, however, we shift our attention from the prison, perceived as an isolated institution, to the set of relationships that comprise the prison industrial complex, it may be easier to think about alternatives. In other words, a more complicated framework may yield more options than if we simply attempt to discover a single substitute for the prison system. The first step, then, would be to let go of the desire to discover one single alternative system of punishment that would occupy the same footprint as the prison system.

Since the 1980s, the prison system has become increasingly ensconced in the economic, political and ideological life of the United States and the transnational trafficking in U.S. commodities, culture, and ideas. Thus the prison industrial complex is much more than the sum of all the jails and prisons in this country. It is a set of symbiotic relationships among correctional communities, transnational corporations, media conglomerates, guards' unions, and legislative and court agendas. If it is true that the contemporary meaning of punishment is fashioned through these relationships, then the most effective abolitionist strategies will contest these relationships and propose alternatives that pull them apart. . . .

An abolitionist approach . . . would require us to imagine a constellation of alternative strategies and institutions, with the ultimate aim of removing the prison from the social and ideological landscapes of our society. In other words, we would not be looking for prisonlike substitutes for the prison, such as house arrest safeguarded by electronic surveillance bracelets. Rather, positing decarceration as our overarching strategy, we would try to envision a continuum of alternatives to imprisonment—demilitarization of schools, revitalization of education at all levels, a health system that provides

Angela Y. Davis, "Alternatives to the Prison Industrial Complex" (editor's title, originally excerpted and reprinted from "Imprisonment and Reform" and "Abolitionist Alternatives") from *Are Prisons Obsolete?* (New York: Seven Stories Press, 2003).

free physical and mental care to all, and a justice system based on reparation and reconciliation rather than retribution and vengeance....

To reiterate, rather than try to imagine one single alternative to the existing system of incarceration, we might envision an array of alternatives that will require radical transformations of many aspects of our society. Alternatives that fail to address racism, male dominance, homophobia, class bias, and other structures of domination will not, in the final analysis, lead to decarceration and will not advance the goal of abolition....

...Recognize that "punishment" does not follow from "crime" in the neat and logical sequence offered by discourses that insist on the justice of imprisonment, but rather punishment—primarily through imprisonment (and sometimes death)—is linked to the agendas of politicians, the profit drive of corporations, and media representations of crime.

READING

Speech in Favor of Capital Punishment (1868)

JOHN STUART MILL

MindTap°   For more chapter resources and activities, go to MindTap.

Study Questions

As you read the excerpt, please consider the following questions:
1. Why does Mill suggest that capital punishment is less cruel than other punishments?
2. Why does Mill claim that we can't judge whether the death penalty fails to work?
3. What does Mill mean by suggesting that the purpose of penal justice is to deter?

When there has been brought home to any one, by conclusive evidence, the greatest crime known to the law; and when the attendant circumstances suggest no palliation of the guilt, no hope that the culprit may even yet not be unworthy to live among mankind, nothing to make it probable that the crime was an exception to his general character rather than a consequence of it, then I confess it appears to me that to deprive the criminal of the life of which he has proved himself to be unworthy—solemnly to blot him out from the fellowship of mankind and from the catalogue of the living—is the most appropriate as it is certainly the most impressive, mode in which society can attach to so great a crime the penal consequences which for the security of life it is indispensable to annex to it. I defend this penalty, when confined to atrocious cases, on the very ground on which it is commonly attached—on that of humanity to the criminal; as

beyond comparison the least cruel mode in which it is possible adequately to deter from the crime. If, in our horror of inflicting death, we endeavour to devise some punishment for the living criminal which shall act on the human mind with a deterrent force at all comparable to that of death, we are driven to inflictions less severe indeed in appearance, and therefore less efficacious, but far more cruel in reality. Few, I think, would venture to propose, as a punishment for aggravated murder, less than imprisonment with hard labor for life; that is the fate to which a murderer would be consigned by the mercy which shrinks from putting him to death.

John Stuart Mill, *The Collected Works of John Stuart Mill*, Volume XXVIII - Public and Parliamentary Speeches Part I November 1850–November 1868, ed. John M. Robson and Bruce L. Kinzer (Toronto: University of Toronto Press, London: Routledge and Kegan Paul, 1988). 11/20/2015. http://oll.libertyfund.org/titles/262#lf0223-28_label_1257

But has it been sufficiently considered what sort of a mercy this is, and what kind of life it leaves to him? If, indeed, the punishment is not really inflicted—if it becomes the sham which a few years ago such punishments were rapidly becoming—then, indeed, its adoption would be almost tantamount to giving up the attempt to repress murder altogether. But if it really is what it professes to be, and if it is realized in all its rigour by the popular imagination, as it very probably would not be, but as it must be if it is to be efficacious, it will be so shocking that when the memory of the crime is no longer fresh, there will be almost insuperable difficulty in executing it. What comparison can there really be, in point of severity, between consigning a man to the short pang of a rapid death, and immuring him in a living tomb, there to linger out what may be a long life in the hardest and most monotonous toil, without any of its alleviations or rewards—debarred from all pleasant sights and sounds, and cut off from all earthly hope, except a slight mitigation of bodily restraint, or a small improvement of diet? Yet even such a lot as this, because there is no one moment at which the suffering is of terrifying intensity, and, above all, because it does not contain the element, so imposing to the imagination, of the unknown, is universally reputed a milder punishment than death—stands in all codes as a mitigation of the capital penalty, and is thankfully accepted as such. For it is characteristic of all punishments which depend on duration for their efficacy—all, therefore, which are not corporal or pecuniary—that they are more rigorous than they seem; while it is, on the contrary, one of the strongest recommendations a punishment can have, that it should seem more rigorous than it is; for its practical power depends far less on what it is than on what it seems. There is not, I should think, any human infliction which makes an impression on the imagination so entirely out of proportion to its real severity as the punishment of death. The punishment must be mild indeed which does not add more to the sum of human misery than is necessarily or directly added by the execution of a criminal. As my hon. Friend the Member for Northampton (Mr. Gilpin) has himself remarked, the most that human laws can do

to anyone in the matter of death is to hasten it; the man would have died at any rate; not so very much later, and on the average, I fear, with a considerably greater amount of bodily suffering. Society is asked, then, to denude itself of an instrument of punishment which, in the grave cases to which alone it is suitable, effects its purposes at a less cost of human suffering than any other; which, while it inspires more terror, is less cruel in actual fact than any punishment that we should think of substituting for it. My hon. Friend says that it does not inspire terror, and that experience proves it to be a failure. But the influence of a punishment is not to be estimated by its effect on hardened criminals. Those whose habitual way of life keeps them, so to speak, at all times within sight of the gallows, do grow to care less about it; as, to compare good things with bad, an old soldier is not much affected by the chance of dying in battle. I can afford to admit all that is often said about the indifference of professional criminals to the gallows. Though of that indifference one-third is probably bravado and another third confidence that they shall have the luck to escape, it is quite probable that the remaining third is real. But the efficacy of a punishment which acts principally through the imagination, is chiefly to be measured by the impression it makes on those who are still innocent; by the horror with which it surrounds the first promptings of guilt; the restraining influence it exercises over the beginning of the thought which, if indulged, would become a temptation; the check which it exerts over the graded declension towards the state–never suddenly attained—in which crime no longer revolts, and punishment no longer terrifies. As for what is called the failure of death punishment, who is able to judge of that? We partly know who those are whom it has not deterred; but who is there who knows whom it has deterred, or how many human beings it has saved who would have lived to be murderers if that awful association had not been thrown round the idea of murder from their earliest infancy? Let us not forget that the most imposing fact loses its power over the imagination if it is made too cheap. When a punishment fit only for the most atrocious crimes is lavished on small offences until human feeling recoils from it, then, indeed, it ceases to intimidate, because it ceases to be believed in. The failure of capital punishment in cases of theft is easily accounted for; the thief did not believe that it would be inflicted. He had learnt by experience that jurors would perjure themselves rather than find him guilty; that Judges would seize any excuse for not sentencing him to death, or for recommending him to mercy; and that if neither jurors nor Judges were merciful, there were still hopes from an authority above both.

When things had come to this pass it was high time to give up the vain attempt. When it is impossible to inflict a punishment, or when its infliction becomes a public scandal, the idle threat cannot too soon disappear from the statute book. And in the case of the host of offences which were formerly capital, I heartily rejoice that it did become impracticable to execute the law. If the same state of public feeling comes to exist in the case of murder; if the time comes when jurors refuse to find a murderer guilty; when Judges will not sentence him to death, or will recommend him to mercy; or when, if juries and Judges do not flinch from their duty, Home Secretaries, under pressure of deputations and memorials, shrink from theirs, and the threat becomes, as it became in the other cases, a mere *brutum fulmen* [futile threat]; then, indeed, it may become necessary to do in this case what has been done in those–to abrogate the penalty. That time may come—my hon. Friend thinks that it has nearly come. I hardly know whether he lamented it or boasted of it; but he and his Friends are entitled to the boast; for if it comes it will be their doing, and they will have gained what I cannot but call a fatal victory, for they will have achieved it by bringing about, if they will forgive me for saying so, an enervation, an effeminancy, in the general mind of the country. For what else than effeminancy is it to be so much more shocked by taking a man's life than by depriving him of all that makes life desirable or valuable? Is death, then, the greatest of all earthly ills? *Usque adeone mori miserum est* [is it so wretched then to die]? Is it, indeed, so dreadful a thing to die? Has it not been from of old one

chief part of a manly education to make us despise death—teaching us to account it, if an evil at all, by no means high in the list of evils; at all events, as an inevitable one, and to hold, as it were, our lives in our hands, ready to be given or risked at any moment, for a sufficiently worthy object? I am sure that my hon. Friends know all this as well, and have as much of all these feelings as any of the rest of us; possibly more. But I cannot think that this is likely to be the effect of their teaching on the general mind. I cannot think that the cultivating of a peculiar sensitiveness of conscience on this one point, over and above what results from the general cultivation of the moral sentiments, is permanently consistent with assigning in our own minds to the fact of death no more than the degree of relative importance which belongs to it among the other incidents of our humanity.

The men of old cared too little about death, and gave their own lives or took those of others with equal recklessness. Our danger is of the opposite kind, lest we should be so much shocked by death, in general and in the abstract, as to care too much about it in individual cases, both those of other people and our own, which call for its being risked. And I am not putting things at the worst, for it is proved by the experience of other countries that horror of the executioner by no means necessarily implies horror of the assassin. The stronghold, as we all know, of hired assassination in the 18th century was Italy; yet it is said that in some of the Italian populations the infliction of death by sentence of law was in the highest degree offensive and revolting to popular feeling.

Much has been said of the sanctity of human life, and the absurdity of supposing that we can teach respect for life by ourselves destroying it. But I am surprised at the employment of this argument, for it is one which might be brought against any punishment whatever. It is not human life only, not human life as such, that ought to be sacred to us, but human feelings. The human capacity of suffering is what we should cause to be respected, not the mere capacity of existing. And we may imagine somebody asking how we can teach people not to inflict suffering by ourselves inflicting it? But to this I should answer—all of us would answer—that to deter by suffering from inflicting suffering is not only possible, but the very purpose of penal justice. Does fining a criminal show want of respect for property, or imprisoning him, for personal freedom? Just as unreasonable is it to think that to take the life of a man who has taken that of another is to show want of regard for human life. We show, on the contrary, most emphatically our regard for it, by the adoption of a rule that he who violates that right in another forfeits it for himself, and that while no other crime that he can commit deprives him of his right to live, this shall. There is one argument against capital punishment, even in extreme cases, which I cannot deny to have weight—on which my hon. Friend justly laid great stress, and which never can be entirely got rid of. It is this—that if by an error of justice an innocent person is put to death, the mistake can never be corrected; all compensation, all reparation for the wrong is impossible. This would be indeed a serious objection if these miserable mistakes—among the most tragical occurrences in the whole round of human affairs—could not be made extremely rare. The argument is invincible where the mode of criminal procedure is dangerous to the innocent, or where the Courts of Justice are not trusted. And this probably is the reason why the objection to an irreparable punishment began (as I believe it did) earlier, and is more intense and more widely diffused, in some parts of the Continent of Europe than it is here. There are on the Continent great and enlightened countries, in which the criminal procedure is not so favorable to innocence, does not afford the same security against erroneous conviction, as it does among us; countries where the Courts of Justice seem to think they fail in their duty unless they find somebody guilty; and in their really laudable desire to hunt guilt from its hiding places, expose themselves to a serious danger of condemning the innocent. If our own procedure and Courts of Justice afforded ground for similar apprehension, I should be the first to join in withdrawing the power of inflicting irreparable punishment from such tribunals.

But we all know that the defects of our procedure are the very opposite. Our rules of evidence are even too favorable to the prisoner; and juries and Judges carry out the maxim, "It is better that ten guilty should escape than that one innocent person should suffer," not only to the letter, but beyond the letter. Judges are most anxious to point out, and juries to allow for, the barest possibility of the prisoner's innocence. No human judgment is infallible; such sad cases as my hon. Friend cited will sometimes occur; but in so grave a case as that of murder, the accused, in our system, has always the benefit of the merest shadow of a doubt. And this suggests another consideration very germane to the question. The very fact that death punishment is more shocking than any other to the imagination, necessarily renders the Courts of Justice more scrupulous in requiring the fullest evidence of guilt. Even that which is the greatest objection to capital punishment, the impossibility of correcting an error once committed, must make, and does make, juries and Judges more careful in forming their opinion, and more jealous in their scrutiny of the evidence. If the substitution of penal servitude for death in cases of murder should cause any declaration in this conscientious scrupulosity, there would be a great evil to set against the real, but I hope rare, advantage of being able to make reparation to a condemned person who was afterwards discovered to be innocent. In order that the possibility of correction may be kept open wherever the chance of this sad contingency is more than infinitesimal, it is quite right that the Judge should recommend to the Crown a commutation of the sentence, not solely when the proof of guilt is open to the smallest suspicion, but whenever there remains anything unexplained and mysterious in the case, raising a desire for more light, or making it likely that further information may at some future time be obtained. I would also suggest that whenever the sentence is commuted the grounds of the commutation should, in some authentic form, be made known to the public. Thus much I willingly concede to my hon. Friend; but on the question of total abolition I am inclined to hope that the feeling of the country is not with him, and that the limitation of death punishment to the cases referred to in the Bill of last year will be generally considered sufficient. The mania which existed a short time ago for paring down all our punishments seems to have reached its limits, and not before it was time.

We were in danger of being left without any effectual punishment, except for small of offences. What was formerly our chief secondary punishment—transportation—before it was abolished, had become almost a reward. Penal servitude, the substitute for it, was becoming, to the classes who were principally subject to it, almost nominal, so comfortable did we make our prisons, and so easy had it become to get quickly out of them. Flogging—a most objectionable punishment in ordinary cases, but a particularly appropriate one for crimes of brutality, especially crimes against women—we would not

hear of, except, to be sure, in the case of garotters, for whose peculiar benefit we reestablished it in a hurry, immediately after a Member of Parliament had been garrotted. With this exception, offences, even of an atrocious kind, against the person, as my hon. and learned Friend the Member for Oxford (Mr. Neate) well remarked, not only were, but still are, visited with penalties so ludicrously inadequate, as to be almost an encouragement to the crime. I think, Sir, that in the case of most offences, except those against property, there is more need of strengthening our punishments than of weakening them; and that severer sentences, with an apportionment of them to the different kinds of offences which shall approve itself better than at present to the moral sentiments of the community, are the kind of reform of which our penal system now stands in need. I shall therefore vote against the Amendment.

READING

A Theory of Just Execution

LLOYD STEFFEN

MindTap For more chapter resources and activities, go to MindTap.

Study Questions

As you read the excerpt, please consider the following questions:
1. What is the basic natural law assumption that guides Steffen's discussion of the death penalty?
2. What are the nine criteria that Steffen outlines for the justification of the death penalty?
3. Explain why Steffen concludes that current execution practice does not live up to the standards of the theory.

Execution is a direct and intended killing, yet framing a moral debate over capital punishment in the American political context has proved a difficult task, even when most Americans are now aware that capital punishment does not deter crime and the legal machinery and processes involved in execution are known to be highly error prone. Since 1973, 140 individuals convicted and sentenced to death have been exonerated, that is, proven to be actually innocent of the crime for which they were

convicted and sentenced to die.[1] American citizens continue to support capital punishment in large numbers, and that support seems to rest on the assumption that any problems that attend the capital punishment system are practical or technical and thus can be corrected. Specific problems, such as wrongful conviction, while acknowledged to be morally provocative, have not led the majority of Americans to rethink their moral assessment of the execution practice and demand of their political leaders an immediate halt to executions. Instead, the assumption appears to be widespread that there is nothing morally problematic about the death penalty per se, and moral controversy has apparently sunk beneath a sea of consensus on this point.

But is there some kind of common agreement that we can point to for guidance on the question of capital punishment? Can we devise a theory of "just execution" on the model of just war, identifying a moral presumption that constitutes a common agreement to which rational people of goodwill could be expected to assent and then consider whether or how capital punishment might be justified as a reasonable exception to that common agreement? And in our effort to reconcile thought and experience, can we demonstrate the practicality of the "common agreement" approach to ethics we have been discussing by finding experiential confirmation that this way of thinking is actually being used and relied upon because it is a useful and practical way to consider relevant justice issues? These are the questions at issue in this chapter. The focus of attention here will be the way the legal system has attempted to fashion policy around what looks to be a kind of "just execution" theory. We shall note, however, by way of critique, that a common agreement "just execution" ethic will direct critical attention to a disparity between thought and practice, so that what "just execution" might make possible on the one hand is taken away by the failure to satisfy the demands of justice on the other. We shall conclude with a consideration of the broader question concerning just punishment, which then has deeper social policy implications. What would a "just criminal justice system" look like were we to evaluate it in light of our common agreement ethic?

JUST EXECUTION

A common agreement ethic concerning "just execution" begins by acknowledging a basic intrinsic good—the good of life.[2] Natural law gives prescriptive force to the claim that life is a basic good, so that it follows that life ought to be preserved and promoted, protected, and advanced, not destroyed. A theory of just execution based on a natural law tradition is committed in the first instance to this claim, namely, that life ought to be promoted and protected and not destroyed.

But the natural law common agreement ethic I am advancing says more than this. Life, as we all know, is messy, and the moral life may be riddled with conflicts. Basic goods can come into conflict with one another; and moral quandaries, even actual dilemmas, can arise. Life itself is a good of life, but it is not an absolute good that is unaffected by relations to other goods of life. If sufficiently strong moral requirements are advanced, a natural law ethic grounded in honoring the basic goods of life may allow the prohibition on destroying life to be lifted, but this is not done idly or without compelling reasons. We saw how this emphasis on developing a common moral agreement functions along with justice-related criteria that might, in exceptional cases, allow an exception to the prohibition on the use of force, or physician-assisted suicide, or nontreatment of severely disabled neonates. We continue to look back to the just war model and to the ethic *behind* just war thinking, even as we look ahead *beyond* just war to another important life and death issue where we are seeking to reconcile ethical thought and moral experience.

If construed as a natural law-based moral perspective wherein reason affirms the goods of life, including the basic good of life itself, a just execution theory in the first instance would affirm that the state ought ordinarily to refrain from killing its citizens. I put the matter this way because this identifies the real moral presumption at stake in capital punishment; and this statement gathers both death penalty supporters and death penalty opponents under a basic reasoned point of common moral agreement. Whatever disputes may arise about particulars, there ought to be no disagreement about the moral presumption behind capital punishment. If states ought ordinarily to refrain from killing citizens and capital punishment in one way states actually do kill citizens, then we must be clear that at the heart of any capital punishment debate is a moral presumption that the state should not resort to a death penalty. Our common moral agreement behind the issue of state-sponsored execution is *a presumption opposing the practice.*

But we note once again that the theory being advanced in these pages and now on this issue is not absolutist. As a moderate theory, the question is legitimately asked: Are there ever circumstances that would allow the state to use lethal force against a citizen? Put this way, examples immediately come to mind, such as the emergency situation where an aggressor is placing innocent civilians in imminent danger of loss of life. Police action to stop such killing, action that as a last resort includes deadly force against the aggressor, would, on the face of it, allow a justifiable lifting of the presumption against the state killing a citizen. So some exceptions to our common moral agreement come quickly to mind, and these exceptions do not seem especially controversial.

But now the question turns to execution. Is capital punishment a justifiable use of lethal force against a citizen? Could it be an exception to the moral presumption that ordinarily states ought not to kill their citizens?

To answer this question, let us construct a theory of just execution on the *model* of just war. Let us say that in order for the moral presumption against capital punishment to be lifted, various criteria would have to be met, The tests or criteria that would constrain the state in the interests of justice yet conceivably permit a use of lethal force would be nine in number:

1. The execution power must be legitimately authorized.
2. Just cause for the use of the death penalty must be established.
3. The motivation for applying lethal punishment must be justice, not vengeance.
4. Executions must be administered fairly, without accidental features such as race, religion, class,

or sex affecting administration of the death penalty.
5. The death penalty is to be used as an expression of cherished values, and it must not subvert the goods of life but promote and advance the value of life.
6. Executions ought not to be cruel.
7. Execution ought to be a last resort, with no other response to the offender except execution adequately serving the interests of justice.
8. Execution ought to restore a value equilibrium distorted and upset by the wrongdoing committed by the person on whom execution is visited.
9. Execution should be a response proportionate to the offense committed.[3]

This natural law-based theory of just execution says this: if all nine of these criteria are satisfied, the presumption against the state using capital punishment as a legitimate mode of lethal force against a citizen can be lifted, and an execution can go forward as a morally justifiable act. Having laid out the theory of just execution, what I want now to consider is how this common agreement moral theory has found its way into American law, and to what effect. The point here is not so much to analyze the merits of capital punishment per se but to make the case that the common agreement ethic has actually been used to deliberate issues involved in the death penalty and this way of addressing moral problems is accessible and helpful. People actually use this way of moral thinking and analysis in their lives, thereby connecting thought with experience, and such connection has been a point stressed in this book as a justification for this particular ethics project, which seeks to articulate the hybrid ethic that this mode of analysis expresses. And this way of thinking about difficult social problems can and has found its way into legal as well as moral deliberations. The value of looking at the capital punishment issue is that we can see here again that the common agreement approach to ethics helps us reconcile our ethical thinking with our moral experience. Let us begin by examining the question of the moral presumption against capital punishment.

THE APPEAL TO A JUST EXECUTION ETHIC IN AMERICAN LAW

On the Moral Presumption against Capital Punishment

It is beyond question that the legal debate over capital punishment in the United States is grounded in a moral presumption against the use of capital punishment. Not only opponents of capital punishment but supporters too would affirm this common agreement. The reason for this claim is that in the United States each year there are anywhere from 14,000 to 23,000 criminal homicides. If a simple retribution ethic were in play legally—by that I mean an ethic that said that those who unjustly take a life must necessarily forfeit their own—we should expect to have thousands of executions each year. We do not. We sentence a little over 1 percent of murderers to death every year and execute not thousands, but only a handful. The number of executions comes nowhere near the number of murders:[4] 37 executions out of 14,180 murders in the United States in 2008 (0.27 percent)[5] and 46 executions out of 14,748 murders in 2010 (0.3 percent).[6] The American legal system has refused to endorse mandatory death sentences, and it has not called for the expansion of execution to cover every instance of wrongful killing. On the contrary, American law has limited the use of the execution power by imposing on it various conditions and restrictions. It is important to keep in the forefront of the moral debate over execution that the American legal system— through the courts and legislatures and the safety net of executive clemency power—affirms a moral presumption *against* the use of the death penalty. The low number of executions relative to the high number of criminal homicides or other capital crimes establishes this as an unmistakable datum of moral relevance.

But executions are assigned and carried out. American law has devised a system of justice checks that have as their purpose establishing tests of justice—again, the criteria—that must be met and satisfied if state power is going to be used to kill a citizen and if the execution is going to be deemed not only lawful but morally justified. The criteria that are relevant to the idea of just execution articulate restraints on the execution power, and these restraints are publicly exposed in American law. The American legal system accepts that ordinarily states ought not to execute citizens, even for murder, and this common agreement can be discerned in the appeal to statistics—the number of executions divided by the number of homicides. The numbers provide convincing evidence that the very system that claims power to execute and does execute also abides by the common agreement that states ordinarily ought not to execute their citizens.

The Nine Criteria for Lifting the Presumption against Capital Punishment

But the state does execute its citizens. From the moral point of view, the simple fact that executions do take place indicates that a theory of just execution is in play, providing a system of authorization and justification for an execution. From a moral point of view, whenever an execution takes place, it does so because good and sufficient reasons have been made to justify lifting the presumption against execution. Would a theory of just execution justify this lifting of a presumption against execution? Before offering a moral critique of the execution practice, let us consider what would be included in the legal appeal to a "just execution" ethic.

On the criterion of legitimate authority: Although the state reserves the right to punish criminal offenders and will neither sanction lethal acts of vigilantism nor condone individual vengeance against criminal offenders, it does not endorse an unqualified execution power. The federal judiciary has ruled that the legitimate authority for execution rests with the states and the federal government. In *Gregg v. Georgia* (1976) the court held that because capital punishment "does not invariably violate the Constitution," legal authorities are free to devise execution laws or not; it then specified legal restraints on use of that power, such things as requiring objective standards for juries to follow in their deliberations about sentencing, requiring mandated appeals, and insisting on jury consideration of mitigating circumstances in assessing capital punishment eligibility. American law certainly recognizes the legitimacy of the execution power, but it subjects that power to oversight so that it conforms to the United States Constitution, which, from a legal standpoint, is the ultimate legal authority for the execution practice in the United States. This first criterion establishes the justification for the state claim to the execution power while also restricting any socially organized use of lethal force against citizens outside the system of legal protections, so that extralegal community execution practices such as lynching are expressly prohibited.

Second, on the idea of just cause: the United States Supreme Court has held in *South Carolina v. Gathers* (490 U.S. 805) the unremarkable opinion that punishment in criminal law is based on an "assessment of [the] harm caused by the defendant as a result of the crime charged." This idea is relevant to proportionality (discussed later in this chapter) but here can be cited as also allowing that criminal wrongdoing is itself a just cause for the legal authority to sanction punishment, one such authorized punishment being the death penalty. Through legislative and court action, the American legal system has restricted the crimes for which execution may be imposed, although the list of crimes has been expanded significantly in recent years.[7] In general, however, the crime for which one may receive the death penalty is aggravated murder. Whether aggravated murder is just cause for invoking a punishment of death has been related to a long-standing legal discussion regarding the Eighth Amendment prohibitions on cruel and unusual punishment and how that prohibition is directly tied to the standards of decency held by the American people....

Third, the motivation for applying lethal punishment must be justice, not vengeance. As Kant, a great death penalty retributivist, argued, hatred-filled vengeance is a vicious motivation that does not accord with the dispensing of justice,[8] and any theory of just execution will be presented as motivated by a concern for justice. On the legal front, the courts seek to satisfy this criterion when they take action to prevent arbitrariness or inflamed jury opinion from affecting verdicts or when they demand that decisions about imposing death be formed through a rational process of deliberation. Jurors are to reach their conclusions not through passion but by the application of objective criteria....[9]

Fourth, executions must be administered fairly, without accidental features such as race, religion, class, or sex affecting who gets the death penalty. This is, of course, a major justice issue at stake when imposing the death penalty, and the 1972 *Furman v. Georgia* decision, which imposed what turned out to be a four-year halt to executions, was in fact a court recognition that the death sentence had been imposed in an arbitrary, capricious, even freakish manner. All subsequent rulings by the Court were designed to extirpate discrimination and require evenhandedness in death sentencing.

Fifth, the death penalty is to be used as an expression of cherished values, and it must not subvert the goods of life but promote and advance the value of life. "Capital punishment is our society's recognition of the sanctity of life," Senator Orrin Hatch says.[10] The courts have acknowledged that standards of decency determine whether or not we have a death penalty, and the idea of killing an offender in conformity to those standards affirms how highly life is cherished, which can be summarized as follows: life is cherished so highly that persons who unjustly take a life risk losing their own.

Sixth, executions ought to be carried out in line with a prohibition on cruelty. Every change in execution method has been advanced as a way of killing more humanely from the invention of the guillotine to Edison's first electric chair to lethal injection. This criterion has come into play in various incidents, including challenges to the state of Florida over its unreliable and malfunctioning electric chair. The cruelty challenge was stopped by the Florida legislature, which met in special session to authorize what it believed was the more humane option of using lethal injection as the authorized mode of dispatching capital offenders. The legal system has sought to conform to this criterion without doubt.

Seventh, since executions take a life and life is so highly regarded in our moral community, execution ought to be a last resort, meaning that no other response but execution will serve the interests of justice. The legal system seems to acknowledge this criterion in its restrictive application of the death penalty—that there are only certain cases that merit the death penalty, that they are special, and that they are and should be relatively rare. Therefore, the logic would seem to go as follows: those individuals who receive a death sentence do so as a judgment on the part of the justice system that execution is the appropriate penalty, that no other penalty would be adequate and hence, de facto, we satisfy last resort. Last resort seems to be involved in dispensing death sentences against the backdrop of a legal system where different jurisdictions dispense different punishments and open different options for eventual release, even after so serious a crime as murder, which can at times warrant a seven-year—sometimes shorter—prison term.[11] Imposing capital punishment in capital cases where the killing is deemed especially egregious seems to some to have the effect of preventing a particularly dangerous murderer from reentering society and threatening it, so execution could be thought to ensure societal protection and juries do act in line with this justification, even in jurisdictions where a life sentence for murder means no possibility of parole. This particular appeal to last resort does affect juries, but note that this kind of reasoning points to a problem involving failures of the criminal justice system to assure citizens of protection rather than being a death penalty justification per se.

Eighth, execution ought to aim at restoring a value equilibrium distorted and upset by an offender's wrongdoing. Restorative justice efforts at this point are deemed inappropriate in aggravated murder cases. Retributive justice, however, has been appealed to as the means whereby the scales of justice, upset by the murderer's unjust act, have their equilibrium put back in balance, or so society seems to have adjudged the matter. The fact that laws have been written to allow surviving victims to witness executions is some legal recognition that the law is concerned that the retributive act of execution serve the end of satisfying the victim survivors that justice has been done, so such laws would provide evidence of support for this criterion in the legal system.

And ninth, execution should be a proportionate response to the offense committed. For the sake of argument, we shall adopt a Kantian standpoint and stipulate that execution is a proportionate response to only one crime, aggravated murder. In decision after decision, the Supreme Court has addressed the issue of proportionality, and certain crimes have been proscribed as inappropriate for execution....

In all these matters—in court decisions, in statutes passed by legislatures—the legal system is shown straining to preserve capital punishment as legal action consistent not only with constitutional principles but with moral ideals of permissible action and necessary restraint, especially in light of the fact that at issue in capital punishment is the morally weighty matter of the state acting intentionally and willfully to extinguish a human life. The decisions above appeal not only to the constitution and a legal system but to a moral theory—a common agreement-based theory of just execution, a theory that holds an execution is permissible only if it meets certain criteria of justice.

THE VALUE OF THE THEORY

Noting that the legal system makes an implicit appeal to a just execution theory does not settle the moral debate over capital punishment. The purpose of the appeal to such a theory is, rather, to frame the moral issues and make conversation and debate possible. The value of the theory lies in its articulation of those moral concerns relevant to the notion of justice, which reasonable people can be expected to affirm without undue controversy. The just execution framework structures debate and insists that engagement over moral issues proceed from a common affirmation of moral meaning. And even though contemporary debate over capital punishment does not make formal appeal to the theory *as a theory*, no important conversation about the moral meaning of the death penalty proceeds without appealing, at least implicitly, to the particulars of the theory. The criteria just discussed identify justice issues that guide moral deliberation around a common agreement, namely, that ordinarily the state ought not to kill its citizens, not even by capital punishment. We have identified the empirical warrants that support this claim. Persons on both sides of the death penalty debate can and do appeal to just execution criteria in the course of the debate. The criteria appear in deliberations over particular issues in particular cases. And I have broached the theory of just execution through a discussion of the legal system to suggest that developments that have occurred in American law around the issue of capital punishment have not taken place in a moral vacuum. In fact, the law on capital punishment has developed over the years in response to justice challenges to execution practices that fail to meet the "just execution" guidelines, with the 1972 *Furman* decision going so far as to halt executions altogether because of the injustices associated with discriminatory imposition practices. That "just execution" theory, grounded in natural law ethics, can be invoked to explain the review of capital punishment in the American legal system as that system has addressed the serious moral question of capital punishment and the exercise of the state execution power.

In case after case over the course of the past forty years, the law has affirmed the moral presumption that the state ordinarily ought not to kill its citizens. Legal review has also attended to questions about fair imposition and other justice problems in the capital punishment system such that justice-related criteria have developed in the law to govern the execution practice. The legal developments, whether brought about by legislatures or by court review, are fraught with moral meaning, and, as I have argued here, they demonstrate that the legal system itself is seeking to conform to an implicit moral theory—a "just execution" theory grounded in a common moral agreement opposed to the death penalty. The value of pointing out that American law appeals implicitly to a theory of

just execution is that once such a theory is articulated and can be seen as the legal embodiment of a moral theory, the theory can then be used as the bar of justice against which the execution practice can be evaluated. *In other words, we can test the American execution practice against the very standards of justice that the practice recognizes as the requirements of justice.* A moral theory, we have been arguing, must be reconciled to our moral experience, and we can investigate the execution practice to see whether the way we actually apply the death penalty is consistent with the standards of justice articulated in the theory and to which the law itself is making implicit appeal. We can then find ourselves in a position to discern the moral meaning of the American practice of execution. The judgments we shall make about the practice of execution in light of that moral theory will not be idiosyncratic or grounded in a religious or political ideology. They will, rather, be framed around the concerns for justice that invite all reasonable persons into reflection, deliberation, and conversation around a commonly accepted structure of moral meaning.

. . . As long as the death penalty exists, every effort must be made to observe not only constitutional safeguards but also the moral requirements laid out in the just execution framework to which that constitutional-legal system appeals. Execution is a killing, and a killing will always require the most strenuous kind of justification process. The moral presumption in capital punishment is against using state power to kill, and tests have been devised—inscribed in law actually—which to meet could lift the presumption against capital punishment. Failure to lift that presumption locates execution in the moral arena of wrongful homicide, even murder.

The ultimate moral question to come out of debate over the possibility of just execution is whether capital punishment is an exception to the moral presumption with which we started—is it ever permissible for the state to kill its own citizens? The question is whether capital punishment qualifies as a particular way of killing citizens that meets the requirements of justice and is thus morally constituted as a justifiable mode of state killing.

My objective here has been to lay out the structure for a theory of just execution that is grounded in natural law ethics but that functions today as a moral theory to which American law has made implicit appeal. I have elsewhere presented my views as to how well the American execution practice conforms to the moral ideals enshrined in just execution,[12] and although I shall not reiterate them all again here, I will share that I find the execution practice at odds with the theory. Thought and experience do not meet in the *practice* of execution and it is the common agreement ethic articulated here as "just execution" that exposes this problem. Serious deficiencies can be found when the practice of execution is measured against the action guides of the just execution criteria, and failure at the point of one criterion suffices to deny the death penalty moral legitimacy. There are, I believe, significant issues to raise with all nine criteria, and let me point out how one influential person appealed implicitly to a "just execution" criterion to condemn the execution practice. Several years ago in a speech in St. Louis, Pope John Paul II condemned the death penalty on natural law grounds.[13] He implicitly appealed to what I have here called a criterion of *last resort*. His comment was that because societies are now able to provide protection against those who engage in terrible criminal wrongdoing, such as aggravated murder, capital punishment is not necessary for such societal protection—we have other means today to assure public safety. We do not need to do this. The Pope's remarks provide evidence for the fact that in debates over capital punishment, we inevitably argue over capital punishment at the justice points of the "just execution" criteria. Articulating those criteria, which has been my purpose, may help to facilitate the debate, narrow the moral issues worthy of attention, and result in more informed voices entering into the conversation over the moral meaning of the death penalty.

Just execution theory does not itself provide the resources to answer specific questions about such things as discrimination, last resort, or whether the value of life is enhanced or diminished by execution. What just execution theory does is organize inquiry and establish common ground for engaged conversation and debate. People of goodwill debate this issue, and much is at stake. For this theory holds that if any criterion fails the test, an execution is rendered impermissible. My own examination of the death penalty has led me to conclude that given the strict requirements of the theory, no execution in America as part of the execution system can possibly meet all of the criteria, so no execution is morally justified. What is significant about this statement is that it represents a morally moderate conclusion, since one can oppose capital punishment yet still affirm that there are situations where the state can act to kill a citizen and do so justifiably. The point is that execution does not happen to be a form of state killing that meets the test of moral justification. Just execution theory convinces me that where capital punishment is concerned, the presumption against the state killing its own citizens should remain in place and stay undisturbed.

If the practice of execution is evaluated in light of the moral guidelines of just execution theory, that theory will itself contribute to sounding the death knell of capital punishment. The practice will be exposed as unjust and unjustifiable, for the execution practice will necessarily fail to meet the stringent demands of reason and justice. That end will come about only if we also engage in vigorous debate over the death penalty practice and if citizens enter that debate having become educated about how our legal system operates to put persons to death. That process is mysterious and unknown to most Americans. Yet just execution makes a contribution at just this point, for it calls citizens to take responsibility for engaging in informed conversation about a legal and public policy issue of deep moral significance. Just execution theory, then, this product of natural law that has found its way at least implicitly into American law, is a spur to citizen education; and the increase of educated citizens is finally the best evidence we have for avowing the reality of an "evolving standard of decency"—that moral ideal embedded in American law.

NOTES

1. Death Penalty Information Center, "Fact Sheet," accessed September 9, 2010, http://www.deathpenaltyinfo.org/documents/FactSheet.pdf The numbers cited will of course change, but they are accurate as of this writing, and current figures may be consulted at the Death Penalty Information Center.

2. A preeminent good in virtue of the fact that the good of life is required for the pursuit or enjoyment of other goods, life is itself a good of life and it is a good in relation, and therefore potentially in conflict, with other goods of life.

3. For a complete discussion of these criteria, see Lloyd Steffen, *Executing Justice: The Moral Meaning of the Death Penalty* (Eugene, OR: Wipf & Stock, 2006).

4. Death Penalty Information Center, "Fact Sheet," accessed September 9, 2010, http://www.deathpenaltyinfo.org/documents/FactSheet.pdf; Federal Bureau of Investigation, accessed September 14, 2010, http://www.fbi.gov/ucr/cius2008/documents/expandhomicidemain.pdf

5. Death Penalty Information Center, "Fact Sheet," accessed September 9, 2010, http://www.deathpenaltyinfo.org/documents/FactSheet.pdf; the number of 2008 murders is from "United States Crime Rates," accessed September 9, 2011, disastercenter.com/crime/uscrime.htm

6. Death Penalty Information Center, "Fact Sheet," accessed November 2011, http://www.deathpenaltyinfo.org/documents/FactSheet.pdf; the number of 2010, murders is from "United States Crimes Rates," accessed November 2011, http://disastercenter.com/crime/uscrime.htm

7. The Antiterrorism and Effective Death Penalty Act of 1996, provisions of which were upheld in *Felker v. Turpin* (116S. Ct. 2333 [1996]), expanded the list of federal crimes that would be eligible for the death penalty to more than sixty, mainly involving drug-related issues. But even so, the connections of death penalty-eligible crimes can be traced to the act of aggravated murder.

8. Immanuel Kant, *The Metaphysic of Morals*, trans, and ed. J. W. Semple (Edinburgh: Thomas Clark, 1836), p. 307. Kant writes that "no punishment ought to be inflicted out of hatred."

9. The case could be made that when the 1991 *Payne v. Tennessee* decision was made, allowing victim impact statements into the penalty phase of capital cases, the U.S. Supreme Court actually turned from the historical understanding that punishments ought to be justice related and deal with wrongs rather than with harms. The difference is important. Evaluating a crime and just punishment has historically allowed a jury to assume that those who lose a loved one to a crime such as aggravated murder are harmed by that loss, so that the idea of dispensing justice was tied to the wrong committed and then addressing that wrong. By allowing harms to be presented to juries, the jury shifts attention to addressing harms, which is a natural incitement to vengeance. *Payne v. Tennessee* is a watershed in moving away from the idea that capital punishment, in order to be just, must focus on justice rather than vengeance. I preserve this criterion as stated because the weight of judicial history is on the side of justice rather than vengeance, and punishment incited by vengeance is at least inadequate, but more likely reprehensible from a moral point of view.

10. This quotation is widely available. See for instance, That Religious Studies Website, "Capital Punishment," accessed September 3, 2010, http://www.thatreligiousstudieswebsite.com/Ethics/Applied_Ethics/Capital_Punishment/capital_punishment.php

11. For references to concerns with state paroling that would release a convicted murderer after seven years of imprisonment, see Richard C. Dieter, "Sentencing for Life: Americans Embrace Alternatives to the Death Penalty," posted February 09, 2003, accessed November 2010, http://www.deathpenaltyinfo.org/sentencing-life-americans-embrace-alternatives-death-penalty

12. See Steffen, *Executing Justice,* passim.

13. Pope John Paul II called capital punishment "cruel and unnecessary" in a papal mass homily in St. Louis, Missouri, January 27, 1999, saying, "Modern society has the means of protecting itself, without definitively denying criminals the chance to reform." Quoted in Catholics against Capital Punishment, "What the Vatican Has Said," accessed November 2010, http://www.cacp.org/vaticandocuments.html

REVIEW EXERCISES

1. What essential characteristics of legal punishment distinguish it from other types of punishment?
2. What is the significance of the idea of decarceration, and what is the goal of critics of mass incarceration?
3. What is the difference between the mechanisms of deterrence and prevention? Given their meanings, does the death penalty prevent murders? Deter would-be killers? How?
4. If legal punishment works as a deterrent, then how does it work? For whom would it work? For whom would it likely not work?
5. How do the retributivist arguments differ from the deterrence arguments?
6. Explain the idea of restorative justice and the possibility of alternatives to incarceration.
7. What is the *lex talionis* view of punishment? How does it differ from the proportional view?
8. Discuss the arguments for and against the identification of retributivism with revenge.
9. Why is the notion of responsibility critical to the retributivist view of legal punishment? How does the insanity defense fit in here?
10. Discuss the use of deterrence arguments for the death penalty. Also summarize opponents' criticisms of these arguments.
11. Discuss the use of retributivist arguments for the death penalty. Also summarize opponents' criticisms of these arguments.
12. Discuss the idea that even if the death penalty can be justified, the current system of execution may not live up to the standards of the theory of justified execution.

DISCUSSION CASES

1. **Imprisonment.** Steven's mother was imprisoned for drug possession with intent to distribute when Steven was just a baby. Steven grew up visiting his mother in prison. Steven has since become politically active and has been advocating on campus for alternatives to incarceration. Steven asks an acquaintance from his philosophy class, Janelle, to sign a petition that aims to provide more state funding for rehabilitation and drug treatment. Janelle is opposed to this. She says, "I have no sympathy for criminals. They get what they deserve." Steven replies, "But consider my mom's case. She's not really a bad person. She had a drug addiction problem, and she sold drugs to support her own habit. Her addiction could have been treated by rehab. But she ended up in prison, which meant pretty hard times for me and my sisters." "Well, she should have thought about that before she committed the crime," Janelle says. "If we start letting the drug dealers out of prison, all hell will break loose." Steven responds, "Well, growing up with a mom in prison was pretty much hell for me. And now that she's out of prison, she's having a hard time getting a job and an apartment. She feels like it's harder than ever to make ends meet, and I worry she's going to turn back to drugs or even dealing. How did her imprisonment help her or society?"

   Whose side are you on? Is prison an appropriate punishment for nonviolent drug crimes? Does it matter whether a criminal has a family that is impacted by imprisonment? Why or why not?

2. **Doctors and Execution.** Dr. Kaur has been asked to serve as a consultant for the state as it is revising its protocol for use of lethal injection in executions. Dr. Kaur is not personally opposed to the death penalty, but he knows that the American Medical Association and other doctors' groups object to the involvement of doctors in executions. These organizations argue that doctors take an oath to preserve life and thus should not be accessories to the taking of life. But Dr. Kaur thinks it is important to find humane ways to execute people. And he figures that it would be better if doctors, who understand how the lethal injection protocol works, were involved in the process. He agrees to work with the state as it reviews and revises its lethal injection protocol.

   Is Dr. Kaur doing the right thing? Should doctors be involved in finding humane ways to execute convicted criminals? Why or why not?

3. **Death Penalty Cases.** Suppose you are a member of a congressional committee that is determining the type of crime that can be punishable by death. What kinds of cases, if any, would you put on the list? The killing and sexual assault of a minor? War crimes? Killings of police officers or public figures? Multiple murderers? Mob hits or other cases in which someone gives an order to kill but does not carry it out himself or herself? Others? What about the premeditated killing of a physically abusive spouse?

   Why would you pick out just those crimes on your list as appropriately punished by death or as the worst crimes? What ethical values can you cite to justify your choices?

MindTap®   For more chapter resources and activities, go to MindTap.

Environmental Ethics

Learning Outcomes

After reading this chapter, you should be able to:

- Describe current environmental challenges, including pollution, climate change, and wilderness preservation.
- Explain the difference between anthropocentric and ecocentric or biocentric ideas about environmental ethics.
- Clarify the difference between intrinsic value and instrumental value.

- Explain how cost–benefit analysis applies in thinking about environmental issues.
- Recognize environmental justice concerns.
- Outline basic differences between ecofeminism and deep ecology.
- Defend a thesis with regard to environmental issues and the value of nonhuman nature.

iStockphoto.com/maakenzi

MindTap° For more chapter resources and activities, go to MindTap.

On May 31, 2013, the widest tornado ever recorded on the planet (measuring 2.6 miles across) tore a 16.2-mile path across Oklahoma near El Reno, outside of Oklahoma City. Wind speeds reached 295 miles per hour, and the storm was rated an EF-5, the highest possible rating on the Enhanced Fujita scale. Eighteen people were killed.[1] This storm came barely a week after another EF-5 tornado hit Oklahoma, striking Moore and its surrounding areas, flattening entire neighborhoods and killing twenty-four people. Oklahoma is in the area of the United States known as "Tornado Alley," where tornadoes most frequently occur. But even in this tornado-prone area, two EF-5s back-to-back was unusual. In addition to record-strength tornadoes, the United States has also been hit with especially damaging hurricanes in recent years. In 2005, Hurricane Katrina killed more than 1,800 people and caused massive damage along the coast of the Gulf of Mexico. It was the most expensive storm in the U.S. history, with devastating destruction of infrastructure as well as long-term damage to jobs and the economy. In 2012, Hurricane Sandy hit the East Coast, killing 285 people and causing billions of dollars of damage; it was the country's second most expensive storm in history.

There have always been deadly storms. Some worry that storms such as these are warning signs, harbingers of our changing climate. Others dispute the idea that climate change could be blamed for particular tornadoes or hurricanes. But behind that dispute is the fact that natural disasters can quickly destroy lives. And this points toward the question of the value of nature and our place within it. Is the natural world something to be revered and cherished? Or is Mother Nature to be feared and dominated? And what sort of impact should human beings have on the environment?

These sorts of questions must be confronted as the human population continues to expand. Earth's human population is approaching 7.5 billion.[2] The human population is expected to increase through this century—up to 9.7 billion by 2050 and 11.2 billion by the end of the century.[3] At the same time, standards of living are increasing, which creates greater demand for energy, more pollution, and related environmental impacts. The Organisation for Economic Co-operation and Development concluded in a 2012 report that if we continue developing at the current pace, there will be serious and irreversible environmental impacts that could "endanger two centuries of rising living standards." Among the issues indicated as problems in the report are climate change, loss of biodiversity, water pollution and depletion, and high urban air pollution.[4]

The air pollution problem is particularly severe in developing countries. Poor air quality reportedly contributed to 1.2 million premature deaths in China in 2010.[5] In Beijing and other cities, the air is often so thick with smog that it is difficult to see the tops of skyscrapers. Even in the United States, air pollution remains a problem. California's Central Valley has some of the worst air pollution in the country. It also has a high number of children with asthma and other respiratory problems. Studies in the Central Valley show that air pollution rates are correlated with asthma attacks, heart attacks, and emergency room visits for pneumonia and bronchitis.[6]

We can see from just these few examples that our environment affects us greatly. Some may argue that this is not really an ethical issue, since it is not clear that we have ethical obligations to something as abstract as "the environment." Others will argue that we do have obligations to the environment, as well as to animal species (we will discuss obligations to animals in more detail in Chapter 17). Regardless, most would agree that we ought to be concerned about the negative impacts that environmental problems cause for people, especially the vulnerable poor

House along the Jersey Shore partially swept away by the wall of water created by Hurricane Sandy in 2012.

David Grossman/Alamy Stock Photo

who are often most adversely affected by pollution and natural disasters. We may also have obligations to future generations: to leave a livable world to our children and grandchildren.

THE ENVIRONMENT AND ITS VALUE

To answer the question of whether we have moral obligations with regard to the environment, we should first define our terms. The word *environment* comes from *environs*, which means "in circuit" or "turning around in" in Old French.[7] From this comes the common meaning of environment as surroundings; note its spatial meaning as an area. However, we have also come to use the term to refer to what goes on in that space—that is, the climate and other factors that act on living organisms or individuals inhabiting the space. We can think of the environment as a systematic collection of materials with various physical and chemical interactions. Or we can think of it in a more organic way, giving attention to the many ways in which individual life forms are interdependent in their very nature. From the latter viewpoint, we cannot even think of an individual as an isolated atomic thing because its environment is a fundamental part of itself. From this point of view, the environment stands in relation to the beings within it—not externally, but internally.

What does it mean for people to value the environment? Certainly, most people realize the important effects that their environment has on them. Those things that produce benefit are good; those that cause harm are bad. Most of the time, it is a mixture of both. Growth is generally good, and poison is bad. But where does this positive or negative value come from? Is "badness" somehow there in the poison? Is "goodness" contained in the idea of growth? This is a considerably difficult metaphysical and moral problem. Does a thing have value in the same sense that it has hair or weight? This does not seem to be so because a thing's value does not seem to be something it possesses. When we value something, we have a positive response toward it. One way to explain this is to think that the value of things is a matter of our preferences or desires.

But we also want to know whether we *should* prefer or desire them. Is there something about the things that we value—some attributes that they have, for example—that provide a legitimate basis for our valuing them? In answering this sort of question, we should bear in mind our earlier discussions (in the first half of this book) of the objectivity of values and the relation between the facts of nature and value judgments. Is it possible to derive an "ought" with regard to the environment? Is there a natural state of affairs that we ought to value? Or are our environmental values merely tastes or preferences?

One distinction about value plays a particularly significant role in environmental ethics: that between intrinsic and instrumental value. Things have **intrinsic value**, sometimes referred to as, **inherent value**, when they have value or worth in themselves. We value things that have intrinsic value for their own sake and not for what we can get or do with them. Something has **instrumental value** if it is valued because of its usefulness for some other purpose and for someone. Some environmentalists believe that trees, for example, have only instrumental and not intrinsic value. They think that trees are valuable because of their usefulness to us. Other environmentalists believe that plants and ecosystems have value in themselves.

Another term sometimes used in discussions about environmental ethics is *prima facie value*. (As we saw in our discussion of W. D. Ross's concept of *prima facie duties* in Chapters 3 and 7, *prima facie* means "at first glance" or "at first sight.") Something has prima facie value if it has the kind of value that can be overcome by other interests or values. For example, we might think that a rainforest has some sort of prima facie value but that if the local population needed more land on which to cultivate food, people might be justified in cutting some of the trees to make room for crops.

These considerations about the nature of value and distinctions between different kinds of value play a key role in judging ethical matters that relate to the environment. This is exemplified by two quite different perspectives in environmental ethics.

One is *anthropocentrism*, and the other *ecocentrism* or *biocentrism*. A moderate or centrist position might combine elements of each, in what we might call a mixed view.

ANTHROPOCENTRISM

The terms **anthropocentrism** and **anthropocentric** refer to a human-centered perspective. A perspective is anthropocentric if it holds that humans alone have intrinsic worth or value. According to the anthropocentric perspective, things are good to the extent that they promote the interests of human beings. Thus, for example, some people believe that animals are valuable only insofar as they promote the interests of humans or are useful to us in one or more of a variety of ways. (More discussion of this is found in Chapter 17 on animal ethics.) For example, animals provide nutritional, medical, protective, emotional, and aesthetic benefits for us. People who hold an anthropocentric view also may believe that it is bad to cause animals needless pain, but if their pain is necessary to ensure some important human good, then it is justified. We do obtain useful products from the natural world. For example, taxol is a drug synthesized from the bark of the Pacific yew tree and is useful in treating ovarian and breast cancers. In the most basic and general sense, nature provides us with our food, shelter, and clothing.

According to an anthropocentric perspective, the environment or nature has no value in itself. Instead, its value is measured by how it affects human beings. Wilderness areas are instrumentally

Outline of Moral Approaches to Environmental Ethics			
	Non-Anthropocentrism	**Moderate or Mixed View**	**Anthropocentrism**
Thesis	Biocentric or ecocentric focus of deep ecology	Balancing human and non-human interests	Environmental issues must be resolved in terms of human interests
Corollaries and Implications	Nonhuman entities (species, ecosystems, etc.) have intrinsic value that cannot be reduced to human interests; focus on wilderness preservation	Recognizes intrinsic and instrumental value of non-human beings; sustainable development and environmental justice balance human needs with respect for nature	Human profit, health, and happiness are primary; denies intrinsic value of nonhuman beings (they only have instrumental value); environmental justice for humans only
Connections with Moral Theory	Deontological focus on duties generated by intrinsic value of nature and respect for nature; consequentialist analysis extended to include consequences for nonhuman beings	Deontological concern for nonhuman beings in connection with respect for human interests; consequentialist analysis may balance human and non-human concerns	Deontological and consequentialist concern is focused only on human beings; duties to nature are indirectly based in respect for human property rights or preventing human suffering
Relevant Authors/ Examples	Bill Devall and George Sessions	Ramachandra Guha	William Baxter

valuable to us as sources of recreation and relax-ation, and they provide natural resources to meet our physical needs, such as lumber for housing and fuel. Estuaries, grasslands, and ancient forests also purify our air and clean our water. Sometimes anthropocentric values conflict. For instance, we cannot both preserve old growth forests for their beauty or historical interest and use them for lum-ber. Therefore, we need to think about the relative value of aesthetic experiences and historical appre-ciation as compared with cheaper housing, lumber-ing jobs, and the impact of lumbering on erosion, climate change, forest fire risks, and so on. Consider the value of 2,000-year-old sequoia trees. Touching one of these giants today connects us to the begin-ning of the Common Era. We can imagine all of the major events in history that have occurred during the life of this tree and, in doing so, gain a greater appreciation of the reality of those events and their connection to us and the world as we experience it. How would the value of this experience compare with the value of the tree's wood on the lumber market? Cost–benefit analyses present one method for making such comparisons.

Cost–Benefit Analysis

Because many environmental issues appeal to diverse values and involve competing interests, we can use a technique known as *cost–benefit analysis* to help us think about how to approach any given environmental problem. If we have a choice between various actions or policies, then we need to assess and compare the various harms (or costs) and ben-efits that each entails in order to know which is the better action or policy. Using this method, we should choose the option that has the greater net balance of *benefits* over harms (or *costs*). This is connected to utilitarian reasoning. For example, suppose we are considering whether to hold industrial polluters to stricter emissions standards. If emissions were reduced, acid rain and global warming would be curtailed—important benefits. However, this would also create increased costs for the polluting com-panies, their employees, and those who buy their products or use their services. We should consider whether the benefits would be worth those costs. We would also need to assess the relative costs and ben-efits of alternative policies designed to address acid rain and global warming.

Involved in such analyses are two distinct ele-ments. One is an assessment or description of these factual matters as far as they can be known. What exactly are the likely effects of doing this or that? The other is evaluation, or the establishment of rela-tive values. In cost–benefit analyses, the value is generally defined in anthropocentric terms. But we still need to clarify which values matter most—clean air, economic development, and so forth. In addition, if we have a fixed amount of money or resources to expend on an environmental project, then we know that this money or these resources will not be avail-able for projects elsewhere. Thus, every expenditure will have a certain *opportunity cost*. In being willing to pay for the environmental project, we will have some sense of its importance in comparison with other things that we will not then be able to do or have. However, if we value something else just as much or more than cleaner air or water, for example, then we will not be willing to pay for the cleaner air or water.

In making such evaluations, we may know what monetary costs will be added to a particular forest product, such as lumber, if limits on logging were enacted. However, we are less sure about how we should value a tree that is two thousand years old. How do we measure the historical appreciation or the aesthetic value of the tree (or the animals that live in the tree)? How do we measure the recreational value of the wilderness? What is beauty or the life of a tree worth? The value of these "intangibles" is dif-ficult to measure because measuring implies that we use a standard means of evaluation. Only if we have such a standard can we compare, say, the value of a breathtaking view to that of a dam about to be built on the site. Sometimes, we use monetary valu-ations, even for such intangibles as human lives or life years. For example, in insurance and other con-texts, people attempt to give some measure of the value of a life.[8] Doing so is sometimes necessary, but it is obviously also problematic.

Environmental Justice

Another concern from the anthropocentric perspective is how environmental costs are distributed. This is connected to the issues of social justice and economic justice (as discussed in Chapter 14). One central and difficult issue is the question of how our activities will affect future generations. Do we have an obligation to leave them a clean environment? It is difficult to figure out what justice requires for future generations. But the more pressing issue is the distribution of benefits and harms for actual persons living in the present.

Environmental justice is a mainstream idea, which the EPA defines as "the fair treatment and meaningful involvement of all people regardless of race, color, national origin, or income with respect to the development, implementation, and enforcement of environmental laws, regulations, and policies."[9] It may seem odd that we would need to emphasize that environmental issues should contain an element of social justice and equity. But in reality, it is often the poor and disenfranchised who end up suffering most from environmental degradation. For example, consider the fact that affluent nations with established and efficient infrastructure will be able to respond to the changing climate in ways that poorer nations will not. Poor people tend to live closer to polluted lands and toxic waste dumps because more affluent people can move away and can use their resources to fight against pollution in their areas. This is not only a concern within the United States, where poor people suffer most from the effects of pollution, but it is also a concern across the globe. Environmental regulations are often nonexistent or are loosely enforced in developing countries.

One notorious case that frequently comes up in discussions of environmental justice is the gas leak at the Union Carbide plant in Bhopal, India, in 1984. More than 3,000 people died within the first days of the poisonous gas leak. The final death toll is estimated to be at least 15,000, with the health of more than 600,000 people affected.[10] Amnesty International puts the death toll higher: 22,000 killed with at least 150,000 still battling diseases of the lungs or liver that are attributed to the toxic waste.[11] In addition to the human casualties, the disaster left behind polluted land and water, which is still not cleaned up. The local managers responsible for the disaster received minor fines and punishments after being found guilty of criminal negligence in the case. However, the former chairman of Union Carbide, Warren Anderson, never received any punishment. In 2012, an American court dismissed a lawsuit filed by Bhopal residents against Anderson and Dow Chemical, which owns Union Carbide. The dismissal protected Anderson and the company from claims for environmental remediation at the disaster site.[12] This case is remarkable because of the numbers affected and the relatively minor punishments meted out to responsible parties, and because it pushes our understanding of what counts as "the environment." Often we think of environmentalism as focused on wild natural settings. But the air and water of urban landscapes are also part of the environment. The Bhopal case reminds us that pollution can cause death and that it is often poor people who suffer the most from the impacts of industrial accidents.[13]

There are a variety of issues that come under the rubric of environmental justice, including where waste dumps are located, whether farm workers and farming communities are properly protected from the effects of fertilizers and pesticides, how uranium is mined, how hunting and fishing is regulated and enforced, who pays for environmental remediation efforts, and who guarantees that polluters are punished. These concerns are connected to other social justice concerns and are entirely anthropocentric. This has led some to complain that the focus on environmental justice is a distraction from the larger concern for the value of ecosystems, in themselves, apart from human interests. One scholar of environmentalism, Kevin DeLuca, laments this anthropocentric focus, concluding, "Abandoning wilderness-centered environmentalism is a disastrous error. The finest moments of environmentalism often involve humans exceeding self-concern and caring for wilderness and other species because of their intrinsic being."[14] This view points us toward the ecocentric or biocentric approach to environmental ethics.

ECOCENTRISM

According to the anthropocentric perspective, environmental concerns ought to be directed to the betterment of people, who alone have intrinsic value. In contrast with this view is **ecocentrism** (or **biocentrism**), which holds that it is not just humans who have intrinsic worth or value, but also such things as plants, animals, and ecosystems. There are variations within this perspective, with some theorists holding that individual life forms have such intrinsic worth and others stressing that it is whole systems or ecosystems that have such value. In this view, ethical questions related to the environment involve determining what is in the best interests of these life forms, or what furthers or contributes to (or is a satisfactory fit with) some ecosystem.

Ecocentrists are critical of anthropocentrists. Why, they ask, do only humans have intrinsic value while everything else has merely instrumental value for us? Some fault the Judeo-Christian tradition for this view. In particular, they single out the biblical mandate to "subdue" the earth and "have dominion over the fish of the sea and over the birds of the air and every living thing that moves upon the Earth" as being responsible for this instrumentalist view of nature and other living things.[15] Others argue that anthropocentrism is a reductionist perspective. According to this view, all of nature is reduced to the level of "thing-hood." The seventeenth-century French philosopher René Descartes is sometimes cited as a source of this reductionist point of view because of his belief that the essential element of humanity is the ability to think ("I think, therefore I am," etc.) and his belief that animals are mere biological machines.[16] Early evolutionary accounts also sometimes depicted humans as the pinnacle of evolution or the highest or last link in some great chain of being. We can ask ourselves whether we place too high a value on human beings and our powers of reason and intelligence. Ecocentrists criticize the view that we ought to seek to understand nature so that we can have power over it because it implies that our primary relation to nature is one of domination.

Ecocentrists hold that we ought rather to regard nature with admiration and respect because nature and natural beings have intrinsic value. Let us return to our example of the 2,000-year-old sequoia tree. You may have seen pictures of trees large enough for tunnels to be cut through, allowing cars to pass. In the 1880s, such a tunnel was cut through a giant sequoia near Wawona, California, on the south end of what is now Yosemite National Park. Tourists enjoyed driving through the tunnel. However, some people claimed that this was a mutilation of and an insult to this majestic tree. They said that the tree itself had a kind of integrity, intrinsic value, and dignity that should not be invaded lightly. Another way to put it would be to say that the tree itself had moral standing.[17] What we do to the tree itself matters morally, they insisted.

On what account could trees be thought to have this kind of moral standing? All organisms, it might be argued, are self-maintaining systems.[18] Because they are organized systems or integrated living wholes, organisms are thought to have intrinsic value and even moral standing. The value may be only prima facie, but nevertheless, they have their own value, in themselves, and are not just to be valued in terms of their usefulness to people. According to this perspective, the giant sequoias of Wawona should not merely be thought of in terms of their tourist value.

Further, there are things that can be good and bad for the trees, themselves. For example, the tunnel in the Wawona tree eventually weakened the tree, and it fell during a snowstorm in 1968. Although trees are not **moral agents**—beings who act responsibly for moral reasons—they may still be thought of as moral patients. A **moral patient** is any being for which what we do to it matters, in itself. A moral patient is any being toward whom we can have *direct duties*, rather than simply *indirect duties*. If a tree is a moral patient, then we ought to behave in a certain way toward the tree for its sake, and not just indirectly for the sake of how it will eventually affect us. Ecocentrists may argue that there are things that are in the best interests of trees, even if the trees take no conscious interest in them.

In addition to those ecocentrists who argue that all life forms have intrinsic value, there are others who stress the value of ecosystems. An *ecosystem* is an integrated system of interacting and interdependent parts within a circumscribed locale. They are loosely structured wholes. The boundary changes and some members come and go. Sometimes, there is competition within the whole—as in the relation between predators and prey in a given habitat. Sometimes there is *symbiosis*, with each part living in cooperative community with the other parts—as in the relationship between flowers and the bees that pollinate them. The need to survive pushes various creatures to be creative in their struggle for an adaptive fit. There is a unity to the whole, but it is loose and decentralized. Why is this unity to be thought of as having value in itself?

One answer is provided by the environmental philosopher Aldo Leopold. In the 1940s, he wrote in his famous essay "The Land Ethic" that we should think about the land as "a fountain of energy flowing through a circuit of soils, plants, and animals."[19] Look at any environment supporting life on our planet, and you will find a *system* of life—intricately interwoven and interdependent elements that function as a whole. Such a system is organized in the form of a *biotic pyramid*, with myriad smaller organisms at the bottom and gradually fewer and more complex organisms at the top. Plants depend on the earth, insects depend on the plants, and other animals depend on the insects. Leopold did not think it amiss to speak about the whole system as being healthy or unhealthy. If the soil is washed away or abnormally flooded, then the whole system suffers or is sick. In this system, individual organisms feed off one another. Some elements come and others go. It is the whole that continues. Leopold also believed that a particular type of ethics follows from this view of nature—a biocentric or ecocentric ethics. He believed that "a thing is right when it tends to preserve the integrity, stability, and beauty of the biotic community. It is wrong when it tends to do otherwise."[20] The system has a certain *integrity* because it is a unity of interdependent elements that combine to make a whole with a unique character. It has a

certain *stability*, not in that it does not change, but that it changes only gradually. Finally, it has a particular *beauty*. Here beauty is a matter of harmony, well-ordered form, or unity in diversity.[21] When envisioned on a larger scale, the entire Earth system may then be regarded as one system with a certain integrity, stability, and beauty. Morality becomes a matter of preserving this system or doing only what befits it.

The kind of regard for nature that is manifest in biocentric views is not limited to contemporary philosophers. Native American views on nature provide a fertile source of biocentric thinking. For example, Eagle Man, an Oglala Sioux writer, emphasizes the unity of all living things. All come from tiny seeds and so all are brothers and sisters. The seeds come from Mother Earth and depend on her for sustenance. We owe her respect, for she comes from the "Great Spirit Above."[22] Also, certain forms of European and American Romanticism imbue nature with spiritual value. The transcendentalists Ralph Waldo Emerson and Henry David Thoreau fall into this category. Transcendentalism was a movement of romantic idealism that arose in the United States in the mid-nineteenth century. Rather than regarding nature as foreign or alien, Emerson and Thoreau thought of it as a friend or kindred spirit. Acting on such a viewpoint, Thoreau retreated to Walden Pond to live life to its fullest and commune with nature. He wanted to know its moods and changes and all its phenomena. Although Thoreau and Emerson read the "lessons" of nature, they also read Eastern texts and were influenced by the history of Western philosophy. Some have characterized aspects of their nature theory as idealism, the view that all is idea or spirit; others characterize it as pantheism, the doctrine that holds that God is present in the whole of nature. The transcendentalists influenced John Muir, the founder of the Sierra Club. Muir held a similar view of the majesty, sacredness, and spiritual value of nature.[23] Muir transformed his love of nature into practical action, successfully petitioning Congress for passage of a national parks bill that established Yosemite and Sequoia national parks.

Romantic and idealistic ideas provide a stark contrast to anthropocentric views of a reductionist type. However, they also raise many questions. For example, we can ask the transcendentalist how nature can be spirit or god in more than a metaphorical sense. And we can ask proponents of views such as Aldo Leopold's the following question: Why is it that nature is good? Nature can be cruel, at least from the point of view of certain animals, and even from our own viewpoint as we suffer the damaging results of typhoons or volcanic eruptions. And, more abstractly, on what basis can we argue that whatever exists is good?

Deep Ecology

Another variant of ecocentrism is the deep ecology movement. Members of this movement wish to distinguish themselves from mainstream environmentalism, which they call "shallow ecology" and criticize as fundamentally anthropocentric. The term *deep ecology* was first used by Arne Naess, a Norwegian philosopher and environmentalist.[24] Deep ecologists take a holistic view of nature and believe that we should look more deeply to find the root causes of environmental degradation. The idea is that our environmental problems are deeply rooted in the Western psyche, and radical changes of viewpoint are necessary if we are to solve these problems. Western reductionism, individualism, and consumerism are said to be the causes of our environmental problems. The solution is to rethink and reformulate certain metaphysical beliefs about whether all reality is reducible to atoms in motion. It is also to rethink what it is to be an individual. Are individuals separate and independent beings? Or are they interrelated parts of a whole?

According to deep ecologists, solving our environmental problems requires a change in our views about what is a good quality of life. The good life, deep ecologists assert, is not one that stresses the possession of things and the search for satisfaction of wants and desires. Instead, a good life is one that is lived simply, in communion with one's local ecosystem. Arne Naess lived his message. He retreated to a cabin in the mountains of Norway, which he built with his own hands. He lived a modest life until his death at age ninety-six in 2009.

In addition to describing the need for radical changes in our basic outlook on life, the deep ecologist platform also holds that any intrusion into nature to change it requires justification. If we intervene to change nature, then we must show that a vital need of ours is at stake.[25] We should be cautious in our actions because the results of our actions may be far-reaching and harmful. And we should view nature *as it is* as good, right, and well balanced. Deep ecology also includes the belief that the flourishing of nonhuman life requires a "substantial decrease in the human population."[26] George Sessions argues that "humanity must drastically scale down its industrial activities on Earth, change its consumption lifestyles, stabilize" and "reduce the size of the human population by humane means."[27]

Some critics maintain that deep ecologists are misanthropic because of their interest in reducing the human population or suggest that they are advocating totalitarian methods for achieving a reduction in human population. Some go so far as to malign deep ecology as "eco-fascism," equating it with fascist plans to create an ecological utopia through population control. Others worry that there may be implicit eugenic and imperialistic agendas when affluent Americans and Europeans advocate population control (see the Ramachandra Guha reading at the end of this chapter). However, deep ecologists would reply that they recognize that population reduction can be achieved only through humane methods such as the empowerment of women and making contraception available.

The members of the deep ecology movement have been quite politically active. Their creed contains the belief that people are responsible for Earth. Beliefs such as this often provide a basis for the tactics of groups such as Earth First! Some radicals advocate direct action to protect the environment, including various forms of "ecosabotage"—for example, spiking trees to prevent logging and cutting power lines.[28] It is important to note that Arne Naess, himself, was interested in nonviolence. He wrote extensively about Gandhi's nonviolent methods, and he conceived his commitment to the environment in conjunction with Gandhian ideas about the interconnectedness of life. And he employed nonviolent methods in his own protests—such as chaining himself to a boulder to protest a project aimed at building a dam on a river.

Critics of deep ecology describe aggressive forms of environmental protest as "ecoterrorism."[29] Of course, there are important distinctions to be made between nonviolent protest, civil disobedience, and more violent forms of protest. Nonetheless, deep ecologists maintain that the stakes are high and that action should be taken to change the status quo— even if this action is only at the level of personal lifestyle choices. On a philosophical level, the view that all incursions into nature can be justified only by our vital needs seems to run counter to our intuitions. The implication here is that we must not build a golf course or a house patio because these would change the earth and its vegetation, and the need to play golf or sit on a patio is hardly vital. Do natural things have as much value as people and their interests? The view that nature, itself, has a "good of its own" or that the whole system has value, in itself, raises complex metaphysical and psychological questions. However we may feel about these issues, deep ecologists provide a valuable service by calling our attention to the possible deep philosophical roots and causes of some of our environmental problems.

Ecofeminism

Another variant of ecological ethics is called *ecofeminism* or *ecological feminism*.[30] It may be seen as part of a broader movement that locates the source of environmental problems not in metaphysics or worldviews, as deep ecologists do, but in social practices. *Social ecology*, as this wider movement is called, holds that we should look to particular social patterns and structures to discover what is wrong with our relationship to the environment. Ecofeminists believe that the problem lies in a male-centered view of nature—that is, one of human domination over nature. According to Karen Warren, a philosopher and environmental activist, ecofeminism is "the position that there are important connections... between the domination of women and the domination of nature, an understanding of which is crucial

to both feminism and environmental ethics."[31] Note here that deep ecologists and ecofeminists do not necessarily agree. The deep ecologists may criticize ecofeminists for concentrating insufficiently on the environment, and ecofeminists may accuse deep ecologists of the very male-centered view that they believe is the source of our environmental problems.[32]

A variety of ecofeminist views are espoused by diverse groups of feminists.[33] One version celebrates the ways that women differ from men. This view is espoused by those who hold that women—because of their female experience or nature—tend to value organic, non-oppressive relationships. They stress caring and emotion, and they seek to replace conflict and assertion of rights with cooperation and community. This idea has obvious connections with the work of those interested in the feminist ethics of care (as discussed in Chapter 9). From this perspective, a feminine ethic should guide our relationship to nature. Rather than use nature in an instrumentalist fashion, they urge, we should cooperate with nature. We should manifest a caring and benevolent regard for nature, just as we do for other human beings. One version of this view would have us think of nature, itself, as in some way divine. Rather than think of God as a distant creator who transcends nature, these religiously oriented ecofeminists think of God as a being *within* nature. Some also refer to this God as "Mother Nature" or "Gaia," after the name of a Greek goddess.[34]

Another version of ecofeminism rejects the dualism often found in the Western philosophical tradition. They hold that this tradition promotes the devaluing and domination of both women and nature. Rather than divide reality into contrasting elements—the active and passive, the rational and emotional, the dominant and subservient—they encourage us to recognize the diversity within nature and among people. They would similarly support a variety of ways of relating to nature. Thus, they believe that even though science that proceeds from a male-oriented desire to control nature has made advances and continues to do so, its very orientation causes it to miss important aspects of nature.

If, instead, we also have a feeling for nature and a listening attitude, then we might be better able to know what actually is there. They also believe that we humans should see ourselves as part of the community of nature, not as distinct, non-natural beings functioning in a world that is thought to be alien to us. Some versions of ecofeminism emphasize the way that women understand their bodies and their reproductive power, maintaining that women have a closer relationship with the body and thus with the natural world. Others view feminine categories as socially constructed, albeit in a way that emphasizes the female connection with nature (and the male as liberated from, and thus able to dominate, nature).

It is sometimes difficult to conceive the practical upshots of ecocentrism, ecological feminism, and deep ecology. We noted previously that Naess and the deep ecologists emphasize living simply and in connection with the local environment. Ecofeminists might add that a sense of justice and equality also requires that we attend to the ways in which environmental destruction impacts women and the way that male-dominant gender roles tend to reinforce exploitation and domination of nature. Ecofeminism and deep ecology both pose a serious challenge to the status quo and its anthropocentric and dominating approach to the natural world.

Ethical anthropocentrists will advocate wise and judicious use of nature, one that does not destroy the very nature that we value and on which we depend. But nonanthropocentrists maintain that we must care for and about nature for its own sake and not just in terms of what it can do for us. This debate is about the very place of human beings within the natural world.

CURRENT ISSUES

We can now take these anthropocentric and ecocentric theories and examine how they might apply to environmental issues confronting us today. We will consider the following problems: climate change, ozone depletion, waste disposal and pollution, and wilderness preservation. We will also consider international environmental conventions as a possible means of addressing global environmental issues.

And finally, we will consider the vexing problem of sustainable development and a problem known as "the tragedy of the commons."

Climate Change

The great majority of scientists now agree that our modern industrial society has created a potentially deadly phenomenon known as the *greenhouse effect*, *global warming*, or *climate change*. There is no denying that the global climate is changing, as the level of carbon dioxide in the atmosphere has increased during the past century. In the spring of 2013, the concentration of carbon dioxide (CO_2) in the atmosphere was measured at a new high of 400 parts per million (or ppm). In 2016, NASA reported that global CO_2 concentration was now at 403 ppm.[35] This level of CO_2 concentration had not been seen on Earth since the Pliocene epoch, 2.5 million years ago, when Earth was three degrees Centigrade warmer than it is today and when sea levels were five meters higher.[36] Coastlines are crumbling as the climate changes and sea levels rise.[37] There is substantial, albeit complicated, evidence that storms are increasing in severity as a result of climate change heating up the oceans.[38] And there is no question that the Arctic ice cap is melting, with ever-larger swaths of ice disappearing during the summer months. In the summer of 2012, the seasonal Arctic melt reached a new low, with the ice covering only about 24 percent of the Arctic Ocean. In the 1970s, coverage during this season was around 50 percent.[39] In the winter of 2013, NASA indicated that the winter maximum (the maximum extent of Arctic sea ice) was the fifth lowest sea-ice maximum measured in the past thirty-five years. According to NASA, "some models predict that the Arctic Ocean could be ice-free in the summer in just a few decades."[40] Melting Arctic ice is not only a *sign* of climate change; it is also a *contributor* to the process. The white Arctic ice reflects the sun, so the more ice there is, the more heat is reflected without being absorbed by the ocean. As the ice melts, however, the dark blue water of the ocean absorbs the solar rays no longer being reflected by the ice, which, in turn, warms the nearby air. The warmer air melts more ice, and so on, creating a feedback loop.

The Arctic ice cap is not the only significant melting process associated with climate change. The ice that covers Antarctica and Greenland has also been melting at an alarming rate and slipping into the sea. In 2012, there was a rapid melting event that caused 97 percent of the Greenland ice sheet to shed water. If Greenland's 680,000 cubic miles of ice melted, it would raise sea levels by up to 20 feet.[41] NASA reports that Greenland has been losing 287 billion metric tons of ice per year, while Antarctica has been losing 134 billion metric tons per year.[42] While most experts think it is unlikely that this massive rise in sea levels will happen for several hundred years, some experts believe that sea levels could rise by up to three feet by 2100.[43] The U.S. Environmental Protection Agency (EPA) predicts that by 2100, global temperatures will rise from 2°F to 11.5°F and sea levels will rise about two feet.[44] Climate change has also caused the oceans to become more acidic as carbon dioxide is absorbed into the oceans. This process has already had negative impacts on delicate marine life, such as the oysters of the Pacific Northwest: oyster shells don't form properly in more acidic water.[45] There will be adverse impacts on fish and corals as the oceans become more acidic.

Melting Arctic ice may also change patterns of ocean currents that have been stable for the past 10,000 years. For example, the Gulf Stream pulls warm water north from near the equator and into the north Atlantic, where some of it evaporates. As the water evaporates, the ocean becomes saltier and heavier and the denser water sinks, cooling and starting a return path to the south. Changing temperatures could alter this process. Shifts in the Gulf Stream could cause weather and climatic changes in Europe and North America, although scientists disagree about what these impacts might be. Some warn that Europe would cool if the Gulf Stream shifted, and others think this is unlikely.[46] While this dispute is an indication of the difficulty of making predictions about climate change, the vast majority of scientists agree that the atmosphere and the oceans are changing.[47]

Climate change may produce hundreds of millions of environmental refugees, which is an environmental justice concern. Those refugees may be displaced by rising tides, storm damage, and changes in agricultural production.[48] Residents of low-lying islands—such as Kiribati, the Maldives, and the Seychelles—and low, flood-prone countries—such as Bangladesh—may be dislocated as sea levels rise and river floods become harder to control.[49]

Some skeptics dispute whether the changes are entirely man-made, but the vast majority of experts believe that one of the major causes of climate change is the burning of fossil fuels, which are the primary energy source for modern societies. The resulting gases—carbon dioxide, methane, fluorocarbons, and nitrous oxide, among others—are released into the atmosphere. There, these gases combine with water vapor and prevent the sun's infrared rays from radiating back into space. The trapped solar radiation contributes to increased air temperature. In this way, the gases function in much the same way as the glass panes of a greenhouse. Newly released gases will remain in the atmosphere for thirty to a hundred years; since greenhouse gas emissions continue to rise, their buildup in the atmosphere is expected to increase over time. Automobile exhaust, along with industrial power plants and agricultural operations, produce most of the gases that lead to climate change. Deforestation also contributes to the warming because there are fewer trees and other plant life to absorb carbon dioxide before it reaches the atmosphere.

According to the EPA, carbon dioxide accounts for 82 percent of U.S. greenhouse gas emissions.[50] Carbon dioxide (CO_2) is emitted when fossil fuels are burned to produce electricity or to fuel cars and other forms of transportation. CO_2 is also produced as a by-product of industrial processes and, along with methane, as a result of animal agriculture. Scientists have warned that global emissions should be limited and reduced. When civilization originally developed, the atmosphere contained about 275 ppm of CO_2. Many have argued that we ought to limit global CO_2 levels to 350 parts per million.[51] And at one point, the aim was to reach peak emissions in 2015 and reduce them thereafter. As we have seen, we passed the 350 ppm threshold, and emissions continue to increase. The 350 ppm target was intended to limit climate change to 2°C. It seems unlikely now that the global temperature increase will be limited to 2°C. In light of ongoing emissions increases, some are calling the 2°C goal a fantasy.[52]

Although the bulk of greenhouse gases emitted since the start of the Industrial Revolution have come from Europe, the United States, and other developed regions, recent increases in carbon dioxide levels are often attributed to growth in the developing world, especially in China.[53] According to the EPA (based upon 2011 data), the main CO_2 producers as a share of the world's total CO_2 emitted are China (28 percent), the United States (16 percent), and the European Union (10 percent).[54]

Climate changes have occurred throughout Earth's history, and while they have usually been gradual, that has not always been the case. Sixty-five million years ago, the dinosaurs are thought to have been wiped out by a dramatic and rapid change in climate caused by a giant meteorite that hit Earth near Mexico's Yucatán Peninsula. The meteorite may have put so much dust into the air that it blocked much of the sun's light, causing temperatures to drop and plants to die—which, in turn, brought about the demise of the dinosaurs. Within the time span of human existence, climate changes have usually occurred over several generations, allowing people to adapt. If these changes occur rapidly, however, such adaptation becomes more difficult. For example, food supplies could be severely stressed. Reduced land fertility could also pose a threat to international security. If crop yields decrease and water shortages increase, peoples and nations suffering severe shortages may resort to violence. These people may migrate to urban slums, causing overcrowding, widespread poverty, and infrastructure breakdown.[55] All of the issues listed above are anthropocentric concerns—they are focused on how climate change may impact human beings. These issues might also be supplemented with a more ecocentric focus on the species and ecosystems that may be disrupted by climate change.

How do we know that present-day global warming is not just a part of a natural pattern? Scientists have determined that recent temperatures and the increased levels of carbon dioxide in the atmosphere are dramatically greater than anything that has occurred in the past. Scientists have drilled deep into the ice and brought up cylindrical *ice cores* that have markings similar to the rings inside of trees. They can read the age of the ice cores and analyze the chemicals and air bubbles in them to determine the average temperature of each year, as well as the carbon dioxide levels during each year. Samples as old as six hundred thousand years have been obtained, and from these samples, scientists know that the temperature and greenhouse gases have increased with unprecedented speed in the past decades. From this, they can also predict how temperatures will continue to rise unless emissions are controlled.[56]

Scientists still disagree about how much Earth will warm, how quickly it will happen, and how different regions will be affected. However, evidence is now accumulating for the acceleration of this effect in the form of receding glaciers, rising sea levels, and the spreading of plant and animal species farther north and to higher altitudes that were previously too cold to support such life. Some European butterfly and bird species have moved their habitats northward of their previous ranges. Unfortunately, some studies show that not all species are able to keep pace with rapidly changing climate zones. During the past twenty years, some butterfly species have failed to keep pace with changing climate zones by a magnitude of approximately 85 miles; some birds are now living 130 miles from their natural climate range.[57] When we consider the problem of animals unable to adapt quickly enough to the planet's changing climate zones, should we focus on the intrinsic value of butterflies and birds, or should we focus on what this may portend for human beings as global temperatures continue to rise?

Further evidence of an accelerated global warming can be seen in the melting of mountain glaciers.[58] While some ecocentrists may argue that mountain glaciers have a kind of intrinsic value, the loss will also have a practical impact on human communities that depend upon glaciers for their water supply. The melting of mountain glaciers can also produce more severe flooding during the rainy season, along with less regular flows of water during the rest of the year.[59]

Some people may benefit from climate change—say, those living in northern latitudes. But it is most likely that changing crop yields and lost coastlines will have negative impacts on billions of human beings. Returning us to the concerns of environmental justice, it is important to note that those who are historically most responsible for climate-changing emissions are the least likely to be harmed. Affluent people living in developed countries will be able to adapt and respond to climate change, while poor people in developing countries are most likely to be harmed. Moreover, the cost to future generations must also be considered. How much we worry about the impact on our descendants will depend on the expected severity of the effects. Those who calculate the costs and benefits must also factor in the uncertainties that are involved.

What can be done about global warming? And is it too late? Scientists generally believe that we may still have time to prevent radical climate change. But they tend to agree that we need to reduce the emission of greenhouse gases now. And some warn that we may be too late. James Hansen, the former head of the NASA Goddard Institute for Space Studies, has sounded a significant alarm. In 2012, Hansen warned that disintegrating ice sheets would accelerate climate change. As a result, "Sea levels would rise and destroy coastal cities. Global temperatures would become intolerable. Twenty to fifty percent of the planet's species would be driven to extinction. Civilization would be at risk."[60] Hansen's argument is ultimately anthropocentric: he means *human* civilization is at risk. In 2016, Hansen and other climate scientists updated this warning, arguing that melting ice would cause a rapid sea-level rise of up to several meters. This could inundate all coastal cities by the end of this century. Hansen states, "That would mean the loss of all coastal cities, most of the world's largest cities, and all of their history."[61] Because Hansen views the risk as so great and the

consequences so dire, he opposes new fossil fuel projects that would ultimately lead to more CO_2 emissions—including the development of tar sands in Canada and new pipelines to transport crude oil. From Hansen's perspective, remaining fossil fuel reserves should stay buried in the ground, no matter how profitable or useful they may prove in the short term.

Among the means of reducing greenhouse gases are better mileage standards for cars and expanded public transportation options. Other methods include alternative sources of power, such as wind, solar, and nuclear. European countries have taken the lead in this effort. For example, Germany has made a commitment to abandon fossil fuels by 2050 and, in recent years, has made great strides toward replacing its fossil fuel infrastructure with renewable energy sources.[62] According to Stanford professor Mark Z. Jacobsen: "It's absolutely not true that we need natural gas, coal, or oil—we think it's a myth. . . . You could power America with renewables from a technical and economic standpoint. The biggest obstacles are social and political—what you need is the will to do it."[63] Opponents of alternative energy sources argue that the economic costs would be prohibitive and would place great burdens on taxpayers. Whether or not this is true, the position points to a different set of values and a different assessment of costs and benefits.

Instead of, or in addition to, greater fuel efficiency standards and alternative energy sources, some suggest imposing a carbon tax on people and companies that burn fossil fuels. This tax could be used, for example, to reimburse or give tax credits to homeowners who use solar cells or energy-efficient appliances; the tax could also be used to fund research into possible means of capturing carbon dioxide and preventing it from being released into the atmosphere. A small tax could yield some $50 billion for such purposes. Former Vice President Al Gore even proposes that such a tax be used in place of payroll taxes for Social Security and Medicare.[64]

Other proposed solutions to climate change involve so-called "geo-engineering" projects. These technological solutions include proposals to remove carbon from the atmosphere and store it underground, as well as proposals to protect Earth from the sun—either by building shades in space or by stimulating volcanoes to produce ash, which would reflect sunlight. These geo-engineering solutions aim to fix the problem without addressing the underlying issues of consumption and pollution. From the standpoint of deep ecology, such an approach looks like another example of human hubris. But proponents of geo-engineering argue that it is too late to halt climate change by returning to the sort of simple, eco-friendly living espoused by deep ecologists. Furthermore, as the climate continues to change, environmental justice concerns will point in the direction of plans to mitigate the damage that climate change will create for vulnerable human populations.

Ozone Depletion

A second environmental problem—and one about which activists and scientists have been concerned for decades—is ozone depletion. In the 1970s, scientists detected holes or breaks in the layer of ozone at the upper reaches of the stratosphere. This layer of ozone protects Earth from the damaging effects of excessive ultraviolet radiation from the sun, which can cause skin cancer and cataracts. The holes in the ozone layer were determined to be caused by chlorine-bearing pollutants such as the chlorofluorocarbons, which were widely used in fire extinguishers and as refrigerants, cleaning agents, and spray propellants. Climate change is also a factor in ozone depletion, as the heating of the lower atmosphere has an impact on ozone in the upper atmosphere.

Like global warming, ozone depletion negatively impacts both humans and wildlife. For example, fish in waters around Great Britain "are suffering sunburn and blisters caused by the thinning ozone layer," and such effects threaten some fish species with extinction.[65] And the ozone hole over the South Pole has affected the circulation of ocean waters in the Southern Ocean.[66] This will cause further changes in ocean temperatures, which will impact global climate. The good news is that the

international community worked together to ban the use of the chlorofluorocarbons (CFCs). The Montreal Protocol (1987) called for many developed countries to phase out their use by 1996. This is a hopeful sign of international cooperation. However, given current rates of depletion and the amount of CFCs in the atmosphere, it may take fifty years for the ozone layer to repair itself.[67]

From a cost–benefit perspective, we should ask whether the cost to us from decreasing or eliminating the causes of ozone depletion is worth the savings in human lives. Here, again, we come up against the issue of how to value human life. The greater its value, the more surely we ought to stop using these chemicals, and the harder we ought to work to find alternatives. The issue of ozone depletion may be viewed as one example of the way that international cooperation based on cost–benefit analysis can work to solve some environmental problems.

Waste Disposal and Pollution

Another issue of environmental concern is waste disposal and pollution. Like global warming and ozone depletion, the negative impacts of these problems on humans and animals are far-reaching. Humans produce tons of garbage each year that must be put somewhere. Just how much garbage is there? According to the EPA, based on 2012 data, "Americans generated about 251 million tons of trash and recycled and composted almost 87 million tons of this material, equivalent to a 34.5 percent recycling rate. On average, Americans recycled and composted 1.51 pounds out of our individual waste generation rate of 4.38 pounds per person per day."[68] While the United States has the world's highest rate of per capita garbage production, China is quickly catching up. According to the World Bank, China has the fastest growing rate of waste production.[69]

Typical American trash includes a variety of disposable items. According to the Clean Air Council, every year, Americans use one billion shopping bags, which create tons of landfill waste. Less than 1 percent of plastic bags are recycled each year.[70] The problem with plastic shopping bags is that they do not biodegrade, or break down, in landfills.

Instead, they break into small pieces, which contaminate the soil and water. Cities across the country have considered banning plastic bags or imposing a use tax on them. Proponents of the ban argued that the plastic bags make up a majority of marine debris and cost millions to dispose of. But critics pointed out that paper bags are not really that much better—since they take up more space in landfills.[71] Many say the preferred option is reusable cloth bags; however, some maintain that reusable cloth shopping bags are unsanitary and spread disease, citing a study that showed that foodborne illness increased in San Francisco after the city banned plastic bags in 2007.[72]

We also generate a lot of garbage through the use of disposable cups and food service items. The Clean Air Council reports that the average American office worker uses about 500 disposable cups every year.[73] Americans use over one billion Starbucks cups per year.[74] Starbucks has worked to find ways to make sure that those cups are recyclable and has recently introduced reusable cups as an alternative. But garbage generated by fast-food restaurants still remains a common feature of urban litter.[75]

So-called e-waste is also becoming a major problem. This includes outdated cellphones, computers, TVs, and printers. Over 40 million tons of this waste is discarded globally per year, with two countries—China and the United States—accounting for one-third of the world's electronic waste.[76] Such items contain huge amounts of toxins: beryllium, cadmium, chromium, lead, mercury, and so on. Some electronics companies are working hard to find less harmful ways to deal with electronic waste. But too often, there are environmental justice issues involved, as electronic waste is commonly sent to countries in Africa and Asia, where it is dumped, often at the expense of local populations and pollution of the local environment.[77] One recent study indicates that people living near an electronic waste dump in China face elevated cancer risks, as a result of exposure to hazardous chemicals. Residents were melting down scavenged electronic products in their homes and backyards in order to extract precious metals concealed within those products, with health

hazards resulting from exposure to toxic fumes produced during this process.[78]

One obvious solution to the e-waste problem is recycling. Indeed, the solution to the problem of waste disposal, in general, is recycling. For example, recycled bottles and cans can be turned into reusable metal and glass, as well as roads, bike parts, and even carpets.[79] Americans use more than eighty billion aluminum beverage cans every year, recycling over sixty billion of them.[80] The energy used to recycle aluminum is 95 percent less than the cost of manufacturing cans from virgin materials. Recycling one aluminum can saves enough energy to keep a 100-watt bulb burning for nearly four hours.[81]

Recycling, in fact, is tackling a wide variety of problems related to waste disposal and pollution. One promising idea is to find ways to convert food and plant waste into fuel. Organic material converted to fuel is known as *biomass fuel* or *biofuel*. Methane gas can be collected from landfills. And plants can be converted directly into usable forms of energy—such as corn that is converted into ethanol. Biomass fuels can be produced in ways that contribute to pollution and to climate change, but when done right—using waste products, rather than growing plants only for fuel consumption—they could hold one of the keys to a sustainable future. One promising idea is to use switchgrass—a common grass native to North America—to produce biofuels in the form of pellets that can be burned in stoves or in the form of ethanol, which can run combustion engines.[82]

While the use of recycling and the development of biomass fuels offer solutions to the problem of waste and pollution, these approaches remain firmly within the anthropocentric approach that emphasizes minimizing costs and maximizing benefits for human beings. A simpler solution, and one that is espoused by advocates of ecocentrism, would be to cut down on consumption, in general. From this perspective, it is not enough to recycle or to drive a biofuel vehicle—since recycling, itself, uses resources and energy and the biofuel vehicle still contributes its share of pollution. A more ecocentric approach would encourage people to ask, for example, whether it is necessary to use aluminum cans at all (not just whether it is necessary to recycle them) or whether it is possible to cut down on driving. The anthropocentric approach is not necessarily opposed to cutting down on consumption; however, it is in favor of finding ways to maximize our ability to consume while minimizing the ecological impact of consumption.

Wilderness Preservation

The use and preservation of the planet's wild and undeveloped areas is an issue of enduring ethical concern. According to the University of Montana's Wilderness.net information site, in 2015, the United States had 765 designated wilderness areas, encompassing over 109 million acres in forty-four states and Puerto Rico. That means that about 5 percent of the United States is protected as wilderness—an area that is slightly larger than the state of California. Much of this wilderness is in Alaska. Within the lower forty-eight states, about 2.7 percent of land is preserved as wilderness—an area about the size of Minnesota.[83] If these wilderness areas were not set aside and protected, their natural resources—including oil reserves, minerals, and forests—would almost certainly be developed. But we also value these wilderness areas for our own recreation, including fishing and hunting, as well as for the habitats they provide to various animal species.

One example of the controversy over protecting wilderness is the question of drilling for oil in Alaska's Arctic National Wildlife Refuge. The refuge is the last part of Alaska's Arctic coastline not open for oil production; its ecosystem includes a number of birds and animals in a tundra area. We might have an ecocentric concern for protecting this fragile ecosystem. Opponents of oil development in the refuge argue that such development would hurt the ecosystem. It might also have a negative impact on the humans who hunt the animals that live there. By contrast, those who argue in favor of drilling point out that the refuge contains large oil deposits that could benefit the economy. As the price of gasoline and other petroleum products goes up, we are looking for new, unexplored oil reserves—the refuge is just such a site, they argue. Advocates of drilling

maintain that efforts to protect sensitive wilderness areas are preventing necessary economic development.[84] Opponents argue that oil development would create unacceptable environmental costs, accelerating climate change and harming animals and natural ecosystems.

Related issues include the construction of oil pipelines and the use of *fracking*, a process for oil and gas extraction that uses hydraulic fracturing (or "fracking") of subterranean rock formations to release gas and oil. The procedure allows extractors to reach reserves that are inaccessible through other drilling technologies. Opponents of fracking argue that the chemicals used in the process are hazardous, and that these chemicals can migrate and contaminate groundwater. Opponents have also argued that fracking can cause earthquakes, even in seismically stable regions. Defenders of the process argue that such risks are negligible and that the benefits of recovering more fossil fuels outweigh the risks.

The means of extraction isn't the only controversial issue related to oil and gas development. Also a subject of intense debate is the way these resources are transported to market. One contentious prospective project is the Keystone XL Pipeline, which aimed to deliver petroleum products from Alberta, Canada, to the United States. The U.S. Congress approved the pipeline in 2015, but President Obama vetoed the project. The pipeline would have carried 830,000 barrels of petroleum daily from the tar sands of Alberta to the Gulf Coast. The route for the proposed pipeline has been changed to avoid sensitive environmental areas, such as the Sand Hills of Nebraska, but environmentalists argued that these modifications are insufficient. Furthermore, environmentalists are opposed to the development of petroleum products from the tar sands of Alberta because of the large-scale destruction of forests and other ecosystems involved in the process. They argue that instead of producing more fossil fuels in wild places, the burning of which contributes to climate change, we should be investing in alternative energy sources.[85] The National Wildlife Federation, for example, says, "Tar sands oil is one of the dirtiest, costliest, and most destructive fuels in the world. Unlike conventional crude oil, unrefined tar sands is hard to extract, and in order to mine this resource, oil companies are digging up tens of thousands of acres of pristine forest in Alberta, Canada and leaving behind a toxic wasteland."[86] But on the other hand, the demand for oil continues to rise: the development of tar sand deposits and fracking are driven by the market demand for petroleum products. Alberta's oil reserves are the third largest on Earth, with current production of about 1.6 million barrels per day.[87] If we want to continue driving gasoline-fueled cars the way we do, we might need that oil.

Forests and wilderness areas are valuable for many reasons. They can provide beneficial new technologies—such as cures for diseases derived from wild species of plants and animals. Forests also provide habitats for wildlife, including threatened species. They provide us with leisure and relaxation, and with recreational opportunities such as whitewater rafting, fishing, hiking, and skiing. They also provide aesthetic and religious experiences, and a chance to commune with the wider world of nature. But the question remains: Are we preserving wilderness for its own sake—or should wilderness areas be viewed as resource reserves, which ought to be developed when and how humans need them?

MindTap° For more chapter resources and activities, go to MindTap.

International Environmental Conventions
Because of widespread concerns about these and other environmental issues, many international meetings and conventions have been held over the past several decades. One example is Earth Summit, the U.N. Conference on Environment and Development, which was held in Rio de Janeiro, Brazil, in 1992. Its focus was the interrelation between environmental issues and sustainable development. At its conclusion, the conference issued, among other documents, a Framework Convention on Climate Change, a Convention on Biological Diversity, and a Statement of Forest Principles. The Framework

Convention on Climate Change went into force in March 1994 and had as its primary objective "stabilization of greenhouse gas concentrations in the atmosphere." The United States, along with many other nations, signed this agreement—updated in Kyoto, Japan, in 1997, under an agreement known as the Kyoto Protocol. Key provisions of the protocol included mandatory restrictions on greenhouse gas emissions to "at least 5 percent below levels measured in 1990" by the year 2012.[88] The protocol also allowed the thirty-five industrialized countries that were covered by it to "earn credits toward their treaty targets by investing in emissions cleanups outside their borders," a so-called *cap-and-trade* system.[89] Developing countries, such as India and China, were exempt from the controls so as to give them a better chance to catch up economically with the more developed nations. Although the United States helped develop this agreement, Congress refused to pass it, and President George W. Bush pulled out of the agreement when he took office in 2001, holding that it was flawed and would hurt the U.S. economy. (Even though the United States did not ratify the treaty, the mayors of more than five hundred U.S. cities pledged to meet its targets.[90]) The Kyoto Protocol was ratified by 141 other nations and took effect on February 16, 2005.

Despite its broad international acceptance, the Kyoto Protocol has not achieved its goals because some developed countries have not met their lowered emissions targets. And from its inception, a significant problem for the Kyoto Protocol was the exemption for developing countries. For example, China has become an emissions titan; since the Kyoto Protocol was signed, China's emissions have nearly tripled and India's have doubled.[91] The United States continues to increase emissions as well. In 2011, Canada officially rejected the Kyoto Protocol, arguing that it was not working to impose limits on the two largest producers of greenhouse gases, the United States and China, and that there was no way to meet the Kyoto targets without serious economic dislocation in Canada.[92] Nevertheless, international negotiations to reduce greenhouse gas emissions continue. The most recent round of climate talks in

2015 took place in Paris, where the international community agreed to work to keep climate change below 2°C.

In addition to the negotiation of the Kyoto Protocol, various other global summits and meetings have been held in the twenty years since the original Earth Summit in Rio de Janeiro. The most recent was the Rio+20 Earth Summit, held in Rio de Janeiro in 2012. Global leaders, such as the UN Secretary General Ban Ki-moon and U.S. Secretary of State Hillary Clinton, declared the Rio+20 meeting a success for clarifying global aspirations for a sustainable future.[93] But environmentalists decried the meeting. The executive director of Greenpeace, Kumi Naidoo, criticized its lack of binding agreements and described it as a meeting full of "empty rhetoric and greenwash from world leaders."[94]

Such conflicts indicate the nature of the divide between those who want radical action to fix environmental problems and politicians and business leaders, who advocate a more cautious approach. At issue here is a substantial difference of opinion about fundamental values. On the one hand, people value the success of short-term business ventures. But on the other hand, long-term environmental sustainability is also important to human well-being—not to mention the well-being of animals, plants, and ecosystems. What is the extent of our obligation to curb emissions and preserve forests and other wilderness areas, especially in light of the fact that these efforts often have a negative effect on other human interests, such as the ability of many people to make a living?

Global Justice and the Tragedy of the Commons

The preservation of the environment is a global issue. Although many problems are specific to certain areas of the world, others, such as global warming, are shared in common. As we have noted, poor people in developing countries may be the most negatively impacted by climate change. However, just as in the developed world, many in developing countries are more concerned with economic growth and development than they are with the environment.

In fact, some people in poor nations even view the environmentalist movement as an example of Western elitism (see the Ramachandra Guha reading that follows). Only wealthy Westerners, they suggest, can afford to preserve unchanged an environment or wilderness that the poor need to use and change in order to survive. From this perspective, poor people who are struggling to survive should not be asked to curtail their own development while citizens of affluent nations enjoy goods unobtainable in the poorer countries.

The concern for environmental justice, which we discussed previously, will tell us that we ought to consider social justice concerns as we deal with environmental issues. Is it fair that those in affluent nations are able to live comfortable lives, while generating a disproportionately large share of waste and pollution? Most environmentalists agree that a sustainable solution to current environmental crises will have to deal with remaining social inequalities across the globe. As we've seen, international agreements regulating greenhouse gases contain variances that attempt to accommodate the inequalities between developed and developing countries.

While alternative fuels, recycling, and other environmentally friendly technologies seem to offer promising solutions to our environmental problems, they do not address the problem of inequality and egoistic rationality. Those in the poorer parts of the world want to have the goods that those in the affluent nations have. And those in affluent countries do not want to give up their current standard of living. However, there are not enough resources available for everyone to enjoy the standard of living of an average American. One solution is to find ways for those in developing regions to raise living standards in ways that create minimal impact on the environment; economic growth that is environmentally sustainable is referred to as *sustainable development*. But those in the affluent countries cannot reasonably expect poorer nations to do their part for the environment while the affluent countries fail to control their own growth and consumption. It might be necessary, in the name of global environmental justice, for affluent countries to radically scale back their level of consumption. Paul and Anne Ehrlich, influential demographers who have been warning about overpopulation for decades, warn: "if we fail to bring population growth and over-consumption under control, then we will inhabit a planet where life becomes increasingly untenable."[95] The problem is not only that the human population has exceeded seven billion, but also that everyone wants to consume as much as the average American.

Who has a right to consume the world's resources? Issues surrounding resource consumption and allocation may make it impossible to create a stable system of global environmental justice. One concern is based upon claims about property rights and capitalism. According to this perspective, landowners have a natural right to develop the resources they possess. To maintain that certain landowners (or countries) should not develop their land or resources appears to be a violation of basic property rights. Furthermore, there is no guarantee that common areas not owned by anyone—the so-called "commons"—will be adequately protected. The oceans and the atmosphere are vast commons. Since they belong to no one, they are easy prey for exploitation and they are also used as vast sinks into which we flush our waste. The American ecologist Garrett Hardin warns that self-interested individuals will tend to take advantage of unprotected common areas, according to a concept that he calls "the tragedy of the commons." (For more on Hardin, see Chapter 20.) Hardin also points out the ethical challenge of global environmental justice in his discussion of what he calls "life-boat ethics." According to Hardin, we should imagine that we are each floating in an isolated lifeboat, competing with one another to survive. Our lifeboats have a limited carrying capacity, so our obligation is to take care of ourselves first—to manage our own resources. Hardin's perspective leaves us with a world of isolated nation-states, each struggling to survive as the growing human population continues to strain the earth's limited resources. Moreover, Hardin's tragic conclusion is that if this is the way we conceive the world, we may not be able to fend off the collapse of the commons, since each of us will try to exploit

what's left for our own benefit.[96] This is a form of the prisoner's dilemma that results from egoism (as discussed in Chapter 4): as each pursues his own self-interest in a world of self-interested people, we may soon end up with unwanted outcomes.[97] From this perspective, which is firmly anthropocentric and even egocentric, the most rational short-term strategy may be to find ways to exploit the environment and enrich oneself before the true impact of the environmental crisis is upon us, to build up our reserves so that we can ride out the coming environmental storm.

This sort of short-term and self-interested reasoning is criticized by both anthropocentric and ecocentric environmentalists. Ecocentrists maintain that we have an obligation to the ecosystem not to overexploit it. Anthropocentrists point out that we have a humanitarian obligation to help others who are suffering, as well as an obligation to future generations to make sure we don't destroy the commons and overexploit the ecosystem. Both note that short-term self-interest can lead to disastrous consequences, as evidenced by "collapsed" or failed societies such as the Rapa Nui on Easter Island and the Maya in the Yucatán.[98] In each case, unsustainable growth led to the downfall of an entire civilization. Societies that collapse do so because they are unable to restrain their own development and unable to focus on the long-term sustainability of their practices. It may be that this is simply part of the natural cycle of life. Organisms grow, reproduce, and consume until they outstrip their resource base. When the resource base is overexploited, the population dies back. But the stakes are quite high now that environmental impacts have created truly global problems. And those who suffer the most from environmental degradation will be the most vulnerable among us. An environmental justice perspective will tell us that we have an obligation to protect those vulnerable people.

We have seen in this chapter that there are a variety of environmental problems confronting us today: from urban pollution to climate change. Some may view these problems from an anthropocentric perspective, focused on cost–benefit analysis or a concern for environmental justice. Others will point toward a deeper set of ecocentric concerns that emphasize the intrinsic value of wilderness and natural systems. The ethical issues to be considered here are complex, as are the causes and possible solutions to environmental challenges.

The first reading for this chapter is a short excerpt from William Baxter who argues that anthropocentrism is the only possible approach to environmental questions and concludes that we should accept an "optimal" pollution level for human beings. In the second reading, Bill Devall and George Sessions explain the key elements of the non-anthropocentric approach of deep ecology. Finally, Ramachandra Guha raises questions about deep ecology from the perspectives of the developing world and Indian and German environmentalism.

NOTES

1. Jason Samenow, "Deadly El Reno, Okla. Tornado Was Widest Ever Measured on Earth, Had Nearly 300 MPH Winds," *The Washington Post*, June 4, 2013, accessed March 29, 2016, http://www .washingtonpost.com/blogs/capital-weather-gang/ wp/2013/06/04/deadly-el-reno-okla-tornado-was-widest-ever-measured-on-earth-had-nearly-300-mph-winds/

2. Worldometers, "Population FAQ," accessed March 25, 2016, http://www.worldometers.info/

3. United Nations, "World Population Projected to Reach 9.7 Billion by 2050," July 29, 2015, accessed March 25, 2016, http://www.un.org/en/ development/desa/news/population/2015-report .html

4. Organisation for Economic Co-operation and Development, *OECD Environmental Outlook to 2050: The Consequences of Inaction*, accessed March 29, 2016, http://www.oecd.org/environment/indicators-modelling-outlooks/49846090.pdf

5. Edward Wong, "Air Pollution Linked to 1.2 Million Premature Deaths in China," *The New York Times*, April 1, 2013, accessed March 29, 2016, http:// www.nytimes.com/2013/04/02/world/asia/air-pollution-linked-to-1-2-million-deaths-in-china .html

6. Central Valley Health Policy Institute, *The Impacts of Short-Term Changes in Air Quality on Emergency Room and Hospital Use in California's San Joaquin Valley*, accessed March 29, 2016, http://www.fresnostate.edu/chhs/cvhpi/documents/ snapshot.pdf

7. Ernest Weekley, *An Etymological Dictionary of Modern English* (New York: Dover, 1967), pp. 516, 518.

8. Safety regulation needs to make use of such monetary equivalencies, for how else do we decide how safe is safe enough? There is no such thing as perfect safety, for that would mean no risk. Thus, we end up judging that we ought to pay so much to make things just so much safer but no more. The implication is that the increased life years or value of the lives to be saved by stricter regulation is of so much but no more than this much value. See Barbara MacKinnon, "Pricing Human Life," *Science, Technology and Human Values* (Spring 1986), pp. 29–39.

9. United States Environmental Protection Agency, "Environmental Justice," accessed March 29, 2016, http://www.epa.gov/environmentaljustice/

10. Andrew North, "Legacy of Bhopal Disaster Poisons Olympics," *BBC News*, May 30, 2012, accessed March 29, 2016, http://www.bbc.co.uk/news/ world-asia-18254334

11. "28 Years Later, Women in Bhopal Still Waiting for Justice," Amnesty International, December 3, 2012, accessed May 13, 2016, http://www.amnestyusa .org/news/news-item/28-years-later-women-in-bhopal-still-waiting-for-justice

12. Bob Van Voris and Patricia Hurtado, "Union Carbide Wins Dismissal of Suit over Bhopal Plant," *Bloomberg*, June 28, 2012, accessed March 29, 2016, http://www.bloomberg.com/news/2012-06-27/union-carbide-wins-dismissal-of-suit-over-bhopal-plant.html

13. See Kristin Shrader-Frechette, *Environmental Justice: Creating Equity, Reclaiming Democracy* (Oxford: Oxford University Press, 2002), p. 10.

14. Kevin DeLuca, "A Wilderness Environmentalism Manifesto: Contesting the Infinite Self-Absorption of Humans," in *Environmental Justice and Environmentalism: The Social Justice Challenge to the*

Environmental Movement, eds. Ronald D. Sandler and Phaedra C. Pezzullo (Cambridge, MA: MIT Press, 2007), p. 49.

15. Genesis 1:26–29. Others will cite St. Francis of Assisi as an example of the Christian with a respectful regard for nature.

16. René Descartes, *Meditations on First Philosophy*. However, it might be pointed out that for Descartes this was not so much a metaphysical point as an epistemological one; that is, he was concerned with finding some sure starting point for knowledge and found at least that he was sure that he was thinking even when he was doubting the existence of everything else.

17. See Christopher Stone, *Do Trees Have Standing? Toward Legal Rights for Natural Objects* (Los Altos, CA: William Kaufmann, 1974).

18. Holmes Rolston III, *Environmental Ethics: Duties to and Values in the Natural World* (Philadelphia, PA: Temple University Press, 1988), p. 97.

19. Aldo Leopold, "The Land Ethic," in *Sand County Almanac* (New York: Oxford University Press, 1949).

20. Ibid., p. 262.

21. See John Hospers, *Understanding the Arts* (Englewood Cliffs, NJ: Prentice Hall, 1982).

22. Ed McGaa (Eagle Man), "We Are All Related," in *Mother Earth Spirituality: Native American Paths to Healing Ourselves and Our World* (San Francisco, CA: Harper & Row, 1990), pp. 203–09.

23. See Stephen R. Fox, *The American Conservation Movement: John Muir and His Legacy* (Madison, WI: University of Wisconsin Press, 1981), p. 5.

24. Arne Naess, *Ecology, Community, and Lifestyle*, trans. David Rothenberg (Cambridge: Cambridge University Press, 1989).

25. Paul Taylor, *Respect for Nature* (Princeton, NJ: Princeton University Press, 1986).

26. Naess, *Ecology, Community, and Lifestyle*, op. cit.

27. George Sessions, ed., *Deep Ecology for the 21st Century: Readings on the Philosophy and Practice of the New Environmentalism* (Boston, MA: Shambhala Publications, 1995), p. xxi.

28. On the tactics of ecosabotage, see Bill Devall, *Simple in Means, Rich in Ends: Practicing Deep Ecology* (Layton, UT: Gibbs Smith, 1988).

29. See Michael Martin, "Ecosabotage and Civil Disobedience," *Environmental Ethics* 12 (Winter 1990), pp. 291–310.

30. According to Joseph des Jardins, the term *ecofeminism* was first used by Françoise d'Eaubonne in 1974 in her work *Le Feminisme ou la Mort* (Paris: Pierre Horay, 1974). See des Jardins, *Environmental Ethics*, op. cit., p. 249.

31. Karen J. Warren, "The Power and Promise of Ecological Feminism," *Environmental Ethics* 9 (Spring 1987), pp. 3–20.

32. I thank an anonymous reviewer for this point.

33. See the distinctions made by Allison Jaggar between liberal (egalitarian) feminism, Marxist feminism, socialist feminism, and radical feminism. *Feminist Politics and Human Nature* (Totowa, NJ: Rowman & Allanheld, 1983).

34. See Carol Christ, *Laughter of Aphrodite: Reflections on a Journey to the Goddess* (San Francisco, CA: Harper & Row, 1987).

35. NASA, "Global Climate Change: Vital Signs of the Planet," accessed March 25, 2016, http://climate.nasa.gov/

36. David Biello, "400 PPM: Carbon Dioxide in the Atmosphere Reaches Prehistoric Levels," *Scientific American*, May 9, 2013, accessed March 29, 2016, http://blogs.scientificamerican.com/observations/2013/05/09/400-ppm-carbon-dioxide-in-the-atmosphere-reaches-prehistoric-levels/

37. Elizabeth Rosenthal, "As the Climate Changes, Bits of England's Coast Crumble," *The New York Times*, May 4, 2007, accessed May 13, 2016, http://www.nytimes.com/2007/05/04/world/europe/04erode.html?_r=0.

38. John McQuaid, "Hurricanes and Climate Change," Nova, November 15, 2012, accessed March 29, 2016, http://www.pbs.org/wgbh/nova/earth/hurricanes-climate.html

39. Justin Gillis, "Ending Its Summer Melt, Arctic Sea Ice Sets a New Low That Leads to Warnings," *The New York Times*, September 19, 2012 accessed March 29, 2016, http://www.nytimes.com/2012/09/20/science/earth/arctic-sea-ice-stops-melting-but-new-record-low-is-set.html

40. NASA, "2013 Wintertime Arctic Sea Ice Maximum Fifth Lowest on Record," April 3, 2013, accessed

March 29, 2016, http://www.nasa.gov/topics/earth/features/arctic-seaicemax-2013.html

41. Climate Central, "Ice Is Flowing Slower on Greenland Than Many Feared," May 3, 2012, accessed March 29, 2016, http://www.climatecentral.org/news/ice-is-flowing-slower-on-greenland-than-many-feared-study-says/

42. NASA, "Global Climate Change: Vital Signs of the Planet," accessed March 25, 2016, http://climate.nasa.gov/

43. John Roach, " 'Horrible' Sea Level Rise of More Than 3 Feet Plausible by 2100, Experts Say," *NBC News*, January 6, 2013, accessed March 29, 2016, http://science.nbcnews.com/_news/2013/01/06/16369939-horrible-sea-level-rise-of-more-than-3-feet-plausible-by-2100-experts-say?lite

44. United States Environmental Protection Agency, "Future Climate Change," accessed March 29, 2016, http://www.epa.gov/climatechange/science/future.html

45. Dan Vergano, "How Climate Change Threatens the Seas," *USA Today*, March 28, 2013, accessed March 29, 2016, http://www.usatoday.com/story/news/nation/2013/03/27/climate-change-seas/2024759/

46. Stephen C. Riser and M. Susan Lozier, "New Simulations Question the Gulf Stream's Role in Tempering Europe's Winters," *Scientific American*, February 1, 2013, accessed March 29, 2016, http://www.scientificamerican.com/article.cfm?id=new-simulations-question-gulf-stream-role-tempering-europes-winters&page=2

47. Al Gore, *An Inconvenient Truth* (New York: Rodale, 2006), pp. 148–51.

48. Gore, op. cit., pp. 194–209; Andrew Revkin, "Climate Panel Reaches Consensus on the Need to Reduce Harmful Emissions," *The New York Times*, May 4, 2007, accessed May 13, 2016, http://www.nytimes.com/2007/05/03/science/04climatecnd.html; Tim Appenzeller, "The Big Thaw," *National Geographic*, June 2007, accessed May 13, 2016, http://ngm.nationalgeographic.com/2007/06/big-thaw/big-thaw-text.

49. Randy Astaiza, "11 Islands That Will Vanish when Sea Levels Rise," *Business Insider*, October 12, 2012, accessed March 29, 2016, http://www.businessinsider.com/islands-threatened-by-climate-change-2012-10?op=1 #ixzz2VU4tcYVu

50. United States Environmental Protection Agency, "Overview of Greenhouse Gases" (2013), accessed March 28, 2016, https://www3.epa.gov/climatechange/ghgemissions/gases.html

51. See www.350.org (accessed March 28, 2016).

52. Jeff Tollefson, "Is the 2°C World a Fantasy?" *Nature* November 24, 2015, accessed March 28, 2016, http://www.nature.com/news/is-the-2-c-world-a-fantasy-1.18868

53. "U.S. Scientists Report Big Jump in Heat-Trapping CO_2," *AP News*, March 5, 2013, accessed May 13, 2016, https://www.yahoo.com/news/us-scientists-report-big-jump-183612249.html?ref=gs

54. United States Environmental Protection Agency, "Global Greenhouse Gas Emission" (published 2015—based on 2011 data), accessed March 28, 2016, https://www3.epa.gov/climatechange/ghgemissions/global.html

55. Thomas Homer-Dixon, "Terror in the Weather Forecast," *The New York Times*, April 24, 2007, p. A25, accessed May 13, 2016, http://www.nytimes.com/2007/04/24/opinion/24homer-dixon.html; Celia W. Dugger, "Need for Water Could Double in 50 Years, U.N. Study Finds," *The New York Times*, August 22, 2006, p. A12, accessed May 13, 2016, http://www.nytimes.com/2006/08/22/world/22water.html; Jane Kay, "Report Predicts Climate Calamity," *San Francisco Chronicle*, May 7, 2007, p. A1, accessed May 13, 2016, http://www.sfgate.com/green/article/Report-predicts-climate-calamity-All-continents-2604480.php

56. Gore, op. cit., pp. 60–67.

57. Wapeningen University and Research Centre, "Butterflies and Birds Unable to Keep Pace with Climate Change in Europe," *Science Daily*, January 18, 2012, accessed March 29, 2016, http://www.sciencedaily.com/releases/2012/01/120118111742.htm

58. Gore, op. cit., Tim Appenzeller, "The Big Thaw," *National Geographic*, June 2007, accessed May 13, 2016, http://ngm.nationalgeographic.com/2007/06/big-thaw/big-thaw-text.

59. United Nations Environment Programme, *High Mountain Glaciers and Climate Change* (2010),

accessed March 29, 2016, http://www.unep.org/pdf/himalayareport_screen.pdf

60. James Hansen, "Game Over for the Climate" *The New York Times*, May 9, 2012, accessed March 29, 2016, http://www.nytimes.com/2012/05/10/opinion/game-over-for-the-climate.html

61. Graham Readfearn, "Has Veteran Climate Scientist James Hansen Foretold the 'Loss of All Coastal Cities' with Latest Study?" *The Guardian*, March 24, 2016, accessed March 29, 2016, http://www.theguardian.com/environment/planet-oz/2016/mar/24/has-veteran-climate-scientist-james-hansen-foretold-the-loss-of-all-coastal-cities-with-latest-study

62. Elisabeth Ponsot, "Will Germany Banish Fossil Fuels Before the US?," *Mother Jones*, January 23, 2013, accessed March 29, 2016, http://www.motherjones.com/environment/2013/01/video-germany-will-banish-fossil-fuels-renewable-energy

63. Quoted in Elizabeth Rosenthal, "Life after Oil and Gas," *The New York Times*, March 23, 2013, accessed March 29, 2016, http://www.nytimes.com/2013/03/24/sunday-review/life-after-oil-and-gas.html?ref=opinion

64. Michael Riordan, "Time for a Carbon Tax?," *San Francisco Chronicle*, March 23, 2007, p. B11.

65. "Study: Fish Suffer Ozone Hole Sunburn," *San Francisco Sunday Examiner and Chronicle*, November 12, 2000, p. A20.

66. Johns Hopkins, "Ozone Thinning Has Changed Ocean Circulation," *Science Daily*, January 31, 2013, accessed March 29, 2016, http://www.sciencedaily.com/releases/2013/01/130131144106.htm

67. "Ozone Depletion," *National Geographic*, accessed March 29, 2016, http://environment.nationalgeographic.com/environment/global-warming/ozone-depletion-overview/

68. United States Environmental Protection Agency, "Municipal Solid Waste Generation, Recycling, and Disposal in the United States: Facts and Figures for 2012," accessed March 28, 2016, https://www3.epa.gov/epawaste/nonhaz/municipal/pubs/2012_msw_fs.pdf

69. Sarah Zhang, "Charts: What Your Trash Reveals about the World Economy," *Mother Jones*, July 16, 2012, accessed March 29, 2016, http://www.motherjones.com/environment/2012/07/trash-charts-world-bank-report-economy; based upon World Bank report, *What a Waste* (March 1, 2012).

70. Clean Air Council, "Waste and Recycling Facts," accessed May 13, 2016, http://www.cleanair.org/program/waste_and_recycling/recyclenow_philadelphia/waste_and_recycling_facts

71. Jon Brooks, "Are Paper Bags Really that Much Better than Plastic?," *KQED*, June 5, 2013, accessed March 29, 2016, http://blogs.kqed.org/newsfix/2013/06/05/paper-bags-vs-plastic/

72. Jonathan Klick and Joshua D. Wright, "Grocery Bag Bans and Foodborne Illness" (University of Pennsylvania, Institute for Law & Economics research paper no. 13-2, November 2, 2012), accessed March 29, 2016, available at SSRN: http://ssrn.com/abstract=2196481 or http://dx.doi.org/10.2139/ssrn.2196481

73. Clean Air Council, "Waste and Recycling Facts," accessed May 13, 2016, http://www.cleanair.org/program/waste_and_recycling/recyclenow_philadelphia/waste_and_recycling_facts

74. Leslie Kaufman, "Where Does That Starbucks Cup Go?," *The New York Times*, November 30, 2010, accessed March 29, 2016, http://green.blogs.nytimes.com/2010/11/30/what-next-after-tossing-a-starbucks-cup/

75. Clean Water Council, "*Taking Out the Trash*" (2011), accessed March 29, 2016, http://www.cleanwateraction.org/files/publications/ca/TakingOuthteTrash%20monitoring%20results.pdf

76. United Nations University, "Global E-Waste Volume Hits New Peak in 2014: UNU Report," April 20, 2015, accessed March 28, 2016, http://unu.edu/news/news/ewaste-2014-unu-report.html

77. "Ghana: Digital Dumping Ground," *PBS's Frontline*, January 23, 2009, accessed March 29, 2016, http://www.pbs.org/frontlineworld/stories/ghana804/video/video_index.html

78. Oregon State University, "Residents Near Chinese E-Waste Site Face Greater Cancer Risk," *Science Daily*, January 23, 2013, accessed March 29, 2016, http://www.sciencedaily.com/releases/2013/01/130123101615.htm

79. *Sierra Club Magazine*, November–December 2005, pp. 42–47.

80. A Recycling Revolution, "Aluminum Recycling Facts," accessed March 29, 2016, http://www.recycling-revolution.com/recycling-facts.html; Earth911, "What We Really Save by Recycling," accessed March 29, 2016, http://earth911.com/news/2012/10/17/how-much-energy-water-saved-by-recycling/

81. Earth911, "What We Really Save by Recycling," accessed March 29, 2016, http://earth911.com/news/2012/10/17/how-much-energy-water-saved-by-recycling/

82. National Resources Defense Council, "Biomass Energy and Cellulosic Ethanol," accessed March 29, 2016, http://www.nrdc.org/energy/renewables/biomass.asp

83. "Fast Facts," Wilderness.net, accessed March 28, 2016, http://www.wilderness.net/NWPS/fastfacts

84. See "Making the Case for ANWR Development," Arctic National Wildlife Refuge, accessed May 13, 2016, http://anwr.org/2013/08/making-the-case-for-anwr/

85. See "When to Say No," *The New York Times*, March 10, 2013, accessed March 29, 2016, http://www.nytimes.com/2013/03/11/opinion/when-to-say-no-to-the-keystone-xl.html?smid=pl-share&_r=0

86. National Wildlife Federation, "Tar Sands," accessed March 29, 2016, http://www.nwf.org/What-We-Do/Energy-and-Climate/Drilling-and-Mining/Tar-Sands.aspx

87. Alberta Government, "Alberta's Oil Sands," accessed March 29, 2016, http://oilsands.alberta.ca/resource.html

88. Larry Rohter and Andrew C. Revkin, "Cheers, and Concern, for New Climate Pact," *The New York Times*, December 13, 2004, accessed May 13, 2016, http://www.nytimes.com/2004/12/13/world/americas/cheers-and-concern-for-new-climate-pact.html.

89. Ibid.

90. Mayors Climate Protection Center, "U.S. Conference of Mayors Climate Protection Agreement," accessed March 29, 2016, http://www.usmayors.org/climateprotection/agreement.htm

91. Quirin Schiermeier, "The Kyoto Protocol: Hot Air," *Nature*, November 28, 2012, accessed March 29, 2016, http://www.nature.com/news/the-kyoto-protocol-hot-air-1.11882

92. Ian Austen, "Canada Announces Exit from Kyoto Climate Treaty," *The New York Times*, December 12, 2011, accessed March 29, 2016, http://www.nytimes.com/2011/12/13/science/earth/canada-leaving-kyoto-protocol-on-climate-change.html

93. Jonathan Watts and Liz Ford, "Rio+20 Earth Summit: Campaigners Decry Final Document," *Guardian*, June 22, 2012, accessed March 29, 2016, http://www.guardian.co.uk/environment/2012/jun/23/rio-20-earth-summit-document

94. Greenpeace International, "Greenpeace Press Statement: Rio+20 Earth Summit—A Failure of Epic Proportions," June 22, 2012, accessed March 29, 2016, http://www.greenpeace.org/international/en/press/releases/Greenpeace-Press-Statement-Rio20-Earth-Summit-a-failure-of-epic-proportions/

95. Paul and Anne Ehrlich, "Too Many People, Too Much Consumption," *Environment 360*, August 4, 2008, accessed May 13, 2016, http://e360.yale.edu/feature/too_many_people_too_much_consumption/2041/

96. Garrett Hardin, "The Tragedy of the Commons," *Science* 162 (1968), pp. 1243–48; also see Garrett Hardin, "Lifeboat Ethics: The Case against Helping the Poor," *Psychology Today*, September 1974.

97. See Andrew Fiala, "Nero's Fiddle: On Hope and Despair and the Ecological Crisis," *Ethics and the Environment* 15, No. 1 (Spring 2010).

98. Jared Diamond, *Collapse* (New York: Viking Press, 2005).

READING

People or Penguins: The Case for Optimal Pollution

WILLIAM F. BAXTER

MindTap® For more chapter resources and activities, go to MindTap.

Study Questions

As you read the excerpt, please consider the following questions:
1. What are the four criteria or goals that Baxter suggests? In what ways are these people-oriented criteria?
2. Does he believe that people-oriented criteria will necessarily be bad for the penguins or other elements of our environment? Why or why not?
3. Why does he believe that there is no right level of pollution?

My criteria are oriented to people, not penguins. Damage to penguins, or sugar pines, or geological marvels is, without more, simply irrelevant.... Penguins are important because people enjoy seeing them walk about rocks; and furthermore, the well-being of people would be less impaired by halting use of DDT than by giving up penguins. In short, my observations about environmental problems will be people-oriented, as are my criteria. I have no interest in preserving penguins for their own sake.

It may be said by way of objection to this position, that it is very selfish of people to act as if each person represented one unit of importance and nothing else was of any importance. It is undeniably selfish. Nevertheless I think it is the only tenable starting place for analysis for several reasons. First, no other position corresponds to the way most people really think and act—i.e., corresponds to reality.

Second, this attitude does not portend any massive destruction of nonhuman flora and fauna, for people depend on them in many obvious ways, and they will be preserved because and to the degree that humans do depend on them.

Third, what is good for humans is, in many respects, good for penguins and pine trees—clean air for example. So that humans are, in these respects, surrogates for plant and animal life.

Fourth, I do not know how we could administer any other system....

I reject the proposition that we *ought* to respect the "balance of nature" or to "preserve the environment" unless the reason for doing so, express or implied, is the benefit of man.

I reject the idea that there is a "right" or "morally correct" state of nature to which we should return. The word "nature" has no normative connotation. Was it "right" or "wrong" for the earth's crust to heave in contortion and create mountains and seas? Was it "right" for the first amphibian to crawl up out of the primordial ooze? Was it "wrong" for plants to reproduce themselves and alter the atmospheric composition in favor of oxygen? For animals to alter the atmosphere in favor of carbon dioxide both by breathing oxygen and eating plants? No answers can be given to these questions because they are meaningless questions....

...It follows that there is no normative definition of clean air or pure water—hence no definition of polluted air—or of pollution—except by reference to the needs of man. The "right" composition of the atmosphere is one which has some dust in it and some lead in it and some hydrogen sulfide in it—just those amounts that attend a sensibly organized society thoughtfully and knowledgeably pursuing the greatest possible satisfaction for its human members.

The first and most fundamental step toward solution of our environmental problems is a clear recognition that our objective is not pure air or water but rather some optimal state of pollution.

READING

Deep Ecology

BILL DEVALL AND GEORGE SESSIONS

MindTap® For more chapter resources and activities, go to MindTap.

Study Questions

As you read the excerpt, please consider the following questions:
1. How do the authors describe the alternative presented by deep ecology?
2. How do the authors contrast the view of deep ecology with what they describe as the dominant worldview?
3. Explain briefly each of the eight basic principles of the platform of the deep ecology movement.

REFORM ENVIRONMENTALISM

Environmentalism is frequently seen as the attempt to work only within the confines of conventional political processes of industrialized nations to alleviate or mitigate some of the worst forms of air and water pollution, destruction of indigenous wildlife, and some of the most short-sighted development schemes.

One scenario for the environmental movement is to continue with attempts at reforming some natural resource policies. For example, ecoactivists can appeal administrative decisions to lease massive areas of public domain lands in the United States for mineral development, or oil and gas development. They can comment on draft Environmental Impact Reports; appeal to politicians to protect the scenic values of the nation; and call attention to the massive problems of toxic wastes, air and water pollution, and soil erosion. These political and educational activities call to the need for healthy ecosystems.

However, environmentalism in this scenario tends to be very technical and oriented only to short-term public policy issues of resource allocation. Attempts are made to reform only some of the worst land use practices without challenging, questioning or changing the basic assumptions of economic growth and development. Environmentalists who follow this scenario will easily be labeled as "just another special issues group." In order to play the game of politics, they will be required to compromise on every piece of legislation in which they are interested.[1]

Generally, this business-as-usual scenario builds on legislative achievements such as the National Environmental Policy Act (NEPA) and the Endangered Species Act in the United States, and reform legislation on pollution and other environmental issues enacted in most industrialized nations.

This work is valuable. The building of proposed dams, for example, can be stopped by using economic arguments to show their economic liabilities. However, this approach has certain costs. One perceptive critic of this approach, Peter Berg, directs an organization seeking decentralist, local approaches to environmental problems. He says this approach "is like running a battlefield aid station in a war against a killing machine that operates beyond reach and that shifts its ground after each seeming defeat."[2] Reformist activists often feel trapped in the very political system they criticize. If they don't use the language of resource economists—language which converts ecology into "input-output models," forests into "commodity production systems," and which uses the metaphor of human economy in referring to Nature—then they are labeled as sentimental, irrational, or unrealistic.

Murray Bookchin, author of *The Ecology of Freedom* (1982) and *Post-Scarcity Anarchism* (1970), says the choice is clear. The environmental/ecology movement can "become institutionalized as an appendage of the very system whose structure and

From Bill Devall and George Sessions, *Deep Ecology: Living as If Nature Mattered*, (Peregrine, 1985). Reprinted by permission.

methods it professes to oppose," or it can follow the minority tradition. The minority tradition focuses on personal growth within a small community and selects a path to cultivating ecological consciousness while protecting the ecological integrity of the place.[3]

DEEP ECOLOGY AND CULTIVATING ECOLOGICAL CONSCIOUSNESS

In contrast to the preceding scenarios, deep ecology presents a powerful alternative.

Deep ecology is emerging as a way of developing a new balance and harmony between individuals, communities and all of Nature. It can potentially satisfy our deepest yearnings: faith and trust in our most basic intuitions; courage to take direct action; joyous confidence to dance with the sensuous harmonies discovered through spontaneous, playful intercourse with the rhythms of our bodies, the rhythms of flowing water, changes in the weather and seasons, and the overall processes of life on Earth. We invite you to explore the vision that deep ecology offers.

The deep ecology movement involves working on ourselves, what poet-philosopher Gary Snyder calls "the real work," the work of really looking at ourselves, of becoming more real.

This is the work we call cultivating ecological consciousness. This process involves becoming more aware of the actuality of rocks, wolves, trees, and rivers—the cultivation of the insight that everything is connected. Cultivating ecological consciousness is a process of learning to appreciate silence and solitude and rediscovering how to listen. It is learning how to be more receptive, trusting, holistic in perception, and is grounded in a vision of nonexploitive science and technology.

This process involves being honest with ourselves and seeking clarity in our intuitions, then acting from clear principles. It results in taking charge of our actions, taking responsibility, practicing self-discipline and working honestly within our community. It is simple but not easy work. Henry David Thoreau, nineteenth-century naturalist and writer, admonishes us, "Let your life be a friction against the machine."

Cultivating ecological consciousness is correlated with the cultivation of conscience. Cultural historian Theodore Roszak suggests in *Person/Planet* (1978), "Conscience and consciousness, how instructive the overlapping similarity of those two words is. From the new consciousness we are gaining of ourselves as persons perhaps we will yet create a new conscience, one whose ethical sensitivity is at least tuned to a significant good, a significant evil."[4]

We believe that humans have a vital need to cultivate ecological consciousness and that this need is related to the needs of the planet. At the same time, humans need direct contact with untrammeled wilderness, places undomesticated for narrow human purposes.

Many people sense the needs of the planet and the need for wilderness preservation. But they often feel depressed or angry, impotent and under stress. They feel they must rely on "the other guy," the "experts." Even in the environmental movement, many people feel that only the professional staff of these organizations can make decisions because they are experts on some technical scientific matters or experts on the complex, convoluted political process. But we need not be technical experts in order to cultivate ecological consciousness. Cultivating ecological consciousness, as Thoreau said, requires that "we front up to the facts and determine to live our lives deliberately, or not at all." We believe that people can clarify their own intuitions, and act from deep principles.

Deep ecology is a process of ever-deeper questioning of ourselves, the assumptions of the dominant worldview in our culture, and the meaning and truth of our reality. We cannot change consciousness by only listening to others, we must involve ourselves. We must take direct action.

Organizations which work only in a conventional way on political issues and only in conventional politics will more or less unavoidably neglect the deepest philosophical-spiritual issues. But late industrial society is at a turning point, and the social and personal changes which are necessary may be aided by the flow of history....

The trick is to trick ourselves into reenchantment. As Watts says, "In the life of spontaneity, human consciousness shifts from the attitude of strained, willful attention to *koan*, the attitude of open attention or contemplation." This is a key element in developing ecological consciousness. This attitude forms the basis of a more "feminine" and receptive approach to love, an attitude which for that very reason is more considerate of women.[5]

In some Eastern traditions, the student is presented with a *koan*, a simple story or statement which may sound paradoxical or nonsensical on the surface but as the student turns and turns it in his or her mind, authentic understanding emerges. This direct action of turning and turning, seeing from different perspectives and from different depths, is required for the cultivation of consciousness. The *koan*-like phrase for deep ecology, suggested by prominent Norwegian philosopher Arne Naess, is: "simple in means, rich in ends."

Cultivating ecological consciousness based on this phrase requires the interior work of which we have been speaking, but also a radically different tempo of external actions, at least radically different from that experienced by millions and millions of people living "life in the fast lane" in contemporary metropolises. As Theodore Roszak concludes, "Things move slower; they stabilize at a simpler level. But none of this is experienced as a loss or a sacrifice. Instead, it is seen as a liberation from waste and busywork, from excessive appetite and anxious competition that allows one to get on with the essential business of life, which is to work out one's salvation with diligence."[6]

. . . . Quiet people, those working on the "real work," quite literally turn down the volume of noise in their lives. Gary Snyder suggests that, "The real work is what we really do. And what our lives are. And if we can live the work we have to do, knowing that we are real, and that the world is real, then it becomes right. And that's the real work: to make the world as real as it is and to find ourselves as real as we are within it."[7]

Engaging in this process, Arne Naess concludes, people ". . . will necessarily come to the conclusion that it is not lack of energy consumption that makes them unhappy."[8]

One metaphor for what we are talking about is found in the Eastern Taoist image, the *organic* self. Taoism tells us there is a way of unfolding which is inherent in all things. In the natural social order, people refrain from dominating others. Indeed, the ironic truth is that the more one attempts to control other people and control nonhuman Nature, the more disorder results, and the greater the degree of chaos. For the Taoist, spontaneity is not the opposite of order but identical with it because it flows from the unfolding of the inherent order. Life is not narrow, mean, brutish, and destructive. People do not engage in the seemingly inevitable conflict over scarce material goods. People have fewer desires and simple pleasures. In Taoism, the law is not required for justice; rather, the community of persons working for universal self-realization follows the flow of energy.[9]

> To study the Way is to study the self.
> To study the self is to forget the self.
> To forget the self is to be enlightened by all things.
> To be enlightened by all things is to remove the barriers between one's self and others.
>
> —Dogen

As with many other Eastern traditions, the Taoist way of life is based on compassion, respect, and love for all things. This compassion arises from self-love, but self as part of the larger *Self*, not egotistical self-love.

DEEP ECOLOGY

The term *deep ecology* was coined by Arne Naess in his 1973 article, "The Shallow and the Deep, Long-Range Ecology Movements."[10] Naess was attempting to describe the deeper, more spiritual approach to Nature exemplified in the writings of Aldo Leopold and Rachel Carson. He thought that this deeper approach resulted from a more sensitive openness to ourselves and nonhuman life around us. The essence of deep ecology is to keep asking more searching questions about human life, society, and Nature as in the Western philosophical tradition of Socrates. As examples of this deep questioning, Naess points out "that we ask why and how, where others do not. For instance ecology as a science does not ask what kind of a society would be the best for maintaining a particular ecosystem—that is considered a question for value theory, for politics, for ethics." Thus deep ecology goes beyond the so-called factual scientific level to the level of self and Earth wisdom.

Deep ecology goes beyond a limited piecemeal shallow approach to environmental problems and attempts to articulate a comprehensive religious and philosophical worldview. The foundations of deep ecology are the basic intuitions and experiencing of ourselves and Nature which comprise ecological consciousness. Certain outlooks on politics and public policy flow naturally from this consciousness. And in the context of this book, we discuss the minority tradition as the type of community most conducive both to cultivating ecological consciousness and to asking the basic questions of values and ethics addressed in these pages.

Many of these questions are perennial philosophical and religious questions faced by humans in all cultures over the ages. What does it mean to be a unique human individual? How can the individual self-maintain and increase its uniqueness while also being an inseparable aspect of the whole system wherein there are no sharp breaks between self and the *other*? An ecological perspective, in this deeper sense, results in what Theodore Roszak calls "an awakening of wholes greater than the sum of their parts. In spirit, the discipline is contemplative and therapeutic."[11]

Ecological consciousness and deep ecology are in sharp contrast with the dominant worldview of technocratic-industrial societies which regards humans as isolated and fundamentally separate from the rest of Nature, as superior to, and in charge of, the rest of creation. But the view of humans as separate and superior to the rest of Nature is only part of larger cultural patterns. For thousands of years, Western culture has become increasingly obsessed with the idea of *dominance*: with dominance of humans over nonhuman Nature, masculine over the feminine, wealthy and powerful over the poor, with the dominance of the West over non-Western cultures. Deep ecological consciousness allows us to see through these erroneous and dangerous illusions.

For deep ecology, the study of our place in the Earth household includes the study of ourselves as part of the organic whole. Going beyond a narrowly materialist scientific understanding of reality, the spiritual and the material aspects of reality fuse together. While the leading intellectuals of the dominant worldview have tended to view religion as "just superstition," and have looked upon ancient spiritual practice and enlightenment, such as found in Zen Buddhism, as essentially subjective, the search for deep ecological consciousness is the search for a more objective consciousness and state of being through an active deep questioning and meditative process and way of life.

Many people have asked these deeper questions and cultivated ecological consciousness within the context of different spiritual traditions—Christianity, Taoism, Buddhism, and Native American rituals, for example.

While differing greatly in other regards, many in these traditions agree with the basic principles of deep ecology.

Warwick Fox, an Australian philosopher, has succinctly expressed the central intuition of deep ecology: "It is the idea that we can make no firm ontological divide in the field of existence: That there is no bifurcation in reality between the human and the non-human realms...to the extent that we perceive boundaries, we fall short of deep ecological consciousness."[12]

From this most basic insight or characteristic of deep ecological consciousness, Arne Naess has developed two ultimate norms or intuitions which are themselves not derivable from other principles or intuitions. They are arrived at by the deep questioning process and reveal the importance of moving to the philosophical and religious level of wisdom. They cannot be validated, of course, by the methodology of modern science based on its usual mechanistic assumptions and its very narrow definition of data. These ultimate norms are *self-realization* and *biocentric equality*.

SELF-REALIZATION

In keeping with the spiritual traditions of many of the world's religions, the deep ecology norm of self-realization goes beyond the modern Western self which is defined as an isolated ego striving primarily for hedonistic gratification or for a narrow sense of individual salvation in this life or the next. This socially programmed sense of the narrow self or social self dislocates us, and leaves us prey to whatever fad or fashion is prevalent in our society or social reference group. We are thus robbed of beginning the search for our unique spiritual/biological personhood. Spiritual growth, or unfolding, begins when we cease to understand or see ourselves as isolated and narrow competing egos and begin to identify with other humans from our family and friends to, eventually, our species. But the deep ecology sense of self requires a further maturity and growth, an identification which goes beyond humanity to include the nonhuman world. We must see beyond our narrow contemporary cultural assumptions and values, and the conventional wisdom of our time and place, and this is best achieved by the meditative deep questioning process. Only in this way can we hope to attain full mature personhood and uniqueness.

A nurturing nondominating society can help in the "real work" of becoming a whole person. The "real work" can be summarized symbolically as the realization of "self-in-Self" where "Self" stands for organic wholeness. This process of the full unfolding of the self can also be summarized by the phrase, "No one is saved until we are all saved," where the phrase "one" includes not only me, an individual human, but all humans, whales, grizzly bears, whole rain forest ecosystems, mountains and rivers, the tiniest microbes in the soil, and so on.

BIOCENTRIC EQUALITY

The intuition of biocentric equality is that all things in the biosphere have an equal right to live and blossom and to reach their own individual forms of unfolding and self-realization within the larger Self-realization. This basic intuition is that all organisms and entities in the ecosphere, as parts of the interrelated whole, are equal in intrinsic worth. Naess suggests that biocentric equality as an intuition is true in principle, although in the process of living, all species use each other as food, shelter, etc. Mutual predation is a biological fact of life, and many of the world's religions have struggled with the spiritual implications of this. Some animal liberationists who attempt to side-step this problem by advocating vegetarianism are forced to say that the entire plant kingdom including rain forests have no right to their own existence. This evasion flies in the face of the basic intuition of equality.[13] Aldo Leopold expressed this intuition when he said humans are "plain citizens" of the biotic community, not lord and master over all other species.

Biocentric equality is intimately related to the all-inclusive Self-realization in the sense that if we harm the rest of Nature then we are harming ourselves. There are no boundaries and everything is interrelated. But insofar as we perceive things as individual organisms or entities, the insight draws us to respect all human and nonhuman individuals in their own right as parts of the whole without feeling the need to set up hierarchies of species with humans at the top.

Dominant Worldview	Deep Ecology
• Dominance over Nature	• Harmony with Nature
• Natural environment as resource for humans	• All nature has intrinsic worth/biospecies equality
• Material/economic growth for growing human population	• Elegantly simple material needs (material goals serving the larger goal of self-realization)
• Belief in ample resource reserves	• Earth "supplies" limited
• High technological progress and solutions	• Appropriate technology; nondominating science
• Consumerism	• Doing with enough/recycling
• National/centralized community	• Minority tradition/bioregion

The practical implications of this intuition or norm suggest that we should live with minimum rather than maximum impact on other species and on the Earth in general. Thus we see another aspect of our guiding principle: "simple in means, rich in ends."...

A fuller discussion of the biocentric norm as it unfolds itself in practice begins with the realization that we, as individual humans, and as communities of humans, have vital needs which go beyond such basics as food, water, and shelter to include love, play, creative expression, intimate relationships with a particular landscape (or Nature taken in its entirety) as well as intimate relationships with other humans, and the vital need for spiritual growth, for becoming a mature human being.

Our vital material needs are probably more simple than many realize. In technocratic-industrial societies there is overwhelming propaganda and advertising which encourages false needs and destructive desires designed to foster increased production and consumption of goods. Most of this actually diverts us from facing reality in an objective way and from beginning the "real work" of spiritual growth and maturity.

Many people who do not see themselves as supporters of deep ecology nevertheless recognize an overriding vital human need for a healthy and high-quality natural environment for humans, if not for all life, with minimum intrusion of toxic waste, nuclear radiation from human enterprises, minimum acid rain and smog, and enough free flowing wilderness so humans can get in touch with their sources, the natural rhythms and the flow of time and place.

Drawing from the minority tradition and from the wisdom of many who have offered the insight of interconnectedness, we recognize that deep ecologists can offer suggestions for gaining maturity and encouraging the processes of harmony with Nature, but that there is no grand solution which is guaranteed to save us from ourselves.

The ultimate norms of deep ecology suggest a view of the nature of reality and our place as an individual (many in the one) in the larger scheme of things. They cannot be fully grasped intellectually but are ultimately experiential....

As a brief summary of our position thus far, Figure 1 [on page 447] summarizes the contrast between the dominant worldview and deep ecology.

BASIC PRINCIPLES OF DEEP ECOLOGY

In April 1984, during the advent of spring and John Muir's birthday, George Sessions and Arne Naess summarized fifteen years of thinking on the principles of deep ecology while camping in Death Valley, California. In this great and special place, they articulated these principles in a literal, somewhat neutral way, hoping that they would be understood and accepted by persons coming from different philosophical and religious positions.

Readers are encouraged to elaborate their own versions of deep ecology, clarify key concepts and think through the consequences of acting from these principles.

Basic Principles

1. The well-being and flourishing of human and non-human Life on Earth have value in themselves (synonyms: intrinsic value, inherent value). These values are independent of the usefulness of the nonhuman world for human purposes.
2. Richness and diversity of life forms contribute to the realization of these values and are also values in themselves.
3. Humans have no right to reduce this richness and diversity except to satisfy *vital* needs.
4. The flourishing of human life and cultures is compatible with a substantial decrease of the human population. The flourishing of nonhuman life requires such a decrease.
5. Present human interference with the nonhuman world is excessive, and the situation is rapidly worsening.
6. Policies must therefore be changed. These policies affect basic economic, technological, and ideological structures. The resulting state of affairs will be deeply different from the present.
7. The ideological change is mainly that of appreciating *life quality* (dwelling in situations of inherent value) rather than adhering to an increasingly higher standard of living. There

will be a profound awareness of the difference between the big and the great.

8. Those who subscribe to the foregoing points have an obligation directly or indirectly to try to implement the necessary changes.

NOTES

1. The most informative recent book on reformist environmentalism in the context of British society is Philip Lowe and Jane Goyder's *Environmental Groups in Politics* (London: George Allen, 1983). Sociological explanations of the environmental movement in North America are found in Craig R. Humphrey and Frederick R. Butell's *Environment, Energy and Society* (Belmont, CA: Wadsworth, 1983); Allan Schnaiberg's *The Environment: From Surplus to Scarcity* (New York: Oxford, 1980); Lester Milbrath's *Environmentalists* (Albany: State University of New York Press, 1984); "Sociology of the Environment," *Sociological Inquiry 53* (Spring 1983); Jonathon Porritt, *Green: The Politics of Ecology Explained* (New York: Basil Blackwell, 1985).

2. Peter Berg, editorial, *Raise the Stakes* (Fall 1983).

3. Murray Bookchin, "Open Letter to the Ecology Movement," *Rain* (April 1980), as well as other publications.

4. Theodore Roszak, *Person/Planet* (Garden City, NY: Doubleday, 1978), p. 99.

5. ———. *Nature, Man and Woman* (New York: Vintage, 1970), p. 178.

6. Roszak, p. 296.

7. Gary Snyder, *The Real Work* (New York: New Directions, 1980), p. 81.

8. Stephen Bodian, "Simple in Means, Rich in Ends: A Conversation with Arne Naess," *Ten Directions* (California: Institute for Transcultural Studies, Zen Center of Los Angeles, Summer/Fall 1982).

9. Po-Keung Ip, "Taoism and the Foundations of Environmental Ethics," *Environmental Ethics 5* (Winter 1983), pp. 335–344.

10. Arne Naess, "The Shallow and The Deep, Long-Range Ecology Movements: A Summary," *Inquiry 16* (Oslo, 1973), pp. 95–100.

11. Theodore Roszak, *Where the Wasteland Ends* (New York: Anchor, 1972).

12. Warwick Fox, "Deep Ecology: A New Philosophy of Our Time?" *The Ecologist*, v. 14, 506, 1984, pp. 194–200. Arne Naess replies, "Intuition, Intrinsic Value and Deep Ecology," *The Ecologist*, v. 14, 5–6, 1984, pp. 201–204.

13. Tom Regan, *The Case for Animal Rights* (New York: Random House, 1983). For excellent critiques of the animal rights movement, see John Rodman, "The Liberation of Nature?" *Inquiry 20* (Oslo, 1977). J. Baird Callicott, "Animal Liberation," *Environmental Ethics 2*, 4 (1980); see also John Rodman, "Four Forms of Ecological Consciousness Reconsidered" in T. Attig and D. Scherer (Eds.), *Ethics and the Environment* (Englewood Cliffs, NJ: Prentice Hall, 1983).

READING

Radical American Environmentalism and Wilderness Preservation: A Third World Critique

RAMACHANDRA GUHA

MindTap® For more chapter resources and activities, go to MindTap.

Study Questions

As you read the excerpt, please consider the following questions:

1. Why does Guha think the emphasis on wilderness preservation is harmful?
2. What problems does he have with the invocation of Eastern religions?
3. How does he believe that elements of deep ecology favor the rich and urban elite in the third world?

The respected radical journalist Kirkpatrick Sale recently celebrated "the passion of a new and growing movement that has become disenchanted with the environmental establishment and has in recent years mounted a serious and sweeping attack on it—style, substance, systems, sensibilities and all."[1] The vision of those whom Sale calls the "New Ecologists"—and what I refer to in this article as deep ecology—is a compelling one. Decrying the narrowly economic goals of mainstream environmentalism, this new movement aims at nothing less than a philosophical and cultural revolution in human attitudes toward nature. In contrast to the conventional lobbying efforts of environmental professionals based in Washington, it proposes a militant defence of "Mother Earth," an unflinching opposition to human attacks on undisturbed wilderness. With their goals ranging from the spiritual to the political, the adherents of deep ecology span a wide spectrum of the American environmental movement....

In this article I develop a critique of deep ecology from the perspective of a sympathetic outsider.... I speak admittedly as a partisan, but of the environmental movement in India, a country with an ecological diversity comparable to the U.S., but with a radically dissimilar cultural and social history.... Specifically, I examine the cultural rootedness of a philosophy that likes to present itself in universalistic terms. I make two main arguments: first, that deep ecology is uniquely American, and despite superficial similarities in rhetorical style, the social and political goals of radical environmentalism in other cultural contexts (e.g., West Germany and India) are quite different; second, that the social consequences of putting deep ecology into practice on a worldwide basis (what its practitioners are aiming for) are very grave indeed.

THE TENETS OF DEEP ECOLOGY

... Adherents of the deep ecological perspective in [America], while arguing intensely among themselves over its political and philosophical implications, share some fundamental premises about human-nature interactions. As I see it, the defining characteristics of deep ecology are fourfold:

First, deep ecology argues that the environmental movement must shift from an "anthropocentric" to a "biocentric" perspective. In many respects, an acceptance of the primacy of this distinction constitutes the litmus test of deep ecology. A considerable effort is expended by deep ecologists in showing that the dominant motif in Western philosophy has been anthropocentric—i.e., the belief that man and his works are the center of the universe—and conversely, in identifying those lonely thinkers (Leopold, Thoreau, Muir, Aldous Huxley, Santayana, etc.) who, in assigning man a more humble place in the natural order, anticipated deep ecological thinking. In the political realm, meanwhile, establishment environmentalism (shallow ecology) is chided for casting its arguments in human-centered terms. Preserving nature, the deep ecologists say, has an intrinsic worth quite apart from any benefits preservation may convey to future human generations. The anthropocentric-biocentric distinction is accepted as axiomatic by deep ecologists, it structures their discourse, and much of the present discussions remains mired within it.

The second characteristic of deep ecology is its focus on the preservation of unspoilt wilderness—and the restoration of degraded areas to a more pristine condition—to the relative (and sometimes absolute) neglect of other issues on the environmental agenda.... Morally, [this] is an imperative that follows from the biocentric perspective; other species of plants and animals, and nature itself, have an intrinsic right to exist.... The preservation of wilderness also turns on a scientific argument—viz., the value of biological diversity in stabilizing ecological regimes and in retaining a gene pool for future generations. Truly radical policy proposals have been put forward by deep ecologists on the basis of these arguments. The influential poet Gary Snyder, for example, would like to see a 90 percent reduction in human populations to allow a restoration of pristine

Ramachandra Guha, "Radical American Environmentalism and Wilderness Preservation: A Third World Critique," *Environmental Ethics* 11 (Spring 1989). Reprinted with permission from the Author.

environments, while others have argued forcefully that a large portion of the globe must be immediately cordoned off from human beings.

Third, there is a widespread invocation of Eastern spiritual traditions as forerunners of deep ecology. Deep ecology, it is suggested, was practiced both by major religious traditions and at a more popular level by "primal" peoples in non-Western settings. This complements the search for an authentic lineage in Western thought. At one level, the task is to recover those dissenting voices within the Judeo-Christian tradition; at another, to suggest that religious traditions in other cultures are, in contrast, dominantly if not exclusively "biocentric" in their orientation. This coupling of (ancient) Eastern and (modern) ecological wisdom seemingly helps consolidate the claim that deep ecology is a philosophy of universal significance.

Fourth, deep ecologists, whatever their internal differences, share the belief that they are the "leading edge" of the environmental movement. As the polarity of the shallow/deep and anthropocentric/biocentric distinctions makes clear, they see themselves as the spiritual, philosophical, and political vanguard of American and world environmentalism.

TOWARD A CRITIQUE

Although I analyze each of these tenets independently, it is important to recognize, as deep ecologists are fond of remarking in reference to nature, the interconnectedness and unity of these individual themes.

1. Insofar as it has begun to act as a check on man's arrogance and ecological hubris, the transition from an anthropocentric (human-centered) to a biocentric (humans as only one element in the ecosystem) view in both religious and scientific traditions is only to be welcomed. What is unacceptable are the radical conclusions drawn by deep ecology, in particular, that intervention in nature should be guided primarily by the need to preserve biotic integrity rather than by the needs of humans. The latter for deep ecologists is anthropocentric, the former biocentric. This dichotomy is, however, of very little use in understanding the dynamics of environmental degradation. The two fundamental ecological problems facing the globe are (i) overconsumption by the industrialized world and by urban elites in the Third World and (ii) growing militarization, both in a short-term sense (i.e., ongoing regional wars) and in a long-term sense (i.e., the arms race and the prospect of nuclear annihilation). Neither of these problems has any tangible connection to the anthropocentric-biocentric distinction. Indeed, the agents of these processes would barely comprehend this philosophical dichotomy. The proximate causes of the ecologically wasteful characteristics of industrial society and of militarization are far more mundane: at an aggregate level, the dialectic of economic and political structures, and at a micro-level, the life-style choices of individuals. These causes cannot be reduced, whatever the level of analysis, to a deeper anthropocentric attitude toward nature; on the contrary, by constituting a grave threat to human survival, the ecological degradation they cause does not even serve the best interests of human beings! If my identification of the major dangers to the integrity of the natural world is correct, invoking the bogy of anthropocentrism is at best irrelevant and at worst a dangerous obfuscation.

2. If the above dichotomy is irrelevant, the emphasis on wilderness is positively harmful when applied to the Third World. If in the U.S. the preservationist/utilitarian division is seen as mirroring the conflict between "people" and "interests," in countries such as India the situation is very nearly the reverse. Because India is a long settled and densely populated country in which agrarian populations have a finely balanced relationship with nature, the setting aside of wilderness areas has resulted in a direct transfer of resources from the poor to the rich. Thus, Project Tiger, a network of parks hailed by the international conservation community as an outstanding success, sharply posits the interests of the tiger against those of poor peasants living in and around the reserve. The designation of tiger reserves was made possible only by the physical displacement of existing villages and their inhabitants; their management requires the continuing exclusion of peasants and livestock. The initial impetus for setting up

parks for the tiger and other large mammals such as the rhinoceros and elephant came from two social groups, first, a class of ex-hunters turned conservationists belonging mostly to the declining Indian feudal elite and second, representatives of international agencies, such as the World Wildlife Fund (WWF) and the International Union for the Conservation of Nature and Natural Resources (IUCN), seeking to transplant the American system of national parks onto Indian soil. In no case have the needs of the local population been taken into account, and as in many parts of Africa, the designated wildlands are managed primarily for the benefit of rich tourists. Until very recently, wildlands preservation has been identified with environmentalism by the state and the conservation elite; in consequence, environmental problems that impinge far more directly on the lives of the poor—e.g., fuel, fodder, water shortages, soil erosion, and air and water pollution—have not been adequately addressed.

Deep ecology provides, perhaps unwittingly, a justification for the continuation of such narrow and inequitable conservation practices under a newly acquired radical guise. Increasingly, the international conservation elite is using the philosophical, moral, and scientific arguments used by deep ecologists in advancing their wilderness crusade. A striking but by no means atypical example is the recent plea by a prominent American biologist for the takeover of large portions of the globe by the author and his scientific colleagues. Writing in a prestigious scientific forum, the *Annual Review of Ecology and Systematics*, Daniel Janzen argues that only biologists have the competence to decide how the tropical landscape should be used.... Janzen exhorts his colleagues to advance their territorial claims on the tropical world more forcefully, warning that the very existence of these areas is at stake: "if biologists want a tropics in which to biologize, they are going to have to buy it with care, energy, effort, strategy, tactics, time, and cash."[2]

This frankly imperialist manifesto highlights the multiple dangers of the preoccupation with wilderness preservation that is characteristic of deep ecology. As I have suggested, it seriously compounds the neglect by the American movement of far more pressing environmental problems within the Third World. But perhaps more importantly, and in a more insidious fashion, it also provides an impetus to the imperialist yearning of Western biologists and their financial sponsors, organizations such as the WWF and IUCN. The wholesale transfer of a movement culturally rooted in American conservation history can only result in the social uprooting of human populations in other parts of the globe.

3. I come now to the persistent invocation of Eastern philosophies as antecedent in point of time but convergent in their structure with deep ecology. Complex and internally differentiated religious traditions—Hinduism, Buddhism, and Taoism—are lumped together as holding a view of nature believed to be quintessentially biocentric. Individual philosophers such as the Taoist Lao Tzu are identified as being forerunners of deep ecology. Even an intensely political, pragmatic, and Christian-influenced thinker such as Gandhi has been accorded a wholly undeserved place in the deep ecological pantheon. Thus the Zen teacher Robert Aitken Roshi makes the strange claim that Gandhi's thought was not human-centered and that he practiced an embryonic form of deep ecology which is "traditionally Eastern and is found with differing emphasis in Hinduism, Taoism and in Theravada and Mahayana Buddhism."[3] Moving away from the realm of high philosophy and scriptural religion, deep ecologists make the further claim that at the level of material and spiritual practice "primal" peoples subordinated themselves to the integrity of the biotic universe they inhabited.

I have indicated that this appropriation of Eastern traditions is in part dictated by the need to construct an authentic lineage and in part a desire to present deep ecology as a universalistic philosophy.... As it stands, [this reading] does considerable violence to the historical record. Throughout most recorded history the characteristic form of human activity in the "East" has been a finely tuned but nonetheless conscious and dynamic manipulation of nature. Although mystics such as Lao Tzu did reflect on the spiritual essence of human relations with nature, it must be recognized that such ascetics and their reflections were supported by a society of cultivators whose relationship with nature was a far more *active* one. Many agricultural communities do have a sophisticated knowledge of the natural environment that may equal (and sometimes surpass) codified "scientific" knowledge; yet, the elaboration of such traditional ecological knowledge (in both material and spiritual contexts) can hardly be said to rest on a mystical affinity with nature of a deep ecological kind....

In a brilliant article, the Chicago historian Ronald Inden points out that this romantic and essentially positive view of the East is a mirror image of the scientific and essentially pejorative view normally upheld by Western scholars of the Orient. In either case, the East constitutes the Other, a body wholly separate and alien from the West; it is defined by a uniquely spiritual and nonrational "essence," even if this essence is valorized quite differently by the two schools. Eastern man exhibits a spiritual dependence with respect to nature—on the one hand, this is symptomatic of his prescientific and backward self, on the other, of his ecological wisdom and deep ecological consciousness. Both views are monolithic, simplistic, and have the characteristic effect—intended in one case, perhaps unintended in the other—of denying agency and reason to the East and making it the privileged orbit of Western thinkers....

4. How radical, finally, are the deep ecologists?...To my mind, deep ecology is best viewed as a radical trend within the wilderness preservation movement. Although advancing philosophical rather than aesthetic arguments and encouraging political militancy rather than negotiation, its practical emphasis—viz., preservation of unspoilt nature—is virtually identical. For the mainstream movement, the function of wilderness is to provide a temporary antidote to modern civilization. As a special institution within an industrialized society, the national park "provides an opportunity for respite, contrast, contemplation, and affirmation of values for those who live most of their lives in the workaday world."[4] Indeed, the rapid increase in visitations to the national parks in postwar America is a direct consequence of economic expansion....

Here, the enjoyment of nature is an integral part of the consumer society. The private automobile (and the life style it has spawned) is in many respects the ultimate ecological villain, and an untouched wilderness the prototype of ecological harmony; yet, for most Americans it is perfectly consistent to drive a thousand miles to spend a holiday in a national park. They possess a vast, beautiful, and sparsely populated continent and are also able to draw upon the natural resources of large portions of the globe by virtue of their economic and political dominance. In consequence, America can simultaneously enjoy the material benefits of an expanding economy and the aesthetic benefits of unspoilt nature. The two poles of "wilderness" and "civilization" mutually coexist in an internally coherent whole, and philosophers of both poles are assigned a prominent place in this culture. Paradoxically as it may seem, it is no accident that Star Wars technology and deep ecology both find their fullest expression in that leading sector of Western civilization, California.

Deep ecology runs parallel to the consumer society without seriously questioning its ecological and socio-political basis....The archetypal concerns of radical environmentalists in other cultural contexts are in fact quite different. The German Greens, for example, have elaborated a devastating critique of industrial society which turns on the acceptance of environmental limits to growth. Pointing to the intimate links between industrialization, militarization, and conquest, the Greens argue that economic growth in the West has historically rested on the economic and ecological exploitation of the Third World.

[Hence] the roots of global ecological problems lie in the disproportionate share of resources consumed by the industrialized countries as a whole *and* the urban elite within the Third World. Since it is impossible to reproduce an industrial monoculture worldwide, the ecological movement in the West must begin by cleaning up its own act....The expansionist character of modern Western man will have to give way to an ethic of renunciation and self-limitation, in which spiritual and communal values play an increasing role in sustaining social life....

Many elements of the Green program find a strong resonance in countries such as India, where a history of Western colonialism and industrial development has benefited only a tiny elite while exacting tremendous social and environmental costs. The ecological battles presently being fought in India have as their epicenter the conflict over nature between the subsistence and largely rural sector and the vastly more powerful commercial-industrial sector. Perhaps the most celebrated of these battles concerns the Chipko (Hug the Tree) movement, a peasant movement against deforestation in the Himalayan foothills. Chipko is only one of several movements that have sharply questioned the non-sustainable demand being placed on the land and vegetative base by urban centers and industry. These include opposition to large dams by displaced peasants, the conflict between small artisan fishing and large-scale trawler fishing for export, the countrywide movements against commercial forest operations, and opposition to industrial pollution among downstream agricultural and fishing communities.

Two features distinguish these environmental movements from their Western counterparts. First, for the sections of society most critically affected by environmental degradation—poor and landless peasants, women, and tribals—it is a question of sheer survival, not of enhancing the quality of life. Second, and as a consequence, the environmental solutions they articulate deeply involve questions of equity as well as economic and political redistribution. Highlighting these differences, a leading Indian environmentalist stresses that "environmental protection per se is of least concern to most of these groups. Their main concern is about the use of the environment and who should benefit from it." They seek to wrest control of nature away from the state and the industrial sector and place it in the hands of rural communities who live within that environment but are increasingly denied access to it. These communities have far more basic needs, their demands on the environment are far less intense,

and they can draw upon a reservoir of cooperative social institutions and local ecological knowledge in managing the "commons"—forests, grasslands, and the waters—on a sustainable basis. If colonial and capitalist expansion has both accentuated social inequalities and signaled a precipitous fall in ecological wisdom, an alternate ecology must rest on an alternate society and polity as well.

This brief overview of German and Indian environmentalism has some major implications for deep ecology. Both German and Indian environmental traditions allow for a greater integration of ecological concerns with livelihood and work. They also place a greater emphasis on equity and social justice (both within individual countries and on a global scale) on the grounds that in the absence of social regeneration environmental regeneration has very little chance of succeeding, Finally, and perhaps most significantly, they have escaped the preoccupation with wilderness preservation so characteristic of American cultural and environmental history.

A HOMILY

In 1958, the economist J. K. Galbraith referred to overconsumption as the unasked question of the American conservation movement. There is a marked selectivity, he wrote, "in the conservationist's approach to materials consumption. If we are concerned about our great appetite for materials, it is plausible to seek to increase the supply, to decrease waste, to make better use of the stocks available, and to develop substitutes. But what of the appetite itself? Surely this is the ultimate source of the problem. If it continues its geometric course, will it not one day have to be restrained? Yet in the literature of the resource problem this is the forbidden question. Over it hangs a nearly total silence."[5]

The consumer economy and society have expanded tremendously in the three decades since Galbraith penned these words; yet his criticisms are nearly as valid today. I have said "nearly," for there are some hopeful signs. Within the environmental movement several dispersed groups are working to develop ecologically benign technologies and to encourage less wasteful life styles. Moreover, outside the self-defined boundaries of American environmentalism, opposition to the permanent war economy is being carried on by a peace movement that has a distinguished history and impeccable moral and political credentials...A truly radical ecology in the American context ought to work toward a synthesis of the appropriate technology, alternate life style, and peace movements. By making the (largely spurious) anthropocentric-biocentric distinction central to the debate, deep ecologists may have appropriated the moral high ground, but they are at the same time doing a serious disservice to American and global environmentalism.

NOTES

1. Kirkpatrick Sale, "The Forest for the Trees: Can Today's Environmentalists Tell the Difference," *Mother Jones* 11, No. 8 (November 1986): 26.
2. Daniel Janzen, "The Future of Tropical Ecology," *Annual Review of Ecology and Systematics* 17 (1986): 305–306; emphasis added.
3. Robert Aitken Roshi, "Gandhi, Dogen, and Deep Ecology," reprinted as appendix C in Bill Devall and George Sessions, *Deep Ecology: Living as if Nature Mattered* (Salt Lake City: Peregrine Smith Books, 1985).
4. Joseph Sax, *Mountains Without Handrails: Reflections on the National Parks* (Ann Arbor: University of Michigan Press, 1980), 42.
5. John Kenneth Galbraith, "How Much Should a Country Consume?" in Henry Jarrett, ed., *Perspectives on Conservation* (Baltimore: Johns Hopkins Press, 1958), pp. 91–92.

REVIEW EXERCISES

1. Why is the notion of *value* problematic when discussing environmental ethics?
2. What are the differences among intrinsic, instrumental, and prima facie values? Give an example of each.
3. What is anthropocentrism? How is it different from ecocentrism?
4. How do cost–benefit analyses function in environmental arguments? Give an example of an environmental problem today and how a cost–benefit analysis could be used to analyze it.
5. Explain how the concept of environmental justice can be used to provide a critical analysis of the impact of pollution.
6. Describe two different types of ecocentrism.
7. What is Aldo Leopold's basic principle for determining what is right and wrong in environmental matters?
8. What is deep ecology? According to this view, what are the root causes of our environmental problems?
9. Summarize the different ecofeminist views described in this chapter.
10. What is the problem of the tragedy of the commons, and how is it connected to capitalism and the idea of property rights?

DISCUSSION CASES

1. **Climate Change**. Carla and Greg are debating climate change. Carla believes that climate change is nothing to worry about. "Even if the scientists could ever really establish that burning fossil fuels causes climate change, there's no need to worry. Scientists will find ways to fix the problem. And we can always move to higher ground or just move north, where it's cooler." Greg laughs out loud. "Ha! That's easy for you to say," Greg replies. "Americans will probably be able to survive the changing climate. But people in other parts of the world are really going to suffer. And anyway, it's not just about the humans. We should also be concerned about the value of natural things like glaciers and forests." Carla shakes her head. "I don't really get you environmentalists. First, you say that poor people will suffer. Then, you say that glaciers and forests will suffer. But aren't people more important than glaciers? And if we had to melt all the glaciers to provide drinking water for poor people, wouldn't that be the right thing to do?"

   Whom do you agree with here? Explain your answer with reference to philosophical concepts such as anthropocentrism and ecocentrism.

2. **Preserving the Trees**. XYZ Timber Company has been logging forests in the Pacific Northwest for decades. It has done moderately well in replanting areas it has logged, but it has also been logging in areas where some trees are hundreds of years old. Now, the company plans to build roads into a similar area of the forest and cut down similarly ancient trees. An environmental group, "Trees First," is determined to prevent this. Its members have blocked the roads that have been put in by the timber company and have also engaged in the practice known as *tree spiking*—in which iron spikes are driven into trees to discourage the use of power saws. Loggers are outraged because tree spiking can make logging extremely dangerous. When a saw hits these spikes, it becomes uncontrollable, and loggers can be seriously injured. Forest rangers have been marking trees found to be spiked and have noted that some spikes are not visible and will present a hidden danger for years to come. People

from Trees First insist that this is the only way to prevent the shortsighted destruction of old-growth forests. They argue that XYZ Timber Company has too much political power and has ignored public protests against their logging practices. The only way to get the company's attention, they say, is to put their employees at risk.

What is your assessment of the actions of the XZY Timber Company and the actions of Trees First? Is it ever justifiable to use extreme protest methods such as tree spiking that put lives at risk? Why or why not?

3. **Sustainable Development**. The people of the Amazon River basin, who live in rural poverty, have begun burning and clearing large sections of the forest. They are doing so to create farmland in order to earn a living for themselves and their families. But the burning and deforestation destroys ecosystems of rare plants and animals and contributes to global warming. As a result, representatives from environmental groups in the United States and other wealthy countries have traveled to the region seeking to persuade the locals to cease this practice and pursue a more sustainable livelihood based on ecotourism. The people of the Amazon River basin are offended by these proposals. They point out that North Americans already have destroyed much of their own forests and become prosperous. "Who are you to criticize us?" they ask. "It is a luxury to worry about what the weather will be like a hundred years from now. We have to worry about what we will eat tomorrow."

Whose position do you find more persuasive here—the environmentalists or the people of the Amazon River basin? How would you balance global concerns about deforestation and global warming against the subsistence needs of cultures in environmentally sensitive areas?

MindTap® For more chapter resources and activities, go to MindTap.

Animal Ethics

Learning Outcomes

After reading this chapter, you should be able to:

- Describe current issues in animal ethics including hunting, vegetarianism, animal research, and endangered species protection.

- Explain the difference between a concern for animal welfare and a concern for animal rights.

- Define *speciesism* and articulate criticisms of this idea.

- Explain the idea of "equal consideration" and what that might mean for animal ethics.

- Articulate anthropocentric and non-anthropocentric criticisms of animal cruelty.

- Explain Peter Singer's notion of animal liberation and how the idea might apply in thinking about animal research or industrial farming.

- Defend a thesis with regard to animal ethics.

Jose Gi/iStock/Thinkstock

> MindTap®   For more chapter resources and activities, go to MindTap.

Gray wolves were once hunted to the brink of extinction in the United States. By 1970, only two states—Alaska and Minnesota—still had viable gray wolf populations. During the 1970s, various subspecies of gray wolf were given protection from hunting under the Endangered Species Act. For some subspecies—the Texas wolf, for example—it was too late. The Texas wolf and other subspecies have disappeared forever. By 1978, all gray wolf subspecies in the lower forty-eight states were protected against hunting.[1] In 1995, wolves captured in Canada were reintroduced to the western United States, in an effort to regenerate the U.S. wolf population. Western ranchers feared that these wolves would prey upon their livestock, and in some places, they were permitted to shoot wolves that had killed their sheep or cattle. By 2009, the population of wolves had grown large enough that the U.S. Fish and Wildlife Service removed the gray wolf from the list of endangered species. This move prompted some states to legalize wolf hunting. Controversially, this included wolf hunting near Yellowstone National Park—a practice that raised objections because the national parks are supposed to protect animals from hunting. In 2012, wolf hunting was allowed in Wyoming, and by 2013, there had been wolf hunts in Wisconsin, Minnesota, Idaho,

Wolf hunting raises moral questions about animal ethics.

Wyoming, and Montana. The wolf hunts (or "harvests") of 2012–13 resulted in more than 1,000 wolves killed.[2] Subsequent litigation resulted in cancelled wolf hunts.

Opponents of wolf hunts criticize the language used to describe these hunts, complaining that it is a euphemism to use the word "harvest" to describe such killing. This points to the question of whether a wolf is a creature with a right to life or something more like a crop to be managed and harvested. Some view wolves as noble symbols of a vanishing wilderness. Others see them as animals very similar to the dogs we keep as pets. Still others view wolves as dangerous predators that pose a risk to sheep and other herd animals. Such perspectives reflect different answers to the question: What is the value of a wolf—or any other animal?

Is there a humane way to kill a wolf or another nonhuman animal? During the wolf harvest, the animals could be shot or trapped. Animal welfare advocates have been especially critical of using leg traps to kill wolves. One anti-trapping group, Footloose Montana, argues that trapping is cruel because it causes excessive suffering and is not in line with the "fair chase" ethos of hunting.[3] Leg traps are intended to hold the wolf until the hunter arrives to finally kill it. Trappers insist that they check their traps often and kill the animals quickly. But some animals are caught in traps for long periods of time. Some die of hypothermia. Others chew off their own legs or are attacked by other predators. Another problem with trapping is that it is indiscriminate. A 2012 report about a trapping program employed by the Wildlife Services in California indicated that traps in California have killed 50,000 unintended animals since 2000, including protected species such as bald eagles and more than one thousand dogs.[4] A 2016 report claims, "In 2014, Wildlife Services killed 322 wolves, 61,702 coyotes, 2,930 foxes, 580 black bears, 796 bobcats, five golden eagles, and three bald eagles."[5] The report stated that the animals were trapped or poisoned. Poison is a common way of dealing with household pests such as rats and mice—along with sticky traps and glue boards. Critics complain that these are inhumane ways of killing pest animals: poison causes internal hemorrhaging and dehydration, while glue boards keep animals immobile until they succumb to dehydration and starvation. For this reason, some argue that snap traps—the old fashioned mousetrap—are the most humane way to kill mice and rats because the trap kills instantly. Others worry that there is no humane way to kill an animal.

A further question is whether trapping and poisoning lives up to the standards of "fair chase." The idea of fair chase in hunting ethics is that the animal should stand some chance and the hunter requires some skill and good luck. According to one definition, fair chase involves a balance between the hunter and the hunted animal "that allows hunters to occasionally succeed, while animals generally avoid being taken."[6] The concept of fair chase might be used to criticize the practice of "rigged" hunting, in which companies obtain "trophy" animals and confine them in certain ways so that hunters have a much better chance at a kill. Such companies often buy their animals from dubious suppliers, including exotic animal auctions, and their hunts have been known to include "zebras, camels, ostriches, kangaroos, and lion cubs."[7] Other problematic forms of hunting include the use of bait to attract animals to be shot. For example, the practice of baiting bears is banned in eighteen of the twenty-eight states in which bear hunting is legal. The former governor of Minnesota, Jesse Ventura, once said of bear baiting, "that ain't sport, that's an assassination."[8] However, the state of Alaska allows and even promotes bear baiting, publishing a bear baiters "code of ethics."[9]

The question of hunting ethics burst into public consciousness with the killing of Cecil the Lion in Zimbabwe in 2015. Cecil was an iconic lion—a local favorite who inhabited the Hwange National Park, where he was protected against hunting. According to media reports, Cecil was lured out of the park with bait and then shot with a bow and arrow by a dentist from Minnesota, who reportedly paid $50,000 for the opportunity. Some reports maintained that Cecil was not killed by the arrow—and that he survived for forty hours, while the hunters tracked him down and finally killed him with a gunshot. Across the globe, there was outraged reaction to the fact that a protected lion was killed for sport and without regard for fair chase hunting ethics.[10] In response to the outrage over Cecil's killing, the U.S. Fish and Wildlife Service announced that it would list the African lion as an endangered species, which would prevent lion trophies from being imported in the United States.[11]

In addition to baiting animals and luring them out of protected areas, other controversial practices include hunting wolves and other animals from helicopters or small planes, such as occurs in Alaska. According to one report, aerial wolf hunts in Alaska kill several hundred wolves every winter.[12] This practice is not only a matter of sport hunting, but also a way of balancing predator and prey populations—which is the only legal reason for such hunts under federal law. Critics of airborne hunting consider it cruel and inhumane because the plane or helicopter is used to chase animals across the snow until they are exhausted and because shots fired from the air rarely result in a clean kill.[13] In 2008, when the former governor of Alaska, Sarah Palin, was a candidate for vice president of the United States, aerial wolf hunting in Alaska became a political issue, since Governor Palin had championed the program of shooting wolves from the air.

The debate over hunting points toward several complex ethical questions. Should we be concerned for the welfare of wild animals and endangered species? Do such animals have a right to live their lives free from human interference? Is it acceptable to "harvest" them, as long as we kill them humanely? Is hunting part of an ancient predator–prey dynamic that defines the rest of the natural world, or do humans have greater moral responsibilities than other animals? How and why should human beings care about the well-being of individual animals or animal species, or about ecosystems that include both predators and prey animals?

These sorts of questions point toward fundamental issues concerning the ontological and moral status of animals. They also point toward fundamental questions about being human and the extent to which we are similar to and different from nonhuman animals. Human beings are animals, after all. But we are also the only animals that raise questions about the morality of killing other animals. Does this make us superior to nonhuman animals; or does it give us a greater responsibility? Anthropocentric (or human-centered) answers to these questions will maintain that humans are superior or that human concerns matter most. Non-anthropocentric answers will reject such claims, maintaining that we also ought to consider things from a standpoint that takes the interests and welfare of nonhuman animals seriously. The distinction between anthropocentric and non-anthropocentric approaches showed up in our discussion of environmental ethics (in Chapter 16). It returns here with a specific focus on the value of nonhuman animals.

CURRENT ISSUES
Moral Vegetarianism

There are a variety of concrete issues that arise in discussing animals and their welfare. Perhaps the most obvious issue is whether we ought to raise and kill animals for food. The discussion of hunting overlaps with discussions of eating animals. Although wolves are not hunted for their meat, harvesting wolves is intended to protect domesticated animals such as cattle and sheep and to protect wild herds of elk, caribou, moose, and deer, which are hunted for their meat. This raises the interesting question about which animals we eat and which animals we don't, and evokes the philosophical issue of cultural relativism (as discussed in Chapter 3). Some cultures eat dogs; others don't. Some cultures eat pigs; others don't. Do these differences reflect moral truths of some kind, or mere cultural conventions and taboos?

Some cultures and individuals don't eat animals at all. The ancient Greek philosopher Pythagoras and his followers were vegetarians, as are some Hindus, Buddhists, and Jains in varying degrees. The nineteenth-century Russian novelist Leo Tolstoy was a vegetarian. Tolstoy maintained that those who are "really and seriously seeking to live a good life" will abstain from animal food because "its use is simply immoral, as it involves the performance of

an act which is contrary to moral feeling—killing."[14] Tolstoy's ideas had an influence on Mohandas Gandhi (discussed in Chapter 2), whose vegetarianism was also connected to his Hindu religion and culture. In his autobiography, Gandhi describes witnessing a ceremonial sacrifice of a lamb. When a friend explained to him that a lamb does not feel anything while being slaughtered, Gandhi replied that if the lamb could speak, it would tell a different tale. Gandhi concludes,

> To my mind the life of a lamb is no less precious than that of a human being. I should be unwilling to take the life of a lamb for the sake of the human body. I hold that, the more helpless a creature, the more entitled it is to protection by man from the cruelty of man.[15]

There are degrees of vegetarianism. All vegetarians avoid eating animals, although some may eat eggs, dairy products, or even fish. Vegans avoid consuming both animals and animal products, including eggs, dairy, and, in some cases, honey. Some people observe vegetarian diets for health reasons—because of a food allergy or in an effort to follow a high-fiber, low-fat diet. But many vegetarians avoid eating animals for ethical reasons. The deep ethical question is whether there are good moral reasons to avoid meat and animal products or whether the consumption of animals is morally justified.

Most meat eaters think that there is nothing wrong with consuming animals and animal products. Meat eating is deeply rooted in custom and tradition. One traditional idea holds that animals are given to us by God for our use. A related idea maintains that there is a hierarchy of beings, with humans at the top, and this entitles us to use the animals below us. Others may assume that animals do not feel pain when they are slaughtered, or that animals are not moral "persons" because they do not have the sort of consciousness that would give them an interest in living. (You might want to compare such positions to other cases where moral status is in question, such as human fetuses or brain-dead adults.) Another argument holds that vegetarianism is supererogatory: that it might be admirable to abstain from eating animals but that there is no duty to do so.[16] Still others argue that the morality of eating meat depends upon the way the meat is raised—whether it is produced on industrial farms or in a "cruelty-free" manner (including free-range or cage-free animals). This issue has even shown up on state ballots: in California in 2008, voters approved the Prevention of Farm Animal Cruelty Act, which aimed to prevent cruelty in the treatment of veal calves, pigs, and chickens. Similar laws have been established in several other states and in the European Union.

A strictly utilitarian account of animal ethics would be focused on whether causing animal suffering can be justified by some account of the greater good. If we are primarily focused on human good, we might say that animal suffering is outweighed by the human interest in nutritious and delicious meat and other animal products. Another utilitarian argument might point out that by raising animals for food and clothing, we produce animals that otherwise would never have been born—so even though these animals are used and killed, they enjoy pleasures while alive that they would not have enjoyed if not for animal agriculture. Unless their lives involve a greater amount of pain than pleasure, we may have done these animals a favor by raising them.

But critics of industrialized agriculture will argue that "factory farms" produce animals that live miserable lives and are then killed for human purposes. While such farms are not intentionally cruel, they employ practices that would certainly appear to be cruel if viewed from the perspective of the animals. Animals are branded, force-fed, and confined, frequently without enough space to exercise or even turn around. They are kept in close proximity to other animals, which makes them susceptible to infectious diseases—and prompts industrial farms to pump them full of antibiotics. Industrialized agriculture also uses breeding technologies, including genetic engineering and cloning, which aim to maximize meat production. For example, these processes create animals that are bred to be large, and then, they are fed so much that eventually they cannot stand up. Chickens packed into close quarters often

have their beaks and claws removed to prevent injury to themselves and other chickens. And some animals—for example, veal cattle or geese raised for foie gras—are kept in cages that prevent almost all movement and force-fed in ways that negatively impact their health. Tasty veal comes from anemic calves; and delicious foie gras comes from diseased goose liver.

Animals are crowded into trucks and transported for slaughter in ways that often result in significant stress, with thousands of animals dying on the way.[17] In the slaughterhouses, there are assembly-line processes by which animals are stunned and killed. Some animals are severely injured before they are slaughtered. Animal welfare advocates have posted videos of "downer cattle" (cattle who can't or won't walk under their own power to the slaughterhouse) who are dragged or forklifted into the killing line. Federal law requires that mammals be stunned before killing. But in some cases, there may be a problem in properly stunning the animals. Peter Singer and Jim Mason conclude, "it is probable that anyone who eats meat will, unknowingly, from time to time be eating meat that comes from an animal who died an agonizing death."[18] There are legal and ethical standards that regulate the meat production industry. But the industrial meat production process is focused on speed and efficiency. This is necessary because of the great demand for meat among the general public. In the United States in 2013, the meat industry processed 93 billion pounds of meat, produced from 8.6 billion chickens, 33.2 million cattle, 239.4 million turkeys, 2.3 million sheep and lambs, and 112 million hogs.[19]

The appetite for meat is growing worldwide, with global meat production tripling between 1980 and 2002, and meat production is expected to double again by 2050.[20] There will likely be substantial environmental costs from more extensive meat production. But defenders of industrial agriculture argue that if we want to feed a human population of seven billion and counting, we need intensified agricultural procedures. Indeed, if the demand for meat continues to grow, we will need to develop even more efficient and productive ways of raising animals for meat: the global population cannot be fed on meat from free-range farms.

Vegetarian critics of factory farming and the growing appetite for meat argue that there are nutritious and delicious alternatives to meat. They also point out that animal agriculture is hard on the environment. The animals that we consume eat grains, require fresh water, and produce waste. Vegetarians argue that it would be more efficient and less wasteful to feed the growing human population if we ate lower on the food chain. This would leave a smaller ecological footprint and make more grain and other food available to fight human hunger around the world.[21]

Vegetarianism is also connected with other political and moral ideas. Some feminists argue that meat eating is connected to male dominance and the oppression of women; other feminists argue that the idea of care ethics should encompass care for animals.[22] Vegetarians often cite medical studies that indicate eating meat is not necessary for human health. This is especially true in much of

Chicks being processed on a conveyor belt in an industrial agriculture operation.

iStockphoto.com/SensorSpot

the developed world, where nutritious alternatives are easily found in the typical supermarket. If meat eating is not necessary for human health, then meat becomes a luxury good. And then, we may ask whether it is morally justified to cause animal suffering in support of a human indulgence. On the other hand, however, many will argue that human interests matter more than animal interests and that eating meat is easily justified by appealing to basic human interests.

Animal Experimentation

Another issue is the use of animals in scientific and industrial research. Some animal rights advocates claim that it is cruel and unnecessary to use animals in scientific and industrial research. Defenders of animal experimentation argue that most of the gains we have made in terms of modern medicine and in safety for modern industrial products are the results of experiments performed on animals.

Animal research has a long history. In the third century BCE in Alexandria, Egypt, animals were used to study bodily functions.[23] Aristotle cut open animals to learn about their structure and development. The Roman physician Galen used certain animals to show that veins do not carry air, but blood. And in 1622, William Harvey used animals to exhibit the circulation of the blood. Animals were used in 1846 to show the effects of anesthesia and in 1878 to demonstrate the relationship between bacteria and disease.[24]

In the twentieth century, research with animals made many advances in medicine possible, from cures for infectious diseases and the development of immunization techniques and antibiotics, to the development of surgical procedures. For example, in 1921, an Ontario doctor and his assistant severed the connection between the pancreases and digestive systems of dogs in order to find the substance that controlled diabetes. In so doing, they isolated insulin and thus opened the possibility for treating the millions of people who have that disease.[25] During the development of a polio vaccine, hundreds of primates were killed, but as a result of these experiments, today polio is almost eradicated

in the developed world. In 1952, there were fifty-eight thousand cases of this crippling disease in the United States, and in 1984, there were just four. Now, there are few reported cases.[26] AIDS researchers have used monkeys to test vaccines against HIV, and animal research has been an important part of the study of human paralysis. In 2000, "researchers at the University of Massachusetts Medical School [took] immature cells from the spinal cords of adult rats, induced them to grow, and then implanted them in the gap of the severed spinal cords of paralyzed rats."[27] Soon, the rats were able to move, stand, and walk. This research has given hope to the three hundred thousand to five hundred thousand people in the United States, and more people around the world, who suffer from spinal-cord damage. It is part of a growing field of tissue engineering in which scientists grow living tissue to replace damaged parts of the human body (see further discussion of biotechnologies in Chapter 18).

Today, laboratory researchers are using leopard frogs to test the pain-killing capacity of morphine, codeine, and Demerol. Japanese medaka fish are being used as a model to determine the cancer-causing properties of substances that are released into rivers and lakes. And research using the giant Israeli scorpion has found a way to use the scorpion venom to treat brain tumors, called gliomas.[28] Other promising research creates genetically modified animals to use as drug-producing machines. For example, scientists have spliced human genes into the DNA of goats, sheep, and pigs. These mammals then secrete therapeutic proteins in their milk, which can be used to treat hemophilia and cystic fibrosis.[29]

Opposition to animal research dates back to at least the nineteenth century. *Antivivisectionists* campaigned against dissecting live animals and other common practices that inflicted pain on animals. In 1876, the British Parliament passed the first animal welfare act, the Cruelty to Animals Act. A few states in the United States passed anticruelty laws in the nineteenth and early twentieth centuries, but it was not until 1966 that the United States instituted a federal law regulating animal research. The Animal Welfare Act of 1966 (AWA) came about, in part, in response to a national outcry over a family dog, Pepper, who had become a stray and ended up being euthanized in a hospital after being subjected to a laboratory experiment. The AWA set minimum standards for handling cats, dogs, nonhuman primates, rabbits, hamsters, and guinea pigs. It also sought to regulate the use of dogs and cats so that pets like Pepper did not end up in lab experiments.[30] In a 1976 amendment, Congress exempted rats, mice, birds, horses, and farm animals from the protections of the AWA because of problems with enforcement and funding.[31] Such exclusions were reinforced in 2002, in an amendment to the annual farm bill, and subsequent efforts to revoke it have failed in Congress. So while the Animal Welfare Act requires careful treatment of some animals used in research, such as dogs, it does not cover the vast majority of laboratory animals. It is estimated that 95 percent of animals used in laboratory research are mice, rats, and birds, all of which the AWA does not cover.[32] The Animal Legal Defense Fund argues that these animals deserve protection: "Modern science has established that birds, mice, and rats are sentient: capable of experiencing pain, fear, distress, and joy. Recent studies show mice feel pain individually and for others. Yet current AWA exclusions mean researchers are not obligated to consider any alternatives to the unnecessary suffering of these animals."[33]

The Humane Society estimates that some twenty-five million animals in total are used in animal experiments each year in the United States.[34] Opponents of animal research argue that this is too much cruelty in the name of research. Groups like People for the Ethical Treatment of Animals (PETA), the American Society for the Prevention of Cruelty to Animals (ASPCA), and the Humane Society continue to question the need for animal research and argue that alternatives are being neglected. Johns Hopkins University's Center for Alternatives to Animal Testing maintains that "the best science is humane science."[35]

The AWA requires laboratories to report the number of animals used. On university campuses, animal use is monitored by Institutional Animal Care and Use Committees (IACUCs). If you do scientific research involving animals as a student, you may have to learn how to prepare a protocol for approval by an IACUC. According to the U.S. Department of Agriculture—which also monitors the use of animals in research—in 2014, there were more than 21,000 cats, nearly 60,000 dogs, and almost 58,000 primates being used in animal research in the United States.[36] Not all of these animals were subjected to painful intervention: they were used in a variety of experiments involving different levels of pain and experimental treatment. One particularly controversial type of medical research involves chimpanzees, an intelligent species of ape that is a close relative of human beings. In 2013, the National Institutes of Health announced that it was going to end chimpanzee research, in part, as a result of ethical concerns.[37] The Humane Society and PETA applauded this move. The NIH had planned to keep fifty chimpanzees in reserve in case they were needed for future research. But in late 2015, the NIH announced that even this reserve cohort of chimpanzees would be retired.[38]

A basic question here is whether we are justified in using nonhuman animals for research that may benefit human beings (and that may also benefit animals, as in veterinary research). A utilitarian approach that focused only on human interests and concerns would claim that if human beings benefit, then such research is justified. A broader utilitarian position that takes animal suffering into account would explore the question of whether the benefits of animal research outweigh the harms of such research on the animals involved.

While opponents of animal research criticize the large numbers of animals used in research, defenders of animal research point out that these numbers are best interpreted in comparison with other uses of animals. The advocacy group Speaking of Research defends the use of animals in research as follows:

Scientists in the US use approximately 12-25 million animals in research, of which only less than 1 million are not rats, mice, birds or fish. We use fewer animals in research than the number of ducks eaten per year in this country. We consume over 1800 times the number of pigs than the number used in research. We eat over 340 chickens for each animal used in a research facility, and almost 9,000 chickens for every animal used in research covered by the Animal Welfare Act. For every animal used in research, it is estimated that 14 more are killed on our roads.[39]

One important moral question is whether the use of animals is really *necessary* to facilitate the medical advances of the past two centuries. Even if it was once necessary, is the use of animals still necessary in today's medical research, given dramatic technological advances? Animal rights activists argue that other sources of information can now be used, including population studies or epidemiology, monitoring of human patients, noninvasive medical imaging devices, autopsies, tissue and cell cultures, in vitro tests, and computer models. Activists also argue that the use of animals as experimental subjects has sometimes actually delayed the use of effective treatment. One example cited in this regard is the development of penicillin for the treatment of bacterial infections. When Alexander Fleming tested penicillin on infected rabbits, it proved ineffective, and thus, he put it aside for a decade, not knowing that rabbits—unlike humans—excrete penicillin in their urine.[40]

Further, activists argue that those who hold we can use animals in experimentation are inconsistent because they claim both that animals are sufficiently different from humans to be ethically used in experiments, and that they are sufficiently like humans to make the experimental results apply to us. Proponents of animal research answer this criticism by pointing out that mice, although quite different from humans, make very good models for the study of human health, simply because we share so many genes with them.[41] Furthermore, they contend, cell culture and computer studies are insufficient. If we moved directly from these cell or computer studies to the use of these drugs or treatments in humans, we would put patients at risk. Take the case of the drug thalidomide, an antinausea drug that was insufficiently tested on animals and ended up causing more than ten thousand babies to be born with birth defects when it was prescribed to pregnant women in the 1950s.

Whether using animals is necessary for various medical advances or whether other kinds of studies can be substituted is an empirical matter. However, most likely, some animal research is redundant or simply unnecessary, and other methods could serve just as well or better. For example, longitudinal human epidemiological studies provide better and more reliable data than many animal studies—even though human epidemiological studies are harder and more costly to conduct.

A primary ethical concern about the use of nonhuman animals in research involves the extent to which pain is inflicted on these experimental subjects. Sometimes, pain is a necessary part of the experiment, such as in pain studies in which the purpose is to find better ways to relieve pain in humans. Those who oppose animal research cite other examples of cruelty to animal subjects. It is not only the physical pain of the experiments they point to, but also psychological pains, such as those that stem from being caged for long periods of time. This is especially true, they argue, for intelligent social animals.

There are at least three positions on the use of nonhuman animals in research. One opposes all use of animals. At the other end of the spectrum is the position that nonhuman animals have no rights or moral standing and thus can be used as we choose. In the middle is the belief that animals have some moral status and thus limits and restrictions should be placed on conducting research with these creatures. But even many who support animal rights agree that the use of animals in experimentation can sometimes be ethically justified. In this view, animal research may be justified if it does, in fact, help us develop significant medical advances, if it provides information that cannot be obtained in any other way, and if experiments are conducted with as little discomfort for the animals as possible. The ethical status of animal experiments for other less vital purposes, such as cosmetics development, is an even more controversial issue.

Endangered Species

International efforts to protect animals often aim to prevent animals from going extinct or losing their natural habitats. International conferences, such as the United Nations Convention on International Trade in Endangered Species, held in November 2002, in Santiago, Chile, try to address these problems. Among the issues discussed in Santiago was whether certain African nations should be allowed to sell elephant ivory, which they had stockpiled in the decades before elephants became a legally protected species. The United States prohibits imports of ivory through laws that include the African Elephant Conservation Act of 1989. But ivory remains in demand in various parts of the world, fueled by the illegal hunting, or *poaching*, of elephants. According to a 2016 report, elephant populations are declining in Africa. Forty years ago, there were an estimated 1 million elephants in the wild—with as many as five million specimens a century ago. Today, there are fewer than one hundred thousand forest elephants and fewer than four hundred thousand savannah elephants left in Africa.[42] In the United States, there is a movement to classify these African elephants as endangered species, which would strengthen protections for these animals.

In addition, the Ringling Bros. and Barnum & Bailey circus has announced that it will retire its elephants by May 2016. Critics have complained that the elephants—and other animals used in circuses—are abused, that they are manipulated by electric prods and metal hooks, beaten, and kept in unhealthy conditions. Circus trainers deny the accusations. The circus elephants used are typically Asian elephants, which are endangered in the wild. These elephants live long lives (up to 65 years) in social groups and families. Critics contend that making animals perform in the circus is abusive and unnatural, and that using endangered species in the circus violates the idea of protecting the species. In its defense, Ringling Bros. maintains that

its elephant retirement plan is part of its effort to conserve the species: it will keep its retired elephants at a facility in Florida, where it will breed them.[43]

In the United States, the protection of wild animals is handled by a patchwork of laws and agencies. For example, the Marine Mammal Protection Act of 1972 "establishe[d] a moratorium on the taking and importation of marine mammals, including parts and products." The Department of the Interior is charged with enforcing the management and protection of sea otters, walruses, polar bears, dugong, and manatees. The 1973 Endangered Species Act protects species that are threatened with extinction and those that the secretaries of the interior or commerce place on a list of endangered species. As we saw at the outset of this chapter, this has been a successful endeavor in the case of the gray wolf, which has increased to a self-sustaining population in the United States.

But the news is not good for other species. In the United States, as of March 2016, 687 animal species are listed as either endangered or threatened. This includes 98 mammalian species, such as bears, foxes, manatees, ocelots, otters, panthers, rats, and whales.[44] The International Union for Conservation of Nature (IUCN) produces a "red list" of animal and plant species that are endangered around the world. As of 2014, IUCN had assessed some 73,600 species. It concludes that 33 percent of reef building corrals are threatened with extinction, along with 41 percent of amphibians, 13 percent of birds, and 25 percent of mammals.[45] Some species, such as the Sumatran rhino, are on the verge of extinction—with fewer than 100 living specimens left in 2015.[46] On the other hand, there has been some good news. After many years of conservation efforts, the mountain gorillas in Eastern Africa are making a comeback. When the renowned primatologist Diane Fossey arrived in Rwanda in 1967, there were only 240 gorillas left in the wild. Today, there are 880 gorillas. That's still a small number. But it provides evidence that species can be preserved with concerted human effort to protect habitat and curb poaching.[47]

Some of the successes are due to the fact that there are more protected areas in the world, including wildlife refuges and reserves. Destruction of animal habitat may be the most potent threat to animal species. Although animals can often adapt to gradual changes in their environment, rapid change often makes such adjustment impossible. Many human activities—such as cutting down trees, damming rivers, mining, drilling, and pipeline building—can cause such rapid change. Another cause of species loss is when humans introduce non-native species into an environment, thus upsetting a delicate ecological balance. Overexploitation of animal populations is also a source of extinction. For example, many species of sharks are being fished into extinction by fishermen—who only want their fins for the Asian delicacy shark-fin soup.[48] The commercial fishing industry threatens not only the species it harvests for food, but also other species caught as "by-catch." Whales, dolphins, and other marine mammals are also threatened by commercial fishing operations. Marine mammals caught in gill nets drown, trapped under water, unable to reach the surface to breathe. According to a 2014 report from National Public Radio, 650,000 marine mammals are killed every year in commercial fishing operations, including 300,000 dolphins and whales and 350,000 seals and sea lions.[49] This so-called "by-catch," accidental entrapment in fishing nets intended to catch other fish, could be remedied by the use of other fishing technologies.

Some point out that species go extinct naturally without human intervention. Through the course of evolution, the species that have been lost have been replaced at a higher rate than they have disappeared, which helps explain the wondrous diversity of our planet's species. But the rate of replacement may no longer be able to keep up because of the accelerated pace of species loss. Those who are concerned about the global ecosystem worry about this loss of biodiversity—both because they value different species for their own sake as having intrinsic value (as we discussed in Chapter 16) and because they see biodiversity as good for the larger ecosystem and thus good for human beings.

While some hold that individual animals have rights or a particular moral status, others believe it is animal species that we ought to protect, not individual animals. It may seem obvious that we have good anthropocentric reasons for preserving animal as well as plant species. We have aesthetic interests in a variety of different life forms. Naturalists, hikers, hunters, and bird watchers know the thrill of being able to observe rare species. The diversity and strangeness of nature are themselves objects of wonder. We also have nutritional and health interests in preserving species. Some species may now seem to have no value for humans, but examples such as the medaka fish and the giant Israeli scorpion, discussed previously, should remind us how important seemingly "minor" species can prove to be for human needs. Loss of species leaves us genetically poorer and more ignorant about the natural systems to which we belong. Animals tell us about ourselves, our history, and how natural systems work or could work. "Destroying species is like tearing pages out of an unread book, written in a language humans hardly know how to read, about the place where they live," writes environmental ethicist Holmes Rolston.[50] If we destroy the mouse lemur, for example, we destroy the modern animal that is closest to the primates from which our own human line evolved.[51]

However, when we ask whether animal species have *moral standing* or *intrinsic value* or even *rights*, we run into puzzling issues. An animal species is not an individual. It is a collection and, in itself, cannot have the kind of interests or desires that may be the basis for the moral standing or rights of individual animals. Thus, according to philosopher Nicholas Rescher, "moral obligation is…always interest-oriented. But only individuals can be said to have interests; one only has moral obligations to particular individuals or particular groups thereof."[52] If we can have duties to a group of individuals and a species is a group, then we may have duties to species. Still, this does not imply that the species has rights.

Some people challenge the very notion of species and question whether a species is identical to the individuals it includes. Consider just what we might mean by a *species*. Is it not a concept constructed by humans as a way of grouping and comparing organisms? Charles Darwin wrote, "I look at the term species, as one arbitrarily given for the sake of convenience to a set of individuals closely resembling each other."[53] If a species is but a class or category of things, then it does not actually exist as an individual thing. If it does not exist, then how could it be said to have interests or rights? However, consider the following possibility, suggested by Holmes Rolston: "A species is a living historical form (Latin *species*), propagated in individual organisms, that flows dynamically over generations."[54] As such, species are units of evolution that exist in time and space. According to Rolston, "a species is a coherent, ongoing form of life expressed in organisms, encoded in gene flow, and shaped by the environment."[55] If we think of species in this way, it may be intelligible to speak of our having duties to an animal species, as forms of life that span millions of years through their genetic legacies. Our duties, then, would be to a dynamic continuum, a living environmental process, and extinction would be wrong because it ends a "lifeline" or a "unique story." Or, finally, as Rolston writes, "A duty to a species is more like being responsible to a cause than to a person. It is commitment to an *idea*."[56] Although Rolston's explanation of the nature of species and his arguments for the view that we have duties to them are often metaphorical ("story," "lifeline"), nevertheless, his reasoning is intriguing. It also raises metaphysical and ontological questions: What kinds of beings exist or have worth?

Those who support animal rights as the rights of individual animals to certain treatment do not always agree in concrete cases with those who believe that it is species that ought to be protected. Suppose, for example, that a certain population of deer is threatened because its numbers have outstripped the food supply and the deer are starving to death. In some such cases, wildlife officials have sought to thin herds by euthanizing animals or allowing for limited hunting. It is thought to be for the sake of the herd that these animals are killed. Those who

seek to protect species of animals may endorse such "thinning" if it does, in fact, help preserve the species. But animal rights activists might criticize such an approach and argue that ways should be found to save each of the deer. The animal rights scholar Tom Regan has referred to such holistic claims about animals and ecosystems as a sort of "environmental fascism."[57] By using this phrase, Regan means to connect the idea of controlling animal populations to the policies of fascist governments such as Nazi Germany. If individual animals are thought to have rights, then it would be wrong to cull them for the well-being of the whole.

APPROACHES TO ANIMAL ETHICS

The ethical questions raised by animals are all around us. The moral question of which animals we eat (or do not eat) is something we confront three times a day as we make choices about food. We also likely consume products tested on animals every day. We may occasionally go to zoos, circuses, and rodeos. Some of us own pets or raise domesticated animals. Our lives are intertwined with the lives of animals, both wild and domesticated. The U.S. legal system contains extensive regulations for animal care and to prevent cruelty to animals, and we generally see ourselves as caring about their proper treatment. However, most Americans do not often reflect on the moral status of animals. We are often unclear about the underlying reasons for what we see as acceptable or unacceptable ways of treating them.

One way to get a clearer sense of these reasons is to consider the different ways in which we might value animals. For example, some people find pleasure in animals as pets or companions. Others have an economic interest in them, raising and selling them as commodities. Animals are sources of food and clothing. We benefit from them when they are used in experiments to test the safety and effectiveness of drugs, detergents, and cosmetics. Some people enjoy fishing and hunting. Even ecotourism depends upon animals, as people travel to appreciate and photograph animals in their natural habitats. Animals are also sources of pleasure and wonder because of their variety, beauty, and strength.

This suggests the wide range of reasons that animals may be viewed as having value. The most obvious is that animals satisfy human needs: they feed us, clothe us, work for us, and allow some of us to make money. A perspective that focuses on human need and satisfaction is *anthropocentric* (a term we encountered in Chapter 16, when we discussed environmental ethics). It is possible to develop a theory of animal welfare from within anthropocentric concerns. Many farmers, horse racers, and pet owners say they get more out of their animals when they treat them well. Thus, concern for the health and welfare of animals allows us to profit from them. In this view, there is more profit in humane animal treatment than in cruel treatment (although critics of modern industrial farming may disagree). Those who manage herds of wildlife and those who raise and kill animals for human consumption view animals as members of species and as commodities to be managed and controlled.

A further anthropocentric position is that learning to care for animals and treat them well is a natural and normal part of human experience—that humans developed among other animals and in specific relations to them. From a virtue ethics standpoint, one could argue that there are important virtues developed in properly relating to animals. The ethics of hunting mentioned previously may be described in virtue ethics terms: virtuous hunters allow for fair chase, kill in moderation, and kill cleanly and without cruelty. A similar idea can be found in the writing of Immanuel Kant. Kant did not think that animals had any value in themselves, since nonhuman animals are not rational beings. But Kant thought that cruelty to animals was a breeding ground for callousness and indifference to suffering, which tended to make human beings treat each other more cruelly.[58] From this perspective, moral duties to animals are only indirect: the treatment of animals matters in terms of its impact, or potential impact, on other humans. We might also recall here that animals are often considered to be property—and that damaging another person's pets or livestock is frequently viewed as a property crime.

A different approach to animal ethics focuses on non-anthropocentric accounts of the value of animals. Such approaches ask about what is in the interest of the animals themselves, apart from human interests. One non-anthropocentric approach focuses on nonhuman animals as *sentient* creatures, which means that they can feel pleasure and pain just as we do. Indeed, many animals, especially the primates that are genetically closest to us, display striking similarities to human beings in their emotions, communication, relationships, and social groups. In this view, we may be obliged to ask whether we are ever justified in causing them physical or psychological suffering, or killing them. A second approach focuses on nonhuman animals as individuals who have interests and rights. Those who focus on animal sentience and welfare tend to operate with a framework that can be defined in consequentialist or utilitarian terms, while those who focus on animal rights more typically appeal to non-consequentialist or deontological theories of value. From the sentience/welfare perspective, we may have to balance the interests of different sentient beings according to some version of the utilitarian calculus: perhaps some nonhuman animals could be killed or used in a cruelty-free fashion for the well-being of a greater number of human animals. But from the animal rights perspective, there is a positive duty to respect the rights of animals—and, more controversially, there may be an active duty to prevent them from being harmed.

Sentience, Equal Consideration, and Animal Welfare

According to some philosophers, sentience is the key to the ethical status of animals. If animals have the capacity to feel and sense, then it makes sense to talk about their welfare or well-being, and we should take their sentience into account. This tradition dates back at least to the utilitarian Jeremy Bentham, who wrote that to know the ethical status of animals, we need only ask if they can suffer.[59] Besides feeling pleasure and pain, many animals—especially highly social mammals—seem to experience other types of emotions, such as fear, grief, and anger. While philosopher René Descartes thought that animals were mere machines devoid of an inner sense or consciousness, the welfare approach views animals as sentient, suffering beings. The assumption of sentience is one of the reasons we have laws that protect animals from cruelty. However, what counts as cruelty is disputed. For example, many people disagree about whether caging certain animals is cruel.

People also disagree about the reasons we shouldn't be cruel to animals. Some believe—as Kant did—that animal cruelty is wrong because of the effect of cruelty on those who are cruel. They argue that if one is cruel to a sentient animal, then one is more likely to be cruel to people as well. We might also note that those who witness cruelty to animals may be affected by it. They may suffer from seeing an animal suffer, as Gandhi reported previously, after seeing a lamb slaughtered.

However, unless one believes that human suffering is the only suffering that can be bad, then the most obvious reason not to be cruel to animals is that the suffering of the animals is bad for *them*. Whether or not something is cruel to an animal might be determined by the extent of the pain and the purpose for which it is caused. We might speak of some veterinary medical procedures as causing "necessary" pain to heal a sick animal; cruel farming practices might be said to cause animals "unnecessary" pain. Not all pain is bad, even for humans. Pain often tells us of some health problem that can be fixed. The badness of suffering also may be only prima facie bad. The suffering may be worth it—that is, overcome by the good end it will achieve. Doing difficult things is sometimes painful, but we think it is sometimes worth the pain. In these cases, we experience not only the pain, but also the benefit. In the case of animals, however, they often experience the pain of, say, an experiment performed on them without understanding it or enjoying its potential benefit. Is this ever justified?

In discussions of animal sentience, we also have to ask whether animals have different capacities to feel pain. Nonhuman animals with more developed and complex nervous systems and brains will likely have more capacity to feel pain as well as pleasure of various sorts. To fully decide this question,

we would need to think carefully about the physiology of various animals. For example, it might be that horses have thick skin; so kicking a horse with spurs may not hurt the horse the way it would hurt a human.

One significant point of emphasis for the discussion of sentient animals and their welfare is the question of what sorts of experiences are normal and good for animals. For example, the pain of childbirth in humans is frequently considered part of a productive and joyful activity. But defenders of animal welfare will argue that much of the pain and suffering animals are subjected to—especially in intensive animal agriculture—does not produce any benefit for the animals. Indeed, some argue that the process of intensive animal agriculture as a whole is wrong because it continuously violates the normal functioning of the animals. This happens, for example, when animals are kept confined in small spaces, packed together in intensive feeding operations, and when their bodies are altered. Previously, we discussed practices such as cropping chickens' beaks, removing cattle's horns, confining veal calves and feeding a diet that makes them anemic, and force-feeding geese a diet that sickens them in order to produce foie gras. These operations do not respect what philosopher Martha Nussbaum calls "the dignity of the species." Nussbaum claims that sentient animals should be given the opportunity to live according to the natural dignity of their species. Nussbaum concludes: "No sentient animal should be cut off from the chance for a flourishing life, a life with the type of dignity relevant to that species...all sentient animals should enjoy certain positive opportunities to flourish."[60] Of course, there is an open and complex question about what it means for an animal to flourish. Should domesticated cats and dogs be allowed to reproduce unchecked; in other words, does spaying and neutering prevent them from flourishing? If we don't spay and neuter our pets, how will we deal with overpopulation? Further, should animals be allowed to roam freely, or is it permissible to confine them? And so on. What counts as living according to the natural dignity of a species remains open to debate.

In the wild, it is a fact of life that animals feed on and cause pain to one another. Predation prevails. Carnivores kill for food. The fawn is eaten by the cougar. Natural processes such as floods, fires, droughts, and volcanic eruptions also contribute to animal suffering and death. If animal suffering is important, then are we ethically obligated to lessen it in cases where we could do so? For example, in 1986, the Hubbard Glacier in Alaska began to move, and in a few weeks, it had sealed off a fjord. As freshwater runoff poured into the enclosed water, its salinity decreased, threatening the lives of porpoises and harbor seals that were trapped inside by the closure. Some people wanted to rescue the animals, while others held that this was a natural event that should be allowed to run its course.[61]

We tend to think that we have a greater obligation not to *cause* pain or harm than we do to *relieve* it. In special cases, however, we may have a duty to relieve pain or prevent the harm. A lifeguard may have an obligation to rescue a drowning swimmer that the ordinary bystander does not. A parent has more obligation to prevent harm to his or her child than a stranger does. In the case of nonhuman animals, do we have similar obligations to prevent harm? Do we feel constrained to prevent the pain and deaths of animals in the wild? In general, it would seem that although we may choose to do so out of sympathy, we may not be obligated to do so. At least the obligation to prevent harm seems less stringent than the obligation not to cause a similar harm. But if there is this moral difference between preventing and causing harm, then while we may be justified in *allowing* animals in the wild to die or suffer pain, it does not follow that we are justified in *causing* similar pain or harm to them. Just because nature is cruel does not necessarily give us the right to be so.

The animal welfare focus is most closely associated with the work of the influential ethicist Peter Singer, whose 1975 book, *Animal Liberation*, is excerpted as a reading for this chapter. Singer maintains that since animals are sentient, their interests should be given equal consideration to those of humans. Singer does not mean that animals should be treated as exactly equal to humans but, rather, that animal interests should be taken into account. Animals may have different interests than we do, but that does not mean that their interests may be ignored. Philosopher David De Grazia has explained the idea of equal consideration as follows: "equal consideration, whether for humans or animals, means in some way giving equal moral weight to the relevantly similar interests of different individuals."[62] De Grazia goes on to explain that if we don't consider relevantly similar interests equally, we are guilty of creating a differential hierarchy of moral status that is elitist and resembles caste systems or aristocracies.

Singer rejects such an elitist or hierarchical account of animal interests as the result of a self-interested and arbitrary way of drawing moral lines. Singer maintains that not giving equal consideration to the interests of animals is **speciesism**, an objectionable attitude similar to racism or sexism. Speciesism is objectionable because it involves treating animals badly simply because they are members of a different species and giving preference to members of our own species simply because we are human beings.[63] But on what grounds is this objectionable? According to Singer, having interests is connected to the ability to feel pleasure and pain, because pleasure is derived from the satisfaction of interests. Thus, from Singer's standpoint, animal interests should be considered because there is no non-speciesist way to draw the line between animal interests and human interests. Both humans and animals seek pleasure and avoid pain; valuing human pleasure over animal pleasure, for example, is arbitrary and unjustifiable. (Animals are different from plants in this regard. Plants have things that are *in their interest* even though they do not *have interests*.) Singer concludes that among animals that have relevantly similar interests, these interests should be given equal consideration. Not everyone accepts this idea, of course. In one of the readings for this chapter, Bonnie Steinbock argues that it is appropriate to give preference to the interests of humans. Her argument focuses on specific mental capacities that human beings have, which

Outline of Moral Approaches to Animal Ethics

	Animal Rights	Animal Welfare	Anthropocentrism
Thesis	Nonhuman animals have rights that generate duties	The interests of nonhuman animals ought to be taken into account	Human beings are the only objects of moral concern
Corollaries and Implications	The claim that nonhuman animals have inherent value results in radical/abolitionist criticism of animal experimentation and animal agriculture; to claim that only human beings have rights is speciesism	The claim that animal welfare—suffering, harm, flourishing, and enjoyment—ought to be taken into account results in substantial critique of animal agriculture and animal experimentation; to deny the importance of animal suffering or flourishing is speciesism	Defends animal agriculture and experimentation in the name of human interests; cruelty to animals is condemned based upon its tendency to debase human beings; rejects the accusation of speciesism and defends human interests as more important than those of animals
Connections with Moral Theory	Deontological focus on the rights of animals and corollary duties not to harm or use them	Consequentialist focus on harms, interests, and preferences of nonhuman animals in comparison with human interests	Consequentialism focuses only on human interests, harms, and benefits; deontological respect for rights only applies to human beings
Relevant Authors/ Examples	Tom Regan	Peter Singer and Jeremy Bentham	Bonnie Steinbock and Immanuel Kant

she views as superior to the mere sentience of nonhuman animals. She writes, "certain capacities, which seem to be unique to human beings, entitle their possessors to a privileged position in the moral community."[64] Among those capacities may be the ability to think about morality and to act on moral responsibility—which seems to involve more than the bare ability to experience pleasure and pain and to have interests.

Animal Rights

It is one thing to say that the suffering of a nonhuman animal is a bad thing, in itself. It is another to say that nonhuman animals have a *right* not to be caused to suffer or feel pain. To consider the question of animal rights, we need to first review our discussions about what a right is and what it means to have a right. A *right* is generally defined as a strong and *legitimate claim* that can be made by a claimant against someone. Rights claims are often grounded in ideas about what is natural or fitting, as we saw in our discussion on natural law and natural rights in Chapter 7. Thus, if I claim a right to freedom of speech, I am asserting my legitimate claim against anyone who would prevent me from speaking out, and I am claiming that there is something about me as a human being that makes my freedom of speech essential. A person can claim a right to have or be given something (a positive right) as well as a right not to be prevented from doing something (a negative right). Legal rights are claims that the law recognizes and enforces. However, we also hold that there are moral rights—in other words, things we can rightly claim, even if the law does not enforce the claim.

Just who can legitimately claim a moral right to something, and on what grounds? One might think that to be the kind of being who can have rights, one must be able to claim them and understand them. If this were so, then the cat who is left money in a will would not have a right to it because the cat does not understand that it has such a right and could not claim that its rights have been violated if the money is withheld. But if the capacity to understand or claim a right is the only thing that matters, then we might have to conclude that human infants have no rights—to inherit money or be protected from abuse and neglect—because they cannot understand or claim them. But we generally think that infants have a right to care from their parents, even if they do not understand this right and cannot claim it. We make similar claims for the rights of the developmentally disabled, who are also often unable to claim or understand their rights. One might think that only **moral agents**—those beings who can make and act upon moral judgments—have rights. According to this view, a person only has rights if he or she is a full member of the moral community, with duties and responsibilities. On the other hand, it is not unreasonable to think that this is too stringent a requirement. Perhaps it is sufficient for one to be a moral patient in order to be the type of being who can have rights. A **moral patient** is an object of moral concern, the kind of being who matters morally. Moral patients have rights, but they do not have correlated responsibilities. Thus, children have rights but are not considered to be full moral agents; we ought not harm them, but they are viewed as less than fully responsible. As we considered in the Chapter 16, some may think that trees could be considered as moral patients. But does it make sense to say that trees have rights? If this does not seem to be correct, then what other reasons can be given for why a being might have rights?

We could argue that it is just because they can feel pain that sentient beings have a *right not to suffer*, or at least not to suffer needlessly. This would mean that others have a *duty* with regard to this claim. However, we may have duties not to needlessly hurt animals, even if they don't have the *right* to be treated in ways that never cause them pain. We have many duties that are not directly a matter of respecting anyone's rights. For example, I may have a duty not to purchase and then destroy a famous and architecturally important building—but not because the building has a right to exist. Thus, from the fact that we have duties to animals—not to make them suffer needlessly, for example—we cannot necessarily conclude that they have rights. If we want to argue for this view, then we would need to make a clearer connection between duties and rights or we would need to show why some particular duties also imply rights. Not all duties are a function of rights, as I might have a duty to develop my talents, even though no one has a right that I do so. However, having a right seems to entail that someone has a duty to protect that right.

As we have seen, some philosophers have pointed to the fact that animals have *interests* as a basis for asserting that they have rights. To have an interest in something is usually thought to require consciousness of that thing as well as desire for it. A being that has a capacity for conscious desire is a being that can have rights, according to this position. Thus, the philosopher Joel Feinberg says that it is because nonhuman animals have "conscious wishes, desires, and hopes; . . . urges and impulses" that they are the kind of beings who can have rights.[65] It is these psychological capacities that make animals capable of having rights to certain treatment, according to this view. Similarly, Tom Regan argues that nonhuman animals have rights, just as we do, because they are what he calls the "subject of a life."[66] This idea is similar to Feinberg's because it states that because animals have an inner life, which includes conscious desires and wants, they have the status of rights possessors. Nonhuman animals differ among themselves in their capacity to have these various psychological experiences, and it probably parallels the development and complexity of their nervous systems. A dog may be able to experience fear, but, most likely, the flea on its ear does not. In more ambiguous cases, however, drawing such distinctions may prove difficult in practice, when we would have to determine the character of a particular animal's inner life. The more serious challenge for such views is to support the more basic claim that inner psychic states are a moral foundation for rights.

We noted previously that Peter Singer maintains that because the interests of animals are similar to ours, they ought to be given equal weight. This does not mean, in his view, that they have a *right* to whatever we have a right to. It would make no sense to say that a pig has a right to vote because it has no interest in voting and lacks the capacity to vote. However, according to Singer, it would make sense to say that we ought to give equal consideration to the pig's suffering. Pigs shouldn't be made to suffer needlessly to satisfy human whims. But Singer is reluctant to say that animals have rights. As a utilitarian, Singer avoids speaking of rights (you might recall from Chapter 7 that the utilitarian Jeremy Bentham described rights as "nonsense on stilts"). This can lead to some confusion. For example, Singer has explained that the "animal rights movement" does not need the concept of rights.[67] The point here is that the phrase "animal rights" is sometimes used in popular parlance as an umbrella term that encompasses a variety of philosophical perspectives, including both utilitarian and nonconsequentialist positions.

Others argue that animals need not be treated as equal to humans and that their interests should not be given equal weight with ours. It is because of the difference in species' *abilities* and *potentialities* that animals are a lesser form of being, according to these views. (The Bonnie Steinbock reading for this chapter presents such a view.) However, this does not mean that animals' interests should be disregarded. It may mean that peripheral or minor interests of human beings should not override more serious interests of animals. It is one thing to say that animals may be used, if necessary, for experiments that will save the lives of human beings, but it is quite another thing to say that they may be harmed in testing cosmetics or other things that are not necessary for human life. Whether this position would provide a sufficient basis for vegetarianism might depend on the importance of animal protein to human health, for example, and whether animals could be raised humanely for food.

In this chapter, we have raised many questions about animal ethics, including questions about the ethics of hunting, vegetarianism, the use of animals in research, and the moral status or rights of animals as individuals and as species. This chapter's readings, present different ideas about whether human beings and nonhuman animals deserve to be given equal consideration. The first reading is from Peter Singer, one of the most important authors writing about animal welfare and what he calls "speciesism." His 1975 book, *Animal Liberation*, is a foundational text for those concerned with animal ethics. The second reading, from animal rights defender Tom Regan argues that animals have inherent value and that animal experimentation and animal agriculture ought to be abolished. The third reading, from bioethicist Bonnie Steinbock, argues for a more anthropocentric idea of value. She argues that it is not wrong to prefer the interests of humans over the interests of animals.

NOTES

1. Peter Steinhart, *The Company of Wolves* (New York: Random House, 1996), Chapter 7.
2. Combining numbers from the following sources: Wisconsin Department of Natural Resources (DNR), "Wolf Hunting and Trapping," accessed March 30, 2016, http://dnr.wi.gov/topic/hunt/wolf.html; Minnesota DNR, "Wolf Hunting," accessed March 30, 2016, http://www.dnr.state.mn.us/hunting/wolf/index.html; Kim Murphy, "More than 550 Wolves Taken by Hunters and Trappers in Rockies," *Los Angeles Times*, March 6, 2013, accessed March 30, 2016, http://articles.latimes.com/2013/mar/06/nation/la-na-nn-wolves-idaho-montana-hunt-trap-20130305; Idaho Fish and Game, "Wolf Harvest," accessed March 30, 2016, http://fishandgame.idaho.gov/public/hunt/?getPage=121

3. Footloose Montana, "Trapping is Not Fair Chase," accessed March 28, 2016, http://www.footloosemontana.org/about-us/the-issue/trapping-vs-hunting/

4. "The Killing Agency: Wildlife Services' Brutal Methods Leave a Trail of Animal Death," *Sacramento Bee*, April 29, 2012, accessed May 15, 2016, http://www.sacbee.com/news/investigations/wildlife-investigation/article2574599.html

5. Christopher Ketcham, "The Rogue Agency," *Harper's Magazine*, March 2016, accessed March 28, 2016, https://harpers.org/archive/2016/03/the-rogue-agency/

6. Jim Posewitz, *Beyond Fair Chase* (Guilford, CT: Globe Pequot, 1994), p. 57.

7. Wayne Pacelle, "Stacking the Hunt," *The New York Times*, December 9, 2003, accessed May 15, 2016, http://www.nytimes.com/2003/12/09/opinion/09PACE.html

8. The Humane Society of the United States, "Fact Sheet on Bear Baiting," November 2, 2009, accessed March 30, 2016, http://www.humanesociety.org/issues/bear_hunting/facts/bear-baiting-fact-sheet.html

9. Alaska Department of Fish and Game, "Online Bear Baiting Clinic: Ethics and Responsibilities," accessed March 30, 2016, http://www.adfg.alaska.gov/index.cfm?adfg=bearbaiting.ethics

10. Michael E. Miller, "Did Walter Palmer give Cecil the Lion a 'Fair Chase'? We Asked a Hunter/Philosopher," *The Washington Post*, July 31, 2015, accessed March 30, 2016, https://www.washingtonpost.com/news/morning-mix/wp/2015/07/31/did-walter-palmer-give-cecil-the-lion-a-fair-chase-we-asked-a-hunterphilosopher/

11. Erica Goode, "After Cecil Furor, U.S. Aims to Protect Lions Through Endangered Species Act" *The New York Times*, December 20, 2015, accessed March 30, 2016, http://www.nytimes.com/2015/12/21/science/us-to-protect-african-lions-under-endangered-species-act.html?smid=tw-share&_r=1

12. Defenders of Wildlife, Protect America's Wildlife (PAW) Act, *Aerial Hunting FAQs*, accessed March 30, 2016, http://www.defenders.org/sites/default/files/publications/aerial_hunting_q_and_a.pdf,

13. Ibid.

14. Leo Tolstoy, "The First Step," in *Cultural Encyclopedia of Vegetarianism*, ed. Margaret Puskar-Pasewicz (Santa Barbara, CA: ABC-CLIO), p. 248.

15. Mohandas K. Gandhi, *An Autobiography: The Story of My Experiments With Truth* (Boston, MA: Beacon Press, 1993), p. 235.

16. Michael Martin, "A Critique of Moral Vegetarianism," *Reason Papers* No. 3 (Fall 1976), pp. 13–43.

17. See Erik Marcus, *Meat Market: Animals Ethics, and Money* (Boston, MA: Brio Press, 2005), p. 33.

18. See Peter Singer and Jim Mason, *The Ethics of What We Eat: Why Our Food Choices Matter* (New York: Rodale, 2006), pp. 67–68.

19. North American Meat Institute, "The United States Meat Industry at a Glance," accessed March 30, 2016, https://www.meatinstitute.org/index.php?ht=d/sp/i/47465/pid/47465

20. United Nations Educational, Scientific, and Cultural Organization, *Livestock in a Changing Landscape*, April 2008, accessed March 30, 2016, http://unesdoc.unesco.org/images/0015/001591/159194e.pdf

21. See James Rachels, "Vegetarianism and 'the Other Weight Problem,'" in *World Hunger and Moral Obligation,* eds. William Aiken and Hugh LaFollette (Englewood Cliffs, NJ: Prentice Hall, 1977).

22. See Carol J. Adams, *The Sexual Politics of Meat: A Feminist-Vegetarian Critical Theory* (New York: Continuum, 1990) or Josephine Donovan and Carol J. Adams, eds., *The Feminist Care Tradition in Animal Ethics: A Reader* (New York: Columbia University Press, 2007).

23. Jerod M. Loeb, William R. Hendee, Steven J. Smith, and M. Roy Schwarz, "Human vs. Animal Rights: in Defense of Animal Research," *Journal of the American Medical Association* 262, No. 19 (November 17, 1989), pp. 2716–20.

24. Ibid.

25. John F. Lauerman, "Animal Research," *Harvard Magazine* (January–February 1999), pp. 49–57.

26. Ibid.; see also World Health Organization, accessed March 30, 2016, http://apps.who.int/immunization_monitoring/globalsummary/timeseries/tsincidencepolio.html

27. Holcomb B. Noble, "Rat Studies Raise Hope of Conquering Paralysis," *The New York Times*,

January 25, 2000, p. D7, accessed May 15, 2016, http://www.nytimes.com/2000/01/25/health/rat-studies-raise-hope-of-conquering-paralysis.html?pagewanted=all

28. Health Physics Society, "Radioactive Scorpion Venom for Fighting Cancer," *Science Daily*, June 27, 2006, accessed March 30, 2016, http://www.sciencedaily.com/releases/2006/06/060627174755.htm

29. Tom Abate, "Biotech Firms Transforming Animals into Drug-Producing Machines," *San Francisco Chronicle*, January 25, 2000, p. B1, accessed May 15, 2016, http://www.sfgate.com/business/article/Biotech-Firms-Transforming-Animals-Into-2783363.php

30. U.S. Department of Agriculture, "Legislative History of the Animal Welfare Act," updated June 2014, accessed May 15, 2016, https://awic.nal.usda.gov/legislative-history-animal-welfare-act-table-contents

31. Lauerman, "Animal Research," op. cit., p. 51.

32. People for the Ethical Treatment of Animals (PETA), "Rats, Mice, and Birds Deserve Protection under the Animal Welfare Act," accessed March 30, 2016, http://www.peta.org/features/unc-awa.aspx

33. Animal Legal Defense Fund (ALDF), "Animal Legal Defense Fund Urges Support of House Bill to Restore Animal Welfare Act," December 20, 2012, accessed May 15, 2016, http://aldf.org/press-room/press-releases/animal-legal-defense-fund-urges-support-of-house-bill-to-restore-animal-welfare-act/

34. The Humane Society of the United States, "Biomedical Research," accessed May 15, 2016, http://www.humanesociety.org/issues/biomedical_research/

35. John Hopkins University, Center for Alternatives to Animal Testing, accessed March 30, 2016, http://caat.jhsph.edu/

36. U.S. Department of Agriculture, Animal and Plant Health Inspection Service, *Annual Report Animal Usage by Fiscal Year* (2014), accessed March 30, 2016, https://www.aphis.usda.gov/animal_welfare/downloads/7023/Animals%20Used%20In%20Research%202014.pdf

37. James Gorman, "Agency Moves to Retire Most Research Chimps," *The New York Times*, January 22, 2013, accessed March 30. 2016, http://www.nytimes.com/2013/01/23/science/nih-moves-to-retire-most-chimps-used-in-research.html?_r=0

38. Jocelyn Kaiser, "NIH to End All Support for Chimpanzee Research," *Science*, November 18, 2015, accessed March 30, 2016, http://www.sciencemag.org/news/2015/11/nih-end-all-support-chimpanzee-research

39. Speaking of Research, "US Statistics," accessed March 30, 2016, http://speakingofresearch.com/facts/statistics/

40. See C. Ray Greek and Jane Swingle Greek, *Sacred Cows and Golden Geese: The Human Cost of Experiments on Animals* (London: Continuum, 2001), pp.73–7.

41. Lauerman, "Animal Research." op. cit.

42. Center for Biological Diversity, "Africa's Two Elephant Species Move Closer to Endangered Species Protection" March 15, 2016, accessed March 30, 2016, https://www.biologicaldiversity.org/news/press_releases/2016/african-elephants-03-15-2016.html

43. Susan Ager, "Here's Where Ringling Bros. Is Sending Its Circus Elephants to Retire" *National Geographic*, September 17, 2015, accessed March 30, 2016, http://news.nationalgeographic.com/2015/09/150916-ringling-circus-elephants-florida-center/

44. U.S. Fish and Wildlife Service, Environmental Conservation Online System, "Listed Species Summary," accessed March 28, 2016, https://ecos.fws.gov/tess_public/reports/box-score-report

45. IUCN, "The IUCN Red List of Threatened Species," accessed March 30, 2016, http://cmsdocs.s3.amazonaws.com/IUCN_Red_List_Brochure_2014_LOW.PDF

46. IUCN, "Sumatran Rhino Likely To Go Extinct Unless Action Is Taken Urgently, Warns IUCN," September 22, 2015, accessed March 30, 2016, http://www.iucn.org/media/news_releases/?21904/Sumatran-Rhino-likely-to-go-extinct-unless-action-is-taken-urgently-warns-IUCN

47. Drew Kann, "Endangered Mountain Gorillas Making a Comeback," *CNN*, March 29, 2016, accessed March 30, 2016, http://www.cnn.com/2016/03/29/us/iyw-dian-fossey-gorilla-fund/index.html

48. *The Washington Post*, "Fishing Is Pushing Sharks Closer to Extinction," March 1, 2013, accessed

March 30, 2016, http://articles.washingtonpost.com/2013-03-01/national/37365646_1_fin-soup-shark-species-juliet-eilperin

49. Richard Harris, "Whales, Dolphins Are Collateral Damage in Our Taste for Seafood," *NPR*, January 8, 2014, accessed March 30, 2016, http://www.npr.org/sections/thesalt/2014/01/07/260555381/thousands-of-whales-dolphins-killed-to-satisfy-our-seafood-appetite

50. Holmes Rolston III, *Environmental Ethics* (Philadelphia, PA: Temple University Press, 1988), p. 129.

51. Ibid.

52. Nicholas Rescher, "Why Save Endangered Species?," in *Unpopular Essays on Technological Progress* (Pittsburgh, PA: University of Pittsburgh Press, 1980), p. 83. A similar point is made by Tom Regan, *The Case for Animal Rights* (Berkeley, CA: University of California Press, 1983), p. 359; and Joel Feinberg, "Rights of Animals and Unborn Generations," in *Animal Rights and Human Obligations*, eds. Tom Regan and Peter Singer (Englewood Cliffs, NJ: Prentice Hall, 1976), pp. 55–56.

53. Charles Darwin, *The Origin of Species* (Baltimore, MD: Penguin, 1968), p. 108.

54. Holmes Rolston III, op. cit., p. 135.

55. Ibid., p. 136.

56. Ibid., p. 145.

57. Tom Regan, *The Case for Animal Rights* (Berkeley, CA: University of California Press, 1983), pp. 361–62.

58. See Immanuel Kant, "Duties to Animals and Spirits," in *Lectures on Ethics* (Cambridge: Cambridge University Press, 1997); and see Regan's discussion in *The Case for Animal Rights*.

59. Jeremy Bentham, *Introduction to the Principles of Morals and Legislation* (1789), Chapter 17.

60. Martha C. Nussbaum, *Frontiers of Justice: Disability, Nationality, and Species Membership* (Cambridge, MA: Harvard University Press, 2006), p. 351.

61. Reported by Holmes Rolston III in *Environmental Ethics: Duties to and Values in the Natural World* (Philadelphia: Temple University Press, 1988), p. 50.

62. David De Grazia, *Taking Animals Seriously: Mental Life and Moral Status* (Cambridge: Cambridge University Press, 1996), p. 46.

63. Peter Singer, *Animal Liberation: A New Ethic for Our Treatment of Animals* (New York: Random House, 1975). Singer was not the first to use the term *speciesism*. Ryder also used it in his work *Victims of Science* (London: Davis-Poynter, 1975).

64. Bonnie Steinbock, "Speciesism and the Idea of Equality" *Philosophy* 53, No. 204 (April 1978), p. 253.

65. Joel Feinberg, "The Rights of Animals and Unborn Generations," op cit., p. 195.

66. Tom Regan, *The Case for Animal Rights* (Berkeley, CA: University of California Press, 1983).

67. Peter Singer, "Animal Liberation at 30," *The New York Review of Books*, May 15, 2003, accessed March 30, 2016, http://www.nybooks.com/articles/archives/2003/may/15/animal-liberation-at-30/?pagination=false#fn5-501709338

READING

All Animals Are Equal

PETER SINGER

MindTap° For more chapter resources and activities, go to MindTap.

Study Questions

As you read the excerpt, please consider the following questions:

1. Does equal consideration imply identical treatment? Why or why not, according to Singer?
2. What is *speciesism*? According to Singer, how does it parallel racism and sexism?
3. Why does Singer prefer the principle of equal consideration of interests to concerns about whether or not certain beings have rights?

"Animal liberation" may sound more like a parody of other liberation movements than a serious objective. The idea of "The Rights of Animals" actually was once used to parody the case for women's rights. When Mary Wollstonecraft, a forerunner of today's feminists, published her *Vindication of the Rights of Woman* in 1792, her views were widely regarded as absurd, and before long an anonymous publication appeared entitled A Vindication of the Rights of Brutes. The author of this satirical work (now known to have been Thomas Taylor, a distinguished Cambridge philosopher) tried to refute Mary Wollstonecraft's arguments by showing that they could be carried one stage further. If the argument for equality was sound when applied to women, why should it not be applied to dogs, cats, and horses? The reasoning seemed to hold for these "brutes" too; yet to hold that brutes had rights was manifestly absurd. Therefore the reasoning by which this conclusion had been reached must be unsound, and if unsound when applied to brutes, it must also be unsound when applied to women, since the very same arguments had been used in each case.

In order to explain the basis of the case for the equality of animals, it will be helpful to start with an examination of the case for the equality of women. Let us assume that we wish to defend the case for women's rights against the attack by Thomas Taylor. How should we reply?

One way in which we might reply is by saying that the case for equality between men and women cannot validly be extended to nonhuman animals. Women have a right to vote, for instance, because they are just as capable of making rational decisions about the future as men are; dogs, on the other hand, are incapable of understanding the significance of voting, so they cannot have the right to vote. There are many other obvious ways in which men and women resemble each other closely, while humans and animals differ greatly. So, it might be said, men and women are similar beings and should have similar rights, while humans and nonhumans are different and should not have equal rights.

The reasoning behind this reply to Taylor's analogy is correct up to a point, but it does not go far enough. There are obviously important differences between humans and other animals, and these differences must give rise to some differences in the rights that each have. Recognizing this evident fact, however, is no barrier to the case for extending the basic principle of equality to nonhuman animals. The differences that exist between men and women are equally undeniable, and the supporters of Women's Liberation are aware that these differences may give rise to different rights. Many feminists hold that women have the right to an abortion on request. It does not follow that since these same feminists are campaigning for equality between men and women they must support the right of men to have abortions too. Since a man cannot have an abortion, it is meaningless to talk of his right to have one. Since dogs can't vote, it is meaningless to talk of their right to vote. There is no reason why either Women's Liberation or Animal Liberation should get involved in such nonsense. The extension of the basic principle of equality from one group to another does not imply that we must treat both groups in exactly the same way, or grant exactly the same rights to both groups. Whether we should do so will depend on the nature of the members of the two groups. The basic principle of equality does not require equal or identical treatment; it requires equal consideration. Equal consideration for different beings may lead to different treatment and different rights.

So there is a different way of replying to Taylor's attempt to parody the case for women's rights, a way that does not deny the obvious differences between human beings and nonhumans but goes more deeply into the question of equality and concludes by finding nothing absurd in the idea that the basic principle of equality applies to so-called brutes. At this point such a conclusion may appear odd; but if we examine more deeply the basis on

Peter Singer, *Animal Liberation*, 2nd ed. (New York: New York Review, 1990). Reprinted with permission from the Author.

which our opposition to discrimination on grounds of race or sex ultimately rests, we will see that we would be on shaky ground if we were to demand equality for blacks, women, and other groups of oppressed humans while denying equal consideration to nonhumans. To make this clear we need to see, first, exactly why racism and sexism are wrong. When we say that all human beings, whatever their race, creed, or sex, are equal, what is it that we are asserting? Those who wish to defend hierarchical, inegalitarian societies have often pointed out that by whatever test we choose it simply is not true that all humans are equal. Like it or not we must face the fact that humans come in different shapes and sizes; they come with different moral capacities, different intellectual abilities, different amounts of benevolent feeling and sensitivity to the needs of others, different abilities to communicate effectively, and different capacities to experience pleasure and pain. In short, if the demand for equality were based on the actual equality of all human beings, we would have to stop demanding equality.

Still, one might cling to the view that the demand for equality among human beings is based on the actual equality of the different races and sexes. Although, it may be said, humans differ as individuals, there are no differences between the races and sexes as such. From the mere fact that a person is black or a woman we cannot infer anything about that person's intellectual or moral capacities. This, it may be said, is why racism and sexism are wrong. The white racist claims that whites are superior to blacks, but this is false; although there are differences among individuals, some blacks are superior to some whites in all of the capacities and abilities that could conceivably be relevant. The opponent of sexism would say the same: a person's sex is no guide to his or her abilities, and this is why it is unjustifiable to discriminate on the basis of sex.

The existence of individual variations that cut across the lines of race or sex, however, provides us with no defense at all against a more sophisticated opponent of equality, one who proposes that, say, the interests of all those with IQ scores below 100 be given less consideration than the interests of those with ratings over 100. Perhaps those scoring below the mark would, in this society, be made the slaves of those scoring higher. Would a hierarchical society of this sort really be so much better than one based on race or sex? I think not. But if we tie the moral principle of equality to the factual equality of the different races or sexes, taken as a whole, our opposition to racism and sexism does not provide us with any basis for objecting to this kind of inegalitarianism.

There is a second important reason why we ought not to base our opposition to racism and sexism on any kind of factual equality, even the limited kind that asserts that variations in capacities and abilities are spread evenly among the different races and between the sexes: we can have no absolute guarantee that these capacities and abilities really are distributed evenly, without regard to race or sex, among human beings. So far as actual abilities are concerned there do seem to be certain measurable differences both among races and between sexes. These differences do not, of course, appear in every case, but only when averages are taken. More important still, we do not yet know how many of these differences are really due to the different genetic endowments of the different races and sexes, and how many are due to poor schools, poor housing, and other factors that are the result of past and continuing discrimination. Perhaps all of the important differences will eventually prove to be environmental rather than genetic. Anyone opposed to racism and sexism will certainly hope that this will be so, for it will make the task of ending discrimination a lot easier; nevertheless, it would be dangerous to rest the case against racism and sexism on the belief that all significant differences are environmental in origin. The opponent of, say, racism who takes this line will be unable to avoid conceding that if differences in ability did after all prove to have some genetic connection with race, racism would in some way be defensible.

Fortunately there is no need to pin the case for equality to one particular outcome of a scientific investigation. The appropriate response to those who claim to have found evidence of genetically based differences in ability among the races or between the sexes is not to stick to the belief that the genetic explanation must be wrong, whatever evidence to the contrary may turn up; instead we should make it quite clear that the claim to equality does not depend on intelligence, moral capacity, physical strength, or similar matters of fact. Equality is a moral idea, not an assertion of fact. There is no logically compelling reason for assuming that a factual difference in ability between two people justifies any difference in the amount of consideration we give to their needs and interests. The principle of the equality of human beings is not a description of an alleged actual equality among humans: it is a prescription of how we should treat human beings.

Jeremy Bentham, the founder of the reforming utilitarian school of moral philosophy, incorporated the essential basis of moral equality into his system of ethics by means of the formula: "Each to count for one and none for more than one." In other words, the interests of every being affected by an action are to be taken into account and given the same weight as the like interests of any other being. A later utilitarian, Henry Sidgwick, put the point in this way: "The good of any one individual is of no more importance, from the point of view (if I may say so) of the Universe, than the good of any other." More recently the leading figures in contemporary moral philosophy have shown a great deal of agreement in specifying as a fundamental pre-supposition of their moral theories some similar requirement that works to give everyone's interests equal consideration—although these writers generally cannot agree on how this requirement is best formulated.[1]

It is an implication of this principle of equality that our concern for others and our readiness to consider their interests ought not to depend on what they are like or on what abilities they may possess. Precisely what our concern or consideration requires us to do may vary according to the characteristics of those affected by what we do: concern for the well-being of children growing up in America would require that we teach them to read; concern for the well-being of pigs may require no more than that we leave them with other pigs in a place where there is adequate food and room to run freely. But the basic element—the taking into account of the interests of the being, whatever those interests may be—must, according to the principle of equality, be extended to all beings, black or white, masculine or feminine, human or nonhuman.

Thomas Jefferson, who was responsible for writing the principle of the equality of men into the American Declaration of Independence, saw this point. It led him to oppose slavery even though he was unable to free himself fully from his slaveholding background. He wrote in a letter to the author of a book that emphasized the notable intellectual achievements of Negroes in order to refute the then common view that they had limited intellectual capacities:

> Be assured that no person living wishes more sincerely than I do, to see a complete refutation of the doubts I myself have entertained and expressed on the grade of understanding allotted to them by nature, and to find that they are on a par with ourselves...but whatever be their degree of talent it is no measure of their rights. Because Sir Isaac Newton was superior to others in understanding, he was not therefore lord of the property or persons of others.[2]

Similarly, when in the 1850s the call for women's rights was raised in the United States, a remarkable black feminist named Sojourner Truth made the same point in more robust terms at a feminist convention:

> They talk about this thing in the head; what do they call it? ["Intellect," whispered someone nearby.] That's it. What's that got to do with women's rights or Negroes' rights? If my cup won't hold but a pint and yours holds a quart, wouldn't you be mean not to let me have my little half-measure full?[3]

It is on this basis that the case against racism and the case against sexism must both ultimately rest; and it is in accordance with this principle that the attitude that we may call "speciesism," by analogy with racism, must also be condemned. Speciesism—the word is not an attractive one, but I can think of no better term—is prejudice or attitude of bias in favor of the interests of members of one's own species and against those of members of other species. It should be obvious that the fundamental objections to racism and sexism made by Thomas Jefferson and Sojourner Truth apply equally to speciesism. If possessing a higher degree of intelligence does not entitle one human to use another for his or her own ends, how can it entitle humans to exploit nonhumans for the same purpose?[4]

Many philosophers and other writers have proposed the principle of equal consideration of interests, in some form or other, as a basic moral principle; but not many of them have recognized that this principle applies to members of other species as well as to our own. Jeremy Bentham was one of the few who did realize this. In a forward-looking passage written at a time when black slaves had been freed by the French but in the British dominions were still being treated in the way we now treat animals, Bentham wrote:

> The day may come when the rest of the animal creation may acquire those rights which never could have been withholden from them but by the hand of tyranny. The French have already discovered that the blackness of the skin is no reason why a human being should be abandoned without redress to the caprice of a tormentor. It may one day come to be recognized that the number of the legs, the villosity of the skin, or the termination of the os sacrum are reasons equally insufficient for abandoning a sensitive being to the same fate. What else is it that should trace the insuperable line? Is it the faculty of reason, or perhaps the faculty of discourse? But a full-grown horse or dog is beyond comparison a more rational, as well as a more conversable animal, than an infant of a day or a week or even a month, old. But suppose they were otherwise, what would it avail? The question is not, Can they reason? *nor* Can they talk? *but,* Can they suffer?[5]

In this passage Bentham points to the capacity for suffering as the vital characteristic that gives a being the right to equal consideration. The capacity for suffering—or more strictly, for suffering and/or enjoyment or happiness—is not just another characteristic like the capacity for language or higher mathematics. Bentham is not saying that those who try to mark "the insuperable line" that determines whether the interests of a being should be considered happen to have chosen the wrong characteristic. By saying that we must consider the interests of all beings with the capacity for suffering or enjoyment Bentham does not arbitrarily exclude from consideration any interests at all—as those who draw the line with reference to the possession of reason or language do. The capacity for suffering and enjoyment is a prerequisite for having interests at all, a condition that must be satisfied before we can speak of interests in a meaningful way. It would be nonsense to say that it was not in the interests of a stone to be kicked along the road by a schoolboy. A stone does not have interests because it cannot suffer. Nothing that we can do to it could possibly make any difference to its welfare. The capacity for suffering and enjoyment is, however, not only necessary, but also sufficient for us to say that a being has interests—at an absolute minimum, an interest in not suffering. A mouse, for example, does have an interest in not being kicked along the road, because it will suffer if it is.

Although Bentham speaks of "rights" in the passage I have quoted, the argument is really about equality rather than about rights. Indeed, in a different passage, Bentham famously described "natural rights" as "nonsense" and "natural and imprescriptable rights" as "nonsense upon stilts." He talked of moral rights as a shorthand way of referring to protections that people and animals morally ought to have; but the real weight of the moral argument does not rest on the assertion of the existence of the right, for this in turn has to be justified on the basis of the possibilities for suffering and happiness. In this way we can argue for equality for animals without getting embroiled in philosophical controversies about the ultimate nature of rights.

In misguided attempts to refute the arguments of this book, some philosophers have gone to much trouble developing arguments to show that animals do not have rights.[6] They have claimed that to have rights a being must be autonomous, or must be a member of a community, or must have the ability to respect the rights of others, or must possess a sense of justice. These claims are irrelevant to the case for Animal Liberation. The language of rights is a convenient political shorthand. It is even more valuable in the era of thirty-second TV news clips than it was in Bentham's day; but in the argument for a radical change in our attitude to animals, it is in no way necessary.

If a being suffers there can be no moral justification for refusing to take that suffering into consideration. No matter what the nature of the being, the principle of equality requires that its suffering be counted equally with the like suffering—insofar as rough comparisons can be made—of any other being. If a being is not capable of suffering, or of experiencing enjoyment or happiness, there is nothing to be taken into account. So the limit of sentience (using the term as a convenient if not strictly accurate shorthand for the capacity to suffer and/or experience enjoyment) is the only defensible boundary of concern for the interests of others. To mark this boundary by some other characteristic like intelligence or rationality would be to mark it in an arbitrary manner. Why not choose some other characteristic, like skin color?

Racists violate the principle of equality by giving greater weight to the interests of members of their own race when there is a clash between their interests and the interests of those of another race. Sexists violate the principle of equality by favoring the interests of their own sex. Similarly, speciesists allow the interests of their own species to override the greater interests of members of other species. The pattern is identical in each case.

ANIMALS AND RESEARCH

Most human beings are speciesists. . . . Ordinary human beings—not a few exceptionally cruel or heartless humans, but the overwhelming majority of humans—take an active part in, acquiesce

in, and allow their taxes to pay for practices that require the sacrifice of the most important interests of members of other species in order to promote the most trivial interests of our own species . . .

The practice of experimenting on nonhuman animals as it exists today throughout the world reveals the consequences of speciesism. Many experiments inflict severe pain without the remotest prospect of significant benefits for human beings or any other animals. Such experiments are not isolated instances, but part of a major industry. In Britain, where experimenters are required to report the number of "scientific procedures" performed on animals, official government figures show that 3.5 million scientific procedures were performed on animals in 1988.[7] In the United States there are no figures of comparable accuracy. Under the Animal Welfare Act, the U.S. secretary of agriculture publishes a report listing the number of animals used by facilities registered with it, but this is incomplete in many ways. It does not include rats, mice, birds, reptiles, frogs, or domestic farm animals used in secondary schools; and it does not include experiments performed by facilities that do not transport animals interstate or receive grants or contracts from the federal government.

In 1986 the U.S. Congress Office of Technology Assessment (OTA) published a report entitled "Alternatives to Animal Use in Research, Testing and Education." The OTA researchers attempted to determine the number of animals used in experimentation in the U.S. and reported that "estimates of the animals used in the United States each year range from 10 million to upwards of 100 million." They concluded that the estimates were unreliable but their best guess was "at least 17 million to 22 million."[8]

This is an extremely conservative estimate. In testimony before Congress in 1966, the Laboratory Animal Breeders Association estimated that the number of mice, rats, guinea pigs, hamsters, and rabbits used for experimental purposes in 1965 was around 60 million.[9] In 1984 Dr. Andrew Rowan of Tufts University School of Veterinary Medicine estimated that approximately 71 million animals are used each year. In 1985 Rowan revised his estimates to distinguish between the number of animals produced, acquired, and actually used. This yielded an estimate of between 25 and 35 million animals used in experiments each year.[10] (This figure omits animals who die in shipping or are killed before the experiment begins.) A stock market analysis of just one major supplier of animals to laboratories, the Charles River Breeding Laboratory, stated that this company alone produced 22 million laboratory animals annually.[11]

The 1988 report issued by the Department of Agriculture listed 140,471 dogs, 42,271 cats, 51,641 primates, 431,254 rabbits, and 178,249 "wild animals": a total of 1,635,288 used in experimentation. Remember that this report does not bother to count rats and mice, and covers at most an estimated 10 percent of the total number of animals used. Of the nearly 1.6 million animals reported by the Department of Agriculture to have been used for experimental purposes, over 90,000 are reported to have experienced "unrelieved pain or distress." Again, this is probably at most 10 percent of the total number of animals suffering unrelieved pain and distress—and if experimenters are less concerned about causing unrelieved pain to rats and mice than they are to dogs, cats, and primates, it could be an even smaller proportion.

Other developed nations all use larger numbers of animals. In Japan, for example, a very incomplete survey published in 1988 produced a total in excess of eight million.[12] . . .

Among the tens of millions of experiments performed, only a few can possibly be regarded as contributing to important medical research. Huge numbers of animals are used in university departments such as forestry and psychology; many more are used for commercial purposes, to test new cosmetics, shampoos, food coloring agents, and other inessential items. All this can happen only because of our prejudice against taking seriously the suffering of a being who is not a member of our own species. Typically, defenders of experiments on animals do not deny that animals suffer. They cannot deny the animals' suffering, because they need to stress the similarities between humans and other animals in order to claim that their experiments may have some relevance for human purposes. The experimenter who forces rats to choose between starvation and electric shock to see if they develop ulcers (which they do) does so because the rat has a nervous system very similar to human beings', and presumably feels an electric shock in a similar way.

There has been opposition to experimenting on animals for a long time. This opposition has made little headway because experimenters, backed by commercial firms that profit by supplying laboratory animals and equipment, have been able to convince legislators and the public that opposition comes from uninformed fanatics who consider the interests of animals more important than the interests of human beings. But to be opposed to what is going on now it is not necessary to insist that all animal experiments stop immediately. All we need to say is that experiments serving no direct and urgent purpose should stop immediately, and in the remaining fields of research, we should whenever possible, seek to replace experiments that involve animals with alternative methods that do not. . . .

When are experiments on animals justifiable? Upon learning of the nature of many of the experiments carried out, some people react by saying that all experiments on animals should be prohibited immediately. But if we make our demands absolute as this, the experimenters have a ready reply: Would we be prepared to let thousands of humans die if they could be saved by a single experiment on a single animal?

This question is, of course, purely hypothetical. There has never been and never could be a single experiment that saved thousands of lives. The way to reply to this hypothetical question is to pose another: Would the experimenters be prepared to carry out their experiment on a human orphan under six months old if that were the only way to save thousands of lives?

If the experimenters would not be prepared to use a human infant then their readiness to use nonhuman animals reveals an unjustifiable form of discrimination on the basis of species, since adult apes, monkeys, dogs, cats, rats, and other animals are more aware of what is happening to them, more self-directing, and, so far as we can tell, at least as sensitive to pain as a human infant. (I have specified that the human infant be an orphan, to avoid the complications of the feelings of parents. Specifying the case in this way is, if anything, over-generous to those defending the use of nonhuman animals in experiments, since mammals intended for experimental use are usually separated from their mothers at an early age, when the separation causes distress for both mother and young.)

So far as we know, human infants possess no morally relevant characteristic to a higher degree than adult nonhuman animals, unless we are to count the infants' potential as a characteristic that makes it wrong to experiment on them. Whether this characteristic should count is controversial—if we count it, we shall have to condemn abortion along with the experiments on infants, since the potential of the infant and the fetus is the same. To avoid the complexities of this issue, however, we can alter our original question a little and assume that the infant is one with irreversible brain damage so severe as to rule out any mental development beyond the level of a six-month-old infant. There are, unfortunately, many such human beings, locked away in special wards throughout the country, some of them long since abandoned by their parents and other relatives, and, sadly, sometimes unloved by anyone else. Despite their mental deficiencies, the anatomy and physiology of these infants are in nearly all respects identical with those of normal humans. If, therefore, we were to force-feed them with large quantities of floor polish or drip concentrated solutions of cosmetics into their eyes [as has been done in experiments using animals], we would have a much more reliable indication of the safety of these products for humans than we now get by attempting to extrapolate the results of tests on a variety of other species. . . .

So whenever experimenters claim that their experiments are important enough to justify the use of animals, we should ask them whether they would be prepared to use a brain-damaged human being at a similar mental level to the animals they are planning to use. I cannot imagine that anyone would seriously propose carrying out the experiments described in this [article] on brain-damaged human beings. Occasionally it has become known that medical experiments have been performed on human beings without their consent; one case did concern institutionalized intellectually disabled children, who were given hepatitis. When such harmful experiments on human beings become known, they usually lead to an outcry against the experimenters, and rightly so. They are, very often, a further example of the arrogance of the research worker who justifies everything on the grounds of increasing knowledge. But if the experimenter claims that the experiment is important enough to justify inflicting suffering on animals, why is it not important enough to justify inflicting suffering on humans at the same mental level? What difference is there between the two? Only that one is a member of our species and the other is not? But to appeal to that difference is to reveal a bias no more defensible than racism or any other form of arbitrary discrimination. . . .

We have still not answered the question of when an experiment might be justifiable. It will not do to say "Never!" Putting morality in such black-and-white terms is appealing, because it eliminates the need to think about particular cases; but in extreme circumstances, such absolutist answers always break down. Torturing a human being is almost always wrong, but it is not absolutely wrong. If torture were the only way in which we could discover the location of a nuclear bomb hidden in a New York City basement and timed to go off within the hour, then torture would be justifiable. Similarly, if a single experiment could cure a disease like leukemia, that experiment would be justifiable. But in actual life the benefits are always more remote, and more often than not they are nonexistent. So how do we decide when an experiment is justifiable?

We have seen that experimenters reveal a bias in favor of their own species whenever they carry out experiments on nonhumans for purposes that they would not think justified them in using human beings, even brain-damaged ones. This principle gives us a guide toward an answer to our question. Since a speciesist bias, like a racist bias, is unjustifiable, an experiment cannot be justifiable unless the experiment is so important that the use of a brain-damaged human would also be justifiable.

This is not an absolutist principle. I do not believe that it could never be justifiable to experiment on a brain-damaged human. If it really were possible to save several lives by an experiment that would take just one life, and there were no other way those lives could be saved, it would be right to do the experiment. But this would be an extremely rare case. Admittedly, as with any dividing line, there would be a gray area where it was difficult to decide if an experiment could be justified. But we need not get distracted by such considerations now.... We are in the midst of an emergency in which appalling suffering is being inflicted on millions of animals for purposes that on any impartial view are obviously inadequate to justify the suffering. When we have ceased to carry out all those experiments, then there will be time enough to discuss what to do about the remaining ones which are claimed to be essential to save lives or prevent greater suffering....

NOTES

1. For Bentham's moral philosophy, see his *Introduction to the Principle of Morals and Legislation*, and for Sidgwick's see *The Methods of Ethics*, 1907 (the passage is quoted from the seventh edition; reprint, London: Macmillan, 1963), p. 382. As examples of leading contemporary moral philosophers who incorporate a requirement of equal consideration of interests, see R. M. Hare, *Freedom and Reason* (New York: Oxford University Press, 1963), and John Rawls, *A Theory of Justice* (Cambridge, MA: Harvard University Press, Belknap Press, 1972). For a brief account of the essential agreement on this issue between these and other positions, see R. M. Hare, "Rules of War and Moral Reasoning," *Philosophy and Public Affairs* 1(2) (1972).

2. Letter to Henry Gregoire, February 25, 1809.

3. Reminiscences by Francis D. Gage, from Susan B. Anthony, *The History of Woman Suffrage*, vol. 1; the passage is to be found in the extract in Leslie Tanner (Ed.), *Voices From Women's Liberation* (New York: Signet, 1970).

4. I owe the term "speciesism" to Richard Ryder. It has become accepted in general use since the first edition of this book, and now appears in *The Oxford English Dictionary*, 2nd ed. (Oxford, UK: Clarendon Press, 1989).

5. Introduction to the *Principles of Morals and Legislation*, chapter 17.

6. See M. Levin, "Animal Rights Evaluated," *Humanist* 37, p. 14–15 (July/August 1977); M. A. Fox, "Animal Liberation: A Critique," *Ethics* 88, pp. 134–138 (1978); C. Perry and G. E. Jones, "On Animal Rights," *International Journal of Applied Philosophy* 1, pp. 39–57 (1982).

7. *Statistics of Scientific Procedures on Living Animals*, Great Britain, 1988, Command Paper 743 (London: Her Majesty's Stationery Office, 1989).

8. U.S. Congress Office of Technology Assessment, *Alternatives to Animal Use in Research, Testing and Education* (Washington, D.C.: Government Printing Office, 1986), p. 64.

9. Hearings before the Subcommittee on Livestock and Feed Grains of the Committee on Agriculture, U.S. House of Representatives, 1966, p. 63.

10. See A. Rowan, *Of Mice, Models and Men* (Albany: State University of New York Press, 1984), p. 71; his later revision is in a personal communication to the Office of Technology Assessment; see *Alternatives to Animal Use in Research, Testing and Education*, p. 56.

11. OTA, *Alternatives to Animal Use in Research, Testing and Education*, p. 56.

12. *Experimental Animals* 37, 105 (1988).

READING

The Case for Animal Rights

TOM REGAN

MindTap® For more chapter resources and activities, go to MindTap.

Study Questions

As you read the excerpt, please consider the following questions:

1. What is the basic similarity between human and nonhuman beings that is the focus of Regan's account?
2. How does Regan understand the inherent value of nonhuman animals?
3. How does his view of the equality of inherent value lead to an abolitionist conclusion with regard to animal experimentation and commercial animal agriculture?

Animals, it is true, lack many of the abilities humans possess. They can't read, do higher mathematics, build a bookcase or make baba ghanoush. Neither can many human beings, however, and yet we don't (and shouldn't) say that they (these humans) therefore have less inherent value, less of a right to be treated with respect, than do others. It is the similarities between those human beings who most clearly, most non-controversially have such value...not our differences, that matter most. And the really crucial, the basic similarity is simply this: we are each of us the experiencing subject of a life, a conscious creature having an individual welfare that has importance to us whatever our usefulness to others. We want and prefer things, believe and feel things, recall and expect things. And all these dimensions of our life, including our pleasure and pain, our enjoyment and suffering, our satisfaction and frustration, our continued existence or our untimely death—all make a difference to the quality of our life as lived, as experienced, by us as individuals. As the same is true of those animals that concern us (the ones that are eaten and trapped, for example), they too must be viewed as the experiencing subjects of a life, with inherent value of their own.

Some there are who resist the idea that animals have inherent value. 'Only humans have such value,' they profess. How might this narrow view be defended? Shall we say that only humans have the requisite intelligence, or autonomy, or reason? But there are many, many humans who fail to meet these standards and yet are reasonably viewed as having value above and beyond their usefulness to others. Shall we claim that only humans belong to the right species, the species Homo sapiens? But this is blatant speciesism....

Well, perhaps some will say that animals have some inherent value, only less than we have. Once again, however, attempts to defend this view can be shown to lack rational justification. What could be the basis of our having more inherent value than animals? Their lack of reason, or autonomy, or intellect? Only if we are willing to make the same judgment in the case of humans who are similarly deficient. But it is not true that such humans—the retarded child, for example, or the mentally deranged—have less inherent value than you or I. Neither, then, can we rationally sustain the view that animals like them in being the experiencing subjects of a life have less inherent value. All who have inherent value have it equally, whether they be human animals or not....

Having set out the broad outlines of the rights view, I can now say why its implications for farming and science, among other fields, are both clear and uncompromising. In the case of the use of animals in science, the rights view is categorically abolitionist....

As for commercial animal agriculture, the rights view takes a similar abolitionist position.

In Peter Singer, ed., *In Defense of Animals,* (New York: Basil Blackwell, 1985).

READING

Speciesism and the Idea of Equality

BONNIE STEINBOCK

> MindTap® For more chapter resources and activities, go to MindTap.

Study Questions

As you read the excerpt, please consider the following questions:

1. Is Steinbock right in claiming that there are morally relevant differences between human beings and nonhuman animals?
2. What is the point of Steinbock's claim about choosing to feed a hungry child before feeding your hungry dog?
3. How does Steinbock argue for the justification of some animal experimentation?

We do not subject animals to different moral treatment simply because they have fur and feathers, but because they are in fact different from human beings in ways that could be morally relevant. It is false that women are incapable of being benefited by education, and therefore that claim cannot serve to justify preventing them from attending school. But this is not false of cows and dogs, even chimpanzees.... Feeding starving children before feeding starving dogs is just like a Catholic charity's feeding hungry Catholics before feeding hungry non-Catholics. It is simply a matter of taking care of one's own, something which is usually morally permissible. But whereas we would admire the Catholic agency which did not discriminate, but fed all children, first come, first served, we would feel quite differently about someone who has this policy for dogs and children.... I might feel much more love for my dog than for a strange child—and yet I might feel morally obliged to feed the child before I fed my dog. If I gave in to the feelings of love and fed my dog and let the child go hungry, I would probably feel guilty.... Human beings have a different moral status from members of other species because of certain capacities which are characteristic of being human. We may not all be equal in these capacities, but all human beings possess them to some measure, and nonhuman animals do not. For example, human beings are normally held to be responsible for what they do. In recognizing that someone is responsible for his or her actions, you accord that person a respect which is reserved for those possessed of moral autonomy, or capable of achieving such autonomy. Secondly, human beings can be expected to reciprocate in a way that nonhuman animals cannot....

...Certain capacities, which seem to be unique to human beings, entitle their possessors to a privileged position in the moral community. Both rats and human beings dislike pain, and so we have a *prima facie* reason not to inflict pain on either. But if we can free human beings from crippling diseases, pain and death through experimentation which involves making animals suffer, and if this is the only way to achieve such results, then I think that such experimentation is justified because human lives are more valuable than animals' lives....

My point is not that the lack of the sorts of capacities I have been discussing gives us a justification for treating animals just as we like, but rather that it is these differences between human beings and nonhuman animals which provide a rational basis for different moral treatment and consideration.... It is certainly not wrong of us to extend special care to members of our own species, motivated by feelings of sympathy, protectiveness, etc. If this is speciesism, it is stripped of its tone of moral condemnation.

Bonnie Steinbock, "Speciesism and the Idea of Equality" from *Philosophy* 53, No. 204 (April 1978).

REVIEW EXERCISES

1. In your view, is it acceptable to hunt animals? If yes, then which animals: bears, wolves, elephants, or whales? Does the method matter? Is trapping or aerial hunting acceptable? Justify your answers using concepts from this chapter.

2. Evaluate moral arguments in defense of vegetarianism. Are these arguments persuasive?

3. What counts as cruelty to animals? What's wrong with cruelty to animals?

4. What is the meaning of the term *rights*? Does it make sense to apply this term to animals? Why or why not?

5. For a being to have rights, is it necessary that it is able to claim them? That it be a moral agent? Why or why not? What about infants and cognitively disabled humans?

6. Do animals have interests? Are these interests worth consideration? Support your answer, drawing on the discussion of interests in this chapter.

7. Describe the issues involved in the debate over whether nonhuman animals' interests ought to be treated equally with those of humans.

8. List some anthropocentric reasons for preserving animal species.

9. What problems does the meaning of the term *species* raise for deciding whether animal species have moral standing of some sort?

10. What reasons do supporters give for using nonhuman animals in experimental research? What objections to this practice do their opponents raise? Be sure your answer makes reference to issues such as the extent and purpose of pain.

DISCUSSION CASES

1. **Animal Experimentation**. Antonio wants to become a doctor and is pursuing a premed major. He has dissected frogs and worms in some of his biology classes. He knows that animal research has produced good outcomes for human beings, including antibiotics and other cures for diseases. Antonio's roommate, Joseph, is a vegetarian who is opposed to all animal research. One night, as Joseph is cooking some tofu, he says, "Look, Antonio, there are all kinds of healthy alternatives to eating meat. There are also alternatives to using animals in research. You can now use computer models to accomplish most of the same outcomes." Antonio disagrees. "Maybe vegetarian food can be nutritious. But even if there were other ways to do medical research, I'd want to be sure that a drug or treatment really worked on an animal before I used it on a human being."

   Whose position is closest to your own? Which ways of treating animals do you find acceptable, and which do you find unacceptable? Is animal experimentation ever justified? If so, on what grounds? What about eating meat?

2. **People Versus the Gorilla**. Many of the world's few remaining mountain gorillas are located in the thirty-thousand-acre Parc des Volcans in the small African country of Rwanda. Rwanda has the highest population density in Africa. Most people there live on small farms. To this population, the Parc des Volcans represents valuable land that could be used for farming to feed an expanding human population. Opening the park to development could support thirty-six thousand people on subsistence farms. But it would have an adverse impact on the gorilla population.

   Should the park be maintained as a way to preserve the gorillas, or should it be given to the people for farming? To what extent, if any, do humans have an obligation to look for new and creative ways to meet their own needs in order to protect the interests of animals?

3. **What Is a Panther Worth?** The Florida panther is an endangered species. Not long ago, one of these animals was hit by a car and seriously injured. He was taken to the state university veterinary medical school, where steel plates were inserted in both legs, his right foot was rebuilt, and he had other expensive treatments. The panther was one of dozens that had been injured or killed on Florida's highways in recent years. As a result, some members of the Florida legislature introduced a proposal that would allocate $27 million to build forty bridges that would allow panthers to move about without the threat of car injuries and death. Those who support the measure point out that the Florida panther is unique and can survive only in swampland near the Everglades. Those who oppose the measure argue that the money could be better spent on education, needed highway repairs, or other projects.

   Should the state spend this amount of money to save the Florida panther from extinction? Why or why not?

MindTap® For more chapter resources and activities, go to MindTap.

18 Biotechnology and Bioengineering

Learning Outcomes

After reading this chapter, you should be able to:

- Describe current issues in biotechnology and bioengineering, including athletic and cognitive enhancements, stem cell research, cloning, genetic engineering, and genetically modified organisms.

- Draw connections between the ethical challenges of biotechnology and ethical issues related to abortion, animal welfare, and personal privacy.

- Examine the difference between a therapy and an enhancement, in connect with

- various applications of biotechnology and bioengineering.

- Apply consequentialist arguments about costs and benefits to bioengineering and biotechnology.

- Critically examine moral objections to "playing God" and the idea of the "wisdom of repugnance."

- Defend a thesis about biotechnology and bioengineering.

MindTap For more chapter resources and activities, go to MindTap.

For two decades, Jan Scheuermann has suffered from a degenerative brain disease that has left her paralyzed from the neck down. In 2012, however, a revolutionary new technology allowed Scheuermann to use a robotic arm to feed herself for the first time in years. By implanting special electrodes in Scheuermann's brain, her doctors were able to create a "brain-computer interface" and connect it to the robotic arm. With practice, Scheuermann learned to control the arm using only her thoughts. This technological feat might sound like science fiction. But it is part of a set of rapidly advancing technologies produced by engineers and doctors who are finding ways to cure disease and improve human capacities. Scheuermann's skill at working with the brain-computer interface improved so much that by 2015, she was able to control a flight simulator through this neurosignaling technique.[1] Scientists have been able to expand the use of brain–computer interfaces in amazing ways. Robotic exoskeletons—devices that allow paralyzed people to stand and walk—have been controlled through mind–machine interfaces. In 2014, Juliano Pinto, a paraplegic, controlled a robotic exoskeleton and kicked a soccer ball at the opening of the World Cup in Brazil.[2]

Scientists are working on a range of technologies that aim to improve the lives of disabled people. For example, they are developing artificial eyes and other devices that

Ingram Publishing/Thinkstock

University of Pittsburgh Medical Center

Jan Scheuermann feeds herself using a robotic arm attached to a brain–computer interface.

allow blind people to see, including so-called bionic eyes, retinal implants, and cameras that bypass the eye and interface directly with the brain's visual cortex.[3] Other surgeries and interventions allow us to radically alter our bodies, including, for example, sex reassignment surgery. In the future, regenerative medicine and genetic interventions may be able to extend our life spans, screen out deadly genetic mutations, or allow us to grow replacement organs. Performance- and mood-enhancing drugs may make us stronger, improve memory and concentration, and help us achieve better emotional health. Other biotechnologies may make it possible to extend our physical capacities—to walk, run, or swim—as the human body has never done before.

While many emerging biotechnologies have obvious therapeutic applications that will benefit people with diseases and disabilities, some worry that these technologies will be abused in ways that are unethical. Others argue that a new form of humanity is looming on the horizon—one that is genetically, chemically, and mechanically enhanced. Some view the "transhuman" or "posthuman" future as a positive development; others worry that we are not wise

or virtuous enough to properly handle these new technologies.

Consider, for example, the speed and variety of recent advances in mind–computer interfacing. It is now possible to wire one brain to another to create "brain-to-brain communication." For instance, a volunteer used his thoughts to trigger a muscle movement in the finger of another volunteer and played a video game using the other person's fingers.[4] In another experiment, one rat controlled the actions of another rat by way of implants connecting the two animals' brains.[5] Harvard researchers have connected human brain waves—detected by electrodes placed on the human's skull—to the nerves of a rat so that the human subject is able to make the rat's tail move by thought power.[6] While such experiments raise concerns from the standpoint of animal ethics, they also suggest other moral issues. What if biotechnology and bioengineering could be used in ways that provide control over other human beings? Some oppose human cloning with that worry in mind; the idea of engineering or creating human beings for the purpose of organ harvesting or other usages is morally repugnant. We might worry about so-called mind-hacking on similar grounds: there is something morally repellant about reading the thoughts of another person or manipulating their thoughts. And yet, there are obvious therapeutic benefits to mind–computer interfacing: paralyzed or brain-damaged people could communicate and interact in new ways. New technologies not only create new therapies but also new ethical worries. A primary concern is that, in our pursuit of medical advancement, we will lose sight of those features of humanity that give life its worth and dignity.

Among the technologies that we ought to think carefully about are reproductive technologies. Scientists are now able to create a human embryo from three different "parents," by combining mitochondrial DNA from one mother with regular DNA from another mother along with a father's contribution; and in the United Kingdom, scientists have been permitted to do research involving human gene editing.[7] These technologies have potential therapeutic benefits. The three-parent process would provide a remedy for diseases connected to mitochondrial DNA. Gene editing could help delete genetic codes that result in disease. We seem to be on the way toward producing "designer babies," even if the potential for designing our offspring is not yet a reality. These technologies may produce good consequences, which utilitarians would applaud; or they may be decried as a violation of ethical ideas associated with the natural law tradition, which are damaging to human dignity.

Biotechnology can be broadly defined as the manipulation of biological systems and organisms through technological means. Biotechnology includes performance-enhancing drugs, stem cell research, genetic engineering, cloning, and genetic screening. These technologies can be applied in human reproduction to select or even engineer desired offspring. They can also be applied to animals, in scientific breeding practices to increase meat production. And plants grown for food can be genetically modified in ways that improve crop yields. **Bioengineering** applies biological science to design machines and alter biological systems for a range of purposes, including the use of machines to supplement or enhance biological organisms, as in the case of the brain–computer interface discussed previously.

Some biotechnologies produce strikingly therapeutic effects, for example, giving paralyzed people the ability to feed themselves. A **therapy** is an intervention that helps restore normal function to an organism that is suffering from an impairment due to disease or injury. But other technologies may be viewed as enhancements, which may be seen to give some people fair, or unfair, advantages over others. An **enhancement** is the result of a technology that provides better than merely normal function. One of the ethical questions to be discussed here is whether anything is wrong with enhancements. While we might accept such uses of technology out of respect for individuals' rights to control their own bodies, some biotech enhancements appear to raise serious ethical questions about what is "natural" and about the value and nature of human life.

CURRENT ISSUES
Athletic and Cognitive Enhancement

Steroid use by athletes who want to bulk up muscle and build strength is an enhancement rather than a therapy. There have been a number of controversies regarding the use of performance-enhancing substances by some of the biggest names in sports, such as baseball superstar Barry Bonds, Olympic sprinter Marion Jones, and tennis star Maria Sharapova. In 2013, cyclist Lance Armstrong admitted that he had used performance enhancements, including blood doping (a procedure that artificially increases the number of red blood cells in the body), in his seven triumphs in the Tour de France. Most athletic organizations view performance enhancements as immoral, undermining fair play and allowing some athletes with sufficient money and connections to buy their victories. But consider the case of athletes such as Oscar Pistorius, who runs on artificial legs—carbon-fiber blades. Should those athletes be allowed to compete against non-impaired athletes? After some controversy, the International Olympic Committee permitted Pistorius to run the 400-meter race in the 2012 London Olympics. Critics complained that Pistorius's prosthetic legs gave him an unfair advantage. *Scientific American* examined the issue and concluded that Pistorius used less energy due to the elastic action of the blades.[8] His lower "legs" are lighter than those of other runners, and they do not tire. On the other hand, Pistorius must compensate for the light springiness of his blades by bearing down on his prostheses in a way that no other runner must do. In 2016, the issue of blade-wearing athletes was focused on Markus Rehm, who is called "the blade jumper." One of Rehm's legs was amputated, and he competes in the long jump by leaping off a blade. Rehm's jumps have reached 8.4 meters, a distance that would have won a gold medal in the 2012 London Olympics. In 2016, he was asked to compete in the Rio Olympics. The question of whether Pistorius or Rehm obtains an *unfair* advantage is not easy to answer. The distinction between therapy and enhancement is vague. Are these blades a therapeutic treatment, or do they enhance abilities in unfair ways?

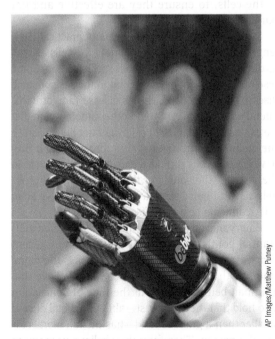

Biotechnology creates amazing new opportunities and unprecedented ethical challenges.

AP Images/Matthew Putney

There is no denying that therapeutic technologies can be used or abused in ways that enhance performance. One controversial development is in the field of so-called cognitive enhancements or smart drugs. Drugs such as Ritalin and Adderall, which are prescribed for diseases such as ADHD, can be used by healthy people in ways that may improve performance at school and at work. It is illegal to use these drugs to enhance performance in this way, and critics warn that such nontherapeutic use is addictive and dangerous. At least one suicide has been connected with abuse of Adderall.[9] But defenders argue that these drugs can provide an advantage in highly competitive fields, such as academia and business. Others argue that smart drugs are less like steroids than they are like caffeine or nicotine. In any case, there is no clear proof that such drugs actually work to consistently improve cognitive performance. "As useful as they may be during the occasional deadline crunch, no study has linked Ritalin or Adderall use in people without ADHD to sustained increases in things like grades or performance reviews."[10]

Nevertheless, other non-pharmaceutical technologies have been developed that purport to stimulate cognitive ability. One such technology is *transcranial direct-current stimulation*—the application of electric current to the brain. This technology has therapeutic applications, for example, treating depression or helping cognitive recovery after a stroke. But apparently electric stimulation of the brain can also be used to enhance the cognitive abilities of healthy individuals. Some studies suggest that transcranial stimulation can aid memory and learning, producing, for example, a greater capacity to learn a new language or mathematical skill.[11] Would it be ethical to use such a technology to enhance your ability to learn new information?

Stem Cell Research

An important current issue in bioethics is stem cell research. Stem cells are found in bone marrow and in other parts of the body. These cells are of interest for biomedical research because they have not yet developed into specific skin, muscle, or other types of body cells and tissues. In recent years, several public figures have made public appeals for the funding of stem cell research, citing its potential for treating or curing certain serious diseases. For example, Mary Tyler Moore, who has type I (insulin-dependent) diabetes and chairs the Juvenile Diabetes Foundation, brought children with this condition to testify in hearings before Congress. These children are not able to produce enough insulin to change nutrients into the energy needed for life; they must monitor their blood sugar levels and inject manufactured insulin. Other advocates hope that stem cell research could lead to a cure for Alzheimer's disease. In addition, the actor Michael J. Fox has promoted stem cell research as a possible cure for Parkinson's disease, a condition he lives with. And *Superman* star Christopher Reeve lobbied during his lifetime for stem cell research as a possible treatment for spinal cord injuries like his own.

Stem cell research is part of the field of *regenerative medicine*. One long-term goal of such research is to produce new cells, tissues, and organs that can be used to treat disease or injury. Certain stem cell therapies have been around for some time. One example is transplanting bone marrow stem cells to treat certain forms of leukemia. Another more recent example is the extraction from cadavers of certain parts of the human pancreas for an experimental treatment of diabetes.[12]

In 2012, scientists were able to find a way to grow a replacement windpipe for a patient with a tracheal tumor. They induced stem cells from the patient's own bone marrow to grow on an artificial windpipe scaffolding, which ensured that the plastic scaffolding would not be rejected by the body's immune response. The stem cells went on to develop into the kind of tissue that is found in normal windpipes. The patient recovered with the plastic scaffolding in place, the stem cells developing into the appropriate form of tissue.[13] A similar procedure has been employed to grow a replacement windpipe for a two-year-old girl born without a windpipe—the youngest person ever to undergo the procedure and the first in the United States.[14] Unfortunately, the child died of complications in July 2013.[15] More recently, scientists have been able to grow "organoids" from stem cells—tissues for rudimentary organs such as intestines and kidneys.[16]

The most potent, flexible type of stem cells are *embryonic* stem cells, or the undifferentiated cells of the early embryo in the first weeks of development, called a *blastocyst*. In human beings, these cells remain undifferentiated for approximately five to seven days after an egg is fertilized. They can be removed and placed in a culture where they will continue to divide, becoming the cells from which all of the body's organs develop. However, once removed in this manner, these cells can no longer develop into a fetus.

In the case of these embryonic stem cells, researchers hope to control the process of differentiation in order to provoke the cells to become, for example, the insulin-producing beta cells of the pancreas or neurons for the treatment of spinal cord injuries. Stem cells themselves cannot be directly implanted into the pancreas, however, because they can cause cancerous tumors to develop. Thus it is necessary to take steps to direct the development of the cells, to ensure they are effective and not harmful.

Stem cell treatments present many practical challenges, such as efficiently obtaining the cells as well as directing and controlling their specialization. Some researchers have pointed out that in the case of some diseases, such as Lou Gehrig's disease (amyotrophic lateral sclerosis, or ALS) and other autoimmune diseases, replacing damaged cells may not help because the cellular environment is the problem, and any newly added cells could become damaged as well. In these cases, the source of the problem would probably need to be addressed before regenerative stem cell treatments could be effective.[17]

Embryonic stem cell research has generated substantial political and ethical controversy in recent years. Among the central ethical issues is the moral status of the early embryo. Those who believe that a human being exists from the time of conception also hold that the blastocyst—although a ball of cells smaller than a grain of sand—has the full moral status of a person. Therefore, they believe it wrong to interrupt the development of such embryos, even to save another life. (See Chapter 11 on abortion for the arguments regarding the moral status of the embryo.) Supporters of stem cell research, however, point out that leftover embryos now stored in fertility clinics (approximately half a million are now frozen in the United States) could be used because they are often otherwise destroyed, and using these embryos could do some good. New techniques have also been developed to "reprogram" adult stem cells to behave like embryonic stem cells, which may defuse some of the controversy.[18]

Cloning

A separate but related issue is cloning. In 2014, scientists successfully created human embryo clones from adult human cells.[19] The purpose of this research is ultimately aimed at creating embryonic stem cells from these clones that could be used in regenerative medicine. We are not yet at the stage of full-blown reproductive cloning—indeed, many have questioned the morality of producing human babies through cloning technology. But the ethical questions are complicated, even at the stage of embryonic clones. Is a cloned human embryo a person? How does our thinking about cloned embryos connect with our thinking about other embryos created by natural reproductive techniques?

A clone is a genetically identical copy, produced asexually from a single living being. Since the birth of Dolly the sheep at the Roslin Institute near Edinburgh, Scotland in March 1996, people have wondered whether it also would be possible to produce humans by cloning. Dolly was a clone or generic copy of a six-year-old ewe. She was created by inserting the nucleus of a cell from the udder of this ewe into a sheep egg from which the nucleus had been removed. After being stimulated to grow, the egg was implanted into the uterus of another sheep, from which Dolly was born. Dolly was produced from a somatic cell of an adult sheep with already-determined characteristics. Because the cells of an adult are already differentiated, that is, they have taken on specialized roles—scientists had previously assumed that cloning from such cells would not be possible. Now, for the first time, producing

an identical, although younger, twin of an already existing human being seemed possible.

The type of cloning described earlier is called *somatic cell nuclear transfer* (SCNT) because it transfers the nucleus of a somatic or bodily cell into an egg whose own nucleus has been removed. Cloning can also be done through *fission*, or cutting, of an early embryo. Through this method it may be possible to make identical human twins or triplets from one embryo.

In recent decades, many higher mammals have been produced through cloning, including cows, sheep, goats, mice, pigs, rabbits, and a cat named "CC" for "carbon copy" or "copy cat." CC was produced in a project funded by an Arizona millionaire, John Sperling. The company that he and his team of scientists established, Genetic Savings and Clone, was based in Sausalito, California, and Texas A&M University at College Station, Texas.[20] In 2004, it charged $50,000 for a cloned cat and $295 to $1,395 to store genetic material from a cat. Two kittens, Tabouli and Baba Ganoush, who were cloned from the same female Bengal tiger cat, were displayed at the annual cat show at Madison Square Garden in October 2004. According to the owners, the kittens have personality similarities as well as differences.[21] Genetic Savings and Clone shut down in 2006.[22] However, Sperling established a new company, BioArts, in 2007. He cloned a dead pet dog, producing three puppies born in February 2008. Sperling said that "cloning techniques had become more efficient over the years" such that "1 percent to 4 percent of embryo transfers now result in a puppy."[23] Cloned animals have themselves produced offspring in the natural way. Dolly had six seemingly normal lambs. Unfortunately, animal cloning has not always been efficient or safe. In the case of Dolly, for example, 277 eggs were used but only one lamb was produced. Moreover, cloned animals also have exhibited various abnormalities. In February 2003, Dolly was euthanized because she had developed an infectious and terminal lung disease.

Some cloning proponents argue that cloning animals might help farmers to more efficiently produce livestock herds. Others argue that cloning could provide a way to save endangered species. Critics argue against animal cloning by appealing to beliefs about animal welfare and animal rights (see Chapter 17). These critics argue that animal clones have high rates of abnormalities and that the risk of animal suffering and illness outweighs potential benefits.[24]

Given the controversy surrounding animal cloning, it is not surprising that human cloning is subject to even more scrutiny. However, proponents of human cloning point to potential benefits for both therapeutic and reproductive goals. **Therapeutic cloning** is cloning for medical purposes. One therapeutic use of cloning might be in conjunction with stem cell therapy, to help avoid the immunological rejection by a patient's body of "foreign" tissues or organs grown from stem cells. In this type of cloning, the nucleus of a somatic or bodily cell from the patient, such as a skin cell, would be inserted into an unfertilized egg that had its own nucleus removed. The egg would then be stimulated to develop into an embryo. The stem cells in this blastocyst would be genetically identical with the patient and tissue grown from them might not then be rejected by the patient's immune system as foreign. The ethical issues raised by this type of cloning mirror those of stem cell research, especially the moral question of the status of the human embryo.

Reproductive cloning aims to produce a new human being who would be the genetic twin of the person whose cell was used in the process. Reproductive cloning is one of several reproductive technologies developed in recent decades. Among these are artificial insemination, in vitro fertilization, donated and frozen embryos and eggs, and the use of surrogate mothers. Although these other methods of reproduction have been accepted, there is almost universal objection to reproductive cloning, even among those countries that allow and support stem cell research or therapeutic cloning. Some countries have laws prohibiting reproductive cloning while still actively supporting therapeutic cloning. Japan, China, Singapore, and South Korea have similar laws. However, Germany, Austria, France, and the Netherlands have banned both types of cloning. Countries in South America, the Middle East, and Africa also have a diversity of regulation. In the United States, there is no federal law banning cloning, but several states have banned the practice. Meanwhile, one of the leading scientists in the field, John Gurdon—the 2012 co-winner of the Nobel Prize for medicine—has predicted that we will be able to safely clone human beings within fifty years.[25] Gurdon suggests that one reason to develop such techniques would be so that parents of children who die could replace their lost child with a copy. Gurdon further suggests that just as the public has gotten used to in vitro fertilization, the public will eventually come to accept the practice of reproductive cloning.

Others worry that such concepts of "replacing" individuals through cloning could lead to a devaluation of human life and a mechanistic "mass production" of babies. They point to the growing acceptance of paying surrogate mothers to bear children and argue that we are already commercializing reproduction, allowing (often wealthy and Western) couples to "rent" the wombs of women (often poor and in the developing world). When combined with cloning, such practices might seem to spring from the dystopia of Aldous Huxley's novel *Brave New World*, in which the production of children was outsourced and managed for sinister eugenic purposes. Huxley's novel is often invoked as a cautionary tale about the totalitarian dangers of cloning and technologized reproduction.

Genetic Engineering and Genetic Screening

Developments in modern genetics can create new ethical problems. The controversial history of the eugenics movement mentioned previously is an important concern. **Eugenics** is the science of improving the genetic components of a species. Livestock breeders have worked for centuries to create such genetic changes in animals. But eugenic practices become more problematic when attempted with human beings, especially given the history of human eugenics efforts, which includes forced sterilizations and abortions and other practices that violated people's liberty in the name of producing good offspring. There is a long history of eugenic projects, going back to Plato's plan for breeding good citizens in the *Republic*. Eugenic laws were enforced in the United States in the early part of the twentieth century, including the forced sterilization of thousands of people deemed "mentally defective." Nazi Germany took eugenic projects to another level of cruelty. The immoral effort to "purify" the Aryan race involved the killing of more than 200,000 people—many of them children—who were deemed disabled, degenerate, homosexual, or insane by Nazi doctors and therefore "unworthy of life."[26] Hundreds of thousands more were sterilized against their will. And eventually millions of people were deemed "unworthy" were slaughtered in the Holocaust.

For the most part, contemporary societies view eugenics as fundamentally immoral. But contemporary genetic research may open the door toward a different form of eugenic outcome—such parents selecting the genes of their children. We mentioned at the outset in a brief discussion of "designer babies" that it is possible to edit genes—and that three-parent combinations are possible, which eliminate defective mitochondrial DNA. Consider what decisions you might make if it were possible for you to engineer a "designer baby" or to screen out an embryo with an unwanted genetic mutation—and how those decisions relate to your ideas about the value of natural reproduction, your view of disability, and your ideas about harms and benefits.

One genetic manipulation process is known as *preimplantation genetic screening*, by which embryos with harmful or perhaps even simply unwanted genetic mutations can be selected out during the in vitro fertilization process. This seems like a prudent step to take, in cases where the risk of genetic diseases, such as Huntington's disease, could be eliminated through a pre-implantation genetic test. But consider the controversy surrounding a Maryland couple—both born deaf—who opted to increase the likelihood that their child would also be born deaf. The couple (two women who had been together for eight years) sought out a sperm donor with hereditary deafness out of a conviction that deafness is not a disability and that they wanted to share deaf culture with their children. "A hearing baby would be a blessing," one of the mothers said. "A deaf baby would be a special blessing."[27] After one of the women did, in fact, give birth to a deaf baby, some critics argued that the selection of a deaf donor was an abuse of genetic screening practices. But one of the mothers argued in reply that if black parents were able to choose black sperm donors, a deaf mother should be allowed to choose a deaf sperm donor.[28]

Many of the ethical controversies surrounding genetic engineering and screening have been intensified by the great progress scientists have made in recent decades in understanding the human genetic structure. The Human Genome Project, an effort to map the entire human genome, was completed in the summer of 2000 and its results first published in early 2001. The project found that humans have approximately twenty thousand genes—roughly the same number as most other animals—and helped scientists determine that "we have only 300 unique genes in the human [genome] that are not in the mouse."[29] However, although humans have approximately the same number of genes as a spotted green puffer fish, it is surmised that human capacity comes from "a small set of regulatory genes that control the activity of all the other genes." These would be different in the puffer fish.[30]

Two entities competed in the race to map the entire human genome. One was a public consortium of university centers in the United States, Great Britain, and Japan. It made its findings publicly available and used the genome from a mosaic of different individuals. The other research was done by Celera Genomics, a private company run by Dr. Craig Venter. It used a "shotgun" strategy, with genetic source material from Venter and four others. Celera performed an analysis of the DNA—identifying where the genes lay in the entire DNA sequence—and in 2007 Venter published his entire genetic sequence.[31] Although initially the cost to have one's complete genome sequenced was quite high, the cost has dropped to under $10,000.[32] A few companies, such as 23 and Me, have begun charging much less, sometimes less than a couple hundred for genetic screening, which can also tell you something about your ancestry.

Since the initial mapping of the human genome, various scientific projects have attempted to determine the precise role that hereditary elements, including the genes, play in human development, health, personality, and other characteristics. In this effort, one focus has been on individual differences. The human genome, "a string of 3 billion chemical letters that spell out every inherited trait," is almost identical in all humans—99.99 percent. But some differences, so-called genetic misspellings that are referred to as *single nucleotide polymorphisms* (SNPs or "snips"), can be used to identify genetic diseases. The SNPs give base variations that contribute to individual differences in appearance and health, among other things. Scientists look for differences, for example, by taking DNA samples of five hundred people with diabetes and a similar number from people without the disease and then look for contrasting DNA patterns.[33] SNPs also influence how people react differently to medications. Some people can eat high-calorie and high-fat foods and still not put on weight while others are just the opposite. Some have high risks of heart disease, whereas others do not. With genetic discoveries based on the Human Genome Project and more recent efforts, one hope is that diets can be tailored to individual human genetic makeups.

Since the early 2000s, an international consortium of scientists has been working on the "hapmap" project, a $100 million endeavor "to hasten discovery of the variant genes thought to underlie common human diseases like diabetes, asthma, and cancer."[34] Scientists have used the Human Genome Project map as a master reference and compare individual genomes to it. Some diseases are caused by single genes, such as that producing cystic fibrosis, but others are thought to be caused by several genes acting together.

Other efforts are directed to finding genes that relate to certain beneficial human traits. For example, some scientists are working on locating what they call the "skinny gene." Using mice from whom a single gene has been removed, scientists

at Deltagen, a company in Redwood City, California, have been able to produce mice that remain slim no matter how much they are fed.[35] According to geneticist David Botstein, the impact of the Human Genome Project on medicine "should exceed that 100 years ago of X-rays, which gave doctors their first view inside the intact, living body."[36]

Our growing knowledge of the human genome may lead to powerful new medical treatments but also raise new ethical questions. Consider, for example, gene therapies that could impact the growth of muscle. Myostatin is a hormone that curbs the growth of muscles. Gene therapies might be able to block myostatin, which could promote muscle growth. As a therapy this could be useful for treating muscular dystrophy or frailty in older persons. Myostatin mutations are already responsible for the development of a breed of cattle called the Belgian Blue that has huge muscles and very little fat. And some human beings have a myostatin mutation, which promotes muscle growth—a natural abnormality that has helped produce exceptional athletes, including a gold medalist in cross-country skiing.[37] While myostatin treatments could save lives, there is also concern that athletes and other healthy individuals might purchase them to gain an advantage in competition or for cosmetic purposes. Such genetic enhancements might not leave traces in urine or blood the way that other performance-enhancing drugs do. However, in recent years the World Anti-Doping Agency has begun to develop new blood tests to detect so-called gene doping, including other genetic enhancements that allow the human body to produce extra red blood cells.[38]

Ethical issues have also arisen over new genetic screening procedures made possible by the genome map. While such screenings may benefit health, insurers and prospective employers might also use genetic screening to their own advantage but not necessarily to the advantage of the person being screened. Although the procedures may be new, the ethical issues are similar to those raised by other types of screening, including drug screening. While we may agree that athletes and airline pilots should have their blood and urine screened for the use of performance enhancements and recreational drugs, do we also agree that students or retail employees should be subject to similar screenings? Related to this is the question of whether insurance companies or employers should be able to obtain information about an individual's genetic code. In 2013, scientists published the results of a study that showed that it was finally possible to identify individuals based upon an analysis of genetic codes in comparison with publicly available databases containing the genetic information of individuals whose genes have been sequenced.[39] This technology could be useful for tracing out genealogies. But it could also raise privacy concerns, for example, among people who fear being stigmatized because of a genetic abnormality or disease.

Genetically Modified Plants and Animals

During the past few decades, a lively debate has sprung up in the United States and beyond about **genetically modified organisms**, or GMOs. While, strictly speaking, humans have been modifying the genes of plants and animals for centuries—through such practices as plant hybridization and selective animal breeding—GMOs are created through new biotechnologies such as gene splicing, radiation, or specialized chemicals. These technologies often change the genetics of plants and animals that humans grow for food, in an attempt to make them hardier, larger, more flavorful, or more resistant to drought or freezing temperatures. Although some of these traits could be established through traditional breeding methods, some could not, and a highly profitable new industry now revolves around creating (and usually patenting) these new forms of life.

Critics of GMOs argue that they open a "Pandora's box" of potential risks to ecosystems and to human health. (In Greek mythology, Pandora's seemingly minor act of opening a beautiful box releases a host of evils into the world.) In 2004, the National Academy of Sciences determined that, "genetically engineered crops do not pose health risks that cannot also arise from crops created by other techniques, including conventional breeding."[40] It is not the method of production that should be of concern, the

NAS argued, but the resulting product. Nevertheless, there is much that the general public does not understand about so-called genetically modified food.

Strictly speaking, genetic engineering involves inserting a specific gene from one organism into another in order to produce a desired trait. In a broader sense, "nearly every food we eat has been genetically modified" as crops and domesticated animals have been bred by humans for centuries.[41] Cross-breeding crops "involves the mixing of thousands of genes, most unknown," and trying to select desirable mutations.[42] In the case of some contemporary GMOs, such mutations are now often caused by "bombarding seeds with chemicals or radiation" and seeing what comes of it. For example, lettuce, beans, and grapefruit have been so modified.[43]

An increasing number of crops have been genetically modified in recent decades. A report of the International Service for the Acquisition of Agri-Biotech Applications concludes, "In 2014, the global area of biotech crops continued to increase for the 19th year at a sustained growth rate of 3 to 4% or 6.3 million hectares (~16 million acres), reaching 181.5 million hectares or 448 million acres."[44] According to the Non-GMO Project, "In North America, 80 percent of our foods contain GMOs."[45] The Non-GMO Project has spearheaded a campaign to certify foods that do not contain GMOs. In 2013, the grocery chain Whole Foods announced that it would label products that contain GMOs in its stores.[46] While some are pushing back against GMOs, mainstream science tends to hold that these products are beneficial or at least not harmful. GMO crops are easier and cheaper to grow and can provide more food from less land. They may be engineered to survive the use of herbicides and insecticides or to be more resistant to pests. Critics argue, however, that herbicide- and pesticide-resistant crops will lead to more toxic chemicals in agriculture, which may have long-term negative impacts on the environment and human health. One article claims that the use of genetically modified crops has unleashed a "gusher" of pesticides.[47] But proponents of GMOs explain things differently. One technique has inserted *Bacillus thuringiensis* (B.t.) genes into corn, which enables it to resist a devastating pest called the corn borer. With this mutation, the use of environmentally damaging herbicides intended to combat the corn borer can then be reduced.

Other benefits of GMOs include the possibility of engineering crops so that they contain more nutritional value. New strains of rice have been developed specifically to combat famine and to reduce a vitamin A deficiency that commonly causes blindness and other infections among the world's poorest children. Plans for GMOs include "edible vaccines" in fruits and vegetables that would make them more easily available to people than injectable ones.[48] Perhaps most significant for global public health, genetically modified foods offer a chance to "produce more food on less land—using less water, fewer chemicals, and less money."[49] And opposition to GMOs in the wealthy West may have negative consequences for developing countries where famine and malnutrition are serious problems. For example, opposition to genetically modified food has led Uganda to prohibit efforts to develop a fungus-resistant banana, even though fungus has seriously damaged its banana crop, one of its most important.[50]

At the same time, protests against genetically modified foods have increased, especially in Europe and Japan, but also in the United States. One significant concern is food allergies that could result from products containing new genetic information.[51] Although some of the criticism may be based on ungrounded fears about new technologies, some GMO-related hazards may be real. There is some evidence, for example, that crops genetically modified for antibiotic resistance may transfer that resistance to humans who eat them raising serious health concerns.[52] There is also evidence that herbicide-resistant crops may help create "superweeds" that require ever more toxic chemicals to try to control them. Neighboring non-GMO crops may become contaminated by GMO crops which has, ironically, allowed giant GMO producers such as Monsanto to sue farmers for patent infringement when pollen from GMO crops blows onto their land. It may well be possible to reduce some of these risks, for example, by creating sterile plants that do not produce pollen. But clearly we are in the early days of human experimentation with GMOs. So far, many of the dangers that people associate with GMOs have not materialized, but this does not prove their safety for humans and the environment.

MindTap® For more chapter resources and activities, go to MindTap.

LEGAL AND ETHICAL ISSUES

A variety of legal and ethical issues arise in thinking about biotechnology and bioengineering. In general, there is a tension between valuing our liberty to pursue biotechnologies for their immediate utility, on the one hand, and concerns over the potential negative impacts of such technologies in the long run. Some consequentialists will argue in favor of the benefits of these technological innovations; others will urge caution, appealing to a "**precautionary principle**," which holds that we ought to do our best to avoid risks and harms when exploring new technologies. There are also tensions between the liberty of individuals and groups to modify biology and concerns about the moral problems involved in such modification, including the risk of "playing God." There is also a concern that new technologies will diminish human dignity by turning human beings into products that are created and engineered. One significant argument, associated with the work of bioethicist Leon Kass (whose work is excerpted in the Readings section of this chapter), is that there is a kind of wisdom in our repugnance for certain forms of bioengineering. When a new technology makes us pause and say "yuck," we may be tapping into a deeper insight about human nature. Of course, others reject such repugnance as little more than taste and inclination without any deeper moral basis. Indeed, some theorists argue that what one generation finds disgusting is easily accepted by the next generation, as people get used to new norms and new ideas about what is natural and possible. We might organize ethical judgments about biotechnologies along a continuum from progressive to conservative. Progressives put great hope in the advantages of biotechnology, with some imagining embracing technologies that enhance human life, while imagining a radically altered transformation that could result in a transhuman or posthuman future. Conservatives are not so sanguine about the promise of biotechnological enhancement, even though they would likely admit that therapeutic applications of biotechnology are beneficial.

The following table provides an outline of moral approaches to biotechnology.

Athletic and Cognitive Enhancement

The issues arising around athletic and cognitive enhancement involve the conflict between liberty and negative consequences. In terms of liberty, defenders of biotechnology will argue that individuals have a right to do whatever they want to their

own bodies, a right to enhance their performance, a right to use technology to choose their own offspring, and a right to find ways to profit and benefit from technology so long as they do not hurt other people. Therapeutic technologies can be defended in terms of their immediate positive impact on impaired and disabled people. Those who want to use these technologies beyond mere therapy will argue that the benefits are obvious and that individuals should be free to take the risks that might be associated with the use of performance-enhancing drugs. Arguments along these lines might parallel ethical considerations regarding the use of other drugs, such as marijuana or nicotine. Defenders will argue that so long as no one else is harmed, individuals should be allowed to choose to use these substances because of a basic right to do what one wants with one's own body.

Outline of Moral Approaches to Biotechnology

	Progressive	Moderate	Conservative
Thesis	Embrace and explore the advantages of biotechnologies	Biotechnologies are neither all good nor all bad	Need for careful reflection about biotechnology (and prohibition in some cases)
Corollaries and Implications	Pro-enhancement; natural systems can be improved through human intervention; negative consequences outweighed by benefits/advantages; there are no inherent moral limits to human freedom to innovate through biotechnology; aspiration to transcend current limits	Balancing need for therapy with desire for enhancement; precautionary principle employed to counsel prudence with regard to harms and benefits biotech innovation; respect for autonomy and innovation balanced with recognition of stability of social and natural systems	Anti-enhancement (although not necessarily opposed to therapeutic interventions); Strict risk-averse application of precautionary principle; fear of "playing God" and eugenics; need to respect the inherent dignity of natural processes including aging, disability, and death
Connections with Moral Theory	Optimistic consequentialism; respect for Liberty	Moderate consequentialism balanced with respect for autonomy/dignity	Natural law; concerns for human dignity
Relevant Authors/ Examples	Bostrom, transhumanism and posthumanism		Kass

On the other hand, critics will argue that the benefits are not obvious. Steroid use by athletes has been proved to produce long-term negative health effects. Athletes may need to be protected from competitive or organizational pressures to alter their bodies in ways that are not healthy. Indeed, the international agreements that prohibit the use of performance enhancements in sport are partly intended to benefit the athletes themselves. If steroid use were allowed, for example, there is a worry that there would be an "arms race" among athletes, which might increase performance but would result in serious health problems. Furthermore, critics of performance enhancements argue that these drugs and technologies create unfairness, as those who are willing to use these drugs (or those who can afford them) will have an unfair advantage over those who restrict themselves to developing their own natural talents and abilities. There is a worry, for example, that affluent students will benefit from smart drugs, giving them an unfair advantage over less fortunate students.

Furthermore, critics will argue that we may not yet understand the potential long-term impacts of these biotechnologies. Just as genetically modified organisms may produce food allergies and contribute to the growth of superweeds, so too, the use of performance enhancements may create future impacts that we might come to regret. Critics may also argue with regard to biotechnology and bioengineering in general that we are not wise enough or benevolent enough to be entrusted with technologies that could be easily abused. This is related to a naturalistic argument, which suggests that we ought to leave natural things alone and not risk dangerous perversions of nature.

Stem Cell Research

As we have seen, ethical debate over stem cell research is often—but not always—rooted in the contentious moral debate about the status of the human embryo. In 2001, President George W. Bush introduced a ban on federally funded research using stem cells from new embryos, stating that, "[l]ike a snowflake, each of these embryos is unique, with

the unique genetic potential of an individual human being."[53] In 2009, President Obama expanded the number of stem cell lines available for use and allowed federal grant money to be used for research on these lines. These stem cell lines are to be derived from excess embryos created in fertility clinics and donated for research purposes with the consent of the donor. (If not used in this way, these excess embryos would be thrown away.) In 2013, the U.S. Supreme Court overruled a lower court decision that would have prevented federal funding for embryonic stem cell research. The plaintiff in that case, Dr. James Sherley, said that his goal was to "emancipate human embryos from research slavery."[54]

To overcome such ethical concerns about the status of the early embryo, some people have suggested that only adult stem cells be used in research. Adult stem cells exist in bone marrow and purportedly in other parts of the body such as the brain, skin, fat, and muscle. The therapeutic use of these cells seems to work in some situations, such as the case of the reconstructed windpipe mentioned previously. Adult stem cells have been used to grow different types of cells, including heart cells, which could be useful for treating heart disease.[55] However, adult stem cells may be limited in their ability to develop into tissues. They may only be *multipotent* rather than pluripotent.

Nevertheless, some recent scientific developments suggest that researchers may find a way out of the moral impasse over embryonic stem cells. Several studies have found that the stem cells present in amniotic fluid (the fluid that surrounds the fetus in the uterus) can be used for many of the same therapies as embryonic stem cells. This would constitute a plentiful source of stem cells and would perhaps be less controversial than obtaining the cells directly from embryos. In 2012, the Nobel Prize for Medicine was given to two researchers, Shinya Yamanaka and John Gurdon (mentioned previously), whose work showed how mature cells could be "reprogrammed" into an immature state capable of growing into various kinds of tissue—a capacity that resembles the pluripotency of embryonic stem cells.[56] Such new techniques may change the ethical conversation about stem cells, especially if it is possible to create therapies that use adult cells instead of embryonic cells. Such work would circumvent the complaints of those who view embryos as incipient human life that ought not be destroyed in the name of research. Scientists continue to make rapid progress along these lines. In April 2013, scientists announced that they had perfected a technique for creating and growing induced pluripotent cells that allows for successful cultivation of large numbers of these cells.[57]

Not all moral concerns about stem cell research, however, are narrowly focused on the individuality and potential personhood of the human embryo. Another significant concern raised, for example, in the National Academy of Sciences (NAS) recommendations for stem cell research is the possible creation of *chimeras*, or new creatures that cross species borders. The NAS guidelines prohibit research in which human embryonic stem cells "are introduced into nonhuman primate blastocysts or in which any embryonic stem cells are introduced into human blastocysts." Furthermore, the guidelines maintain, "no animal into which human embryonic stem cells have been introduced such that they could contribute to the germ line should be allowed to breed."[58]

The possibility of creating and breeding partially human or cross-species genetic mutants raises a number of serious ethical worries about how such creatures might be treated, about just *how* human such beings would need to be to deserve human rights and personhood, and, more generally, what it means for scientists to "play God" and create unprecedented new life forms. Such moral questions are not merely speculative or limited to the realm of science fiction. Some medical therapies already do include tissues and genes taken from animals. For example, pig heart valves that contain some human cells have been used to treat human patients with cardiac diseases. While recommending that these therapies and research programs be allowed, the NAS also recommended that: (1) chimeric animals not be allowed to mate because, if human cells invaded the sperm and eggs of an animal host, this could lead to the remote possibility of a being with

human DNA being conceived in a non-human host; (2) human stem cells not be allowed to become part or all of an animal's brain and not be injected into other primates because this could have the possible result of a human mind trapped in a non-human body; (3) embryos used in stem cell research should not be allowed to develop for more than fourteen days; and (4) women who donate eggs not be paid in order to avoid financial inducement.[59]

In 2007, a task force of the International Society for Stem Cell Research published its own guidelines for embryonic stem cell research. These guidelines were developed by ethicists, scientists, and legal experts from fourteen countries. Like the NAS recommendations, these guidelines do allow some research on chimeric animals—those that could carry human gametes—but only if such research passes the review of an oversight committee. The guidelines also affirm the fourteen-day limit for embryo development, arguing that it is not until this point in the development of a "primitive streak" that the embryo "has begun to initiate organogenesis."[60] The idea is that prior to that point, the embryo has not yet reached a point of development that would qualify it for moral concern—a claim that is connected to the discussion of the ethics of abortion (see Chapter 11).

Cloning

Perhaps no issue related to biotechnology raises more ethical controversy than the prospect of cloning human beings. Although much of the reaction to cloning humans has been the product of both hype and fear, serious ethical questions also have been raised. One of the most serious concerns is that cloning might produce medical problems for the individuals produced in this way, just as it has in some cases of animal cloning. For this reason alone, we might raise ethical objections to human cloning. Some have pointed out, though, that fertility clinics have had broad experience in growing human embryos, and thus cloning humans might actually be less risky than cloning animals. However, moral objections to cloning are also based on other considerations.

One classic objection to human cloning is that it amounts to "playing God." The idea is that only God can and should create a human life. Those who hold this view might use religious reasons and sources to support it, but although this looks like a religious position, it is not necessarily so. For example, it might simply suggest that the coming to be of a new person is a *creation*, rather than a making or production. According to this view, the creation of a human is the bringing into being of an individual, a mysterious thing and something that we should regard with awe. When we take on the role of *producing* a human being, as in cloning, we become makers or manipulators of a product that we control and over which we have some kind of power. Another version of this objection stresses the significance of nature and the natural. In producing a human being through cloning, we go against human nature. For example, in humans, as in all higher animals, reproduction is sexual. Cloning, by contrast, is asexual reproduction, and thus may be seen to go beyond the "natural" boundaries of human biology. Leon Kass, whom we mentioned earlier, is one of the strongest proponents of the view that in cloning someone, we would wrongly seek to escape the bounds and dictates of our sexual nature. According to another related criticism, attempting to clone a human being demonstrates *hubris*, an arrogant assumption that we are wise enough to know and handle its potential consequences. Tampering with a process as fundamental as human reproduction should only be undertaken with the utmost caution, this argument claims. Above all, we should avoid doing what unknowingly may turn out to be seriously harmful for the individuals produced as well as for future generations.

Those who defend human cloning respond to this sort of objection by asking how cloning is any different from other ways we interfere with or change Nature in accepted medical practices such as in vitro fertilization, for example. Others argue from a religious perspective that God gave us brains to use, and that we honor God in using them, especially for the benefit of humans and society. Cloning advocates also point out that in using technology to assist reproduction, we do not necessarily lose our awe at the arrival of a new being, albeit one who comes into being with our help.

A second objection to the very idea of cloning a human being is that the person cloned would not be a *unique individual*. He or she would be the genetic copy of the person from whom the somatic cell was transferred, the equivalent of an identical twin of this person, although years younger. Moreover, because our dignity and worth are attached to our uniqueness as individuals, this objection suggests that cloned individuals would lose the unique value we believe persons have. We might find that the difficulties that clones have in maintaining their individuality would be a more confusing and troubling version of the difficulties that identical twins sometimes face. For example, often identical twins are expected to act alike. The implication is that they do not have the freedom or ability to develop their own individual personalities. A related objection is sometimes expressed as the view that a cloned human being would not have a soul, or that he or she would be a hollow shell of a person. The idea is that if we take on the role of producing a human being through cloning, then we prevent God or nature from giving it the spiritual component that makes it more than a material body.

One response to this objection points out how different the cloned individual would be from the original individual. Identical twins are more like each other than a clone would be to the one cloned. This is because twins develop together in the same mother's body in addition to sharing the same genetic code. Clones would develop in different uteruses and would have different mitochondria—the genes in the cytoplasm surrounding the renucleated cell that play a role in development. They would also likely grow up in very different circumstances and environments. Developmental studies of plants and animals give dramatic evidence of how great a difference the environment makes. The genotype (the genetic code) does not fully determine the phenotype (the genes' actual physical manifestations). CC, the cloned cat mentioned previously, does not quite look like its genetic donor, Rainbow. They have different coat patterns because genes are not the only things that control coat color. They exhibit other differences. "Rainbow is reserved. CC is curious and playful. Rainbow is chunky. CC is sleek."[61] Although genes do matter, and thus there would be similarities between a human clone and the person who was cloned, they would not be identical. On the matter of soul, cloning defenders ask why could God not give each person, identical twin or clone, an individual soul; any living human being, cloned or not, would be a distinct being and so could have a human psyche or soul, they suggest.

Another objection to human cloning is that while any person born today has a *right to an open future*, a cloned human being would not. He or she would be expected to be like the originating person and thus would not be free to develop as he or she chose. The genetic donor (or his or her life story) would be there as the model of what he or she would be expected to become. Even if people tried not to have such expectations for the one cloned, they would be hard-pressed not to do so. Critics of this argument point out that while there might indeed be certain expectations for a clone, this undue influence is a possibility in the case of all parents and children, and thus a possibility that is not limited to clones. Parents select their children's schools and other formative experiences and promote certain activities, perspectives, and tastes. Thus any child, cloned or sexually reproduced, would seem to run the risk of being unduly influenced by those who raise them or contribute to their genetic makeup.

Related to the previous objection to cloning is one that holds that cloned children or adults would tend to be *exploited*. If one looks at many of the potential motivations for cloning a person, the objection goes, they indicate that cloning would often be undertaken for the sake of others, rather than for the sake of the new cloned person. For example, the cloned child could be viewed as a potential organ or blood donor—a so-called "savior sibling"—or to "replace" a child who has died. A more far-fetched scenario might include making clones who were specifically produced for doing menial work or fighting wars. We might want to clone certain valued individuals,

such as stars of the screen or athletics. In all of these cases, the clones would neither be valued for their own selves nor respected as unique persons. They would be valued for what they can bring to others. Kant is cited as the source of the moral principle that persons ought not simply be used but ought to be treated as ends in themselves, and such practices would seem to be condemned by Kantian ethics.

Critics of these objections could agree with Kant but still disagree that a cloned human being would be more likely than anyone else to be used by others rather than valued as an individual. Just because a child was conceived to provide bone marrow for a sick sibling would not prevent her from also being loved for her own sake. Furthermore, the idea that we would create and confine a group of human beings while training them to be workers or soldiers must presuppose that we abandon a host of legal protections against such treatment of children or other individuals. Equally far-fetched, these critics say, is the notion of a eugenic "brave new world" in which children are produced only through cloning.

Some people believe that if human cloning were widely practiced, then it would only add to the *confusion within families* that is already generated by the use of other reproductive technologies. When donated eggs and surrogate mothers are used, the genetic parents are different from the gestational parents and the rearing parents, and conflicts have arisen regarding who the "real" parents are. Cloning, objectors contend, would create even more of a problem, adding to this confusion the blurring of lines between generations. The birth mother's child could be her twin or a twin of the father or someone else. What would happen to the traditional relationships with the members of the other side of the family, grandparents, aunts, and uncles? And what would be the relationship of a husband to a child who is the twin of his wife or of a wife to a child who is the twin of her husband?

Critics of these arguments respond that, although there is a traditional type of family that, in fact, varies from culture to culture, today there are also many different kinds of nontraditional families. Among these are single-parent families, adopted families, blended families, and lesbian and gay families. It is not the type of family that makes for a good loving household, they argue, but the amount of love and care that exists in one.

A final objection to human cloning goes something as follows: Sometimes we have a *gut reaction* to something we regard as abhorrent, and we are offended by the very thought of it. We cannot always give reasons for this reaction, yet we instinctively feel that what we abhor is wrong. Many people react to human cloning in this way. The idea of someone making a copy of themselves or many copies of a celebrity is simply bizarre, revolting, and repugnant, and these emotional reactions tell us there is something quite wrong with it, even if we cannot explain.

Any adequate response to this argument would entail an analysis of how ethical reasoning works when it works well. Emotional reactions or moral intuitions may indeed play a role in moral reasoning. However, most philosophers would agree that adequate moral reasoning should not rely on intuition or emotion alone. Reflections about why one might rightly have such gut reactions are in order. People have been known to have negative gut reactions to things that, in fact, are no longer regarded as wrong—interracial marriage, for example. It is incumbent on those who assert that something is wrong, most philosophers believe, that they provide rational arguments and well-supported reasons to justify these beliefs and emotional reactions.

There is currently no federal law banning human cloning, although as we saw previously, several laws have been proposed to ban the practice or to prohibit federal funding for research that involves it. Under President George W. Bush, the President's Council on Bioethics recommended a moratorium on all types of human cloning. In 2009, President Barack Obama replaced the council with the Presidential Commission for the Study of Bioethical Issues, chaired by philosopher Amy Gutmann and focused on specific policy recommendations.[62] This commission has yet to issue a specific recommendation on cloning. Meanwhile state legislatures have weighed in on the issue. As of 2011, eight states

ban human cloning for any purpose, while ten other states explicitly allow research in which clones are created and destroyed for therapeutic purposes.[63]

Some critics of state cloning laws argue that it is too difficult to ban one type of cloning without the other. For example, if reproductive cloning were prohibited but research or therapeutic cloning were allowed, it would be difficult to know for certain that cloned embryos were not being produced for reproductive purposes. With regard to proposed federal bans, some have pointed out that if there are no federal funds provided for research cloning, then there also will be no oversight. We will not know what types of cloning that corporations or other private entities engage in. Scientists also point out how essential federal research funds have been for new developments in biotechnology.

Genetic Engineering and Genetic Screening

The ethical debate over the genetic engineering of human offspring overlaps substantially with the debate outlined previously about reproductive human cloning. Opponents of "designer babies" argue that exercising control over these aspects of traditional human reproduction would be both unnatural and an affront to human dignity. Those on the other side argue on consequentialist grounds for giving parents the opportunity to choose to produce the healthy children they desire, even if that involves selection of preferred physical and mental characteristics beyond the merely healthy. So long as there is no coercion involved and no one is harmed in the process, one might think that people should be free to reproduce in accord with their own interests and in ways that would be beneficial to society. Again, the worry is that this could easily slide toward a eugenic project in which reproduction is regulated in more insidious ways. Defenders of genetic engineering will respond by claiming that the slope is not really that slippery.

There are some obvious benefits to human genetic engineering. If it were possible to use gene therapy to activate, replace, or change malfunctioning genes before a baby is born, then this could greatly reduce human suffering from genetic diseases. Using genetic techniques to manipulate cells or organisms in order to provide human blood-clotting factor for hemophiliacs, manufactured human insulin for diabetics, human growth hormone for those who need it, and better pain relievers for everyone is surely desirable and ethically defensible. However, use of the technology also raises ethical concerns. Among these questions are those related to the risks that exist for those who undergo experimental genetic therapies and the issue of informed consent in such experiments.[64]

Related to the issue of informed consent are a variety of ethical questions that arise with regard to genetic screening, the process of searching for and screening out genetic defects. For example, what limits should be placed upon the ways that genetic information is used? Do people have a right to know their own genetic predispositions? And is there a right to privacy regarding genetic information?

We also should be concerned about access to these procedures and whether only the well-off will benefit from them. The biotechnology industry continues to grow. Should information and products of great medical benefit be kept secret and patented by biotech companies and developers? For example, the company Myriad Genetics found a gene linked with breast cancer and attempted to patent the gene.[65] In another example, therapeutic techniques now allow the alteration of genes in sperm, which affect not the individual himself but his offspring and thus alter human lineage.[66] It is one thing to do this in the interest of preventing genetic disease in one's offspring, but it is quite another to add new genetically based capabilities for one's children or to the human race. Such capabilities raise serious moral concerns. Are we wise enough to do more good than harm with these methods? Can we legitimately deny access to such technologies to individuals who may benefit from them, without also violating those individuals' rights to do what they want with their own bodies and reproductive capabilities?

The Value of Privacy As in our discussion of abortion in Chapter 11, arguments about our rights to employ biotechnologies in our own bodies often involve the value of privacy. We might want to say that decisions that people make about their own health and reproductive lives is no one's business but their own. We think that people generally have a right to privacy, but we are less sure what this means and what kinds of practices would violate privacy. Suppose, for example, that a technology existed that could read a person's mind and the condition of various parts of her body, or could hear and see what goes on in one's home—his bedroom or bathroom—and could record all of these in a data bank that would be accessible to a variety of interested parties. What, if anything, would be wrong with this?[67] One of the things that we find problematic about others having access to this knowledge is that they would have access to matters that we would not want anyone else to know. According to Thomas Scanlon, this is what the right to privacy is—a right "to be free from certain intrusions."[68] Some things, we say, are just nobody else's business.

If this definition of privacy seems reasonable, then we can ask for reasons why we would not want certain intrusions like those in the hypothetical example. Many reasons have been suggested, and you may sympathize with some more than others. Four are provided here.

The first concern is the basic idea of shame. Shame and embarrassment are feelings we have when certain private things become known or observed—one's thoughts, bathroom behavior, or sexual fantasies, for example. Some private thoughts and behaviors are thought to be shameful—something that should remain private and not shared in public. Could there be reasons to be ashamed of our genetic inheritance or genetic disease susceptibilities, for example?

A second reason why we might want certain things kept to ourselves is our desire to control information about us and to let it be known only to those to whom we choose to reveal it. Such control is part of our ability to own our own lives. We speak of it as a form of autonomy or self-rule. In fact, the loss of control over some of these more personal aspects of our lives is a threat to our very selfhood, some say. For example, in his classic study of what he calls "total institutions," such as prisons and mental hospitals, the sociologist Erving Goffman describes the way that depriving a person of privacy is a way of mortifying (literally killing) the self.[69] Having a zone of privacy around us that we control helps us define ourselves and marks us off from others and our environment. Perhaps our genetic endowment should be kept private so that we have a zone of control in this sphere.

Third, privacy helps in the formation and continuation of personal relations. We are more intimate with friends than with strangers, and even more so with lovers and spouses than with mere acquaintances. The private things about ourselves that we confide to those closest to us are an essential part of those relationships. According to legal theorist Charles Fried, "privacy is the necessary context for relationships which we would hardly be human if we had to do without—the relationships of love, friendship, and trust."[70] Sexual intimacies are thus appropriate in the context of a loving relationship because they are private sharings that also help to establish and further that relationship. It may be that our genetic heritage is only the business of our potential sexual partners, those with whom we may choose to have children. Potential mates might actually have a right to access our genetic information, in this view.

Fourth, we want to keep certain things private because of the risk that the knowledge might be used against us to cause us harm. Screening procedures in particular come to mind here. Drug screening, HIV testing, or genetic disease scans all make information available to others that could result in social detriment. For example, we could be harmed in our employment or our ability to obtain medical insurance. The problem of data banks is also at issue here. Our medical records, records of psychiatric sessions, histories of employment, and so forth could be used legitimately by certain people. However, they also may be misused by those who have no business having access to them. In a particularly problematic example, the managed care company that was paying for the psychological counseling of one patient asked to inspect his confidential files. The psychologist was concerned. "The audit occurred, they rifled through my files," he said, and "made copies and went. But it changed things. He [the patient] became more concerned about what he was saying.... A few visits later he stopped coming."[71] Another notorious case is also illustrative of the harm that can be caused by the invasion of privacy. During a contentious New York congressional campaign, someone obtained a copy of the hospital records of one of the candidates and sent them anonymously to the press. *The New York Post* published the material, including notes about the candidate's attempt to kill herself with sleeping pills and vodka. Despite this, the candidate won the election and she successfully sued the hospital for invasion of privacy.[72] Similar concerns about privacy and reputation may arise with regard to genetic information.

Screening and Conflicting Interests As we have seen, the value of privacy is particularly relevant in the context of genetic screening and screening procedures in general. Ethical debates over screening often revolve around a conflict between the privacy interests of those being screened, on the one hand, and the legitimate interests of others in obtaining relevant information, on the other. An employer may have a legitimate interest in having a drug-free workplace, for example. It may have a valid economic interest, for employees may not be able to do an effective job if they have drug-use problems. Public transportation passengers may also have a legitimate interest in whether or not those who build and operate the bus, train, or plane function well and safely. Airline passengers may have an interest in having other passengers and their bags scanned to prevent dangerous materials from being carried on board. Drug screening in professional athletics might be justified with reference to the interests of several different parties. In some cases, it may be in the legitimate economic interests of the owners; in collegiate athletics and nonprofessional competitions such as the Olympics it might be justified by the fans' interests in fair competition as well as by an interest in the health of the athletes themselves. But in all of these cases, we also need to consider the privacy interests of the parties being screened.

In cases of conflicting interests generally, as in the more specific examples given here, we want to know on which side the interest is stronger. In the case of drug testing of airline pilots, the safety of the passengers seems clearly to outweigh the legitimate interest that pilots might have in retaining their privacy. In many other cases of employee drug screening, it is not so clear that employers' economic interests outweigh the employees' privacy interests. In these cases, one might well argue that unless there is observable evidence of inefficiency, drug testing should not be done, especially mandatory random drug testing. In the case of genetic screening by life or health insurance providers, the answer also seems less clear. If a person has a genetic defect that will cause a disease that will affect his life expectancy, is his interest in keeping this information secret more important than the financial interests of the insurer knowing that information? A person's ability to obtain life insurance will affect payments to others on his or her death. In the case of health insurance coverage, where it is not socially mandated or funded, the stronger interest might seem to lie with the person to be insured rather than the insurer—in part because being able to afford health care or not plays such a major role in a person's health and well being. In fact, some state legislatures have moved to prevent health insurers from penalizing individuals who are "genetically predisposed to certain diseases."[73] In arguing for these laws, supporters sometimes frame them as a matter of preventing "genetic discrimination." The phrase is apt in the sense that it seeks to prevent people from being singled out and penalized for things that are not in their power to control—their genes. On a national level, the "Genetic Information Nondiscrimination Act…makes it illegal for insurers and employers to discriminate against people with genetic markers for diseases like cancer, Alzheimer's disease, and diabetes." This act took full effect on November 21, 2009.[74]

With genetic screening, as with many other controversial issues, ethical analysis of conflicting interests can be consequentialist, deontological, or some mixture of the two. On consequentialist grounds, we might ask whether mandatory screening in a particular situation would really produce more harm than good, or more good than harm, overall. We might weigh the harm done to individuals through intrusions into their privacy against the benefits to the public or employers. On deontological grounds, we might compare the rights of individuals to be "free from certain intrusions" with their duties as employees, soldiers, or citizens. Or we might factor in both consequentialist and deontological concerns as we try to determine whose interest is stronger or more important morally.

Genetically Modified Organisms

In general, the ethical debate over genetically modified food and crops has involved a consequentialist analysis of costs and benefits. Cost–benefit analysis first involves estimating risks and potential benefits—an empirical matter—and then a comparative evaluation in which one tries to analyze and weigh the various values involved. Longer and healthier lives for more people clearly belong on the positive side, and risks to longevity and health belong on the negative side, but we must also try to determine the relative value of life, health, wellbeing, and so on. There is also the problem of how to count speculative and unknown risks. If we are risk-averse and come down on the side of conservatism, then we may avoid unknown risks but also eliminate possible benefits, including saving lives.

Such problems are particularly vexing when it comes to GMOs, which appear to have striking potential benefits—such as increased crop yields in the developing world—as well as some potential risks—such as increased resistance to herbicides or antibiotics. As we saw previously, benefits to genetically modifying animals can include the production of "pharmaceutical" milk from cows, sheep, and goats that can provide more effective treatments for cystic fibrosis and hemophilia.[75] And through *xenotransplantation*, animal organs (such as those from pigs as described previously) may be modified with human genes and given to humans with reduced risk of immune rejection. In other cases, GMOs may promote economic efficiency, as animals are modified to produce more meat or meat with less fat or to have better resistance to disease. Still, GMOs may also pose risks. For example, some critics worry that farm-raised and genetically altered salmon, if released into the wild, might harm other species of fish.[76] Weighing potential benefits and risks of GMOs will likely be an ongoing process in the decades to come—one that may reach different conclusions about different techniques of modifying organisms along the way.

A different ethical debate over GMOs involves the idea that humans should not modify or interfere with the fundamental design of nature. Shouldn't the world of plant and animal species as we find them inspire our respect and awe and place some limits on our efforts to manipulate or change them? One problem with this line of criticism is that it is difficult to distinguish good forms of manipulating nature from unacceptable ones. Some critics of GMOs argue that we ought to leave species as we find them, and that it is the cross-species transfers of genetic material involved in some GMOs that make them unacceptable. One problem with this objection is that similar transfers have occurred in nature—from basic plant genetics to the long-term patterns of evolution.

In addition, the "yuck" objection introduced earlier is sometimes also raised in this context. For example, just the thought of having a pig heart or lung within one's own body might provoke this reaction in some people. As with similar objections to human cloning, however, we must question whether such reactions are, by virtue of their intuitive force alone, legitimate moral insights. Even more important, in the case of genetically modified animals, is the question of their ethical or humane treatment and potential violations of their dignity or rights. This may involve not only the engineering of such animals but also their suffering and death as in the case of pigs whose organs would be transplanted or mice who would be given a human cancer. Animal welfare and rights arguments (as discussed in Chapter 17) should be considered with regard to such cases.

As we have seen in this chapter, biotechnology and bioengineering raise a host of ethical issues—something that should probably come as no surprise. With every new scientific advance and development come new ethical problems, for new questions arise about what we ought and ought not to do. To judge well with regard to these issues, we need to understand the facts, including facts about possible benefits and adverse consequences. We also need to clarify our values about issues such as autonomy, liberty, and privacy. And we need to consider whether there is anything wrong with "playing God" and using technology to alter natural beings, including ourselves.

The readings for this chapter begin with "The Transhumanist Declaration," which is a manifesto drafted by a number of authors including Nick Bostrom, a futuristically oriented bioethicist and director of the Future of Humanity Institute at Oxford University. The next reading by the bioethicist Leon Kass reflects on the question of new technologies. Kass is a prominent geneticist and physician who once served as the chairman of the President's Council on Bioethics under President George W. Bush. Kass is deeply concerned about the way that technologies are impacting our understanding of human nature and human values; he argues for greater humility with respect to our "given" biological life and respect for our intuitive repugnance at altering it. In response to Kass, the chapter concludes with a short excerpt from an article by Nick Bostrom, which defends the idea of "transhumanism" and advocates using technology to improve human nature.

NOTES

1. "A Paralyzed Woman Flew an F-35 Fighter Jet in a Simulator—Using only Her Mind," *Washington Post*, March 3, 2015, https://www.washingtonpost.com/news/speaking-of-science/wp/2015/03/03/a-paralyzed-woman-flew-a-f-35-fighter-jet-in-a-simulator-using-only-her-mind/ (accessed April 1, 2016).
2. "'We Did It!' Brain-Controlled 'Iron Man' Suit Kicks Off World Cup," *NBC News*, June 12, 2014, http://www.nbcnews.com/storyline/world-cup/we-did-it-brain-controlled-iron-man-suit-kicks-world-n129941 (accessed April 1, 2016).

3. Judy Lin, "Farsighted Engineer Invents Bionic Eye to Help the Blind," *UCLA Today*, March 21, 2013, accessed April 11, 2013, http://today.ucla.edu/portal/ut/wentai-liu-artificial-retina-244393.aspx; "This Bionic Eye Could Help the Blind See—From the Back of Their Head," *Fortune*, January 6, 2016, http://fortune.com/2016/01/06/bionic-eye-monash/ (accessed April 1, 2016).

4. "Why Brain-to-Brain Communication Is No Longer Unthinkable," *Smithsonian*, May 2015, http://www.smithsonianmag.com/innovation/why-brain-brain-communication-no-longer-unthinkable-180954948/?no-ist (accessed April 4, 2016).

5. James Gorman, "In a First, Experiment Links Brains of Two Rats," *New York Times*, February 28, 2013, accessed April 11, 2013, http://www.nytimes.com/2013/03/01/science/new-research-suggests-two-rat-brains-can-be-linked.html?_r=0

6. "Man Wriggles Rat's Tail Using Only His Thoughts," *Discovery News*, April 9, 2013, accessed April 11, 2013, http://news.discovery.com/tech/biotechnology/man-wriggles-rats-tail-using-thoughts-130409.htm

7. "US Panel Deems 'Three Parent Babies' Ethical to Test," *Smithsonian*, February 8, 2016, http://www.smithsonianmag.com/smart-news/us-panel-deems-three-parent-babies-ethical-test-180958057/?no-ist (accessed April 7, 2016).

8. Rose Eveleth, "Should Oscar Pistorius's Prosthetic Legs Disqualify Him from the Olympics?" *Scientific American*, July 24, 2012, accessed April 22, 2013, http://www.scientificamerican.com/article.cfm?id=scientists-debate-oscar-pistorius-prosthetic-legs-disqualify-him-olympics

9. Alan Schwarz, "Drowned in a Stream of Prescriptions," *New York Times*, February 2, 2013, accessed April 22, 2103, http://www.nytimes.com/2013/02/03/us/concerns-about-adhd-practices-and-amphetamine-addiction.html

10. Will Oremus, "The New Stimulus Package," *Slate*, March 27, 2013, accessed April 22, 2013, http://www.slate.com/articles/technology/superman/2013/03/adderall_ritalin_vyvanse_do_smart_pills_work_if_you_don_t_have_adhd.2.html

11. Will Oremus, "Spark of Genius," *Slate*, April 1, 2013, accessed April 22, 2013, http://www.slate.com/articles/technology/superman/2013/04/tdcs_and_rtms_is_brain_stimulation_safe_and_effective.html

12. *Scientific American*, July 2005, A6–A27.

13. Henry Fountain, "A First: Organs Tailor-Made with Body's Own Cells," *New York Times*, September 15, 2012, accessed April 11, 2013, http://www.nytimes.com/2012/09/16/health/research/scientists-make-progress-in-tailor-made-organs.html?_r=1&pagewanted=all

14. Henry Fountain, "Groundbreaking Surgery for Girl Born without Windpipe," *New York Times*, April 30, 2013, accessed May 8, 2013, http://www.nytimes.com/2013/04/30/science/groundbreaking-surgery-for-girl-born-without-windpipe.html?pagewanted=all&_r=0

15. "Young Girl Given Bioengineered Windpipe Dies" *New York Times*, July 7, 2013, accessed July 25, 2013, http://www.nytimes.com/2013/07/08/science/young-girl-given-bioengineered-windpipe-dies.html

16. "Researchers grow Kidney, Intestine from Stem Cells," *NBC News,* October 8, 2015, http://www.nbcnews.com/health/health-news/researchers-grow-kidney-intestine-stem-cells-n441066 (accessed April 4, 2016).

17. Carl T. Hall, "Stem Cell Research Opens New Doors," *San Francisco Chronicle*, April 16, 2007, A1, A9.

18. "Stem Cell Information," National Institutes of Health, accessed June 16, 2013, http://stemcells.nih.gov/info/pages/faqs.aspx#besttype

19. "Scientists Make First Embryo Clones from Adults," *Wall Street Journal*, April 17, 2014, http://www.wsj.com/articles/SB10001424052702303626804579507593658361428 (accessed April 4, 2016).

20. Jason Thompson, "Here, Kitty, Kitty, Kitty, Kitty, Kitty!" *San Francisco Chronicle*, February 24, 2002, D6.

21. *New York Times*, October 8, 2004, A24.

22. Peter Fimrite, "Pet-Cloning Business Closes—Not 'Commercially Viable,'" *San Francisco Chronicle*, October 11, 2006, B9.

23. James Barron, "Biotech Company to Auction Chances to Clone a Dog," *New York Times*, May 21, 2008, A17.

24. "Fast Facts about Animal Cloning," End Animal Cloning.org, accessed April 22, 2013, http://www.endanimalcloning.org/factsaboutanimalcloning.shtml

25. Nick Collins, "Human Cloning 'within 50 Years,'" *Telegraph*, December 18, 2012, accessed April 22, 2013, http://www.telegraph.co.uk/science/science-news/9753647/Human-cloning-within-50-years.html.

26. "Close-up of Richard Jenne, the Last Child Killed by the Head Nurse at the Kaufbeuren-Irsee Euthanasia Facility," United States Holocaust Memorial Museum, accessed June 16, 2013, http://tinyurl.com/ke3kj6e

27. Discussed in Michael J. Sandel, *The Case Against Perfection: Ethics in the Age of Genetic Engineering* (Cambridge, MA: Harvard University Press, 2009), Chapter 1.

28. "Couple 'Choose' to Have Deaf Baby," *BBC*, April 8, 2002, accessed April 22, 2013, http://news.bbc.co.uk/2/hi/health/1916462.stm. Also see Darshak M. Sanghavi, "Wanting Babies Like Themselves, Some Parents Choose Genetic Defects," *New York Times*, December 5, 2006, accessed June 15, 2013, http://www.nytimes.com/2006/12/05/health/05essa.html?_r=0

29. Tom Abate, "Genome Discovery Shocks Scientists," *San Francisco Chronicle*, February 11, 2001, A1.

30. *New York Times*, October 21, 2004, A23.

31. "In the Genome Race, the Sequel Is Personal," *New York Times*, September 4, 2007, accessed July 25, 2013, http://www.nytimes.com/2007/09/04/science/04vent.html?pagewanted=all&_r=0

32. Wetterstrand K.A. "DNA Sequencing Costs: Data from the NHGRI Genome Sequencing Program (GSP)," accessed July 25, 2013, www.genome.gov/sequencingcosts

33. Tom Abate, "Proofreading the Human Genome," *San Francisco Chronicle*, October 7, 2002, E1; Nicholas Wade, "Gene-Mappers Take New Aim at Diseases," *New York Times*, October, 30, 2002, A21.

34. Wade, "Gene-Mappers."

35. "Decoding the Mouse," *San Francisco Chronicle*, February 24, 2002, G2.

36. Nicholas Wade, "On Road to Human Genome, a Milestone in the Fruit Fly," *New York Times*, March 24, 2000, A19.

37. Nicholas D. Kristof, "Building Better Bodies," *New York Times*, August 25, 2004, accessed April 22, 2013, http://www.nytimes.com/2004/08/25/opinion/building-better-bodies.html

38. "WADA-Funded Researchers Achieve Gene Doping Breakthroughs," World Anti-Doping Agency, accessed April 22, 2013, http://www.wada-ama.org/en/Media-Center/Archives/Articles/WADA-Funded-Researchers-Achieve-Gene-Doping-Breakthroughs/

39. "Genetic Privacy," *Nature*, January 17, 2013, accessed April 22, 2013, http://www.nature.com/news/genetic-privacy-1.12238

40. "Panel Sees No Unique Risk From Genetic Engineering," *New York Times*, July 28, 2004, A13.

41. "Facing Biotech Foods Without the Fear Factor," *New York Times*, January 11, 2005, D7.

42. "Panel Sees No Unique Risk From Genetic Engineering," *New York Times*, July 28, 2004, A13.

43. "Facing Biotech Foods Without the Fear Factor," *New York Times*, January 11, 2005, D7.

44. International Service for the Acquisition of Agri-Biotech Applications, "Global Status of Commercialized Biotech/GM Crops: 2014," accessed April 7, 2016, http://www.isaaa.org/resources/publications/pocketk/16/

45. "GMOs and Your Family," Non-GMO Project, accessed April 7, 2016, http://www.nongmoproject.org/learn-more/gmos-and-your-family/

46. Stephanie Strom, "Major Grocer to Label Foods with Gene-Modified Content," *New York Times*, March 8, 2013, accessed April 22, 2013, http://www.nytimes.com/2013/03/09/business/grocery-chain-to-require-labels-for-genetically-modified-food.html?pagewanted=all&_r=0

47. Tom Philpott, "How GMOs Unleashed a Pesticide Gusher," *Mother Jones*, October 3, 2012, accessed April 22, 2013, http://www.motherjones.com/tom-philpott/2012/10/how-gmos-ramped-us-pesticide-use

48. See "Genetically Modified Foods: Harmful or Helpful," *ProQuest*, http://www.csa.com/discoveryguides/gmfood/overview.php

49. *New York Times*, January 1, 2005, D7.

50. Ibid.

51. "Genetically Engineered Foods May Cause Rising Food Allergies—Genetically Engineered Soybeans," Institute for Responsible Technology, accessed April 22, 2013, http://www.responsibletechnology.org/gmo-dangers/health-risks/articles-about-risks-by-

jeffrey-smith/Genetically-Engineered-Foods-May-Cause-Rising-Food-Allergies-Genetically-Engineered-Soybeans-May-2007

52. Sean Poulter, "Can GM Food Cause Immunity to Antibiotics?," *Daily Mail*, accessed June 25, 2013, http://www.dailymail.co.uk/health/article-128312/Can-GM-food-cause-immunity-antibiotics.html

53. "Text: Bush Announces Position on Stem Cell Research," accessed June 28, 2013, http://www.washingtonpost.com/wp-srv/onpolitics/transcripts/bushtext_080901.htm

54. Meredith Wadman, "High Court Ensures Continued US Funding of Human Embryonic-Stem-Cell Research," *Nature*, January 7, 2013, accessed April 20, 2013, http://www.nature.com/news/high-court-ensures-continued-us-funding-of-human-embryonic-stem-cell-research-1.12171

55. "Adult Stem Cells: A Piece of My Heart, From Cells in My Arm," *ABCNews*, January 28, 2013, accessed July 25, 2013, http://abcnews.go.com/Health/stem-cells-bill-weir-nightline-sees-cells-turned/story?id=18252405

56. "Nobel Prize in Physiology or Medicine," Nobelprize.org, press release, October 8, 2012, accessed April 20, 2013, http://www.nobelprize.org/nobel_prizes/medicine/laureates/2012/press.html

57. "New Protocol to Ready Clinical Applications of Induced Pluripotent Stem Cells," *Science Daily*, April 3, 2013, accessed April 20, 2013, http://www.sciencedaily.com/releases/2013/04/130403092655.htm

58. "Final Report of The National Academies' Human Embryonic Stem Cell Research Advisory Committee and 2010 Amendments to The National Academies' Guidelines for Human Embryonic Stem Cell Research" (2010), Appendix C, p. 23, National Academies Press, accessed April 20, 2013, http://www.nap.edu/openbook.php?record_id=12923&page=23#p2001b5399970023001

59. "Group of Scientists Drafts Rules on Ethics for Stem Cell Research," *New York Times*, April 27, 2005, accessed July 25, 2013, http://www.nytimes.com/2005/04/27/health/27stem.html?pagewanted=print&position=

60. George Q. Daley et al., "The ISSCR Guidelines for Human Embryonic Stem Cell Research," *Science*, February 2, 2007, 603–04.

61. "Copied Cat Hardly Resembles Original," *CNN.com*, January 21, 2003.

62. The Commissions website is found here: http://www.bioethics.gov/

63. Bioethics Defense Fund, *Human Cloning Laws: 50 State Survey*, 2011, accessed April 22, 2013, http://bdfund.org/wordpress/wp-content/uploads/2012/07/CLONINGChart-BDF2011.docx.pdf

64. See Barbara MacKinnon, "How Important Is Consent for Controlled Clinical Trials?," *Cambridge Quarterly of Healthcare Ethics* 5, no. 2 (Spring 1996): 221–27.

65. Reported in *New York Times*, May 21, 1996.

66. *New York Times*, November 22, 1994, A1.

67. This is modeled after a "thought experiment" by Richard Wasserstrom in "Privacy," *Today's Moral Problems*, 2nd ed. (New York: Macmillan, 1979), 392–408.

68. Thomas Scanlon, "Thomson on Privacy," in *Philosophy and Public Affairs* 4, no. 4 (Summer 1975): 295–333. This volume also contains other essays on privacy, including one by Judith Jarvis Thomson on which this article comments. W. A. Parent offers another definition of privacy as "the condition of not having undocumented personal knowledge about one possessed by others." W. A. Parent, "Privacy, Morality, and the Law," *Philosophy and Public Affairs* 12, no. 4 (Fall 1983): 269–88.

69. Erving Goffman, *Asylums* (Garden City, NY: Anchor Books, 1961).

70. Charles Fried, *An Anatomy of Values: Problems of Personal and Social Choice* (Cambridge, MA: Harvard University Press, 1970), 142.

71. "Questions of Privacy Roil Arena of Psychotherapy," *New York Times*, May 22, 1996, A1.

72. "Who's Looking at Your Files?," *Time* (May 6, 1996): 60–62.

73. "Bill in New Jersey Would Limit Use of Genetic Tests by Insurers," *New York Times*, June 18, 1996, A1.

74. Tracey Neithercott, "A Victory for Your Genes," *Diabetes Forecast*, August 2008, 35.

75. Tom Abate, "Biotech Firms Transforming Animals into Drug-Producing Machines," *San Francisco Chronicle*, January 17, 2000, B1.

76. See www.greennature.com

READING

Transhumanist Declaration

VARIOUS AUTHORS

MindTap° For more chapter resources and activities, go to MindTap.

Study Questions

1. What sorts of problems does this declaration imagine being solved through science and technology?
2. Is this manifesto hopeful or fearful about the use of technology in the future?
3. How does this manifesto appeal to ideas about autonomy, individual rights, and freedom of choice?

Humanity stands to be profoundly affected by science and technology in the future. We envision the possibility of broadening human potential by overcoming aging, cognitive shortcomings, involuntary suffering, and our confinement to planet Earth.

We believe that humanity's potential is still mostly unrealized. There are possible scenarios that lead to wonderful and exceedingly worthwhile enhanced human conditions.

We recognize that humanity faces serious risks, especially from the misuse of new technologies. There are possible realistic scenarios that lead to the loss of most, or even all, of what we hold valuable. Some of these scenarios are drastic, others are subtle. Although all progress is change, not all change is progress.

Research effort needs to be invested into understanding these prospects. We need to carefully deliberate how best to reduce risks and expedite beneficial applications. We also need forums where people can constructively discuss what should be done, and a social order where responsible decisions can be implemented.

Reduction of existential risks, and development of means for the preservation of life and health, the alleviation of grave suffering, and the improvement of human foresight and wisdom should be pursued as urgent priorities, and heavily funded.

Policy making ought to be guided by responsible and inclusive moral vision, taking seriously both opportunities and risks, respecting autonomy and individual rights, and showing solidarity with and concern for the interests and dignity of all people around the globe. We must also consider our moral responsibilities towards generations that will exist in the future.

We advocate the well-being of all sentience, including humans, non-human animals, and any future artificial intellects, modified life forms, or other intelligences to which technological and scientific advance may give rise.

We favour allowing individuals wide personal choice over how they enable their lives. This includes use of techniques that may be developed to assist memory, concentration, and mental energy; life extension therapies; reproductive choice technologies; cryonics procedures; and many other possible human modification and enhancement technologies.

---

http://humanityplus.org/philosophy/transhumanist-declaration/

READING

Ageless Bodies, Happy Souls

LEON R. KASS

MindTap® For more chapter resources and activities, go to MindTap.

Study Questions

1. How does Kass call into question the distinction between therapy and enhancement?
2. What sorts of things stimulate "repugnance" in Kass's account? Is Kass right to identify a sort of wisdom in this sort of repugnance?
3. Why does Kass celebrate humility and modesty in the face of the "givenness" of life and acceptance of our aging bodies?

Let me begin by offering a toast to biomedical science and biotechnology: May they live and be well. And may our children and grandchildren continue to reap their ever tastier fruit—but without succumbing to their seductive promises of a perfect, better-than-human future, in which we shall all be as gods, ageless and blissful.

As nearly everyone appreciates, we live near the beginning of the golden age of biotechnology. For the most part, we should be very glad that we do. We are many times over the beneficiaries of its cures for diseases, prolongation of life, and amelioration of suffering, psychic as well as somatic. We should be deeply grateful for the gifts of human ingenuity and cleverness, and for the devoted efforts of scientists, physicians, and entrepreneurs who have used these gifts to make those benefits possible. And, mindful that modern biology is just entering puberty, we suspect that the finest fruit is yet to come.

Yet, notwithstanding these blessings, present and projected, we have also seen more than enough to make us anxious and concerned. For we recognize that the powers made possible by biomedical science can be used for non-therapeutic or ignoble purposes, serving ends that range from the frivolous and disquieting to the offensive and pernicious. These powers are available as instruments of bioterrorism (e.g., genetically engineered drug-resistant bacteria or drugs that obliterate memory); as agents of social control (e.g., drugs to tame rowdies or fertility blockers for welfare recipients); and as means of trying to improve or perfect our bodies and minds and those of our children (e.g., genetically engineered super-muscles or drugs to improve memory). Anticipating possible threats to our security, freedom, and even our very humanity, many people are increasingly worried about where biotechnology may be taking us. We are concerned about what others might do to us, but also about what we might do to ourselves. We are concerned that our society might be harmed and that we ourselves might be diminished, indeed, in ways that could undermine the highest and richest possibilities of human life.

The last and most seductive of these disquieting prospects—the use of biotechnical powers to pursue "perfection," both of body and of mind—is perhaps the most neglected topic in public and professional bioethics. Yet it is, I believe, the deepest source of public anxiety about biotechnology, represented in the concern about "man playing God," or about the Brave New World, or a "post-human future." It raises the weightiest questions of bioethics, touching on the ends and goals of the biomedical enterprise, the nature and meaning of human flourishing, and the intrinsic threat of dehumanization (or the

Leon Kass, "Ageless Bodies, Happy Souls" *The New Atlantis* 1 (Spring 2003). Reprinted by permission.

promise of super-humanization). It compels attention to what it means to be a human being and to be active as a human being. And it gets us beyond our often singular focus on the "life issues" of abortion or embryo destruction, important though they are, to deal with what is genuinely novel and worrisome in the biotechnical revolution: not the old crude power to kill the creature made in God's image, but the new science-based power to remake him after our own fantasies.

This is, to be sure, a very difficult topic and one not obviously relevant to current public policy debate. Compared with other contemporary issues in bioethics, the questions connected with biotechnological "enhancement" seem abstract, remote, and too philosophical, unfit for political or other action. The concerns it raises are also complicated and inchoate, hard to formulate in general terms, especially because the differing technologically based powers raise different ethical and social questions. Finally, bothering oneself about this semi-futuristic prospect seems even to me precious and a touch self-indulgent, given that we live in a world in which millions are dying annually of malaria, AIDS, and malnutrition for want (in part) of more essential biotechnologies, and when many of our fellow Americans lack basic healthcare. Yet this push toward bio-engineered perfection strikes me as the wave of the future, one that will sneak up on us before we know it and, if we are not careful, sweep us up and tow us under. For we can already see how the recent gains in health and longevity have produced not contentment but rather an increased appetite for more. And, from recent trends in the medicalization of psychiatry and the study of the mind, it seems clear that the expected new discoveries about the workings of the psyche and the biological basis of behavior will greatly increase the ability and the temptation to alter and improve them. Decisions we today are making—for instance, what to do about human cloning or sex selection and genetic selection of embryos, or whether to get comfortable prescribing psychotropic drugs to three-year-olds, or how vigorously to pursue research into the biology of senescence—will shape the world of the future

for people who will inherit, not choose, life under its utopia-seeking possibilities. It is up to us now to begin thinking about these matters....

THE PROBLEM OF TERMINOLOGY

...Among the few people who have tried to address our topic, most have approached it through a distinction between "therapy" and "enhancement": "therapy," the treatment of individuals with known diseases or disabilities; "enhancement," the directed uses of biotechnical power to alter, by direct intervention, not diseased processes but the "normal" workings of the human body and psyche (whether by drugs, genetic engineering, or mechanical/computer implants into the body and brain). Those who introduced this distinction hoped by this means to distinguish between the acceptable and the dubious or unacceptable uses of biomedical technology: therapy is always ethically fine, enhancement is, at least prima facie, ethically suspect. Gene therapy for cystic fibrosis or Prozac for psychotic depression is fine; insertion of genes to enhance intelligence or steroids for Olympic athletes is not. Health providers and insurance companies, by the way, have for now bought into the distinction, paying for treatment of disease, but not for enhancements.

But this distinction, though a useful shorthand for calling attention to the problem, is inadequate to the moral analysis. Enhancement is, even as a term, highly problematic. Does it mean "more" or "better," and, if "better," by what standards? Can both improved memory and selective erasure of memory both be "enhancements"? If "enhancement" is defined in opposition to "therapy," one faces further difficulties with the definitions of "healthy" and "impaired," "normal" and "abnormal" (and hence, "super-normal"), especially in the area of "behavioral" or "psychic" functions and activities. "Mental health" is not easily distinguished from "psychic well-being" or, for that matter, from contentment or happiness. And psychiatric diagnoses—"dysthymia," hyperactivity, "oppositional disorder," and other forthcoming labels that would make Orwell wince and Soviet psychiatry proud—are notoriously vague. Furthermore, in the many human qualities (like height or IQ) that distribute themselves "normally," does the average also function as a norm, or is the norm itself appropriately subject to alteration? Is it therapy to give growth hormone to a genetic dwarf but not to a very short fellow who is just unhappy to be short? And if the short are brought up to the average, the average, now having become short, will have precedent for a claim to growth hormone injections. Needless arguments about whether or not something is or is not an "enhancement" get in the way of the proper question: What are the good and bad uses of biotechnical power? What makes a use "good," or even just "acceptable"? It does not follow from the fact that a drug is being taken solely to satisfy one's desires that its use is objectionable. Conversely, certain interventions to restore what might seem to be natural functioning wholeness—for example, to enable postmenopausal women to bear children or 60-year-old men to keep playing professional ice hockey—might well be dubious uses of biotechnical power. The human meaning and moral assessment are unlikely to be settled by the term "enhancement," any more than they are settled by the nature of the technological intervention itself.

This last observation points to the deepest reason why the distinction between healing and enhancing is of limited ethical or practical value. For the human whole whose healing is sought or accomplished by biomedical therapy is by nature finite and frail, medicine or no medicine. The healthy body declines and its parts wear out. The sound mind slows down and has trouble remembering things. The soul has aspirations beyond what even a healthy body can realize, and it becomes weary from frustration. Even at its fittest, the fatigable and limited human body rarely carries out flawlessly even the ordinary desires of the soul. Moreover, there is wide variation in the natural gifts with which each of us is endowed: some are born with perfect pitch, others are born tone-deaf; some have flypaper memories, others forget immediately what they have just learned. And as with talents, so too with desires and temperaments: some crave immortal fame, others merely comfortable preservation. Some are sanguine, others

phlegmatic, still others bilious or melancholic. When Nature deals her cards, some receive only from the bottom of the deck. Conversely, it is often the most gifted and ambitious who most resent their limitations: Achilles was willing to destroy everything around him, so little could he stomach that he was but a heel short of immortality.

As a result of these infirmities, human beings have long dreamed of overcoming limitations of body and soul, in particular the limitations of bodily decay, psychic distress, and the frustration of human aspiration. Dreams of human perfection—and the terrible consequences of pursuing it—are the themes of Greek tragedy, as well as (by the way) "The Birthmark," the Hawthorne short story with which the President's Council on Bioethics began its work. Until now these dreams have been pure fantasies, and those who pursued them came crashing down in disaster. But the stupendous successes over the past century in all areas of technology, and especially in medicine, have revived the ancient dreams of human perfection. Like Achilles, the major beneficiaries of modern medicine are less content than worried well, and we regard our remaining limitations with less equanimity, to the point that dreams of getting rid of them can be turned into moral imperatives. For these reasons, thanks to biomedical technology, people will be increasingly tempted to realize these dreams, at least to some extent: ageless and ever-vigorous bodies, happy (or at least not unhappy) souls, and excellent human achievement (with diminished effort or toil).

Why should anyone be worried about these prospects? What could be wrong with efforts to improve upon human nature, to try, with the help of biomedical technology, to gain ageless bodies and happy souls? A number of reasons have been offered, but looked at closely, they do not get to the heart of the matter.

THREE OBVIOUS OBJECTIONS

Not surprisingly, the objections usually raised to the uses of biomedical technologies that go "beyond therapy" reflect the dominant values of modern America: health, equality, and liberty.

In a health-obsessed culture, the first reason given to worry about any new biological intervention is safety, and that is certainly true here. Athletes who take steroids will later suffer premature heart disease. College students who take Ecstasy will damage dopamine receptors in their basal ganglia and suffer early Parkinson's disease. To generalize: no biological agent used for purposes of self-perfection will be entirely safe. This is good conservative medical sense: anything powerful enough to enhance system A is likely to be powerful enough to harm system B, the body being a highly complex yet integrated whole in which one intervenes partially only at one's peril. Yet many good things in life are filled with risks, and free people if properly informed may choose to run them, if they care enough about what is to be gained thereby. If the interventions are shown to be highly dangerous, many people will (later if not sooner) avoid them, and the FDA or tort liability will constrain many a legitimate purveyor. It surely makes sense, as an ethical matter, that one should not risk basic health trying to make oneself "better than well." On the other hand, if the interventions work well and are indeed highly desired, people may freely accept, in trade-off, even considerable risk of later bodily harm. Yet, in the end, the big issues have nothing to do with safety; as in the case of cloning children, the real questions concern what to think about the perfected powers, assuming that they may be safely used. And the ethical issue of avoiding risk and bodily harm is independent of whether the risky intervention aims at treating disease or at something beyond it.

A second obvious objection to the use of personal enhancers, especially by participants in competitive activities, is that they give those who use them an unfair advantage: blood doping or steroids in athletes, stimulants in students taking the SATs, and so on. Still, even if everyone had equal access to brain implants or genetic improvement of muscle strength or mind-enhancing drugs, a deeper disquiet would remain. Not all activities of life are competitive: it would matter to me if she says she loves me only because she is high on "erotogenin," a new brain-stimulant that mimics perfectly the feeling of falling in love. It matters to me when I go to a seminar that the people with whom I am conversing are not psychedelically out of their right minds.

The related question of distributive justice is less easily set aside than the unfairness question, especially if there are systematic disparities between who will and who will not have access to the powers of biotechnical "improvement." The case can be made yet more powerful to the extent that we regard the expenditure of money and energy on such niceties as a misallocation of limited resources in a world in which the basic health needs of millions go unaddressed. As a public policy matter, this is truly an important consideration. But, once again, the inequality of access does not remove our disquiet to the thing itself. And it is, to say the least, paradoxical in discussions of the dehumanizing dangers of, say, eugenic choice, when people complain that the poor will be denied equal access to the danger: "The food is contaminated, but why are my portions so small?" It is true that Aldous Huxley's Brave New World runs on a deplorable and impermeably rigid class system, but would you want to live in that world if offered the chance to enjoy it as an Alpha (the privileged caste)? Even an elite can be dehumanized, and even an elite class can dehumanize itself. The central matter is not equality of access, but the goodness or badness of the thing being offered.

A third objection, centered around issues of freedom and coercion, both overt and subtle, comes closer to the mark. This is especially the case with uses of biotechnical power exercised by some people upon other people, whether for social control—say, in the pacification of a classroom of Tom Sawyers—or for their own putative improvement—say, with genetic selection of the sex or sexual orientation of a child-to-be. This problem will of course be worse in tyrannical regimes. But there are always dangers of despotism within families, as parents already work their wills on their children with insufficient regard to a child's independence or real needs. Even partial control over genotype—say, to take a relatively innocent example, musician parents selecting a child with genes for perfect pitch—would add to existing social instruments of parental control and its risks of despotic rule. This is indeed one of the central arguments against human cloning: the charge of genetic despotism of one generation over the next.

There are also more subtle limitations of freedom, say, through peer pressure. What is permitted and widely used may become mandatory. If most children are receiving memory enhancement or stimulant drugs, failure to provide them for your child might be seen as a form of child neglect. If all the defensive linemen are on steroids, you risk mayhem if you go against them chemically pure. As with cosmetic surgery, Botox, and breast implants, the enhancement technologies of the future will likely be used in slavish adherence to certain socially defined and merely fashionable notions of "excellence" or improvement, very likely shallow, almost certainly conformist....

...But, once again, important though this surely is as a social and political issue, it does not settle the question for individuals. What if anything can we say to justify our disquiet over the individual uses of performance-enhancing genetic engineering or mood-brightening drugs? For even the safe, equally available, non-coerced and non-faddish uses of these technologies for "self-improvement" raise ethical questions, questions that are at the heart of the matter: the disquiet must have something to do with the essence of the activity itself, the use of technological means to intervene in the human *body* and mind not to ameliorate disease but to change and (arguably) improve their normal workings. Why, if at all, are we bothered by the voluntary self-administration of agents that would change our *bodies* or alter our minds? What is disquieting about our attempts to improve upon human nature, or even our own particular instance of it?

It is difficult to put this disquiet into words. We are in an area where initial repugnances are hard to translate into sound moral arguments. We are probably repelled by the idea of drugs that erase memories or that change personalities; or of interventions that enable 70-year-olds to bear children or play professional sports; or, to engage in some wilder imaginings, of mechanical implants that enable men to nurse infants or computer-body hookups that would enable us to download the Oxford English Dictionary. But is there wisdom in this repugnance? Taken one person at a time, with a properly prepared set of conditions and qualifications, it is going to be hard to say what is wrong with any biotechnical intervention that could give us (more) ageless bodies or happier souls. If there is a case to be made against these activities—for individuals—we sense that it may have something to do with what is natural, or what is humanly dignified, or with the attitude that is properly respectful of what is naturally and dignifiedly human....

THE ATTITUDE OF MASTERY

A common man-on-the-street reaction to these prospects is the complaint of "men playing God." An educated fellow who knows Greek tragedy complains rather of hubris. Sometimes the charge means the sheer prideful presumption of trying to alter what God has ordained or nature has produced, or what should, for whatever reason, not be fiddled with. Sometimes the charge means not so much usurping God-like powers, but doing so in the absence of God-like knowledge: the mere playing at being God, the hubris of acting with insufficient wisdom.

The case for respecting Mother Nature, and the critique of rushing in where angels fear to tread in order to transform her, has been forcefully made by environmentalists. They urge upon us a precautionary principle regarding our interventions into all of nature—usually, by the way, with the inexplicable exception of our own nature. Go slowly, they say, you can ruin everything. The point is certainly well taken. The human body and mind, highly complex and delicately balanced as a result of eons of gradual and exacting evolution, are almost certainly at risk from any ill-considered attempt at "improvement." There is not only the matter of unintended consequences already noted, but also the question about the unqualified goodness of our goals—a matter to which I shall return.

But for now, I would observe that this matter about the goodness of the goals is insufficiently appreciated by those who use the language of "mastery," or "mastery and control of nature," to describe what we do when we use knowledge of how nature works to alter its character and workings. Mastery of the means of intervention without knowing the goodness of the goals of intervening is not, in fact, mastery at all. In the absence of such knowledge of ends, the goals of the "master" will be set rather by whatever it is that happens to guide or move his will—some impulse or whim or feeling or desire—in short, by some residuum of nature still working within the so-called master or controller. To paraphrase C. S. Lewis, what looks like man's mastery of nature turns out, in the absence of guiding knowledge, to be nature's mastery of man. There can, in truth, be no such thing as the full escape from the grip of our own nature. To pretend otherwise is indeed a form of hubristic and dangerous self-delusion....

...Modesty born of gratitude for the world's "givenness" may enable us to recognize that not everything in the world is open to any use we may desire or devise, but it will not by itself teach us which things can be fiddled with and which should be left inviolate. The mere "giftedness" of things cannot tell us which gifts are to be accepted as is, which are to be improved through use or training, which are to be housebroken through self-command or medication, and which opposed like the plague.

The word "given" has two relevant meanings, the second of which Sandel's account omits: "given," meaning "bestowed as a gift," and "given" (as in mathematical proofs), something "granted," definitely fixed and specified. Most of the given bestowals of nature have their given species-specified natures: they are each and all of a given sort. Cockroaches and humans are equally bestowed but differently natured. To turn a man into a cockroach—as we don't need Kafka to show us—would be dehumanizing. To try to turn a man into more than a man might be so as well. We need more than generalized appreciation for nature's gifts. We need a particular regard and respect for the special gift that is our own given nature (and, by the way, also that of each of our fellow creatures).

In short, only if there is a human givenness, or a given humanness, that is also good and worth respecting, either as we find it or as it could be perfected without ceasing to be itself, does the "given" serve as a positive guide for choosing what to alter and what to leave alone. Only if there is something precious in the given—beyond the mere fact of its giftedness—does what is given serve as a source of restraint against efforts that would degrade it. When it comes to human biotechnical engineering, only if there is something inherently good or dignified about, say, natural procreation, human finitude, the human life cycle (with its rhythm of rise and fall), and human erotic longing and striving; only if there is something inherently good or dignified about the ways in which we engage the world as spectators and appreciators, as teachers and learners, leaders and followers, agents and makers, lovers and friends, parents and children, and as seekers of our own special excellence and flourishing in whatever arena to which we are called—only then can we begin to see why those aspects of our nature need to be defended. (It is for this reason why a richer bioethics will always begin by trying to clarify the human good and aspects of our given humanity that are rightly dear to us, and that biotechnology may serve or threaten.) We must move from the hubristic attitude of the powerful designer to consider how the proposed improvements might impinge upon the nature of the one being improved. With the question of human nature and human dignity in mind, we move to questions of means and ends.

"UNNATURAL" MEANS

...We believe—or until only yesterday believed—that people should work hard for their achievements. "Nothing good comes easily." Even if one prefers the grace of the natural athlete, whose performance deceptively appears to be effortless, we admire those who overcome obstacles and struggle to try to achieve the excellence of the former, who serves as the object of the latter's aspiration and effort and the standard for his success or failure. This matter of character—the merit of disciplined and dedicated striving—though not the deepest basis of our objection to biotechnological shortcuts, is surely pertinent. For character is not only the source of our deeds, but also their product. People whose disruptive behavior is "remedied" by pacifying drugs rather than by their own efforts are not learning self-control; if anything, they are learning to think it unnecessary. People who take pills to block out from memory the painful or hateful aspects of a new experience will not learn how to deal with suffering or sorrow. A drug to induce fearlessness does not produce courage.

Yet things are not so simple, partly because there are biotechnical interventions that may assist in the pursuit of excellence without cheapening its attainment, partly because many of life's excellences have nothing to do with competition or adversity. Drugs to decrease drowsiness or increase alertness, sharpen memory, or reduce distraction may actually help people interested in their natural pursuits of learning or painting or performing their civic duty. Drugs to steady the hand of a neurosurgeon or to prevent sweaty palms in a concert pianist cannot be regarded as "cheating," for they are not the source of the excellent activity or achievement. And, for people dealt a meager hand in the dispensing of nature's gifts, it should not be called cheating or cheap if biotechnology could assist them in becoming better equipped—whether in body or in mind. Even steroids for the proverbial 97-pound weakling help him to get to the point where, through his own effort and training, he can go head-to-head with the naturally better endowed.

Nevertheless, there is a sense that the "naturalness" of means matters. It lies not in the fact that the assisting drugs and devices are artifacts, but in the danger of violating or deforming the deep structure of natural human activity. In most of our ordinary efforts at self-improvement, either by practice or training or study, we sense the relation between our doings and the resulting improvement, between the means used and the end sought. There is an experiential and intelligible connection between means and ends; we can see how confronting fearful things might eventually enable us to cope with our fears. We can see how curbing our appetites produces self-command. Human education ordinarily proceeds by speech or symbolic deeds, whose meanings are at least in principle directly accessible to those upon whom they work. Even where the human being is largely patient to the formative action—say, in receiving praise and blame, or reward and punishment—both the "teacher" and the "student" can understand both the content of the means used and their relation to the conduct or activity that they are meant to improve. And the further efforts at self-improvement, spurred by praise and blame, will clearly be the student's own doing.

In contrast, biomedical interventions act directly on the human body and mind to bring about their effects on a subject who is not merely passive but who plays no role at all. He can at best feel their effects without understanding their meaning in human terms. (Yes, so do alcohol and caffeine and nicotine, though we use these agents not as pure chemicals but in forms and social contexts that, arguably, give them a meaning different from what they would have were we to take them as pills.) Thus a drug that brightened our mood would alter us without our understanding how and why it did so—whereas a mood brightened as a fitting response to the arrival of a loved one or an achievement in one's work is perfectly, because humanly, intelligible. And not only would this be true about our states of mind. All of our encounters with the world, both natural and interpersonal, would be mediated, filtered, and altered. Human experience under biological intervention becomes increasingly mediated by unintelligible forces and vehicles, separated from the human significance of the activities so altered. (By contrast, the intelligibility of a scientific account of the mechanism of action of the biological agent would not be the intelligibility of human experience.) The relations between the knowing subject and his activities, and between his activities and their fulfillments and pleasures, are disrupted. The importance of human effort in human achievement is here properly acknowledged: the point is less the exertions of good character against hardship, but the manifestation of an alert and self-experiencing agent making his deeds flow intentionally from his willing, knowing, and embodied soul. The lack of "authenticity" sometimes complained of in these discussions is not so much a matter of "playing false" or of not expressing one's "true self," as it is a departure from "genuine," unmediated, and (in principle) self-transparent human activity....

"Personal achievements" impersonally achieved are not truly the achievements of persons. That I can use a calculator to do my arithmetic does not make me a knower of arithmetic; if computer chips in my brain were to "download" a textbook of physics, would that make me a knower of physics? Admittedly, this is not always an obvious point to make: if I make myself more alert through Ritalin or coffee, or if drugs can make up for lack of sleep, I may be able to learn more using my unimpeded native powers in ways to which I can existentially attest that it is I who is doing the learning. Still, if human flourishing means not just the accumulation of external achievements and a full curriculum vitae but a lifelong being-at-work exercising one's human powers well and without great impediment, our genuine happiness requires that there be little gap, if any, between the dancer and the dance.

This is not merely to suggest that there is a disturbance of human agency or freedom, or a disruption of activities that will confound the assignment of personal responsibility or undermine the proper bestowal of praise and blame. To repeat: most of life's activities are non-competitive; most of the best of them—loving and working and savoring and learning—are self-fulfilling beyond the need for praise and blame or any other external reward. In these activities, there is at best no goal beyond the activity itself. It is the deep structure of unimpeded, for-itself, human being-at-work-in-the-world, in an unimpeded and whole-hearted way, that we are eager to preserve against dilution and distortion.

In a word, one major trouble with biotechnical (especially mental) "improvers" is that they produce changes in us by disrupting the normal character of human being-at-work-in-the-world, what Aristotle called energeia psyches, activity of soul, which when fine and full constitutes human flourishing. With biotechnical interventions that skip the realm of intelligible meaning, we cannot really own the transformations nor experience them as genuinely ours. And we will be at a loss to attest whether the resulting conditions and activities of our bodies and our minds are, in the fullest sense, our own as human. To the extent that we come to regard our transformed nature as normal, we shall have forgotten what we lost....

DUBIOUS ENDS

How are we to think about the goals themselves—ageless bodies and happy souls? Would their attainment in fact improve or perfect our lives as human beings? These are very big questions, too long to be properly treated here. But the following initial considerations seem to merit attention.

The case for ageless bodies seems at first glance to look pretty good. The prevention of decay, decline, and disability, the avoidance of blindness, deafness, and debility, the elimination of feebleness, frailty, and fatigue, all seem to be conducive to living fully as a human being at the top of one's powers—of having, as they say, a "good quality of life" from beginning to end. We have come to expect organ transplantation for our worn-out parts. We will surely welcome stem cell-based therapies for regenerative medicine, reversing by replacement the damaged tissues of Parkinson's disease, spinal cord injury, and many other degenerative disorders. It is hard to see any objection to obtaining a genetic enhancement of our muscles in our youth that would not only prevent the muscular feebleness of old age but would empower us to do any physical task with greater strength and facility throughout our lives. And, should aging research deliver on its promise of adding not only extra life to years but also extra years to life, who would refuse it? Even if you might consider turning down an ageless body for yourself, would you not want it for your beloved? Why should she not remain to you as she was back then when she first stole your heart? Why should her body suffer the ravages of time?

To say no to this offer seems perverse. But I want to suggest that it may not be—that there are in fact many human goods that are inseparable from our aging bodies, from our living in time, and from the natural human life cycle by which each generation gives way to the one that follows it. Because this argument is so counterintuitive, we need to begin not with the individual choice for an ageless body, but with what the individual's life might look like in a world in which everyone made the same choice. We need to make the choice universal, and see the meaning of that choice in the mirror of its becoming the norm.

What if everybody lived life to the hilt, even as they approached an ever-receding age of death in a body that looked and functioned—let's not be too greedy—like that of a 30-year-old? Would it be good if each and all of us lived like light bulbs, burning as brightly from beginning to end, then popping off without warning, leaving those around us suddenly in the dark? Or is it perhaps better that there be a shape to life, everything in its due season, the shape also written, as it were, into the wrinkles of our *bodies* that live it? What would the relations between the generations be like if there never came a point at which a son surpassed his father in strength or vigor? What incentive would there be for the old to make way for the young, if the old slowed down little and had no reason to think of retiring—if Michael could play until he were not forty but eighty? Might not even a moderate prolongation of life span with vigor lead to a prolongation in the young of functional immaturity—of the sort that has arguably already accompanied the great increase in average life expectancy experienced in the past century? One cannot think of enhancing the vitality of the old without retarding the maturation of the young.

I have tried in the past to make a rational case for the blessings of finitude. In an essay entitled "L'Chaim and Its Limits: Why Not Immortality?," I suggest that living with our finitude is the condition of many of the best things in human life:

engagement, seriousness, a taste for beauty, the possibility of virtue, the ties born of procreation, the quest for meaning. Though the arguments are made against the case for immortality, they have weight also against even more modest prolongations of the maximum lifespan, especially in good health, that would permit us to live as if there were always tomorrow. In what I take to be the two most important arguments of that essay, I argue that the pursuit of perfect bodies and further life-extension will deflect us from realizing more fully the aspirations to which our lives naturally point, from living well rather than merely staying alive. And I argue that a concern with one's own improving agelessness is finally incompatible with accepting the need for procreation and human renewal: a world of longevity is increasingly a world hostile to children. Moreover, far from bringing contentment, it is arguably a world increasingly dominated by anxiety over health and the fear of death. . . .

. . . Those who propose adding years to the human lifespan regard time abstractly, as physicists do, as a homogeneous and continuous dimension, each part exactly like any other, and the whole lacking shape or pattern. Yet, the "lived time" of our natural lives has a trajectory and a shape, its meaning derived in part from the fact that we live as links in the chain of generations. For this reason, our flourishing as individuals might depend, in large measure, on the goodness of the natural human life cycle, roughly three multiples of a generation: a time of coming of age; a time of flourishing, ruling, and replacing of self; and a time of savoring and understanding, but still sufficiently and intimately linked to one's descendants to care about their future and to take a guiding, supporting, and cheering role.

What about pharmacologically assisted happy souls? Painful and shameful memories are disquieting; guilty consciences disturb sleep; low self-esteem, melancholy, and world-weariness besmirch the waking hours. Why not memory blockers for the former, mood brighteners for the latter, and a good euphoriant—without risks of hangovers or cirrhosis—when celebratory occasions fail to be jolly? For let us be clear: if it is imbalances of neurotransmitters—a modern equivalent of the medieval doctrine of the four humors—that are responsible for our state of soul, it would be sheer priggishness to refuse the help of pharmacology for our happiness, when we accept it guiltlessly to correct for an absence of insulin or thyroid hormone.

And yet, there seems to be something misguided about the pursuit of utter psychic tranquility, or the attempt to eliminate all shame, guilt, and painful memories. Traumatic memories, shame, and guilt, are, it is true, psychic pains. In extreme doses, they can be crippling. Yet they are also helpful and fitting. They are appropriate responses to horror, disgraceful conduct, and sin, and, as such, help teach us to avoid them in the future. Witnessing a murder should be remembered as horrible; doing a beastly deed should trouble one's soul. Righteous indignation at injustice depends on being able to feel injustice's sting. An untroubled soul in a troubling world is a shrunken human being. More fundamentally, to deprive oneself of one's memory—including and especially its truthfulness of feeling—is to deprive oneself of one's own life and identity.

Second, these feeling states of soul, though perhaps accompaniments of human flourishing, are not its essence. Ersatz pleasure or feelings of self-esteem are not the real McCoy. They are at most shadows divorced from the underlying human activities that are the essence of flourishing. Not even the most doctrinaire hedonist wants to have the pleasure that comes from playing baseball without swinging the bat or catching the ball. No music lover would be satisfied with getting from a pill the pleasure of listening to Mozart without ever hearing the music. Most people want both to feel good and to feel good about themselves, but only as a result of being good and doing good.

Finally, there is a connection between the possibility of feeling deep unhappiness and the prospects for achieving genuine happiness. If one cannot grieve, one has not loved. To be capable of aspiration, one must know and feel lack. As Wallace Stevens put it: Not to have is the beginning of desire. There is, in short, a double-barreled error in the pursuit of ageless bodies and factitiously happy souls: human fulfillment depends on our being creatures of need and finitude and hence of longings and attachment.

I have tried to make a case for finitude and even graceful decline of bodily powers. And I have tried to make a case for genuine human happiness, with satisfaction as the bloom that graces unimpeded, soul-exercising activity. The first argument resonates with Homeric and Hebraic intuitions; the second resonates with the Greek philosophers. One suspects that they might even be connectable, that genuine human flourishing is rooted in aspirations born of the kinds of deficiencies that come from having limited and imperfect bodies. To pursue this possibility is work for another day.

A flourishing human life is not a life lived with an ageless body or untroubled soul, but rather a life lived in rhythmed time, mindful of time's limits, appreciative of each season and filled first of all with those intimate human relations that are ours only because we are born, age, replace ourselves, decline, and die—and know it. It is a life of aspiration, made possible by and born of experienced lack, of the disproportion between the transcendent longings of the soul and the limited capacities of our bodies and minds. It is a life that stretches towards some fulfillment to which our natural human soul has been oriented, and, unless we extirpate the source, will always be oriented. It is a life not of better genes and enhancing chemicals but of love and friendship, song and dance, speech and deed, working and learning, revering and worshipping. The pursuit of an ageless body is finally a distraction and a deformation. The pursuit of an untroubled and self-satisfied soul is deadly to desire. Finitude recognized spurs aspiration. Fine aspiration acted upon is itself the core of happiness. Not the agelessness of the body, nor the contentment of the soul, nor even the list of external achievement and accomplishments of life, but the engaged and energetic being-at-work of what Nature uniquely gave to us is what we need to treasure and defend. All other perfection is at best a passing illusion, at worst a Faustian bargain that will cost us our full and flourishing humanity.

READING

In Defense of Posthuman Dignity

NICK BOSTROM

MindTap° For more chapter resources and activities, go to MindTap.

Study Questions

1. How does Bostrom explain the transhumanist view of morphological freedom and reproductive freedom?
2. Explain why Bostrom says that "nature's gifts are sometimes poisoned" and how this relates to the goals of transhumanism.
3. To what extent is Bostrom right that we would appear as "posthuman" to our hunter-gatherer ancestors?

Transhumanism . . . can be viewed as an outgrowth of secular humanism and the Enlightenment. It holds that current human nature is improvable through the use of applied science and other rational methods, which may make it possible to increase human health-span, extend our intellectual and physical capacities, and give us increased control over our own mental states and moods. . . .

Transhumanists promote the view that human enhancement technologies should be made widely available, and that individuals should have broad discretion over which of these technologies to apply to themselves (morphological freedom), and that parents should normally get to decide which reproductive technologies to use when having children (reproductive freedom). Transhumanists believe that, while there are hazards that need to be identified and avoided, human enhancement technologies will offer enormous potential for deeply valuable and humanly beneficial uses. Ultimately, it is possible that such enhancements may make us, or our descendants, 'posthuman', beings who may have indefinite health-spans, much greater intellectual faculties than any current human being—and perhaps entirely new sensibilities or modalities—as well as the ability to control their own emotions. The wisest approach vis-à-vis these prospects, argue transhumanists, is to embrace technological progress, while strongly defending human rights and individual choice, and taking action specifically against concrete threats, such as military or terrorist abuse

of bioweapons, and against unwanted environmental or social side-effects. . . .

Nature's gifts are sometimes poisoned and should not always be accepted. Cancer, malaria, dementia, aging, starvation, unnecessary suffering, and cognitive shortcomings are all among the presents that we would wisely refuse. Our own species-specified natures are a rich source of much of the thoroughly unrespectable and unacceptable—susceptibility for disease, murder, rape, genocide, cheating, torture, racism. . . . Rather than deferring to the natural order, transhumanists maintain that we can legitimately reform ourselves and our natures in accordance with humane values and personal aspirations. . . .

If the alternative to parental choice in determining the basic capacities of new people is entrusting the child's welfare to nature, that is blind chance, then the decision should be easy. Had Mother Nature been a real parent, she would have been in jail for child abuse and murder. . . .

In the eyes of a hunter-gatherer, we might already appear 'posthuman'. Yet these radical extensions of human capabilities—some of them biological, others external—have not divested us of moral status or dehumanized us in the sense of making us generally unworthy and base. Similarly, should we or our descendants one day succeed in becoming what relative to current standards we

Nick Bostrom, "In Defense of Post-Human Dignity" *Bioethics* 19, no. 3 (2005).

may refer to as posthuman, this need not entail a loss dignity either.

From the transhumanist standpoint, there is no need to behave as if there were a deep moral difference between technological and other means of enhancing human lives. By defending post-human dignity we promote a more inclusive and humane ethics, one that will embrace future technologically modified people as well as humans of the contemporary kind.

REVIEW EXERCISES

1. What is the basic difference between a therapy and an enhancement?
2. How do bioengineering and biotechnology provide opportunities for disabled people? How might these techniques point toward a posthuman future?
3. How does your thinking about animal ethics, the ethics of abortion, and even sexual ethics connect with your thinking about the ethics of biotechnologies? What concepts overlap among these issues?
4. Summarize the arguments for and against cloning and other reproductive technologies based on the idea that it would be "playing God" and would undermine human dignity.
5. Summarize the idea that cloning might pose a threat to the clone's individuality.
6. Summarize the arguments regarding human cloning related to exploitation, confusion of families, and the "yuck" factor.
7. Summarize arguments for and against genetic screening and genetic engineering of offspring.
8. What ethical issues have been raised regarding the production and use of genetically modified plants and crops?
9. Discuss the value of privacy and how it relates to genetic and other types of screening.
10. Should we pursue a "posthuman" future or are there reasons to remain conservatively connected to more traditional ideas about human nature? Why or why not?

DISCUSSION CASES

1. **Human Cloning**. Victor and Jenny have one son, Alan, who was hit by a car at age four and then lapsed into a coma. The prognosis is bleak for Alan, but Jenny cannot bear to see him die and so they have kept him on life support. Victor has heard that scientists working at a secret lab have been successfully cloning human beings. Victor suggests that they contact the scientists to see if they can clone Alan—using Alan's DNA to grow a new baby, which would be a genetic copy of him. Jenny is appalled at this idea. "But it wouldn't be Alan. It would be a totally different person." But Victor suggests that the clone would be very similar. "The new baby would be created to honor Alan. Of course it wouldn't literally be *him*. But we could honor Alan's memory and keep Alan's unique genetic gifts alive by cloning him."

   What do you think? To what extent would a clone be the same person as the original? Would it be unethical to clone Alan? Why or why not?

2. **Smart Drugs**. Ramsey has obtained a "smart drug" from someone else in the dorms. He's heard that it may be possible to increase cognitive ability through the use of this drug and hopes it will help him on his upcoming finals. He knows it is illegal to use the drug in this way. But he does not believe that it would be unethical. "I think they ought to legalize marijuana too," he says to his roommate, Marc. "That's not the same, man," Marc replies. "Marijuana is just for fun. You're talking about using a drug to get an edge over other people on tests and in studying. That's just not fair. It's cheating." Ramsey rolls his eyes. "That's ridiculous. It's not really cheating," he says. "The drug won't make me smart. I still have to study. The drug will just make me more effective at studying. It's like coffee but stronger. Besides, the guy I got the drugs from has a prescription for them because he's got ADHD. If he gets to use the drugs to improve his performance, why can't I?"

   Who do you agree with here: Ramsey or Marc? Is it "cheating" to use a "smart drug"? Explain your answer using concepts discussed in the chapter.

3. **Designer Babies**. Steven and Marisol are a young married couple who are concerned about passing genetic diseases on to their children. Members of Steven's family have been diagnosed with Huntington's disease, an incurable genetic disorder that causes cognitive problems, difficulties with movement that ultimately require full-time nursing care, and reduced life expectancy. Members of Marisol's family have tested positive for a mutation of the BRCA genes that are strongly associated with breast and ovarian cancer. At a family reunion, they are discussing their decision to use in vitro fertilization and preimplantation genetic screening of embryos. Steven's cousin, Valerie, is appalled. She is opposed to the idea of in vitro fertilization and to the entire idea of genetic screening. Valerie says, "You can't just choose the babies you want to have. God will only give you the challenges that He knows you can handle. And if a child is born with a disease, your job is to love that child, no matter what." Steven is speechless. But Marisol is not. "But if we can guarantee that our child is healthy and will live a happy life, shouldn't we do that? We don't want to raise a child who is doomed to genetic diseases." Valerie shakes her head. "There is no way to know," she says. "Kids get sick and die. Some who have diseases get better. You can't control everything. And besides, that test-tube baby stuff is really expensive. How can you afford it?" Now Steven replies, "We want to invest in this procedure now because it might save money in the long run. I've seen how much Huntington's costs a family—so have you. I'd rather pay to prevent it now than have to deal with the costs later." Valerie responds, "That sounds really rude. It sounds like you resent people who get sick and need your help. The whole thing is very selfish."

   Whom do you agree with here: Steven and Marisol or Steven's cousin, Valerie? Is it wrong to want to prevent genetic disease? Is it a wise investment? Is it selfish to want to control your child's genes? Explain your answer.

MindTap® For more chapter resources and activities, go to MindTap.

19 Violence and War

Learning Outcomes

After reading this chapter, you should be able to:

- Describe issues arising in the context of the war on terrorism including the use of drones and targeted assassination, and the morality of terrorism and torture.

- Articulate arguments for pacifism.

- Articulate arguments for realism.

- Explain the distinction made in just war theory between *jus ad bellum* and *jus in bello*.

- Explain and apply key terms employed in the just war tradition, including *just cause*,

- *legitimate authority*, *discrimination*, and *noncombatant immunity*.

- Demonstrate how the doctrine of double effect applies within the just war theory to deal with the problem of collateral damage.

- Understand the history and concept of war crimes and crimes against humanity.

- Defend your own ideas about the ethics of war.

MindTap   For more chapter resources and activities, go to MindTap.

For most Americans, terrorism became an inescapable moral issue after September 11, 2001. On that day, Al Qaeda terrorists crashed loaded passenger jets into the World Trade Center in New York, the Pentagon in Washington, D.C., and a field near Shanksville, Pennsylvania, killing nearly three thousand people. The U.S. administration of President George W. Bush came to call its response to these attacks "the war on terrorism," a war that has grown and changed in a variety of ways. It began as the United States and its allies invaded Afghanistan in late 2001, in an unsuccessful effort to capture or kill the leadership of the Al Qaeda terrorist group, including Osama bin Laden. Afghanistan was viewed both as a failed state being ruled by an extremist religious faction—the Taliban—and as the haven from which Al Qaeda masterminded the September 11 attacks. Within two years, another front in the war on terrorism opened in Iraq, as the United States invaded the country in March 2003. Although Iraq had nothing to do with the September 11 terrorist attacks, President George W. Bush argued that the leader of Iraq, Saddam Hussein, was a malicious dictator who was a threat to stability in the region, that he had used chemical weapons against his own people, and—quite controversially—that he was currently stockpiling other weapons of mass destruction or WMDs. After the U.S.

invasion of Iraq, no such weapons were ever found, but the country did descend into a bloody and destructive civil war, which has continued to destabilize the region. The rise of the so-called "Islamic State in Iraq and Syria" (ISIS) can be traced back through the war on terror under the administration of President Barack Obama, battles in the war on terror were waged in other countries such as Libya, Yemen, and Pakistan, fought by drone aircraft and special operations forces, which target specific terrorists or terrorist groups.

Terrorism remains an issue of grave concern throughout the world. As of this writing, Syria remains embroiled in a brutal civil war, which has involved the use of chemical weapons. ISIS terrorists and sympathizers have publicly beheaded some victims, burned others alive, and have waged attacks in cities in Europe and North America. Recent and ongoing conflicts in Israel, Lebanon, Libya, Pakistan, Mali, and Egypt have been marked by high civilian death tolls, both as a result of terrorist attacks and the actions of conventional armies. More than a decade of war in the Middle East and North Africa has had a profound impact on the world. Estimates for civilians killed in the war on terrorism range from 150,000 up to over 1.3 million. Military deaths include nearly 10,000 American and coalition forces killed, tens of thousands of enemy fighters killed, and many more injured and disabled soldiers.[1] Instability remains across the region.

Terror attacks continue. In Paris, in November of 2015, ISIS sympathizers killed 130 people. In San Bernardino, California, in December 2015, 14 people were killed by ISIS sympathizers. Other ISIS inspired attacks have occurred in Brussels, Orlando, Nice, and elsewhere. While those attacks demonstrate ISIS's global reach, the primary victims of ISIS and other terrorist groups reside in North Africa and the Middle East, where members of minority religions have persecuted, women have been forced into marriages, and communities have been decimated by violence. We continue to worry about attacks on water supplies, transportation systems, computer systems, and fuel depots in Europe and North America. Attacks in Europe, the Middle East,

and Asia have targeted civilians in crowded markets, shopping malls, and buses. While Americans remain concerned about terrorism employed by foreigners, we should note that terrorism can be employed by homegrown domestic terrorists. One of the brothers involved in the Boston Marathon bombing was a naturalized American citizen; the perpetrator of the far deadlier Oklahoma City bombing, in 1994, was a native-born citizen. Terrorists do not need complicated or high-tech mechanisms to cause serious damage and widespread fear. And terrorists do not wear uniforms or announce their plans in advance.

Some claim that it is difficult to define terrorism, pointing out that one person's "freedom fighter" is another person's "terrorist." But terrorism is generally agreed to involve violent acts that deliberately intend to inflict harm on those who do not deserve to be harmed. We'll discuss this further later in this chapter. But note that according to that definition, school shootings—such as the one that occurred at Sandy Hook Elementary School in Newtown, Connecticut, in 2012 and at Virginia Tech University in 2007—can be described as terrorism. These acts may not have been politically motivated. But they certainly inflicted harm on the innocent. Most would agree that violence of this sort is wrong. And many would also agree that the police and the military are justified in using violent force to kill those who kill children. But are there moral limits on how much violence might be employed in such circumstances?

Most people assume that there is a right to use violence in self-defense. And many also think that we are *permitted* (some may say *required*) to use violence in defense of innocent children. The natural law tradition maintains that individuals have a right to life and liberty—and that violence can be employed to defend life and liberty against those who threaten it, including the life and liberty of defenseless and innocent others. A consequentialist argument could also be used here. More happiness will be produced for more people when such threats are eliminated. For a strict consequentialist, if the goal is to eliminate threats, the means employed are irrelevant. If war or other forms of violence work to produce good outcomes, then these can be used as a tool to defend social welfare.

In this chapter, we discuss three alternative approaches to the justification of violence. One maintains that violence is always wrong—this is **pacifism**. Another approach, often called **realism**, maintains that there are no *moral* limits on violence in warfare, even though there may be *pragmatic* or *strategic* reasons to limit violence. In the middle between these two extremes is an idea known as **just war theory**, which holds that violence can be justified when it is employed in limited and focused ways. The just war theory is grounded on a fundamental claim about the justification of violence in self-defense, and it extends this to a consideration of violence used in defense of others. While the just war theory is not directly applicable to the issue of domestic law enforcement, there are clear parallels between the idea that war can be justified and the idea that violence can be employed by armed guards

to defend people against domestic criminals and terrorists. If we have a right to use violence to defend ourselves against those who would do violence to us, then we can also delegate defense to others—the police or the army. Furthermore, we might claim that while we are entitled to defend ourselves against violence, we are also entitled (or even obliged) to defend innocent and defenseless others from those who would do them harm. Realists will claim that in such circumstances, anything goes. We are entitled to pursue our own interests and defense in whatever way works. Pacifists have a difficult choice to make about the right to use violence in self-defense. But they tend to maintain that nonviolent alternatives should be developed and employed in a sustained and deliberate fashion.

Central to the discussion of the justification of violence is the question of what violence is. Violence is generally thought of as the use of physical force to cause injury to another. Physical assaults, shooting, and bombing are examples. However, we

Violence and war continue to afflict us, while raising complicated moral questions.

Eric J. Tilford/ZUMAPRESS/Newscom

would not say that someone who pushed another out of the way of an oncoming car had been violent or acted violently. This is because violence also implies infringement of another in some way as well as the intent to do harm. It also has the sense of something intense or extreme. A small injury to another may not be considered an act of violence. Whether some sports—for example, football—can be considered violent games is something to think about. But we would certainly want to say that the destruction and harm of war is violent. The three moral approaches to thinking about the justification of violence—realism, pacifism, and the just war theory—are primarily focused on the morality of war, which may be defined as sustained and organized political violence. But the arguments presented here can be expanded and applied to the justification of other sorts of violence (for example, as Lloyd Steffen did in his discussion of the death penalty in

Chapter 15). To get a better sense of these implications, let's turn to a more detailed exposition of realism, pacifism, and just war theory.

REALISM

Realism is the idea that in the "real world" of social and political life, violence is one tool among others to be employed strategically to get things done. Realists tend to be consequentialists, who are primarily focused on outcomes and results—and who are not as concerned with the morality of the means employed to achieve such results. Realism is often characterized as holding an "anything goes" approach to the question of violence. The idea of realism has roots in the thinking of Thucydides, the ancient Greek historian of the Peloponnesian War. In his account of a battle between the Athenians and the inhabitants of the island of Melos, Thucydides describes an attempted negotiation prior to the battle.

Outline of Moral Approaches to War

	Pacifism	Just War	Realism
Thesis	War is never justified	War can be justified	Moral judgment does not apply to war
Corollaries and Implications	Creative and active *nonviolence* should be employed	War should be limited by the moral concerns of *jus ad bellum* and *jus in bello*; violations of these limits are "war crimes"	We should do what is necessary in war to achieve victory and maximize our interests; there can be no crimes in war
Connections with Moral Theory	*Deontological* prohibition against killing; or *consequentialist* claim that war causes more harm than good and that nonviolence can produce good outcomes	Combination of *deontological* concerns (e.g., right intention, noncombatant immunity) and *consequentialist* concerns (proportionality); connected with natural law tradition and need for defense of life, liberty, and other rights	*Consequentialist* concern with victory can be focused on national self-interest or on the need for balance of power and international stability; tends to focus on cost-benefit analysis and pragmatic or strategic concerns
Relevant Authors	Mohandas Gandhi, Martin Luther King Jr; Andrew Fitz-Gibbon	Thomas Aquinas, Michael Walzer	Thucydides

The Athenians argue that since they have the more powerful military, the Melians ought to surrender, since it is useless for them to fight. The Athenians explain that the stronger party does whatever it can get away with, while the weaker party is prudent to acquiesce. The Athenians go on to say that the strong sometimes have to use violence to establish their supremacy and as a warning against those who might challenge them. The Melians do not submit to the Athenian threat. The Athenians attack, killing or enslaving all of the inhabitants of the island of Melos. One moral of this story is that it is better to be strong than to be weak. Another moral is that there are no limits in war. From this perspective, war is understood as an existential struggle for supremacy. Perhaps it is possible to achieve a balance of power between equal powers. But if another power is threatening you, the realist would argue that in a life or death struggle it is necessary to do whatever it takes to defend against the threat of annihilation. Realists are opposed to the idea that there are inherent or intrinsic moral limits on the justification of violence. Indeed, they may argue that adherence to limitations on violence can make a nation look weak and ineffectual and produce more harm than good.

Realism is sometimes related to "militarism," a social and ethical system that celebrates martial power and military might. Some militarists argue that the highest glory is to be found in military adventures—an idea with a deep history that goes back to Achilles, the warrior hero in Homer's *Iliad*. Achilles and other heroes in warrior cultures view warfare as a test of manhood, which produces virtues such as loyalty, courage, and steadfastness (see Chapter 8's discussion of virtue). Some continue to celebrate this spirit of masculine sacrifice and the glory of military service. But in modern culture, we have also expanded the definition of service and sacrifice to include gender-neutral virtues: it is not manhood that is tested but dedication and valor. Indeed, in the American military, women have been active participants for decades and a recent policy change allows women to serve in combat.

Critics of militarism argue that there should be nonviolent ways to produce the same sorts of virtues. In his essay "The Moral Equivalent of War," American pragmatist philosopher William James called for a substitute for war. He wanted to find a way to develop virtues such as heroism and loyalty without the destruction of armed conflict.[2] But James was generally an opponent of war—especially the expansive American war in the Philippine islands. He and other philosophers—including the American feminist and pacifist author Jane Addams—were actively involved in the antiwar movement during the early part of the twentieth century.

Realists generally deny that moral ideas can be applied in warfare or that moral concerns should inhibit us from doing what is necessary to achieve victory. If we must bomb civilians or use torture to win a war, then that is what we must do. But realists are not simply bloodthirsty. They might agree that there are good pragmatic reasons to limit the use of violence. Violence can provoke a backlash (as enemies fight harder and unite against a dominant power). For realists, the central question is about what works. If terror bombing works, then it should be used, but if it does not work, then it should be avoided. Realists also have to consider the costs and benefits of warfare. War can be expensive. Realists do not advocate war at any cost. Instead, realists want to be strategic about the use of violence. It is imprudent to get involved in battles that cannot be won or that are so costly that they leave us in a weakened state. Note here that realism is focused on the question of prudence, strategy, and pragmatism—it is a consequentialist approach that is not concerned with moral questions about the means employed. From a utilitarian perspective, war may be employed as a way of pursuing the greatest happiness for the greatest number of those living within a polity. (Note that such a use of the utilitarian calculus ignores suffering on the other side.) Realism may also be criticized as being amoral, as when it simply denies that morality applies in the context of war. This version of realism will hold that "all's fair in love in war" or that "war is hell"—both clichés point in the direction of the realist idea that in war there is no morality at all.

PACIFISM

Pacifism lies on the opposite end of the spectrum from realism. While extreme realists argue that there are no moral limits in warfare, extreme pacifists argue that war is always wrong. Pacifism is often grounded in a deontological claim that focuses on the morality of killing. Deontological pacifists will maintain that there is an absolute moral rule against killing. Pacifism is also grounded in a more positive commitment to active nonviolence. Some forms of pacifism extend the idea of nonviolence in a very general way that condemns violence done to sentient beings in general, including nonhuman animals. Other forms of pacifism are narrowly focused on a condemnation of war as the most horrible form of violence, which must be opposed. Not all pacifists oppose the use of all types of force. After all, there are nonphysical means of exerting force and even nonviolent social protest is a way of mobilizing social force. One can think of there being degrees of pacifism—that is, in terms of the degree and type of force thought acceptable. Some pacifists may reluctantly allow the use of physical and even lethal physical force when it is absolutely necessary, such as to defend oneself.

Pacifists generally maintain that nonviolent alternatives to violence are preferable and should be actively pursued in a creative and sustained fashion. Prominent pacifists include Mohandas Gandhi and Martin Luther King Jr., whose ideas we encountered in Chapter 2. Both were actively engaged in trying to change the world by using nonviolent social protest, including nonviolent civil disobedience. While King is best known as a civil rights activist, he was also a critic of war. He opposed the Vietnam War, for example, arguing that using war to settle differences is neither just nor wise.[3]

The reasons given in support of pacifism vary. Some—like Gandhi and King—grounded their commitment to nonviolence in a religious perspective. Gandhi was dedicated to the idea of *ahimsa* (Sanskrit for nonviolence), which is a common value in South Asian traditions such as Hinduism, Buddhism, and Jainism. King developed his ideas about nonviolence from reading Gandhi. But as a Baptist minister, he also appealed to a pacifist interpretation of the Christian Gospels, an interpretation that is shared by such groups as Mennonites and Quakers. These Christians view Jesus as a pacifist who maintained (in the Sermon on the Mount found in the Gospel of Matthew 5, for example) that peacemakers are blessed, that one should not return evil for evil, and that we should love even our enemies.

Nonreligious arguments for pacifism can also be found—many derived from consequentialist considerations. Consequentialist pacifists believe that nonviolent means work better than violence to produce social goods. Violence does more harm than good, they argue, because violence begets violence. How can we determine whether or not this is true? We can look to see whether historical examples support the generalization. We also can inquire whether this may result from something in human nature. Are we overly prone to violence and bloodlust? Are we able to restrain ourselves when we turn to war? Our judgments will then depend on adequate factual assessments. We should note that it is difficult to weigh the benefits and costs of war—because we would have to engage in counter-factual speculation, asking what would have happened if we had (or had not) gone to war. War does cause substantial damage; however, it is an open question as to whether the damage of war is worse than the damage that would result if we did not use war to respond to aggressive dictators or genocidal regimes.

Most pacifists argue that killing is wrong. But critics of this view argue that if killing is wrong, there may be times when we need to kill to prevent killing from occurring. Consider, for example, whether it is justifiable to kill those who threaten the innocent. Should an exception to the rule against killing be made to prevent such killing? Would it be acceptable to kill in self-defense? Or in defense of innocent children, such as the children killed at Sandy Hook Elementary School? Or in defense of those who are being slaughtered by genocidal or racist governments? Pacifists must address the criticism that it seems inconsistent to hold that life is of the highest value and yet not be willing to use force to defend it. One way they might address this objection is to clarify that pacifism is not passive—pacifists do not advocate doing nothing in response to atrocity. Rather, pacifists can be committed to active, creative, and sustained efforts to help people and defend the innocent, so long as such efforts do not involve killing. Pacifists will also argue that the problem of war is that innocent people are accidentally killed even by the "good guys" and that it is very difficult to focus the destructive power of war in a way that does not harm the innocent.

JUST WAR THEORY

Intermediate between pacifism and realism is the idea that the use of force, including military force, is justified in limited and specific circumstances. The just war theory attempts to clarify when it is justifiable to resort to the use of lethal force. The just war approach is more or less the mainstream theory of the American military and political system. While some critics may argue that American military strategy includes a realist element—that the United States is engaged in asserting force and displaying strength around the globe—the rhetoric used to explain American military power is generally grounded in just war language. President Barack Obama defended this idea when he delivered his Nobel Peace Prize acceptance speech. According to Obama, philosophers and theologians developed the just war idea over time as they attempted to find moral language to criticize and limit the destructive power of war. "The concept of a 'just war' emerged, suggesting that war is justified only when certain conditions were met: if it is waged as a last resort or in self-defense; if the force used is proportional; and if, whenever possible, civilians are spared from violence."[4]

As Obama noted, the just war theory is not new. Indeed, the just war theory has a long history. Its origins can be traced to the writings of Augustine, one of the ancient fathers of the Catholic Church. Augustine wanted to reconcile traditional Christian views about the immorality of violence with the necessity of defending the Roman Empire from invading forces.[5] He asked what one should do if one sees an individual attacking an innocent, defenseless victim.

His response was that one should intervene and do whatever is necessary (but only so much as was necessary) to protect the victim, even up to the point of killing the aggressor. Further developments of the theory were provided by Thomas Aquinas, who provides a natural law justification of the violence used in self-defense. Medieval codes of chivalry also have something in common with just war ideas. But the theory gets its most systematic exposition in the work of early modern theologians and jurists such as Francisco de Vitoria, Francisco Suarez, and Hugo Grotius. In more recent times, just war ideas have been instituted in international law, which asserts the right of a nation to defend itself against aggression, while also calling for protections for civilians and prisoners of war. These ideas can be found in international conventions, as well as in the Charter of the United Nations and other treaties signed by world powers.

There is general agreement that just war theory includes two basic areas: principles that would have to be satisfied for a nation to be justified in using military force, or initiating a war, and principles governing the conduct of the military action or war itself. These have been given the Latin names of *jus ad bellum* (the justness of going to war) and *jus in bello* (justness in war).

Jus ad Bellum

Just Cause To use force against another nation, there must be a serious reason to justify it. Defense of one's territory against an invader is a prime example of a just cause for war. Nations have the right to defend themselves against aggression. But war is not justified to right a minor wrong or to respond to an insult. A newly developing concept of just cause includes the idea of intervening to prevent another nation from harming its own population. This idea is known as humanitarian intervention—the idea of using limited military force for humanitarian purposes. The United Nations has expanded this idea recently under the idea of a "responsibility to protect" (sometimes called "R2P"). The R2P idea holds that the international community has a responsibility to intervene to protect people from their own governments and to prevent war crimes and crimes against humanity (which we discuss in more detail later in this chapter).

Other causes for war have been proposed. Could war be employed to prevent the spread of communism, to rid another country of a despotic leader, to prevent a nation from obtaining nuclear weapons, or to protect the world's oil supply? These may be viewed as cases of self-defense, using a broad definition of what is in a nation's vital interest. But the just war theory in general attempts to limit the causes of war.

One contentious issue related to just cause is the justification of preventive and preemptive strikes. If a neighboring nation is about to invade one's territory, preemptive defense against threatened aggression would seem to be a just response. A nation need not wait to be attacked when it knows an invasion is impending. The principle of "only if attacked first" may be too strict. Traditionally, preemptive attacks were thought to be justified if an attack was *imminent*. However, in the age of terrorists with weapons of mass destruction, some have argued that to wait until an attack is imminent is to wait too long. This logic has been employed to justify a variety of attacks. For example, Israel has attacked weapons sites in Iraq (in 1981) and in Syria in more recent years in an effort to prevent its enemies from developing deadly weapons. The 2003 U.S. invasion of Iraq was justified as an attempt to prevent Iraq from using, developing, and disseminating weapons of mass destruction. While some just war theorists supported this invasion, others argued that preventive war was an immoral use of war.[6] The danger of preventive war is that it can cause an escalation in violence, as each side may feel justified in attacking first.

Legitimate Authority If we assume that we can agree upon the question of what counts as a just cause for war, another concern is the question of who has the authority to declare war. Traditionally, it was thought to be the sovereign power who had the right to declare war. In the era of kings and princes, it was the monarch who declared war. In democracies, however, we presume that the power to declare war rests in the hands of the duly elected government. In the United States, there has been some concern about where the power to declare war resides: in Congress or in the president. The Constitution (Article I, Section 8, Clause 11) stipulates that the power to declare war rests in the hands of the Congress. However, in recent decades, the president has sent military forces into battle without explicit declarations of war. Leaving aside this constitutional question, we might wonder whether it makes sense for the civilian leadership to declare war. Wouldn't it be wiser to let the military decide when and where to fight? After all, soldiers are the experts in war. However, the idea of civilian control of the military is a central idea for democratic nations, which believe that warfare must be approved by the people through duly elected representatives. This can lead to a difficulty, however, as military priorities may conflict with the concerns of the civilian leadership.

The issue of legitimate authority points toward other problems. Who has a claim to legitimate authority in a civil war or a revolution? That's a difficult question to answer. Another problem has to do with the development of international institutions such as the United Nations. Should the United States defer to the judgments of the United Nations Security Council about wars and interventions? Or do the United States and other nations have the right to "go it alone" when it comes to war? In 2004, the secretary-general of the United Nations, Kofi Annan, declared that the United States had violated the United Nations Charter by going to war against Iraq and that the war was illegal.[7] But the United States maintained that it had a moral right to go to war without United Nations approval. The issue of legitimate authority remains an important concern for thinking about the justification of war.

Proportionality Not only must the cause be just, according to the theory, but also the probable good to be produced by the intervention must outweigh the likely evil that the war will cause. Before engaging in warfare, we should consider the probable costs and benefits and compare them with the probable costs and benefits of doing something else or of doing nothing. Involved in this utilitarian calculation are two elements: one assesses the likely costs and benefits, and the other weighs their relative value. The first requires historical and empirical information, whereas the second involves ethical evaluations. In making such evaluations, we might well compare lives that are likely to be saved with lives lost, for example. But how do we compare the value of freedom and self-determination, or a way of life with the value of a life itself? How do we factor in the long-term impacts of war, including the possibility of post-traumatic stress for soldiers and civilians? Moreover, there is the difficulty of assessing costs and benefits with regard to a complex and chaotic activity such as fighting a war.

Last Resort The just war theory holds that war should be a last resort. Military interventions are extremely costly in terms of suffering, loss of life, and other destruction, so other means must be considered first. They need not all be tried first, for some will be judged useless beforehand. However, nonviolent means should be attempted, at least those that are judged to have a chance of achieving the goal specified by the just cause. Negotiations, threats, and boycotts are examples of such means. When is enough finally enough? When have these measures been given sufficient trial? There is always something more that could be tried. This is a matter of prudential judgment and therefore always uncertain.[8]

Right Intention Military action should be directed to the goal set by the cause and to the eventual goal of peace. Thus, wars fought to satisfy hatred and bloodlust or to obtain wealth are unjustified. The focus on intentions is a deontological element in the *jus ad bellum* consideration. Recall that Kant's deontological theory focused on the intention behind an act (what Kant called the "good will" and the nature of the maxims of action). In thinking about going to war, this principle would remind us that we ought to intend good things even as we employ violent means. The right intention principle seems

to imply that there should be no gratuitous cruelty such as would follow from malicious intentions. This moves us into discussion of the conduct of a war, the second area covered by the principles of just war theory.

Jus in Bello

Even if a war were fought for a just cause and by a legitimate authority, with the prospect of achieving more good than harm, as a last resort only, and with the proper intention, it still would not be fully just if it were not conducted justly or in accordance with certain principles or moral guidelines. The *jus in bello* part of the just war theory consists of several principles.

Proportionality The principle of proportionality stipulates that in the conduct of the conflict, violence should be focused on limited objectives. No more force than necessary should be used. And the force or means used should be proportionate to the importance of the particular objective for the cause as a whole. This principle is obviously similar to the principle of proportionality discussed previously in thinking about *jus ad bellum*; however, within the *jus in bello* consideration of proportionality, the cost–benefit analysis is focused on limited war aims and not on the question of the war itself.

Discrimination Just warriors should not intentionally attack noncombatants and nonmilitary targets. While this principle sounds straightforward, there are complex issues to sort out in terms of what counts as a nonmilitary target or who is a noncombatant. Are roads, bridges, and hospitals that are used in the war effort military targets? The general consensus is that the roads and bridges are targets if they contribute directly and in significant ways to the military effort, but that hospitals are not legitimate targets. The principle to be used in making this distinction is the same for the people as for the things. Those people who contribute directly are combatants, and those who do not are not combatants. There is some vagueness here. Is a soldier at home on leave a legitimate target? One writer suggests that persons who are engaged in doing what they do ordinarily as persons are noncombatants, while those who perform their functions specifically for the war effort are combatants.[9] Thus, those who grow and provide food would be noncombatants, whereas those who make or transport the military equipment would be combatants.

Note, too, that although we also hear the term *innocent civilians* in such discussions, it is noncombatants who are supposed to be out of the fight and not people who are judged on some grounds to be "innocent" in a deeper moral sense. Soldiers fighting unwillingly might be thought to be innocent but are nevertheless combatants. Those behind the lines spending time verbally supporting the cause are not totally innocent, yet they are noncombatants. The danger of using the term *innocents* in place of *noncombatants* is that it also allows some to say that no one living in a certain country is immune because they are all supporters of their country and so not innocent. However, this is contrary to the traditional understanding of the principle of discrimination.

One way of describing the discrimination principle is to say that noncombatants should have immunity from harm. The idea of *noncombatant immunity* says that noncombatants should not be intentionally harmed. Combatants are not immune because they are a threat. Thus, when someone is not or is no longer a threat, as when they have surrendered or are incapacitated by injury, then they are not to be regarded as legitimate targets. The discrimination principle does not require that no noncombatants be injured or killed, but only that they not be the direct targets of attack. Although directly targeting and killing civilians may have a positive effect on a desired outcome, this would not be justified. The principle of discrimination is a deontological principle that stipulates a duty not to deliberately target noncombatants.

Nonetheless, some noncombatants are harmed in modern warfare—as bombs go astray and battles rage within cities. Noncombatant harms can be permitted by application of the *principle of double effect* (also discussed in Chapter 10). Noncombatant harms can be permitted if they are the foreseen but unintended and accidental result of a legitimate war aim. Not only must the noncombatants not be directly targeted but also the number of them likely to be injured when a target is attacked must not be disproportionately great compared to the significance of the target. Thus if a bomb goes astray and kills some children, this could be permitted by the principle of double effect if the intended target was a legitimate one, if the numbers harmed were minimal, and if the death of the children was not directly intended. In such a case, these children would be described as *collateral damage*, that is, as harms that are accidental and unintended.

Intrinsically Evil Means   A final concern of *jus in bello* is a strictly deontological prohibition on the use of means that are viewed as being evil in themselves (or *mala in se*, as this is expressed in Latin). One obvious inherently evil act is rape. Rape has long been a weapon of war, employed by conquering armies as a way of degrading and terrorizing a conquered people. But just warriors ought not engage in rape. We should also prohibit slavery as a means of warfare—for example, forcing captured enemies to engage in hard labor or using them as human shields. We might also think that the use of poisons—including poison gas—is intrinsically wrong. And most just war accounts maintain that torture is intrinsically wrong, although (as we shall see) in recent years there has been an open debate about the morality of torture in American war-making. To say that these things are wrong in themselves creates a deontological prohibition on such weapons and actions: just warriors may not use such weapons even if they might work to produce good outcomes.

According to just war theory, then, for a war or military intervention to be justified, certain conditions for going to war must be satisfied, and the conduct in the war must follow certain principles or moral guidelines. We could say that if any of the principles are violated, that a war is unjust, or we could say that it was unjust in this regard but not in some other aspects. Just war ideas have become part of national and international law, including the U.S. Army Rules for Land Warfare and the UN Charter. Its principles appeal to common human reason and both consequentialist and non-consequentialist concerns.

Realists will maintain that the moral limits imposed by the just war theory can get in the way of victory and the goal of establishing power and supremacy. Pacifists will maintain that the just war theory is too permissive. Pacifists might reject, for example, the way that the doctrine of double effect allows noncombatants to be harmed. To evaluate realism, pacifism, and the just war theory, you must think about how you evaluate the various consequentialist and deontological principles and ideas appealed to by each approach. Let's apply these principles to some current issues.

MindTap°   For more chapter resources and activities, go to MindTap.

CURRENT ISSUES

Terrorism

Terrorism would be condemned by pacifists, along with other acts of killing. Just war theory would condemn terrorism that kills noncombatants as violating the *jus in bello* principle of discrimination. Realists may argue that terrorism is acceptable if it works as a strategy.

We can describe an act of violence as terrorism when this violent act causes or intends to cause widespread terror. Usually this terrifying act has a political goal (although there may be nihilistic terrorists who blow up things just for fun). Some maintain that terrorism is a politically loaded term, employed to denigrate one's enemies. Some say that one person's terrorist is another person's freedom fighter. But the common element in a definition of terrorism is the use of attacks on noncombatants. The first known use of the term *terrorism* was during the French Revolution for those who, like Maximilien Robespierre, used violence *on behalf* of a state. Only later was the term used to categorize violence *against* a state. The U.S. Code of Justice (Title 22, section 2656f(d)) defines terrorism as "premeditated, politically motivated violence perpetrated against noncombatant targets by subnational groups

or clandestine agents, usually intended to influence an audience." The FBI defines terrorism as, "the unlawful use of force or violence against persons or property to intimidate or coerce a government, the civilian population, or any segment thereof, in furtherance of political or social objectives."[10]

By combining these definitions, we see that terrorism is, first of all, a particular kind of violence with particular aims and goals. The more immediate goal is to create fear. This is why civilians simply going about their daily routines are targeted at random. The more distant goals vary. Terrorists may use such violence to achieve some political goal such as independence from a larger national unit or to fight back against occupying armies or to protest against particular injustices. A terrorist may be motivated by religious or political ideology. Although we often read about Islamic militants employing terror tactics, it is important to note that terrorism can be employed by people from a variety of religions, and it can be used by secularly minded political groups. Christians have employed terror tactics (as in the struggles in Northern Ireland or as in the antiapartheid violence in South Africa). And Marxist revolutionaries have employed terrorism in pursuit of atheistic and communistic goals.[11] One could argue that the Ku Klux Klan used terrorism to subjugate the black population in the American South. And black militants in the 1960s advocated terrorism against white supremacy. One could argue that Native Americans used terrorism against the white settlers of the American West. And one could argue that colonial powers used terror tactics against the Natives. And so on. Any time there is an attempt to manipulate a political situation by applying indiscriminate force, it is possible that there is terrorism. We might even suspect that the use of firebombing and atomic bombing during the Second World War was a sort of terrorism—terror bombing that aimed to force the enemy to surrender by indiscriminately bombing civilian population centers.

Some terrorists commit suicide while killing others. We hear quite a bit about Muslim terrorists who employ the tactic of suicide attack. But we should note that suicide attacks have been employed by a variety of religious (and nonreligious) groups. The Japanese kamikaze pilots of World War II were, for example, suicide attackers (although since they attacked military targets, they may not be considered terrorists). Indeed, we might note that those American soldiers who launched themselves on the beach of Normandy on D-Day also were involved in a kind of suicidal attack—although again, such a military onslaught is not terrorism. Suicidal terrorism is especially frightening, however, because the suicide bomber is not subject to a rational calculus of deterrence. The suicidal bomber is willing to die and wants to kill others in order to produce terror. Most suicide bombers are young (as are most soldiers) and thus may be more idealistic and easily influenced and manipulated. While some blame fundamentalist preaching and religious schools for the rise of suicidal terrorism, those who have investigated the background of known terrorists find that most of them are at least middle class and most often well educated.[12] Some terrorists are more rational in their goals than others, in having sufficient historical and political sense to know what will and will not work. In other cases, it seems that terrorists simply strike out in frustration, not caring about the long-term strategic consequences of their actions.

Terrorists seem to lack the ability to empathize with the innocent victims of their attacks. Terrorists may demonize entire nations and peoples, killing out of hatred. But terrorists may also be engaged in a consequentialist calculation that has much in common with the thinking of realism. From a realist perspective, there is nothing inherently wrong with targeting innocent civilians for attack. And if one is on the losing end of a military conflict, it might be necessary to resort to terror attacks as a way of continuing the fight. Those who resort to terror may be motivated by political or religious ideology. But they may also feel they have no other way to influence the state of affairs than to resort to terrorism.

In evaluating terrorism, we might reject it outright as a form of unjustified killing. From this standpoint, terrorism is like murder—by definition wrong. Terrorism would be condemned in this way by pacifists, who maintain that all violence is wrong. Pacifists would also maintain that a war against terrorism is also wrong, since pacifists maintain that war is wrong. Pacifists may also view terrorism as an example of what is wrong with war and violence—it tends to spread toward the deliberate targeting of noncombatants. Moreover, pacifists might point out that terrorism produces backlash and escalation, which only tends to beget more violence.

Could there be an ethical justification of terrorism? The reasoning that supports terrorism is most often basically consequentialist. This is connected with the realist approach to the justification of violence, which holds that the end justifies the means. If one supported this type of reasoning, then one would want to know whether, in fact, the benefits outweighed the harm and suffering caused by the means. One could do empirical studies to see whether terrorism actually produces desired outcomes. Did the terror bombing of Japan during World War II result in the surrender of the Japanese? Did the September 11 attacks bring down the U.S. government or change its international behavior? Did terror attacks on American military forces in Iraq and Afghanistan lead Americans to retreat? These sorts of questions point toward the primary realist concern, which is the prudential and strategic application of power.

One might, however, question the consequentialist nature of realist reasoning by appealing to the just war theory's ideas about noncombatant immunity and discrimination. Indiscriminate violence can be rejected on realist grounds as simply being an inefficient use of power and resources. But in the just war tradition, the principle of discrimination is a non-consequentialist or deontological prohibition. Noncombatants cannot be intentionally or directly targeted, their deaths being used to send a message to others (no matter the importance of justification of the cause for which we are fighting). International law also condemns terrorism. The Geneva Conventions, including the fourth (adopted on August 12, 1949—more than sixty years ago), enunciated principles that aim to protect civilian populations from the worst effects of war. These conventions hold that civilians should not be directly attacked. From the standpoint of international law and the just war theory, terrorism is a war crime.

Targeted Killing and Drones

Terrorists are not necessarily part of any recognized state. Often they are loosely affiliated, acting alone or organized in small cells. They may be motivated by radical ideology read online or viewed in videos. And terrorists do not declare war or put on uniforms that distinguish them as combatants. For these reasons, some argue that the weapons and rules of traditional just war theory may not apply. Others argue that terrorists are simply criminals and that domestic and international law enforcement should be employed to bring them to justice.

Should terrorists be viewed as criminals, who ought to be captured if possible and put on trial so that they might be punished? Or are terrorists *enemy combatants* who may be killed or captured without a trial and held as prisoners of war until an eventual peace treaty is concluded? Or are terrorists *unlawful combatants* whose actions and ideology put them outside of the established moral and legal framework for dealing with enemy combatants? The term *unlawful combatant* has been employed by the United States to indicate that the normal rules for dealing with criminals and enemy fighters do not apply to those suspected of terrorism. For example, American policy is that terrorist suspects can be killed without trial. And when captured, terrorism suspects have been held without trial in extraterritorial prisons such as the American prison at Guantanamo Bay in Cuba (discussed in Chapter 7). Terror suspects have been tortured. And Americans have engaged in targeted killing of terrorists, hunting them down in foreign lands (often in violation of the sovereignty of foreign nations).

The most famous case of targeted killing is that of Osama bin Laden. Osama bin Laden was the leader of Al Qaeda at the time of the September 11 attacks. He was killed by an American military attack on his compound in Abbottabad, Pakistan, on May 2, 2011. The operation that killed him was in violation of Pakistani sovereignty. When he was killed, he was accompanied by his wives and children. He was not actively engaged in military operations. Some claim that he was unarmed, with a recent book by one of the Navy SEALs involved in the raid maintaining that Bin Laden was shot in the head as he peered down a dark hallway and again in the chest as he lay convulsing in a pool of his own blood.[13] The SEALs feared bin Laden could have had a booby trap or suicide vest at his disposal. President Obama explained in a speech to the nation celebrating the death of bin Laden that there was a firefight, which led to bin Laden being killed.

Whether bin Laden posed an active threat to the Navy SEAL team that attacked him or not, Obama and others maintain that the killing of bin Laden was justified. Obama explained that bin Laden was responsible for killing Americans and that he was also, as Obama explained, "a mass murderer of Muslims." Obama concluded, "[H]is demise should be welcomed by all who believe in peace and human dignity."[14] Eric Holder, the attorney general of the United States, further explained, "The operation against bin Laden was justified as an act of national self-defense. It's lawful to target an enemy commander in the field."[15] Critics objected that the killing was a violation of international law and that Americans had an obligation to work to try to extradite bin Laden and put him on trial. Critics might also object to Holder's claim that bin Laden was a "commander in the field." Is a terrorist who is resting at home in the middle of the night a commander in the field?

The justification of the killing of bin Laden points toward the broader question of whether it is morally and legal permissible to employ targeted killing as a method of warfare. The larger question from the standpoint of the just war theory is whether it is permissible to target an enemy commander or other soldier who is not actively engaged in fighting. The just war idea of discrimination may encourage us to distinguish between soldiers who are actively fighting and those who are in hospitals, on leave, or engaged in nonlethal support operations. One reason to avoid targeting soldiers behind the lines is to keep violence contained on the battlefield. But some may argue that this convenient distinction between combatants who are fighting and soldiers on leave does not hold in the war on terrorism where there are no specified fields of battle and where terrorists themselves refuse to adhere to the distinction between combatants and noncombatants. A realist would have no problem with targeting a terrorist mastermind or a political leader, except for pragmatic concerns about potential blowback from such attacks. The just war theory may also permit assassinations of terrorist masterminds and political leaders, if such attacks are discriminate and proportional. One concern, however, is that by employing targeted assassination, the door is open for similar attacks coming from the other side. Could Al Qaeda make similar arguments in attempting to justify attacks on American political or military leaders? The presumption here is that the "good guys"—those who fight justly and who have a just cause—are permitted to employ targeted killing, while the "bad guys" are not.

The issue of targeted killing has come to prominence lately with regard to the use of unmanned drones. Drone aircraft, piloted by remote control, can attack terrorist suspects around the world, easily crossing borders. Drones have been used to attack targets in a variety of countries. One advantage of drones is that they are more precise than the use of other sorts of bombing, allowing for more discriminate and proportional killing. However, civilian noncombatants have been killed by the use of drones. One estimate from the Bureau of Investigative Journalism claims the United States has killed at least five thousand people in Yemen, Afghanistan, Somalia, and Pakistan with drone strikes (as of spring 2016), including at least five hundred to six hundred civilians.[16] At one point, early in the drone program in Pakistan, nearly half of the casualties were noncombatants. But the drone program has become more precise, with civilian deaths accounting for only 10 to 15 percent of casualties from more recent drone attacks.[17] Such killing may be justifiable on just war grounds as collateral damage. But they are still morally troubling. In April of 2016, President Obama admitted the difficulty, saying of the drone war, "It wasn't as precise as it should have

been, and there's no doubt civilians were killed that shouldn't have been. . . . We have to take responsibility where we're not acting appropriately, or just made mistakes."[18]

Another advantage of using drones is that drones are cheaper than manned aircraft. And they do not put pilots at risk. However, they return us to the problem of who counts as a combatant. Would the remote control drone pilots, who fly these drones from facilities based in the United States and who thus never come near the battlefield, be considered "combatants"? One worry along these lines is that remote control piloting of drones extends our idea of what counts as "the battlefield" in a way that undermines the just war effort to constrain violence to a confined space of battle.

Defenders of drones will argue that they are an essential response to terrorism. The war on terrorism is not a traditional war, with armies fighting each other on clearly marked battlefields. Terrorists do not wear uniforms. Indeed, they try to blend into to the local populace. And they employ mundane objects and camouflaged devices as part of their weaponry: car bombs, suicide vests, and most notoriously commercial jet airliners. Perhaps the rules have changed for a war on terrorism, which leads to a changed evaluation of the use of targeted killing. And since terrorists plan their operations in cities and villages around the globe, it might be necessary to use drones to cross borders and kill terrorists where they are doing their planning.

Another problem arises when we think about the justification of targeted killing of terrorists—whether by drones or by other means—and that is the question of preventive violence. We might think that the killing of Osama bin Laden is justifiable because he was responsible for terrorist attacks in the past. But the drone and targeted killing policy of the United States allows for targeted killing of terrorists who have not themselves committed terrorism and who may not be an imminent threat. A Justice Department memo outlining the justification of targeted killing explains that the policy "does not require the United States to have clear evidence that a specific attack on U.S. persons and interests will take place in the immediate future."[19] In other words, it may be enough to be thinking about terrorism to be liable for targeted killing. Such an idea might make sense from a standpoint that advocates preventive warfare, as discussed previously. If the U.S. invasion of Iraq was justified as a war aiming to prevent Iraq from obtaining or using weapons of mass destruction to terrorize the world, couldn't a drone attack on a terrorist in Yemen be justified by the same logic? A defender of the drone program will argue that it is better to prevent terrorist attacks before they happen. But a critic will argue that it is a disproportionate escalation of hostilities.

The discussion of drones has become even more contentious due to the government policy of allowing targeted killing of American citizens. The Department of Justice memo mentioned earlier was used to justify the killing of American citizens who are actively involved in Al Qaeda and who are residing in foreign countries. This policy was employed in the killing of four Americans in Yemen and Pakistan in 2011.[20] Among those killed was a radical Muslim cleric, Anwar Al-Awlaki, who was born in New Mexico and attended college in Colorado. He was killed along with his son and another American associate. The U.S. government claims that Al-Awlaki was actively involved in planning terrorist operations against the United States and thus that his killing was justified. Such a justification might appeal to just war ideas about the killing of aggressive combatants. Or targeted killing might be justified by realists as part of the struggle for supremacy in the world of power and politics. Critics have argued that it is illegal for the government to execute American citizens without attempting to capture them and put them on trial, perhaps maintaining that domestic and international law enforcement standards should be employed. But President Obama defended the drone program by maintaining that it was part of a just war against terrorism, which is discriminate and proportional in its approach to targeted killing.[21]

Weapons of Mass Destruction

One of the central concerns of the war on terrorism is the issue of weapons of mass destruction. Recall that the proliferation of weapons of mass destruction was a primary reason given by George W. Bush as a cause for the invasion of Iraq in 2003. The Bush administration maintained that the invasion was necessary to prevent Saddam Hussein from obtaining weapons of mass destruction, especially nuclear weapons. The issue of weapons of mass destruction remains a concern with regard to Iran and North Korea. International sanctions against Iran were directed against Iran's nuclear program. And the Korean peninsula remains tense due to North Korea's nuclear capabilities. In 2013, there was evidence that the Syrian government had used chemical weapons against rebels. This was widely condemned by the international community, leading to a change in the U.S. policy toward the civil war in Syria. As a result of the chemical weapons attacks, the United States began actively arming rebel forces in Syria, while also threatening a military strike on the country.

The category of weapons of mass destruction usually includes biological, chemical, and nuclear weapons. Biological weapons are living microorganisms that can be used as weapons to maim, incapacitate, and kill. Among these weapons is anthrax, which infects either the skin or the lungs. Breathing only a small amount of anthrax causes death in 80 to 90 percent of cases. Smallpox, cholera, and bubonic or pneumonic plague are other biological agents that might be used. Genetic engineering may also be used to make more virulent strains. There have been no proven usages of biological weapons in modern wars. One hundred sixty-three states have ratified the Biological Weapons Convention (1975), which prohibits the production, stockpiling, and use of such agents as weapons.

Chemical weapons include blister agents such as mustard gas, which is relatively easy and cheap to produce. It produces painful blisters, and it incapacitates rather than kills. Iraq used mustard gas in its 1980 to 1988 war with Iran as well as some type of chemical weapon on the Kurdish inhabitants of Halabja in 1988. Through low-level repeated airdrops, as many as five thousand defenseless people in that town were killed. Phosgene is a choking agent, and hydrogen cyanide "prevents transfer of oxygen to the tissues." Large quantities of the latter, however, would be needed to produce significant effects.[22] Hydrogen cyanide is a deadly poison gas, as is evidenced by its use in executions in the gas chamber. Sarin is called a nerve "gas," but it is actually a liquid. It affects the central nervous system and is highly toxic. In 1995, the Japanese cult group Aum Shinrikyo deployed sarin in the Tokyo subway. It sickened thousands and killed twelve people. Sarin is the gas employed in attacks in Syria that killed more than 1,000 people. Chemical weapons were also used in both world wars. For example, in World War I, the Germans used mustard gas and chlorine, and the French used phosgene. Although it might not be usually classified as the use of a chemical weapon, in 1945 American B-29 bombers "dropped 1665 tons of napalm-filled bombs on Tokyo, leaving almost nothing standing over 16 square miles." One hundred thousand people were killed in this raid, not from napalm directly but from the fires that it caused.[23] One hundred and eighty-eight nations are party to the Chemical Weapons Convention (1994). Because such weapons can be made by private groups in small labs, however, verifying international compliance with the convention is highly problematic.

Nuclear weapons, including both fission and fusion bombs, are the deadliest weapons. They produce powerful explosions and leave radiation behind that causes ongoing damage. The effects were well demonstrated by the U.S. bombings of Hiroshima and Nagasaki in August 1945. It is estimated that 150,000 people perished in these two attacks and their immediate aftermath, with an eventual total of nearly 300,000 deaths caused by these bombs (as survivors died of subsequent maladies attributed to the bombing).[24] Among the casualties at Hiroshima were American citizens—including American prisoners of war and Japanese Americans who were unable to escape from Japan once the war began. Some 3,000 Japanese Americans were in Hiroshima when the bomb was dropped; 800 to 1,000 survived and returned to the United States.[25]

Since the bombings of Hiroshima and Nagasaki, no other nation has ever employed nuclear weapons in wartime. Perhaps we learned a moral lesson from the sheer destructive power of these bombings. But for many decades after World War II, we continued to stockpile weapons. The world's nuclear arsenals grew to include unimaginable destructive power throughout the Cold War. Recognizing that nuclear weapons were pointing toward the nihilistic conclusion of mutually assured destruction, the nuclear powers have attempted to limit nuclear arsenals. There have been many nuclear weapons treaties designed to limit nuclear stockpiles and prevent proliferation. Nations known to have nuclear weapons now include China, France, India, Israel, North Korea, Pakistan, Russia, the United Kingdom, and the United States. Although some dream of complete disarmament, we are a far from a nuclear free world. On the other hand, there has been some progress made regarding the agreement to reduce nuclear stockpiles. On April 8, 2010, in a new START treaty, the US and Russia agreed to limit the number of nuclear warheads in each arsenal to 1,550.[26]

The global community continues to be concerned about nuclear proliferation. There is a worrisome global black market in nuclear materials and know-how. These weapons are difficult but not impossible to make. And many fear so-called "loose nukes," nuclear weapons that are not carefully guarded (for example in the former Soviet Union) and that are sold on the black market to terrorists. There was an attempt to confine possession of nuclear weapons to the original nuclear powers: the United States, the UK, France, the Soviet Union (now Russia), and China. But in recent decades nuclear weaponry has been developed by Israel and India, with Pakistan joining the nuclear club in 1998. North Korea successfully detonated a nuclear device in 2006 and claimed to have tested a hydrogen bomb in early 2016, an act that provoked outrage in the international community. Other states have agreed not to pursue nuclear weapons by signing on to the Nuclear Non-Proliferation Treaty. At least one state has voluntarily given up its nuclear weapons: South Africa dismantled its nuclear weapons in the 1990s.

In calling these nuclear, chemical, and biological devices *weapons of mass destruction*, we imply that they are of a different order of magnitude than the usual means of modern warfare. It is clear why nuclear weapons are labeled in this way, but it is not so clear why the others are. Even when used somewhat extensively in World War I, "fewer than 1 percent of battle deaths" during that war were caused by gas, and only "2 percent of those gassed during the war died, compared with 24 percent of those struck by bullets, artillery shells, or shrapnel."[27] For gas to work well, there can be no wind or sun, and it must be delivered by an aircraft flying at very low altitude. If delivered by bombs, the weapons would be incinerated before they could become effective. Today's gas masks and antibiotics and other preventives and treatments lessen the lethality of such weapons even more. In 1971, smallpox accidentally got loose in Kazakhstan but killed only three people; and in 1979, a large amount of anthrax was released through the explosion of a Soviet plant, but only sixty-eight people were killed.[28] There have been subsequent scares with regard to chemical and biological agents. In 2001, Americans were frightened by anthrax scares, as suspicious white powder was sent by the mail. In 2013, federal authorities arrested domestic terrorists who sent letters laced with the poison ricin through the mail to judges and politicians, including one to the president. Ricin is made from castor beans and it is quite deadly: a dose about the size of a grain of salt can cause death.

Realists would have no moral problem with weapons of mass destruction, provided that they work. One concern is that such weapons are difficult to use without harming your own soldiers. The wind can blow chemical and biological weapons in the wrong direction, and nuclear weapons leave deadly radiation that can harm one's own troops. On the other hand, just war theorists may argue that weapons of mass destruction are *mala in se* or evil in themselves (and so prohibited). But we need not appeal to intrinsic qualities of the weapons to form a moral critique of weapons of mass destruction. Principles from the just war theory that are used to evaluate terrorism and other warfare can be employed to evaluate the use of weapons of mass destruction. The principle of discrimination tells us that it is morally wrong to deliberately target innocent civilians with firebombs, nuclear bombs, or chemical weapons. And massive destruction caused by these weapons might fail the proportionality test as well. One wonders, however, whether ordinary bombs and bullets that explode and kill many more people than biological or chemical weapons are less objectionable. During the Second World War, more civilians were killed by conventional bombs than were killed by atomic bombs. And land mines continue to be a cause of harm—left behind in battlefields to harm civilians after conflicts end. Nevertheless, people seem to fear biological and chemical weapons more than conventional weapons. Possibly it is the thought of being killed by something invisible—radiation sickness or poison gas—that makes them so feared and is behind the desire to call them weapons of mass destruction, with the implication that they are morally abhorrent and are intrinsically evil.

War Crimes and Universal Human Rights

One of the difficulties of thinking about the morality of war is that, as the realists may insist, there is no international authority that could regulate behavior in war. Realists will argue that victors dispense so-called "victor's justice." Usually the term *victor's justice* is thought of as an accusation of unilateral and hypocritical judgment, as the victors punish the losers, while failing to prosecute or condemn their own unjust or immoral actions. Consider, for example, a scene from the 2003 documentary *The Fog of War* in which former Defense Secretary Robert S. McNamara is interviewed about his participation in the bombing of Japan during World War II. McNamara worked with General Curtis LeMay to coordinate the bombing of Japan. In addition to the atomic bomb attacks mentioned previously, American planes dropped incendiary bombs on a large number of Japanese cities, causing massive damage and killing millions. As McNamara reflects on this in the film, he acknowledges that the bombing would have been viewed as a war crime if the Americans had lost. He said that LeMay suggested,

"If we had lost the war, we'd all have been prosecuted as war criminals." McNamara continued, "And I think he's right. He...and, I'd say, I...were behaving as war criminals. LeMay recognized that what he was doing would be thought immoral if his side had lost. But what makes it immoral if you lose and not immoral if you win?"[29] The realist will argue that this shows us that moral judgments do not apply in wartime and that the goal is to win so that one can be the victor dispensing victor's justice.

On the other hand, there is a growing consensus in the international community that moral judgment should apply to behavior in war. International agreements, treaties, and institutions have developed in the past centuries that aim to limit warfare and prosecute immoral actions done in war. These efforts in international law are grounded upon ideas that are closely connected to ideas found in the just war theory—most important, the idea that civilians should not be targeted and the idea that certain actions—rape, for example—are always immoral. Many of the elements of the laws of war and the nature of war crimes have been developed in the various declarations of the Geneva Conventions and in other international treaties and agreements. For example, the 1984 UN Convention against Torture, which was ratified by the United States, requires that all signatory nations avoid cruel, inhuman, or degrading treatment.[30]

Those who violate these conventions and protocols may be held to be guilty of "war crimes." One important source for the conventions regarding war crimes were the war crimes tribunals conducted after World War II—both the Nuremberg trials and the Tokyo trials. There have been questions about the legal procedures and standards of proof employed in these trials. But in general, they are viewed as examples of the developing moral consensus about the rules of war. The Nuremberg trials established three categories of crimes: *crimes against the peace* (involving aggression and preparation for war), *war crimes* (including murder, maltreatment of prisoners, etc.), and *crimes against humanity* (involving racial, religious, or political persecution of civilians). The last category, *crimes against humanity* included

a newly developed concept—that of *genocide*, the deliberate effort to exterminate a people. As is well known, the Nazis were engaged in a genocidal campaign of extermination against Jews, Gypsies, and others. Nazi death camps were employed in an efficient and mechanized effort to annihilate the Jewish people, resulting in the deaths of six million Jews (out of a prior population of nine million Jews in the German-controlled parts of Europe). This event is referred to as the Holocaust. The mass extermination of civilians is a war crime and a crime against humanity.

The idea of a crime against humanity and of war crimes in general can be understood in relation to the natural law and natural rights theories discussed in Chapter 7. Certain actions violate the natural value and dignity of persons, and all human beings should know this based upon a common moral sense, no matter what orders they receive. The important point here is that soldiers cannot be excused for criminal behavior by claiming that they are merely following orders. Principle IV of the Nuremberg trials stipulates, "The fact that a person acted pursuant to order of his Government or of a superior does not relieve him from responsibility under international law, provided a moral choice was in fact possible to him."[31] Moreover, Principle III of the Tribunal stipulated that heads of state and other political leaders were not excused from prosecution. The Nuremberg trials put twenty-two Nazi leaders on trial (Hitler, Himmler, Goebbels, and other Nazi leaders were already dead), resulting in convictions for nineteen of them and death sentences for twelve. While the Nuremberg trials are viewed as an important step in the development of war crimes tribunals and international law, some still worry that they remained examples of victor's justice—since there was no similar accounting for war crimes committed by the Allied powers.[32]

Since Nuremberg, the international community has worked to create a more impartial system for dealing with war crimes and crimes against humanity, including the development of an International Criminal Court in The Hague. But egregious attacks on civilians continue to occur, attacks that are referred to as "ethnic cleansing" or genocide. These attacks have occurred in Kosovo, in Rwanda, in Sudan, in Syria, and elsewhere. The international community condemns such atrocities. But it is often at a loss as to what to do about them. Military intervention is risky—and pacifists will argue for nonviolent responses. A significant problem is whether a war of intervention intended to rescue civilians will produce more harm than good in the long run. Although there is a developing international consensus about war crimes, the world is still not able to agree on strategies for responding to such crimes.

Torture

Torture is viewed as a criminal activity, outlawed by the Geneva Conventions and by other international treaties such as the UN Convention against Torture. But some have argued that torture could be justified in the fight against terrorism. And others in the U.S. government have sought to justify techniques that have traditionally been viewed as torture, in part by calling them "enhanced interrogations methods." In congressional testimony in February 2007, the director of the CIA, Michael Hayden, admitted that the United States has used waterboarding on prisoners. Waterboarding is a technique in which a prisoner's head is strapped to a board with his face drenched in water to produce a sensation of drowning. The CIA admitted that it used waterboarding on one particular terror suspect, Khalid Shaikh Mohammed, 183 times; another suspect was waterboarded 83 times.[33] These prisoners were subjected to other so-called "enhanced interrogation techniques": they were kept disoriented, naked, and cold. We have learned that prisoners were slammed against walls, given suppositories, prevented from sleeping, and kept in stress positions. The Red Cross concluded that this treatment was torture and that it was cruel, inhuman, and degrading.[34]

But the government under George W. Bush argued that this use of torture was justified. Former Vice President Dick Cheney explained,

> No moral value held dear by the American people obliges public servants to sacrifice innocent lives to spare a captured terrorist from unpleasant things. And when an entire population is targeted by a terror

network, nothing is more consistent with American values than to stop them. The interrogations were used on hardened terrorists after other efforts had failed. They were legal, essential, justified, successful, and the right thing to do.[35]

Cheney's justification of torture is a straightforwardly utilitarian justification: it works to prevent terrorism and should not be prohibited by a "moral value." The Bush administration's legal staff provided legal and moral justifications of torture. The Office of Legal Counsel in the Justice Department issued a number of memos suggesting that certain methods of trying to extract information from prisoners suspected of terrorism were not torture. The author of a number of these memos, John Yoo, argued that "inflicting physical pain does not count as torture unless the interrogator specifically intends the pain to reach the level associated with organ failure or death."[36] This definition was given to allow certain enhanced interrogation techniques while avoiding the legal prohibition on torture. According to this definition, waterboarding—simulated drowning—does not count as torture. Critics complained loudly that waterboarding was indeed torture and that this was not consistent with American law or international law and that the use of torture was contrary to American values.[37] For example, the U.S. Uniform Code of Military Justice makes "cruelty, oppression, or maltreatment of prisoners a crime."[38] Senator John McCain—who was himself tortured as a prisoner of war in Vietnam—spoke out against torture. And when Barack Obama became president, he banned the use of these "enhanced interrogation methods."

Pacifists will condemn torture as another example of unjustified violence. They may also point out that this episode from recent history indicates the ugly logic of war—that we can end up betraying our own values in the name of victory and power—and that this shows us why war is a corrupting and immoral force. Realists may nod in agreement with Dick Cheney's consequentialist justification of torture. Realists are not opposed to using supposedly immoral means to achieve other goals. Indeed, realists may also add that our enemies are not opposed to using torture and to employing other cruel techniques, including beheading prisoners. Realists may argue that the best way to fight cruelty is to employ cruelty in return. Just war theorists will not agree to that line of reasoning. Instead, they may argue that torture ought to be considered as one of those actions that are considered as evil in themselves and that are prohibited by principles of *jus in bello*. They may argue that even if torture works, there are some things we simply ought not do in pursuit of justified causes.

In the readings in this chapter, we have selections representing pacifism and just war theory. First, we will read an essay by Andrew Fitz-Gibbon, a philosopher who explains pacifism and nonviolence with reference to the legacies of Gandhi and King. Next, Michael Walzer—the leading exponent of the just war theory—evaluates some key elements of the theory.

NOTES

1. Physicians for Social Responsibility (http://www.psr .org/assets/pdfs/body-count.pdf); (http://costsofwar .org; www.icasualties.org; www.iraqbodycount.org; and Wikipedia

2. William James, "The Moral Equivalent of War," *Popular Science Monthly*, October 1910.

3. Martin Luther King Jr., "Beyond Vietnam" (speech from April 4, 1967) at Martin Luther King Papers Project (Stanford), accessed May 21, 2013, http:// mlk-kpp01.stanford.edu/index.php/encyclopedia/ documentsentry/doc_beyond_vietnam/

4. "Remarks by the President at the Acceptance of the Nobel Peace Prize," The White House, press release, December 10, 2009, accessed May 21, 2013, http://www.whitehouse.gov/the-press-office/ remarks-president-acceptance-nobel-peace-prize

5. Robert W. Tucker, *The Just War* (Baltimore, MD: Johns Hopkins University Press, 1960), 1.

6. See Andrew Fiala, *The Just War Myth* (Lanham, MD: Rowman & Littlefield, 2008), Chapter 6.

7. "Lessons of Iraq War Underscore Importance of UN Charter—Annan," *UN News Centre*, September 16, 2004, accessed July 25, 2013, http://www.un.org/ apps/news/story.asp?NewsID=11953&#. UfMBmWTEo_s

8. We might consider this particular principle as what is called a regulative rather than a substantive

principle. Instead of telling us when something is enough or the last thing we should try, it can be used to prod us to go somewhat further than we otherwise would.

9. James Childress, "Just-War Theories," *Theological Studies* (1978): 427–45.

10. Both definitions found at "Terrorism," National Institute of Justice, September 12, 2011, accessed May 21, 2013, http://www.nij.gov/topics/crime/ terrorism/

11. Max Rodenbeck, "How Terrible Is It?" *New York Review of Books*, November 30, 2006, 35.

12. Peter Bergen and Swati Pandey, "The Madrassa Myth," *New York Times*, June 14, 2005, A19.

13. Mark Owen, *No Easy Day: The Firsthand Account of the Mission That Killed Osama Bin Laden* (New York: Dutton, 2012).

14. "Remarks by the President on Osama Bin Laden," The White House, press release, May 2, 2011, accessed May 21, 2013, http://www.whitehouse. gov/the-press-office/2011/05/02/remarks-president-osama-bin-laden

15. Erik Kirschbaum and Jonathan Thatcher, "Concerns Raised over Shooting of Unarmed bin Laden," *Reuters*, May 4, 2011, accessed May 22, 2013, http://www.reuters.com/article/2011/05/04/ us-binladen-legitimacy-idUSTRE74371H20110504

16. Adding low-end estimates from Bureau of Investigative Journalism, https://www.thebureauinvesti-gates.com/category/projects/drones/drones-graphs/ (accessed April 7, 2016).

17. Peter Bergen and Jennifer Rowland, "9 Myths about Drones and Guantanamo," *CNN*, May 22, 2013, accessed May 22, 2013, http://www.cnn. com/2013/05/22/opinion/bergen-nine-myths-drones-gitmo/index.html

18. "Obama: 'No Doubt' U.S. Drones Have Killed Civilians," *CNN*, April 1, 2016, http://www.cnn .com/2016/04/01/politics/obama-isis-drone-strikes-iran/ (accessed April 7, 2016).

19. "Department of Justice White Paper," (published by *NBC News* February 2013), accessed May 22, 2013, http://msnbcmedia.msn.com/i/msnbc/ sections/news/020413_DOJ_White_Paper.pdf

20. "Obama, in a Shift, to Limit Targets of Drone Strikes," *New York Times*, May 22, 2013, accessed

July 26, 2013, http://www.nytimes.com/2013/05/23/us/us-acknowledges-killing-4-americans-in-drone-strikes.html?_r=0

21. "Obama Speech on Drone Policy," *New York Times*, May 23, 2013, accessed May 23, 2013, http://www.nytimes.com/2013/05/24/us/politics/transcript-of-obamas-speech-on-drone-policy.html?pagewanted=all&_r=0

22. "Introduction to Chemical Weapons," Federation of American Scientists, www.fas.org/cw/intro.htm

23. Howard W. French, "100,000 People Perished, but Who Remembers?" *New York Times*, March 14, 2002, A4.

24. John W. Dower, "The Bombed: Hiroshimas and Nagasakis in Japanese Memory," in *Hiroshima in History and Memory*, ed. Michael J. Hogan (Cambridge: Cambridge University Press, 1996).

25. Rinjir Sodei, *Were We the Enemy?: American Survivors of Hiroshima* (Boulder, CO: Westview Press, 1998).

26. U.S. State Department, "New START" http://www.state.gov/t/avc/newstart/index.htm (accessed July 26, 2013)

27. Gregg Easterbrook, "Term Limits, The Meaninglessness of 'WMD,' " *New Republic*, October 7, 2002, 23.

28. Ibid.

29. Errol Morris, *The Fog of War*: Transcript, accessed May 21, 2013, http://www.errolmorris.com/film/fow_transcript.html

30. "UN Convention against Torture and Other Cruel, Inhuman or Degrading Treatment or Punishment (December 1984)," Audiovisual Library of International Law, accessed May 21, 2013, http://untreaty.un.org/cod/avl/ha/catcidtp/catcidtp.html

31. "Principles of the International Law Recognized in the Charter of the Nüremberg Tribunal and the Judgment of the Tribunal, 1950," Principle IV, at International Committee of the Red Cross, accessed May 21, 2013, http://www.icrc.org/applic/ihl/ihl.nsf/ART/390-550004?OpenDocument

32. See Michael Biddiss, "Victors' Justice? The Nuremberg Tribunal," *History Today* 45, no. 5 (1995), accessed May 21, 2013, http://www.historytoday.com/michael-biddiss/victors-justice-nuremberg-tribunal

33. Scott Shane, "Waterboarding Used 266 Times on 2 Suspects," *New York Times*, April 19, 2009, accessed June 16, 2013, http://www.nytimes.com/2009/04/20/world/20detain.html

34. Mark Danner, "U.S. Torture: Voices from the Black Sites," *New York Review of Books*, April 9, 2009, http://www.nybooks.com/articles/22530

35. Dick Cheney speaking on *The McLaughlin Group*, May 22, 2009, accessed June 18, 2013, http://www.mclaughlin.com/transcript.htm?id=725

36. David Luban, "The Defense of Torture," *New York Review of Books*, March 15, 2007, 37–40.

37. Ibid.

38. Uniform Code of Military Justice Sec. 893, Art. 93 accessed May 21, 2013, http://www.au.af.mil/au/awc/awcgate/ucmj2.htm

READING

Peace

ANDREW FITZ-GIBBON

MindTap® For more chapter resources and activities, go to MindTap.

Study Questions

1. Summarize Fitz-Gibbon's account of the history of nonviolence.
2. How does Fitz-Gibbon describe the difference between comprehensive approaches to nonviolence and less selective approaches?
3. What are the three main types of pacifism that Fitz-Gibbon discusses?

Despite the predominance of war in political affairs, peace and nonviolence were central ideas behind much political activism in the twentieth century. M. K. Gandhi was the first to use techniques of nonviolent resistance, first in South Africa (1893–1914) and then in India (1915–1947). For Gandhi, nonviolent protest required as much courage as warfare. The *satyagrahis*—those who practice *satyagraha*, "truth force" or "love-force"—were to resist oppressive sanctions by absorbing the violence of their oppressors in their own persons (2001, 3ff). In time the oppressor would cease violence, having had a fill of it. He called this the "law of self-sacrifice," the "law of nonviolence," and the "law of suffering." Just as the requirement of the military is training in how to use violence effectively, *satyagrahis* needed to be trained in how not to be violent (ibid., 92 ff). Gandhi even called for an official "non-violent army" of trained volunteers numbering the thousands who could put themselves in harmful way to end violence (ibid., 86).

Martin Luther King, Jr relied extensively on Gandhi's developed nonviolent techniques (see his "Pilgrimage to Nonviolence" in King 1986, 54–62). In his "My Trip to the land of Gandhi," King says, "True nonviolent resistance is not unrealistic submission to evil power. It is rather a courageous confrontation of evil by the power of love, in the faith that it is better to be a recipient of violence than the inflictor of it, since the latter only multiplies the existence of violence and bitterness in the universe, while the former may develop a sense of shame in the opponent, and thereby bring about a transformation and change of heart" (1986, 44).

King's understanding of nonviolence led him eventually to oppose all war and to make significant protest of the Vietnam War. He said, "I have come to the conclusion that the potential destructiveness of modern weapons of war totally rules out the possibility of war ever serving as a negative good. If we assume that mankind has a right to survive then we must find an alternative to war and destruction" (ibid., 60). Gandhi and King held in creative tension of the notions that nonviolence was a "good," an end in itself—something akin to love or truth—with

the notion of nonviolent resistance as a political strategy. In other words, nonviolence was not merely a political technique, but the outworking of a deeper metaphysics.

Since King, nonviolence as a political tool has been developed most especially by Gene Sharp (1973a-c, 2005). Sharp analyzed different techniques for using nonviolent protest as a means of achieving political ends. He suggested 198 different methods of nonviolent action in order to bring about social change. Peter Ackerman and Jack Duvall (2000) built on the pioneering work of Sharp. Ackerman and Duvall analyzed 12 different movements in the twentieth century which accomplished social and political change by direct nonviolent action. On close analysis, many of the movements were not as clearly nonviolent as Ackerman and Duvall suggest. Such change is accomplished by seizing the initiative to control a conflict to make the opposition give-in to demands against their will. In practice, nonviolent direct action is far from "peaceful." Nonetheless, their conclusion is persuasive: nonviolent direct action is a powerful means of social and political change. Their organization, the International Center on Nonviolent Conflict, through its publications and DVDs was influential in the overthrow of Serbian leader Slobodan Milosevic in 2000, and Ukrainian leader Viktor Yanukovych in 2004–2005. Their techniques were extensively used in the Arab Spring revolutions of 2010–2011 (see Gan, 2013, 70).

However, some on the Left criticize nonviolent direct action as politically ineffective and not going far enough. Ward Churchill in his *Pacifism as Pathology* says, "Pacifism as a strategy of achieving social, political, and economic change can only lead to the dead end of liberalism" (Churchill and Ryan, 2007, 33). Yet, in Eastern Europe, it was just such liberalism that the masses pursued as Soviet Communism faded.

Those who see nonviolence as more than a sociopolitical strategy also have criticized the direction

Andrew Fitz-Gibbon, *Peace* in Andrew Fiala, ed., The Bloomsbury Companion to Political Philosophy (London: Bloomsbury Publishing, 2015).

that Sharp, Ackerman, and Duvall have taken. Barry L. Gan notes a distinction between "selective nonviolence" and "comprehensive nonviolence" (2013, 73 ff). Selective nonviolence rejects the use of violence for pragmatic reasons in order to accomplish a political aim. The "good" is not nonviolence itself, but rather the political goal. If violence could achieve the goal more effectively and quickly, then violence would be used. However, some selective nonviolentists consider nonviolence as always a better strategy than violence, and so make no resort to violent tactics. Nonetheless, nonviolence is still considered merely a tool to use toward some other goal. Comprehensive nonviolence is the rejection of violence in all its forms; nonviolence being considered a good in itself. A comprehensive nonviolentist will attempt to practice nonviolence in all aspects of personal, social, and political life. Comprehensive nonviolentists reject some of the techniques suggested by Sharp as being inherently violent.

Gan also suggests that between the extremes of selective and comprehensive nonviolence is a wide spectrum of understandings and practices. He places Tolstoy, Gandhi, and King toward the pole of comprehensive nonviolence, and Sharp, Ackerman, and Duvall toward the pole of selective nonviolence.[1]

Feminism has contributed to understandings of peace through the Ethics of Care and other feminist philosophical writing (see Ruddick, 1990, Noddings, 2003, Held, 2007). Ethicists of care argue that it is, in part, the impersonal masculinist themes of political philosophy and ethics (contracts, rights, and duties) that allow even the contemplation of war as a good. The ethics of care, focused on networks of personal caring relationships, would make war and violence less likely than other ethical schemes.

Notable organizations involved in pacifism and antiwar are the Fellowship of Reconciliation, founded in 1914 as a Christian antiwar movement. It has since become an interfaith organization involving all faiths and includes those who have no formal faith commitment (see the collection of writings from the Fellowship of Reconciliation, Wink, 2000).

In some recent political philosophy, a distinction has been made between "negative peace" and "positive peace." Negative peace is the mere absence of war. Positive peace has taken on a more full conceptualization, a condition more akin to the Jewish notion of Shalom and is a state of well-being, free from violence. In different presentations, positive peace is a eudemonic, or else, a loving state. Duane L. Cady says of positive peace, "the point is always to build on and broaden our sense of community by stressing interdependence, respect, tolerance, common aspirations, and understanding" (2010, 86).

Johan Galtung analyzes negative peace as: (a) the absence of violence of all kinds (physical and psychological; (b) structural violence (violence embedded in institutions); and (c) cultural violence (attitudes and values that tolerate harm) (1996, 31). In moving the discussion of violence beyond the bounds of physical violence (to psychological, structural, and cultural harm), Galtung moves the discussion of negative peace beyond the notion of the absence of war. Although a nation may not be at war, its citizens may be subject to internal strife and various harms that Galtung classifies as violence. Positive peace, then, is not only the absence of war together with these diverse violent harms, but also a different kind of human interaction. Michael Allen Fox suggests that positive peace includes four aspects: (a) subjective (a state of well-being); (b) objective (a goal with a process to reach the goal); (c) cosmic (unity with a larger whole—not merely peace between human beings, but with other sentient beings and with the environment); and (d) prescriptive/visionary (guiding principles and outlook) (2014, 188–193).

HISTORICAL AND MULTICULTURAL PRECEDENTS

From ancient times, war has been an accepted part of human interaction. In the ancient world, arguments against war are few and far between, though in the *Crito* Plato argues that we should never return evil for evil. One interpretation of Plato would be to say that retaliation is morally wrong. As the conduct of war is largely retaliatory, often with extreme violence, Plato's argument might be taken as an early argument against war (2011, *Crito* 48b-c). However, even if this is a true construction, Plato's suggestion is a mere drop of war resistance in a bucketful of the political acceptance of, and justifications for, war.

It is not that notions of peace were absent from the ancient world. The Epicureans pursued *ataraxia* as the goal of human life—a state of tranquility untouched by the chances and changes of life— hence peace. Yet *ataraxia* belongs to peace as an inner state. The pursuit of *ataraxia* was engaged in with the knowledge that the world is one of conflict and war. There was no Epicurean antiwar movement in any political sense.

Ancient Buddhism and Jainism share the concept of *ahimsa*—nonharm—and from the sixth-century BCE onward had a direct influence on Hindu thought. Yet, in Buddhist thought the notion that all of life is suffering, and that the eightfold path leads one away from suffering have tended toward a social conservatism and individualism. As suffering will be always a part of the human condition, why try to eradicate it? The best hope is to become personally nonattached, and hence avoid suffering. The political attempts to embrace Buddhism as public policy, and hence antiwar, have been few and far between. A notable exception is Aśoka who ruled most of India from c. 265 to 238 BCE (see Cortwright, 2008, 186). However, more recently a new tradition, known as engaged Buddhism, has taken the Buddhist notion of *metta*—loving-kindness, as a starting point for engaged social action to alleviate suffering and protest war. Vietnamese monk Thich Nhat Hanh (1992) and the Dalai Lama (1999) are notable in this regard.

The Western world had to wait for the early Christian movement for its first brief hiatus looking toward an antiwar philosophy. For its first 250 years of existence, Christianity was a pacifist movement (Hershberger, 1981, 64–70). Christians were forbidden from being soldiers in the army of empire until around 174 CE, under the reign of Marcus Aurelius, though it must be remembered that early Christianity was a movement composed of slaves, women, and subaltern Jewish males. However, when Constantine embraced Christianity in the early fourth-century CE, the pacifist religion became the favored religion of Empire and began its own justifications

for war. Besides some elements of monasticism and a few minor sects in the medieval period, Christianity was at ease with violence, either enacted by the state against other states in war, or in pogroms, inquisitions, and crusades. Some Christians returned to pacifist roots, but not until the early sixteenth century.

Modern philosophers built their understanding of human nature—whether fundamentally aggressive or pacifistic—from a careful reading of ancient texts, by observation of human behavior, and sometimes because a certain view of human nature matched well with a religious or ideological viewpoint. However, recent developments in brain science have challenged the often-held view that human beings are ineluctably aggressive by nature. Suggestions, backed by science, that human beings are an empathic species have caused some controversy (see Rifkin, 2009). At the very least psychologists seem to have established that the human being rather than being either always aggressive, or else pacifistic, has the potential for predation, vengeance, and violence on the one hand, and for compassion, reason, and peacefulness on the other (see Pinker, 2011, 483–696).

PACIFISMS

Pacifism is generally taken to mean something like "opposition to war." However, there is no single understanding of pacifism in the literature. Scholars note these main types of pacifism: (a) principled opposition to war in all its forms, but not to all forms of violence; (b) principled opposition to all kinds of violence, which includes war; (c) principled opposition to some kinds of war, such as in nuclear pacifism, but not to "conventional" war. However, Duane L. Cady (2010) suggests a moral continuum from warism to pacifism, with the different versions of pacifism melding into each other with no clear boundaries.

The early sixteenth century saw profound changes in the political and social landscape of Europe. Besides the major reforms produced by Martin Luther, Ulrich Zwingli, John Calvin, and others, a number of small radical sects arose—loosely termed Anabaptist—in part in the wake of the breaking of the hegemony of the Roman church, and in part as a reaction to the slow progress of reform by the magisterial reformers. Once characterized as violent revolutionaries (in some tellings as proto-Marxist), the sixteenth-century radicals were rebranded as pacifists in the historiography of Mennonite scholars from the 1940s onward (see Estep, 1963, Hershberger, 1981). Careful, and nonpartisan, scholarship places the radicals somewhere in between. The beginning of religious and political freedom in the sixteenth century was fertile ground in which many varieties of religious and political groups thrived. Some radicals were truly revolutionary, though more often than not of an apocalyptic bent, while some embraced the pacifism of a nonviolent Christ (Stayer, 1976). Those groups that gradually embraced pacifism were historically longer lived as movements than the violent revolutionaries. Although both types of radical were persecuted by both Catholic and Protestant state authorities, the peaceful sects continued through migration, first to Eastern Europe, and then to the new world. These groups we know now as the Amish, the Mennonites, and the Hutterites, the historic peace churches. They have been largely pacifist groups who see themselves as islands of holiness in the vast sea of godlessness—what Stayer terms "separatist nonresistance." Those within the radical communities see themselves as within "the perfection of Christ." The rest of society is outside "the perfection of Christ." The world is characterized mostly by violence, which the Anabaptists eschew. Although pacifists, the Anabaptists had a generally pessimistic view of society and of political authority, though most viewed the government as God-given. They did not expect society to become more peaceful (Brock, 1981, 20). Nonetheless, the peaceful sixteenth-century radicals influenced the pacifist groups of the seventeenth century—most notably the Quakers—and many pacifists since. Whereas the Anabaptists tended to withdraw from society, the Quakers under William Penn's leadership attempted the "holy experiment" of a pacifist colony in the new world—Pennsylvania. The pacifist colony was in part successful (in relationships with native Americans and in its generally humanitarian

approach to law), but following Penn's death Pennsylvania gradually moved away from its pacifist roots (Brock, 1981, 43–46).

Anabaptist pacifism was of an absolute kind and has been termed nonresistance, based on an interpretation of the gospel text where Jesus says, "Do not resist evil." The text was interpreted to include not only opposition to war or any government violence—"the sword"—but also any interpersonal violence. The Anabaptists took the injunction to "turn the other cheek" quite literally. Even self-defense was considered morally wrong. Although few have followed the Anabaptist extreme of nonresistance, most notably Leo Tolstoy embraced such radical pacifism in the late nineteenth century (1984). Tolstoy differed from the Anabaptists in holding a more hopeful view of the world. The Anabaptists considered the world unredeemable until some great apocalyptic event. Hence they did not try to change society, and simply withdrew into closed communities. Tolstoy, on the other hand, argued that all in society should embrace nonresistance.

The Anabaptist stance has often been considered politically irrelevant—though in the twentieth century Anabaptist were also conscientious objectors (see Brock and Young, 1999). However, scholars have used Anabaptist-like arguments, that is religious, to protest war (see, e.g. Hauerwas, 1983, 2004, Yoder, 1994, 1996, 1997).

A different argument against war and for a peaceful life is the brief but influential tract by Henry David Thoreau, *On The Duty of Civil Disobedience* written originally in 1849, in part as protest both to slavery and to the Mexican war. Thoreau's basis is not a religious one, but is based on the inviolability of the individual conscience. Government has no right to demand anything from citizens (for Thoreau the best form of government is no government at all). As government demand citizens to enter the military, it is the citizen's duty to resist, to disobey government nonviolently. Thoreau's view is significant for political philosophy in its direct challenge of the legitimacy of government. Libertarians and anarchists alike have used Thoreau as a justification for an antigovernment stance.

Thoreau (along with other New England pacifists) influenced Tolstoy. In turn, Thoreau and Tolstoy's work had a direct effect on the young Mohandas Gandhi, then in South Africa, and later on Martin Luther King Jr. In process of time, the religious argument of the teaching of the New Testament—to not resist evil, to love enemies, and to bless persecutors—was conjoined with Thoreau's notion of civil disobedience, based on conscience, to become the social political strategy of nonviolent resistance, sometimes termed simply nonviolence.

NOTES

1. For an extended essay on the implementation of non-violence, see Nagler (2004). For the history of peace movements, see Cortwright (2008). For an eclectic collection of essays on non-violence, see Zinn (2002). For the history of non-violence, see Kurlansky (2009). For a general introduction to peace studies, see Fox (2014). For an historical collection of essays on non-violence, see Holmes and Gan (2005).

WORKS CITED

Ackerman, P. and Duvall, J. (2000), *A Force More Powerful: A Century of Nonviolent Conflict.* Palgrave: New York.

Brock, P. (1981), *The Roots of War Resistance: Pacifism from the Early Church to Tolstoy.* Nyack: The Fellowship of Reconciliation.

Brock, P. and Young, N. (1999), *Pacifism in the Twentieth Century.* Toronto: University of Toronto Press.

Cady, D. L. (2010), *From Warism to Pacifism: A Moral Continuum.* Philadelphia, PA: Temple University Press.

Churchill, W. and M. Ryan (2007), *Pacifism as Pathology: Reflections on the Role of Armed Struggle in North America.* Oakland: A.K. Press.

Cortwright, D. (2008), *Peace: A History of Movements and Ideas.* Cambridge: Cambridge University Press.

Estep, W. R. (1963), *The Anabaptist Story.* Grand Rapids, MI: Wm. B. Eerdmans.

Fox, M. A. (2014), *Understanding Peace: A Comprehensive Introduction.* New York and London: Routledge.

Galtung, J. (1996), *Peace by Peaceful Means: Peace and Conflict, Development and Civilization.* Oslo: PRIO International Peace Research Institute, and London: SAGE.

Gan, B. L. (2013), *Violence and Nonviolence: An Introduction.* Lanham: Rowman & Littlefield.

Gandhi, M. K. (2001), *Non-Violent Resistance (Satyagraha).* Mineola, NY: Dover.

Hanh, T. N. (1992), *Peace in Every Step: The Path of Mindfulness in Every Day Life.* New York: Bantam.

Hauerwas, S. (1983), *The Peaceable Kingdom: A Primer in Christian Ethics.* Notre Dame: University of Notre Dame Press.

—(2004), *Performing the Faith: Bonhoeffer and the Practice of Nonviolence.* Grand Rapids, MI: Brazos Press.

Held, V. (2007), *The Ethics of Care: Personal, Political And Global.* Oxford: Oxford University Press.

Hershberger, G. F. (1981), *War, Peace, and Nonresistance; A Classic Statement of a Mennonite Peace Position in Faith and Practice.* Scottdale: Herald Press.

Holmes, R. L. and Gan, B. L. (2005), *Nonviolence in Theory and Practice.* Longrove, IL: Waveland.

King, M. L., Jr (1986), *I Have a Dream: Writings and Speeches that Changed the World*, J. M. Washington (ed.). San Francisco: Harper.

Kurlansky, M. (2009), *Non-Violence: The History of a Dangerous Idea*, foreword by His Holiness the Dalai Lama. New York: The Modern Library.

Lama, D. (1999), *Ethics for a New Millennium.* New York: Berkley.

Nagler, M. N. (2004), *The Search for a Nonviolent Future: A Promise of Peace for Ourselves, Our Families, and Our World.* Maui, HI: Inner Ocean Publishing.

Noddings, N. (2003), *Caring: A Feminine Approach to Ethics and Moral Education.* Berkeley, CA: University of California Press.

Pinker, S. (2011), *The Better Angels of Our Nature: Why Violence Has Declined.* London: Penguin.

Plato (2011), *The Last Days of Socrates.* London: Penguin.

Rifkin, J. (2009), *The Empathic Civilization: The Race to Global Consciousness in a World of Crisis.* New York: Jeremy P. Tarcher/Penguin.

Ruddick, S. (1990), *Maternal Thinking: Towards a Politics of Peace*. London: Women's Press.

Sharp, G. (1973a), *The Politics of Nonviolent Action: Part One Power and Struggle*. Boston, MA: Porter Sargent.

—(1973b), *The Politics of Nonviolent Action: Part Two The Methods of Nonviolent Action*. Boston, MA: Porter Sargent.

—(1973c), *The Politics of Nonviolent Action: Part Three The Dynamics of Nonviolent Action*. Boston, MA: Porter Sargent.

—(2005), *Waging Nonviolent Struggle: 20th Century Practice and 21st Century Potential*. Boston, MA: Porter Sargent.

Stayer, J. M. (1976), *Anabaptists and the Sword*. Lawrence, KS: Coronado Press.

Tolstoy, L. (1984), *The Kingdom of God is Within You: Christianity Not as a Mystic Religion but as a New Theory of Life*, trans. C. Garnett. Lincoln: University of Nebraska Press.

Wink, W. (ed.) (2000), *Peace is the Way: Writings on Nonviolence from the Fellowship of Reconciliation*. Maryknoll, NY: Orbis Books.

Yoder, J. H. (1994), *The Politics of Jesus*. Grand Rapids, MI: Eerdmans.

—(1996), *When War is Unjust: Being Honest About Just War Thinking*. Maryknoll, NY: Orbis.

—(1997), *For the Nations: Essays Public and Evangelical*. Grand Rapids, MI: Wm. B. Eerdmans.

Zinn, H. (Introduction) (2002), *The Power of Nonviolence: Writings by Advocates of Peace*. Boston, MA: Beacon Press.

READING

The Triumph of Just War Theory (and the Dangers of Success)

MICHAEL WALZER

MindTap For more chapter resources and activities, go to MindTap.

Study Questions

1. What role did "the national interest" play in the new realism of the 1950s and 1960s, according to Walzer?
2. According to Walzer, in what way has moral theory about just war triumphed?
3. What two responses to this position does Walzer describe, and what are his criticisms of each?

In the 1950s and early 1960s, when I was in graduate school, realism was the reigning doctrine in the field of "international relations." The standard reference was not to justice but to interest. Moral argument was against the rules of the discipline as it was commonly practiced, although a few writers defended interest as the new morality. There were many political scientists in those years who preened themselves as modern Machiavellis and dreamed of whispering in the ear of the prince; and a certain number of them, enough to stimulate the ambition of the others, actually got to whisper. They

practiced being cool and tough-minded; they taught the princes, who did not always need to be taught, how to get results through the calculated application of force. Results were understood in terms of "the national interest," which was the objectively determined sum of power and wealth here and now plus the probability of future power and wealth. More of both was almost always taken to be better; only a

Michael Walzer, "The Triumph of Just War Theory (and the Dangers of Success)," *Social Research* (Winter 2002): 925–933. Reprinted by permission of The New School for Social Research.

few writers argued for the acceptance of prudential limits; moral limits were, as I remember those years, never discussed. Just war theory was relegated to religion departments, theological seminaries, and a few Catholic universities. And even in those places, isolated as they were from the political world, the theory was pressed toward realist positions; perhaps for the sake of self-preservation, its advocates surrendered something of its critical edge.

Vietnam changed all this, although it took a while for the change to register at the theoretical level. What happened first occurred in the realm of practice. The war became a subject of political debate; it was widely opposed, mostly by people on the left. These were people heavily influenced by Marxism; they also spoke a language of interest; they shared with the princes and professors of American politics a disdain for moralizing. And yet the experience of the war pressed them toward moral argument. Of course, the war in their eyes was radically imprudent; it could not be won; its costs, even if Americans thought only of themselves, were much too high; it was an imperialist adventure unwise even for the imperialists; it set the United States against the cause of national liberation, which would alienate it from the Third World (and significant parts of the First). But these claims failed utterly to express the feelings of most of the war's opponents, feelings that had to do with the systematic exposure of Vietnamese civilians to the violence of American war-making. Almost against its will, the left fell into morality. All of us in the antiwar camp suddenly began talking the language of just war—though we did not know that that was what we were doing…

What happened then was that people on the left, and many others too, looked for a common moral language. And what was most available was the language of just war. We were, all of us, a bit rusty, unaccustomed to speaking in public about morality. The realist ascendancy had robbed us of the very words that we needed, which we slowly reclaimed: aggression intervention, just cause, self-defense, noncombatant immunity, proportionality, prisoners of war, civilians, double effect, terrorism, war crimes. And we came to understand that these words had meanings. Of course, they could be used instrumentally; that is always true of political and moral terms. But if we attended to their meanings, we found ourselves involved in a discussion that had its own structure. Like characters in a novel, concepts in a theory shape the narrative or the argument in which they figure.

Once the war was over, just war became an academic subject; now political scientists and philosophers discovered the theory; it was written about in the journals and taught in the universities—and also in the (American) military academies and war colleges. A small group of Vietnam veterans played a major role in making the discipline of morality central to the military curriculum. They had bad memories. They welcomed just war theory precisely because it was in their eyes a critical theory. It is, in fact, doubly critical—of war's occasions and its conduct. I suspect that the veterans were most concerned with the second of these. It is not only that they wanted to avoid anything like the My Lai massacre in future wars; they wanted, like professional soldiers everywhere, to distinguish their profession from mere butchery. And because of their Vietnam experience, they believed that this had to be done systematically; it required not only a code but also a theory. Once upon a time, I suppose, aristocratic honor had grounded the military code; in a more democratic and egalitarian age, the code had to be defended with arguments.

And so we argued. The discussions and debates were wide-ranging even if, once the war was over, they were mostly academic. It is easy to forget how large the academic world is in the United States: there are millions of students and tens of thousands of professors. So a lot of people were involved, future citizens and army officers, and the theory was mostly presented, though this presentation was also disputed, as a manual for wartime criticism. Our cases and examples were drawn from Vietnam and were framed to invite criticism. Here was a war that we should never have fought, and that we fought badly, brutally, as if there were no moral limits. So it became, retrospectively, an occasion for drawing a line—and for committing ourselves to the moral casuistry necessary to determine the precise location of the line. Ever since Pascal's brilliant denunciation, casuistry has had a bad name among moral philosophers; it is commonly taken to be excessively permissive, not so much an application as a relaxation of the moral rules. When we looked back at the Vietnamese cases, however, we were more likely to deny permission than to grant it, insisting again and again that what had been done should not have been done.

But there was another feature of Vietnam that gave the moral critique of the war special force: it was a war that we lost, and the brutality with which we fought the war almost certainly contributed to our defeat. In a war for "hearts and minds," rather than for land and resources, justice turns out to be a key to victory. So just war theory looked once again like the worldly doctrine that it is. And here, I think, is the deepest cause of the theory's contemporary triumph: there are now reasons of state for fighting justly. One might almost say that justice has become a military necessity.

There were probably earlier wars in which the deliberate killing of civilians, and also the common military carelessness about killing civilians, proved to be counterproductive. The Boer war is a likely example. But for us, Vietnam was the first war in which the practical value of *jus in bello* became apparent. To be sure, the "Vietnam syndrome" is generally taken to reflect a different lesson: that we should not fight wars that are unpopular at home and to which we are unwilling to commit the resources necessary for victory. But there was in fact another lesson, connected to but not the same as the "syndrome": that we should not fight wars about whose justice we are doubtful, and that once we are engaged we have to fight justly so as not to antagonize the civilian population, whose political support is necessary to a military victory. In Vietnam, the relevant civilians were the Vietnamese themselves; we lost the war when we lost their "hearts and minds." But this idea about the need for civilian support has turned out to be both variable and expansive: modern warfare requires the support of different civilian populations, extending beyond the population immediately at risk. Still, a

moral regard for civilians at risk is critically important in winning wider support for the war... for any modern war. I will call this the usefulness of morality. Its wide acknowledgement is something radically new in military history.

Hence the old spectacle of George Bush (the elder), during the Persian Gulf war, talking like a just war theorist. Well, not quite: for Bush's speeches and press conferences displayed an old American tendency, which his son has inherited, to confuse just wars and crusades, as if a war can be just only when the forces of good are arrayed against the forces of evil. But Bush also seemed to understand—and this was a constant theme of American military spokesmen—that war is properly a war of armies, a combat between combatants, from which the civilian population should be shielded. I do not believe that the bombing of Iraq in 1991 met just war standards; shielding civilians would certainly have excluded the destruction of electricity networks and water purification plants. Urban infrastructure, even if it is necessary to modern war-making, is also necessary to civilian existence in a modern city, and it is morally defined by this second feature. Still, American strategy in the Gulf war was the result of a compromise between what justice would have required and the unrestrained bombing of previous wars; taken overall, targeting was far more limited and selective than it had been, for example, in Korea or Vietnam. The reasons for the limits were complicated: in part, they reflected a commitment to the Iraqi people (which turned out not to be very strong), in the hope that the Iraqis would repudiate the war and overthrow the regime that began it; in part, they reflected the political necessities of the coalition that made the war possible. Those necessities were shaped in turn by the media coverage of the war—that is, by the immediate access of the media to the battle and of people the world over to the media. Bush and his generals believed that these people would not tolerate a slaughter of civilians, and they were probably right (but what it might mean for them not to tolerate something was and is fairly unclear). Hence, although many of the countries whose support was crucial to the war's success were not democracies, bombing policy was dictated in important ways by the demos.

This will continue to be true: the media are omnipresent, and the whole world is watching. War has to be different in these circumstances. But does this mean that it has to be more just or only that it has to look most just, that it has to be described, a little more persuasively than in the past, in the language of justice? The triumph of just war theory is clear enough; it is amazing how readily military spokesmen during the Kosovo and Afghanistan wars used its categories, telling a causal story that justified the war and providing accounts of the battles that emphasized the restraint with which they were being fought. The arguments (and rationalizations) of the past were very different; they commonly came from outside the armed forces—from clerics, lawyers, and professors, not from generals— and they commonly lacked specificity and detail. But what does the use of these categories, these just and moral words, signify?

Perhaps naively, I am inclined to say that justice has become, in all Western countries, one of the tests that any proposed military strategy or tactic has to meet—only one of the tests and not the most important one, but this still gives just war theory a place and standing that it never had before. It is easier now than it ever was to imagine a general saying, "No, we can't do that; it would cause too many civilian deaths; we have to find another way." I am not sure that there are many generals who talk like that, but imagine for a moment that there are; imagine that strategies are evaluated morally as well as militarily; that civilian deaths are minimized; that new technologies are designed to avoid or limit collateral damage, and that these technologies are actually effective in achieving their intended purpose. Moral theory has been incorporated into war-making as a real constraint on when and how wars are fought. This picture is, remember, imaginary, but it is also partly true; and it makes for a far more interesting argument than the more standard claim that the triumph of just war is pure hypocrisy. The triumph is real: what then is left for theorists and philosophers to do?

This question is sufficiently present in our consciousness that one can watch people trying to respond. There are two responses that I want to describe and criticize. The first comes from what might be called the postmodern left, which does not claim that affirmations of justice are hypocritical, since hypocrisy implies standards, but rather that there are no standards, no possible objective use of the categories of just war theory. Politicians and generals who adopt the categories are deluding themselves—though no more so than the theorists who developed the categories in the first place. Maybe new technologies kill fewer people, but there is no point in arguing about who those people are and whether or not killing them is justified. No agreement about justice, or about guilt or innocence, is possible. This view is summed up in a line that speaks to our immediate situation: "One man's terrorist is another man's freedom fighter." On this view, there is nothing for theorists and philosophers to do but choose sides, and there is no theory or principle that can guide their choice. But this is an impossible position, for it holds that we cannot recognize, condemn, and actively oppose the murder of innocent people.

A second response is to take the moral need to recognize, condemn and oppose very seriously and then to raise the theoretical ante—that is, to strengthen the constraints that justice imposes on warfare. For theorists who pride themselves on living, so to speak, at the critical edge, this is an obvious and understandable response. For many years, we have used the theory of just war to criticize American military actions, and now it has been taken over by the generals and is being used to explain and justify those actions. Obviously, we must resist. The easiest way to resist is to make noncombatant immunity into a stronger and stronger rule, until it is something like an absolute rule: all killing of civilians is (something close to) murder; therefore any war that leads to the killing of civilians is unjust; therefore every war is unjust. So pacifism reemerges from the very heart of the theory that was originally meant to replace it. This is the strategy adopted, most recently, by many opponents of the

Afghanistan war. The protest marches on American campuses featured banners proclaiming, "Stop the Bombing!" and the argument for stopping was very simple (and obviously true): bombing endangers and kills civilians. The marchers did not seem to feel that anything more had to be said.

Since I believe that war is still, sometimes, necessary, this seems to me a bad argument and, more generally, a bad response to the triumph of just war theory. It sustains the critical role of the theory vis-à-vis war generally, but it denies the theory the critical role it has always claimed, which is internal to the business of war and requires critics to attend closely to what soldiers try to do and what they try not to do. The refusal to make distinctions of this kind, to pay attention to strategic and tactical choices, suggests a doctrine of radical suspicion. This is the radicalism of people who do not expect to exercise power or use force, ever, and who are

not prepared to make the judgments that this exercise and use require. By contrast, just war theory, even when it demands a strong critique of particular acts of war, is the doctrine of people who do expect to exercise power and use force. We might think of it as a doctrine of radical responsibility, because it holds political and military leaders responsible, first of all, for the well-being of their own people, but also for the well-being of innocent men and women on the other side. Its proponents set themselves against those who will not think realistically about the defense of the country they live in and also against those who refuse to recognize the humanity of their opponents. They insist that there are things that it is morally impermissible to do even to the enemy. They also insist, however, that fighting itself cannot be morally impermissible. A just war is meant to be, and has to be, a war that it is possible to fight.

REVIEW EXERCISES

1. Why is the just war theory considered a middle path between realism and pacifism?
2. List and explain the basic principles of *jus ad bellum* and *jus in bello*.
3. What are the challenges for thinking about the application of just war principles in the contemporary world?
4. Can terrorism or torture be justified? On what grounds?
5. How does the principle of double effect apply in just war thinking?
6. What counts as a "war crime" or a "crime against humanity"?

DISCUSSION CASES

1. **Military Service**. Although military service is no longer compulsory in the United States, American males age eighteen to twenty-five have to register with the Selective Service. If you do not register, you may be denied benefits and employment opportunities. James recently turned eighteen. He is opposed to war and is considering not signing up. He is explaining this to his parents. James says, "Look, I don't want to support a system that fights unjust wars and I won't fight in one. So I'm not going to sign up." James's father is a military veteran. He responds, "We've all got a duty to serve our country, whether just or unjust. And anyway, you're wrong to claim we fight unjust wars. Our military fights justly. Do your duty and register." James's brother has a different opinion. He says, "Your moral principles don't apply in war. There are no just or unjust wars. There are only winners and losers. It's better to be on the winning side. You should register because you want the benefits and don't want to get busted."

   Whom do you agree with here: James, his father, or his brother? Should a person register to fight if he doesn't believe in the justice of the wars that are being fought? How should moral principles apply in this case?

2. **Terrorism.** Marta has expressed sympathy for rebels fighting in country X. These rebels have been fighting against an unjust and malicious regime. The regime has killed innocent civilians and has an awful record of human rights violations. The rebellion started as a nonviolent protest in the streets. But now the rebels have taken up arms and are actively fighting government forces. They have begun to employ terror tactics, exploding car bombs in the city center in the capital. Marta supports the rebel cause and has even bought a T-shirt with a slogan from the rebel campaign on it. Marta's roommate, Andrea, is appalled. Andrea tells her, "How can you wear a T-shirt celebrating terrorists? They kill innocent people. Even if their cause is just, the rebels have crossed the line. They're murderers. All terrorists are simply murderers." Marta replies, "That's easy for you to say because you're not suffering under a repressive government. The rebels are justified in doing whatever it takes to bring down the government. The government forces are ruthless and strong—the rebels have to use terrorism: it's their only tool."

   Whom do you agree with: Marta or Andrea? Is terrorism justified as a tool of last resort? Or is terrorism always murder? Explain your answer, making use of concepts employed in discussions of realism, just war theory, and pacifism.

3. **Military Intervention**. The ruler of country Z has a terrible record of human rights violations. He has ordered the slaughter of civilians and has threatened to invade neighboring states. He has been working with known arms dealers to develop his military capacity. And he has worked to spread his influence by supporting insurgent fighters and terrorist groups in other countries. Three students are debating this case and what the United States should do in response. Roxanne is a realist. She argues that we should attack country Z with massive force as soon as possible with the goal of decapitating the regime. "That's what we did in Japan during World War II. And now Japan is a peaceful and stable ally." Patrick is a pacifist. He disagrees. "You know that we dropped atomic weapons on Japan and firebombed cities. It was immoral to do that. The end doesn't justify the means. We have to find nonviolent alternatives to deal with Z." Justin advocates limited use of military force. He says, "The just war tradition might allow for preemptive force and may allow for limited war in defense of human rights. But we have to be careful not to kill civilians." Roxanne shakes her head. "Sorry, but you can't win a war without killing civilians. And the faster you win, the better for everyone." Patrick sighs. "Have we even tried all of the nonviolent alternatives?" Justin shrugs. "If we go to war, it can only be a last resort. But, Roxanne, you can't just kill the innocent. You've got to win hearts and minds, as well."

   Whom do you agree with in this debate? Why? What do you suggest we do about brutal dictators and aggressive regimes?

MindTap® For more chapter resources and activities, go to MindTap.

20 Global Justice and Globalization

valentina angiuli photografie/Moment/Getty Images

Learning Outcomes

After reading this chapter, you should be able to:

- Recapitulate contemporary debates over global justice.
- Explain the ideas of ethical consumerism and fair trade.
- Apply concepts such as utilitarianism, justice, and rights to global issues.
- Explain criticisms and defenses of economic globalization.
- Describe connections between globalization and the challenges posed by cultural diversity and relativism.
- Evaluate levels of international aid and the role of international institutions.
- Defend a thesis about the ethical issue of global poverty.

MindTap® For more chapter resources and activities, go to MindTap.

In recent years, it has become obvious that the globe is increasingly integrated. Ebola outbreaks in West Africa have caused health scares in North America and elsewhere. European youth have traveled to the Middle East to fight on behalf of ISIS—the so-called Islamic State. Terrorists with ties to ISIS and other radical groups have attacked Europe and North America. Refugees from Middle Eastern conflicts have fled to Europe. Immigrants from South and Central America continue to travel across the border into the United States. Climate change and other global environmental problems threaten all of us. A downturn in the market in one part of the world can have an impact on prices in faraway lands. Oil, electronics, books, films, music, airplanes, and people flow across borders in ways previously unimaginable.

An old story holds that a butterfly flapping its wings in one part of the world may be a contributing cause to a hurricane in another part of the world. One recent book warns that this so-called butterfly effect becomes dangerous in a world that is not prepared to respond to the interconnected systems of our global era. The authors of *The Butterfly Defect* argue that the ethical justification of globalization rests upon its promise to improve living conditions and life prospects for people around the world—but also that this justification is undermined when globalization does not deliver on this promise.[1] This basic justification of globalization appeals to consequentialism: globalization is thought to be good if it produces good outcomes. A different question focuses on rights and obligations. Do we have obligations to care for others across the globe—those who live in poverty, for example? And how ought we to respond to the challenges produced by global integration, including the demand to admit refugees and the need to respect the rights of indigenous cultures? There are a variety of connected issues to be discussed here. We cannot focus on all of them. Instead we will focus on a few issues, reminding ourselves that similar issues—economic opportunity, social justice, respect for rights, and the challenge of cultural relativism—have been addressed in prior chapters.

Let's begin with the question of where our food and clothing comes from. There is a good chance that at least some of the food you ate for breakfast today was either produced in a foreign country or was processed by immigrants. The same is true for the clothes on your back. Take a look at the labels on your clothing and other consumer goods: chances are that your clothes, electronics, furniture, and toys are produced in places such as China, Sri Lanka, or Bangladesh. One reason for this is that it is cheaper to manufacture goods in these places. But cheap manufacturing is not without social costs and ethical challenges. In 2013, a garment factory in Bangladesh collapsed, killing more than 1,120 workers. The previous year, a fire at another Bangladeshi garment factory resulted in more than a hundred deaths. In 2013, a shoe factory caved in on workers in Cambodia, killing two and injuring dozens of others.[2] In 2011, two explosions at plants manufacturing iPads in China killed four workers, injured seventy-seven others, and raised serious questions about safety conditions throughout Apple's supply chain.[3] These industrial disasters prompted calls for more equitable and just treatment of workers across the globe. The Walt Disney company announced that it was going to stop producing Disney brand products in developing countries that have lax labor standards and poor regulation, including Bangladesh, Pakistan, Belarus, Ecuador, and Venezuela.[4] Some viewed this as a good move on the part of Disney, motivated by a sense of moral responsibility. But critics worry that if big corporations pull out of the developing world,

it will cause unemployment and create negative outcomes for the workers there. Some brands and retail chains are working with local labor and business leaders in the developing world to forge agreements on fire codes and other safety codes for the factories they do business with.

Of course, if working conditions in the developing world are improved, consumer prices in the developed world may rise. While rising prices of consumer goods would create hardship for many, some consumers may not mind paying more for products that are produced and traded in nonexploitative markets. Indeed, some people conscientiously choose to pay more for clothing and other products that are not produced in sweatshops, pursuing a path called variously, *ethical consumption, ethical consumerism,* or *shopping with conscience.* This approach to consumption aims to channel consumer choices in morally responsible and sustainable directions. Would you be willing to pay more for a product to ensure that the product is not produced in a sweatshop or by other exploitative labor practices?

One concept associated with the idea of ethical consumerism is the idea of *fair trade practices.* Fair trade aims to help disadvantaged people in the developing world by buying goods that are produced in beneficial and nonexploitative conditions.[5] You may have seen fair trade items advertised in stores or on websites. Fair trade coffee, for example, is typically certified by one of several nonprofit organizations (such as Fair Trade USA) to be grown and harvested by workers who are able to earn a living wage under safe working conditions. (See the discussion of living wage in Chapter 14.) But some critics worry that the fair trade label simply makes consumers feel good, while being used as a marketing ploy by big corporations.[6] Similar worries have been voiced about contributions to aid organizations. How can we be sure that those we intend to help actually receive the help we intend to give? There is an important practical question here, one that does not, however, change the moral question of whether we should help others in need—especially very poor people in other parts of the globe.

Globalization creates moral questions about global justice, including decent working conditions for people across the globe.

Not everyone agrees we should go out of our way to help others. And many will argue that it is perfectly fine to maximize one's own self-interest by seeking out bargains no matter how they are produced, or by refusing to donate to charities. For many, it just does not seem rational to pay more for fair trade coffee or sneakers or T-shirts, when cheaper products can be found. Why should we be concerned with the deaths of garment workers in distant countries? Why should we care whether foreign peasants earn a living wage? Those questions are part of a larger question about the sorts of obligations we have to those who suffer and die in distant lands. These sorts of ethical questions arise in the context of thinking about globalization; they are the concerns of global justice.

Globalization is the process through which the world's business, cultural, and political systems are becoming more integrated. **Globalization** can be defined as a historical process that includes the growing interconnection of local and national economies from all corners of the world, which occurs as capital, goods, services, labor, technology, ideas, and expertise move across international borders. Globalization is a fact; the world is increasingly integrated. **Global justice** is focused on the moral question of the underlying fairness and justice of the current globalized situation. Proponents of global justice are focused broadly on the question of what sort of concern we ought to have for all human beings, regardless of national status or citizenship. In this sense, global justice is *cosmopolitan*—directed toward the universal concerns of all citizens of the world. We discussed cosmopolitan concerns in Chapter 2, where we dealt with the problem of relativism and religious difference. Those issues remain in the background of the consideration of global justice. Is there a moral framework that can encompass the entire globe, despite global diversity? Or is the world fragmented into rival nations, economies, and civilizations that each ought to fend for themselves? What sorts of obligations do individuals have toward each other in the context of a world that is controlled by national governments, international treaties, nongovernmental organizations, and multinational corporations?

One of the issues of concern from the standpoint of global justice is poverty and gross inequalities across the globe. This topic is connected to our discussion of economic justice and inequality in Chapter 14. But the issue of global economic inequality is complicated by the fact that many current inequities can be traced to past colonial and imperial injustices. Some nations have built up their present economic power by exploiting other nations. A further problem is the presence of national and cultural differences, as well as local governments of various types, which operate as intermediaries between individual citizens and the demands of global justice. We have to figure out which theory of economics and politics makes sense in thinking about global justice. We also have to figure out how that moral theory should be applied in a world of vast cultural differences.

MindTap   For more chapter resources and activities, go to MindTap.

MORAL ARGUMENTS ABOUT GLOBAL POVERTY

In 2013, the president of the World Bank, Jim Yong Kim, announced the goal of eliminating extreme poverty across the globe by the year 2030. He linked the moral goal of eliminating global poverty to the goal of sustainable development for all peoples: "Assuring that growth is inclusive is both a moral imperative and a crucial condition for sustained economic development."[7] Kim suggested that sustainable development for everyone requires us to address global poverty and inequality—and that it is beneficial for those in affluent nations when those in the developing world are also doing better. But Kim also used strong moral language, claiming that helping the global poor is a moral imperative. If there is a moral duty to help the poor, then it would be wrong not to help them. And if it is wrong not to help the poor, then we should feel guilty if we do not help them. With billions of people living on a few dollars per day, should we feel guilty if we are enjoying a $5 café latte or ice cream treat? For the price of one of those luxuries, we could be helping children who might die from poverty. If you don't feel guilty when you enjoy your tasty treat, is there something morally wrong with you?

A critic may reply that the fact that we do not feel guilty about our indulgences is a sign that there is no moral obligation to care about the suffering of distant people. Of course, it might be that our feelings are poor guides for morality and we really should feel guilty. A further argument is needed. The critic might provide one by claiming that our individual choices can have little effect on something as complex as the global economy. There is no guarantee that by donating to charity instead of enjoying a luxury good, we will actually help anyone. And besides, the critic may continue, the old saying holds that if you give a man a fish, you only feed him for a day but when you give a man a fishing pole, you feed him for a lifetime. Following that line of reasoning, the critic may argue that giving to the poor only makes them dependent on handouts. It is better, from this perspective, to buy commodities produced by the poor than to give to them directly,

since trading on the market is the key to long-term economic well-being.

Another criticism of the idea of donating to the poor focuses on the nature of obligation and duty. Many feel that although it would be nice to help poor people, charity is supererogatory—something that goes above and beyond what is required. And furthermore, some might argue, charity should begin at home, as the saying goes. In this view, we have obligations to care for our close relations, our friends, and our co-citizens, and those obligations are more important than any charitable obligation we might have to suffering foreigners. These critics may also argue that global poverty is simply not our fault. Guilt and responsibility are appropriate if you have done something wrong. But there is nothing wrong with buying a latte or a pair of sneakers, and my consumer choices do not actively harm the poor. In fact, some may argue, by buying sneakers produced in sweatshops in Cambodia, we are helping the Cambodians who produce them by purchasing their products. Without the purchases of consumers in affluent countries, those workers might have no jobs at all.

One response to that argument has been given by the philosopher Thomas Pogge, an important proponent of the idea of global justice. Pogge argues that the international system violates the rights of the world's poor. He claims that the international system is rigged against the poor—as large corporations and conditions created by historical injustices contribute to the continuing plight of the disadvantaged. Pogge acknowledges that there is a difference between failing to save people and actively killing them. But he claims that we are not merely failing to save the poor; he also claims that we are actively perpetuating their predicament because historical and international structures create a "massive headwind" that the poor cannot overcome. He concludes that affluent nations and citizens of affluent nations owe compensation to the poor.[8] He has proposed, for example, a "global resource dividend" as one aspect of a global scheme for compensating the poor. This is a sort of tax on resources that would be used to help the poor. One example he proposes is a $3 per barrel charge on oil. This would raise the price of oil by about 7 cents per gallon; but the revenue generated would create sufficient funding to eradicate world hunger within a few years.[9] Practical and political details remain to be worked out for such a proposal. For example, how do we institute and collect such resource dividends? But the practical concerns do not change the nature of Pogge's moral claim—that we owe compensation to the poor and that we ought to find ways to help alleviate world hunger.

A similar argument has been made by the utilitarian philosopher Peter Singer—an author whom we've discussed in previous chapters (with regard to animal welfare, for example, in Chapter 17). Singer maintains that giving to victims of famines is not charity but, rather, a duty. Singer stipulates that, "if it is in our power to prevent something very bad from happening, without thereby sacrificing anything morally significant, we ought, morally, to do it." Singer uses an analogy of saving a child from drowning in a mud puddle to make his point: "if I am walking past a shallow pond and see a child drowning in it, I ought to wade in and pull the child out. This will mean getting my clothes muddy, but this is insignificant, while the death of the child would presumably be a very bad thing."[10] Singer maintains that proximity does not matter—if the dying child is far away or nearby, we still have the same obligation. And he denies that our individual responsibility can be diffused by the fact that there are lots of others who could also help; each should help, whether there are others who could help or not. Singer believes that we have an obligation to help those less well off than ourselves to the extent that helping them leaves us less well off than they are. He explains that we ought to give up to the point of "marginal utility," that is up to the point at which giving causes us to suffer significantly so that by giving we end up in as bad a state as those we are trying to help.

Singer's idea is demanding. It implies that I must always justify spending money on myself or my family or friends. Whether I am justified in doing so, in this view, depends on whether anything I do for myself or others is of comparable moral importance to saving the lives of others who are starving and lacking in basic necessities. But Singer's arguments

have resonated with a number of people. The *Washington Post* reported on a number of people who have pursued big salaries on Wall Street and in other ventures with the goal of earning lots of money precisely so they can give much of it away to help the poor. The phenomenon has been described as "earning to give." Several of the individuals who are "earning to give" explain that they were motivated by Singer's concerns.[11]

Of the opposite point of view is Garrett Hardin (whose work is excerpted below), who believes that we have no obligation to give to the poor because to do so will do no good.[12] We discussed Hardin (in Chapter 16) with regard to the problem of the tragedy of the commons—the problem that arises when everyone pursues their own self-interest without regard for common environmental goods. Hardin's ideas about global justice are linked to a related worry about growing populations and lack of adequate resources to feed everyone. Hardin maintains that the nations of the world are struggling for existence as if each nation is an individual lifeboat on a stormy sea. Each of these lifeboats has a limited carrying capacity and is subject to environmental threats, which means that the members of each lifeboat have to look out for themselves by building up reserves and avoiding overuse of their own resources. Hardin further suggests that famine relief only postpones the inevitable—death and suffering. According to Hardin, this is because overpopulation produced by famine relief will lead to more famine and even worse death in the future. From Hardin's perspective, there is a natural process of boom and bust, binge and purge that follows along lines outlined by Thomas Malthus, the eighteenth-century author and economist. Malthus predicted that populations grow until they outstrip their resources, after which they die back. Hardin maintains—as Malthus did—that it is wrong to help starving people because such help only causes them to live longer and reproduce, which will produce more mouths to feed and more suffering and a worse population crash in the future.

Whether Hardin's Malthusian predictions are correct is an empirical matter. These predictions would need to be verified or supported by observation and historical evidence. And many factors must be considered. For example, will all forms of famine relief, especially when combined with other aid, necessarily do more harm than good as Hardin predicts? Is it possible to provide assistance to the impoverished while also encouraging birth control, responsible farming practices, liberation for women, and sustainable industrial development—all of which would prevent overpopulation and subsequent die-back?

Answering such questions is difficult because it requires knowledge of the effects of aid in many different environmental, cultural, and political circumstances. It is worthwhile reflecting, however, on the consequentialist nature of these arguments. The primary focus of most discussions of global poverty is a sort of global utilitarianism, which is concerned with the suffering of mass numbers of the global poor. A different sort of concern can be grounded in the natural law tradition associated with the Catholic Church. Thomas Aquinas suggests, for example, that when people are in severe need, they have a natural right to be fed and that it is immoral for those with a superabundance of food to withhold assistance to the needy: "whatever certain people have in superabundance is due, by natural law, to the purpose of succoring the poor." Aquinas quotes St. Ambrose, who says of rich people who hoard their wealth: "It is the hungry man's bread that you withhold."[13] Claims about the need to alleviate poverty can also be derived from other non-consequentialist arguments that rely on notions of justice and fairness. Objections to these sorts of arguments may also appeal to non-consequentialist concerns such as concern for property rights. My right to my own property, for example, might trump another person's entitlement to be helped. Other non-consequentialist considerations may involve claims about the importance of proximity and relatedness. For example, I may have stronger obligations to my own kin or to members of my own country than I do to distant strangers.

Before we move on to examine the practical implications of this debate, let's consider in greater detail a few other basic ethical ideas that could be appealed to in thinking about global poverty and global justice.

Self-Interest

On the one hand, our own interests may dictate that we should do something to lessen the gap between rich and poor nations and alleviate the conditions of the less fortunate. In terms of trade alone, these nations can contribute much to our economic benefit by the goods they could purchase from us. Moreover, the worldwide problems caused by the migration of desperate people from poorer to wealthier countries could be moderated. Furthermore, the problem of terrorism might be dramatically reduced if we could reduce poverty and suffering abroad. Some critics argue that it is not poverty that breeds terrorism but "feelings of indignity and frustration."[14] Nonetheless, poverty is destabilizing and inequality breeds resentment. In the long run, other people's poverty can have negative consequences for our own self-interested concerns.

In terms of self-interest, we may also be concerned about the impact of global poverty on the environment and with regard to other social issues that affect us. Global poverty causes stress on the environment. Poor people in the Amazon region, for example, cut down trees to make farms and charcoal to sell. Impoverished people burning wood for cooking and warmth produce pollution. Because we are all affected by damage to the environment, it is in our best interest to find ways to eliminate the poverty that leads to some of this damage. Furthermore, new infectious diseases often break out in impoverished areas, which can then spread across the globe. And mass migrations of the poor and dispossessed can put pressure on political and social institutions, as affluent nations are forced to deal with the needs of so-called economic refugees.

Justice

Apart from self-interest, there may be requirements of justice that tell us we ought to care for the poor. Justice is not charity. It may well be that *charity* or altruistic concern for the plight of others ought to play a role in how we relate to distant peoples. Charity is certainly an ethically important notion, but a more difficult consideration is whether we have any obligation or duty to help those in need in faraway places. Charity, in some sense, is optional. But if we are obligated to help others, then this is not an optional matter. Are we under any obligation to help those faraway persons in need, and why or why not? Recall from Chapter 14 that considerations of justice play a role in evaluating the distribution of goods. In that chapter, we discussed this in relation to such a distribution within a society. However, it can also be used to evaluate the distribution of goods in the human community as a whole. We can then ask whether a particular distribution of goods worldwide is just. As noted in Chapter 14, there are differences of opinion as to how we ought to determine this.

One idea of justice is the *process view*, according to which any distribution can be said to be just if the process by which it comes to be is just. In other words, if there was no theft or fraud or other immoral activity that led to the way things have turned out, then the resulting arrangement is just. In applying this at the global level, we can ask whether the rich nations are rich at least partly because of wrongful past actions, such as colonialism, the slave trade, or other forms of exploitation. If affluent nations caused poverty in poor nations through colonial exploitation, then the affluent countries might owe some sort of reparation to the poor. But a critic may respond by saying that even if past exploitation was wrong, at some point history is over and we have to move forward.

Another idea of justice is called *end-state justice*. According to this view, the end state, or how things have turned out, is also relevant. Egalitarians argue that the gap between rich and poor is something wrong in itself because we are all members of the same human family and share the same planet. On the one hand, some argue that it is morally permissible for some people to have more than others if the difference is a function of something like the greater effort or contributions of the affluent. From this perspective, those who work harder and who are thrifty are entitled to what they have. They sacrificed and saved while others did not. On the other hand, if the wealth of some and the poverty of others result instead from luck and fortune (or exploitation of the poor), then it does not seem fair that the lucky have so much and the unlucky so little. Is it not luck that one nation has oil and another does not? But the primary concern for the defenders of end-state justice is the actual distribution of things; if it is too unequal, then it is wrong.

Justice is also a matter of *fairness*. People in affluent nations consume a much larger proportion of goods and resources than people in less affluent nations. According to one estimate, people in affluent nations such as the United States, Japan, and countries in Western Europe consume on average thirty-two times more resources per person than do people in underdeveloped countries.[15] The ecological footprint of affluent nations is also larger than that of underdeveloped countries. People in affluent countries consume more, use more resources, and produce more pollution. We could ask whether this is a fair distribution. How would we determine an equal or fair share of resource use or pollution production, while also taking into account global diversity? Do people in very hot or very cold climates deserve more or less energy usage? Are people in cities entitled to more or less pollution than people who live in rural or in wilderness areas? To address this issue more fully would require complex analysis of the idea of fair shares of world resources.

As a preliminary, let's note that in Chapter 14 we discussed the idea of justice as fairness, which is associated with the ideas of John Rawls. Rawls's account is primarily focused on distributive justice within the domestic arena. Late in his career, Rawls extended his considerations toward global issues in a book called *The Law of Peoples*.[16] In that text, Rawls outlined a way of approaching what we might call *international distributive justice*—the question of how we ought to distribute goods among nations. One important point to note here is that when we focus on the issue as one of "international" concern we assume a framework based upon agreements among nations. In other words, from this point of view the concerns of global justice are mediated by the nations of the world. While someone like Peter Singer may direct our attention to the question of what affluent individuals ought to do about starving others, a liberal internationalist approach is focused more on the question of what nations (or as Rawls calls them, "peoples") owe one another. Applying this framework, Rawls concludes, among other things: "peoples have a duty to assist other peoples living under unfavorable conditions that prevent their having a just or decent political and social regime."[17] We should note that Rawls's account seems to agree with the mainstream approach of institutions such as the World Bank, which want to approach the alleviation of global poverty within the framework on existing international institutions and nation-states.

Rights

Most Western governments and international organizations agree that political freedoms, civil rights, and labor standards are not separable from economic progress. They stress that prohibitions on child labor, enforcement of women's rights, prevention of deforestation and pollution, and the enhancement of intellectual property rights, freedom of the press, and other civil liberties must be central to economic development. As the global economy is becoming more integrated, many would argue that this integration must be based upon ideas about human rights, which are supposedly universally valid and applicable.

Outline of Moral Approaches to Globalization

	Global justice	Moderate Internationalism	Self-Interest
Thesis	The demands of global justice are primary and universal	Respect international agreements and pursue international justice as fairness	National interest and self-interest are primary
Corollaries and Implications	We have obligations to the global poor including refugees; we ought to avoid exploitative international economic arrangements; we ought to engage in fair trade and pursue ethical consumption; former colonial powers may owe compensation to the global poor	Globalization ought to produce benefits for all parties; but national self-determination remains important; goal of international agreements to help the poor combined with aspects of capitalist globalization including free markets and political liberalization	Primary obligation is to ourselves and our own posterity; charity toward global poor creates dependence and population pressures which exacerbate problems; developed nations do *not* owe compensation or reparation to the poor
Connections with Moral Theory	*Utilitarian* concern for *global application* of the idea of greatest happiness for the greatest number; prior violations of the *rights* of the global poor require reparation and compensation; *positive right* to subsistence	*Utilitarian* concern to balance national productivity and profit with global concern; *right* of nations to their own product balanced with the need to help the poor within *modern liberal* economic and political theory	*Egoism*; at the national level, *utilitarianism* focused *domestically*; *libertarian* economic theory views global economy as a struggle limited only by *negative rights*
Relevant Authors/ Institutions	Singer, Pogge	World Bank; Rawls	Malthus, Hardin

The issue of rights is not that simple. There are positive rights—to welfare—and negative rights—to liberty and property (as discussed in Chapter 14). Some proponents of globalization will argue that every person has a positive right to subsistence—a basic right to clean water, basic food, and freedom from want. It is not enough, from this perspective, to avoid harming others or exploiting them. Rather, such a positive right to subsistence implies a positive obligation on the part of those who have surplus wealth. Others will maintain that the negative rights to liberty and property are primary. From this perspective, we only have an obligation not to exploit others, steal their property, or enslave them.

PRACTICAL CONSIDERATIONS

Responses to global poverty should be guided by moral concepts, such as the ones we've discussed previously. But, as we've seen with regard to many of the applied topics in this book, moral questions also depend on circumstantial and factual matters. This is especially true with regard to consequentialist reasoning, where the goal is to produce good outcomes in the world. If we are going to produce good outcomes, we have to understand the circumstances and empirical issues. Here are some issues to consider.

Global Inequality

At the heart of many arguments about the need to help the poor is the claim that gross inequalities across the globe are unjustified. A related claim is that there is an obvious moral demand for the affluent to respond to the abject suffering of those who are on the bottom. Singer, Pogge, and others argue that our relative wealth means that we can alleviate lots of suffering for a minor cost—an empirical claim that should prompt us to examine the severity of global inequality.

Consider, for example, that workers in the Bangladeshi garment factories that have burned and collapsed typically earn between $37 and $50 per month—that amounts to just over a dollar per day.[18] This means that if you donate a dollar and change per day, you could double someone's income. We have made progress in reducing global poverty. The World Bank claims that in 2015, global poverty rate fell below 10 percent, with "only" about 700 million people now living in extreme poverty. This is a landmark achievement and marks progress toward the World Bank's goal of eliminating extreme poverty by 2013. Given long decades of double-digit poverty rates, a poverty rate in the single digits is something to be celebrated.[19] Of course, such data need interpretation. One significant consideration is the fact that the World Bank has redefined what it counts as extreme poverty. Prior to 2008, it defined extreme poverty as an income of less than $1 per day; after 2008, it redefined extreme poverty as income of less than $1.25 per day. As of 2015, the World Bank defines it as an income of less than $1.90 per day; under the older definition, back in 2012, there were over 900 million people living in extreme poverty (12.8% of the global population).[20] It could be that changing the numbers allows us to feel that we are making progress. But at any rate, whether you live on one dollar per day or two, let's admit that you are poor; and the fact remains that hundreds of millions of people are extremely poor.

Extreme poverty is also "poverty that kills." People in extreme poverty are "chronically hungry, unable to get health care, lack safe drinking water and sanitation, cannot afford education for their children, and perhaps lack rudimentary shelter...and clothing."[21] Children of the global poor are particularly vulnerable, dying from various causes including easily preventable diseases and illnesses.[22] For example, hundreds of millions of people come down with malaria every year and hundreds of thousands die. In 2015, there were 214 million malaria cases and 438,000 malaria deaths.[23] People living in the poorest countries and children in those countries are especially vulnerable to malaria, which can be easily prevented by the use of mosquito nets and other prophylactic measures. There has been an improvement over past mortality rates as a result of an active campaign to prevent and treat malaria. Nonetheless, the disease still preys upon the poor.

Poverty in the developing world undermines opportunities. It is connected to a variety of issues including the oppression of women, illiteracy, governmental corruption, and so on. There are vast inequalities across the globe. One obvious measure of inequality is found in mortality rates and life expectancy. Life expectancy in rich countries is substantially higher than in poor countries. In Japan, Switzerland, Germany, and Norway, life expectancy is above 80 years. In the United States, life expectancy is 79 years. But in Kenya, life expectancy is 63 years; it is 70 years in Bangladesh; and 64 years on Cambodia. The country of Chad has the lowest life expectancy, 49 years.[24] Those who argue that we ought to take action to alleviate global poverty will point out the injustice of these sorts of inequalities. Is it fair that Americans and Europeans live long and live well while others suffer and die young?

Another measure of inequality is in economic terms. According to the World Bank, the United States is the world's richest country in terms of gross domestic product (GDP), with China, Japan, Germany, and France following. The GDP in the United States in 2014 was over $17.4 trillion, compared, for example to Kenya, with a GDP of $60 billion or with some smaller nations such as the Marshall Islands, with a GDP of $187 million.[25] A more precise measure of inequality is to compare per capita GDP, which divides the gross domestic product of a nation by its population. Using that measure, Malawi had the lowest per capita GDP in 2014, at $255. By comparison, Kenya's per capita GDP in 2014 was $1,358 and Chad's was $1,024. The per capita GDP for Bangladesh was $1,086, while in the United States, per capita GDP was $54,629. The per capita GDP in the United States was lower than that of a number of other countries, including Sweden, Denmark, Switzerland, and Norway.[26]

Levels of International Aid

The rich nations of the world do allocate some of their budgets to the alleviation of global poverty and inequality. Most affluent nations acknowledge that there is some need to help the poor, either because they see a moral imperative to help or believe that helping is in everyone's interest, since poverty and inequality are destabilizing forces in the global economy. International agreements have established a goal for rich countries to donate 0.7 percent of their gross national product (GNP) to alleviate poverty. (GNP is calculated in ways that are similar to GDP, or gross domestic product.) This international effort has been established in a variety of treaties in recent decades including the UN Millennium Development Project and the Monterrey (Mexico) Conference on Financing for Development and a subsequent agreement in Johannesburg, South Africa.[27] One of the difficulties for discussing foreign aid is that many Americans think that the United States gives much more in aid. A poll in 2014 reported that the average American thinks that around 25 percent of the federal budget goes to foreign aid.[28] When asked what they considered the appropriate amount of foreign aid to be, the typical response was about 10 percent of the budget—which is actually ten times the amount of aid actually allocated in the federal budget.[29]

Only 1 percent of the U.S. budget goes to foreign aid. Out of $4 trillion budget that is a significant amount.[30] But even at 1 percent of the federal budget, the United States falls short of the 0.7 percent of GNP target set by the United Nations. The United States continues to be the world's largest donor in raw terms, giving a total of over $32 billion in 2014; at 0.19% of GNP, this is still a long way from the UN target.[31] This means that U.S. aid donations amount to about 19 cents for every $100 of income, while the United Nations' target would have the United States donating 70 cents for every $100. If the United States hit the 0.7 percent target, its aid budget would increase from its current $32 billion to around $100 billion. That extra $70 billion could go a long way toward solving the problem of global poverty.

Some rich nations have made an effort to reach the target of donating 0.7 percent, with European nations in the lead. The Organization for Economic Cooperation and Development reports that in 2014, the world's largest donors in raw terms were the United States, the UK, Germany, France, and Japan. Some nations exceed the UN.'s 0.7 percent target: Denmark, Luxembourg, Norway, and Sweden—with the United Kingdom joining the list in 2014 (and the

Netherlands falling of the list for the first time in a number of years)[32]. Indeed, the UK passed a law in 2015 making a commitment to the 0.7 percent target, which made it the first G7 country to make such a commitment (the G7 countries—the "group of seven" countries—are the leading industrial nations of the world: Canada, France, Germany, Italy, Japan, the UK, and the United States).[33]

Causes of Global Poverty

The causes of extreme poverty and lack of development in a nation are many and complicated. Among them are said to be geographic isolation, epidemic disease, drought and other natural disasters, lack of clean water, poor soil, poor physical infrastructure, lack of education and a decent health care system, civil war and corruption, and the colonial and trade practices of Western nations.

Colonialism   In one view, it is colonialism that has been the cause of poverty in many of the world's poorest countries. Among those who hold this to be the case is Frantz Fanon, a North African intellectual who was born in the Caribbean. Fanon's work *The Wretched of the Earth* is a seminal text in postcolonial studies.[34] Fanon's idea is that the Western nations stole the riches of their colonies, thus enhancing their own wealth while depressing the wealth of the colonies. According to Fanon, "European opulence is literally scandalous, for it has been founded on slavery, it has been nourished with the blood of slaves and it comes directly from the soil and from the subsoil of that underdeveloped world. The well-being and the progress of Europe have been built up with the sweat and the dead bodies of Negroes, Arabs, Indians, and the yellow races."[35] From this standpoint, the poverty of much of the world is due to a long history of European intervention, colonial domination, slavery, and theft. Moreover, the argument continues, deprivation in what Fanon calls the "third" or underdeveloped world can be attributed to continued exploitation of the poor by the rich. Even though outright colonialism ended in the twentieth century, as former colonies gained their independence, Fanon argues that the

institutions, corporate structures, military treaties, and trade relations left behind continue to favor the First World to the detriment of the Third World.

One response to this sort of argument is to claim that colonialism was not the evil it is made out to be. Dinesh D'Souza—an Indian-born American intellectual—has argued, for example, that "colonialism has gotten a bad name in recent decades."[36] D'Souza maintains that in some ways colonialism may have been good for the colonized countries. In a book in which he accuses President Obama of being a proponent of Fanon-style anticolonialism, D'Souza concludes,

> When the British came to India and Kenya, they came for selfish reasons: they came to rule and to benefit from that rule. Nevertheless, in order to rule effectively the British introduced Western ideas and Western institutions to the subject peoples. Eventually those people used British ideas of self-determination and freedom to combat British rule. As a native-born Indian, I have to say that even our freedom was a consequence of what we learned from our Western captors.[37]

D'Souza has also pointed out that Western colonialism is only part of a much larger history that includes a long litany of colonial interventions, including colonizing by the Egyptians, the Persians, and so on. D'Souza concludes that to blame European colonialists for stealing and exploitation in the Third World is to "relieve the Third World of blame for its wretchedness."[38] From D'Souza's perspective, the corruption, injustice, and poverty found in the Third World are not the result of European exploitation. Rather, it is the result of insufficient Westernization. D'Souza argues that the solution is further expansion of Western European ideas about human rights, technology, and free markets.

Farm Subsidies and Other Trade Barriers   Subsidies for the farms of Western countries have also been blamed by some critics for the poverty in developing countries. In the United States, these subsidies originally were intended to help farmers hurt by the Great Depression. But they have been maintained and expanded. Between 1995 and 2012, farmers in the United States received $292.5 billion in subsidies—both by direct payments and through crop insurance.[39] In other countries, subsidies are given to small specialty farms, for example, those in the grape-growing or cheese-producing regions of France. Such distortions of the international agriculture market can make it extremely difficult for poor farmers in Mexico or in sub-Saharan Africa to compete. Moreover, in some cases (especially in the United States) such subsidies go to large industrialized farms that then produce huge crop surpluses for cheap export—undercutting the sale of local agricultural products in the developing world. Substantial evidence suggests that reducing subsidies and removing trade barriers would help end poverty. Economist Gary S. Fields points out, "Agricultural subsidies by the United States, Europe, and Japan total $350 billion a year—seven times the foreign aid provided by all developed countries." He concludes that ending farm subsidies could lift 140 million people out of poverty.[40] Other people argue, however, that there is no guarantee that eliminating these subsidies would help poor farmers. Moreover, perhaps all nations should have a right to protect and support their own farmers, whatever the consequences abroad.

One of the issues with regard to subsidies is fairness. The International Monetary Fund and the World Bank often ask developing countries that receive loans and other aid to eliminate subsidies for their exports. However, developed countries such as the United States continue to subsidize their own agricultural products. As a result, foreign farmers frequently cannot compete on the global market with products grown on U.S. farms. At the same time, U.S. producers lobby against trade barriers enacted by foreign countries, which prevent Americans from selling U.S. products in foreign markets. It makes sense for nations to want to protect their own farmers and producers. And it also makes sense that farmers and producers would want to have access to markets abroad. The reality of globalized business is complicated and there is a constant struggle to maximize profit and minimize risk. All of this results in unequal outcomes across the globe. Consider the North American Free

Trade Agreement (NAFTA), which links Canada, Mexico, and the United States in a Free Trade Zone. As a result of this agreement, Mexico was flooded with cheap corn and corn products from the United States, such as animal feed. (Corn is one of the most heavily subsidized crops in the United States.) This had a devastating impact on small Mexican farmers. According to one estimate, nearly two million farm jobs were lost in Mexico as a result. Many of these small farmers abandoned their fields and headed north to work as illegal laborers in the United States. The general cross-border economy is doing well. But the chief beneficiaries of NAFTA have been big companies, while the small operations have been hurt.[41] The moral ideal of fair competition is certainly relevant in such discussions. Just how to make competition fair is, however, a matter for debate.

Institutional Issues   Debate also continues about the role played by international financial institutions. The International Monetary Fund (IMF) and World Bank were both established in 1944 to preserve international financial stability. A newer international organization is the World Trade Organization (WTO), and there are other organizations such as the G7 mentioned above, which represents the interests of eight of the world's largest economies, accounting for more than half of global GDP. (The G7 expanded to include Russia at one point, becoming the G8—but Russia was suspended from the organization in 2014).[42] The G20 includes twenty finance ministers and central bank governors and represents the financial interest of nations that account for about 80 percent of world trade. In recent years, there have been massive protests at meetings of these organizations and others like them. Pro-labor and environmental groups have protested against economic globalization at meetings of the WTO, the G8, the G20, the IMF, and the World Bank. These antiglobalization protests culminated in police crackdowns, mass arrests, vandalism, and street fighting in Seattle, Washington, in 1999; in Genoa, Italy, in 2001; and in Geneva in 2009. In Toronto, in 2010, more than 1,100 people were arrested in anti-G20 protests.[43]

The antiglobalization protesters have a variety of specific concerns. But among them is a feeling that economic decisions are being made by bureaucrats and bankers without concern for the interests of working people. Canadian journalist and author Naomi Klein has explained the antiglobalization movement as developing out of a perceived "crisis of democracy."[44] Critics of the economic institutions of globalization insist that they are not opposed to international integration and cooperation. Rather, they say that they are opposed to that type of globalization that is more concerned about the rights of investors than the rights of workers. Noam Chomsky, a well-known critic of globalization and of American foreign policy, argues, "the term 'globalization' has been appropriated by the powerful to refer to a specific form of international economic integration, one based on investors rights, with the interests of people incidental."[45] The alternative would be a form of economic integration that was more concerned with human development and the concerns of ordinary people than with the bottom line of banks and corporations.

In response, defenders of the international finance and business system argue that investing in and supporting the current economic system is the best (and possibly only) way to help poor people around the world—by using banks and other global economic infrastructure to invest in opportunities for the impoverished. We've already seen that the World Bank is concerned with poverty reduction across the globe. And international agreements (such as the 0.7 percent aid target) are aimed at reducing poverty by increasing foreign aid.

However, some criticize the methods employed by international institutions such as the World Bank, IMF, and WTO. According to Joseph Stiglitz, a Nobel Prize–winning economist, the key to problems in developing nations has been these international financial institutions' ideological support of strict capitalism. He argues that free markets and global competition are not the solution to all problems. And he worries about the lack of representation of poorer countries: "these institutions are not representative of the nations they serve."[46] Some

IMF and World Bank policies, for example, have harmed rather than helped the development of Third World countries. High interest rates harmed fledgling companies, trade liberalization policies made poorer countries unable to compete, and liberalization of capital markets enabled larger foreign banks to drive local banks out of business. Privatization of government-owned enterprises without adequate local regulation also contributed to the increasingly desperate situation of some developing countries. According to Stiglitz, these international financial institutions have ignored some of the consequences of their policies because of their belief in unfettered capitalism. He writes:

> Stabilization is on the agenda; job creation is off. Taxation, and its adverse effects, are on the agenda; land reform is off. There is money to bail out banks but not to pay for improved education and health services, let alone to bail out workers who are thrown out of their jobs as a result of the IMF's macroeconomic mismanagement.[47]

In response to Stiglitz and others, defenders of the international economic system have argued that these worries are overblown and based on a limited analysis that does not take economic realities into account. Moreover, defenders of economic globalization argue that the critics of globalization have actually made things worse by encouraging developing countries to feel that they are being taken advantage of and that the global institutions that are the best hope for development are hypocritical and mercenary. The economist Jagdish Bhagwati has argued, for example, that globalization actually does have a human face. He argues that economic globalization—by promoting competition in wages across international borders—has benefited women by equalizing gender-based wage disparities, which were more typical of countries where the wage gap was protected against global competition.[48] To assess these arguments would require a much deeper examination of economic issues.

A further criticism should be mentioned here, which is the concern for corruption and self-interest. Just as the antiglobalization movement suspects that the global financial sector is interested only in profit, a similar suspicion is held by some who worry that local governments and aid organizations are corrupt. Not all financial aid given to poor countries actually gets directly to the people. Much of it, for example, covers consultants, administrative costs, and debt relief. Furthermore, aid dollars are used to purchase supplies and expertise that are manufactured in the developed world. Journalist Loretta Napoleoni argues that "foreign aid is mostly beneficial to those who give it" because aid creates a market for Western products.[49] One of the difficult practical challenges to be confronted is how we can best provide aid in a global economy that includes corrupt local politicians as well as international corporations and banks that are seeking to make a profit.

Poor countries suffer from serious political problems; continuing civil wars and corrupt and unstable governments. Corruption and mismanagement have contributed not only to the poverty of the people but also to the hesitancy of wealthy countries to give aid. Any solution to the issue of global poverty will have to deal with a variety of concerns: the problem of local corruption, the challenge of making sure that aid is effective, and the concern that large multinational banking and corporate concerns are seeking profit. But it is important to note that none of these empirical concerns changes the moral question of whether we ought to be concerned about the suffering of others in distant lands.

Solutions and Progress

The issues discussed in this chapter are complex. It will be difficult to solve issues like global poverty and to deal with the ongoing cultural, political, and economic conflicts that are part of the era of globalization. Nonetheless, some thinkers argue that there are some fairly obvious solutions to the most pressing issues, such as poverty. We saw that Thomas Pogge proposed a resource tax and that Peter Singer thought that we have a duty to donate to charity. Development economist Jeffrey Sachs has argued that we should focus on five "development interventions": (1) boosting agriculture, with improvements

in fertilizers and seeds; (2) improving basic health, in particular through bed nets and medicines for malaria and treatments for AIDS; (3) investing in education, including meals for primary school children; (4) providing power, transportation, and communications technologies; and (5) providing clean water and sanitation.[50] Others argue that changing intellectual property laws and freeing up patents would help to make new technologies—such as better seeds for growing crops or beneficial medicines—available to poor people who could use them.[51] Some suggest that money is the most basic solution and that rich nations should live up to the standard of donating 0.7 percent of GNP.

The global poverty numbers have been improving, thanks to a concerted effort by international organizations such as the United Nations and the World Bank. As noted above we are making progress in dealing with other issues such as malaria control, AIDS, and education. The rate of extreme poverty has dropped below 10 percent. But we still have a long way to go when hundreds of millions of the people on earth live in extreme poverty. If we are going to make further progress, we will have to take the problem of global justice seriously. But as we've seen, there are others who think that helping the global poor is not a matter of justice but only a matter of charity. And there are other critics, such as Hardin, who appeal to Malthusian logic to argue that it is not a good idea to help the poor.

GLOBALIZATION AND ITS CRITICS

Questions of global justice are complicated by the fact of globalization. As the world's economic and cultural forces become more interconnected, our understanding of our obligations to distant others may be shifting in a more global direction. But one might argue, to the contrary, that our primary obligations to members of our own nation or culture remain more important than obligations to distant others. To think about global justice, it is useful to understand the causes and effects of globalization.

One key causal factor in globalization is the development of technologies that improve economic efficiency and allow for broader economic and cultural influence. According to the journalist and scholar Robert Wright, "globalization dates back to prehistory, when the technologically driven expansion of commerce began."[52] Technological innovations—from roads and boats to writing, airline travel, and the Internet—allow for commercial and cultural interchanges among formerly isolated peoples. The journalist Thomas Friedman described globalization as a process that has made the world "flat."[53] People around the world are now connected in ways unimaginable twenty years ago, and the playing field in which they operate is now more even—provided that they have access to computers, Internet connections, and e-mail. This increases opportunities for collaboration and development. It also changes the nature of the economy.

According to Jan Scholte, a leading expert on globalization, there are at least five different interpretations of globalization, some of which are overlapping: internationalization, liberalization, universalization, modernization or Westernization, and deterritorialization or respatialization.[54] *Internationalization* refers to "cross-border relations between countries." Among these are trade, finance, and communication, which create international interdependence among nations and peoples. *Liberalization* focuses on the free and "open, borderless world economy." Trade and foreign exchange, as well as travel barriers, are abolished or reduced, making it possible to participate in the world as a whole. *Universalization* refers to the various ways in which a synthesis of cultures has taken place. This covers such things as having a common calendar; shared communication technologies; and similar methods of manufacturing, farming, and means of transportation. *Modernization* or *Westernization* refers to the ways that "the social structures of modernity"—capitalism, science, movies, music, and so forth—have spread throughout the world. Among the characteristics of modernity is an emphasis on scientific rational thought in combination with technological innovation—as well as a move toward secular institutions that are independent of traditional religious organization. *Deterritorialization* or *respatialization* refers to the fact that in the globalized

world "social space is no longer wholly mapped in terms of territorial places...and borders."[55] Thus corporations as well as nongovernmental organizations transcend local geographic constraints.

Sometimes the processes of globalization have increased people's understanding and sympathy for other peoples, while fostering tolerance, respect, and concern for human equality. The economic integration of isolated communities often brings with it greater peace as people of different races and cultures trade and rub shoulders with one another. But this globalizing process can also be the basis of resentment and antipathy. One source of complaint is the way that globalization affects local economies. Another complaint involves the problem of cultural diversity.

Economic Impacts

Many argue that globalization will increase productivity and produce profit and innovation. But others complain that this produces certain costs that may not be outweighed by such benefits. *Outsourcing* is one example. Outsourcing occurs when part of a process—say, tax preparation or customer service information—is contracted out to workers in other countries where labor costs are cheaper. A related issue is *offshoring*. This differs from outsourcing in that rather than taking some specific function and hiring it out, entire factories or operational units are moved to cheaper offshore locations. Outsourcing and offshoring may help to produce profit and lower the price of commodities. But they also undermine opportunities in countries that lose jobs to cheaper countries. Furthermore, if jobs are allowed to go where the lowest-priced workers are located, this produces a "rush to the bottom" in which labor, safety, and environmental standards are constantly undermined. Defenders of these practices argue that in the long run globalization is good for everyone as products become cheaper, capital flows toward labor markets, and jobs and wealth are created.

Globalization will be evaluated in different ways by those who think in different ways about economic and political issues. Proponents of free-market capitalism see globalization as a further stage of economic development as markets go global and capital, labor, and commodities are free to flow around the world. Others worry that the development of global capitalism will come at the expense of social welfare and the interests of the global poor and working classes. Some praise the development of cosmopolitan social concern and international laws that regulate wars, environmental impacts, and economic development. Others rue the demise of state sovereignty and the autonomy of the more traditional nation-state. Another critical perspective is more concerned that the development of global culture poses a threat to traditional familial, cultural, and religious values.

Cultural Diversity

This last issue points toward cultural problems created by modernization, Westernization, and secularization. Some have argued that there is a clash of civilizations in the world today—most notably between secular Westernized democracies and more conservative, traditional societies.[56] Those who focus on such civilizational conflict may argue that there are deep cultural and historical values found in various "civilizations." From this perspective, the process of globalization will be fraught with conflict, instead of being a process of harmonious integration and global development.

One supposed civilizational fissure is that between Western and Asian values. But some have argued that "Asian values" do not fit well with the values of Western liberal democracy and capitalism. Defenders of "Asian values" may claim, for example, that the welfare of society and economic development ought to come first before political rights. They may claim that human rights may temporarily be put on hold for the sake of economic growth. Thus it would be better, they say, to give a starving person a loaf of bread than a crate on which to stand and speak his mind. This idea was propounded in the 1990s by Lee Kuan Yew, the former prime minister of Singapore. Lee maintained that Asian values were founded on a communitarian approach that could be traced back to Confucian ethics. (See the discussion of communitarianism in Chapter 14.) He held that

there was a social pyramid with a good leader at the top, good executives in the middle, and civic-minded masses at the bottom.[57]

Some critics worry that these sorts of relativist appeals to culturally specific value systems provide a justification for the continued exploitation of oppressed groups within countries that are reluctant to democratize and modernize. Criticism of democratic values may be used to serve the ideological purposes of those in charge and those who benefit from inequality. Others maintain that an idea such as "Asian values" is so broad and obscure as to be meaningless. The economist Amartya Sen concludes, for example, that we must recognize diversity within different cultures and that we should avoid simplifying concepts such as "Western civilization," "African cultures," or "Asian values." He concludes, "the grand dichotomy between Asian values and European values adds little to our understanding, and much to the confounding of the normative basis of freedom and democracy."[58] There are liberal-democratic and capitalist elements in Asian cultures just as there are anti-liberal and authoritarian strands in Western cultures.

Another line of supposed civilizational conflict is that between the Arab/Muslim world and the European/Christian world. Some claim that "Islamic values" do not fit within the increasingly globalized and Westernized economic system. Proponents of Islamic values claim that Western market-oriented economics does not help the poor and that the secular nation-states of the West sacrifice a more valuable religiously structured social system. Some argue that Islamic culture emphasizes a more collectivist and communitarian approach to social norms and structures and is thus is at odds with Western individualism.[59]

A more concrete issue is whether there are cultural or "civilizational" issues that exacerbate inequality and the challenge of global poverty. Maybe cultural values can help explain differences that exist across the globe. Consider, for example, that the combined gross domestic product of all twenty-two countries in the Arab League was about $2.87 trillion with a population of more than 385 million.[60]

By comparison, Germany's GDP is higher at around $3.9 trillion with a much smaller population of approximately 81 million.[61] This wealth disparity may help explain why poverty and food insecurity are problems in some parts of the Arab world. Of course, one might respond by pointing out that even within the richest nation on earth—the United States—there are gross inequalities, hungry people, and people living in poverty (we discussed some of this in Chapter 14). It may be that cultural differences do not make all that much difference when it comes to economics.

A further problem may have to do with political institutions. Poverty and food insecurity may have been exacerbated by political instability since the "Arab Spring" (revolutions across the Arab world in 2011). One recent report indicates that official poverty numbers are untrustworthy and that economic inequality including high unemployment was a chief cause of the uprising of Arab people in 2011. At any rate, the turmoil in the Arab world has resulted in violence, unrest, and civil war. Among the most prominent development is the civil war in Syria and the development of the Islamic State in Syria and Iraq (known as ISIS or ISIL). Political turmoil has led to even further unemployment, food insecurity, and a growing refugee crisis. Youth unemployment is at 50 percent in a number of Arab nations.[62] Political instability makes it difficult to develop natural resources, create educational opportunities, and build businesses.

The resulting war and dislocation has caused a flood of refugees to attempt to leave the Middle East and head for European countries such as Germany. While some refugees have been admitted, in other cases these refugees have confronted closed borders and have been turned back. Some have drowned in boats used to cross the sea; others remain in refugee camps. While some European countries have welcomed limited numbers of refugees from Syria and the Middle East, in some cases, refugees have faced discrimination. And European countries remain wary about admitting terrorists with allegiances to ISIS or other radical ideologies. We discussed recent terror attacks in Europe in Chapter 19. Difficult questions arise about whether the terrorist threat represents a fundamental clash of values and about how European nations ought to respond to instability in the Middle East and the refugee problem.

Defenders of the clash of civilization idea argue that there are cultural reasons that unemployment is high and the economy is shaky in Muslim and Arab countries. As an example, some cite a 2002 report from the United Nations Development Programme in coordination with the Arab Fund for Economic and Social Development, which held that Arab countries have not advanced economically in modern times because of "a shortage of freedom to speak, innovate, and affect political life, a shortage of women's rights, and a shortage of quality education."[63] That report criticized education in the Arab world with remaining illiteracy and educational gaps. Literacy in the Arab world has hovered at around 70 percent compared to the literacy rate of the developed world, which is around 95 percent. Some will attribute these kinds of disparities to cultural and religious differences. And similar disparities and challenges are found in other parts of the world, with literacy rates in sub-Saharan Africa even lower than rates in the Arab world—at around 65 percent.

The general issue of cultural relativism shows up here. Are we employing Eurocentric values when thinking about development issues? Is it possible to focus on helping impoverished people and political refugees, while also respecting cultural practices that may be contributing to poverty and instability? And how can we encourage and support indigenous cultural values that can help deal with these problems? Muslims practice *zakat*, or alms-giving, for example. How can aid to the poor be coordinated with traditional religious practices such as this? A further problem involves cultural and political conflicts of the past. Will predominantly Muslim countries welcome aid that comes from the United States, when, in the past, this aid has been used to prop up unpopular governments. In Egypt, for example, the United States supported the former president, Hosni Mubarak, who was driven from power by the Egyptian people who gathered in protest during the Arab Spring. The United States had a difficult relationship with the short-lived government of the Muslim Brotherhood, which was driven from power in a 2013 coup. The United States has subsequently supported the government of the former general Abdel Fattah el-Sisi. Similar political and historical problems haunt aid efforts in the rest of the world, with former colonial powers in the developed world dealing with residual political issues as they also try to fulfill obligations to assist. Do the British have more of an obligation to help in India or do the French have more of an obligation to help in North Africa because of their past colonial relations? And how will assistance be perceived by former colonies?

There is no denying that Western values dominate global culture. Western-style clothing, advertising, and products are becoming more and more pervasive. Coca-Cola, McDonald's, American pop music, and American computer and Internet technologies seem to be everywhere. Do people around the world admire or want U.S. goods? Or are these goods somehow foisted upon them by the forces of corporate globalization?

There is also cultural backlash against the values of Western consumerism and individualism. These values are viewed with antipathy and resentment by some people who hold other traditional cultural or religious values. For example, some traditional cultures reject the lack of modest dress in women and graphic and sexualized forms of popular entertainment and music. Clearly, there are criticisms to be made of some elements of Western societies that are showing up around the world. On the other hand, we may want to argue that other elements of modern culture ought to become universally accepted. Take, for example, the position of women. Should modern notions of individual rights and freedoms and equality for women become the norm? There are those who argue against this. They would retain individual cultural and religious practices regarding the position of women. Is it colonialist or Eurocentric to want to encourage development toward a more secular and liberal social and political system?

Can we actually judge the practices of another culture? Are one culture's values as good as any other? This is the issue of ethical relativism

discussed in Chapters 2 and 3. We surely want to say that if some culture has a practice of enslaving some of its members, this is not morally acceptable. Which elements of globalization are good and bad is not always an easy matter to judge. Hopefully, however, the ethical signposts, values, and principles discussed here and elsewhere in this text can help determine the way we should go in a world that is, in ever-increasing ways, becoming one.

Let's conclude this section by mentioning the conflict between modernization and globalization and traditional religion. The modernized world is a secular one, which keeps traditional religious values distinct from the public values of the political sphere. While religions have "gone global" during the past millennia—spreading around the globe through conquest and missionary work, economic and political globalization poses a threat for traditional religion. The modern Western nation-state is grounded upon basic claims about human rights including the right of freedom of religion. And the modern economy is a 24/7 activity oriented toward progress and development, ignoring the ritual time frames and Sabbath days of rest in traditional religions.

Some critics of globalization, modernization, and secularization will argue that all of this is heading in the wrong direction. Some will want to return to tradition—as religious fundamentalists do—withdrawing from the global economy and finding a separate peace with the secular, modern world. Some other fundamentalists may take up arms against the global system—as religious terrorists do. Others will want to find ways to humanize and universalize traditional religious values. And others will insist that the way forward must be to find universal human values that can transcend cultural and religious differences and that can be used to deal with the difficult challenges of the future, such as those we have discussed in this book.

In the readings in this chapter, utilitarian philosopher Peter Singer argues that the affluent have a moral obligation to help those who are living at subsistence levels. An article by Garret Hardin makes a different argument—against the idea of helping the poor.

NOTES

1. Ian Goldin and Mike Mariathasan, *The Butterfly Defect: How Globalization Creates Systematic Risks, and What to Do About it* (Princeton, NJ: Princeton University Press, 2014).

2. Thomas Fuller, "Deadly Collapse in Cambodia Renews Safety Concerns," *New York Times*, May 16, 2013, accessed June 25, 2013, http://www.nytimes.com/2013/05/17/world/asia/cambodia-factory-ceiling-collapse.html?_r=0

3. Charles Duhigg, "In China, Human Costs Are Built into an iPad," *New York Times,* January 25, 2012, accessed July 14, 2013, http://www.nytimes.com/2012/01/26/business/ieconomy-apples-ipad-and-the-human-costs-for-workers-in-china.html?pagewanted=all

4. Peter Grier, "The Walt Disney Company Pulls Out of Bangladesh: Will That Make Workers Safer?," *Christian Science Monitor*, May 3, 2013, accessed June 25, 2013, http://www.csmonitor.com/USA/2013/0503/The-Walt-Disney-Company-pulls-out-of-Bangladesh-Will-that-make-workers-safer

5. See Alex Nicholls and Charlotte Opal, *Fair Trade: Market Driven Ethical Consumption* (London: SAGE Publications, 2005).

6. See Peter Griffiths, "Ethical Objections to Fair Trade," *Journal of Business Ethics* 105 (2012): 357–73.

7. "Within Our Grasp: A World Free of Poverty—World Bank Group President Jim Yong Kim's Speech at Georgetown University," April 2, 2013, accessed June 25, 2013, http://www.worldbank.org/en/news/speech/2013/04/02/world-bank-group-president-jim-yong-kims-speech-at-georgetown-university

8. Thomas Pogge, "Are We Violating the Human Rights of the World's Poor?," *Yale Human Rights & Development Journal* 14, no. 2 (2011): 1–33.

9. Thomas Pogge, *World Poverty and Human Rights* (Cambridge: Polity Press, 2008), 211–12.

10. Peter Singer, "Famine, Affluence, and Morality," *Philosophy and Public Affairs* 1, no. 3 (1972): 231.

11. Dylan Matthews, "Join Wall Street, Save the World," *Washington Post*, May 31, 2013, accessed June 25, 2013, http://www.washingtonpost.com/blogs/wonkblog/wp/2013/05/31/join-wall-street-save-the-world/

12. Garrett Hardin, "Living on a Lifeboat," *Bioscience* 24 (1974): 561–68.

13. Thomas Aquinas, *Summa Theologica*, trans. by the Fathers of the English Dominican Province, Online Edition Copyright © 2008 by Kevin Knight, II–II, Q 66, Art. 7, http://www.newadvent.org/summa/3066.htm (accessed July 26, 2013).

14. Alan B. Krueger and Jitka Maleckova, "Does Poverty Cause Terrorism?" *New Republic*, June 24, 2002, 27.

15. Jared Diamond, "What's Your Consumption Factor?" *New York Times*, January 2, 2008, accessed June 25, 2013, http://www.nytimes.com/2008/01/02/opinion/02diamond.html?pagewanted=all

16. John Rawls, *The Law of Peoples* (Cambridge, MA: Harvard University Press, 2001).

17. Ibid., 37.

18. Jim Yardley, "Made in Bangladesh: Export Powerhouse Feels Pangs of Labor Strife," *New York Times*, August 23, 2012, accessed June 20, 2013, http://www.nytimes.com/2012/08/24/world/asia/as-bangladesh-becomes-export-powerhouse-labor-strife-erupts.html?pagewanted=1; "Worker Safety in Bangladesh and Beyond," *New York Times*, May 4, 2013, accessed June 20, 2013, http://www.nytimes.com/2013/05/05/opinion/sunday/worker-safety-in-bangladesh-and-beyond.html

19. World Bank, "World Bank Forecasts Global Poverty to Fall Below 10% for First Time; Major Hurdles Remain in Goal to End Poverty by 2030," October 4, 2015, http://www.worldbank.org/en/news/press-release/2015/10/04/world-bank-forecasts-global-poverty-to-fall-below-10-for-first-time-major-hurdles-remain-in-goal-to-end-poverty-by-2030 (accessed April 12, 2016).

20. "World Bank: 'Extreme Poverty' to Fall Below 10% of World Population for First Time," *The Guardian*, October 5, 2015, http://www.theguardian.com/society/2015/oct/05/world-bank-extreme-poverty-to-fall-below-10-of-world-population-for-first-time (accessed April 12, 2016).

21. "The End of Poverty," *Time*, March 14, 2005, 47.

22. World Health Organization, "Ten Facts on Malaria," November 2015, http://www.who.int/features/factfiles/malaria/en/ (accessed April 12, 2016).

23. Central Intelligence Agency, "The World Factbook: Life Expectancy at Birth," 2015, https://www.cia.gov/library/publications/the-world-factbook/rankorder/2102rank.html (accessed April 12 2016).

24. World Bank, "Gross Domestic Product 2014," April 11, 2016, http://databank.worldbank.org/data/download/GDP.pdf (accessed April 12, 2016).

25. World Bank, "Per Capita GDP," http://data.worldbank.org/indicator/NY.GDP.PCAP.CD?order=wbapi_data_value_2014+wbapi_data_value+wbapi_data_value-last&sort=asc (accessed April 12, 2016).

26. See "The 0.7% Target: An In-Depth Look," Millennium Project, accessed June 25, 2013, http://www.unmillenniumproject.org/press/07.htm

27. "Guess How Much of Uncle Sam's Money Goes to Foreign Aid. Guess Again!" *NPR*, February 10, 2015, http://www.npr.org/sections/goatsandsoda/2015/02/10/383875581/guess-how-much-of-uncle-sams-money-goes-to-foreign-aid-guess-again (accessed April 12, 2016).

28. Ken Hackett, "Surprise! Americans Want to 'Slash' Foreign Aid – to 10 Times Its Current Size," *Christian Science Monitor*, March 7, 2011, accessed June 30, 2013, http://www.csmonitor.com/Commentary/Opinion/2011/0307/Surprise!-Americans-want-to-slash-foreign-aid-to-10-times-its-current-size

29. Ibid.

30. Organization for Economic Cooperation and Development, "Net Official Development Assistance," April 2015, http://www.oecd.org/dac/stats/documentupload/ODA%202014%20Tables%20and%20Charts.pdf (accessed April 12, 2016).

31. Ibid.

32. "UK Passes Bill to Honour Pledge of 0.7% Foreign Aid Target," *The Guardian*, March 9, 2015, http://www.theguardian.com/global-development/2015/mar/09/uk-passes-bill-law-aid-target-percentage-income (accessed April 12, 2016).

33. Frantz Fanon, *The Wretched of the Earth* (New York: Grove Press, 1968).

34. Ibid., 96.

35. Dinesh D'Souza, "Two Cheers for Colonialism," *Chronicle of Higher Education*, May 10, 2002.

36. Dinesh D'Souza, *Obama's America: Unmaking the American Dream* (Washington, D.C.: Regnery Publishing, 2012), 219.

37. D'Souza, "Two Cheers for Colonialism."

38. "United States Summary Information," Environmental Working Group, Farm Subsidies, accessed July 16, 2013, http://farm.ewg.org/region.php?fips=00000

39. Gary S. Fields, *Working Hard, Working Poor: A Global Journey* (Oxford: Oxford University Press, 2011), 114.

40. Tim Johnson, "Free Trade: As U.S. Corn Flows South, Mexicans Stop Farming," *McClatchy News*, February 1, 2011, accessed June 25, 2013, http://www.mcclatchydc.com/2011/02/01/107871/free-trade-us-corn-flows-south.html#.UcyNyz7Eo_s#storylink=cpy

41. "U.S., Other Powers Kick Russia out of G8," *CNN*, March 24, 2014, http://www.cnn.com/2014/03/24/politics/obama-europe-trip/ (accessed April 12, 2016).

42. Adrian Morrow, "Toronto Police Were Overwhelmed at G20, Review Reveals," *Globe and Mail*, June 23, 2011, accessed July 1, 2013, http://www.theglobeandmail.com/news/toronto/toronto-police-were-overwhelmed-at-g20-review-reveals/article2073215/

43. Naomi Klein, interview on PBS, April 21, 2001, accessed July 1, 2013, http://www.pbs.org/wgbh/commandingheights/shared/minitext/int_naomiklein.html

44. Noam Chomsky, quoted in Jack Lule, *Globalization and Media: Global Village of Babel* (Lanham, MD: Rowman & Littlefield, 2012), 11.

45. Joseph E. Stiglitz, *Globalization and Its Discontents* (New York: Norton, 2003), 19.

46. Ibid., 80–81.

47. Jagdish Bhagwati, *In Defense of Globalization* (Oxford: Oxford University Press, 2007), see especially the Afterword.

48. Loretta Napoleoni, *Rogue Economics* (New York: Seven Stories Press, 2011), 195.

49. Jeffrey Sachs, *The End of Poverty: Economic Possibilities for Our Time* (New York: Penguin Press, 2005), Chapter 12.

50. See Thomas Pogge, *World Poverty and Human Rights* (op. cit.), Section 9.2.

51. Robert Wright, "Two Years Later, a Thousand Years Ago," *New York Times*, Op-Ed., September 11, 2003.

52. Thomas L. Friedman, *The World Is Flat: A Brief History of the Twenty-First Century* (New York: Farrar, Straus, and Giroux, 2005), 8.

53. Jan Scholte, *Globalization: A Critical Introduction*, 2nd ed. (New York: Palgrave MacMillan, 2005), 15–17.

54. Ibid.

55. Samuel P. Huntington, *The Clash of Civilizations* (New York: Simon and Schuster, 1996).

56. Michael D. Barr, *Cultural Politics and Asian Values: The Tepid War* (London: Routledge, 2002), Chapter 3.

57. Amartya Sen, *Human Rights and Asian Values* (New York: Carnegie Council on Human Rights, 1997), 31.

58. See essays in Ali Mohammadi, *Islam Encountering Globalization* (London: Routledge, 2002).

59. World Bank Data, http://data.worldbank.org/country/ARB (accessed April 13, 2016).

60. World Bank Data, http://data.worldbank.org/country/germany (accessed April 13, 2016).

61. International Food Policy Research Institute, "Beyond the Arab Awakening: Policies and Investment for Poverty Reduction and Food Security," February 2012, accessed June 30, 2013, http://www.ifpri.org/sites/default/files/publications/pr25.pdf

62. Thomas L. Friedman, "Arabs at the Crossroads," *New York Times,* July 3, 2002, A19.

63. "Human Development Data for the Arab States," United Nations Development Programme, accessed July 2, 2013, http://www.arab-hdr.org/data/indicators/2012-18.aspx

READING

The Singer Solution to World Poverty

PETER SINGER

MindTap° For more chapter resources and activities, go to MindTap.

Study Questions

1. Explain how Singer's reasoning is "utilitarian."
2. Does it matter that there are lots of people who could help and who need help?
3. How does Singer differentiate between luxury goods and the basic needs of the poor?

In the Brazilian film "Central Station," Dora is a retired schoolteacher who makes ends meet by sitting at the station writing letters for illiterate people. Suddenly she has an opportunity to pocket $1,000. All she has to do is persuade a homeless 9-year-old boy to follow her to an address she has been given. (She is told he will be adopted by wealthy foreigners.) She delivers the boy, gets the money, spends some of it on a television set and settles down to enjoy her new acquisition. Her neighbor spoils the fun, however, by telling her that the boy was too old to be adopted—he will be killed and his organs sold for transplantation. Perhaps Dora knew this all along, but after her neighbor's plain speaking, she spends a troubled night. In the morning Dora resolves to take the boy back.

Suppose Dora had told her neighbor that it is a tough world, other people have nice new TV's too, and if selling the kid is the only way she can get one, well, he was only a street kid. She would then

---

Peter Singer, "The Singer Solution To World Poverty," *The New York Times Magazine*, September 5, 1999. Reprinted by permission of the author.

have become, in the eyes of the audience, a monster. She redeems herself only by being prepared to bear considerable risks to save the boy.

At the end of the movie, in cinemas in the affluent nations of the world, people who would have been quick to condemn Dora if she had not rescued the boy go home to places far more comfortable than her apartment. In fact, the average family in the United States spends almost one-third of its income on things that are no more necessary to them than Dora's new TV was to her. Going out to nice restaurants, buying new clothes because the old ones are no longer stylish, vacationing at beach resorts—so much of our income is spent on things not essential to the preservation of our lives and health. Donated to one of a number of charitable agencies, that money could mean the difference between life and death for children in need.

All of which raises a question: In the end, what is the ethical distinction between a Brazilian who sells a homeless child to organ peddlers and an American who already has a TV and upgrades to a better one—knowing that the money could be donated to an organization that would use it to save the lives of kids in need?

Of course, there are several differences between the two situations that could support different moral judgments about them. For one thing, to be able to consign a child to death when he is standing right in front of you takes a chilling kind of heartlessness; it is much easier to ignore an appeal for money to help children you will never meet. Yet for a utilitarian philosopher like myself—that is, one who judges whether acts are right or wrong by their consequences—if the upshot of the American's failure to donate the money is that one more kid dies on the streets of a Brazilian city, then it is, in some sense, just as bad as selling the kid to the organ peddlers. But one doesn't need to embrace my utilitarian ethic to see that, at the very least, there is a troubling incongruity in being so quick to condemn Dora for taking the child to the organ peddlers while, at the same time, not regarding the American consumer's behavior as raising a serious moral issue.

In his 1996 book, *Living High and Letting Die*, the New York University philosopher Peter Unger presented an ingenious series of imaginary examples designed to probe our intuitions about whether it is wrong to live well without giving substantial amounts of money to help people who are hungry, malnourished or dying from easily treatable illnesses like diarrhea. Here's my paraphrase of one of these examples:

Bob is close to retirement. He has invested most of his savings in a very rare and valuable old car, a Bugatti, which he has not been able to insure. The Bugatti is his pride and joy. In addition to the pleasure he gets from driving and caring for his car, Bob knows that its rising market value means that he will always be able to sell it and live comfortably after retirement. One day when Bob is out for a drive, he parks the Bugatti near the end of a railway siding and goes for a walk up the track. As he does so, he sees that a runaway train, with no one aboard, is running down the railway track. Looking farther down the track, he sees the small figure of a child very likely to be killed by the runaway train. He can't stop the train and the child is too far away to warn of the danger, but he can throw a switch that will divert the train down the siding where his Bugatti is parked. Then nobody will be killed—but the train will destroy his Bugatti. Thinking of his joy in owning the car and the financial security it represents, Bob decides not to throw the switch. The child is killed. For many years to come, Bob enjoys owning his Bugatti and the financial security it represents.

Bob's conduct, most of us will immediately respond, was gravely wrong. Unger agrees. But then he reminds us that we, too, have opportunities to save the lives of children. We can give to organizations like UNICEF or Oxfam America. How much would we have to give one of these organizations to have a high probability of saving the life of a child threatened by easily preventable diseases? (I do not believe that children are more worth saving than adults, but since no one can argue that children have brought their poverty on themselves, focusing on them simplifies the issues.) Unger called up some experts and used the information they provided to offer some plausible estimates that include the cost of raising money, administrative expenses and the cost of delivering aid where it is most needed. By his calculation, $200 in donations would help a sickly 2-year-old transform into a healthy 6-year-old—offering safe passage through childhood's most dangerous years. To show how practical philosophical argument can be, Unger even tells his readers that they can easily donate funds by using their credit card and calling one of these toll-free numbers . . . (Oxfam can be found at www.oxfam.org; Unicef can be found at http://www.supportunicef.org/).

Now you, too, have the information you need to save a child's life. How should you judge yourself if you don't do it? Think again about Bob and his Bugatti. Unlike Dora, Bob did not have to look into the eyes of the child he was sacrificing for his own material comfort. The child was a complete stranger to him and too far away to relate to in an intimate, personal way. Unlike Dora, too, he did not mislead the child or initiate the chain of events imperiling him. In all these respects, Bob's situation resembles that of people able but unwilling to donate to overseas aid and differs from Dora's situation.

If you still think that it was very wrong of Bob not to throw the switch that would have diverted the train and saved the child's life, then it is hard to see how you could deny that it is also very wrong not to send money to one of the organizations listed above. Unless, that is, there is some morally important difference between the two situations that I have overlooked.

Is it the practical uncertainties about whether aid will really reach the people who need it? Nobody who knows the world of overseas aid can doubt that such uncertainties exist. But Unger's figure of $200 to save a child's life was reached after he had made conservative assumptions about the proportion of the money donated that will actually reach its target.

One genuine difference between Bob and those who can afford to donate to overseas aid organizations but don't is that only Bob can save the child on the tracks, whereas there are hundreds of millions of people who can give $200 to overseas aid

organizations. The problem is that most of them aren't doing it. Does this mean that it is all right for you not to do it?

Suppose that there were more owners of priceless vintage cars—Carol, Dave, Emma, Fred and so on, down to Ziggy—all in exactly the same situation as Bob, with their own siding and their own switch, all sacrificing the child in order to preserve their own cherished car. Would that make it all right for Bob to do the same? To answer this question affirmatively is to endorse follow-the-crowd ethics—the kind of ethics that led many Germans to look away when the Nazi atrocities were being committed. We do not excuse them because others were behaving no better.

We seem to lack a sound basis for drawing a clear moral line between Bob's situation and that of any reader of this article with $200 to spare who does not donate it to an overseas aid agency. These readers seem to be acting at least as badly as Bob was acting when he chose to let the runaway train hurtle toward the unsuspecting child. In the light of this conclusion, I trust that many readers will reach for the phone and donate that $200. Perhaps you should do it before reading further.

Now that you have distinguished yourself morally from people who put their vintage cars ahead of a child's life, how about treating yourself and your partner to dinner at your favorite restaurant? But wait. The money you will spend at the restaurant could also help save the lives of children overseas! True, you weren't planning to blow $200 tonight, but if you were to give up dining out just for one month, you would easily save that amount. And what is one month's dining out, compared to a child's life? There's the rub. Since there are a lot of desperately needy children in the world, there will always be another child whose life you could save for another $200. Are you therefore obliged to keep giving until you have nothing left? At what point can you stop?

Hypothetical examples can easily become farcical. Consider Bob. How far past losing the Bugatti should he go? Imagine that Bob had got his foot stuck in the track of the siding, and if he diverted the train, then before it rammed the car it would also amputate his big toe. Should he still throw the switch? What if it would amputate his foot? His entire leg?

As absurd as the Bugatti scenario gets when pushed to extremes, the point it raises is a serious one: only when the sacrifices become very significant indeed would most people be prepared to say that Bob does nothing wrong when he decides not to throw the switch. Of course, most people could be wrong; we can't decide moral issues by taking opinion polls. But consider for yourself the level of sacrifice that you would demand of Bob, and then think about how much money you would have to give away in order to make a sacrifice that is roughly equal to that. It's almost certainly much, much more than $200. For most middle-class Americans, it could easily be more like $200,000.

Isn't it counterproductive to ask people to do so much? Don't we run the risk that many will shrug their shoulders and say that morality, so conceived, is fine for saints but not for them? I accept that we are unlikely to see, in the near or even medium-term future, a world in which it is normal for wealthy Americans to give the bulk of their wealth to strangers. When it comes to praising or blaming people for what they do, we tend to use a standard that is relative to some conception of normal behavior. Comfortably off Americans who give, say, 10 percent of their income to overseas aid organizations are so far ahead of most of their equally comfortable fellow citizens that I wouldn't go out of my way to chastise them for not doing more. Nevertheless, they should be doing much more, and they are in no position to criticize Bob for failing to make the much greater sacrifice of his Bugatti.

At this point various objections may crop up. Someone may say, "If every citizen living in the affluent nations contributed his or her share I wouldn't have to make such a drastic sacrifice, because long before such levels were reached, the resources would have been there to save the lives of all those children dying from lack of food or medical care. So why should I give more than my fair share?" Another, related, objection is that the Government ought to increase its overseas aid allocations, since

that would spread the burden more equitably across all taxpayers.

Yet the question of how much we ought to give is a matter to be decided in the real world—and that, sadly, is a world in which we know that most people do not, and in the immediate future will not, give substantial amounts to overseas aid agencies. We know, too, that at least in the next year, the United States Government is not going to meet even the very modest United Nations-recommended target of 0.7 percent of gross national product; at the moment it lags far below that, at 0.09 percent, not even half of Japan's 0.22 percent or a tenth of Denmark's 0.97 percent. Thus we know that the money we can give beyond that theoretical "fair share" is still going to save lives that would otherwise be lost. While the idea that no one need do more than his or her fair share is a powerful one, should it prevail if we know that others are not doing their fair share and that children will die preventable deaths unless we do more than our fair share? That would be taking fairness too far.

Thus this ground for limiting how much we ought to give also fails. In the world as it is now, I can see no escape from the conclusion that each one of us with wealth surplus to his or her essential needs should be giving most of it to help people suffering from poverty so dire as to be life-threatening. That's right. I'm saying that you shouldn't buy that new car, take that cruise, redecorate the house or get that pricey new suit. After all, a $1,000 suit could save five children's lives.

So how does my philosophy break down in dollars and cents? An American household with an income of $50,000 spends around $30,000 annually on necessities, according to the Conference Board, a nonprofit economic research organization. Therefore, for a household bringing in $50,000 a year, donations to help the world's poor should be as close as possible to $20,000. The $30,000 required for necessities holds for higher incomes as well. So a household making $100,000 could cut a yearly check for $70,000. Again, the formula is simple: whatever money you're spending on luxuries, not necessities, should be given away.

Now, evolutionary psychologists tell us that human nature just isn't sufficiently altruistic to make it plausible that many people will sacrifice so much for strangers. On the facts of human nature, they might be right, but they would be wrong to draw a moral conclusion from those facts. If it is the case that we ought to do things that, predictably, most of us won't do, then let's face that fact head-on. Then, if we value the life of a child more than going to fancy restaurants, the next time we dine out we will know that we could have done something better with our money. If that makes living a morally decent life extremely arduous, well,

then that is the way things are. If we don't do it, then we should at least know that we are failing to live a morally decent life—not because it is good to wallow in guilt but because knowing where we should be going is the first step toward heading in that direction.

When Bob first grasped the dilemma that faced him as he stood by that railway switch, he must have thought how extraordinarily unlucky he was to be placed in a situation in which he must choose between the life of an innocent child and the sacrifice of most of his savings. But he was not unlucky at all. We are all in that situation.

READING

Living on a Lifeboat

GARRETT HARDIN

MindTap®   For more chapter resources and activities, go to MindTap.

Study Questions

1. Is earth best described as a spaceship or a lifeboat—what is Hardin's explanation for his answer to this question?
2. How does Hardin explain and utilize the idea of the tragedy of the commons?
3. How does Hardin respond to the claim that his view is ethnocentric and bigoted?

No generation has viewed the problem of the survival of the human species as seriously as we have. Inevitably, we have entered this world of concern through the door of metaphor. Environmentalists have emphasized the image of the earth as a spaceship—Spaceship Earth. Kenneth Boulding (1966) is the principal architect of this metaphor. It is time, he says, that we replace the wasteful "cowboy economy" of the past with the frugal "spaceship economy" required for continued survival in the limited world we now see ours to be. The metaphor is notably useful in justifying pollution control measures.

Unfortunately, the image of a spaceship is also used to promote measures that are suicidal. One of these is a generous immigration policy, which is only a particular instance of a class of policies that are in error because they lead to the tragedy of the

commons (Hardin 1968). These suicidal policies are attractive because they mesh with what we unthinkingly take to be the ideals of "the best people." What is missing in the idealistic view is an insistence that rights and responsibilities must go together. The "generous" attitude of all too many people results in asserting inalienable rights while ignoring or denying matching responsibilities.

For the metaphor of a spaceship to be correct the aggregate of people on board would have to be under unitary sovereign control (Ophuls 1974). A true ship always has a captain. It is conceivable that a ship could be run by a committee. But it could not possibly survive if its course were determined

BioScience, Vol. 24, No. 10 (Oct. 1974), pp. 561–568. Published by Oxford University Press on behalf of the American Institute of Biological Sciences, URL: http://www.jstor.org/stable/1296629.

by bickering tribes that claimed rights without responsibilities.

What about Spaceship Earth? It certainly has no captain, and no executive committee. The United Nations is a toothless tiger, because the signatories of its charter wanted it that way. The spaceship metaphor is used only to justify spaceship demands on common resources without acknowledging corresponding spaceship responsibilities.

An understandable fear of decisive action leads people to embrace "incrementalism"—moving toward reform by tiny stages. As we shall see, this strategy is counterproductive in the area discussed here if it means accepting rights before responsibilities. Where human survival is at stake, the acceptance of responsibilities is a precondition to the acceptance of rights, if the two cannot be introduced simultaneously.

LIFEBOAT ETHICS

Before taking up certain substantive issues let us look at an alternative metaphor, that of a lifeboat. In developing some relevant examples the following numerical values are assumed. Approximately two-thirds of the world is desperately poor, and only one-third is comparatively rich. Metaphorically, each rich nation amounts to a lifeboat full of comparatively rich people. The poor of the world are in other, much more crowded lifeboats. Continuously, so to speak, the poor fall out of their lifeboats and swim for a while in the water outside, hoping to be admitted to a rich lifeboat, or in some other way to benefit from the "goodies" on board. What should the passengers on a rich lifeboat do? This is the central problem of "the ethics of a lifeboat."

First we must acknowledge that each lifeboat is effectively limited in capacity. The land of every nation has a limited carrying capacity. The exact limit is a matter for argument, but the energy crunch is convincing more people every day that we have already exceeded the carrying capacity of the land. We have been living on "capital"- stored petroleum and coal-and soon we must live on income alone.

Let us look at only one lifeboat—ours. The ethical problem is the same for all, and is as follows. Here we sit, say 50 people in a lifeboat. To be generous, let us assume our boat has a capacity of 10 more, making 60. (This, however, is to violate the engineering principle of the "safety factor." A new plant disease or a bad change in the weather may decimate our population if we don't preserve some excess capacity as a safety factor.)

The 50 of us in the lifeboat see 100 others swimming in the water outside, asking for admission to the boat, or for handouts. How shall we respond to their calls? There are several possibilities.

One. We may be tempted to try to live by the Christian ideal of being "our brother's keeper," or by the Marxian ideal (Marx 1875) of "from each according to his abilities, to each according to his needs." Since the needs of all are the same, we take all the needy into our boat, making a total of 150 in a boat with a capacity of 60. The boat is swamped, and everyone drowns. Complete justice, complete catastrophe.

Two. Since the boat has an unused excess capacity of 10, we admit just 10 more to it. This has the disadvantage of getting rid of the safety factor, for which action we will sooner or later pay dearly. Moreover, *which* 10 do we let in? "First come, first served?" The best 10? The neediest 10? How do we *discriminate*? And what do we say to the 90 who are excluded?

Three. Admit no more to the boat and preserve the small safety factor. Survival of the people in the lifeboat is then possible (though we shall have to be on our guard against boarding parties).

The last solution is abhorrent to many people. It is unjust, they say. Let us grant that it is.

"I feel guilty about my good luck," say some. The reply to this is simple: *Get out and yield your place to others.* Such a selfless action might satisfy the conscience of those who are addicted to guilt but it would not change the ethics of the lifeboat. The needy person to whom a guilt-addict yields his place will not himself feel guilty about his sudden good luck. (If he did he would not climb aboard.) The net result of conscience-stricken people relinquishing their unjustly held positions is the elimination of their kind of conscience from the lifeboat. The lifeboat, as it were, purifies itself of guilt. The ethics of the lifeboat persist, unchanged by such momentary aberrations.

RUIN IN THE COMMONS

The fundamental error of the sharing ethics is that it leads to the tragedy of the commons. Under a system of private property the man (or group of men) who own property recognize their responsibility to care for it, for if they don't they will eventually suffer. A farmer, for instance, if he is intelligent, will allow no more cattle in a pasture than its carrying capacity justifies. If he overloads the pasture, weeds take over, erosion sets in, and the owner loses in the long run.

But if a pasture is run as a commons open to all, the right of each to use it is not matched by an operational responsibility to take care of it. It is no use asking independent herdsmen in a commons to act responsibly, for they dare not. The considerate herdsman who refrains from overloading the commons suffers more than a selfish one who says his needs are greater. (As Leo Durocher says, "Nice guys finish last.") Christian-Marxian idealism is counterproductive. That it *sounds* nice is no excuse. With distribution systems, as with individual morality, good intentions are no substitute for good performance.

A social system is stable only if it is insensitive to errors. To the Christian-Marxian idealist a selfish person is a sort of "error." Prosperity in the system of the commons cannot survive errors. If *everyone* would only restrain himself, all would be well; but it takes *only one less than everyone* to ruin a system of voluntary restraint. In a crowded world of less than perfect human beings-and we will never know any other–mutual ruin is inevitable in the commons. This is the core of the tragedy of the commons.

One of the major tasks of education today is to create such an awareness of the dangers of the commons that people will be able to recognize its many varieties, however disguised. There is pollution of the air and water because these media are treated as commons. Further growth of population and growth in the per capita conversion of natural resources into pollutants require that the system of the commons be modified or abandoned in the disposal of "externalities."

"But it isn't their fault! How can we blame the poor people who are caught in an emergency? Why must we punish them?" The concepts of blame and punishment are irrelevant. The question is, what are the operational consequences of establishing a world food bank? If it is open to every country every time a need develops, slovenly rulers will not be motivated to take Joseph's advice. Why should they? Others will bail them out whenever they are in trouble.

Some countries will make deposits in the world food bank and others will withdraw from it: there will be almost no overlap. Calling such a depository-transfer unit a "bank" is stretching the metaphor of *bank* beyond its elastic limits. The proposers, of course, never call attention to the metaphorical nature of the word they use.

THE RATCHET EFFECT

An "international food bank" is really, then, not a true bank but a disguised one-way transfer device for moving wealth from rich countries to poor. In the absence of such a bank, in a world inhabited by individually responsible sovereign nations, the population of each nation would repeatedly go through a cycle of the sort shown in Figure 1. P_2 is greater than P_1, either in absolute numbers or because a deterioration of the food supply has removed the safety factor and produced a dangerously low ratio

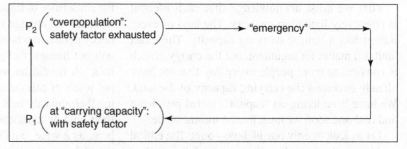

Fig. 1. The population cycle of a nation that has no effective, conscious population control, and which receives no aid from the outside. P_2 is greater than P_1.

of resources to population. P_2 may be said to represent a state of overpopulation, which becomes obvious upon the appearance of an "accident," e.g., a crop failure. If the "emergency" is not met by outside help, the population drops back to the "normal" level—the "carrying capacity" of the environment—or even below. In the absence of population control by a sovereign, sooner or later the population grows to P_2 again and the cycle repeats. The long-term population curve (Hardin 1966) is an irregularly fluctuating one, equilibrating more or less about the carrying capacity.

A demographic cycle of this sort obviously involves great suffering in the restrictive phase, but such a cycle is normal to any independent country with inadequate population control. The third century theologian Tertullian (Hardin 1969a) expressed what must have been the recognition of many wise men when he wrote: "The scourges of pestilence, famine, wars, and earthquakes have come to be regarded as a blessing to overcrowded nations, since they serve to prune away the luxuriant growth of the human race."

Only under a strong and farsighted sovereign—which theoretically could be the people themselves, democratically organized—can a population equilibrate at some set point below the carrying capacity, thus avoiding the pains normally caused by periodic and unavoidable disasters. For this happy state to be achieved it is necessary that those in power be able to contemplate with equanimity the "waste" of surplus food in times of bountiful harvests. It is essential that those in power resist the temptation to convert extra food into extra babies. On the public relations level it is necessary that the phrase "surplus food" be replaced by "safety factor."

But wise sovereigns seem not to exist in the poor world today. The most anguishing problems are created by poor countries that are governed by rulers insufficiently wise and powerful. If such countries can draw on a world food bank in times of "emergency," the population *cycle* of Figure 1 will be replaced by the population *escalator* of Figure 2. The input of food from a food bank acts as the pawl of a ratchet, preventing the population from retracing its steps to a lower level. Reproduction pushes the population upward, inputs from the world bank prevent its moving downward. Population size escalates, as does the absolute magnitude of "accidents" and "emergencies." The process is brought to an end only by the total collapse of the whole system, producing a catastrophe of scarcely imaginable proportions.

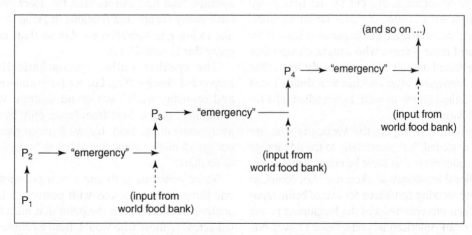

Fig. 2. The population escalator. Note that input from a world food bank acts like the pawl of a ratchet, preventing the normal population cycle shown in Figure 1 from being completed. P_{n+1} is greater than P_n, and the absolute magnitude of the "emergencies" escalates. Ultimately the entire system crashes. The crash is not shown, and few can imagine it.

Such are the implications of the well-meant sharing of food in a world of irresponsible reproduction.

World food banks move food to the people, thus facilitating the exhaustion of the environment of the poor. By contrast, unrestricted immigration moves people to the food, thus speeding up the destruction of the environment in rich countries. Why poor people should want to make this transfer is no mystery: but why should rich hosts encourage it? This transfer, like the reverse one, is supported by both selfish interests and humanitarian impulses.

The principal selfish interest in unimpeded immigration is easy to identify: it is the interest of the employers of cheap labor, particularly that needed for degrading jobs. We have been deceived about the forces of history by the lines of Emma Lazarus inscribed on the Statue of Liberty:

Give me your tired, your poor
Your huddled masses yearning to breathe free,
The wretched refuse of your teeming shore,
Send these, the homeless, tempesttossed, to me:
I lift my lamp beside the golden door.

The image is one of an infinitely generous earth-mother, passively opening her arms to hordes of immigrants who come here on their own initiative. Such an image may have been adequate for the early days of colonization, but by the time these lines were written (1886) the force for immigration was largely manufactured inside our own borders by factory and mine owners who sought cheap labor not to be found among laborers already here. One group of foreigners after another was thus enticed into the United States to work at wretched jobs for wretched wages.

At present, it is largely the Mexicans who are being so exploited. It is particularly to the advantage of certain employers that there be many illegal immigrants. Illegal immigrant workers dare not complain about their working conditions for fear of being repatriated. Their presence reduces the bargaining power of all Mexican-American laborers. Cesar Chavez has repeatedly pleaded with congressional committees to close the doors to more Mexicans so that those here can negotiate effectively for higher wages and decent working conditions. Chavez understands the ethics of a lifeboat.

The interests of the employers of cheap labor are well served by the silence of the intelligentsia of the country. WASPS—White Anglo-Saxon Protestants—are particularly reluctant to call for a closing of the doors to immigration for fear of being called ethnocentric bigots. It was, therefore, an occasion of pure delight for this particular WASP to be present at a meeting when the points he would like to have made were made better by a non-WASP speaking to other non-WASPS. It was in Hawaii, and most of the people in the room were second-level Hawaiian officials of Japanese ancestry. All Hawaiians are keenly aware of the limits of their environment, and the speaker had asked how it might be practically and constitutionally possible to close the doors to more immigrants to the islands. (To Hawaiians, immigrants from the other 49 states are as much of a threat as those from other nations. There is only so much room in the islands, and the islanders know it. Sophistical arguments that imply otherwise do not impress them.)

Yet the Japanese-Americans of Hawaii have active ties with the land of their origin. This point was raised by a Japanese-American member of the audience who asked the Japanese-American speaker: "But how can we shut the doors now? We have many friends and relations in Japan that we'd like to bring to Hawaii some day so that they can enjoy this beautiful land.

The speaker smiled sympathetically and responded slowly: "Yes, but we have children now and someday we'll have grandchildren. We can bring more people here from Japan only by giving away some of the land that we hope to pass on to our grandchildren some day. What right do we have to do that?"

To be generous with one's own possessions is one thing; to be generous with posterity's is quite another. This, I think, is the point that must be gotten across to those who would, from a commendable love of distributive justice, institute a ruinous system of the commons, either in the form of a world food bank or that of unrestricted immigration. Since every speaker is a member of some ethnic group it is always possible to charge him with ethnocentrism. But even after purging an argument of ethnocentrism the rejection of the commons is still valid and necessary if we are to save at least some parts of the world from environmental ruin. Is it not desirable that at least some of the grandchildren of people now living should have a decent place in which to live?

THE ASYMMETRY OF DOOR-SHUTTING

We must now answer this telling point: "How can you justify slamming the door once you're inside? You say that immigrants should be kept out. But aren't we all immigrants, or the descendants of immigrants? Since we refuse to leave, must we not, as a matter of justice and symmetry, admit all others?"

It is literally true that we Americans of non-Indian ancestry are the descendants of thieves. Should we not, then, "give back" the land to the Indians; that is, give it to the now-living Americans of Indian ancestry? As an exercise in pure logic I see no way to reject this proposal. Yet I am unwilling to live by it; and I know no one who is. Our reluctance to embrace pure justice may spring from pure selfishness. On the other hand, it may arise from an unspoken recognition of consequences that have not yet been clearly spelled out.

Suppose, becoming intoxicated with pure justice, we "Anglos" should decide to turn our land over to the Indians. Since all our other wealth has also been derived from the land, we would have to give that to the Indians, too. Then what would we non-Indians do? Where would we go? There is no open land in the world on which men without capital can make their living (and not much unoccupied land on which men with capital can either). Where would 209 million putatively justice-loving, non-Indian, Americans go? Most of them—in the persons of their ancestors—came from Europe, but they wouldn't be welcomed back there. Anyway, Europeans have no better title to their land than we to ours. They also would have to give up their homes. (But to whom? And where would *they* go?)

Clearly, the concept of pure justice produces an infinite regress. The law long ago invented statutes of limitations to justify the rejection of pure justice, in the interest of preventing massive disorder. The law zealously defends property rights—but only *recent* property rights. It is as though the physical principle of exponential decay applies to property rights. Drawing a line in time may be unjust, but any other action is practically worse.

We are all the descendants of thieves, and the world's resources are inequitably distributed, but we must begin the journey to tomorrow from the point where we are today. We cannot remake the past. We cannot, without violent disorder and suffering, give land and resources back to the "original" owners—who are dead anyway.

We cannot safely divide the wealth equitably among all present peoples, so long as people reproduce at different rates, because to do so would guarantee that our grandchildren—everyone's grandchildren—would have only a ruined world to inhabit.

MUST EXCLUSION BE ABSOLUTE?

To show the logical structure of the immigration problem I have ignored many factors that would enter into real decisions made in a real world. No matter how convincing the logic may be it is probable that we would want, from time to time, to admit a few people from the outside to our lifeboat. Political refugees in particular are likely to cause us to make exceptions: We remember the Jewish refugees from Germany after 1933, and the Hungarian refugees after 1956. Moreover, the interests of national defense, broadly conceived, could justify admitting many men and women of unusual talents, whether refugees or not. (This raises the quality issue, which is not the subject of this essay.)

Such exceptions threaten to create runaway population growth inside the lifeboat, i.e., the receiving country. However, the threat can be neutralized by a population policy that includes immigration. An effective policy is one of flexible control.

Suppose, for example, that the nation has achieved a stable condition of ZPG, which (say) permits 1.5 million births yearly. We must suppose that an acceptable system of allocating birth-rights to potential parents is in effect. Now suppose that an inhumane regime in some other part of the world creates a horde of refugees, and that there is a widespread desire to admit some to our country. At the same time, we do not want to sabotage our population control system. Clearly, the rational path to pursue is the following. If we decide to admit 100,000 refugees this year we should compensate for this by reducing the allocation of birth-rights in the following year by a similar amount, that is downward to a total of 1.4 million. In that way we could achieve both humanitarian and population control goals. (And the refugees would have to accept the population controls of the society that admits them. It is not inconceivable that they might be given proportionately fewer rights than the native population.)

In a democracy, the admission of immigrants should properly be voted on. But by whom? It is not obvious. The usual rule of a democracy is votes for all. But it can be questioned whether a universal franchise is the most just one in a case of this sort. Whatever benefits there are in the admission of immigrants presumably accrue to everyone. But the costs would be seen as falling most heavily on potential parents, some of whom would have to postpone or forego having their (next) child because of the influx of immigrants. The double question *Who benefits? Who pays?* suggests that a restriction of the usual democratic franchise would be appropriate and just in this case. Would our particular quasi-democratic form of government be flexible enough to institute such a novelty? If not, the majority might, out of humanitarian motives, impose an unacceptable burden (the foregoing of parenthood) on a minority, thus producing political instability.

Plainly many new problems will arise when we consciously face the immigration question and seek rational answers. No workable answers can be found if we ignore population problems. And—if the argument of this essay is correct—so long as there is no true world government to control reproduction everywhere it is impossible to survive in dignity if we are to be guided by Spaceship ethics. Without a world government that is sovereign in reproductive matters mankind lives, in fact, on a number of sovereign lifeboats. For the foreseeable future survival demands that we govern our actions by the ethics of a lifeboat. Posterity will be ill served if we do not.

REFERENCES

Anonymous. 1974. *Wall Street Journal* 19 Feb.

Borlaug, N . 1973. Civilization's future: a call for international granaries. *Bull. At. Sci.* 29: 7–15.

Boulding, K. 1966. The economics of the coming Spaceship earth. *In* H. Jarrett, ed. Environmental Quality in a Growing Economy. Johns Hopkins Press, Baltimore.

Buchanan, W. 1973. Immigration statistics. *Equilibrium* 1(3): 16–19.

Davis, K. 1963. Population. *Sci. Amer.* 209(3): 62–71.

Farvar, M. T., and J. P. Milton. 1972. The Careless Technology. Natural History Press, Garden City, N.Y.

Gregg, A. 1955. A medical aspect of the population problem. Science 121: 681–682.

Hardin, G. 1966. Chap. 9 *in* Biology: Its Principles and Implications, 2nd ed. Freeman, San Francisco.

——. 1968. The tragedy of the commons. *Science* 162: 1243–1248.

——. 1969a Page 18 *in* Population, Evolution, and Birth Control, 2nd ed. Freeman, San Francisco.

——.1969b. The economics of wilderness. *Nat. Hist.* 78(6): 20–27.

——. 1972a. Pages 81–82 in Exploring New Ethics for Survival:The Voyage of the Spaceship *Beagle*. Viking, N.Y.

——. 1972b. Preserving quality on Spaceship Earth. *In* J. B. Trefethen, ed. Transactions of the Thirty-Seventh North American Wildlife and Natural Resources Conference. Wildlife Management Institute, Washington, D.C.

——. 1973. Chap. 23 *in* Stalking the Wild Taboo. Kaufmann, Los Altos, Cal.

Harris, M. 1972. How green the revolution. *Nat. Hist.* 81(3): 28–30.

Langer, S. K. 1942. Philosophy in a New Key. Harvard University Press, Cambridge.

Lansner, K. 1974. Should foreign aid begin at home? *Newsweek*, 11 Feb., p. 32.

Marx, K. 1875. Critique of the Gotha program. Page 388 *in* R. C. Tucker, ed. The Marx-Engels Reader.Norton, N.Y., 1972.

Ophuls, W. 1974. The scarcity society. *Harpers* 248(1487): 47–52.

Paddock, W. C. 1970. How green is the green revolution? *BioScience* 20: 897–902.

Paddock, W., and E. Paddock. 1973. We Don't Know How. Iowa State University Press, Ames, Iowa.

Paddock, W., and P. Paddock. 1967. Famine-1975! Little, Brown, Boston.

Wilkes, H. G. 1972. The green revolution. *Environment* 14(8): 32–39.

REVIEW EXERCISES

1. What are some of the current contrasting conditions between rich and poor nations described in the text?
2. Explain how the history of colonialism might be connected to current inequalities. Explain a criticism of this idea.
3. What self-interested reasons can be given for doing something to remedy the situation of poor countries?
4. What is justice, and what role does it play in determining what ought to be done about global poverty?
5. Why is cultural relativism a concern when thinking about global justice?
6. Why might we think that we have obligations to be concerned with the suffering of those in distant lands? Explain one criticism of this idea.
7. Contrast Singer's and Hardin's views on how we ought to deal with famine.
8. Summarize different meanings of *globalization* given in the text.
9. Describe some positive and some negative aspects of globalization.

DISCUSSION CASES

1. **Ethical Consumption.** Chris is an advocate of ethical consumption. He tries to buy only fair-trade products, and he is willing to pay more for an item when he is certain that the item is produced without exploitation. This means that he often pays 10 to 25 percent more for certain products. His father thinks this is a bad idea. He tells Chris, "You could buy cheaper stuff and with the money you save, you could save for your own future and retirement. Heck, you could even give that money to the poor." Chris is not concerned with his retirement fund. But he is concerned about alleviating poverty. He's puzzled by his father's response.

   Should Chris try to find the cheapest products and save money, which he would then donate to charity? Or should he continue to seek out fair trade items, which would leave him with less to donate to charity? What is the solution to this problem? Explain your thinking.

2. **Which Poverty Matters?** Madison is a successful businessperson who has become convinced that she ought to give a substantial amount of her earnings to help those in extreme poverty in the developing world. Her brother, Thomas, a local college student, is not persuaded that such donations are a good idea. "It just makes people ask for more handouts later," he says. "And besides," he adds, "there are a lot of poor people here in our city: homeless people living on the streets. And I'm not doing too well myself. You ought to give me some of your charity so I can pay for college. I'm going to be swamped with student loan debt."

   How should Madison reply? Does she have an obligation to help her brother pay for school, to help the homeless in her city, or to help those in poverty in other countries? Should her proximity or relationship to these various people make a difference here? Or is Thomas right that handouts don't help?

3. **Global Culture.** Sam and Jane have been arguing about the effects of globalization as a form of modernization or Westernization of the world.

Sam points out all of globalization's crass and commercialized aspects—the same McDonald's, consumer electronics, and pop culture icons all over the world—and the negative impact that Western culture has on local and indigenous cultures. Jane argues that Western personal and political freedoms ought to be made universal and that a more homogenous culture is a small price to pay for democracy and the liberation of women and minority groups.

   With whom do you agree, Sam or Jane? Can economic and political modernization be divorced from cultural globalization?

4. **Colonialism and Globalization.** Robert is excited about the recent focus on global justice within institutions such as the United Nations and the World Bank. His family emigrated from Africa to the United States to escape the poverty and political instability of his home country. He thinks these new initiatives will be helpful to those they left behind. But his brother, Daniel, is not convinced. Daniel complains, "Nobody helps without asking for something. Most of those international organizations serve the interests of the countries who caused our unhappiness to begin with. The rich countries are always taking advantage of the poor. They enslaved and marginalized lots of us and exploited our countries' resources. Then they left us with a mess." Robert disagrees. "I don't know why you blame others for the poverty back home. Anyway, I'm glad that the rich countries are finally helping. Our people need any help they can get." Daniel responds, "They owe us for what they did to us. But I still don't trust them."

   What do you think? Do rich countries owe something to poor countries? Do rich countries offer their help without strings attached? Or is Daniel right to be cynical?

MindTap® **For more chapter resources and activities, go to MindTap.**

Glossary

A

Absolutism metaethical idea that there are eternal and unchanging values and rules (versus relativism).

Act utilitarianism utilitarian theory that focuses on judging whether individual acts create the greatest happiness for the greatest number (compare: *rule utilitarianism*).

Active euthanasia actively killing someone for the benefit of the one being killed (versus *passive euthanasia*).

Actuality ontological consideration focused on what a thing is at the present moment (versus what it has the potential to become); often employed in discussions of the ethics of abortion; see also *ontological status* and *potentiality*.

Ad hominem a phrase meaning "to the person"; ad hominem arguments are (usually) fallacious arguments that attack a person rather than the person's idea or logical reasoning.

Advance directive a health care directive that stipulates in advance what sort of care a patient wants or does not want in case of incapacity; see also *living will* and *durable power of attorney*.

Aesthetics the study of beauty and taste.

Affirmative action social programs that take positive steps to remedy past injustice and inequality (usually racial); for example: *preferential treatment*; criticized as *reverse discrimination*.

Ahimsa term meaning nonviolence; associated with South Asian traditions such as Hinduism and Buddhism.

Akrasia see *weakness of will*.

Altruism behavior that is oriented toward the well-being of others (versus egoism); see also *pro-social behavior*.

Animal rights idea that individual animals have an interest in their lives and a corresponding right not to suffer or be killed (associated with Regan); see also *animal welfare*.

Animal welfare idea that animal suffering matters and that we should not cause unnecessary harm to animals (associated with *utilitarianism* and Singer); see also *animal rights*.

Anthropocentrism approach to environmental ethics (and *animal welfare*) that maintains that human interests alone are the proper focal point (versus *biocentrism* and *ecocentrism*).

Arguments from analogy arguments based upon a comparison between items; relevant similarities among things are intended to incline us to accept conclusions about these things that are also relevantly similar.

Autonomy self-determination, self-control, independence, and freedom of action.

B

Begging the question a fallacious argument in which the conclusion is assumed in the premises (also called a *circular argument*).

Biocentrism approach to environmental ethics that is

focused on the value of biotic systems and all life (versus *anthropocentrism*); see also *ecocentrism*.

Bioconservativism idea that we should not be "playing God" with regard to biotechnologies, sometimes based upon repugnance toward new technologies (associated with Kass).

Bioengineering projects aiming to develop mechanical supplements for biological systems, which can be used for therapy or enhancement.

Biotechnology interventions and manipulations of biological systems and organisms through the use of technological means including genetic engineering, cloning, the use of drugs, surgeries, and so on.

Biotic pyramid the interrelated food chains that unite plants, grazing animals, prey animals, predators, and human beings (associated with Leopold's *land ethic*).

C

Capitalism a social and economic system based on private property and freedom to make profit; see also *laissez-faire capitalism* (versus *socialism* and *communism*).

Cardinal virtues primary virtues; the four cardinal virtues in the ancient Greek tradition are justice, wisdom, moderation, and courage.

Care ethics ethical theory that emphasizes nurturing relationships, while downplaying

autonomy and individualism (associated with Noddings).

Categorical imperative Kantian idea about the universal form of the moral law, which is not based on hypothetical or conditional interests; Kant's formulation: "act only according to that maxim, whereby you can will that it should also be a universal law" (versus *hypothetical imperative*).

Circular argument a fallacious argument that assumes what it seeks to prove (also called *begging the question*).

Cisgender someone who identifies with the sexual/gender identity they were assigned at birth or with traditional gender roles (as opposed to *transgender*).

Civil disobedience breaking a law in a civil manner that retains fidelity to the system of justice and accepts punishment as an act of protest.

Civil union a legally recognized relationship between same-sex partners, similar but not identical to marriage (also called *civil partnership* or *domestic partnership*).

Collateral damage term used in just war ethics to describe unintended noncombatant harm that is justified by application of the *principle of double effect*; see also *noncombatant immunity*.

Communism a social and economic system focused on communal ownership of the means of production, radical

equality, and the abolition of social classes; see also *socialism* (versus *capitalism*).

Communitarianism a theory of society that emphasizes communal belonging and is critical of the individualistic focus of *liberalism* and *libertarianism*.

Consequentialism normative theories that focus on the consequences of actions; examples include *egoism*, *altruism*, *utilitarianism* (versus *non-consequentialism*).

Contractarianism normative theory that holds that moral norms arise from a contract or agreement between rational parties (associated with Hobbes and Rawls); see also *reciprocal altruism*.

Cosmopolitanism idea that there are (or ought to be) universal norms that unite people across the globe.

Criminal justice justice that is focused on punishment and correction (versus *social justice*); see also *retributive justice*, *deterrence*, *restorative justice*.

D

Decarceration the idea of eliminating prisons or radically reducing the role of incarceration in punishment.

Deep ecology extreme ecocentric idea in environmental ethics that emphasizes human belonging to nature and the intrinsic value of natural things (associated with Devall and Sessions).

Deontological ethics normative theory that morality ought to be focused on duties and adherence to rules and imperatives (associated with Kant).

Descriptive claims propositions that state true or false claims about facts in the world.

Descriptive egoism (defined under egoism).

Descriptive relativism descriptive claim that values differ depending upon culture and perspective.

Deterrence a focal point for consequentialist approaches to *criminal justice*, which is concerned with deterring criminals from committing crime (versus *retributive justice* and *restorative justice*).

Discrimination (in just war) principle of the just war theory that stipulates that just warriors should target only combatants and protect noncombatants; see also *noncombatant immunity.*

Discrimination (as injustice) to treat someone unfairly and unequally based upon racial, ethnic, gender, or other identity claims (not to be confused with discrimination in just war theory).

Distributive justice a theory of justice concerned with the fair distribution of benefits and harms within society (versus *retributive justice* and *procedural justice*).

Divine command theory idea that ethical norms are ultimately based upon the authoritative decrees of God.

Double effect the principle or doctrine of double effect is the idea in deontological ethics that holds that if the intention behind an action is morally appropriate, unintended (but foreseen and accidental) negative effects may be permissible.

Durable power of attorney used to appoint or empower someone to make health care decisions for you in the case of incapacity; see also *advance directive* and *living will.*

E

Ecocentrism approach to environmental ethics that is focused on the value of the ecosystem as a whole and not merely on its relation to human beings (versus *anthropocentrism*); see also *biocentrism.*

Ecofeminism a critical version of environmental ethics that emphasizes the way that patriarchal systems have abused nature and a more productive feminine connection with nature.

Ecosystem a concept used in environmental ethics that refers to the broad integrated, coordinated, and organized whole, including plants, animals, and human beings.

Egoism normative or *ethical egoism* claims that we ought to pursue our own self-interest; *descriptive egoism* (also called *psychological egoism*) maintains that as a matter of fact we can pursue only our own self-interest (versus *altruism*).

Embryonic stem cells cells removed from a developing embryo, which can develop into multiple tissues; controversial because the embryo is destroyed to harvest them.

Emotivism metaethical idea that ethical propositions express emotional states (associated with Stevenson).

Enhancement an intervention that goes beyond natural/ normal function and creates superior performance, employed in discussions of biotechnology (versus therapy).

Enlightenment period of fertile development of Western culture and philosophy, during the seventeenth and eighteenth centuries.

Environmental ethics field of ethical inquiry that is concerned with the question of the value of ecosystems, the natural environment, and the distribution of benefits and harms in relation to the environment.

Environmental justice a concern in environmental ethics that is focused on the fair distribution of harms and benefits to human beings in relation to environment impacts such as pollution (related to *distributive justice* and *social justice*).

Epicureanism theory of Epicurus, which holds that pleasure and happiness are primary (also called *hedonism*).

Epistemology theory of knowledge.

Ethical egoism see *egoism*.

Eudaimonia Greek term for human flourishing and happiness that is more than simply pleasure; associated with Aristotle and *virtue ethics*.

Eugenics goal of producing genetically superior offspring, either through genetic screening or through more forceful interventions including forced sterilization.

Eurocentrism attitude or practice of interpreting the world from a perspective that focuses primarily on European interests, values, and history.

Euthanasia literally good death; also called mercy killing; forms include *active*, *passive*, *voluntary*, *involuntary*, and *nonvoluntary*.

Exoneration to be found innocent of a crime for which one was previously convicted and found guilty.

Extraordinary measures in discussion of end of life care and euthanasia, extraordinary measures are medical interventions that are not proven to be reasonably beneficial—may include, for example, experimental treatments or risky interventions (versus *ordinary measures*).

F

Fair chase idea in hunting ethics that the animal should stand some chance and the hunter requires some skill and good luck.

Female genital mutilation removal of parts of the female genitals (includes a variety of procedures); also called *female circumcision*.

Feminism intellectual commitment and a political movement that seeks justice for women and the end of sexism in all forms.

Feminist ethics a critical theory of ethics that rejects male-dominant ideas, can include "feminine" ethics emphasizing community and caregiving (associated with Noddings).

Fundamentalism idea that truth is grounded in religious texts, traditions, and prophets.

G

Gay marriage marriage of homosexual couples, also called same-sex marriage; see also *civil union*.

Genetic screening process of choosing embryos based on their genetic assets prior to implantation; can include efforts to modify genes to eliminate disease or produce enhanced capacities.

Genetically modified organisms plants or animals that have been genetically altered by scientists in an effort to improve the stock and increase yield.

Global justice concern for distributive justice, environmental justice, and social justice across the globe.

Globalization process of increasing integration of global markets and ideas, by way of growing international cooperation and international business.

Golden Mean idea associated with virtue ethics that virtue is found in the middle between excess and deficiency.

Golden Rule idea that one ought to love one's neighbor as oneself or do unto others as we would have them do unto us.

Greatest happiness principle utilitarian idea that we ought to work to achieve the greatest happiness for the greatest number of people; see also *principle of utility*.

H

Hate crime a crime that is accompanied by bias (racial, religious, gender, sexuality) against the individual who is the victim of the crime.

Hedonism theory that holds that pleasure is the highest good; as a normative theory tells us we ought to pursue pleasure; see also *Epicureanism*.

Hippocratic Oath medical ethics pledge rooted in ancient Greek tradition; primary tenet is to do no harm.

Human rights rights that are basic to human beings, often described in universal terms that transcend national and cultural differences; see also *rights, natural rights*.

Humanism orientation to human concerns and interests (as opposed to theistic or religious orientation); see also *secular ethics*.

Hume's law the claim (derived from David Hume's thinking) that it is illegitimate to derive an "ought" from an "is"; see also *naturalistic fallacy*.

Hypothetical imperative Kantian idea of a conditional rule that governs prudential behaviors and skilled activities aimed at procuring or producing some conditional good (versus *categorical imperative*).

I

Implicit bias unconscious prejudices and attitudes, based upon stereotypical ideas, which affect our judgments and behaviors without conscious awareness.

Imperfect/meritorious duties Kantian idea about duties of virtue that are admirable and praiseworthy but not always necessary (versus *perfect/ necessary duties*).

In vitro fertilization a process by which egg and sperm are united outside of the uterus, the consequent embryo is implanted into the uterus—a way to create pregnancy for infertile couples.

Individual relativism idea that ethical claims are relative to an individual's values and perspectives; see also *subjectivism*.

Inherent worth/value value residing by nature in something and without reference to any other value or good; see also *intrinsic value*.

Institutional racism see *structural racism*.

Instrumental value/goods things that are useful or good as tools or as means toward some other good (versus *intrinsic goods*).

Intrinsic value/goods things that have value in themselves and not merely as tools or means (versus *instrumental goods*); see also *inherent worth*.

Intrinsically evil means concept in just war theory that rules out some weapons and methods of war as being evil in themselves (or mala in se).

Intuitionism metaethical idea that ethical truths are objective and irreducible and can be known by faculty of intuition (associated with Moore).

Involuntary euthanasia euthanasia that is done against an individual's will (versus *voluntary euthanasia* and *nonvoluntary euthanasia*).

J

Jus ad bellum just war concern for ethical issues arising in deciding to go to war, including *just cause, legitimate authority*, and *proportionality*.

Jus in bello just war concern for ethical issues arising within

warfare, including *proportionality, discrimination*, and prohibition on *intrinsically evil means*.

Just cause concern of jus ad bellum, which holds that a war is justified only if there is a just cause, including defending the innocent or repelling aggression.

Just war theory a theory about the justification of war that maintains that war should be limited by moral concerns; see also *jus ad bellum* and *jus in bello*.

K

Kingdom of ends Kantian ideal of rational, moral society in which persons are respected as ends in themselves.

L

Laissez-faire **capitalism** form of economic and social organization that emphasizes leaving the market alone to regulate itself.

Land ethic an ecocentric idea in environmental ethics that views the land as a whole and claims that good actions contribute to the well-being of the whole (associated with Leopold).

Law of peoples idea of international law that transcends national borders.

Legitimate authority concern of jus ad bellum that holds that a war is justified only if the entity declaring war holds power legitimately.

Lex talionis an idea of *retributive justice* that is focused on equivalence or proportionality between the crime and the punishment, often described as "eye for an eye" justice.

LGBT acronym standing for "lesbian, gay, bisexual, and transgendered" (can be extended to include other sexual identities, sometimes abbreviated as LGBT+).

Liberalism a political theory that emphasizes a combination of concern for liberty and concern for social justice and distributive justice (associated with Rawls) (versus *libertarianism* and *socialism*).

Libertarianism a political theory about both the importance of liberty in human life and the limited role of government (associated with Rand) (versus *liberalism* and *socialism*).

Liberty rights see *negative rights.*

Living wage a minimum wage standard indexed to the cost of living (versus *minimum wage*).

Living will a form of advance health care directive; see also *advance directive* and *durable power of attorney.*

M

Metaethical relativism metaethical claim that there are no objective or nonrelative values that could mediate disputes about ethics.

Metaethics study of moral concepts and the logic of ethical language.

Minimum wage legally mandated minimum hourly wage for labor (versus *living wage*).

Modernization theory of development that emphasizes increased secularization, spread of capitalism, and liberalization of economics and politics.

Moral agent a being who is able to express ethical concern and take responsibility for behaviors, attitudes, and actions (versus *moral patient*)

Moral patient an object of ethical concern, a recipient of moral concern, or a being that is viewed as having value (versus *moral agent*).

Moral pluralism see *value pluralism.*

Moral realism idea that there are ethical facts and that moral judgments can be said to be true or false; see also *objectivism.*

N

Natural law a theory of law that is grounded in claims about nature; natural law ethics is a normative theory that holds that reason can discover objective ethical norms by examining natural human functions (associated with Aquinas).

Natural rights rights or entitlements that we have by nature, which are not created by positive laws and which create a

limit to legal intervention; see also *rights, human rights.*

Naturalistic fallacy argument that inappropriately derives normative claims from descriptive claims (associated with Moore); see also *Hume's law.*

Negative rights rights of noninterference and prevention of harm, often called *liberty rights* (as opposed to *welfare rights* and *positive rights*).

Nepotism showing favoritism toward one's relatives.

Noncombatant immunity idea in just war theory that noncombatants should not be deliberately targeted; see also *collateral damage.*

Non-consequentialism normative theories that do not focus on consequences of actions but instead on intentions, rules, or principles; examples include deontology, divine command, and natural law (versus *consequentialism*).

Nonvoluntary euthanasia euthanasia that is done when the patient is incapacitated and unable to express her wishes or give consent (versus *voluntary euthanasia* and *involuntary euthanasia*).

Normative ethics study of prescriptive accounts of how we ought to behave.

Normative judgments evaluative or prescriptive claims about what is good, evil, just, and the like.

O

Objectivism metaethical idea that ethical propositions refer to objective facts (versus *subjectivism*); see also *moral realism.*

Ontological status related to a theory of being (ontology); questions about the moral status of things (fetuses, ecosystems, etc.) depend upon deciding what sorts of beings these things are; see also *actuality* and *potentiality.*

Ontology theory of being or beings; an account of what exists or about the sort of being a thing is.

Ordinary measures in discussions of end of life care and euthanasia, ordinary measures are those medical interventions that are proven to be reasonably beneficial in most cases (vs. *extraordinary measures*).

Original position idea used in John Rawls's theory of justice that asks us to imagine ourselves as original or founding parties to the social contract; see also *veil of ignorance.*

Original sin Christian idea that human beings inherit a tendency to do evil from the original sin of Adam and Eve.

P

Pacifism commitment to nonviolence and opposition to war (associated with Gandhi and King).

Palliative care health care that is aimed at pain management and dealing with suffering.

Palliative sedation sedation employed to provide pain management at the end of life (related to *terminal sedation*).

Paradox of hedonism problem for hedonism: when pursuing pleasure directly, we fail to obtain it; but pleasure occurs when we do not directly pursue it.

Paradox of toleration problem of whether one should tolerate those who are intolerant or who reject the idea of toleration.

Passive euthanasia allowing someone to die ("letting die") for the benefit of the one who is dying (versus *active euthanasia*).

Perfect/necessary duties Kantian idea about duties of justice that we always ought to do or that we always ought to avoid (versus *imperfect/meritorious duties*).

Persistent vegetative state a condition of permanent brain damage, characterized by lack of awareness and loss of higher brain functions; patient remains alive but has lost cognitive function; see also *whole brain death.*

Perspectivism relativist idea that there are only perspectives and interpretations, which cannot be reduced to a fundamental fact of the world.

Physician-assisted suicide closely related to euthanasia; doctors prescribe lethal medication but patients take the medication, killing themselves.

Positive rights rights of entitlement to basic subsistence and other means of living sometimes called *welfare rights* (as opposed to *liberty rights* and *negative rights*).

Post-structuralism a philosophical movement of the late twentieth century that emphasizes the social construction of categories of thought.

Potentiality ontological consideration focused on what a thing has the potential to become; often employed in discussions of the ethics of abortion; see also *ontological status* and *actuality.*

Precautionary principle an idea used in environmental ethics and in thinking about biotechnology that emphasizes avoiding risk when considering innovations.

Preferential treatment a form of affirmative action that intends to give preference to members of groups who were previously unjustly discriminated against; see *affirmative action.*

Premises the reasons given in an argument that provide support for the argument's conclusion.

Prima facie term meaning "on the face of it" or "at first glance."

Prima facie duties pluralist idea that there are several duties, each of which is valuable but which can end up in conflict (associated with Ross).

Principle of equality idea that we should treat equal things in equal ways and that we ought to treat different things in unequal ways.

Principle of utility utilitarian idea that what matters is the pleasure produced by an action, especially the pleasure produced for the greatest number of people; see also *greatest happiness principle*.

Prisoner's dilemma problem for rational self-interest and social contract: self-interested parties who do not trust one another will be unable to cooperate and thus will end up with less than optimal outcomes.

Problem of evil argument against the existence of God that claims that a good God would not permit evil but since evil exists, God must not exist (versus *theodicy*).

Procedural justice a theory of justice focused on the fairness of the procedures used to distribute benefits and harms (versus *distributive justice*).

Proportionality concern of just war theory that maintains that war should be a proportional last resort and that limited and proportional means should be employed during the course of war.

Pro-social behavior behaviors that intend to help others (versus antisocial behavior).

Psychological egoism (defined under *egoism*).

Q

Queer theory a post-structuralist approach to thinking about gender and sexuality that maintains that sex and gender roles are socially constructed (associated with Butler).

Quickening the point in pregnancy at which the mother is able to detect movement of the fetus; sometimes viewed as the time when the fetus attains moral status.

R

Racial profiling law enforcement technique that targets individuals based upon suspicion resulting from the individual's racial or ethnic identity.

Racialism idea that there are firm biological distinctions between human beings based on racial categories (critiqued by Appiah).

Racism unjust use of racial or ethnic categories to classify individuals and distribute social benefits and harms.

Realism view on ethics of war that maintains that limits on warfare are merely pragmatic or prudential and that the goal is strength and victory.

Reciprocal altruism idea that altruistic behavior is traded with others in a mutually beneficial exchange; see also *contractarianism*.

Regenerative medicine an approach to medical therapy that aims to regrow damaged tissues and organs using stem cells—both embryonic stem cells and other forms of stem cells.

Relativism a variety of claims that deny the objectivity of values including: *descriptive relativism*, *individual relativism* (or *subjectivism*), *metaethical relativism*, and *social or cultural relativism*.

Relativism, social or cultural idea that ethical claims are relative to a social or cultural matrix.

Religious pluralism idea that diverse religions provide multiple paths toward a common truth (associated with Gandhi).

Reproductive cloning a cloning procedure that aims to develop an individual organism as a substitute for ordinary reproduction (versus *therapeutic cloning*).

Restorative justice an approach to *criminal justice* that seeks to make criminals take responsibility and make amends, while restoring the community that they have broken (versus *retributive justice* and *deterrence*).

Retributive justice a theory of *criminal justice* that focuses on giving criminals what they deserve and forcing them to pay back what they owe to victims or to society (versus *restorative justice* and *deterrence*); see also *lex talionis*.

Reverse discrimination an idea used to criticize affirmative action that claims that actions aiming to help those who were previously discriminated against result in discrimination against those who were the beneficiaries of past discrimination.

Rights basic entitlements that ordinarily cannot be taken away or overridden; can be positive entitlements (*positive rights*) or negative protections (*negative rights*) (associated with Locke); see also *natural rights* and *human rights*.

Rule utilitarianism utilitarian theory that focuses on postulating general rules that will tend to produce the greatest happiness for the greatest number (versus *act utilitarianism*).

S

Secular ethics approach to ethics that locates ethical norms in nonreligious principles acceptable to people from a variety of religions (versus *divine command theory*); see also *humanism.*

Secularization movement away from religious culture and toward a nonreligious public sphere; see also *modernization.*

Sentience the ability to feel, perceive, and be conscious of the world, used in discussions of animal welfare and abortion in considering the moral status of animals and fetuses.

Sex trafficking trading sex for money; also called prostitution.

Sexting sending and receiving sexually explicit messages via cell phones.

Sex-selective abortion abortion performed for the purpose of selecting the gender of the baby.

Skepticism questioning and doubting attitude.

Social contract theory idea that social norms and political agreement are derived from a mutually beneficial contract to which the parties would consent (associated with Hobbes, Locke, and Rawls).

Social Darwinism idea of applying Darwinian evolution to society as a way of improving the genetic stock of humanity (widely repudiated as immoral).

Social justice an approach to justice that is concerned with the fair distribution of goods in society, often associated with natural law theories (versus *criminal justice*).

Socialism a social and economic system focused on developing shared social assets and a social safety net; see also *communism* (versus *capitalism*).

Sociobiology a field of study that applies evolutionary and comparative biology to understanding social phenomena, including ethical behaviors.

Sound argument a valid argument with true premises.

Speciesism a pejorative term used to describe anthropocentrists,

who maintain that human beings are superior to nonhuman animals (associated with Singer).

Stem cell research a promising line of research that could help to regenerate damaged tissues; controversial when it employs human *embryonic stem cells.*

Stoicism theory of ancient Stoic philosophers, which holds that obedience to natural law and duty is essential (despite pain).

Straw man argument fallacious argument that describes an opponent's position in such a way as to easily dismiss it.

Structural racism idea that social structures are constituted in ways that create disparate racial outcomes (also called *institutional racism*).

Subjectivism metaethical idea that ethical propositions refer to subjective dispositions or values (versus *objectivism*); see also *individual relativism, descriptive relativism, metaethical relativism.*

Supererogatory a term used to describe actions that go above and beyond the call of duty.

T

Teleological adjective used to describe ideas and theories that are focused on goals, purposes, or outcomes (related to *consequentialism*).

Terminal sedation use of sedatives in palliative care that aims to reduce suffering at the end of life but may also contribute to death and be considered as part of euthanasia.

Theodicy theoretical explanation of why a good God would permit evil; response to the *problem of evil*.

Therapeutic cloning a cloning procedure that is used to grow stem cells or tissues that could be used for organ donation or regenerative medicine (versus *reproductive cloning*).

Therapy an intervention employed to return something to natural/normal function, employed in discussions of biotechnology (versus *enhancement*).

Toleration attitude of forbearance or permissiveness for attitudes or behaviors that are disapproved; an open and nonjudgmental attitude.

Totipotent term describing the ability of embryonic stem cells to develop into any kind of tissue; see also *stem cell research*.

Tragedy of the commons worry about degradation of common resources when no one owns them, associated with concerns for environmental degradation (associated with Hardin).

Transgender persons who do not feel comfortable with or who do not identify with the traditional sex/gender roles assigned to them (see *cisgender*).

Transhumanism a movement aiming to improve human abilities, extend human life span, and increase cognitive capacity; sometimes referred to as *post-humanism* (associated with Bostrom).

U

Utilitarianism normative theory that we ought to concern ourselves with the greatest happiness for the greatest number of people (associated with Bentham and Mill).

V

Valid argument an argument in which the conclusion necessarily follows from the premises.

Value pluralism the metaethical idea that there is more than one objective value (associated with Ross); see also *prima facie duties*.

Vegetarianism commitment to avoiding eating meat including veganism, which avoids consuming any animal product including eggs, milk, and leather.

Veil of ignorance idea used in John Rawls's version of the social contract that asks us to ignore concrete facts about our own situation as we imagine the ideal social contract.

Viability the point at which a fetus might live outside of the womb if delivered early; sometimes used as a criteria for determining the permissibility (or not) of abortion.

Virtue ethics normative theory that maintains that the focus of morality is habits, dispositions, and character traits (associated with Aristotle).

Voluntary euthanasia euthanasia that is done with the consent of the one being killed or dying (versus *involuntary euthanasia* and *nonvoluntary euthanasia*).

W

Weakness of will problem in moral psychology: we sometimes will things that we know are not in our own self-interest or are unable to do things we know are good (also called *akrasia*).

Welfare rights see *positive rights*.

Whole brain death legal criteria for death focused not on respiration and heartbeat but on the presence of brain activity; see also *persistent vegetative state*.

Index